THE ROUTLEDGE COMPANION
TO NINETEENTH CENTURY PHILOSOPHY

The nineteenth century is a period of stunning philosophical originality, characterised by radical engagement with the emerging human sciences. Often overshadowed by twentieth century philosophy which sought to reject some of its central tenets, the philosophers of the nineteenth century have re-emerged as profoundly important figures.

The Routledge Companion to Nineteenth Century Philosophy is an outstanding survey and assessment of the century as a whole. Divided into seven parts and including thirty chapters written by leading international scholars, the *Companion* examines and assesses the central topics, themes, and philosophers of the nineteenth century, presenting the first comprehensive picture of the period in a single volume:

- German Idealism
- Philosophy as political action, including young Hegelians, Marx, and Tocqueville
- Rethinking the subject, including Schopenhauer, Kierkegaard, and Nietzsche
- Engaging naturalism, including Darwinism, philosophy of race, experimental psychology, and Neo-Kantianism
- Utilitarianism and British Idealism
- American Pragmatism and Idealism
- New Directions in Philosophy of Mind and Logic, including Brentano, Frege, and Husserl.

The Routledge Companion to Nineteenth Century Philosophy is essential reading for students of philosophy, and for anyone interested in this period in related disciplines such as politics, history, literature, and religion.

Dean Moyar is Associate Professor of Philosophy at Johns Hopkins University. He works primarily in German Idealism and has strong interests in political philosophy and in ethics.

Routledge Philosophy Companions

Routledge Philosophy Companions offer thorough, high-quality surveys and assessments of the major topics and periods in philosophy. Covering key problems, themes, and thinkers, all entries are specially commissioned for each volume and written by leading scholars in the field. Clear, accessible, and carefully edited and organised, *Routledge Philosophy Companions* are indispensable for anyone coming to a major topic or period in philosophy, as well as for the more advanced reader.

Forthcoming:

PRAISE FOR THE SERIES

The Routledge Companion to Aesthetics

'This is an immensely useful book that belongs in every college library and on the bookshelves of all serious students of aesthetics.' – *Journal of Aesthetics and Art Criticism*

'The succinctness and clarity of the essays will make this a source that individuals not familiar with aesthetics will find extremely helpful.' – *The Philosophical Quarterly*

'An outstanding resource in aesthetics ... this text will not only serve as a handy reference source for students and faculty alike, but it could also be used as a text for a course in the philosophy of art.' – *Australasian Journal of Philosophy*

'Attests to the richness of modern aesthetics...the essays in central topics – many of which are written by well-known figures – succeed in being informative, balanced and intelligent without being too difficult.' – *British Journal of Aesthetics*

'This handsome reference volume ... belongs in every library.' – *Choice*

'The *Routledge Companions* to philosophy have proved to be a useful series of high quality surveys of major philosophical topics and this volume is worthy enough to sit with the others on a reference library shelf.' – *Philosophy and Religion*

The Routledge Companion to Philosophy of Religion

'... a very valuable resource for libraries and serious scholars.' – *Choice*

'The work is sure to be an academic standard for years to come... I shall heartily recommend *The Routledge Companion to Philosophy of Religion* to my students and colleagues and hope that libraries around the country add it to their collections.' – *Philosophia Christi*

The Routledge Companion to Philosophy of Science

'With a distinguished list of internationally renowned contributors, an excellent choice of topics in the field, and well-written, well-edited essays throughout, this compendium is an excellent resource. Highly recommended.' – *Choice*

'Highly recommended for history of science and philosophy collections.' – *Library Journal*

This well-conceived companion, which brings together an impressive collection of distinguished authors, will be invaluable to novices and experience readers alike.'
– *Metascience*

The Routledge Companion to Twentieth Century Philosophy

'To describe this volume as ambitious would be a serious understatement ... full of scholarly rigor, including detailed notes and bibliographies of interest to professional philosophers ... Summing up: essential.' – *Choice*

The Routledge Companion to Philosophy and Film

'A fascinating, rich volume offering dazzling insights and incisive commentary on every page ... Every serious student of film will want this book ... Summing up: highly recommended.' – *Choice*

The Routledge Companion to Metaphysics

'The *Routledge Philosophy Companions* series has a deserved reputation for impressive scope and scholarly value. This volume is no exception ... Summing up: highly recommended.' – *Choice*

THE
ROUTLEDGE COMPANION
TO NINETEENTH CENTURY
PHILOSOPHY

Edited by
Dean Moyar

Routledge
Taylor & Francis Group

LONDON AND NEW YORK

First published 2010 by Routledge
Firs published 2013 in paperback by Routledge
2 Park Square, Milton Park, Abingdon, Oxon OX14 4RN

Simultaneously published in the USA and Canada
by Routledge
711 Third Avenue, New York, NY 10017

Routledge is an imprint of the Taylor & Francis Group, an informa business

Typeset in Goudy Oldstyle Std 10.5/13pt by
Fakenham Photosetting Ltd, Fakenham, Norfolk

British Library Cataloguing in Publication Data
A catalogue record for this book is available from the British Library

Library of Congress Cataloging in Publication Data
The Routledge companion to nineteenth century philosophy / edited by Dean Moyar.
p. cm. -- (Routledge philosophy companions)
Includes bibliographical references and index.
1. Philosophy, Modern--19th century. I. Moyar, Dean.
B803.R68 2010
190.9'034--dc22
2009035627

ISBN13: 978-0-415-40450-1 (hbk)
ISBN13: 978-0-415-40451-8 (pbk)
ISBN13: 978-0-203-85658-1 (ebk)

CONTENTS

LIST OF CONTRIBUTORS

Keith Ansell-Pearson is Professor of Philosophy at the University of Warwick. He is author and editor of books on Nietzsche, Bergson and Deleuze. Recent publications include: *Bergson Key Writings* (2002), *The Nietzsche Reader* (2006) and *A Companion to Nietzsche* (2006).

Robert Bernasconi is Edwin Erle Sparks Professor of Philosophy at Pennsylvania State University. He has written extensively on nineteenth- and twentieth-century continental philosophy and in critical philosophy of race. He has edited a number of books on race, including *Race, Miscegenation, and Hybridity* (2005), *Race and Anthropology* (2003) and *Race* (2001). His most recent book is *How to Read Sartre* (2008).

Christian Beyer studied philosophy, linguistics and the history of science in Bielefeld and Hamburg, where he also took his PhD (1999). He was a visiting scholar at Stanford University (1994–5), served as Temporary Lecturer in Philosophy at the University of Sheffield (2000) and as *Wissenschaftlicher Mitarbeiter* (assistant professor) at the University of Erfurt (2000–5), where he earned his *Habilitation* (accreditation to teach in higher education). In 2005 he was awarded a Heisenberg Scholarship of the German Research Foundation, and he has recently been appointed as Professor of Theoretical Philosophy at the Georg-August-Universität Göttingen. He is the author of *Von Bolzano zu Husserl* (1996), *Intentionalität und Referenz* (2000), *Subjektivität, Intersubjektivität, Personalität* (2006) and co-editor of *Philosophical Knowledge* (2007).

David Boucher is Professor of Political Theory at the School of European Studies, Cardiff University, and Adjunct Professor of International Relations at the University at the Sunshine Coast, Australia. He is the Director of the Collingwood and British Idealism Centre, Cardiff University, and chairman of the trustees of the Collingwood Society. He has published widely in idealist-related studies, including *The Social and Political Thought of R. G. Collingwood* (1989), *A Radical Hegelian: The Political and Social Thought of Henry Jones* (1993, with Andrew Vincent) and *The Limits of Ethics in International Relations*. He has edited three works by R. G. Collingwood, the most recent of which is *The Philosophy of Enchantment* (2006), and two collections of idealist writings. He is currently writing *British Idealism: A Guide for the Perplexed*, with Andrew Vincent.

Robert Burch received his BA in mathematics from Rice University in 1965 and his PhD in philosophy from Rice University in 1969. He has taught philosophy at Rice University, Queens College CUNY, the Russian State University for the Humanities, University of Southampton (England) and Texas A&M University. He is currently Professor of Philosophy at Texas A&M University. His areas of special interest include the history of logic, American philosophy, graphical logic, and non-deductive logic. Included in his publications is A *Peircean Reduction Thesis: Foundations of Topological Logic* (1991).

Stewart Candlish of the University of Western Australia is a Fellow of the Australian Academy of the Humanities and Editor of the *Australasian Journal of Philosophy*.

Vincent Colapietro is a Liberal Arts Research Professor in the Department of Philosophy at Pennsylvania State University. He has published extensively on American pragmatism and, in particular, C. S. Peirce. One of his principal goals is to show in detail how the pragmatic perspective is a unique outlook of abiding relevance and broad significance. Subjectivity, agency, discourse, meaning, normativity and history are among the topics to which he has devoted his attention.

Jon Elster is the Robert K. Merton Professor of Social Science at Columbia University and also holds the Chaire de Rationalité et Sciences Sociales (Philosophical and Sociological Sciences) at the Collège de France. His recent publications include *Explaining Social Behavior* (2007), *Le Désintéressement* (2009) and *Alexis de Tocqueville: The First Social Scientist* (2009).

Ken Gemes is a Reader in Philosophy at Birkbeck College, University of London, and at Southampton University. His published research is in general philosophy of science and on aspects of Nietzsche's philosophy and appears in various journals, including the *Journal of Philosophy*, the *Journal of Philosophical Logic*, *Philosophy of Science*, the *British Journal for the Philosophy of Science*, *Noûs*, *Philosophy and Phenomenological Research*, the *European Journal of Philosophy*, *Erkentniss*,and *Synthese*. He is co-editor, with Simon May, of *Nietzsche on Freedom and Autonomy* (2009).

Gary Hatfield teaches philosophy at the University of Pennsylvania. He has published *The Natural and the Normative: Theories of Spatial Perception from Kant to Helmholtz* (1990) and *Descartes and the Meditations* (2003), as well as numerous articles in the philosophy and history of psychology. He translated Kant's *Prolegomena* (2nd edn, 2004). Some of his essays are collected in *Perception and Cognition: Essays in the Philosophy of Psychology* (2009).

Dietmar H. Heidemann earned his PhD from Cologne, in 1997, and his Dr (phil. habil.) (accreditation for teaching in higher education) from Cologne 2005, and in 2006 became an Assistant Professor of Philosophy at Hofstra University, New York. Since 2009 he has been a Professor of Philosophy at the University of Luxembourg, with specialisation in the study of epistemology, Kant, German Idealism, and history of modern philosophy. He has written *Der Begriff des Skeptizismus* (2007), *Kant und das Problem des metaphysischen Idealismus* (1998), edited the *Kant Yearbook* (2009–), and co-edited *Hegel und die Geschichte der Philosophie* (2007) and *Warum Kant heute?* (2004).

Scott Jenkins is Assistant Professor of Philosophy at the University of Kansas. His work has appeared in *History of Philosophy Quarterly* and the *Journal of the History of Philosophy*.

Stephan Käufer is Associate Professor of Philosophy at Franklin and Marshall College.

Philip Kitcher was born in London (UK). He received his BA from Cambridge University and his PhD from Princeton. He has taught at several American Universities, and is currently John Dewey Professor of Philosophy at Columbia. He is the author of ten books on topics ranging from the philosophy of mathematics, to the philosophy of biology, the growth of science, the role of science in society, Wagner's *Ring* and Joyce's *Finnegans Wake*. He has been President of the American Philosophical Association (Pacific Division) and editor-in-chief of *Philosophy of Science*. A Fellow of the American Academy of Arts and Sciences, he was also the first recipient of the Prometheus Prize, awarded by the American Philosophical Association for work in expanding the frontiers of science and philosophy. He has been named a Friend of Darwin by the National Committee on Science Education, and received a Lannan Foundation Notable Book Award for *Living with Darwin*.

Kevin C. Klement is Associate Professor of Philosophy at the University of Massachusetts, Amherst. He is the author of *Frege and the Logic of Sense and Reference*, and has published articles on Frege, Russell, the history of analytic philosophy, the history of logic, and informal logic. He is currently engaged in a research project regarding the development of Bertrand Russell's philosophical logic.

Jane Kneller is Professor of Philosophy at Colorado State University. Her publications include *Kant and the Power of Imagination* (2007), and *Novalis: Fichte Studies* (2003). She is also co-editor, with Sidney Axinn, of *Autonomy and Community: Readings in Contemporary Kantian Social Philosophy* (1998).

Sebastian Luft has studied in Freiburg, Heidelberg, SUNY Stony Brook and Wuppertal. He received his MA in Heidelberg and his PhD in Wuppertal. He has been editorial assistant at the Husserl Archives in Louvain 1998–2002, visiting assistant professor at Emory University 2002–4, and is currently Associate Professor of Philosophy at Marquette University. He is the author of *"Phänomenologie der Phänomenologie": Systematik und Methodologie der Phänomenologie in der Auseinandersetzung zwischen Husserl und Fink* and editor of Husserliana, vol. 34, *Zur phänomenologischen Reduktion: Texte aus dem Nachlass (1926–35)*; book review editor of Husserl Studies, and recipient of fellowships from DFG (Deutsche Forschungsgemeinschaft, German Research Foundation), FWO (Fonds voor Wetenschappelijk Onderzoek, Fund for Scientific Research, Belgium), Alexander von Humboldt Foundation, the Mellon Foundation and the National Endowment for the Humanities. He has written articles on figures from the Phenomenological Movement and the Marburg School of neo-Kantianism. He has co-edited a volume, with Rudolf A. Makkreel, entitled *Neo-Kantianism in Contemporary Philosophy*. He has also co-edited a volume with Pol Vandevelde, entitled *Epistemology, Archeology, Ethics. Current Investigations of Husserl's Corpus*. He is working on another, with Dermot Moran, *The Neo-Kantian Reader*, and he is working with Thane M. Naberhaus on a translation of Edmund Husserl's lecture-course *Erste Philosophie* (1923/24).

Rudolf A. Makkreel, Charles Howard Candler Professor of Philosophy at Emory University, is the author of *Dilthey, Philosopher of the Human Studies; Imagination and Interpretation in Kant: the Hermeneutical Import of the "Critique of Judgment"*; co-editor of *Dilthey's Selected Works*; editor of the *Journal of the History of Philosophy* (1983–98) and recipient of fellowships from the NEH (National Endowment for the Humanities), DAAD (Deutscher Akademischer Austauschdienst, German Academic Exchange Service), Alexander von Humboldt Foundation, Thyssen Stiftung (Thyssen Foundation) and Volkswagen Stiftung (Volkswagen Foundation). He is currently writing a book entitled *Critical Hermeneutics and Historical Judgment*.

Dean Moyar is Associate Professor in the Department of Philosophy at Johns Hopkins University. He received his BS from Duke University and his PhD from the University of Chicago. His essays have appeared in (among others) the *Journal of Moral Philosophy* and *Hegel-Studien*. He is the co-editor (with Michael Quante) of *Hegel's Phenomenology of Spirit: A Critical Guide* (2007) and the author of the forthcoming *Hegel's Conscience* (2010).

Michael Quante is Professor of Practical Philosophy in the Department of Philosophy at the Westfälische Wilhelms-University. He is Associated Editor of the journal *Ethical Theory and Moral Practice*. Books (in English): *Hegel's Concept of Action* (2004, paperback, 2007), *Enabling Social Europe* (2005; co-authored with Bernd von Maydell et al.), *Hegel's Phenomenology of Spirit: A Critical Guide* (2008, co-edited with Dean Moyar), *Moral Realism* (2004, co-edited with Jussi Kotkavirta) and *Pragmatic Idealism* (1998, co-edited with Axel Wüstehube). Books (in German): *Menschenwürde und Personale Autonomie* (2010), *Karl Marx: Ökonomisch-Philosophische Manuskripte* (2009), *Person* (2007), *Einführung in die Allgemeine Ethik* (2003, 3rd edn *Personales Leben und menschlicher Tod* (2002), 2008), *Ethik der Organtransplantation* (2000, co-authored with Johann S. Ach and Michael Anderheiden) and *Hegels Begriff der Handlung* (1993).

Richard A. Richards Associate Professor of Philosophy at the University of Alabama, received his PhD from Johns Hopkins University under the supervision of Peter

Achinstein. He writes on a variety of topics in the history and philosophy of biology: Darwin, taxonomy, phylogenetic inference, species and naturalistic theories of value. In a former life he was a professional ballet dancer.

Robert C. Scharff teaches philosophy at the University of New Hampshire, is the former editor of *Continental Philosophy Review* (1994–2005), author of *Comte after Positivism*, and co-editor of *The Philosophy of Technology: The Technological Condition*. He publishes on nineteenth- and twentieth-century Continental philosophy, the history of positivism, and the philosophy of technology. He is currently finishing a book manuscript, *How History Matters to Philosophy*, and editing a *Blackwell Guidebook* on Heidegger's *Being and Time*.

David P. Schweikard is assistant Professor in the Department of Philosophy at the Westfaelische Wilhelms University, Münster (Germany). He works and publishes on philosophy of action, social philosophy and applied ethics, as well as on German idealism and Pragmatism. He is co-editor of *Robert Brandom – Analytic Pragmatist* (2008) and *Kollektive Intentionalität – Eine Debatte über die Grundlagen des sozialen* (2009).

Peter Simons studied mathematics and philosophy at Manchester. He taught in Salzburg and Leeds before moving to Trinity College Dublin in 2009. His research interests include metaphysics and ontology, philosophy of logic and mathematics, philosophy of engineering, and the history of logic and philosophy in Central Europe. His publications include *Parts* (1987), *Philosophy and Logic in Central Europe from Bolzano to Tarski* (1992) and over 200 articles.

Tony Smith is Professor at the Department of Philosophy and Religious Studies at Iowa State University. His books include *The Logic of Marx's Capital, Technology and Capital in the Age of Lean Production*, and *Globalisation: A Systematic Marxian Account*.

Chris Sykes is a graduate student currently completing his PhD at Birkbeck College, University of London. His forthcoming publications include 'Nietzsche on the Illusion of Meaning' (co-authored with Ken Gemes) in the volume *Nietzsche on Art and Aesthetics* edited by Daniel Came (2010).

Dieter Wandschneider was Professor for Philosophy at Tübingen University, Germany (1983–1987); and Chair for Philosophy and Philosophy of Science at Aachen University RWTH, Germany (1988–2004). His books include: *Raum, Zeit, Relativität. Grundbestimmungen der Physik in der Perspektive der Hegelschen Naturphilosophie* (1982); *Grundzüge einer Theorie der Dialektik. Rekonstruktion und Revision dialektischer Kategorienentwicklung in Hegels 'Wissenschaft der Logik'* (1995); *Das Problem der Dialektik* (ed. 1997); *Technikphilosophie* (2004); *Das Geistige und das Sinnliche in der Kunst. Ästhetische Reflexion in der Perspektive des Deutschen Idealismus* (ed. 2005) and *Naturphilosophie* (2008).

David E. Wellbery is the LeRoy T. and Margaret Deffenbaugh Carlson University Professor in the Departments of Germanic Studies and Comparative Literature and the Committee on Social Thought at the University of Chicago. His books include: *Lessing's Laocoon: Semiotics and Aesthetics in the Age of Reason* (1984, paperback, 2009); *The Specular Moment: Goethe's Early Lyric and the Beginnings of Romanticism* (1996); *Schopenhauers Bedeutung für die moderne Literatur* (1998), and *Seiltänzer des Paradoxalen: Aufsätze zur ästhetischen Wissenschaft* (2006). He is editor-in-chief of *A New History of German Literature* (2005).

Merold Westphal is Distinguished Professor of Philosophy at Fordham University in New York City. He has served as President of the Hegel Society of America and of the Søren Kierkegaard Society and as Executive Co-Director of the Society for Phenomenology and Existential Philosophy. He is the author of *History and Truth in Hegel's Phenomenology*; *Hegel, Freedom and Modernity*; *Kierkegaard's Critique of Reason and Society*; *Becoming a Self: A Reading of Kierkegaard's Concluding Unscientific Postscript*; *God, Guilt, and Death: An Existential Phenomenology of Religion*; *Suspicion and Faith: The Religious Uses of Modern Atheism*; *Overcoming Onto-Theology*; *Transcendence and Self-Transcendence: An Essay on God and the Soul*; *Levinas and Kierkegaard in Dialogue*, and *Whose Community? Which Interpretation? Philosophical Hermeneutics for the Church*.

Fred Wilson has a BSc from McMaster University in Hamilton, Ontario, Canada, and received his PhD from the University of Iowa in 1965. He was subsequently appointed to the Philosophy Department at the University of Toronto, where he is now Professor Emeritus. He has published extensively in the philosophy of science, ontology and the history of philosophy. In the last, his major interests have been David Hume, John Stuart Mill and the British idealists. His books include *Psychological Analysis and the Philosophy of John Stuart Mill* (1990) and, most recently, *The External World and Our Knowledge of It: Hume's Critical Realism, an Exposition and a Defense* (2008). His *The Logic and Methodology of Science in Early Modern Thought* won the 2003 Canadian Philosophical Association/Broadview Press book prize. He was elected a Fellow of the Royal Society of Canada in 1994.

Allen W. Wood is Ward W. and Priscilla B. Woods Professor at Stanford University. In 2008–9 he was Professor of Philosophy at Indiana University. He studied at Reed College (1960–4) and Yale University (1964–8). Before assuming his present position at Stanford, he taught at Cornell University (1968–96) and Yale University (1996–2000). He also held visiting appointments at the University of Michigan (1973), and the University of California at San Diego (1986), and he was Isaiah Berlin Visiting Professor at Oxford University in 2005. He has also spent sabbatical years at the Free University, Berlin (1983–4) and the University of Bonn (1991–2). He is author of *Kant's Moral Religion* (1970, reissued 2009), *Kant's Rational Theology* (1978, reissued 2009), *Karl Marx* (1981, 2nd edn 2004), *Hegel's Ethical Thought* (1990), *Kant's Ethical Thought* (1999), *Unsettling Obligations* (2002),

Kant (2004), and *Kantian Ethics* (2008). His books have been translated into Hebrew, Iranian, Portuguese and Turkish. He is co-general editor of the Cambridge Edition of the Works of Immanuel Kant. While at Cornell University he frequently edited the *Philosophical Review*, and is currently on the editorial boards of *Ethics*, *Kantian Review*, *Kant-Studien*, *Owl of Minerva* and *Journal of the History of Philosophy*.

Rachel Zuckert is Associate Professor at Northwestern University. She received BA degrees from Williams College and Oxford University, and her MA and PhD from the University of Chicago. She has also taught at Bucknell University and Rice University. Her research primarily concerns eighteenth- and nineteenth-century philosophy, with a specific focus on the history of aesthetics. She has published a number of essays in (among others) the *Journal of Aesthetics* and *Art Criticism*, *Kant-Studien*, and *Journal of the History of Philosophy*, and a book, *Kant on Beauty and Biology* (2007).

ACKNOWLEDGEMENTS

I would first of all like to thank my fellow contributors to the volume for their hard work in delivering a remarkable set of essays. The volume itself would never have gotten started without the initiative of Tony Bruce, who provided intellectual and moral support throughout the project. I am also grateful to the many anonymous reviewers recruited by Tony to comment on various versions of the proposal and individual chapters. In the early stages these comments led to many important additions to the volume, and in the later stages they led to major improvements in the readability and focus of the essays.

For providing an environment very conducive to extended projects such as this, I would like to thank the members of the Johns Hopkins Philosophy Department. Of the many teachers and advisers who have shaped my thought, I want to thank two in particular as the most important for my understanding of the nineteenth century. Terry Pinkard, whose published work on German philosophy is indispensable reading for students of the period, has been a crucial source of guidance and encouragement. Robert Pippin's writings and courses have been central to my intellectual development, and his breadth of interest and openness to diverse philosophical traditions has been an inspiration for this volume. My final and deepest thanks go to my wife, Sharlyn Rhee, for her patience throughout the long gestation of this volume.

INTRODUCTION

Dean Moyar

1

Changes in the English-speaking philosophical community in the last twenty years make this an auspicious moment for a new companion to nineteenth-century philosophy. The narrowness and territoriality that accompanied the division between so-called analytic and continental philosophy for many years has given way to an openness marked by a plurality of approaches to philosophical problems. For the study of the history of philosophy, this shift has been nowhere more important than for the appropriation of nineteenth-century thinkers. While philosophical respectability in Anglo-American philosophy used to end with Kant and resume with Frege and Russell, there is now serious attention being paid at all levels of the profession to the thinkers represented in this companion. To take only the example closest to my heart, the last thirty years have seen a dramatic increase in attention to post-Kantian German Idealism. Inquiry into Fichte and Hegel, as well as into the many other figures in the immediate Kantian aftermath, has matured as a field of historical study, and has inspired a number of important appropriations by analytically oriented philosophers.

Accounts of the nineteenth century are usually oriented by the century's great thinkers, whose diversity makes studying the century as a whole seem unmanageable. The originality of the views, along with the assumption by many of these thinkers that the reader has extensive knowledge of the history of philosophy, make this period especially challenging. Another reason the century intimidates is that philosophers still had the sense that philosophy should be able to get a grip on the whole of human knowledge and practice. There are those thinkers who actually ventured a synoptic account, such as Hegel, and those who despaired at the loss of the meaningful whole that the new science implied. Exclusive attention to the great thinkers, or to the overall philosophical movements of the century, tends to exaggerate the singular personalities or the impersonal forces that shaped the context of thought. Consonant with the century's intellectual character, the approach taken here is eclectic. First, the crucial period of German Idealism is structured according to its major themes. The main advantage of this approach is that it allows multiple tellings of the crucial progression from Kant to Hegel, with all the complex issues involved. Since the debates between those two thinkers structure much of the century's issues, a full fifth of the book is devoted to that period. The rest of the companion mixes chapters devoted to great thinkers (fourteen chapters focus on a single author) with key topics, many of which have been neglected in earlier accounts (ten chapters cover topics or schools of thought). In this way the volume is able to capture important new fields of inquiry (psychology, race) while doing justice to the originality and complexity of individual thinkers.

The contributors to this volume were selected based on their expertise in their historical fields and on their willingness to engage (here and/or in their previous work) with contemporary debates in systematic fields of inquiry. Though they were given broad leeway in their treatments of the specific thinkers, they were encouraged to tie their discussions into the themes (discussed in the second section of this Introduction) that characterize the period as a whole. They were instructed to pitch the essays at a level of difficulty suitable for philosophically minded readers coming to these authors for the first time. Yet because there was room for longer essays than in most historical companions, and because of the still-developing nature of the scholarly debates, authors were also encouraged to include their own interpretations and more advanced material. The task set for the contributors led one referee for the initial proposal to worry that too much was being asked of the contributors. This is no doubt the case, yet every author has risen to the task. The result is a volume that will engage new students of the period and provide an impetus for further research by scholars already working in specific fields in the period.

Though most of the contributors to this volume are members of philosophy departments, the material is naturally of interest to a broad range of students and scholars in the humanities and social sciences. Nineteenth-century philosophy is marked by explorations across traditional boundaries, for the disciplines we know today were still taking shape and the era of specialization and professionalization had not truly set in. Many of the thinkers covered here worked outside of the university setting and were thus less constrained by accepted standards of what does and does not count as philosophy.

These thirty chapters push the limits of the content that will fit in a single-volume companion, yet there are nonetheless significant omissions. On the thematic level, philosophy of religion and philosophy of history get shortchanged, given their importance for nineteenth-century thought as a whole. Both subjects are engaged in Michael Quante's essay on the young Hegelians, yet his essay is temporally and geographically restricted and thus does not survey the contributions throughout the century. I am also conscious that the Companion is heavily oriented towards German- and English-speaking philosophy. Certainly more French philosophy, as well as an engagement of Russian thought, would have been desirable. Even within the English-speaking world important thinkers were left out, especially those writing in a more literary style. I especially regret that the commissioned chapter on Emerson and Thoreau did not make it to publication.

2

I will let the chapters speak for themselves, since no summary would helpfully capture the incredible variety and depth of inquiry represented here. As a rough guide I will present six problems that provide some coherence or unity to the century's different strands of thought. These problems can all be traced back to Kant's critical philosophy. The shape in which they were inherited by the bulk of the nineteenth century was largely formed through Hegel's development of them. For each of the six problems, I will first give the rough outlines of the issue with reference to Kant and German Idealism. This will of course involve a good deal of simplification (as will be immediately apparent in reading the accounts of German Idealism in Part I of the Companion). In each case Kant's innovation was radicalized by Fichte and incorporated in that radicalized form into Hegel's system. The Hegelian project turned out to be quite fragile, as the radicality of the ideas at the heart of his method would seem to his successors inconsistent with the content of the developed system itself. In a second step, then, I will discuss briefly how philosophers after Hegel would be drawn towards two opposite extremes. We can roughly characterize these extremes in each case as *reductionism* and *constructivism* (I do not mean this term in the sense used by Kantian moral philosophers today). These extremes have often been associated with the thinkers covered in this volume, though usually in order to establish a caricature of the author's position than to genuinely understand it. Though no philosopher fully embraces these extremes, it is instructive to see how the extremes became attractive in the aftermath of German Idealism.

(1) Perhaps the most fundamental issue is how to negotiate the distinction between the natural and the normative. At the heart of Kant's theoretical philosophy is the idea that all thinking is judging, and that judgment is essentially normative, a matter of *correctly* employing concepts. In theoretical philosophy this contrast is most vivid as a contrast between receptivity and spontaneity in perception. On a version of the classical empiricist theory of knowledge, individuals stand in a straightforward causal relationship to perceived entities. We are exposed to impressions from the world that cause us to have the representations we have of those entities. This is a naturalist theory because it assumes that we register the world in quite the same way that any animal registers it, namely through dispositions to respond in certain ways to certain stimuli. On the contrasting picture advocated by Kant and radicalized by Fichte, what is given in experience is a manifold of intuition that is only discriminated (into objects, etc.) through the subject's activity of judging. An object in Kant's sense is the result of a synthesis by a subject of a sensory field (i.e., a manifold of intuition), where that field is "united" under a concept that picks out certain features as constituting that object. The activity of the subject is *spontaneous* in that it is not determined by the sensory inputs themselves, but has its source within the subject herself. Most importantly, it depends on the activity of self-consciousness, which in Kant goes by the name "the unity of apperception."

While Kant clearly maintained an element of receptivity in his account, Fichte and Hegel jettisoned the doctrine of sensible intuition, seemingly leaving all the work to the mind's spontaneous conceptual capacities. Their positions can seem radically *constructivist* in the sense that with nothing meaningful given by the world of sense, the mind must simply construct a world of concepts and objects for itself. This move makes *everything* normative, which means we alone are *responsible* for getting the world right. But it also seems to imply that our conceptual activity is *unconstrained* by the world, and thus seems to leave arbitrary and ungrounded just what getting it right means. When confronted by the extreme of the spontaneous subject imposing his concepts upon the world, a natural philosophical reaction is to go to the other extreme and embrace a kind of *reductionism* whereby causal interaction with the world is all that matters. Progress in the natural sciences over the course of the nineteenth century made such reductionism an increasingly attractive option to many.

(2) The second issue arises from the mind applying the natural/normative distinction to itself. Do the rules governing our judgment *describe* the operation of our minds, or do they hold, have normative validity, independent of their instantiation in brains like ours? This is the question of the relation of *psychology* and *logic*. Kant's transcendental logic certainly relied on an account of the faculties of the mind, and thus despite his emphasis on the normative he could justly be accused by Hegel of being a psychological idealist. Many philosophers today would not see this psychological aspect to be a liability. But given that the rational relations of logic are supposed to form a self-contained, and in some conceptions self-grounded, system of thought, it has seemed to many philosophers that logic should not be tied to the workings of the human brain. This contrast is clearest in thinking about mathematics, for mathematical truths (2 + 2 = 4) do not seem to depend on human psychology. Rules for other kinds of judgment are trickier, but the basic point remains the same. The opposing view, often labeled "psychologism," holds that a descriptive study of the workings of the human mind can determine standards of correctness.

Once again, on the logic–psychology question two extremes present themselves. One is to *reduce* logic and rationality to descriptive psychology and anthropology. On this view it is *because* our minds work in a certain way that various rules and norms have the validity that they do. The other extreme is a kind of Platonism in which concepts and numbers exist in another domain of truth independent of whether anyone ever thinks about them. This latter extreme can still be considered a kind of constructivism since we know the realm of truth only insofar as we can *construct* it with a self-consistent system/proof. While a psychological account held sway for much of the century, with Frege and the neo-Kantians the century closed on an emphatically anti-psychologistic note. The fundamental issue was not actually resolved, for it remains very much with us today, but the major options in the debate were explored for the first time.

(3) Kant claimed that we can only have knowledge in the strict sense of appearances, namely of what comes in the form of spatio-temporal intuition. We cannot make claims about substance, the soul, or God, comparable to our claims about the spatio-temporal world. Kant's claims certainly did not stop philosophers from doing metaphysics, but they did alter the character of that metaphysics. Fichte develops a metaphysics of subjectivity that reproduces metaphysical categories based on the activity of the I. The young Schelling would then use Fichte's innovation to reinterpret Spinoza's monism in post-Kantian terms. Hegel combined the fields of logic and metaphysics, claiming that Kant was right to free metaphysics from spatio-temporal conditions, but also maintaining that as logic, or an account of the categories

of thinking, metaphysics could continue its work. Having dismissed Kant's conception of things-in-themselves beyond the conditions of thought, Hegel could claim that his was as robust a metaphysics as we could desire.

The extremes on this issue have to do with the role of philosophy in relation to the natural sciences, on the one hand, and theology, on the other. On the *reductive* side, it could seem that philosophy henceforth is just a handmaiden to the natural sciences, clarifying the concepts used to study the spatio-temporal world. If the domain of facts in the extended world is all we have, it is a waste of time to think of anything beyond what can be verified by science. But, on the other side, one should always remember that Kant intended to "make room" for faith by restricting the domain of knowledge-claims. Science cannot rule out the claims of ethics and theology since those claims lie outside the domain of science (of knowledge in the strict sense of the term). So, at the other extreme, there is the possibility of *constructing* a theology beyond the world of science, and even beyond the realm of traditional metaphysics, since that metaphysics was infected in just the way Kant diagnosed in his Trascendental dialectic.

(4) Kant himself offered a way to make claims about the supersensible, namely through *practical philosophy*. Thus he invoked God and immortality as necessary postulates that derive from the moral law. Beyond these specific claims, Kant made freedom the "keystone" of his system, which thus appeared to be grounded as a whole on practical activity. This practical turn was then radicalized by Fichte, who takes the activity of the I as philosophy's first principle and the moral law as our only evidence for the reality of that principle. Fichte also conceives of his dialectical method as a series of experiments for the acting subject, and he famously implored his students from the lectern, "Act! Act!" While Hegel is often thought to absorb the practical into the theoretical, the activity of the I and of Spirit are also fundamental to his method. In the *Phenomenology of Spirit* in particular, Hegel follows the action of self-consciousness and Spirit as they pass through stages on the way to self-knowledge.

The idea that philosophy can only have a practical basis, given our inability to intuit theoretically the supersensible, found its clearest expression in the American pragmatists. The extreme constructivist side of this move to the practical is epitomized for many by William James' idea of a "will to believe," which seems to imply that belief and knowledge are simply up to our voluntary capacities. It would be the classic "analytic" paradigm of Moore and Russell that would go to the opposite extreme, and would succeed for half a century in suppressing attention to the pragmatist and idealist traditions. The reduction of philosophy to analysis of the meaning of concepts is about as far from the idea of grounding philosophy on ethics as one could get. Even Moore's *Principia Ethica*, a book on moral philosophy, makes practical judgment of the good look like a theoretical knowledge of a certain property. With the demise of classic analytic philosophy, practice-oriented idealism and pragmatism itself are now once again living options in philosophy.

(5) The shift towards practice brought another shift in its wake, namely away from the lone individual of Descartes' *Meditations* towards a *social conception of rationality*. Though there are elements of a social conception in Kant (the ethical common-wealth, the "common sense" of the *Critique of Judgment*), for the most part he supposed

that each individual is in possession of the same human reason and thus that each individual could be conceived as the locus of theoretical and practical rationality. One of Hegel's main innovations was to place the source of normativity in the community (this is the meaning of his shift from self-consciousness to Spirit). But this innovation seemed to come at a cost to the individual, who seemed to lose thereby the sense of independence that the Enlightenment had fought so hard to attain. After Hegel the individual–community relation becomes a central *problem* for philosophy, especially in the domains of ethical and political philosophy.

One extreme on this issue is the *reduction* of individual human beings to their social world, such that nothing remains for the individual to be other than a product of his environment. The rise of anthropology and of social theory that took individual agents to be unimportant in themselves was the theoretical correlate of the large-scale industrialization and the growing nationalism in Europe. At the political level American democracy seemed to threaten a "soft despotism" of the "tyranny of the majority," as Tocqueville put it. The reactions from the constructivist side of individualism to these developments were equally extreme. The birth of existentialism is a reaction against the hegemony of social conditioning. Nietzsche's claim for an overman who could create or reorder all values was a reaction to the threat of the "last man" and the herd mentality.

(6) If norms of thought and action are a function of social practice, they are clearly also bound to a specific time, leading to our final issue of *historicism*. The boundedness of knowledge by temporally specific horizons was not new with the nineteenth century. In most previous incarnations, however, the thesis was accompanied by the idea that the search for knowledge was futile or that the timeless truth was finally at hand. Even with Hegel's famous lines from the Preface to the *Philosophy of Right* that "every philosophy is a child of its times," and the "Owl of Minerva only flies at dusk," Hegel himself preserves the idea of a final truth finally discovered. Hegel's self-understanding would not hold, however, as his followers historicized his own thought after his death, and the ideas of radical contingency and finitude led to the characteristic nineteenth century melancholy pathos.

The extremes on this issue have to do not so much with the nature of the historicist claims (though there certainly is a wide variety there), but rather with the nature of the reaction to historicism. In Marx's hands historicism fueled the turn to a *revolutionary* task for philosophy. Though enough of a Hegelian to find a necessity in the course of previous history, the new goal for philosophy had to be revolutionary action rather than retrospective interpretation. At another extreme, Nietzsche saw in historicism the danger of nihilism, the loss of meaning. The reduction of every human existence to a temporally specific instant threatened to rob life of purpose. Nietzsche himself countered this threat with his difficult doctrines of *amor fati* (love of fate), and the eternal return of the same. These are ways of coming to terms with our temporality and finitude without the illusion that we can radically recreate the conditions of our being.

All of these issues persisted, sometimes above and sometimes below the surface of the increasingly professionalized philosophical debates of the twentieth century. Even the two most original thinkers of the early twentieth century, Heidegger and

Wittgenstein, were both deeply influenced by central figures and debates of the nineteenth century. The century's two main revisionary movements, ones that dominated Anglo-American philosophy for a good part of the century, British analytic philosophy and Austrian logical positivism, were both born from an engagement with German Idealism. Moore and Russell were reacting against the Hegelianism of the British idealists. Carnap and other logical positivists were relying on essentially neo-Kantian ideas. Both pragmatists in the United States and idealists in Britain were on the run for much of the twentieth century, but were both reborn in the last decades of the century following the criticism of the analytic paradigm by Quine and Sellars. Largely thanks to P. F. Strawson, Kant began to receive increasing scholarly attention, and thanks to Richard Rorty and Hilary Putnam (among others) pragmatism won new life. The ongoing work of Robert Brandom, to mention just one of the prominent recent inheritors of the tradition, resuscitates Hegel as a pragmatist in the service of a post-analytic semantics.

It is worth focusing so much on the German Idealist legacy in large part because the attitude towards Kant and Hegel have undergone so many striking reversals in the past 150 years. But the other story to tell is of the thinkers who have become so much a part of our philosophical culture that we hardly notice their influence. The works of Darwin, Frege, Mill, and Nietzsche form so much of the background of how we think of a host of issues that we often take their thought for granted. Other thinkers, especially Marx and Comte, represent movements whose heyday has passed, but whose central problems continue to resurface in ever more-pressing forms. If there is one thing that we realize now, at the outset of the twenty-first century, it is that the twentieth century largely deferred rather than resolved the central problems that were bequeathed to us by the Enlightenment and that were wrestled with in the nineteenth century. My hope is that on the basis of this companion, we can more self-consciously engage with those problems anew.

Part I
GERMAN IDEALISM

1

SELF-CONSCIOUSNESS, SYSTEM, DIALECTIC

Scott Jenkins

The problems that would shape early nineteenth-century European philosophy arose out of Immanuel Kant's realization, early in 1772, that his conception of metaphysics rested upon a problematic assumption. Two years earlier, upon his appointment to the chair of logic and metaphysics at the University of Königsberg, he had outlined his central philosophical views in his Inaugural Dissertation in which he distinguished between sensible knowledge and knowledge possible through pure thought, which he believed to be capable of disclosing the fundamental features of things and relations that are not themselves present to the senses. Like his rationalist predecessors, such as Leibniz and Wolff, Kant took for granted that we are capable of producing such a metaphysics. When he realized that this assumption stood in need of justification, the trajectory of modern European thought underwent a fundamental change. The *Critique of Pure Reason* was Kant's attempt to demonstrate that metaphysics is in fact possible. The work both introduced a new philosophical methodology and generated a radically new theory of knowledge and its limitations. The Idealist philosophers who followed Kant, figures such as Karl Reinhold, J. G. Fichte, Friedrich Schelling, and G. W. F. Hegel, all regarded the *Critique* as the starting point of philosophical activity. But while some saw the completion of Kant's project as the central task of philosophy, others saw in Kant's critical philosophy errors and ungrounded assumptions so significant that the method of the *Critique* had to be abandoned.

In this chapter, I begin with the emergence of Kant's new philosophical method in order to provide a context for the Idealist innovations that followed. I then consider, in part two, the work of Reinhold and Fichte, who regarded themselves as adhering to the spirit of Kant's critical philosophy while changing its central terms. In their work on the central Kantian notions of representation and self-consciousness, respectively, Reinhold and Fichte aim to provide a firm foundation for the claims of the first *Critique*. This project leads them to introduce into European thought radically new methodological ideals, such as systematicity in relation to a first principle of philosophy, which give rise to new methods of doing philosophy, such as phenomenological description. The work of Reinhold and Fichte also had a significant effect upon Hegel, and in the third part I consider how Hegel's rejection of the methodological assumptions of his predecessors can be seen as a development of the same basic concern about the possibility of metaphysics that led to Kant's *Critique*, twenty-five years earlier. In order to account for Hegel's turn to a new, dialectical method in philosophy, I consider in part three how his most innovative work, the *Phenomenology of Spirit*, can function as an argument for the claim that pure reason is not limited in its scope.

Kant's critical thought

In a letter to his friend Marcus Herz dated 21 February 1772, Kant states that his plan to produce a book to be entitled "The Limits of Sense and Reason" has been frustrated by the discovery that he, like all metaphysicians before him, had overlooked an essential problem of metaphysics. This problem, he says, can be summed up in the question, "What is the ground of the relation of that in us we call 'representation' to the object?" (Kant 1999: 133).[1] Kant notes that in some cases this question appears easy to answer. In perception, for example, there exists a causal relation between a subject's representation of an object and that object itself. The passive subject is affected by an object, resulting in a particular modification of the mind, one characteristic of subjects and objects of those particular kinds. Thus the product of this affection counts as a representation of the object, Kant asserts, due to the regular causal relation between objects of sensibility and the sensory capacities of the subject. We can also conceive of a relation of representation grounded in a causal relation in which the subject is causally active. God, for example, does not need to be affected by objects in order to have cognition of those objects. As an archetypal intellect, God's cognitions are immediately reality. Such a capacity does not exist in finite beings, however, and except in the case of agency our cognitions do not serve as archetypes for reality.

In light of these considerations, it would appear that sensory affection is the only ground of a relation of representation for finite subjects such as ourselves. Such a result would yield a generally empiricist account of mental content, according to which our thoughts relate exclusively to entities that can be presented to us in sensory experience. Kant was troubled by this result since he, like his rationalist predecessors, had taken for granted relations of representation that are not compatible with such an understanding of representational content. The objects of traditional metaphysical discourse, such as God and the soul, are not possible objects of sensory experience. Accordingly, if no ground of a relation of representation can be produced in the case of those mental entities Kant had previously termed "intellectual representations," then it is not at all clear that we have a right to regard those mental entities *as contentful representations*. They would, instead, be mere subjective determinations of the mind, and claims in which they appear would be lacking not just in empirical evidence, but in cognitive content.

Looking back on this period of thought, Kant in 1783 characterized himself as operating within a "dogmatic slumber" from which he awoke only with the assistance of David Hume's investigations into our notion of cause (Kant 1997b: 10). It was Hume, of course, who argued that the notion of a necessary connection between events has its origin in the subjective faculty of imagination. On his view, the human mind constructs the notion of a necessary connection between events only once we have observed the constant conjunction in space and time of events of particular kinds and come to anticipate that this regularity will continue in the future. The subjective ground of this feeling of anticipation, which Hume terms "custom," is thus the source of our tendency to expect that a stationary billiard ball, for example, will begin to roll across the table once it is struck by another billiard ball. Without such a subjective ground, we would not possess the notion of a necessary connection between objects. On this analysis, it is not at all clear what right we have to claim that there exist causal relations between objects. The notion of cause has its origin in a subjective mental tendency and seems to be nothing more than a way in which we are constrained to think of objects.

Kant's realization that he had been operating within a dogmatic slumber receives its first expression in the letter to Herz. There he states of the pure concepts of the understanding (by which he understands those concepts that do not arise from a sensible affection) "if such intellectual representations depend on our inner activity, whence comes the agreement that they are supposed to have with objects – objects that are nevertheless not possibly produced thereby?" (Kant 1999: 133). This question, he notes, was answered in a "merely negative way" in the Inaugural Dissertation, where he stated that intellectual representations are not the product of a sensible affection – they are instead "given in a fundamental fashion by the pure understanding itself" (Kant 1992: 406). But this answer of course fails to address the question of our *right* to assert that representations that are not products of sensible affection nevertheless relate to objects and can figure in contentful thought about those objects. As a result, a skepticism concerning the relation between our minds and the world threatens. While our distinctively metaphysical reflections might appear to make progress in elucidating the basic structure of existence, it appears that we have no right to assert that the basic concepts and axioms of that metaphysics are in fact contentful.

Kant's own scepticism did not last long, and in the letter to Herz he states that he has already succeeded in demonstrating that there exist mental entities that originate in the mind independent of any particular affection but nevertheless refer to objects. The demonstration of this result, he announced, would appear in the theoretical part of a work to be entitled the "Critique of Pure Reason." Its subject matter would, accordingly, be "the sources of metaphysics, its methods and limits" (Kant 1999: 135). Confident in his solution to the problem he had discovered, Kant states that he expects to publish his results in just three months. It would be nine years, however, until the first edition of the *Critique of Pure Reason* would appear in print. This so-called "decade of silence" was a result of the magnitude, and innovative nature, of Kant's task.

The method of Kant's Critique

In order to motivate the project of the *Critique of Pure Reason*, Kant begins his work with a preface to the reader designed to make clear the need for a consideration of the issues discussed in the letter to Herz. The question of the ground of the relation of a representation to its object – which in fact does not make an appearance in the *Critique* until the end of the Introduction to the work, and then only implicitly – is cast as the key to making progress in a self-examination of reason itself. And this self-examination, Kant thinks, is required by the sorry state of metaphysics in his time. While rationalists and empiricists continually disagree concerning the nature and limits of knowledge, no progress is made in resolving these disputes. Rationalists continue to employ metaphysical principles such as the principle of sufficient reason, empiricists deny the legitimacy of such principles, and philosophy continually falls short of its goal of generating a secure doctrine of knowledge. Consequently, Kant proposes to examine the faculty of reason as a means to resolving these endless disputes.

But how does one carry out such a critique of reason itself? While Kant has a compelling answer to this question, one that shaped the trajectory of philosophy through the nineteenth century, that answer is obscured, in part, by Kant's own attempts to make clear the revolutionary nature of his work. In the Preface to the second edition of the *Critique*, Kant likens his investigation to that of Copernicus, whose heliocentrism finally put the science of astronomy on a stable footing.

> We must … make trial whether we may not have more success in the tasks of metaphysics, if we suppose that objects must conform to our knowledge. This would agree better with what is desired, namely, that it should be possible to have knowledge of objects *a priori*, determining something in regard to them prior to their being given. We should then be proceeding precisely on the lines of Copernicus' primary hypothesis. (Bxvi)

There are at least three potential problems with Kant's analogy. First, Kant appears to be getting Copernicus exactly wrong. While Copernicus made progress in astronomy by assuming that Earth does not stand at the center of the universe, Kant's suggestion that we take up the hypothesis that objects conform to our knowledge seems to involve the opposite relation; it seems to put us at the center of the epistemological universe. A second, related worry concerns Kant's employment of the notion of knowledge, or cognition. Since our common understanding of knowledge involves the idea that something within us (a belief, image, etc.) corresponds to reality by conforming to reality, Kant's talk of an object conforming to our faculties of representation can sound like a perversion of that concept of knowledge. We tend to think that the world is the way it is, regardless of what we think of it, and that an inner state counts as a state of knowledge by matching up with the way the world is. Finally, Kant's presentation of his "Copernican revolution" should give one pause. The claim that objects conform to our representational capacities (and not the other way around) appears to be a mere assertion lacking any grounding. We might wonder, then, why we ought to employ just this assumption as a fundamental principle of metaphysics.

Kant has a response to all three worries, though as we will see, the third of these will reappear in various forms in the work of his successors. Taking them in order, Kant's understanding of Copernicus can be defended by considering the geocentric framework that Copernicus abandoned. On this view, the observed motion of celestial bodies is to be explained exclusively through appeal to their actual motion relative to the stationary Earth. A heliocentric model of the universe, on the other hand, requires that the observed motion of celestial bodies be explained, in part, through appeal to the Earth's revolution around the sun. Similarly, Kant's understanding of cognition requires that we abandon the assumption that the observed properties of objects are to be explained exclusively through appeal to properties that they possess in themselves. His new 'heliocentric' model of cognition explains our experience of objects in part through appeal to an activity of the subject, making the analogy with Copernicus' innovation rather apt.

The second worry concerning Kant's Copernican analogy – that Kant has perverted our concept of knowledge – involves a misunderstanding of Kant's notion of knowledge, or cognition (as some translators render the German "Erkenntnis"). If Kant were claiming that knowledge is a matter of the world conforming to whatever we happen to believe, he would indeed be employing a bizarre notion of knowledge. The claim is, rather, that the world, somehow, conforms to our cognitive capacities. Whether any empirical particular belief is true is always, Kant thinks, dependent upon the state of the world.

The final worry to consider concerns Kant's right to his new Copernican framework. Even if such a framework does make possible the distinctively metaphysical claims that Kant aims to establish, the question remains, Why should we assume that objects do conform to our representational capacities? We cannot, after all, judge the legitimacy of Kant's understanding of cognition through appeal to its epistemological consequences. In response, Kant would assert that his new, Copernican standpoint is both supported by independent argument and a part of a venerable philosophical tradition. In the first edition of the *Critique*, Kant praises the "celebrated Locke" who attempted a "*physiology of the human understanding*" designed to determine the scope of our knowledge (Aix). Convinced that it was a mistake to "let loose our thoughts into the vast ocean of Being" before we were assured that our understanding was suited to such inquiries, Locke proceeded to examine our capacities for understanding themselves (Locke 1959: 31). Similarly, Kant's goal in the *Critique* is to determine the legitimate domain of reason by considering the way in which the mind operates. His examination of our cognitive capacities is meant to establish that objects do in fact conform to those capacities, a conclusion that would both make possible distinctively metaphysical claims – claims that are both synthetic and *a priori* – and show the limits of metaphysics.

Kant terms this kind of knowledge of our cognitive faculties "transcendental" – a term he defines in the first edition of the *Critique* as follows: "I entitle *transcendental* all knowledge which is occupied not so much with objects as with our *a priori* concepts of objects in general" (A11). This definition is not immediately transparent, and to make matters worse, Kant altered this definition in the second edition of the *Critique*, yielding the following: "I entitle *transcendental* all knowledge which is occupied not so much with objects as with the mode of our knowledge of objects in so far as this mode of knowledge is to be possible *a priori*" (B25). While this change is instructive, Kant's philosophical methodology and plan for the *Critique* is much clearer if we consider the first edition definition alone. To begin with, it should be clear that Kant is attempting to separate his investigation into reason from metaphysics proper, a commitment evident in his statement that transcendental knowledge is concerned "not so much" with objects. Kant does not mean to put forward a doctrine of objects such as God, the world whole, or the soul, since the possibility of such doctrines is precisely what is in question. Instead, Kant means to examine the mental entities that make possible thought about such entities, which he terms "concepts of objects in general." It is essential to note that in this definition Kant is not using the term "concept" with the narrow sense that the term takes on later in the work, where it picks out a mental representation that is general and a product of the intellect. The term "concept," in the definition of "transcendental," is synonymous with "representation," and Kant's proposal is to examine those representations of objects that we possess *a priori*, that is, independent of any particular experience.

The central aims of the *Critique* are to demonstrate that there do exist *a priori* representations and to determine their role in our cognition. If the project were to fail – that is, if Kant could find no argument establishing the existence of *a priori* representations – then there would exist no transcendental knowledge. All of our representations would then be a product of experience, and we would be left with empiricism. Following the letter to Herz, such a result would obviously provide us with a basis for maintaining the contentfulness of many representations. They would relate to their objects as effect to cause. However, an empiricism such as Hume's is obviously incompatible with metaphysical claims of the sort that Kant aimed to establish (such as a doctrine of universal causation).

If there in fact exist *a priori* representations, then some central empiricist doctrines are false. But such a result would not yet establish Kant's Copernican revolution, because it must be demonstrated, in addition, that objects *conform* to those representations. And at this point, the problem that Kant sketched in his letter to Herz comes to the fore. The central challenge is to demonstrate that *a priori* representations, which exist in the mind independent of any particular experience, are not merely subjective constraints on our thinking. They must be shown that they relate to objects by virtue of the fact that objects conform to those representations. And because they cannot relate to objects as cause to effect – after all, we are not gods, capable of bringing objects into existence merely by thinking of them – it is mysterious how an *a priori* representation could nevertheless relate to an object. Kant's second-edition definition of transcendental knowledge gives us a preview of his strategy for demonstrating that *a priori* representations nevertheless relate to objects. His talk of *a priori* conditions of our mode of knowledge (or cognition) of objects suggests that he intends to show that at least some *a priori* representations are a condition of our cognition of objects.

The execution of Kant's Copernican revolution

The structure of the *Critique* is easy to understand in light of this rough sketch of Kant's intentions. The bulk of the work, what Kant terms the "Doctrine of Elements," is divided into two main parts, a "Transcendental Aesthetic" dealing with *a priori* representations of sensibility, and a "Transcendental Logic" dealing with *a priori* representations of the intellect. The latter division is further divided into a "Transcendental Analytic" and a "Transcendental Dialectic," yielding three main parts of the *Critique*. Each of these has the same structure. Kant first demonstrates that there exist *a priori* representations associated with a particular faculty of the mind and then proceeds to examine the role played by those representations in our cognition of objects. As we will see, Kant concludes that while some representations play a constitutive role in our cognition of objects, others do not.

The question remains, How exactly does Kant respond to the problem he first expressed in the letter to Herz? The following passage from the *Critique*, reminiscent of his letter nine years earlier, outlines Kant's answer: "There are only two possible ways in which synthetic representation and its objects can establish connection, obtain necessary relation to one another, and, as it were, meet one another. Either the object alone must make the representation possible, or the representation alone must make the object possible" (A92/B124–5). The causal relation between a subjective entity and an object that grounds the relation of representation in the letter to Herz is here replaced by talk of "making possible." Kant draws attention to this change by noting that the representation "does not produce its object in so far as *existence* is concerned." He then continues, "... the representation is *a priori* determinant of the object, if it be the case that only through the representation is it possible to *know* anything *as an object*" (A92/B125). How are we to understand talk of "making possible" an object of representation, if not as a causal relation?

Kant's view is perhaps easiest to grasp in connection with his discussion of sensibility in the Transcendental Aesthetic. There Kant argues that our representations of space and of time are *a priori* and make possible our experience of objects. While the details of this argument lie beyond the scope of this essay, the two stages of Kant's argument are easy to sketch. First, Kant attempts to show that there exist *a priori* representations associated with sensibility by arguing that our representations of space and time could not be acquired empirically through attending to spatial or temporal relations. The representation of such relations is possible, Kant maintains, only within a representation of a space or time in which such relations obtain. And since Kant assumes that any account of empirical acquisition must appeal to an experience of spatial or temporal relations, all such accounts are circular. If we are persuaded by Kant's argument, we must conclude that our representations of space and time are *a priori* representations (of a sort Kant terms intuitions). This conclusion leads directly to the second major claim of the Aesthetic, that our *a priori* representations of space and time *make possible* the objects of sensible awareness. Insofar as all objects of perception are spatial, and space is an *a priori* representation that determines the form of all perception of objects, the objects we experience are essentially determined by our representational capacities. This does not mean that our perception creates its objects; Kant is careful to emphasize that the objects of perception are empirically real. They are nevertheless *transcendentally* ideal since they are, nevertheless, dependent upon our *a priori* representational capacities.

Much of Kant's critical account of space and time was already present in his 1770 Inaugural Dissertation. The strikingly new element in the *Critique of Pure Reason* is

9

Kant's attempt, in the Transcendental Logic, to extend his account of the objective validity of *a priori* sensible representations (i.e. space and time) to the case of intellectual representations. He concludes that only some of those representations, twelve *a priori* concepts of the understanding he terms "categories," actually have objective validity. Other intellectual representations, termed the "ideas" of reason, cannot be demonstrated to have any objective validity and thus play only a regulative role in thought. This distinction is grounded in Kant's argument for the claim that only the categories do in fact *make possible* objects of our cognition. Showing that this is the case is the task of Kant's Transcendental Deduction of the Categories, an argument modeled on the notion of a legal deduction, which was common in Kant's time (Henrich 1989). The argument is intended to convince the reader of our right to claim that intellectual representations that have their origin in the mind alone are nevertheless valid of objects.

The challenge of the Deduction can be appreciated through considering two points. First, Kant argues for the existence of the categories by considering the various forms of judgment constitutive of our thought. This "Metaphysical Deduction" establishes that any being that judges as we do will also employ the categories in any thought whatsoever. Second, Kant notes that a quite natural notion of sense experience makes mysterious any *a priori* agreement between the objects of experience and these *a priori* forms of thought.

> That objects of sensible intuition must conform to the formal conditions of sensibility which lie *a priori* in the mind is evident, because otherwise they would not be objects for us. But that they must likewise conform to the conditions which the understanding requires for the synthetic unity of thought, is a conclusion the grounds of which are by no means so obvious. Appearances might very well be so constituted that the understanding should not find them to be in accordance with the conditions of its unity. Everything might be in such confusion that, for instance, in the series of appearances nothing presented itself which might yield a rule of synthesis and so answer to the concept of cause and effect. The concept would then be altogether empty, null, and meaningless. (A90/B122–3)

Since it appears that our capacity for sense experience is in no way dependent upon our intellectual capacities, the project of demonstrating the objective validity of subjective intellectual representations would seem to be doomed. Kant's challenge is, accordingly, to demonstrate that our prereflective notion of sense experience is false. It must be the case that appearances *cannot* be so constituted that the understanding would not find them to be in accordance with *a priori* forms of thought, such as the concept of cause.

The Transcendental Deduction aims to establish this conclusion through demonstrating that essential features of our experience would not be possible unless appearances conform to our subjective conditions of thought. The argument itself is incredibly complex and abstract, and to make matters even more challenging Kant completely rewrote the argument for the second edition of the *Critique*. Nevertheless, it is possible to isolate and describe two strands in Kant's anti-empiricist argument. In places, especially in the first-edition Deduction, the argument appears to turn on the notion of an object of representation. That sensibility offers up to us distinct entities that admit of comparison in thought already presupposes, Kant argues, that those entities have been combined, ordered, or "synthesized" in accordance with our *a priori* concepts, the categories. Even space and time, as *a priori* intuitions, are subject to the categories as conditions under which they appear to us unified, divisible entities. Thus any appearances in space and time must be subject to the categories, and the most basic sensory experience that all empiricists take for granted already presupposes the activity of the intellect which makes possible the objects of experience.

In both editions of the deduction Kant indicates that this argumentative strategy must be supplemented by another, which employs the premise that all of our sensory experience is the experience of a self-conscious subject. The relation between these two premises in the deduction is a matter of dispute, but many commentators see the self-consciousness as the starting point of any plausible deduction of the categories (see Henrich [1994] for a clear statement of this position). Regardless of how we understand the relation between these two premises, it should be clear that appeal to self-consciousness can also serve as the starting point in an anti-empiricist argument. All empiricists take for granted self-conscious experience of objects, and if self-consciousness requires that those objects of awareness conform to our *a priori* concepts the categories' objective validity is established. Kant's formulation of this premise is clearest in the second edition of the *Critique*: "It must be possible for the 'I think' to accompany all of my representations …" (B131). By this Kant means that it must be possible for a subject to attend to its states *as* its own states. It is essential to note that Kant does not maintain that we are explicitly aware of all of our mental states as our own states; his talk of the necessity of the *possibility* of ascribing all of our states to ourselves is compatible with there being states that we as a matter of fact do not self-ascribe.

My concern here is not with the details of Kant's notion of self-consciousness, but instead with the role played by this notion of self-consciousness in Kant's attempt to demonstrate the objective validity of the categories. The deduction proceeds by considering the conditions under which the ascription of diverse representations to an identical subject is possible. Kant argues that because we have no direct, inner awareness of a subject of representations, awareness of the identity of the subject requires that we combine our representations in one act of thought. Such combination must take place according to *a priori* rules of thought, however, since only *a priori* rules could guarantee the ability to make a transition from one total representational state to another. At this point Kant is able to appeal to his theory of judgment in order to argue that in the case of beings such as ourselves, those rules just are the forms of judgment with their associated *a priori* concepts, the categories. From this point the conclusion of the deduction is relatively easy to attain. As noted above, our unified representations of space and time are themselves subject to the categories, from which follows the anti-empiricist conclusion that the categories apply to all objects given in sensibility. In other words, no objects of awareness are merely given since our *a priori* concepts *make possible* the objects of self-conscious experience. Due to the relation of dependence between these objects and our mental capacities, Kant's position is an idealist one. But since those capacities merely make such objects possible, Kant terms his view *transcendental* idealism.

Kant's deduction of the categories enables him to enumerate a collection distinctively metaphysical (i.e. synthetic *a priori*) judgments valid of objects of experience, which judgments he terms "principles." For example, from the fact that the category of cause and effect is constitutive of objects of experience he concludes that any change in state of an object occurs in accordance with a causal law. All such judgments rest upon the claim, established in the deduction, that "the conditions of the *possibility of experience* in general are likewise conditions of the *possibility of the objects of experience*, and for this reason they have objective validity in a synthetic *a priori* judgment" (A158/B197). Thus Kant has shown how metaphysics is possible, and the remainder of the *Critique* is dedicated to demonstrating its limits. Having shown how *a priori* representations make possible objects of experience, Kant concludes that metaphysical judgments are limited to such "appearances" or "phenomena." While we can certainly conceive of entities that are not possible objects of experience, such as God, or the world as it is in itself, independent of our representational capacities, we can have no knowledge of entities that are not objects of sensible intuition. Kant refers to such objects as "noumena" in order to emphasize that they are *merely* objects of thought, which is to say that they are not entities about which anything can be known and thus are not legitimate topics of metaphysical investigation. Such things – termed "things-in-themselves" – constitute a limit on the legitimate realm of reason.

This conclusion shapes Kant's examination of the final class of *a priori* representations he locates in the mind. These are the so-called "concepts of reason," or as Kant terms them, "ideas" of the soul, of a world whole, and of God. Since God, freedom, and immortality constitute a significant part of traditional metaphysics, Kant's limitation of knowledge to appearances serves to exclude from the realm of metaphysics much of its previous territory. Kant would, of course, assert that ceding this territory is a small price to pay for the assurance that metaphysics rests on the firm foundation supplied by transcendental philosophy, and his investigation into the role played by these ideas in our thought also serves to alleviate worries concerning our right to employ these ideas in our thought. While we cannot, strictly speaking, have any knowledge concerning these entities, Kant believes that the idea of a world whole, for example, serves a regulative function in our thought by providing us with a goal for our scientific investigation into the world. And in the practical realm, the ideas play an even more significant role. In the *Critique of Practical Reason*, Kant abides by the limits on knowledge established in the *Critique of Pure Reason* but also aims to establish a "primacy of the practical" through demonstrating that our practical, moral interest in the existence of God, freedom, and the soul gives us a right to believe in the existence of these entities (Kant 1997a: 100). Nevertheless, our *knowledge* is limited, as theoretical reason is limited in accordance with the results of the first *Critique*.

Throughout Kant's critical philosophy that followed upon the *Critique of Pure Reason*, he aimed to elucidate the knowledge possible for us within the constraints established in the first *Critique*. As we will see, Kant's Idealist successors believed that he actually showed the possibility, or even the necessity of transcending those limits. Nevertheless, it would be a mistake to regard Kant's aim in his critical system as anything other than the application to other areas of thought of the theory of cognition and its constraints established in the first *Critique*. To be sure, Kant does at times take distinctively metaphysical judgments for granted in order to illustrate for the reader how such judgments are possible. The "analytic" method of the *Prolegomena to Any Future Metaphysics*, for example, aims to make clear how Kant's views on cognition account for the right we assume we have to synthetic *a priori* judgments in mathematics and natural science (Kant 1997b: 13, 118). This method is opposed to the "synthetic" method of the first *Critique* which cannot, of course, take for granted any right to synthetic *a priori* judgments since the possibility of metaphysics is originally in question. This synthetic method, and the results of the *Critique of Pure Reason*, set the agenda for the Idealism that followed Kant.

The first stage of Idealism: Grounding the *Critique*

Kant's development of his critical system set the stage for an unprecedented enthusiasm concerning the prospects for philosophy. While Kant worked to extend the theory of cognition of the first *Critique* to the spheres of ethics, aesthetics, and teleology, his successors recognized the importance of his revolution in method and believed that the essential features of an enduring philosophical system could be laid out in short order. Thus there arose a race, of sorts, to complete philosophy on the foundation established by Kant. Kant himself was suspicious of the work of his Idealist successors, and even went so far as to declare publicly that he viewed Fichte's system of philosophy as "totally indefensible" (Kant 1999: 559). The system in question was Fichte's attempt to provide a firm foundation for Kantian thought, which in his view was lacking in the *Critique* itself. This worry appeared first in the work of Karl Leonhard Reinhold, which constitutes the first step in the development of German Idealism.

The concept of representation

Reinhold's *Letters on the Kantian Philosophy* were largely responsible for introducing Kantian thought to the late eighteenth-century intellectual scene. Primarily a supporter of the critical philosophy, Reinhold aims in his letters to demonstrate its consistency with traditional ethical and religious thought. In these letters there is also a hint of Reinhold's most important contribution to post-Kantian philosophical methodology, his attempt at providing a sure foundation for the critique of reason itself. This foundation was to be found in the concept of representation, which as we have seen plays a central role in Kant's notion of transcendental philosophy. Reinhold believed that if this notion did not admit of elucidation, the *Critique* as a whole rested on shaky ground. Reinhold's attempt to make clear what had been obscure in Kant's work thus began the attempt to complete philosophy on Kantian terms.

In the *Critique* Kant does make a number of illuminating remarks concerning the notion of representation. He distinguishes between "pure," or *a priori*, representations that owe nothing to sensation and those that are, in part, products of affection (A20/B34). He also provides a taxonomy of representations, both implicitly, in his arguments for the existence of particular *a priori* representation types that open the three parts of the Doctrine of Elements, and explicitly, in a division of the genus of a representation in general (A320/B376–7). Reinhold recognizes these features of Kant's work and praises them in his *Foundation of Philosophical Knowledge* (Reinhold 2000: 62), but he worries that in taking for granted the notion of representation itself Kant fails to provide the kind of foundation for metaphysics he was seeking. Kant's transcendental philosophy, with its distinction between objects of cognition and the forms of cognition itself, would be completed on Reinhold's view only once we "proceed from the concept of representation as such, and exhaustively identify its essential characteristics ..." (Reinhold 2000: 69). Such an account of representation would determine what the species of representation have in common, in virtue of which they can form the subject matter of Kant's "special science" of transcendental philosophy. We might think of Reinhold as aiming to make as clear as possible the limits of the domain of discourse for transcendental philosophy. This process would enable the transcendental philosopher to elucidate the difference between metaphysical discourse and the claims of transcendental philosophy, which are "not so much" about objects (A11). Doing so would also have the added benefit of presenting the essential aspects of Kant's thought in a new, scientific form, with all of the central assumptions of the work resting on a single claim concerning the nature of representation.

Reinhold's search for a first principle of philosophy

Reinhold believed that he was in possession of a single principle upon which philosophy can rest. He expresses that principle, the "principle of consciousness," as the claim that "in consciousness representation is distinguished through the subject from both object and subject and is referred to both" (Reinhold 2000: 70). This principle is not immediately intelligible, and Reinhold never provides a detailed discussion of its sense. As we will see, this feature of Reinhold's work is explained, at least in part, by his views concerning philosophical methodology. But there are two aspects of the principle that should be comprehensible in light of Kant's views in his Transcendental Deduction. First, Reinhold's talk of the subject referring a representation to itself should bring to mind the central premise of the deduction, the necessity of the possibility of self-ascribing representations. The role played by the subject in producing representations that have objective purport can also be seen in Reinhold's proposition in the relation of representation to its object, which is due to the subject. Of course, many questions remain – What kind of referring is in play here? What is meant by "subject" or "object"? – and in addition, we might wonder whether the principle is terribly original, given its connection with the central tenets of Kant's

Critique. Nevertheless, the methodological function of the principle is innovative and constitutes Reinhold's central contribution to questions of methodology in post-Kantian thought.

Reinhold's understanding of the role that the principle of consciousness is to play in his work is rooted in a concern shared with many of his successors, namely that Kant's first *Critique* relies upon claims that are borrowed from elsewhere (e.g. that there are twelve forms of judgment) or assumed with no right (e.g. that experience begins with affection). This concern might be expressed more generally as relating to the very possibility of a critique of reason. It might seem that such a critique must either begin with definitions and empirical claims alone (which would make impossible any progress in such a critique) or with contentful claims concerning consciousness, self-consciousness, or objectivity (which would themselves stand in need of a new critical assessment). Kant's awareness of these worries appears in the *Critique* itself in his insistence, for example, that the self-ascription principle that serves as the premise for the Transcendental Deduction of the categories is, in fact, analytic (B135). Reinhold likely regarded such claims an inadequate and unnecessary due to the fact that it is possible to begin with a proposition that is neither a definition nor an empirical claim. And while it may appear that such a claim stands in need of justification, just as Kant's synthetic *a priori* principles do, Reinhold nevertheless maintains that the principle of consciousness need not be justified through a kind of meta-critique.

Reinhold believes that his proposition of consciousness can be both contentful and self-evidently true since it, and it alone, serves only to express a basic fact of consciousness familiar to any subject of experience. Our "consciousness of an *actual fact* [Tatsache]" is the true starting point of Reinhold's system (Reinhold 2000: 70); all philosophy is to proceed from this fact, as expressed in the principle of consciousness, giving rise to a well-grounded doctrine of knowledge and experience. Reinhold goes so far as to label the proposition of consciousness "self-determined" in order to draw attention to the fact that in order to serve its function as the starting point of all philosophy it must be impossible, strictly speaking, for any other claim to be offered in support of the proposition. It must be self-evident. This fact explains Reinhold's reluctance to provide an extended discussion of the sense of the proposition of consciousness; if it is the kind of principle that Reinhold claims it to be, no such discussion should be necessary. Furthermore, if the principle were to gain support from an appeal to logic, language, or empirical psychology, such support would immediately disqualify the proposition as a first principle of philosophy. Thus Reinhold maintains that "it is not through any inference of reason" that we know the principle of consciousness to be true (Reinhold 2000: 70). Mere reflection upon the "actual fact" of consciousness, which involves the process of "ordering together [*Vergleichung*]" what is found in this reflection, is to provide the philosopher with a basis for the principle of consciousness. Thus, the true starting point of Reinhold's so-called Philosophy of the Elements is the fact expressed by the principle of consciousness, not the principle itself.

The only way to gain a more complete understanding of the proposition is to consider what follows from it, and if Reinhold's project is to have any hope, the proposition of consciousness must have as its consequences all of the grounding assumptions of the critical philosophy. It must show not only that the mind is best regarded as a "faculty of representation" but that representations have particular properties. It must, for example, underlie Kant's assertion in the Transcendental Aesthetic that the matter of our experience, sensation, is a product of affection by an object, while the formal qualities of experience such as its spatiotemporal structure are due to the mind alone. It should also provide a foundation for Kant's distinction between sensibility and the intellect. And in fact, Reinhold believes that he can derive all of these assumptions. Most of Reinhold's contemporaries found these derivations obscure, but the principle of consciousness itself, and Reinhold's project of providing a foundation for philosophical reflection, had a profound effect on the development of Idealist thought.

Fichte's first principle

J. G. Fichte picked up the challenge of completing Kantian philosophy and, strangely enough, arrived at a very different first principle of philosophy primarily through his attempt to defend Reinhold's work against the attack of G. E. Schulze, a self-proclaimed skeptic who wrote under the pseudonym "Aenesidemus" (a name often used to denote the work as well). Schulze was not concerned so much with Reinhold's attempt to provide a systematic form for the critical philosophy, but rather with the nature of the claims that figure in that attempt. His central charge in this context is that in order to describe their most basic theoretical views both Reinhold and Kant must make use of concepts such as causation, thereby employing the concept in a manner that the first *Critique* itself classifies as illegitimate. Schulze states of Reinhold's work, for example, that "by deriving actual representations from a faculty which it takes to be something objectively actual, and by defining it as the cause of the representations, contradicts its own principles as well as the results of the *Critique of Reason*" (Schulze 2000: 109). The charge is serious since Reinhold's first principle, as the ultimate ground of Kantian thought, certainly cannot beg any questions concerning our right to employ the concept of cause.

Schulze assumes that in order for us to make sense of Reinhold's claim that the human faculty of representation does anything at all, we must think of it as an actual thing with causal powers. Doing so of course requires that we employ the categories, so it would be surprising if Reinhold had made just this mistake. In fact, Reinhold at times goes out of his way to emphasize that his remarks on the faculty of representation should not be understood in this way (though his work does occasionally lend the impression that the faculty of representation is a peculiar sort of thing). In the second edition of Reinhold's *Letters*, published two years before Schulze's attack, he states that a theory of the capacities of a representing subject "is not a science of representing *power* and even less a science of the *substance* to which the mere faculty of representation belongs" (Reinhold 2005: 200). In other words, Reinhold does not intend his remarks about representational capacities as metaphysical claims; they are neutral with regard to the ontological status of that which represents. Thus, like Kant's transcendental claims, they are "not so much" about objects (to use Kant's phrase from the definition of transcendental knowledge). In his review of *Aenesidemus* Fichte makes just this point in a more confrontational manner, describing Schulze as one who "as soon as he hears the words 'faculty of representation,' can think only of some sort of thing (round or square?) which exists as a thing in itself, *independently of its being represented*, and indeed, exists as a thing which *represents*" (Fichte 1988: 66–7). Nevertheless, Fichte's defense of Reinhold is limited. Due to lingering doubts concerning the relation between the principle of consciousness and the fact it is said to express, he asserts that no mere fact of consciousness can underlie our tendency to assent to the principle. All such facts are objects of empirical observation, and the validity of the principle simply could not be grounded in an act of abstraction from a set of such facts.

His project of understanding the authority of the principle of consciousness leads Fichte to a set of claims that would underlie his own system of philosophy. First, he maintains in the review of *Aenesidemus* that the principle of consciousness must be grounded in, and derivable from, a still more basic principle. And to the question of how *this* principle is to be grounded, he maintains that "...such a principle does not have to express a fact; it can also express an Act [*Tathandlung*]" (Fichte 1988: 64). Fichte's coinage of the term "*Tathandlung*" – which could be translated as act, actual deed, or fact-act – is motivated by the desire to deny that the first principle of philosophy could express a mere fact present to reflection. He offers a partial explanation of this new vocabulary in his claim that the subject is never merely given to itself in empirical intuition, but is instead "posited" intellectually. In expressing himself in this way Fichte has adopted distinctively logical vocabulary; one says that a judgment is posited when, for example, it is taken to follow from premises that one accepts. Fichte is thus denying that the most basic relation of a subject to itself is the generally observational relation we find in Reinhold. While he certainly would not deny that there are self-conscious states in which we simply find ourselves in a determinate state, with all of its associated facts, he means to deny that this is the most basic relation of a subject to itself. In place of this generally reflective model of self-consciousness, Fichte offers us a picture of a subject as originally relating to itself, even creating itself.

Fichte's self-positing doctrine constitutes a significant change in our understanding of the nature of self-consciousness, one that he believes most of us will resist. He goes so far as to state that most people would rather regard themselves as a "piece of lava in the moon" than as a subject, or a self-positing 'I' (Fichte 1970: 175); a piece of lava in the moon is, after all, a thing, a possible object of observation. But Fichte believes that an understanding of subjectivity as self-positing is necessary both for a proper understanding of subjectivity and for the possibility of generating a system of philosophy (for the details of Fichte's views on self-consciousness see the second chapter in this volume). His own attempt to provide a foundation for philosophy, in his *Groundwork of the Entire Doctrine of Science*, starts with the familiar claim that philosophy must begin with a principle that does not admit of proof. In this case, the principle serves only to express this basic positing activity of the subject. This principle is "the self [or, the 'I'] begins by an absolute positing of its own existence"

(Fichte 1970: 99). Fichte proceeds by deriving from this principle two additional principles, which are conditioned by the first and together with it are to generate the entire foundation of philosophy. These two principles are that the 'I' posits a not-I in opposition to itself, and that the 'I' also posits in itself a divisible 'not-I' that is opposed to its divisible self. By this Fichte means to say that the mere act of self-positing is incomplete and thus impossible without these additional acts of positing, or equivalently, that the self-positing principle has these two additional principles as its immediate consequences. Of course, Fichte's method suggests a number of questions, foremost among them a question concerning the nature of the derivation of these two further principles from the original one. Their relation is familiar to any Kantian, since Kant's Transcendental Deduction of the categories aims to show that from the mere idea of self-consciousness we can derive the claims that our experience is of objects, and that this objective experience is a result of the subject's activity. But of course Fichte cannot appeal to Kant in order to justify these transitions. His three principles are supposed to underlie Reinhold's principle of consciousness, and thus the notion of representation in general, and true to his intention Fichte offers a derivation of representation later in the *Groundwork*. Since Reinhold's principle is still more basic that Kant's starting point in the deduction, Fichte's methodology can appear mysterious.

Fichte does offer the reader some account of these crucial transitions in the *Foundations* of the Entire Science of Knowledge. In the case of the second principle he maintains that it is conditioned by the first as to its content, while the second is conditioned as to its form. This is likely meant to indicate that while the second principle introduces a new element into the activity of self-positing, the third only specifies the relation between subject and object. Fichte also introduces distinctively logical notions into his derivation of these principles, claiming a relation between the first principle and the logical relation A=A, for example. But these considerations are not sufficient to generate the second and third principles of Fichte's system, and in fact, Fichte would likely admit that no appeal to logic or notions of matter and form can make possible the progress from the first principle that he has in mind. Since the progress in principles is supposed to mirror acts of the positing subject, it is to those acts themselves that we must turn in order to understand Fichte's methodology.

The emergence of phenomenology

While Fichte and Reinhold disagree concerning the nature of the first principle of philosophy and its relation to the notion of representation, they share a methodological assumption that plays a significant role in Hegel's thought and influenced philosophy well beyond the nineteenth century. In insisting that philosophy must begin with a principle that expresses some feature of our experience, both Fichte and Reinhold are engaging in a process that is explicitly phenomenological. However we understand the relation between a first principle and the fact or act that it expresses, the principle is taken to be valid solely in virtue of some manifest quality of the subject that is engaged in philosophical reflection.

This emphasis on describing experience in general does not arise from nowhere. In the first *Critique* Kant follows Locke's model and often appeals to examples of particular experiences or acts, such as the act of drawing a line in thought, in order to motivate his claims concerning the acts of the mind that underlie consciousness and self-consciousness. Furthermore, Kant often notes that he understands the *Critique* on analogy with a lawyer's argument to a judge or jury (Axxi, Bxiii, A84/B116). His thought is that we, his readers, must test his claims against our own experience in order to judge the *Critique* as a whole, just as a judge or juror must appeal to her own experience in human affairs in order to determine the plausibility of a particular construal of the evidence in a court case. Similarly, Reinhold's account of the fact of consciousness is plausible only if his readers find such a fact within themselves.

These considerations point to a way of understanding the very abstract opening moves of Fichte's *Foundations*. Fichte's goal there can be regarded as the production of a series of experiences in the reader, experiences which themselves warrant the assertion of the second and third principles that serve to structure the rest of the *Foundations*, including the derivation of the notion of representation. That the 'I' posits in opposition to itself a 'not-I' would then find its support in the felt insufficiency of the first principle concerning the self-positing activity of the 'I.' We, as readers of Fichte, would simply come to recognize the validity of the second and third principles in virtue of being led to have the right experience. (In this context it should also be kept in mind that Fichte's *Foundations* derives from a set of notes for his students in Jena and would have been supplemented by personal engagement with Fichte himself.) But Fichte must regard this appeal to experience in general as compatible with the naïve reader's unwillingness to agree with his doctrine of subjectivity. He believes, after all, that most of us are much more comfortable thinking of ourselves as moon rocks than as self-positing subjects. Thus Fichte's method anticipates the views of Martin Heidegger, for example, who as an existential phenomenologist maintains both that philosophy begins with description and that we systematically misdescribe our own experience. Unlike Heidegger, Fichte does not aim to uncover the motivation behind a tendency to misdescribe and thus misunderstand ourselves. Instead, he simply aims to combat it through guiding his readers through the acts that underlie the principles of his work. One gets a sense for this aspect of Idealist thought through considering passages such as the following, from Fichte's applied work in ethics.

> The easiest way to guide someone toward learning to think and to understand the concept I in a determinate manner is as follows: think for yourself of some object, e.g., the wall in front of you, your desk, or something similar. In doing this you undoubtedly assume a thinker or thinking subject [*ein Denkendes*], and this thinker is you yourself. (Fichte 2005: 24)

Fichte's goal here is clearly to provide the reader with a sense for the concept I through directing the reader to consider the activity of thinking that exists, but is often overlooked, in the most mundane acts of thought. His assumption is that we know very well what is designated by "I" but nevertheless have trouble associating the term with its referent. This is not to say that simple thought exercises such as this are sufficient for us to become acquainted with all mental acts and entities; like many twentieth-century phenomenologists, he believes that training and practice are required in order for us to attend to the phenomena in a responsible manner. Furthermore, such exercises cannot be sufficient to guide the reader to the first principle of the *Foundations*. The activity described there cannot be the object of inner awareness since it is that which is to make possible all awareness. It must be only implicit in other mental acts. Nevertheless, Fichte believes that all of his central claims can be grounded by the philosopher through attending to his own acts and experiences. This is what Fichte primarily has in mind when he insists that claims concerning the 'I' are valid only for the 'I' itself, or that the 'I' is what it is only *for itself*. This peculiarity concerning claims about the subject of experience lead Fichte to speak of there being, in subjectivity, a "double series of being and seeing" (Fichte 1970: 17). While objects merely *are*, an I, or a subject, is what it is *for itself*, instantiating the double series that makes possible the unique awareness that grounds Fichte's methodology. Thus it is certainly difficult to draw a strict line between the method that Fichte employs and his denial that talk of facts of consciousness does justice to subjectivity, a peculiarity that will resurface in Hegel's account of the method of the *Phenomenology of Spirit*.

Fichte on the unity of theoretical and practical philosophy

In considering the multiplicity of acts required for the mere self-positing of the subject, Fichte arrives at the conclusion that self-positing has a distinctively practical dimension. This claim takes a number of different forms over the course of Fichte's development, and Fichte provides us with at least two different accounts of why a self-conscious subject must be, in some sense, practical. In the *Foundations* he argues that we can understand the limit between the 'I' and 'not-I' only as the result of a check on an activity characteristic of the subject. Objectivity, he claims, is fundamentally a practical phenomenon. As Fichte puts it:

> The result of our inquiry so far is therefore as follows: in relation to a possible object, the pure self-reverting activity of the self is a striving; and as shown earlier, an infinite striving at that. This boundless striving, carried to infinity, is the condition of the possibility of any object whatsoever; no striving, no object. (Fichte 1970: 231)

Even representation, he later argues, rests on this basic activity of striving. In connection with Fichte's critique of Reinhold, this claim suggests that we ought to understand the striving doctrine as a development of Fichte's original claim that we cannot understand subjectivity without employing the notion of an activity or deed (*Tathandlung*). So understood, the claim bears a strong resemblance to Kant's thesis that a self-consciousness requires the acts of judgment involved in self-ascription and objective representation. But Fichte is also clear that he understands this practical dimension of self-positing as entailing that a subject must have a will, be embodied, and find itself subject to norms of ethics and right.

These claims figure prominently in Fichte's deductions of the norms of ethics and right in his works following the *Foundations*. Both the *System of Ethics* and the *Foundations of Natural Right* begin with a proof of the practical nature of the subject, and in this context we find an easily recognized notion of the practical. The *System of Ethics* turns on the claim that "I find myself as myself only as willing," which Fichte uses to derive the authority of ethical norms, arguing that the conditions of such an experience of self include the recognition of the authority of ethical norms (Fichte 2005: 24). Similarly in the *Foundations of Natural Right*, Fichte asserts that the "practical faculty is the innermost root of the I; everything else is placed upon and attached to this faculty" (Fichte 2000: 21). In this context he argues that practical activity requires the recognition of subjects other than oneself, who serve to limit one's practical activity through instantiating relations of right. This claim concerning the essentially intersubjective nature of self-consciousness had a profound effect on modern European philosophy, beginning with Hegel's discussion of self-consciousness and extending into the twentieth century with Heidegger's and Sartre's phenomenological accounts of our relations to others.

Unlike in the *Foundations*, where the argument for the existence of practical capacities in the subject begins with the notion of objective experience, in the works on ethics and right Fichte argues that practical capacities are a condition of experiencing *oneself*. If we were not practical, he argues, we would never be aware of ourselves as subjects existing in a determinate state. It is only in agency that the activity essential to subjectivity in general takes a determinate form. Fichte argues for this claim in two different ways. First, he appeals to generally phenomenological considerations in maintaining that we are not aware of ourselves in sense perception: "activity in intuiting the world cannot be posited by the rational being as such, for this world-intuiting activity, by its very concept, is not supposed to revert into the intuiter ..." (Fichte 2000: 19). In other words, Fichte believes that perception does not appear to the subject as a case of self-determination or activity. These considerations are supplemented, especially in the *System of Ethics*, with a more abstract argument for the claim that willing just is a state in which a subject's activity exists in a determinate state. For this reason, if I find myself in a determinate state, I am aware of myself as willing.

The need for a system of philosophy

Fichte's arguments for the practical nature of a subject in general lend his work a systematic form different from what we find in Kant's critical system. Fichte's thought begins with the self-positing doctrine of the *Foundations* and aims to establish that both theoretical and practical claims, ranging from very general claims about the nature of subjectivity to quite particular claims concerning ethical norms in special circumstances (e.g. within the context of a marriage), follow from this one principle. This systematicity is a defining mark of post-Kantian Idealist thought, which is explained in large part through Idealist interest in Spinoza's thought (see Franks 2005

21

for an account of this aspect of the Idealist's concern with systematicity). Of course Kant is often (and quite rightly) described as having produced a system of philosophy. By this philosophers usually mean that the epistemological results of the *Critique of Pure Reason* underlie Kant's accounts of moral, scientific, aesthetic, historical, and religious knowledge in the many works that followed the first *Critique*. Kant believes that no claim in those works is incompatible with the limitation of knowledge to appearances, and his positive account of knowledge in those fields is grounded in the understanding of our cognitive faculties laid out in the first *Critique*. For example, in the *Critique of Practical Reason* Kant appeals to the table of categories in order to provide an account of the structure of the practical field of action, what he terms the object of pure *practical* reason. In places within the critical system this employment of the categories can appear forced, a feature of his work (and that of the Idealists as well) that later led Friedrich Nietzsche to assert "the will to a system is a lack of integrity" (Nietzsche 1982: 470). While some contemporary readers would likely agree with Nietzsche that Kant and the Idealists place too much weight on the systematic form of their work, Kant's critical philosophy ought to be viewed as an attempt to work within the methodological constraints established in the first *Critique*.

In the case of Fichte, two concerns guided these systematic aspirations. First, Fichte believed that in subjectivity itself theoretical and practical capacities are essentially interdependent. To consider questions concerning objectivity, knowledge, and representation independent of issues in practical philosophy necessarily leads to an inaccurate account of subjectivity itself. In Fichte's view, a merely theoretical subject is nothing but a philosopher's abstraction. Thus in order to produce an adequate account of subjectivity Fichte aims, wherever possible, to connect his work in what might seem to be unrelated areas of philosophy. But the systematic form of Fichte's work is not simply a result of his understanding of the nature of a subject. Like Reinhold, Fichte was of course concerned with showing the relation between central claims in his work and a first principle of philosophy, which he regarded as their only possible ground. Similarly, Friedrich Schelling's *System of Transcendental Idealism*, deeply influenced by Fichte's thought, presents in a single volume a theory of self-consciousness, objective experience, practical activity, moral reflection, history, and aesthetic experience. Each aspect of the system derives from the thought of the 'I' separating into subject and object, as in the opening sections of the *Foundations*. Accordingly, Schelling states that his goal in the work is, "simply this, to enlarge transcendental idealism into what it really should be, namely a system of all knowledge" (Schelling 1978: 1). Schelling's work took many different forms over the course of his life, however, and this structure was soon replaced by others (see Chapter 3 of this volume for an account of Schelling's contribution to these issues).

The Idealist concern with producing a system of philosophy was realized in Hegel's work, especially in his *Encyclopedia of the Philosophical Sciences*. Hegel explicitly states his systematic aims in the Preface to the work that he later characterizes as the introduction to his system, the *Phenomenology of Spirit*. There he asserts directly that "the true shape in which truth exists can only be the scientific system of such truth" (Hegel 1977: 3). While the claim is familiar, his reasons for maintaining that philosophy must be systematic are new. The system of philosophy, he maintains, is simply the only possible candidate for truth, or as he puts it, "the true is the whole" (Hegel 1977: 11). First principles considered by themselves cannot, therefore, be true – a fact Hegel expresses with the paradoxical claim that any first principle considered merely as such is both true and false (Hegel 1977: 13). These claims concerning the importance of systematicity appear not just radical, but also self-undermining. One wants to ask about *their* status. It is likely for this reason that Hegel's *Phenomenology* begins with the self-referential claim that there is something inappropriate about attaching a preface to a work of philosophy. To understand Hegel's new emphasis on systematicity we need to consider the methodological innovations that shape the Hegel's *Phenomenology*, which are rooted in his engagement with the methodological assumptions of his predecessors.

Hegel's completion of German Idealism

Hegel's opposition to Kant's critical methodology is evident in his essay "Faith and Knowledge," where he aims to demonstrate that we need not settle for faith, or mere belief, in areas of thought where we seek knowledge. Thus while Kant famously asserted that he had to limit knowledge in order to make room for faith, Hegel maintains that the need for faith results from nothing more than a misunderstanding of knowledge or cognition. The misunderstanding he diagnoses concerns what he terms the "culture of reflection," which he regards as reaching its apex with Locke's theory of ideas and as first starting to come apart in Kant's radicalization of Locke's project in the first *Critique*. This culture of reflection is characterized by the "one self-certifying certainty … that there exists a thinking subject, a reason affected with finitude; and the whole of philosophy consists in determining the universe with respect to this finite reason" (Hegel 1975a: 64). By this Hegel means that the assumption that reason is finite, that is, essentially limited in its capacities, leads to a system of philosophy in which this mere assumption appears to be confirmed. In the case of Kant, the charge is that the methodology in the *Critique* already determines his conclusions concerning the limits of metaphysics, and thus the limits of reason.

But where, exactly, does Kant go astray in his critical examination of reason? Hegel's central claim, both in "Faith and Knowledge" and more explicitly in the Introduction to the *Phenomenology*, is that in grounding his investigation in the notion of representation – as he clearly does in his conception of transcendental philosophy – Kant uncritically accepts a Lockean limitation on knowledge that should be asserted only as the conclusion of an investigation into the limits of reason. Hegel opens the Introduction with the claim "It is a natural assumption that in philosophy, before we start to deal with its proper subject-matter, namely the actual cognition of what truly is, one must first of all come to an understanding about cognition, which is regarded either as the instrument to get hold of the absolute, or as the medium through which one discovers it" (Hegel 1977: 46). The reference to Kant's *Critique* – and to Kantianism in early Idealism – should be clear. It was Kant who determined that metaphysics requires a preparatory investigation into cognition, and his investigation determined that we ought to think of our representational capacities as consisting in the activity of thought (Hegel's 'instrument') and the forms of intuition (Hegel's 'medium'). Hegel seeks to demonstrate in the Introduction that Kant's attempt to avoid errors in metaphysics should be regarded as a kind of error itself, in fact a "fear of truth," insofar as it presupposes that our capacities for thought separate us from the way the world is in itself.

This criticism of Kant is not limited to his explicit use of the notion of representation. More generally, Hegel sees in Kant an uncritical willingness to accept from elsewhere claims that ought to be established only within philosophy. For example, while our everyday reflection on the nature of experience may present us with a picture of cognition as the ordering of sensory information given in experience, such unreflective assumptions should not ground a philosophical investigation. But this is what Kant does: "Kant has simply no ground except experience and empirical psychology for holding that the human cognitive faculty essentially consists in the way it appears" (Hegel 1975a: 89). In connection with Kant's logic, the charge is that merely deriving the categories from the forms of judgment, which are themselves taken from the work of logicians, involves accepting as "valid presuppositions" claims concerning the function of thought that ought to be the content of a philosophical system (Hegel 1969: 595). Such an uncritical acceptance of foundational claims strikes Hegel as incompatible with the aspirations of philosophy: "to pick up the plurality of categories again in some way or other as a welcome find, taking them, e.g., from the various judgments and complacently accepting them so, is in fact to be regarded as an outrage on Science" (Hegel 1977: 142). Thus Hegel maintains that Kant's critical investigation into the capacities of reason, and the theories of knowledge and subjectivity that rise from it, are infected by the presence of mere assumptions that can never be grounded within the system. For this reason, he takes Kant's limitations of reason to be illegitimate.

On the other hand, Hegel actually agrees with Kant that we cannot simply assume that the legitimate realm of reason is unlimited. Hegel sees this assumption both in traditional metaphysics and in the work of his colleague Friedrich Schelling, who maintained that philosophy must begin with the intuition that subject and object are originally one, a starting point from which the reciprocal relations between subject and object are to be derived. Hegel's opposition to such a view appears in the Preface to the *Phenomenology* where he complains that such a starting point in philosophy resembles the night in which "all cows are black," i.e. a point lacking any discernible way forward (Hegel 1977: 9). Hegel's unwillingness to accept any such starting point also appears in his assertion that even Fichte's first principle, "I=I," which expresses the self-positing of the subject, requires a demonstration within philosophical reflection (Hegel 1977: 140). The truth of Schelling's or Fichte's views is not in question here. Hegel is fundamentally concerned with the issue of how one goes about producing a system of philosophy.

Hegel's transformation of Idealist methodology

Thus the problem that confronts us concerns the starting point of philosophy in general. What seems to be required is a presuppositionless science capable of demonstrating the possibility of metaphysics and, at the same time, generating that system of knowledge. The task seems impossible to carry out. Hegel's confrontation with this problem has three parts. First, he simply denies that an investigation into the nature and limits of our cognitive faculties must take the form of a Lockean, or Kantian, examination of those faculties prior to a development of metaphysics as a system of knowledge. This denial appears most clearly in his discussion of Kant's categories in the *Encyclopedia Logic*.

> Kant undertook to examine how far the forms of thought were capable of leading to the knowledge of truth. In particular he demanded a criticism of the faculty of cognition as preliminary to its exercise. That is a fair demand, if it means that even the forms of thought must be made an object of investigation. Unfortunately, there soon creeps in the misconception of already knowing before you know – the error of refusing to enter the water until you have learnt to swim. True, indeed, the forms of thought should be subjected to a scrutiny before they are used: yet what is this scrutiny but *ipso facto* a cognition? (Hegel 1975b: 66)

This unflattering portrait of Kant's critical concerns, reminiscent of the "fear of truth" charge, suggests that Kant's error consists in taking for granted that a determination of the legitimate scope of reason must take the form of a special science of transcendental philosophy. Hegel is claiming that due to the inevitable use of reason in such an investigation, it is a serious mistake to regard an investigation into cognition as separable from metaphysics itself. Thus he opposes the separation between critique and metaphysics that Kant regarded as his central methodological innovation. This opposition (and its development in the *Phenomenology*) completes the gradual disintegration of the distinction between transcendental philosophy and metaphysics in the work of Kant's successors.

The second aspect of Hegel's account of the proper starting point in philosophy follows from the necessity of examining cognition by using those same cognitive capacities. Hegel assumes that the outcome of such an investigation will be determined by the actual powers of those capacities. In particular, he believes that if our cognitive faculties are in principle capable of comprehending all aspects of reality, they should also be capable of demonstrating this fact about their scope. They should be capable of showing, in other words, that their validity is not limited to the human point of view, as Kant had assumed (B145–6). Such a demonstration would involve showing that doubts about the legitimacy of our forms of cognition, when examined in the proper manner, can be shown to be without ground. This aspect of Hegel's methodology has recently reappeared in Robert Brandom's attempt to demonstrate that our logical capacities are sufficient to show their own status as the capacities of a discursive being in general – a project that he describes as "animated by the ideal of the systematic philosophers of old" (Brandom 1994: xxiii).

All of this may seem to miss the central question of how one actually *begins* such a process. What claims are accepted as true, and with what right? In the *Phenomenology* Hegel is keenly aware of the ancient problem of presupposing a criterion for knowledge in such a way that it undermines the authority of any epistemology that follows from it, and he sets out to answer this problem directly. While I will not examine the details of that answer (for such an account, see Chapter 2 of this volume), it is essential to consider the central feature of Hegel's answer, which constitutes the third aspect of Hegel's methodology. He maintains that there exists a feature of the cognitive capacities of any being interested in assessing the legitimate scope of those capacities that ensures the existence of a starting point in philosophy that is not question-begging. That feature is expressed as a claim about the essential nature of consciousness: "…consciousness is, on the one hand, consciousness of the object, and on the other, consciousness of itself; consciousness of what for it is the true, and consciousness of its knowledge of the truth" (Hegel 1977: 54). By this Hegel means that awareness of an object carries with it, at least implicitly, a distinctive form of self-awareness. As cognizing subjects we are always capable of making explicit what we take to be the essential features of an object of knowledge and what we take knowledge of such an object to consist in.

In order for Hegel's notion of consciousness to serve as the foundation of his method in the *Phenomenology*, it must express an aspect of our experience that no one would deny. It would be a mistake, however, to regard Hegel's claim about consciousness as requiring the same kind of justification as Reinhold's principle of consciousness. Hegel criticizes Reinhold's use of the principle in the Preface to the *Phenomenology*, and he appeals to no inner fact in describing the principle, so it should be clear that Hegel, at least, sees this claim as having a ground different from that of the principle of consciousness. We can understand this difference by considering two points concerning Hegel's notion of consciousness. First, Hegel should not be read as claiming that in every case, consciousness's "consciousness of itself" is accurate and complete. In fact, he maintains that we systematically misconstrue our relation to objects of knowledge. Thus the claim is rather weak. Second, Hegel is not making this claim concerning consciousness on the basis of some inner experience. It is simply intended as to draw our attention to the mundane fact that we are capable of reflecting upon our own views concerning cognition, a fact that no one interested in the subject matter of the *Phenomenology* could possibly deny. Thus Hegel's most general claim in the Introduction is that if our conceptual capacities are not limited by any alien thing-in-itself, this fact is demonstrable through some activity of consciousness. His goal is to provide us with a demonstration of such activity.

The science of the experience of consciousness

The *Phenomenology* presents the reader with a series of forms of consciousness – that is, ways in which a subject understands objects and knowledge of those objects – that form an idealized path of reflection taking us from our everyday understanding of knowledge to the point of view of what Hegel terms "science." We, Hegel's readers, are to follow that path, confirming the various steps along the way, and thereby arrive at the conclusion that our cognitive abilities are not in principle limited and are in this sense infinite. This proof of science lies in our realization that the way in which we have progressed through this series of forms of consciousness itself deserves to be regarded as science, that our cognitive capacities were, prior to the investigation, already implicitly what we hoped them to be. This path of reflection begins with a form of consciousness Hegel terms "sense certainty," which is intended to express the essential assumptions of our day-to-day point of view. This so-called "natural consciousness" takes its relation to reality to be one of passive reception of sensory information, and it understands the objects of its cognition as completely independent of that cognition. To use Kant's terminology, natural consciousness presumes that objects of experience are in no way "made possible" by our cognitive capacities. Hegel is presuming that such a view of cognition in general will be recognizable to all readers, but he need not convince us of the authority of this particular starting point for the path of reflection. In principle, his argument could begin with any form of the assumption that there exists a lack of identity between our forms of cognition and world.

Hegel's understanding of the way in which one form of consciousness gives rise to another is the most important aspect of his method in the *Phenomenology*. He maintains that when examined closely, any form of consciousness that denies an identity between cognition and its objects will reveal internal inconsistencies that demonstrate its inadequacy as an understanding of cognition. The key to Hegel's method lies in his assertion that such inconsistencies provide a blueprint of sorts for the construction of a superior understanding of cognition, one that retains central features of the old view but at the same time approaches closer to the truth of the matter. As he puts it, if "…the exposition of the untrue consciousness in its untruth is not a merely *negative* procedure," then a "determinate negation" enables us to isolate the problems associated with a failed conception of knowledge and improve upon them (Hegel 1977: 50–1). Such a determinate negation generates both a new conception of knowing and a new conception of what that knowledge is knowledge *of* – it generates in this sense a new object of knowledge, and thus a new understanding of that in virtue of which our cognition is true. As Hegel expresses the idea, "*Inasmuch as the new true object issues from it*, this *dialectical* movement which consciousness exercises on itself and which affects both its knowledge and its object, is precisely what is called experience" (Hegel 1977: 55). The experience of consciousness, so construed, provides the methodological basis for Hegel's demonstration of mind– world identity and for his later metaphysics itself. Thus it should not be surprising that Hegel's early title for the work we have today was "The Science of the Experience of Consciousness." This notion of the experience of consciousness both gives rise to the point of view of science and, at the same time, enables us to grasp that activity of experience itself as science.

Of course, such a dialectical activity of consciousness is not what we commonly have in mind under the heading of "experience." Hegel is well aware of this fact. Since the point of view of natural consciousness is the starting point of all reflection, we naturally think that any inadequacy in an understanding of an object must be due to a failure to capture what an object is in itself. But Hegel's goal is precisely to get us to give up this pre-reflective attitude. In addition, in our everyday experience we certainly do not encounter anything like the movement of thought Hegel terms "dialectical," an activity that involves the free development of forms of thought independent of empirical constraint. Again, though, the essential claim is not that this activity is an aspect of our day to day experience, but that a path of reflection upon our cognition of objects reveals such an activity to underlie our most basic awareness of ourselves and the world around us. Thus Hegel must supplement descriptions of our experience of the inadequacy of various forms of consciousness with an account of how a new form of consciousness could emerge from them (or, since the *Phenomenology* is in part an account of how our forms of cognition emerged through history, how new forms of knowing did in fact emerge). Thus the *Phenomenology* as a whole takes the form of a series of forms of consciousness that we, with Hegel's help, are to recognize as a demonstration that we currently inhabit the cognitive standpoint of science. In claiming that the structure of this path of experience "is something contributed by us," Hegel is appropriating from Fichte and Schelling the idea of a point of view of a philosophical observer who sees acts of the subject in a manner different from the subject itself, but in Hegel this point of view becomes constitutive of the activity of philosophy itself (Hegel 1977: 55).

Hegel's argument stands or falls depending on his ability to convince us, the observers of the progression, that each transition from one form of consciousness to the next is necessary, in the sense that the successor view responds to, and improves upon, a real deficiency in the predecessor. If we are convinced by his presentation of this series of forms of consciousness, we will have to conclude both that our cognitive capacities are essentially unlimited and that those capacities are the result of a historical process of development. Spirit – Hegel's notion of the socially determined conceptual structure that underlies our cognition – appears as a condition of the simple reflective cognition of an object described at the beginning of the *Phenomenology*. The next task for Hegel is to elucidate those most basic forms of thought that are constitutive of cognition, a task for reason itself that Hegel assigns to his *Science of Logic*.

Hegel's Logic and the end of Idealist thought

Following the path of experience in the *Phenomenology* leads the reader to an understanding of cognition very different from the Kantian view of cognition as a representational medium. As Hegel puts it in the *Phenomenology*, "in thinking, the object does not present itself in representations but in concepts..." (Hegel 1977: 120). Such concepts, or "notions" (as the term "*Begriffe*" is sometimes translated) are the subject matter of Hegel's work in logic. He regards the *Phenomenology* as an introduction to his *Science of Logic*, which is to exhibit in detail the basic structure of thought responsible for our cognition of ourselves and the world. In this discussion of the basic forms of thought Hegel has left behind the relation to an object of knowledge constitutive of the progression of the *Phenomenology*. What remains is "pure thoughts" which requires an activity of "spirit thinking its own essential nature" (Hegel 1969: 28). Such an activity of thought thinking about itself is, for Hegel, the content of logic.

Hegel's notion of logic thus differs radically from Kant's, for whom the forms of judgment and of syllogism are taken as basic. While even the most basic features of Hegel's logic lie beyond the scope of this essay, in this context a few points concerning his methodology in the *Science of Logic* are relevant. Hegel's goal there is to demonstrate how such forms of thought come into being through the unlimited activity of thought itself (Hegel 1970: 613). This requires a dialectical activity of thought that determines the nature of the forms of judgment or inference independent of any reliance on empirical claims concerning human tendencies in thought or a theory of inference or judgment. The activity of thought thinking itself is to begin with the simple thought of being, of there being something at all (a starting point similar to that of the *Phenomenology*, but repeated at the level of thought alone). Progress is made through the activity of thought itself since Hegel maintains that this simple thought of being can be seen by us to be incomplete, insofar as it is in itself contradictory. The thought of mere being carries with it the thought of nothing, and does so in such a way that it is correct to say that "*pure being* and *pure nothing* are, therefore, the same" (Hegel 1970: 82). This claim surely appears baffling at first glance, but it illustrates the central feature of Hegel's method in the *Science of Logic*. Just as in the *Phenomenology*, this investigation is to progress through considering implicit contradictions in overly simple presentations of its subject-matter and resolving them through the construction of new entities (in this particular case, a new notion of becoming).

Hegel's *Science of Logic* proceeds by considering the relations between these central concepts, demonstrating that these concepts are the concepts they are only in virtue of their relations to others in the activity of thought. The result of the investigation is to be the realization of a system of thought in general that is, equally, the structure of reality itself. We might say that in his *Science of Logic* Hegel takes himself to have completed the Kantian project of demonstrating that our thinking determines the form of reality, and that it does so without a remainder of a thing-in-itself, but of course for Hegel the sense of this claim concerning a relation between thought and reality has shifted rather radically. Hegel now understands the forms of thought not as representations, but as interdetermining concepts. And those logical forms do not make possible the objects of experience in virtue of serving an ordering function in sense experience. Nevertheless, even in the *Science of Logic* Hegel notes his debt to Kant, and in particular, to his Transcendental Deduction of the Categories which first took up the challenge of establishing the objective validity of our forms of thought (Hegel 1970: 590). Kant's central methodological innovation of transcendental philosophy did not survive the developments of German Idealism, but without his attempt to provide a secure foundation for metaphysics the movement known as Idealism would never have occurred.

Note

1 All references will be made within the text in Author, Year, Page format, with the exception of references to the *Critique of Pure Reason*, where the usual A/B page designations will be employed.

References

Brandom, R. (1994) *Making It Explicit: Reasoning, Representing, and Discursive Commitment*, Cambridge, MA: Harvard University Press.

Fichte, J. G. (1970) *Foundations of the Entire Science of Knowledge*, edited, trans. P. Heath and J. Lachs, New York: Appleton.

—— (1988) "Review of Aenesidemus," in *Early Philosophical Writings*, edited, trans. D. Breazeale, Ithaca: Cornell University Press.

—— (2000) *Foundations of Natural Right*, edited by F. Neuhouser, trans. M. Baur, Cambridge: Cambridge University Press.

—— (2005) *The System of Ethics*, edited, trans. D. Breazeale and G. Zöller, Cambridge: Cambridge University Press.

Hegel, G. W. F. (1969) *Science of Logic*, trans. A. V. Miller, Atlantic Highlands: Humanities Press International.

—— (1975a) *Faith and Knowledge*, edited, trans. W. Cerf and H. S. Harris, Albany, NY: SUNY Press.

—— (1975b) *The Encyclopaedia of the Philosophical Sciences Part I: Science of Logic*, Oxford: Clarendon Press.

—— (1977) *Phenomenology of Spirit*, trans. A.V. Miller, Oxford: Oxford University Press.

Henrich, D. (1989) "Kant's Notion of a Deduction and the Methodological Background of the First Critique," in E. Förster (ed.) *Kant's Transcendental Deductions*, Stanford: Stanford University Press.

—— (1994) "Identity and Objectivity: An Inquiry into Kant's Transcendental Deduction," trans. J. Edwards, in R. Velkley (ed.) *The Unity of Reason*, Cambridge: Harvard University Press.

Kant, I. (1965) *Critique of Pure Reason*, edited, trans. N. Smith, New York: St Martin's Press.

—— (1992) "On the Form and Principles of the Sensible and the Intelligible World," in D. Walford (ed. and trans.) *Theoretical Philosophy 1755–1770*, Cambridge: Cambridge University Press.

—— (1997a) *Critique of Practical Reason*, edited, trans. M. Gregor, Cambridge: Cambridge University Press.

—— (1997b) *Prolegomena to Any Future Metaphysics*, edited, trans. G. Hatfield, Cambridge: Cambridge University Press.

—— (1999) *Correspondence*, edited, trans. A. Zweig, Cambridge: Cambridge University Press.

Locke, J. (1959) *An Essay Concerning Human Understanding*, vol. 1, edited by A. Fraser, New York: Dover.

Nietzsche, F. (1982) *Twilight of the Idols*, trans. W. Kaufmann, in Kaufmann (ed.) *The Portable Nietzsche*, New York: Viking Press.

Reinhold, K. L. (2000) *The Foundation of Philosophical Knowledge*, trans. G. di Giovanni, in H. S. Harris and G. di Giovanni (eds) *Between Kant and Hegel*, Indianapolis, IN: Hackett.

—— (2005) *Letters on the Kantian Philosophy*, edited by K. Ameriks, trans. J. Hebbeler, Cambridge: Cambridge University Press.

Schelling, F. W. J. (1997) *System of Transcendental Idealism*, trans. P. Heath, Charlottesville: University Press of Virginia.

Schulze, G. E. (2000) *Aenesidemus*, trans. G. di Giovanni, in H. S. Harris and G. di Giovanni (eds) *Between Kant and Hegel*, Indianapolis, IN: Hackett.

Further reading

F. Beiser's *The Fate of Reason* (Cambridge: Harvard University Press, 1987) provides an overview of the period between Kant and Fichte. D. Henrich's *Between Kant and Hegel*, edited by D. Pacini (Cambridge: Harvard University Press, 2003) is a very accessible series of lectures on Kant, Hegel, and figures in between. P. Franks' *All or Nothing* (Cambridge: Harvard University Press, 2005) is a study of post-Kantian thought focusing on issues of methodology and systematicity. F. Neuhouser's *Fichte's Theory of Subjectivity* (Cambridge: Cambridge University Press, 1990) offers an accessible account of the theory of subjectivity that underlies Fichte's theoretical and practical philosophy. R. Pippin's *Hegel's Idealism* (Cambridge: Cambridge University Press, 1989) offers an interpretation of Hegel as an idealist in the Kantian-Fichtean tradition.

2
EPISTEMOLOGY IN GERMAN IDEALISM

Dietmar H. Heidemann

Introduction

It is not at all clear whether there is anything like 'epistemology' in Kant and German Idealism. According to a widespread view, Kant wasn't interested in epistemology in the narrow, contemporary sense of the word as theory of knowledge. His focus, as is argued sometimes, was rather on a systematic critique of metaphysical knowledge claims. Since the German Idealists – in particular Fichte, Schelling, and Hegel – in many ways react to Kant, and develop philosophical systems of their own, in part by re-establishing metaphysics, one wouldn't expect them to deal with epistemology either. What one can find in Kant and German Idealism therefore would be, at most, an interest in epistemological questions in the negative rather than in the positive sense. Over the last two decades, research on Kant and German Idealism has revised this view as one-sided. Nowadays, many scholars agree that Kant and the German Idealists in fact did show a strong interest in epistemology and even made substantial contributions to this core philosophical discipline. Still one has to be careful, since on the other hand metaphysics looms large in Kant and German Idealism. In what follows it will become obvious that Kant's and the German Idealists' dedication to epistemological themes is compatible with the systematic role these authors devote to metaphysics, be it that they criticize or vindicate metaphysical knowledge claims. Nevertheless, one has to be cautious about describing eighteenth- and nineteenth-century epistemology with the help of canonical contemporary categories such as internalism, externalism, social epistemology, etc. Moreover, for Kant and the German Idealists the central concept of 'idealism' is not to be understood in terms of 'skepticism', though their individual conceptions of 'idealism' differ fundamentally from each other. The following outline takes the various doctrines of 'idealism' as the guide to theory of knowledge in Kant and German Idealism. In the various stages of the development of classical German philosophy we will see what each kind of idealism amounts to, and in particular how it is different from skepticism.

Kant's transcendental idealism

Kant's epistemology is best known under the title "transcendental idealism." Kant defines "transcendental idealism" as the doctrine according to which "everything intuited in space or in time, hence all objects of an experience possible for us, are nothing but appearances, i.e. mere representations, which, as they are represented, as extended beings or series of alterations, have outside our thoughts no existence grounded in itself" (CPR: B518–19). Much of the criticism and misinterpretation of Kant's philosophy derives from this rather ambiguous definition of transcendental idealism as the alleged view that external objects are nothing over and above representations, and do not exist outside the perceiving subject. Moreover, the fact that Kant has chosen the concept of 'idealism' to designate his doctrine seems to indicate that his epistemological views are rather odd since 'idealism' is traditionally associated with skepticism and therefore regarded as a controversial philosophical concept. However, Kant specifies his idealism as '*transcendental* idealism', and this suggests that he has a more specific kind of idealism in mind. That Kant's transcendental idealism indeed diverges fundamentally from traditional philosophical theories and skeptical versions of idealism becomes clear once one considers the initial motivation and meaning of his *critique* of pure reason. Thus the first step to understand transcendental idealism is to understand Kant's *critique* of metaphysics.

Critique of metaphysics

Kant didn't develop his theory of knowledge out of the blue. Like most philosophers he got engaged with specific views of his precursors and contemporaries, and the critical engagement with these views motivated the development of transcendental idealism. To fully grasp Kant's epistemological project one has to bear in mind his critique of metaphysics. Though the young Kant was in many respects positive about metaphysics as the traditional philosophical science of the super-sensible, he over the years started to question metaphysics' entitlement to the role of the "queen of all the sciences" (CPR: Aviii). The reason why Kant began to take up a critical stance towards metaphysics is a systematic one. Around 1769/70 it became clear to him that metaphysics' pretension of being a science is incompatible with the fact of there being "endless controversies" (CPR: Aviii) in metaphysics. It was not so much that there were disputes in metaphysics about specific problems since in every science there is disagreement with respect to certain questions. The problem with metaphysics rather was that there was ongoing disagreement about the most fundamental philosophical issues, such as the possibility to prove the substantiality of the soul, the finiteness or infiniteness of the universe, or the existence of God. Kant therefore famously called metaphysics the "dialectical battlefield" (CPR: B450; see also CPR: Aviii, Bxv) of fruitless, unproductive disputes. For Kant the fundamental disagreement in metaphysics was not due to the fact that metaphysics hasn't been carried out in the correct way. Metaphysics' misery rather originated from the deficiency of never having asked itself whether it is at all possible as a science.

According to Kant, it is an intrinsic feature of scientific cognition and of reason itself that it "has insight only into what it itself produces according to its own design" (CPR: Bxiv). Being able to "cognize of things *a priori* only what we ourselves have put into them" (CPR: Bxviii) is a distinctive way of circumscribing how reason functions as source of *a priori* knowledge. However, if reason should be a source of *a priori* cognition it must meet a necessary epistemological condition of the possibility of *a priori* cognition. This precondition is not that "our cognition must conform to the objects" but "the objects must conform to our cognition" (CPR: Bxvi). Kant argues that the latter possibility hasn't been accurately taken into account though it is the only way to explain how cognition *a priori* – to be more precise, cognition *a priori* that extends our knowledge of objects – is possible. To change our "ways of thinking" (CPR: Bxvi) from the object-dependence of all cognition to the cognition-dependence of all objects of cognition as Copernicus famously did with respect to the explanation of "celestial motions" (CPR: Bxvi) is a necessary condition of the possibility of *a priori* cognition. For if our cognition would be completely determined through its conformity to the objects, everything we could possibly know would previously have to be given to us, given through our senses, and what we know through our senses is by definition empirical, not *a priori* knowledge. Kant transfers this picture to the possibility of *a priori* cognition in metaphysics. Hence, *a priori* cognition in metaphysics is only possible if the given objects conform to the "constitution of our faculty of intuition" (CPR: Bxvii). Thus if, as many philosophers believe, metaphysics is a science of reason, the question is how exactly it can be ascertained that *a priori* cognition in metaphysics is possible under the condition that objects conform to cognition (on Kant's idea of the 'Copernican revolution', see the previous article in this volume).

Kant answers this question by distinguishing between the sources *a priori* and *a posteriori* of cognition, sensibility (sense-perception) and understanding, on the one hand, and the analytic and synthetic nature of judgments that derive from, or that are justified through, these sources, on the other. Accordingly, cognition *a priori* is defined as "cognition independent of all experience and even of all impressions of the senses"; cognition *a posteriori* is defined as cognition which has its "sources ... in experience" (CPR: B2). Hence, what is *a posteriori* cannot be known without experience, as its justificatory origin is empirical; whereas what is *a priori* cannot be known through experience, since its justificatory origin is independent of sense-perception. Kant identifies two marks "by means of which we can securely distinguish a pure cognition from an empirical one": "necessity" and "universality." To cognize a proposition "with its necessity" (CPR: B3) means being constrained to cognize it exactly the way it is and not otherwise such as cognizing that '1 + 1 = 2', not '3', or that every alteration is causally determined. The concept of "universality" does not characterize the manner of cognizing something but the cognized proposition itself. To know that the mark of "universality" in the strict, non-comparative sense pertains to a proposition means to know *a priori* that that proposition, like mathematical propositions or laws of nature, does not allow for any exception. Not allowing for any exception simply means not being refutable by experience. To sum up, cognition *a priori* is independent of experience, necessary, and strictly universal whereas cognition *a posteriori* is dependent on experience, not necessary, and not strictly universal.

The distinction between analytic and synthetic does not pertain to the sources of knowledge but to the nature of judgments that are justified through these sources. If metaphysics is a science of reason, Kant argues, it must be able to inform us about super-sensible reality, and consequently to justify its knowledge claims *a priori*. It is one of Kant's major epistemological achievements to have clarified this through the distinction between analytic and synthetic judgments. In general, judgments represent "the relation of a subject to the predicate" (CPR: B10), and they do so in two possible ways: "Either the predicate B belongs to the subject A as something that is (covertly) contained in this concept A; or B lies entirely outside this concept A, though to be sure it stands in connection with it" (CPR: B10). Hence, with respect to the subject–predicate-relation there are two types of judgments, analytic judgments, as in the first case, and synthetic judgments, as in the second (for an in-depth discussion of analytic and synthetic judgments or propositions, see Hanna 2001: Chs 3–5). This distinction is basically about the question of whether a particular judgment solely *clarifies* or *amplifies* our knowledge. Following Kant, analytic judgments are "judgments of clarification" (CPR: B11) because they solely elucidate, or explicate, what is implicitly thought of as being identical in the relation between the predicate- and subject-term. E.g. the judgment, "All bodies are extended," is analytic because the predicate-term "extension" is 'covertly contained' in the subject-term "body," and therefore their relation is thought through "identity" (CPR: B11; see *Prolegomena* [Kant 2002] §§2–3). To see this one only has to analyze the concept of "body," and to, merely through analysis, become aware of the fact that – because of intensional "identity" – "extension" is 'covertly contained' in the concept of "body." By contrast, the judgment, "All bodies are heavy," is synthetic because the predicate-term "heavy" (or weight) is not 'covertly contained' in the subject-term "body." It is rather added to the subject-term, since "heavy" (or weight) cannot be extracted from "body" through the analysis of that term. Similar to the distinction between cognition *a priori* and *a posteriori* it is not sufficient to know that analytic judgments clarify and that synthetic judgments amplify knowledge in order to be able to determine whether or not a predicate-term is 'covertly contained' in a subject-term. The way analytic and synthetic judgments can be distinguished essentially involves the way in which we acquire knowledge, i.e. the distinction between cognition *a priori* and *a posteriori*. Knowledge that "extension" is 'covertly contained' in "body" is knowledge *a priori* because we know this through mere analysis of the term "body," and that means independently of experience, though "body" itself is an empirical concept. The necessary and sufficient test-criterion for analytic judgments therefore is the principle of non-contradiction (PNC) (see CPR: B189–93). Simply by negating the predicate-term "extension" we can find out that the judgment, "All bodies are extended," is analytic because it is not possible to conceive of bodies that are not extended, i.e. the thought of a non-extended body is contradicting the very concept of "body." Analytic judgments therefore are *a priori*, namely necessary and universal, since they are independent of experience and cannot be empirically refuted (see Allison 2004: 89–93).

Synthetic judgments are different in that we cannot know whether they are true solely by means of PNC, i.e. we cannot know whether a synthetic judgment is true through merely analyzing the terms it involves. Although synthetic judgments also must obey PNC this principle is not sufficient for cognizing their truth. In the case of the synthetic judgment, "All bodies are heavy," this is easy to see since the predicate-term "heavy" (or "weight") is not analytically contained in the subject-term "body" for we can without contradiction think of bodies that do not have weight, e.g. bodies in space. That there are bodies that do have weight is for that reason something we only know through experience. Synthetic judgments of this kind therefore depend on experience, are not necessary, and are not strictly universal, since they allow for exceptions, i.e. they are *a posteriori* because experience is the source by means of which we determine their truth. Synthetic judgments *a posteriori* are in this sense "judgments of amplification" (CPR: B11). They do not clarify but rather extend our knowledge through adding something to the subject-term that is not analytically contained in it.

The crucial question now is whether all synthetic judgments are judgments *a posteriori*, or whether there are also synthetic judgments *a priori*. Synthetic judgments *a priori* are judgments that are informative about the world without experience being the source by means of which we determine their truth. If there are synthetic judgments *a priori* it must be possible for us to get access to them just through rationalizing about the world. Metaphysics essentially depends on this possibility since metaphysics claims to be a science that is not grounded in experience but provides *a priori* information about what the world is like. It follows that metaphysics cannot for the most part consist of analytic judgments, because analytic judgments do *not* inform us about the world; they are true no matter what the status of the world is like. Nor can metaphysics refer to synthetic judgments *a posteriori*, since the knowledge it claims to provide is not contingent upon empirical facts. Thus for metaphysics to be possible at all synthetic judgments *a priori* must be possible.

That there are synthetic judgments *a priori* in particular sciences is obvious for Kant from the examples of mathematics and natural science (physics) (CPR: B14–18; see *Prolegomena* §§6–39; for details, see Hanna 2001: Ch. 5). Similar to mathematics and the natural sciences also metaphysics seems to contain synthetic judgments *a priori*. For metaphysics is concerned with amplifying our cognition in a non-empirical manner. The judgment, "The world must have a first beginning" (CPR: B18), is a classical example of a synthetic judgment *a priori* in metaphysics. It is not an analytic judgment because the analysis of the concept "world" does not reveal that the world has necessarily "a first beginning" for the concept of a "world" that does not have a "first beginning" is not contradictory. The term "first beginning" is rather a predicate that is *a priori* added to the subject-term "world" and that makes the statement necessary and universal. From the fact that the judgment, "The world must have a first beginning," is synthetic *a priori* it does not, however, automatically follow that this judgment is authorized. Since we know that PNC determines a judgment to be analytic, and that experience justifies synthetic judgments *a posteriori* the question arises what it is that warrants synthetic judgments *a priori*. Kant famously phrases the question in the following way: "How are synthetic judgments *a priori* possible?" (CPR:

B19). His answer to this question is that if synthetic judgments *a priori* are possible they must be justified through pure intuition as the representation *a priori* of sensibility in combination with the understanding. It is therefore the theory of sensibility and understanding that carries the heaviest burden in Kant's theory of knowledge.

Sensibility and understanding: the dual-compositional theory of knowledge

Unlike in Gettier's famous article "Is Justified True Belief Knowledge?" (1963) the point of departure in Kant's epistemology is not the analysis of the concept of knowledge but the examination of the sources of knowledge. The primary focus of transcendental idealism is therefore not on what cognition consists in but on what makes cognition possible. Kant's epistemology can be characterized as a dual-compositional theory of knowledge according to which cognition is only possible through the cooperation of sensibility and understanding as the sources of knowledge, or intuition and concept, respectively. This is the idea behind the often-cited quote: "Thoughts without content are empty, intuitions without concepts are blind" (CPR: B75). To explain the possibility of cognition on the basis of a dual-compositional theory of knowledge requires exploring the faculties that make knowledge possible, i.e. cognitive faculties as exhibited through the subject of knowledge. For Kant it "comes along with our nature" (CPR: B75) and therefore is a fact about our cognitive capacities that for humans sensibility and understanding are the sole sources of knowledge. Whereas sensibility is the "capacity (receptivity) to acquire representations through the way in which we are affected by objects," understanding is the capacity by means of which objects "are thought" (CPR: B 33). Sensibility affords intuitions, while concepts arise from the understanding, and neither faculty is reducible to the other.

The first step to demonstrate the irreducibility of sensibility and understanding is taken in the transcendental aesthetic of the first *Critique* (CPR: B33–73). In general, Kant calls "all cognition transcendental that is occupied not so much with objects but rather with our mode of cognition of objects insofar as this is to be possible *a priori*" (CPR: B25). Consequently the transcendental aesthetic is a theory of *pure* sensibility rather than the contents of phenomenal experience. As Kant demonstrates in the first *Critique* through five equally brief and demanding arguments (see Paton 1965: 93ff.) space and time are not actual objects but forms of *a priori* intuition; they can nonetheless be represented as pure spatial (like next to and behind each other) and temporal (like succession and simultaneity) relations. However, this does not mean that they are not real. Space and time are empirically real insofar as all objects that can ever be given to us in intuition must accord with them as conditions of our intuition; and we can known this *a priori*. But they are transcendentally ideal inasmuch as they are nothing for us if we do not consider them as subjective determinations of our mode of intuiting (CPR: B44; 52–3). The fact that human sensibility as a receptive, and for that reason passive, faculty of intuition is conditioned through space and time as forms implies that given objects are represented as "appearances" (CPR: B43, 50–1), a term Kant introduces in order to indicate that cognizable objects are contingent upon transcendental conditions of experience, not that they are illusions. According to his transcendental dual-compositional account of knowledge, sensible intuition is nevertheless only *one* component that makes up cognition.

In parallel with the theory of pure sensibility Kant develops a theory of pure understanding. His aim is to show that the pure understanding, like pure sensibility, contains elements *a priori* determining its self-reliance as a source of knowledge. Whereas sensibility, or intuition, respectively, is passive (receptive), dependent on sensuous affection, direct-referential with respect to its objects, and therefore able only to represent particular objects such as *this* chair or *this* table, the understanding is spontaneous, based on "functions" as logical rules of ordering representations, indirect-referential with respect to its objects, and therefore able only to represent conceptual universals such as 'chair' or 'table' (CPR: B92–4). It is obvious that though sensibility and understanding are self-reliant faculties they cannot produce full-fledged cognition on their own. This seems to be true especially of sensibility since intuition represents objects according to subjective sensuous conditions, at the same time being unable to conceptualize the given sensible object for "the senses are not capable of thinking anything" (CPR: B75). Likewise the understanding is "not capable of intuiting anything" (CPR: B75) because it is the discursive, not intuitive mode of representation. A discursive representation is a concept, i.e. an analytic, universal representation of marks shared by particular objects such as the concept of "chair," which contains specific marks ('being a furniture', 'seat', 'backrest' etc.) that make it possible to apply it to actual chairs. Thus concepts refer to objects indirectly because their reference is mediated through the representation of specific marks (CPR: B94; Allison 2004: 78–82). For Kant's dual-compositional account of knowledge this finding is decisive since it necessitates the cooperation of sensibility and understanding to allow for the conceptualization of the intuitively given and therewith to cognize objects.

Through the "analysis of the faculty of understanding" (CPR: B90) Kant claims to be able to demonstrate that the only way the understanding can make use of concepts is "that of judging by means of them," and that all judgments are "functions of unity among our representations" (CPR: B93–4). Abstracting from all content of a judgment yields all "functions of thinking" as the purely formal, logical modes of ordering representations in judgments. No matter what the content of a judgment might be there are four classes of "logical functions of the understanding in judgments" (quantity, quality, relation, and modality, each containing three titles) (CPR: B95). Additionally, Kant maintains that it is possible to deduce from these purely formal "functions of unity among our representations" an equal number of categories that give "unity to the mere synthesis of different representations in an intuition" (CPR: B105; *Prolegomena* §21). That is, the determination of intuition through categories is analogous to the way the understanding determines representations in judgments through logical functions. The cognition, e.g. that an object x has a certain property F corresponds to the logical function of the categorical form of judgment, 'x is F'. Therefore categories or pure concepts can be applied to intuition in accordance with logical rules. To be more precise, categories are logical rules of unity by means of which the understanding synthesizes what is given in intuition.

Now, showing that pure concepts can be applied to intuition seems to imply that the pure concepts of the understanding can determine all kinds of intuition. However, this is not the case for the human mind. In principle, it is possible to distinguish between non-sensible and sensible intuition. Human intuition is sensible intuition but it is not just this. It is sensible intuition that has space and time as its forms. For this reason it has to be proven that the pure concepts of human understanding have objective reality, i.e. do refer to real objects, if and only if these objects are possible objects of our sensible, spatio-temporal intuition. Referring the categories to objects that are not possible objects of this specific kind of intuition means they are concepts void of objective reality, and thus unable to yield cognition. Kant demonstrates this in the notorious 'Transcendental Deduction of the categories' of the first *Critique* (this article refers to the revised version in the second edition, CPR: B116–69; see Allison 2004: 159–201). The very idea of the Transcendental Deduction is that since a given manifold of representations in an intuition is only cognizable as a synthesized manifold, and since synthesis requires rules of combination, namely categories, applied through the pure apperception or self-consciousness in judgments, the "manifold in a given intuition ... stands under categories" (CPR: B143) on Kant's theory of apperception in more detail, see the previous article in this volume. However, this only shows that sensible "intuition in general" (CPR: B148) stands under categories rather than specifically human, i.e. *spatio-temporal* sensual intuition. In a complex line of argument Kant therefore argues that for the human mind the categories have objective reality only if they are applied to "objects of experience" (CPR: B146). Because only objects as possible things in space and time are possible objects of our sensible intuition, categories cannot be legitimately applied to objects of a non-human kind of intuition. Such application would yield only "empty concepts of objects" (CPR: B149). This insight completes the Transcendental Deduction as one of the most disputed systematic elements of Kant's epistemology. The restriction concerning the objective reality of the categories to possible objects of experience does not, however, inform us about how pure concepts (categories) refer to intuitions. For that reason Kant provides a theory, the "schematism of the pure concepts of the understanding" (CPR: B176–87), by means of which it is possible to show what conditions intuitions must satisfy in order for the categories to objectively apply to them. These applicability conditions of concepts to intuition allow for the mediation between sensibility and understanding. The capstone of the overall argument finally is the "System of all Principles of Pure Understanding" (CPR: B187–294; see Guyer 1987: Pt 3). On the basis of the theories of pure intuition and understanding Kant here finally develops the synthetic principles *a priori* of pure understanding specifying in detail how categories are objectively applicable to intuition. The principles are formulated as synthetic judgments *a priori*, as the only judgments the understanding has at its disposal as synthetic cognition *a priori*. It is only these judgments that independently of experience provide objective information about the world. From this cognitive limitation, i.e. from the dual-compositional account of knowledge, naturally follows the doctrine of appearance and thing-in-itself which is constitutive of transcendental idealism.

Appearance and thing-in-itself

Transcendental idealism is defined in terms of the distinction between appearance and thing-in-itself. It is not surprising that one of the major difficulties with Kant's epistemology lies in the question of how to understand this distinction. For Kant confronts the reader with a variety of rather ambiguous explanations of what transcendental idealism means, such as "the transcendental idealism of all appearances [is] the doctrine that they are all together to be regarded as mere representations and not as things in themselves" (CPR: A369). On the other hand, he is well aware that *transcendental* idealism can be mistaken as idealism. He therefore at the same time draws the line: "Idealism consists in the claim that there are none other than thinking beings; the other things that we believe we perceive in intuition are only representations in thinking beings, to which in fact no object existing outside these beings corresponds" (*Prolegomena* 84). By contrast, *transcendental* idealism is the theory, that "[t]here are things given to us as objects of our senses existing outside us, yet we know nothing of them as they may be in themselves, but are acquainted only with their appearances, i.e. with the representations that they produce in us because they affect our senses" (*Prolegomena* 84). Nevertheless, at first glance it looks as if according to transcendental idealism we do not perceive real objects in space and time but representations of objects as opposed to things in themselves as real objects. However, we cannot know whether the latter really exist. There is a long history of controversies over whether or not this doctrine amounts to skepticism. The aforementioned arguments for transcendental idealism as a dual-compositional theory of knowledge suggest that it does not. The distinction between appearance and thing-in-itself is an epistemological one since it is introduced with respect to sources of knowledge rather than with respect to different types of objects. Kant presents it as a natural consequence of the make-up and epistemic cooperation of our cognitive faculties, sensibility and understanding, that we "can have cognition of no object as a thing in itself, but only insofar as it is an object of sensible intuition, i.e. as an appearance; from which follows the limitation of all even possible speculative cognition of reason to mere objects of experience" (CPR: Bxxvi). According to the transcendental aesthetic, in sensibility we refer to singular objects since intuition is the only way in which we are able to directly refer to sensually given objects, and intuition is *repraesentatio singularis*, singular representation. There are pure intuitions, as in geometry, and empirical intuitions, as in sense perception. Only the latter can represent "appearances," i.e. the "undetermined object of an empirical intuition" (CPR: B34). 'Appearance' in this sense does not have a diminutive or relativizing meaning like appear words do such as 'looks like', 'sounds like', 'feels like', 'tastes like', etc. Hence, in transcendental idealism, it is not possible to conceive of an appearance as "mere illusion" (CPR: B69), because both concepts, appearance and illusion, are used in different ways, and in fact refer to different objects. The concept of "appearance" refers to objects and their properties depending on the kind of intuition of the subject "in the relation of the given object to it" (CPR: B69). Since, in this sense, what appears, the object and its properties, is really given we can attribute the predicates of appearances like color or smell to objects in space. The concept of "illusion," by contrast, cannot be attributed to the object because "illusion" is something that refers to the subject's cognitive capacities. Though transcendental idealists can, of course, be under an illusion, appearances, in Kant's epistemology, cannot be reduced to illusions.

Kant's use of the concept 'thing-in-itself' is equally vexing. It is introduced in the transcendental aesthetic as well. In general, Kant distinguishes between thing-in-itself in the empirical sense and thing-in-itself in the non-empirical sense. Thing-in-itself, in the empirical sense, is the object existing in space, having properties and causing representations in us. Kant calls it 'appearance' because we represent it according to subjective conditions of sensibility. Although our way of perceiving depends on our subjective conditions of sensibility, we can at least conceive of objects that might be perceived in a way that is totally different from perception under conditions of space and time as forms of our intuition. In this case we are not conceiving the thing-in-itself in the empirical sense but the thing-in-itself in the non-empirical sense. For the most part Kant just calls it 'thing-in-itself'. Things-in-themselves in the non-empirical sense do not exist in space. They do not inhibit properties we could perceive and therefore they do not cause appearances. Kant further specifies that the non-spatial thing-in-itself is the noumenon or object of thought. He distinguishes between the "noumenon in the negative sense" and the "noumenon in a positive sense" (B307). The "noumenon in positive sense" is the "object of a non-sensible, ... a special kind of intuition, namely intellectual intuition, which, however, is not our own, and the possibility of which we cannot understand" (CPR: B307). What Kant has in mind here are objects of traditional metaphysics like God, unextended simple parts, the spiritual soul, monads, etc. According to transcendental idealism, our intuition is a sensible, not intellectual intuition. We therefore cannot cognize these objects, though this does not mean that it is unreasonable to conceive of them, or even that the concept of such an object is contradictory. "Noumenon in the negative sense" is the thing insofar as it is not an object of our sensible intuition, i.e. a thing "the understanding must think without this relation to our kind of intuition" (CPR: B307). In the case where we abstract from space and time as forms of intuition we, likewise, cannot cognize such an object, for our intuition is spatio-temporal. Thus, in transcendental idealism, the concept 'thing-in-itself' breaks up into the thing-in-itself in the *empirical* sense and the thing-in-itself in the *non-empirical* sense. The thing-in-itself in the *non-empirical* sense is the *noumenon*. It is, again, subdivided into the noumenon in the *positive* sense and the noumenon in the *negative* sense (Figure 2.1).

Ever since the first *Critique*, it has been argued that in transcendental idealism the status of the thing-in-itself, especially its relation to 'appearance', is fundamentally unclear. The standard criticism is that, contrary to what the transcendental idealist maintains things-in-themselves must be interpreted as the underlying grounds of appearances, i.e. as objects in space outside us that affect our senses and thereby produce appearances in us. Indeed, there seems to be some textual evidence in support of this causal account of the relation between appearance and thing-in-itself in Kant's work: "In fact, if we view the objects of the senses as mere appearances, as is fitting, then we thereby admit at the very same time that a thing in itself underlies them, although

41

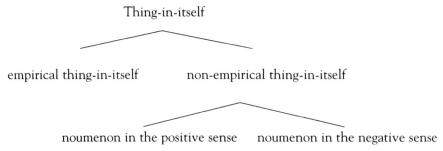

Figure 2.1

we are not acquainted with this thing as it may be constituted in itself, but only with its appearance, i.e. with the way in which our senses are affected by this unknown something. Therefore the understanding, just by the fact that it accepts appearances, also admits to the existence of things in themselves, and to that extent we can say that the representation of such beings as underlie the appearance, hence of mere intelligible beings, is not merely permitted but also unavoidable" (*Prolegomena* 107f.). Statements like this one seem to suggest that, in transcendental idealism, the distinction between appearances and things-in-themselves must be construed in terms of a causal relation between cause (thing-in-itself) and effect (appearance). On this understanding, it seems, that transcendental idealism couldn't avoid skeptical consequences. If our knowledge of the existence of external objects were due to a causal inference from the perceptual representation of an external object to the actually existing external object in itself outside us, then this knowledge would be uncertain because causal inferences of this sort are doubtful. For in this case the "cause of given perceptions" (CPR: A366), the external object, could, in principle, be a mere product of the imagination. However, according to Kant, transcendental idealism cannot be misconceived as "common idealism that itself doubts or denies the existence of external things" (CPR: B519), since the transcendental idealist does not causally infer the existence of external objects from inner perceptions. In transcendental idealism, Kant argues, external objects are rather "immediately perceived" (CPR: A371) because space and time are forms of intuition and not "something given in themselves," i.e. "independent of our sensibility" (CPR: A369; see Heidemann 2010). By the same token this makes the transcendental idealist a realist. Transcendental idealists are realists of a specific kind. They are empirical realists who affirm the reality of "extended beings" (CPR: B520) as they are intuited in space. This is not phenomenalism, the view that external reality is a construction out of perceived sense data. Transcendental idealists and empirical realists, rather, hold that objects do exist in "world-space even if no human being has ever perceived them or ever will perceive them" (CPR: B524). Empirical realism isn't indirect realism either, the view that representations in us function as mental mediators between mind and independently existing external reality. For in transcendental idealism external reality is mind-dependent in that we cannot cognize external objects independently of the conditions *a priori* of the possibility of knowledge.

That Kant succeeds in establishing an epistemological option that integrates idealism and realism was already disputed by his contemporaries. In the Refutation of

Idealism (CPR: B 274–9) he therefore responds to the criticism that his theory in the end is identical with external-world skepticism. There Kant argues that the fact of the "empirically determined, consciousness of my own existence" proves "the existence of objects in space outside me" (CPR: B275; see Guyer 1987: 279–329, and Heidemann 1998). Since the argument starts off with an empirical fact, namely self-consciousness or internal experience, to demonstrate that empirical self-consciousness is possible only on the condition of external experience, i.e. through the fact that there is an external world that affects our senses and thus makes it possible to determine our existence in time, it has, in more recent times, been regarded as the prototype of a transcendental argument (see Strawson: 1966). In a way it is symptomatic of the fate of transcendental idealism that Kant's efforts to repudiate charges of skepticism didn't convince the majority of his contemporaries or German Idealists. It is almost schizophrenic that, on the other hand, those philosophers did take transcendental idealism as an original source for their own epistemological ideas.

The early debate about transcendental idealism

In the immediate aftermath of the publication of the first *Critique* and the subsequent debate about transcendental philosophy the academic discussions in Germany were dominated to a large extent by two themes, pantheism and skepticism. Pantheism designates a metaphysical problem closely associated with Spinozism, atheism and determinism. It had been revived by F. H. Jacobi's book *On the Doctrine of Spinoza in Letters to Mr. Moses Mendelssohn* (1785). The so-called pantheism- or Spinozism-controversy resulting from that publication had an enormous impact on the development of German romanticism, early nineteenth-century philosophy, and especially of German Idealism (for details see Beiser 1987: 44–126). 'Skepticism', by contrast, designates specifically the epistemological problem of the justifiability of knowledge. In a way skepticism was the natural counter to the strong epistemological claims raised by Kant. Since many critics reproached Kant's system with being incomplete the debate about skepticism as it emerged from these claims took basically two forms. On the one hand, (early) adherents of transcendental idealism such as Reinhold and Fichte attempted to advance the theory by means of epistemological foundationalism to safeguard it from skeptical attacks. On the other hand, critics of transcendental idealism, such as Schulze and Maimon, insisted on unavoidable skeptical conclusions to be drawn from Kant's theory and its foundationalist reinterpretation. In the course of this complex debate many of its participants, e.g. Reinhold, and later Schelling, modified their views, or even changed sides. For that reason it would be inadequate to depict the situation just in black and white. Anyway, the emergence of German Idealism as such would be difficult to imagine without these oscillating epistemological discussions (see Beiser 1987; Giovanni and Harris 2000: 3–36).

Karl Leonard Reinhold's foundationalist account of transcendental idealism was of great importance for the further development of epistemology towards and within German Idealism. Epistemological foundationalism is the view that the structure of the justification of knowledge is hierarchical, exhibiting a basic belief, or principle, at the bottom that the edifice of knowledge builds upon. A widespread criticism of Kant that Reinhold responds to was that transcendental idealism fails because the dualism of sensibility and understanding lacks a unifying foundation. Reinhold became widely renowned through the publication of his *Letters on Kantian Philosophy* (1786/7). In the *Letters* he not only very successfully elucidated Kant's philosophy for the wider academic public; he also responded to the pantheism controversy (see the introduction to Reinhold 2005). Reinhold's significance from the point of view of systematic thought, however, is grounded in his theory of the faculty of representation that is supposed to provide the foundation of transcendental idealism through the "actual fact" or principle that: "Representation is that which is distinguished in consciousness by the subject from object and subject, and is referred to both" (Reinhold 2000: 72; see also 70, 78; for details of Reinhold's theory, see Chapter 1 of this volume). A modified version of this foundationalist idea re-emerges in Fichte's *Doctrine of Science*.

In part responsible for Fichte's appreciation of foundationalism is another important figure, who plays an active role in the early debate about transcendental idealism, Gottlob Ernst Schulze, the subsequent teacher of Schopenhauer. Schulze became known through his anonymously published book *Aenesidemus* (1792). The *Aenesidemus* – being not only a criticism of Reinhold but also of Kant – argues that the principle of consciousness is synthetic and therefore cannot serve as the unanalyzable foundation of knowledge, and moreover that the theory of the faculty of representation "contradicts its own principles" (Schulze 2000: 109; see also Beiser 1987: 272–9). It is interesting to see that Schulze's skepticism in the *Aenesidemus*, on the one hand, attacks the possibility of acquiring knowledge of metaphysical objects as well as *a priori* conditions of knowledge while, on the other hand, not denying the epistemological intelligibility of the concept of representation. This changes fundamentally in his major work, the *Critique of Theoretical Philosophy* (*Kritik der theoretischen Philosophie*) (1801). Radicalizing skepticism Schulze here argues that the cardinal mistake in philosophy is to believe "that all cognition of external objects is mediated through mere representations" (Schulze 1801: vol. 2, 8; my translation). The only certainties we have are "facts of consciousness" as immediate intuitions of these objects. Any further-going epistemic claim would be subject to skeptical doubt (Schulze 1801: vol. 1, 57–8, 63–4 my trans.). It was Schulze's skepticism of the *Aenesidemus* that had a major impact on the development of Fichte's foundationalist theory of knowledge in his *Doctrine of Science*.

Fichte's subjective idealism

Johann Gottlieb Fichte (1762–1814), the first major protagonist of German Idealism, started his philosophical career as an admirer not of Kant's theoretical, but of his practical, philosophy. In a letter dated from late summer 1790 he proclaims: "I have been living in a new world ever since reading the *Critique of Practical Reason*" (Fichte 1988: 357). It is therefore not surprising that Fichte first gained fame through a work in practical philosophy, more specifically in philosophy of religion respectively through his *Attempt at a Critique of All Revelation* (1792). The development of his work in the field of theoretical philosophy emerged from the engagement in the debate especially between Reinhold and Schulze on Kant's transcendental philosophy. To a certain extent Fichte's epistemological views were strongly influenced by that controversy inasmuch it shaped the systematic point of departure of his theory. Fichte calls this theory the *Doctrine of Science* (or *Science of Knowledge*). This title suggests that his intention was not to develop a theory of knowledge but a foundational conception that precedes such a theory, by exhibiting the basic structures of what it means at all to have knowledge. Like Kant, Fichte does not focus on the analysis of the concept but of the possibility of knowledge, on the question of what makes it possible to know something as such. This meta-theoretical approach differs from Kant in three major respects: First, Fichte's theory of knowledge as it is presented in the *Doctrine of Science* is to be seen in the tradition of *prima philosophia*, though he does not understand it in terms of traditional "pure metaphysics" (Fichte 1988: 97). Unlike Descartes he does not have an ontological interest in the ultimate essence of the epistemic subject. By contrast, Kant does not understand transcendental philosophy as *prima philosophia*, not least because his epistemology is not grounded on a unique foundational principle. Second, since Fichte aims at a foundational theory of knowledge in the aforementioned sense he had to conceive it as a theory of subjectivity. A theory of subjectivity explains the possibility of knowledge through the subject's cognitive activities. Accordingly, every element that is needed to give an account of the possibility of knowledge derives from the subject's basic cognitive activities. This is incompatible with Kant's departure from sources of knowledge. Third, unlike for Kant there is for Fichte an original unity of theoretical and practical philosophy depending on the structures of the I's cognitive activities (see Zöller 2002).

The foundation of knowledge

Fichte takes a major step towards the *Doctrine of Science* in his "Review of *Aenesidemus*" (1794). Still acknowledging Kant and Reinhold as major philosophical authorities but also partly agreeing with *Aenesidemus'* (Schulze's) criticisms of them (Fichte 1988: 59f.), he, in this essay, sets out to develop a new theory. Since Fichte accepts transcendental idealism while claiming Kant didn't justify it through adequate reasons, and since he renounces Reinhold's attempt to provide such reasons, he develops a version of transcendental idealism that had a foundational principle other than Reinhold's principle of consciousness as its basis. The central task of this theory is to explicate the new foundation as first principle. Since the theory's object is the most fundamental principle of all possible knowledge the theory itself had to be the most fundamental theory, i.e. the *Doctrine of Science* as "science of science as such" (Fichte 1988: 105). It is obvious that such a theory cannot justify the first principle from higher order principles for in this case the alleged first principle would be a subordinate principle. Fichte therefore conceives the *Doctrine of Science* as *philosophia prima*, as the theory of the highest principles pertaining not just to specific but to all philosophical, and even scientific areas. This "science of all sciences" (Fichte 1988: 114) has to meet certain requirements. Fichte mentions them in *Concerning the Concept of the Wissenschaftslehre*

(1794). The *Wissenschaftslehre* must begin with a proposition that is intrinsically certain and "communicates its certainty to the other propositions" thereby constituting "one science." This proposition is the "first principle" every science requires (Fichte 1988: 103–4). Fichte describes his epistemological project in terms of "a sound building" (Fichte 1988: 104) having the first principle as its foundation upon which a hierarchical systematic whole, the theory, can rest. Thus the first principle "cannot be demonstrated within that science itself" (Fichte 1988: 107), it has to be demonstrated independently of it. Consequently, Fichte entitles the book that for the first time establishes the first principle not just *Doctrine of Science* but *Foundations of the Entire Doctrine of Science* (1794/95). Clearly alluding to Kant's project of analyzing the possibility of particular sciences such as mathematics, the natural sciences, and metaphysics in particular, he, in a more radical way than Kant, formulates the *Foundations'* leading question in the following way: "[H]ow is science possible?" (Fichte 1988: 105). He explains the possibility of science as such through the doctrine of the self-positing I, and the three principles. This doctrine accomplishes the task of laying the foundation of the *Wissenschaftslehre*, i.e. of explaining how a scientific account of knowledge is possible. For Fichte it is self-evident that one can arrive at such a foundational theory only by departing from consciousness, because the possibility of knowing something depends in the first place on the subject's most fundamental cognitive activities; and any factual knowledge whatsoever already presupposes these activities. The *Wissenschaftslehre* is therefore 'idealism', i.e. a theory that makes subjectivity, or self-consciousness the principle by means of which the complete set of basic epistemic components necessary to explain the possibility of knowledge can be deduced. This form of idealism is subjective because it grounds the justification of knowledge on the cognitive activities of the *finite* I. However, subjective idealism cannot be associated with skepticism or even solipsism, since Fichte does not question external reality. His theory even presupposes the independent existence of physical objects as well as other rational minds. As we will see, skepticism indeed becomes a problem for Fichte's idealism.

The *Foundations of the Entire Doctrine of Science* starts off with the somewhat striking remark that the "absolutely unconditioned first principle of all human knowledge … can be neither proved nor defined" (Fichte 1970: 93). This is due to the status of the *Doctrine of Science*, as science of all sciences, not allowing for any principle or definition from which the first principle could be deduced. The theory's systematic starting point cannot be a "fact" ("Tatsache") either. First, since facts are usually construed as truth-makers of propositions, the first principle would depend on a fact as something its truth depends on; but this would be unacceptable for a *first* principle. Second, unlike facts the first principle cannot be proven. Third, to know facts already presupposes the first principle of knowledge. For these reasons the theory's systematic basis is the "*Act*" ("Tathandlung") expressing the first principle as something that "cannot appear among the empirical states of our consciousness" (Fichte 1970: 93). The insight that the *Act* lies at the basis of all consciousness can be achieved through abstracting from given facts as much as possible. What we cannot abstract from is thought, because without thought it would not be possible to give an account of the possibility of knowledge at all. Thinking is an *activity* performed through the reflecting subject thereby knowing itself as the object of thought. This knowledge is self-consciousness as the identity of knowing subject and known object, namely, the I. Hence, unlike Descartes, Fichte is not claiming that the self is a thinking substance. He rather contends that we cannot go behind the activity of thinking, and that the required unity of thought yields self-consciousness as the I's knowing itself. This irreducible, spontaneous activity at the basis of consciousness, or any knowledge whatsoever, gives rise to the first principle. Since it is a principle, a 'fundamental proposition' (in German: "Grundsatz"), it takes propositional shape: "The I posits itself" (Fichte 1970: 97). Though Fichte specifies that the I "posits its own existence" (Fichte 1970: 97) the first principle does not say that the I creates itself, or its objects. To interpret Fichte's idealism in a creationist manner would be fundamentally misleading. In Fichte's philosophy 'positing' rather denotes becoming conscious of x through reflecting on x. Thus, the I positing itself, i.e. its own existence, means that the act of reflection of the I yields at once what the I *is*, namely, self-consciousness. To put it another way, the I or self is at the same time "agent and the product of action" (Fichte 1970: 97), and thus knows itself.

Because self-consciousness is the identity-expression of the subject and object of consciousness Fichte claims that the first principle deduces the logical law of identity ("A = A") (Fichte 1970: 94). The original identity of self-consciousness, however, cannot fully explain the possibility of knowledge, since knowledge includes the basic difference between knowing subject and known object. To account for the idea of difference within knowledge Fichte introduces the second principle: "[A] not-I is opposed absolutely [posited in opposition] to the I" (Fichte 1970: 104). This proposition says that knowledge cannot be construed just as the homogeneous unity of self-consciousness, since to know means to know something, i.e. a known object that is different from the knowing, and thus far limits the sphere of the knowing. Therefore the self-positing of the I is only possible through the posited not-I; and as opposed, both are independent of each other. According to Fichte, from the second principle the logical law of non-contradiction can be deduced. Since the unity of consciousness, i.e. self-consciousness is indispensable for knowledge I and not-I have to "be thought together" (Fichte 1970: 108). This is accomplished through the third principle: "In the self I oppose a divisible not-self to the divisible self" (Fichte 1970: 110). The third principle, from which the logical law of sufficient reason is deducible, thinks I and not-I together by dividing the overall unity of the I up into two mutually limiting spheres: The I knows itself by being limited through the not-I, and the not-I can be known by being limited through the I. This complex epistemic structure constitutes the unity of self-consciousness and hence the very possibility of knowledge. The early *Wissenschaftslehre* is thus a developmental theory of self-consciousness and knowledge because the "Science of Knowledge is to be a pragmatic history of the human mind" (Fichte 1970: 198–9). From Fichte onwards the history of self-consciousness became a significant meta-theoretical conception in German Idealism aiming at the explanation of the possibility of (self-)knowledge. The term 'history of self-consciousness' does not designate the empirical coming into being of the human mind in the course of real history. 'History of self-consciousness' rather is a developmental theory designed to demonstrate how a systematic deduction of logical and epistemic concepts, faculties and claims is possible, starting from a basic principle, namely subjectivity, that itself is proved to be an objective principle within the 'historical' process of the self's epistemic self-realization. In the *Doctrine of Science* the "pragmatic history of the human mind" constructs the development of self-consciousness as a trajectory that gradually enriches the I's cognitive and epistemic capacities. At the end-point of that ideal trajectory the I's fully developed cognitive scale, and with it the explanation of the possibility of knowledge, is realized. There are early forms of that conception in Platner, Reinhold, and Maimon that Fichte was familiar with (Breazeale 2001).

In Fichte's theory of knowledge the self's original independence demonstrates that the I is the unifying ground of theoretical as well as practical philosophy, the foundation that is missing in Kant's philosophy. For since the I posits itself as I it accomplishes not only its own theoretical spontaneity but at the same time also its practical freedom as self-determining will. Subsequent to the exposition of the three principles, the *Foundations of the Entire Doctrine of Science* analyses in greater detail the "Foundation of theoretical Knowledge" in terms of the systematic deduction of categories as well as cognitive faculties such as interdetermination, causality, substance, imagination, representation, intuition, understanding, judgment and reason. The third part, on the "Foundation of knowledge of the practical," does the same with respect to the 'practical' components of knowledge such as striving, drive and feeling. It is one of Fichte's central claims that the I can become aware of its self-positing and the structure of its cognitive activities through "intellectual intuition." "Intellectual intuition" is a non-sensible, holistic "act" of spontaneous self-knowledge "by means of which the I originates": It "is the immediate consciousness that I act and of what I do when I act" (Fichte 1994: 46; see also 42, 47–51). However, the I's original activity has to be motivated through "a mere check" ("Anstoß") (Fichte 1970: 190–1) as the limiting factor of knowledge that activates its positing. The "check" originally belongs to the I, for the second and third principles show that its self-positing necessarily involves limitation, i.e. the "check" is not a merely contingent limitation of the I but an epistemic constituent of self-consciousness. This multilayered conception of self-positing as a whole makes Fichte's theory especially vulnerable to charges of skepticism.

Dogmatism, idealism, and skepticism

Because of its strong idealist claims the *Doctrine of Science* seems to leave no room for a realist account of the external world, i.e. an account of external reality as being independent of the epistemic subject. The skeptical concern that Fichte cannot satisfactorily explain how external-world beliefs are about real external objects is even amplified through his attempt to conclusively deduce the external world, or to be more precise, our conception of the external world, from the I. In the *Foundations of Natural Right* (1796) he presents an argument according to which external reality is the condition of the possibility of the practical I's self-consciousness inasmuch the practical I posits the external world to limit its activity, thereby making external reality dependent on the I's positing. In a similar manner Fichte likewise attempts to deduce the person's body from the I's activity of positing. These arguments are led by the general idea that "the entire system of objects for the I must be produced by the I itself" (Fichte 2000: 27). Fichte was well aware of the possible misunderstanding of his theory as being opposed to realist accounts of our knowledge about the external world. Recapitulating the main ideas of the *Foundation of the Entire Doctrine of Science* in a more accessible way, in the "First Introduction" (1797/98) he juxtaposes in opposition the "systems" of "idealism" and "dogmatism" as "the only ones possible," the first one regarding external world representations as "products of the intellect," the latter as "a product of the thing in itself" (Fichte 1994: 11). Both "systems" aim at "displaying the foundation of experience"; however, to accomplish this task idealism and dogmatism must likewise presuppose their "system." For that reason neither of the "two systems can directly refute the opposing one" (Fichte 1994: 15). From this Fichte draws the often-misconstrued conclusion: "The kind of philosophy one chooses thus depends upon the kind of person one is" (Fichte 1994: 20). It is not Fichte's view that the choice of a system is an arbitrary one but that the *free* opt for idealism, the system of freedom, whereas the *unfree* opt for the system of deterministic dogmatism.

The idealist spirit of this line of argument in favor of the I as foundation of all knowledge turned out to be grist for the mill of those critics who attacked Fichte in connection with the atheism controversy of 1798/99. The most severe attack on his system was launched by F. H. Jacobi who reproached him with nihilism (see Beiser 2002: 223–6). In the sequel, Fichte was forced to respond to this criticism, and he did so by clarifying and modifying his philosophy in several works. Illuminating – especially with respect to dogmatism, idealism and the problem of skepticism – is the *Vocation of Man* (1800) because Fichte here summarizes his position in a particularly clear way. The work's first book ("Doubt") examines nature according to specific categories such as thing and property, the principle of complete determination, causality, as well as substance and force. The examination yields the insight that nature is, as Fichte says, "an unbroken chain of appearances, since each link is determined by the one preceding it and determines the one following it" (Fichte 1987: 7). The theory characterized here is Spinozism as the position of rationalist-dogmatic determinism. For according to dogmatism the I along with its cognitive capacities is a product of effective natural forces because it is "a link in this chain of strict necessity" (Fichte 1987: 11). By means of practical arguments Fichte confronts the Spinozist system with the theoretical possibility that the I possesses an original awareness of its freedom, on the basis of which it is able to determine itself to free action. Hence, book 1 of the *Vocation of Man* ends with the unsolvable conflict or "disagreement" (Fichte 1987: 23) between the systems of dogmatism (realism) and idealism.

Book 2 ("Knowledge"), set up as a dialogue between the I and Spirit, discusses idealism. The dialogue reconstructs basic ideas of the *Doctrine of Science* focusing on the problem of knowledge of the external world. By means of the aforementioned categories Fichte first analyzes the capacity of sensation as a reliable source of knowledge about external reality. The result of that analysis is that external-world knowledge cannot solely rely on sensation. Next the examination moves on to intuition. As Fichte argues, perception of external objects is nothing but external intuition, i.e. the I's self-intuition: "In all consciousness I intuit myself; for I am I: for the subjective, that which is conscious, it is intuition" (Fichte 1987: 50–1). Eventually thought endows intuition with sensation by synthesizing both: "The *property* of the thing has its origin in the sensation of my own condition, and *space*, which it fills, has its origin in intuition. The two are connected by thought" (Fichte 1987: 56). This synthesis, however, is nothing over and above an immanent product of consciousness. Hence, consciousness of external objects is nothing but the product of the I's representational capacity. Therefore the external world itself proves to be nothing but the I's representation. In this context an instructive analysis of external-world skepticism and its consequences emerges. The I now claims that there is "nothing, absolutely nothing but presentations; determinations of consciousness as mere consciousness" (Fichte 1987: 60). From this claim it follows that the external world is nothing but mere representation, a "mere image, only a shadow of a reality" (Fichte 1987: 60). The uncertainty of our external-world beliefs is not the major issue here. On the condition of strong representationalism "I myself disappear no less than it, I become a mere presenting without sense and without purpose" (Fichte 1987: 60). This holds equally true for the I's body ("Körper," "Leib") and the I as "mental being." For if all external objects are nothing over and above representations then this also goes for my own body as a physical object in space. However, the thinking I itself equally turns out to be nothing but "a product of my thinking, something purely and entirely thought up ..." (Fichte 1987: 61). According to Fichte's argument, the I's access to its own mental states is mediated through representations, and, consequently, also the idea of an existing, thinking I collapses for it turns out that even the I is "a pure invention" (Fichte 1987: 63). In the *Vocation of Man* Fichte seems to claim that, in the proper sense of the word, there is no I as the permanent, mental reference point of all representations. The analysis of the I's cognitive capacities shows that we are not allowed to state "I think;" but at the same time we are likewise not allowed to use the impersonal formulation *"there is thinking"* either. The only thing we can state about our own mental states is *"thought appears*: the thought *that* I feel, intuit, think" (Fichte 1987: 63). From this it results that the "I think" is mere fabrication rather than a persisting mental substratum as the point of unity of mental states, i.e. as the representing, the *I*. Consciousness dissolves into a disconnected change of images, without there being an observer who visualizes them. Fichte formulates this in a powerful way: "There are *images*: they are all that exists and they know about themselves in the manner of images – images which drift by, without there being anything by which they drift; images which hang together through images; images which do not represent anything, without meaning and purpose. I myself am one of these images. No, I am not even that, but only a distorted image of these images" (Fichte 1987: 63–4). From this Fichte draws a skeptical conclusion, a skeptical conclusion that is even more radical than the one put forward in the Cartesian dream argument: "All reality is transformed into a fabulous dream, without there being any life the dream is about, without there being a mind which dreams" (Fichte 1987: 64).

There are two problems with this line of argument. First, it seems to be unreasonable to develop external-world skepticism into what one might call 'internal-world skepticism'. For it is obviously unintelligible to doubt one's own mental states in terms of disputing the reality of the representing I. Second, it is unclear what Fichte intends to show with the aid of this kind of skepticism. It looks as if he uses radical skeptical doubt about the existence of the representing I in order to show, as a response to Jacobi's reproach of nihilism, that the theoretical I is unable to secure our knowledge of the external world, and that we have to open up the practical dimension of subjectivity to see how we can secure such knowledge. This is reflected in book 3 ("Faith") of the *Vocation*, where Fichte shows how the practical I determines itself as practical reason through the awareness of its freedom. Accordingly, man's vocation is "faith" as expressed though moral will and human conscience. The only way to assure us of external reality is through our awareness as moral beings acting in accordance with God's law as the moral foundation. Appealing to the reality of practical reason Fichte attempts to repudiate objections according to which the *Doctrine of Science* favors skepticism, and even nihilism. This appeal foreshadows a fundamental change in his theory. The various versions of the *Wissenschaftslehre* after 1800 move towards a metaphysical intuitionism of the divine and depart from the original epistemological project of grounding transcendental idealism; that is, in his later work Fichte seems to give up early subjective idealism. Considering the development of German Idealism it indeed looks as if epistemology, around 1800, is superseded by the re-establishment of metaphysical accounts of reality.

Hegel's absolute idealism

At first glance this view gets support from the rise of Hegelian idealism, not least because Hegel begins his academic career in close collaboration with his old friend and full-fledged metaphysician Friedrich Wilhelm Joseph von Schelling (1775–1854) in Jena. Within German Idealism Schelling is undoubtedly the most famous as a proponent of philosophy of nature and metaphysics rather than of a theory of knowledge. However, it is noteworthy that before Schelling got engaged in speculative metaphysics, particularly in his philosophy of identity after 1800, he participated in the early idealist debate about foundational problems of knowledge. His thematic interest in the justification of knowledge arose from his encounter with Kant's philosophy, on the one hand, and his initial admiration of Fichte, on the other. Similar to Fichte the early Schelling (1794-1800) started off with the basic criticism according to which Kant's philosophical project is uncompleted, because it does not offer a unifying superior principle of transcendental idealism (see Schelling 1980: 64–6). In *Of the I as Principle of All Philosophy* (1794) Schelling argues in line with Fichte that there must be an "original ground of reality," i.e. a "real ground of all our knowledge" (see Schelling 1980: 71–2). The justificatory model he has in mind complies with classical epistemological foundationalism. Accordingly, conditional knowledge depends on unconditional knowledge, and since we have conditional knowledge there must be unconditional knowledge. From this Schelling eventually concludes that the "unconditional" of human knowledge "can lie only in the *absolute I*" and "intellectual intuition" (see Schelling 1980: 74–5, 81, 85). Though the early Schelling agrees with the major ideas of the *Doctrine of Science* he does not accept Fichte's teachings all along the line. This becomes evident in the *Philosophical Letters on Dogmatism and*

Criticism (1795). Here Schelling argues, like Fichte, for the superiority of "criticism" over "dogmatism" because the latter does not allow for "my freedom." On the other hand, he postulates "freedom" in criticism and "necessity" in "dogmatism" (realism) to "be united in the absolute" (cf. Schelling 1980: 191, 189). This move already indicates how Schelling begins to distance himself from the *Doctrine of Science*, especially because of the claim that nature is independent of the positing I, a claim unacceptable for Fichte. Having given up epistemological interests as such, after the publication of the *System of Transcendental Idealism* (1800) Schelling dedicated his philosophical efforts to the development of an idealist metaphysics of nature.

It is not surprising that, when Hegel arrived in Jena in 1801, he initially worked with Schelling on a common philosophical project that one might call "absolute metaphysics" (see Düsing 1988). The project's aim was to demonstrate the possibility of rational cognition of the absolute. However, this project didn't commit Hegel to ignoring epistemological problems for the rest of his philosophical career. By contrast, there can be no doubt that in the history of philosophy Georg Wilhelm Friedrich Hegel (1770–1831) is among those philosophers who made significant contributions to theory of knowledge. Hegel's account of knowledge is especially vital in three respects: First, he challenges the idea of epistemology as first philosophy. Second, he regards a knowledge as the product of *historical* development. Third, he aims to keep skepticism under control by integrating it into the concept of knowledge formation, thereby allowing for a restitution of metaphysics within absolute idealism. Although Hegel dedicates much of his philosophical work to the concept of knowledge, he is in particular opposed to theory of knowledge in terms of the Kantian critical analysis of cognitive faculties as well as the transcendental proof of the elements of knowledge. The works that are most representative of Hegel's views on knowledge are the *Phenomenology of Spirit* (1807) and the *Encyclopedia of the Philosophical Sciences* (1817–30). The celebrated *Science of Logic* (1812–31) is a book on ontology, i.e. on the dialectical development of categories as pure determinations of thought, although it contains several references to problems of cognition. Hegel's dialectic as such cannot, in the first place, be regarded as an epistemological conception. 'Dialectic' is rather a methodological concept explaining the development of categories in his ontology.

Justifying knowledge without first epistemic principles

Hegel's main concern about the theory of knowledge is the claim raised by many traditional epistemologists that before cognition can legitimately be acquired the concept or possibility of knowledge has to be justified. Directed against Kant's *critical* project of investigating "our *faculty of cognition*" before employing it, Hegel objects that "to want to have cognition *before* we have any is as absurd as the wise resolve of Scholasticus to learn to *swim before he ventured into the water*" (Hegel 1991: 34; see also Hegel 1977b: 46–8). For Hegel such a project must fail because the examination of knowledge cannot be accomplished by making use of epistemic principles that the examination has yet to examine. Hegel does not deny that beliefs have to be justified to count as knowledge; however, he abolishes the possibility of doing so on the basis of a preceding theory of justification that appeals to an allegedly unquestionable epistemic starting point. In this respect his critique of epistemology targets two major approaches: First, the *intuitionist* approach of founding knowledge by appealing to something intuitive, i.e. directly given, as Schelling, Jacobi and the romantics claimed. Second, the *individualist* approach of grounding knowledge on the individual I and its cognitive performances. According to Hegel, it is especially Descartes, Kant, Reinhold, and Fichte who favor this approach.

Hegel is not just interested in a criticism of the theoretical status of epistemology. There is another, more deeply rooted reason why he distances himself from the traditional project of the theory of knowledge. Although Hegel respects Kant as a major philosophical authority, he believes that Kant's criticism of metaphysics is mistaken from the very beginning. Without paying much attention to the motivation of critical philosophy and the transcendental meaning of the question of whether synthetic judgments *a priori* are possible, the Jena Hegel, in *Faith and Knowledge* (1802) reinterprets central elements of the theory of apperception and judgment of the first *Critique*. He objects that Kant confines himself to an empiricist "investigation of the finite intellect," therefore being unable to see that "rational insight" into infinite, metaphysical ideas preceding finite cognition is possible (Hegel 1977a: 70-71). Contrary to Kant, Hegel firmly believes in the possibility of metaphysics as science, though not in the pre-critical sense of a theory of the soul, world and God. This line of argument and objection to Kant's criticism of metaphysics looms throughout his work. It was after his first publications that Hegel became more and more aware that his rejection of any theory of knowledge as first philosophy, together with Kant's criticism of metaphysics, required Hegel to offer an epistemological alternative. His first book, the *Phenomenology of Spirit* (1807), is supposed to provide this alternative.

It would be short-sighted to take the *Phenomenology* as an isolated, independent project. The work must rather be conceived against the backdrop of the metaphysical views Hegel held around 1800. In roughly 1797 Hegel became an adherent of Hölderlin's (and Sinclair's) metaphysics of unification. According to this conception, the absolute cannot be rationally cognized, since as divine union that precedes finite opposition it is the object of religious faith. On the one hand, finite understanding's only way to apprehend absolute, divine union is intellectual intuition. On the other hand, divine union manifests itself within finite understanding by way of (conceptual) oppositions that are characteristic of the cognitive limitations of the human mind. This is why Hegel at this time believed religion to be superior to metaphysics. Philosophical reason only unsuccessfully strives to achieve absolute union that precedes finite opposition. It is important to see that, according to Hegel's early metaphysical conception, there is an irreconcilable conflict or opposition within the finite, and that the absolute or divine cannot be rationally cognized, since it is the object of religious faith. However, around 1800/1 Hegel changes his position. He now replaces religion with metaphysics, and assigns logic the function of introducing metaphysics. In this new conception, logic is supposed to fulfill the function of a preparatory introduction to metaphysics by showing the immanent deficiencies of finite cognition, i.e. by exhibiting contradictions inherent in reflection. The method logic applies is the skeptical procedure of counter-positing that guides reason in producing antinomies. In establishing antinomies, skepticism reaches beyond finite reflection, Hegel argues, and touches upon speculative reason as the negative side of the cognition of the absolute. The negative side of the cognition of the absolute presupposes its positive side that is itself cognized through intellectual intuition. The logic Hegel has in mind is not formal or symbolic logic. Logic as a preparatory introduction to metaphysics rather is the logic of finite cognition. With respect to the internal contradictions of finite cognition Hegel particularly refers to Kant's antinomies and, moreover, to the paradoxes of the *Parmenides*. According to the *Skepticism* essay (Hegel 2000), antinomies and paradoxes document internal contradictions of finite cognition that arise when assessing the cognitive capacities of finite understanding. Like Schelling, and following Spinoza's philosophy, Hegel, at around 1801, conceived of the absolute as substance. However, around 1804 he realized that to conceive of the absolute as substance is to leave it underdetermined (see Düsing 1995: Ch. 3). He became aware specifically of the problem that the absolute is not a static object of thought (substance) but rather comprises complex logical relations that can only be developed in an independent discipline. It is this independent discipline that finally became the speculative science of logic. After having given up the earlier idea of religion being superior to metaphysics, then replacing religion with metaphysics and assigning logic the function of introducing metaphysics, he finally converts logic itself into metaphysics as the science of the absolute. As mentioned earlier, this science is not a theory of knowledge but of ontology. It is the *Phenomenology of Spirit* that now takes on the function of introducing metaphysics.

The *Phenomenology*'s aim is the justification of knowledge, i.e. to demonstrate "*actual* knowing" as "insight into what knowing is" (Hegel 1977b: 3, 17). Hegel argues that beliefs or epistemic claims initially count as an "appearance of knowledge," and that the *Phenomenology* examines step by step whether and how they comply with the concept of "true knowledge" (Hegel 1977b: 48–9). Most important is that the theoretical transformation of provisional knowledge into "true knowledge," i.e. the justification of knowledge, is supposed to be possible without presupposing (unjustified) first epistemic principles. In the *Phenomenology* Hegel directs this claim against the *intuitionist* and *individualist* approaches in epistemology. Accordingly, intuitionism claims to have "immediate knowledge of the Absolute." This knowledge claim is, however, unjustified because in intuitionism "the absolute is not supposed to be comprehended, it is to be felt or intuited" (Hegel 1977b: 4). Individualism in epistemology basically faces the same problem. Descartes' *primo cognitio*, Kant's transcendental apperception, or Fichte's principles lay claim to the epistemic status of a "universal" philosophical "beginning" without conceptually developing this. Such an epistemic starting point consequently lacks justification since one can only dogmatically ensure its truth, by relying on "a dogmatism of self-certainty" (Hegel 1977b: 13, 33; see also Heidemann 2008). Because of these flaws Hegel argues for an anti-intuitionist and anti-individualist account of knowledge. According to this account, true epistemic claims result from a process of epistemic justification conceived as the "path of education." "Education" or "Bildung" is to be understood in terms of an epistemic process of "coming-to-be of *Science as such* or of *knowledge*" proceeding from basic forms of epistemic consciousness, such as sensory knowledge, to "genuine knowledge" (Hegel 1977b: 15–16). The *Phenomenology* is in this sense a theory of epistemic justification not relying on presupposed, unjustified first principles, thereby avoiding the short-comings of intuitionism and individualism in epistemology. Hegel is not denying that this theory would require principles of justification; he rather emphasizes that these principles emerge within the process of justification itself and cannot be taken from somewhere else. The achievement of true knowledge at the end of the process then opens access to metaphysics. The epistemological method that is supposed to make this possible is the history of self-consciousness (Hegel 1977b: 15–16).

Idealist history of self-consciousness

For Hegel the problem of justifying knowledge is essentially a skeptical problem. Its solution is made possible through the history of self-consciousness, more precisely, through the combination of the history of self-consciousness and what he calls "thoroughgoing [self-fulfilling, D.H.] skepticism" (Hegel 1977b: 50). In the intro-duction to the *Phenomenology* Hegel prepares his argument by alluding to Agrippa's trilemma according to which the justification of a criterion or "standard" of knowledge involves either circularity, dogmatism or infinite regress (Hegel 1977b: 52–3; see Heidemann 2007: Ch. 3). To overcome this trilemma he introduces the concept of an emerging science that reforms itself as truth by turning against the mere appearance of knowledge in consciousness and thereby abdicating its provisional status. The transformation takes the form of a skeptical examination of fundamental knowledge claims. The standard required in order to carry out this examination, Hegel argues, falls into the sphere of the examined consciousness, for "truth" and "knowledge" are "abstract determinations" of consciousness itself (Hegel 1977b: 52). The examination of knowledge specifically consists in a comparison of consciousness with what it takes to be true. Consequently, an epistemic claim meets the standard of true knowledge if consciousness corresponds to what it takes to be true. In this manner the knowing consciousness itself produces the standard of knowledge, and does not have to presuppose it. The history of self-consciousness is the coherent application of this highly abstract method.

Hegel adapts this method from Fichte and Schelling, and coins it "history of the *education* of consciousness itself to the standpoint of Science" (Hegel 1977b: 50), i.e. not a history of empirical events but of ideal epistemic stages. Its purpose is to explain how the human mind develops epistemic claims as a "series of forms" of consciousness (Hegel 1977b: 50–1), and how these claims are transformed into true knowledge. A form of consciousness is an idealized epistemic shape or structure of consciousness with respect to specific fields of knowledge such as sense certainty, perception, reason or spirit. The exposition of forms of consciousness explains the specific epistemic claims involved in sense certainty, perception, etc., and answers the question of whether consciousness meets these claims so as to acquire *true* knowledge. Each form of consciousness must have its own standard by means of which it is possible to determine whether an epistemic claim is satisfied. The standard is intrinsic to each form of consciousness and set up by consciousness itself. According to this conception, no shape of consciousness meets its standard or "criterion" except "absolute knowing" as the fully developed form of self-consciousness or self-knowledge. Hegel's examination of the "criterion of what knowledge is" (Hegel 1977b: 55) is notoriously difficult to grasp. An easier way to understand how this methodological procedure works is to look at two concrete examples of its application in the *Phenomenology*: "sense certainty" and "perception."

"Sense certainty" and "perception" are the two shapes of consciousness the *Phenomenology* examines first. The examination starts off with sense certainty because sense certainty, Hegel argues, seems to provide the most secure knowledge since it is non-conceptual as well as immediate knowledge. It is knowledge of something that is, "merely because it is" (Hegel 1977b: 58–9). As Hegel points out, immediacy therefore is the standard that knowledge has to meet in sense certainty. Knowledge is immediate if it is acquired through the senses, and not achieved through conceptual inferences. Now the *Phenomenology*'s skeptical analysis examines whether sense certainty meets its own standard. The analysis takes three steps. In the first step the analysis examines sense certainty's claim to have immediate sensory knowledge of spatio-temporal objects. The linguistic equivalents of such knowledge are "Now" and "Here" (Hegel 1977b: 60). *Prima facie* both of these indexicals seem to express the immediate epistemic relation between the knowing consciousness and the cognized object, such as in the statement '*Now* is x, and *here* is y.' But Hegel shows that because of their invariant sense, indexical terms are indeed not capable of establishing such a direct relation. "Now" denotes arbitrary points in time (e.g. morning, night, noon) while "Here" denotes arbitrary spatial locations (e.g. tree, house, chair). Sense certainty consequently cannot represent *immediate* knowledge, because "Now" and "Here" are universal linguistic representations (indexicals) and do not by nature pick out particular objects. For this reason the universal rather than the particular has to be regarded as the truth of sense certainty. The second step therefore examines whether the "I" as the knowing subject is capable of establishing epistemic immediacy, because "the immediacy of my seeing, hearing, and so on" seems to be beyond doubt (Hegel 1977b: 61). This move fails for the same reason the first step falls through: The term "I" is a universal, an indexical that cannot successfully ensure immediate reference to its object, the "I" of cognitive performances, for the term "I" does not individuate a particular "I." Thus, in sense certainty, knowledge of the "I" does not represent *immediate* knowledge of myself. In the third step, the question is whether it is possible to establish epistemic immediacy in sense certainty by taking sensory knowledge as "a pure act of intuiting" (Hegel 1977b: 63). The idea is to stick to *one* immediate point in sense experience. Maintaining, e.g. the proposition "Now is day," as an immediate relation means to point to a single instance as a temporal singularity. As the skeptical analysis shows again it is not possible to establish sense certainty's relation of immediacy, for "Now" is many "Nows" since the "Now" as day contains hours, minutes, seconds and so on. The same holds true as well for the "Here" (Hegel 1977b: 64). Consequently, in "Sense certainty" consciousness cannot satisfy its standard of epistemic immediacy.

According to the *Phenomenology*'s method of self-fulfilling skepticism, consciousness must give up sense certainty and its standard in favor of a new shape of consciousness that sets up its own standard of knowing. The new shape of consciousness is "perception" and its "criterion of truth is ... self-identity" (Hegel 1977b: 70). Sense certainty and perception are not completely unrelated, though, for in perception the immediate sensual is now conceived as "property." This is due to Hegel's principle of "*determinate* negation" (Hegel 1977b: 51) according to which skeptical doubt does not completely destroy a shape of consciousness but takes over the positive outcome of its predecessor to the following stage of consciousness. In perception the problem is that things have many properties, and the perceiving consciousness therefore has to conceive of things as unities of properties. This only seems to be possible if a thing is the self-identical bearer of its properties. Hegel again carries out a three-step analysis examining whether in perception consciousness meets the criterion of self-identity. The examination eventually demonstrates that perception is likewise incapable of meeting its standard, and that it must be abandoned.

Whether and how the *Phenomenology*'s shapes of consciousness subsequent to the "Perception" chapter can be reconstructed in the same way, and whether Hegel succeeds in showing that "Absolute Knowing" is its end-point is a question of detailed analysis (see Forster 1998). In fact, in his later writings, in particular in the *Encyclopedia*, Hegel advocates a different account of knowledge. Though different from the *Phenomenology*'s skeptical procedure of knowledge acquisition. It still remains skeptical in nature.

Skepticism, dialectic, and absolute idealism

Though after 1807 Hegel no longer pursues the project of the *Phenomenology* he still, in the *Encyclopedia of the Philosophical Sciences* (1817, 1827, and 1830), holds onto the critical views of traditional epistemology he developed in his early writings. He claims, first, that unlike in Kant, knowledge does not rely on the basic distinction of sources of knowledge. Second, it is not possible to examine the nature of knowledge by means of knowledge. Third, contrary to what the standard analysis of knowledge as justified true belief tells us, we cannot specify conditions beliefs must satisfy to count as knowledge. Fourth, epistemic justification does not conduce to the transformation of beliefs into truth, i.e. unlike what the majority of modern epistemologists claim, true knowledge does not rely on a procedure that distinguishes between a set of tools of knowledge acquisition, on the one hand, and the application of these tools to true knowledge, on the other. By contrast, Hegel argues for a conception of knowledge that does justice to both skepticism and dialectic, the latter being a key component of absolute idealism. Similar to his procedure in the *Phenomenology* in the opening chapters of the *Logic* (the first of three constitutive parts of the *Encyclopedia*) Hegel rejects the possibility of "immediate knowledge" as an epistemically inappropriate idea. However, he explicitly concedes the requirement to give an account of what knowledge is. The first possibility for meeting this requirement would be to start with an epistemological analysis of knowledge, e.g. as a theory of epistemic justification. As mentioned earlier, this is what he takes to be systematically question-begging. The second possibility would be to introduce a specific concept of knowledge as a working hypothesis. This in fact would be dogmatic, for such a beginning, e.g. with the "category of immediacy," would have to rely on unjustified "[a]ssurances" instead of "proofs" (Hegel 1991: 6, 24), and is therefore vulnerable to skeptical attacks. Thus starting with the analysis of knowledge and beginning by presupposing an initial concept of knowledge would be equally futile.

To escape this difficulty Hegel develops the idea of knowledge starting from the conception of philosophy as the "thinking consideration of objects" (Hegel 1991: 24). He believes this to be the legitimate point of departure since the "scientific cognition of truth" can only be carried out through thinking, and this means, for Hegel, essentially by means of "concepts" as the only way of grasping what the content of our consciousness such as "feeling, intuition, image, etc." *is* (Hegel 1991: 26). Philosophy's task is therefore to "raise itself above the natural, sensible, and argumentative consciousness into its own unadulterated elements," i.e. concepts, and to free itself from what is just given in consciousness (Hegel 1991: 35). Hegel claims that the true *philosophical* use of concepts is different from the common use of them as analytic, abstract representations. The *philosophical* use of concepts "in the speculative sense" has, of course, to be "justified" (Hegel 1991: 33). It is one of Hegel's central arguments against *traditional* epistemology that this kind of justification cannot be assigned to the theory of knowledge as a discipline that precedes *philosophy* as speculative science of concepts, because the justification of philosophical science is itself "philosophical cognition, and therefore it can only fall within philosophy" (Hegel 1991: 33-34). Consequently, epistemology cannot be carried out as a "preliminary explanation," namely as a theory of epistemic justification that conduces to the transformation of beliefs into truth, for such a theory would have to work from an unjustified basis. The science of *philosophy* is therefore different from sciences like physics or mathematics in that it does not simply find but produces its object, i.e. thinking. That thinking as mental activity is philosophy's 'immediate' object is for Hegel an unquestionable *fact* (Hegel 1991: 54). However, the insight into the *fact* that thinking is 'immediate' is itself mediated through thinking; it is not a given content of consciousness like empirical or non-empirical representations. As such the self-mediation of pure thinking is the object of *Logic*. The *Logic* thereby demonstrates that "questions about the nature of cognition" can be reduced to "simple determinations of thought" (Hegel 1991: 65). Hence, analyzing knowledge means to develop the complexity of thinking as such, as opposed to formulating conditions of cognition, or examining sources of knowledge. In the *Encyclopedia* Hegel claims to provide such an account of knowledge, although from the outset the methodological requirement of presuppositionslessness confronts him with the problem of skepticism.

The problem of "presuppositionlessness" (Hegel 1991: 124) is subsequent to the problem of a systematic introduction to metaphysics. For Hegel it is clear that the demonstration of "Science" (Hegel 1991: 124) must not make any unjustified presuppositions. Applying skeptical doubt as the method of a systematic introduction to science would be question-begging since Science itself is supposed not to rely on any preceding justification. The demonstration of Science can therefore not be construed as a procedure of skeptical justification. Consequently, the *Phenomenology* and its method of self-fulfilling skepticism can no longer function as a systematic introduction to metaphysics (see Heidemann 2007: 327–39). Hegel responds to this difficulty with the claim that we can get access to Science without relying on presuppositions, "by the freedom that abstracts from everything, and grasps its own pure abstraction, the simplicity of thinking – in the resolve to think purely" (1991: 124). Hegel believes that the "resolve" represents the appropriate procedure to make it possible for an individual to get immediate access to the proper content of Science by pure thought. He thereby denies that skeptical doubt is threatening to "Science," since skepticism is contained within philosophy as "the dialectical moment" (Hegel 1991: 128–30). Here one has to bear in mind that, according to speculative idealism, logic represents "the pure truth itself" (Hegel 1991: 45–8). As such, it contains "objective thoughts" that "express the essentialities of the things," however, not as a collection of abstract terms but as dialectically evolving "thought-determinations." Since Hegel's logic is to be construed in traditional terms of ontology, it "coincides with metaphysics" (Hegel 1991: 56).

Now to establish the claim that truth can be cognized through pure thought one must show that the finite "forms of cognition" are deficient, for otherwise logic or metaphysics wouldn't represent the *only* possible "Science" of "the pure truth itself" (Hegel 1991: 46). This is demonstrated by the nullification of the finite "forms of cognition" through skeptical doubt: "The high skepticism of antiquity accomplishes this by showing that every one of those forms contained a contradiction within itself" (Hegel 1991: 61). At this point skepticism intersects with dialectic. For according to Hegel, "every genuine philosophy" has a "negative side," i.e. a "free side" (Hegel 2000: 324f). This "negative" or "free side" is skepticism, to be more precise, skepticism understood in terms of dialectic. By integrating skepticism qua dialectic into philosophy, Hegel pursues the strategy of immunizing metaphysics or, more broadly, philosophy against skeptical doubt. The alliance between skepticism and dialectic is systematically motivated. The finite mind, Hegel argues, cognitively amounts to nothing more than the fixation of its concepts, i.e. Kantian or Fichtean categories. On the other hand, the mere fixation of finite concepts is one-sided. To overcome one-sidedness, the determinations of finite understanding have to be opposed, as they are in Kant's antinomies, and finally sublated by their unification through speculative thought. The *Encyclopedia* describes this procedure in the order of three steps as "three sides" the "logical has": (a) "the side of abstraction or of the understanding," (b) "the dialectical or negatively rationale side," and (c) "the speculative or positively rational one" (Hegel 1991: 125). Within this sequence skepticism's systematic place is the "dialectical moment": "The dialectical, taken separately on its own by the understanding, constitutes skepticism, especially when it is exhibited in scientific concepts. Skepticism contains the mere negation that results from the dialectic" (Hegel 1991: 128). It is the concept "negation," i.e. contradiction that explains the connection between skepticism and dialectic. Skepticism is not identical with dialectic though. Dialectic demonstrates the "one-sidedness and restrictedness of the determinations of the understanding" (Hegel 1991: 128), hence, their "negation."

Negating is what the skeptic does by raising doubts and thereby opposing epistemic claims. Unlike dialectic, skepticism does not go any further than demonstrating the "negation" of the "determinations of the understanding." Nevertheless, skepticism is capable of recognizing the positive content of its "negation." Consequently, skepticism and dialectic coincide only in as much as both reveal finite understanding's intrinsic negativity. Even so, finite understanding is not aware of dialectic itself but exclusively of the skeptical negation of epistemic claims. Since finite understanding is incapable of reaching dialectical insights, it has to accept skepticism as a fundamental threat to knowledge. By contrast, "genuine philosophy" itself is not affected by skeptical doubts: "Skepticism should not be regarded merely as a doctrine of doubt; rather, it is completely certain about its central point, i.e. the nullity of everything finite … But then philosophy does not stop at the merely negative result of the dialectic, as is the case with skepticism. The latter mistakes its result, insofar as it holds fast to it as mere, i.e., abstract, negation" (Hegel 1991: 130f.). Hence, skepticism and dialectic are in accord with respect to "negation" while at once being vitally distinct. Though both likewise rely on "negation," skepticism performs "abstract negation" by simply doubting, i.e. nullifying epistemic claims, whereas from the point of view of dialectic the "result" of the "negation" preserves the positive content, "what it resulted from." This idea draws on the *Phenomenology*'s distinction between two kinds of negation. Skepticism's, i.e. finite understanding's ("abstract") negation confines itself to "wait[ing] to see whether something new comes along and what it is, in order to throw it too into the same empty abyss" (Hegel 1977b: 51). By contrast, true, "determinate negation" realizes that "nothingness is, in a determinate fashion, specifically the nothingness of that from which it results. For it is only when it is taken as the result from which it emerges, that it is, in fact, the true result; in that case it is itself a determinate nothingness, one which has a content" (Hegel 1977b: 51).

In absolute idealism it is the method of counter-position or negation that makes skepticism dialectical, i.e. an integrative element of human rationality. From the immanent point of view of human understanding, skeptical counter-position or negation of epistemic claims has destructive consequences for human rationality since finite understanding's cognitive performances naturally lead to skeptical doubt. For finite understanding it therefore looks as if the skeptic, by means of counter-position or negation, is able to keep the human mind from successfully achieving positive metaphysical knowledge. Hegel does not deny the devastating consequences skepticism has for finite understanding. However, he criticizes this destructive view of skepticism as one-sided. For him, the true, positive meaning of skepticism is the "dialectical moment," i.e. skepticism's ability to nullify finite reflection by means of skeptical doubt in order to promote speculative knowledge, speculative knowledge itself being achieved, though, through absolute reason. In fact it is important to see that Hegel is not operating with two distinct types of skepticism, destructive (negative) skepticism, on the one hand, and constructive (philosophical) skepticism, on the other. On the contrary, destructive and constructive skepticism are two sides of the same coin. It is one and the same skeptical doubt that in the domain of finite understanding nullifies reflection while, in terms of dialectic, promoting metaphysical knowledge. The distinction itself is, of course, made from the metaphysical point of view of logic, i.e. it is an insight that cannot be achieved from within finite reflection. This is how Hegel, in his idealism, connects skepticism and dialectic. Though skeptical doubt as such is negative with respect to finite knowledge claims, it is productive with respect to "Science" in that it positively contributes to insight into metaphysical truth. Hence, Hegel does not deny that skepticism is a fundamentally epistemological problem for finite reflection. But from a dialectical angle skeptical doubt has to be taken as the documentation of true philosophical knowledge.

The systematic importance that both the *Phenomenology of Spirit* and the *Encyclopedia* credit, in particular, the problem of skepticism proves that Hegel was not ignorant of epistemological questions. Obviously Hegel's discussion of epistemological themes such as skepticism looks very different from the one in Kant or Fichte. Transcendental and subjective idealism offer constructive accounts of knowledge, i.e. Kant by starting off from the analysis of sources of knowledge, and Fichte by grounding knowledge on the I. By contrast, Hegel basically gives a diagnosis of the problem of knowledge as such. That is, unlike Kant, Hegel is not so much interested in how sensibility and understanding cooperate in order to make cognition possible, or how, like in Fichte, the I actively produces knowledge. Hegel's epistemological approach is much broader in that it takes into account the allegedly mistaken presuppositions of traditional theory of knowledge as well as contingent components of belief-building processes. Even though this does not necessarily mean that Hegel relativizes epistemic claims, absolute idealism has undeniably a tendency towards historicizing knowledge.

The legacy of idealist epistemology

Whether or not one regards the development of idealist epistemology as a linear, conclusive progression from transcendental to absolute idealism (see e.g. Pippin 1989; Beiser 2002) it is unquestionable that the trajectory of the various accounts of knowledge in philosophy from Kant to Hegel shows a significant move towards the historicizing of the problem of knowledge as such. Thus Kant's non-empirical fixation of conditions *a priori* of knowledge was superseded by Fichte's idea of an evolutionary conception of cognitive capacities, although not in terms of an empirical coming into being of knowledge but as rational formation. Hegel, on the other hand, conceives of knowledge in terms of its historical development, both empirically as well as non-empirically. As we have seen, Hegel regards, e.g. skepticism, as a historical phenomenon that occurred in full strength especially in antiquity; but he likewise considers it a purely systematic, ahistorical philosophical problem that can be interpreted in terms of dialectic. The oscillation between Kant's transcendental theory of knowledge and Hegel's historical explanation of how knowledge comes into being and what it amounts to is nowadays reflected in the legacy of idealist episte- mology, particularly in the pragmatist tradition. It is Wilfrid Sellars who paved the way for the pragmatist reconsideration of idealist conceptions of knowledge. In his influential *Empiricism and Philosophy of Mind* (1997; originally a set of lectures given 1956) he praised Hegel for his insight that anything immediately "given" cannot have any justificatory force. Despite various allusions to Hegel's critique of episte-mological immediatism however, Sellars, philosophizes rather in the spirit of Kant, most obviously in *Science and Metaphysics: Variations on Kantian Themes* (1968). In this work he explicitly applauds the dual-compositional account of knowledge, albeit rejecting idealism. The early pragmatist sympathy for transcendental philosophy was vehemently disapproved of by Richard Rorty. In his *Philosophy and the Mirror of Nature* (1979) he holds Kant's transcendental theory of knowledge responsible for major misconceptions in modern philosophy. Accordingly, it was Kant who made epistemology the leading discipline that fatally dominated philosophy for two hundred years by establishing the *a priori* criteria by means of which philosophers distinguish between cognition and mere belief. In Rorty's eyes the one-sided, transcendental account of knowledge was devastating inasmuch it explicitly ignored historical condi-tions of knowledge formation such as cultural or social facts. For that reason Rorty almost enthusiastically appreciates Hegelian idealism since Hegel considers what Kant ignored, namely the historical side of human rationality. It is therefore not surprising that Robert Brandom dedicates his widely praised book *Making It Explicit* (1994) to Sellars and Rorty. For Brandom it is Hegel, not Kant, who promotes the crucial insight that we are not allowed to understand epistemic claims as theoretically isolated but as claims that stand in complex inferential relations with other claims. Brandom conceives of himself as contemporary heir of a linguistically advanced version of Hegelian philosophy, a version that is supposed to do justice to semantic and social elements of representing, or knowing respectively. Whereas Brandom sees himself as a modernized Hegelian, John McDowell appears as an updated Kantian. Though playing with Hegelian ideas, McDowell, in *Mind and World* (1994), clearly opts for the Kantian account of knowledge. However, McDowell presents a rather idiosyncratic version of Kant's dual-compositional theory of knowledge. Accordingly, to explain objective reference of thought we have to conceive of sensibility as being intrinsically rational, i.e. conceptual, a claim that seems to violate Kant's original separation of the sources of knowledge. It seems as if this more recent reappraisal of, especially, Kant's and Hegel's accounts of knowledge goes the same way as the idealist discussion. As work in progress it is open to future modifications.

References

Allison, H. E. (2004) *Kant's Transcendental Idealism: An Interpretation and Defense*, 2nd edn, New Haven; London: Yale University Press.

Beiser, F. (1987) *The Fate of Reason: German Philosophy from Kant to Fichte*, Cambridge, MA; London: Harvard University Press.

Beiser, F. (2002) *German Idealism: The Struggle against Subjectivism 1781–1801*, Cambridge, MA; London: Harvard University Press.

Brandom, R. (1994) *Making It Explicit: Reasoning, Representing, and Discursive Commitment*, Cambridge, MA: Harvard University Press.

Breazeale, D. (2001) "Fichte's Conception of Philosophy as a 'Pragmatic History of the Human Mind' and the Contribution of Kant, Platner, and Maimon," *Journal of the History of Ideas* 62: 685–703.

Düsing, K. (1988) *Schellings und Hegels erste absolute Metaphysik (1801–1802): Zusammenfassende Vorlesungsnachschriften von I. P. V. Troxler*, Köln: Dinter.

—— (1995) *Das Problem der Subjektivität in Hegels Logik*, 3rd edn, Bonn: Bouvier.

Fichte, J. G. (1970): *Foundations of the Entire Science of Knowledge*, in *Science of Knowledge*, edited, trans. P. Heath and J. Lachs, New York: Appleton.

—— (1987) *The Vocation of Man*, trans. with introduction and notes by P. Preuss, Indianapolis, IN; Cambridge, MA: Hackett.

—— (1988) *Fichte. Early Philosophical Writings*, edited, trans. D. Breazeale, Ithaca; London: Cornell University Press.

—— (1994) *Introductions to the Wissenschaftslehre and Other Writings (1797–1800)*, edited, trans., with an Introduction and notes, by D. Breazeale, Indianapolis, IN; Cambridge, MA: Hackett.

—— (2000) *Foundations of Natural Right*, edited by F. Neuhouser, trans. M. Baur, Cambridge: Cambridge University Press.

Forster, M. N. (1998) *Hegel's Idea of a Phenomenology of Spirit*, Chicago: University of Chicago Press.

Gettier, E. L. (1963) "Is Justified True Belief Knowledge," *Analysis* 23: 121–3.

Giovanni, G. di, and H. S. Harris (2000) *Between Kant and Hegel: Texts in the Development of Post-Kantian Idealism*, Indianapolis, IN: Hackett.

Guyer, P. (1987) *Kant and the Claims of Knowledge*, Cambridge: Cambridge University Press.

Hanna, R. (2001) *Kant and the Foundations of Analytic Philosophy*, Oxford: Clarendon Press.

Hegel, G. W. F. (1977a) *Faith and Knowledge*, trans. W. Cerf and H. S. Harris, Albany, NY: SUNY Press.

—— (1977b) *Phenomenology of Spirit*, trans. by A. V. Miller, Oxford: Oxford University Press.

—— (1991) *The Encyclopedia Logic* (= *Encyclopedia*, pt 3, 1830), trans., with introduction and notes, by T. F. Geraets, W. A. Suchting and H. S. Harris, Indianapolis, IN; Cambridge, MA: Hackett.

—— (2000) *On the Relation between Skepticism and Philosophy*, in Giovanni and Harris (2000).

Heidemann, Dietmar H. (1998) *Kant und das Problem des metaphysischen Idealismus*, Berlin; New York: Walter de Gruyter.

—— (2007) *Der Begriff des Skeptizismus: Seine systematischen Formen, die pyrrhonische Skepsis und Hegels Herausforderung*, Berlin; New York: Walter de Gruyter.

—— (2008) "Substance–Subject–System: The Justification of Science in Hegel's *Phenomenology of Spirit*," in D. Moyar and M. Quante (eds) *Hegel's "Phenomenology of Spirit": A Critical Guide*, Cambridge: Cambridge University Press, 1–20.

—— (2010) "Appearance, Thing-in-Itself and the Skeptical Hypothesis," in D. Schulting and J. Verburgt (eds) *Kant's Idealism: New Interpretations of a Controversial Doctrine*, Dordrecht: Springer.

Kant, I. (1998) *Critique of Pure Reason*, edited, trans. Paul Guyer and Allen W. Wood, Cambridge: Cambridge University Press.

—— (2002) *Prolegomena to Any Future Metaphysics*, trans. Henry Allison, in *Immanuel Kant: Theoretical Philosophy after 1781*, edited by Henry Allison and Peter Heath, Cambridge: Cambridge University Press.

McDowell, J. (1994) *Mind and World*, Cambridge, MA: Harvard University Press.

Paton, H. J. (1965) *Kant's Metaphysic of Experience: A Commentary on the First Half of the "Kritik der reinen Vernunft*," vol. 1, 4th edn, London: George Allen & Unwin.

Pippin, R. B. (1989) *Hegel's Idealism: The Satisfaction of Self-Consciousness*, Cambridge: Cambridge University Press.

Reinhold, K. L. (2000) *The Foundation of Philosophical Knowledge* (1791), in Giovanni and Harris (2000).

—— (2005) *Letters on the Kantian Philosophy*, edited by K. Ameriks, trans. J. Hebbeler, Cambridge: Cambridge University Press.

Rorty, R. (1979) *Philosophy and the Mirror of Nature*, Princeton, NJ: Princeton University Press.

Schelling: F. W. J. (1980) *The Unconditional in Human Knowledge: Four early essays 1794–6*, trans. and commentary by F. Marti, Lewisburg, PA: Bucknell University Press.

Schulze, G. E. (2000) *Aenesidemus*, in Giovanni and Harris (2000).

—— (1801) *Kritik der theoretischen Philosophie*, 2 vols, Hamburg: Bohn.

Sellars, W. (1969) *Science and Metaphysics: Variations on Kantian Themes*, London: Routledge & Kegan Paul; New York: Humanities Press.

—— (1997) *Empiricism and Philosophy of Mind*, Cambridge, MA: Harvard University Press.

Strawson, P. F. (1966): *The Bounds of Sense: An essay on Kant's Critique of Pure Reason*, London: Methuen.

Zöller, G. (2002) *Fichte's Transcendental Philosophy: The Original Duplicity of Intelligence and Will*, Cambridge: Cambridge University Press.

3

THE PHILOSOPHY OF NATURE OF KANT, SCHELLING AND HEGEL

Dieter Wandschneider

Translated by Patrick Leland

Introduction

Man, though himself a child of nature, is – in Herder's words – a *freed man of nature*. Through reason he is able to disentangle himself from natural compulsions and adapt nature to his needs. Admittedly, that also means his *relation to nature* is not thoroughly determined by nature but rather is precariously open. Reason is thus continuously required to clarify and justify anew man's relation to nature. In other words, it is constitutive of man that he has a concept of nature and hence also a fundamental need for a philosophy of nature. It is no accident that in the Ionian world the philosophy of nature was "the form in which philosophy as such was born" (Wahsner 2002: 9).

In this respect, it is surprising that the present age, which more than any previous era is determined by the results and applications of scientific research, has not developed a thoroughgoing philosophy of nature. Instead, it is the *philosophy of science*, or philosophical reflection on the foundations of natural science, which – prepared already in the second half of the nineteenth century – has attained a truly epochal status during the twentieth century and continues to dominate contemporary philosophy. As the latter has allowed the philosophy of science to supersede the philosophy of nature, it has neglected to develop a concept of nature adequate for our time. Yet the sheer number of popular publications on cosmogony, elementary particle physics, chaos theory, etc., up to theories of biogenesis, evolution, ecology, neurophysiology, and brain science (even including freedom of the will) are all indicative of an immense *epistemic need*. But popular scientific commentary, however interesting and commendable, does not amount to a philosophy nature. It reports and explains the results of scientific research, but it is not a philosophical reflection on the "principle nature."

In this situation, it is only natural that our gaze turns back so as to inquire of the philosophical tradition and to clarify the extent to which the enormous intellectual achievements of the past might still be of use. The present investigation brings into view the philosophy of nature of German Idealism, a philosophical movement which emerged around the beginning of the nineteenth century. German Idealism appropriated certain motivations of the Kantian philosophy and developed them further in a "speculative" manner (Engelhardt 1972, 1976, 2002). This powerful philosophical movement, associated above all with the names of Fichte, Schelling and Hegel – and moreover having nothing whatsoever to do with the "subjective idealism" of George Berkeley – was replaced by philosophical positions designated roughly as metaphysics of the will, Marxism, life-philosophy, phenomenology and existentialism, as well as positivism, empiricism, philosophy of science, the linguistic turn, and analytic philosophy. These philosophical positions more or less still shape us today. German Idealism amounts to a virtual intellectual-historical antithesis to these movements and thus presents itself in retrospect as a striking alternative.

The basis of Idealism – in its various respective forms – is *the ideal* <*Ideelle*>, and thus the opposite of that which is real. It continually takes as its task explaining the real in terms of the ideal, and this is especially true of the Idealists' philosophy of nature.[1] Is this a hopeless undertaking? Does Idealism not lack an empirical basis? Can one secure any solid ground whatsoever in the ether of the ideal? In what follows, I explain how, more than anyone else, Schelling and Hegel sought to handle this problem and to cope with it. By way of anticipation, a clear preference for the *Hegelian* philosophy of nature will emerge in what follows, a preference which may come as some surprise considering how much controversy has surrounded the significance of that view. The project of renewing a thoroughgoing philosophy of nature can meaningfully begin here.

My presentation begins with *Kant's* philosophical project, which played a key role in understanding German Idealism, and then considers in detail the philosophical approaches developed by Schelling and Hegel. Without doubt, the true initiator of German Idealism is Fichte. However, following Kant, Fichte's primary interest concerns exclusively the Transcendental Philosophy. Although within that framework one finds various remarks about nature, Fichte did not develop his own philosophy of nature. For this reason, his work is only mentioned here in passing. Commensurate with his significance, however, are four articles in the present volume which discuss Fichte's philosophy in detail.

Numerous other thinkers are to be included among the German Idealists – the more or less central being Friedrich Heinrich Jacobi (1743–1819), Karl Leonhard Reinhold (1758–1823), Friedrich Schleiermacher (1768–1834), Friedrich Hölderlin (1770–1843), Novalis (1772–1801) and Friedrich Schlegel (1772–1829). However, in the present context it seems appropriate to restrict the scope of investigation to the central positions.

Kant

As stated earlier, one cannot conceive of German Idealism independently of Kant's philosophy, and so it is at a minimum necessary to outline the main features of the latter. Here, emphasis is naturally placed on those of Kant's arguments which are the most relevant for the philosophy of nature. I begin with the groundwork for the theoretical philosophy as it was developed in the *Critique of Pure Reason* (1781), followed by a few brief remarks on Kant's *Metaphysical Foundations of Natural Science* (1786). Then, and of particular importance, is the *Critique of Judgment* (1790), a work which contains essential insights of enduring significance regarding the essence of life and which was itself extremely important for the development of German Idealism. Finally, I consider Kant's *Opus Postumum*. Though this work was first published in 1936 and thus could not have had any direct influence on German Idealism, it is nevertheless investigated here with respect to the far-reaching philosophical motives contained therein. It is interesting that Kant's thought, as is shown, has in the end already moved in the direction of Idealism.

Critique of Pure Reason

In the *Critique of Pure Reason*, Kant asserts – in opposition to Hume's empiricism – that the *lawfulness* of nature can be explained thoroughly, though not by means of experience alone. Experience "certainly tells us what is there, but it does not tell us what must necessarily be one way and not another" (KVR: A1). In order to explain the possibility of natural laws, Kant performs a revolutionary reinterpretation, a "Copernican Turn," as it were. Accordingly, knowledge need not simply conform to nature; on the contrary, nature must itself, in a certain sense, conform to knowledge. The object of knowledge is understood not as something already fully determined and available for empirical assimilation; rather, it is only by means of the subject that it is first determined what the object is. Kant is certainly of the opinion, which he carefully outlines, that the subject is "affected" by an external "thing in itself." However, the still chaotic sense-data which the subject receives in this way are, according to Kant, given order and form by the subject. First, they are ordered through the *forms of intuition*, namely space and time, which already lie in the subject and confer on the sense-data the character of spatial-temporal intuitions. The sense-data are clasped in the *unity of self-consciousness* to the "synthetic unity of apperception" (KVR: B131–9) and then determined further by means of the *categories* of the understanding which similarly already lie within the subject – categories such as "quantity," "causality," and "substance." In this way, the spatial-temporal ordering of intuitions is imprinted with an additional structure. Two successive events, such as "A spark descended into the powder keg" and "An explosion occurs" are linked together by means of the category of causality, and only then can they be understood as linked with respect to a causal law: "*Because* a spark descended into the powder keg, *therefore* an explosion was triggered." The spark is conceived as the *cause* and the explosion as its *effect*. It is only through such categorial determinations, such as that of causality, that natural being becomes available for knowledge, as for example in the aforementioned case of knowledge of *causal* relations. With that a *principle of pure understanding* is formulated which is constitutive for all experience. Accordingly, the law-like regularity of nature is essentially the result of the formative activity of the subject. This is emphasized in Kant's famous *dictum*: "The understanding does not draw its laws (a priori) from nature, but rather prescribes them to it" (PR: §36; the original text in italics).

With respect to the above example, this means that any natural being which I encounter is in principle causally conditioned. Of this I am certain prior to all experience – "*a priori.*" Certainly, *how* the causal principle is realized in concrete natural laws is variable, for example as the law of gravity, as the law of the refraction of light, etc. Thus, with respect to their *specific determinateness* the natural laws cannot originate in the subject.

Kant names the view he develops "*transcendental.*" The transcendental philosophy is "the system of all principles of pure reason" (KVR: B27). With that, he wants to distance himself terminologically from a philosophy which accepts any kind of *transcendent* authority lying "beyond," and thus unavailable to, the subject. By contrast, according to the transcendental view the formal elements of nature reside in the *subject* prior to all experience: these are the forms of intuition, namely *space* and *time*, as well as the twelve *categories of the understanding*, which further determine the intuitions. We thus never have knowledge of "*things in themselves,*" that is, things "as they in themselves might be." Rather, we have knowledge of *appearances*, i.e. of how things *appear* to us with respect to our forms of intuition and categories – whereby Kant explicitly remarks that "appearance" <*Erscheinung*> should not be equated with "fiction" <*Schein*> (KVR: B69–71). Since, however, the appearances are determined by our own forms (i.e. the forms of intuition and the categories), we can have *a priori* knowledge of the appearances *in advance of all experience*, for example that nature is constituted spatio-temporally and causally. Kant's transcendental approach thus renders valid *a priori* determinations of experience, and without these the scientific experience of law-like regularities of nature would be impossible. The aim of the *Critique of Pure Reason* is to make visible such "transcendental conditions of the possibility of experience" which exist within the subject from the outset.

A fundamental problem with Kant's fascinating proposal is admittedly the concept of the *thing-in-itself.* This must be entirely unrecognizable, since it is in no way liable to any subjective formation. It is nevertheless constitutive of Kant's position, for, as stated earlier, the *thing-in-itself* must "affect" the subject and deliver to it by means of this effect the "raw material of sensible perception." If the spatio-temporal and categorial *forms* which enable knowledge lie in the subject, then, in contrast, the *sensible content* must originate in a *thing-in-itself* which, for its part, must in principle lie beyond the reach of knowledge. Nevertheless Kant argues with this concept. He attributes existence to it, characterizes it as unknowable and yet claims to know that the thing-in-itself affects the subject. That, however, means that it has an effect, and "effect" presupposes the category of causality, which sure enough has no application with respect to things-in-themselves. In short, with regard to the thing-in-itself nothing is compatible. It is thus no surprise that Fichte, who succeeded Kant and was in thorough agreement with the principle of the transcendental, set out to resolve this *aporia*.

Though not aporetic, it is nevertheless a further serious defect that, though Kant certainly provided justifications within the scope of his claim, he unfortunately left the claim itself unjustified. The unaccounted assumption of a thing-in-itself is but *one* facet of the problem. The assumption of *a priori* "forms of intuition" and categories is no more justified, and this leads directly to such questions as: Why are there spatial and temporal forms of intuition? Why are there forms of intuition at all, and why are there exactly two? Why does the faculty of the understanding possess categories, and why are there exactly twelve? Here, Kant himself recognized the need for an explanation and, at any rate, tried to provide a rationale. He ascribed the categories to the capacity to judge (which itself is admittedly in need of justification) and sought to provide arguments for why there are exactly twelve (on this issue, see Reich 1932).

Of particular significance for the development of German Idealism are those observations which Kant developed under the title of a "*transcendental dialectic*." With *intuition* attached to space and time, and the *understanding* grounded on the capacity to judge, Kant sees in *reason* the capacity to bring the rules of the understanding under a *principle* (KVR: A302/B359), i.e. to find the *unconditioned* for that which is conditioned in multiple respects (A307/B364) and in this way to think of an ultimate "absolute totality" (A326/B383). Such a concept, generated by reason, is called a "transcendental idea" (A311/B368) and appears concretely in three forms – soul, world and God. Since they exceed the bounds of experience, such ideas have a *transcendent* character and so, Kant explains, can only function regulatively, i.e. they cannot lead to "hard" empirical results but rather can only guide scientific research. If this restriction is not born in mind, then thought inevitably becomes ensnared in dialectical *aporias*, as for example in the question of whether or not the world has a beginning: as Kant demonstrated, the affirmative and the negative response each leads to an antinomy (for critical analysis on this see Wandschneider 1989).

While holding the "hard," empirically oriented knowledge of the understanding in the highest esteem, Kant clearly also allowed for the concerns of reason and, in particular, the question concerning the *unconditioned*. It is with respect to the latter that Kant substantially influenced the development of the "speculative" philosophy of German Idealism. (Of interest with respect to this point is Hegel's presentation of Kant's "critical philosophy" in the context of the "Encyclopedia," Hegel Werke: 8.§§40–60.)

Metaphysical foundations of natural science

Published in 1786, Kant's *Metaphysical Foundations of Natural Science* seeks to work out more clearly the consequences of the transcendental approach with respect to the natural sciences (here in particular see Plaass 1965; Schäfer 1966; Hoppe 1969: esp. Ch. 2; Falkenburg 1987: Ch. 2). One can only speak of a *real science of nature*, according to Kant, "if the natural laws, which it takes as its basis, are known a priori and not as mere laws of experience" (MA: 468). What Kant has in mind is a *metaphysics* of nature (469), which consequently "is drawn from the essence of thought itself and is in no way a fictitious invention on account of not being borrowed from experience" (472). With that, Kant is thinking of the "*principles of pure understanding*," such as the universal principle of causality, which were developed in the *Critique of*

Pure Reason under the guidance of the categories. The system of principles "provides the schema for the metaphysics of nature" (Schäfer 1966: 24) and, with that, forms the general background for the empirical science of nature. For its part, however, this assumes collaterally the empirical *existence* of things and the *intuition* thereof. It thus presupposes space and time and accordingly, as Kant emphasizes, *mathematics* (geometry and arithmetic) as that which is conceptually commensurate to space and time – such that "in every doctrine of nature there is only so much proper science, ... as there is that to which mathematics is applicable" (MA 470). Mathematical physics is thus distinguished from all other natural sciences. Its fundamental concept is a concept of matter, understood as "movable in space." This general concept, which nevertheless contains an empirical element (i.e. existence), is developed further by Kant in accordance with the categories and in a purely conceptual manner: into a pure doctrine of motion ("phoronomy"), a doctrine of the filling of space by forces ("dynamics"), a doctrine of the interaction of material bodies ("mechanics"), and a doctrine of motion with respect to the perceiving subject ("phenomenology"). With that, the "metaphysical foundations" of natural science are delineated, though admittedly restricted to physics. Kant's doctrine of forces was repeatedly taken up in German Idealism, whereby the spatial reality of matter was said to be constituted by the opposing forces of attraction and repulsion (MA: Ch. 2).

Critique of Judgment

The *Critique of Judgment*, published in 1790, is devoted to organic nature. It may at first come as a surprise that this work also contains Kant's philosophy of art. The two themes are connected by the concept of purposiveness, which is central for Kant's explanation of artistic beauty, as well as for his understanding of organic systems. Both parts became significant for the development of German Idealism. For present purposes, it is only the second part, the "Critique of Teleological Judgment," which is germane.

Kant here distinguishes between "external" and "internal" purposiveness (KU: §63–7, §82). *External purposiveness* means that the determination of an object as a medium is a determination which is *external* to that object. Thus, either the determination is *accidental* – as sandy soil is certainly "conducive" for forests of spruce trees, though it is certainly not there for the sake of the forests (KU: 280–1); or the determination is bestowed on the object *from without* by means of a conscious intention of *thought* and thus represents in principle a *technical determination of aims* (KU: 285–6, 289–90, 291–2). By contrast, *inner purposiveness* means a coherent functioning which is in itself purposive and whose purposive organization is not even "externally purposive," i.e. neither accidental nor technical but rather, as it were, consisting "of nature." Thus, Kant also speaks of an "end of nature" <*Naturzweck*> (KU: 286). It preserves its final character entirely on its own, independent of accidental factors or technical determinations of aims. The inner purposiveness of an end of nature is thus nothing other than its self-preservation. Thereby, the organs are means for the preservation of the entire organism. Yet the organs themselves also belong to the organism.

Self-preservation thus means that the organism is conversely a means for the preservation of the organs – basically, a familiar matter of fact: on the one hand, heart, lungs, kidneys, etc., are necessary for the functioning of the organism, and, on the other hand, the organism serves to ensure the functioning of these (and all remaining) organs. It is in this sense that Kant comes to the immediately plausible definition of inner purposiveness, according to which everything in an organic system "is an end and reciprocally also a means" (KU: 296, originally italicized). Or, in another formulation, the parts of an organism "relate to one another through the unity of a whole, such that they are interdependently the reciprocal cause and effect of their form" (KU: 291). According to Kant, this thoroughgoing *reciprocal relationship* in the function of an organic totality is to be understood as the characteristic of inner purposiveness.

With regard to *realization conditions* of inner purposiveness, Kant admittedly seems confronted with what appear to be insurmountable difficulties. He considers a *causal explanation* impossible, and that above all for two reasons: the causal relation is *asymmetrical*, i.e. unilaterally directed from cause to effect, whereas the *reciprocity* of cause and effect which is substantial for the structure of inner purposiveness would imply a cause which is likewise an effect and an effect which is likewise a cause (KU: 289). Kant further asserts that causal processes are *blind* (270, 326), i.e. they do not trend in pursuit of a goal, since they alone are determined by factors which lie in the past and not by a goal which is first realized in the future, as is obviously the case for the self-preservation of an organism. One could object that even a causally determined process is goal-directed insofar as a future stage of the process is clearly determined by the past stages of that process (so e.g. Sachsse 1979: 13–18). To this one can respond that causally determined processes are *interrupted* by external influences, i.e. they are sidetracked from their original "goal," whereas organic behavior seeks to conform to its particular goal even *against external disturbances*.

Kant is, however, also fundamentally skeptical with regard to his own characterization of the organic in terms of the *concept of purposiveness*, since this is not a *category* which is *constitutive of experience* (in the sense of KRV), as is the case with the category of causality. So, according to Kant, we can indeed be *a priori* certain that every object we encounter in experience is an object which is causally determined, whereas there are certainly objects which do not exhibit the inner purposiveness of an organism. Correspondingly, Kant says "purposiveness" should be *merely* a "*subjective* principle (maxim) of judgment" which, as such, guarantees nothing with respect to the qualities of *objects* (KU: xxxiv). It is "a mere idea" (318), a *regulative* and not a constitutive principle (see e.g. 301, 331), which can only serve to "reflect" on nature but not determine its objective being (e.g. xxvi–xxviii, 345).

The reason for the merely subjective-regulative character of the principle of purposiveness can be seen, for Kant, in the involvement of the *concept of an end*. Whoever judges organisms to be purposive ultimately considers them to be the result of an *intentional, thinking* goal-directed activity and thus as analogous to technical creations (269, 309, 333–8, 345–6, 374). And this is akin to the model of *external* purposiveness which, as technical, presupposes a *rational positing of ends*.

So neither the concept of causality nor the concept of an end (which is presupposed in the principle of purposiveness) is, in Kant's view, sufficient for explaining the *reali-zation conditions* of inner purposiveness. In view of the incontestable facts of physical structures, which nevertheless suggest a compelling purposive explanation, Kant entertains the speculative thought of a *supersensory substratum* of nature, i.e. that of *reason inhering in nature itself* (KU: xx, lvi, 304, 316–17, 352–3, 357–63, 374 – here, see Bartuschat 1972: 215–17, 253–5; Düsing 1968: 108–10, 116–18). The starting-point here is the moral philosophical consideration that the will which is determined by practical reason should also be able to manifest itself in real action and thus ultimately in physical relations. That, however, is only possible, Kant suspects, if nature itself is not ultimately exempt from reason. Consequently, there should be "a ground for the *unity* of the supersensory which grounds nature with that which is contained in the practical concept of freedom" (xx). Accordingly, *reason* would no longer be a mere subjective instance but rather, as it were, a "supersensory real ground [*Realgrund*] for nature, ... to which we ourselves belong" (352). It would thus no longer be merely the foundation of thinking but rather the foundation of *all beings*; reason would no longer have merely moral relevance but rather would possess *ontological* relevance in the sense of a *logos* which underlies subject and object alike. From there it would at least be plausible that, on the one hand, natural objects could be organized purposively in the sense of "inner" purposiveness and, on the other hand, the subject's reason could be capable of adequately grasping the purposiveness of nature. With respect to Kant's difficulties with the realization conditions of inner purposiveness, the ontological thought of a rational substratum of nature must have seemed exceptionally attractive. And nowhere is he closer to the thought of German Idealism, in particular the kinds of "objective idealism" advocated by Schelling and Hegel, than here.

With that, Kant admittedly abandoned the transcendental view of the *Critique of Pure Reason*, a view which had deprived reason of an ontological status and accorded it the sole function of regulating knowledge. Kant shied away from this consequence. Commensurate with a concept of knowledge which is restricted to knowledge of nature, Kant is convinced that, with respect to a possible supersensory-rational substratum of nature, we can have "for theoretical purposes not the slightest affirmative determinate concept" (KU: 358). The ontological thought of a *logos* which underlies nature was again withdrawn, and thus the possibility of grasping the inner purposiveness of the organic as a reason which inheres in nature itself was discarded (see Heintel 1966). The only form in which *we* are capable of thinking of organic purposiveness is thus the *teleological* explanation, which remains oriented to a technical model – thus it is as if organisms were constructed by a "highest architect" (354). It is clear that one thus only arrives at an *external* purposiveness, which as such presupposes an ideal antici-pation of an end. Kant expressed this *aporia* in terms of the impossibility of a "Newton of the blade of grass" (338, also 353), he thus expresses regret that the principle of inner purposiveness possesses the status of a *merely regulative idea* for human thought, a regulative idea for which no realization conditions are assignable and thus which facilitates *no scientific knowledge* of the organic.

In the *Critique of Pure Reason*, as well as in both the *Metaphysical Foundations* and the *Critique of Judgment*, there remains open a fundamental question which

71

was clearly articulated in the last of these works: namely, the question touched on earlier concerning empirical laws of nature, such as the law of gravitation. According to Kant, what is determined transcendentally is only the *general* character of its law-likeness, not its specific content. The reason for this undoubtedly is Kant's assumption that in the process of experience the subject is first "affected" by a thing-in-itself which delivers empirical content. In doing so, the thing-in-itself remains subjectively *inaccessible* and therewith anyway transcendentally inexplicable. In the *Critique of Judgment*, this is in principle addressed in the distinction between *determinant* and *reflective judgment*: "If the universal (i.e. the rule, the principle, the law) is given, then the judgment, which subsumes the particular under it, is ... *determinant*. If, however, only the particular is given, for which it must find the universal, then the judgment is merely reflective." In other words, reflective judgment can only establish an "as if principle" through which it gives "only a law unto itself and not a law of nature" (xxviii). It is ultimately the previously mentioned thing-in-itself which is problematic for the Kantian system.

Opus Postumum

Kant did not let this problem rest but rather continually circled it and sought to resolve it, as can be seen in the *Opus Postumum*. I have only a few remarks on this point. Certainly, the *Opus Postumum* could not have had a direct influence on German Idealism since it was first published in 1936–8 – aside from Kant's public declarations concerning Fichte's *Wissenschaftslehre*. Nevertheless, it is a document of the historical-intellectual situation within which German Idealism arose, and, as it demonstrates, Kant himself was already *en route* to an idealistic position (instructive here is Mathieu 1989; Tuschling 1995).

Here, reflective judgment no longer appears to have only an "as if principle" through which it can create only a system unto itself. Rather, as Vittorio Mathieu noticed, this "in point of fact is claimed *categorically* as a system which is concerned with reality itself, and the judgment which erects the system gives the law not only 'unto itself' but also 'to nature'" (Mathieu 1989: 44). That which earlier was asserted to be empirically valid has now become an "a priori given matter" which "is not concerned with the senses but rather with reason" (Kant, *Opus Postumum*, cited in Mathieu 1989: 276). The empirical ultimately resolves itself into mere relationships, i.e. the form becomes the "object itself" (Mathieu 1989: 276–7). Burkhard Tuschling notes that in the *Opus postumum* Kant, as it were, reverts to Spinoza and Leibniz. Schelling named Kant "the Leibniz of our epoch" and understood his Transcendental Idealism as Spinozism (Tuschling 1995: 209). This is an astonishing about-face of the once most critical Kant which only illustrates the historical-intellectual trend initiated by Kant himself: namely, that one must think further both with and against Kant, and that the consistent elaboration of his project must lead to German Idealism.

Schelling

The inclusion of nature

In fact this development began during Kant's lifetime. Johann Gottlieb Fichte (1762–1814) was emphatically persuaded of the fundamental correctness of the Kantian view. Its greatest shortcoming – the assumption of a thing-in-itself – Fichte considered reparable, and his entire system is in effect an attempt to realize Kant's transcendental thought without the ominous thing-in-itself (Fichte Werke: 1:420). Fichte referred to Kant's concept of *transcendental apperception* and from there undertook an *ultimate justification from the I*. For Fichte, the I can in no way be circumvented, because every attempt at a derivation of the I already presupposes the I. In the immediate awareness of the I's self-performing one can find the ground of being which cannot be derived from anywhere else and from which the transcendental philosophy must originate.

This is also true of Fichte's claims about *nature*, for which the perspective of the transcendental philosophy is consistently determinant and, with that, the relation to the I. So, for Fichte there arises from the moral constitution of human beings the *ontological* demand that nature must exist in such a way as to allow for the existence and moral action of the I. It is in this sense that one should understand the famous claim that the world is "nothing more than ... the sensualized material of our duty; this is what is actually real in things, the true elementary material of all appearance" (5:184–5). Significantly, there is from Fichte no monograph on the philosophy of nature. Apparently, there was a plan for such a monograph, but it was never carried out (Widmann 1982: 131). Fichte's "scattered remarks" on nature (Lauth 1984: xvii) were compiled and presented by Reinhard Lauth.

Originally a strong adherent to Fichte's philosophy, Schelling eventually raised fundamental objections against it. Some of these took a polemical form (e.g. Schelling Werke: 7:23), but very soon he emphasized the necessity for a philosophy of nature in its own right and criticized Fichte for having totally failed to provide one.

Chronologically, Schelling (1775–1854) follows Hegel (1770–1831). But from an intellectual-historical standpoint, Schelling is positioned prior to Hegel. The latter's publishing activity begins later, and his writings presupposed Schelling's philosophical perspective.

Above all, Schelling's early work is concerned with nature. The reasons for this are manifold. On the one hand, Kant is a leading figure, and his transcendental interpretation had opened up an entirely new perspective on nature. This is especially true of Kant's "transcendental dialectic" (Jacobs 1998: 69, 77), the *Metaphysical Foundations of Natural Science* (Matsuyama 2000), and the "Critique of Teleological Judgment" (Düsing 1985: 203–7; Franz 1998: 86–8). On the other hand, Fichte's transcendental philosophy was significant for Schelling, though he soon noticed problems with that approach, in particular Fichte's sweeping characterization of nature as a *non-I*: "It is as if Fichte perceived in the external world no differences whatsoever. For him, nature so fades away into the abstract, mere limiting concept <*eine bloße Schranke bezeichnenden Begriff*> of the non-I, of a completely empty object, ... that he no longer thinks a deduction which extends beyond this concept is necessary" (10:90–1). As can be seen from Schelling's university notes his path to the transcendental philosophy also proceeded by way of an intensive engagement with Plato's interpretation of nature in the *Timaeus* (1794) (Sandkaulen-Bock: 1990, 19–21; Franz 1998: 60–4; Jantzen 1998: 85–6). Here, what admittedly concerned Schelling was not the thematic of nature but rather the idea of transcendental philosophy: in the "divine understanding" of the demiurge he sees "in nuce already manifest the model of an 'absolute I'," and that remarkably "several months *before* the appearance of Fichte's programmatic work *On the Concept of a Science of Nature*" (Franz 1998: 63; see also Jantzen 1998: 85–6). Schelling's philosophical orientation nevertheless went in a completely different direction from that of Fichte. As Wilhelm G. Jacobs has shown, in contrast to Fichte what was of primary interest to Schelling was not Kant's theory of the transcendental constitution of objects but rather Kant's problem of the transcendental dialectic: in the product of nature as a conditioned – Spinoza's *natura naturata* – he saw a reference to the idea of an unconditioned (Wieland 1967: 416), of a divine self-producing nature, thus in the sense of Spinoza's *natura naturans* (Jacobs 1998: 69, 77), in which nature itself acquires the character of an absolute subject: "*Nature* considered as a mere *product* (*natura naturata*) is what we call nature as *object* (this alone is the object of all empirical investigation). *Nature* considered as *productivity* (*natura naturans*) is what we call *nature as subject* (this alone is the object of all theoretical inquiry)" (3:284) which is, for Fichte, an unthinkable position.

Schelling's first great work on the philosophy of nature, entitled *Ideas for a Philosophy of Nature*, appeared in 1797 and was followed by additional works on this subject: *On the World-Soul* (1798), *First Draft of a System of the Philosophy of Nature* (1799), *Introduction to the Draft of a System of the Philosophy of Nature* (1799), *Universal Deduction of the Dynamic Processes or of the Categories of Physics* (1800). And even though the philosophy of nature is not implied in the title of Schelling's *System of Transcendental Idealism* (1800), it is nevertheless a central theme of that work. Additional writings on the philosophy of nature followed, now within the framework of Schelling's meanwhile conceived "*philosophy of identity*": *On the True Concept of the Philosophy of Nature and the Correct Method for Solving its Problems* (1801) and *Presentation of My System of Philosophy* (1801). Additional works which treat extensively of the philosophy of nature include: *Bruno, or On the Divine and Natural Principle of Things* (1802), *Further Presentations from the System of Philosophy* (1802), the essay *On the Relation of Philosophy of Nature to Philosophy, in General* (1802), *System of the Entire Philosophy and of the Philosophy of Nature, in Particular* (1804), *Presentation of the True Relation of the Philosophy of Nature to the Emended Doctrine of Fichte* (1806), *Aphorisms for an Introduction to the Philosophy of Nature* (1806), and *Aphorisms on the Philosophy of Nature* (1806). A subsequent work marks a turning-point, namely, *Philosophical Investigations on the Essence of Human Freedom and its related Objects* (1809), in which Schelling addresses the origin of *evil*. Nevertheless, the philosophy of nature remains a constitutive part of Schelling's philosophical framework, as is apparent in the *Private Lectures in Stuttgart* (1810) and in the lectures given in Munich entitled, *On the History of the New Philosophy* (1827).

Admittedly, one cannot speak of a continuity of argument. The dynamic of his "eruptive thinking" leads Schelling to ever new, "interwoven" schemes (Wieland 1967: 408) to such an extent that it is difficult to claim any one of these works represents *the* philosophy of nature of Schelling. Thus, it is only in its historical development that an appropriate presentation could be given of Schelling's philosophy of nature (as is done by Jantzen 1998) – or perhaps not even in this manner (Wieland 1967: 408). Since in the present context describing the historical development is not even remotely possible, another approach must be found. It seems reasonable to orient the presentation in terms of the later statements which Schelling formulated in retrospect of his own development and the continually broadening philosophical horizon, such as those claims advanced in the above mentioned lectures from Stuttgart and Munich. The earlier writings, however, must also be kept in view.

The way out of the absolute

Schelling's thought systematically takes as its point of departure the question as to *why* nature exists, at all. It is at the same time a question about the *absolute* which preoccupied Schelling throughout his life (Wieland 1967: 419). Birgit Sandkaulen-Bock (1990) has demonstrated in impressive detail how complex and varied the argumentative structure of Schelling's early thought is. Given the chosen methodological principle, I will instead here consider Schelling's reflections from the Munich lectures *On the History of the New Philosophy* (1827, published from the hand-written *Nachlass*).

In "complete independence from Fichte" – Schelling is clearly referring to his later positions – it is not the finite, human I which constitutes the original point of departure but rather the "infinite subject" which *qua* infinite "can *never* cease to be subject" (10:99). As *subject*, however, it is "as it were, natural" for it also to "will [itself] as object" (10:99), "for it is only subject *in that* it becomes an object unto itself, since it is assumed there is nothing *external* to it which could become an object for it" (10:101). The subject becomes object for itself and, in so doing, first becomes *something*: this is the *primum Existens*, the first being. It is essential, however, that in its "becoming an object it never ceases to be subject." For this reason, it must be an "*infinite* self-positing" (10:101): "Insofar as it is *something*, it is also immediately once more that which goes beyond itself" (10:103). In other words, it posits itself as finite so that, in the continually renewed sublation of the finite, it can grasp itself *as infinite* (10:101–2), so to speak on "a second level or potency" (10:102). Through this *potentizing* <*Potenzierung*>, it is no longer only subject (A) but rather now *explicitly* determined *as subject*: A *qua* A, or as Schelling characterized it, A^2 (10:103). The self-finitizing subject posits itself as *something real* in order to know itself in this positing as subject, and this knowledge is itself something *ideal* (10:103–4).

According to Schelling, that "first being" is nothing other than *matter*: "*This* matter, which itself is only the first existing something, is certainly not *the* matter which we now see before us, the formed, … already corporeal matter." On the contrary, it is "the matter of this matter, the matter of that which is already formed and a sensible object of knowledge for us, … its stuff, its foundation" (10:104) which, as such, can assume a *spatial* form and so is like an "original *filling of space*" (Heckmann 1985: 303). The *ideal* which stands opposite this real is fundamentally a "knowing" and is identified by Schelling as *light*, and that apparently because the latter represents the fact that matter can be known. "Compared with matter the light is as nothing and yet it is not nothing; that which, in matter, is as something is, in the light, as nothing; and to that extent it is admittedly also something, yet something different, posited as the pure *ideal*. The light is apparently not matter, to which earlier hypotheses had reduced it." On the contrary, as ideal the light is "the objectively self-positing" "*concept* of matter" (10:105).

That the infinite subject thus realizes itself in original matter and light is, for Schelling, the rationale for the existence of *nature*. I use this formulation for the time being in order to first characterize Schelling's line of thought in its context. It is essential for "this philosophy" that it "begins from nature" (10:106–7). The philosophy of nature is accordingly its "first part, or the foundation of the whole." What also arises from this is the quasi-ambivalent character of nature: more objective in the form of original matter, more subjective in the form of light. Directed against Fichte, the claim is that nature is not merely a non-I, something merely objective, but rather something – such as light – which always also has an ideal, subjective character. "Nowhere, in no sphere is there a merely subjective or a merely objective but rather always the unity of both. ... Only against a still higher ideal, e.g. against human knowledge, and thus in general only relative, does the light belong respectively to the real world" (10:106). To this extent, this philosophy can be characterized neither as idealism nor as realism but only properly as "real-idealism" (10:107). Both the real and the ideal arise from an *identical* root, namely from that "single ultimate subject" (10:107). So understood, the philosophy of nature, as Schelling himself presents it, evidently amounts to a *philosophy of identity* (10:107).

This position was initially set out in Schelling's *System of Transcendental Idealism* (1800). The title suggests a proximity to Fichte. However, that absolute subject presented by Schelling is no longer the pure self-consciousness from which Fichte had started but rather an absolute which underlies every conditioned. In this, Schelling's affinity to Spinoza becomes visible – with the qualification, however, that this absolute is no longer thought Spinozistically as a highest *being* but rather as a *subject*. As finite subjects, we can only have knowledge of this by means of *intellectual intuition*, that is, through an immediate, non-sensible, holistic apprehension of the absolute (of the kind which is imparted paradigmatically by works of *art* (3:625); on the problematic of intellectual intuition, see Wieland 1967: 417–20). And this must take the form of a single *identity* which encompasses the ideal and the real and which lies ahead of each; an identity which Schelling also characterizes as *indifference* because it is neither the one nor the other. For this reason, according to Schelling, the subject never has only an ideal character, but also always has a real character. Similarly, the object never has only a real but also an ideal character: "neither is ever separate, rather they are originally together (also in nature) (4:87; 6:204–10). Conditioned through the identity realized in the absolute, everything is both subject and object, *subject–object*, as it were – though with a preponderance of the subjective in the subjects and a preponderance of the objective in the objects: the subject as subjective subject–object and the object as objective subject–object. Correspondingly, philosophy must necessarily pursue two opposed directions: as *transcendental philosophy* it commences from the ideal in order to explain the real in terms of it – this is essentially still Fichte's program. As *philosophy of nature* it commences from the real in order to explain the ideal in terms of it – this is new and contrary to Fichte, who could only shake his head disapprovingly: "Nature is the product of intelligence, so how can it be, without entering an obvious circle, that intelligence is the product of nature?" (Fichte GA: II/5:421–2). Within the framework of the *system of identity* which Schelling developed in the period from 1801 to 1806, both philosophies belong constitutively together. However, in the justificatory essay *On the True Concept of the Philosophy of Nature and the Correct Method for Solving its Problems* (1801) Schelling emphasized the "priority" of the philosophy of nature: "because this first allows for the *standpoint* of idealism to arise and by means of this creates a secure, *pure* theoretical foundation for idealism" (4:92), so that "knowledge ... only proceeds through the gates of the knowledge of nature to the knowledge of the divine principle" (4:424). The philosophy of nature provides something like "a *physical explanation of idealism*. ... Come here to physics and recognize what is true!" (4:76; 3:378) – by "physics" Schelling here means that which he also refers to as "*speculative physics*," thus philosophy of nature (3:274–82; Wieland 1967: 435–6; Krings 1985; Meyer 1985), or the "depth grammar of nature," as it were (Kanitschneider 1985: 246). And the system of philosophy should prove "that without the philosophy of nature no philosophy, i.e. knowledge and science of the absolute, obtains at all, and that the former is a necessary and essential part of the latter" (4:424). This is "the only thinkable idealism" which is namely "simultaneously a complete realism" (4:148). Birgit Sandkaulen-Bock has made clear the implicit *aporias* of this position (1990: 95–8).

The fundamental structures of nature

Fichte's "complete manslaughter of nature" (7:445) is, for Schelling, a philosophically unacceptable defect which the *philosophy of nature* shall now remedy. In his writings, Schelling offers various arguments to explain the *concrete structures* of nature. The aforementioned *doctrine of potency* is, however, a relatively consistent methodological approach. I focus here on the detailed statement offered in the 1801 published work *Presentation of My System of Philosophy* (Werke: Vol. 4,), in which Schelling also continually refers to arguments advanced in the earlier published *System of Transcendental Idealism* (Werke: Vol. 3). A modified version of the potency doctrine can also be found in the *Stuttgart Private Lectures* (1810) (Werke: Vol. 7) and in the Munich Lectures from 1827 (Werke: Vol. 10).

As already expounded, Schelling argues that the pure subject, symbolized by A, must become objective for itself, symbolized by B, thus in sum A=B, though not in the sense of a mathematical equation but rather as the self-objectification of A: "It *wills* itself, and so becomes another, unlike itself" (10:102). Therewith exists a first, original being, an original matter, a subject–object A=B, through which A and B appear as *polar forces*: B as an "infinite expansive force," A as "an opposed, negative impeding force" corresponding to the "limiting activity of the I" (3:441; 4:145–8). These forces are said to *constitute* matter and thus are not merely properties *of* matter (Jantzen 1998: 91). The synthesis of both forces should – in contrast to Kant (Matsuyama 2000: 59–62) – be a third, force constitutively combined with matter, namely the *gravitational force* (3:444; 4:145–8), "which expresses nothing other than the infinite striving of nature to return to that absolute identity out of which nature, through the initial rupture, was torn" (4:7). From the threefold nature of these forces Schelling believes he is able to derive the *three-dimensional nature* of matter (3:444–9; modified in 7:447; Ziche 2004).

Schelling explains (4:149-51) that A is first determined *as A, as subjective*, through its opposition to B, and this is symbolized as A^2. But this subjective being exists on the (A=B)-level of the original matter, as a "subjective-material," so to speak. This is a (relatively) immaterial being which, as stated earlier, Schelling identifies with *light*. It is, as it were, the representative of absolute identity in reality ("In light, the absolute identity itself arises and in reality," Werke: 4:163) – or more generally as *form* which as such has an immaterial character. Therewith emerges a new polarity between subjective and objective, namely that of light/form (A^2), on the one hand, and of materiality (A=B), on the other. This new polarity is symbolized by A^2=(A=B); again, this should not be understood as a mathematical equation but rather in terms of the described subject–object-schema. This new subject–object thus represents the combination of materiality and immaterial form, and, according to Schelling, this is – in contrast to the still formless original matter – the formed, different matter. The formation processes of matter thus operate at the level which is determined by A^2=(A=B), which Schelling refers to as the level of *dynamic processes*. Differentiated matter appears at this level and, with that, novel polarities: the inseparable polarity of *magnetism*, the separable polarity of *electrical* charges, and the combination of both – as Schelling suggests – in the *chemical process*. He explains these as polarities in the determination of identity, duplicity and totality. The magnetic, the electrical, and the chemical are thus said to be the three fundamental categories of differentiated, formed matter (10:109) whose dynamic results from the striving for the sublimation of the polar difference: "Nature strives necessarily in dynamic processes toward the absolute indifference" (4:181, italicized in original).

All of this is scarcely comprehensible in the way of argument. Empirically, however, it is not necessarily absurd. In Jena, Schelling had made the acquaintance of the physicist Johann Wilhelm Ritter (1776–1810) and became interested in the latter's research. Additionally, Schelling's *"dynamic"* conception of natural phenomena (Jantzen 1998: 91–2; Matsuyama 2000) received an essential impulse from his studies of the mechanical-atomistic physics of the Swiss natural scientist Georges-Luis Le Sage (1724–1803) (Küppers 1992: 68–73). Beyond that, Schelling was familiar with contemporary empirical research (Wieland 1967: 436; Engelhardt 1985: 40–6). However, Schelling's attempts to ground this systematically and to interpret it in natural philosophical terms nevertheless come across as improvised and *ad-hoc*.

It is through the relation A^2=(A=B), which is determinant at the dynamic level, that, in Schelling's terminology, the subjective instance again *as such* becomes concrete in the higher potency A^3 (4:200). This is said to be the *organism* (4:202;

10:110; Frank 1998). The level of *animate nature* is characterized accordingly in the formula $A^3=(A^2=(A=B))$ (4:205). With that, the life-process presupposes the level of the dynamic process $(A^2=(A=B))$ but surpasses it through the efficacy of the organismic principle A^3, by means of which the organism is essentially *subject*. The pronounced subjective moment prevents the difference which preserves the life process from becoming indifference and thus from coming to rest, as is the case with a dynamic process (such as a chemical reaction) (2:500, 3:150, 322–5). "Matter is thus no longer considered as substance; in fact, the organism does not exist as such through material substance, which continually changes, but rather only through the type or form of its material being – is it an organism. ... For life, it is the *form* which has become essential ..., the preservation of substance in this form, in which it is even the form of existence of a higher potency (A^3)" (10:110; 7:451). Stated in contemporary terms, the organism is a self-preserving and self-organizing *system*. Indeed, like a stone or a machine, it consists of "normal" matter. However, what is characteristic of an organism is not the elementary lawfulness of matter but rather the *lawfulness of the system*; building on the elementary laws which first become visible at the level of the system, at which point it "emerges." To this extent, Schelling here has already caught sight of an *emergence-theoretical* perspective. The organism is "the higher potency of the category of interaction" (3:495). Drawing on Kant's notion of teleological judgment, Schelling thus attributes to the organism *inner* purposiveness (a product in which "everything is reciprocally means and end," Werke: 3:186). The categories of magnetism, electricity, and the chemical have been determinant for the dynamic process with respect to identity, duplicity, and totality. Now – drawing on the analyses of Albrecht von Haller and Carl Friedrich Kielmeyer (Jantzen 1998: 98) – *sensibility* (organization of the senses), *irritability* (an organism-specific reaction) and *power of reproduction* (self-preservation in a dynamic process) are the analogous determinations for the life-process (e.g. 3:155–240, 3:325, 7:452; Engelhardt 1985: 48–9). Accordingly, "organic nature [is] nothing other than the inorganic repeating itself at a higher potency" (4:4). For Schelling, the plant represents a preliminary stage of life, whereas the animal represents that of a true organism (2:495).

Finally, in the life-process which is characterized by $A^3=(A^2=(A=B))$, the subjective instance A^3 again becomes concrete *as such* and thus appears as a yet higher potency A^4, which Schelling also characterized as the "absolute A^2." The reason for this is that, by comparison, the organic and the inorganic opposed to A^4 have again thereby assumed the fundamental position of B (7:455). This, according to Schelling, is "the point of transfiguration of nature" (7:454): A^4 "is external or *above* nature, but it is nevertheless efficacious *within* nature; it is not cut-off from nature but rather stands in contrast to it as the universal stimulus <*Erregende*> of nature" (7:455). This is said to be "the birth of man, with which *nature* as such is complete, and a new world – a completely new series of developments – begins," namely, in the medium of "*knowledge*" (10:112, for more on this see the following subsection, "Potentizing as the Ground for the Gradual Structure of Nature"). At the same time, it is clear that this highest level of subjective potency presupposes all of the lower levels, "for the subsequent moment must always retain the preceding moment as its immediate basis"

(10:113). While knowledge is related to all of its preceding levels, it is at the same time assigned the task of apprehending these and therewith of providing an *explanation* on the basis of transcendental principles. This process of cognition is thus "parallel" to the progressive gradation process of nature: "But the difference is that everything which there is real here proceeds only in the ideal" (10:114).

Corresponding to the trio of polarity, duplicity and totality there is at the spiritual level, and thus for humans, a series of henceforth spiritual potencies. For the *mind*, Schelling mentions: *longing, desire, feeling*; for the *spirit* (in the narrow, personal sense): *egoism, understanding, will*; and for the *soul*, which is understood to be supra-personal and divine: *art, philosophy* (later: *religion*), *morality* (later: *philosophy* – the later structuring is thus equivalent to that of the *absolute spirit* in Hegel). Here, it is worth mentioning that on the basis of these topics Schelling also developed a theory of illnesses and, in particular, of mental illnesses (e.g. "melancholy") (Engelhardt 1984a).

Schelling's conception of an original *identity* which both precedes the real and the ideal, alike, and underlies the potency doctrine also implies that *the whole of nature* possesses not only the character of an object but *also the character of a subject*. It is not only *natura naturata*, or nature as product, but also – in opposition to the Cartesian concept of nature – essentially animate, creating nature, *natura naturans*. Schelling took as the title of his 1798 published work on the philosophy of nature a concept from ancient philosophy, namely, that of the *world-soul*. The finite and the infinite are accordingly "united" such that they "constitute only one and the same irresolvable absolute" (2:370, 46–7). The protagonist of the *romantic* philosophy formulated the matter in complete conformity with "*hen kai pan*" (oneness of all), the motto of the three friends – Schelling, Hegel, Hölderlin – studying in the Tübingen Stift: "the whole of nature [is] connected to a universal organism," and in "that being, which the most ancient philosophy [had considered] the *common soul of nature*" (2:569) Schelling saw the "world-soul" (2:369). Nature is thus also an appearance of the absolute; matter is "nothing other than the unconscious part of God" (7:435), "the *extinguished spirit*," as it were (3:182; 453), "the embodiment of divine forces and the first image of the universe" (7:210); nature in its entirety is "the visible spirit," and spirit conversely is "the invisible nature" (2:56). It is clear that in this idealisti-cally turned Spinozism – Leibniz is also repeatedly mentioned in this context (e.g. at 2:20; see also Holz 1984; Matsuyama 2000: 65–8) – there lies the decisive difference between Schelling's and Fichte's understanding of the absolute as I (instructive on this point is Sandkaulen-Bock 1990).

Spirit at last arrives at the knowledge that the entirety of nature is the work of that self-recognizing "one subjectivity" which precedes everything. It comes to realize that it therefore only understands nature as something *external* to itself because nature – although a product of subjectivity – is produced *unconsciously*, not consciously and deliberately: *that* would be an absurd "subjective idealism" à la Fichte, for even "the most thoroughgoing idealist cannot avoid thinking of the I, concerning its ideas of the external world, as something *dependent*" (10:92; 7:445). Thus, the productive activity of the I can only "be a blind productive activity which is grounded not in the *will* but rather in the *nature* of the I." Philosophy must therefore "assume a region beyond that of the *now existing* consciousness and an activity which itself no longer comes directly to consciousness but rather only through its result." This then "is just the external world of which the I can become conscious, not as something which it has itself produced but rather as something which exists simultaneous with it." It is in this sense that Schelling speaks of "the history of self-consciousness" (4:78) and of "the *transcendental past* (italics added) which precedes *real*, or empirical, consciousness" (10:93). Thus understood, nature is, "as it were, a fossilized intelligence" (4:77) which is then reconstructed in the consciousness of the philosopher (Wieland 1967: 421–6; Krings 1985: 116).

Potentizing as the ground for the gradual structure of nature

In the potency doctrine, the fundamental ideas of Schelling's philosophy of nature are contained, as it were, *in nuce*. The "potentizing" is supposed to ground the gradual construction of nature – though admittedly not as an evolutionary process (Jantzen 1998: 101). Its principle is as follows: "that which was posited subjectively on a previous level itself always becomes objective on the subsequent level" (10:108).

The elementary contrast between subject and object thereby forms the *original duality*, i.e. the original identity experiences a rupture which strives for a sublation and a return to identity. Duality is accordingly "*the condition of all formation*" (3:299), the ground of all activity (3:325), its goal is the return to identity. Thus, identity and duality form the basic structure of natural phenomena. With this, Schelling has in mind a kind of *dialectic of nature* which results from the potency doctrine and which makes comprehensible the gradual structure of nature. Every level arises from the opposition between the subjective and the objective. However, in this opposition the subject is again posited *as such*, i.e. it is reflected in itself and, through this "potentizing," again generates a higher level.

The potentizing thus appears as a *heightening*, mediated by the objectification of the subjective moment of a level which in this way becomes increasingly explicit. It is the process of the self-objectification of the subjective which generates these levels and repeats itself at each one. At the lowest level of matter, the subjective is still obscure. At the level of the dynamic process, it appears as light. In the organism, it is the active, self-preserving universal of its species. And as spirit it is the subjective itself as such, admittedly also here in its opposition to the objective world – from this perspective, it is nature. Accordingly, spirit and nature belong substantially together. Nature appears as de-potentized spirit, and spirit as potentized nature. Moreover, for spirit as the highest level, all of the preceding lower levels remain presupposed.

With what right can Schelling claim that the spirit (A^4) which follows upon the organic level is the *highest*? How does this form the *conclusion* of the process of potentizing? Why is the *process of nature* completed in this way? Schelling explains it is brought to conclusion in that "intelligence is compelled [here] to intuit itself as identical with itself" (3:497), and thus the subject in potency A^4 to material being has "still only an *ideal* relation" (10:112; 7:455), "thus [is] *pure* knowing, i.e. pure spirit, ... *because* it already has the entire being outside of itself, for *in itself* it is not another but is rather the same subject which in its first and immediate activity became matter, and then in a higher potency appears as light, and in a still higher one as the principle of life" (10:113). The goal and culmination of this movement is thus "the most perfect object." Its perfection arises from the fact that the subject has finally become wholly objective: the "subject posited as such" is "that which is no longer *able* to become objective (because all forms are realized)." "The subject has the necessary tendency toward the objective, and in this it exhausts itself" (10:108).

Admittedly, this argument that already "all forms are realized" (10:108) actually explains nothing, for it is only the repeating of the claim in a different form. Now, the potentizing of the organic process means that the active, animate principle of the organism, and thus its subjectivity *as such*, becomes objective. Assuming that this is an *ideal*, the sphere of materiality is in fact left behind. Here, one can think of the emerging dominance of the principle of form, biologically of the universal of species, and thus of the system-lawfulness as such which Schelling has in view when he emphasizes the independence of constantly changing matter (10:110; 7:451). However, that is conceived more *intuitively* through the *experience* of the organism and is not actually "deduced."

Criticism

This is in general characteristic of Schelling's procedure. He draws upon a powerful intuition. Providing a thorough and systematic explanation of this intuition, however, is not one of Schelling's proper strengths. Rather, Schelling too easily succumbs to the tendency to rashly appropriate the empirical data of contemporary natural scientific research for philosophical purposes (Meyer 1985: 136–7; Mutschler 1990: 93–108), and this occasionally leads him to adventurous interpretations. That "electricity never becomes active without having been created through either rubbing or some other cause of asymmetrical heating" (2:476); that "the general tendency of chemical processes" is "to transform all matter into water" (4:196; italicized in the original); that "water [is] *completely de-potentized iron*" (4:197); that plants and animals are opposing poles among which gravitational force appears (4:202): these are but a few of the various examples of nonsense in Schelling's writings on the philosophy of nature.

In contrast to this, his great achievement lies in his overcoming of Fichte's *subjective* idealism. The philosophy of nature confronts the transcendental philosophy on equal footing. Nature is recognized as existing in its own right, and, with that, Fichte's absurd asymmetry between the I and nature is rectified. Correspondingly, for Schelling, nature and spirit are ultimately "not two distinct worlds but rather only *one* and the same" (4:102; 6:204–8). This is intuitively much more plausible than the pre-eminence which Fichte accords to the I.

Philosophically, however, *reasons* are also required. Schelling seeks to develop a concept of nature which has as its ground the absolute. This he determines as an original *identity* – or also as an indifference – of subject and object which externalizes itself into the duality of subject and object, though only insofar as both are *likewise* subject and object, thus *subject–object*, with a mere excess of either the subjective or the objective. The fundamental problem with this construction is this: why does absolute identity *externalize* itself, at all? Why does it not simply remain as identity? (Küppers 1992: 50).

Now, as Hegel stated in his early essay *On the Difference Between the Systems of Philosophy of Fichte and Schelling* (1801), the whole is "represented as a self-construction of the absolute" (Hegel Werke: 2.111). The process of self-externalization must accordingly proceed from the absolute itself. Schelling takes this into account when, as we saw earlier, he retrospectively presents his own argument in the Munich lectures (1827): the absolute is essentially *subject*. In order to grasp itself *as subject*, however, it is "as it were natural" that it also "will itself as object" (10:381), "for only *in this* is it subject, that it becomes an object unto itself, since it is presupposed that there is nothing *external* to it which could become an object for it" (10:383). Schelling thus seeks to explain the externalization of the absolute by attributing to it a *subjective character*.

This admittedly raises questions: the pretended absolute *identity* of subject and object ultimately appears again as *subject*. On the one hand, this is so because the absolute – in true Fichtean form – can only be thought as *self-positing*. This is a constitutive condition of its absoluteness, and in this manner Spinoza's error of a dogmatically claimed absolute *being* is avoided. On the other hand, it is *qua* subjective character that the movement of the absolute out of itself becomes conceivable. This recourse to subjectivity means that difference is always already implicitly put into the purported identity (Lauth 1984: 224) and thus that the basic approach of the philosophy of identity cannot be maintained. Instead, it again veers off in a Fichtean direction whereby the subject is understood Spinozistically as a divine unconditioned. The evidence of self-certainty is only available to the individual I, which, as Schelling is convinced, is an instance of the absolute, and so does not come into question, anyway. A supra-individual, truly absolute subject, however, has a *hypothetical* character and thus needs its own justification. Schelling does not provide this but rather, as Hegel criticizes in the *Phenomenology of Spirit* (though admittedly without mentioning Schelling's name), "begins with absolute knowing like the shot out of a pistol" (Hegel Werke: 3.31).

With regard to the status of the absolute, Schelling waivers till the end. Insofar as in his later philosophy he considered it discursively incomprehensible (Burbidge 1984), Schelling approaches the "critique of reason" endorsed by his contemporary, Friedrich Heinrich Jacobi (1743–1819) (Sandkaulen-Bock 1990: e.g. 34–7, 40–3, 178–9). Schelling's construction of the absolute, which is supposed to underwrite the entire approach of the philosophy of nature, is very much up in the air with regard to its theoretical justification. What Schelling has provided is a wealth of ingeniously conceived ideas; inspiring, often even plausible, visions on which natural philosophical reflection and systematic philosophical thinking can work further.

Schelling's reflections in *On the Essence of Human Freedom* (1809) are interesting with regard to the increasingly problematic relation between humans and nature. This work, which does not have the philosophy of nature as its object in a narrow sense, thematizes the *self-empowerment* of the human being, which accompanies his coming to conscious awareness and thus also his emancipation from nature. Although itself a child of nature, a human being can disentangle itself from, oppose, and deform nature (see Wandschneider 2005a: 206–12). Schelling sees that human freedom inevitably brings with it the possibility of *evil* in the world (Schulz 1975b: 333–5). One could take Schelling to have in mind the arrogance of technologies hostile to nature when he speaks of "the hunger of egoism" in which "it renounces the whole and the unity" (7:390) and which "denies the bonds characteristic of finite creatures, and on account of pride in being everything plunges into nothingness" (7:391). With that, the eco-ethical side of the human relation to nature is in principle already addressed (Schmied-Kowarzik 1985).

The fact that Schelling was obviously not pleased with the recourse to an absolute *subject* is evident in, on the one hand, the admittedly ineffectual recourse to an "identity" which underlies subject and object and, on the other hand, the incidental reference to *reason* as absolute instance. This is evident in the text *System of the Entire Philosophy and of the Philosophy of Nature, In Particular* (1804): "Reason, as reason, … is the absolute identity of all the effects of God, just as the absolute universe itself" (6:207; italicized in the original). And: "Incidentally, by no means do I here understand reason as that which merely expresses itself in human beings but rather reason, insofar as it is universally distributed, as the true essence, which is the substance of everything and which inhabits the entire universe" (6:208) – a reprise, as it were, of the Kantian hypothesis of a *supersensory substratum of nature*. It was not until his *later philosophy* that Schelling tried to thematize the problem of reason in a fundamental way, to solve it by means of the dual conception of *"negative"* and *"positive"* philosophy, and, as it were, to think above and beyond reason (instructive on this point is Schulz 1954a: 242–50; 1954b: 344–7; 1975a: Chs 3–4; Burbidge 1984). It is precisely this which *Hegel* considered to be impossible. For him, reason alone can be the true essence of the universe and simultaneously the uncircumventable foundation on which a philosophical system can be established.

Hegel

Georg Wilhelm Friedrich Hegel (1770–1831), a colleague of Schelling's from the *Tübingen Stift*, initially considered himself a comrade of Schelling. In his first great philosophical publication, *On the Difference between Fichte's and Schelling's Systems of Philosophy* (1801), Hegel followed Schelling's philosophical project, which he opposed to Fichte's philosophy. However, during their subsequent years together in Jena, Hegel gradually developed his own position. The culmination of this development was the *Phenomenology of Spirit* (1807), which led to a separation from, and ultimately a break with, Schelling. The philosophical approach advanced in the *Phenomenology* was developed further and presented systematically in Hegel's *Encyclopedia of the Philosophical Sciences* (1817). In what follows, I take the completed version of the "Encyclopedia" from 1830 as the basis for my exposition.

After Hegel's death in 1831, and in view of the triumphant ascendancy of the empirical sciences and their related technologies, the fascination with Hegel's philosophy subsided. It was not until eighty years later, at the beginning of the twentieth century, that Hegel's philosophy was, as it were, rediscovered – sure enough with the exception of Hegel's philosophy of nature. The "Hegel renaissance" of that day was primarily oriented toward the humanities and thus appeared to confirm a common preconception according to which Hegel was not only far removed from the natural sciences but actually usurping them on account of "systematic constraints." The number of damning verdicts is legion. Even such a sympathetic interpreter of Hegel as Heinrich Scholz could ultimately find in Hegel's philosophy of nature reason to believe that "a great mind, when it errs, is not content with small errors." "The Hegelian philosophy of nature is an experiment, which, instead of advancing the philosophy of nature, set it back by hundreds of years and reduced it to the level it possessed during the time of Paracelsus …. Hegel's philosophy of nature merely plays with concepts and will never again be taken seriously" (Scholz 1921: 38). Ernst Cassirer reached a similar conclusion (III: 374–7). And in Charles Taylor's enormous monograph on Hegel (1983) barely 17 of the total 749 pages are devoted to the philosophy of nature.

Hegel's philosophy of nature has thus fallen almost entirely out of view. Michael John Petry noted that "until 1970 … there was hardly anyone among the Hegelians, let alone among the philosophers of science, who was prepared to recognize Hegel's philosophy of nature as an area of research worth taking seriously" (Petry 1981: 618).

This decidedly negative evaluation gradually began to change with the appearance of Petry's English translation of the Hegelian *Philosophy of Nature* in 1970, together with a detailed commentary which elucidated the significance of this part of Hegel's system for an understanding of his entire philosophy (Petry 1970). With that the ice was broken, and the way was cleared for an intense reception of Hegel's philosophy of nature (documented in Neuser 1987b; Petry 1988). After the rediscovery of Hegel's philosophy of spirit at the beginning of the century, his philosophy of nature was – with half-a-century's delay – similarly received (e.g. Buchdahl 1973). Decisive for this were the detailed scientific-historical investigations by Dietrich von Engelhardt on the intellectual context around 1800 (Engelhardt 1972, 1976), as well as the continuing efforts of Michael J. Petry (e.g. 1981, 1987, 1993b, 2004) and many others after him. A further important contribution in this area was the publication of various discovered transcripts of Hegel's lectures on the philosophy of nature (e.g. Hegel 1980, 2000). The transcripts made possible a comparison of variants such that the meanings of opaque passages – of which there is in the *Philosophy of Nature* no shortage – could often be deciphered more easily.

Thanks to such intensive efforts in research on the primary sources, the negative image of Hegel as a philosopher of spirit, removed from the natural sciences and subordinating empirical facts to the constraints of his own system, must today be recognized as wholly inappropriate. Hegel was continually occupied with physics, chemistry, geology, biology and mathematics, as is evidenced, among other things, by the numerous relevant works utilized by him and retained in his library (Bronger 1993; Mense 1993; Neuser 1987a, 2000: 199–205; Petry 1993a). Vittorio Hösle remarked that Hegel is "surely the last thinker who surveyed all of the sciences of his day which fell outside the purview of philosophy – certainly and especially the natural sciences" (Hösle 1987b: 279). On the other hand, there is without doubt in Hegel a certain carelessness in his engagement with the already exuberant empiricism of his day, whereby he succumbed not infrequently to attempts at hasty systematizations.

Nevertheless, Hegel's philosophy of nature is, in my eyes, of paramount importance. His version of an *objective idealism* – the philosophical counterpart to Cartesianism, so to speak – leads to a formidable and explanatorily powerful concept of nature. In order to explain this, it is first necessary to sketch briefly the place of nature in the Hegelian system (here, see Hösle 1987b: Ch. 5; Wandschneider 1985, 1987b, 1990).

The place of nature in Hegel's overall system

In contrast to Schelling's continual reformulation of his philosophy, Hegel's philosophical conception forms a consistent, reasoned system, at least with respect to its construction. It is divided into *Logic*, *Philosophy of Nature* and *Philosophy of Spirit*. These parts are related essentially to one another and so constitute a systematic unity. *Logic* – understood as a *fundamental* logic and not as a special calculus construct – forms the uncircumventable foundation. Stated briefly, logic is incircumventable because the refutation of such a fundamental logic would itself require an appeal to *logic*, and thus appeal precisely to that whose refutation is sought. Every such attempt thus ends in a sublation of itself. This argument is familiar from recent discussions concerning "ultimate justification" and, since antiquity, has occupied a place in the repertoire of responses to skepticism. It is in this sense – briefly explained – that Hegel conceives of logic as *absolute*, as an ideal with absolute character, or, in Hegel's idiom, as the *absolute idea*. By this is meant the *totality* of the logical, which, since it encompasses the entirety of logic, must also include its justification and so must be conceived as *self-justifying*. *Self*-justification means that a *cyclical* structure of justification is operative (Rockmore 1993). Normally, a circular justification is to be avoided, on the grounds that circular reasoning cannot serve as an explanation. However, with regard to the borderline case of logic *in its entirety* this circle cannot be avoided. It is a *necessary circle* to which *qua* circle admittedly belongs not a *justifying* but rather an *explicative* character, in the sense that traversing this circle makes the internal structure of logic visible and rationally comprehensible (Wandschneider 2005b).

In the consummation of logic in the absolute idea, says Hegel, *nature* is represented as having been posited therewith, such that the idea which is consummated in itself "*decides* itself in the absolute truth of itself, … the *immediate idea* as its reflection, freely *discharging* itself *out of itself* as *nature*" (8.393). Hegel's statements on this point could not be more meager. It is therefore no surprise that Hegel's purported transition from logic to nature has been a subject of controversy from Schelling to the present (e.g. Volkmann-Schluck 1964; Brinkmann 1976; Falkenburg 1987: Ch. 1, §2; Wandschneider 1990b; Drees 1993) – even more so since the transition is accorded a key role in Hegel's overall project. What is decisive here is the extent to which nature is still capable of being established on the basis of logic and, in this sense, *idealistically*.

Here, I would like to make do with an argument from plausibility: insofar as logic ultimately determines itself as *absolute* idea and thus, as it were, as the *self-supporting, self-justifying* system of the logically ideal in its entirety, it is thereby implied that logic is *not* determined through something which is not ideal. In other words, in the determining of an unconditioned ideal there is simultaneously a negative referring back to a *non-ideal*. In this respect, ideal and non-ideal belong logically together. Insofar as the system of logic completes itself, insofar as it determines itself as absolute and thus as ideal, it simultaneously reveals itself as non-ideal, as non-absolute. With this interpretation, that obscure dictum of Hegel concerning the self-externalization of the absolute idea into nature acquires – in the form of a *dialectic of consummation*, as one might call it – a comprehensible meaning (Wandschneider 1985, 1990a, 1992).

But what *is* the *non-ideal*? If the principal feature of the *ideal*, understood as the "absolute idea," is to be seen in continuous logical mediation, i.e. in a logical-conceptual coherence (e.g. 6.572, 8.§237, and *zusatz* 8.§§242–3), then the non-ideal must be characterized through a "sublation of the mediation" (6.572), i.e. through individuation, or as Hegel also said, *being-apart <Außereinandersein>* or *externality*, as it appears empirically in the spatial-temporal structure of *nature*. Insofar as the logical realizes and consummates itself as absolute idea, it must – just as much for logical reasons – come out of itself and posit itself as *externality*, as nature. The unavoidable question which essentially remains open in Spinoza and Leibniz, and as seen earlier, also in Fichte and Schelling, is *why* an absolute should go out of itself, at all, and externalize itself into the finitude of nature. Within the framework of the Hegelian system, this question finds an answer which is derived from the concept of the absolute itself: it is, as it were, the philosophical "proof ... that nature exists necessarily," as Hegel himself formulated it (9.10 *zusatz*). As far as I can see, Hegel's philosophy is the only one which undertakes a *rational justification* for the existence of nature. It is therefore of particular interest for those interested in appropriating the available intellectual efforts of the past for the project of renewing the philosophy of nature. Those concrete consequences which arise from Hegel's concept of nature must now be considered in greater detail.

Hegel's objective-idealistic concept of nature

The logical justification which Hegel asserts is *logic itself*. With that – and in contrast to Cartesian self-certainty – Hegel utilizes not only a subjective, private authority but the objectively binding validity of logic. The Hegelian form of idealism is accordingly an *objective idealism* which differs fundamentally from other types of idealistic systems which take as their justificatory basis either self-certainty (Descartes), individual perception (Berkeley), the subject (Kant), the I (Fichte), or a hypothetical "absolute identity" (Schelling) (see also Solomon 1974; cf. Maker 1998). As seen earlier, the defect of these approaches consists in the fact that the underlying principle either is only asserted but not demonstrated; or it has ultimately a subjectively certain character and is thus not objectively binding: the typical deficiency of every *subjective idealism*. In contrast, only that which itself has a *logical* status can be capable of being *justified* – and this is a condition which, because it takes logic as its basis, Hegel's *objective idealism* fulfills.

As described, Hegel's concept of nature permits an answer to the question of the *existence* of nature: in the absoluteness of the logical ideal, the *non-ideal*, nature, is simultaneously posited therewith. Here, "posited therewith" means that what is attributed to nature is *not unconditioned* but rather derived existence: the non-ideal presupposes the ideal, and, admittedly, the ideal conversely does not exist without the non-ideal. With Hegel, it becomes possible to develop the view according to which nature is understood as the, as it were, *eternally attending phenomenon* of the ideal. Leibniz designated as the fundamental problem of metaphysics the question: "Why is there something rather than nothing?" Hegel's reply is: to the ideal, because it is unconditioned, belongs necessary existence and, with that, then also to the non-ideal, nature, as the eternally attending phenomenon of the ideal.

From the concept of nature characterized above there arises a fundamental *ambivalence* in the existence of nature: it is a non-ideal which however, as non-ideal, remains tied to the ideal. In other words, in its appearance nature is a non-ideal which nevertheless takes as its essential basis the ideal. What Kant in the *Critique of Judgment* tentatively assumed and then admittedly discarded, namely, the idea of a *supersensory substratum* of nature as its underlying reason, is here declared as the *essence* of nature. Hegel formulates this point as follows: nature is "the idea in the form of *other-being*" (9.24). It is certainly "in itself the idea" (9.25), i.e. its *essence* is the "inner idea which constitutes the ground of nature" (9.31); however, it *appears* as a not-ideal (Wahsner 1996: Ch. 1, §1; Neuser 2004). In nature, essence and appearance fall apart.

The thought of an ideal underlying nature may at first appear outlandish. There is, however, good reason for this idea in view of the *law-like* character of nature. For the natural law which governs a stone is, for its part, not a stone. The law of electromagnetism is not itself electromagnetic. The law-like regularity of nature is, for its part, not a real natural object or a natural process but rather something akin to a *logic* underlying natural being. One cannot abut against a law-like regularity, as if against a stone, but one can conceive of such a regularity and formulate it mathematically. Science aims at nothing other than the acquisition of this logic of nature (Wahsner and Borzeszkowski 2004; critically, Wetzel 2004: 18). To this extent, science, though admittedly without reflecting on it, has fundamentally an objective-idealistic concept of nature. In fact, it is this which uniquely allows one to explain how natural phenomena are determined by natural laws which serve as their underlying logic; how natural reality "is in itself law-like" (3.121–2).

This being the case, it then becomes understandable how it is that nature is *knowable*: if thought and existence – in roughly Descartes' sense – belonged to separate worlds; if nature was thus utterly foreign to thought; then nature would not be accessible to thought, and knowledge of nature would be impossible. If, however, the existence of nature in its *essence* is logical, then the logical no longer belongs exclusively to thought; rather, there is from the outset an affinity between thought and nature. Thus the question as to how natural being can be known, i.e. can be taken up into thought, contains no *aporia* for such an account (critically, Onnasch 2004). Ultimately, the foundation for a consistent epistemology can only be an idealistic ontology of nature.

Furthermore, if the ideal is characterized in terms of its conceptual coherence, then nature, as the non-ideal, is determined as *being-apart*, as *externality* and, with that – and in contrast to the logical necessity of the conceptual – through something which is in principle *contingent* (Webb 1980). Externality is the way in which the existence of nature *appears*; however, its underlying *essence* is the logical-ideal through which it remains implicitly determined. This *discrepancy* between appearance and essence is, according to Hegel, characteristic of the existence of nature.

The *tension* which is thus contained in the existence of nature is said, following Hegel, to express itself in the tendency to overcome the discrepancy, i.e. to assimilate the appearance to the underlying ideal essence. Nature exhibits, as it were, a trend towards coherence, towards the sublation of *being-apart*, right up to the *ideality* of its underlying logic: as a *telos* which is immanent to nature and yet admittedly never obtainable for it.

Here and in what follows it is important to bear in mind that Hegel certainly does not understand this "trend" in the sense of a real *natural process* but rather as something "*categorial*," i.e. as a main feature of the *conceptual* development, not of nature but rather of the *categories* of nature. Thus, what is meant is *natural philosophical reasoning* and not a spatial-temporal evolutionary process, the assumption of which Hegel repudiates (although there are good – and thoroughly Hegelian – reasons for the latter; see "The Philosophy of the Organic," in this section, below).

Space and time – motion and mass

The first determination of nature in Hegel's sense is the pure, still fully undetermined *being-apart*. Here, one can already see the immanent tendency of nature to sublate itself and to form coherent structures, i.e. the category of *being-apart* requires further categories for its implementation, which includes an increase in structure. Hegel's reasoning for the development of the categories of *being-apart* is admittedly barely conceivable and thus, to a considerable extent, in need of clarification. I have provided an interpretation of these issues elsewhere (Wandschneider 1982, 2009: Ch. 4, §1). Here, I restrict myself to the task of making visible Hegel's intention with regard to this matter.

In accordance with the law of dialectic, there belongs to the category of *being-apart* also that of the *not-being-apart*, the latter understood as the determinate negation of *being-apart*. This is the category of the point. The unfolding of this dialectic proceeds via the determinations of lines and surfaces, and ultimately to those of a spatial element, i.e. a space which is limited by surfaces. Hegel sees in this three-tiered development a consequence of logic which underlies nature, in particular the three "conceptual moments" of singularity, particularity, and universality. Therein lies simultaneously an argument for the three-dimensional nature of space, which would thus provide an *a priori* explanation. Philosophically, this claim is certainly inevitable. For all *empirical* arguments for the three-dimensional nature of space ultimately amount to a *petitio principii*, insofar as an empirical natural being is always already structured three-dimensionally. An example for many is Peter Janich's idea that grinding real bodies shows "that only three planes can be cut pair-wise rectangularly" (Janich 1989: 219). Kant, on the other hand, assumes that an *a priori* spatial structure is *given a priori* (KVR: A25, B40–1) without accounting for this argumentatively. To this extent, Hegel's conceptual development – which admittedly remains to be worked out in detail (Halper 1998) – represents, from the standpoint of theoretical justification, a significant *novum* with respect to the philosophy of nature.

Hegel's reasoning leads further to the category of *time* and its characteristic structure of past, present, and future: the spatial element is determined by boundaries. Now, the boundary itself is nothing other than the point of *transition* from one space to another, thus the ending and new beginning of space. It is without extension but is yet not nothing: something *occurs*, namely the *passing* from the one into the other, and that is only possible in the temporal ordering of *succession* and not in spatial juxtaposition. Correctly understood, the boundary is not only a spatial position but more properly also an *event*: a process having a *temporal* sense (discussed in detail in Wandschneider 1982: Ch. 3). "The existence of this continuous self-sublation" is, according to Hegel, time (9.48 *zusatz*; Richli 2002).

Already, this line of reasoning makes clear how *relations of coherence*, in the sense of the spatial-temporal structure of natural beings, are derivable from the assumption of a completely amorphous *being-apart*. This affects, first, the dimensional relations of space and time and, second, the essential togetherness of space and time (Inwood 1987).

Involved with the categories of space and time are, according to Hegel, the categories of *motion*, *rest* and – at first perhaps somewhat surprisingly – *mass*. Here I also provide only a brief summary of Hegel's reasoning (see 9.§261), or more precisely a reconstructive interpretation of it (Wandschneider 1982: Ch. 6; also 1987, 1990a).

The *explication* of the – at first only inner – togetherness of space and time necessitates, according to Hegel, the introduction of the category of *motion*. Now, motion is only meaningful relative to something which is not in motion, i.e. the category of motion always implies the category of *rest* (on Hegel's concept of motion, see Wandschneider 1982: Ch. 4; Ihmig 1989: Ch. 4; on the *dialectic* of this concept, see De Laurentiis 2004). Only that can be at rest whose identity is preserved in motion and which defines through this a *determinate, single place* as the instance of reference of the motion. According to Hegel, such a *singular* thing whose *identity* is *preserved* in motion is *mass* (9.§261). However, insofar as mass is singular, there can be in principle many instances of mass (Wandschneider 1982: 210; Février 2000: 156), which are *distinct* from one another and yet as individuals are *also similar*. This tension, which is contained intrinsically in matter, is said to express itself as *gravitational force*, i.e. as the striving of instances of mass to each other; that is, as the tendency to sublate their heterogeneity (9.§262; Winfield 1998).

The category of mass is thus implied through the "logic" of the concept of motion: that is, as an identity-preserving individual through which first and foremost "place" is realized, in the sense of an instance of reference which is necessary for motion and which as such represents non-motion, or "rest." One mass can itself naturally also be moved relative to another mass. In this case, the relation of motion is symmetrical: each of the two masses can equally be considered as either at rest or in motion (Hegel JEN: 258–9, 361). In fact, Hegel thereby formulates a *principle of relativity of motion*, which in this form implies: *motion of mass is equivalent with relative motion*.

Relative motion and the absoluteness of the motion of light

This relationship has – independently of Hegel – the notable consequence that the movement of a *non-mass* is a *non-relative movement*: *qua* movement it is certainly related to a mass, but *qua* non-relative it is independent of the particular instance of reference and so is related to *every* mass in the *same* way. In other words: a non-relative motion has the *same* velocity in relation to *all* masses. Moreover, such a non-mass – in accordance with its concept – cannot be in a state of rest but rather can *only be in motion* – a very peculiar phenomenon which in point of fact has been realized empirically in the form of the motion of light.

But how should one understand the concept of a non-mass? Hegel asserted that in nature there must be something which is identified with *light* and to which is attributed the *absolute* (and thus non-relative) character of the movement of light (9.111–12 *zusatz*). As mentioned, empirically, this applies to light, a fact which led Einstein to the development of the ("special") theory of relativity. Naturally, it would be absurd to say that Hegel had anticipated Einstein's theory, for the latter is above all a complex *mathematical* theory whose real value consists in its demonstration of the compatibility of relative and non-relative motion. Nevertheless, following Hegel, the elementary idea is in point of fact derivable from the "logic of the concept of motion." In this regard, John N. Findlay was not wrong when he claimed there is "a flavour of relativity-physics in some of the things Hegel says about Light" (Findlay 1964: 279). In point of fact, the interpretation of Hegel developed here admits the possibility of a *natural philosophical explanation* of the relation between relative and absolute motion: *the relativity of bodily motion and the non-relativity of non-bodily motion are accordingly expressions of two strictly opposed forms of matter – body and light* – which, according to Hegel, are derivable from the "logic" of the concepts of motion and matter. The philosophical interpretation of the principle of relativity offered here yields a necessary and non-trivial consequence: namely, that not only does a non-relative motion not contradict the principle of the relativity of motion, it is actually implicated in that principle. This may be conceived as a fundamental natural philosophical insight (discussed in detail in Wandschneider 2009: Ch. 4, §9).

Here, striking *possibilities for the updating* of an Hegelian natural philosophical line of reasoning become visible in the sense of a *philosophy of modern physics*: the thought developed here should be understood as a contribution to the philosophical exploration of the theory of relativity, the likes of which was not achieved in the exceedingly sophisticated investigations of Ernst Cassirer (1972) and Hans Reichenbach (1924, 1928).

Light already belongs under the second heading in the Hegelian *Philosophy of Nature*. The first part, entitled "Mechanics," takes as its object the material existence of nature and does so without further qualification. The second part, which Hegel designates as "Physics," thematizes the different qualitative determinations of matter and begins with light (9.§275; Falkenburg 1993) – whereby Hegel's interpretation is manifestly tied to the thoughts of the early Schelling (see Schelling Werke: 4:162–6, 169, 174; vol. 7, 358). Additional consideration is given also to other physical issues, such as the (classical) elements of cohesion, caloric, electricity, magnetism, and chemical phenomena (on Hegel's account of chemistry, see Engelhardt 1976, 1984b, 1993; Burbidge 1993, 1996, 2001). The assertions of this chapter – being to a certain extent empirically oriented and thus related to the state of the just emerging natural science of that time – are often reflective of an earlier period and consequently have been surpassed to a considerable extent. Polemics against Hegel's *Philosophy of Nature* were drawn significantly from this second part. For the philosophy of nature, however, the fundamental idea underlying this chapter is still of significance: namely, that the qualitative material determinations – e.g. from acid and base in chemistry – are mutually related to one another and in their qualitative existence consist only in this intrinsic *relationality* (9.§112, §274 *zusatz*).

Philosophy of the organic

Deserving of particular interest is the *third part* of the Hegelian *Naturphilosophie*, the subject of which is the philosophy of the *organic* (Ilting 1987; Brinkmann 1996; Neuser 2000b; Frigo 2001; Bach 2004; Breidbach 2004). What is characteristic of organisms, according to Hegel, is that they possess *subject character* <Subjektcharakter> (9.337, 339–42 *zusatz*), and for Hegel that means: the structure of a *concept* (339 *zusatz*). The earthworm is, so to speak, a concept which works its way through the soil! Decisive for this view is the fact that the organism shows itself to be *self-preserving* in the sense that it automatically seeks to preserve itself in its specific nature, i.e. in the *universality of its species*. The life process of a fly is at the same time a continuous striving towards the preservation of the "fly-like characteristics" which it realizes, simply because the organism, according to Hegel, is intrinsically a universal which strives to preserve its identity in its specifications – and this, for Hegel, is clear evidence of a *teleologically* structured nature (Dahlstrom 1998). Therewith, the fly is in point of fact something like a concept which has become acting, hence a *subject*. The concept, which according to the objective-idealistic view underlies the entirety of nature, itself appears in the organism in, as it were, a physical form: "What heretofore was only our cognition has now entered into existence" (340 *zusatz*). "Here, nature has thus achieved the existence of a concept" (336 *zusatz*); "life is the concept which has come to its manifestation" (37 *zusatz*).

Here, one must ask to what extent this "speculative" view admits of *empirical conditions of realization*. Today, a categorical answer is possible within the framework of *systems theory*. According to W. Ross Ashby, one of the early protagonists of cybernetics, an organism can only be a self-preserving system insofar as it, howsoever, contains a control agent which controls and regulates the system's functioning in terms of self-preservation. It is, as it were, a representation of itself, a *self-agent-instance*. Accordingly, organic self-preservation should in principle be understood in the sense that the self-regulation of the system is steered by the *set points of the system existence itself*, and thus by the constitutive physiological parameters of the system: such a system strives to preserve its own existence (Ashby 1966: esp. Chs 7 and 9). In this way, Hegel's account of the organism as an existing concept can be reconstrued in terms of systems theory.

With regard to the claimed tendency towards coherence and idealization which Hegel attributes to nature, the organism is evidently the most advanced. Now, can this be understood as the result of an *evolution of nature*? According to Hegel, nature in general is "to be considered as a *system of levels*, wherein one necessarily proceeds out of another." However, one should "not think that these levels would be generated *naturally*" (9.31). Hegel rejects the idea of a *real evolution* of forms of nature (Breidbach 1987; Drees 1992) about which there is for us today no doubt. The reason for Hegel's verdict is the earlier discussed "categorial" view of development which attributes *development* to the "concept," alone (8.308–9 *zusatz*). Elsewhere I have shown that precisely within the framework of the Hegelian ontology of nature one can also argue for a temporally real *layering process* <Aufstufungsprozess> of nature, without requiring for that argument Hegel's concept of development (in the sense of a *conceptual* development) (Wandschneider 2001).

Higher levels mean an *increase in complexity* and thus, in principle, require more complex organisms. Plants, for example, are *autotrophic*, i.e. they are in the position to produce organic substance *itself* out of the materials dissolved in the ground at their locations by converting these into system-like organismic substances. By contrast, animals are *heterotrophic*, i.e. they require organic substance which is produced by *other* living organisms, e.g. plants. This at first seemingly inessential fact nevertheless has decisive consequences for the organization of animals, a point to which Hegel also alluded (9.430–1): not only must an animal be equipped with an appropriate set of teeth and digestive system for the intake and processing of nourishment; it must above all and from the outset be able to find such nourishment. To this end, the animal must be able to move about and orient itself in its environment. And this requires an *organization of the senses*, a *nervous system* and – in principle – a central agent for guiding and controlling, a *brain*; both for the processing of sense data, as well as for coordinating and monitoring vital external action. This is in contrast to the plant whose internal functions are merely a matter of biochemical regulation. The organization of an animal is necessarily more complex than that of plants. Thus in the course of biological evolution *something new* continuously arises – how should that be understood with respect to the *ontology of nature*?

Let us first consider the question of novelty from an *empirical-scientific* standpoint. Modern systems theory invokes the concept of *emergence*. This explains the occurrence of qualitatively new characteristics on the basis of the formation of the system, i.e. as a *holistic phenomenon*. Emergent qualities are qualities of the system which relate to it in its entirety and for that reason can be completely novel with respect to the qualities of the subsystems. At the same time, that which arises through emergence is always already contained within the existence of nature as a *possibility*. This is latent in the elementary matter, but it is in the system's formation that the possibilities which lie within the system become manifest. This is an immediate consequence of the fact that matter underlies the *laws of nature*. System formation is nothing other than an inter-connection of elementary natural laws into a more complex form of lawfulness, even system laws which can thus lead to the emergence of qualitatively new phenomena. In other words, the existence of nature is not limited to its primitive phenotype but rather contains intrinsically *possibility* which, for its part, stems from the natural laws and becomes apparent in emerging phenomena. So this *dimension of possibility* which is tied to the natural being is of decisive significance for an understanding of system formation, evolution, and, of course, technology. Their basis is to be recognized in laws of nature.

Here, one can again see the fruitfulness of the Hegelian concept of nature. According to the objective-idealistic explanation, the laws of nature are an expression of the logic underlying nature. This being the case, the central assumption of every theory of evolution can now be substantiated, in that nature does not run out in its actual state but rather contains *possibility* which increasingly becomes manifest, or "emerges," in the process of evolution. A persuasive ontological foundation for the theory of evolution is only possible within the framework of an objective-idealistic ontology of nature, even when, as mentioned earlier, Hegel himself denies the possibility of a real evolutionary process. Despite this untimely repudiation of evolu-tionary thought, Hegel's approach has an eminent explanatory value with respect to an *ontology of nature concerning evolution*. It is in this sense that Findlay explains, "If any philosopher is a philosopher of evolution, that philosopher is Hegel ... Had the Darwinian and later data been available, he would almost certainly have acknowl-edged the historical trends in nature that he admits in the realm of spirit" (1964: 272; similarly, see Harris 1998: 206).

Emergence of the psychic from nature

However great the full range of possibility inherent in nature might be, it ultimately reveals itself in the emergence of the *psychic*. To clarify this, I will first pursue the line of argument from the *system-theoretical* interpretation I have developed and then show that, from that vantage point, Hegel's explanation of feeling can be reconstructed. This is related both to what was presented earlier, as well as to some of my other work (Wandschneider 1987b, 1999, 2009: Ch. 7). I first briefly present again that line of argument.

As explained earlier, organisms have a subject-character in the sense of an actively self-preserving universal in the life process. Considered system-theoretically, this means, as already indicated, that there is a kind of agent which controls and regulates the self-preservation of the organism. In terms of the traditional concept, there is a self-instance, or a *self*. This is structured differently in the case of plants and animals. For the autotrophic plant, it is a matter of the self-regulation of biochemical functions, and it is in this sense that I will speak of a *function-self*. Over and above that, the heterotrophic animal has – on the basis of the earlier mentioned organization of nerves and senses – the capacity to control and coordinate actions and, correspondingly, possesses not only a function-self but also an *action-self*, as I will call it. Thus, from a system-theoretical perspective, what is characteristic of the animal subject is a *double structure* of the function-self and the action-self.

Now, such a "doubled self" is also asserted by Hegel: in contrast to plants, it is characteristic of animals that they possess a "doubling of subjectivity" in their "unity" (9.430 *zusatz*), quasi a "self–self" (432 *zusatz*), i.e. a "self which is for the self" (430 *zusatz*, also 432 *zusatz*, 465 *zusatz*). In other words, the self has "itself as an object" (432 *zusatz*). This *"finding itself in itself"* of the subject is, according to Hegel, *"feeling"* (342 *zusatz*, my italics; see also 432 *zusatz*).

Hegel does not explain in greater detail the subjective double-structure which underlies feeling. This concept is, however, immediately evident in the *system-theoretical reconstruction* provided above. Similarly, the structure of feeling is comprehensible in system-theoretical terms: what is obviously essential for the characteristic duality of the function-self and action-self is that both *cooperate* for the organism's self-preservation. The function-self represents the physiological needs of the organism which then prescribes a norm to the steering activity of the action-self. This is especially the case for the action-self's *perception* which is always *two-sidedly* oriented. On the one hand, it is external perception, on the other hand it is also internal perception, i.e. perception of the physiological situation of the organism. For example, the perception of temperature contains at the same time information about the extent to which the perceived temperature is *conducive* for the organism itself; or insofar as I have a tactile impression of an object, I at once have a tactile impression of myself (see 9.466 *zusatz*). Thus, in principle, animal perception includes – namely, increasingly with the stage of development – a subjective element. In the perception of what is external, the perception of what is internal is, as it were, superimposed. The subjective affectivity is thus not merely an organic state but rather also appears additionally in *perception*. This *subjectivized perception* is, in Hegel's formulation, the subject's finding-itself-in-itself, or *feeling*.

In this elementary form of the psychic in nature, I think one can see a concrete starting-point for a further clarification of the body–soul-problem. To some extent, contemporary discussion of the "mind–body relation" begins at too "high" a level. In the abstract opposing of body and mind, the contrast is so crass that it scarcely seems surmountable (for an interpretation of the psychic within the framework of the Hegelian philosophy of *mind*, see Wolff 1992).

Similarly, those characteristics of the psychic to which Hegel refers, such as *non-localness* (9.431 *zusatz*), *inwardness* (9.377 *zusatz*, also 10.20 *zusatz*) and *self-identity* (9.430 *zusatz*, 10.97 *zusatz*), find within the framework of the developed *system-theoretical* model an explanation. Insofar as the psychic is constituted in the fusion of external and internal perception, as was shown earlier, it is *not localizable* in some particular place in the body. Rather, the psychic is present equally in *all* feelings.

Moreover, this means that in the occurrence of feelings a *subjective, inner horizon* extends itself at once in perception; it is a private sphere of *"inwardness"* which is only accessible to the subject itself. Finally, it is in this inwardness that the subject is continuously with itself in the diversity of feelings. Not only does the subject preserve its identity amid the continually changing feelings, but it has moreover a *perception* of this identity and thus an identity for itself, or a *self-identity*.

I think it is in this manner that a system-theoretical reconstruction of Hegel's account of feeling is possible and thus also an empirical-scientific concretizing of Hegel's approach (presented in detail in Wandschneider 1999, 2009: Ch. 7). It is as an emergent phenomenon that the psychic becomes explicable, and the tendency for idealizing nature emphasized by Hegel likewise manifests itself with the utmost clarity: in the non-localness, the inwardness, the self-identity, and therewith also the ideality of psychic existence it becomes apparent that the existence of nature realizes itself not in dull materiality but rather always already contains the possibility of *ideality* (9.465 *zusatz*). "The progress of nature itself consists in bringing to light what is internal; to go into itself and to become subjective, and to do this by overcoming its externality and positing it as ideal" (Hegel 1980: 11).

With the appearance of subjectivity, perception and feeling, a natural evolutionary tendency toward cognition and self-perception becomes visible. Ultimately, this culminates in the appearance of *spirit* and, with that, *culture* (Burbidge 1996: 210–11; Wandschneider 2005a: 206–12; on the organic and psychic dimension of illness in Hegel's account, see Engelhardt 1984c). Hegel's *philosophy of nature* also ends with the transition to spirit: "[With that], nature's last *externality* is sublated, and the Concept which in nature is only *in itself* thus becomes *for itself*" (9.537), i.e. the Concept *recognizes itself* in nature.

Also, from an *evolutionary perspective*, nature has developed in the form of spirit a kind of organ, as it were, which now can turn back on nature and recognize it: in this manner, so to speak, "nature is realized in spirit" (Breidbach 2004: 226). In the knowledge of nature, spirit adds something to it which is not realized within its own horizon, namely the knowledge of its own underlying ideality. Hegel's dictum – "Nature presupposes spirit; spirit is nature's end. The result of the *philosophy of nature* is: reconciliation of spirit with nature, by knowing in nature the idea which spirit itself is in the form of self-consciousness" (Hegel 1980: 145) – this dictum can also be interpreted evolutionary-theoretically: the ideal essence of nature sets in motion an evolutionary process which ultimately manifests this ideal. It is by means of evolution that the ideal, as it were, carries out its own self-revelation. This, ultimately, must be the answer to the question of the direction and goal of evolution – spirit, as "the goal to which nature itself aims" (Quante 2002: 119).

The relevance of the Hegelian philosophy of nature

In the *reconstructive interpretation* offered here, Hegel's philosophy of nature provides an impressive comprehensive view of nature (Schmied-Kowarzik 1998; Fulda 2006):

a *continuous relation* of natural phenomena in the form of a sequence of levels which exhibits a tendency towards increasing coherence and ideality – from elementary being-apart to the quasi-ideality of the psychic. Accordingly, the existence of nature is not taken up with the facticity of the material but rather contains essentially *possibility*, and in particular the possibility of the *psychic*, which thus no longer appears as some remote realm cut off from the physical.

Such a unified view of nature is contained in *materialism*, or, from a scientific perspective, *physicalism*. Certainly, here a fundamental difference becomes clear: these positions are of limited import for the philosophy of nature because they are not equipped with a sufficient ontology of nature; they are not in a position to explain the law-like character of nature which they nevertheless presuppose. It is only within the framework of an objective-idealistic ontology of nature – for which there are good reasons, as shown earlier – that this can be achieved.

On the other side, this line of reasoning must also be supplemented by arguments concerning the *conditions for the realization* of natural phenomena. Insofar as these belong to the real world, considerations of realizibility cannot be ignored, and in this sense the integration of *empirical-scientific* arguments becomes unavoidable. The system-theoretical connections raised here are an example of this. Hegel explains feeling in terms of the self–self-structure of animal subjectivity, admittedly without providing a justification for this peculiar double structure. At the same time, he also points to *empirical* conditions for the kind of existence which animals exhibit (self-motion, interrupted intake of food, nervous systems, etc., see 9.430–1). The system-theoretical considerations developed here assimilate essentially this line of argument and simply pursue its consequences.

In point of fact, it is also of *philosophical* interest to clarify whether, to what extent, and in what way the "self–self-structure" is *really possible*, and what *consequences* follow from that. Among these consequences is the ability to reconstruct feeling in terms of systems theory. In this regard, one can say that Hegel's line of reasoning not only *allows for* an actualization, in the sense of empirical conditions of realization, but also *requires* such an actualization; that the natural philosophical argumentation not only can accommodate empirical-scientific considerations but moreover must do so.

Conversely, the emergence of the psychic can be explained only within the framework of an ontology of nature of the Hegelian type, whereby the *ideal* is the essence which underlies physical existence and which can manifest itself through emergence. It is by means of this that the empirical system-theoretical line of argument first gains an *ontological foundation*.

In essence, Hegel's philosophy of nature proves itself to be of amazing contemporary relevance – even despite some mistakes and misinterpretations reflective of its historical period. It aims at an integrated view of nature *via* its conception of an intrinsic *unity of nature*, which offers a persuasive alternative to both Cartesian reductionism and Kantian dualism. In my view, it is in Hegel's philosophy of nature that we have the most sophisticated concept of nature in philosophy (similarly, Rinaldi 2002: 248). Now it is our turn to utilize this enormous philosophical labor, sedimented in Hegel's project. On the one hand, it is as an *empirical-scientific concretization* of

Hegelian arguments with respect to the conditions for the realization of that which constrains the integration of empirical-scientific issues. On the other hand, conversely, it provides an *ontological foundation* for empirical-scientific lines of argument on the basis of an objective-idealistic ontology of nature. In this reciprocal interweaving and illumination of natural scientific and idealistic approaches, the opportunity for a contemporary concept of nature and, with that, a renewal of an autonomous philosophy of nature, becomes visible.

Note

1 Angle brackets (< >) distinguish the translators interpolations.

References

Ashby, W. Ross (1966) *Design for a Brain*, London: Chapman & Hall.
Bach, Thomas (2004) "Leben als Gattungsprozess: Historisch-systematische Anmerkungen zur Unterscheidung von Pflanze und Tier bei Hegel," in Neuser and Hösle (2004), pp. 175–90.
Bartuschat, Wolfgang (1972) *Zum systematischen Ort von Kants "Kritik der Urteilskraft,"* Frankfurt am Main: Klostermann.
Borzeszkowski, Horst-Heino von (2004) "Gibt es eine Logik der Physik als Vorstufe zur Hegelschen Begriffslogik?" in Neuser and Hösle (2004), pp. 51–77.
Braun, Hermann, and Manfred Riedel (eds) (1967) *Natur und Geschichte: Karl Löwith zum 70. Geburtstag*, Stuttgart: Kohlhammer.
Breidbach, Olaf (1987) "Hegels Evolutionskritik," *Hegel-Studien* 22 (1987): 165–72.
—— (2004) "Überlegungen zur Typik des Organischen in Hegels Denken," in Neuser and Hösle (2004), pp. 207–27.
Breidbach, Olaf, and Dietrich von Engelhardt (eds) (2001) *Hegel und die Lebenswissenschaften*. Berlin: Verlag für Wissenschaft und Bildung.
Brinkmann, Klaus (1976) "Schellings Hegel-Kritik," in Hartmann (1976), pp. 117–210.
—— (1996) "Hegel on the Animal Organism," in *Laval Théologique et Philosophique* 52: 135–53.
Bronger, Patrick (1993) "Hegel's Library: The Newton Editions," in Petry (1993b), pp. 711–19.
Buchdahl, Gerd (1973) "Hegel's Conception of 'Begriffsbestimmung' and his Philosophy of Science," in *Studies in Logic and the Foundations of Mathematics* 74: 943–55.
Burbidge, John W. (1984) "Contraries and Contradictories: Reasoning in Schelling's Late Philosophy," *Owl of Minerva* 16, no. 1: 55–68.
—— (1993) "Chemistry and Hegel's Logic," in Petry (1993b), pp. 609–17.
—— (1996) *Real Process: How Logic and Chemistry Combine in Hegel's Philosophy of Nature*, Toronto: University of Toronto Press.
—— (2001) "Hegel und die Chemie: Drei Auseinandersetzungen mit der chemischen Orthodoxie," in Breidbach and Engelhardt (2001), pp. 43–53.
Cassirer, Ernst (1972) *Zur modernen Physik*. Darmstadt: Wissenschaftliche Buchgesellschaft.
—— (III) *Das Erkenntnisproblem in der Philosophie und Wissenschaft der neueren Zeit*, 4 vols, vol. 3, Darmstadt: Wissenschaftliche Buchgesellschaft, 1974.
Cohen, Robert S., and Marx W. Wartofsky (eds) (1984) *Hegel and the Sciences*, Dordrecht: Springer.
Dahlstrom, Daniel O. (1998) "Hegel's Appropriation of Kant's Account of Teleology in Nature," in Houlgate (1998), pp. 167–88.
De Laurentiis, Allegra (2004) "The Tenacity of Contradiction. Hegel on Ancient and Modern Views of Paradox," in Hüning et al. (2004), pp. 405–38.
Drees, Martin (1992) "Evolution and Emanation of Spirit in Hegel's Philosophie of Nature," *Bulletin of the Hegel Society of Great Britain* 26 (Autumn/Winter): 52–61.
—— (1993) "The Logic of Hegel's Philosophy of Nature," in Petry (1993b), pp. 91–102.

Drüe, Hermann, Annemarie Gethmann-Siefert, Christa Hackenesch, Walter Jaeschke, Wolfgang Neuser, and Herbert Schnädelbach (2000) Hegels "Enzyklopädie der philosophischen Wissenschaften" (1830), Ein Kommentar zum Systemgrundriss, Frankfurt am Main: Suhrkamp

Düsing, Klaus (1968) Die Teleologie in Kants Weltbegriff. Bonn: Bouvier.

—— (1985) "Teleologie der Natur: Eine Kant-Interpretation mit Ausblicken auf Schelling," in Heckmann et al. (1985), pp. 187–210.

Engelhardt, Dietrich von (1972) "Grundzüge der wissenschaftlichen Naturforschung um 1800 und Hegels spekulative Naturerkenntnis," in Philosophia Naturalis 13: 290–315.

—— (1976) Hegel und die Chemie: Studien zur Philosophie und Wissenschaft der Natur um 1800, Wiesbaden: Guido Pressler.

—— (1984a) "Schellings philosophische Grundlegung der Medizin," in Sandkühler (1984), pp. 305–25.

—— (1984b) "The Chemical System of Substances, Forces and Processes in Hegel's Philosophy of Nature and the Science of his Time," in Cohen and Wartofsky (1984), pp. 41–54.

—— (1984c) "Hegel's Philosophical Understanding of Illness," in Cohen and Wartofsky (1984), pp. 123–41.

—— (1985) Die organische Natur und die Lebenswissenschaften in Schellings Naturphilosophie, in Heckmann et al. (1985), pp. 39–57.

—— (1993) "Hegel on Chemistry and the Organic Sciences," in Petry (1993b), pp. 657–65.

—— (2002) "Natural Philosophy and Natural Science around 1800," in Fabio Bevilacqua and Lucio Fregonese (eds) Nuova Voltiana: Studies on Volta and His Times, vol. 4, Milano: Ulrico Hoepli, 11–27.

Falkenburg, Brigitte (1987) Die Form der Materie: Zur Metaphysik der Natur bei Kant und Hegel, Frankfurt am Main: Athenäum.

—— (1993) "Hegel on Mechanistic Models of Light," in Petry (1993b), pp. 531–46.

Février, Nicolas (2000) "Das syllogistische Bild des Sonnensystems in der absoluten Mechanik Hegels" (1830), in Jahrbuch für Hegelforschung 4–5: 143–70.

Fichte, Johann Gottlieb (GA) (Akademie-Ausgabe) Gesamtausgabe der Bayerischen Akademie der Wissenschaften, edited by Reinhard Lauth, Erich Fuchs, and Hans Gliwitzky, ca. 40 vols Stuttgart 1962–. (GA I/2:431 refers to Gesamtausgabe ser. I, vol. 2, p. 431.)

—— (Werke) Sämmtliche Werke, 8 vols, edited by Immanuel Hermann Fichte, Berlin: Veit, 1845–46. ("1:482" refers to vol. 1, p. 482.)

Findlay, John N. (1964) Hegel: A Re-Examination. London: George Allen & Unwin.

Frank, Manfred (1998) "Schellings spekulative Umdeutung des Kantischen Organismus-Konzepts," in Vieweg (1998), pp. 201–18.

Franz, Michael (1998) "Die Bedeutung antiker Philosophie für Schellings philosophische Anfänge," in Sandkühler (1998), pp. 50–65.

Frigo, Gian Franco (2001) "Die Welt der lebenden Natur bei Hegel," in Breidbach and Engelhardt (2001), pp. 107–20.

Fulda, Hans Friedrich (2006) "Methode und System bei Hegel: Das Logische, die Natur, der Geist als universale Bestimmungen einer monistischen Philosophie," in Fulda and Krijnen (2006), pp. 25–50.

Fulda, Hans Friedrich, and Christian Krijnen (eds) (2006) Systemphilosophie als Selbsterkenntnis: Hegel und der Neukantianismus, Würzburg: Königshausen & Neumann.

Halper, Edward (1998) "The Logic of Hegel's Philosophy of Nature. Nature, Space and Time," in Houlgate (1998), pp. 29–49.

Harris, Errol E. (1998) "How Final Is Hegel's Rejection of Evolution?" in Houlgate (1998), pp. 189–208.

Hartmann, Klaus (ed.) (1976) Die ontologische Option: Studien zu Hegels Propädeutik, Schellings Hegel-Kritik und Hegels Phänomenologie des Geistes, Berlin; New York: Walter de Gruyter.

Heckmann, Reinhard (1985) "Natur–Geist–Identität: Die Aktualität von Schellings Naturphilosophie im Hinblick auf das moderne evolutionäre Weltbild," in Heckmann et al. (1985), pp. 291–344.

Heckmann, Reinhard, Hermann Krings, and Rudolf W. Meyer (eds) (1985) Natur und Subjektivität: Zur Auseinandersetzung mit der Naturphilosophie des jungen Schelling, Stuttgart: Frommann-Holzboog.

Hegel, Georg Wilhelm Friedrich (1980): Naturphilosophie, vol. 1 of Die Vorlesung von 1819/20, ed. Manfred Gies, in association with Karl-Heinz Ilting, Naples: Bibliopolis.

—— (2000) Vorlesung über Naturphilosophie Berlin 1823/24, edited by Gilles Marmasse, postscript by K. G. J. von Griesheim, Frankfurt am Main: Peter Lang.

—— (JEN) *Jenenser Logik, Metaphysik und Naturphilosophie*, Hamburg: Meiner, 1967.

—— (Werke) *Werke*, 20 vols, edited by Eva Moldenhauer and Karl Markus Michel, Frankfurt am Main: Suhrkamp, 1969–. ("9.15" refers to vol. 9, p. 15, and "9.§4" to vol. 9, section 4; *zusatz* refers to an inserted addition.)

Heidemann, Dietmar H., and Christian Krijnen (eds) (2007) *Hegel und die Geschichte der Philosophie*, Darmstadt: Wissenschaftliche Buchgesellschaft.

Heintel, Erich (1966) "Naturzweck und Wesensbegriff," in Dieter Heinrich and Hans Wagner (eds) *Subjektivität und Metaphysik: Festschrift für Wolfgang Cramer*, Frankfurt am Main: Klostermann, 163–87.

Hogrebe, Wolfram (ed.) (1995) *Fichtes Wissenschaftslehre 1794: Philosophische Resonanzen*, Frankfurt am Main: Suhrkamp.

Holz, Hans Heinz (1984) "Der Begriff der Natur in Schellings spekulativem System: Zum Einfluss von Leibniz auf Schelling," in Sandkühler (1984), pp. 202–26.

Hoppe, Hansgeorg (1969) *Kants Theorie der Physik: Eine Untersuchung über das Opus postumum von Kant*, Frankfurt am Main: Klostermann.

Hösle, Vittorio (1987a) "Pflanze und Tier," in Petry (1987), pp. 377–422.

—— (1987b) *Hegels System: Der Idealismus der Subjektivität und das Problem der Intersubjektivität*, vol. 2: *Philosophie der Natur und des Geistes*, Hamburg: Felix Meiner.

Hösle, Vittorio, Peter Koslowski and Richard Schenk (eds) (1999) *Jahrbuch für Philosophie des Forschungsinstituts für Philosophie Hannover*, Band 10, Wien: Passagen Verlag.

Hösle, Vittorio, and Christian Illies (eds) (2005) *Darwinism and Philosophy*, Notre Dame, IN: University of Notre Dame Press.

Houlgate, Stephen (ed.) (1998) *Hegel and the Philosophy of Nature*, Albany, NY: SUNY Press.

Hüning, Dieter, Karin Michel, and Andreas Thomas (eds) (2004) *Aufklärung durch Kritik: Festschrift für Manfred Baum zum 65. Geburtstag*, Berlin: Duncker & Humblot.

Ihmig, Karl-Norbert (1989) *Hegels Deutung der Gravitation. Eine Studie zu Hegel und Newton*. Frankfurt am Main: Athenäum.

Ilting, Karl-Heinz (1987) "Hegels Philosophie des Organischen," in Petry (1987), pp. 349–76.

Inwood, Michael (1987) "Kant and Hegel on Space and Time," in Priest (1987), pp. 49–64.

Jacobs, Wilhelm G. (1998) "Schelling im Deutschen Idealismus: Interaktionen und Kontroversen," in Sandkühler (1998), pp. 66–81.

Janich, Peter (1989) *Euklids Erbe: Ist der Raum dreidimensional?* Munich: Beck.

Jantzen, Jörg (1998) "Die Philosophie der Natur," in Sandkühler (1998), pp. 82–108.

Kanitscheider, Bernulf (1985) "Über Schellings 'spekulative Physik' und einige Elemente einer idealistischen Epistemologie in der gegenwärtigen Kosmologie," in Heckmann et al. (1985), pp.239–63.

Kant (MA) *Metaphysische Anfangsgründe der Naturwissenschaft* (Akademie edn, vol. 4).

—— (KRV) *Kritik der reinen Vernunft*, A edn (1st edn 1781) and B edn (2nd edn, 1787).

—— (KP) *Kritik der praktischen Vernunft* (Akademie edn, vol. 5).

—— (KU) *Kritik der Urteilskraft*, 3rd original edn, Berlin, 1799.

—— (PR) *Prolegomena* (Akademie edn, vol. 4).

Krings, Hermann (1985) "Natur als Subjekt: Ein Grundzug der spekulativen Physik Schellings," in Heckmann et al. (1985), pp. 111–28.

Küppers, Bernd-Olaf (1992) *Natur als Organismus: Schellings frühe Naturphilosophie und ihre Bedeutung für die moderne Biologie*, Frankfurt am Main: Klostermann.

Lauth, Reinhard (1984) *Die transzendentale Naturlehre Fichtes nach den Prinzipien der Wissenschaftslehre*, Hamburg: Felix Meiner.

Maker, William (1998) "The Very Idea of the Idea of Nature, or Why Hegel is not an Idealist," in Houlgate (1998), pp. 1–27.

Mathieu, Vittorio (1989) *Kants "Opus postumum,"* ed. Gerd Held, Frankfurt am Main: Klostermann.

Matsuyama, Juichi (2000) "Mechanisch versus dynamisch – Zur Bedeutung des dynamischen Naturverständnisses und zum Vergleich der Materiekonstruktion bei Kant und Schelling," in Matsuyama and Sandkühler (2000), pp. 41–69.

Matsuyama, Juichi, and Hans Jörg Sandkühler (eds) (2000) *Natur, Kunst und Geschichte der Freiheit: Studien zur Philosophie F. W .J. Schellings in Japan*, Frankfurt am Main: Peter Lang.

Mense, André (1993) "Hegel's Library: The Works on Mathematics, Mechanics, Optics and Chemistry," in Petry (1993b), pp. 669–709.

Meyer, Rudolf W. (1985) "Zum Begriff der spekulativen Physik bei Schelling," in Heckmann et al. (1985), pp. 129–55.

Mutschler, Hans-Dieter (1990) Spekulative und empirische Physik: Aktualität und Grenzen der Naturphilosophie Schellings. Stuttgart: Kohlhammer.

Neuser, Wolfgang (1987a) "Die naturphilosophische und naturwissenschaftliche Literatur aus Hegels privater Bibliothek," in Petry (1987), pp. 479–99.

—— (1987b) "Sekundärliteratur zu Hegels Naturphilosophie (1802–1985)," in Petry (1987), pp. 501–42.

—— (2000a) "Darstellung der Hegelschen Naturphilosophie" in Drüe et al. (2000), pp. 139–205.

—— (2000b) "Der systematische Ort des Hegelschen Organismusbegriffs und dessen Wandel," Jahrbuch für Hegelforschung 4–5: 115–42.

—— (2004) "Das Anderssein der Idee, das Außereinandersein der Natur und der Begriff der Natur," in Neuser and Hösle (2004), pp. 39–49.

Neuser, Wolfgang, and Vittorio Hösle (eds) (2004) Logik, Mathematik und Natur im objektiven Idealismus: Festschrift für Dieter Wandschneider zum 65. Geburtstag, Würzburg: Königshausen & Neumann.

Onnasch, Ernst-Otto (2004) "System und Methode in der Philosophie Hegels," in Neuser and Hösle (2004), pp. 79–89.

Petry, Michael John (1970) Hegel's Philosophy of Nature, edited, trans., with an introduction and explanatory notes, London; New York: George Allen & Unwin.

—— (1981) "Hegels Naturphilosophie – Die Notwendigkeit einer Neubewertung," Zeitschrift für Philosophische Forschung 35: 614–28.

—— (ed.) (1987) Hegel und die Naturwissenschaften, Stuttgart: Frommann-Holzboog.

—— (1988) "Hegel's Philosophy of Nature: Recent Developments," in Hegel-Studien 23: 303–26.

—— (1993a) "Hegel's Library: The Works on Mathematics, Mechanics, Optics and Chemistry," in Petry (1993b), pp. 669–710.

—— (ed.) (1993b) Hegel and Newtonianism. Dordrecht: Springer.

—— (2004) "Physik und Mathematik um 1790: Hegel und Schelling als Schüler Pfleiderers," in Neuser and Hösle (2004), pp. 145–55.

Plaass, Peter (1965) Kants Theorie der Naturwissenschaft: Eine Untersuchung zur Vorrede von Kants "Metaphysischen Anfangsgründen der Naturwissenschaft," Göttingen: Vandenhoek & Ruprecht.

Priest, Stephen (ed.) (1987) Hegel's Critique of Kant, Oxford: Clarendon Press.

Quante, Michael (2002) "Schichtung oder Setzung? Hegels reflexionslogische Bestimmung des Natur-Geist-Verhältnisses," in Hegel-Studien 37 (2002): 107–21.

Reich, Klaus (1932) Die Vollständigkeit der Kantischen Urteilstafel, Hamburg: Meiner, 1986.

Reichenbach, Hans (1924) Axiomatik der relativistischen Raum–Zeit–Lehre. Braunschweig: Friedrich Vieweg & Sohn.

—— (1928) Philosophie der Raum-Zeit-Lehre, Berlin; Leipzig: Walter de Gruyter.

Richli, Urs (2002) "Der wahrhafte Punkt· Bemerkungen zu Hegels Bestimmung der Zeit als selbstbezüglicher Negation," in Wahsner and Posch (2002), pp. 80–100.

Rinaldi, Giacomo (2002) "Zur gegenwärtigen Bedeutung von Hegels Naturphilosophie," Jahrbuch für Hegelforschung 6–7, 219–52.

Rockmore, Tom (1993) Before and after Hegel: A Historical Introduction to Hegel's Thought, Berkeley: University of California Press.

Sachsse, Hans (1979) Kausalität – Gesetzlichkeit – Wahrscheinlichkeit, Darmstadt 1979.

Sandkaulen-Bock, Birgit (1990) Ausgang vom Unbedingten: Über den Anfang in der Philosophie Schellings, Göttingen: Vandenhoek & Ruprecht.

Sandkühler, Hans Jörg (ed.) (1984) Natur und geschichtlicher Prozess. Studien zur Naturphilosophie F. W. J. Schellings, Frankfurt am Main: Suhrkamp.

—— (ed.) (1998) F. W. J. Schelling, Stuttgart; Weimar: Metzler.

Santoro-Brienza, Liberato (1992) "Aristotle and Hegel on Nature," Bulletin of the Hegel Society of Great Britain 26 (Autumn/Winter): 13–29.

Schäfer, Lothar (1966) Kants Metaphysik der Natur, Berlin: Walter de Gruyter.

Schelling, Friedrich Wilhelm Joseph (Werke). *Werke*, 13 vols, edited by Manfred Schröter, based on the original edn by K. F. A. Schelling, Munich: Beck, 1927–. ("7:23" refers to vol. 7, p. 23.)

Schmied-Kowarzik, Wolfdietrich (1985) "Die existentiell-praktische Einheit von Mensch und Natur: Zur Bedeutsamkeit der Naturphilosophie Schellings für die Ökologiedebatte," in Heckmann et al. (1985), pp. 375–89.

—— (1998) "Die frühen Abweichungen Hegels von der Naturphilosophie Schellings und ihre Folgen für das absolute System," in Vieweg (1998), pp. 231–49.

Scholz, Heinrich (1921) *Die Bedeutung der Hegelschen Philosophie für das philosophische Denken der Gegenwart*, Berlin: Reuther & Reichard.

Schulz, Walter (1954a) "Die Vollendung des Deutschen Idealismus in der Spätphilosophie Schellings," *Studia Philosophica* (Separatum) 14: 239–55.

—— (1954b) "Das Verhältnis des späten Schelling zu Hegel," *Zeitschrift für Philosophische Forschung* 8: 336–52.

—— (1957) Introduction to Schelling, *System des transzendentalen Idealismus*, Hamburg: Felix Meiner.

—— (1975a) *Die Vollendung des Deutschen Idealismus in der Spätphilosophie Schellings*, Pfullingen: Neske.

—— (1975b) "Anmerkungen zu Schelling," in *Zeitschrift für Philosophische Forschung* 29: 321–36.

Siemek, Marek J. (1995) "Fichtes und Husserls Konzept der Transzendentalphilosophie," in Hogrebe (1995), pp. 96–113.

Solomon, Robert C. (1974) "Hegel's Epistemology," *American Philosophical Quarterly* 11: 277–89.

Taylor, Charles (1983) *Hegel*, Frankfurt am Main: Suhrkamp.

Tuschling, Burkhard (1995) "System des traszendentalen Idealismus bei Kant? Offene Fragen der – und an die – Kritik der Urteilskraft," *Kant-Studien* 86: 196–210.

Vieweg, Klaus (ed.) (1998) *Hegels Jenaer Naturphilosophie*, Munich: Fink.

Volkmann-Schluck, Karl-Heinz (1964) "Die Entäußerung der Idee zur Natur," *Hegel-Studien Beiheft* 1: 37–44.

Wahsner, Renate (1996) *Zur Kritik der Hegelschen Naturphilosophie: Über ihren Sinn im Lichte der heutigen Natuerkenntnis*, Frankfurt am Main: Peter Lang.

—— (2002) "Ist die Naturphilosophie eine abgelegte Gestalt des modernen Geistes?" in Wahsner and Posch (2002), pp. 9–40.

Wahsner, Renate, and Borzeszkowski, Horst-Heino von (2004) "Gibt es eine Logik der Physik als Vorstufe zur Hegelschen Begriffslogik?" in Neuser and Hösle (2004), pp. 51–77.

Wahsner, Renate, and Thomas Posch (eds) (2002) *Die Natur muss bewiesen werden: Zu Grundfragen der Hegelschen Naturphilosophie*, Frankfurt am Main: Peter Lang.

Wandschneider, Dieter (1982) *Raum, Zeit, Relativität: Grundbestimmungen der Physik in der Perspektive der Hegelschen Naturphilosophie*, Frankfurt am Main: Klostermann.

—— (1985) "Die Absolutheit des Logischen und das Sein der Natur. Systematische Überlegungen zum absolut-idealistischen Ansatz Hegels," *Zeitschrift für Philosophische Forschung* 39: 331–51.

—— (1987a) "Die Kategorien 'Materie' und 'Licht' in der Naturphilosophie Hegels," in Petry (1987), pp. 293–321.

—— (1987b) "Anfänge des Seelischen in der Natur in der Deutung der Hegelschen Naturphilosophie und in systemtheoretischer Rekonstruktion," in Petry (1987), pp. 443–75.

—— (1987c) "Die Stellung der Natur im Gesamtentwurf der hegelschen Philosophie," in Petry (1987), pp. 33–64.

—— (1989) "Der überzeitliche Grund der Natur. Kants Zeit-Antinomie in Hegelscher Perspektive," *Prima Philosophia* 2: 381–90.

—— (1990a) "Prinzipientheoretisches zur Speziellen und zur Allgemeinen Relativitätstheorie," *Prima Philosophia* 3: 82–95.

—— (1990b) "Das Problem der Entäußerung der Idee zur Natur bei Hegel," *Hegel-Jahrbuch* (1990): 25–33.

—— (1992) "Nature and Dialectic in Hegel's Philosophy of Nature," *Bulletin of the Hegel Society of Great Britain* 26 (Autumn/Winter): 30–51.

—— (1999) "Das Problem der Emergenz von Psychischem – im Anschluss an Hegels Theorie der Empfindung," in Hösle et al. (1999), pp. 69–95.

—— (2001) "Hegel und die Evolution," in Breidbach and Engelhardt (2001), pp. 225–40.

—— (2005a) "On the Problem of Direction and Goal in Biological Evolution," in Hösle and Illies (2005), pp. 196–215.

—— (2005b) "Letztbegründung unter der Bedingung endlichen Wissens. Eine Hegelsche Perspektive," in Wulf Kellerwessel, Wolf-Jürgen Cramm, David Krause, and Hans-Christoph Kupfer (eds) *Diskurs und Reflexion: Wolfgang Kuhlmann zum 65. Geburtstag*, Würzburg: Königshausen & Neumann, 353–72.

—— (2007) "Die Bedeutung Hegels für eine zeitgemäße Naturphilosophie," in Heidemann and Krijnen (2007), pp. 260–89.

—— (2009) *Naturphilosophie*, Bamberg: Buchner.

Webb, Thomas R. (1980) "The Problem of Empirical Knowledge in Hegel's Philosophy of Nature," *Hegel-Studien* 15 (1980): 171–86.

Wetzel, Manfred (2004) "Objektiver Idealismus und Prinzip Subjektivität in der Philosophie der Natur," in Neuser and Hösle (2004), pp. 9–22.

Widmann, Joachim (1982) *Johann Gottlieb Fichte: Einführung in seine Philosophie*, Berlin; New York: Walter de Gruyter.

Wieland, Wolfgang (1967) "Die Anfänge der Philosophie Schellings und die Frage nach der Natur," in Braun and Riedel (1967), pp. 406–40.

Winfield, Richard Dien (1998) "Space, Time and Matter: Conceiving Nature without Foundations," in Houlgate (1998), pp. 51–69.

Wolff, Michael (1992) *Das Körper–Seele-Problem: Kommentar zu Hegel, Enzyklopädie (1830), §389*, Frankfurt am Main: Klostermann.

Ziche, Paul (2004) "Raumdimension und Prinzipiendeduktion: Beweise für die Dreidimensionalität des Raumes bei Schelling und Hegel," in Neuser and Hösle (2004), pp. 157–73.

4

THE MORAL THEORY OF GERMAN IDEALISM

Allen W. Wood

Below I will trace the development of German idealist thinking about moral theory from Immanuel Kant through Gottlieb Fichte to G. W. F. Hegel. The exposition will focus on the theoretical structure of German idealist theories about morality in the narrower sense, mostly leaving aside what these thinkers would call "right" (*Recht*) (and Hegel would call 'abstract right'), especially the aspects of right that deal with legal and political theory.

   In comparing these thinkers it has been customary to emphasize points of disagreement – as if, for instance, we were faced with an inevitable choice between Kant and Hegel, whose basic views present us with something like mutually exclusive (if not jointly exhaustive) alternatives. But I think the development is much better understood if we focus on the continuity within the tradition, and view the disagreements as presenting us with interesting variations on a common position. Most of the important developments within this tradition took place between Kant and Fichte; Hegel's contributions, though original and highly significant, consisted mainly in new ways of appropriating Fichte's insights. Fichte, however, did not see his theory as fundamentally at odds with Kant's, and I think he was right – from which it follows that Hegel's theory is not fundamentally at odds with it either.

Kant

Freedom

The ethics of German idealism is most fundamentally an ethics of *freedom*. This is true both in the sense that it depends on regarding the human will as free in a fairly strong sense of the term, and on locating basic moral value in certain ways of exercising freedom of the will. All three philosophers realized, however, that 'freedom' is a term with multiple (if interconnected) meanings. They were of course not entirely of one mind about how 'freedom' is to be conceived, and the structure of different capacities, activities and values falling under the concept are to be theoretically organized. But the starting point for any understanding of the moral theory of any of them must begin with the theory of freedom.

Kant distinguishes 'practical freedom' (the freedom we ascribe to ourselves as agents) from 'transcendental freedom' – which is the metaphysical idea of a cause whose activity is independent of the necessitation by other causes outside it. Kant thinks that we cannot ascribe practical freedom to ourselves unless we think of ourselves as transcendentally free. (He does not think of practical freedom as excluding the influence on us of objects outside us, only of our being *necessitated* by such causes.) Of practical freedom, Kant forms two concepts: a negative one and a positive one. Practical freedom in the negative sense is the absence of necessitation of our will by sensuous impulses or empirical desires (inclinations); practical freedom in the positive sense is the capacity to act according to principles one gives oneself – normative principles belonging to one's own rational faculty, not imposed on one by anything outside it (whether natural or supernatural, or indeed, by something simply passively 'given' in our own nature rather than actively generated by our exercise of reason) (G: 4:446–7). Freedom in this sense is the capacity for *autonomy*, that is, action according to a self-given law.

The moral law

There are two kinds of principles, however, through which a free being exercises its freedom: *maxims* and *laws*. A maxim is a rule arbitrarily adopted by an agent for the governance of its actions (G: 4:400n). Maxims are rationally binding on me only subjectively – only because and for as long as I adopt them. People may adopt maxims and then either follow them or not follow them. A law, by contrast, is a principle given by my reason that is objectively binding on me – that is, it is rationally binding on me simply as a rational being (hence binding on all rational beings equally). Kant actually thinks there are also rational principles universally binding on rational beings that are not laws. One of these is the principle that if you set an end, you are bound to take the necessary means to it (this principle of technical or instrumental reason is binding because it is analytic). The other is the pragmatic or prudential principle that from my empirical inclinations I should form an idea of overall satisfaction or happiness and prefer happiness to any limited satisfactions that would frustrate my happiness. Both the technical and pragmatic principles of reason, however, are conditional or "hypothetical" in the special sense that they presuppose ends adopted on the basis of impulses or inclinations not given by reason alone.

The only principle that is not so conditioned, hence "categorical," is the moral principle, which is rational independently of (and where necessary, even in opposition to) all my inclinations. To finite and imperfectly rational beings such as human beings, principles of reason are "imperatives" because they constrain a will that does not by its nature necessarily act according to them. It follows from this that the only genuine law of reason is the moral law, which for us humans is a *categorical imperative*. For a being that must rationally constrain itself in this way, 'duty' is Kant's term for those actions to which it is constrained by the moral law (MS: 6:379; G: 4:400).

Kant thinks of the moral law, or supreme principle of morality, as a single principle underlying all particular moral duties. This supreme principle is the foundation of moral theory. Because the principle is given by our reason alone, independently of all sensuous desires, it is *a priori*. And because 'metaphysics' is Kant's name for any theory consisting in *a priori* principles, he calls the foundations of moral philosophy the 'metaphysics of morals.' It is important, however – as well as often overlooked – that there is a lot more to moral philosophy for Kant than these metaphysical foundations. The *a priori* or metaphysical principle of morality must further be applied to empirical human nature in order to generate the moral rules or duties of which moral philosophy proper consists (G: 4:388, 429). Kant even incorporates this stage of empirical application into the 'metaphysics of morals' in his work with that title (MS: 6:216–17).

In the Second Section of the *Groundwork*, where the topic is solely the fundamental principle of morality, Kant formulates this principle in three principal ways, two of which have more "intuitive" variants:

First formula:

FUL   *The Formula of Universal Law:* "Act only in accordance with that maxim through which you at the same time can will that it become a universal law" (G: 4:421; cf. G: 4:402);

with its variant,

FLN   *The Formula of the Law of Nature:* "So act, as if the maxim of your action were to become through your will a **universal law of nature**" (G: 4:421; cf. G: 4:436).

Second formula:

FH   *The Formula of Humanity as End in Itself:* "So act that you use humanity, as much in your own person as in the person of every other, always at the same time as an end and never merely as a means" (G: 4:429; cf. G: 4:436).

Third formula:

FA   *Formula of Autonomy:* "… the idea *of the will of every rational being as a will giving universal law*" (G: 4:431; cf. G: 4:432) or "Not to choose otherwise than so that the maxims of one's choice are at the same time comprehended with it in the same volition as universal law " (G: 4:440; cf. G: 4:432, 434, 438).

with its variant,

FRE   *The Formula of the Realm of Ends:* "Act in accordance with maxims of a universally legislative member for a merely possible realm of ends" (G: 4:439; cf. G: 4:433, 437, 438).

In that discussion, Kant provisionally assumes that moral obligations are categorical imperatives, that is, principles constraining the will whose rational bindingness is not dependent on the setting of any prior end, to which action would be rational as a means. He intends to redeem the claim that there is a categorical imperative in the Third Section. Much of the argument of the Second Section consists in a derivation of these formulas from the concept of a categorical imperative. This argument represents the formulas as a developmental progression, from the more formal and more provisional formulas (FUL and FLN) through the formula that is based on the substantive value providing the rational motive for obedience to a categorical imperative (FH) to the definitive or "universal" formula of the moral law (FA and its more intuitive variant FRE) (G: 4:436). The three main formulas are said to be formulas of "the very same law," and *one* of them – presumably, FA (cf. G: 4:431) – is said "of itself to unite the other two in itself" (G: 4:436). The argument for these formulas is then completed in the Third Section, where it is argued that in both theory and practice, we must presuppose (though we cannot theoretically demonstrate or transcendentally deduce) that the human will is free, and that if the will is free, then it is a law to itself, hence stands under FA (G: 4:446–8). (Some think that Kant abandoned this argument three years later in the *Critique of Practical Reason*, resting the moral law instead solely on our alleged immediate awareness of moral obligation and the bare assertion that the moral law is a "fact of reason" (KpV: 5:31–3.).)

Duties of virtue

Both the *Groundwork* and the second Critique are focused solely on the foundations of moral philosophy, and we learn relatively little from them about the shape and content of the moral principles and duties that might answer the questions most of us bring to the inquiry into moral theory. This fact, and its having too often gone unnoticed or unappreciated, has done quite a bit of mischief in the reception of Kant's moral philosophy, as readers of these two works have attempted to infer from Kant's foundational pronouncements how he would answer the questions that most concern them. In fact, Kant seems to have been reluctant to present anything like a system of moral philosophy, and did so only at the end of his career, in the *Metaphysics of Morals* (1797–8). What he provided there is in fact in some respects rather different from what readers tend to infer from their reading (or misreading) of the earlier foundational works. From the beginning, in fact, the reception of Kant's moral philosophy has often been determined more by misreadings of the foundational works than by a proper comprehension of what Kant actually proposed to build on these foundations.

For example, from the start it has often been assumed that Kant's chief contribution to moral philosophy is the first formula of the moral law (FUL, or its variant, FLN, which in many discussions are not clearly distinguished from one another). (Fixation on this merely preliminary and provisional formulation of the law, that approach the law one-sidedly from the standpoint of its mere *form*, has also determined the common caricatures of Kantian ethics as "formalistic," and the basic misunderstanding involved in this also vitiates most of the resulting criticisms directed at Kantian ethics.) In deriving ethical duties in the *Metaphysics of Morals*, however, Kant appeals to universalizability tests for maxims only once, in connection with the duty of beneficence (MS: 6:389, 451–3), while eleven of the remaining fifteen ethical duties discussed in the Doctrine of Virtue are grounded on FH (on the worth of humanity), and the other four are grounded on it by implication. Another important feature of Kant's moral system in the *Metaphysics of Morals*, is the division of morals (*Sitten*) into two basic divisions: right (*Recht*) and ethics (*Ethik*), with many of the duties philosophers are often most interested in (those involving promising, lying, and punishment, for instance) being assigned wholly or partly to the sphere of right and not that of ethics.

Critics and even sympathizers of Kantian ethics have very seldom appreciated the far-reaching implications of this fundamental division. A third feature of Kant's system is the centrality to ethics of the idea of virtue (the system of ethical duties is called the 'Doctrine of Virtue'). Kant does not think of virtue, of course, in the same way that Aristotelian or Humean 'virtue ethics' does, but his emphasis on virtue as the basis of ethics suffices to discredit standard readings of Kantian ethics as primarily focused on the "rightness" of actions and with whether the maxim of a given action is "universalizable." Finally, standard images of Kantian ethics as 'deontological' (or even the paradigm case of a "deontological" moral theory) is called into question by the fact that Kant's entire system of ethical duties, is conceptualized *teleologically*; it is based on the pursuit of two fundamental "duties of virtue" (or "ends that are duties"), namely, our own perfection and the happiness of others.

Most of these features of Kantian ethics are prefigured clearly enough in the *Groundwork*, at least if we attend to the right things in it; but none of them are precisely what we might have expected from what Kant says in the *Groundwork*, especially when it is read on the basis of assumptions people often bring unreflectively to the reading of that work. For example, in his four famous illustrations of FLN (G: 4:421–5, 429–30), Kant presents the taxonomy of ethical duties (to oneself/to others, perfect/imperfect) around which he organizes the duties of virtue presented in the Doctrine of Virtue. He discusses the same duties as illustrating both FLN and FH, and a perceptive reader might see that the latter discussion is the deeper-going of the two, and actually justifies the duties in question, rather than merely arguing for the impermissibility of certain maxims on which someone might be tempted to violate them. In his discussion of promising under FH, Kant explicitly distinguishes issues about the rights of human beings (G: 4:430), and the third and fourth illustrations focus on the two basic duties of virtue (to include one's own perfection and the happiness of others among one's ends) (G: 4:422–3, 430). But a reader of the *Groundwork* alone could easily be forgiven for entertaining some quite erroneous expectations about a Kantian system of ethics, including many of the errors common among philosophers who have read only Kant's foundational works on ethics or whose reading of the *Metaphysics of Morals* has been so shaped by prejudices derived from their encounter with these works that they have become unable to appreciate the points made in the previous paragraph.

The realm of ends

Kant's most definitive statement of the moral law is FA, and the spirit of the Kantian moral principle is thus best conveyed by the intuitive variant of FA, namely FRE. By a 'realm' (*Reich*) Kant means "a systematic combination of various rational beings through communal laws," or again, "a whole of all ends in systematic connection" (G: 4:433). The term 'realm of ends' refers to an ideal community with all rational beings as its members, one involving a systematic harmony among the ends of all the members of the community. The terms Kant uses most often to express the relationship between the rational beings that are members of a realm of ends are 'system' (*System*) and 'combination' (*Verbindung*). A collection of *ends* constitutes a 'realm' if these ends are not in conflict or competition with one another, but are combined into a mutually supporting system. The *laws* of a realm of ends are those which, if followed, would *combine* all the rational beings, as ends in themselves, and all the ends they set, into a mutually supporting *system* of shared collective ends. Thus at the end of *Anthropology from a Pragmatic Point of View*, Kant describes historical progress as "the progressive organization of citizens of the earth in and to the species as one system, cosmopolitically combined" (VA: 7:333).

The basic idea of the realm of ends is that human beings should not relate to one another as enemies or opponents, but should shape their ends so that they mutually support and further one another. Forms of human competition are compatible with the realm of ends only when they rest on and promote a deeper convergence of human ends. In a friendly game of cards, for instance, each player seeks to win, and this end is in competition with that of the friend, who is trying to win. But both players choose this activity in common as a way of spending time together and enjoying each other's company. Their competition in the game is grounded on this deeper shared end.

The realm of ends is not fundamentally a result or consequence of actions, a *state of affairs* to be brought about. It is rather a kind of community, a mode of interpersonal action among rational beings. Kant sometimes suggests that friendship is a social relationship exemplifying what it would be to act according to the idea of a realm of ends (VE: 27: 428, 675). For Kant, it belongs to the natural sociability of human beings that they have a powerful need to communicate their thoughts and desires to others, even with no ulterior purpose or further end to be served by this act of self-revelation (MS: 6:471). This need is so great that Kant thinks a human life shut up within itself and involving no sharing or disclosure to others would not be worth living. But our unsociable sociability and the competitiveness arising from it make such acts of self-revelation risky, since others may treacherously use our self-disclosures against us. Friendship for Kant is grounded on the mutual trust necessary for free and honest intimate communication between people. According to Kant, friendship is "the human being's refuge in this world from the distrust of his fellows, in which one can reveal his disposition to another and enter into community with him; this is the whole human end, through which he can enjoy his existence" (VE: 27:428). Friendship depends on equality, without which mutual respect and mutual trust are not possible. Friends share their thoughts, including their ends. Thus true friends do not each pursue their own good independently, but share a common end, in which the happiness of both friends is "swallowed up" (MS: 6:469–473; cf. VE: 27:426–9).

Kantian ethics is often described as "individualistic." Perhaps the most valid reason for this characterization is Kant's emphasis on individual rights, dignity and responsibility. At the same time, I think the term "individualism" reflects an all-too-common tendency to read Kant through the lens of certain ideas about Western morality and a moralistic attitude toward the world, of which Kant is assumed (not arbitrarily, to be sure, but all too hastily) to be the paradigm representative. On many subjects, this leads people to ignore important themes in Kantian ethics, and to misread others. In the case of Kant's supposed "individualism," I think the use of this term is nearly always based either on overlooking or misunderstanding the full implications of the idea of the realm of ends. In this way, the social or communal orientation of the ethics of Fichte and Hegel, that we will see presently, derives its pedigree quite legitimately from its Kantian sources.

Kant, however, thinks that all ethical duties are grounded in a "metaphysics of morals" that results from applying the moral law to human nature in general. He acknowledges duties grounded in particular social institutions or relations to others, but thinks that an adequate "doctrine of duties" can be presented without detailing them – or, therefore, employing the moral principle of freedom to outline the structure of a rational society (MS: 6:468–9). We will see in due course that Fichte – and following him, Hegel – strongly disagree on this point. Fichte thinks that a conception of social roles and responsibilities should belong to any "doctrine of duties," while Hegel appears to think it should supersede such a doctrine altogether.

Autonomy

From early on, it was appreciated that a fundamental idea characteristic of Kant's ethics was that of *autonomy* – the idea that the moral law in Kant's theory is not a principle advising us how to achieve some prior end, such as happiness or perfection, and also that it does not come from some alien source, such as social custom or the divine will, but has its foundation instead in each human being's own will. Further, it was appreciated that this radical new idea was also basic to Kant's reconceptualization of the freedom of the will, which is now grasped as the will's capacity to legislate to itself or to be a law unto itself. But there is more than one way to understand the concepts of 'law' and 'legislation', and Kant's conception of the autonomy of the will employs these concepts in a different sense from the one that has, by and large, dominated the reception of Kant.

The most familiar concept of legislation is what Kant calls "positive" or "arbitrary" law (MS: 6:227). This is a command issued by someone who is in a position to enforce the law through the imposition of sanctions. The person whose will determines the content of the law is called its 'author' (*Urheber*), and the person who commands through the law (by providing the sanctions) is called the 'legislator' (*Gesetzgeber*). This, however, is not the concept of legislation that Kant uses in moral philosophy. There he employs a different concept of law, which he calls 'natural legislation'

(VE: 27:261). Here the term 'law' (*Gesetz*) does not refer to an arbitrary command with sanctions to back it up, but instead means an objective principle of reason (G: 4:401n). That is, a law in this sense is a principle that is binding in itself on the rational will as such. It does not owe its content to the positive act of any will, and its bindingness is independent of any sanctions that any will might impose.

Natural laws, then, do not properly speaking have either an author or legislator. In particular, Kant denies that God is either the author or the legislator of moral laws. If they are to be categorical imperatives, natural laws must obligate *directly* or *by nature*, not through the sanctions imposed by a legislator: "*Obligatio naturalis* is *directa*: I must not lie, [not] because God has forbidden it, but because it is [bad] in itself" (VE: 27:261–2). For the same reason, natural laws also have no author: "God is not the author of morality, since otherwise it would come through his will and we would not come to know it through nature as well. It lies in the essence of things" (VE: 29:633–4). Moral laws, for Kant, are natural laws in this sense. Their content comes from no will, but "lies in the nature of things." And the grounds for obeying them are universal and objective, not lying in a set of sanctions imposed by a will. Moral laws, then, have neither an author nor a legislator. Not only are they neither authored nor legislated by God, but the human will is also neither the author nor the legislator of them. Instead of having an author, whether human or divine, the moral law is "practically necessary" (VE: 27:282) – it commands regarding what is "[good or] bad in itself" (VE: 27:262).

But if this is really Kant's view, we are bound to ask, what becomes of his doctrine of autonomy? After all, in introducing the idea of the autonomy of the will, or "the idea of the will of every rational being as giving universal law," Kant declares: "The will is thus not solely subject to the law, but is subject in such a way that it must be regarded also *as legislating to itself*, and precisely for this reason as subject to the law (of which it can consider itself as the author)" (G: 4:431). I suggest that we must attend very carefully to Kant's wording here. In this first statement of the doctrine of autonomy, he does not say that the human will *is* the legislator or the author of the moral law, but rather that "it must be regarded" as the legislator of the moral law, and "may consider itself" the law's author. In other words, we should understand Kant as saying that there are compelling reasons for considering the will as standing in the relation of legislator and author to the moral law, even though strictly speaking it has neither a legislator nor an author.

What might these reasons be? We *may consider* our will the author of the moral law because of the precise nature of that in which its content lies. The "thing" in whose nature the content of morality lies is the rational will itself: "Morals is precisely the science of all the ends that are *established through the nature of the will* and that prescribe the objective laws of the will, and according to which we direct and exert our faculties" (VA: 25:438). Our will does not lay down the law in the manner of the author of a positive law, as if its content were determined by some arbitrary choice of ours, but its content is determined by the nature of rational will, hence our own rational will, rather than by (say) the arbitrary will of the king, or God, or a set of contingent facts about what is conducive to human perfection or happiness, or by a transcendent order of values, such as a realm of heavenly Platonic forms.

For similar reasons, we *must regard* our will as the legislator of the law, not because it imposes sanctions that bind us to obey the law, but rather because it is solely our own faculty of practical reason that is capable of recognizing, and offering us, the objective reasons that obligate us to follow the moral law. (I owe this insightful thought to Assaf Sharon.) Moreover, a will that responds to these objective reasons and conforms itself on principle to the moral law – which Kant calls the "absolutely good" will (G: 4:437) – in obeying the law, is also in effect giving itself the law, rather than being given the law from some source outside its own rational will. The absolutely good will, therefore, in these respects acts "as" or "as if" it were both the author and legislator of the moral law (G: 4:431, 432, 438). This is why, even though the law has neither an author nor a legislator, the will of the moral agent (especially the will which is absolutely good) must regard itself as the legislator of the law, and may consider itself the law's author.

If this account is correct, then Kant's conception of the autonomy of the will has been widely misunderstood, and its subsequent reception has probably reflected these misunderstandings far more often than it has the actual meaning of Kant's doctrine. This applies to all those who think of Kantian autonomy in voluntaristic terms, whether as the "Promethean" assertion of a "human-made" morality, in the Nietzschean or existentialist form of a will that "creates values, or as the "constructivist" idea that Kantian ethics denies every conception of "values in themselves" or in the nature of things: and instead places the sole "source of normativity" in human "acts of legislative will" that "confer value" both on human beings as ends in themselves and on their ends and other objects of choice.

Fichte

Autonomy is freedom, conceived as self-legislation. The big question about how to understand it, as we have just seen, is whether the law of freedom is regarded as belonging to the nature of the free will or as created by an act of the free will. Kant, as I have been arguing, and contrary to most of the reception of his idea of autonomy, clearly opts for the former alternative. With Fichte, it is difficult to decide where he stands, owing to his radical reconceptualization of the free will and the I whose will it is. The Fichtean I, like the Kantian rational will, has a nature, and is even conceptualized as a rational faculty, but the I is also nothing but an act – so its nature, as ground of the moral law, is nothing beyond an original act through which the law is posited.

Ethics and the Wissenschaftslehre

Fichte's entire philosophy – not only his moral theory – is based on this radical conception of the I as an act of freedom. Fichte's transcendental method begins with a first principle, which Fichte takes to be present to us in every consciousness, but also capable of generating, through a method something like a Kantian Transcendental Deduction, the entire system of philosophy. His technical name for the fundamental science grounding this system is 'doctrine of science' (*Wissenschaftslehre*). This starting point is our immediate awareness of our own agency, which constitutes, according to Fichte, that direct or immediate consciousness of itself that belongs necessarily to every conscious state. The I is simply an acting, not a thing that acts, or a being of any kind. This is the technical sense that Fichte gives to the word 'I' (*Ich*).

Fichte's claim is not, of course, that this acting could ever actually occur simply by itself, divorced from any agent – or, for that matter, separately from an objective world toward which the acting is directed. On the contrary, such a supposition would be quite incoherent. The point is rather that beginning with the I, a critical philosophy must advance (by transcendental arguments) to other concepts, whose instantiation proves to be transcendentally necessary for the self-conscious acting of the I. These include the material body which is the substantial agent of the I's action, the not-I or external material world which is the object of its actions, and even other I's, which Fichte argues are necessary for the I to form a concept of its own acting as a determinate acting of a definite acting self. Similarly, in the Transcendental Deduction of the categories and the principles of pure understanding, Kant argues that it is incoherent to suppose a self-identical subject conscious of the manifold of its own sensible states through time unless you take it to have an ordered experience made up of objects thought through the categories, even material substances distinct from these conscious states whose alterations follow causal laws and which reciprocally act on one another, constituting an entire law-governed material world. Fichte radicalizes this strategy, beginning only with the I as a free self-conscious acting, which is never found in isolation, but is nevertheless always present in our conscious experience as that from which we can least of all ever coherently abstract, and hence constitutes the necessary transcendental ground of any possible conception of an experienced world.

The first science with practical implications that Fichte undertakes to construct is the science of right, presented in his *Foundations of Natural Right* (1796). Fichte draws an even clearer distinction than Kant does between "right" and "ethics," and even seems to regard right as a purely theoretical science, or at least a merely technical-practical science. It specifies the conditions under which a relation of free beings to one another might be established, but it can supply no grounds why it ought to be established (GNR: 3:10). The science of right is based on a transcendental argument to the effect that it is a fundamental condition for the I's self-awareness that it should be aware of other I's. This awareness takes the form of what Fichte calls a "summons" (*Aufforderung*): the representation coming from outside of some possible action or omission as to be done. Fichte argues that the I cannot regard such a representation as simply given along with its self-awareness, any more than the I can represent itself as acting without representing a not-I (an external or material world) on which it acts, and which limits or resists its activity. The relation of right results from the most basic summons two I's could possibly issue to one another: namely to be allowed an external sphere of action free from the interference of the other (GNR: 3:41–3). This is the relation of mutual recognition (*Anerkennung*) (GNR: 3:44–7).

Fichte's entire theory of self-consciousness thus depends on the idea that there could be no such thing as a single I. Every I is always addressed by other I's and stands in reciprocal interaction with them: "The concept of individuality is a reciprocal concept, a concept that can be thought only in relation to another thought ... This concept can exist in a rational being only if it is posited as *completed* by another rational being. Thus this concept is never *mine*; rather it is … *mine and his, his and mine*; it is a shared concept within which two consciousnesses are unified into one" (GNR: 3:47–8). The relation of right is the basis of Fichte's entire theory of right – including property, justified coercion and the political state. For Fichte this is entirely independent of the theory of ethics – which arises solely from the I's free self-determination. This intersubjectivity of the I is emphasized right at the beginning of the theory of right, but not at the beginning of the system of ethics. However, we will see that it is still basic to Fichte's ethics as well.

Will and the deduction of the moral law

The science of ethics for Fichte is another particular science based on the fundamental principle of the I. This science he attempts to present systematically in his *System of Ethics* (1798). Ethics is grounded on the thinking of the I not simply in general, as is the *Wissenschaftslehre*, but the I thought under a certain special condition, to which Fichte applies the term 'finding oneself' (*sich finden*). This is the awareness of oneself as already actively engaged, but it is not itself the standpoint of active engagement, only a mere "apprehending" of oneself in this engagement (SL: 4:19); and it is also an awareness in which the finder and that which is found are to be one and the same, so that in self-finding one abstracts from whatever one thinks of as other than oneself. The problem, he says, is to "think oneself merely as oneself, i.e. separated from everything that is not oneself." In answer to the problem, Fichte's claim is: "I find myself only as willing" (SL: 4:18).

Fichte begins by declaring that it is impossible to give a real definition of "willing." In the course of his later exposition, however, it becomes clearer what Fichte means by "willing," and also some of the radical theses to which Fichte thinks we must assent in being conscious of ourselves only as willing. Willing is always directed toward some object outside itself; it presupposes an external, material world to which it is directed (SL: 4:23). At the same time, the will is also directed at itself, but in such a way that at each moment it experiences itself as producing itself anew – which Fichte describes by saying that the will "tears itself away from itself" (SL: 4:32). Whatever the will has been in the past, in willing it freely makes itself anew. Using language that anticipates Sartre's famous slogan that "existence precedes essence," Fichte says that the will must "exist in advance of its nature," it is "supposed to be before it is determined" (SL: 4:35–6). Fichte's chief formula for the will's freedom is that "willing is an absolutely free transition from indeterminacy to determinacy, accompanied by a consciousness of this transition" (SL: 4:158).

Nevertheless, Fichte insists that the will has a "true essence," an "essential character" or "original being" (SL: 4:24, 29, 30). This, however, is not a state of being but rather a "tendency" – which he describes as "a tendency to self-activity for self-activity's sake" (SL: 4:29). In ordinary consciousness, Fichte thinks, we recognize this tendency in moral obligation, where we find ourselves inwardly constrained to do certain things simply for the sake of doing them, apart from any extrinsic ends (SL: 4:13). But in transcendental philosophy we become conscious of the tendency in a way that is more original and more abstract, as a "drive toward the entire I" (SL: 4:41–2). As to its form, it is not a "feeling" (that is, a passivity in relation to the not-I) but only a "thought" or "concept" – that is, an act of thinking that we hold over against what exists, as a norm to which it ought to conform (SL: 4:43–7). In its content, the thought arising from this drive is that of a "legislation" (*Gesetzgebung*) carrying with it an absolute necessity (SL: 4:48–51). Here Fichte considers Kant's claim in the second Critique that the moral law and freedom reciprocally imply each other (KpV: 5:29) – which he rejects, or at least modifies. "Freedom does not follow from the law any more than the law follows from freedom. These are not two thoughts, one of which can be thought to depend upon the other; rather this is one and the same thought" (SL: 4:53).

Deduction of the applicability of the law

This is a thought Fichte takes himself to have transcendentally deduced from the very concept of the I, when it is thought under the condition that it is "found" as willing. The next stage in Fichte's systematic development of ethics is to demonstrate that this thought has applicability, in other words, that it relates objectively to our actions and determines what we ought to do. It is at this stage that Fichte runs through the basic conditions of the I's existence, viewing them specifically in their relation to willing. These conditions consist, first, in the I's relation to a not-I or objective material world; second, in the I's necessary embodiment in a part of that world (one's own body, which must be conceived as a living organism); and third, the existence of a future in which several actual and determinate actions are always open to it, and its possession of a power of freedom to bring about one of these actions, exercising an actual causality on the world outside itself (SL: 4:76–91).

Out of these considerations Fichte draws a transcendental or formal conception of the basic drives characterizing the I. These are fundamentally twofold, since the I is both self-active and self-active in its (passive) relation to external objective reality, including the needs of its own organic body. The basic drives of the I are therefore (1) the "natural drive" and (2) the "pure drive" (SL: 4:149). If we reach this stage in Fichte's theory and are under the influence of the thought that Fichte is basically a Kantian (and especially if we are influenced by some familiar simplistic misreadings of Kant), then we are apt think we know already what must be coming: The natural drive is going to represent "sensuousness" or "inclination" (and will be "bad," or at best morally indifferent), while the "pure drive" will be "reason" or "duty" and will turn out to be "good." But if we do think this, then we are in for a big surprise. For Fichte's position is that truly free action, hence moral action, is possible only through a "synthesis" of the two drives, each of which, taken independently from the other, is incomplete and even morally harmful. The natural drive, separated from the pure drive, yields maxims that are unworthy, because they reflect only the I's passivity to the not-I (SL: 4:182–4). But the pure drive, separated from the natural drive, is also evil, because it represents only a "blind and lawless drive to self-sufficiency," and "the maxim of unrestricted and lawless dominion over everything outside us" (SL:

4:185–90). This is the kind of person who esteems himself above all, prides himself on his own inherent goodness, and readily sacrifices others to his own dogmatic self-conceit. The person subject only to the natural drive is "the publican and sinner" while the one subject only to the pure drive is the "Pharisee," whose way of thinking is "even more dangerous than the first, merely sensible way of thinking" (SL: 4:190).

Thus the ethical drive is neither the natural drive nor the pure drive, taken separately. The ethical is possible only if the two drives are not opposed, but can be made to coincide. "The ethical drive," therefore, "is a mixed drive. It obtains its material, toward which it is directed, from the natural drive … All [it] obtains from the pure drive is its form" (SL: 4:152). Fichte is therefore among those – even perhaps, the *first* among those – who think one must "go beyond Kant" in ethics by rejecting the sharp duality between reason and sense, duty and inclination.

Conviction and conscience

These views have far-reaching implications for moral epistemology, and radical implications for moral psychology, that may surprise or even shock those who accept his critique of Kant. For moral epistemology, Fichte thinks they mean the supreme principle of morality is merely formal. "The moral law is purely formal and must receive its content from elsewhere" (SL: 4:166). Those who complain that no deter-minate actions can be derived from Kant's moral principle are correct in what they say, but wrong in complaining. They err in supposing that it was ever the function of the formal principle to provide the content of our duty. Fichte formulates the purely formal principle as follows: "Act purely and simply in accordance with your conviction concerning your duty" (SL: 4:163). As a moral agent, I find out what my duty is through a theoretical inquiry, which involves an examination of my practical situation, including a comparison of all my convictions for their coherence, and a consideration of the convictions of others. The result is an objective "conviction" (*Überzeugung*) about what my duty is, accompanied by a subjective feeling of certainty, which is the feeling of a "complete harmony of our empirical I with the pure I" (SL: 4:169). This immediate consciousness of our determinate duty is "conscience" (SL: 4:173). The conviction involved in conscience is objective (directed to a determinate external action that is objectively right), but the criterion for its correctness is an inner, not an outer one (SL: 4:170). Conscience, says Fichte, cannot err, for if it could, then it might be a mere matter of chance whether the final criterion of duty tells us what our duty really is, and if that could be a matter of chance, then it would be only a matter of luck whether we could ever do what is right, and we could therefore not be held responsible for what we do (SL: 4:174).

Fichte's rigorism

The result of moral conviction is always a synthesis of the pure drive with the natural drive. This entails also an important thesis in moral psychology: The ethical for Fichte can permit no Kantian "dualism" of sense and reason or duty and inclination. Instead, the natural drive provides the end or content of the action, while the pure drive provides its motivation or form. The pure drive supplies the necessary moral motive, but the content of duty is supplied only by the natural drive. Either without the other would be incomplete, encumbered by the absence of the other, hence unfree. In any truly free action, the two drives must be in complete harmony. Many critics of Kant – Schleiermacher, for instance, or Hegel – would agree with this point, but they would not draw from it a set of shocking consequences – all fairly obvious, I think, when you reflect on them – that Fichte does draw. (Fichte's philosophy is characterized above all by a ruthless resolve to be *consequent*, even to draw conclusions to the bitter end which more faint-hearted philosophers would try to avoid.)

First, Fichte concludes that of any two alternative actions, one must be a duty, while the other is contrary to duty (SL: 4:195). For in any situation, only one action among our practical options could ever perfectly unite the pure drive with the natural drive, and this action alone is truly free, or truly ethical. Consequently, there can be no indifferent or merely permissible actions, and no merely wide, meritorious or imperfect duties in Kant's sense. The result is that the moral law sets out for each of us a determinate series of actions which ought to be performed; the failure to perform any of them is wrong, blamable and a culpable failure of our free agency (SL: 4:150–1).

Second, every action that is not done from the motive of duty (even if it is the action our conscience tells us is our duty) is morally wrong and blamable (SL: 4:156). For a determinate action, whose content is given by the natural drive, becomes ethical only when this drive is united with the pure drive, which supplies its rational motive, and this is precisely the motive of duty. So for Fichte there can be no actions that are merely *pflichtmäßig*, without being done *aus Pflicht*. For Kant there *are* such actions, and they are even "dutiful and amiable," "deserving of praise and encouragement" (certainly not moral blame) (G: 4:398). For Fichte, however, not to be motivated by the pure drive is to be in disharmony with oneself, therefore to be unfree, unethical, in the wrong.

Third, the only permissible attitude toward oneself is to treat oneself as a means of morality, an instrument or tool in service of the moral law (SL: 4:236). We may treat others as ends in themselves in the sense that it may be part of the end of morality to promote their good (though others too, as rational beings are really only so many tools of the moral law). But the only meaning Fichte allows the phrase "end in itself" regarding ourselves is that since our dignity consists in promoting the end of reason, we honor our dignity only by treating ourselves as mere means for realizing that end (SL: 4:256).

Finally, all "enjoyment" (*Genuß*) – that is, the satisfaction of a natural drive simply for its own sake, not for the sake of morality – is *wrong* (SL: 4:128, 216). Every pursuit of our own satisfaction merely for its own sake is morally forbidden. Every action, of course, moral and immoral actions alike, does satisfy some natural drive; and the ethical drive not only permits such satisfaction but even requires it. But no action can be ethical unless it, and even the natural satisfaction involved in it, can be seen as a way of making ourselves more effective tools of the moral law. Even our natural drives, therefore, must in the end be satisfied only for the sake of morality: "Eat and drink in order to honor God. A person to whom such an ethics appears austere and painful is beyond help, for there is no other ethics" (SL: 4:216).

It is important to realize where these shocking conclusions come from, and that Fichte's rigorism means something entirely different from what Kant would have meant if he had claimed (as he most certainly did not) that the only permissible actions are those required by duty and that it is blameworthy to act on any motive except duty. Modern day critics of "the system morality," such as Bernard Williams, frequently saddle traditional moral philosophers (chiefly the utilitarians and Kant) with a number of extravagant views they never held (see Williams 1985: esp. Ch. 10). If Williams wanted to find someone who really agrees with them about the extreme demands morality makes on us, then he ought instead to read Fichte. He would then find not only someone who exemplifies "the system morality" as he attacks it, but who draws these extreme conclusions from precisely the same starting point as his own.

Fichte (and Williams), unlike Kant, cannot accept that we are bound to be (to some degree) alienated from our empirical desires, and therefore from any projects that are rooted only in them. For Kant, it is often permissible for us to base our projects on empirical desires, but we should not frame our "ground projects" solely on them, without attention to morality. When our projects run directly contrary to morality, we should give them up. But we cannot always determine in advance when this will happen, so the relation between morality and our projects will always be to some extent uneasy. All this for Kant is simply our human condition, not anything we should try to evade or abolish.

Williams, by contrast, fears that the unity and integrity of our moral agency will be compromised if we permit morality to alienate us from those desires and projects that have a fundamentally non-ethical origin. He should have noticed, however, that this end of complete self-harmony could be achieved more directly if we identified our ground project itself directly with moral obligation, so that the only morally permissible actions are those that express my authentic self and its precious harmony and integrity. Fichte's terrifying moral austerity arises solely from taking Williams' horror of self-alienation to a relentlessly logical conclusion. The moral of the story is that when you oppose Kantian "dualisms" of reason and sense, morality and nature, duty and inclination – wishing for complete integrity and self-harmony – you had better watch out. You might just get what you wish for – a self so beautifully unified with the demands of the ethical that you may feel suffocated by morality, as if the claims of duty have buried you alive.

The intersubjectivity of reason

It is at this point in his systematic exposition of ethics that Fichte explicitly introduces the intersubjectivity of the I – the summons, and the thesis that the concept of a rational being is essentially a plural concept – there cannot be one rational being unless there is a plurality of rational beings, in interaction with one another. Since ethics is a higher science than right, moreover, Fichte claims that the approach to intersubjectivity at this point is "conducted on the basis of some higher principle"

(SL: 4:218). This principle appears to be that the very act of being aware of oneself as an individual depends on the summons to free action that comes from others. In effect, it is only through the summons to free action that I can acquire the concepts of a practical possibility to become a determinate individual and of a reason for me to actualize one possibility rather than another. It is through the summons that I acquire the concept of a determinate action, and of a determinate end of action. Hence if the mere not-I, the material world, is the ground in general for limits on my freedom, the summons from another I is the ground in general for my freedom as an individual (SL: 4:220–5).

At this point, however, Fichte thinks we are threatened with a contradiction, one of the contradictions whose resolution permits transcendental philosophy to make an essential advance, by deducing a concept that is indispensable to us. The existence of others, as free agents setting their own ends, is a condition for the existence of any individual I and its ability to set ends. Moreover, from the relation of right we know that each individual summons every other to act in such a way as to leave that individual free to pursue its own ends. However, the actions of others, and their ends, may conflict with mine. So I seem to be freed by others yet also limited by them. I must set my own ends, subordinating everything in the external world to them, but I must not limit others or subordinate their ends, since they are free beings like myself. Fichte's resolution is that we must presuppose that the true ends of all rational beings do not conflict, but that "all free beings necessarily share the same end" (SL: 4:231). This end is the end of reason, to which every rational being ought to conform the ends it sets. And this end is therefore the end of the moral law. I am free only in pursuing this common or shared end. Fichte puts it this way: as I rational being I cannot be in harmony with myself unless I am in harmony with others (SL: 4:234–5)

Clearly, Fichte's conception here has a strong affinity with Kant's conception of the realm of ends. But the sharing of ends for Fichte has to be something more than an ideal, or an ideal way of representing the moral laws that each individual must follow. Fichte interprets the idea that the ends of all rational beings must be shared as involving an obligation to communicate with others, so as to determine in common with them what ends can and should be shared. "Kant's proposition talks only about the idea of an agreement and by no means about any actual agreement" (SL 4:234). Fichte would not be content, for example, with the present-day contractualist thought that we must treat others only in ways, and pursue only ends, to which no one could reasonably object. That would not be enough. In fact, I think he is best understood as holding that there is no fact of the matter about what one could reasonably object to, or reasonably consent to, apart from an actual process of free rational communication, mutual give-and-take, that aims at empirical agreement on the end of reason that is to be shared by all rational beings. Ethical inquiry, therefore – and practical convictions – require that we also seek actual agreement with others, and ends that all may actually share. Our ethical convictions thus in effect always represent the best provisional conception of this that we are capable of at any given time. Hence in Fichte's system this phase of ethics leads directly into a lengthy consideration of the social conditions under which people may freely and rationally communicate with the aim of reaching shared practical convictions (SL: 4:234–4; SW: 6:307–11). And this leads, as we will presently see, to the idea that it is indispensable, in considering even the most basic of our duties, how social relationships between rational beings might be rationally structured.

The doctrine of duties

Fichte distinguishes sharply between moral duties as the agent experiences them, and as they may be scientifically comprehended by a systematic theory of ethics. The former way of considering duties is the one we have looked at so far, involving conviction and conscience. But Fichte thinks that the deliverances of conviction and conscience can also be summarized systematically, in the form of an "ethics in the proper sense of the term," that is, a "doctrine of duties" (SL: 4:254). This is in effect a taxonomy of the kinds of duties we have, including the specification of their content and scope (for example, Fichte's insistence that the duty not to lie is virtually without exceptions, and what is covered precisely by the ethical duties to respect the lives and property of others).

In the Doctrine of Virtue, Kant also presents us with a taxonomy of duties: The basic division is between duties to oneself and duties to others. Under each heading, some duties are narrow (requiring specific actions or omissions and exposing us to blame if we do what we shouldn't or leave undone what we should). Others are wide or meritorious: We have a duty to make our own perfection and the happiness of others our ends, or rather specific instances of these, but the choice of which instances is more or less up to us. Action in pursuit of these ends is meritorious, but omission of such actions is not blameworthy unless it involves the failure to set the end at all, or the setting of a contrary (hence forbidden) end. Kant's taxonomy extends only as far as the scope of the "metaphysics of morals" – that is, to those basic duties that result from the application of the principle of morality to empirical human nature, and the circumstances of human life, in general. Kant also recognizes duties beyond the scope of a "metaphysics of morals" – these are duties contingent upon the more particular circumstances of others or our relations to them.

Fichte's taxonomy is bound to be different from this, simply because of what I have called the ferocious rigorism that results directly from his refusal to tolerate the infamous Kantian "dualism" between reason and sense or duty and inclination. So there is no division between narrow and wide, or perfect and imperfect duties, because all duties are narrow or perfect; there is no latitude in Fichte's ethics for the meritorious or the merely permissible. The basic division instead is between *universal* duties, duties that apply in the same way to all people, and *particular* duties, that apply to a person in virtue of their estate (*Stand*) or profession (*Beruf*) (SL: 4:327; cf. SW: 6:312–23). Both admit of another division that cuts across this one. This is the division between immediate or unconditioned duties and mediate or conditioned duties. The former are duties to do or omit actions because these are directly required by the end of reason and conscience. The latter are duties to shape our own abilities and character so as to make ourselves into better tools of the moral law. This category corresponds roughly to Kant's "duties to oneself," but Fichte cannot accept that formula, because it means (and Kant intends) that its ground is the value of oneself as an end. But as we have seen, Fichte regards the only acceptable attitude toward myself as one that treats me as a means or tool of morality (SL: 4:254–8).

Fichte's system of particular duties in effect sketches the structure of a rational society, in terms of its familial, economic and cultural roles. Much of this is worked out in much greater detail in the *Foundations of Natural Right*, where his concern is social justice rather than the ethical disposition of individuals toward their social calling. In his treatment of the economic and cultural orders, Fichte is insistent that all citizens, and all social vocations, must be regarded as equal in social and moral status – and his highly egalitarian economic proposals bear out the implications of this position. In his social philosophy as well as his treatment of personal morality, the spirit of Fichte's theory is radical discontent with the present, and his aim is to instil in his readers an enthusiasm for the infinite ethical striving that he takes to be the human condition. Early in his career Fichte was a notorious defender of the French Revolution, and he does not share Kant's squeamish attitude toward revolution, or Kant's controversial defense of the duty to obey even the unjust commands of rulers (as long as they do not command you to do what is wrong). Nevertheless, Fichte's general attitude toward social progress is similar to Kant's: namely, that it is best achieved by gradual reform of the state from within rather than by revolutionary upheavals. But his general stance is the reverse of conservative or quietistic. "In summary, every state constitution is rightful and can be served with good conscience, so long as it does not make it impossible to progress toward what is better … The only constitution that is utterly contrary to right is a constitution the end of which is to preserve everything just as it now is" (SL: 4:361).

Hegel

The task of philosophy

The philosophy of Hegel is an attempt to appropriate the entire Western philosophical tradition in light of the philosophical revolution incited by Kant, begun by Fichte and carried forward by Schelling. Because Hegel's writings are so notoriously difficult, and because in his appropriation of all past philosophy he is concerned to point out the one-sidedness of each contribution and to synthesize it with its perceived opposite, there is a temptation to view Hegel as having fashioned some new and startlingly original philosophical standpoint from which the stance of any earlier philosopher, and especially his relatively direct predecessors, Kant and Fichte, is to be rejected and condescended to. But I think this is precisely the wrong way to look at Hegel's contribution, and especially its relation to the German idealist tradition, of which he was (I think correctly) seen both in its own day and since, as the completion. Rightly regarded, the continuities between Hegel and these two predecessors are far more significant than their squabbles, and what they have in common – what separates them from pre-Kantian rationalist or modern empiricist approaches to philosophy – is far more significant than the points on which they disagree.

Hegel's philosophy might be seen as attempting a reinterpretation of the fundamental concepts and viewpoints of the Western metaphysical tradition in terms of what we might now call their "existential" significance. The final aim of his philosophy was to attain to a kind of philosophical wisdom that reconciles us, intellectually and emotionally, to the whole of reality by means of its rational comprehension. This means that ethical concerns, broadly speaking, are present in Hegel's philosophy at every stage, but the tasks of "ethical theory" (in some narrower sense) are always subordinated to his larger aims. Further, Hegel's ethical views were always closely related to his philosophy of society and history, and these views went through a number of distinct stages from his early Tübingen, Bern, and Frankfurt periods through his Jena period, culminating in his mature philosophy as presented after his return to university life in Heidelberg and then finally in Berlin. The account I will give here follows that given in Hegel's last major work, *Elements of the Philosophy of Right* (1821), which is also the work whose concerns are closest to the traditional aims of ethical theory.

The *Philosophy of Right* occupies a definite place in Hegel's system as a whole. The first stage of the system, speculative logic, deals with the systematic exposition of the "thought-determinations" that simultaneously constitute the inventory of the rational mind's resources for understanding reality and the basic structure of that reality itself. The remainder of the system consists in the comprehension of the real in terms of them. The second part of the system is the philosophy of nature, which follows the levels of comprehension of nature from its simplest elements in mechanistic physics up through more complex structures to organic life, and then returns to the rational itself in the third stage, the philosophy of *spirit* (*Geist*). Hegel divides the philosophy of spirit into three stages: subjective, objective and absolute, which (translated out of Hegelese) refer roughly to the individual mind, society and God. The *Philosophy of Right* begins (in its Introduction) at the highest stage of subjective spirit, the free will, and the main body of that work deals with the structure of objective spirit – in effect, developing a systematic conception of the structure of a rational society, as we are able to comprehend it with the philosophical resources of modernity, and reaching completion in our comprehension of world history.

Hegel's real aim in all this is to comprehend the "rationality of the actual" – to display the inner intelligibility of the "core" of modern social order that lies beneath the transitory, contingent "brightly colored covering in which consciousness resides," so that we may be philosophically reconciled to ourselves and the common life in which we participate (PR: Preface). But we may also look at the *Philosophy of Right* (to some extent in defiance of its explicit aims) as a contribution to "ethical theory," as an exposition of the normative structure of modern life and as rational grounding of the norms belonging to it.

Freedom and right

As with both Kant and Fichte, the basis of all these norms is *freedom*, and this is why the starting point of the *Philosophy of Right* is the free will (PR: §4). Much of Hegel's development of the free will follows closely the account given of it by Fichte in part 3, §§13–14, of the *System of Ethics* (compare PR: §§5–16, with SL: 4:153–63). But the conception of freedom that emerges at the end of this development represents a partial rejection, or at least a carefully considered revision, of Fichte's basic conception of the practical freedom of the I. For Fichte, the relation of the I to the not-I is initially negative – the not-I resists the striving of the I – but the essential being of the I is a tendency to wholeness, unity, agreement, which therefore means bringing the not-I into agreement with the I by transforming it according to the I's ends or practical concepts (SL: 4:71, 90–3; SW: 6:298–305) – a process Fichte takes to be infinite and never finally achievable (SL: 4:131, 150, 229). Hegel's reaction to these doctrines is to say that freedom must not be conceived as activity in opposition to objectivity or otherness, but rather as the achievement of harmony or agreement between the rational agent and otherness. His preferred formula for freedom, therefore, is "Being with oneself in another" (*Beisichselbstsein in einem Andern*) (PR: §23; cf. PhG: ¶799; EL: §24A; EG: §382, A). By this Hegel means that we achieve freedom when something that counts as "other" in relation to our own agency comes to be in harmony with it, for example, as an enabling condition of it or a fulfillment of its aims. Then this "other" no longer limits us or poses any resistance to our agency, and it is this unlimitedness of our agency that constitutes its freedom. Since Hegel thinks we do achieve such freedom in many different ways, he does not see the striving of freedom as infinite in the sense of uncompletable (hence insatiable, and in a sense pointless and absurd, as it seems to him it is in Fichte). But he agrees with Fichte that the truly free will is the will that wills its own freedom "merely for freedom's sake" (SL: 4:139) or "the free will that wills the free will" (PR: §27). The free will does this when it "cancels the contradiction between subjectivity and objectivity" (PR: §28) by relating itself to some existent other in which it is "with itself" in the sense just explained.

This leads Hegel to his formula for "right" (*Recht*), which is the fundamental conception of the *Philosophy of Right* as a whole: "*Right* is any existence in general which is the *existence* of the *free will*" (PR: §29). The importance of this highly abstract and technical notion of "right" for this work as a whole, and for an "ethical theoretic" interpretation of it, cannot be overemphasized. And both the structure and the development of the *Philosophy of Right* are to be comprehended by understanding the kinds of "existence" which are the "existence of the free will," the corresponding kinds of free will which gives itself existence (or is "with itself") in them, and the developmental series of these forms as Hegel presents them systematically.

Abstract right

At the first or most immediate stage, the will is free in its relation to the external or material world. The free will is grasped as the *person* (PR: §35), and freedom gives itself existence as *property* (PR: §40). 'Property' is to be understood here in a broad sense, as Fichte's "external sphere" for the exercise of arbitrary choice (PR: §41). But whereas Fichte understands all property rights as, strictly speaking, rights to actions (rejecting the whole idea of a "right" to *things*) (GNR: 3:210), and Kant understands property as a right to things that must be postulated in order to secure external freedom of action (MS: 6:250), Hegel understands property directly as free will objectified in a thing (PR: §43), so that the person's ownership over it is "essentially free and complete" (PR: §62, cf. §52). This includes ownership over one's own body, and hence also the right to free status (PR: §§47, 57). In fact, these rights, along with the basic right to own property, are regarded as essential to personality itself, hence inalienable and imprescriptible (PR: §66).

Property becomes a relation to other wills through the possibility of alienating it (PR: §§65–7). This requires us to make explicit the role of (Fichtean) "recognition" in abstract right (PR: §71) and leads to the category of contracts, in which we can distinguish the private arbitrary will of a contractor from the *common will* established by the contract (PR: §75). This category of common will, however, leads us to see that right has always been grounded in a *universal will* or "will in itself" to which the individual will may be opposed. This opposition constitutes the category of "wrong" (*Unrecht*) (PR: §82). Wrong can take the form of unintentional or ingenuous (*unbefangenes*) wrong (PR: §84), as in civil law, or as "deception" (or fraud) in which wrong masquerades as a recognition of right (PR: §87), but it becomes fully explicit in the form of the direct attempt to coerce the free will in "crime" (PR: §95).

Hegel argues that crime, as the free will attempting to annul the free will, is inherently null (*nichtig*), and calls for the manifestation of this nullity in the form of the cancellation of the crime, or punishment, which *actualizes* right by reaffirming it out of its own negation (PR: §99). Hegel's theory of punishment is therefore *retributive*, in the sense that he thinks that the criminal act in itself requires a response to the crime which involves a negation or cancellation of the criminal's will. More specifically, he holds that the criminal will, as inwardly null, implicitly wills its own negation – in other words, it wills that its own right should be infringed to just that extent that it has attempted to infringe the right of another will, and this means that punishment should always be "equal" to the crime (PR: §§100–1). Later it becomes clear that Hegel does not understand this "equality" in any crude or literal sense, but rather as the idea that crimes have a determinate gravity and punishments a determinate severity, both as functions of the ethical life of a determinate civil society, so that the measure of just punishment is a function of that ethical life (PR: §218, R).

Morality

The opposition of the universal and particular will found in crime, and its cancellation in punishment, lead to the development of a new category of right, even a new conception of the free will and its corresponding objectification. This is the idea of the moral *subject*, which encompasses both a universal will (a moral law) and a particular will (which ought to conform to it), and the expression of this will in external actions.

In many treatments of Hegel, this "moral" phase is thought to be Hegel's conception of an abstractly individualistic (Kantian) ethics, which Hegel rejects in the name of an ethics of social custom or "ethical life" (*Sittlichkeit*). This picture may correspond at least approximately to Hegel's views during his Jena period (1801–7) but it provides a hopelessly distorted image of the role of morality in the *Philosophy of Right*. There morality, along with abstract right, are essential phases of, or stages in the development of the concept of free will toward, ethical life. The moral subject, moreover, turns out to be one of the essential identities of the free will within modern ethical life, especially in its most characteristic institution, civil society (PR: §207). So it would be a serious error to hold that in Hegel's mature thought morality and ethical life are fundamentally opposed. Morality finds its completion in ethical life, but modern ethical life is what it is – that is, truly rational – only due to the role of morality in it.

The moral subject's freedom attains to existence in its actions in three basic ways: in its responsibility for them (PR: §§115–18), in the actualization of its individual good or "welfare" (PR: §§119–28) and in its pursuit of the universal good by following its conscience (PR: §§129–40). Hegel's theory of responsibility is distinctive in that it makes agent directly responsible for external deeds in the world, rather than regarding them as primarily responsible for subjective states (such as inner volitions or intentions) which may then be causally responsible for external deeds. I am responsible for my "purpose" (*Vorsatz*), as that portion of my deed that fell within my "cognizance" (*Kenntnis*) (PR: §132) – that is, for what I knew, or should have known, would occur as a result of my action. This Hegel calls the "right of knowledge" (PR: §117), using "right" in his technical sense – for it is knowledge that makes a subject's deed an existence of its freedom. The purpose is further imputed to me in light of the universal concept under which I will it (what we might also call its "desirability characterization" for the agent) – which Hegel calls my "intention" (*Absicht*). The "right of intention" is to be understood, however, as falling under an equal "right of objectivity" – it is the universal under which the subject as a thinking agent should have known its action will be understood (PR: §§120). The subject itself, Hegel says, is nothing but the series of its actions (PR: §124) – a formulation that was later famously borrowed by Sartre. In other words, purely inner or unrealized "good intentions" without deeds are without moral significance. No appeal to "good intentions" (realized or unrealized) can justify an action which is objectively wrong (PR: §126). The result is a theory of moral responsibility for actions and consequences that is original, insightful and rather hard-headed in its implications.

Hegel accepts the idea that duty should be done for duty's sake, in the sense that the thought of duty should belong to the intention from which it is done (PR: §133). But like Fichte, he rejects the idea (which he attributes to Kant) that we may perform actions solely for duty's sake and with no satisfaction of any of our empirical desires or "the particular aspect" of our intention (PR: §122). So all action includes, and ought to include, the subjective satisfaction of the agent: Hegel follows Fichte in thinking that it is only this side of the action that saves the Kantian moral law from emptiness in its content (PR: §135). Also Fichtean is Hegel's immediate transition from this to the concept of conscience, regarded as "particularity" of the will's awareness of its duty (PR: §136). But Hegel distinguishes the "true conscience" which accords with objective ethical principles (which cannot be specified determinately within the sphere of morality) from "formal conscience" which may claim moral validity independently of the objective sphere of ethical life (PR: §137). Only the former has even moral validity; the attempt by various forms of moral subjectivism – such as Jesuitical "probabilism," the "ethics of conviction" of J. F. Fries, and (most diabolical of all) the theory of Romantic irony championed by Friedrich Schlegel – represent (successively) the unrelenting descent of the moral will into evil (PR: §§139–40, R, A).

It is noteworthy that each sphere of right ends in a determination which seems to be its negation – abstract right ends with wrong, morality ends with the evil will. These negations, moreover, involve the development to its extreme of an inner opposition within the sphere – between the "will in itself" and the particular will in the case of crime, and between the universal or objective aspect of the subjective will and its merely subjective or particular aspect in the case of evil. Advance to a new sphere involves a new determination in which the opposites are brought together or creatively harmonized. In the case of the evil will of morality, these opposites are the objective rationality of universal laws and institutions (PR: §144) and the subjective self-consciousness through whose actions these laws and institutions become actual (PR: §146).

Ethical life

Hegel's term *Sittlichkeit* tends to connote moral customs, so to Hegel's critics it comes to represent deference to an unreflective, uncritical or even unthinkingly dogmatic acceptance of traditions. This impression is possibly reinforced by Hegel's idealization, both in his early writings of the 1790s and during the Jena period, of ancient Greek ethical life, as a beautiful harmony and "naïve simplicity" (*Gediegenheit*) of the relation between the will and interests of individuals and the common good of the community. In the *Philosophy of Right*, however, Hegel's theme is modern ethical life, which is taken to include the distinctive aspects of modernity, and also the way Hegel thinks modern life and consciousness represent a higher kind of freedom than was possible in the ancient world.

The basic meaning of "ethical" for Hegel is this substantial unity of objectively rational social institutions with the individual self-consciousness that knows itself to be in harmony with them. (For this reason, Hegel thinks that the "oriental realm" – he is thinking mainly of the ancient Persian empire – because it lacked the value of individuality, was pre-ethical; the ethical emerged only in the Greek realm, along with the idea of "beautiful individuality" (PR: §§355–6).) But Hegel thinks that the unity of individual consciousness with social institutions can exist on several different levels of self-consciousness: the undeveloped and unreflective level of simple identity, the naïve self-consciousness of faith and trust, the partial or one-sided "insight" of those who justify social institutions by appealing to various particular interests or values they serve, and finally the complete philosophical comprehension that reveals modern institutions to reason as ends in themselves (PR: §147). In all these phases, but more in this last than any of the others, the will becomes free by being "with itself" in the institutions of a modern ethical order, and the ethical duties of this order, so that it is precisely in the performance of ethical duty that the will finds its liberation (PR: §149). In place of the "doctrine of duties" we find in Kant and Fichte, Hegel quite consciously puts the system of "relations" constituted by the institutions of modern ethical life (PR: §148, R). In effect, he thinks it will suffice if we confine ourselves to what Fichte called the system of "particular duties," and treat these not merely in terms of the subjective disposition of those who fulfill them (though Hegel does a lot of that too) but more basically in terms of the social relationships they involve.

It is important to keep in mind that in this discussion Hegel is assuming we are talking about a modern social order in its actuality (*Wirklichkeit*), not merely in its contingent existence (*Dasein*). The latter always involves contingent defects and bad behavior by individuals, and is therefore always open to criticism and correction (PR: §257A). If we do not realize this, we will think Hegel is glorifying an uncritical or merely submissive attitude toward existing institutions and traditions when he is in fact doing nothing of the kind. It is true that Hegel's position of seeking philosophical comprehension of the modern ethical order – and hence rational and emotional reconciliation with it insofar as he takes this order to be fundamentally rational – precludes any form of social radicalism that would fundamentally overturn the prevailing ethical order (at least as long as this order corresponds to the latest historical stage of spirit's rationality). But he also acknowledges that an alienation from the social order, in times of decadence or historical transition is sometimes the rational attitude (PR: §138R), and he sees revolution as historically (though not morally or ethically) justified in tumultuous times of historical transition (PR: §§344–5). Hegel's project of seeking reconciliation with the modern state is therefore always based on the *historical* judgment that he is living in a time of stable and mature ethical institutions, which may be imperfect in their existence and may need contingent reform, but at their core are fundamentally rational and represent the highest stage spirit has yet achieved.

Civil society as the key to modern ethical life

Modern ethical life for Hegel has three fundamental institutions: the family, civil society and the state. The state is the highest of these and "the actuality of concrete freedom" (PR: §260). But we will learn more about both the family and the state, in their modern forms, and about the ethical values that underlie Hegel's *Philosophy of Right*, if we concentrate attention primarily on the uniquely modern institution that Hegel calls "civil society."

The basis of civil society is a distinctively modern way that people relate to one another in their economic life. Individuals in the modern world understand themselves as particulars existing on their own, freely determining their own way of life. This is the source of the modern conceptions of the *person* (in the sphere of abstract right) and of the *subject* (in the sphere of morality). At the same time, both these spheres involve universal standards – of arbitrary freedom, property and mutual recognition in the sphere of right, and of responsibility, welfare, the good and conscience in morality. The fact that individuality also involves certain normatively regulated relations to others is what makes civil society a species of ethical life at all (PR: §§182–6).

We may consider civil society in terms of the Hegelian concept of right as the existence of freedom, and the variations in the corresponding relation between the conception of the *free will* and the corresponding *existence* or "otherness" in which the will is "with itself." The free will simply as a member of civil society (*bürgerliche Gesellschaft*) in general is the 'citizen' (*Bürger*) in the determinate sense of the French word *bourgeois* (as distinct from *citoyen*, who is instead a member of the political state). But there are three levels of this bourgeois existence: (1) As a member of the economic realm properly speaking, the "system of needs," (2) as a person before the law in the system of justice, and (3) as a member of a determinate branch of civil society, to which Hegel gives the name "corporation" (*Korporation*) (PR: §188). Each corresponds to a way in which the bourgeois is "with himself" or achieves freedom in relation to a determinate institutional form in civil society.

The greatest contribution of Adam Smith's *Wealth of Nations* was to show how the relations between people in what he called "commercial society" express, and also actualize, a certain conception of human individuality and dignity that is characteristically modern and corresponds to values like individual freedom and personal independence that belong to post-Enlightenment culture. According to Hegel, people receive education (*Bildung*) for this new kind of society from the *labor* they do in civil society (PR: §187). This labor makes them part of a "system of needs." Civil society, however, is far more than merely the market system. For in Hegel's view, the division of labor educates each person to a distinctively different ways of life, and to a determinate social group, for which he uses Fichte's term "estate" (*Stand*) (PR: §201). For Hegel, there are three basic estates, the "substantial" (rural, agricultural) estate, the "formal" (urban manufacturing and commercial) estate, and the universal (or civil service) estate (PR: §202).

Especially in the "formal" estate, people achieve a determinate sense of identity and honor (*Standesehre*) through being a specific kind of professional or tradesman (*Gewerbsmann*) (PR: §252–3). This sense of identity grounds membership in the state as a community that takes universal responsibility for all members of civil society – the function Hegel refers to as the "police" (*Polizei*) – which in his day referred not only to law-enforcement but also more generally to the state's provision of public services, ranging from public roads and streets to poor-relief (PR: §§230–42). In this connection, Hegel shows remarkable insight into some of the contradictions involved in the inequality and poverty in civil society (PR: §§243–9). But the social identity of an estate also grounds membership in a *corporation* – not in the sense of a limited liability firm but more like a guild or professional organization, which both takes collective responsibility for performing a determinate service in civil society and also serves as a kind of "second family" to its members, providing them with economic security and a determinate ethical home in civil society (PR: §§250–6).

The sense of self-identity as *bourgeois* is the real ethical basis of both the person of abstract right and the subject of morality (PR: §207). It also determines the specifically modern form of the other two traditional ethical institutions – the family and the state. It means that the family must be the bourgeois nuclear family, rather than the extended family or "kinship group" of feudal society (PR: §§161–72, 177). It requires the modern state to have representative institutions or 'estates' – Hegel favors political representation through one's economic group rather than through abstract geographical regions (PR: §§307–19). Hegel thinks it also requires *monarchy* as a political form, in order that the state itself may be represented as a single person (PR: §279).

Concluding remark

The fundamental thought running through the moral theories of Kant, Fichte and Hegel is that there are two fundamental goods: individual *freedom* (or rational autonomy) and *community* (the shared end of reason, the ethical life of society) – which, however, must not be thought of as distinct (much less opposed) values, but must rather be grasped together as a single value. If we think freedom and community are at bottom different values, which we must "balance" or between which we must choose, then that is merely because we do not understand the real meaning of either one. We are also unlikely to reach either one in practice to an acceptable degree, and whatever we do reach will probably be a perversion of freedom or a perversion of community.

This is seen already in Kant's treatment of FA and FRE as variations of the same formula of the moral law (and variations of the most developed or definitive formula at that). In Fichte it is presented as the identity of the I's drive to absolute self-activity with the end of reason that must be shared by all rational beings; in Hegel we see it in the idea of ethical life as the highest kind of freedom, and especially in Hegel's conception of the state, which is not (as in other modern theories) a fundamentally coercive institution, but rather the "actuality of concrete freedom" (PR: §260) and at the same time the explicitly rational form of the collective life of society – the individual leading a universal life (PR: §258R).

Nevertheless, there is development from Kant to his later idealist followers. Fichte is dissatisfied with the "dualism" of reason and sense, or duty and inclination, in Kantian ethics, and develops a conception of ethical freedom in which the two are to be united. Fichte also thinks of "particular duties" (hence the rational structure of society) as indispensable to any doctrine of duties. Here too he was followed by Hegel, who presented a far more detailed and historically sophisticated social theory than either Kant or Fichte ever attempted. On both points, the decisive development came with Fichte, though Hegel developed the Fichtean insights in original ways. The same powerful ethical conception is developed differently by each of these three great moral philosophers.

References

Fichte (GNR) *Foundations of Natural Right*, trans. Michael Baur, edited by F. Neuhouser, Cambridge: Cambridge University Press, 2000.

—— (SL) *System of Ethics*, trans. D. Breazeale and G. Zöller, Cambridge: Cambridge University Press, 2006.

—— (SW) *Fichtes Sammtliche Werke*, edited by I. H. Fichte. Berlin: deGruyter, 1970. (Cited by volume: page number.)

Hegel, G. W. F. (EG) *Philosophy of Spirit*, trans. W. Wallace and A. V. Miller, Oxford: Oxford University Press, 1977. (Cited by paragraph [§] number.) Werke 12.

—— (EL) *The Encyclopedia Logic*, trans. T. F. Geraets, W. A. Suchting, and H. S. Harris, Indianapolis, IN: Hackett, 1991. (Cited by paragraph [§] number.) Werke 10.

—— (PhG) *Phenomenology of Spirit*, trans. A. V. Miller. Oxford: Oxford University Press, 1975. (Cited by paragraph [¶] number in this translation.) Werke 3.

—— (PR) *Elements of the Philosophy of Right*, trans. H. B. Nisbet, edited by A. Wood, Cambridge: Cambrige University Press, 1991. (Cited by paragraph [§] number.) Werke 7.

—— (Werke) *Werke*. Theorie Werkausgabe. Frankfurt: Suhrkamp, 1970. (Cited by volume.)

Kant (Ak) *Immanuel Kants Schriften*, edited by Königlich preussischen Akademie der Wissenschaften, Berlin: Walter de Gruyter, 1902–. (Unless otherwise footnoted, writings of Immanuel Kant will be cited by volume:page number in this edition.)

—— (Ca) *Cambridge Edition of the Writings of Immanuel Kant*, New York: Cambridge University Press, 1992–. (This edition provides marginal Ak volume:page citations. Specific works will be cited using the following system of abbreviations [works not abbreviated below will be cited simply as Ak volume:page].)

—— (G) *Grundlegung zur Metaphysik der Sitten* (1785), Ak 4; *Groundwork of the metaphysics of morals*, Ca Practical Philosophy.

—— (KpV) *Kritik der praktischen Vernunft* (1788), Ak 5; *Critique of practical reason*, Ca Practical Philosophy.

—— (MS) *Metaphysik der Sitten* (1797–8), Ak 6; *Metaphysics of morals*, Ca Practical Philosophy.

—— (R) *Religion innerhalb der Grenzen der bloßen Vernunft* (1793–4), Ak 6; *Religion within the boundaries of mere reason*, Ca Religion and Rational Theology.

—— (VA) *Anthropologie in pragmatischer Hinsicht* (1798), Ak 7; *Anthropology from a Pragmatic Point of View*, Ca Anthropology, History and Education

—— (VA 25) *Vorlesungen über Anthropologie*; *Lectures on Anthropology*, Ca Lectures on Anthropology.

—— (VE) *Vorlesungen über Ethik*, Ak 27, 29; *Lectures on Ethics*, Ca Lectures on Ethics.

Williams, Bernard (1985) *Ethics and the Limits of Philosophy*, Cambridge, MA: Harvard University Press.

Further reading

For further reading on this topic, see Marcia Baron, *Kantian Ethics (Almost) Without Apology* (Ithaca, NY: Cornell University Press, 1995); Frederick C. Beiser, *The Fate of Reason* (Cambridge, MA: Harvard University Press, 1987); *Enlightenment, Revolution, Romanticism* (Cambridge, MA: Harvard University Press, 1992); *Hegel*. London: Routledge, 2005); Stephen Darwall, *The Second-Person Standpoint* (Cambridge, MA: Harvard University Press, 2006); Paul Guyer, *Kant's Groundwork for the Metaphysics of Morals: Critical Essays* (Lanham, MD: Rowman & Littlefield, 1998); Thomas Hill Jr, *Dignity and Practical Reason* (Ithaca, NY: Cornell University Press, 1992); Christine Korsgaard, *Creating the Kingdom of Ends* (New York: Cambridge University Press, 1996); Frederick Neuhouser, *Fichte's Theory of Subjectivity* (Cambridge: Cambridge University Press, 1990); *Foundations of Hegel's Social Theory* (Cambridge, MA: Harvard University Press, 2000); Andreas Wildt, *Autonomie und Anerkennung* (Stuttgart: Klett-Cotta, 1982); Allen Wood, *Hegel's Ethical Thought* (New York: Cambridge University Press, 1991); *Kant's Ethical Thought* (New York, Cambridge University Press, 1999); *Kantian Ethics* (Cambridge: Cambridge University Press, 2008).

5

THE POLITICAL THEORY OF KANT, FICHTE AND HEGEL

Dean Moyar

Modern political philosophy

The cloud of suspicion that hung over the political philosophy of German Idealism for much of the twentieth century has almost fully dissipated. The connections, real and imagined, to communism and to German nationalism no longer stand in the way of a sober assessment of the texts of these thinkers. I focus in this essay on the major works of the three most important idealists, Kant, Fichte and Hegel, and on the extent of their continuity with the classical liberal tradition. Their ideas are developed from the tradition of modern political philosophy, and each of them critiques and extends that tradition. In this introductory section I lay out four of the main themes of modern political philosophy. This will allow me in the rest of the essay to analyze the moves in the idealists' texts as appropriations and transformations of these themes.

One of the defining moves of modern political philosophy is to *separate political right from morality*. Machiavelli tried to separate the question of political freedom from a Christian morality that urges people to care more for their souls in the afterlife than their freedom in this life. In *The Prince* he wrote that politics should be oriented by how we actually live, and by the general unreliability of humans to do the right thing, rather than by philosophical theories or religious teachings of how we ought to live. This is not only advice to rulers who want to secure their power, but it is also an assumption Machiavelli thought necessary for securing republican freedom. He writes in the *Discourses on Livy*, "it is necessary to whoever disposes a republic and orders laws in it to presuppose that all men are bad, and that they always have to use the malignity of their spirit whenever they have a free opportunity for it" (Machiavelli 1996; 15). Rather than basing politics on trust and morality, a political order should instead be based on coercive laws and the motives of self-interest and fear of punishment. In Hobbes and Locke, the separation of political right from morality is less oriented by an antipathy to religion in general (though one can certainly detect that in Hobbes), and more from a concern that religious differences make orderly political life impossible. Writing in the context of the English Civil War, Hobbes sought to build a political system on the basic human passions, with the idea that if the basis of political authority could be traced to the (amoral) desires common to all humans, there could be no grounds for civil discord based on scriptural interpretation or moral ideals. John Locke also had religious discord in the forefront of his thoughts in his "Letter Concerning Toleration," in which he sought to distinguish the purview of government from that of religion. On Locke's view the commonwealth has to do with securing the private property of each individual and with regulating trade and industry. It is not the business of the government to legislate matters of faith or private morality, but only to adjudicate the external conditions of freedom.

Two more themes come out quite clearly in the social contract theory of Hobbes's *Leviathan*. Hobbes's argument begins with an account of the human passions and of the pre-political "state of nature." This state is characterized by a war "of every man against every man," in which there is "continual fear and danger of violent death, and the life of man, solitary, poor, nasty, brutish, and short" (Hobbes 1994: 76). There is no justice, no right or wrong, and no morality in the state of nature. The first and second "laws of nature" are to seek peace and contract with others for peace. There is no moral basis for the move from the state of nature to civil society, but rather simply the strategic concern that one's life will be longer and better: "the motive and end for which this renouncing and transferring of right is introduced, is nothing else but the security of a man's person, in his life and in the means of so preserving life as not to be weary of it" (Hobbes 1994: 82). To gain this security one seeks agreement with others to constitute a coercive power that gives efficacy to the contract by instituting a system of punishments. This "motive and end" defines the *second* major theme of modern political philosophy, which I call *securing property through a common coercive force.*

The coercive force is administered by a sovereign political authority with the power to legislate and judge the legality of particular actions. The *third* main theme concerns how individual freedom is embodied or expressed in the action of the sovereign, especially in the action of making laws. I call this theme *personal freedom through the will of the sovereign.* According to Hobbes, once I have given my consent to the social contract, every action of the sovereign is by definition also my action, so in obeying the sovereign I am obeying myself. Hobbes relies on this claim in arguing against the right of resistance. He holds that the sovereign must be granted absolute power, for otherwise there would always be the possibility of war and a return to the state of nature. There can be no rightful rebellion or resistance to the sovereign, for there is no judge above the sovereign who could say whether a claim against the sovereign's authority is legitimate. We are to accept this result because of the absolute misery of the state of nature, which makes the relative misery of living under a bad sovereign tolerable.

The social contract theorist with the greatest impact on German Idealism is Jean-Jacques Rousseau. His influence on the idealists stems from the importance he places on freedom and his analysis of the social conditions that make freedom possible. The focus on freedom is evident in his basic formulation of the challenge of political philosophy: "To find a form of association that will defend and protect the person and goods of each associate with the full common force, and by means of which each, uniting with all, nevertheless obeys only himself and remains as free as before" (Rousseau 1997: 49–50). Rousseau's formulation captures neatly the goals of *securing property through a common coercive force* and *personal freedom through the will of the sovereign*. Rousseau's answer to this challenge is a social contract in which each individual *completely* alienates his powers to the sovereign "general will." The general will has "full common force," and since the general will is also the universal will of the individual, obedience to the sovereign will of the united whole is a form of *self*-obedience. Though republican and egalitarian, Rousseau's theory shares many structural features with Hobbes' account of absolute sovereignty. Like Hobbes's sovereign, Rousseau's general will is infallible and has complete power over an individual's property and even over the individual's life. The general will has this power because it expresses the will of each individual considered as a *citizen*. Each person is subject to the law as a person, and each is *author* of the law as a citizen possessing a general will. Rousseau admits that these two perspectives can diverge, and he requires that "whoever refuses to obey the general will shall be compelled to do so by the whole body. This means nothing less than that he will be forced to be free" (Rousseau 1997: 53). One is free when the laws treat everyone equally and state action is oriented by the good of all. Rousseau's general will is an ideal standard of political legitimacy, and a government which did not follow the general will can for Rousseau (unlike for Hobbes) be legitimately resisted by the sovereign power of the people. Yet the statement that one can "be forced to be free" is worrisome for liberals because it puts personal freedom too much in the hands of the collective will. Rousseau gives some indications of how this will is determined, such as through democratic voting procedures, but for many liberal political theorists he does not do enough to secure the rights of individuals *against* the collective will. It seems that one exercises personal freedom only *in* willing the general will, which leaves the individual's particular attachments and projects in a precarious position under the authority of the whole.

Whereas the Hobbesian (and Lockean) model of a state that sets external boundaries between individuals left personal morality outside the purview of public power, Rousseau's conception of the general will and his requirements for a healthy polity pull him away from modern political philosophy's strict divide of morality and right. Rousseau moralizes about the selfishness and corruption of modern bourgeois agents, which he takes to be a major obstacle to the genuine political freedom available under the general will. In his "Discourse on the Origins of Inequality," he takes Hobbes to task for modeling natural man on the Englishmen of his day rather than on truly natural, primitive man. The most prominent feature of Rousseau's natural man, and of the young Emile in his book on education, is a *wholeness* and *integrity* that Rousseau thinks is missing in the bourgeois man. The bourgeois civilized man has a split personality because he cares primarily for himself and his own interests, while having to look to other agents in society for confirmation of who he is. But Rousseau does not give up on civilized man, and he argues for the malleability of human nature and the transformation of human nature within civil society. One of Rousseau's revolutionary ideas is that individuals are *constituted* as free moral beings by entering the social contract and submitting themselves to the general will. This is our *fourth* major theme, which I call the *social constitution of free agency*. Individuals who enter the social contract do not remain the same as they were before, for entering "the civil state produces a very remarkable change in man, by substituting justice for instinct in his conduct" (Rousseau 1997: 53). Rousseau introduces an alternative strand in modern political philosophy in giving social conditions the role of constituting free agency. The main significance of this move is that it provides another motive, potentially even more important than securing property, for entering and remaining in society. He holds out the promise of a society in which one finds moral fulfillment in the public sphere because through public action one's deepest values are realized in a way that is affirmed by others. This strand in Rousseau's thought stands in obvious tension with our first two themes (separating morality from right), for it highlights the alienating and inegalitarian tendencies of a non-moral politics based exclusively on protecting private property.

The moral dimension of Rousseau's view comes out most clearly in his claims about the need for a polity to have good customs if the general will is to actually be expressed in the community's actions. To achieve this condition, Rousseau invokes the "lawgiver" as a mythic character, modeled on the great founders of peoples in ancient societies, who unites a people by instilling common customs. Rousseau was clear that only a small city-state or commonwealth with shared values could realize his ideal. Yet large-scale revolutionary movements, beginning with the French Revolution, have attempted to recreate society and citizens along Rousseauian lines. The German idealists were generally sympathetic to Rousseau and to the French Revolution's ideals, but each in his own way attempted to correct for the deficiencies of Rousseau's conceptions of freedom and self-determination. Kant and Fichte were truest to Rousseau's ideas in their elevation of morality to the highest point in philosophy. In their mature political philosophies, however, they both returned to a Hobbesian line about the separation of morality and right, and both strongly emphasized securing property through a common coercive power. They are not oriented by a social condition of shared value, but rather they take right to be an "external" relationship of mutual constraint, a set of rules for restricting actions that is neutral to specific moral values. Hegel rejects Rousseau's contract theory, but he is much closer to Rousseau in thinking of ethics (which for Hegel includes politics) as public action that expresses shared values. There are legitimate liberal concerns about Hegel's rejection of the right/morality dichotomy, but his theory remains among the best resources for thinking through liberalism's hopes and discontents.

The foundations of Kantian right

Kant's political philosophy has long been overshadowed by his moral philosophy. His only systematic presentation of his political philosophy, in his "Doctrine of Right," is embedded within the enigmatic *Metaphysics of Morals*, and to many readers it lacks the intuitive appeal of the *Groundwork*'s presentation of the moral philosophy. Yet Kant's political philosophy is an important contribution to the liberal tradition, and deserves the attention it has now begun to receive. The most accessible outline of the theory of right actually comes in the essay "On the Common Saying: That may be correct in theory, but it is of no use in practice," where Kant presents three *a priori* principles of the "rightful condition": the freedom of all as human beings, the equality of all as subjects, and the independence of all as citizens (UG: 8:291). Though independence introduces an illiberal element into his theory (only male property owners can vote because only they are truly independent), his main claims are oriented by equality and especially by freedom. The most pronounced liberal dimension of Kant's theory is his vehement rejection of *paternalism*. A paternalistic government would be one that takes its business to be determining the happiness of the individuals. He writes,

> No one can coerce me to be happy in his way (as he thinks of the welfare of other human beings); instead, each may seek his happiness in the way that seems good to him, provided he does not infringe upon that freedom of others to strive for a like end which can coexist with the freedom of everyone in accordance with a possible universal law (i.e., does not infringe upon this right of another). (UG: 8:290)

One's action must leave sufficient room for the actions of others and not obstruct the exercise of their freedom. The good and happiness are left up to the individual, whereas right (and the coercion that it authorizes) is restricted only to regulating certain external conditions. Kant stands firmly in the liberal tradition of viewing the function of the law as primarily to limit individual freedom in the service of that freedom. A system of right defines the social space in which individuals may pursue their interests without interference by others. The universalization criterion for right is a test of whether it is possible for others to "strive for a like end." The criterion is whether the maxim of action could be a universal law governing actions that would allow for the freedom of action of all. My maxim to cheat on my taxes would violate the freedom of others because if everyone cheated on their taxes the government could not function.

The central issue in coming to terms with Kant's theory of right is understanding how, if at all, the foundations of right depend on Kant's much better known (and more fully developed) claims about pure practical reason and morality. This issue is so important because the dependence relation tracks Kant's thinking on the theme of the *separation of morality and right*. Kant exhibits tendencies in both directions – towards a strict separation and towards a unification of the two. Like the moral theory, the theory of right is oriented by the concept of a universal law (as in the passage above). But Kant explicitly rules out from the theory of right the source of moral worth, namely the good will that wills duty for its own sake. This leaves it unclear just where the value of right comes from, or whether it is a "value-neutral" conception of boundary-setting between individuals to secure their pursuit of happiness, whatever that may be. Kant is clear that *from the perspective of morality*, one's actions on the right are duties, and that they are therefore "indirectly ethical" (MS 6:221). But the *determination* of what is rightful is independent in some sense of the moral law.

Kant's various claims on the morality/right issue have in fact sparked a controversy about the independence of the theories of right and morality. The two main camps that have emerged in this debate are the "derivationists," who represent the widespread view that the theory of right is in fact derived from the basics of Kant's moral theory, and the "separationists," who hold that right is independent from the moral theory (for a summary of the debate, see Pippin 2006). After briefly presenting the main points on each side, I will suggest that the irresolvable nature of this debate indicates that there is a fundamental problem with Kant's thinking about right. I then discuss aspects of his view that could be the basis of a solution to this problem, but that Kant never brought to final fruition.

The *derivationist* case is largely based on Kant's general definitions and statements in the introduction to the *Metaphysics of Morals* and in the introduction to the "Doctrine of Right." He refers to *all* "laws of freedom" as "*moral* laws," before subdividing these laws into the "juridical" and "ethical" (MS: 6:214). He also includes under the concepts common to both the "Doctrine of Right" and the "Doctrine of Virtue" the concepts of obligation, categorical imperative, and duty; these concepts seem to require the arguments for transcendental freedom and all that entails in Kant's moral theory (MS: 6:222–3). The derivationist case is strengthened by Kant's claim later in the introduction that the moral imperative is an imperative "from which the capacity for putting others under obligation, that is, the concept of a right, can afterwards be explicated" (MS: 6:239). So too, the references to the universal law in the passage cited above and in Kant's "Universal Principle of Right" (MS: 6:231) make it seem that right is just a specific application of the moral law (Rosen 1993). Perhaps the most significant point in the derivationists' favor is that Kant claims that there is an obligation to enter the social contract, a categorical imperative of pure practical reason. Instead of mere fear of a violent death as a prudential motive, we enter the social state from an original obligation. Such an obligation must be grounded, it seems, in the freedom established in the moral philosophy. These claims run counter to the thrust of modern political philosophy because they presume moral capacities rather than just passions and desires as the basis for claims of political justification.

The starting point for the *separationist* case is Kant's distinction between two kinds of "lawgiving," an internal moral lawgiving and an external lawgiving of right (important statements of this position are Willaschek 1997 and 2002). Whereas morality essentially involves taking duty to be the "internal incentive of action," the external lawgiving of right can only have external incentives (MS: 6:219). The external incentive of right is "pathological," namely that provided by the fear of coercion. The authorization to use coercion is not derived from an obligation of right, but is analytically contained within the *concept* of right itself. This counts strongly in favor of right being separated from morality (see Wood 2002), for no authorization to coerce others can be derived from the moral law (Willaschek 2008). Some of Kant's descriptions of right seem to make right a purely external, mechanical affair of reciprocal coercion, of action and reaction, that is very far indeed from the internal freedom of the moral law. What Kant calls "strict right" does not regulate choice by any sort of appeal to self-legislation, but "rests instead on the principle of its being possible to use external constraint that can coexist with the freedom of everyone in accordance with universal laws" (MS: 6:232). This idea of strict right is behind Kant's claim that the problem of establishing a rightful condition can be solved even for a "nation of devils" (EF: 8:366). It is a problem only of the "mechanism of nature," of self-interest and prudence, and therefore it does not require any assumptions about the disposition behind the actions (which we can assume are evil). To some (Pogge 2002) this reference to right among devils is decisive evidence that Kant's view of right can be detached from his theory of moral agency (see also Höffe 1992 on this issue).

The fundamental problem with Kant's political philosophy, and the reason why his claims cannot be rendered fully consistent, is that he does not have a way to think of the *expression* of the moral value of inner freedom in external, public actions (Kant's lack of a concept of expression was noted by Rawls 1971: 255). The source of the bindingness of right should be the same rational self-legislation that is the source of normativity in the moral domain. Yet Kant relegates this to an "internal freedom" distinct from the "external freedom" of strict right. The question that remains unanswered is how specific forms of external freedom express the subject's internal freedom. How is my nature as a moral being expressed in the laws and institutions of a state based on right? Because Kant lacks an answer to this question, it is hard to see how his *Rechtstaat* embodies substantive moral ideals. As the separationists argue, it looks much more like a minimal state designed primarily to protect property claims and keep the peace.

There is a third alternative, distinct from the derivationist and separationist readings, that suggests a Kantian answer to the expression problem. We can call this the *value* reading, since it takes the external freedom of right to have value based on the "supreme moral principle of the absolute value of freedom" (Guyer 2002: 64). This interpretation draws strength from Kant's reference at a crucial point in the "Doctrine of Right" to an innate right of freedom (MS: 6:237). The value interpretation gives us a way of thinking of morality and right in Kant as distinct and yet united in a single source. Though reading Kant as primarily concerned with realizing the value of freedom seems to run counter to the traditional stress on Kant as a deontologist, the value reading has become increasingly widespread. The reading captures a fundamental dimension of Kant's view, but the shift to value does not by itself solve the problem of expression. After all, the main slogan of value readings is the claim that only the good will has unconditional value, and it is just this internally free will that is not supposed to be at issue in strict right. The question of how the value of freedom is realized in right in more than a minimal sense remains unanswered.

Kant's argument for entry into civil society proceeds from a claim about the possession of things. The argument turns on treating each other in a way that enables individuals to own things. Insofar as ownership is an expression of the will in external actions, one could argue that the property relation is a mode of expressing value in a public way. Through property claims I make my will manifest for others, and the property relation could therefore be the missing link in Kant's argument (see Pippin 2006). Kant argues that it would be a practical contradiction if there were external objects that could not become someone's property. It is a "postulate of practical reason with regard to rights" (MS: 6:246) to treat each other in a way that allows objects to become property (to be intelligibly possessed, in Kant's terminology). This postulate is the basis in practical reason of Kant's argument for an obligation to leave the state of nature to enter into a condition in which property rights are secured. Kant writes,

> When I declare (by word or deed), I will that something external is to be mine, I thereby declare that everyone else is under obligation to refrain from using that object of my choice, an obligation no one would have were it not for this act of mine to establish a right. This claim involves, however, acknowledging that I in turn am under obligation to every other to refrain from using what is externally his; for the obligation here arises from a universal rule having to do with external rightful relations. I am therefore not under obligation to leave external objects belonging to others untouched unless everyone else provides me assurance that he will behave in accordance with the same principle with regard to what is mine. (MS: 6:255–6)

The universal rule is established *a priori* through the postulate of right. But the entitlement to property involves a reciprocal obligation and a mutual assurance that each will follow the same principle. Because *external* freedom is at stake, the obligation must have external conditions and the assurance must be given the form of external law with coercive force. Kant's argument for the civil condition employs a version of the *securing property through a common coercive power* strategy. Kant concludes, "So it is only a will putting everyone under obligation, hence only a collective general (common) and powerful will, that can provide everyone this assurance" (MS: 6:256). This is only possible in a civil condition. Only in such a condition do agents have a common assurance about the status of their property, and therefore a reciprocal obligation to respect each other's property. In the absence of such a condition, individuals do not have the obligation to respect each other's property.

Property claims are an expression of the will, and the agent's action in making such a claim produces a claim on another. Property thus points to a distinctive kind of intersubjectively generated obligation that could bridge the claims of internal and external freedom, of morality and right. But Kant's exposition of the acquisition of property shows that he thinks of property as valuable quite apart from moral considerations. Property does not really solve the problem of expression because there are no substantive moral claims implied by the property relation. Kant does not follow Rousseau in arguing that the individual completely alienates his property rights to the general will conceived as a collective moral authority. Rather, Kant argues for a "*provisionally rightful* possession" (MS: 6:257) that accords individuals claims with genuine normative force already in the state of nature. He writes that "if external objects were not even *provisionally* mine or yours in the state of nature, there would also be no duties of right with regard to them and therefore no command to leave the state of nature" (MS: 6:312–13). It is because the free will is capable of "intelligible possession" that we have an obligation to leave the state of nature. He writes that "a civil constitution is just the rightful condition, by which what belongs to each is only secured, but not actually settled and determined" (MS: 6:256). This suggests a Lockean picture of inalienable pre-social rights that are merely protected and administered by the state. In entering the civil condition one is simply securing the possessions that had been determined provisionally under the pre-civil condition. Kant claims that "provisional acquisition is true acquisition" (MS: 6:264), and that one can provisionally acquire as much land as one is capable of defending. The picture that emerges is that might makes right in provisional acquisition, and that the civil condition simply secures the holdings that were already acquired. This shows that the will's expression in property acquisition does not generate moral claims, and that right is a matter of external freedom, minimally conceived. Property is certainly an expression of the value of freedom, but it remains a narrow expression that cannot generate substantive moral principles of justice. Kant does have resources for generating such claims, as we shall see in the next section, but they fall outside of strict right.

Kantian political freedom

Kant's lack of a clear account of the public expression of the moral will is reflected in his treatment of our third theme, *personal freedom through the sovereign will*. Kant's arguments invoke the *rational consent* of individuals. The state's actions are legitimate because one *could have* rationally consented to them according to a universal law. Kant also claims that any government must be obeyed simply because it secures the conditions of choice in general by keeping the peace, regardless of the further characterization of its actions (as the possible objects of rational consent). There is thus a marked tension between Kant's aim of providing a moral criterion for political legitimacy through the idea of moral freedom, and his aim of securing the minimal conditions of personal freedom under a state that demands absolute obedience.

On the one hand, Kant clearly supports rational consent in endorsing a version of Rousseau's general will, according to which political authority is legitimate for each individual because each individual can see himself as the author of the law. Like Rousseau, Kant thinks of the general will as an ideal of sovereign legislative action that is a standard for the legitimacy of state action. Kant does not think that this authorship claim entails that each person must be given a direct vote about each law, or even that there be an actual assembly to first form society through an act of all joining the social contract. Kant writes of the original contract that it need not "be presupposed as a *fact*," because it is "*only an idea* of reason, which, however, has its undoubted practical reality, namely to bind every legislator to give his laws in such a way that they *could* have arisen from the united will of a whole people and to regard each subject, insofar as he wants to be a citizen, as if he has joined in voting for such a will" (UG: 8:297). To be a citizen means to want to be governed by the laws of the general will. He also writes, "Properly speaking, the original contract is only the idea of this act, in terms of which alone we can think of the legitimacy of a state" (MS: 6:315). The contract is ideal and hypothetical. It is supposed to provide a critical standard by which to judge the legitimacy of legislation. Indeed, because of Kant's lack of emphasis on *voluntary* consent, some commentators have questioned whether Kant should be classified as a social contract theorist at all (Kersting 1992; Pippin 2006). Kant writes of one's freedom in one's dependence on the laws in the civil condition that "this dependence arises from his own lawgiving will" (MS: 6:316). Right flows from the nature of the rational will rather than from the sheer voluntary choice to enter into the contract.

When it comes to the actual functioning of the sovereign legislative will, however, Kant holds with Hobbes that the actions of the sovereign who is in power are by definition the actions of individuals living under that sovereign. In making these claims, Kant assumes a mere voluntary consent (actual or tacit) to whatever the actual sovereign does. By continuing to live under the government, one has consented to obey the laws and commands of the sovereign, whether they meet the standards of the general will or not.

The tension between the rational and voluntary models of consent is apparent in his rather confusing discussion of the sovereign. Kant sets out requirements on the sovereign legislator that seem to be thoroughly republican, but in his elaborations on how the sovereign authority functions in practice, Kant makes it clear that his claims for the general will and for the legislative authority as the sovereign authority of the state are compatible with any number of forms of legislative authority. So though he claims that "only the general united will of the people can be legislative" (MS: 6:313–14), he then describes cases in which the people and the legislative authority are opposed. He writes that "the presently existing legislative authority ought to be obeyed, whatever its origin" (MS: 6:319), and "a people cannot offer any resistance to the legislative head of a state" (MS: 6:320). Is Kant simply contradicting himself here?

To make sense of Kant's claims about the sovereign, it is necessary to think of Kant as distinguishing between *de jure* and *de facto* sovereignty (Rosen 1993). The people have sovereign legislative authority *de jure* (*by right*) since the general will is best expressed through the people's representative assemblies. Yet even if the sovereign is not in fact the people and is not in fact just, one must obey because one has consented to this condition by living under the sovereign. Because security under the law is the minimal condition of personal freedom, the de facto sovereign is legitimate even if one's rational freedom is not expressed in the sovereign's acts.

Kant's split between the de facto and de jure, between voluntary and rational consent, is part of a complicated dance to accommodate the real conditions of political authority and the ideal claims of justice. This dance is quite evident in the Theory/Practice essay, where Kant distances himself from Hobbes's view that the sovereign has no obligation to the people. He writes that "the people too has its inalienable rights against the head of state, although these cannot be coercive rights" (UG: 8:303). The rights of the people are not *reducible* to the positive laws and existing institutions, yet the ideal "inalienable rights" also cannot justify any coercive action against the existing authorities.

The question of whether there is a *moral* basis in the rational will from which to resist existing political institutions has different answers depending on the perspective that one takes. From within the perspective of strict right, Kant is very clear that no resistance can be justified. In "Perpetual Peace" he argues against a right of resistance based on a practical contradiction that arises with the principle of *publicity*. Kant puts it in characteristic terms of a practical contradiction: "the maxim of rebellion, if one *publicly acknowledged it as* one's maxim, would make one's own purpose impossible" (EF: 8:382). There would be a practical contradiction in setting up as a public law a proviso undermining the authority of the state (see Holtman 2002 on the nature of these contradictions). It has long been a matter of dispute whether Kant is thereby inconsistent in his attitude towards revolution (see Seebohm 1981). Kant consistently rejects the right of resistance in the most forceful terms, yet he also praises the ideals of the French Revolution and the reaction of those who sympathized with the revolution. In a much-discussed passage from Kant's 1798 *Conflict of the Faculties*, he highlights the morality of the observers of the Revolution:

> It is simply the mode of thinking [*Denkungsart*] of the spectators which reveals itself *publicly* in this game of great revolutions, and manifests such a universal yet disinterested sympathy for the players on one side against those on the other, even at the risk that this partiality could become very disadvantageous for them if discovered. Owing to its universality, this mode of thinking demonstrates a character of the human race at large and all at once; owing to its disinterestedness, a moral character of humanity, at least in its predisposition ... this revolution, I say, nonetheless finds in the hearts of all spectators (who are not engaged in this game themselves) a wishful participation that borders closely on enthusiasm, the very expression of which is fraught with danger; this sympathy, therefore, can have no other cause than a moral predisposition in the human race. (SF: 7:85)

Kant takes heart from the response by the onlookers, not from the actions of the revolutionaries themselves. Of course Kant had to believe that the ideals of the French Revolution were genuine ideals, but his excitement about the reaction to these events does not really touch on the question of whether the actions of the revolutionaries are justified (see Nicholson 1992).

His differing claims are made from two different *perspectives* and thus are not simply inconsistent The passage above comes as part of a positive answer to the question, "Is the Human Race Continually Improving?," which is a question posed from the perspective of moral anthropology. Moral anthropology studies how moral ideals are expressed in practice and whether we can hope for the more adequate realization of these ideals in the future. This mode of inquiry does address the expression problem, though it does so only by moving to a perspective outside that of the agents themselves. By moving to the level of the onlookers, Kant is shifting the question away from the agent's own perspective on the rightness of resistance. From *within* the civil condition and the principles of right established therein, no resistance is rightful even if one's ideals are moral and the existing government is despicable. Yet when the question is whether the moral vocation of humanity can be realized, Kant holds that in the progress of history we can look at revolutionary events and the reaction to them for signs that such a realization is in fact possible. In the case of the French Revolution, the decisive sign for Kant was that, unlike in all other revolutions, the goals were not defined by party interests but by the universal ideals of freedom (see Seebohm 1981). It tells us something about the human species, Kant thinks, that people would respond in such a disinterested way to the struggle to achieve these ideals. Though we are limited in what we can say and do from within a state about how it ought to change, philosophy can use the idea of morality to interpret history as developing towards political goals of justice.

The bearing of Kant's moral anthropology on political questions is also evident in "Perpetual Peace," where he investigates the evidence *within nature* that humans and the world have been created so as to bring about peace within and between nations, and eventually morality within individuals. In the section "On the guarantee of perpetual peace" (EF: 8:360), Kant discusses "providence," the idea of a creating God behind the operation of nature and history and the evidence we can find in nature and history gives us hope that peace is possible. It is in this discussion that Kant invokes the "nation of devils" in order to show the resources even with non-moral nature for instituting right and thereby peace, and thus ultimately for the development of morality.

It is through this anthropological and historical lens that Kant addresses the fourth theme, Rousseau's theme of the *social constitution of free agency*. Kant makes little of this theme from within the perspective of right, where he assumes that individuals can possess property and relate to each other on the basis of an inherent freedom and equality. But within the teleological lens of moral anthropology, Kant is concerned with how moral agency develops through political institutions. He thus writes in "Perpetual Peace" that "the good moral education of a people is to be expected from a good state constitution" (EF: 8:366). Kant imagines a productive interplay between the reformation of states and the development of morality, such that the more that peace and freedom are secured by a constitution, the better are the conditions for morality to develop. In turn, the development of morality cannot help but lead to more peace and external freedom (see Kleingeld 2006). Agents under existing circumstances (in Kant's time) cannot will the republican constitution or perpetual peace *directly*, but they do have reason to hope that these will come about gradually through rightful reform.

Kant's split perspective view can be seen as a sensible compromise on the role of moral ideals in practical politics. But the deferral to history, and the lack of any definite sense (beyond the procedural claim of legislative sovereignty) of the morality expressed in the rightful condition, do not put enough pressure on the institutions themselves to realize moral ends rather than just to secure the existing conditions (and inequalities) of external freedom. It is not enough to say that philosophers can simply watch and hope, without granting any authority to agents themselves to challenge unjust political conditions.

Fichte's argument for right as mutual recognition

Fichte's most lasting contribution to political philosophy is the theory of mutual recognition that he developed in his 1796 *Foundations of Natural Right*. His derivation

142

of right as a relation of mutual recognition was a pivotal spur for Hegel's development, and continues to be an important type of argument in political philosophy and in ethics (see especially Darwall 2006). Fichte's mutual recognition argument foregrounds the *social constitution of free agency* by showing that individual free agency is conditioned by interaction with other free agents. This move promises to solve the expression problem by making the legitimacy of determinate social and political institutions a function of their ability to foster and secure free agency. Laws and institutions express free agency in so far as they allow individuals to interact in just those ways that lead to the development and exercise of free agency itself. The generality of the recognition argument for mutual dependence makes it a very powerful tool for social and political theory. But as we shall see in the following section, Fichte does not capitalize on this generality, giving recognition a restricted negative role in his theory of public right, which thus suffers from some of the same shortcomings as Kant's theory.

Since the basics of Fichte's conceptions of philosophy and of freedom have been laid out in earlier chapters (Chapters 1, 2, and 4), I will proceed here straight to Fichte's argument in the *Foundations*. Fichte sets out his argument of right as an argument for the conditions of finite rational willing, and in doing so attempts to generate the relevant features of the political subject and of claims of *right* from the ground up. Fichte derives from self-consciousness the finite subject's capacities, the world in which subjects interact, and the nature of the relationship of right that holds between subjects. Fichte sets up the argument for recognition through an initial argument for a "summons" to freedom. The argument is an excellent example of his transcendental form of deductive argument. The first *theorem* states "A *finite rational being cannot posit itself without ascribing a free efficacy to itself*" (GNR: 3:17). The first constructive step in Fichte's argument is to state that free activity is only possible as *limited* activity in a world that is opposed to that activity. He then notes that there is a contradiction here between the individual's free activity and the requirement that the activity be limited by an *object* in the sensible world. To overcome this contradiction, the subject must find an object and his own efficacy united "in one and the same undivided moment" (GNR: 3:30). The only way for this to occur is if the object is the subject's efficacy itself, and if this objective version of the subject's efficacy determines or constrains the subject in an external manner. The solution is that we must think of "a *being-determined of the subject to self-determination*, a summons [*Aufforderung*] of the subject to resolve (himself) to an efficacy" (GNR: 3:32–3).

Fichte's formulation is purposely paradoxical. In setting and resolving an apparent contradiction of being determined to self-determination, Fichte generates further conditions for the individual's efficacy. The next step is to show that the source of this summons must be something that can take the agent's free efficacy as the purpose of its activity. Such a purposive entity cannot be in nature, but can only be another rational being (GNR: 3:38–9) in the sensible world who summons the self to free activity. Fichte has thus derived another free agent as the condition of the possibility of self-consciousness. The role of this argument in first *constituting* the free agent is clear when Fichte writes that "The human being (like all finite beings in general) becomes a human being only among human beings" (GNR: 3:39), and "Only free, reciprocal interaction by means of concepts and in accordance with concepts, only the giving and receiving of knowledge, is the distinctive character of humanity, by virtue of which alone each person undeniably confirms himself as a human being" (GNR: 3:40). With this basic summoning relationship established, Fichte is ready to derive the relation of right as the mutual recognition of two subjects.

A crucial move in Fichte's argument is to distinguish universal self-consciousness or free agency from individual free agency, or the capacities for freedom of a determinate embodied individual. An agent can only be an individual if the agent is compared to and distinguished from other individuals. Fichte calls the relationship at issue a "*process of distinguishing through opposition*" (GNR: 3:42), which refers to the process of taking another subject to be a constraint on one's activity (opposed to it) by distinguishing one's own sphere of activity from that of another subject. The distinguishing action must determine the individual's concept of himself as free and must also take account of the other as a free being. I must set an end for myself while at the same time reserving a sphere for the action of another. The relationship of recognition, which is the relation between the spheres of action of two individuals, depends on a shared knowledge of *practical self-limitation*. The knowledge in question takes the form of an *expectation* of how others will behave towards me. My recognition of others is the condition of my *entitlement* to holding that expectation.

With the recognition relationship in hand, Fichte presents the argument for the concept of right through a three-part syllogism. The first premise states the dependence of my expectation of recognition on my treatment of the other:

> (I) *I can expect from a determinate rational being that he recognize me as a rational being only in so far as I myself treat him as a rational being.* (GNR: 3:44)

Fichte stresses that recognition is irreducible to the ordinary ways of thinking of other agents in a moral or political community. He writes of the first half ("the conditioned," separated from "the condition" by "only") that the other's act should be understood neither as a recognition of me in his conscience nor as a recognition of me in front of others. Rather, I expect another to recognize me according to our "common consciousness." Recognition is thus not a moral relationship (conscience), nor is it a relationship through a third-party authority (other subjects or the state). The realm of recognition is that of the second person, of the "Thou," which serves as a bridge from first-person moral autonomy to third-person public power. Fichte qualifies the second half of the proposition, the condition, in writing that the I must treat the other as free in a definite *practical* way. I do not merely *form a concept* of the other subject as a generic rational being. Rather, I have to actually act to come into contact with him, for my mere thoughts can never be anything *for him*. It cannot be that I merely refrain from violating the concept of him as a rational being, but I actually have to act in a way that impinges on the activity of the other individual.

The second premise in the argument affirms the condition in (I) as a necessary condition of individuality. Fichte writes, "(II) *But in every possible case, I must expect that all rational beings outside me recognize me as a rational being*" (GNR: 3:45). Only with that expectation "in every possible case" can I be an individual, for only with that recognition by others is my distinct sphere of activity secured. Notice in (II) that Fichte has switched to "all rational beings" from "a determinate rational being." He is not thereby abandoning his claim that this relationship is between two definite individuals, but he is arguing that the relationship must hold between *any* two individuals who come into contact. To establish that point, Fichte argues for a rational constraint that governs the *thinking* of all subjects. His argument for this constraint, which he calls the "law of thought," follows a pattern familiar from the social contract tradition. He imagines a conflict between agents akin to the mutual antagonism in the state of nature, and he then attempts to determine a common basis of appeal for restoring a condition of right. To avoid a mere reciprocation of the action (an act of force to which I would be entitled), I must raise myself out of my individuality and refer to a law that is valid for both of us. I posit myself as the judge above him, but I invite him to judge along with me according to the shared "law of thought," that is, according to the demand of logical consistency. Fichte uses the law of thought as a shared external conception of normativity, of rational bindingness, based on the two subjects' common consciousness. He is very explicit that this is not a matter of *moral obligation*, but that the law of thought does place a normative *demand* on others. To be *consistent*, an agent cannot claim a sphere of free activity for himself (for his own individuality) while denying it to others (more on the nature of this demand below).

In the final step in the argument for the principle of right, Fichte infers the temporal persistence of recognition as a condition of the subject's *efficacy* in carrying out his intentions. The recognition relationship of right must extend beyond this immediate point in time into the future. I must be able to expect that others will leave a sphere open for my freedom in the future so that I can rely on stable conditions for implementing my intentions. Fichte thus arrives at the statement of the principle of right: "(III) ... *I must in all cases recognize the free being outside me as a free being, i.e. I must limit my freedom through the concept of the possibility of his freedom*" (GNR: 3:52). With this principle, Fichte provides the basis for an account of political institutions that are legitimate because they are stable contexts for inherently equal subjects who strive to develop their individuality through distinct projects and interests. It is the mutual determination of individuals as both the same and as opposed that sets the dynamics of equality and difference that are the basis of the discourse of recognition today.

From recognition to a politics of mistrust

Although it is natural to think of mutual recognition as a moral relationship, Fichte advocates a strict *separation of right and morality*. He maintains in no uncertain terms that the right based on recognition has to do only with external relations between individuals, and nothing at all to do with the realm of morality. These two branches of practical philosophy are not merely separable, but they "are, already originally and without our involvement, separated through reason, and are completely opposed" (GNR: 3:55). Fichte in effect radicalizes the split in Kant between internal and external lawgiving. Just as Kant emphasized the difference in the "incentives" in the two domains, Fichte too claims that right can be determined without referring to the moral disposition. He puts the point succinctly: "The good will has nothing to do with the sphere of Natural Right. Right must be able to be enforced, even when no person has a good will ... Physical power, and that alone, is what sanctions right in this sphere" (GNR: 3:54). When moral considerations are categorically excluded from politics, there is nothing left but the threat of force to provide motivation. In one sense Fichte's theory is a return to Hobbes' strict line on the separation of morality and right from Rousseau's attempt to bring the two domains back together (see Neuhouser 1994 for an account of Fichte's earlier Rousseauian views). This return is rather surprising given the appeal to the "common consciousness" in the argument for recognition. While in Hegel's hands recognition will be a tool to remoralize the political, for Fichte it is a theoretical tool for the construction of right as a domain fully distinct from morality. In actual practice, according to Fichte, we do not rely on mutual recognition, which has an implicit moral aspect that cannot be relied upon in the actual system of right.

The cardinal distinction that underwrites Fichte's morality/right split is the distinction between universality and individuality. Though Fichte's theory of right and his theory of ethics contain arguments for the importance of both universal and individual dimensions of human activity, universality is clearly the basis and goal of the moral theory while individuality is the basis and goal of right. Fichte's philosophical system begins with the non-individual I of original self-consciousness, and its completed goal is the achieved overcoming of individuality in a world in which all individuals agree and there are no obstacles, in nature or reason, to pure universality. He thus writes in the *Sittenlehre*, "Each [subject] becomes the pure depiction [*Darstellung*] of the ethical law in the sensible world precisely through his entire individuality disappearing and being destroyed; actual pure *I* through free choice and self-determination" (SL 4:256). At such an endpoint there is no need for a state, since the state's job is to adjudicate the differences between our individual ends. While in morality we strive to free ourselves from all dependence on anything outside of Reason, in relations of right individual finitude and limitation are assumed as given, and the goal is to work out the maximum "freedom" of individual action compatible with the freedom of other individuals. Though individuality is the ground and purpose of right, it is not at all clear that Fichte takes individuality itself to be intrinsically valuable. Frederick Neuhouser (1994) has argued that we should see Fichte's theory of right as demarcating a domain, based on the concept of the person, in which individuality and personal freedom are given a distinct value. But although we can see Fichte staking out here a conception of personal freedom distinct from moral freedom, he simply does not give a defense of individuality that accords it value comparable to the universal value of morality. So in the above passage Fichte claims that morality is directed towards the disappearance of individuality, which implies that individuality itself cannot positively express moral agency.

Fichte takes the split between right and morality to be obvious from the difference between the nature of rights and duties. While duties command one to act in certain ways, rights are merely *permissive*. A duty says what you *must* do while a right only says what you *may* do. This point comes up already in the Introduction to the *Foundations*, where Fichte compares his approach to Kant's claims in "Perpetual Peace" (Kant's "Doctrine of Right" had not yet been published). Echoing commentators to this very day, Fichte writes that "it is not possible to see clearly whether Kant derives the law of right from the moral law" (GNR: 3:13). Fichte takes as evidence that Kant did *not* derive right from the moral law the claims in "Perpetual Peace" about permissive laws (EF: 8:348). Such laws do not command or prohibit, but simply give one a claim on others, a right against others, that one may or may not exercise. Fichte sharpens the contrast between right and duty in the following passage:

> The moral law commands duty categorically: the law of right only permits, but never commands, that one exercise one's right. Indeed, the moral law very often forbids a person to exercise his right, and yet – as all the world acknowledges – that right does not thereby cease to be a right. In such a case one judges that the person may well have had a right to something but that he ought not to have exercised it in this situation. In that case, then, is not the moral law (which is one and the same principle) at odds with itself, simultaneously granting and denying the same right in the same situation? (GNR: 3:54)

Fichte's question is rhetorical. The idea of the moral law standing in conflict with itself in this way is unthinkable for him. Yet rather than actually proving Fichte's point, this passage shows that the strict separation of right and morality depends more on Fichte's own conception of morality than it does on the nature of the normative claims themselves. Most moral theories acknowledge the possibility of conflicting moral claims. The argument is only compelling if one accepts Fichte's controversial argument that the moral law commands a single action categorically in every case, so that it can never be "at odds with itself."

Fichte's other main argument for separating morality and right stems from his claim that rights, as opposed to duties, govern only *actual* relations between individual rational agents. While as an individual I may have moral qualms about certain actions, and may indeed have obligations to act in certain ways in my conscience, the concept of right is inappropriate for describing the nature of these obligations. Fichte writes, "The concept of right is the concept of a relation between rational beings. Thus, it arises only under the condition that rational beings are thought in relation to one another. It is nonsense to talk about a right to nature, to land, to animals, etc., considered only on their own or in direct relation to a human being" (GNR: 3:55). This claim is a consequence of the recognition relation that defines the concept of right. Only free beings can recognize each other, and therefore only free beings can make claims of right. Within a *moral* perspective we may have obligations to the planet and to animals, but talk of animal rights is completely out of order on Fichte's picture. This aspect of Fichte's view also limits the kinds of rights that individuals can claim from each other and from the state. He writes,

> Rational beings enter into reciprocal interaction with one another only through actions, expressions of their freedom, in the sensible world: thus the concept of right concerns only what is expressed in the sensible world: whatever has no causality in the sensible world – but remains inside the mind instead – belongs before another tribunal, the tribunal of morality. Thus it is nonsense to speak of a right to the freedom of thought, freedom of conscience, and so forth. There is a capability for these inner actions, and there are duties, but no rights, with respect to them. (GNR: 3:55)

Fichte's claims here would be reasonable enough if freedom of thought were just the freedom to think and to believe in one's mind, cut off from every expression in the sensible world. The problem is that it is completely unreasonable to treat freedom of thought and freedom of conscience as thus separated from expression (as separated, for instance, from the rights of freedom of speech and freedom of worship). This unwillingness to link such "internal" capacities to expressions in external actions highlights that Fichte has an untenably sharp divide between the internal freedom of morality, which has supreme value, and a circumscribed realm of right as the domain of those actions that can be subjected to coercion.

Because he claims that rights only apply to actual relationships between individuals, Fichte sometimes comes close to denying that a theory of individual right can provide ideal standards for assessing actual political institutions. That is, he comes close to saying that there are no "original" individual rights that a political system must respect. Fichte insists that "there is no condition in which original rights exist; and no original rights of human beings" (GNR: 3:112). According to Fichte the "original right" of persons simply as such is a necessary theoretical fiction that we theorize by *abstracting from* the conditions of the rights of agents within a commonwealth. This position seems to bring Fichte closer to Hobbes and to distance him from the Kantian position of the real status of provisional rights in the state of nature. Yet Fichte does use original right as the (fictional) basis for theorizing right within the state. Fichtean original right is "the absolute right of the person to be *only a cause* in the sensible world (and purely and simply never something caused)" (GNR: 3:113). Original right therefore guarantees bodily integrity and the integrity of the relationship of one's intentions to the physical world. Though Fichte asserts the fictional character of these rights, he does use them to make arguments about the rights of individuals within the social contract. Thus he claims that the state secures not only whatever the person brings to the contract, but also a minimal ability of individuals to support themselves through their work (GNR: 3:213).

On the basis of original right, Fichte uses the *securing property through common coercive power* strategy to move from the principle of right to the commonwealth in which that right is secured. Fichte's argument for a "right of coercion" against someone who has violated one's original right closely resembles the arguments in other social contract theorists about what happens in situations of conflict in the state of nature. One is entitled to exercise a right of coercion over someone who has violated one's original right, though the mere fact that one is entitled to coerce another does not entail that this right can be successfully employed in practice to restore a condition of mutual recognition. The failure of mutual recognition in practice leads to the introduction of new means to secure personal freedom. One can only be satisfied in one's assertion of one's right of coercion if one is convinced of "the other person's sincere subjection to the law of right," but "his attestation of regret, his promise of better behavior in the future, his voluntary subjection to authority, his offer of compensation, etc." (GNR: 3:98) do not suffice as grounds for thinking he has now adopted the law. There is no "mutual restoration of freedom" (GNR: 3:99) unless the other has actually proven over time that he would never violate one's right, which would just assume what the argument is supposed to prove (i.e. how such future behavior could be guaranteed). Fichte uses this conflict over property claims to show that no argument merely from mutual recognition between two agents is sufficient to establish secure property claims. After demonstrating that two agents can at best declare their property claims with words and physical signs, Fichte writes that "this agreement presupposes that each trusts that the other will keep his word ... it presupposes that each will trust that the other has made keeping his word an inviolable law for himself" (GNR: 3:138). Since honesty and trust are moral factors that rely on the good will of each to remain committed to the law, this is an inadequate basis for the mutual security required for personal freedom.

While mutuality is the hallmark of recognition as characteristic of non-moral right in theory, Fichte argues that in practice mutual recognition is implicitly moral and therefore incapable on its own of sustaining secure relationships of right. Fichte introduces the *law* of coercion, a law that operates with "mechanical necessity" to return coercive punishment for violations of right, as the only route to guarantee security when "honesty and trust have been lost" (GNR: 3:139). The importance of this moment and its solution for Fichte's overall theory becomes clear later when he writes that the state "is constructed on the premise of universal mistrust" (GNR: 3:244). This move has been the source of criticism of Fichte's political philosophy because with it he seems to *replace* the relationship of recognition with the law of coercion (Williams 2002). Recognition may be the basis of *natural* right, but positive right in a commonwealth is based on the *failure* of recognition, and coercive laws are needed to do the work in ensuring rightful action that the good will would otherwise accomplish. Fichte concludes that "there is no *natural right* at all in the sense often given to that term" (GNR: 3:148) because a rightful relation only exists in a commonwealth under positive coercive laws. Mutual recognition is a fictional basis for theorizing right, but it cannot be relied upon in practice.

If the mutual regard for each other's freedom is not the source of the bindingness of right in the commonwealth, how does Fichte think of *personal freedom through the will of the sovereign*? Clarifying an ambiguity in Kant's conception of right, Fichte insists that the bindingness of right stems not from a necessary obligation constitutive of rationality itself, but rather solely from the individual's voluntary consent. He thus departs from Kant's view that there is a categorical imperative *of right*, an obligation, to leave the state of nature, writing, "I live in community specifically with them as a result of my free decision, not through any obligation" (GNR: 3:14). Fichte takes pains to highlight this voluntary aspect of the political in contrast to the original obligation of morality:

> I am in conscience, through my knowledge of how things ought to be, bound to limit my freedom. But this moral obligation is not at issue in the doctrine of right; each is only bound through the voluntary decision to live in society with others, and if someone does not at all want to limit his free choice, then within the field of the doctrine of right, one can say nothing further against him, other than that he must then remove himself from all human community. (GNR: 3:10–11)

The doctrine of right does not contain grounds for obligating individuals to remain in human community, but only grounds for saying how they must act *if* they have decided to live with others. The law of right thus has "hypothetical validity" (GNR: 3:89), commanding how you must act *if* you will human community, for such a community is possible only under the conditions of right. This hypothetical rather than categorical validity is closely related to the claim in the recognition argument that *theoretical consistency* is the basis of appeal in the pre-civil condition. The hypothetical law demands that *if* you act in a certain way you must also act in another way (if you expect recognition from others you must recognize others in turn). Though within the recognition argument Fichte presents the law of thought as a constitutive condition of individuality, in practice this law is not inherently binding on the will. As Fichte puts it, "consistency here depends on the freedom of the will, and it is not clear why someone should be consistent, when he *need* not be; it is just as unclear why he should *not* be consistent" (GNR: 3:86). A theoretical rule does carry obligation with it, so the theoretical consistency of recognition and right depends for its practical validity on the free decision of individuals to remain in relations with one another.

Given his claims that one enters the state from mutual distrust and through a purely voluntary act, it is surprising (and often overlooked) that Fichte presents an argument that the commonwealth should be considered an *organic whole*. After taking what looks to be a highly individualistic turn, Fichte endorses a strong individual–whole unity, though again this is a unity that does not have a moral basis. Fichte writes that "the real bond that unites the different individuals" is the "uncertainty as to which individual will first be transgressed against" (GNR: 3:203). Since each individual does not know if his property will be the first to be violated, or if he will be the first to need protective assistance in defending his property, and since all individuals are in the same boat, they are unified by the common contingency of their property and thus come to a mutual understanding of their dependence on the whole. This is the basis of what Fichte calls the "*unification contract*," through which "the individual becomes a part of an organized whole, and thus melts into one with the whole" (GNR: 3:204). It is striking, given Hegel's attack on Fichte as a prototypical individualist, that Fichte contrasts his own account of an organic unity with an account "of an ideal aggregation of individuals" (GNR: 3:207). In the organic whole, each part has its particular function through which it helps maintain the whole, and each part is dependent on the whole for its continued existence. The problem with this argument is that the strong unity claim in this organic relation does not accord well with Fichte's voluntarism or with his emphasis on coercion as the only motivation for individuals to follow the laws of right. Most importantly, Fichte does not provide a convincing account of *personal freedom under the sovereign will* because the obligations within the state are a function of the pure freedom of voluntary choice. One's individuality is realized within the state, to be sure, but it remains obscure how that determinate individuality expresses one's universal freedom and the value of one's humanity.

Hegel's critique of social contract theory

For Hegel, Fichte's theory of right crystallized much of what had gone wrong with modern political philosophy. The extreme voluntarism of Fichte's contract theory and the assumption that no trust exists are two main symptoms for Hegel of the modern tendency to presume an atomistic individualism and thereby to render genuine freedom impossible. Hegel's criticisms of modern political philosophy derive from his conception of the unity of self-consciousness. While Kant and Fichte also oriented their philosophies by the unity of self-consciousness, Hegel reconceives this unity – which he describes as "being with oneself in otherness" – in order to establish an identity of the subject and the world. For our purposes, the essential move is to establish a unity of subject and world in action such that there is no sharp divide between internal and external freedom. Kant and Fichte fail to capture this unity in their political theories in failing to conceptualize the outer *expression* of inner moral freedom. Hegel's theory of objective Spirit (*Geist*) builds on Fichte's concept of recognition, but goes beyond Fichte in conceiving of Spirit as a context of successful recognition of freedom in action. Before examining that theory more closely, I first present the motivation of Hegel's views in his critique of social contract theory.

We can approach the criticism of social contract theory through Hegel's conception of the disrupted condition of the individual that he calls *alienation*. An individual is alienated when he cannot identify with his desires or actions as expressions of himself, of whom he takes himself to be. Alienation is a pervasive problem under modern social conditions because social relations are less fixed than in pre-modern times. Individuals are free to choose their own course in life, and social contract theory is on the surface quite attractive because it places an act of individual choice at the center of political legitimacy. For Hegel this consent masks rather than overcomes the alienation of modern individuals. Hegel thinks there is a constructive role of alienation as a liberation from the "immediacy" of mere convention and natural inclination (see Moyar 2008), but he also thinks that modern political philosophy threatens to entrench alienation in public life and to undermine those public values that are crucial to overcoming alienation. On all four of the themes of modern political philosophy, Hegel critiques social contract theory for failing to show how, in the public sphere of right, actions are valued as expressions of the deepest concerns of individuals.

Hegel criticized the sharp separation in modern political philosophy between right and morality from the beginning of his engagement with political philosophy. In action on ethical norms properly conceived, the individual's ethical will is not simply private or inner, and the public bindingness of right is not primarily a function of the physical force of coercive laws. He writes in the early "Natural Law" essay of Fichte's separation of right and morality, "neither legality nor morality is absolutely positive or genuinely ethical. And since each of them is just as positive as the other, both are absolutely necessary; and the possibility that the pure concept and the subject of right and duty are *not* one must be posited unalterably and without qualification" (W: 2.470; N: 442). In Hegel's language at this time, the "positive" is what is binding on the will. The "pure concept" is the activity of self-consciousness that he takes to be the ground of all freedom and normativity. If there are two separate domains that each bind the will in different and irreconcilable ways, then the subject as a whole can never completely express the concept of freedom in her action. The "genuinely ethical" is binding on the will without remainder, such that the individual can express free subjectivity completely in action.

The possibility of a non-alienating unity of the individual and social is foreclosed, according to Hegel, when *securing property through common coercive power* is the basis of the political system and fear of coercion is the fundamental motivational force in the lives of individuals. Hegel objects to Fichte's assumption of universal mistrust because it makes a social order based on shared value impossible. In the "Natural Law" essay Hegel writes,

> Fichte expresses the matter in a more popular way as the presupposition that "honesty and trust have been lost." On this presupposition a system is built whereby both the concept and the individual subject of ethical life are supposed to be united despite their separation, though the unity is on this account only formal and external, and this relation between them is called "coercion." In this way the external character of oneness is utterly fixed and posited as something with absolute being-in-itself; and thereby the inner life, the rebuilding of the lost honesty and trust, the union of universal and individual freedom, and ethical life itself, are made impossible. (W: 2.471; N: 442–3)

When Hegel writes of "the concept and the individual subject of ethical life," he is referring to the universal ground of normativity (the concept, self-consciousness) and the subjectivity of particular individuals. They are supposed to be united in Fichte's system because self-consciousness is supposed to be the ground of norms binding on the individual subject. But for Fichte coercion is what in fact binds the will to act on right. Further, it is the threat of punishment by the state that holds society together, and the union of different individuals is external in the sense that only an outside force binds different individuals together. What Hegel calls "the union of universal and individual freedom" is the leading characteristic of Hegel's own conception of Ethical Life. It is the non-alienated condition in which individuals act on particular purposes that are simultaneously realizations of the universal. A state based on universal mistrust, as Fichte's is, can never hope to overcome the mistrust both between individuals and between the individuals and the state.

Hegel's critique of social contract theories for basing authority on the individual will is largely a critique of the model's failure to adequately capture the *freedom through the will of the sovereign*. He finds fault with the contract view of the state for making the sheer decision of the individual the entire basis of allegiance to the state. In the *Philosophy of Right* Hegel singles out Rousseau and Fichte for criticism:

> [They] regarded the universal will not as the will's rationality in and for itself, but only as the *common element* arising out of this individual will *as a conscious will*. The union of individuals within the state thus becomes a *contract*, which is accordingly based on their arbitrary will and opinions, and on their express consent given at their own discretion; and the further consequences which follow from this, and which relate merely to the understanding, destroy the divine [element] which has being in and for itself and its absolute authority and majesty. (PR: §258)

Basing political legitimacy on "the conscious will" rather than on the "will's rationality in and for itself" means leaving it up to the arbitrary will of the individual to decide whether or not he owes any allegiance to the state. Hegel's argument here does not really do justice to the resources of social contract theory (see Neuhouser 2000), which can account for the rationality of the will as stemming from universal goods secured by the state. Yet even if a more robust rationality is available to social contract theory, Hegel's main charge, which is that the contract model cannot capture the objective value that undergirds social relations, still holds.

On the last of our four themes, the *social constitution of free agency*, Hegel is very emphatic that individuals only come to be who they are within society. He differs from Rousseau and Fichte because he takes this fact to count decisively *against* the social contract model. There is no question for Hegel of individuals choosing to enter society from a state of nature outside of the actual state, and this lack of choice makes the entire idea of a social contract unintelligible. Hegel writes against thinking of the state as a contract, "But in the case of the state, this is different from the outset, for the arbitrary will of individuals is not in a position to break away from the state, because the individual is already by nature a citizen of it" (PR: §75A). In a business contract one can think of opting out of the agreement, but this is not the case with the state, because "the individual is already by nature a citizen" of the state. One might respond to this objection that the social contract is only hypothetical, and serves as a standard for judging laws regardless of whether an actual act of contract did take place or could have taken place. Hegel would say that this move to the hypothetical is just a further symptom of the tendency to look past the existing norms within the state to a formal model of rationality that abstracts from the way citizens actually live and the values that enable societies to flourish.

Property and ethical value in Hegel's *Philosophy of Right*

Expositions of Hegel's practical philosophy often set out from his conception of Spirit, and take as a central task unpacking the claims about the self-realization of Spirit in history. While I do not want to deny the importance of Spirit for Hegel's account, I want to emphasize that Hegel's theory involves the realization of ethical *value*. The overarching value for Hegel is freedom, and he holds that free agents realize a multiplicity of values in ethical action. The concepts of individuality and recognition drive the dialectical development of right in Hegel, just as they did in Fichte, yet in Hegel's hands these concepts are put in the service of a conception of value and of the expression of value in action. Though Hegel preserves many of Fichte's key distinctions, including that between right and morality, the distinctions are relativized and ultimately overcome in the account of *Sittlichkeit* or ethical life.

Central to Hegel's *Philosophy of Right* is the idea of the "free will" (see also Wood's account in the previous chapter), which he analyzes in terms of the three logical moments of universality, particularity, and the comprehensive moment of individuality. Hegel identifies the first moment with the French Revolution: it is the moment of abstract universality, which Hegel calls the "absolute freedom" of abstracting from all given determinations of the will. The second moment of the will is its particularity, the willing of something *determinate*, the capacity to commit oneself to a definite action with a definite goal. The third, integrative moment is that of individuality, the "self-referring negativity" (PR: §7) that incorporates the other two moments and represents the full concept of the free will. The will's individuality, is the capacity to identify with determinate actions *as expressions of universal freedom*. Hegel's example is friendship (PR: §7A), a commitment to a specific person that limits one's willing while realizing a common, universal relationship. One remains "with oneself" in the relationship because friendship is mutual recognition in which one sees oneself reflected in the other. Hegel does not base his political theory on the model of friendship, which remains at the level of "feeling," but he does think of the reciprocity of friendship as continuous with the more concrete institutionalized reciprocity of family and citizenship. In the latter case our relationships are mediated through universal laws, but the idea that we are *expressing* our individuality in acting within the state remains the same.

A major challenge in reading the *Philosophy of Right* is that, by contrast to Hobbes's *Leviathan* or even Fichte's *Foundations*, the underlying account of the human subject is assumed rather than given in the text. The account is nothing less than the "Philosophy of Subjective Spirit" that forms the first part of the *Philosophy of Spirit* (including anthropology, phenomenology, and psychology). For our purposes the most important dimension missing from the *Philosophy of Right* is the phenomenological account of the generation of "universal self-consciousness" and personhood through the struggle for recognition. Hegel sums up this account in writing of the person as "his own property" (PR: §57),

The point of view of the free will, with which right and the science of right begins, is already beyond that untrue point of view whereby the human being exists as a natural being and as a concept which has being only in itself, and is therefore capable of enslavement. This earlier and false appearance is associated with the spirit which has not yet gone beyond the point of view of its consciousness; the dialectic of the concept and of the as yet only immediate consciousness of freedom gives rise at this stage to the *struggle for recognition* and the relationship of *lordship* and *servitude*. (PR: §57)

In the *Philosophy of Right* Hegel assumes the concept of the person that he first developed in the *Phenomenology of Spirit's* account of the struggle to the death over recognition and the master-servant relationship (see Wood 1990 on the systematic place of that struggle in Hegel's ethics). The struggle for recognition is the social constitution of the *person* as a being capable of expressing his will in the external world, and thus as a being capable of owning property.

In Hegel's terminology, the capacity of personhood is the distinctive moment of the *universality* of the free will. Persons distinguish themselves from each other through their property-claims, but these claims say nothing distinctive about the *individual* person, who has a title to property sheerly by virtue of the capacity of personhood that is identical for all. Recognition is implicit throughout the *Philosophy of Right*, and explicit at certain key junctures, such as in the transition from property to contract within "Abstract Right." Hegel makes the transition from property to contract in writing "This relation of will to will is the true distinctive ground in which freedom has its *existence*" (PR: §71). It is important for Hegel, and for understanding his take on the theme of *securing property through coercion*, that contract and the recognition relationship are developed independently of coercion. It is not through coercion that we first can claim a right, but rather we claim a right on the basis of the capacity of the will to relate to other agents as free. Hegel notes that his view differs from others that define right in terms of coercion: "To define abstract right – or right in the strict sense – from the start as a *right* which justifies the use of coercion is to interpret it in the light of a consequence which arises only indirectly by way of wrong" (PR: §94). The right for Hegel is "the *existence* of the *free will*" (PR: §29), and the coercive element of right is just one (very important) determination of right. To think it is part of the concept of right itself is to misconstrue the freedom and recognition that define right.

Some of the most important conceptual moves in Hegel's *political* theory come in "Morality," the second major sphere of right presented in the *Philosophy of Right*. He introduces the concept of the *subject* as a *particular* agent with rights defined in terms of his own particular perspective (for a full account of the opening description of "Morality," see Quante 2004). Though there is an inner dimension to the moral capacities, Hegel's conception of morality is aimed at overcoming the merely interior character of morality by developing an account of action on intersubjectively available values. The intention of an individual in action includes a description that captures the value the individual aims to realize in that action. In the section "Intention and Welfare," Hegel emphasizes that modern freedom includes valuing individuals in their particularity and respecting their particular choices. The "right of the subject's *particularity* to find satisfaction" (§124) is a right to realize ethical value in one's own particular way.

Hegel's most dramatic move in uniting the claims of morality and right is his endorsement of the *right of necessity*, which is the right to take someone else's property if that is the only way to stay alive. One has a legitimate claim to take another's property when one's life is at stake. Hegel defends the right of necessity on the grounds that to deny someone's right to live is to deny someone's right completely (PR: §127). Recognizing every individual's right to exist is the fundamental imperative of right, so that even a property claim cannot be upheld at the expense of an individual's right as a person. The right of necessity reveals the "contingency of both right and welfare, of the abstract definite existence of freedom as distinct from the existence of the particular person, and of the sphere of the particular will as distinct from the universality of right" (PR: §128). This "right of necessity" relation between the two agents cannot be sustained, however, and requires that right be determined so that such justified breaches of mutual recognition do not occur. The contrast of this conflict with the conflict over property claims in the state of nature account reveals the fundamental difference between Hegel and the social contract tradition. Hegel's conflict is between two clearly justifiable rights rather than between a malevolent usurper and the rightful property owner. The goals of the two accounts are also clearly different. Rather than mere security as the goal of the new determination of right, the resolution of the conflict between two legitimate rights is a comprehensive conception of value that can underwrite a shared conception of justice.

From the need to overcome the right of necessity Hegel develops an overarching moral purpose that he calls "the Good." Although the immediate context of Hegel's introduction of the Good is to define a moral purpose for the individual moral agent, as *"the absolute final purpose of the world"* (PR: §129) the Good is also the abstract purpose of political institutions. Hegel's political institutions are oriented towards achieving value rather than simply securing rights-claims. This emphasis on value brings him closer to utilitarian conceptions of ethics and politics, though the idea of a simple maximization rule is quite foreign to his conception of right. The Good actually formulates *as a purpose* all the previous claims of right, so that no real dichotomy holds between the deontological rights-claims and consequentialist value-maximization. Hegel is also emphatic that he will not sanction violations of individual right for the good of the many.

Hegel's reliance on this Good as the basis of his ethical institutions, including the state, might seem (and has seemed to many) to place Hegel outside of the liberal trajectory of modern political thought, for he seems to reinstate the picture of a paternalistic state that decides what is best (i.e. what conforms to the Good) in the lives of individuals. But this is not Hegel's aim. The state does not legislate a specific morality or institute a specific religion. Hegel's Good is a version of what Rawls has called a "thin theory of the good" (Rawls 1971: 92–3; see also Neuhouser 2000: 266–9, for a discussion of Hegel's conception of the Good as a "thin theory"). It is also the case that Hegel gives no set of essential ends that all individuals must pursue. The requirement that Hegel most often invokes when discussing the state's authority over individuals is the requirement of military service in wars of self-defense. This duty to the state does not depend on specific morality, but rather on the defense of a basic condition of freedom (it is significant in this regard that he is willing to grant exceptions for religious objections to military service).

The abstract idea of the Good does not determine actions directly, but is only "actual" through individuals and their actions on specific purposes. In the *Philosophy of Right* Hegel identifies conscience with the moment of *particularity* (PR: §136) because it is the specific practical judgment of individuals about what is right and good in particular cases. It is crucial for understanding Hegel's use of conscience to understand that it is a concept of *action*, rather than simply a matter of *belief*. The objection to conscience as a source of public authority, an objection canonized by Hobbes (1994: 212), is that conscience undermines all public laws because it allows the individual to set up his own authority in competition with the authority of the laws. Hegel distinguishes between the "formal" conscience of the individual's own claim to authority, and "true" conscience as the willing of what is actually good (PR: §137), which might lead one to think that he agrees with Hobbes that the laws define what has public authority and conscience is good only to the extent that it agrees with those laws. But for Hegel the direction of authority-conferral runs both from the individual to the social as well as from the social to the individual. Hegel holds that the laws, and the public institutions generally, are indirectly determined through the practice of conscience. Individuals cannot directly claim authority over a public norm because their conscience objects to it. But those norms are modern norms because they enable individuals to act in specific situations on their conscience, and do not systematically undermine the self-identification of individuals with their actions. Individuals have an indirect claim over public norms because they are free to realize those norms in particular ways, through particular actions that are recognized as valuable.

Hegel's institutionalism and holism

Hegel's abstract descriptions of Ethical Life and the state seem to place all the authority in the hands of the institutional powers. His claims that individuals are "accidents" of the institutional "substance" (§145A) that has "an absolute authority and power" (§146), seem at first sight simply opposed to the emphasis on the rights of individuals in liberal political theory. Yet Hegel's claims about the institutional powers are balanced with claims about the authority of individuals within those institutions. Hegel views Ethical Life primarily as a system of value, but within that system individuals are themselves valuable and are sources of transformation of existing values. For every claim that the social substance must be conceived as prior to the individual there is a corresponding claim that the individual must be able to affirm institutional values as his own.

The key to a proper appreciation of Hegel's view is to understand how the subject-oriented rights laid out in "Morality" do real work in determining the institutions of Ethical Life. These rights include the right of self-consciousness, of intention, of subjective freedom, of particularity, and of insight into the good. Hegel writes of individuals as "ruled" by institutional powers (PR: §145) because the meaningfulness of individuals' lives is sustained by the institutional system of value. But it is not accidental to the institutions that there are individuals who are self-conscious, who identify with particular actions, and who develop particular interests and projects. Hegel takes Fichte's point about the generation of individuality through social relations to its logical conclusion, yet Hegel also is able, because of his more expansive conceptions of right and recognition, to think of the claims of individuals as expressions of value rather than as coercive rights against other agents. His account of civil society, and especially his account of the state, have the goal of overcoming Fichte's divide of morality and right, and thus of restoring the idea of a public morality expressed in institutions.

In his treatment of the legal system (which, according to his division of spheres of institutional authority, is part of civil society) Hegel brings moral and legal considerations together while respecting the distinctive claims of the moral subject. He dismisses with astonishing brevity the right of positive law over an individual's morality. He writes, "Since morality and moral precepts concern the will in its most personal [*eigensten*] subjectivity and particularity, they cannot be the object [*Gegenstand*] of positive legislation" (PR: §213). This restriction reflects the right to conscience that Hegel claims the State must respect – "conscience is a sanctuary which it would be *sacrilege* to violate" (PR: §137). Hegel's bark about the restrictions on conscience's authority is thus worse than his bite, for he explicitly bars legislation that would require moral action or that would make one's moral disposition the court's business.

On the side of integrating morality and right, Hegel endorses a legal institution, a "court of arbitration" or a "court of equity," that brings moral considerations to bear on legal cases in a way that overcomes the sharp split of morality and right. He writes, "*Equity* involves a departure from formal right in the light of moral or other considerations, and relates primarily to the *content* of the legal action" (PR: §223). While the legal system is primarily a realm of procedural justice, here Hegel acknowledges that there may be other (moral) factors that warrant departing from strict procedure. The point of such a court is to take account of circumstances in which there are claims that should override the strict claim of a certain law.

A more striking departure from Fichte's separation of morality and right comes in Hegel's thesis of the close interrelationship of rights and duties. Fichte had set up a sharp opposition between the two, mainly relying on the prescriptive character of duty and the permissive character of right. Hegel departs from this conception when he writes that in Ethical Life "*duty* and *right* coincide in this identity of the universal and the particular will, and in the ethical realm, a human being has rights in so far as he has duties, and duties in so far as he has rights" (PR: §155). As opposed to the realm of "Abstract Right," where the individual has a right and other individuals have the duty to respect that right, in the institutional contexts of Ethical Life one's right, the existence of one's freedom, is always connected to a duty. So one has the rights of a father over one's children in so far as one also has the duty to raise them to live independent lives.

The claim that duty and right coincide is worrisome in the context of political rights because it seems to imply that an individual's rights within the state are coextensive with his duties towards the state. This would seem to mean that one only has the right to do one's duty to the state. But the unity that Hegel espouses is not so far from liberal conceptions as it may seem. The complexity of Hegel's position comes out in his discussion of the individual's relationship to the state. After writing that individuals "have *duties* towards the State to the same extent as they also have rights," he continues,

> in the process of fulfilling his duty, the individual must somehow attain his own interest and satisfaction or settle his own account, and from his situation within the State, a right must accrue to him whereby the universal cause becomes *his own particular* cause. Particular interests should certainly not be set aside, let alone suppressed; on the contrary, they should be harmonized with the universal, so that both they themselves and the universal are preserved. The individual, whose duties give him the status of a subject, finds that, in fulfilling his duties as a citizen, he gains protection for his person and property, consideration for his particular welfare, satisfaction of his substantial essence, and the consciousness and self-awareness of being a member of the whole. (PR: §261)

The rights and duties are not strictly identical, but rather one does one's duties to the state (which can be as little as paying one's taxes) with the awareness that one's rights ("protection for his person and property ...") are secured through the state. The decisive strength of the modern state comes from the harmonization of these elements (see also Wood's analysis in the previous chapter). In this harmonization one's freedom is indirectly expressed through public authority, because one's obligation to the state is motivated and justified by the relation of the state to one's own individuality.

In Hegel's conception one achieves *personal freedom through the will of the sovereign* not only through the particular right achieved through the state (outlined in the passage above), but through the operation of the state powers as well. The separate powers in the constitution of the Hegelian state are the sovereign monarch, the executive government ministers, and the legislative representative assemblies. These correspond to the three logical moments of individuality (monarch), particularity (executive), and universality (legislative). In so far as this structure reproduces the structure of the agent's own will, the agent can recognize his own authority in the authority of the state. The most obvious sense in which the concept of individuality informs Hegel's views on the state is in his theory of sovereignty and constitutional monarchy. Though the theory of monarchy may seem not fully modern to us today, Hegel took it to be the clearest expression of the distinctive modernity of his view. The sovereign monarch himself is the power of ultimate decision, the "I will," which expresses the modern achievement of self-determining subjectivity. Hegel contrasts the modern sovereign monarch with the governments of ancient cities that made major decisions based on omens or the signs of birds (PR: §279). We moderns take our fate to be in our own hands, and we thus take the authority over decisions to lie within the self-conscious individual.

The trouble with Hegel's view of monarchy is that he infers from the principle of individual authority a monarch who is not accountable for his decisions, who *cannot* be held accountable because he stands at the apex of the state. There is reason to doubt, however, that Hegel invests much actual authority in the monarch. Despite his elevated rhetoric about the sovereign in the published text of the *Philosophy of Right*, in the lecture notes published after his death we find many statements to the effect that the monarch usually just signs his name to the decision determined by his ministers and advisors. In a "fully organized state" (PR: §280A) the rationality of state action is secured through the laws and the technical expertise of a well-trained bureaucracy (the executive).

Hegel also has a role for representative bodies within his fully organized state, though it is a lesser role than citizens of democracy would like. One of their main functions is their role in securing the accountability of those officials, namely, "the expectation of criticism, indeed of public criticism" (PR: §301). It is as a force of *publicity* and transparency in the operation of the executive that the representative assemblies serve their most important function. This publicity ensures that their deliberation is more thorough and more explicit. For the everyday operations of the state, however, Hegel is much more confident in the professional civil servants than in the people or their representatives.

The final way that Hegel takes personal freedom to be expressed in public activity is "public opinion," which is the most democratic activity in the Hegelian state. Hegel is skeptical that the marketplace of opinion can play a role in governing, but he does think of it as a bearer of ethical rationality. He writes,

> Public opinion therefore embodies not only the eternal and substantial principles of justice – the true content and product of the entire constitution and legislation and of the universal condition in general – in the form of *common sense* (the ethical foundation which is present in everyone in the shape of prejudices), but also the true needs and legitimate tendencies of actuality. (PR: §317)

In other words, ethical content and justice arise through the collective interaction of concretely situated individuals acting on and debating the issues of the day. Hegel's reference here to "the true needs and legitimate tendencies of actuality" indicates his dynamic conception of truth and actuality.

This dynamic conception is at the root of Hegel's philosophy of world history, which is often taken to be a quasi-theological conception of the unfolding of cosmic spirit. But Hegel's philosophy of history, and its relation to his politics, is not so different from Kant's speculations in moral anthropology about the progress of the human race. Hegel too finds an inner telos in human action, leading to the progressive development of human freedom, where freedom involves progressively greater particularization and differentiation. By concluding his *Philosophy of Right* (and the section of the *Encyclopedia* called "Objective Spirit") with "World History," Hegel in effect brings Kant's speculations about the human species into a more concrete form. World history has the highest right in Hegel's system because it captures, retrospectively, the actual existence of states in their rise and fall. The trajectory of history is towards the greater self-consciousness of freedom. Hegel does not think that world peace is a possibility or even an ideal, for he is a realist about the pervasiveness of conflict among nation-states. Within those states the realization of moral values is essential, but Hegel thinks that the concern for one's own state and its moral well-being does not flow continuously into regard for other states and their citizens.

An open-ended legacy

The political philosophy of German Idealism had an immediate impact in Europe, especially in the 1830s and 40s (see Quante essay below), and in so far as Marx is an outgrowth of Fichte's and Hegel's dialectical philosophy, the influence on actual events over the last two centuries has been massive indeed (see Smith essay below). The influence of their ideas has been more prominent in the last forty years than at any time since 1848, for they have been a central resource in the renewed push to find a philosophical grounding for liberalism. They have been a major influence on the most prominent recent German democratic political philosophers, Jürgen Habermas and Karl-Otto Apel, who define their work in dialogue with the idealists. In the English-language literature, the main line of influence has come through the work of Rawls, on the one hand, and those Hegelian thinkers, such as Alasdair MacIntyre and Charles Taylor, who argue for a communitarian counterposition to Rawls. I close this essay with a brief exposition of the influence on Rawls and a few words on his critics.

There are both Kantian and Hegelian themes in Rawls's masterwork, *A Theory of Justice*. The Kantian aspects draw more from Kant's moral philosophy than from the specific elements of the "Doctrine of Right." In the section entitled "The Kantian Interpretation of Justice as Fairness," Rawls presents his conception of "the original position" as an interpretation of Kant's idea of moral legislation for an ethical commonwealth (Rawls 1971: 251–7). The leading feature of Rawls's original position is the "veil of ignorance," which restricts the knowledge of the agents within the hypothetical contract situation of rational choice. Rawls conceives of this restriction as guaranteeing the *autonomy* of the choice, claiming that a choice based on the knowledge of one's own specific circumstances would be *heteronomous*. Rawls understands his two principles of justice as categorical imperatives in Kant's sense, for they apply "to a person in virtue of his nature as a free and equal rational being" (Rawls 1971: 253). In this interpretation of his theory of justice as fairness, Rawls combines into a single conception the moral, political, and anthropological elements of Kant's view. He is in effect molding together Kant's different levels, and Kant's ambiguities over the separation of morality and right, into a single whole that is suitable for a public *expression* of justice. Though this moralized politics is a departure from Kant's theory in the "Doctrine of Right," it certainly captures the spirit and complexity of Kant's practical philosophy as a whole.

The original position is focused on the rational choice of the single moral individual, yet Rawls also advocates a strongly social conception of justice that draws on elements from Hegel. The "subject" of social and political justice is the *basic structure* of society. This structure includes the major social and political institutions, including the family, and thus resembles the system of institutions that Hegel calls "Ethical Life." Rawls' normative goal is not simply to secure principles of justice, but rather to present a picture of a "well-ordered society" that is structured by those principles. One of the "primary goods" in such a society is the "social bases of self-respect" (Rawls 1971: 440–6), which ties the justness of institutions to the recognition that individuals achieve therein. His theory thus presents institutions as forms of intersubjectivity akin to Hegel's configurations of the free will in contexts of mutual recognition. Finally, in his late "Restatement" of his position, Rawls specifically mentions Hegel's theme of reconciliation as a goal of political philosophy (Rawls 2001: 3–4). The task for Rawls is to illuminate the rational within modern social organization, to show why we should accept the political order in roughly the form that it has taken even though it does not live up to anyone's ideal of justice.

Despite the Hegelian elements in Rawls, the communitarian attack on Rawlsian liberalism has drawn a good deal of ammunition and inspiration from Hegel's conception of Ethical Life. The main point of contention is the *priority* relationship between the individual and the social "substance." Hegel is very clear that he parts company with social contract theories in thinking of the social substance as prior to the individual will. The communitarian charge is that the abstract detached conception of the individual contractor is a fiction that is positively harmful in that it asks individuals to distance themselves from the very sources of meaning that make life worth living. The charge is that the idea of a value-neutral or value-free procedure that generates determinate answers to real political questions is an illusion. Either no such answers are generated, or certain liberal values are illicitly given precedence over all others. To the extent that Rawls does endorse substantive values (such as autonomy), he is committing himself to elements that are bound to be unacceptable to some citizens. The costs of adopting the self-image of liberal individualism, according to this line of attack, include alienation, social fragmentation and loss of meaning. In its extreme form, communitarianism eschews the language of rights altogether, a move that would certainly not have found favor with Hegel. Most communitarians today are not willing to part company with liberalism on the question of certain inalienable individual rights, and like Hegel they seek instead to reorient our thinking about those rights to emphasize their dependence on forms of sociality.

Partly in response to worries that his conception of the Good was too restrictive, in his *Political Liberalism* Rawls (1993) abandoned the strong Kantian interpretation of justice as fairness is favor of a narrow *political* interpretation. A theory is comprehensive for Rawls if it "applies to all subjects and covers all values" (Rawls 2001: 14), while it is political if it is limited to the context of political cooperation. Rawls came to this position as a way to deal with what he calls "the fact of reasonable pluralism," the idea that there are many reasonable and yet mutually incompatible moral, religious and philosophical views, and that the political order should not impose one such a view on all citizens. Rawls's distinction in his later work between a political and a comprehensive theory of justice draws him closer to Kant's specifically political theory of external freedom. Recently Thomas Pogge (2002) has mapped Rawls' distinction onto Kant's "Doctrine of Right" and claimed that Kant's distinction between the moral and the right makes Kant's view "political," or non-comprehensive. If the question of right can be solved even for a nation of devils, in Kant's phrase, then right does not presume any allegiance to a moral view and it can therefore be considered purely political.

Though Fichte's work has received the least attention in English-speaking countries, his concept of recognition is the most promising conceptual tool for the development of modern liberalism. The communitarian reaction was largely a worry about forms of human relatedness, and to counter this attack liberals have been stressing the compatibility of liberal rights with thick forms of community. Liberals have rightly insisted that they do not need to deny Fichte's claim that humans only become humans with other humans, nor to deny that we should foster institutional structures that make mutual recognition possible. The liberal defense of basic rights is a defense of the basic efficacy that Fichte referred to as "original right," which is secured through the mutual recognition of one another's claims to a sphere of activity and to the capability to act within it. Hegel already showed in his transformation of Fichtean recognition how we can think of individual freedom and ethical community as two complementary aspects of a single conception of public action. The challenge then for theorizing further forms of mutual recognition is to understand which social conditions are necessary to sustain our efficacy as agents living lives that are both meaningful and open to the claims of others.

References

Darwall, S. (2006) *The Second-Person Standpoint: Morality, Respect and Accountability*, Cambridge, MA: Harvard University Press.

Fichte (GNR) *Foundations of Natural Right*, trans. Michael Baur, edited by F. Neuhouser, Cambridge: Cambridge University Press, 2000.

—— (SL) *System of Ethics*, trans. D. Breazeale and G. Zöller, Cambridge: Cambridge University Press, 2006.

Guyer, P. (2002) "Kant's Deductions of the Principle of Right," in Timmons (2002), 23–64.

—— (ed.) (2006) *The Cambridge Companion to Kant and Modern Philosophy*, Cambridge: Cambridge University Press.

Hegel, G. W. F. (N) "Uber die wissenschaftliche Behandlungsart des Naturrechts, seine Stelle in der praktischen Philosophie und sein Verhältnis zu den positiven Rechtswissenschaften," in *Werke* 2; "The Scientific Ways of Treating Natural Law," in *Hegel's Political Writings*, trans. T. M. Knox, Oxford: Clarendon Press, 1998.

—— (PR) *Elements of the Philosophy of Right*, trans. H. B. Nisbet, edited by A. Wood, Cambridge: Cambridge University Press, 1991. (Cited by paragraph (§) number.) Werke 7.

—— (W) *Werke*, 20 vols, Frankfurt: Suhrkamp, 1986.

Hobbes, T. (1994) *Leviathan*, edited by Edwin Curley, Indianapolis, IN; Cambridge, MA: Hackett.

Höffe, O. (1992) "'Even a Nation of Devils Needs the State': The Dilemma of Natural Justice," in Williams (1992), pp. 120–42.

Holtman, S. (2002) "Revolution, Contradiction, and Kantian Citizenship," in Timmons (2002), pp. 209–32.

Kant (Ak) *Immanuel Kants Schriften*, edited by Königlich preussischen Akademie der Wissenschaften, Berlin: Walter de Gruyter, 1902–. (Unless otherwise footnoted, writings of Immanuel Kant will be cited by volume:page number in this edition.)

—— (Ca) *Cambridge Edition of the Works of Immanuel Kant*, New York: Cambridge University Press, 1992–. (This edition provides marginal Ak volume:page citations. Specific works will be cited using the following system of abbreviations [works not abbreviated below will be cited simply as Ak volume:page].)

—— (EF) "Zum ewigen Frieden" (1796), Ak 8; "Toward Perpetual Peace," Ca Practical Philosophy.

—— (MS) *Metaphysik der Sitten* (1797–8), Ak 6; *Metaphysics of Morals*, Ca Practical Philosophy.

—— (SF) *Der Streit der Fakultäten* (1798), Ak 7; *The Conflict of the Faculties*, trans. Mary Gregor, New York: Abaris Books, 1979.

—— (UG) "Über den Gemeinspruch: Das mag in der Theorie richtig sein, taugt aber nicht für die Praxis" (1793), Ak 8; "On the Common Saying: That May Be Correct in Theory, But It Is of No Use in Practice," Ca Practical Philosophy.

Kersting, W. (1992) "Kant's Concept of the State," in Williams (1992), pp. 143–65.

Kleingeld, P. (2006) "Kant's Theory of Peace," in Guyer (2006), pp. 477–504.

Machiavelli, N. (1996) *Discourses on Livy*, trans. H. Mansfield and N. Tarcov, Chicago: University of Chicago Press.

Moyar, D. (2008) "Self-completing Alienation: Hegel's Argument for Transparent Conditions of Free Agency," in D. Moyar and M. Quante (eds), *Hegel's Phenomenology of Spirit: A Critical Guide*, Cambridge: Cambridge University Press, pp. 150–72.

Neuhouser, F. (1994) "Fichte and the Relationship between Right and Morality," in Daniel Breazeale and Tom Rockmore (eds) *Fichte: Historical Context/Contemporary Controversies*, Atlantic Highlands, NJ: Humanities Press, pp. 158–80.

—— (2000) *Foundations of Hegel's Social Theory: Actualizing Freedom*, Cambridge, MA: Harvard University Press.

Nicholson, P. (1992) "Kant, Revolution and History," in Williams (1992), pp. 249–68.

Pippin, R. (2006) "Mine and thine? The Kantian state," in Guyer (2006), pp. 416–46.

Pogge, T. (2002) "Is Kant's *Rechtslehre* a 'Comprehensive Liberalism'?," in Timmons (2002), pp. 133–58.

Quante, M. (2004) *Hegel's Concept of Action*, trans. Dean Moyar, Cambridge: Cambridge University Press.

Rawls, J. (1971) *A Theory of Justice*, Cambridge, MA: Harvard University Press.

—— (1993) *Political Liberalism*, New York: Columbia University Press.

—— (2001) *Justice as Fairness: A Restatement*, Erin Kelly (ed.), Cambridge, MA: Harvard University Press.

Rosen, A. (1993) *Kant's Theory of Justice*, Ithaca, NY, and London: Cornell University Press.

Rousseau, J.-J. (1997) *The Social Contract and Other Late Political Writings*, edited by Victor Gourevitch, Cambridge: Cambridge University Press.

Seebohm, T. (1981) "Kant's Theory of Revolution," *Social Research* 48: 555–87.

Timmons, M. (ed.) (2002) *Kant's Metaphysics of Morals: Interpretive Essays*, Oxford: Oxford University Press.

Willaschek, M. (1997) "Why the *Doctrine of Right* does not belong in the *Metaphysics of Morals*: On some Basic Distinctions in Kant's Moral Philosophy," *Jahrbuch für Recht und Ethik* 5: 205–27.

—— (2002) "Which Imperatives for Right? On the Non-Prescriptive Character of Juridical Laws in Kant's *Metaphysics of Morals*," in Timmons (2002), pp. 65–88.

—— (2008) "Right and Coercion: Can Kant's Conception of Right Be Derived from his Moral Theory?" *International Journal of Philosophical Studies* 17: 49–70.

Williams, H. (ed.) (1992) *Essays on Kant's Political Philosophy*, Chicago: University of Chicago Press.

Williams, R. (2002) "The Displacement of Recognition by Coercion in Fichte's *Grundlage des Naturrechts*," in Daniel Breazeale and Tom Rockmore (eds), *New Essays on Fichte's Later Jena Wissenschaftslehre*, Evanston: Northwestern University Press, pp. 47–64.

Wood, A. (1990) *Hegel's Ethical Thought*, Cambridge: Cambridge University Press.

—— (2002) "The Final Form of Kant's Practical Philosophy," in Timmons (2002), pp. 1–22.

6

THE AESTHETICS OF SCHELLING AND HEGEL

Rachel Zuckert

Synopsis

Hegel and Schelling understand art to be a central human activity, one that models, rivals, or even supersedes the accomplishments of philosophy. This exalted status attributed to art rests upon a novel conception of art as a distinctive metaphysical and cognitive achievement: art presents the Absolute, ultimate being, in sensible or finite form. Their theories of art are the source, in the history of aesthetics, of the influential claim that artistic value resides in the "unity of form and content" and are also the first philosophies of art that treat art systematically, differentiated both by media (art forms) and in historical periods.

This essay concentrates on Hegel and Schelling, alone, because Fichte pays little attention to aesthetics, and because the central concern of Kant's aesthetic theory – the justification of judgments of taste – fits squarely within the eighteenth-century project of philosophical aesthetics (the investigation of taste) and is quite alien to Hegel's and Schelling's shared dominant concerns and methods. For this reason, Kant's aesthetics will be discussed in the "historical background" section; various aspects of Kant's aesthetic theory that were influential on Hegel and Schelling will also be noted.

Historical background

Though philosophers in the West had long discussed art and beauty, philosophical attention focused intensively upon aesthetics in the eighteenth century. Eighteenth-century Europe saw the foundation of public institutions dedicated to the arts such as art galleries, museums, and concert halls, as well as the development of a growing public market for artworks. The category of the fine or "beautiful" arts was also first formulated, to include the arts of literature ("poetry"), painting, sculpture, architecture, dance, landscape gardening, and music (see Kristeller 1951 and 1952, and Shiner 2001). In the Germanic countries, this was also a period of great artistic flourishing – the age of Lessing, Schiller, and Goethe, of Haydn, Mozart, and Beethoven, as well as of the origins of art history in Winckelmann's work on the art of ancient Greece.

In part because of these historical developments, and in part for philosophical reasons, philosophers in Britain (Shaftesbury, Hutcheson, Hume, Burke), France (Batteux, du Bos, Diderot, Rousseau) and Germany (Baumgarten, Mendelssohn, Herder, Kant, Schiller) devoted extensive attention to matters aesthetic. These philosophers mostly concentrated on questions concerning "taste." They understood beauty to be identified by the pleasurable responses of spectators or auditors to objects; indeed many claimed that beauty *consisted* in an object's disposition to cause such responses. Thus they aimed to identify what, phenomenologically or functionally, is distinctive about these responses, and which characteristics of an object are likely to occasion them. They attempted as well to determine which responses, by which people, are "valid" for all others, or establish a "standard of taste." These investigations were of philosophical interest in their own right, as they purport to define the beautiful, as (usually) subjective, i.e. as dependent upon the individual's response to objects. But they were also turned to broader philosophical purposes, for example to contribute to the Enlightenment "science of man" by providing an account of human capacities for feeling and perception, or to identify resources – shared sentiments aroused by art – for promoting moral behavior and social unification in democratic societies.

As will be discussed below, Hegel and Schelling reject this project – the investigation of taste – vehemently. Though they admit this less openly, however, they are also deeply influenced by their predecessors, particularly those in the German aesthetic tradition. We may identify three chief claims as influential upon them: (a) the representation of beauty is intermediate between "mere" sense experience and rational cognition and thereby perhaps may serve as sensible representation of rational ideas; (b) human *pleasure* in beauty is intermediate between sensible pleasures and rational, moral approval, and thus might be educative towards morality; (c) aesthetic or artistic value is to be understood (in part) in historical terms, as proposed by Schiller and Herder. (On many of these points, Hegel and Schelling were immediately influenced by the Romantics; on the Romantics, see Chapter 10 of this volume; on their relation to Hegel's and Schelling's aesthetics, see Schaeffer 2000, and in response to Schaeffer, Ameriks 2006.)

Characteristic of the German tradition in aesthetics beginning with Baumgarten is the view that the experience of beauty comprises representation that is both sensible – gained through the senses, of particular objects – and yet also akin to rational representation of universals, or of objects as governed by conceptually articulated connections and order. Baumgarten and other German rationalists (including Lessing and Mendelssohn) understood this kinship to rationality as the "perfection" of the objects of aesthetic experience: the beautiful object is (and is sensibly represented as) superlatively ordered; every part, every property, has a reason for belonging to the whole. Correspondingly, the perceiving subject is in a state of perfection itself: in apprehending such objects, the subject has orderly representations, or is in a state of proto-rationality itself.

In the *Critique of Judgment* – a work deeply influential on both Hegel and Schelling – Kant expands upon and reinterprets these claims. Like the German rationalists, Kant understands our representation of the beautiful to be similar to, but distinct from, conceptual cognition of objects: in representing an object as beautiful, on Kant's view, we experience it as unified and intelligible, but without using the conceptual rules that guide our comprehension of objects in ordinary cognition. Thus – and importantly for Hegel and Schelling – Kant claims that in experiencing the beautiful, our imaginations (or capacities for sensible representation more broadly) are "free" both from causally induced association and from conceptual determination, free to perceive new, fresh order in the perceived object; likewise, artistic creation of the beautiful consists, in part, in the free, creative power of the imagination. Moreover, particularly in his discussion of the beauty of fine art, Kant suggests that the order we represent in the beautiful transcends – is richer in content, more complex, than – the order we represent in cognized objects. Artworks present to us "aesthetic ideas" or "representation[s] of the imagination that occasion much thinking though without it being possible for any determinate thought, i.e., concept, to be adequate to it, which, consequently, no language fully attains or can make intelligible" (Kant 2000: 192). Therefore, Kant suggests, artworks may represent imaginatively or in sensible form "ideas of reason," ideas of that which lies beyond sensible experience or description by (mere) concepts, such as "the kingdom of the blessed, the kingdom of hell, eternity, creation" (*ibid.*).

Thus Kant introduces the conception of art, expanded upon by Hegel and Schelling, as not simply similar (in its beauty) to rational representation, but as a representation of rational, transcendent ideas. Kant suggests, too, that beauty might "bridge" a central Kantian "gulf" of great concern to Hegel and Schelling (as to nearly all post-Kantians): between nature and freedom or morality. Kant claims that beauty is a "symbol of morality" or a "transition" to morality: in appreciating beauty, we recognize nature as suitable to our purposes (including moral purposes), and we feel a disinterested pleasure that may move us towards the disinterested commitment required for moral action, a pleasure that is – as is morality – free from our natural needs and desires (Kant 2000: 225–8).

In his *Letters on Aesthetic Education*, Friedrich Schiller expands upon this Kantian suggestion, adding intra- and extra-personal historical dimensions. Like Kant, Schiller suggests that the experience of the beautiful is educative towards morality: in appreciating the beautiful, we feel our freedom from natural need and material necessity, but we do so not as purely rational, autonomous individuals, separate from the natural order. Rather, we find the beautiful object to be freely ordered within sensibility – and we are and sensibly feel ourselves to be free and harmonious in having this experience (Schiller 1982: 100–9). This state prepares the individual for rational freedom, for moral action even in conflict with sensible inclination, and thus is part of the individual's developmental process from natural neediness to rational, free self-rule (Schiller 1982: 138–43, 160–9).

Schiller suggests that this developmental transition from beauty to rational morality may also be traced in Western history: the Greeks lived harmonious, beautiful lives, in which the claims of sensibility and rationality were immediately united. The chief difference between us moderns and the Greeks is that we have come to recognize the distinctiveness of rationality, of freedom and morality, as potentially opposed to sensible inclination and as corrective of the given natural order. But this opposition between rationality and sensibility, between freedom and nature, is also alienating, leading to disunified individuals and societies (Schiller 1982: 32–43). (In another influential essay, "On Naïve and Sentimental Poetry," Schiller suggests that this break between ancients and moderns is reflected in poetry as well, as a distinction between "naïve" poetry that joyously celebrates the intelligibility of nature and one's union with it, and the "sentimental" poetry of reflection, yearning, or alienation.) On Schiller's view, as for many after him, the French Revolution exemplifies both the achievements and the dangers of modern (Kantian) moral rationality: the revolutionaries admirably attempted to transform the world in light of a self-legislated, rational moral conception, but the degeneration of the French Revolution into fanaticism also demonstrates the dangers of reason's alienation from nature, our inability – without some sort of "transition" – to leave our sensible natures behind, to act purely in accord with reason. In light of this catastrophic event, Schiller proposes that a social return to beauty and artistic idealization might provide such a "transition" and address this alienation by bringing nature and freedom together once more (1982: 7–9, 42–7, 214–19).

Like Schiller, Johann Gottfried Herder contrasts the experience and production of art with the alienation – of rationality from sensibility, of abstract concepts from lived experience and individuality – characteristic of modern society. Art, he claims, is both produced and experienced by human beings employing all of their capacities in harmonious balance (Herder 2006: 309, 331). More strongly than Schiller, however, Herder emphasizes that art may overcome the alienation of the individual from society because it expresses the life and world view of its society, thus allowing individuals to recognize their connections to their community, their shared values. More than Schiller, therefore, Herder celebrates the historical and social diversity of artistic works: artworks not only do, but should, reflect the diversity and specificity of societies' ways of life (Herder 2006: 292–8). Unlike Schiller's suggestions concerning the promise of a return to beauty and an aesthetically unified future society, moreover, Herder's conception of historical change is less optimistic: he argues that because modernity is characterized by increasing specialization and rational abstraction (as Schiller argues as well), there may be no harmonious art expressive of modern life (Herder 2006: 246–56). We, as moderns, may have lost the holism – of individual capacities, of societal values and practices – expressed in truly great art. These conceptions of the historical function of art – as expressing historically changing social values, as a source of future reconciliation, or as a lost locus of harmony – are central to Hegel's and Schelling's philosophies of art, to which we shall now turn.

Philosophy of art

Schelling and Hegel treat aesthetics in two contexts: as part of their systematic philosophies as a whole – respectively, in the *System of Transcendental Idealism* (of 1800) and in the *Encyclopedia of the Philosophical Sciences*, part 3: *The Philosophy of Spirit* (of 1830) – and, in greater detail, in lectures on the philosophy of art, given by Schelling in 1802–3, and by Hegel in 1820–1, 1823, 1826 and 1828–9. In these treatments, Schelling and Hegel propose doctrines concerning the nature of beauty and art. In the lectures, they develop these general theoretical claims into accounts of the different art forms – architecture, music, sculpture, painting, literature – claiming, ambitiously, that their theories can account for the specific character of these art forms and their historical developments.

Before turning to discuss their claims, two notes concerning these texts are in order. First, Schelling's treatments of art span his transition from the Fichtean position of the *System* to the more Spinozistic position of his identity-philosophy; some differences between these phases in Schelling's career will be noted, but they cannot be discussed in detail here (on the phases in Schelling's philosophical career, see White 1983). Second, the edition of Hegel's lectures that has been most studied is that edited by his disciple, Hotho, and published posthumously in 1835 (and translated in Hegel 1975). New editions of transcripts of Hegel's lecture courses have been published, which suggest that Hotho may have altered Hegel's lecture notes (see Hammermeister 2002: 89–90, 228). Because Hegel's central claims in the lectures appear to remain constant and because the Hotho edition is still the most available, however, this edition alone will be cited here.

Criticism of their predecessors: from taste to art

As noted above, Hegel and Schelling emphatically reject their predecessors' philosophical aesthetics of taste. Neither denies that we respond emotionally to artworks, and both endorse a common eighteenth-century claim concerning this feeling and/or its object, namely, disinterestedness: art (and our response to it) does not serve external ends, is not the object of desire or use, but is valuable in itself (Schelling 1978: 223, 227; Hegel 1975: 35–7, 55). But they deny that these responses alone can define or substantively characterize art. Schelling objects that eighteenth-century theories "tried to explain beauty using empirical psychology, and in general treated the miracles of art the same way one treated ghost stories and other superstitions: by enlightening us and explaining them away" (Schelling 1989: 12). Hegel argues that personal taste is arbitrary and diverse – and so (he jokes) it should be, as each husband's taste for his wife as the most beautiful woman is much better than an agreed-upon, universal taste; thus taste cannot determine the (objective, universal) value of art (Hegel 1975: 1, 16, 44–5). Moreover, a doctrine that defines beauty or art as arousing feelings is superficial, Hegel argues, because it disregards their determinate character: feeling is an "indefinite dull region of the spirit ... [D]ifferences between feelings are ... completely abstract, not differences in the thing itself ... .[Feeling] is capable of receiving into itself the most varied and opposite contents" (*ibid.*: 1, 32–3).

Hegel's and Schelling's objections to the philosophy of taste can be glossed as objections to aesthetic "subjectivism" in several meanings of this term: if one concentrates on taste, one understands artistic value to reside merely in felt responses – not in the object itself. These responses are, moreover, arbitrary, individualized, and insufficiently reflective of the characteristics of the object. One can, Hegel suggests, feel different emotions towards the same object, and one can feel the same emotion (e.g. anger) toward many different things. The episodes of anger themselves – though perhaps qualitatively and quantitatively somewhat different – are largely similar, and thus do not reflect the possibly vast differences among their objects. (This objection may have particular weight against the common eighteenth-century proposal that the beautiful occasions pleasure, a broadly defined and variously caused feeling.) As the quotation above from Schelling suggests, this philosophical approach is seen not only as inadequate to its subject matter (art) because it concentrates on external response, but also as reductive, denying the "miracle," the greatness, of art, by treating it as a mere feeling-producer (cf. Hegel 1975: 34). And indeed by contrast to all of their predecessors in philosophical aesthetics, Hegel and Schelling concentrate nearly exclusively on art (as opposed to natural beauty) as a fundamental human activity and distinctive product, not merely as a source of pleasure. Correspondingly, in their lectures on the philosophy of art, they investigate, to a degree unmatched by previous or (arguably) subsequent aesthetic theorists, an enormous range of artworks.

Method and aims

Hegel and Schelling aim to articulate the essential character of art as a human activity and product. Both purport to provide definitions of art as such, but, by contrast to previous and subsequent aestheticians, neither claims that this definition ought to apply to any object said to be "art." Hegel claims that though art (like thought) may be used in many frivolous ways, he is concerned solely with "true" and "free" art, that which is valuable in itself and "fulfils its supreme task" (Hegel 1975: 7). Schelling criticizes the "liberal use of ...'work of art'" that would identify even any "epigram which preserves a momentary sensation" as an artwork (Schelling 1978: 231); he is also willing to identify objects that fit his definition as art, even if they are not standardly so considered, e.g. the Catholic church (Schelling 1989: 81).

Instead of surveying objects already labeled as "art," therefore, both Schelling and Hegel attempt to define art within their systematic accounts of the nature of being or of self-determining self-consciousness – within, that is, their systematic accounts of the "Absolute." (I shall use the term "Absolute" to refer to what they conceive to be the ultimate being or the object of philosophical knowledge because this term is shared by both, and can be used to refer, somewhat indeterminately, to the various conceptions they propose concerning the character of ultimate being.) Only such a systematic account, they claim, can provide a properly philosophical account of the essence of art, as opposed to the merely contingent and open-ended results of empirical induction (Schelling 1989: 12; Hegel 1975: 15).

Though an account of their philosophical systems as a whole – and of the Absolute as allegedly known therein – lies beyond the scope of this essay, we may note broadly that both Hegel and Schelling attempt to provide comprehensive accounts of all aspects of being, within an organized totality. In particular, they attempt to reconcile

Kantian oppositions that prevent a comprehensive understanding of being as a whole: between subjects (or self-consciousness) and objects, between human freedom and natural necessity, between universals (concepts, laws, ideals) and particulars (sensible objects, individual human beings), between sensibly appearing objects and supersensible things in themselves.

Kant had argued that nature (or objects of knowledge) was governed by causal laws *only as* experienced by human subjects, who employ universal concepts (such as cause and effect) to interpret sensible experience. We – as subjects of knowledge – cannot be understood to be objects (these are always objects *for* a subject), nor can such sensibly perceived objects be understood to exhaust all aspects of reality, which may include supersensible entities as well. Thus we human beings "in ourselves," not as objects of experience, may be free (not causally determined) – as indeed may God (who, if He exists, is not an object of experience). Like post-Kantians generally, Hegel and Schelling found this account unsatisfactory, chiefly (for our purposes) because it does not provide an integrated account of human subjectivity and freedom as arising out of and operative within non-human nature (as Schelling argues), or because (as Hegel argues) it does not give an account of being as a whole, of which both subject and object, mind and nature, are components (Hegel 1971: 314–15). (This aspiration of Schelling's is emphasized in Bowie 2003.) Indeed the Kantian free and knowing subject itself lies in some ways beyond knowledge or self-knowledge. Both object as well that Kant cannot account for the consonance between universals and particulars, whether in cognition or in morality: Kant's universal laws of morality or concepts for cognition are too abstract and formal fully to determine the character of particulars or even, perhaps, definitively to apply to particulars. Specifically, the Kantian conception of morality sets up a "contradiction" between universal, rational laws of the will and particular, sensuous drives or needs: the self-determining universal will is always opposed to, but demands reconciliation with, sensuous human nature (Hegel 1975: 52ff.). Unlike the Romantics, who are also deeply concerned with these Kantian oppositions, Hegel and Schelling aspire to reconcile all of these oppositions in one, overarching, philosophically articulated system.

As we shall see, these aims are at work in their treatment of art. Most generally, Hegel and Schelling characterize art by assigning it a place within their systems in accord with two of these desiderata. Both argue, first, that artworks are or present unities of universal and particular: in artworks, universal truths or values – such as laws of nature, ideals of romantic love, moral virtues – are presented in sensible, particular form, e.g. as symbolized by gods or instantiated in characters, gestures, or actions. Second, the most central systematic "place" of art is as a form of human self-consciousness, a part of the project of self-knowledge that they take to be ruled out, at least in part, by Kant. In producing and appreciating art, we render our own commitments, nature, feelings, connection to and place within the world "objective," i.e. we become the objects of our own consciousness (Schelling 1978: 230–1). Hegel understands such objectification as an activity of expression, of externalizing "inner," spiritual ideals in an "outer," perceptible medium, in which human beings can "recognize" themselves (Hegel 1975: 30–1). The language of the first person plural is important here: though Hegel and Schelling claim that individual artists engage in such activity, they do not mean that art is an individualistic, narrowly artist-centered activity or product. They argue that art renders "objective" the nature of human self-consciousness as such, or (like Herder) that it expresses the character of communally shared values or world views; thus, they claim, art renders others, the audience or society at large, "self-conscious" as well.

Hegel and Schelling purport, then, to provide systematically derived, ontological conceptions of art on the basis of their comprehensive philosophical systems. Insofar as these definitions can also explain the variations among art forms and historical change in the arts, they may, too, be endorsed for systematic reasons, namely, of providing a comprehensive account of art in its various manifestations. Thus, though Hegel and Schelling reject the empirical method of surveying so-labeled "art" objects, they do take it to be confirmation of their doctrines that they can articulate the nature and value of many artworks taken to be paradigms (see Hegel 1975: 22–5; Schelling 1989: 17–19, 53–4 – for statements of these systematic theoretical aspirations).

In accord with the exaltative "idealistic" attitude expressed in passages quoted above, then, Hegel and Schelling also aim to characterize great, paradigmatic art, to explain why it is "miraculous," of great human significance. Thus, they propose what are now called "evaluative" theories of art, i.e. they do not attempt to describe *all* things referred to as "art," but understand art in normative terms: objects that do not have the requisite character – the sensible, particular, or finite presentation of the Absolute (as will be discussed in a moment) – do not, on their view, properly count as art as such or are understood as objects "that merely ape the character of a work of art" (Schelling 1978: 225). Such evaluative definitions of art – Hegel's predominantly among them – are in disrepute these days, because (it is claimed) such theories prescribe what artists ought to do, or exclude from consideration certain works of art in a dictatorial way, from the heights of philosophical speculation (e.g. Schaeffer 2000: 8). Though both Hegel and Schelling base their aesthetic theories upon philosophical premises, and do exclude objects from celebration as "art proper," however, their evaluative theories are not to be dismissed so quickly. One may note, first, that such criticisms are based on metaphysical and evaluative commitments of their own – e.g. concerning the reality and value of the free creativity of artists, an aspect of art that Hegel himself emphasizes. Moreover, one might take evaluative definition to be not only accurate to, but also respectful toward, the aspiration of artists and the function of art in past and present society: artworks are taken not to be mere objects, but to be valuable – desirable, lovable, informative – and artists aim to produce objects of value and take this to be a serious enterprise, at which they could fail. Indeed Hegel anticipates this very objection and responds indirectly by alleging that it rests on a misunderstanding, namely, "that [the] life of nature and spirit [here: art] is marred and killed by comprehension … instead of being brought nearer to us by conceptual thinking" (Hegel 1975: 12). Correspondingly, Hegel denies that his evaluative definition is prescriptive for artists; it aims, rather, to elucidate the pre-existing value of art (Hegel 1975: 18). In any case, even if one endorses a "descriptive" definition of art – one that attempts to describe any object taken to be an artwork, even if bad

– one may still ask what the value of *good* works of art might be, and we will now turn to Hegel's and Schelling's responses to this question, in the form of their evaluative definitions.

Art: the presentation of the absolute in sensible form

Hegel and Schelling not only derive their characterization of art from their systematic accounts of the Absolute, but also propose that art is a revelation – a presentation or instantiation – of that Absolute. Hegel claims that beautiful art is the "sensuous presentation of the Absolute" or of "the Idea" (Hegel 1975: 70) and Schelling defines art as "the infinite finitely displayed" (Schelling 1978: 225) or as the "representation" of the unity of "universal and the particular within the particular" (Schelling 1989: 45, 83). Schelling's definition refers to his conception of the Absolute as a reconciliation of basic, apparently opposed characteristics of beings or "antitheses" – infinite and finite, universal and particular, subjective or conscious ("ideal") and material ("real"); Hegel likewise claims that the Idea is "the *unity* of universal and particular, freedom and necessity, spirit and nature" (Hegel 1975: 62). But both gloss this represented content of art – the Absolute – in more familiar terms as well: as the "divine" or as "Ideas" (in the Platonic sense), i.e. that which is – or is conceived by human consciousness or the artist's society as – the pre-eminent being(s), the essences of things and actions that identify their nature, value, and meaning.

In the broadest sense, then, Hegel and Schelling hold that artworks *mean* something, indeed mean the highest things; art "bring[s] to our minds and express[es] the *Divine*, the deepest interests of mankind, and the most comprehensive truths of the spirit" (Hegel 1975: 7). Art is fundamentally representational or, perhaps better, "presentational" (rather than mimetic). Art does not merely reproduce – or, as on a traditional theory widely held prior to and during the eighteenth century, "imitate" – particular objects we find around us in experience. Such imitation, Hegel argues, would be not only "superfluous," but also "presumptuous" and "deceptive" in producing *mere* copies of real things, praiseworthy only for the skill involved in producing them (Hegel 1975: 42–3; cf. Schelling 1989: 129). Rather, art presents the ultimate metaphysical character of those objects, of being as such, and of human existence in particular. Like Aristotle and the neo-Platonists – and like Schopenhauer – Hegel and Schelling thus repudiate Plato's accusation against the arts, namely, that they merely copy the appearance of particular sensible objects, which are themselves dependent beings or copies of the Ideas, in explicitly Platonic terms: art presents the Ideas, universal truths and ultimate being (Hegel 1975: 8–9, 42–3; Schelling 1989: 4–5).

Art has, therefore, deep philosophical significance, indeed is a model or rival for philosophical knowledge. Like philosophy, art is a form of self-conscious understanding of ultimate truths and values. Thus Schelling claims that art is "a magic and symbolic mirror" showing the "inner essence" of philosophy (Schelling 1989: 8) and Hegel identifies art as a mode of "absolute spirit," like philosophy (Hegel 1971: 292f.). Accordingly, both draw upon art in their philosophical works (not merely in their philosophies of art) to inform their claims. Schelling, for example, explains the character of unconscious mental activity by adverting to the case of an artist "lost in his work" (Schelling 1978: 75), and in the *Phenomenology of Spirit* Hegel draws upon literary works, most famously the *Antigone*, to articulate the historically changing shapes of human self-consciousness. (Such use of art as philosophically significant material does not distinguish Hegel and Schelling from many other philosophers, but, again like the Romantics, they are distinctive in promulgating aesthetic theories that explain such use.)

Art is, however, different from philosophy, they argue, because it presents the Absolute in sensible, particular, finite form, rather than in universal, rational, or conceptual form. In Schelling's terms, art is "aesthetic intuition" of the Absolute, namely, as presented in a particular, finite object (the artwork), as contrasted to the "intellectual intuition" characteristic of philosophy, the rational cognition of the Absolute (Schelling 1978: 229; cf. Schelling 1989: 45). In Hegel's terms, "the work of art should put before our eyes a content, not in its universality as such, but one whose universality has been absolutely individualized and sensuously particularized" (Hegel 1975: 51). Therefore, on Hegel's view, art is a preliminary, not completely satisfactory model for true, philosophical understanding of the Absolute; because it presents the Idea in sensible form, art is "limited to a specific content," namely, what can be so presented (Hegel 1975: 9, 1971: 294 – hence Hegel's infamous claim, to be discussed below, that art is at an end). Schelling's comparative ranking of art and philosophy is more ambiguous. In the lectures, Schelling appears to concur with Hegel's judgment: as a "real" rather than "ideal" presentation of the Absolute, art presents less clearly the truths that are the subject matter of philosophy (Schelling 1989: 6). In his earlier *System*, however, Schelling suggests that art can transcend the achievements of philosophy: it is the "*one* everlasting revelation" of the Absolute (Schelling 1978: 223) and thus "is ... the only true and eternal organ and document of philosophy, which ever and again continues to speak to us of what philosophy cannot depict in external form" (Schelling 1978: 231).

Thus for Hegel and Schelling, art not only has deeply significant, philosophical meaning (the Absolute or Ideas), but also is distinct from philosophy in that it presents that meaning in sensible or particular form – stone, paint, shapes, sounds. On this point, Hegel and Schelling differ from those of their contemporaries – the Romantics, Schopenhauer – who similarly claim that art is revelatory of ultimate truths, but less clearly distinguish art from philosophy (often quite purposefully). This distinction is, however, not only philosophically plausible (art and philosophy do seem to be importantly different from one another), but also fruitful for the analysis of art. For it generates Hegel's and Schelling's most influential claim concerning art: that artistic representation is distinctive not only because of its form, but because of the relationship between meaning and form of representation, i.e. the "unity" of form and its content, specifically of *sensible* form (the configuration of a particular medium, the composition and character of the art object as a particular thing) with *ideal*, metaphysical content.

Artistic representation: the unity of form and content

On Schelling's view, the distinctive artistic mode of representation is the "symbol," which he elucidates by contrasting it to the "schema" and the "allegory" (Schelling 1989: 46). Each of these modes of representation comprises a relationship between universal and particular: the schema is the use of a universal to mean (designate, interpret) a particular – as, e.g. when children use a flashcard image of a triangle to learn to recognize particular, triangularly shaped objects – while allegory is the use of a particular to mean (refer to, indicate) a universal, as when the Euclidean geometer uses a drawing of a particular triangle to show truths about the essence of triangles. The symbol combines these two modes of representation: the particular means the universal, *and* vice versa; therefore, Schelling concludes (rather strongly), the symbol both has meaning and *is* its meaning (Schelling 1989: 49). Schelling's chief examples of symbols are the Greek gods, which are both particulars – individual agents with specific characters – and universals, whether aspects of nature that belong to many phenomena (e.g. light), aspects of human practices (e.g. warlikeness, invention), or virtues (e.g. wisdom). These gods may be interpreted as allegorical – Apollo stands for (the idea of) healing – or schematic – Athena, as goddess of form, can identify the common element among philosophy and the productive arts, thus allowing us to recognize and class them. But both interpretations are falsifying, missing the fundamental union of universal and particular in them, as suggested by the reversibility of the "direction" of interpretation; Apollo *is* both a particular god and the power of healing (Schelling 1989: 43).

These distinctions concern, first and foremost, the content of art (e.g. Greek mythology), and Schelling suggests that symbolic content itself distinguishes artistic representation. But Schelling also (albeit not entirely consistently) iterates his distinctions at the level of artistic form: the artwork as a particular object may be allegorically or symbolically (or possibly schematically) related to its content, which is in turn itself symbolic. Like the Greek gods, the art object that represents such content – when it achieves full symbolic status – does not merely "signify" it, but "is" its meaning (Schelling 1989: 83, 147).

Hegel contrasts artistic representation to other representations somewhat similarly. Ordinary representations – "mere signs" – do not, Hegel claims, comprise a unity of representation and represented, but indicate their content or object merely by convention, as, e.g. "snow" and "neige" both refer to snow, according to different conventions. By contrast, artistic representations instantiate or exemplify their meaning (as, e.g. white paint instantiates or exemplifies whiteness) and thus are not merely linked to, but unified with, the universal they instantiate. On Hegel's view, artistic representations may, however, attain to different degrees of "unity" with their content. (Schelling also in practice takes there to be such degrees of unity, but does not treat this issue directly.) The complete unity of form and content is, on Hegel's view, to be found in Greek art or "the Ideal," in which sensible form perfectly expresses, and is thoroughly determined by, its ideal meaning (Hegel 1975: 763–4). But art also takes two other forms: the Symbolic (primarily characterizing art made in civilizations prior to the Greeks) and the Romantic (characterizing Christian and post-Christian art), in which the characteristic Ideas are not perfectly, seamlessly expressible in sensible form. Such Ideas are (respectively) too abstract and all-encompassing to be presented in a particular form, or concern the "inward," "subjective" or "reflective" that cannot be adequately expressed in external, sensible form (Hegel 1975: 75–80, 1971: 295–7). Thus, in these types of art, the Idea represented is more evoked or suggested than directly presented, or is presented *as* beyond this particular, sensible representation.

It is probably not coincidental that Hegel chose "symbol," Schelling's term for art as such, to denote art that reaches for representation of something that is in principle not so representable. Though Schelling himself does *not* use "symbol" to describe a work aiming to present an always ungraspable (conception of the) Absolute – quite the contrary – on Hegel's view, Schelling's conception of the Absolute is in fact ungraspable both for human thought and in sensible representation. Likewise, Hegel's use of "Romantic" to denote the striving, never fully externalized nature of modern art (and subjectivity) is, surely, meant to evoke the Romantics and their conception of the Absolute and the never-quite-knowable or representable nature of the subject.

Though Hegel does mean to suggest that Symbolic and Romantic art fail to attain to the full, complete essence or value of art, these are nonetheless not pejorative or exclusionary terms: both are, still, valuable exemplars of art. (Hegel reserves his pejorative, exclusionary scorn for Romantic irony, which he takes to be the self-assertion of mere, negative subjectivity, the mere denial of one's endorsement or identity with any claim or value.) Specifically, the sensible forms of Symbolic and Romantic artworks are, on Hegel's view, nonetheless distinct both from mere "signs" and from philosophical representation. For the particular character of the artwork is expressive of the Idea – even of the beyond-ness of that Idea – not merely indicative of a meaning entirely separable (and independently conceivable) from itself. Thus, Hegel claims that the "abstractness" of the Symbolic Idea entails and is shown in the "unrest," "exaggeration," "indefiniteness," "immensity" and "diffuseness" of sensible forms (Hegel 1975: 76). The Symbolic artist does not, that is, merely *say* (as a negative theologian might) that the One (God) is both the source of being for all things and unfathomable, beyond all particular objects or specific description, but shows it through elevated "extravagance" of forms.

This claim concerning the unity of form and content is both appealing and somewhat puzzling, particularly in its more extreme formulations, e.g. that the content is in no way referred to, but exists solely *within*, that object (as the Greek gods perhaps were understood to "inhabit" their sculptural representations). (For discussion of the difficulties of this doctrine in Hegel, see Geuss 1983.) This claim cannot, moreover, be understood to mean the *identity* of form and content, as both Hegel and Schelling emphasize: in order to be meaningful, to be (re)presentational at all, the particular sensible object must indicate something beyond and (in some sense) different from, its character simply as a particular object. Nonetheless, we may say, first, that such unity is understood to mean that the sensible properties of the object are not conventionally, but intrinsically, connected to the Idea represented; thus they suggest (respectively) that Egyptian pyramids symbolize death (the organizing Idea of Egyptian society) or the "eternal immutability" of the elements of nature because they are inorganic and rigid in shape and material (Hegel 1975: 654; Schelling 1989: 172). Moreover, as both emphasize, there are no superfluous, inexpressive properties in the artwork; all are determined by the Idea. Correspondingly, the Idea represented in an artwork is not (fully) articulable without reference to the particular artistic representation. Thus one might say that *Romeo and Juliet* expresses the essence of romantic love – and one cannot characterize such love without reference to the actions, characters, images, specific language, by which it is portrayed in the drama. Hence the difficulty of translation of literary works, or one's need to experience an artwork directly in order fully to appreciate its meaning. (This claim is, however, complicated by the claim that art presents – in some sense – the "same" content as does philosophy, namely, the Absolute.)

In any case, and importantly for both Hegel and Schelling, as such unity of form and content, the artwork inhabits an intermediary position between mere sensibility or particularity and that which is beyond sensible particulars (universal ideas of being, virtue, or value) (Hegel 1975: 35, 38). This claim constitutes a chief continuity between their aesthetic theory and the prior German tradition begun with Baumgarten, with the addendum suggested by Kant – namely, the doctrines that beauty is characteristic of representations both akin to yet different from pure rational representation, and that it is therefore suited to represent transcendent, metaphysical, rational ideas. Also like their German predecessors, Hegel and Schelling use this doctrine to characterize the traditionally identified value of art: beauty.

Beauty in art and nature

As noted above, Hegel's and Schelling's definition of art – the sensible presentation of the Absolute – is an evaluative definition. They do provide metaphysical definitions of art – they attempt to identify what art is (as opposed, for example, to many eighteenth century aestheticians, who attempt to explain, rather, why we like it) – and these definitions also *refer* to metaphysical truths (art presents these). Nonetheless, "art" is used as a normative concept: it identifies objects that are of value (because they present metaphysical truths), and only objects that do so will count as artworks proper. The evaluative character of this concept of art is shown even more distinctly in their assimilation of it to the concept of beauty. Schelling usually identifies the character of art (as symbolic, the presentation of the infinite in the finite, etc.) with beauty (Schelling 1978: 225–6, 1989: 29, 160). Hegel's account is more nuanced: all art presents the Absolute in sensible form. Beauty is, in turn, the *perfectly adequate* presentation of the Absolute in sensible form; this is accomplished in the "Ideal" (classical Greek art). Unlike Schelling, then, Hegel explicitly leaves room for non-beautiful works of art, for degrees of artistic beauty, and for other aesthetic values such as sublimity or expressiveness (which characterize Symbolic and some Romantic art on his view). This nuance is, in fact, theoretically necessary for both Hegel's and Schelling's treatments of the art forms in their lectures. For, like Hegel, Schelling argues that some works, because of the constraints of their content or medium, present the Absolute less completely (are less beautiful), but he nonetheless understands them to be art.

In so defining beauty, Hegel and Schelling return to the neo-Platonic conception of beauty (as propounded, for example, by Plotinus): the immediately perceivable presence of an Idea in a particular, sensible object, the recognition of which can educate the individual towards direct, purely intellectual apprehension of the Ideas themselves. Unlike the neo-Platonists, however, Hegel and Schelling take this conception of beauty to establish the superiority of artistic beauty over natural beauty. Explicitly inverting the traditional view (that art imitates nature), Schelling claims that "what art creates in its perfection is the principle and norm for the judgment of natural beauty" (Schelling 1978: 227). Hegel, likewise, asserts that art is "higher" than natural beauty, which is a mere "reflection" of artistic beauty (Hegel 1975: 2).

This judgment appears, in part, to be motivated by their great appreciation for art and estimation of its value by comparison to that of natural beauty; e.g. music appears *prima facie* to be more valuable than natural arrangements of sound, even birdsong. Both Hegel and Schelling argue more explicitly, however, that natural beauty is inferior to artistic beauty for two, related reasons: natural objects have no "content" or meaning (and/or such meaning is not easily discerned), and they are only contingently beautiful (not as a result of their essential natures). Both of these reasons rest upon the different ontological status of natural objects as opposed to artworks: natural objects are not purposefully addressed to conscious recognition and enjoyment by human beings.

In appreciating natural beauty, they suggest, human beings merely project ideal significance or human interest onto natural things. Thus human beings appreciate natural beauty as "in harmony with" emotional moods, but "here significance does not belong to the objects as such, but must be sought in the emotional mood they arouse" (Hegel 1975: 131; cf. Schelling 1989: 86–7). More generally, though natural objects are determined by the Absolute or Ideas – e.g. material objects are essentially governed by rationally articulated laws – they are understood to be such externally, by theoretical intelligence.

The consequences of this view for the comparative beauty of art and nature may be read in a weaker or stronger way. More weakly: natural objects are less easily perceived to have significance, to be determined in their character by universal laws, than are artworks. Thus, Hegel writes, "Human interest, the spiritual value possessed by an event, an individual character, an action ... is grasped in the work of art and blazoned more purely and ... transparently than is possible on the ground of ... non-artistic things" (Hegel 1975: 29). By contrast to the possibly opaque significance of natural objects, the "external shape" of the work of art is that "whereby the [ideal] content is made visible and imaginable" (Hegel 1975: 71; cf. Schelling 1989: 190). As Hegel suggests, however, this claim may also be read more strongly: natural objects do not merely have less discernible significance, but have *no* meaning or content; they do not *refer* to the laws that govern them. By contrast, art has content, can mean something, can present Ideas *as* their meanings – none of which needs, then, to be merely projected by the viewer.

Artworks have and present such meaning "purely and transparently" because they are the product of conscious, communicative activity. Unlike natural objects, artworks are not "naively self-centered" but are "essentially a question, an address to the responsive breast, a call to the mind and spirit" (Hegel 1975: 71). In Schelling's more abstract terms, unlike art, natural objects are only contingently (found) beautiful (Schelling 1978: 227). It is coincidental (not a necessary result of the laws that govern them) that the essences of natural objects are transparent for perception, or that they are found beautiful, whatever one might understand beauty to be. By contrast, artworks are *essentially* a "call to a responsive breast"; in being (found) beautiful, artworks fulfill their intended characters, are adequate to their essences.

Though these arguments contain some persuasive observations, they appear to beg the question concerning the priority of artistic over natural beauty. For they employ a conception of beauty derived from a consideration of art (as meaningful, as a product of "spirit" made for conscious recognition). More broadly, they seem to rest on prior philosophical commitments to the ontological and normative superiority of the creations of "spirit" over mere nature (e.g. Hegel 1975: 2). By contrast – as Kant among others had argued – one might value natural beauty more than artistic beauty precisely because it is contingent: such contingency might not only intensify the unexpected order and delight therein that might define beauty, but also might be of philosophical, human significance because thereby – unexpectedly, not by our design – nature is shown to be amenable to human purposes. (This possibility is indeed noted at Schelling 1989: 49.)

These difficulties might be avoided somewhat by reframing Hegel's and Schelling's claims. Despite their reference to "beauty," it might be more accurate to understand them to be the first modern aestheticians to concentrate on *artistic* (rather than aesthetic) value, on that which is left unregarded by theories of beauty in general, e.g. as Hegel suggests, the "human interests" portrayed in artworks. Indeed Danto, a neo-Hegelian philosopher of art, claims that Hegel's importance as a philosopher of art lies in his recognition that beauty is "inessential to art" (Danto 2000: xii). Their proposed understanding of beauty in turn might be understood to identify the central *artistic* value as the unity of form and content, whether or not this is identified with beauty. And, though neither Hegel nor Schelling suggests so, their conception of artistic value does seem to accommodate great art that is not (obviously) beautiful. Thus, to take an anachronistic example, Anselm Kiefer's paintings might be understood as successful art because they are terrifying, bleak presentations of the essence of war, as horrible destruction, i.e. not because they are beautiful, but because they unite form and content. Hegel's and Schelling's own deep appreciation of Greek tragedy might suggest such a view as well: tragedies may well be great, but also not clearly characterized by the harmony and tranquility characteristic of beauty (Schelling 1978: 225; Hegel 1975: 85).

We shall now turn, however, to more detailed consideration of their claims concerning artistic activity and artworks. As we have seen, Hegel and Schelling (in the *System*) conceive of art both as a form of self-consciousness and as a presentation of the Absolute, Ideas, or the Divine. These two conceptions of art are united because, they argue, the Absolute is best understood as a form of (non-individualized) self-consciousness (Hegel 1975: 8, 1971: 298; Schelling 1978: 7). The correct understanding of the Absolute – of the nature of being as a systematic totality – must be reflexive: it must be conceived as including, within itself, cognizance and explanation of the possibility of that very theoretical conception of it (i.e., of consciousness and self-consciousness). Correlatively, they argue that human self-consciousness is best understood in terms of one's conception of the "divine": one understands oneself in recognizing the universal moral laws, socially shared norms, unconditional truths, etc., to which one is most deeply committed, on which one acts, which identify one's place in the world and society (Hegel 1975: 65–8) or, more abstractly, one recognizes one's true being in recognizing one's connection to the "all" (Schelling 1989: 34). For our purposes, however, these aspects of their theories are better discussed separately: their doctrines concerning art as self-consciousness concern the structure of artistic activity and reception in general, whereas their claims concerning the presentation of the Absolute in sensible, particular form concern artistic subject matters and media.

Art as self-consciousness: creativity and reception

According to Hegel and Schelling, art "presents" the Absolute in part performatively, not by its signified content, but by instantiating the Absolute (as self-consciousness) in artistic processes and products: the creation and reception of art instantiates human self-consciousness as self-objectifying or self-productive.

Schelling: unity of conscious and unconscious, finite and infinite

On Schelling's view in the *System* (but not in the lectures), the Absolute is understood as self-producing, self-intuiting self-consciousness, which oscillates between two opposed activities, unconscious "productive" activity and conscious, free, knowing activity. The self is, however, fundamentally identical; it is both of these activities. The self attempts to gain self-consciousness – to recognize its own identity – by striving to overcome the opposition between its two activities, to recognize itself in its unconscious productivity. Artistic activity and its products are of signal importance for this project of self-consciousness, as its most fulfilled instance.

Artistic activity

Following Kant, Schelling understands artistic creativity or "genius" to combine activity in accord with conscious intentions – to produce a work of a certain kind – and unconscious activity ruled by "nature": the artist does not produce a work in accord with her conceptually worked out scheme alone, but also is (in traditional terms) inspired, pressed to create from an involuntary, obscure "feeling of inner contradiction" (Schelling 1978: 222). In the product of this activity – the work of art – the contradiction between conscious and unconscious activity (obscurely felt by the artist) is reconciled, the ultimate unity of the two is revealed. For the artwork is not merely a hodgepodge, an awkward combination of conscious elements and unconscious, accidental elements, but rather a unity, weaving together the artist's conscious planning, learned skills and "industry" with unplanned, inspired touches, which "involuntarily impart...unfathomable depth" to the work "which he does not understand himself, and whose meaning is infinite" (Schelling 1978: 223–4).

In the successful work of art, therefore, one can apprehend the unity of unconscious and conscious activity, thereby realizing the goal proposed by the project of self-consciousness (Schelling 1978: 219, 221, 225). In particular, artistic activity comprises the unification of freedom and necessity, of voluntary, conceptually guided activity and compulsion, and thereby exemplifies the unification of these that must be attributed to ultimate reality (Schelling 1978: 236).

Reception and interpretation

In the *System*, Schelling focuses on artistic activity rather than upon reception of artworks, but his view entails some conclusions about the latter as well. The audience, like the artist, can perceive the union of freedom and necessity in the artwork; such unity is revelatory not simply of the artist's self-consciousness, but of the workings of self-consciousness more generally, in which the audience, as well, participates. And, just as the artist engages and "objectifies" all aspects of human self-consciousness, so too does the artwork address and engage the "whole man" in the recipient, feeling and reason, perception and thought (Schelling 1978: 233).

Moreover, precisely because the artist has "instinctively...depicted [in the work] an infinity, which no finite understanding is capable of developing to the full" (Schelling 1978: 225), the artist and audience are in the same position: like the audience, the artist comes to perceive that which she did not intend, which is beyond her conscious cognizance, in the work. Every artwork, Schelling writes, is "capable of being expounded *ad infinitum*, as though it contained an infinity of purposes, while yet one is never able to say whether this infinity has lain within the artist ... or resides ... in the work of art" (Schelling 1978: 225). This moment of reception – of disentangling the complex, never completely articulated content of the artwork – is a performative "presentation" of the infinite in the finite: artworks are finite objects that provoke an infinite elaboration of possible interpretations. (This connotation of Schelling's "infinite" is inherited from the Kantian concept of "aesthetic ideas"; it is emphasized in Hammermeister 2002.)

On the view of the *System*, in sum, art is the "organ" of philosophy, even superior to philosophy, because it does not merely *describe* (conceptually) the unity of nature and freedom in the Absolute, but *instantiates* and "objectifies" this unity in both artist and recipient; it engages and makes us conscious of unconscious activity in unity with conscious activity, and as our own. In Schelling's later, more Spinozistic lectures, the Absolute is reconceived as "God," the ultimate, primal being, which unites within itself, is "indifferent" between, the fundamental antitheses (subject and object, finite and infinite, etc.) that characterize particular entities, which "indifference" is more portrayed in art than instantiated in it. Artistic activity is, therefore, no longer conceived here as the paradigmatic activity of human self-consciousness and thereby the revelation of the Absolute, but rather as God "working through" human beings

(Schelling 1989: 84). Schelling continues, however, to hold that artistic activity comprises a combination of "ideality" and "reality," of knowledge and (unconscious) activity (Schelling 1989: 28, 30) and that the infinity in artworks is thus present as infinite interpretability (Schelling 1989: 50).

Hegel: freedom and expression

Hegel concurs with Schelling that artistic activity requires both natural gifts and conscious intent or learned technique: to produce vivid, sensuously concrete representations of Ideas (i.e. art), the artist cannot solely employ universal rules, learned technique, and knowledge of the "deep interests" of human beings – though such skills and knowledge are necessary – but must also have the natural gift of creative imagination (Hegel 1975: 26, 39–41). Unlike Schelling, then, Hegel appears to hold that the content of artistic representation is planned and conscious, whereas "nature" is required to give this content an appropriate sensible form. But more important for Hegel is the free "self-production" characteristic of artistic activity (Hegel 1975: 31).

In general terms, Hegel, like Schiller, understands human theoretical and practical consciousness as developmental in structure. The subject is most immediately immersed in sensible, natural particularity, but can (then) "criticize" that given nature in light of universal norms or concepts – asking, e.g. should I act upon these desires? What is the essence or ultimate reality underlying that particular appearance? – thus freeing itself from unquestioning determination by given nature. By articulating "the depth of a suprasensuous world which thought pierces and sets up at first as a *beyond* in contrast with immediate consciousness and present feeling, ... the freedom of intellectual reflection ... rescues itself from the *here* and now, called sensuous reality and finitude" (Hegel 1975: 8). Comprehensive knowledge and realized freedom comprise, finally, a reconciliation of such theoretical and practical demands with naturally given particularity, i.e. an account of the essential nature of objects as determining the particular characteristics of the object (in Hegel's terms, understanding that object as an "individual"), and a self-determining transformation of given natural desires or one's environment in light of universal ethical norms (as, e.g. in political institutions) (see Hegel 1971: 299–300, 1975: 68).

This realized knowledge and freedom comprise, moreover, *self*-knowledge and self-realization. Only through the "negation" of particular givenness, is one a self at all – a subject distinct from the objects of its regard, free to determine itself, rather than simply a particular among others. But the self's "demand" for a "beyond" utterly distinct from, and indeterminate in application to, the world of particulars is insufficient for either self-knowledge or self-realization, for this demand is empty, the self simply an abstraction, having no substantive character or effects (Hegel 1975: 96). Thus, only through applying and realizing universal concepts or ethical demands (in theoretical claims or actions), can the self not only recognize her own substantive commitments and desires, but also be truly, effectively free, or indeed come to be a self in the fullest sense (Hegel 1975: 31–2).

Insofar as artistic activity comprises at once a free formulation of Ideas, meant to be the "inner" significance, value, or nature of things or of human life, and the presentation of such ideas in sensible form, artistic activity exemplifies the structure of absolute knowledge or realized freedom. The closer an artwork comes to the "Ideal," the more it succeeds in being and showing itself to be an "individual," a particular item thoroughly informed by a universal, its parts thoroughly unified and inter-dependent. Following Kant, Hegel takes such order to be analogous to the unity of organisms, in which the parts are what they are only in the context of the organism as a whole, or (somewhat metaphorically) in which the Idea unifies the object as the "life" or "soul" of the external shape (Hegel 1975: 982–4). (Schelling also follows Kant in suggesting various analogies between art and organisms; e.g. Schelling 1989: 9, 1978: 219.)

On Hegel's view, artistic activity, as expression, is also an activity of self-reali-zation. By presenting universal norms or ideals in particular, sensible form, art both renders them more determinate and thereby makes "inner" commitments "external," recognizable. Thus through art one's commitments are not only known, but also (in part) thereby "produced" – made concrete and rendered explicitly, self-consciously valuable. (Charles Taylor has emphasized this clarificatory and productive character of expression, as understood both by Hegel and by Herder; see Taylor 1975. It is also central to the conception of art as expression proposed by the twentieth-century aesthetician, R. J. Collingwood.) As such expression, artistic activity is also an exercise of human freedom; it comprises both the self-determining demand for necessary truths or universal norms and the transformative "return" to the sensible, natural world – here the transformation of sensible materials *into* representational "form." As noted above, such activity is not, for Hegel, fundamentally individualist, expressing the artist's own, idiosyncratic feelings or attitudes; the achievement of the artist is an achievement of and for the artist's community at large, expressing its ideals, norms, values, world views, thus rendering the community as a whole self-conscious, aware of its metaphysical and normative commitments. (Here Hegel is quite different from later expressivists such as Collingwood.) Thus Hegel writes concerning Greek art: "the artists became for the Greeks the creators of their gods, i.e., the artists gave the nation a definite idea of the behaviour, life, and effectiveness of the Divine ... . And it was not as if these ideas ... were already there, *in advance* of poetry, in an abstract mode of consciousness ... and then later were only clothed in imagery by artists ... . on the contrary, the mode of artistic production was such that what fermented in these poets they could work out *only* in this form of art" (Hegel 1975: 102).

Presentation of the absolute in the arts: art forms, content and history

The preceding characterizations of artistic process apply to all works of art – in the *System*, Schelling indeed claims that "there is properly speaking but one absolute work of art" (Schelling 1978: 231). But because they also understand art to *present* the Absolute, they attend in detail, systematically, to art objects themselves, to differences of content (conceptions of the Absolute), form, and historical change.

Artistic content

Hegel and Schelling attend more searchingly to the represented content of artworks as fundamental to their nature and value, and as definitive of artistic periods or styles, than nearly any other aesthetic theorist before or since. (For a representative contrasting view, see Schiller 1982: 154–7.) Their understanding of artistic representation – as the unity of form and content – dictates this focus and entails some conclusions about appropriate artistic content: it must be conceived as sufficiently individualized (a unity of universal *and* particular, in Schelling's terms) to be representable in and by a particular object (the artwork). Thus, for example, a fully articulated theory of physics – which could constitute an aspect of the fully worked out Idea or the Absolute – might not be susceptible to artistic representation (at least without considerable artistic reformulation). But they also suggest two further, related conditions governing appropriate artistic content: it should reflect the comprehensive world views of the historical period and society in which it is made, and it must be *worthy* of representation, as an Idea of the fundamental character of being or highest values.

For Hegel and Schelling, therefore, art is intimately connected to religion – a society's comprehensive, evaluative world view; artistic content is understood, as we have seen, either as "the divine" (Hegel) or "mythology" (Schelling). (On both views, religion may also include non-representational practices, e.g. confession, and other forms of representation, but artistic representation may be the primary form of representation within many religions.) This understanding of art renders their philosophies of art – unlike many eighteenth-century (and later) theories of art as autonomous – more accurate to the origin, function and character of many canonical artworks of the Western tradition, and indeed in non-Western society (though Hegel deems the latter "defective" art, and Schelling dismisses it without much consideration). Not only classical Greek art, but also Bach's *Passions*, Gothic cathedrals, Michelangelo's *Pieta*, Milton's *Paradise Lost*, Rumi's poetry, Maori carvings, and Egyptian pyramids are informed by, and receive their meaning within, the religious views and practices of their originating societies. As Hegel and Schelling aver – and as has been an ongoing source of debate concerning the rightfulness of museum exhibition of such objects – the religious content and social function of these objects seem not only to be constitutive of them, but also (at least in part) to ground the high estimation of their value not only within their original societies, but for others as well, as reflective of specific ways of life, and as expressive of our highest aspirations and comprehensive understandings of the human place in the world (Hegel 1975: 30).

This focus on artistic content allows Hegel and Schelling, then, to account not only for the traditional embeddedness of artworks within societal practices and world views, but also thereby for historical and cultural variations in artistic content *and* style (or manner of representation), as (at least in part) determined by the varying religious conceptions of those societies. So Hegel analyzes Symbolic form, as noted above. One might suggest, similarly, that anthropomorphic religions, such as classical Greek religion, employ idealizing yet also "naturalist" modes of artistic representation (e.g. physically ideal human bodies), whereas Christianity – with its emphasis upon spirituality as separate from the body – would engender anti-realist forms of representation, in order to convey the non-materiality of that which is of ultimate value, as, e.g. the elongated figures in El Greco's painting suggest spiritual alteration and transcendence of the body. Thus – as against crude conceptions of historical progress in the arts, grounded on the conception of art as "imitation" – Hegel argues that often the "abandonment and distortion of natural formations is not unintentional lack of technical skill ... but intentional alteration which ... is demanded by what is in the artist's mind" (Hegel 1975: 74).

This view of art thus accounts not only for philosophical, but also anthropological, historical and art-historical attention to artworks as revelatory of societal practices and values (Hegel 1975: 7). But both Hegel and Schelling understand these varying conceptions not simply to be historical facts about different societies, but also as contributions – albeit incomplete – to the (development of their own) comprehensive knowledge of the Absolute. (Thus, although Hegel may be understood as the progenitor of twentieth-century Marxist and of "institutional" theories of art, he does not hold that art is *simply* to be identified with whatever objects a society identifies as art, or embeds in relevant institutions; art must also contribute to our understanding of the Absolute.) Hegel and Schelling interpret the Greek gods (for example) not as purported entities (in the existence of which the Greeks believed, and we do not), but rather as coalesced, individualized instantiations of the union of natural forces and human virtues (Schelling) or the presence of "spirit," as free, within the natural world (Hegel), i.e. of the reconciled unity between freedom and nature that must characterize the Absolute. Indeed they transpose Schiller's arguments about the effects of beauty and art – it educates towards freedom, may train recipients to harmonize rational freedom and nature – into their characterization of the content of art: art "unveils the truth" because it "set[s] forth the reconciled opposition" between nature and freedom (Hegel 1975: 55).

Hegel and Schelling therefore conceive of "divine" content more extensively than might originally appear, to include less explicitly religious content. For Hegel "God" – the Absolute – is in, works through, self-determining human beings (Hegel 1975: 30); thus the representation of realized human freedom constitutes "divine" content even more than does the representation of gods as external to human existence. That is, religious conceptions of gods are rightly understood as formulated by human beings, as part of human self-understanding; however, such an understanding does not devalue those religious conceptions, but rather reveals the "divinity," the absolute value, of human free self-conception. Schelling's view in the *System* might entail similar conclusions concerning artistic content (which is not extensively discussed there). On the conception of the Absolute in the lectures (as the indifferent union of antithetical attributes), it may be represented not only by mythological gods, but also (for example) in paintings representing light and color as, at once, natural and belonging to material objects ("real"), and as perceived, shown appearance ("ideal").

As a result, this conception of art can also characterize artworks in the modern period that express an individual's own feelings or distinctive world view (in contrast to pre-modern artistic portrayal of socially shared values and conceptions). For Hegel and Schelling argue that these works (and corresponding theories of art) reflect the characteristic, socially shared and articulated norms, ideals, and ways of life of Western modernity: the (secularized Christian) valuation of the individual person as an "end in himself" (to use a Kantian phrase), of individual moral struggle and resignation. Thus, for example, Schelling suggests that by contrast to traditional, socially shared and socially created conceptions of mythology, modern literature presents unique "worlds" created by distinctive individuals, drawing upon their own experience and their own creative originality (Schelling 1989: 75). In a typically reflexive way, then, Hegel and Schelling identify art in the modern period as "individualized" both in artistic content *and* in the practice and conception of art itself.

Hegel's and Schelling's concentration on artistic content also engenders illuminating discussions of artworks, by contrast to aesthetic theories of response or imitation. For example, tragedy was much discussed in the eighteenth century, as giving rise to a puzzle about audience response – why do we enjoy seeing suffering and other troubling events? – to which question theorists proposed various psychological explanations (sympathy, Schadenfreude). By contrast, Hegel argues that tragedy portrays the conflict of objective goods, an argument that is justly famous both as an analysis of the structure and content of tragedy and (thereby) as an articulation of crucial problems for human ethical action (Hegel 1975: 1194–9, 1208–37). Less famously, Schelling argues that Greek tragedies – taking *Oedipus Rex* rather than Hegel's favored *Antigone* as his central case – portray the Absolute as the "indifference" of freedom and necessity (clearly shown also, nonetheless, to be opposed or antithetical). In tragedy, human, freely chosen action is shown to be opposed to an oppressive, inescapable necessity, fate. Such freedom is also, however, shown to be compatible with that necessity: human beings can "freely accept misfortune" by assuming responsibility and voluntarily atoning even for fated guilt (as when Oedipus blinds himself). Thus, Schelling suggests, the tragic hero's free moral character, far from being destroyed by fate, is even "victorious" over it (Schelling 1989: 250–5, 89). Correspondingly, tragedies support ("indifferently") interpretations that emphasize the fatedness or the moral freedom of actions, and, through the representation of the chorus, both impose necessary reactions upon spectators as the appropriate ones *and* thereby liberate the spectators to reflect upon those reactions (Schelling 1989: 259–60). Such treatments of tragedy are, precisely as Hegel and Schelling claim, considerably closer to the character of the objects, which are taken to have cognitive, depictive value in themselves, than the explanations of human psychological responses (pleasures in tragedy) proffered by their predecessors.

Similarly, Hegel suggests a provocative reading of Dutch still life painting, which would seem, *prima facie*, to be the paradigm achievement of art as imitation (for which reason Schelling deems it not very important art). Hegel suggests that the value of these beautiful imitations may be explained not only by their mimetic accuracy and the skill required to produce it, but because the paintings thereby "recreate … the existent and fleeting appearance of nature as something generated afresh [and rendered permanent] by man" (Hegel 1975: 162–3). These paintings have historical-social meaning as well, for they reflect the struggles of the Dutch for religious, commercial, and political freedom: "the citizenship, this love of enterprise, in small things as in great ... this painstaking as well as cleanly and neat well-being, this joy ... in their ... sense that for all this they have their own activity to thank, all this is what constitutes the general content of their pictures" (Hegel 1975: 169).

System of the arts

Their conception of art likewise leads Hegel and Schelling to attend to the material or sensible character of artworks, as elaborated in their systematic accounts (in the lectures) of the different art forms. The details of these accounts are too numerous to be treated here, and some aspects of them – notably Hegel's attempt to conjoin art forms with historical periods (he claims that architecture is pre-eminently Symbolic, sculpture classical, and the three other arts Romantic) – have been much criticized. We may note here, however, several central points.

First, the detailed, differentiated treatment of artistic media is dictated by the definition of art as unity of form and content: the sensible or particular form, its medium – words, three dimensional material forms, colored surface, sound – is, on this view, essential to the art object. The differences among these media are significant because they therefore can present different contents (different construals or aspects of the Absolute) (Hegel 1975: 73; Schelling 1989: 48, 162). More specifically, Hegel's differentiation among the media is based on their different sensible properties, because he conceives of art as the sensible presentation of the Idea. By contrast, because Schelling defines art as a particular that represents the unity of universal and particular (the symbol), he differentiates art forms – the character of the object as a particular – in accord with one of his fundamental antitheses, that between "real" and "ideal": poetry alone is an ideal art because language, its medium, is ideational, universal and cognitive, whereas the other art forms employ material media (stone, paint, sound) (Schelling 1989: 98–103, 201–2).

Thus Hegel's and Schelling's views can incorporate ways to differentiate artworks common in the more applied study of the arts, and renders attention to medium important for understanding particular artworks (more than is warranted or accomplished in nearly all other aesthetic theories) (see, for example, Hegel's treatment of the various sculptural media and their meanings in Hegel 1975: 775–7). The systematic treatment of different art forms also, however, brings to the forefront two *prima facie* problems for their general conception of art: how to accommodate art forms that are not clearly representational (of an Idea or otherwise) and how to understand art forms that do not seem to employ *sensible* means of representation or are not obviously composed of particular elements as such, namely literature, which employs language, i.e. conventional and discursive signs.

Schelling and (more explicitly) Hegel respond to these paired difficulties, first, by ordering the art forms in a spectrum, from one semiotic extreme to another: both end their treatments of art forms with literature, suggesting that literature is a limit-case of artistic production (closest to philosophy or conceptual representation), and begin their treatments with art forms that represent ideal content only in a limited way. Specifically, Hegel identifies architecture, Schelling music, as initial, more "sensible" or "real" modes of artistic representation. Hegel claims that architecture does not by itself present spiritual meaning. Rather, it reforms the natural environment to produce a "place" for spiritual, human practices (primarily of religious worship and community) and to become more "akin" to spirit in having intellectually recognizable order (e.g. symmetry) (Hegel 1975: 84). Schelling claims that music represents the Absolute – as a unity of universal and particular – abstractly as the unity of multiplicity in rhythm and melody (quantitatively and qualitatively unified sequences of particular tones, respectively) and in harmony (a single sound that also unifies many). Thus, Schelling suggests, music may be understood to represent the most basic characteristics of both matter and mind – the continuity of motion and the persistence of self-consciousness through temporal change. And, in accord with his analysis of artistic representation, Schelling argues that musical works not only *mean* such unity (of motion and consciousness) but *are* motion (these sounds are vibrations of objects and of air) and (as heard) unified consciousness (Schelling 1989: 109, 111, 116). (Schelling provides a more complex version of the Hegelian proposal concerning architecture, while Hegel takes music, as non-spatial, primarily to represent subjective, internal states such as moods and feelings.)

On the other hand, both Hegel and Schelling attempt to identify "sensible" or "poetic" aspects of linguistic presentation in order to distinguish literary representation from mere "prose." Both claim that poetic representation is distinct from much other linguistic representation because of its content (as discussed above), but also emphasize the sonorous characteristics of poetic language such as rhyme and meter. Hegel argues as well that figurative uses of language (primarily metaphor) are a "sensible" medium because they appeal to the imagination or call forth images (Hegel 1975: 1000–34; cf. Schelling 1989: 204–6). Such concerns also lead them to identify drama as the highest literary genre, where a "complete and specific action" is given a "fully visible presentation" (Hegel 1975: 1192; cf. Schelling 1989: 261).

This treatment of art forms in a "spectrum" is not only meant to be a comprehensive account of the similarities and differences among the arts, but also, like their general definition of art, is evaluative: each art form is judged in accord with the norm for art in general, and therefore ranked in accord with its ability to present the highest content (i.e. the most complete portrayal of the Absolute) sensibly or in a particular. Because of the resources of linguistic representation, both judge that poetry (literature) is most able to portray a complete world view, but it is also the least "sensible" art form (Hegel), or presents least the "real" character of the Absolute (Schelling). Thus, both claim that the "mean" between the two extremes – sculpture, for both, as well as drama, for Schelling – is the best art, the perfect unity of sensible form and ideal content or symbolic "indifference" between ideal and real.

These rankings of the art forms do not have much contemporary interest (though they were a prevalent concern for aestheticians until the twentieth century), and Hegel's and Schelling's ranking of Greek sculpture as the paramount art might well be attributable to the influence of Winckelmann. Their evaluative treatment of the art forms could, however, be fruitful for broader considerations of the systematic differentiation and media-specificity of artistic values. For it is apparent that different artistic values are more or less salient in the discussion of different art forms; expressiveness (particularly of emotion) is a more salient value for music, while realism is more salient for understanding painting and literature. For such reasons, twentieth-century philosophers have suggested that there ought to be "philosophies of the arts" rather than a philosophy of art that would one-sidedly emphasize one or another artistic value (e.g. Kivy 1997). Hegel's and Schelling's accounts might well provide a starting point for a satisfying, systematic account of artistic value, i.e. one that can articulate reasons for these evaluative differences within an overarching account of artistic ontology and value.

Art, history, and modernity

As noted above, Hegel and Schelling focus on an aspect of the human practice of art largely unacknowledged by previous philosophers: its historical development. On their view, art not only does, but through an internal necessity must, develop over the course of human history. This claim may be seen as a result of their conceptions of the Absolute: because Schelling (much of the time) and Hegel conceive of the Absolute as self-developing, they see art – as revelation of that Absolute – as essentially developmental as well.

Hegel and Schelling understand connoisseurship and art history to be concerned with the details of historical and social context that inform the character of particular works (Hegel 1975: 14, 34–5; Schelling 1989: 3). Such critical analysis is consonant with – indeed enjoined by – their conception of art (by contrast e.g. to formalist methods of art criticism that were inspired by Kant's aesthetics or contemporary neurophysiological investigation of aesthetic experience, which might be taken to be the "critical" method consonant with Burke's aesthetics). They conceive of their own task in different terms, however: to articulate the overarching structure of historical development in the arts (Hegel 1975: 12; Schelling 1989: 8–9).

This historical structure is again based upon their identification of art as an attempted unification of form and ("divine") content. Artistic change is understood as the development of new contents for art, a development that occurs hand in hand with that of new formal modes of expression; the major periods in art history are identified both by their distinctive content and by distinctive relations between that content and sensible form. Hegel's classification of art into symbolic, classical and romantic is, as noted above, both historical and semiotic (Hegel 1975: 75). Schelling similarly identifies two artistic periods – ancient (pre-eminently Greek) and modern (pre-eminently Christian) – on broadly semiotic grounds. In the first, mythology "precedes" abstract religious conceptions, and its universal content is nature, while modern religion "precedes" myth, and its universal content is providential history and moral consciousness. More abstractly, in the first case the infinite is taken to be present in all particulars (as parts of universal, infinite nature), while in the second the finite particular aims to realize a universal or infinite (as moral ideal) (Schelling 1989:

59, 61–2, 80–1). Ancient and modern art are distinguished as properly symbolic versus more allegorical (i.e. incomplete) representation. (This is Schelling's official view; in light of his claims that in ancient art "the collective will cultivate itself or develop into the ... particular" [Schelling 1989: 80] and for better symmetry in his account, however, one might identify ancient art as more schematic.)

Perhaps reflecting their conception of art as at once a socially and religiously embedded practice and as of non-instrumental value because it reveals the highest truths, Hegel and Schelling seem to suggest that artistic development is to be understood both as externally imposed upon and as produced within artistic practice. (Their focus on artistic media might have generated an account of univocally internal change through refinement of the handling of media, though they do not exploit this opportunity.) Both claim that the advent of Christianity radically changes the character of artworks, and seem to conceive of this change largely as imposed upon art "from outside" (Schelling 1989: 58–9; Hegel 1975: 80). But because they (particularly Hegel) claim that art articulates and thereby in part establishes a community's religious, moral, or philosophical commitments, such historical change can also be conceived as an internal development in the arts, a search at once for more satisfactory (representable, complete, moving) content, and for the appropriate manner of representation, as Hegel analyzes the stages of Symbolic art, for example (Hegel 1975: 303ff.).

The future of art: new mythology and the end of art

On the basis of their overarching conceptions of art history, both Hegel and Schelling make famous, controversial claims about future artistic practice. Like Schiller and his Romantic contemporaries, and anticipating Heidegger, Schelling calls for a "new mythology" that will provide a holistic conception of the Absolute, and thus address human alienation in nature and society (Schelling 1978: 233). By contrast, Hegel notoriously announces the "end of art": "art, considered in its highest vocation, is and remains for us a thing of the past"; it no longer fulfills our "highest need...which earlier nations sought in it, and found in it alone" (Hegel 1975: 10–11).

These claims – particularly Hegel's – have been the subject of much debate, the full range of which cannot be discussed here. (For a good discussion, see Bungay 1986: 71–89.) We can, however, identify two theses endorsed by both Hegel and Schelling (despite their prognostic differences): that post-Christian art does not fulfill the "highest vocation" of art – unlike Greek art and mythology – and that, despite their view of Greek art as the height of artistic excellence, its achievements are neither still "living" for modern society, nor a model for modern artistic production. (They are both in this way less classicist than many of their predecessors, who often claim that Greek art furnishes general rules or models for modern art.)

Despite continuing furor over Hegel's "end of art" claim, both of these theses are plausible, even uncontroversial. Neither denies that there are still works of art being made, even great ones; both refer to Goethe's *Faust* as a great, distinctively modern work. Rather, they claim that no modern artwork or body thereof unites the functions of Greek art, namely, the complete representation of the Absolute (divine) in particular form, an articulation of the ideals and values to which a society aspires, patterns for action and interpretation of others, and an overarching vision of the natural world and of the human place within it. Moreover, they provide plausible accounts as to why Greek art cannot serve as a model for modern art: though the Greek gods (and artistic representation thereof) do provide a glimpse of the Absolute (correctly conceived) as "indifferent" union of antitheses, or reconciliation of freedom and nature, the thus-glimpsed reconciliation no longer seems possible, given the modern conceptions of both sides of this antithesis.

Specifically, on the one hand (as Schelling argues), neither modern religions nor modern scientific conceptions endow nature with divinity (Schelling 1989: 63–6, 76–7). On the other hand, as both argue, modern (Christian and secularized Christian) conceptions of morality, freedom and subjectivity resist full externalization or symbolization. As Schelling argues, one's inner moral character, one's connection to the (morally conceived) divine, can always be further revealed through subsequent acts (or in historical events more broadly) – no one of which is, therefore, a complete symbol of the divine or infinite, but rather is understood as a transient part of an historical revelation (Schelling 1989: 72–4). Thus, Schelling observes, modern mythological figures – Don Quixote, Don Juan, Faust – are symbols precisely of unquenched desire and incompleteness, the yearning of the finite individual for the infinite, not individuals infinite (in power and blessedness) themselves, as were the Greek gods. On Hegel's view, the modern (secularized Christian) valuation of subjectivity entails that no one work will both sensibly realize that value (through concrete representation e.g. of individual points of view) *and* present that value *as* universal. The universal, shared valuation of all individuals (as such) is better expressed "reflectively," in philosophy, in political ideals such as universal human rights, and the institutions that realize those ideals (Hegel 1975: 10; that human freedom is realized by modern political institutions is the purport of Hegel's *Philosophy of Right*).

One obvious objection to Hegel's and Schelling's claim that modern religion is not susceptible to artistic treatment would seem to be Jesus Christ, who is claimed to be the divine in a particular, sensible being – and is indeed the subject matter of a great deal of art. Both Hegel and Schelling waver, however, as to whether Christ is to be conceived as an artistic subject proper. Against this proposal, they argue that Christ is not a self-contained image of the divine – whether because as suffering and then resurrected by reunion with God, Christ represents the "nullification" of the finite, not the full interpenetration of finite/particular and infinite (Schelling), or because the true meaning of Christ is not Christ the individual and/or representations thereof, but the transformation of every individual's heart, within a community (Hegel).

Hegel's and Schelling's differing claims concerning the future of art, given their (broadly) shared conception of modernity rest, finally, upon their disagreements concerning the nature of the Absolute and historical progress. For Hegel, as is well known, the Absolute is historically progressive, self-producing, intersubjective human self-consciousness. Thus the modern conception of free subjectivity is incontestably superior to pre-modern conceptions of the divine; if this conception is, as Hegel argues, incompletely representable in sensible form, then world-defining art is a necessary sacrifice to human historical self-realization. (Contra Wicks 1993, this claim concerning the decline of art is not inconsistent with Hegel's general conception of dialectical-historical progress. For art is only one form or stage of absolute spirit, the dialectical progress of which culminates in philosophy.) Though modern art is inferior *as* art, namely, as revelation of the Absolute in sensible form, to classical art, it is superior insofar as it represents – albeit only evocatively – a more accurate conception of the Absolute (Hegel 1971: 295).

For Schelling, by contrast, such a historically progressive conception is itself distinctively modern and "one-sided," emphasizing freedom, subjectivity, universality, ideality, over the equally constitutive antithetical aspects of the Absolute. Thus, though Schelling classifies art in historical terms – ancient versus modern – he takes these to be related to one another not progressively, but rather as two possible combinations between the antitheses "indifferently" united in the Absolute (myth may begin with nature or with freedom, with the infinite or with the finite, etc.), which are temporally unfolded (Schelling 1989: 81–2). On Schelling's view, it is therefore not only possible, but indeed dictated by the character of art as a revelation of the Absolute, that modern art should give rise to a "new mythology" that is properly symbolic (not weighted to the allegorical, as is modern art). Such mythology would incorporate nature, just as ancient art began with nature gods but also brought these gods "into" the realm of freedom and history (predominantly in the Homeric epic) (Schelling 1989: 82). By so incorporating nature, the "new mythology" would not only more fully present the character of the Absolute, but also be consolatory for modern human beings, who are "torn loose" from the natural world (Schelling 1989: 59).

Whether Schelling's envisioned new mythological re-enchantment of nature is possible, and whether Hegel's claims concerning the end of art can be defended in light of the vast artistic changes after 1830, are questions we cannot pursue here. What is incontestable, however, is the influence of these prognostications upon their philosophical successors, whether in the form of the re-conception of nature in the "artists' metaphysics" of Nietzsche, Kierkegaard's aesthetics of subjectivity, or Marxist philosophies of art proposed by Lukàcs and Adorno, who apply Hegelian methods and guiding concerns to new art forms (e.g. mass art), and to generate anti-Hegelian conclusions.

References

Ameriks, K. (2006) "Hegel's Aesthetics: New Perspectives on its Response to Kant and Romanticism," in *Kant and the Historical Turn: Philosophy as Critical Interpretation*, Oxford: Oxford University Press.

Bowie, A. (2003) *Aesthetics and Subjectivity from Kant to Nietzsche*, Manchester: University of Manchester Press.

Bungay, S. (1986) *Beauty and Truth: A Study of Hegel's Aesthetics*. Albany, NY: SUNY Press.

Danto, A. (2000) Foreword to J.-M. Schaeffer, *Art of the Modern Age*, Princeton, NJ: Princeton University Press.

Geuss, R. (1983) "A Response to Paul de Man," *Critical Inquiry* 10, no. 2: 375–82.

Hammermeister, K. (2002) *The German Aesthetic Tradition*, Cambridge: Cambridge University Press.

Hegel, G. W. F. (1971) *Philosophy of Mind; Part Three of the Encyclopaedia of the Philosophical Sciences (1830)*, trans. W. Wallace, Oxford: Oxford University Press.

—— (1975) *Aesthetics: Lectures on Fine Art*, trans. T. M. Knox, Oxford: Clarendon Press.

Herder, J. G. (2006) *Selected Writings on Aesthetics*, trans. G. Moore, Princeton, NJ: Princeton University Press.

Kant, I. (2000) *The Critique of the Power of Judgment*, trans. P. Guyer and E. Matthews, Cambridge: Cambridge University Press.

Kivy, P. (1997) *Philosophies of Arts: An Essay in Differences*, Cambridge: Cambridge University Press.

Kristeller, P. O. (1951) "The Modern System of the Arts I," *Journal of the History of Ideas* 12: no. 4: 496–527.

—— (1952) "The Modern System of the Arts II," *Journal of the History of Ideas* 13, no. 1: 17–46.

Schaeffer, J.-M. (2000) *Art of the Modern Age: Philosophy of Art from Kant to Heidegger*, trans. S. Rendall, Princeton, NJ: Princeton University Press.

Schelling, F. W. J. (1978) *System of Transcendental Idealism (1800)*, trans. P. Heath, Charlottesville: University of Virginia Press.

—— (1989) *The Philosophy of Art*, trans. D. W. Stott, Minneapolis: University of Minnesota Press.

Schiller, F. (1982) *On the Aesthetic Education of Man in a Series of Letters*, trans. E. M. Wilkinson and L. A. Willoughby, Oxford: Clarendon Press.

Shiner, L. (2001) *The Invention of Art*, Chicago: University of Chicago Press.

Taylor, C. (1975). *Hegel*, Cambridge: Cambridge University Press.

White, A. (1983) *Schelling: An Introduction to the System of Freedom*, New Haven: Yale University Press.

Wicks, R. (1993) "Hegel's Aesthetics: An Overview," in F. Beiser (ed.) *Cambridge Companion to Hegel*, Cambridge: Cambridge University Press, pp. 348–77.

Part II

PHILOSOPHY AS POLITICAL ACTION

7

AFTER HEGEL: THE ACTUALIZATION OF PHILOSOPHY IN PRACTICE

Michael Quante

Translated by Patrick R. Leland

The history of the debate which led from Hegel to Marx is philosophically the history of the disintegration of the Hegelian school, and socially a time of political stagnation and restoration in Germany. The debate is short-lived, but fierce and in a continual process of fermentation. Its participants are philosophers, publicists, and political thinkers who were excluded from academic life, persecuted politically, and marginalized by a politically restrictive society. To trace the history of a philosophical debate is always, in a certain respect, to tell a *story*. The perspective adopted for the narrative organizes an abundance of material, guides its selection and constitutes its inner logic. Without doubt, it is itself the expression of an epistemic interest or a philosophical thesis, for no history narrates itself. The perspective chosen for this article takes as its protagonist the young Marx. The narrative begins during the early 1830s and ends at the point where Karl Marx and Friedrich Engels take stock and come to terms with their earlier philosophical conscience: with the emergence of the *German Ideology* during the years of 1845–6.

To present the history of the philosophical debate during these fifteen years as a path from Hegel to Marx is neither original nor obligatory. Nevertheless, this article is *not* another contribution to the Marxist historiography of a progressive historical development from a bourgeois Idealism to a mature Marxism. On the contrary, I will present issues that have philosophical potential that has been submerged in the course of societal, political, and philosophical events. Some of these issues are still (or are again) an object of contemporary philosophical discussion, though without any awareness of the relation to the earlier debate. This article aims to bring the earlier debate out of obscurity and make it again available for contemporary thought.

It is the concern of this article to carry out a philosophical-historical review from a systematic perspective. Thus, the presentation does not strictly follow the chronology, but rather pursues the constellation of problems which underlie this debate. In the *first* section, two general themes which are central for the post-Hegelian discussion are presented. The *second* section concerns three models of post-Hegelian philosophy which provided decisive impulses for the formation of Marxist thought: Bruno Bauer's theory of self-consciousness, the philosophical anthropology of Ludwig Feuerbach, and the philosophy of history of Moses Hess. In the *third* section, the Marxist species metaphysics <*Gattungsmetaphysik*> from 1844 is presented as his attempt to overcome definitively the Hegelian and post-Hegelian philosophy.[1] Here, Max Stirner's criticism of post-Hegelian philosophy is shown to be of central importance. His book, *The Ego and Its Own*, was published in 1844 and had a profound effect on Marx's thought. Finally, the *fourth* section outlines the various ways in which the central themes of this debate in the history of philosophy extend to the present day.

Dimensions of the post-Hegelian debate

The multiple points of contention in the post-Hegelian debate can be organized into two problem areas: first, the relation between religion and philosophy and, second, the function of philosophy as both a critique of the present and an instrument of knowledge for the future.

Religion and philosophy

The Life of Jesus by David Friedrich Strauss as catalyst for the Hegelian school In a certain respect, *The Life of Jesus*, which first appeared in two volumes during 1835–6, is not an original book. The thoughts and reflections Strauss compiled in that work were already discussed in both the theological and the historical studies of that time, as well as in the Hegelian school and in philosophy more generally. The constellation of themes which come together in Strauss's thought, as well as the clarity and the uncompromising Hegelian account of the relation between religion and philosophy, together explain the significant attention which this book received from many quarters. The systematic application of the Hegelian philosophy to the interpretation of the Gospels, as well as what that interpretation implied about the relation of the historical person of Jesus to Christology, had a catalytic effect on the Hegelian school and contributed decisively to its disintegration.

The relation between philosophy and religion in Hegel

The account of the relation between church and state, which Hegel offered in a famous footnote to §270 of the *Elements of the Philosophy of Right*, is not the only one in need of and amenable to clarification. His determination of the relation between philosophy and religion also leaves room for interpretation. The absolute knowledge of speculative philosophy is:

the concept – cognized by thought – of art and religion, in which the diverse elements in the content are cognized as necessary and the necessary is cognized as free. (Hegel PhilM: §572; translation modified)

Philosophy "determines itself," as Hegel goes on to say,

> as a cognizing of the necessity of the content of the absolute representation as well as of the necessity of both forms: on the one hand, of immediate intuition and its poetry, and the objective and external revelation presupposed by representation. (Hegel PhilM: §573; translation modified)

Here, Hegel operates with the logic of essence's concepts of reflection of "form and content" (Hegel 1999: 77ff.), whose dialectic is difficult to comprehend. Independent of this speculative-logical explication and *a propos* the relation between philosophy and religion, Hegel says that the Christian religion contains the same content as art and philosophy. In contrast to art and religion, philosophy comprehends both the necessity of those two forms of the cognition of this content *qua* art and religion, as well as the necessity of this content itself: philosophy sublates <*aufheben*> art and religion – in the sense of preserving and elevating them. What is debatable is whether this sublation also contains a negation. In the manuscript on the philosophy of religion which originated with Hegel himself and formed the basis for his lectures, we learn of the specific cognitive achievement of philosophy:

> Now, it is this determination which contributes to the philosophical cognition of the truth; from this however it becomes immediately clear that it is only the entire speculative philosophy which is capable of doing this – and simultaneously that it has absolutely nothing to do with the annihilation of religion, i.e. to claim as though the content of religion could not be truth unto itself; rather, religion is the true content, but only in the form of the representation, and philosophy does not have to provide the substantial truth in the first place. (Hegel 1993: 159)

Whoever adopts the position that religion possesses a content which is distinct from philosophy, or even claims that religious (and theological) knowledge is above philosophy, cannot accept Hegel's account of the relation between religious and philosophical content. And whoever asks from the perspective of cognition how Hegel understood the relation of religion to philosophy must come to the conclusion that religion may very well have had this special content prior to philosophy, although only in a deficient form, and that adequate knowledge of this content is only first attained through speculative philosophy.

One can approach the phenomena of religious convictions, attitudes, and institutions by examining the ways in which cognition of the Absolute (or the self-cognition of God) is accomplished in these phenomena. One must also ask what function religious attitudes, convictions, and institutions have in man's social life. In this respect, Hegel attributes to religion not only independence from, but also a certain superiority to, philosophy. Because the Christian religion apprehends the absolute truth in the medium of representation, it is more accessible for the philosophically untrained subject and can develop more easily a motivational force out of the content which it has cast in the form of images and representations. In this way, the practice of religion functions precisely as a medium which makes the absolute truth into a living ethics. By contrast, philosophical insight into the rational nature of existing circumstances cannot, according to Hegel, be conveyed to all, and is moreover so abstract as to scarcely yield a broadly efficacious motivational foundation.

This functional account of religion is not an adequate reconstruction of the self-conception of religion, but rather paves the way for an ideological-critical inter-pretation of religious phenomenon. What is more, the claimed superiority of Hegelian philosophy is incompatible with the self-conception of religion and theology, and so Hegelian theologians were confronted with the problem of reconciling their own religious and theological praxis with their philosophical convictions.

Strauss' critique of Hegel

In *The Life of Jesus*, Strauss radicalizes that component of the Hegelian philosophy which was critical of religion. More specifically, he interprets the Gospels as the product of the hope for redemption on the part of an original Christian community which appealed to the messianic figure of the Hebrew Bible. The Jesus-mythology is said to express a content which ultimately can be reconstructed philosophically but which lacks any historically revealed truths. The Jesus myth is interpreted as the actualization of the idea of humanity, God is construed pantheistically as the infinite, and personal immortality is understood to be (merely!) an idea.

Strauss thus derives the conclusion from the sublation <Aufhebung> which was suggested by Hegel's speculative construction of form, content, and sublation. It does not depend on either the literal truth or the historical accuracy of the Gospels. Rather, the exclusive aim is to locate in these religious narratives, images, and representations a content which, together with the means of the Hegelian philosophy, can encompass the concept in terms of the speculative logic and thus which can be shown to be rationally, necessarily and absolutely grounded. It is no longer revelation but rather philosophical grounding which is the highest standard to which the Bible is held. Strauss concedes no epistemic value to the mythical apprehension of absolute truth through religious convictions. The philosophically inspired critique of the Gospels is a philosophical process of elucidation and, as such, a "sublation" of their content. Although it is an abiding confidence in the incontrovertible truth of the Hegelian philosophy which motivates Strauss' relentless and uncompromising disenchantment of the New Testament, there is next to the implicit critique of the indecisiveness of Hegel's personal attitude a central point of criticism: namely, Strauss repudiates Hegel's thesis that the absolute truth must be manifested in a single human being. Thus, Strauss concludes *The Life of Jesus* with the claim that the critic of religion is obliged to recognize that:

he commits no sacrilege to the Holy, but rather effects a good and necessary work, if he clears away everything which, though well-intended and perhaps even initially beneficial, is ultimately harmful and a downright pernicious delusion – that is, everything in virtue of which Jesus is said to be a super-human being – and recovers as far as possible the image of the historical Jesus in his ultimately human form. This is the man whom humanity, for the sake of its salvation, posited as the ideal Christ, to which every morally exemplary model refers, several of the principal features of which the historical Jesus was certainly the first to bring to light, the aptitude for which, however, belongs to the dowry of our species, as his further development and perfection can only be the task and work of all of humanity. (Strauss 1864: 627)

The equating of the Absolute, or God, with the Spirit, or the moral legislation of humanity, seizes on a tendency in the philosophies of religion from Kant, Fichte and Hegel. And it was with regard to Hegel that contemporaries referred to this tendency by means of the term 'pantheism'. Alongside this interpretation, which could still be understood as religious, there developed a pronounced atheistic line of thought. Whereas for Bauer this line of interpretation was primarily concerned with the cognitive dimensions of religious convictions, for Feuerbach, by contrast, it was the emotive aspects of religious attitudes which were the principal concern. And while Bauer, like Strauss, proceeded on the assumption that Hegel's philosophy could ultimately only be read in terms of this atheistic line of interpretation, Feuerbach came to the conclusion that Hegel's philosophy represented the last manifestation of theology and so must also be sublated.

Bauer's dramatized critique of Hegel

After what was initially a theologically motivated critique of Strauss from 1838 to 1841, Bauer underwent a difficult and conflicted process of personal development. As a result, Bauer discarded his religious and theological convictions and developed a consistent atheistic philosophical outlook. As his hopes of receiving a professorship in the Prussian state dwindled, he published – at first anonymously – two works which one can designate as dramatized critiques of Hegel: *The Trumpet of the Last Judgment on Hegel, the Atheists, and the Anti-Christians: An Ultimatum* (1841) and *Hegel's Doctrine of Religion and Art, Assessed from the Standpoint of Faith* (1842).

Both of these books assume the perspective of a radical anti-philosophical religious subject who rejects as illegitimate every attempt at a rational reconstruction and justification of the biblical content, on the grounds that every such attempt contains an assault on God, religion, and the divinely sanctioned political order. In the literary form of an *exposé* containing warnings of imminent danger, the narrating subject presents the content of Hegel's own position as having been correctly described by the critical interpreters of religion and their successors. It is claimed that Hegel himself had made merely cosmetic concessions with regard both to the sovereignty of religion and to certain theological suppositions, such as the immortality of the soul and the idea of a personal God, because he feared political reprisals. Moreover, he trusted the careful reader would recognize that the sublation of religion in philosophy is nothing other than the elimination of religion and theology.

With this literary ruse, Bauer succeeded in establishing the atheistic reading as the only correct interpretation of Hegel. In contrast to Strauss, Bauer does not reduce the religious and theological content of (Protestant) Christianity into pantheism, but rather explains this content as the mere product of human self-consciousness. As an adequate interpretation of Hegel, this is in fact problematic, even apart from the question of the relation between religion and philosophy, because Bauer's interpretation presupposes a dualism of subject and object which leads back to the activity of self-consciousness. With that, Bauer underwrites Hegel's concept of Spirit with a Fichtean conception which is ultimately inadequate for Hegel's intended claim. Moreover, on Bauer's interpretation it is difficult to discern how the empirical is related to the transcendental, as well as how the individual relates to the 'I' *qua* genus. Although Bauer's interpretation, which he offers by means of a dramatized critique of Hegel, is in fact problematic, he nevertheless succeeded in persuading many of his contemporaries that this is the correct reconstruction of Hegel's account of the relation between philosophy and religion.

Bauer's assessment of the diverse contributions to the discussion – an appraisal performed under the useful guise of anonymous authorship – was a politically shrewd gambit. Moderate Hegelians were confronted with a dilemma: either they were not in the position to accurately interpret Hegel or, conscious of the truth, they were suppressing their knowledge for either political or personal reasons. By forcing this dilemma Bauer sought to dissolve the mediating position in the Hegelian school, insofar as he pressed Hegelians either to embrace atheism or to do that which critics of Hegel by and large demanded: namely, to abandon Hegel's philosophy altogether. Bauer pushed his political strategy still further by extolling the positive philosophy of Immanuel Fichte and the rationalistic theology of the likes of Schleiermacher precisely because these thinkers sought to confront the Hegelian danger. At the same time, however, Bauer continuously emphasized that even the positions of these thinkers are inconsistent, because they either make concessions to a rationalistic interpretation of the Bible or assert a peaceful coexistence between philosophy and religion. Against these latter alternatives, the anonymous narrator aligns himself with an irrational and anti-enlightenment point of view: the fundamental tenets of the Christian religion are revelations from God which are neither in need of nor capable of human justification. Any concession to the contrary opens a path at the end of which stands the Hegelian *Aufhebung* of religion and theology in a purely immanent, atheistic philosophy; a philosophy which ultimately leads to the destruction of the Christian state.

With this approach, Bauer sought to make it impossible to hold any of the mediating positions owing to their inconsistent standpoints. Thus, there emerges a choice between two diametrically opposed positions: on the one hand, a restorative, irrational religiosity which brings with it the rejection of any justificatory claims in religion and politics; and, on the other hand, an atheistic, anti-constitutional Hegelian philosophy which subverts religion, church, and state. Bauer could claim a twofold success in both having founded this interpretation of Hegel and having brought about the intended polarization. The latter achievement was no doubt aided by the fact that the increasingly reactionary politics of the Prussian state rendered ever more dubious Hegel's claim that the actual Prussian reality can be taken as a manifestation of the rational state.

Feuerbach's critique of religion

Feuerbach's critique of religion is fundamentally different from that of the French Enlightenment because Feuerbach takes religion to be not only fraudulent and deceptive but also to be an essential anthropological feature. His central thesis, namely, that the idea of God is an unconscious projection of the essence of human characteristics, continues to be a central theme in both the philosophy of religion and theology. According to Feuerbach, the individual, who in a finite life riddled with contingencies is unable to realize the essence of what it means to be human, projects essential properties onto a divine being – properties which for Feuerbach as for Strauss are always characteristics of the species.

> I show that religion takes the apparent, the superficial essence of nature and of humanity as its true, inner essence, and thus takes the true, esoteric essence as something else, represented as a special being; and, consequently, that in the determinations which it attributes to God, e.g. the divine word, religion only defines or hypostatizes the true essence of the human word ... . (GW: 5:19)

The individual who is unaware of his capacity for projection actually relates to his own essence in his relation to God. However, because he does not comprehend this externalization, he relates to his own essence in an alienated manner.

> Religion is the unconscious self-consciousness of humanity. In religion, one's own essence is the object, though without one knowing this to be the case; one's own essence is the object *as if it were the essence of another*. (GW: 5:75)

The philosophical unmasking of this religious projection leads, in the sense of the Enlightenment, to the individual appropriating those characteristics assigned to God and consciously ascribing them to himself.

Feuerbach's critique of religion differs from that of Strauss and Bauer in multiple respects, which is why Feuerbach always resisted being associated with them. His primary argument was to constantly refer to his materialistic-anthropological renunciation of Hegel, a renunciation which distinguished him in principle from the continued idealist – and, according to Feuerbach, Hegelian – inspired critique of religion advanced by Strauss and Bauer. Moreover, Feuerbach always emphasized his concern with "religion, as the immediate object, the immediate essence of humanity" (GW: 5:23), and not with biblical theology, as in the case of Bauer, or Christian doctrine, as in the case of Strauss.

Feuerbach's assessment is in principle justified, though it obscures further religio-philosophical differences which go beyond the distinction between idealism and materialism. Whereas Strauss and Bauer were primarily concerned with the cognitive content of religion *qua* theology, it is the emotive aspects of religious attitudes which are central for Feuerbach. In contrast to Bauer, Feuerbach conceives of religion not as an inversion but rather only as the uncomprehended projection of the characteristics of the species. To this extent, there is some similarity with Strauss, insofar as the religious representation of the species is assimilated positively into the correct philosophical viewpoint. What distinguishes Feuerbach from Strauss is that, according to Feuerbach, Hegel's philosophy is not adequate for this assimilation.

The future of philosophy

All of the thinkers belonging to the Hegelian school considered Hegel's philosophy, and in particular his dialectical method, as the incontrovertible, final form of philosophy. In the face of changing political circumstances, this method had to be applied anew to the political situation, and this in turn led to divergent assessments of particular aspects of Hegel's philosophy. This is evident in the claim of Eduard Gans that Hegel's philosophy must itself be seen as an historically situated shape of <the Absolute> Spirit. August von Cieszkowski developed this point further, insofar as he applied Hegel's method to the Hegelian philosophy of history, and ultimately to the Hegelian system generally, so as to incorporate into philosophy the dimension of the future.

The historicization of the Hegelian philosophy

The ever stronger reactionary tendencies in Prussia, already looming during Hegel's lifetime, led to fundamental differences between Hegel and Gans, who gave the lectures on the philosophy of right numerous times during the 1820s. Whereas from 1820 onwards Hegel had placed in the foreground those aspects of his philosophy of right which emphasized conformity to and stability of the political system, Gans emphasized the critical, change-oriented dimension of Hegel's theory. This difference highlights the ambiguity of Hegel's formula concerning the rationality of the actual and the actuality of the rational. Although Gans certainly followed Hegel in designating the role of the monarch as ultimately a representative element, he nevertheless emphasized more clearly the critical components of this conception in the face of restorative tendencies, as for example in his doctrine of opposition (Gans 1971: 136).

Against the background of the unfulfilled promise of Friedrich Wilhelm III to give Prussia a constitution, there occurred a debate over the correct interpretation of the classes. Gans sought to show that Hegel's philosophy of right must be construed progressively as a theory of representative classes which champions not only particular interests but also the general interest. Gans himself clearly spoke out in favor of a representative system and derived from this view the rejection of an electoral process based on corporations. Instead, and in contrast to Hegel, he advocated for an election which is "atomistic according to the populace" (Gans 2005: 227ff.).

By and large, Gans approached and employed his lectures as weapons on behalf of modernization and liberalization. This certainly explains the phenomenal public success of his lectures, for which there were sometimes more in attendance than the number of students in matriculation at the University of Berlin. Above all, it was in his approach to the social question that Gans departed from Hegel. Gans had studied intensively the modern national economy and the developing capitalist market society, and he had integrated this social domain into his philosophy of right within the framework of his account of civil society. Already for Hegel, poverty was a critical problem, though he did not yet proceed on the assumption of class antagonism but rather consolidated the manufacturers and laborers into a social group. In general, Hegel is of the view that the free market society must be controlled by the state, so that its predominant tendencies toward atomization and destruction of the ethical bond can be held in check. In the 1820 *Elements of the Philosophy of Right* the relation between the national economy and the general social structure is developed in only a cursory manner. However, as we know from various transcripts, in the lectures which Hegel delivered on the basis of the published work he treated contemporary phenomena in vastly greater detail. In particular, he sought to explain philosophically the increasing disparity between luxury and destitution in terms of the connections of poverty, work, and the division of labor. Gans sets out in his work a legally and politically mediated balancing of social antagonisms, yet he categorically rejected the socialist Utopia that would overcome all social conflict via the formation of a new society beyond civil society, the political state, and the system of right.

Gans' reflections are informed by his personal encounters with conditions of poverty in England (he sojourned there briefly in 1830 and 1831 while traveling in France), as well as by his familiarity with the theories of the Saint-Simonists in France. Up through his lectures on natural right in 1828–9, Gans' approach to the social question is very similar to that of Hegel. However, after his visit to Paris during the revolutionary year of 1830, Gans expanded his approach to include detailed accounts of the French theories (as, for example, in the lectures from 1832–3), though he had in view the social conditions of industrialized England.

In contrast to the Saint-Simonists, Gans rejected the fundamental socialist idea of the abolishment of private property with regard to the means of production, of rights to inheritance, of the freedom to choose one's occupation, or of marriage, as well as the idea of a radical egalitarianism, on the grounds that such ideas are both utopian and politically incompatible with personal autonomy and the structure of the will of individual persons (see Gans 1971: 216–19). As an alternative, Gans developed out of his synthesis of Hegel and Saint-Simon what to some extent could be considered an early form of the trade union. Gans conceived of this in terms of a "socialization of individuals," i.e. not merely as the representation of economic interests, but rather as educational institutions which should enable the workers to identify with their society and to participate in universal ethical life. Unlike Hegel, Gans sees clearly that the actual state very quickly becomes the means for expressing existing economic interests and cannot by itself fulfill the regulatory function which Hegel attributed to it as the advocate for the general interest. Gans, however, did not simply develop the basic idea of solidarity as a union of workers aimed at asserting their interests, and thus of a "coalition of workers in the cities" (Gans 2005: xxxivff.). In the lectures on the philosophy of history from the winter semester of 1833–4, transmitted in handwritten notes by H. F. W. Jahnke, Gans goes further and claims that the actual social and political development:

> demonstrates that the struggle of humanity is not over, that the lower classes of society will fight for a portion of history, that little by little they will intervene ever more in the state, that the difference between ruler and ruled will disappear ever more, and that the concept of the human, which Christianity has made the basis of all religion, will becomes more and more universal until it is increasingly realized in the lowest circles of society. (Gans 2005: xxxiv)

The conjunction of law, politics, and social processes, as well as the thoroughgoing emphasis on the openness of the future and of future developments, are central motifs with which Gans influenced the thought of subsequent thinkers. Most similar to Arnold Ruge, Gans remained negatively disposed to socialism and communism and instead pressed for the further development of law and politics, though not in terms of a transformation of the bourgeois form of life, as would later occur to Hess and Marx. To this extent, Gans developed further the Hegelian philosophy independently of the question concerning the relation between philosophy and religion, and, unlike Feuerbach, he did not call into question the idealist-rationalist foundation of the Hegelian system. His contribution consists in restoring to philosophy the function of actively shaping contemporary politics.

Gans achieved this only by relativizing the historical philosophical position of Hegel's philosophy. In surveying the existing thought on natural right, Gans acknowledged Hegel's philosophy of right as the historically pre-eminent theory on the subject but nevertheless denied that it was the ultimate and conclusive expression of philosophical knowledge in general. In the preface to his edition of the Hegelian philosophy of right, in the 1833 "circle of friends" edition of Hegel's works, Gans sharpens his assessment:

> As part of the Hegelian system, it will have to rise and fall with the system. It will also perhaps admit of greater elucidation, nuanced developments, and increased clarity. As with the entire system, perhaps it will after many years recede into general consciousness: its distinctive language of art will fall by the wayside, and its profundity will become public property. For, philosophically speaking, its time is over, and it now belongs to history. A new philosophical development, proceeding from the same foundational principles, has occurred; a different conception of a changed actuality. (Gans 1971: 12)

The future as a subject for philosophy
Gans' historicizing of the Hegelian system and the emphasis he placed on the practical aspects of legal and political philosophy indicate two aspects of Hegelian thought which, to those among his successors who were critical of society during a time of political restoration, were considered deficits that must be expunged. Already the external construction of the Hegelian philosophy of history cannot persuade even those who hold Hegel's dialectic to be both methodologically and ontologically convincing. For these reasons, Cieszkowski drew the conclusion that "Hegel's philosophy of history was by no means adequate for his own system" (Cieszkowski 1981: 72). However, according to Cieszkowski, who was employing a figure of thought derived from Hegel's philosophy of history, this deficiency was not only a contingent inconsistency on the part of Hegel, but rather the expression of Hegel's own philosophical self-understanding. Thus, Hegel was:

> … never in the position to elevate himself, because we find him there in the appropriate place, completely true to his universal philosophical position. (Cieszkowski 1981: 73)

We need not concern ourselves in detail with Cieszkowski's substantive reconfiguration of the four philosophical stages into which Hegel divided history. He arranged them into two stages, namely, that of the beautiful (Cieszkowski 1981: 80–91) and that of the philosophical, in which Hegel is located (Cieszkowski 1981: 91–112). A third stage must follow the first two, in accordance with the fundamental structure of dialectical development which Hegel discovered and to which Cieszkowski remains faithful: namely, the realization of philosophy through conscious practice, the realization of the true and the beautiful in the good social life.

The persuasiveness of such a philosophical history of development is, from a contemporary perspective, entirely independent of the question as to whether dialectic is now of little use as a methodological structure. Still, two decisive revisions of the Hegelian philosophy emerge from Cieszkowski's recommended reconstruction of the Hegelian philosophy of history. First, the future is declared to be an appropriate object for historical-philosophical interpretation. With that, Hegel's thesis of the end of all philosophically relevant development is contested and the self-assessment of his system as the consummation of philosophy must be refuted. Since this must occur on the basis of an Hegelian dialectic (which is presupposed as universally valid), the conceptual labor of the Hegelian increases considerably. This first revision entails a second: Hegel's fundamental meta-philosophical assumptions of the priority of thought over volition – of theory over practice – and the priority of being over change must both be abandoned. Cieszkowski clearly and consistently spells out the implications of the transformation of speculative dialectic into a philosophy of practice:

> With Hegel, the practical is still absorbed through the theoretical; the former has not distinguished itself from the latter. It is still considered as, so to speak, a tributary <*Filialausfluss*> of the theoretical. Its true and actual determination

however is to be a separate, a specific, – even the highest – level of Spirit. (Cieszkowski 1981: 120)

Cieszkowski characterizes his own "new teleological standpoint of world history" in the following terms:

> World history is the process of the development of the spirit of humanity in sensation, in consciousness, and in the activity of the beautiful, the true, and the good; it is a process of development which we must know in its necessity, contingency, and freedom. (Cieszkowski 1981: 137)

Hegel's philosophy takes knowing as its standpoint and thus belongs to the second stage of history. Within the framework of Cieszkowski's philosophy of history, the path is thus cleared for Hegel's philosophical system to be integrated as a moment in history. To this extent, Hegel's system is no longer said to represent the completion of all development, in general, but rather only the completion of the philosophical knowledge of the laws of motion of this development. The true consummation of the content of this philosophy occurs not in the medium of knowledge, but rather in the actual realization of this content through philosophically informed action.

This philosophy of practice must invariably repudiate Hegel's thesis that philosophy can only grasp what has come to be in its rationality but cannot know the future; and it must insist on the possibility of scientific knowing of the future:

> Why do we not construct the immaterial entirety of the historical process, in general, out of those parts which have already occurred? And, in particular, why do we not construct the missing future parts which must conform to the past and with this construct the true idea of humanity? The deeds of the past; those are our fossils, our antediluvian remains, out of which we must build the universal life of humanity. (Cieszkowski 1981: 13)

In the idea of developing the entire prehistoric organism out of fossils, Cieszkowski relates the parallels drawn by Condorcet and Saint-Simon to the method of Curviers. And similar to them, Cieszkowski transfers this method to the question of scientific knowability of the future:

> It does not concern guessing this or that idiosyncrasy, or predicting a particular hero or deed. Rather, it concerns the investigation of the unique nature of humanity; of determining the laws of its progress, the manifestations of which can be detected rationally in history; of appreciating the distance implicit in the past and its relation to the future; and ultimately in determining the periods of this continual self-formation with respect to the determinate contents of its types, which are the posited realization of the *virtually* imprinted elements of humanity. And this is precisely the essential concern of philosophy. (Cieszkowski 1981: 12)

Admittedly, Cieszkowski did not reject entirely the Hegelian skepticism of philosophical "instruction" but rather combined his philosophy of the future with a critique of the pure utopianism which he found in the writings of the early socialists:

> In general, the primary defect of a Utopia is that it does not itself develop with actuality but rather wants to enter into actuality. And this it can never do, for as soon as there is a Utopia, there exists an insurmountable divide separating it from actuality. (Cieszkowski 1981: 147)

This criticism arises from the self-confidence that a scientific method is available for the purpose of understanding future developments. For Cieszkowski, the fundamental conceptual structure of historical development is known philosophically through Hegel and moreover is also already adequately realized in the areas of law (the stage of antiquity) and morality (Christianity). The complete realization of philosophy through the objectification of the third stage, however, still remains to be accomplished:

> But ethical life, which as the third concrete sphere must appear in both of the preceding abstract spheres, and yet which finds itself in each in a field which does not correspond to itself; this ethical life is determined so as to begin its true development and to appear in a development as adequate, as is the case with right and morality. (Cieszkowski 1981: 152)

The social relations thus far were still one-sided, such that, according to Cieszkowski, "the actual and absolute consequence still remains to be drawn" (Cieszkowski 1981: 152f.). He describes the result in the following terms:

> The human being thus emerges from abstraction and becomes pre-eminently (*kat' exochen*) a social individual. The naked 'I' abandons its universality and defines itself as a concrete relation-rich person. Simultaneously, the state abandons its abstract isolation and itself becomes a member of humanity and of the concrete family of peoples. The state of nature of peoples is transformed into their social condition, and the heretofore still young law of peoples develops itself into an every richer morality and ethical life of peoples. Lastly, humanity, whose universality scarcely wishes to be present to consciousness and to thought, conceives of itself concretely and vividly, and becomes an organic humanity that can certainly be regarded as a church in its highest significance. (Cieszkowski 1981: 153)

In contrast to the democrats and socialists of his day, Cieszkowski characterized himself as a conservative because he advocated practical change without a one-sided emphasis on negating, and because he did not want to surrender completely the element of philosophical understanding in favor of political and revolutionary practice. The noticeable eschatological features of his philosophy of history derive from the utopian dream of Charles Fourier, which during this time appealed signifi-cantly first and foremost to Catholic thinkers. Moreover, among the utopian-socialist models, Fourier's concept of society was the one which placed the greatest emphasis on the individual and on personal autonomy, which is why the political views of Gans and Cieszkowski were similar to those of Fourier. Thus, Cieszkowski took to Fourier's theory of association, which can be interpreted unproblematically as a collective solidarity of free individuals. Cieszkowski is thus, on the one hand, a critic of the atomistic liberalism which accompanied the rise of capitalistic society; and, on the other hand, and similar to Gans, he disassociates himself sharply from the collectivist conceptions of the early socialists and communists. Both Gans and Cieszkowski are united in rejecting the connection which the Hegelian critics of religion drew between the alienating aspects of capitalism and the fundamental dogmas of Christianity. This adherence to the institutions of the constitutional state, on the one hand, and the continued separation of religious questions from those of political philosophy, on the other hand, which increasingly fell out of view in the thought of Marx from 1843 to 1846, there is an aspect of Cieszkowski's philosophical program which acquired increasing significance: namely, the idea of a scientific knowing and inducement of the future. Certainly, Marx introduced a different bearer of historical development. However, it was Cieszkowski's idea of developing a scientific interpretation of society and of the history of humanity that was always preserved in Marxism, both as a criterion for distinguishing itself from concurrent "Utopias" and as the legitimating basis for its own political agitation.

Laying to rest the Hegelian spirit: three models of post-Hegelian Philosophy

The emancipation of self-consciousness in Bauer

In 1843, Bruno Bauer published *Christianity Exposed*. Very few copies of the book were made available to the public, even before its publication was halted by the censor. The work was eventually considered lost, and it was not until 1927 that the Bauer researcher Ernst Barnikol acquired possession of the book and published a new edition of it. *Christianity Exposed* is without question one of the most radical and scathing critiques of Christianity, and in many respects it anticipates the later critique of Friedrich Nietzsche. It is also one of the clearest presentations of Bauer's critical view of religion and theology:

> Religion is the fixed, intuited, made, desired, and essentialized passivity of the human; the highest suffering which it could inflict on itself; the fear of human beings; the poverty and emptiness of spirit raised to the essence of the human; the sorrow of the world, which is examined, desired, and fixed as its essence. (Bauer 1927: 95)

In sentences which recall Fichte's thesis that the philosophy of freedom presupposes the individual's decision to want to be free, religiosity is construed as *angst* before one's own freedom, as faint-heartedness, and simultaneously as the origin and essence of religion, in general. The sublation of this phenomenon in Bauer's philosophy of radical self-determination can thus be achieved only through the complete negation of religion (see Bauer 1927: 94). The reduction of the origins of religion to ignorance, misery, and misfortune was something which Bauer took over from the French Enlightenment, whose materialist proponents considered the fear of humanity to be the source for the idea of God. Bauer thereby undercuts the complex relation between philosophy and religion which Hegel had developed. For Bauer, the focus on divine revelation is "the self-deception of humanity with regard to its vocation <Bestimmung>," – a vocation which, for Bauer, properly consists in autonomy (Bauer 1927: 98). This self-deception is deemed the cause of all of the social evil which Bauer observes in the world:

> What is a greater source of sadness than the awareness, or the feeling, of having failed in one's true calling? What gives human beings a more irritated disposition, what is a greater cause of injustice against all the interests of life, what does more to alienate humans from society and to make a man a tyrant against his fellow human beings than the voice from within which he must always work to suppress and yet which speaks to him without ceasing: *you are not what you're supposed to be, and you will never become that which you desire?* (Bauer 1927: 98)

Only one year later Marx would locate the cause of this alienation elsewhere, namely in the social organization of the conditions of reproduction. And this, in turn, would serve as the basis for explaining religious consciousness itself. The explanatory paradigm is retained in its essential characteristics; however, a different cause is ultimately identified, and religion, which for Bauer functions as the root cause, is instead interpreted as an effect of this true cause.

The secularization of the state as a project for the emancipation of humanity
There was, moreover, further agreement with respect to the thesis that religion is the opiate of the people, which Bauer had already formulated in 1841:

> The most Christian state is that which is governed by theological statutes. This amounts to real domination, even to absolute domination. That is, it can ultimately exercise its opiate influence to such an extent that no trace of resistance is found, and all the drives of free humanity either fall asleep, or if on occasion they should wake up, these drives are driven to a more dull, sleep-intoxicated crime before which humanity, either having yet to achieve this degree of Christianity or having already left it behind, must tremble. (Bauer 1968: 9ff.)

Following Hegel, and in agreement with Ruge and with Marx before 1844, Bauer conceives of the state as the realization of the freedom of humanity, such that the critique of religion must necessarily lead to a critique of the theological legitimation of political domination:

> It must be granted that even in its most raw form the state is the appearance of freedom and the act <*Tat*> of universal self-consciousness. (Bauer 1968: 7)

At this point, Bauer is convinced that the decisive breakthrough towards both a truly free state and the ultimate liberation from religion and theology is about to occur, and that the site of this decisive battle will be the Prussian state:

> Without having been noticed, the situation has progressed and become very serious. It appears certain that the matter will be decided in Prussia. (Bauer 1968: 37)

Thus, with the publication of two works in 1843, Bauer entered the debate concerning the political emancipation of Jews in a Christian state. Both *The Jewish Question* and *The Ability of Contemporary Jews and Christians to Become Free* express Bauer's appropriation of Hegel's thesis that Christianity must be regarded as the self-overcoming and higher development of religion on the path to (philosophical) reason. These works also advance the thesis – that goes well beyond Hegel – that true emancipation consists in the liberation of humanity from religion:

> The question of emancipation is a universal one: both Jews and Christians want to be emancipated. History, whose ultimate aim is freedom, must and will at least work towards the coming together of Jews and Christians in their longing and striving for emancipation, since there is between them no difference, and since, with respect both to the true essence of humanity and to freedom, Jews and Christians alike must be recognized as slaves. (Bauer 1968: 175)

A state which still recognizes religious privileges and for which religion still plays a significant role, is not a rational state. A state whose basis of legitimacy is drawn from religion or theology is a state which can neither conceive of itself as the product of self-determination nor impart to its members the self-consciousness requisite for being autonomous subjects. Thus, the struggle for emancipation on the part of Jews and Christians must, according to Bauer, be conceived as the struggle for emancipation from religion in general.

Bauer considered his thoughts on the philosophy of religion to be a direct challenge to every state which derives its legitimacy from religion and theology, and it was such thoughts which Bauer introduced into the political debates of his day. At the same time, he was of the opinion that the proper tactic in political struggle can only be that which, by means of a critique of religion and theology, brings about an elucidation of the self-consciousness of one's own striving for freedom. This was the point which Marx attacked foremost in his critique of Bauer's analysis of the Jewish question. In defense of Bauer, one could claim that he only intended to advance the thesis that social and political emancipation would be impossible without such self-elucidation. Yet the characteristic style of his writings suggests the stronger thesis, namely, that for Bauer the emancipation should consist primarily in bringing about this realization by means of analyses in the philosophy of religion.

Bauer's conception of radical self-determination
The reduction of Hegel's 'Spirit' into human self-consciousness

In his writings from 1843, Bauer presented neither a systematic theory of his view of self-consciousness and freedom nor a developed philosophy of history. In order to fill in the gaps of Bauer's account, one must collect the relevant claims from numerous texts and continually have in view Hegel's philosophy of Spirit as the basic intellectual background. In so doing, one should note that Bauer proceeds from a modified form of Hegelianism, one which in important respects resembles Fichte more than Hegel:

> The form which is born in willing and self-consciousness makes and decides everything; without it there is no decision and no demonstration. And if it is missing, that which is nearest cannot find itself, and that which is furthest removed cannot come to an understanding. Indeed, without it there is no nearest, no furthest, no unity, no opposition; without it there is nothing. Out of nothingness it creates everything. (Bauer 1968: 7)

The primacy of will and the emphasis on the side of the subject *vis-à-vis* that of the object bear a greater resemblance to Fichte's dialectic of self-consciousness than to Hegel's concept of Spirit, though Bauer himself does not appear to have noticed this Fichteanization. In the dramatized critique of Hegel which Bauer sought to present as Hegel's true position, there was one explicit shift whereby the Hegelian concept of Spirit is reduced to human self-consciousness and everything which is transcendent for human consciousness is placed in history and thus in objective Spirit. Neither the issue of nature, which would become important for both Feuerbach and Marx, nor any transcendental content tied to concepts of God are recognized. Therewith, Bauer's theory of self-consciousness exhibits a fundamental ambiguity: is the species consciousness conceptualized as a supra-individual social entity, or does Bauer advocate an individualistic approach? From 1844 onwards, Bauer rejected every account which makes individual self-consciousness a subordinate moment in a larger social structure, on the grounds that such an account is a quasi-theological denial of freedom and implies a paternalistic metaphysics of substance. There is, however, nothing in the earlier writings which clarifies whether Bauer overlooked the fact that the Hegelian concept of Spirit transcends individual self-consciousness, or whether Bauer sought to return to the shape of self-consciousness advanced in the *Phenomenology of Spirit*. Marx implied the latter was the case when he characterized Bauer's critique of religious consciousness as simply a copy of Hegel's analysis of unhappy consciousness.

Objectification and dissolution: Bauer's philosophy of history

Every theory which employs the concept of alienation to critically analyze existing phenomena must account for several things: it must explain the source of this alienation; it must determine whether the alienation can in principle be overcome or whether it instead represents a condition of human existence; and, if it can be overcome, it must describe what such an overcoming might look like.

Bauer's answer to these questions rests on an Hegelian philosophy of history, the basic model of which is the path from consciousness to adequate self-knowledge, as described by Hegel in the *Phenomenology*. Thus, Bauer describes the development whereby self-consciousness comes to a realization of its own freedom in terms of a path which necessarily proceeds through the intermediate stage of alienation in the form of religious and theological consciousness.

> Theological consciousness cannot exist without the fracture and disunity of self-consciousness. If, namely, all of the universal determinations which apply to humans and which bind humans to one another are considered by free, human self-consciousness to be the result of its own development and the only worthwhile result of its life; if these determinations are understood by self-consciousness and are held together in its inner, universal, ideal world; religious consciousness has torn away these determinations from the human self, and displaced them to a heavenly realm. And, with that, it has wrought discord between the wandering, wavering, suffering individual 'I' and the universal, true I, the one 'I' which merits the name of the human. (Bauer 1968: 156)

Religious and theological consciousness is not only incapable of overcoming this alienation, but rather it is, according to Bauer, the primary cause of all discord:

> The contradiction, the brokenness, and the alienation thus repeat themselves again in this objective world, for which indeterminate religious consciousness has fashioned itself. This world arose through the first, original activity of reflection, i.e. of theological consciousness. This consciousness, however, neither knows nor understands its own creative power; in relation to the divine it considers itself as merely receptive, i.e. only as religious. (Bauer 1968: 157)

Analogous to the account of consciousness in Hegel's *Phenomenology*, human consciousness, on Bauer's view, contains within itself the criterion and the potential for overcoming the alienation, even if – at the stage of religious and theological consciousness – it still does not possess a clear concept of this:

> There is necessarily in this premonition, in this feeling [i.e. the feeling of the unity of subject and object in the transcendent, or in God], thus also a feeling that consciousness itself is the unity, for it is in itself, in fact, this unity. (Bauer 1968: 162)

For this reason, the alienation in the essence of human consciousness is certainly a necessary intermediate stage to be traversed on the way to the self-actualization of freedom. However, the unity of self-consciousness is simultaneously the guarantor that one does not completely lose oneself in this bifurcation but rather will overcome it:

> In effect, humanity cannot fall so far as to have thrown itself away completely and irretrievably. It can discard itself – religion is itself this very discarding –, but it will learn to again collect itself and respect itself. Humanity will lacerate itself – religion is itself this bloody sacrifice –, but it will again be reconciled with itself. It cannot escape itself, since it is everything, and the nothingness into which – by means of religion – humanity plummets is only its own act, its capriciousness, its own fantasy and evil. (Bauer 1927: 100f.)

So long as religion exists, however, humanity remains outside itself:

> Humanity pushes itself away from itself and again stumbles, in order to discard itself once more and, the next moment, to lift itself <aufzuheben> once again out of this trap; because it is in religion that humanity has lost its true center, its center within itself. (Bauer 1927: 101)

This characterization illustrates the extent to which Bauer construes the Hegelian moment of *Aufhebung* in the sense of a negating and reversing of the extremes. At the same time, the structure of self-consciousness is the conceptual guarantor for the ultimate surmounting of alienation, which, through a process of learning and formation, overcomes the extremes and contradictions by means of which humanity alienates itself:

> These antagonisms however, as unnatural as they are, are nevertheless not unnatural: as much as they contradict the essence of humanity, they are nevertheless a necessary consequence of it. They are the contradiction against humanity itself. However, it lies in the nature and determination of humanity that in its historical development it should generate a contradiction with itself, and that it should press this contradiction to the extreme, before it should attain harmony with itself. (Bauer 1927: 138)

The emancipation of human beings in the anthropology of Feuerbach

Feuerbach's philosophical anthropology

During the time which concerns us here, Feuerbach pursued a philosophical anthropology, and he understood philosophy in general to be Idealism and Hegel's system to be its completion. In Feuerbach's critique of religion there occurred two systematically decisive shifts. First, the difference which Hegel alleged between the structure of finite, empirical self-consciousness and infinite, divine self-consciousness is leveled insofar as the latter is explained as a projection of the former. Since according to Feuerbach's view the latter constitutes the externalization of human characteristics and abilities, the structures which Hegel ascribed to absolute subjectivity are now assigned to the self-consciousness of the species. Second, with Feuerbach, theoretical and practical consciousness collapse into one another, although the latter wins the upper hand, such that from the theoretically constituted Idealism a kind of practical philosophy arises.

According to Feuerbach – and Marx will follow him in this – the theoretical and practical object for human beings is their own species. In the words of Marx: the concrete existence of the species is "universal." With respect to the theoretical dimension of the relation of the species, Feuerbach entirely followed Hegel: in virtue of its cognitive abilities, a human being is in the position to become aware of his own essence, as well as that of other things *qua* concepts. As a consequence of the direction of his critique of religion, Feuerbach simplified the practical dimension of human beings' relation to their species. While Hegel had developed a radically differentiated conception of Spirit which recognized, in addition to the anthropological and social institutions, the self-interpreting media of art, religion, and philosophy as legitimate ways of realizing this character of the species, Feuerbach placed everything in the domain of the anthropological and the social. Moreover, what was for Hegel a differentiated relation between the individual and its species was changed into a dominance of the species, consistent with the assumption that it is only in humanity as a whole that the marks of the species can be actualized.

What in these years was an empiricist philosophy oriented to the empirical sciences was subsequently developed by Feuerbach into part of a larger theory which can no longer be classified in any obvious sense as philosophical but, more plausibly, as natural scientific. To this extent, one could rightly call into question our characterization of the theory advanced in Feuerbach's later writings as *philosophical* anthropology. The consideration of empirical data in philosophical anthropology, which is already observable during the time relevant here, certainly implies a critique of purely *a priori* philosophical theories, but it does not transform a philosophical theory into a natural scientific theory. It is undeniable, however, that many post-Hegelian materialists drew this consequence and turned strongly towards the natural sciences (and this applies not only to Feuerbach but also to Marx and Engels). At any rate, Feuerbach was decisive in his opposition to every form of Idealism which locates the essence of human beings exclusively in their cognitive capacities and in self-consciousness. Against this form of philosophy, which Feuerbach frequently equated with philosophy in general, Feuerbach adopted an empirically oriented, empiricist anthropology, which on first glance appears to represent a turning-away from philosophy. For the assumptions (accepted unreflectively by philosophy) underlying the philosophical questions were themselves subjected to critical examination and rejected, such that Feuerbach appeared to adopt an unphilosophical point of view. This appearance, however, is deceptive, for even this therapeutic position should be regarded as philosophy, since it presents a philosophical answer to philosophical questions. Feuerbach's rejection of certain philosophical lines of inquiry should thus not be understood as a rejection of philosophy in general (see Brudney 1998).

Resisting the misunderstanding of Feuerbach's view as anti-philosophical is made more difficult by the fact that Feuerbach was not only inclined to equate Idealism with philosophy but also to identify the latter with Hegel's system. Because he still conceives of Hegel's philosophy as the ultimate form of theology, to which one must apply the critique of religion, there arises the impression that Feuerbach's anthropology aims to reduce both theology and philosophy equally, and thus that it is no longer philosophy but rather a pure empirical science. This obvious misunderstanding, to which Feuerbach himself perhaps also succumbed, left clear traces in the self-conception of Marx and Engels (at least starting in 1845, with the publication of the *German Ideology*), who took as their point of departure Feuerbach's critique of Idealism.

Feuerbach's critique of Idealism

In his critique of Hegel, published in 1839, Feuerbach rejected the claim that we can grasp things themselves by means of philosophical thinking. Against this claim, he offered his first materialistic thesis, namely, that there is matter independent of thought, given to humans in experience, the existence of which is always already presupposed, such that it cannot itself be captured philosophically.

> Thought cannot extend beyond what exists, because it cannot extend beyond itself; because reason is only the positing of being; because only this or that being can be thought but not the being itself as what has become. (GW: 9:54ff.)

In addition to this, Feuerbach put forth a second materialistic thesis (in this case, one which was simultaneously directed against theology): matter is prior to thought, according to its being. First, the latter is passive and receptive in relation to the former. Second, thought is to be explained in terms of matter and not, as Hegel claimed, conversely. Herein lies the basis for Feuerbach's charge that Hegel makes a dependent predicate into the subject and what is most basic and, conversely, that he makes the subject and what is most basic into a dependent predicate.

> The method of a reformatory critique of *speculative philosophy, in general,* does not distinguish itself from that already applied to the *philosophy of religion.* We are always only allowed to make the *predicate* into the *subject* and so the *subject* into the *object* and *principle* – and thus only to *reverse* the speculative philosophy, and in this manner we have the uncovered, pure, bare truth. (GW: 9:244)

Because Hegel does not recognize the independence and primacy of matter (of being) over thought (of consciousness), his philosophy is, like all Idealism, a last form of theology. Feuerbach classifies Hegel's system as "rational mysticism" (GW: 9:53).

The idea of a subject–predicate transposition suggests a pure inverting of Hegel's conception, which Feuerbach did in effect carry out: in the famous words of Marx, Hegel was turned upside down. This is, however, merely a negation, i.e. a simple counter-position to Hegel's theory, and by no means a dialectical sublation of it through a refined, transformed model. As a consequence, Feuerbach presents a passive-sensualistic concept in place of Hegel's active-idealist epistemology. *Qua* knowing subject, a person is passive, receptive, and experiences the influence of the material external world, whose causal impact the subject processes internally (this is an assumption of the empiricist tradition which runs from Hume to Quine). With that, Feuerbach's epistemology loses the historical dimension, since it aims at an anthropological original condition of the physical animal existence of human beings in a material environment, and not one which is mediated by society and history.

Against this, Marx sought to rescue the historical-philosophical dimension of Hegelian thought: first, in the form of a political philosophy in the sense of Gans and Ruge (see Ruge 1846); and later in the social-economic form motivated by Hess and Engels. The anthropological grounding of philosophy on a materialistic foundation and the emphasis on nature, together, form an enduring Feuerbachian legacy in Marx, to whom also belongs the idea of a subject–predicate transposition as a method of ideological-critical unmasking. The empiricist epistemology, however, would soon become an object of Marxist critique, as is emphasized in the first of the *Theses on Feuerbach*:

> The chief defect of all previous materialism (that of Feuerbach included) is that things <*der Gegenstand*>, reality, sensuousness, are conceived only in the form of the *object* <Objekts>, *or of contemplation* <Anschauung>, but not as *sensuous human activity, practice* <Praxis>, not subjectively. Hence, in contra-distinction to materialism, the *active* side was set forth by idealism – which, of course, does not know real, sensuous activity as such. (CW: 5:3)

Above all, it was the consistent historical-philosophical approach of Hess which helped Marx to develop a critical distance to Feuerbach's philosophy. This led, in the German Ideology, to the following reproach:

> As far as Feuerbach is a materialist he does not deal with history .... . (CW: 5:41)

For this reason, Marx takes aim at the passive conception of reason, which Feuerbach's thought shares with empiricism, when he writes that Feuerbach offers:

> He gives no criticism of the present conditions of life. Thus he never manages to conceive the sensuous world as the total living sensuous *activity* of the individuals composing it. (CW: 5: 41)

By contrast, in his own view, which he had already developed in 1844, Marx sought to combine the active conception of reason, which one finds in Hegel and in Bauer, with his own materialistically oriented anthropology. Before we can present this, however, we must first consider the historical-philosophical model of Hess.

The emancipation of the species in Hess's philosophy of history

The writings of Hess can be viewed as the first manifesto of socialist thought in Germany. Even before Wilhelm Weitling, Hess 'discovered' the proletariat as the significant force in the philosophy of history, the force that would eliminate the existing social misery and attain the next level of societal evolution. In a rejection of Hegelian Idealism, Hess proceeds from the unity of idea and matter, a thought which also plays a fundamental role in Marx's *Manuscripts*. In 1842, Hess wrote contributions for the *Rheinische Zeitung*, whose editor at that time was Marx. In these essays, Hess developed not only his view of species-being <*Gattungswesen*>, but also clearly moves toward a communist position. The latter was met with extreme criticism by Marx, who at this time considered himself a democrat. Hess, however, was first able to persuade Engels of communism, and then subsequently Marx. Until 1845–6, there was most notably between Engels and Hess an active collaboration, as Hess even wrote a chapter for the *German Ideology*.

Hess's contributions to the *Twenty-One Sheets from Switzerland* were extolled by Marx as the most important German work on political economy. The foundation of this work is both the philosophy of practice and the view, taken over from Bauer, that historical progress consists in negation, i.e. a destruction of the existing state of affairs which categorically excludes mediation and positions of compromise. On this basis, Hess sought to provide a philosophical basis for communism as the goal of a social development which has as its aim the free activity of human beings. The thought of Hess is not only marked by a profound indignation against the misery and the injustices of the society of his time, but is also simultaneously the expression of a conception of history in which world events and the development of humanity are interpreted in terms of a salvation history <*Heilsgeschichte*>. This religiously motivated socialism, which was understood as the redemption of a religious promise, was transformed by Marx – by means of Feuerbach's critique of religion – into an atheistic anthropology of species-being. This atheistic transformation does not, however, necessarily demand a modification of the explicit evaluative and normative foundation of the anthropology.

The Hessian philosophy of practice proceeds through three stages. It begins with a conception of history, understood as the consummation of a salvation history through increasing knowledge of both God and self. Hess then proceeds to a theory of consciousness, inspired by Fichte and Bauer, in which the aforementioned historical process is understood as the emancipation of autonomous self-consciousness. In the wake of Feuerbach's critique of religion, Hess is in the position to supplement his philosophy of practice with an anthropology, in which a human being experiences the realization of his species-being not *qua* individual but rather as part of a rationally organized community (see Stuke 1963):

> The purpose of a human being, as that of every being, is to activate itself *completely*. However, as a single individual, a human being *cannot at all activate himself*. The essence of the human activity of living just is *collaboration* with other individuals of the species. Apart from this collaboration – apart from

society –, a human being is incapable of a single specifically human *activity*. (Hess 1961: 275)

In contrast to Marx, Hess's assimilation of Feuerbach's views did not result in a firm criticism of Idealism; rather the appropriation remained without exception within the context of the philosophy of religion.

> The essence of God, according to Feuerbach, is the transcendent essence of the human, and the true doctrine of divine essence is the doctrine of human essence: *theology is anthropology* – this is true – but it is not the *complete* truth. The essence of the human, it must be added, is a social essence, the collaboration of various individuals for one and the same purpose, for entirely identical interests, and the true doctrine of humanity, the true humanism, is the doctrine of human socialization; that is, *anthropology is socialism*. (Hess 1961: 293)

Above all, it was the critique of state and private property which impressed Marx. In the aftermath of Hess, he came to regard these institutions as alienating phenomena. In contrast to the influence of Feuerbach, the most lasting effect of Hess's work is the much more trenchant and consistent historical-philosophical orientation of his theory of species-being. Moreover, it was Hess who advocated the thesis that species-being is realized primarily in economic interaction. "On the Essence of Money" was an article written for the *Deutsch-Französischen Jahrbücher* but unpublished on account of the periodical's financial problems following the first volume. With that article, Hess became the first to apply the method of Feuerbach's critique of religion in the context of an analysis of economic theories and concepts. The programmatic formulation is as follows:

> Then it is self-evident that the essence of money is defined in the same way as that of the essence of God, namely, that it is likewise the transcendent, practically externalized essence of human beings. (Hess 1961: 293)

Through the application of Feuerbach's method for the critique of religion to the analysis of economic phenomena, Hess drew an analogy that is not limited to these two areas. Thus, he writes that:

> ... in our world of shopkeepers ... it is thus practically the case, as it is theoretically the case in the Christian heaven, that the individual is the *goal* of life and the species its *means*. (Hess 1961: 334)

Hess equates the two: "Christianity is *realized* in our world of shopkeepers" (Hess 1961: 338). The essence of the later fetish theory of Marx, who as the editor and publisher in charge of the *Jahrbücher* must have known of this essay, is here anticipated:

> What God is for the *theoretical* life, *money* is for the *practical* life of the inverted world: the *externalized capacity* of human beings, their *vital activity bartered away*. (Hess 1961: 334ff.)

After Bauer's extension of the religio-critical method to the political sphere, Hess completed the transfer with regard to the domain of economic and general social life. For Hess, the species-being of a person realizes itself in practical social activity. The sublation of the existing alienation is only possible through the abolishment of private property, of the state, and of all its institutions. At this point, there emerges the Utopia of social unity and harmony, which both invokes the representations of the utopian Fourier and excludes the exploitation of humans by one another. Hess made this "anarchistic daydream" (Lange 1980: 99) into an essential determination of species-being and, with that, the goal of history: the spontaneous, harmonious, increasingly attuned conscious collaboration of human beings in cooperative production, free from state coercion. With that the theoretical dimension of the relation between individual and species is completely subordinated to the practical sphere. Above all, the focus of the actualization of existence is finally and unilaterally moved to the side of the species: in complete contrast to Hegel and much more strongly than Feuerbach, the individual human being is said to be an exemplar. The cardinal mistake of the criticized position consists in locating the consummation of the human being in the individual, as well as in believing:

> that which the capitalist, who insists on his holy *private property*, consciously and systematically declares or thinks of himself as a private person: namely, that he can possess the love of God, the capacity of the species, *for himself alone*. (Hess 1961: 315)

This tendency then culminates in the aforementioned essay "On the Monetary System," in that the relation between the individual and the species is conceptualized in terms of an organic model, when Hess speaks of the "organic community" (Hess 1961: 347).

In the end, the scholarly and political cooperation between Hess and Marx broke down over two fundamental differences. *First*, Hess continually insisted on the *ethical* foundation of his view and combined it with a philosophy of history constructed in terms of the category of historical inevitability, which is modeled on the idea of the necessity of natural laws. Hess, however, could not resolve the tension which results from this, and so on this point his theory remains unsatisfactory. In the end, Hess underpinned his version of socialism and history with the ahistorical ideal of an ethical humanism, which he augmented with socialist ideas and images of a just social order. *Second*, Hess arrived at an historical philosophical view, according to which the species-being of a person can only first be realized through a history of externalization and alienation. Neither the categorical framework which comprehends species-being philosophically, nor the objective of the historical development itself, however, are brought within the historical process, even if they themselves can only be realized through the historical process.

The *dual* nature of the difference between Marx and Hess consists in the fact that Marx tries to reinforce his historical-philosophical-essentialist view with an historically detailed study of both historical processes and the national economy, and simultaneously to bring this to a philosophical-scientific form of expression with the aid of the Hegelian *Logic*. As a result, the evaluative and normative aspects of the anthropological construct are essentially obscured. Marx is also concerned to show that this essence is an historical product, so as to avoid employing the concept of species-being as an ahistorical, utopian, and thus inevitable evaluative and normative benchmark. The scientific evidence of necessary historical progress should take the place of appeals to morality and should accomplish the actualization of philosophy through revolutionary practice. Whether Marx could make good on this claim must be shown through an analysis of the *Manuscripts* and the *German Ideology*. Ultimately, it may be that the Marxist philosophical construct represents an ethically laden ahistorical figure of thought; one in which historical processes are admitted as processes of the self-development and self-discovery of the species-being of humanity.

The *Aufhebung* of philosophy, or the actualization of philosophy?

We have now gathered together a few of the central building blocks with which Marx, while in Paris in 1844, constructed his first outline of a critical philosophical anthropology. Against Bauer's individualism, Marx aligned himself with Feuerbach and Hess, insofar as he made the foundation of his account the socially constituted nature of humanity as species-being. His critique of religion, however, combined elements from Feuerbach and Bauer. Marx followed Feuerbach by incorporating certain emotive aspects of religious attitudes into his metaphysics of species-being. And he is indebted to Bauer insofar as he conceives of the externalization and alienation of human beings in religion not only as projection, but also as the inversion and distortion of the human essence. In what follows, it will be shown in what manner Marx incorporates these themes into his own version of Hegel's dialectic, and how, under the pressure of Stirner's criticism, he develops it further into a theory which then became efficacious as both historical materialism and a critique of political economy.

The metaphysics of species in Karl Marx

We can here explicate the line of thought advanced in the *Manuscripts* only in terms of Marx's central concepts and premises, or more precisely his theses. I would like to begin by describing the action-theoretical foundation of Marx's account, because it is "the model of externalization, or of objectification, <which forms> the decisive foundational and conceptual resource for the Marxist critique" (Lange 1980: 55).

Objectification: the action-theoretical model

Marx locates the point of difference between the vital activity of human and non-human animals in consciousness, or – as one says today – intentionality, that is, intentional human action (see CW: 3:275). As a theory of intentional action, the model of objectification is anticipated in both Hegel's theory of action and Feuerbach's transformation thereof. Marx himself was fully aware of this:

> The outstanding achievement of Hegel's *Phenomenology* and of its final outcome, the dialectic of negativity as the moving and generating principle, is thus first that Hegel conceives the self-creation of man as a process, conceives objectification as loss of the object, as alienation and as transcendence of this alienation; *that he thus grasps the essence of labour* and comprehends objective man – true, because real man – as the outcome of man's own labour. The real, active orientation of man to himself as a species-being, or his manifestation as a real species-being (i.e., as a human being), is only possible if he really *brings out* all his species-powers – something which in turn is only possible through the cooperative action of all of mankind, only as the result of history – *and treats these powers as objects*: and this, to begin with, is again only possible in the form of estrangement. (CW: 3:332f.; my emphasis)

It is clear that, for Marx, Hegel has already developed an objectification model of action. In fact, it is not only in the *Phenomenology* but also in Hegel's *Philosophy of Right* that one finds a theory of action which shares a number of essential features with the Marxist account (see Quante 2004). There are, however, three important differences. First, in the *Phenomenology* Hegel distinguishes between the externalization and the alienation of self-consciousness, whereas Marx does not differentiate the two. By contrast, in his work on the philosophy of right Hegel speaks primarily of the objectification of a goal through action. Although poetic action, which results in the bringing forth of some object, is a central paradigm in the Hegelian theory of action, he does not confine himself to it. Rather, it is in Feuerbach's materialist-anthropological transformation of Hegel's model of action that one first finds the restriction of action to objectification in the sense of (1) the production of some material; (2) the process of production; and (3) an end-product which can be detached from the action. Second, in contrast to Feuerbach and Marx, Hegel works within a rationalist framework: spatial-temporal objects are from a philosophical view essentially of a conceptual, or – as one says today – propositional nature. Since the intention of the action is also understood as having a propositional shape – what Hegel calls "subjective purpose" – one can recognize as plausible the close relation between an intention and its realization (or what Hegel calls "objective purpose"). Third, the religious and philosophical context of God's creation of the world is systematically fundamental for Hegel's thought. Marx dispenses with this element through Feuerbach's critique of religion, and this in turn has consequences for Marx's theory of alienation and metaphysics of species-being. In a digression on Hegel, Marx clearly acknowledges Feuerbach's influence:

> Feuerbach is the only one who has a serious, critical attitude to the Hegelian dialectic and who has made genuine discoveries in this field. He is in fact the true conqueror of the old philosophy. (CW: 3:328)

One should note that, in the course of his materialist transformation, Feuerbach translates Hegel's talk about purpose, which remains "identical" in relinquishment, into talk about the object, and he conceives of purposes as material objects. A passage from Feuerbach's *The Essence of Christianity* confirms this conceptual reformulation:

> The human being is nothing without an object. Great, exemplary persons – those persons who reveal to us the essence of the human being – confirm this proposition through their lives. The have only one dominant, basic passion: the actualization of a purpose, which was the essential object of their activity. (GW: 5:33)

Now we turn to the Marxist model of action. Marx writes:

> This fact simply means that the object that labour produces, its product, stands opposed to it as something alien, as a power independent of the producer. The product of labour is labour embodied and made material in an object, it is the objectification of labour. The realization of labour is its objectification. (CW: 3:272)

This talk of objects is constricted and systematically deceptive, and it must be translated into talk of facts and states of affairs. On the assumption of this modification, if one distinguishes between labor in the sense of a result (product) and labor in the sense of a process (laboring), there emerges a threefold schema:

(a) I intend (through my action) to bring about the state of affairs p.
(b) Through my action, I bring about (in the sense of a process) the state of affairs p (I actualize p).
(c) The actualization of this process of production is the independent, alien circumstance p, in which my activity has "fixed" itself.

Now, on the plausible premise that the state of affairs and the circumstance p are "identical" (in an action-theoretical sense to be defined more clearly), a plausible reconstruction of our common-sense understanding of actions is as follows: (c) implies that an existing state of affairs, thus a circumstance p, is independent of me. My action h may have been – and it is in this sense that (b) can be reconstrued – a *causal* condition for p to have become a circumstance; therefore the circumstance exists independently of me.

Alienation: Marx's first philosophy of history

The second central theorem of the *Manuscripts* is the theory of alienation. Marx begins with the social fact that, under the national economic conditions of his time, working people are impoverished and immiserated with systematic necessity. The more they contribute to societal prosperity, the more impoverished they become. And the greater the potential power and knowledge of the human species becomes through industry, technology and science, the more the proletariat is reduced to a weakened, passive state.

The cause of this systematically necessary alienation, according to Marx, lies in the social institutions of the division of labor, the private ownership of the means of production, and the commodification of labor. This thesis is explained in terms of the model of objectification, and it is in this model too that Marx locates the origin of alienation:

> Let us now take a closer look at objectification, at the production of the worker, and the estrangement, the loss of the object, of his product, that this entails. (CW: 3:273)

Under capitalistic conditions, the products do not belong to the worker who produced them, because the products are the property of the capitalists. The worker must first acquire the products by means of the wages, which he receives for the selling of his labor. If he has no money, then the products of his labor lie beyond his grasp. Since the means of production are also privately owned, the worker cannot simply employ his own labor in order to produce the things which are necessary for his existence. First, he must successfully sell his labor, so that it can be activated within a process of production. Thus, in a capitalistic system the worker himself is not able to determine the utilization of his labor, since the means of production belong to someone else. The same applies to the products of his labor. The "loss of the object, of his product" consists in the fact that this is the property of another. Marx thus summarizes the point:

> In these two respects, then, the worker becomes a slave of his object; firstly, in that he receives an object of labour, i.e., he receives work, and, secondly, in that he receives means of subsistence. (CW: 3:273)

According to the objectification model, the product of human action is an independent, alien object in relation to the action. Thus, there arises the possibility that a social institution can intervene between the activity and the product. In capitalism, this is the legal institution of private property. By means of this, the producer is cut-off from his products, and the actual contexts of production qua market mechanisms gain the upper hand over the worker and the conducting of his life.

Marx subsequently alters the perspective and inquires into the alienation of the worker from his activity. Thus, the focus is no longer restricted to the product but rather now extends to the act of production – in terms of the objectification model, this is at the level of (a) and (b):

> But estrangement manifests itself not only in the result, but also in the act of production, within the activity of production itself. (CW: 3:274)

True to the idealist model of objectification, which assumes a transfer of the properties of production to those of the product, this dimension of alienation is more basic.

According to Marx, it consists of two aspects: first, in his activity the worker experiences himself as determined by another, and, second, he feels "unhappy." The goal of his activity is specified through the process of production, the product does not belong to him, and the impetus for his activity is the necessity for survival. Labor is not the realization of his existence but rather ultimately only a means to survive. Labor is not the goal of his existence but rather only the means for physically extending his ever weakening, passive state.

Marx wants to "derive a third feature of estranged labour from the two we have already examined" (CW: 3:275). To this end, he introduces a premise of his argument – the species nature of human beings:

> Man is a species-being, not only because he practically and theoretically makes the species – both his own and those of other things – his object, but also – and this is simply another way of saying the same thing – because he looks upon himself as the present, living species, because he looks upon himself as a universal and therefore free being. (CW: 3:275)

This account of species-being is explained still further. Now of particular interest is where both further dimensions of alienation lie:

> Estranged labour not only (1) estranges nature from man and (2) estranges man from himself, from his own function, from his vital activity; because of this, it also estranges man from his species. It turns his species-life into a means for his individual life. Firstly, it estranges species-life and individual life, and, secondly, it turns the latter, in its abstract form, into the purpose of the former, also in its abstract and estranged form. (CW: 3:276)

"But productive life is species-life," and "free conscious activity constitutes the species-character of man" (CW: 3:276). The specific species nature of a human being consists of intentional action in the sphere of production and reproduction.

Now, the Marxist criticism of capitalistic society is that it alienates human beings from their species-being in two ways. Insofar as the realization of his species-being, which for Marx consists in cooperative material production and reproduction, is confronted by an increasingly opaque and controlling market, the individual person is unable to identify with this realization of the species. On account of the inhumane rules of the game, the worker participates in this social or species dimension of his existence only for the sake of securing his own survival. For the worker, labor is not the actualization of his species essence but rather only a means for safeguarding his existence. As Marx summarized the point:

> Estranged labour, therefore, turns man's species-being – both nature and his intellectual species-power – into a being alien to him and a means of his individual existence. It estranges man from his own body, from nature as it

exists outside him, from his spiritual essence, his human existence. (CW: 3:277)

Yet, this third dimension of alienation is only the first inversion of means and end with respect to the individual's relation to his species-being. Marx reminds us that the species-being of a human being manifests itself not only in the relation of the individual to the entirety of his social context, or the productive sector, but also in the relation of individuals to one another, which Marx expresses in good Hegelian fashion:

When man confronts himself, he also confronts other men. (CW: 3:277ff.)

The fourth dimension of alienation consists in the inversion of means and end with respect to the relation of individual persons to one another. Since a single human being does not produce directly for the sake of satisfying the needs of other human beings, he does not recognize in their neediness the species-being of human beings. He therefore cannot himself realize his own species-being – either through acts of exchange or through acts of purchase. The social institutions of the market, of wage labor, and of the private ownership of the means of production, respectively, do not allow for the establishment of relations between persons in the productive sector which could be seen as the realization of the human species-being.

In the *Manuscripts*, Marx accuses the bourgeois national economy of failing to explain "to what extent these external, apparently contingent circumstances are only the expression of a necessary development" (CW: 3:271). At the point in the text where the first, unfinished part breaks off, Marx himself raises the question:

How, we now ask, does man come to *alienate his labour*, to estrange it? How is this estrangement founded in the nature of human development? (CW 3:281)

If one understands the first of these questions as calling for an historical-genetic explanation, then the second formulation can be understood as Marx's search for a philosophical answer which derives alienation from the human essence as a necessary step in its development. This human essence is defined as objective species-being, which both objectifies and realizes its essence in productive activity, where realization also includes conscious activity in the sense of conscious appropriation of objectified characteristics of the species.

The figure of thought which lies at the basis of the Marxist theory of development and, before that, in the Feuerbachian critique of religion to which Marx continually alludes in his analysis of alienation, was a line of thinking which originated in German Idealism. It found its way into Marx's thought by means of Bauer's concept of emancipatory self-consciousness. It was the goal of the philosophical systems of both Fichte and Hegel to explain how self-consciousness can know and actualize itself, or its own essence. Since the essence of self-consciousness is determined as autonomy, a property can only belong to the essence of self-consciousness if it is both produced by self-consciousness itself and recognized by self-consciousness as one of its own properties.

Both the theory of self-consciousness and the epistemology of German Idealism function according to the subject–object model, which of course also underlies the thought of Feuerbach and Marx. In order that a subject might know something, it must relate itself to an object and its properties. The case of self-consciousness is unique in that the known object is identical with the subject, and the subject is aware of this identity. In place of self-consciousness Marx substitutes the sensible, physical human being, and in place of the idealist acts of consciousness Marx substitutes the objectification model of objective species-being. In other words: a person can only realize his species-being insofar as he develops a consciousness of it (a point of contrast with non-human animals: universality and freedom). The latter only occurs insofar as he recognizes his species properties in an object. In order that this object should be the occasion for true knowledge of one's own species-being, the object must be an objectification of the species properties of the subject. For Marx, this is the social context of production. Thus, herein lies the first step towards the objectification and estrangement, or alienation, of the species powers – capitalism as the end point of this alienated objectification. If all of the species properties are worked out in this way, then a person can, in the second step, begin to appropriate practically these species powers through social revolution.

The original condition of human beings in this construct is accordingly not *un*-alienated but rather *pre*-alienated and undifferentiated. The person has not realized his species-being because he is not aware of it. The alienation which occurs in the course of objectification is the necessary intermediate stage which makes possible a conscious appropriation of the species essence. It is not the initial immediate state but rather the sublated alienation, or the sublation of alienation which proceeds through diremption, which is the realization of the human species-being. It is central not only for Hegel but also for Marx that this *Aufhebung* is not merely a regression into the initial state of undifferentiated immediacy but rather is conceived as a productive process of learning, development, and formation. In the sublation of alienation the experience of alienation cannot be forgotten. The quality of sublated alienation consists precisely in the preservation of the knowledge of alienation and its causes.

Species metaphysics: love and recognition

What exactly does Marx mean with the thesis that a human being is an objective species-being? And what potential ethical implications are contained in this Marxist metaphysics?

The Marxist model of species-being can be understood as the synthesis of three things: Feuerbach's anthropological concept, Hess's vision of social unity, and the objectification model of action taken over from Hegel. With Hegel, Marx retains the epistemological subject–object model in order to conceptualize the necessity of alienation. With Feuerbach, he accepts the individual anthropological and the theoretical dimension of the species-being as a subordinate aspect of a primarily social species-being. And, with Hess, Marx criticizes the private ownership of the means of production, wage labor, and the existence of the constitutional state as the expression of alienation, a state of affairs which is to be replaced by immediate or consciously planned and rationally transparent cooperation. Moreover, with Hess, Marx's thought is radically historical in the sense of a necessary process of the development of existence, whereby history proceeds by means of crises and of formation out of opposition. Alongside this historical and social construal of the species-being there comes into play, as an amplification of Feuerbach's anthropology, Hess's image of the unity of matter and spirit. Marx construes the human being as a part of nature, living both in and by means of nature. Simultaneously, nature becomes a part of the human being in the course of the self-actualization of the species. What Marx calls the inorganic body of species-being is nature which has been transformed and appropriated through human activity. Nevertheless, the more precise determination of all of these complex relations remains undeveloped in the unified vision of the *Manuscripts*. Instead of conceptual precision, one finds rhetoric and enthusiasm:

> Thus *society* is the complete unity of man with nature – the true resurrection of nature – the consistent naturalism of man and the consistent humanism of nature. (CW 3:298)

The species metaphysics of Marx, however, contains not only a philosophical determination of the relation between nature and spirit, as well as an essentialist philosophy of history grounded on the objectification model of acting and knowing; the species metaphysics also contains an evaluative dimension. Many passages in the *Manuscripts* can certainly be understood as advancing a line of ethical argumentation. This is most evident in a famous passage following the excerpts from a book by James Mill (*Éléments d'économie politique*), a passage which Marx wrote at approximately the same time as his completion of the *Manuscripts*. There, he writes:

> Let us suppose that we had carried out production as human beings. Each of us would have *in two ways affirmed* himself and the other person. 1) In my *production* I would have objectified my *individuality, its specific character*, and therefore enjoyed not only an individual *manifestation of my life* during the activity, but also when looking at the object I would have the individual pleasure of knowing my personality to be *objective, visible to the senses* and hence a power *beyond all doubt*. 2) In your enjoyment or use of my product I would have the *direct* enjoyment both of being conscious of having satisfied a *human* need by my work, that is, of having objectified *man's* essential nature, and of having thus created an object corresponding to the need of another *man's* essential nature. 3) I would have been for you the *mediator* between you and the species, and therefore would become recognised and felt by you yourself as a completion of your own essential nature and as a necessary part of yourself, and consequently would know myself to be confirmed both in your thought and your love. 4) In the individual expression of my life I would have directly created your expression of your life, and therefore in my individual

activity I would have directly *confirmed* and *realised* my true nature, my *human* nature, my *communal nature*.

Our products would be so many mirrors in which we saw reflected our essential nature.

This relationship would moreover be reciprocal; what occurs on my side has also to occur on yours. (CW 3:277f.)

This striking passage contains in a compressed form all of the elements from the *Manuscripts* which we have treated under the heading of "alienation." Furthermore, Marx here formulates the ontological thesis that an individual cannot realize his species-being in isolation. Realizing one's species-being is much more a task allocated to the constitutive contribution of one or of all of the others. This ontologically unified bond is realized through co-production which is not alienated: A knows and senses B as a necessary part of his own essence. In order for this realization of the essence to occur, however, something more than a causal relation is required. On the contrary, the social cooperation of the participants must be accompanied by the right attitude, even at the level of interpreting both oneself and the other: recognition of the other as a human being with needs, as a bearer of my needs; and also love as the expression of the recognition that, through his activity, the other makes possible the actualization of my own species-being. Both the act of production and the consummation of A and B are necessary components of the proper realization of species essence, which Marx here only negatively describes as the absence of means-end-inversions and the falling away of the mediation of private property, the market, and wage labor. Alongside the ontological dimension of reciprocal dependence, understood as moments of the objective species-being which realizes itself in production, there arises the requirement of a commensurate individual perspective both of this ontological dimension and of correct action in relation to the needs of others. This can certainly be viewed as an implicit ethical norm. The necessity of symmetry ("reciprocal relation") can simultaneously be used as the basis both for the inter-subjective validity of these claims, which ground themselves in the ontological limitation of the individuals in relation to their species nature, and as a criterion for their normative appraisal. With that, there is inscribed in the Marxist metaphysics an ethics; an ethics, moreover, which is not threatened by the consideration that this correct structure of recognition possibly adapts itself to the proper social organization of living together. For, if ethical consciousness is itself dependent on societal existence, then correct ethical consciousness necessarily remains a component of the proper realization of the species-being.

Stirner's fundamental criticism

The end of 1844 witnessed the publication of *The Ego and Its Own*, a book which sparked an extremely heated discussion within the Hegelian school and eventually led to its demise. Stirner's fundamental criticism consisted in the claim that every philosophical construct must work with universal concepts which cannot completely encompass the concrete single individual. Applied to the debate at that time:

> Feuerbach, in the *Principles of the Philosophy of the Future*, is always harping upon *being* <*das Sein*>. In this he too, with all his antagonism to Hegel and the absolute philosophy, is stuck fast in abstraction; for 'being' is abstraction, as is even 'the I'. ... With this, of course, Feuerbach does not get further than to the proof, trivial in itself, that I require the *senses* for everything, or that I cannot entirely do without these organs. (Stirner EO: 300)

On the presupposition of these radically nominalistic premises, every assumption of a human essence (whether *qua* spirit as by Hegel, *qua* self-consciousness as with Bauer, *qua* human being as with Feuerbach, *qua* species as in Hess, or *qua* objective species-being as with Marx) must be recognized as a paternalistic patronization. For every assumption which runs counter to this nominalism leads to an external determination of the individual based either indirectly on essentialist premises or directly on moral ones. Even the historical-philosophical belief in progress leads invariably to an incapacitation of the individual, concrete subject in favor of the progress of the species or of the future society, if this progress is defined in terms of either essentialist or moral categories.

Stirner radically and unequivocally opposes this Utopia of socialization as the means for abolishing alienation. To the question, much discussed by socialists at that time, "How can you live a truly social life so long as even one exclusiveness still exists between you?'," Stirner retorts, "How can you be truly single so long as even one connection still exists between you?" (Stirner EO: 120)

Stirner's criticism, which left clear traces in Marxist thought, is directed against three forms of this paternalism. *First*, he rejects every form of paternalism which proceeds on the assumption of a universal human essence:

> A man is "called" to nothing, and has no "calling," no "destiny," as little as a plant or a beast has a "calling." (Stirner EO: 288)

Even the idea of the species is emphatically rejected by Stirner as a paternalistic deprivation of freedom:

> That society is no ego at all, which could give, bestow, or grant, but an instrument or means, from which we may derive benefit; that we have no social duties, but solely interests for the pursuance of which society must serve us; that we owe society no sacrifice, but, if we sacrifice anything, sacrifice it to ourselves – of this the socialists do not think, because they – as liberals – are imprisoned in the religious principle, and zealously aspire after – a sacred society, such as the State was hitherto. (Stirner EO: 111)

Second, no less clear and fundamental is Stirner's rejection of every form of moral paternalism:

Against *right* one can no longer, as against *a* right, come forward with the assertion that it is 'a wrong'. One can say now only that it is a piece of nonsense, an illusion. If one called it wrong, one would have to set up *another right* in opposition to it, and measure it by this. If, on the contrary, one rejects right as such, right in and of itself, altogether, then one also rejects the concept of wrong, and dissolves the whole concept of right (to which the concept of wrong belongs). (Stirner EO: 93)

Unlike Stirner's radically nominalistic criticism, which Marx cannot incorporate into his view, these remarks by Stirner denote an emphatic immoralism, such as that advocated by Marx and Engels in the *German Ideology*. To this extent, Stirner's criticism radicalizes substantially the critique Marx made against Bauer in *On the Jewish Question*:

It was not the *individual man* – and he alone is *man* – that became free, but the *citizen*, the *citoyen*, the *political* man, who for that very reason is not *man* but a specimen of the human species, and more particularly a specimen of the species Citizen, a *free citizen*. (Stirner EO: 132)

Third, Stirner is also decisively opposed to historical-philosophical paternalism:

In the revolution it was not the *individual* who acted so as to affect the world's history, but a *people*; the *nation*, the sovereign nation, wanted to effect everything. A fancied I, an idea, such as the nation is, appears acting; the individuals contribute themselves as tools of this idea, and act as 'citizens'. (Stirner EO: 100)

Above all, it is the third reproach which is immediately applicable to the role of the proletariat in Marx's thought. Thus, one finds in Stirner's book parallels to the historical role of the proletariat described in Marx's then nascent work *The Holy Family*:

it is not a question of what this or that proletarian, or even the whole proletariat, at the moment *regards* as its aim. It is a question of *what the proletariat is*, and what, in accordance with this *being*, it will historically be compelled to do. Its aim and historical action is visibly and irrevocably foreshadowed in its own life situation as well as in the whole organization of bourgeois society today. (CW: 4:37)

Although he could not have referred to this passage from Marx on account of the chronology of their writings, Stirner's criticism nevertheless hits upon an essential and, from a contemporary perspective, problematic aspect of the Marxist theory of history, one which Stirner opposes with his radical individualism:

I on my part start from a presupposition in presupposing *myself*; but my presupposition does not struggle for its perfection like 'man struggling for his perfection', but only serves me to enjoy it and consume it. (Stirner EO: 135)

Stirner's critique of the combination of essentialism with a teleological philosophy of history speaks to the core of the theory which Marx had just then developed in the *Manuscripts*:

> Enough, there is a mighty difference whether I make myself the starting-point or the goal. As the latter I do not have myself, am consequently still alien to myself, am my *essence*, my 'true essence', alien to me, will mock me as a spook of a thousand different names. Because I am not yet I, another (like God, the true man, the truly pious man, the rational man, the freeman, etc.) is I, my ego. (Stirner EO: 290)

For Bauer, Feuerbach, Hess, or even Marx, the conclusion Stirner draws from his critical exposition of the various attempts to overcome Hegelian philosophy and theology in the pursuit of emancipation is a conclusion which must have been a provocation of the first order, for it sticks a finger in the wound of the unexplained relation between the individual and its species. It is thus not surprising that following the publication of this work, three of those criticized – Bauer, Feuerbach, and Hess – responded immediately. Already in 1845, there followed a response by Stirner. The final round of this debate, in which Bauer and Feuerbach also critically engaged one another, formed the basis of Marx and Engels' criticism of German ideology. Since, however, the work which bore that name was not published, it did not affect the course of the debate.

The formula of Stirner's reply consists in pointing out that his critics proceed on the assumption of something which is designated as absolutely valuable, interesting, or normatively binding. As such, that which is assumed does not depend for its value on the consent or identification of the individual, whereas for Stirner it represents something determined externally:

> Every relation to something which is deemed to be of absolute interest or valuable in and of itself is a religious relation or religion as such. That which is of interest can only be such through its interest for you, and that which is valuable can only be so through your attribution of value; against which what is uninteresting is so despite its interest to you, and what is worthless is so despite its value for you. (Stirner 1976: 358)

Shortly following this, Stirner assumes the role of an anonymous reviewer in order to clarify his own terminology:

> This thing which is of absolute interest, which should be interesting independent of those who take interest in it; this thing which thus, instead of being the concern of the individual, rather seeks to be first a 'vessel of his

honor', or the people, who should be its 'skills and tools'; this thing seeks, according to Stirner, 'the Holy' as such. (Stirner 1976: 359)

Stirner's arguments speak to the core of Marxist thought, since he finds the ethical and philosophical-anthropological self-defense of Feuerbach (GW: 9:427–41) as unconvincing as the idealistic and individualistic position which Bauer contributed to this debate (Bauer 2003: 55–68). The dismissal of Hess's ethical doctrine and the renunciation of Feuerbach's philosophy which Marx and Engels execute in the *German Ideology* should be understood against this background as an implicit recognition of Stirner's objections. Simultaneously, it is obvious that Marx cannot simply incorporate Stirner's fundamental criticisms into his own theory without dissolving them completely. Let us thus see how, in the *German Ideology*, Marx endeavors to extricate himself from this difficult situation.

The overcoming of German ideology?

The critique of Stirner is the largest part of the *German Ideology*. This is clear evidence of the extent to which Marx understood himself to have been affected by Stirner's reasoning. The present essay is not the place for a detailed assessment of Marx's extensive and, at times, purely polemical anti-criticism. Marx does not engage with Stirner's radical nominalism, since he regarded this aspect of Stirner's critique as pure philosophical fantasy and, with that, as something which the human being *qua* theoretical, universal consciousness refutes practically, i.e. through the development of adequate theories. At least, this is what he claimed for the new conception of historical materialism presented in the *German Ideology*:

> Incidentally, when things are seen in this way, as they really are and happened, every profound philosophical problem is resolved, as will be seen even more clearly later, quite simply into an empirical fact. (CW: 5:39)

Marx goes to great lengths, *first*, to prove that the reconstruction of history, or of the philosophy of history, which Stirner had put forth in his book is itself still the expression of an Idealist philosophy of history. On Stirner's account, according to Marx, it is in the place of the philosophy of history that "history runs into the old philosophy, and even then only as Saint Max, following Hegel and Feuerbach, imagines it" (CW: 3:121). Marx criticizes Stirner for examining only "the philosophical relation" (CW: 3:121) of the theoretician to the world and not, as is recommended by the historical materialism of Marx and Engels, the real relation. Through detailed analyses, Marx aims to prove that, because Stirner remains in the paradigm of the Idealist construct of history, Stirner is not in the position to integrate adequately the empirical facts into his philosophy of history. Marx's point is thus that Stirner's theory fails in terms of both his own critique of ideology as well as that of historical materialism.

Second, Marx seizes on the objections which Hess and Feuerbach raised against Stirner's critique of the paternalism implicit in the metaphysics of substance. Marx writes that Stirner's 'I' itself represents a philosophical construct which is not commensurate with the empirically describable human being:

> This "ego," the end of the historical construction, is no "corporeal" ego, carnally procreated by man and woman, which needs no construction in order to exist; it is an "ego" spiritually created by two categories, "idealism" and "realism," a merely conceptual existence. (CW: 5:240)

With that, Marx rejects not only the norm implicit in Stirner's criticism of the paternalism in the positions he critiques, but also the underlying norm which – as a philosophical construct – is not only empirically implausible, but also generates paternalistic effects.

Ultimately, we stand again before the question which we encountered earlier in the Marxist account of alienation and his metaphysics of species-being: How is the relation of individual and species, of the individual 'I' and universal self-consciousness, etc. to be adequately determined in metaphysical and evaluative-normative respects? The debate between Bauer, Hess, Feuerbach and Stirner went around in circles on this point amid the exchange of accusations. Even Marx, in his response to Stirner's critique, did not develop a positive answer to this central question but rather contented himself with the strategy of repudiating the critique through a meta-critique. With that, however, the systematic problem remains unresolved. Even the second side of the Marxist critique of Stirner, his plea for an empirically informed philosophical anthropology, does not address this problem. Thus, even if Marx, with his theory of historical materialism, is successful both in answering a few of the questions left open by the philosophical account advanced in the *Manuscripts* and in rejecting Stirner's fundamental criticism, Marx is nevertheless unable to satisfactorily fill the gaps in his metaphysics of species-being.

The end of the post-Hegelian discussion: Is everything 'dead and gone'?

As hectic and boisterous as this discussion was during the Hegelian school's process of disintegration, it passed just as quickly and was forgotten. There are, however, good systematic reasons to again engage this discussion, because we have the chance to learn something from the history of philosophy. At a time in which religiosity is burgeoning once more and neo-liberalism is asserting itself aggressively worldwide, Western societies and their philosophical traditions stand before questions with which the protagonists of these essays already had to grapple.

As the earlier theorists were concerned with the emancipation of political institutions from forms of religious legitimization, so today political philosophy must shed light on how a secularly legitimated state can circumnavigate religious conceptions in social, political and juridical matters (Habermas 2005). It may be that our questions on this point come from the opposite direction, as it were, when we adopt a suspicious eye towards forces seeking to abolish the separation of church and state. At the time of the post-Hegelians the gradual emancipation of the state from religion was beginning, while today we are experiencing – and questioning – the partial re-theologization of politics. Yet perhaps in our questioning we will also discover, as for example in the context of the disenchantment of human nature which is occurring presently in the biological sciences, the remnants of religious thinking which continue to shape the legitimization of law and state.

Certainly, in the post-Hegelian projects which have provided the material for this essay, one does not find a philosophically satisfying answer to the question as to how one should define the relation between individual and species, existence and essence, and personal autonomy and universal morality. However, the debate which has continued for three decades between liberalism and communitarianism is instructive for us in two respects. First, it shows that the projects which political philosophy has offered heretofore could not provide a satisfying answer. And, second, it appears that the societal conflict which underwrites this debate continues unabated. Processes of globalization, the erosion of the welfare state, and the multifaceted heightened atomization of individuals in Western societies accentuate all the more the problem whose normative content raises – both today and for the post-Hegelians – the question concerning the proper relation between individual self-determination and the social inclusion of human beings.

Presumably, we will find neither decisive answers to, nor formulas for, solving our contemporary questions in the philosophical debate which inflamed tempers in Germany almost two hundred years ago. Nevertheless, we can learn from the philosophical mistakes and the resulting societal failures of that earlier period. Considering the possible costs which errors in these matters could cause for our historical balance sheet, this is anything but insignificant.

Note

1 Angle brackets (< >) distinguish the translators interpolations.

References

Primary literature

Bauer, B. (1843) *Die Judenfrage*, Braunschweig: Otto.
—— (1927) *Das Entdeckte Christentum*, edited by E. Barnikol, Jena: Diederichs.
—— (1968) *Feldzüge der reinen Kritik*, edited by H. M. Sass, Frankfurt am Main: Suhrkamp.
—— (2003) "Charakteristik Ludwig Feuerbachs: *Feuerbach und der Einzige*," in K. W. Fleming (ed.) *Recensenten Stirners: Die Kritik und die Anti-Kritik* (= Stirneriana 24), Leipzig: Max-Stirner-Archiv, 55–68.
Cieszkowski, A. (1981) *Prolegomena zur Historiosophia*, Hamburg: Meiner.
Feuerbach, L. (GW) *Gesammelte Werke*, edited by W. Schuffenhauer, Berlin: Akademie, 1967–. (Cited GW volume:page.).
Gans, E. (1971) *Philosophische Schriften*, edited by H. Schröder, Glashütten am Taunus: Auvermann.
—— (2005) *Naturrecht und Universalrechtsgeschichte*, edited by J. Braun, Tübingen: MohrSiebeck.
Hegel, G. W. F. (1830) *Encyclopädie der philosophischen Wissenschaften im Grundrisse*, Heidelberg: Winter.
—— (1993) *Einleitung in die Philosophie der Religion: Der Begriff der Religion*, Hamburg: Meiner.
—— (1999) *Die Lehre vom Wesen (1813)* (= Gesammelte Werke, vol. 11), Hamburg: Meiner.

—— (PhilM) *Philosophy of Mind*, trans. W. Wallace and A. Miller, Oxford: Clarendon, 1971.

Hess, M. (1961) *Philosophische und sozialistische Schriften (1837–1850)*, edited by A. Cornu and W. Mönke, Berlin: Akademie.

Marx, K., and F. Engels (CW). *Collected Works*, New York: International Publishers, 1975. (Cited as CW volume:page.)

—— (1975–) *Werke*, edited by Institut für Marxismus-Leninismus beim ZK der SED, Berlin: Dietz. [zitiert mit MEW Band, Seite].

Ruge, A. (1846) *Gesammelte Schriften*, pt 3, Mannheim: Grohe.

Ruge, A., and K. Marx (ed.) (1981) *Deutsch-Französische Jahrbücher*, Leipzig: Reclam.

Stirner, M. (1976) *Max Stirner's Kleinere Schriften*, edited by J. H. Mackay, Stuttgart-Bad Cannstatt: Frommann.

—— (EO) *The Ego and Its Own*, trans. David Leopold, Cambridge: Cambridge University Press, 1995.

Strauss, D. F. (1864) *Das Leben Jesu für das deutsche Volk bearbeitet*, 2nd edn, Leipzig: Brockhaus.

Secondary literature

Brudney, D. (1998) *Marx's Attempt to Leave Philosophy*, Cambridge, MA: Harvard University Press.

Habermas, J. (2005) *Zwischen Naturalismus und Religion*, Frankfurt am Main: Suhrkamp.

Hook, S. (1962) *From Hegel to Marx*, Ann Arbor: University of Michigan Press.

Lange, E. M. (1980) *Das Prinzip Arbeit*, Frankfurt am Main: Ullstein.

Quante, M. (2004) *Hegel's Concept of Action*, trans. Dean Moyar, Cambridge: Cambridge University Press.

Further reading

For further reading on this topic, see B. Bauer, *Hegels Lehre von der Religion und Kunst von dem Standpunkt des Glaubens aus beurteilt* (Aalen: Scientia, 1967); *Die Posaune des jüngsten Gerichts über Hegel, den Atheisten und Antichristen* (Aalen: Scientia, 1969); "Die Fähigkeit der heutigen Juden und Christen, frei zu werden," in G. Herwegh (ed.) *Einundzwanzig Bogen aus der Schweiz* (Leipzig: Reclam, 1989), pp. 136–54; G. W. F. Hegel, *Grundlinien der Philosophie des Rechts* (Hamburg: Meiner, 1955); *Phänomenologie des Geistes* (= Gesammelte Werke, vol. 9) (Hamburg: Meiner, 1988); M. Stirner, *Der Einzige und sein Eigentum*, Leipzig: Reclam, 1988 [1882]); W. Breckman, *Marx, the Young Hegelians, and the Origins of Radical Social Thought* (Cambridge: Cambridge University Press, 1999); D. Leopold, *The Young Karl Marx* (Cambridge: Cambridge University Press, 2007); K. Löwith, *Von Hegel zu Nietzsche* (Hamburg: Meiner, 1986); D. McLellan, *The Young Hegelians and Karl Marx* (London: Macmillan, 1969); D. Moggach, *The Philosophy and politics of Bruno Bauer* (Cambridge: Cambridge University Press, 2003); (ed.) *The New Hegelians* (Cambridge: Cambridge University Press, 2006); Z. Rosen, *Bruno Bauer and Karl Marx* (The Hague: Martinus Nijhoff, 1977); *Moses Hess und Karl Marx* (Hamburg: Christians, 1983); H. Stuke, *Philosophie der Tat* (Stuttgart: Klett, 1963); J. E. Toews, *Hegelianism* (Cambridge: Cambridge University Press, 1980); and A. Wood, *Karl Marx* (London: Routledge, 1981). K. Marx, *Ökonomisch Philosophischen Manuskripte*, M. Quante (ed.) (Frankfurt am Main: Suhrkamp, 2009).

8

KARL MARX

Tony Smith

No one would dispute that it is impossible to understand the intellectual and political history of the nineteenth and twentieth centuries without taking Karl Marx (1818–83) into account. Most believe, however, that Marx's legacy was buried once and for all in the rubble of the Berlin Wall. This consensus is mistaken. It would be foolish to assert that Marx anticipated the correct answer to every significant question facing us today. But it would be no less foolish to deny that Marx's work presents a powerful challenge to contemporary political philosophy.

In the first section I shall sketch Marx's early theories of religious and political alienation. The heart of the chapter will then be devoted to Marx's critique of political economy, concentrating on the role of money in capitalist society, the capital/wage labor relation, the limits of democracy in a capitalist order, and the systematic tendencies to uneven development and crises in the world market. The chapter ends with brief comments on the shape of a feasible and normatively attractive alternative to capitalism and Marx's relationship to Hegel.

Marx's early writings

The critique of religion

After the defeat of Napoleon elites in Continental Europe dismissed the French Revolution as a mere interruption in the "natural" state of things. Calls for greater political liberty and constitutional reforms were met with minimal concessions. Kant and Hegel disagreed. While neither endorsed Robespierre's Terror, or Napoleon's empire-building, both insisted that the French Revolution introduced a promise of political emancipation, and that this promise had been merely deferred, not irrevocably defeated. For Kant, political structures and policies that could not be rationally defended were ultimately doomed, given the ineluctable rise of an enlightened public. He also argued that success in geopolitical competition requires economic strength, which favors republics that eliminate the market-distorting privileges of aristocrats and petty despots. Hegel too felt that societies clinging to traditional economic and political arrangements were fated to historical insignificance, given the dynamism of modern market societies and the efficiency of rational state bureaucracies (Losurdo 2004).

The Young (or "Left") Hegelians of Marx's student days felt that neither Kant nor Hegel adequately appreciated the pernicious role religious dogma played in support of the status quo. Religious leaders throughout Germany blessed the restoration of aristocratic and monarchical privileges as divinely ordained, while encouraging political passivity in their flock by diverting attention to the hereafter. The Young Hegelians concluded that the emancipatory promise of the French Revolution would remain deferred without a critique of religious consciousness.

Ludwig Feuerbach's *The Essence of Christianity* (1839) was perhaps the major contribution to this project. Feuerbach did not simply describe the earthly consequences of belief in a heaven "out there." He explained how the supposedly transcendent realm was in fact a projection of life on earth. Predicates describing activities of human subjects (such as knowing or loving) were treated as if they constituted an (absolute) Subject ("God is Knowledge"; "God is Love"). The supposedly transcendent heavenly realm is nothing but the earthly realm in an alien (non-human) form.

Marx accepted Feuerbach's account as far as it went. But he insisted that Feuerbach ignored the most important question: *why* did this alienation take place? Answering this query requires a critical account of the social world from which religious consciousness springs:

> Religion is the self-consciousness and self-esteem of man who has either not yet found himself or has already lost himself again. But *man* is no abstract being encamped outside the world. Man is *the world of man* – the state, society. This state, this society, produce religion, an *inverted world-consciousness*, because they are an *inverted world* ... *Religious* distress is at the same time the *expression* of real distress and also the *protest* against real distress. (Marx 1975c: 175)

It follows that:

> To abolish religion as the *illusory* happiness of the people is to demand their *real* happiness. The demand to give up illusions about the existing state of affairs is the *demand to give up a state of affairs which needs illusions*. (Marx 1975c: 176)

Marx's critique is not applicable to all forms of religious experience. It does not illuminate the role of religion as a spur to social change described in *The Peasant Wars in Germany*, written by Marx's closest collaborator, Frederick Engels. Nor does it apply to recent religious movements associated with liberation theology. In these and many other instances, religious beliefs have not encouraged political quietism. In my view Marx's account also does not address Hegel's philosophy of religion (Smith 1993: Ch. 2; see also the Appendix below). For our purposes, however, the point to stress is that the general framework underlying Marx's critique of the religious orthodoxy of his day is found in his accounts of the state and capital as well.

The critique of the state

Marx initially agreed with Kant, Hegel, and most Young Hegelians that emancipation was identical to dismantling the political rule of aristocrats and petty despots. Fairly soon, however, he came to believe that merely political emancipation would be inadequate. This realization, the pivotal event in Marx's life (Kouvelakis 2003), was developed in the course of early commentaries on Hegel's *Philosophy of Right*.

Hegel is notorious for insisting that the state transcends civil society. But *any* theorist for whom it is the state's responsibility to institutionalize the common good over against the particular interests of individuals and associations holds some version of this view. (This includes even defenders of a "minimal state," who limit the public good to protection against force and fraud.) For Marx the modern state does indeed function as a transcendent power over and above society, analogous to the heavenly realm's relation to earth in orthodox Christianity. And just as for Marx the heavenly realm is nothing but the projection of human activities in an alien and reified form, the state also is nothing but an alienation and reification of social powers. It follows that the pernicious effects following from the transcendental status of the state vis-à-vis civil society (analogous to those following from belief in a heaven transcending the earthly realm) are not due solely to the political privileges of aristocrats and despots. Pernicious effects follow from the dualism of state and society defining the modern state as such, a dualism that allows the "egoistic spirit of civil society" more or less free reign. Marx believed that this could be seen most clearly in the countries that had gone farthest in political emancipation:

> [T]he completion of the idealism of the state was at the same time the completion of the materialism of civil society. Throwing off the political yoke meant at the same time throwing off the bonds which restrained the egoistic spirit of civil society. Political emancipation was, at the same time, the emancipation of civil society from politics, from having even the *semblance* of a universal content ... The *political revolution* resolves civil life into its component parts, without *revolutionizing* these components themselves or subjecting them to criticism. (Marx 1975b: 166–7)

Just as belief in an other-worldly divine realm was generated by material social practices on earth, the existence of the state as an allegedly transcendent power above society is rooted in historically specific social practices as well. And just as "to abolish religion as the *illusory* happiness of the people is to demand their *real* happiness," the abolition of the state as a transcendent power is a demand for a social order which does not require such a state. *The transformation of constitutional forms in the absence of profound social transformation is doomed to be incomplete and inadequate.*

To abolish the state as a transcendent power is not to reduce the political to the social. It is to affirm the social as political. Marx's term for this transformation is "democracy." In so far as radical democracy makes explicit that the supposedly transcendent state is nothing but the powers of society in an alien form, democracy is not merely one political form among many. It is the underlying secret of *all* political forms:

> Democracy is the solved *riddle* of all constitutions. Here, not merely *implicitly* and in essence but *existing* in reality, the constitution is constantly brought back to its actual basis, the *actual human being*, the *actual people*, and established as the people's *own* work. The constitution appears as what it is, a free product of man ... [I]t goes without saying that all forms of state have democracy *for* their truth and that they are therefore untrue insofar as they are not democracy. (Marx 1975a: 29, 31)

Democratization, in other words, cannot be limited to a supposedly separate political realm. It must permeate social life:

> In democracy the *abstract* state has ceased to be the dominant factor ... The *political* republic is democracy within the abstract state form. The abstract state form of democracy is therefore the republic; but here it ceases to be the *merely political* constitution. (Marx 1975a: 31)

This new sort of social theory must be addressed to a new sort of social agent. The call for merely political emancipation could be addressed to citizens in general, an abstract category whose scope ranged from the wealthiest industrialists and financiers to the most abject unemployed laborer. Once it is recognized that emancipation involves socio-economic transformation as well, this no longer suffices. And so the young Marx addressed his theory to a quite different sort of social agent, the *proletariat*, defined in an open-ended fashion as a class "which does not stand in any one-sided antithesis of the consequences but in an all-round antithesis to the premises of the German state" (Marx 1975c: 186).

Marx was well aware that his early writings rested on claims he had not sufficiently established. He knew that he had not developed an adequate understanding of the material social practices of modernity, making do with vague references to "the egoistic spirit of civil society." Marx's immersion in the philosophical debates of his student days did not adequately prepare him to develop the sort of theory he now required. And so he devoted decades to the intensive study of Adam Smith, David Ricardo, other leading classical political economists, and their critics. Marx confronted many obstacles in the course of these studies. He was harassed by political authorities, who forced him to flee from Germany into exile in Paris, Brussels, and, eventually, London. He lacked an academic appointment or any other form of institutional support. He and his family lived most of their lives in poverty, plagued by illnesses and premature deaths. Marx was forced to devote much of his time to journalism to keep creditors away. And he chose to devote great time and effort to social movements of his day. Despite these great challenges Marx maintained an astonishing level of intellectual commitment and energy. The main results of his vast body of writings must now be considered. First, however, some main themes of the classical political economists need to be introduced, themes which continue to be accepted by mainstream social scientists and political philosophers today.

The critique of political economy

The "core thesis" of mainstream social theory

We may begin with the exchange of commodities by property owners, a defining activity of our sort of society. A set of fundamental rights is associated with the generalization of commodity exchange, including the right to own property and the right to freely decide its use (including the right to make contractual exchanges). When owners mutually recognize each other's rights to property and liberty, their formally equal status as persons is affirmed.

Classical political economists asserted that a social order based on generalized commodity exchange generates the material preconditions for human flourishing better than any feasible alternative. Free agreements to exchange tend to occur when mutual benefits can be won, and to continue as long as there are further mutual benefits to be obtained. At the conclusion of any given period, then, everyone will tend to be better off (or at least no worse off) than they were at the beginning. Further, market competition encourages producers to specialize and to introduce technical improvements in the production process, both of which tend to generate advances in productivity. Producers also have incentives to introduce new products that better meet existing wants and needs, or that extend wants and needs in new directions freely chosen by consumers. It follows from all this that markets necessarily tend to generate a greater aggregate satisfaction of wants and needs over time. Adam Smith summarized this point in his famous notion of the "invisible hand": while economic agents in market societies may be motivated primarily by private self-interest, competition operates as an "invisible hand" leading them to further the interests of others.

A system based upon the direct barter of one commodity for another would break down whenever one potential trading partner desired a commodity possessed by someone else, while lacking anything the latter wished to obtain. Money is the solution to this problem. A commodity can be sold for money, which can then be used to purchase a desired commodity from a third agent. The use of money as a means of circulation tremendously extends market opportunities.

We can define a "circuit" as a patterned sequence of exchanges oriented towards a particular end point. In a C–M–C circuit an agent begins with a commodity (C) that he or she does not want, exchanges it for money (M), and then brings the sequence to a close by purchasing a second commodity (C) that is desired. If we consider a series of C–M–C circuits together, M–C–M circuits can be discerned (… C–M–C–M–C …); generalized commodity exchange includes the structural possibility of economic agents choosing to invest money to obtain a monetary return. Such investment would generally be pointless unless returns exceeding the initial investment were possible. They are. Merchants can purchase inventory at one price, and then sell it at higher one; producers can sell commodities for prices exceeding their production costs; savers can loan money in return for interest payments. These are all instances of M–C–M' circuits, with M' exceeding the initial money invested.

The introduction of profit-seeking activities obviously complicates matters. The crucial issue is whether these complications call into question the claim that generalized commodity exchange institutionalizes freedom and equality while providing the material preconditions for human flourishing. According to what I shall term the "core thesis" of mainstream social theory, the answer is no. *Money ultimately remains a merely proximate goal, subordinate in principle to the end of meeting human wants and needs in a manner respecting equality and freedom.* This thesis is implicitly or explicitly accepted by almost all economists and political philosophers today. Even those who strongly disagree with Friedrich Hayek on numerous other points believe he was fundamentally correct on this one:

> [I]n an uncertain world individuals must mostly aim not at some ultimate ends but at procuring means which they think will help them to satisfy those ultimate ends; and their selection of the immediate ends which are merely means for their ultimate ends, but which are all that they can definitely decide upon at a particular moment, will be determined by the opportunities known to them. The immediate purpose of a man's efforts will most often be to procure means to be used for unknown future needs – in an advanced society most frequently that generalized means, money, which will serve for the procurement of most of his particular ends. (Hayek 1976: 8–9)

The view that capitalist markets are normatively acceptable ultimately rests on this thesis.

No serious theorists assert that capitalist markets are normatively acceptable in the absence of appropriate background conditions. The main debates in mainstream social theory concern the precise nature of these conditions. "Classical liberals" like Hayek assert that capitalism functions in an efficient and normatively acceptable manner so long as a coercive state apparatus institutionalizes the "rule of law," protecting agents from force and fraud. The point holds for cross-border trades and investments no less than for economic activities within national borders, and so contemporary "neo-liberals" call for abstract rules enabling a free flow of commodities and investments across borders. "Liberals" in the contemporary sense of the term, in contrast, hold that capitalist markets necessarily tend to generate unreasonable concentrations of economic power and involuntary unemployment, as well as levels of poverty and inequality inconsistent with the satisfaction of basic needs, fair equality of opportunity, and the equal worth of political liberties. Were these tendencies allowed to operate unchecked, normative justifications for capitalist markets would be thoroughly undermined, in their view. And so they insist that the state must do far more than simply protect against force and fraud. Rawls, for example, calls for an allocation branch of government to break up unreasonable concentrations of market power, a stabilization branch to maintain full employment, a transfer branch to eliminate the most pernicious forms of poverty, and a distribution branch to keep economic inequalities within bounds consistent with fair equality of opportunity and the fair worth of political liberties (Rawls 1971: 276–7). Liberal cosmopolitan ethicists agree with Rawls's assessment of markets, but insist that states today lack the capacity to politically regulate globalized markets sufficiently. They therefore call for a new "regime of global governance," based on democratic cosmopolitan law (Held 1995).

From Marx's standpoint, these perspectives share a common flaw: they all lack an adequate concept of capital. And that, as they say, is like *Hamlet* without the Prince.

Value, abstract labor, and money

Marx announces in the first sentence of volume 1 of *Capital* that his object of investigation is a social world in which wealth takes the form of an "immense collection of commodities" (Marx 1976a: 125). This distinguishes our social world from precapitalist societies, where commodity exchange was restricted in scope. To understand *generalized* commodity exchange we must begin with what is *generally* the case, dealing with exceptional cases (the exchange of found objects, art works, etc.) at later stages of the theory. In general, commodities are goods and services that have been produced for exchange, rather than for immediate consumption by their producers. If the labor that has gone into the production of a particular commodity finds a buyer, this privately undertaken labor is validated as "socially necessary" labor. If it does not, the labor has been socially wasted.

Different commodities have diverse concrete properties; otherwise they would not have diverse uses, and exchanging one for the other would be pointless. But commodities that have been exchanged acquire an additional abstract property. The process that socially validates labor establishes that the commodities possess "value," defined simply as the property of "having been produced by privately undertaken labor that has proven to be socially necessary." Or we may define "value" as the property of "exchangeability in definite proportions"; the two definitions refer to the same state of affairs. While the properties that qualitatively distinguish commodities from each other are concrete and heterogeneous, the property of having been produced by socially validated privately undertaken labor is homogeneous and abstract (as is the identical property of "exchangeability in definite proportions"). It follows that the value of one commodity can be distinguished from that of another only quantitatively. More privately undertaken labor may be socially validated in one commodity than another, or, equivalently, one commodity may exchange at higher ratios than another.

In a parallel fashion, one particular act of laboring can be qualitatively distinguished from another by its concrete and heterogeneous properties. But insofar as both acts have been socially validated through exchange, they share the abstract and homogeneous property of being value-creating labor. Marx terms labor considered in this light *abstract labor*, both because abstraction is made from the concrete qualitative determinations of particular acts of laboring, and because these acts are now considered only insofar as they produce value, an abstract property of commodities. Marx describes abstract labor as the "substance" of value, referring to value as "congealed" abstract labor. Like value, and for the same reasons, different instances of abstract labor can be compared only quantitatively.

The next stage of Marx's argument is to note that a socially objective measure of value (or, equivalently, a socially objective representation of abstract labor) is a necessary condition of the possibility of generalized commodity exchange. Without some objective measure of the extent to which the labor devoted to the production of commodities has been socially validated, exchange would be sporadic and contingent, rather than a generalized system capable of being reproduced over time. We cannot measure value in terms of the concrete qualitative properties a commodity may possess, or the concrete wants and needs a commodity with those particular properties might fulfill (its "use-value"). These concrete dimensions of the commodity are heterogeneous and therefore incommensurable. The value dimension, in contrast, is abstract, homogeneous, and commensurable.

Units of labor time are abstract, homogeneous and commensurable, and so may appear to provide an objective measure for the value dimension. But we cannot measure value by simply adding up with a stopwatch the hours of different labors that directly and indirectly produced the product. These labors are, once again, concrete, heterogeneous and incommensurable. Further, some will turn out to have been socially wasted if there is insufficient demand for the product in question, or if competitors have introduced improvements in labor productivity. While units of abstract labor time provide an *immanent* measure of the value of commodities, the only labor times that can be directly measured with a stopwatch are concrete labors.

Some *external* measure is therefore required. This conclusion is reinforced if we recall that value is only potentially created in the privately undertaken production process, becoming actual only when the commodity is successfully exchanged for something external to it. If this external thing is to be a *universal* objective measure, it must have the property of *universal* exchangeability. It must also be as homogenous as the value dimension, and be able to express quantitative differences of value in abstract units. In principle, anything capable of being divided into homogenous units could play this role. But in any given social context one thing (or a very few) must be singled out. That thing, whatever it is, is money (Marx 1976a: Ch. 1, §3).

Once introduced, money's role necessarily extends beyond being the sole socially objective measure of value. It will also serve as a means of sale of commodities (C–M), a means of purchase (M–C), and (taking both together) a means for the circulation of commodities (C–M–C).

The general formula of capital

As we have seen, a system of generalized commodity exchange includes the structural possibility of M–C–M′ circuits, in which agents invest money in order to obtain a monetary return. No one disputes that such circuits are found throughout our social world. But mainstream social theorists explicitly assert (or, more often, implicitly presuppose) that with the proper political regulation money ultimately remains a generalized means, and is at most a merely proximate end. This view fails to take the unrelenting competitive pressure faced by producing units in capitalist markets seriously enough.

It would be difficult to deny that in generalized commodity production almost all units of production must systematically and relentlessly direct their endeavors to monetary returns exceeding their initial investments. Units of production that are not systematically and relentlessly oriented to the appropriation of monetary returns necessarily tend to be pushed to the margins of social life, or disappear entirely. This ceaseless pressure is a historically defining feature of generalized commodity production, distinguishing *societies with markets* from capitalist *market societies*. It is also the single most important factor underlying the unprecedented dynamism of the latter. Productivity advances, for example, are spurred by the drive to obtain above average profits by selling commodities produced at below average costs (Marx 1976a: 431–5) or by decreasing turnover time, the period between investment and the appropriation of the return on that investment (Marx 1978: Ch. 9). Countless C–M–C circuits can be discerned in generalized commodity production, culminating in the consumption of a commodity to satisfy a human want or need. But these transactions necessarily tend to be subordinated within overarching M–C–M′ circuits.

M–C–M′ circuits, no less than C–M–C circuits, consist of nothing but the actions of buyers and sellers, with a special role played by capitalists with a disposition to seek monetary returns. Marx could have made things easy for himself by placing the psychological disposition of capitalists to seek monetary returns at the center of his analysis. He chose instead to talk of capitalists as "character masks" of *capital*, postponing an examination of the subjective agency of capitalists until after the concept of capital had been elaborated. He did this because he believed that "capital" as a principle of social organization is in a sense prior to the intentions and activities of individual agents, however much human agency is responsible for its emergence and maintenance. The unrelenting pressure to invest money for the sake of monetary returns is externally imposed on capitalists themselves, and the force of this external compulsion is missed if priority is given to psychological dispositions.

Marx initially defines capital as "value-in process," with "value" now referring to the principle unifying the different moments of M–C–M′ circuits into a dynamic whole:

> [B]oth the money and the commodity function only as different modes of existence of value itself ... [Value] is constantly changing from one form into the other, without becoming lost in this movement; it thus becomes transformed into an automatic subject ... [V]alue is here the subject of a process in which, while constantly assuming the form in turn of money and commodities, it changes its own magnitude, throws off surplus-value from itself considered as original value, and thus valorizes itself independently. For the movement in the course of which it adds surplus-value is its own movement, its valorization is therefore self-valorization ... [V]alue suddenly presents itself as a self-moving substance which passes through a process of

its own, and for which commodities and money are both mere forms. (Marx 1976a: 255–6)

Marx calls this notion of value-in-process "the general formula of capital." While it directly applies to individual M–C–M' circuits, it also operates as an organizing principle on the level of society as a whole, with M representing the aggregate of money capital initially invested in a given period and M' the aggregate of money accumulated at the end of that period, after the intertwining particular circuits of capital have been completed.

For many, talk of capital as a "subject," as a "self-moving substance" that "valorizes itself" is extremely odd, to say the least. We know what it means to speak of living organisms as "subjects" and "self-moving substances." Does it make any sense to treat "capital" in these terms? I believe Marx uses such provocative language to stress that in our social world it is *as if* a familiar nightmare of science fiction has become true: an alien being ("capital") rules over us, subordinating our goals and activities to its ends, without our even being aware of it. That is not literally the case. Nonetheless, the valorization imperative, the drive to transform M into M', *is* the central organizing principle of capitalist society. Human life is now governed by this alien, non-human, principle, defining a distinct level of social ontology with its own emergent properties.

The first and foremost of these properties is the totalizing drive to subordinate social life to the accumulation of capital. This can be seen in the tendency to systematically neglect human wants and needs that cannot be met through the sale of commodities for a monetary return. It can also be seen in the fact that in this system "demand" for commodities is completely irrelevant *per se*. Only *effective* demand, demand with sufficient purchasing power behind it, counts, because only effective demand contributes to M'. Further, access to the monetary resources required for consumption is generally a function of one's position within, or relation to, units of production forced by ceaseless and all but irresistible competitive pressures to grant priority to the pursuit of monetary returns.

The general formula of capital merely describes the metamorphosis of M into a greater sum, M'. It does not explain this transformation. Marx's explanation forms the heart of his theory.

The capital/wage labor relation

Capitalist societies are not the first societies to generate a *social surplus*, an increase in social wealth beyond what its producers consume. They are the first in which the surplus predominately takes the form of *surplus value*, the difference between M' and M. There are other significant differences as well.

In precapitalist societies the surplus was produced through the forcible extraction of "surplus labor" from an exploited class, that is, labor in excess of the "necessary labor" required to maintain members of the exploited class (and their dependants) in the given socio-historical circumstances. Part of the labor time of slaves in the ancient world, for example, produced the wealth required to keep them and their dependants alive. In the remainder they were forced to produce wealth for their owners. Similarly, serfs in some feudal societies worked a certain number of days of the week on their own fields, producing the wealth required for their own subsistence, and spent the remaining workdays on the lord's estate. In other cases "independent" peasants working on their own land were forced to give up a portion of their production to rulers in the form of tribute. A striking feature of social orders based on slavery, serfdom, or tribute-extraction is the role overt coercion and the threat of coercion played in maintaining these social relations.

Matters appear quite different in capitalism, as we can see if we expand M-C-M′ to M–C–P–C′–M′, with the middle terms referring to commodity inputs to production (C), the production process (P), and the produced commodity outputs (C′) that will (hopefully) be sold for a profit. We can now make explicit what has been merely implicit so far: the units of production with which we are concerned are capitalist firms, in which labor power is purchased as a commodity input to production. Wage contracts, like other contracts, are in principle free agreements among legal equals for the sake of mutual benefits. And, like other contracts, they are rendered void by the sort of overt violence or threat of violence characterizing precapitalist societies, at least in principle. (The qualification is required because violence and the threat of violence against wage laborers have hardly been unknown in the history of capitalism, to put it mildly. At this stage of the argument, however, Marx abstracts from such matters.) According to the terms of these contracts, wage laborers are paid for their entire working day. It would seem that the account of the social surplus in capitalism must be quite different from that appropriate to precapitalist societies.

Standard models in neoclassical economics do not include profits on the grounds that they are the result of temporary monopolies that dissipate in the absence of illegitimate constraints. The returns to owners of non-labor productive resources are not categorized as profits, but simply as compensation for the contributions of these resources, identical in all relevant respects to the returns those who labor receive for their contributions to production. There are two major problems with these models. First, the behavior of capitalist firms continually establishes, and the business press invariably confirms, that profits are an abiding and defining feature of a capitalist order, qualitatively quite distinct from wages. The second difficulty is that returns to the owners of resources are explained here in terms of the physical transformation of inputs into outputs. While the generation of surpluses in capitalism certainly has a physical dimension, so did the generation of surpluses in precapitalist societies. The fact that the surplus predominately takes the monetary form of *surplus value* is historically specific to capitalism, and must therefore be explained in terms of histori-cally specific social forms. And social forms are always underdetermined by physical processes.

This is a point of tremendous general importance for Marx. The physical properties of pieces of gold or paper (or electronic blips allowing zeros and ones to be repre-sented), do not explain why they have the social form of money. The physical properties of labor do not explain why it has social form of wage labor. The physical properties of land do not explain why a rent can be extracted from it. *And the physical properties of raw materials or machinery do not explain why these inputs have the social form of capital investments, or why the results of production have the social form of commodities that can be sold for profit.* Who would dream of explaining the relationship between slave and slave owners, or serfs and feudal lords, or independent peasants and tribute-extracting politico-military elites, by appealing to the physical properties of the tools or raw materials used by these slaves, serfs, or peasants? No one. Explanations of returns to investment that focus on physical matters (the "productive contribution" of machinery, raw materials, etc.) are no more adequate.

What of attempts to explain profits as a reward that investors deserve for a social reason? These accounts avoid the category mistake of treating historically specific social forms as if they were "naturally" tied to physical processes. They also bring out how explanations of profits invariably have a normative component. From Marx's standpoint, however, all such accounts are ultimately question-begging. They affirm that investors deserve a reward for a particular sort of activity, while other activities of the same type are not rewarded in the same fashion.

"Profits are the reward investors deserve for abstaining from personal consumption." But wage laborers routinely abstain from pursuing myriad personal enjoyments during the often long and exhausting time they perform (and recover from) wage labor. One form of abstention does not explain (or justify) the appropriation of profits and the other not, unless we presuppose the issue in question.

"Profits are the reward investors deserve for risking their money." But extremely serious risks are imposed on wage laborers in the workplace, ranging from immediate physical injury to the debilitating long-term effects of stress. One form of risk does not explain (or justify) the appropriation of profits and the other not, unless we presuppose what was to be proven.

"Profits are the rewards investors deserve for allocating funds efficiently." But massive profits can be appropriated even when investors do not make any allocation decisions themselves. All investors need do qua investors is grant permission that funds be allocated. No one today would say that a slave owner's appropriation of the surplus produced by the slave was explained (or justified) by the fact that slaves could not have produced that surplus without their owner's permission. One form of granting permission does not explain (or justify) anything and the other not, unless we presuppose the very question at issue.

Perhaps the strongest mainstream account of the difference between M' and M is the simplest, appealing to the contractual agreements among firms, between firms and wage laborers, and between firms and final consumers. Units of production are free to buy or not buy the output of other firms. Wage laborers, unlike slaves, serfs, or those forced to provide tribute to overlords, are free to choose their occupation and employer, and to accept or reject the terms of a wage contract. Consumers are free to choose what to buy. When all is said and done, profits appear to be simply the result of a series of free choices, culminating in decisions to purchase commodities at prices that both cover production costs and include an increment above these costs.

Marx does not deny that there is a profound sense in which wage laborers in capitalism are free (Marx 1976a: 271). But matters are more complicated than this. Wage labor must be considered in the context of the M–C–P–C'–M' circuit as a totality, each stage of which defines a dimension of the capital/wage labor relation. This relationship is between:

- a class that owns and controls investment funds (M), and one that does not;
- a class that purchases labor power along with other commodity inputs (C), and one that sells its labor power as a commodity;
- a class with the power to initiate and direct changes in the production process (P), and one whose living labor is treated as an object of control in that process;
- a class that after produced commodities (C′) have been sold appropriates the proceeds (M′), an amount generally exceeding its own consumption needs, and a class that must spend most if not all of its wages to gain access to means of subsistence; and, finally,
- a class that at the beginning of the succeeding period owns and controls even more investment funds, and a class that must once again sell its labor power as a commodity to gain access to its necessary means of subsistence.

The valorization process, and the process of reproducing the capital/wage labor relation, are one and the same. At the end of every period wage laborers as a class have merely been able to maintain themselves at the given standard of living, while those who owned their labor power and set it to work in the production process have as a class increased their money capital. For Marx, this state of affairs can only be explained by the difference between the time workers spend producing an amount of value equivalent to what they receive in the form of wages, and the time they spend engaged in surplus labor, producing a value beyond their wages. For all its historical specificity, the capital/wage labor is *analogous* to the slave/owner, serf/lord, peasant/tribute collector relations in one all-important, respect: it is an *exploitative* relation. The valorization process is a process in which a social surplus produced by wage laborers is appropriated by the owners and controllers of capital. This may not be apparent on the surface level of appearances, as it is in precapitalist class societies. It is systematically occluded by the freedom of wage contracts, and the appearance that wage laborers are paid for every moment they work. But it is the essence of the matter nonetheless.

Why would wage laborers agree to the extraction of a social surplus, given that they are "free" and not subject to the direct compulsion underlying slavery, serfdom and tributary systems of exploitation? One factor is surely the lack of transparency that arises when class relations are systematically reproduced *through* choices made by individuals. The most important factor, however, is surely that freedom from direct violence (or its threat) is not the same as freedom from all forms of social coercion. When one class possesses investment capital, and sufficient funds to purchase consumption goods for itself indefinitely, while another lacks these monetary resources, members of the latter class are *forced* to sell their labor power to the members of the former. Survival in minimally acceptable conditions requires access to productive resources and means of subsistence. Once the social forms of capital are in place, such access is denied to the vast majority of people unless they agree to sell their labor power at terms that allow those who own investment capital to appropriate profits from their labor. This is a matter of social *compulsion*, not a mere response to "market opportunities." Social welfare programs may lessen or even remove the most extreme forms of this duress. But as long as capitalism persists they cannot eliminate the *structural coercion* at the heart of the capital/wage labor relation (whenever they have threatened to do so they have soon been weakened). In such circumstances it is hardly surprising that "free" choices are made to accept wage contracts enabling one class to appropriate surplus value from another.

Marx was well aware that the complexity of our social world is not captured in a simple two-class model. In other contexts he discussed domestic laborers, workers in the informal sector, the self-employed, state officials, and various other groups besides capitalists and wage laborers. He also knew, of course, that individual capitalists can go bankrupt, while individual workers may escape their class position through some combination of talent, opportunities, ruthlessness, and luck. Marx realized as well that prices and profits are not simply means to reproduce the capital/wage labor relation. They also play an essential role in mediating relations among units of capital, between units of capital and consumers, between units of capital and the owners of monopolizable inputs, between units of capital and state officials, and so on. Marx explicitly acknowledged that these sorts of matters demand a more complex theory of prices and profits than that developed in volume 1 of *Capital* (Moseley 1993). Such complications, however, do not require a modification of Marx's critique of capital as exploitative.

It is worth noting in passing the parallel between this critique and Marx's earlier analysis of religious consciousness and the state (Murray 1988). For Marx, the transcendent God of orthodoxy that supposedly determines and shapes the world is in fact nothing but an alien (reified) projection of human capacities. The supposedly transcendent state that clearly does determine and shape social life is ultimately nothing but social powers reified in an external form. "Capital" is similarly a sort of transcendent external thing standing above and beyond human society, an alien power shaping and determining social life. In a certain sense, in fact, it can be seen as *the* creative power in the world:

> [E]very increase in the productive powers of labour – leaving aside the fact that it increases use values for capital – is an increase in the productive power of capital and it is only a productive power of labour in so far as it is a productive power of capital. (Marx 1994: 11)

But capital, like the heaven projected by religious consciousness and the state in modern society, is ultimately nothing but an alienated form of human sociality, rooted in historically specific material social practices. From an ontological standpoint, capital is nothing but the creative powers of social labor (and the powers of nature, machinery, science, etc., mobilized by social labor), appearing in an alienated form due to the social practices of generalized commodity production:

> The different means whereby capital creates ... surplus value, raises the productive forces, and increases the mass of products, *are* all social forms of

labour; but they *appear,* even within production, rather as social forms of capital – modes of capital's existence. (Marx 1988: 11; italics added; see also Marx 1976a: 755–6)

At this point we should stop and consider the immense challenge to contemporary political philosophy posed by Marx's concept of capital. Other aspects of this concept will be introduced in the course of this discussion.

Marx and contempory political philosophy

A striking feature of contemporary political philosophy is the extent to which leading theorists, influenced by Kant and John Rawls, defend versions of the same normative principles. Marx's concept of capital calls into question the widespread view that a capitalist order can be justified on the basis of these principles.

The moral equality principle

Many of today's leading political philosophers affirm what may be termed *the moral equality principle*. Jürgen Habermas calls for "equal respect for the human worth of each individual," a view he terms "egalitarian universalism" (Habermas 2001: 94, 103). David Held agrees: "Humankind belongs to a single moral realm in which each person is equally worthy of consideration" (Held 2004: 174). Alan Buchanan has recently written:

> [J]ustice requires respect for the inherent dignity of all persons . . . this notion of dignity includes the idea that all persons are equal, so far as the importance of their basic interests are concerned. (Buchanan 2004: 42)

Thomas Pogge similarly calls for principles that "assign the same fundamental moral benefits (e.g. claims, liberties, powers, and immunities) and burdens (e.g. duties and liabilities) to all," such that "these fundamental moral benefits and burdens [do] not privilege or disadvantage certain persons or groups arbitrarily" (Pogge 2002: 92). This view is echoed by Martha Nussbaum:

> If we agree that citizens are all worthy of concern and respect ... then we ought to conclude that policies should not treat people as agents or supporters of other people, whose mission in the world is to execute someone else's plan of life. It should treat each of them as ends, as sources of agency and worth in their own right, with their own plans to make and their own lives to live, therefore as deserving of all necessary support for the equal opportunity to be such agents. (Nussbaum 2001: 58)

Examples could be easily multiplied. Not all contemporary political philosophers accept "egalitarian universalism." Far from it. But a great number do.

For these authors the next stage in the argument is to derive a theory of human rights from the moral equality principle:

> [T]he implication of the phrase "human rights" is that there are some interests common to all persons that are of such great moral concern that the very character of our most important institutions should be such as to afford them special protection. These interests are shared by all persons because they are constitutive of a decent life; they are necessary conditions for human flourishing. (Buchanan 2004: 127)

(A comprehensive and systematic derivation of rights from the moral equality principle is found in Held [1995].)

The connection between "human rights" and "human flourishing" in the last passage raises one of the most important questions of contemporary political philosophy: are there (or should there be) ends or goals on the level of society as a whole? For liberal political philosophers individuals and groups should have the right to attempt to determine and pursue their own conceptions of the good life, limited only by the right of other individuals and groups to do the same. From this perspective a liberal society does not institutionalize *particular* ends on the level of society as a whole. Nonetheless, a *general* end of social life can be affirmed: human flourishing. The fact that this flourishing can take a wide variety of reasonable forms does not undercut its special status as an end holding on the level of society as a whole.

The vast majority of contemporary liberal political philosophers hold that the moral equality principle, and the principle of neutrality regarding ends on the level of society as a whole, can be adequately institutionalized in a suitably regulated form of capitalism. Debates rage regarding the precise regulations that are necessary, the degree to which a regime of global governance is required to supplement regulation by states, and other immensely important matters (Smith 2005: Chs 1–4). For present purposes, however, these issues may be put to the side.

There has been extensive debate among philosophers concerning Marx's views on moral theory (see Cohen et al. 1980: Pt 1). In many respects he rejected the project of moral philosophy, at least as it has often been practiced. Unlike most philosophers, Marx consistently refused to treat normative principles in abstraction from historical and social contexts. He also held that when we do examine how these principles have functioned in concrete historical contexts, we find that they often served to legitimate oppressive and exploitative regimes. Marx further believed that moral categories should have a relatively limited explanatory role. If, for example, we wish to comprehend capitalism we should not focus primarily on the greediness of capitalists. The major instances of social change in the past have not occurred primarily because of the efficacy of moral appeals, in his view. Nor is it likely to be the case that the efficacy of moral appeals will deserve to be granted the greatest explanatory weight in accounts of major social transformations in the future. In all these respects Marx's *historical materialism* differs sharply from the "idealism" of much moral philosophy. Finally, Marx also wrote sharp polemics against specific moral notions, such as "rights" and "equality." As we have just seen, these notions are at the core of egalitarian universalism. It would seem to follow that there is no point of contact between Marx's work and that of the contemporary moral philosophers who defend egalitarian universalism.

This conclusion would be mistaken. There are numerous places in Marx's writings where he explicitly affirmed normative principles, for example, the texts calling for "a society in which the full and free development of every individual forms the ruling principle," and in which "the free development of each is the condition for the free development of all" (Marx 1976a: 739; Marx and Engels 1976: 506). It is important to note that his critical remarks on "rights" were directed against a particular version of rights theory, widespread in his day and ours, in which rights are conceptualized as properties of self-interested individuals in solely external relations to each other (Marx 1975b: 161–4). The theorists quoted at the beginning of this section all reject this social atomism. Marx's rejection of "equality" was limited to proposals to institute a strict equality in distribution, which he argued did not take differences in social contributions and needs seriously enough (Marx 1989). This is not equivalent to rejecting the quite different principle that "all persons are equal, so far as the importance of their basic interests are concerned," a principle that Marx quite obviously accepted. On the level of normative principles, then, Marx's views are broadly compatible with those of contemporary liberal defenders of egalitarian universalism (Callinicos 2000).

Marx's main challenge to this important stream of contemporary political philosophy concerns instead the essential determinations and structural tendencies of capital. (Marx's challenge to other positions in contemporary political philosophy can easily be extrapolated from the following.)

Capitalism and the question of social ends

Liberal political philosophers today assert that *particular ends* should not be institutionalized on the level of society as a whole. Particular individuals and groups must have the right to freely determine and pursue their own conceptions of the good life, qualified only by the rights of other individuals and groups to do the same. This freedom is consistent with an affirmation of human flourishing as the *general end* of social life. Almost all contemporary political philosophers also hold that a suitably regulated form of capitalism is consistent with – some would say necessary for – a social order in which individuals and groups define their particular ends for themselves, and in which human flourishing is institutionalized as a general end on the level of society as a whole. This claim rests on the (usually implicit) core thesis that money in a capitalist order is ultimately (at least in principle) a generalized means, a thing we use for our practical convenience in order to take advantage of market opportunities.

It is true, of course, that in generalized commodity production, as in other social orders, individuals and groups have conceptions of the good which they try to fulfill as best they can, and that money can play a role in this process. But this is not the historically defining feature of our social world. Nor is it the source of its unprecedented dynamism. Capitalism is more than a complicated form of barter. It is not merely a system in which money is used; it is a historically unprecedented *monetary system* (Campbell 1997; Bellofiore 2005).

On the level of individuals, money is not simply a means that we can choose to employ or not to take advantage of opportunities. The use of money is not a matter of mere convenience. That may be true of precapitalist *societies with markets*. But it is not true of a capitalist *market society*, where individuals are *compelled* to obtain access to money. Money is here the center of the social universe, "the god among commodities" (Marx 1986c: 154). To be without money is to be literally outside this sort of society. As Marx strikingly notes, "[E]ach individual ... carries his social power, as well as his connection with society, in his pocket" (Marx 1986c: 94).

On the level of society as a whole, could anyone deny that investing money for the sake of a monetary return is at the very heart of capitalist societies? The point almost seems too obvious to mention. Nonetheless, most mainstream social theorists (including most political philosophers) treat a social organization of production whose historical specificity and dynamism stems from M–C–M' circuits as if it were ultimately comprehensible in terms of C–M–C circuits. The freedom of individuals and groups in capitalism to select particular ends is the freedom to negotiate within a public order in which *an intrinsic end is already in place*: the accumulation of capital as an end in itself. Humanly created social forms have brought about a bizarre ontological inversion in which an inhuman end has come to have precedence over human ends. Human freedom is subordinate to the freedom of capital; human flourishing is subordinate to the flourishing of capital.

Some ways in which human flourishing is set aside when it fails to further the flourishing of capital have already been mentioned (human wants and needs that cannot be commodified are systematically neglected, as are all wants and needs that lack sufficient purchasing power behind them). Others must now be added to the list, having to do with the capital/wage labor relation, the limits of democracy in capitalism, the crisis tendencies of capitalist market societies, and the systematic tendency to uneven development.

The precarious and partial nature of improvements in workers' consumption

In *Capital* and other writings Marx consistently stressed how capitalism's technological dynamism enables the consumption of use-values by workers to expand over time (Marx 1976a: 275). In fact, he acknowledged a systematic tendency for a historically unprecedented improvement in living standards (Marx 1986c: 213, 337). Nonetheless, Marx insisted that it would be wrong to conclude that capitalism could ever adequately provide access to the material preconditions for human flourishing. The gains enjoyed are *precarious* and *partial* in ways that undermine the claim that the capital/wage labor social relation is compatible with egalitarian universalism (Marx 1976a: Ch. 15).

Gains in real wages are *precarious* even for relatively privileged workers employed by leading firms in the world market. Gains won in firms enjoying high profits as a result of innovations tend to be eroded as these innovations diffuse. If a given unit of capital does maintain its advantages, it may do so through labor-saving innovations that displace previously privileged wage laborers. Or technological change may enable the implementation of effective "divide and conquer" strategies, in which the threat of employing less privileged categories of workers is used to reduce wages and worsen work conditions. The owners and controllers of capital also have an incentive to seek innovations that "deskill" those enjoying relatively high levels of remuneration (scare quotes must be used here since a *generalization* of previously above average skills also makes gains difficult to maintain or expand). In addition, there is an incentive to introduce innovations that allow striking workers to be replaced for extended periods if not permanently, lessening the chances of strikes being successful (and historically strikes have been perhaps the single most effective means of furthering workers' interests).

Gains to workers from technological change in capitalism are *partial* as well. Those laid off due to the introduction of labor-saving machinery hardly can be said to have benefited much. Nor can this be said of those employed by less productive firms resorting to low wages as a competitive strategy. These gains also do not eliminate the physical and psychological harms associated with the extension and intensification of the labor process, accompaniments of technological change in Marx's day and our own. (The faster the rate of technological change, the greater the pressure to extend and intensify the workday in order to minimize the risk of new technologies becoming obsolete before acceptable returns have been won.)

A related problem arises from the fact that in capitalism productivity gains necessarily tend to be used to increase the output of commodities, rather than to reduce work, since the former generally furthers capital accumulation more than the latter. The problem here is not simply that workers often prefer more free time. It is that in many contexts greater free time would better further human flourishing. Increased consumption also does not address the environmental costs associated with ruthlessly using productivity gains to increase output (greater waste, pollution, etc.). A disproportionate share of these costs invariably falls on workers and their communities.

The most important way in which consumption gains are partial, however, is that they do not eliminate the structural coercion underlying the wage contract. Even with expanded consumption, workers as a class still face the social compulsion to return to the labor market to sell their labor power. Gains in consumption also do not eliminate the class exploitation that follows from structural coercion. (All the factors listed above that make these gains precarious provide the mechanisms enforcing this result.) There are individual exceptions, but they do not negate the general rule. A framework of coercion and exploitation is not one in which "all persons are equal, so far as the importance of their basic interests are concerned" (Buchanan 2004: 42), or in which "persons [are] free and equal in the determination of the conditions of their own lives" (Held 1995: 147), even if some of those who sell their labor power are sometimes able to improve their living standards in a precarious and partial fashion.

The limits of democracy

Almost all contemporary political philosophers assert that exercises of authority by state officials are normatively legitimate if and only if they reflect the democratic will of those over whom authority is exercised:

> It can be argued that democracy is itself an important element of justice because justice requires equal regard for persons and this in turn requires that they can participate as equals in determining the most basic social rules and the allocation of the unequal political power that governance inevitably involves. (Buchanan 2004: 278)

In the capitalist work place some adults exercise "governance" over others, with "basic social rules" at stake. Two examples of basic social rules have been alluded to above. One is, "Introduce innovations debasing the creativity and skill level of the work force whenever doing so can be anticipated to lower wage costs (and/or increase management control of the production process) without adversely affecting profits." Here is the other: "Use productivity advances to increase the output of commodities, rather than to increase free time while holding the level of output constant." Alternative "basic social rules" are certainly possible.

Consistency demands, then, that governance in the workplace be categorized as a form of *political* governance, legitimate only if all members of the workplace "participate as equals in determining the most basic social rules and the allocation of the unequal political power that governance inevitably involves." Precisely this is ruled out by the capital/wage labor relation, even in the most extensive schemes of worker participation imagined by capitalist utopians (Smith 2000: Ch. 3).

It is ruled out on the level of the state as well.

While some of Marx's more provocative slogans may suggest otherwise, he did not believe the capitalist state is a mere epiphenomenon, completely determined by economic factors. The discussion in *Capital* of laws restricting the length of the working day, and Marx's many newspaper articles and extended essays on state policies and geopolitical conflicts, discuss a variety of non-economic causal variables, including divergences of interests among economic elites, the self-interests of state officials, the difficulties of forming effective organizations and the variable quality of leadership within them, and the manner in which (socially constructed) differences of race, gender, ethnicity, religion, and nationality can prevent common interests from being recognized, let alone acted upon. As a result of these sorts of considerations the adoption of a particular state policy can never be deduced from a list of economic facts, no matter how extensive. Marx also did not believe that state policies reforming capitalism are impossible in principle, or that it was possible to determine precisely where the limits of reforms are found. And he consistently supported reforms that promised to alleviate human suffering or extend respect for persons, even when they left capitalist social relations in place (see, for example, Marx 1986a). He understood that there are more or less humane variants of capitalism, and that the difference matters. But there were more and less humane slave systems, and more and less humane forms of feudalism. Nonetheless, contemporary political philosophers insist that *no* form of government tied to *any* variant of the master/slave relation or the lord/serf relation could be compatible with "egalitarian universalism." There are good reasons to hold that the same is true of governments essentially tied to the capital/wage labor relation.

The interests of capitalists and of state elites are often too heterogeneous for there to be a direct one-to-one correspondence between the two. But any extended breakdown in the capital accumulation process brings with it the danger of social unrest. And the more the process of capital accumulation slows, the more difficult it is to raise the revenues required by the state apparatus. As a result state officials necessarily tend to implement policies designed to encourage investments, including incentives to discourage units of capital from exercising the exit options granted to them by the property relations of capital. Whatever the fantasies of libertarians might be, capitalist states necessarily tend to further capital accumulation in ways that go far beyond the mere enforcement of property rights. Examples include public funding of research and development (R&D), infrastructure, education, training, and countless other forms of subsidies; various forms of disciplining laborers, the unemployed, households and communities; the political regulation of money; and so on. This does not imply that state policies will never further the interests of any other group besides the owners and controllers of capital. But it does imply that their interests will necessarily tend to have priority over the interests of other individuals and groups. Not always, not everywhere, but "proximately and for the most part," as Aristotle might say. This is a form of systematic discrimination, to which liberal egalitarians are officially opposed:

> By pursuing policies that systematically discriminate against a group in the distribution of wealth, the state is violating a fundamental condition of its legitimacy, failing to function as an institutional structure for mutual benefit under the requirement of equal regard for persons. (Buchanan 2004: 396)

Such discrimination in favor of the owners and controllers of capital must be the *normal* state of affairs in capitalist democracies in so far as the capitalist state is essentially tied to the systematic reproduction of the exploitative capital/wage labor relation. If the latter is not compatible with egalitarian universalism, neither is the former.

Few contemporary political philosophers acknowledge the challenge this state of affairs poses to their views. David Held is a notable exception:

> A government's policies must, thereby, follow a political agenda that is at least favourable to, that is, biased towards, the development of the system of private enterprise and corporate power. Democratic theory and practice are, thus, faced with a major challenge: the business corporation or multinational bank enjoys a disproportionate "structural influence" over the polity and, therefore, over the nature of democratic outcomes ... Democracy is

embedded in a socio-economic system that grants a "privileged position" to certain interests. *Accordingly, individuals and interest groups cannot be treated as necessarily equal, and the state cannot be regarded as a neutral arbiter among all interests.* (Held 1995: 247; italics added)

Unfortunately, Held does not provide any compelling reason whatsoever to think that his proposals for a global capitalist regime based on "democratic cosmopolitan law" would fundamentally transform this state of affairs, as opposed to improving matters at the margin (Smith 2005: Ch. 4).

The choice is reasonably clear. Either the principle that all individuals must "participate as equals in determining the most basic social rules" must be abandoned, or the claim that capitalism can in principle institutionalize this principle must be abandoned. When pressed, most contemporary political philosophers who initially affirmed the principle opt for the former path, retreating to the quite different, and much weaker, imperative to institute a social order in which all individuals enjoy an acceptable minimal level of subsistence. When a shift of this magnitude occurs, it is a clear sign that ideological considerations are at work.

The drive to capital accumulation systematically undermines egalitarian universalism in two other ways important enough to warrant separate consideration. Both have to do with tendencies holding on the level of the capitalist world market, the higher-order unity under which national economies are subsumed.

Crisis tendencies

Mainstream economic models typically abstract from economic instability, at the cost of ignoring crucial aspects of how capitalist markets actually function. Liberal egalitarians understand that capitalist markets left to themselves are regularly susceptible to recessions and depressions severe enough to be incompatible with a social order devoted to the furthering of human flourishing for all. They hold, however, that this tendency can be put out of play through appropriate public policies. Rawls, for example, refers to a "stabilization branch" of government, which "strives to bring about reasonably full employment in the sense that those who want work can find it and the free choice of occupation and the deployment of finance are supported by strong effective demand" (Rawls 1971: 276). Cosmopolitan liberals believe that attaining this goal requires new global institutions (Davidson 2002). For Marx, the crisis tendencies in capitalism doom all such proposals to failure (Marx 1968: 501). Unfortunately, Marx never wrote a systematic account of crisis tendencies in capitalism, and there is not space here to do more than discuss a few central aspects of his position.

Capitalism's technological dynamism stems from the drive to appropriate above average profits. New plants and firms will enter a given sector when they foresee being able to win "surplus profits" from superior products or more efficient production processes (Marx 1976a: 437; 1981: 295–6, 299). But – contrary to an assumption of almost all models in mainstream economics – established firms and plants do not automatically withdraw after the entry of new and more efficient competitors at a rate ensuring an equilibrium of supply and demand (Reuten 1991; Brenner 2006). The fixed capital costs (for, machinery, facilities, etc.) of established producers are already "sunk," and so they may be happy to receive the average rate of profit on their circulating capital alone (investment in raw materials, labor power, etc.). They may also have established relations with suppliers and customers impossible or prohibitively expensive to duplicate elsewhere in any relevant time frame. Further, their management and labor force may have industry-specific skills. And governments may provide subsidies for training, infrastructure, or R&D that would not be available if they were to shift sectors. When a sufficient number of firms and plants do not withdraw from a sector when more efficient competitors enter, the result is an overaccumulation of capital, manifested in excess capacity and declining rates of profit. In Marxian jargon, living labor will fail to produce sufficient surplus value to valorize the given capital investments. When this dynamic unfolds simultaneously in leading sectors, an economy-wide fall in profit rates may result for an extended period.

Once overaccumulation difficulties commence, the rate of industrial investment slows significantly, forming a pool of money capital. (When Central Banks responds to slowdowns in accumulation by increasing liquidity, this pool grows even faster.) These funds seek new sectors with a potential for high future rates of growth. When such sectors appear to emerge, financial capitals throughout the world market stampede to purchase their capital assets (stocks, bonds, etc.). Expectations of future earnings eventually become a secondary matter, and financial assets are purchased in the hope of profits from sales to other financial speculators (Marx 1981: 615–6, 742). This tendency is reinforced when previous (paper) gains in capital assets are used as collateral for borrowings to fund further purchases of financial products, setting off yet more rapid capital asset inflation. Throughout the course of the speculative bubble, it remains the case that financial assets remain in essence nothing but claims on the future production of surplus value. When it becomes overwhelmingly clear that their ever increasing prices are ever less likely to be redeemed by future profits, the speculative bubble collapses and a financial crisis ensues.

When overaccumulation crises break out, previous investments in fixed capital must be devalued if profit rates in industrial sectors are to be restored. When financial crises break out, equity holdings and debt instruments must be devalued if profit rates in the financial sector are to be restored (Marx 1981: 648–9). Every unit of capital attempts to shift the costs of these devaluations onto other units. And those who control capital will invariably mobilize their vast economic, political, and ideological weapons in the attempt to shift as many of the costs as possible onto wage laborers and their communities, through increased unemployment, lower wages, and worsened work conditions.

Neither the benefits of industrial expansions and financial bubbles, nor the burdens of overaccumulation and financial crises, are distributed in a neutral fashion. Those who own and control capital tend to receive a disproportionately high share of the former and a disproportionately low share of the latter, with the reverse holding for those who own little beyond their labor power. This is not a contingent feature of a capitalist global economy. It is part of the "rules of the game" defining this order. How could it be said of such a system that "all persons are equal, so far as the importance of their basic interests are concerned"?

Uneven development

The overwhelming majority of mainstream economists proclaim that any region in the global economy can in principle enjoy economic growth and improved living standards converging with those of advanced regions, if only the right sorts of public policies are consistently pursued (Jones 2002: Ch. 7). Contemporary political philosophers who hold that global capitalism could in principle adequately institutionalize egalitarian universalism are implicitly committed to this view as well. Marx, in contrast, holds that the drive to obtain above average profits through innovations necessarily tends to generate uneven development in the world market, involving levels of severe poverty and inequality beyond what defenders of egalitarian universalism should regard as normatively acceptable (Marx 1981: 344–5). Many dimensions of the world market contribute to this tendency, only one of which will be noted here.

Units of capital with access to advanced R&D are best positioned to enjoy above average profits from innovations. This implies that they are best able to establish a virtuous circle in which these returns provide the funds necessary to continue operating at the scientific-technical frontier, an essential precondition for being able to successfully introduce the next generation of the innovations, and thereby appropriate the next generation of above average returns. In contrast, units of capital without such access to advanced R&D necessarily tend to be trapped in a vicious circle. Their resulting inability to introduce significant innovations prevents them from enjoying above average returns, limiting their ability to participate in advanced R&D in the succeeding period. This in turn limits future innovations and, consequently, future profit opportunities.

Today, 95 per cent of all R&D is undertaken in wealthy regions of the global economy, where advantaged units of capital are clustered (Helpman 2004: 64). This enables those capitals to reproduce their advantages in the global economy over time. In this manner the interests of those owning and controlling these units of capital are systematically advantaged in the capitalist global economy. (If in the future R&D were more diffused, but a relative handful of companies retained privileged access to its commercializable results, little if anything essential would have changed.) Some investors and managers from poorer regions undoubtedly prosper in this arrangement. But they do so only as junior partners. And any gains to workers in these "peripheral" regions will be especially precarious and partial (and will exacerbate the precarious and partial nature of gains won by wage laborers in the "center" of the world market).

It is possible for particular regions to rise or fall in the hierarchy of the world economy. But the fact that some particular regions are able to transcend their initial position does not imply that all can, or that severe inequality and poverty in the global economy is a merely contingent matter. The tendency to uneven development is not a subsidiary matter accidentally linked to the reign of capital. The tendency is inextricably tied to the drive to innovation, which is utterly fundamental ("endogenous") to capital. The more honest contemporary mainstream economists studying economic growth admit this explicitly:

> [I]nvestment in innovation widens the gap between rich and poor countries. The output gains of the industrial countries exceed the output gains of the less-developed countries. We therefore conclude that investment in innovation in the industrial countries leads to divergence of income between the North and the South. (Helpman 2004: 85)

This is an astounding statement, with profound implications for contemporary political philosophy. If the interests of those owning and controlling firms with access to advanced R&D are systematically privileged at the cost of the interests of the vast majority of the globe's population, then the latter can hardly be said to be "equal in the determination of the conditions of their own lives" and global capitalism can hardly be affirmed to a system in which "all persons are equal, so far as the importance of their basic interests are concerned." If we want to understand why the population of global slums is expected to exceed two billion human beings in the next twenty-five years (Davis 2004) – or why the richest 1 per cent of adults in the world owned 40 per cent of global assets in the year 2000 while the bottom *half* owned barely 1 per cent of global wealth (Davies et al. 2006) – the tendency to uneven development in the capitalist world market may not be the entire story. But it is surely the place to start.

This concludes the discussion of Marx's theory of capital. In Marx's view the property and production relations defining capitalism are systematically connected to structural coercion, class exploitation, alienation from our essential capacities, radical economic insecurity, overaccumulation crises, financial crises, and uneven development. No set of social relations with these features and systematic tendencies can institutionalize egalitarian universalism adequately, even in principle. No set of social relations of this sort could pass Kant's universalizability test, or claim to have human flourishing as its end. Rawls' rational individuals behind a veil of ignorance following a maximin rule would not contract for a basic structure with these features, nor would a rational consensus in its favor be reached by participants in the practical discourse anticipating an ideal speech situation to which Habermas refers. Such is the nature of Marx's theoretical challenge to contemporary political philosophy.

But, as Marx famously wrote, "Philosophers have hitherto only interpreted the world in various ways; the point is to change it" (Marx 1976b: 5). What are the prospects for a post-capitalist epoch in world history? And what might a feasible and normatively attractive alternative to capitalism look like? The concluding sections will be devoted to these questions.

The dialectic of world history

Marx discussed the possible transition from capitalism to a post-capitalist order within the theoretical framework of *historical dialectics* (a second form of dialectical social theory, *systematic dialectics*, will be discussed briefly in the appendix). Hegel's lectures on the philosophy of history, tracing an alleged sequence from the Oriental World, through the Greek and Roman Worlds, to the Modern World, provide one example (Hegel 1956). Marxian theories in which modes of production rise and fall in a non-arbitrary order provide others (Cohen et al. 1980: Pt 2; Levine and Wright 1980).

The standard objection to historical dialectics is that it assumes a determinist and teleological view of history. Human agency appears to become all but irrelevant, as one historical stage inexorably gives way to the next. Joseph McCarney has argued persuasively that this is a caricature of Hegel's position (McCarney 2000). Daniel Bensaïd has established that for Marx history is an open-ended process in which human agency is the absolutely crucial factor (Bensaïd 2002). Marx's theory of history does not call into question the contingency and path dependency of history, or the transformative power of human agency (Marx 1977: 570–1). This does not imply, however, that history is a matter of pure contingency. Human agency always operates within particular historical contexts that set limits on what is objectively possible, even if these limits are indeterminate.

The goal of historical dialects is to rationally reconstruct a pattern of development underlying the contingent twists and turns of empirical history. There are, I believe, four main epochs in world history in Marx's account, each of which expands the limits of what is objectively possible in a fundamental fashion:

(1) a "ground zero," so to speak, when productive capacities were not developed enough to provide a significant surplus product;
(2) the millennia in which various *precapitalist class societies* arose and passed away, societies in which productive capacities were developed enough to provide a surplus product that ruling strata, separate from producers, could appropriate;
(3) the centuries of the reign of capital; and
(4) a possible future period in which feasible and normatively attractive alternatives to capitalism emerge.

Marx never suggested that every particular society must necessarily go through each stage in this ordering. (Previously isolated tribes, for example, can be forced to adjust to capitalism without ever having established a precapitalist class society.) This historical dialectic does not rule out historical regressions. (There have been numerous occasions in which ruling elites in precapitalist class societies over-exploited the producers of the social surplus to the point where they could no longer reproduce themselves, leading to "dark ages" in which previous gains in productivity and civilization were lost; see Harman 2008.) Nor does Marx's historical dialectic rule out evolutionary "dead ends" that do not fit neatly under any of the four headings. (The Soviet Union perhaps provides an illustration.) The key point is that the ordering of these four epochs is not random. Each subsequent epoch does not simply count as a fundamental rupture with what went before; each objectively expands the realm of realizable human potential by a major increment. Many other ways of reconstructing world history are legitimate in principle. But if we want a theory of history that orients practical struggles to move beyond capitalism, Marx thought that something along the above lines is what we need.

From this point of view capitalism plays a pivotal role in world history. As a system in which "the self-valorization of capital – the creation of surplus value – is the determining, dominating, and overriding purpose" it counts as the most extensive and intensive system of alienation in history (Marx 1976a: 990). Paradoxically, however, its ontological inversion of ends and means (its subordination of human ends under the alien end of a thing, capital) brings about the greatest expansion of human capacities in world history. The rule of things forces the development of human capacities beyond the limits imposed by the customs and traditions of precapitalist societies:

> [A]t the level of material production …we find … the inversion of subject into object and *vice versa*. Viewed historically this inversion is the indispensable transition without which wealth as such, i.e. the relentless productive forces of social labour, which alone can form the material base of a free human society, could not possibly be created. (Marx 1976a: 990)

In the concluding section I shall sketch one form a "free human society" might take. No one could argue that the "material base" for such a society is absent today. But so what? Does not the implosion of the Soviet Union prove that the dialectic of history ends with capitalism? There are, I believe, three objective features of our contemporary situation that should make us pause before answering yes.

(1) Two of the most important social consequences of the information technology revolution are the rise of "commons-based peer production" and the increasing importance of knowledge products. The former refers to cooperative knowledge work undertaken within information networks outside the capital/wage labor relation (Benkler 2006). A list of Internet applications developed by people engaged in this form of production should be sufficient to convey its contemporary significance:

> Ideas like free Web-based e-mail, hosting services for personal Web pages, instant messenger software, social networking sites, and well-designed search engines emerged more from individuals or small groups of people wanting to solve their own problems or try something neat than from firms realizing there were profits to be gleaned. (Zittrain 2008: 85)

Encryption software, peer-to-peer file-sharing software, sound and image editors, and many other examples can be added to this list. "Indeed, it is difficult to find software *not* initiated by amateurs" (Zittrain 2008: 89).

Capitalist firms are happy to appropriate the creative achievements of social labor outside the capital/wage labor relation as "free gifts." But capitalism is fundamentally based upon profits from the sale of proprietary products. And so the resources devoted to the non-proprietary output of commons-based peer production will inevitably be severely restricted. And the time and energy people have to participate in commons-based production will be severely limited as well, since most of those who do not own and control capital must sell their labor power to capitalist firms and engage in extensive surplus labor for them.

Similarly severe restrictions also afflict the production and distribution of knowledge goods. Many categories of knowledge products (software; information; literary, scientific, and cultural texts; music; videos – etc.) can today be reproduced and distributed within information networks at close to zero marginal cost. In principle, they could be made freely available. But "the self-valorization of capital" requires the sale of commodities. And so massive amounts of monetary and human resources are devoted to technologies whose sole purpose is to *restrict* flows of knowledge products to privately appropriable commodities (Perelman 1998).

Commons-based peer production, and knowledge goods that can be produced and distributed at a marginal cost close to zero, have a tremendous objective potential to develop human capacities and to bring the satisfaction of human wants and needs to new peaks. Much of this potential is doomed to remain undeveloped under a system based on the production and sale of privately owned commodities. The fact that this unprecedented objective potential cannot be fully actualized within the social forms of capital strongly suggests that capitalism should not be taken as the final stage of human history.

(2) There are also good reasons to think that we may now be in a new historical period where "golden ages" of capitalist development are not likely to recur, at least not prior to unimaginable human suffering. As prominent non-Marxian economic historians recognize, "golden ages" have occurred when units of capital in one region in the world system have enjoyed a quasi-monopoly of economic advantages for an extended period of time (Perez 2003). For the first time in human history numerous effective national innovation systems have been established across the globe today (Nelson 1993). These systems greatly contribute to technological dynamism in use-value terms. In value terms, however, they necessarily tend to shorten the period in which innovating firms can appropriate above average profits. As soon as a new sector emerges that shows signs of becoming especially profitable, a multitude of national innovation systems will quickly funnel massive amounts of subsidies and credit to new entrants in that sector, quickly leading to overcapacity problems. No new "golden age" of capitalist growth can be expected to emerge in such circumstances. If another world war were to destroy excess productive capacity and national innovation systems, the preconditions for a new "golden age" would be in place. A major global Depression might also renew the conditions for dynamic growth in the capitalist world market. Short of such catastrophes, however, overaccumulation difficulties can be expected to persist in non-financial sectors, with increasingly desperate attempts by firms in these sectors to maintain profits through lay-offs, lower wages, and intensified (and extended) labor processes (Smith 2007).

In recent decades, massive profits have been won in the financial sector. In fact, the greatest concentration of knowledge workers, the highest private sector investment in information technologies, and the highest rate of product innovation, have been found here. Not coincidentally, there have also been financial bubbles of increasing frequency and scale, and severe financial crises when those bubbles burst. These features of our era cannot be adequately explained by a lack of a political will to regulate finance. On a deeper level they are explained by the fact that when overaccumulation difficulties persist in non-financial sectors, speculating on financial assets provides the greatest opportunities for profits. Or at least it does so until the scale of financial insanity threatens a global financial meltdown (Foster and Magdoff 2009).

Overaccumulation and financial crises have accompanied capitalism from its beginnings (Arrighi 1994). But there are good reasons to think that they now will persist and recur, respectively, to a historically unprecedented degree. If that is indeed an objective feature of the contemporary period, it too strongly suggests that capitalism should not be regarded as the final stage in the dialectic of world history.

(3) There are, finally, also good reasons to think that *environmental crises* now put the place of capitalism in world history into question as well. Capitalist firms face unrelenting pressure to accumulate. They must therefore attempt to produce and sell as many commodities as possible, as rapidly as possible. A tendency follows ineluctably for the technologies of production and distribution to be used in a manner that depletes resources and generates wastes at a faster rate than ecosystems can sustain (Harvey 1996). We may well be at a tipping point today where a social order with different properties is objectively required for humanity's survival.

No set of objective factors is sufficient to bring about a transition to a post-capitalist epoch. A host of subjective conditions must come into play. The single most important subjective factor concerns the capital/wage labor relation. In all societies the reproduction of social life is due to the creative powers of social labor, in the broadest sense of the term. In capitalism, these collective powers can only be brought into play by capital, for the simple reason that the conditions necessary for laborers to actualize and develop these capacities – the productive resources of society and their own means of subsistence – are owned by capital:

> [T]he rule of the capitalist over the worker is nothing but the rule of the independent *conditions of labour* over the *worker*, conditions that have made themselves independent of him ... These embrace not only the objective conditions of the process of production – the means of production – but also the objective prerequisites for the substance and effectiveness of labour-power, i.e. means of subsistence. (Marx 1976a: 989)

As a result the creative powers of social labor appear to be capital's powers, and the products of social labor appear to be capital's products. Marx fully recognized the unprecedented development of human capacities this social organization has brought about. But he also recognized the alienation and exploitation at its heart. Were this recognition to become widespread, the practical consequences would be profound:

> The recognition of the product as its [labor's] own, and its awareness that its separation from the conditions of its realisation is an injustice – *a relationship imposed by force* – is an enormous consciousness ... and just as much the KNELL TO ITS DOOM as the consciousness of the slave that he *could not be the property*

of the another reduced slavery to an artificial, lingering existence, and made it impossible for it to continue to provide the basis of production. (Marx 1994: 246)

The main practical goal of Marx's theory of capital is to make this recognition widespread.

A new consciousness alone, however, does not suffice to bring about a new stage in world history. It requires organizational structures within which radical social change can be effectively pursued in different contexts, structures whose shape cannot be derived *a priori*. Neither can the strategies and tactics to be adopted in specific contexts be deduced by theorists. These are all matters to be determined by the particular agents operating in the concrete circumstances. Marx, however, did assert a few general points. He repeatedly stated that emancipation will not be bestowed by ruling classes as a gift, nor will it be won by the conspiracies of small sects. It can only be achieved through mass social movements from below; the emancipation of the working class must be a process of *self*-emancipation (Marx 1985). Marx also insisted that movements against the reign of capital must have an internationalist orientation, both because capital operates on the level of the world market, and because the effects of nationalism are so often pernicious (Marx 1986a).

It is not possible to pursue these topics further here. Further pursuit would in any case be irrelevant, were there no feasible and normatively attractive alternative to capitalism.

Towards a Marxian alternative

Marx himself did not describe his vision of a post-capitalist society in any detail. But he repeatedly insisted that any acceptable alternative must overcome the dualism separating the supposedly private and non-political realm of "free" agreements (which is in fact the realm of capital, an alien power dominating social life) from the public and political realm of a state supposedly transcending society (but whose very form is essentially shaped by its relationship to capital). When one class extracts a social surplus from another, that is inherently a *political* matter, even if it occurs through "private" and "non-political" contracts among formally free and equal agents enforced by an allegedly "neutral" state.

Most contemporary political philosophers believe that Marx conflated political and economic power, and that this is a recipe for authoritarianism, if not totalitarianism. Such a conflation was, after all, the project of fascism and Stalinism. Whatever the limits of democratic capitalism might be, it institutionalizes a separation of political and economic power that most philosophers regard as an irreplaceable protection against tyranny, no less important than the separation of state powers or the universal franchise.

A first response is to note that Marx insisted on the importance of elections, universal franchise, and representative institutions throughout his life, from his earliest writings on the state through his late essay on the Paris Commune (Marx 1986b).

Intellectual honesty demands that the immense gulf between this commitment and the intellectual foundations of fascism and Stalinism be acknowledged. The most important question, however, is not what Marx intended. It is whether attempts to surpass the limits of democratic capitalism are doomed to produce something far, far worse. Given the horrors of the twentieth century, this issue cannot be dismissed with a blithe reference to Marx's scorn for blueprints of the future. Some sketch of a feasible and normatively attractive alternative to capitalism is required here, however provisional and inadequate it might be (interested readers are urged to consult Schweickart 1993, 2002; Smith 2000: Ch. 7, and 2005: Ch. 8 for extended discussions).

A first requirement is the overcoming of the drive to accumulate money capital as an end in itself, a drive holding on the level of society as a whole, overriding all other social ends. This requires the abolition of capital markets. Decisions regarding the level of overall new investment, the main priorities for new investment, and the overall level of resources to be devoted to public goods, could then be made within democratically elected bodies after extensive public debates. In the absence of compelling reasons to do otherwise, funds for new investment could then be distributed to regions on a per capita basis. The actual allocation of new investment funds to enterprises could then undertaken by community banks, whose boards would include representatives of a broad range of social groups affected by the banks' decisions. With these institutions in place, capital markets could be abolished.

Democratizing decisions regarding the levels and priorities of new investments would allow for greater coordination of investments, removing the systematic tendency to overaccumulation crises. The elimination of "private" markets in capital assets would automatically remove the danger of financial crises. The allocation of new investment funds to regions on a per capita basis is especially crucial. The equal moral worth of all individuals implies that all individuals should have access to the material preconditions for human flourishing. Nothing would further this desideratum more than a social order in which all regions had a (*prima facie*) equal right to a per capita share of new investment funds. A global order founded on this right would not be characterized by a systematic tendency to uneven development. The tendency to uneven development would also be put out of play if all forms of scientific-technological knowledge were treated as the public goods they inherently are, rather than as just another form of private property.

The abolition of labor markets, that is, of wage labor, is also required if we are to ever attain a world in which the "all persons are equal, so far as the importance of their basic interests are concerned." To accomplish this, the production and distribution of goods and services could be undertaken by community-owned worker cooperatives, with managers democratically elected by, and accountable to, those over whom they exercise authority. Workers' share in the fruits of these enterprises could then be allocated in a transparent fashion, with the principles underlying these allocations subject to democratic discussion and approval among members of the workforce themselves.

It is not the mere presence of markets *per se* that establishes the alien power of capital. What makes capitalist market societies so different from precapitalist societies with markets is the society-wide compulsion to place the accumulation of surplus value above all other ends, and the separation of producers from the means of production and subsistence. The democratizing of decisions regarding the levels and priorities of new investments removes the compulsion, and the democratizing of the workplace removes the separation. In other words, what matters most is the abolition of capital markets and labor markets. There could still be an important role for producer and consumer markets in a post-capitalist social order if the central planning of all producer inputs and outputs, and the distribution of all consumer goods, is likely be excessively time-consuming, inefficient, and vulnerable to abuses by the central planners.

Many details of this alternative obviously remain open. And those that have been sketched may well require significant revision (Ollman 1998). The goal of this sketch has simply been to suggest that a dogmatic insistence that there is no feasible and normatively superior alterative to capitalism is just that: dogmatic.

Appendix: a note on the Hegel/Marx connection

In the course of his preparatory studies for *Capital* Marx wrote to Engels that Hegel's *Logic* "was of great use to me as regards *method* of treatment" (Marx 1983: 50). Exactly what Marx meant, and the extent to which he later modified or even rejected this view, remains controversial. There is only space here for a few brief comments.

The above statement alerts us to the importance of Hegel for an understanding of Marx's methodological framework. *The Contribution to the Critique of Political Economy, Capital,* and the preparatory drafts for these works (especially the *Grundrisse* and Marx's *1861–63 Manuscripts*), are complex works. But a unifying thread runs throughout them, the reconstruction in thought of the essential determinations of capital, beginning with the simplest and most abstract ("commodity," "value," "money") and proceeding step-by-step to progressively more complex and concrete determinations. The term for this sort of project is *systematic dialectics*, and from this perspective Hegel was Marx's great predecessor (Smith 1990). The references in this chapter to different levels of abstraction in Marx's theory alluded to this Hegelian legacy in Marx.

While Marx was happy to creatively adopt Hegel's systematic dialectics, he clearly thought that Hegel's own position illustrated the same sort of alienation found in religious consciousness, the state, and the social forms of capital. In Marx's reading, Hegel's "Absolute Thought" ("The Concept"; "The Idea") is an allegedly transcendent subject reigning over us, just as heaven supposedly reigns over the earth, and the state and capital reign over society. This reading has become enshrined in subsequent Marxist thought, with important contemporary Marxian philosophers asserting a strong homology between Hegel's system and the logic of capital (Arthur 2002). In my view, this is an extremely uncharitable reading of Hegel, albeit one for which his idiosyncratic and obscure terminology is greatly responsible. At his best Hegel, like Marx, was a thoroughgoing philosopher of immanence: "philosophy is the apprehension of the present and the actual, not the erection of a beyond, supposed to exist, God knows where" (Hegel 1967: 10). And Hegel, like Marx, was a predecessor of scientific realism. "Absolute Thought" is not some sort of bizarre metaphysical Supersubject, but *our* thought insofar as it is not "subjective thinking applied to some matter externally, but is rather the matter's very soul" (Hegel 1967: 34–5).

There is, however, a major difference between dialectical social theory in Hegel and Marx. In Hegel's major contribution to political philosophy, *The Philosophy of Right*, the fundamental limitations of one theoretical level are resolved as the theory progresses. (In specific, the state resolves the contradictions of civil society to the greatest possible extent.) In contrast, the limitations of the capitalist mode of production explicated at the beginning of Marx's theory are *not* overcome in the course of the theory's development. The same antagonism between human sociality, on the one hand, and alien social forms subsuming human life under inhuman ends, on the other, reappears in ever-more concrete and complex shapes. While the *Philosophy of Right* is an affirmative social theory, *Capital* maintains its critical thrust from first page to last.

Hegel's 'logic of the concept' is designed to capture the intelligibility of dynamic wholes whose different moments are harmoniously reconciled without sacrifice of their particularity. Hegel himself thought the social forms of modern European civil society and the state were "homologous" with this logic, at least in principle. They are not. The fundamental antagonism between capital and wage labor is not resolved in a higher-level totality in which the two opposing poles are transformed and reconciled. Whatever Hegel's own views on the matter, a social world in which systematic antagonisms are overcome has yet to be created.

References

Arrighi, G. (1994) *The Long Twentieth Century*, New York: Verso.

Arthur, C. (2002) *The New Dialectic and Marx's Capital*, Leiden: Brill.

Bellofiore, R. (2005) "The Monetary Aspects of the Capitalist Process in the Marxian System," in F. Moseley (ed.) *Marx's Theory of Money*, New York: Palgrave Macmillan.

Benkler, Y. (2006) *The Wealth of Networks*, New Haven, CT: Yale University Press.

Bensaïd, D. (2002) *Marx for Our Times: Adventures and Misadventures of a Critique*, New York: Verso.

Brenner, R. (2006) *The Economics of Global Turbulence*, New York: Verso.

Buchanan, A. (2004) *Justice, Legitimacy, and Self-Determination*, New York: Oxford University Press.

Callinicos, A. (2000) *Equality*, Malden, MA: Polity Press.

Campbell, M (1997) "Marx's Theory of Money: A Defense," in F. Moseley and M. Campbell (eds) *New Investigations of Marx's Method*, Atlantic Highlands, NJ: Humanities Press.

Cohen, M., T. Nagel, and T. Scanlon (1980) *Marx, Justice and History*, Princeton, NJ: Princeton University Press.

Davidson, P. *Financial Markets, Money and the Real World*, Northhampton, MA: Edward Elgar.

Davies, J., S. Sandstrom, A. Shorrocks, and E. Wolff (2006) "The World Distribution of Household Wealth," World Institute for Development Economics Research of the United Nations University website; available at http://www.wider.unu.edu/research/2006-2007/2006-2007-1/wider-wdhw-launch-5-12-2006/wider-wdhw-press-release-5-12-2006.htm

Davis, M. (2004) "Planet of Slums," *New Left Review* 26: 5–34.

Foster, J. Bellamy, and F. Magdoff (2009) *The Great Financial Crisis*, New York: Monthly Review Press.

Habermas, J. (2001) *The Postnational Constellation*, Cambridge: MIT Press.

Harman, C. (2008) *A People's History of the World: From the Stone Age to the New Millennium*, London: Verso.

Harvey, D. (1996) *Justice, Nature and the Geography of Difference*, Malden, MA: Blackwell.

Hayek, F. (1976) *Law, Legislation, and Liberty*, vol. 2: *The Mirage of Social Justice*, Chicago: University of Chicago Press.

Hegel, G. W. F. (1956) *The Philosophy of History*, New York: Dover.

—— (1967) *Philosophy of Right*, New York: Oxford University Press.

Held, D. (1995) *Democracy and the Global Order: From the Modern State to Cosmopolitan Governance*, Stanford: Stanford University Press.

—— (2004) *Global Covenant: The Social Democratic Alternative to the Washington Consensus*, Malden, MA: Polity Press.

Helpman, E. (2004) *The Mystery of Economic Growth*, Cambridge, MA: Belknap Press.

Jones, C. (2002) *Introduction to Economic Growth*, New York: W. W. Norton.

Kouvelakis, S. (2003) *Philosophy and Revolution: From Kant to Marx*, New York: Verso.

Levine, A., and E. O. Wright (1980) "Rationality and Class Struggle," *New Left Review*, 123: 47–68.

Losurdo, D. (2004) *Hegel and the Freedom of Moderns*, Durham, NC: Duke University Press.

Marx, K. Marx, K. (1968) *Theories of Surplus Value*, pt 2, Moscow: International Publishers.

—— (1975a) "Contribution to the Critique of Hegel's Philosophy of Right," in K. Marx and F. Engels, *Collected Works*, vol. 3: Mar 1843–Aug 1844, New York: International Publishers.

—— (1975b) "On the Jewish Question," in K. Marx and F. Engels, *Collected Works*, vol. 3: Mar 1843–Aug 1844, New York: International Publishers.

—— (1975c) "Contribution to the Critique of Hegel's Philosophy of Law: Introduction," in K. Marx and F. Engels, *Collected Works*, vol. 3: Mar 1843–Aug 1844, New York: International Publishers.

—— (1976a) *Capital*, vol. 1, New York: Penguin Books.

—— (1976b) "Theses on Feuerbach," in K. Marx and F. Engels, *Collected Works*, vol. 5: Apr 1845–Apr 1847, New York: International Publishers.

—— (1977) *Selected Writings*, edited by D. McLellan, New York: Oxford University Press.

—— (1978) *Capital*, vol. 2, New York: Penguin Books.

—— (1981) *Capital*, vol. 3, New York: Penguin Books.

—— (1983) "Marx to Engels, January 16, 1858", in Marx, K. and Engels, F. *Collected Works: Volume 40, Letters 1856–59*, New York: International Publishers.

—— (1985) "Inaugural Address of the Working Men's International Association," in K. Marx and F. Engels, *Collected Works*, vol. 20: 1864–8, New York: International Publishers.

—— (1986a) "First Address of the General Council of the International Working Men's Association on the Franco-Prussian War," in K. Marx and F. Engels, *Collected Works*, vol. 22: 1870–1, New York: International Publishers.

—— (1986b) "The Civil War in France," in K. Marx and F. Engels, *Collected Works*, vol. 22: 1870–1, New York: International Publishers.

—— (1986c) "Outlines of the Critique of Political Economy" ["the Grundrisse'], in K. Marx and F. Engels, *Collected Works*, vol. 28: 1857–61, New York: International Publishers.

—— (1988) "Economic Manuscript of 1861–63," in K. Marx and F. Engels, *Collected Works*, vol. 30: 1861–3, New York: International Publishers.

—— (1989) "Critique of the Gotha Program," in K. Marx and F. Engels, *Collected Works*, vol. 24: 1874–83, New York: International Publishers.

—— (1994) "Economic Manuscript of 1861–63," in K. Marx and F. Engels, *Collected Works*, vol. 34: 1861–3, New York: International Publishers.

Marx, K., and F. Engels (1976) "The Communist Manifesto," in K. Marx and F. Engels, *Collected Works*, vol. 6: 1845–8, New York: International Publishers.

McCarney, J. (2000) *Hegel on History*, London: Routledge.

Moseley, F. (1993) "Marx's Logical Method and the 'Transformation Problem'," in F. Moseley (ed.) *Marx's Method in Capital*, Atlantic Highlands, NJ: Humanities Press.

Murray, P. (1988) *Marx's Theory of Scientific Knowledge*, Atlantic Highlands, NJ: Humanities Press.

Nelson, R. (1993) *National Innovation Systems: A Comparative Analysis*, New York: Oxford University Press.

Nussbaum, M. (2001) *Women and Human Development,* New York: Cambridge University Press.

Ollman, B. (ed.) (1998) *Market Socialism: The Debate among Socialists.* New York: Routledge.

Perelman, M. (1998) *Class Warfare in the Information Age,* New York: St Martin's.

Perez, C. (1993) *Technological Revolutions and Financial Capital: The Dynamics of Bubbles and Golden* Ages, Northhampton, MA: Edward Elgar.

Pogge, T. (2002) *World Poverty and Human Rights,* Malden: Polity Press.

Rawls, J. (1971) *A Theory of Justice,* Cambridge, MA: Harvard University Press.

Reuten, G. (1991) "Accumulation of Capital and the Foundation of the Tendency of the Rate of Profit to Fall," *Cambridge Journal of Economics,* 15, no. 1: 79–93.

Smith, T. (1990) *The Logic of Marx's Capital: Replies to Hegelian Criticisms,* Albany, NY: SUNY Press.

—— (1993) *Dialectical Social Theory and Its Critics,* Albany, N.Y.: SUNY Press.

—— (2000) *Technology and Capital in the Age of Lean Production: A Marxian Critique of the 'New Economy',* Albany, NY: SUNY Press.

—— (2005) *Globalisation: A Systematic Marxian Account,* Leiden: Brill.

—— (2007) "Technological Dynamism and the Normative Justification of Capitalism," in R. Albritton, R. Jessop, and R. Westra (eds) *Political Economy and Global Capitalism,* New York: Anthem Press.

Schweickart, D. (1993) *Against Capitalism,* New York: Cambridge University Press.

—— (2002) *After Capitalism,* New York: Rowman and Littlefield.

Zittrain, J. (2008) *The Future of the Internet,* New Haven, CT: Yale.

9

TOCQUEVILLE, SOCIAL SCIENCE AND DEMOCRACY

Jon Elster

Introduction

Most scholars of Tocqueville think he was a great political theorist, and pay little attention to him as a social scientist.[1] In this chapter I shall offer my reasons for believing that he was a great social scientist, in fact one of the founders of social science. He has not, to be sure, been completely ignored by contemporary social scientists. The "Tocqueville paradox" – revolutions occur when conditions get better, not when they are getting worse – has had a considerable influence on theories of revolutions. It is also generally acknowledged that the equally paradoxical idea of "pluralistic ignorance" that was launched by Floyd Allport in 1924 had a direct precursor in Tocqueville's theory of conformism, although Allport does not refer to him. Yet I believe there are many other equally important insights that have been largely ignored. In this chapter I shall explore some of them.

The ideas of *democracy*, *liberty* and *equality* are at the core of Tocqueville's work. Whereas he believed that the progress of equality was inevitable and irresistible, he argued that French society at his time had the choice between equality with liberty (democracy) and equality without liberty (despotism). *Democracy in America* (2004 [DA], 1969 Lawrence trans. [DAL]) is exclusively devoted to democratic equality. *The Old Regime and the Revolution* (*L'Ancien régime et la révolution*, AR) explains the emergence of the non-democratic egalitarian regimes that existed under the two Napoleons.

In writing about democracy, Tocqueville's main concern was normative. Although hardly a wholehearted advocate of democracy, he believed that one could not set the clock back and recreate the natural hierarchies of the ancien régime. At the same time, he detested despotism for its crushing of individual liberty. Yet in defending democracy he was also drawn, perhaps against his original intentions, into a *causal analysis of the mechanisms of democracy* and a *methodological analysis of social causality*. Although I shall mainly focus on the latter, let me briefly sketch, by way of background, some aspects of the former.

It is generally believed that equality, in the static sense of equality of conditions at any given point in time, is a main independent variable in *Democracy in America*. And it is true that many of Tocqueville's analyses to refer to equality in this sense, notably his discussions of democratic conformism and democratic envy. Yet I believe that the idea of *dynamic equality* – high rate of social, economic mobility – is at least equally important. He argues that the absence of classes in America can be explained by the high turnover rates among groups – from rags to rags, or from shirtsleeves to shirtsleeves, in three generations. If he had been asked why there is no socialism in the United States, that would almost certainly have been his answer. (Interestingly, Marx read and was probably influenced by this analysis.) In his analysis of American politics, Tocqueville also emphasized its high rate of metabolism that made for constant changes in legislatures and administrations. It is a portrait of a society *constantly on the move* that is in many ways inconsistent with the vision of a society based on envy and conformism.

Explaining democracy to the French

In the Preface to his analysis of English capitalism, Marx (1867) told his German readers, "De te fabula narratur" – the story is told about you. And he added, "The country that is more developed industrially only shows, to the less developed, the image of its own future." DA is also a book about a foreign country that is held up to native readers as the image of their future. In the Introduction to the work, Tocqueville tells his readers that "There is no doubt in my mind that sooner or later we will come, as the Americans have come, to an almost complete equality of conditions" (DA: 14).

Tocqueville believed that his French readers would recoil before this prospect. DA as a whole may be read as an attempt to persuade them that their fears were ungrounded. His rhetorical strategy can be represented as follows. "You, my French readers, claim that democracy is pernicious. To support that claim you point to this or that dangerous effect of democratic customs and institutions. For each of these alleged flaws of democracy, I will show you that it rests on one of the following causal fallacies. You misidentify the causes of the facts you cite; you fail to take a sufficiently long time perspective; you ignore how the flaws of democracy are remedied or offset by democracy itself; or you make a fallacious inference from the effects of a marginal practice to the effects that would arise were the practice to become generalized. Once you have seen through these errors, your objections will cease."

I may add that some of his readers might have raised – and almost certainly did raise – an objection that cannot be put to rest in the same way. It refers to the essential mediocrity of democracies, which provide comfort for the many but fail to nourish outstanding achievements in the arts or sciences. Tocqueville acknowledged this fact, and to the extent he remained an aristocrat, deplored it. To the extent he was able to take a more impartial perspective, he embraced it. In his concluding chapter he writes that "It is natural to believe that what is most satisfying to the eye of man's creator and keeper is not the singular prosperity of a few but the greater well-being of all;

what seems decadence to me is therefore progress in his eyes; what pains me pleases him. Equality is less lofty, perhaps, but more just" (DA: 833). In addition to being a methodological individualist, he was an ethical individualist.

Tocqueville's idea of a social equilibrium

The first of the four causal fallacies I listed involves a confusion between transitional effects and equilibrium effects. Usually this implies a confusion between the effects of equalization and the effects of equality, but we shall see that the distinction is more broadly applicable.

First, we need to characterize Tocqueville's idea of a social equilibrium. The French terms he uses, "assiette" and the corresponding verbal form "assis," are not easy to translate, nor is the idea easy to understand. Another phrase used to express the same idea, "the natural state" of a society (e.g. DA: 259, 754), is not very illuminating.

I believe the best entry into the subject is provided by a discussion of why there are so few great ambitions in the United States:

> Desires proportion themselves to means. *Needs, ideas, and sentiments follow from one another.* Leveling is complete; democratic society has finally found its footing [*est enfin assise*]. If we consider a democratic society that has achieved this permanent and normal state ... we will come to the conclusion that if ambition is great while conditions are tending toward equality, it loses that character when equality becomes a fact. (DA: 739; my italics)

Tocqueville clearly intends to assert that America has found this "permanent and normal" state, in which there are no internal tensions that would presage a major social upheaval. In another passage, however, he asserts that American society "has yet to achieve a settled and definitive form" (*une assiette tranquille et définitive*) (DA: 247). On my reading of this text, he is not claiming that the society is unstable, only that the dust has not yet quite settled. Admittedly, while plausible, this interpretation is not compelling. It is supported, however, by a number of texts which taken together imply that Tocqueville viewed the various aspects of American life as *mutually reinforcing each other*. As we shall now see, the idea that "Needs, ideas, and sentiments follow from one another" can be generalized.

Needs, ideas and sentiments belong to the category of *mores*, "habits of the heart" (DA: 331). These constitute one of the three main variables of the analyses in DA, the other two being the *laws* and "the *social state*" of society. The last usually but not invariably refers to equality in either its static form (equality of income or wealth) or its dynamic form (high *de facto* rates of social mobility). Tocqueville makes a number of seemingly contradictory claims concerning the causal relations among these three variables. I shall argue that the contradiction can be resolved if we view him as grappling with the idea of *circular social causality* in which the three main variables "follow from one another."

275

In the title of one chapter, mores are explicitly said to be more important than the laws: "Laws do more to maintain a democratic republic in the United States than physical causes do, and mores do more than the laws" (DA: 352). Towards the end of the chapter he asserts that mores are supremely important (and not just more important than laws): "The importance of mores is a common truth, which study and experience have repeatedly confirmed. It is a truth central to all my thinking, and in the end all my ideas come back to it" (DA: 356). Now, saying that A is more important than B could mean several things. It could mean that A offers an explanation of B, typically through being a cause of B, that A explains more phenomena or more important phenomena than B, or that A contributes more powerfully to the explanation of the phenomena jointly caused by A and B. Whichever of these ways we choose to understand it, the idea that mores are more important than laws is incompatible with a number of other passages that I shall now cite.

Tocqueville writes, "More than once in the course of this book I have sought to explain the prodigious influence that the social state seems to me to exert on the laws and mores of men" (DA: 379). Or consider the opening sentence of the second volume: "The democratic social state of the Americans has naturally suggested certain laws and certain political mores" (DA: 483). But if laws and mores are both the effects of a common cause, one can hardly claim that mores are fundamental. One may still claim, perhaps, that they are more important than laws. That claim, however, is hard to reconcile with passages in which laws are said to shape the mores. Such is the case with the legal institution of slavery, which "explains the mores and the social state of the South" (DA: 35). By giving priority to the social state over the laws, this passage also goes against the two passages cited at the beginning of this paragraph. Another assertion of this priority comes in the discussion of inheritance laws: "I am astonished that ancient and modern writers have not ascribed greater influence over human affairs to the laws governing inheritance. Such laws belong, course, to the civil order, but they should be placed first among political institutions because of their incredible influence on a people's social state" (DA: 53–4).

In these passages, then, we have seen Tocqueville asserting the priority of mores over laws (DA: 352), the priority of the social state over laws and mores (DA: 379), the priority of laws over mores (DA: 35) and the priority of laws over the social state (DA: 53–4). Although some of the passages assert a general priority and others simply the priority in special cases, the overall impression they leave is one of sheer muddle. However, we can dispel the confusion by a simple decoding principle, replacing two or more statements that stipulate causal chains working in different directions by a single statement about circular causality. In equilibrium, social conditions, legal institutions and mores support each other mutually, just as do needs, ideas and sentiments within the mores.

For another example of how apparently contradictory statements may be reconciled by the idea of circular causality, we may consider two of Tocqueville's comments on slavery. On the one hand, he asserts that the slave "finds his joy and pride in a servile imitation of his oppressors" (DA: 367). Slavery, in other words, causes servility. On the other hand, we find him comparing the two oppressed races in America in the following terms: "The Negro would like to blend in with the European, and he cannot. The Indian might to some degree succeed in such an enterprise, but he disdains to attempt it. The servility of the Negro delivers him into slavery and the pride of the Indian leads him to death" (DA: 369). Servility, in other words, causes slavery. Charitably interpreted, the two passages need not contradict each other. We can read them simply as saying that slavery generates mental attitudes in the slaves that tend to stabilize the institution.

A third apparent contradiction can be resolved in the same way. Tocqueville asserts both that "Americans almost always carry the habits of public life over into private life" (DA: 352) and that their "habits of private life carry over into public life" (DA: 245–6). In a social equilibrium, private and public life would tend to mutually support one another. This is not to say that the spillover effect is invariably stabilizing. Tocqueville writes that in the decades prior to the French Revolution "the nation carried these literary propensities over into the political arena" (AR: 147), adding that "what is merit in the writer may well be a vice in the statesman." Because the ban on concrete criticism of the government prevented writers from engaging directly with political matters, they turned to abstract theorizing that the government was willing to tolerate. Later, when they had the opportunity to go into politics, they retained this disastrous propensity to propose general schemes that took no account of facts on the ground.

To complete the picture I ought to add that Tocqueville in various places does suggest some tensions in American democracy that might cause its demise or radical transformation. Some of these are intrinsic to *American* democracy rather than to democracy *per se*, notably the fragmentation of the union and the risk of civil war over the issue of slavery (DA: 752). The rise of a mild and tutelary despotism, sketched in part 4 of volume 2 of DA, probably applies more to France than to democracies in general. There is also the possible emergence of an aristocracy of industrialists that may constitute a danger more specific to democracies. More generally, Tocqueville observes that what strikes participants and observers as stability may only be motion that is too slow to be perceptible (DA: 199–200).

I think it is fair to say, however, that these are minor dissonances in what is otherwise a portrait of a remarkably stable society. In the somewhat disorganized chapter on "Causes that tend to maintain the democratic republic in the United States" we even find an anticipation of Frederick Jackson Turner's "frontier hypothesis," sometimes called "the safety-valve hypothesis":

> I have it on good authority that in 1830 thirty-six members of Congress could trace their birth to the small state of Connecticut. ... Yet the state of Connecticut itself sends only five representatives to Congress. The other thirty-one represent the new states of the West. If those thirty-one people had stayed in Connecticut, they would very likely have remained small farmers instead of becoming wealthy landowners, would have lived in obscurity without any possibility of a political career, and would have become not useful legislators but dangerous citizens. (DA: 325)

By contrast, Tocqueville asserts that French society from the Revolution up to this own time was in constant disequilibrium. In the notes for the second volume of AR we read the following: "I have already heard it said in my lifetime on four occasions that this new society made by the Revolution has now finally found its natural and permanent form (*son assiette naturelle et permanente*). Four times events afterwards proved that people were wrong" (ER: 166). Taking into account regime transitions that occurred before his lifetime, he counts six such occasions:

> The Constitutional Monarchy had succeeded the Ancien Régime; the Republic followed the Monarchy; the Empire the Republic; after the Empire the Restoration; then there had come the July Monarchy. After each of these successive changes it was said that the French Revolution, having finished what was presumptuously called its work, was finished. ... Under the Restoration, I, too, unfortunately hoped for that, and I continued to hope after the Restoration government had fallen. (R: 66)

This passage follows directly upon one in which he asserts that "whatever might be the fate of our posterity, it was our lot to spend a wretched life between alternate swings to license and to oppression" (DA: 65). This gloomy statement echoes a comment on Mexico "lurching from anarchy to military despotism and back again" (DA, 187). More generally,

> For the past quarter of a century, people have been astonished to see the new nations of South America repeatedly convulsed by revolution, and they keep waiting for those countries to return to what they call their natural state. But who can say that, for the Spaniards of South America is not today the most natural state? (DA: 259)

Tocqueville believed that in the United States change due to social mobility was endemic. "[W]ealth circulates there with incredible rapidity, and experience teaches that it is rare for two successive generations to garner its favors" (DA: 57). Or again, "everyone works in order to live, or has worked, or was born to people who worked" (DA: 642), In the intriguing passages I just cited he suggests that in other societies *violent* change may be endemic – that regime change may be, as it were, part of the regime itself. Although he thought stability might be achieved after his lifetime, recent writers have argued that the permanent effect of the French Revolution was to create a cyclical change between Bonapartism and Orleanism (Aron 1962: 292; Lévi-Strauss 1960: 94). But as Chou-en Lai is reported to have said when asked what he thought of the French Revolution, it may be "too early to tell."

Transition effects and equilibrium effects

Be this as it may, Tocqueville warns the reader against confusing the effects of a transition from state A to state B and the effects of state B itself. In most of the examples to be given below B is democracy, but in one it is absolutism. In most of the examples I shall cite, the effects of the transition are negative and those of the final state more positive. There are also, as we shall see, cases in which the transition is more fertile in achievements than the equilibrium state.

Tocqueville formulates the warning very explicitly towards the end of the work: "one must be careful not to confuse the fact of equality with the revolution that is responsible for introducing it into the social state and the laws. Therein lies the reason for nearly all the phenomena that we find surprising" (DA: 814). He proposed a fuller development of this distinction in a review from 1848 of a book *On Democracy in Switzerland*:

> M. Cherbuliez has called his book *On Democracy in Switzerland*, which might give the impression that the author thinks Switzerland can provide the basis for a book treating of the theory of democracy and that that country offers an opportunity to judge democratic institutions in themselves. That is the origin, in my view, of almost all the mistakes in the book. The title should have been *On the Democratic Revolution in Switzerland*. Switzerland has in fact for fifteen years been a country in the state of revolution. ... One can well study there the particular phenomena which go with a state of revolution, but one cannot take it as the basis for a description of democracy in its *permanent and peaceful established state*. (DAL: 637)

Let me mention some examples of the use Tocqueville makes of this distinction, beginning with the following: "If ambition becomes great while conditions are tending toward equality, it loses that character when equality has become a fact" (DA: 739). In a three-stage model of belief formation: "Woe unto those generations that abruptly introduce freedom of the press for the first time!" (DA: 213) By contrast, in an established democracy freedom of the press "is the only cure for most of the ills that equality can produce" (DA: 824). (In a different argument [DA: 600], he appeals to the net effect idea: "the ills [newspapers] cause is ... far less than the ill they heal.") Moreover, whereas democracy generates mutual indifference, the transition causes mutual hatred: "Democracy tends to make men unwilling to approach their fellows, but democratic revolutions encourage them to shun one another and perpetrate in the midst of equality hatreds originating in inequality" (DA: 589). Elsewhere he writes that "If equality of conditions encourages good morals, the social travail that makes conditions equal is very damaging to morality" (DA: 703). And whereas democracy produces conformism, the transition generates diversity: "The more closely I consider the effects of equality on the mind, the more I am persuaded that the intellectual anarchy we see all around us is not, as many people assume, the natural state of democratic peoples. In my view it should be looked upon rather as an accidental consequence of their youth, and it manifests itself only in this era of transition" (DA: 754).

Tocqueville argued that religion was endogenous to democracy. If man "has no faith, he must serve, and if he is free, he must believe" (DA: 503). In a brief aside on the state of affairs in Europe at his time, he asks himself: "Why does this picture not apply to us?" In his answer he first cites the existence of "lukewarm allies and ardent adversaries" of religion, and adds that there are "a small number of believers [who], having seen that the first use their own countrymen made of independence was to attack religion . . ., fear their contemporaries and recoil in horror from the liberty those contemporaries seek" (DA: 347–8). These defenders of religion, therefore, confuse the effects of democratization with the effects of democracy: to defend religion, they think that they must attack democracy.

In some analyses Tocqueville contrasts the effect of the transition from state A to state B with the equilibrium effects of A as well as with the effects of B. Typically, he claims, the transitional stage will be worse than either equilibrium state. In the Introduction to DA a major theme is how, in the transition to democracy, "we have abandoned what was good in our former state without acquiring what useful things our present state might have to offer" (DA: 11).

A more specific development of this idea occurs in a section on "The public spirit in the United States, in which he distinguishes between the "unreflective" patriotism of the ancien régime and the "more rational form of patriotism" which is "born of enlightenment" rather than of passion (DA: 269). In the transition from the one to the other, however, "there may come a time when ancient customs are transformed, mores decay, faiths are shaken, memories lose their prestige, but enlightenment has yet to complete its work. . . . Lacking both the instinctive patriotism of monarchy and the considered patriotism of the republic, [men] find themselves stuck somewhere between the two, surrounded by confusion and misery" (DA: 270).

We find another three-stage comparison in the chapter on "How democracy modifies the relations between servant and master":

> In aristocratic nations, domestic service is commonly an estate that does not debase the soul of those who submit to it, because they neither know nor imagine any other, and the extraordinary inequality they observe between themselves and the master strikes them as a necessary and inevitable consequence of some hidden law of Providence. Under democracy, there is nothing degrading about the estate of domestic service because it is freely chosen and temporarily adopted and because it is not stigmatized by public opinion and creates no permanent inequality between servant and master. During the transition from one social condition to another, however, there is almost always a moment of hesitation between the aristocratic notion of subjection and the democratic notion of obedience. . . . The master is malevolent and mild, the servant malevolent and intractable. (DA: 677)

In these passages, then, Tocqueville tells us that in the turbulence of transition we observe bad morals, intellectual anarchy, irreligion, swelling ambitions, mutual hostility, lack of patriotism, and insolence. In all respects, the end state of the transition is to be preferred. In the two last-cited cases the state prior to the transition is also to be preferred. In one exceptional case, however, the transition to democracy allows for greater achievements than what democracy itself allows for: "Although the French made remarkable progress in the exact sciences at the exact moment they were finishing off what as left of feudal society, that sudden burst of creativity must be attributed not to democracy but to the unprecedented revolution that attended its growth" (DA: 524).

In the chapter on "The Literary Aspects of Democratic Centuries," he turns the master-servant argument on its head, arguing that in the arts the transition from aristocracy to democracy period yielded greater achievements than either of the two equilibrium states. In aristocracies, "style will seem almost as important as substance" and "writers will devote more effort to perfecting their works than to producing them" (DA: 540). In democracies, "Form will usually be neglected and occasionally scorned" and "authors will seek to astonish rather than please" (DA: 542–3). Yet in the transition from one state to the other "there is almost always a moment when the literary genius of democracy encounters that of aristocracy and the two seem to want to reign in harmony over the human spirit. Such periods are fleeting but very brilliant. They are fertile without exuberance and dynamic without confusion. French literature was like that in the eighteenth century" (DA: 543).

Great art can also be produced in the transition to absolutism:

> Almost all of the great works of the human mind were produced during centuries of liberty. It does not seem true that the spirit of literature and of the arts is recharged or that they attain high perfection when liberty is destroyed. Looking closely at what happens, we will see that certain absolute governments inherited certain forms, certain intellectual practices, and the liberty of imagination which free habits and free institutions had created before them. The despots then contributed the sole benefit of absolutism: a degree of tranquility was added to the continued usage of those intellectual treasures acquired from the previous government they had destroyed. It might, therefore, seem that certain absolute governments were spiritually fruitful ones. But this is a false semblance which quickly pales with the passing of time: soon the true face and the true tendency of these absolute governments appears. (ER: 168–9)

Short-term effects and long-term effects

A constant theme of *Democracy in America* is that the advantages of democracy emerge only in the long run, whereas at any given point in time its performance is inferior to aristocratic or monarchical governments. Later, Joseph Schumpeter (1961: 83) made a similar distinction, in the context of comparing capitalist and communist regimes: "A system – any system, economic or other – that at every given point of time fully utilizes its possibilities to the best advantage may yet in the long run be inferior to a system that does so at no given point of time, because the latter's failure to do so may be a condition for the level or speed of long-run performance." Much earlier, it had also been made by Leibniz (1875–90: Vol. 6, 237): "The infinite series of all things may be the best of all possible series, although what exists in the universe at each particular instant is not the best possible." Since the short-term and long-term effects of regimes belong to their equilibrium features, the distinction must not be confused with the previous one.

The most explicit statement of this idea is perhaps the following: "I believe that democratic government must in the long run increase the real strength of society. But at a given time and in a given place it cannot assemble as formidable force as an aristocratic country or an absolute monarchy" (DA: 256). An implication is that "In order for a democratic republic to survive easily in a European nation, all the other nations of Europe would have to establish democratic republics at the same time" (*ibid.*). Along similar lines Tocqueville asserts that "administrative centralization can gather all of a nation's available forces at a specific time or place, but it impedes the reproduction of those forces. It ensures the nation's victory on a day of battle but over the long run diminishes its might" (DA: 98–9). An implication is that "An aristocratic people that does not succeed in destroying a democratic nation in the first campaign of a conflict is always at great risk of being defeated by it" (DA: 776).

Along similar lines, Tocqueville justifies democratic government by its long-term effects on economic growth: "Democracy will often abandon its projects before harvesting their fruits, or it will embark on dangerous adventures. In the long run, however, it achieves more than despotism. It does each thing less well, but it does more things" (DA: 280).

Another application of the distinction concerns the level of public expenditures in democracies:

> Is the government of democracy economical? First we must know what we intend to compare it to. The question would be easy to answer if we wished to establish a parallel between a democratic republic and an absolute monarchy. We would find that public expenditures in the former are considerably higher than in the latter. But this is true of all free states, in contrast to states that are not free. There can be no doubt that despotism ruins men more by preventing them from producing than by depriving them of the fruits of production. It dries up the sources of riches but often respects acquired wealth. Liberty, by contrast, begets far more wealth than it destroys, and in nations familiar with it, the people's resources always increase faster than taxes. (DA: 238–9)

In these passages, Tocqueville compares short-term and long-term effects from the objective standpoint of an outside observer. We may also ask, however, how citizens and politicians assess and compare the two effects from their subjective point of view. If they are unaware of the long-term benefits, or tend to give them little weight in their decisions, the system that works best in the long run may never be established.

In particular, the long-term benefits of liberty are less clear and less motivating than the short-term costs. The following eloquent passage is relevant:

> Nor do I think that a genuine love of freedom is ever born by the sole prospect

of material rewards; indeed, that prospect is often hard to perceive. In the long run freedom always brings to those who know how to retain it comfort and well-being, and often riches. Nevertheless, at some times freedom disturbs for a while the use of these goods, and at other times only despotism can ensure a brief enjoyment of them. In fact, those who prize freedom only for the material benefits it offers have never kept it long. ... Who asks of freedom anything else than itself is born to be a slave. (AR: 168–9)

It is worth to digress a moment on the last remark, which amounts to a claim that the benefits of freedom are *essentially by-products* of the love of freedom for its own sake (Elster 1983: Ch. 2), To exhort people to seek freedom because it leads to prosperity would be self-defeating. For the same reason, it would be self-defeating to publicly recommend the democratic form of government by the argument that, although inefficient as a decision-making system, it generates a valuable spillover to economic life. Nor would it be coherent to encourage jurors to work hard on reaching a correct judgment by the argument that "I do not know if juries are useful to civil litigants, but I do know that they are very useful to the people who judge them" (DA: 316). A similar idea applies to religion: although "Christianity tells us that we must prefer others to ourselves to gain entry to heaven," it also tells us "that we must do good unto our fellow men for love of God" (DA: 614). Love of freedom and love of God have in common that the benefits they produce – prosperity or salvation – are essentially by-products.

In these cases, the point of view of the observer and that of the agent *necessarily* diverge. The causal structure, therefore, is not analogous to other trade-offs between short-term costs and long-term benefits. An observer and an economic agent may both agree that it makes instrumental sense for the agent to consume less today in order to invest and consume more tomorrow. A person may, to be sure, prefer an ascetic life style for its own sake and receive the benefits from saving and investing as a windfall, but that preference is not a *condition* for profit-making. By contrast, the non-instrumental love of freedom or of God *is* a condition for its instrumental value.

Suppose, however, that a political leader, having read DA and the AR, wanted to create political freedom "behind the back" of the subjects for the sake of these instrumental benefits. Tocqueville doubts that the attempt would be successful. "A very civilized society finds it tolerates only with difficulty experiments with local independence. It rebels at the sight of numerous errors and despairs of success before the final result of the experiment is achieved" (DA: 67). As recent French history also suggests, projects of centrally imposed decentralization never go very far. As has been said, "Liberty cannot be granted; it must be taken." In Tocqueville's words, "local independence is beyond the reach of human effort. It is seldom created but in a sense springs up of its own accord" (DA: 68).

Partial effects and net effects

The general pattern of this argument is the following. Tocqueville first observes an effect of democracy that, if taken in isolation, would count against adopting that mode of government. He then goes on to observe that democracy also tends to have other effects that offset or neutralize the danger inherent in the first. When opponents of democracy focus on the partial, negative effects, Tocqueville hopes to persuade them by presenting the full set of consequences and arguing that the net effect is in fact positive. Strictly speaking, the previous distinction between long-term and short-term effects is a special case of this one. Yet because of the crucial importance of the temporal dimension – both objective and subjective – in Tocqueville's work, it seemed appropriate to single it out as a separate category.

The argument has two subvarieties. In the first, the positive effect outweighs the negative one, but does not make it disappear. In the second, the positive effect provides an antidote to the negative one, so that its harmful consequences are no longer felt. A trivial but amusing example of the first is provided by Tocqueville's observation that "Because preventive measures are not taken in the United States, fires are more common than in Europe, but generally they are extinguished more quickly because neighbors are always quick to respond in case of danger" (DA: 853). A more substantial example arises in a comparison of municipal life in France and the United States:

> I see most French *communes*, mired, despite their impeccable bookkeeping, in profound ignorance as to their true interests and in a state of apathy so invincible that society seems to vegetate rather than thrive. Meanwhile, in the same American towns whose budgets are so unmethodical and so utterly lacking in uniformity, I find an enlightened, active, enterprising population; there I contemplate a society that is always at work. .. I wonder, therefore, if it might not be possible to ascribe the prosperity of the American town and the disorderly state of its finances to the same cause, and, likewise conversely, the distress of the French *commune* and the perfection of its budget. In any case, I am suspicious of a good that I find mingled with so many ills and find it easy to console myself for an ill that is compensated by so many goods. (DA: 104n)

In a very different kind of example, Tocqueville draws on the fact that the expected punishment for a political crime is a function both of the severity of punishment if convicted and of the probability of conviction: "One should be *careful not to be misled* by the apparent mildness of American legislation regarding political judgments. ... Although political judges in the United States cannot pronounce sentences as severe as those pronounced by political judges in Europe, there is ... a smaller chance that they will render an acquittal" (DA: 124; my italics). By contrast, "in despotic states ... the sovereign can instantly punish any faults he perceives, but he cannot presume to perceive all he faults that he ought to punish" (DA: 235).

The second subvariety is illustrated by *the desire-opportunity pattern*, a paradigm being the observation that "even as the law allows the American people to do anything and everything, there are some things that religion prevents them from imagining or forbids them to attempt" (DA: 338). A more complex example can be taken from Tocqueville's analysis of political associations in the United States. The argument goes as follows. As Tocqueville often remarks, democracies tend to produce conformism and tyranny of the majority. Fortunately, political associations – also an endogenous product of democracies – provide "a necessary guarantee against the tyranny of the majority" (DA: 218). However, such associations can also be dangerously destabilizing: "Most Europeans still look upon association as a weapon of war, to be organized in haste and immediately tried on some field of battle" (DA: 220). In the United States, however, the danger is contained, as the last step in this "triple negation," by the democratic practice of universal suffrage:

> [O]f all the causes that help moderate the violence of political associations in the United States, the most powerful, perhaps, is universal suffrage. In countries where universal suffrage is allowed, the majority is never in doubt, because no party can reasonably portray itself as the representative of those who did not vote. ... In Europe, there is virtually no association that does not claim to represent, or believe that it does represent, the will of the majority. This claim or belief adds prodigiously to the association's strength and serves marvelously to justify its actions, for what is more excusable than violence in the cause of righteousness oppressed? Thus in the immense complexity of human laws it is sometimes the case that extreme freedom corrects the abuses of freedom and extreme democracy guards against the dangers of democracy. (DA: 221–2)

Marginal effects and global effects

The fourth fallacy Tocqueville denounces is closely related to the fallacy of composition: what may be true for *any* member of a set might be true for *all* the members simultaneously (Elster 1978: Ch. 4). Although I have detected only one instance of this particular denunciation in DA, it is extremely interesting. It arises with respect to the democratic habit of people marrying for love rather than as a by-product of property consolidations. Tocqueville begins by noting that

> Our fathers had a peculiar opinion of marriage. Having observed that what few marriages of inclination were made in their time almost always turned out badly, they resolutely concluded that it was very dangerous to consult one's own heart in such matters. Chance struck them as more clairvoyant than choice. (DA: 700)

He then proceeds to give three arguments against this inference. The first relies on the conjunction of capacities and opportunities, while the second and the third take the form of denouncing a fallacy of composition.

Tocqueville first observes that in this case as in many others, the ills of democracy can be cured by more democracy. If women in democracies were uneducated, love marriages would be disastrous – as they are in effect when they occur in aristocracies. Since, however, the education of women is itself an endogenous effect of democracy, this danger does not arise. Also, in democracies women have the "time to get to know and the capacity to judge" (DA: 701) their future husbands, whereas in aristocracies women are kept so cloistered that they have no occasion to form an opinion about them. Even if marrying for love is disastrous in societies that allow women neither the capacity nor the opportunity to judge we cannot infer that the same effect will be produced in democracies.

Second, Tocqueville shows that the inference rests on a further fallacy. Suppose that in an aristocratic society two young, well-educated and well-acquainted people marry for love. By going against the current they will tend to encounter the hostility of their friends and relatives, a situation that "soon breaks their courage and embitters their hearts" (*ibid.*). In a society in which this practice was general, this effect would not arise.

Third, Tocqueville points to another mechanism that explains why we cannot generalize from exceptional cases to the general case. For a man to marry for love in societies in which this practice is uncommon he must have "a certain violent and adventurous cast if mind, and people of this character, no matter what direction they take, rarely arrive at happiness or virtue" (*ibid.*). And one might add that a marriage of *two* people of this disposition is even less likely to be happy.

The last two arguments are quite remarkable. The first rests on a causal after-effect: the fact of going against the current generates a causal process that has unhappiness as the outcome. The second, by contrast, rests on a selection effect: only those individuals who are destined to become unhappy in any case are likely to go against the current in the first place. The distinction is of fundamental importance for the interpretation of social processes. Tocqueville, characteristically, does not make much of it. It is embedded in the flow of the discussion, and it is left to the reader to appreciate its explanatory potential.

No halfway houses

A frequent theme in DA is in fact that people often – but wrongly – think they can have the best of both worlds. Three examples follow:

> When it comes to freedom of the press … there really is no middle ground between servitude and license. In order to reap the priceless goods that derive from freedom of the press, one must learn to accept the inevitable evils that it breeds. To seek the former without the latter is to succumb to the sort of illusion that sick nations indulge when, tired of fighting and exhausted by their exertions, they seek ways to oblige hostile opinions and contrary principles to coexist within the same territory. (DA: 208–9)

Americans want the Union, but reduced to a shadow: they want it strong in certain cases and weak in all others. They pretend that in time of war it can gather all the nation's forces and all the country's resources in its hands, yet in time of peace that it can cease, as it were, to exist – as if this alternation of debility and vigor existed in nature. (DA: 454)

Democratic mores are so mild that even partisans of aristocracy find them attractive, and after savoring them for a time they are not tempted to revert to the chilly and respectful formalities of the aristocratic family. They would willingly preserve the domestic habits of democracy if only they could reject its social state and laws. But these things go together, and it is impossible to enjoy the one without enduring the other. (DA: 690)

These are all instances of *motivated fallacies* or wishful thinking. Tocqueville also denounces a number of other compromises or "halfway houses," without implying that anyone had actually thought them to be feasible. As he notes, "There are certain great social principles that a people either embraces in every aspect of its existence or roots out entirely" (DA: 686). A halfway house must be distinguished from a transitional state. The concept of transition refers to a temporal succession, that of a halfway house to location on a conceptual scale. Among the examples of halfway houses I have cited and the others I shall give, some are naturally seen as transitional stages between one stable situation and another. Others, such as the idea of having equality within the family but not in society, define situations that are not so much unstable as impossible.

The most important example is the impossibility of a limited extension of (male) suffrage: "Once a people begins to tamper with the property qualification, it is easy to see that sooner or later it will eliminate it entirely. Of the rules that govern societies, this is one of the most invariable" (DA: 64). The reason, arguably, is *envy of privilege*: "The ambition of those who remain below the qualification level is spurred in proportion to the number who stand above it" (*ibid.*). Nor is it possible to use fine-tuning in allowing some political associations while forbidding others: "When certain types of association are prohibited and others permitted, it is difficult to tell in advance to which category a particular association belongs. Being in doubt, people avoid associations in general" (DA: 606). Finally, "between the extreme inequality created by slavery and the complete equality to which independence naturally leads, there is no durable intermediate state" (DA: 418). I believe Tocqueville would have been surprised by the perpetuation into the present of the *de facto* inferiority of descendants of slaves.

The normative argument for democracy

As briefly noted earlier, Tocqueville also wanted to refute the objection to democracy that invokes the mediocrity of the citizens and accomplishments of that regime. Although he often asserted the inefficiency of democracy as a system of political decision-making, this is not the only relevant normative dimension. In a passage I have cited earlier, he praises democracy for promoting "the greater well-being of all"

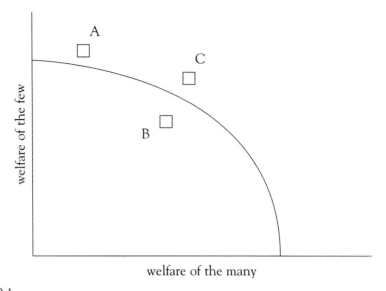

Figure 9.1

rather than "the singular prosperity of a few," a statement that is perfectly compatible with the claim that democracy is an inefficient system.

In Figure 9.1, the distribution of welfare at point A represents an aristocratic society and that of point B a democratic one. The curve represents the technically feasible combinations of welfare of the two groups. Any point that is strictly below the curve is inefficient, since one could in theory make both groups better off by moving to some point on the curve. (Economists refer to such a move as a Pareto-improvement.) While the efficient aristocratic society is very unfair, the inefficient democracy is superior on grounds of fairness. (Economists refer to this as the efficiency–equality trade-off.) The leaders of aristocracies are capable of making efficient decisions, but only to promote the welfare of their own caste. Democratic leaders are mediocre and inefficient, but they care about the common good rather than the interest of a few.

One may ask whether institutions exist that would sustain efficiency *and* fairness, as in point C of the diagram. If that point is, as assumed, feasible, what prevents one from realizing it? A Tocquevillian answer would be that C is technically feasible since there are no *objective* constraints that prevent the citizens of democratic societies from choosing excellent rather than mediocre politicians. (The standard economic illustration is that redistribution through taxes may cause deadweight losses by reducing the labor supply of the most heavily taxed. Although one might in theory overcome this problem by imposing lump-sum taxes rather than taxes that depend on earnings, that solution presupposes an unrealistic ability to assess the skills and labor–leisure trade-off of the citizens.) Yet the psychology of democracy makes it less likely that outstanding candidates will present themselves and, if they do, that the electorate will choose them. In aristocracies, no mechanism of this kind prevents the most competent from exercising power. "Democracy's resources are therefore more imperfect than those of aristocracy. ... But its goals are more utilitarian [*plus utile*]" (DA: 265).

The reason why democracies will tend to promote the general interest is simply that the majority of citizens "may be mistaken but cannot be in conflict with themselves" (DA: 265). Although democratic officials "may often betray their trust and commit grave errors, they will never *systematically* adopt a line hostile to the majority" (DA: 267; my italics). In other words, no group or class can expect a cumulative and sustained advantage from the workings of democracy in the way elites in aristocratic societies can. Also, because a democratic official generally "holds power for a shorter term" (DA: 266) than officials in other regimes, there is less damage he can do. Moreover, Tocqueville asserts that democracies are capable of *learning* from their mistakes.

When one points out such things [popular resistance to good legislation] to people in government, their only response is, "Let time do its work. When people begin to feel the ill, it will enlighten them and make them aware of their needs." This is often true: if democracy is more likely than a king or body of nobles to make a mistake, it is also more likely to correct that mistake once enlightenment arrives, because within democracy there are generally no interests contrary to that of the majority and hostile to reason (DA: 258).

This statement is somewhat obscure, as it seems to imply – contrary to what he says elsewhere – that non-democratic regimes have *more* severe cognitive deficiencies than democracy because of their "hostility to reason." The more important part of the argument is that because people in democracies have good values *and* are able to correct their false beliefs, they will in the long run also make good policy choices. The crucial condition is that they have enough *time* for the learning to take place: they must have "the faculty of committing errors that can be repaired" (DA: 258). The Americans have this enviable faculty because their geographical isolation ensures that they have no enemies who might exploit a momentary weakness (DA: 192–3). "Democracy can discover truth only through experience, and many nations will perish before they had an opportunity to learn from their mistakes" (DA: 258). Even when a regime is free of any tendency to make *systematic* mistakes, a single *large* mistake might, in a hostile environment, may be enough to bring it down.

France or the United States?

It has often been observed that when Tocqueville refers to "democracy," he sometimes means "France," sometimes "America," and sometimes "democracies in general." Although I do not claim to be able to sort out all the textual ambiguities, I believe one may assert, as a first approximation, that the more positive references to the democratic political regime pertain to America, whereas the more critical observations concern the prospects of democracy in France. While the dismal concluding part of the second volume of DA has nothing whatsoever to do with America, I believe it accurately reflects Tocqueville's apprehensions about France. It may have been intended, perhaps, as a self-defeating prophecy. Be this as it may, I believe it may be worthwhile to summarize his analysis, as another instance of his grasp of multifactorial social causality. There are no fewer than *ten distinct paths* by which equality might lead to despotism, many of them mediated by industry, which is itself a natural result of equality (DA: 644).

(1) Equality suggests the *idea* of a "single, uniform and powerful government" (DA: 796), because their delight "in simple and general ideas" inspired by equality easily causes individuals "to imagine a great nation whose citizens all conform to a single model and are directed by a single power" (DA: 789).

(2) Equality also inspires a *taste* "for such a government" (DA: 789), because the hatred "which animates democratic peoples against the most insignificant privileges powerfully encourages the gradual concentration of all political rights in the hands of the sole representative of the state" (DA: 795). The state, by contrast, is too powerful to cause envy.

(3) "On the one hand, the taste for well-being increases steadily, and on the other hand the state increasingly controls all sources of well-being" (DA: 807n). The statement refers to the tendency for private savings associations to be replaced by the state.

(4) At the same time, "the taste for well-being diverts them from participating in government" (*ibid.*), since "private life in democratic times is so active, so agitated, so filled with desires and labors that individuals have virtually no energy or leisure left for political life" (DA: 793). This is a kind of crowding-out or satiation effect.

(5) Industry "exposes men to great and sudden alternations of abundance and misery ... and [6] can also compromise the health or even the life of those who profit from or engage in it. Thus the industrial class needs to be regulated, supervised, and restrained more than other classes, and it thus is natural for the prerogatives of government to grow along with it" (DA: 809).

(7) "As a nation becomes more industrial, it feels a proportionately greater need for roads, canals, ports and other works of a semi-public nature. ... The obvious tendency for all sovereigns nowadays is to assume sole responsibility for undertakings of this kind, thereby constricting the independence of the populations they rule more and more each day" (DA: 811).

(8) The weakness of the individual citizen "causes him on occasion to feel the need of outside help which he cannot expect to receive from any of [his equals] because they are all powerless and cold-hearted. In this extreme, he naturally turns his attention to the one immense being that alone stands out amid the universal abasement" (DA: 794).

(9) Each citizen is opposed to government support to industry, except in his particular case: he wants the government to help him but not others. The result is that "the sphere of the central power expands in every direction, even though each [man] wishes to restrict it" (DA: 794n).

(10) In democratic societies, "all the citizens are constantly on the move and in a permanent state of transformation. Now, it is in the nature of every government to seek to expand its sphere continually. Hence in the long run it is unlikely that it will not succeed in doing so, since it acts with a fixed

thought and a constant will on men whose position, ideas, and desires vary from day to day" (*ibid.*).

Reading these gloomy analyses, one is tempted to say, "Come on! It can't be quite as bad as that." And indeed it can't. No state has acquired all these powers by non-violent means. Yet except for the first and (perhaps more arguably) the second, the ten arguments show a remarkable understanding of the *growth of the public sector in industrial societies*. The state does indeed provide public goods, undertake counter-cyclical measures, and regulate workplace conditions. Citizens easily turn to the state for assistance, and firms for subsidies or protection. Retreat into private life and the subsequent political apathy are common phenomena. Social and geographical mobility can make it harder to organize for collective action against the expansionist tendencies of the government. To be sure, Tocqueville does not describe the interaction among these tendencies, nor does he say much about the counter-tendencies that have prevented the prophecy from coming true. Yet who, in the space of twenty-five pages, has done any better?

Note

1 This chapter draws on my book-length study, *The First Social Scientist: A Study of Alexis de Tocqueville*, Cambridge University Press, 2009.

References

Aron, R. (1962) *Les étapes de la pensée sociologique*, Paris: Gallimard.
Elster, J. (1978) *Logic and Society*, Chichester: Wiley.
Elster, J. (1983) *Sour Grapes*, Cambridge: Cambridge University Press.
Leibniz, G. W. (1875–90) *Gesammelte Schriften*, Hildesheim: Olms.
Lévi-Strauss, C. (1960) *La pensée sauvage*, Paris: Plon.
Marx, K. (1867) *Das Kapital*, Hamburg.
Schumpeter, J. (1961) *Capitalism, Socialism and Democracy*, London: Allen & Unwin.
Tocqueville, A. de (AR) *The old regime and the revolution*, New York: Anchor Books, 1955.
—— (DA) *Democracy in America*, trans. A. Goldhammer, New York: Library of America, 2004.
—— (DAL) *Democracy in America*, trans. G. Lawrence, New York: Anchor Books, 1969. (This translation includes a book review by Tocqueville that is not part of the 2004 edition.)
—— (ER) *The European revolution and correspondence with Gobineau*. Gloucester, MA: Peter Smith, 1986.
—— (R) *Recollections: The French Revolution of 1848*, New Brunswick, NJ: Transaction Books 1990.

Part III

RETHINKING THE SUBJECT

10
EARLY GERMAN ROMANTICISM:THE CHALLENGE OF PHILOSOPHIZING

Jane Kneller

"Romanticism" currently is a term fraught with negative connotations for most philosophers in the anglophone world. To label a philosophical position "romantic" or "neo-romantic" is nearly always a peremptory dismissal of that view. The label carries the implicit message that such views are irrationalist, mystical, idealist, and/or utopian. It has become a code word for worries that the view so labeled lends itself to authoritarian absolutism, intolerance and anti-pluralist views of the state. At the same time it also suggests, somewhat inconsistently, that romanticism is overly individualistic, hyper-subjectivist in its analyses, and hence lacks commitment to objectivity in its claims. Even in more technical literary contexts, "romanticism" is currently used very broadly to label thinkers and artists from the period beginning as early as the 1780s all the way into the early twentieth century. Barzun's classic work is a good case in point, dating romanticism from as early as the 1770s in Germany with Goethe and Schiller's early works, and taking three major nineteenth-century reactions to romanticism (realism in art and materialism in philosophy) from "roughly 1850–1875" as well as impressionism/symbolism and naturalism (1875–1905, roughly) to be variations or "specializations" of romanticism (Barzun 1961: 99, 96–114).

The label as it is now used would be nearly unrecognizable to the close-knit but philosophically diverse group of German intellectuals who first coined it. The term "romanticism" was first used in Jena and Berlin during the 1790s by a small group of friends who wanted to distinguish their own innovative philosophical and poetic work from earlier, more rigidly defined literature. It is this original group of "romanti-sizers" and their philosophy that will be the subject of this essay. It will examine the core views of the founders of the philosophical aspect of that movement with the goal of showing that romanticism as *originally* conceived is well worth a second look. The central figures who shaped the philosophy of this group are Friedrich Schlegel, together with his close friends Friedrich von Hardenberg (known by his pen-name, Novalis) and Friedrich Schleiermacher. Their individual influence in German intellectual history was immense, with Schlegel primarily being known for his literary criticism, Novalis for his poetry and Schleiermacher for his theology. Together their perspectives combined to give rise to an iconoclastic, creative philosophy that challenged and extended existing philosophy at the time. Their work is self-consciously unsystematic and unapologetically collaborative. They influenced each other in conversation, encouraged each other's work and constructed their views in such close discussion with each other that it is often impossible to determine which of them might rightfully lay claim to this or that innovation. Indeed, this was a hallmark of their work. It was profoundly collaborative, and the collaboration itself, which they labeled "symphilosophizing" was a defining feature of the philosophy of romanticism.

Because their work has so often been misunderstood and misrepresented by later generations, (and even by some of their own members in later stages of their lives), it is important to distinguish this philosophical movement, often called the "early romantic" period or *Frühromantik,* from the movements that immediately followed, both in Catholic circles in Heidelberg (Clemens Brentano, Bettina Brentano, Karoline von Günderode, Achim von Arnim and the Grimm brothers) and the "late romantics" (*Spätromantiker*) such as Joseph von Eichendorff, and E. T. A. Hoffmann in Berlin during the Napoleonic wars. These movements in Germany were less philosophical in orientation and certainly far more conservative and nationalist in their politics. The Heidelberg and later Romantics saw art as a vehicle for the preservation of traditions, especially of church and state institutions, and as an antidote to rationalistic tendencies rather than as a complement to rational thought. Art was of course also central to the early romantics' philosophy. For them, however, art was anything but a tool for conservative politics. Rather, it was seen as an all-encompassing human endeavor with the potential to liberate individuals and society, to make room for new forms of social interaction, and generally to make human rational effort more creative.

Unfortunately, the reactionary and anti-rationalist aspects of the late romantics have come to dominate current assessment of early German romanticism as well. The reception of the work of Novalis epitomizes and helps explain this tendency. His work has until recently been associated mostly with his poetry and the unfinished novel *Heinrich von Ofterdingen,* which, taken out of context of his philosophy, might be easily portrayed as anti-Enlightenment in tone. His brilliant use of nocturnal metaphor and imagery, the expressions of longing for transcendence, his use of the trope of an earlier golden age of spirituality together with the chaotic play of themes and character in his work certainly sound a new and very different chord from that of Lessing or even Schiller, Novalis' revered professor and friend. Essays like *Christianity or Europe* with its enthusiastic descriptions of a past era of Catholic medievalism appear to be expressions of naive religious traditionalism at best, and of cultish, proto-fascist nationalism at worst. This reading was facilitated by the first editors of Novalis' collected works, Ludwig Tieck and Friedrich Schlegel. Each had been close friends of Novalis and members of the early romantic circle, but in the years following Novalis' death in 1801, both turned more and more to traditional religion and a politics of reaction in the face of French imperialism. Schlegel and Tieck were at pains to present Novalis' work (and thereby their own earlier work as well) in a way that did not challenge the Christianity and nationalism of their later ideology (O'Brien 1995: Ch. 1). Not surprisingly then, Novalis' highly original philosophical studies, including his notes on Fichte, Kant and other philosophical work has been largely ignored by philosophers. Only recently, thanks largely to the work of Manfred Frank, has Novalis work resurfaced as an innovative philosophical effort (Frank 1989).

Re-examination of these texts, along with those of the early Friedrich Schlegel and Schleiermacher makes clear that the brief period of philosophical ferment and innovation known as the Frühromantik was deeply committed to rational dialogue and argumentation, strongly opposed to dogmatism, to one-sided approaches to philosophical issues, and to authoritarian interference in the process of philosophizing. For Novalis, and all the *early* German romantic thinkers, the goal was not to challenge reason, but to discover and successfully to respond to the challenges that dogmatism and fanaticism of all kinds pose to reason. In this regard, as in many others, they carried on the work of the Enlightenment, and of the philosophical giant who was their immediate predecessor, Immanuel Kant.

Novalis, Friedrich Schlegel and Friedrich Schleiermacher were themselves part of a broader network of artists and literary critics that included at various points Friedrich's brother August Schlegel, his wife Caroline (later married to Schelling), Ludwig Tieck, Friedrich Schelling, Wilhelm Wackenroder and Dorothea Mendelssohn Veit (later married to Fr Schlegel). Of the philosophical figures, only Schelling produced what could be called a philosophical system. For this reason it is Schelling who has traditionally been labeled *the* Romantic philosopher, and who has been canonized, along with Fichte and Hegel, as one of the three great system building idealists following Kant. However, as Ernst Behler reminds us, Schelling was "only loosely connected with the romantic circle and really belonged to the movement called "Idealism" (Behler 1993: 4). In the Anglo-american philosophical tradition, Schleiermacher's work has received some philosophical attention as the founder of modern hermeneutics, Friedrich Schlegel has received an occasional nod from philosophical aesthetics, and only very recently has Novalis' contribution to philosophy been recognized at all. Yet together, Novalis, Friedrich Schlegel and Friedrich Schleiermacher introduced an important new direction for Kantian and post-Kantian philosophy, and their philosophical insights constituted a new approach to doing philosophy that was fed and watered by their mutual friendship and respect for each other. Indeed, it is perhaps one of the few times in the history of philosophy when the free exchange of ideas became not only the occasion for great individual insights, but actually constituted a collective philosophical enterprise. The Frühromantik was above all deeply collaborative, and for this reason the philosophical works of these three central figures must be juxtaposed if we are to understand the movement itself. In what follows I sketch the outlines of the movement, beginning with a description of the political and intellectual soil that allowed it to take root.

Origins

In the *Gespräche über die Poesie*, one of Friedrich Schlegel's fictional interlocutors defends the grotesque in art on the grounds that art is always the product of the soil in which it grows. Great artists who must work in times of spiritual impoverishment or turmoil will produce great art, but one cannot expect beautiful art from them, if by "beauty" is understood the "quiet grandeur and noble simplicity" that Winkelmann used to describe as classical art. Applied to philosophy, Schlegel's point holds also for philosophical romanticism. The conditions in which it developed are essential to understanding its character, its greatness, and ultimately also the short-lived nature of its flourishing.

The early stirrings of this movement were set in motion in response to reactionary attacks on broadly Kantian and Enlightenment values. In 1788, a venerable old seminary in Tübingen in Württemberg, the Tübinger Stift, provided the perfect combination of intellectual stimulation and repressive conservatism from which the seeds of subsequent German literary and philosophical revolution would grow. The early motivations of German romanticism are perfectly symbolized by the early friendship of three seminarians there. All three were destined for stardom in German intellectual history, but at the time of their friendship, Friedrich Hölderlin and Georg Wilhelm Friedrich Hegel, joined by the fiifteen-year-old Friedrich Schelling in 1790, were rebelling against the petty tyranny of their masters. The rebellion took the form of a staunch defense of both Kantian philosophy and the French Revolution. The Stift, a Protestant institution, was founded in 1536 for young men in Württemberg intending to become teachers and/or ministers. In his intellectual biography of Hölderlin, David Constantine describes the situation at the Stift around 1790 as a regime dedicated to a philosophy of breaking the will and the pride of its students, and he comments that such views must have been especially unbearable to students simultaneously experiencing "the heady west winds of Liberty, Equality, and Fraternity blowing across from France" (Constantine 1988: 20). He continues:

> By 1793, Hölderlin's last year there, most of the students were said (by their principle, C.F. Schnurrer) to be *"von dem Freyheits-Schwindel angestekt* [infected by freedom-dizziness]" ... Really there can be no doubt that among the students the preponderance of opinion was enthusiastically revolutionary and pro-French; and consequently impatient of the regime in the *Stift*, which they understood, quite rightly, as being the repressive state in miniature ... the *Stiftler* [Seminarians] founded their political clubs, entered revolutionary slogans in one another's autograph books, erected Liberty Trees, and behaved disrespectfully during the Duke's visitations. He was, after all, the potentate from whom Schiller had fled after writing *Die Räuber,* and [who] had incarcerated the radical publicist Schubart for years in the Asperg .... (Constantine 1988: 20)

The eventual fruit of the close bonds of friendship formed at the Tübinger Stift among Hölderlin, Hegel and Schelling was a politico-philosophical fragment titled

"The Oldest System Programme of German Idealism." It is one of the most intriguing documents to stem from this period of German Philosophy. The manuscript, transcribed in 1795, is in Hegel's handwriting, but its authorship is disputed, and scholars have given persuasive arguments in favor of each of the three friends as sole authors of the text. Whatever its final authorship, it was certainly a collaborative effort at least in its earliest stages, and the message of the essay is clearly in the spirit of the young, "freedom infected" seminarians. Most important for our purposes, it represents the spirit of early German romanticism, and in Frederick Beiser's words, "Whoever the author was, the *Programme* clearly and succinctly presents some of the fundamental themes of the early romantic movement" (Beiser 1996: 3n).

The *System Programme* is a manifesto for a new society, aimed at describing an emancipated social order built upon the ideals of Enlightenment and the French revolution. Its interest lies, however, in the way in which it expands the ideals of liberty, equality and brotherhood to encompass a vision of an emancipated, artistic, anarchist vision of community that transcends the state. Referencing Kant and influenced by Fichte, this brief manifesto begins by claiming that a "complete system of all ideas" will be an all-encompassing moral metaphysics whose first principle "is the representation of myself as an absolute free being." It then raises the central question: "How must a world be constituted for a moral being?" The answer rests on a metaphysics of freedom that begins by embracing a new, non-mechanistic physics with "wings" and ends with a call for social arrangements freed from the mechanical model that defines the state.

Enlightenment political philosophers, including Kant, had often characterized the authoritarian state as a machine. Kant used the example of the hand mill (grinding out subjects) as a common and appropriate symbol of absolutism, and argued that a state ruled by constitutional law would be best symbolized as a living body (Kant 1986: 5:352). Of course, conservatives like Edmund Burke had also characterized the traditional authoritarian monarchy as an organism, but the *System Programme* goes well beyond both to argue that *any* state is mechanical and artificial and that the very idea of the state should be exposed as altogether a "miserable apparatus":

> We must therefore go beyond the state! For every state must treat free human beings as if they were cogs in a machine; but it should not do that; therefore it should *cease* to exist. (Beiser 1996: 4)

The vision of the end of the political state expressed here is by no means a supernatural or religious one. Rather, the *Programme* explicitly demands that all individuals replace superstition, religious authority and the *pretense* of reason with the natural authority of their own intellect. It then goes on to articulate an alternative vision for humanity that is at the heart of early romantic thought: the idea that truth and morality should be united in an artistic vision of beauty and that philosophy is as much an art as it is a science:

> ... the highest act of reason is an aesthetic act since [beauty] comprises all

ideas, and ... truth and goodness are fraternally united only in beauty. The philosopher must possess as much aesthetic power as the poet ... . (Beiser 1996: 4)

The poet and playwright Friedrich Schiller had famously claimed that aesthetic education was necessary to effectively lead people to morality, but again, the *Programme* document is more radical. It argues that philosophy itself must become aesthetic. In this spirit, the *System Programme* calls for a "mythology of *reason*" that will make philosophers comprehensible to everyone else, and raise everyone to the level of enlightened autonomy that is necessary for true equality. When this is achieved its authors say,

> Only then can we expect equal development of *all* powers, of each individual as well as all individuals. No longer will any power be repressed, and then will rule the universal freedom and equality of the spirits! (Beiser 1996: 4)

The *System Programme* does indeed yield headings under which we can subsume the central concerns of the early German romantics: the influence of Kant and the Enlightenment; the critique of mechanism and more broadly of "one-sided" approaches to philosophy and science; the centrality of beauty and artistic creativity; the elevation of poetry and "poeticizing" to the medium for producing the best social order, and the re-visioning of religion as a work of the aesthetic reflective spirit. A closer look at all of these topics and the key figures who theorized them will bring this fascinating period into a clearer light. To begin, however it is important to briefly describe the influence of a few of the philosophical giants whose work served as both soil and seed for early German romanticism.

Philosophical influences

Early German romanticism was deeply indebted to the post-Kantian attempt to defend Kant from conservative detractors, but it was also philosophically indebted to the past. Not only past German philosophy, especially Leibniz, but also Plato's works were of great importance to the early romantics. Socratic irony was Schlegel's initial model for romantic irony, and he and Schleiermacher undertook to translate Plato's works into German – a task that in the end Schleiermacher completed alone, and brilliantly. In what follows we will look briefly at some of the influences on their work that were reshaped and incorporated into the heart of their unique philosophical program.

Kant

That the *System Programme* begins with an oblique reference to Kant is no chance matter. The Revolutionary activism that shook France to the core was mirrored in the theoretical revolution in Germany by Kant's liberal new philosophy. Kant's Copernican revolution constrained knowledge to the conditions that make human experience possible, thereby denying that human knowledge can ever be "absolute," i.e., we can never observe objects as they are "in themselves." At the same time, Kant believed that this recognition of a limitation on human knowledge legitimized rational *belief* in the reality of freedom of human action and choice. Lacking proof of either the reality or irreality of our "absolute" freedom, Kant's ethics are justified by practical necessity: Human beings can do nothing *but* believe in their freedom of choice and in the possibility that their chosen actions will actually make a difference. To that end they must postulate certain "facts." First and foremost they must postulate their own freedom. For Kant, rational belief in human freedom took priority over all individual, religious or social conceptions of the good, and human freedom took the form of a rational self-determining will that made human agency possible *a priori*. The positing of the reality of freedom stood at the very core of his account of what it means to be a human actor in the world.

But this absolute practical freedom, not unlike the new political freedoms in France, came at a cost. Kant's revolution in philosophy depended on a strict bifurcation of human knowledge on the one hand and human agency on the other. We can act only on the condition that we believe in our own freedom, but we can never claim theoretical knowledge of that same freedom. In Kant's terms, human freedom as it is *absolutely*, or "in itself," is problematic – not an object of possible cognition. This led inevitably to charges of incoherence, famously captured by F. H. Jacobi's claim that "Without the thing in itself I cannot enter the Kantian system, and with it I cannot remain" and even, as we saw in the Tübinger Stift, to charges that Kantianism leads to skepticism and atheism. At the same time, Kant himself recognized that even if belief in our own freedom is justified on practical grounds alone, it is not sustainable without at least the occasional cooperation of nature. If all our efforts to transform ourselves and the world into what it ought to be always fail, then acting from duty is simply an act of hopeless desperation (Kant 1986: 5:114). Thus in the *Critique of Practical Reason*, Kant introduced two further postulates: God and immortality, which serve to rationalize our continued efforts to be moral and to bring about a moral world even in the face of perpetual failure. Like the notion of the "thing in itself," Kant's use of postulates of practical reason led to criticism. How could mere *postulation* of God provide the real hope that is required to persevere in the face of moral defeat? How could human beings believe in themselves if their only hope is to depend on another, superior being? Kant himself continued to worry about this, and he claimed that he wrote the *Critique of Judgment* to address the "great gulf" that his account created between nature and the world of experience on the one hand, and human freedom on the other (Kant 1986: 5:195).

On this issue, the early romantics differ from Kant more in degree than in substance. One could say that this Kantian problem became the guiding thread and core of the early romantic philosophical enterprise (Larmore 2006; Eldridge 2001). They too rejected claims to know metaphysical absolutes, and their work expresses a great sense of urgency about finding a solution to the nature/freedom bifurcation. Thus, even though they agree with Kant that knowledge of such an absolute unity was an unattainable ideal, and although they certainly agreed with him that reason by its very nature is driven to attempt to discover the unconditional, absolute truth about the world., nevertheless, the early German romantics were far more insistent about the absolute necessity *consciously to strive* for this ideal in every aspect of human endeavor. For this reason, too, the importance of artistic beauty, that is, beauty created purposively, became the cornerstone of their philosophical enterprise. For Kant, natural beauty is the expression of the human subject's feeling of harmony with the world around her (Kant 1986: 5:219–36). Moreover, Kant maintained, such feelings of harmony carry an intellectual interest for humanity because they "hint" that free, moral beings like ourselves have a place in nature (5:298–303). Given their acceptance of Kant's notion of a perpetual striving of reason for unity and completion, it is clear why the romantics viewed the attempt to *create* beauty in every aspect of human endeavor as a philosophical and existential imperative. Thus, even though Novalis complains of Kant's "one-sided scholasticism" in his *"Kant Studies"* he immediately adds: "Of course, ['Kant's entire way of philosophizing'] is a pinnacle (*Maximum*) of its kind – one of the most remarkable phenomena of the human spirit" (1983: Vol. 3, 392).

The great philosopher's insistence upon the centrality of human freedom combined with his on-going defense of the French revolution was a source of great inspiration and, one would have to say also, of hope, to the young and politically idealistic German intellectuals in the last decade of the eighteenth century. Their philosophy reflects Kant in its insistence on viewing freedom and nature as equally real and significant aspects of human experience, and like Kant they rejected the strategy of their idealist contemporaries, who insisted on uniting these realms by assuming the existence of a metaphysical absolute. Like Kant they adopted a merely regulative or "postulated" higher unity of body and spirit, and of nature and freedom, insisting that this unity was a limit concept only approachable by infinite approximation.

Fichte

As we saw, in the early 1790s defenses of Kantian philosophy became particularly urgent in the context of reactionary intellectual attacks on his views. The first and most influential early defense of Kantian philosophy took place at the University of Jena in the late 1780s and early 1790s where Karl Leonard Reinhold was given a chair in Kantian Philosophy. Reinhold's work attempted to reunite the bifurcated human agent and knower by arguing that human sensibility and understanding on the one hand and practical reason on the other, could both be derived from a single first principle of representation in consciousness (Reinhold 1791). Reinhold himself gave up on this derivational approach and returned to something like a regulative idea in Kant's sense (Frank 1995: 68ff.). In 1794, J. G. Fichte, who had been strongly influenced by Reinhold, replaced him at Jena, and proceeded to resurrect Reinhold's attempt to discover a first principle from which to derive and hence also to unite the divided notion of the self in Kant's philosophy. Fichte took the problems with a Cartesian derivation from first principles of consciousness in Reinhold's philosophy to be rooted in an understanding of consciousness as representation of an object. Fichte argued that a different sort of starting point was required, that is, any first principle in a theory of consciousness would have to make a very different claim about the nature of subjectivity. Thus he argued, the first principle of consciousness from which to derive and account for both the knowing *and* the acting self must tell us that the "I" brings *itself* into being – becomes, as it were, a fact – through its own positing of itself, which is an *act*: He called this act a *Tathandlung*, which translates into English as a "deed-act" (Horstmann 2000: 123ff) or as "fact-act" (Neuhouser 1990: 106ff.). Fichte at first argued for arriving at this fundamental principle via an act of abstractive reflection, and later conceived of it as a kind of creative rational discovery: an intellectual intuition. In either case what is intuited is the original principle that refers to the self as positing itself.

The early romantics rejected any approach based on first principles in favor of a more Kantian, regulative philosophical theory of human consciousness and of nature. But like the younger founders of the early romantic movement, Fichte was an early supporter of the French revolution and its ideals. His philosophy expressed a bold new vision of human subjectivity that was free and creative, and capable of dramatically changing its own world. That vision banished, with a vengeance, the Kantian specter of morally good but impotent will. Even more than Kant's, Fichte's theory served the early romantics as a model of intellectual courage and of philosophy's capacity to feed the flames of justice and emancipation that the French revolution had begun. No wonder then that Friedrich Schlegel, in the first volume of his journal, *Athenaeum*, famously named Fichte's *Doctrine of Scientific Knowledge (Wissenschaftslehre)*, along with the French Revolution and Goethe's *Wilhelm Meister* as "the greatest tendencies of the age" (Schlegel 1967: #216, 198).

The young romantics were as deeply critical of Fichte as they were of Kant, but the productive creativity that Fichte, more than Kant, granted human cognition was a powerful impetus for their own theories. They too affirmed the capacity of individuals for creative, imaginative freedom, Being artists themselves, they saw creative productivity as universally human, and the artist as differing from everyone else simply in the degree to which he or she exercised that capacity. Fichte's philosophy had armed them: Art would be the new weapon and artists the appropriate revolutionaries ushering in a new era of equality, freedom and human solidarity.

Novalis, Schlegel and Schleiermacher each in their own way took this very powerful Fichtean notion of a free imaginative act as springboard to their views. Perhaps most important of all, they retained and took to the very heart of their movement Fichte's invitational approach to *doing* philosophy. The activity of philosophizing as Fichte practiced it is captured in Novalis' famous definition of romanticism as a creative activity that both takes a subject matter to new and transcendent heights and at the same time reduces it to a common, everyday activity. In his *Fichte Studies*, Novalis says,

> Fichtean philosophy is a call to self-activity – I cannot thoroughly explain something to someone unless I refer him to himself, unless I bid him to perform the same action that clarified it for me. I can teach someone to

philosophize when I teach him to do it as *I* do it – when he does what I do, he is what I am, is there, where I am. (Novalis 2003: #567, 169)

For the romantics, Fichte's approach to philosophizing seemed to develop naturally into a social, interactive effort, or in Fichte's own words, "a continually progressing synthesis" (Fichte 1992: 109–10). Sounding very much like Fichte, Schlegel later defined romantic poetry as "progressive universal poetry [*Poesie*]" that is "in touch with philosophy and rhetoric." He transposes Fichte's term "hovering" (*Schweben*) (which Fichte used to refer to the oscillating of consciousness between the sense of its own limitation and its ability to transcend its limitation) to characterize the emerging art of romanticism: "[Romantic poetry] can also – more than any other form – hover at the midpoint between the portrayed and the portrayer, free of all real and ideal self-interest ..." and he also uses Fichte's language of progression to describe romantic poetry:

> Other kinds of poetry are finished and are now capable of being fully analyzed. The romantic kind of poetry is still in the state of becoming; that, in fact, is its real essence: that it should forever be becoming and never be perfected. (Schlegel 1967: #116, 31)

Novalis similarly adopts an account of philosophy as a progressive activity:

> Philosophizing must be a unique kind of thinking. What do I do when I philosophize? I reflect upon a ground. The ground of philosophizing is thus a striving after the thought of a ground. ... All philosophizing must therefore end in an absolute ground. Now if this were not given, if this concept contained an impossibility – then the drive to philosophize would be an unending activity – and without end because there would be an eternal urge for an absolute ground that can be satisfied only relatively – and that would therefore never cease. Unending free activity in us arises through the free renunciation of the absolute – the only possible absolute that can be given us and that we only find through our inability to attain and know an absolute. (Novalis 1983: Vol. 3, #566, 167–8)

What he rejects in Fichte's work is the claim that an absolute, metaphysical or even epistemological ground can be arrived at, or fully discovered. Hence philosophy, like Schlegel's romantic poetry, goes on forever and is never finally perfected. Any philosophy, like Fichte's, that claims to have found its foundation has really only ceased trying to *do* philosophy. In claiming to have found its ground it has stopped *striving* for it, but it is the striving which is the true essence of philosophy:

> Philosophy, the result of philosophizing, arises accordingly through *inter-ruption* of the drive toward knowledge of the ground – through standing still at the point where one is .... (Novalis 1983: Vol. 3, #566, 168)

Spinoza

One other very important influence on early German Romantic philosophy was Spinoza. His unified account of spirit and nature resolved the Kantian problem of a divided human nature, determined and mechanical on the one side, freely acting on the other. Throughout the height of the early romantic period, Novalis, Schlegel and Schleiermacher shared a positive, almost reverential assessment of Spinoza's work. In a famous letter (1796) to Schlegel, Novalis announced that together with his love for Sofie (von Kuhn) he had also fallen head over heels for philosophy: "Philosophy [*Filosofie*] is the soul of my life and the key to my innermost self" he enthused, adding that he owed his inspiration to Fichte. A few sentences later, however, he demonstrated that he was no blind follower. He tells his friend that the "Schöpfungsathem" – the breath of creation – that he finds in Spinoza (and Zinzendorf, the founder of the Moravian Brethren in Germany, the "Herrnhüter") is entirely missing in Fichte. Spinoza's philosophy, he says, possesses "the unending idea of love" and the method for realizing it in the world (Novalis 1983: Vol. 4, 186–8). Schlegel concurred. In a 1798 *Athenaeum*'s fragment he writes "Every philosophy of philosophy that excludes Spinoza must be spurious" (1967: *Athenaeum* fragment [AF] 274).

At the same time, it is important to recognize that Spinoza's naturalism was not seen as supplanting or even overtaking either Fichte or Kant in the romantics' newly developing philosophy. Novalis' famous description of Spinoza as a "God-intoxicated man" (Novalis 1983: Vol. 3, #562, 651) should be read in conjunction with his comment of the same period that "Spinozism is a surfeit of divinity [*Gottheit*]," a description which he contrasts with unbelief (*Unglauben*). The latter is a *direct* form of atheism, he suggests, and Spinoza's pantheism is an *indirect* atheism. The middle point is his aim (Novalis 1983: Vol. 3, #552, 649).

> Schlegel had made a very similar comment in the *Athenaeum* fragment *Ideen* of 1800:

> The piety of philosophers is theory, pure intuition of the divinity, calm and gay in silent solitude. Spinoza is the ideal of the species. The religious state of the poet is more passionate and more communicative . . . . (1967: *Ideen*, #137)

Schleiermacher too defended Spinoza, and this defense from a devout theologian and romantic was no doubt central to both Schlegel and Novalis in their assessment of Spinoza – and religion – at the turn of the century:

> Respectfully offer up with me a lock of hair to the manes of the holy rejected Spinoza! The high world spirit permeated him, the infinite was his beginning and end, the universe his only and eternal love; in holy innocence and deep humility he was reflected in the eternal world and saw how he too was its most lovable mirror; he was full of religion and full of holy spirit . . . . (Schleiermacher 1996: 24)

In short, Spinoza's philosophy, like Fichte's, was important to early romanticism, but not because the romantics completely embraced a Spinozist metaphysics. As we have seen, the early romantic definition of philosophy denied that any metaphysic could ever be established absolutely. Rather, they embraced Spinoza's philosophy for its unified world view. They were enchanted and moved by the "magic circle" of his *ethics* of awe and of beatitude. They admired Spinoza's ideal of contemplative living and its prescription for a purely philosophical approach to walking the "dusty path" of this world. Even so, they did not themselves follow that path, because, for these artistic souls, the color and even the dust of everyday living were the ultimate subject matter of a poeticized philosophy. They were concerned, in Schlegel's words, to philosophize in a way that was "more passionate and more communicative." We might say that they subscribed to Spinoza's vision without endorsing the other-worldly resignation that his contemplative love of God/Nature prescribed.

Schelling

Friedrich W. G. Schelling's work was also deeply indebted to Spinoza's naturalism and pantheism. At the same time Schelling's metaphysics was vitalist and organicist. The combination amounted to a metaphysical system that in effect answered the call of the *System Programme* for a non-mechanistic "physics with wings." There can be no doubt that an account of a universe whose conscious subjects and physical objects are seen as identical was very appealing to Novalis, Schleiermacher and Schlegel, or that Schelling was personally involved with the Jena circle. (He later married August Schlegel's wife, Caroline, after all.)

As already mentioned, Schelling is the "German idealist" philosopher typically identified as the romantic philosopher of the post-Kantian idealist trio that includes Fichte and Hegel. He was the only member of the Jena circle whose work could stand with Fichte's and Kant's in its architectonic scope and aims, and whose ideas decisively influenced Hegel. Schelling's early work is unquestionably an expression of many of the deepest concerns the early romantics raised about Kant and Fichte's philosophies. In the 1797 *Idea for a Philosophy of Nature* and also in the *System of Transcendental Idealism* (1800), nature is reinstated to a level of importance equal to subjectivity and freedom, and artistic creativity is elevated above other human activity. Aesthetics for Schelling is the branch of philosophy that represents the unity of the practical and theoretical, and explains the way in which freedom and nature are connected in human experience. During the last years of the 1700s Schelling was certainly influenced by and influential upon his early romantic friends. His theory of attraction and repulsion propose a dynamic and organic account of nature and subjectivity that makes room for freedom not merely as a postulate but, via artistic activity, as a real manifestation of nature. Even when Schelling moved away from art and towards religion as the key to unifying human freedom and nature, he still retained the *System Programme*'s call for a new mythology expressed by art. In this respect his "absolute idealism" is closer to the early romantics than is that of either Fichte or Hegel.

However, in crucial respects Schelling's work is far removed from Novalis, Schlegel and Schleiermacher's philosophical approach. It is thus fair to say, that Schelling was a peripheral figure in early German romanticism whose work was an influence upon, but not to be identified with the asystematic, even antisystematic work of Friedrich Schlegel, Novalis, and Schleiermacher. Millán-Zaibert correctly characterizes the differences between the German Idealists and the early German romantics in terms of Schlegel's own distinction between Kant and Fichte: it is the difference between a tracking dog (*Spürhund*) and a hunter (*Jäger*): "The idealists go after and believe they have hunted down the Absolute, whereas the early German romantics are convinced that we can be on the trail of the Absolute and get ever closer but never hope to capture it" (Millán-Zaibert 2007: 34).

The early romanticism of Novalis, Schlegel and Schleiermacher simply would not embrace the idealist certainty of Schelling's approach. Schelling's philosophy had to "start with the absolute" (Zöller 2000: 207) and he agreed with Spinoza (and for that matter, also with Fichte) that the "absolute" could be known or at least posited as an axiom – as a real existence. For the early romantics such an open embrace of metaphysical first principles was doomed; it was, in Novalis' words, "like the attempt to square the circle" (Novalis 1983: Vol. 3, #566, 168). Although long characterized as *the* romantic philosopher *par excellence*, Schelling must be seen as methodologically opposed, even in his romantic phase to the characteristic anti-foundationalism of early romantic philosophy. In spite of the substantial overlap with aspects of Schelling's idealism, the views of Novalis, Schlegel, and Schleiermacher, represented a third path in philosophy that was neither fully Kantian nor absolute Idealist.

Early romanticism's alternative path

I have expressed some ideas that point toward the center; I have greeted the dawn in my own way, from my standpoint. Let anyone who knows the way do likewise, in his own way, from his standpoint. (Friedrich Schlegel, *Ideen* [1800], #155)

If Hölderlin, Hegel and Schelling greeted the dawn of a new philosophy in the *System-Programme*, it was Friedrich Schlegel, Friedrich von Hardenberg and Friedrich Schleiermacher who jointly carried it forward, each in their own way, into the full light of day. The appearance of the *System Programme* document in 1795 coincided with Novalis' study of Fichte, and with Schlegel's turn away from classicism and his new use of the label "romantic" to designate a new and positive ideal (Millán-Zaibert 2007: 13; Eichner 1970: 50ff). For Schleiermacher, 1796 marked his entry into the sociable intellectual conversations of the romantic circle in Berlin, where he eventually forged a close friendship with Friedrich Schlegel. The latter's early college friendship with Hardenberg continued and grew. Schleiermacher and Hardenberg did not meet in person, but they were aware of and mutually admired each others' work. Their close friendship with Schlegel and their contributions to his and August's innovative new journal, the *Athenaeum*, insured the cross-pollination of ideas among the three that occasionally made it difficult to distinguish each others' contributions. Each pursued an alternative philosophy, and although each was occupied with his own personal and professional concerns, in the period between 1797 and March 1801, when Novalis died, they constructed their views "symphilosophically", with Friedrich Schlegel facilitating. The *Athenaeum* brought their work together, developing them in the process to the point where a core of overlapping views emerges. It is this *"Zentrum"* (center) to use Schlegel's terminology, that represents the heart of early German romantic philosophy. This section will thus trace the contours of that emergent philosophy as they appeared in core philosophical works of these three thinkers.

Novalis

> Human beings are not only destined for science – They must be *human* – They are destined for humanity. A tendency to the universal is indispensable to the genuine scholar. But one must never, like a phantast, seek something unconditioned – the offspring of fantasy – an ideal. One must simply proceed from determinant task to determinant task … revelation cannot be forced. (Novalis 1983: Vol. 3, 601)

Friedrich von Hardenberg, who adopted the pen name Novalis, was the poet of the three, celebrated to this day for his brilliant and original contributions to German literature. Yet as this passage indicates, he was no enemy of empirical scientific method. At the time of his literary collaborations with the early romantics, he was also a serious and talented student of the natural sciences as well as a skilled mining administrator. His philosophical writings were as much influenced by his commitment to the scientific as to the humanistic aspects of scholarship.

Novalis had begun writing poetry at an early age. His university studies began at Jena and included courses with the Kantian, K. L. Reinhold and with Friedrich Schiller, with whom Novalis had already developed a close personal acquaintance. These studies were broken off to go to law school in Leipzig where he met his lifelong friend Friedrich Schlegel. After eventually obtaining the law degree (progress was impeded by an ill-starred love affair) he entered into the Prussian civil service. In 1796 he was employed in the Directorate of the Saxonian saltworks and met the adolescent girl who was to become his fiancée, the famous "Sophie" whose early death and its effects on Hardenberg have prompted so many caricatures (O'Brien 1995: 27–71). It was in 1797 that Hardenberg enrolled in the Mining Academy in Freiburg and during this time he also undertook a serious study of mathematics, chemistry, physics, and geology.

When Friedrich moved to Jena in 1796 their friendship blossomed into one of the most fruitful artistic and philosophical collaborations in European intellectual history. By this time, too, Novalis had already met Fichte (for one evening, and in the company of Friedrich Hölderlin and Friedrich Niethammer) and determined to study Fichte's philosophy. The result of this effort became known as his "Fichte Studies," a set of over 400 manuscript pages that Manfred Frank has called "the most significant philosophical contribution of early romanticism" (Frank 1989: 248).

The Fichte Studies

As mentioned earlier, the Romantics rejected the view that a first principle as ground of all knowledge could be found. When he turned to Fichte's theory of self-knowledge, Novalis' primary target was Fichte's claim that knowledge of the self rests on a first principle that is not merely representational but is an originary "fact-act" of self-positing in which the mind at once creates and knows itself "absolutely" in a kind of intellectual intuition. Novalis argued that such claims are simply incoherent. He agreed with Kant that the pure activity of the "I" in cognition can only be known representationally (conceptually) and hence that the "I" can never be known as it is "in itself" through mere reflection upon it. Even the concept of not-being is useless, Novalis says: "It just grasps a handful of darkness" (Novalis 2003: 6). Or, as he later claims, the attempt to know self-activity is an act of abstraction, separating what is known from the agent that is "doing" the knowing:

> Abstraction means transposing oneself in the pure I – to separate what [in fact] is not separate ... the form of pure activity of the subject. If the subject reflects upon the pure I – then it has nothing – in that it has something for itself – if on the other hand it does not reflect upon the pure I – then it has nothing for itself, in that it has something. The "for itself" means for itself *only*, for its *particular subjectivity*. (Novalis 2003: #49, 36)

In other words, I can intuit or *feel* my own mental activity immediately, but the moment I *reflect* upon or try to *represent* this feeling, the activity itself is changed. Novalis approaches his subject in the terms he inherited, dating at least as far back as Frances Bacon, of the mind as a mirror of the world outside it. Self-knowledge on this model means that the mind turns on itself in an attempt to "reflect" itself as it would any other object. But Novalis, writing in the shadow of Kantian theories of the mind as *agent*, manipulates the metaphor in various ways. For instance, the "mirror of the mind" for Novalis becomes an activity, a mirroring performed by an agent, and acting mind. Thus he says that self-knowledge poses a dilemma: either the self captures itself as it is "for itself *only*," in which case it simply has a merely private feeling of itself and *represents* ("reflects") nothing or on the other hand, if self-knowing reflects or represents itself it becomes just another object "outside" itself and then the moment of pure *feeling* is lost (the self "has nothing for itself") and all that we grasp is the reflection of it. Trying to "grasp" that reflection yields only another reflection, etc. Immediate intuition cannot represent, and reflection only yields a regress of reflected objects.

Rather than give up the metaphor of reflection as Fichte did when he posited an original act of self-positing that was known immediately by the agent, Novalis insists that human knowing is by its very nature representational. No act of self-positing can give rise to self-knowledge. He addresses the regress problem by extending the reflection analogy: in physical reflection what is reflected is changed – a reflection inverts the object reflected. This, however, can be "corrected" by holding a mirror to the inverted mirror image of the original object. The second, re-inverted reflection of course is not identical with the original object, but nevertheless it does in an important respect set the original inversion "right" by giving us a reflected correction. Novalis uses this phenomenon to symbolize the process of coming to self-knowledge through self-representation. We can, through further reflection, create for ourselves an "ordo inversus" or "reflexive inversion." As Frank points out, this central metaphor of the inverted order serves as the key to Novalis' own account in the *Fichte Studies* (Frank 1989: 257ff). In effect, Novalis argues that self-knowledge is a regulative ideal, and the *process*, a "striving" towards further self-representation built on previous corrections of self-representation, captures a fundamental truth about the nature of human self-knowledge.

Novalis then stretches the metaphor to the breaking point, speaking of the reflective inversion itself as a creative act of *painting* a portrait of the self "in the mirror of reflection." In a long passage in the *Fichte Studies* that has come to be known as "the semiotic fragment," Novalis effectively breaks with the reflection model of self-consciousness in favor of a model involving the *construction* of self out of the attempt to represent self-feeling. Along with the sign and the signified, he introduces an actively signifying agent ("*das Bezeichnende*"). On this *three* place model, the representation (or "sign") itself is not passively mirrored, but is actively created by the "signifying agent":

> Question? How first to recognize this schema and then to be able to orient ourselves by it:
>
>> The first signifier without noticing it will have painted its own picture in the mirror of reflection, not forgetting to paint the feature that the picture is painted in the arrangement that [the first signifier] itself paints.

The "schema" referred to here is of immediate intuition (feeling) being recognized or "taken up" by the signifying agent in a "reflection" of (upon) the feeling. Although on the model Novalis inherited, the overall process of trying to know oneself sets up a regress of representations like the reflections in facing mirrors, Novalis incorporates an element of agency in the very process of reflection that resembles "painting" rather than "mirroring." That is, as reflecting *agents* we can *re-create* our immediate feeling of self in a self-representation that resembles self portraiture as much as it does self-mirroring. Then, because "the image is reality for the I that is conscious of itself" (Novalis 2003: #63, 40) this self-conscious re-presentation itself may be taken up and itself re-created or constituted in an unending series. The process of self-knowledge is thus an unending series, but it is not a *regress* of reflection. It is rather a progressive "raising to a higher power" of past experiences, a series of self-portrayals, each built upon previous senses of our self. The entire series captures the nature of what is unique to human consciousness, namely, its malleability and capacity for reforming itself.

This conception of the self is suggested but not fully worked out in Novalis' early studies of Fichte. It is therefore not entirely surprising that Novalis returns to a study of Kant immediately thereafter. It was Kant, after all, who first argued that the striving of reason for an unattainable absolute is the fundamental condition of human self-consciousness. And of course it was Kant who claimed that we can never *know* our "self" as it is "in itself." In his *Kant Studies*, Novalis' accepts this, on the one hand, and on the other goes beyond Kant's negative pronouncement to embrace this view of human self-knowledge as an unending striving or "grasping" after its own image, modeled on the striving self-corrections of artistic creativity.

Novalis early philosophical sketches on the nature of subjectivity frame the central issues and form the starting point of early romantic thought, so that it is with good reason that Manfred Frank can refer to them as the most significant philosophical contribution of this movement. Yet in another respect they must be seen as only the beginning of a much larger project that Novalis intended to carry out in collaboration with his romantic cohort. His part of that project took shape only shortly before his untimely death.

The Allgemeine Brouillon

The working out of his regulative and creative theory of subjectivity was transposed to the "outer" world of nature during his study of the sciences at the renowned Freiberg Mining Academy. Novalis' work in mathematics, earth sciences, chemistry and physics led him to the conviction that what was true for the self must also be true of the world at large: knowledge of it depended on a series of constructive representations, each a correction and elaboration of the last. In the Fall of 1798 he began a preliminary gathering of materials in the form of notes for a book that would describe a unified method for all arts and sciences and would itself embody the ideal practices of these endeavors to fill methodological gaps: "All good researchers – physicians, observers and thinkers, proceed like Copernicus – They turn the data and methods around, to see whether or not they fit better this way" (Novalis 2007: 92, #517). The *Allgemeine Brouillon* provides a glimpse of Novalis' own free-wheeling efforts to play with puzzle pieces gleaned from the arts and sciences.

"*Allgemeine Brouillon,*" the name attached to the unnamed "romantic encyclopedia" (see Wood, in Novalis 2007: xii) by his early twentieth-century editor means simply "General Notebook." and reveals this brilliant philosopher-poet brainstorming the basis for an "exponential" or "potentialized," higher order philosophizing: As Novalis conceived it, it would both bring scientific process to bear on the arts, and artistic process to the sciences. He called his method "encyclopedistics" and intended it to be no less than a theory of the nature of philosophical inquiry in general. In the *Fichte Studies* he had theorized a notion of subjectivity as an ever-critical ("inverting") reflection upon the nature of reflective activity itself. The task he set himself in the *Brouillon* was a natural extension of this process, aiming to find a way to "get outside the self" in order to unify the outer realm of nature with the inner realm of subjectivity. It was to be a book that would document the aesthetic dimension and artistry of scientific practice at the same time that it explored the way in which these subjective practices themselves reflected natural processes. In the *Brouillon* Novalis repeatedly employed what he elsewhere called the "magic wand of analogy" to explore connections between art, music, and poetry on the one hand, and physics, mathematics, chemistry and other sciences on the other.

Novalis famously and somewhat flamboyantly used terms like "magic" and "love" to describe key aspects of his philosophy of nature, but however startling these terms may be in philosophical context, it must be pointed out that for Novalis they meant no more nor less than the ability to use artistic practices like metaphor, analogy and symbolism to enliven and explore new aspects of nature in the service of an all-embracing concern for truth. Thus practices that traditionally were ignored in scientific method and appear "magical" in that sense, were to be reintroduced. Novalis' famous "magical idealism" claims that the human ability to contribute to nature insofar as the mind shapes phenomena could be consciously exploited to literally construct or create new ways of viewing nature: He proposes for instance, that self-knowledge may also be the model for knowing nature:

> It lets us divine Nature, or the external world, as a human being – It proves that we can and should only understand *everything* as we understand ourselves and our *loved ones*, as we understand us and *you*. (Novalis 2007: 151, #819)

In his studies of Kant, Novalis had called Kant a "one-sided scholastic" for not being able to imagine that science, morality and human creativity could be united in the activity of philosophizing:

> to philosophize is *to scientize* [*wissenschaften*], to think through thoughts, to cognize cognitions – to treat the *sciences* scientifically and *poetically*. Shouldn't [the] practical and [the] poetic be one – and the latter simply be a species of [the] absolutely practical? (Novalis1983: Vol. 3, 390)

Novalis believed Kant's transcendental idealism, and Reinhold's and Fichte's too, had failed to appreciate the scientific value of poeticizing objects. In theorizing the ways in which the data and methods could "be turned around" to find the best fit, they had failed to notice a crucial facet of human knowledge: its creative and imaginative, or in his poetical language, it has a "magical" side. David Wood quite correctly points out that what Novalis called "magical idealism" was an extension of transcendental idealism (in Novalis 2007: xxiii). It was, in other words, a sharper turn of the Copernican revolution.

The "magical" ability to see the world through analogical and other "artistic" lenses, enables us to take on the perspectives of an "other," be it human or not. Such perspectivism was rooted in a Spinozist ideal of "infinite love." As Wood explains in his introduction to the *Allgemeine Brouillon*:

> Love is another essential element of Novalis's philosophy of Magical Idealism. In the *Encyclopedia* [the *Allgemeine Brouillon*], love forms "the highest science" and is the "basis for the possibility of magic" (in Novalis 2007: xxv).

Novalis himself writes that

Love proceeds like philosophy – it is and will be- each and everything to everyone. Therefore love is the ego – the ideal of every endeavor. (Novalis 2007: 153, #835)

This is poetic, to be sure, but it is also philosophically significant: it lays the groundwork for the idea of an I–thou relationship to nature at the same time that it proposes a straightforward philosophical explanation for how that relationship works. Our understanding of the self leads us by analogy to see the "other" as both different and at the same time relevantly similar to ourselves:

> Selfhood is the foundation of all *knowledge* – as the foundation of permanence in change– as well as the principle of utmost *diversity*–(You.) (Instead of the non-ego–You).

In sum, Novalis' brief forays into philosophy were insightful and significant. His emphasis on the fundamentally open-ended and self-creative nature of human subjectivity opened the way for several new directions in philosophical thinking that were immediately put to use. As we just saw, Novalis himself initiated the romantic exploration of natural science, and in social science and literary and art criticism Schleiermacher and Friedrich Schlegel did the same. The romantic model of self-knowledge as a process of constructively "reversing" prior self-representations also opened the door to seeing knowledge of ourselves as determined not only by self-observation but also by seeing ourselves reflected in others' representations of us. Social interactions were seen as integral to knowledge of a "self," for the romantics, and so too were reflections of ourselves in art and in nature. Schleiermacher famously took up the challenge of understanding subjectivity in the context of social interaction, and Friedrich Schlegel dealt extensively with the contribution of art works in shaping human nature.

Schleiermacher

If Novalis was the philosopher of art and science, then Friedrich Schleiermacher might be called the ethicist and metaphysician of early German romanticism. Recent work has underscored this view, even though Schleiermacher is still best known primarily as one of the giants of Protestant Christian theology. In an essay on Schleiermacher's metaphysical commitments, Frank discusses his break with both Fichte and Schelling:

> Schleiermacher was strongly interested in ethical issues from a philosophical perspective. However, he noted the one-sided and foundationalist way in which Fichte resolved them. On the other hand, in Schelling's philosophy of nature he recognized a physicalistic antidote to this praxis-oriented trajectory that did not suit him either. (Frank 2005: 16)

He notes that Schleiermacher's unique philosophical contribution depends in part on his rejection of the possibility of absolute knowledge for human beings on grounds similar to Kant's "problematic but nevertheless clear formulations ... that the content of reality depends upon things in themselves" (Frank 2005: 32). He describes Schleiermacher (as well as Novalis) as a "realist" in this respect, and also as "anti-foundationalist." That is, his philosophy does not ground knowledge in a logical first principle, but rather situates the beginning of knowledge in the midst of experience: "This oscillation between speech and response points to a Kantian regulative Idea, rather than to a preestablished principle, since each understanding attained is revisable" (Frank 2005: 17). Although Frank is referring here to a work written after the dissolution of the Jena Circle, it is clear that in this regard even Schleiermacher's later work retains an important aspect of early romanticism.

Schleiermacher entered the philosophical scene in earnest only after much cajoling from Friedrich Schlegel and his circle of friends to write a book on his views on religion. Schleiermacher's reluctance to write gave way finally to his desire to defend a radical new vision of religion that epitomized the romantics' philosophical orientation. The result, one of the most renowned and permanently influential of early romantic works, was On Religion: Speeches to its Cultural Despisers, published in 1799. The work profoundly influenced Novalis, especially his essay on Europe ("Christenheit oder Europa") (Kneller 2009). Schleiermacher's "On Religion" is a creative, impassioned defense of religious experience that leaves completely open the question of what forms such experience can take. Schleiermacher's own heritage (his grandfather was a radical Herrnhüter [Moravian Brethren] and his father an army chaplain), his close ties to the Jewish intellectual community in Berlin, and his enthusiastic friendships within the Berlin circle of romantics (most of whom at the time were very critical of institutional religions) reinforced his emerging view that religion was a matter of individual feeling and longing for a sense of the infinite. Religion was not a matter of argument or actions but of feeling or "intuition," and hence not a discipline requiring priests, but an aesthetic experience in need of poet-philosophers. The latter serve not to dictate individual behavior but artistically to model their own experiences of connection to divine infinity, and thereby to mediate and translate that experience for others.

Even though his later theological positions appeared more orthodox, Schleiermacher never renounced this early work, whose theological departure from even the liberal views of the Enlightenment was profound. Schleiermacher agreed with Kant's hard-hitting attack on existing institutions and clerics, but his criticism also aimed at what he felt was the lifeless abstraction of the Kantian position, and the failure to recognize that human beings need more than religious *ideas*. Religion arises from a ubiquitous human need and tendency to *see* and *feel* these ideas embodied in their everyday lives and in nature. His theology has often, and misleadingly, been summed up in terms of his view that a feeling of dependence accompanies every religious experience. However, like his conception of the deity, this notion of dependence is extremely elastic: the experience at issue is subject to the perspectival interpretations of the individuals who have these experiences.

Schleiermacher begins his "Speeches" by arguing that human nature is a function of the opposition of two basic human drives – "insatiable sensuality" and restless intellectual enthusiasm for ideas. These two are dangerous only when they take extreme form in people, either on the side of abstraction or its opposite, sensuality. There are special people, however, in every age, who themselves have mediated and combined these natural urges "in a more fruitful manner." These are "equip[ed] with wondrous gifts ... and employe[d] as translators and as mediators of what would otherwise remain eternally separated" (1996: 6). Only those who through self-consciously practiced discipline combine the sensual and the abstract human urges can bring the two human types closer together and thereby perfect humanity:

> They show the inactive, merely speculative idealist ... that this thing is active, which he merely imagined ... and reconcile him with the earth and with his place in it. Merely earthly and sensual people, however, require such mediators even more, who teach them to comprehend that higher elemental force of humanity. (Schleiermacher 1996: 7)

Lest there be any question that these "prophets" are the "cultured despisers" being addressed, namely Schleiermacher's artistic friends, he describes them as follows:

> ... after every flight of their spirit to the infinite they must set down in pictures or words the impression it made on them as an object so as to enjoy it themselves afresh, transformed into another form on a finite scale. They must also instinctively, and, as it were, enrapturedly – for they would do it even if no one were there – represent for others what they have encountered as poets and seers, as orator or as artists. Such people are true priests of the most High. (7)

Freely building on Novalis' definition of romanticism Schleiermacher speaks here of the artist/philosopher's ability to "transform the common life into something higher" (7).

In addition to seeing artists as social mediators between very different social and individual types, Schleiermacher argues for the strict necessity of keeping religion and state separate. He points to the damage done to civil society when religion is used as a tool of civil institutions and asks rhetorically: "To what dark barbarism of unholy times would that return us?" (16). By the same token, combining church and state denigrates the *church*: "It also shows the greatest contempt for religion to wish to transplant it into another realm and expect it to serve and work there" (16). In the second Speech, "On the essence of religion" he lays out his radical experiential account of religion. He grants that religion, along with metaphysics and morals, shares the same object, "namely, the universe and the relationship of humanity to it." But he is insistent that religion is nevertheless distinct from these two on the grounds that it is not about classification and analysis of the universe (metaphysics) nor about how to systematize human obligation and provide moral laws: "Religion's essence is neither thinking nor acting but intuition and feeling" (22):

Thus religion maintains its own sphere and its own character only by completely removing itself from the sphere and character of speculation as well as from that of praxis. Only when it places itself next to both of them is the common ground perfectly filled out and human nature completed from this dimension. Religion shows itself to you as the necessary and indispensable third next to those two, as their natural counterpart … Praxis is an art, speculation is a science, religion is the sensibility and taste for the infinite. Without religion, how can praxis rise above the common circle of adventurous and customary forms? How can speculation become anything better than a stiff and barren skeleton? (23–4)

It is worth noting with Peter Foley, in his interpretive essay on Schleiermacher's unfinished work on sociability (Foley 2006: 108), that this strict division of the realms of science, ethics and religion had immediate practical implications. It supported Schleiermacher's defense of Jewish civil rights in Germany. His "Letters on the Occasion of the Political-Theological Task and the Open Letter from Jewish Heads of Households" was published while he was writing *On Religion*, and reaches its conclusion based on this very separation between religious experience on the one hand and ethical and political laws on the other. Religion's role is at once more removed from public life and higher than it: it is defined by Schleiermacher as that which mediates, through feeling, humanity's relation to "infinite and living nature, whose symbol is multiplicity and individuality" (1996: 24). After describing the religious experience as "heartfelt reverence in the face of the eternal and the invisible," "true unaffected humility," "heartfelt love and affection for all individual human beings," and "heartfelt compassion toward all the pain and suffering," He concludes:

All these feelings are religion, and likewise all others in which the universe is one pole, and your own self is somehow the other pole between which consciousness hovers. (46)

Miracles, revelation, and other typically religious phenomena are all defined by Schleiermacher as forms of feeling ("intuiting") "the immediate relation of a phenomenon to the infinite or universal," and also "to the finite and to nature" (48–9). Religion in all its plurality of forms provides a method for filling in "the common ground" between the two sides of human nature, bringing sensibility together with reason, connecting nature and freedom.

Around the same time that he worked on the *Speeches*, Schleiermacher began an ambitious project to describe the rules and patterns of successful sociable discourse. His unfinished *Essay on a Theory of Sociable Behavior* (*Geselligkeit*) begins with the view that the ideal society requires sociability for its own sake: "… it can aim at nothing other than the free play of thoughts and feelings by means of which all members excite and animate one another" (Foley 2006: 159). Schleiermacher's plan was to give a complete theory of the laws that govern ideal social interactions in "particular actual societies" (1996: 159). Drawing on his experience in the Berlin romantic circle, he is struck by what he calls the practical "contradiction" of social behavior, namely that to further sociability for its own sake, one most both act independently and express one's individuality, but at the same time restrain oneself so as not to derail the conversation. One-sidedly adopting one or the other strategy of self-censorship or domination – or even switching back and forth between the two, is no solution, according to Schleiermacher. Rather a distinction must be recognized between a given subject matter, where restraint and "staying on topic" are required, as is what he calls "manner" or the style in which the discussion is conducted. In the case of manner, individuals should not worry about restraint:

> It really is essential to the perfection of a society that its members diverge from one another in their opinion on the subject, and in their manner of dealing with it in as manifold ways as possible. Only thus can the subject be exhausted and the character of the society entirely developed. Shyness in giving one's own approach free range, even if it should be inferior and faulty, is a stupidity that is highly damaging to society. (164–5)

Of course, he continues, it is not a virtue to be dull or uninformed, but the only way to correct these traits is through practice. Hence it is more important that individuals "strive to make evident what he or she is" and count on the others to "hold one's disagreeable qualities within bounds" (165). The general principle of such societies must be one of thoroughgoing social reciprocity: "each individual's effect should be on the activity of the rest, and the activity of each individual should be his or her influence on the others" (158). The aim of it can be "nothing other than the free play of thoughts and feelings by means of which all members excite and animate one another" and its goal is to "lift a person out of the viewpoint of his or her profession for a time" (168).

It is worth mentioning that at this point that Schleiermacher also inserts a side comment characteristic of the early German romantic circles whose practice so influenced the philosophy of the movement: These circles all included highly gifted intellectual women. He makes a (rather double-edged) comment that women are the better able to facilitate true sociability due to their own lack of a profession and hence of a constraining professional viewpoint:

> For the very reason that they have no status in common with men other than that of an educated person, women thus become the founders of the better society. (169)

Of course, women were stereotyped by their male peers in the romantic movement, but they were at least considered part of it. And although many of the men may have seen them as more decorative than substantial contributors, still the early romantic circles provided educated, confident and articulate women a venue for showcasing their talents. Regardless of how the men viewed them, these women were far more involved in the intellectual discourse of the romantic circles than they had been in earlier Enlightenment discussion groups. More generally, and to its credit, romanticism's deep theoretical commitment to sociable interaction as the ideal *form* of philosophy opened, at least in theory, a space for individuals who were otherwise excluded from academic discourse.

Schleiermacher's unfinished project on sociable conduct was born of the romantic conviction that sociability, like other human creative endeavors, is a progressive, constructive process that when consciously directed is capable of opening hitherto unimagined forms and avenues to human development. Insofar as sociable interaction is such a process it is certainly "practical." But like Novalis, Schleiermacher did not thereby consider it to be *in itself* an ethical enterprise. Like religion, it was seen as furthering or mediating the moral and intellectual sides of humanity; Schleiermacher is at pains to point out that his theory is descriptive – meant to show under what conditions free sociability comes about. The actual results of such practice, however, are not given prior to the outcome: the practice of constructing a higher sociability must rely centrally on a certain degree of contingency, namely the degree of wit, imagination and sensitivity of the participants themselves. The beauty of the process for Schleiermacher and other early romantics is that it begins at the place where people in fact are, for better or worse, and constructively perfects itself from there. It is an intentionally creative, regulative and essentially unending process aimed, like religion, at connecting the individual to the "other" in ways that elevate both.

Peter Foley makes a plausible case for the claim that Schleiermacher's unfinished project on sociability gave way to the *Speeches* on religion as he came to see that the natural desire to communicate our most profound experiences meant that sociability was a necessary component of the religious experience: "Once there is religion, it must necessarily also be social" Schleiermacher says in the fourth Speech (*On Religion*, 1996: 73), not to "make others like ourselves" but simply to "have witnesses for and participants in that which enters [our] senses and arouses [our] feelings." At the same time, Foley suggests, since for Schleiermacher the religious feeling is the most all-encompassing, he came to see religious sociability as the highest form of sociability (Foley 2006: 149ff.). Keeping in mind Schleiermacher's extremely open, pluralist-individualist view of religion we can begin to grasp how Schleiermacher's contribution to romantic philosophy is really a far-reaching humanist metaphysics that is not properly described as realist, idealist, or irrealist. The problem of bridging the gulf between human nature and human freedom, and in the individual between object and subject, is framed as a human problem whose answer hinges on the achievement and perfection of human sociability. That in turn hinges on the development of the capacity of individuals to express their most profound feelings and intuitions in a way that is communicable to others. The result will not embrace metaphysical proof or systems, but will be something more modest, namely, a "hint of a return to a shared center" (Schleiermacher 1996: 81).

Friedrich Schlegel

Novalis and Schleiermacher share the view that philosophizing is regulated by an ideal but does not start from first principles. They understand philosophizing as requiring both contemplation and intimate communication with others. Both are epistemological and metaphysical pluralists who condemn one-sided approaches to philosophizing, and both were able to develop these views to new philosophical heights in collaboration with their mutual close friend, Friedrich Schlegel, who brought them together philosophically. Schlegel shared Novalis' work and insights in discussions that he attended in Berlin with Schleiermacher. In Jena, in the famous romantic circle sessions in the home of Friedrich's brother and sister-in-law, August and Caroline, Novalis learned of Schleiermacher's views. He was especially deeply moved by Schleiermacher's speeches on religion. It was Friedrich Schlegel who urged them both to contribute their work to the *Athenaeum*, publishing it in such a format that the three authors' work was often indistinguishable. During the period of the Berlin and Jena romantic circles, Schlegel shared both Schleiermacher's and Novalis' anti-foundationalist and humanist views. Indeed, the views that each developed are so heavily dependent on inspiration gleaned from each others' work that their collaboration can fairly be called one of the very few truly "joint productions" of a philosophy in the western tradition.

At the same time, Schlegel's contribution, like those of his collaborators, added a unique dimension to their view. In Schlegel's case it was to bring to romantic philosophy a keen, scholarly appreciation of the literary arts. He had begun his career in literary criticism as a diehard neoclassicist. He read Kant's "Critique of Aesthetic Judgment" (the first half of the *Critique of Judgment*) in 1792, two years after it was published, and he initially gave it a negative assessment based on Kant's rejection of rules for judging beauty. Schlegel's immediate reaction was that artists might proceed without self-consciously following rules, but critics by definition require them. Kant was wrong to deny the latter point, he claimed. Four years later, upon reading it again, Schlegel still insisted that criticism requires taste, and that taste cannot be purely subjective, but as Eichner points out "Schlegel's own taste had by now become too catholic to be restrained by rules" (Eichner 1970: 36). In the course of broadening his own literary horizons, in other words, Schlegel came to see that taste required a method, but that no *system* of rules could encompass once and for all the multiplicity of possible styles and types of literature. Critical pronouncements must rest upon credentials, but even so, genuine disagreement among critics exists. The way to adjudicate these differences is not to disprove or prove one side or the other, but to understand what the individual critic sees in the work. It is incumbent upon the critic, in turn, to *characterize* what he or she sees in the work so as to communicate his or her impression of it to others. This requires not only a thorough familiarity with the work, returning to it many times and reading it in many ways, but also a profound, comparative grasp of the cultural and historical context of the work.

Schlegel's theory of criticism is empiricist in many ways, but two aspects of his approach distinguish it from Hume's "standard of taste" and other influential eighteenth-century empiricist accounts. First, Schlegel argues for the possibility of a genuinely *objective* account of taste that emerges from multiple experiences of a work and of cultural and historical scholarship of the work's milieu. The resulting interpretation will then express a kind of center point of the individual critic's many interpretative engagements with the work. Second, unlike Hume, Schlegel views the critic as an artist in his or her own right: *communicating* his or her interpretation requires a high degree of expressive skill and artistic prowess on the part of the critic. The critic's work is itself art:

> Poesie can be criticized only through poesie. A critique which itself is not a work of art, either in content as representation of the necessary impression in the process of creation, or through its beautiful form and in the liberal tone in the spirit of the old Roman satire, has no right of citizenship in the realm of art. (Schlegel 1967: *Lyceum* fragments [LF] #117, 162)

For Schlegel, this creativity was typified by the form of literary "fragments" which he published in two major venues – the *Lyceum of the Fine Arts* (1797) and his own *Athenaeum* (1798–1800). The fragment form was ideally suited for his own approach, which, compared to Schleiermacher's hortatory style, or Novalis' poeticism, tended towards wit and compactness and was thoroughly ironic. In his own famous description, a good fragment is a self-contained organic whole: "A fragment, like a miniature work of art, has to be entirely isolated from the surrounding world and complete in itself like a hedgehog" (Schlegel 1967: AF #206, 197). A perfect fragment is a world unto itself that can give rise to what Novalis, describing philosophy, called "unending free activity."

The image of a hedgehog is apt in another respect: Schlegel delighted in making his thoughts purposely difficult to approach and to "open." Not surprisingly then, the *Athenaeum* was criticized for being "incomprehensible" by some of its readers. Quite characteristically, Schlegel responded with good humor and high irony to this charge in the last volume of the journal. His essay "On Incomprehensibility" is itself a miniature masterpiece, explaining irony ("unironically," he claims) as follows:

> All of the highest truths of every kind are altogether trivial; and for this very reason nothing is more necessary than to express them ever anew, and if possible ever more paradoxically, so that it will not be forgotten that they are still there and that they can never really be entirely expressed. (Schulte-Sasse 1997: 122)

Beyond Schlegel's significant contributions to literary criticism (which, as Eichner points were a century ahead of their time, anticipating Wilde and Lemaître [Eichner 1970: 39]) it is crucial to recognize the broader significance of his theory for philosophy. His demands on the critic to start empirically, from the individual point of view of the critic him- or herself, and through repeated engagement and creative communication to "proceed toward a new kind of objectivity" (Eichner 1970: 39) were from the very start intended for application far beyond the literary realm. If the highest truths require paradoxical expression, and "Irony is the form of paradox" (Schlegel 1967: LF #48, 153), then it is easy to see why he also believed that "Philosophy is the real home of irony, which could be called logical beauty" (LF #42, 152). "Nothing is more rarely the subject of philosophizing than philosophy" is the first of the *Athenaeum* fragments, and #56 suggests it is time to change that:

> Since nowadays philosophy criticizes everything that comes before it, then a critique of philosophy would be nothing more than a proper payback [*Repressalie*]. (Schlegel 1967: 173)

Schlegel was determined to change that situation using the romantics new system-eschewing, collaborative method. Novalis and Schleiermacher each insisted on forcing philosophy on to new, more creative and social paths, and each agreed that philosophy itself need to be done poetically and aesthetically. But Schlegel was perhaps the most unrelenting of the romantics in calling on philosophy to critique itself.

We have seen the romantics' philosophical position taking shape in the works of Novalis and Schleiermacher. Thanks largely to Schlegel's brash efforts to critique systematic philosophy in a new and ironic way in the *Athenaeum*, he was able to distinguish himself and his romantic cohort from their system-building post-Kantian contemporaries. Given the fact that the romantics have for so long been dismissed as philosophers, it is worth emphasizing this difference one more time, and especially to emphasize the importance of seeing Schlegel's recourse to a "system of fragments" in the *Athenaeum* as philosophy, and not merely a matter of personal style. In Millán-Zaibert's words,

> The work of the early German Romantics was not work that awaited completion, even culmination, in Hegel or Schelling. The themes of incompleteness and incomprehension we find in their work are reflected in the literary forms they used to present it: the use of the fragment, for example, was not a result of a lack of resolution, a blameworthy incompleteness, in the sense of something that was meant to be finished and never was. Early German Romantic philosophy is incomplete not because the Romantics failed to finish their work but rather because they were convinced that a complete system could not be built. (Millán-Zaibert 2007: 46)

Subjecting philosophical systems to creative criticism meant that philosophy itself was open to interpretation and artistic representation (quite literally re-presentation). Like the interpretation of a work of art, this task had to begin *in media res -*" in the middle of things" ("Considered subjectively, philosophy, like epic poetry, always begins in the middle" [Schlegel 1967: AF #84, 178]). From there it continues to develop, incorporating the personal points of view of the individual philosopher's many engagements with it. Indeed, Novalis, Schleiermacher and Schlegel all returned more than once to grapple with Kant, Fichte, Spinoza and Plato among others, constructing their own philosophical views in the process.

Like Novalis, Schlegel challenged the system-building trends in the German philosophy of his time, and extolled the importance of a method that did not succumb to the temptation to complete philosophy. His famous claim that "It is just as fatal for a person to have a system as it is to have none" was not a mystification, but a succinct acknowledgment of the problems of philosophical hubris. Like Novalis he held out against "standing still at the place where one is" in philosophy, and with Schleiermacher he saw philosophy as a conversation in progress. Yet Schlegel raised the reflective stakes, or one might say, "exponentialized" both of these qualities: "To philosophize is to seek omniscience together" (Schlegel 1967: AF #344, 226), and, since he considered irony to be native to philosophy, this sociable omniscience-seeking must involve irony carried to a higher power: It must involve romantic irony or what he called "permanent parabasis" (Schlegel 1967: #668, 18:85), that is, permanent interruption. Novalis had defined completed philosophical systems as "interruptions" of the activity of philosophizing, but Schlegel, in a brilliant move, uses the notion of a state of constant "interruption" itself as the ideal artistic tool of philosophizing. In other words, if a philosopher proclaims to have spoken the last word and to have finished the system, the romantic ironic task is to interrupt the stopping of the process by calling it into question and opening the debate again. The *Athenaeum* was an attempt to do just this.

The aftermath of early romanticism

The period of permanent interruption, of "unending free activity" and "free sociability" came to an end, not coincidentally, when Novalis died. Shortly thereafter, Schlegel and Schleiermacher's relations become strained, no doubt due in part to Schlegel's failure to keep his part of the contract to translate Plato with Schleiermacher. Although Novalis had hoped that after his death his friends would continue work on his unfinished novel (*Heinrich von Ofterdingen*), none could bring themselves to do it. More important than the scattering of the romantic circle itself, then, was the breakdown of its collaborative spirit. The movement evaporated, leaving behind an unparalleled legacy of brilliant writings and bold theoretical and social experiments, but its evanescent nature should not detract from its creative impact, nor undermine its very real philosophical breakthroughs.

In *Das Andere der Vernunft*, Gernot and Hartmut Böhme charactize romanticism as an "intermezzo" in what they see as the unimaginative Enlightenment rationalism that dominates European philosophy to this day (Böhme and Böhme 1985: 231). Certainly the romantics, especially the early German romantics that have been the subject of this essay, have been sadly undervalued and, especially in twentieth-century anglophone philosophy, largely ignored. Although they were widely read and often quoted by nineteenth-century philosophers in Europe, Great Britain and America, they typically served philosophers largely as inspiration, rather than as a source of argument and counterargument. Still, they were not without philosophical influence in the nineteenth century in Germany. Frank traces Novalis' influence through Schelling's 1821 lectures to Feuerbach and Marx's notion of an inverted world (*verkehrte Welt*) (Frank: 1989: 257). Schleiermacher and Schlegel of course had great influence in the fields of theology and literary criticism, and Schleiermacher to this day is appreciated internationally for his very contemporary sounding criticism of institutionalized religion and for his positive views on the nature of individual religious experience. The early romantics' work was also influential for American transcendentalism, but the latter has itself been largely viewed by academic philosophy in the US as a peripheral philosophical contribution. And certainly Nietzsche's much vaunted perspectivism owed its roots and much of its development to the early romantics' very strong commitment to truth as a centering of many and diverse perspectives.

At the turn of the twentieth-century early German romanticism was given serious philosophical treatment in the work of Wilhelm Dilthey. Heidegger was clearly influenced by the early romantics and his own philosophy appears to many as a twentieth-century incarnation of romanticism. Members of the Frankfurt school Critical Theorists also helped moved romanticism back from the periphery of philosophy as Adorno and Horkheimer's "Dialectic of Enlightenment" challenged an emaciated instrumental view of Enlightenment reason. Their work set the stage for the re-emergence of the early German romantics' nuanced (and far more appreciative) views on the Enlightenment period in Europe. By the mid-twentieth century a student of theirs, Hans-Georg Gadamer, had reintroduced a generation of philosophers to the early romantics in *Truth and Method*, albeit in a critical and at times one-sided vein. One can see the influence of his interpretation finally in the American Analytic tradition in the later work of Richard Rorty, and more recently the work of Stanley Cavell has drawn on the early romantic insistence on the philosophical importance of the ordinary.

Even more recently, a generation of scholars who came of age during the political and cultural ferment of the 1960s have revived and rejuvenated the early romantics. Much of their work has been mentioned already in this essay, and a great deal more work is emerging as the landmark works of this revival ignite interest in younger scholars. Manfred Frank is certainly at the forefront in Germany at the present time, defending early German romanticism as a forerunner of post-structuralism and as an opposed to the excesses of post-Kantian idealism. In England, Andrew Bowie has done much to establish the enormous relevance of early romantic aesthetic theory for contemporary philosophy, arguing for their significance also as precursors of Critical Theory in the Frankfurt and New School traditions, In the United States, among recent scholars, Frederick Beiser's work has been probably the most far-reaching in scope, covering nearly every aspect of their work and defending their political philosophy against the old charge that they are reactionary. In short, there has been a renaissance of new scholarship in recent years that promises to bring the philosophy of this movement back into academic view.

Current debate

Philosophical controversies among the new interpreters of early German romanticism are at this point not about the value of their contribution. The main point
of contention currently has to do with the nature of the metaphysics of the early
romantics. Beiser contends that in spite of their differences, the early romantics
were united in attempting to "synthesize idealism and realism, and more specifically
the idealism of Fichte and the realism of Spinoza" (Beiser 2003: 131). Their hope,
he claims, was to "marry" the idealism and antinaturalism of Fichte with Spinoza's
realist naturalism in order to capture the "one half of the truth" that each possessed
(131). Beiser sees the romantic solution as hinging on their adoption of Schelling's
organicism with respect to nature, and an embrace of Spinoza's theory of attributes,
that is, the theory that the universe must be viewed under the attributes of both
thought and substance. Their new metaphysics would use the two-attribute view to
reunite idealism (the subjective) with realism (the objective) while redeeming purposiveness (teleology) for philosophy via organicism.

Frank and others, on the other hand, have distanced the early romanticism of
Schlegel, Novalis and Schleiermacher from that of Schelling, pointing to the repeated
insistence on the part of these thinkers on the open-ended nature of the philosophical
enterprise. To embrace a single philosophical system fully, once and for all, would be
anathema – it would violate the very heart of their meta-philosophical project, which
was, as each said in various ways, to characterize philosophical method as an open-
ended and multi-perspectival enterprise. Thus, however much they may have admired
and been inspired by Schelling's new "physics with wings" or Spinoza's "God (or
nature)-intoxicated" metaphysics, they would never have proclaimed to have spoken
the last word in philosophy, or to have discovered its one true system.

A brief comment on this debate might also serve as an appropriate place to end this
essay, and to end it on an appropriately open note: It is surely correct to emphasize
the early romantics abhorrence of one-sidedness in philosophy. No single criticism is
raised more often in the works of all three of the philosopher than is that of being
"one-sided." Often enough this charge is used by the romantics to condemn a failure
on the part of a theory or a theorist to see "the other side" of an issue. But just as
often the problem addressed is not that *the* alternative is being ignored, but that *all the
alternatives* are being ignored. The charge of "one-sidedness" as used by the romantics
is first and foremost a criticism that a *multiplicity* of other perspectives is not being
countenanced, each of which reflects in its own way, and "from its own standpoint"
an aspect of the truth. Thus Beiser is certainly correct to invoke Spinoza's theory
of attributes as a central inspiration for romantic metaphysics, but with one crucial
caveat. We should recall that for Spinoza the number of *actual* attributes was infinite.
That such infinity was incomprehensible to the human mind led Spinoza to assert
an aspect-dualism for human knowledge: thought and extension (matter). But the
romantics weren't so cautious and in this respect did not follow Spinoza. Inclusion of
incomprehensibility – or "systemlessness" – into philosophy was precisely their goal.
Their central insight, one might say, was that only through inclusion of what is at any

given point, or from any given viewpoint appears to be, "unsystematizable," can the possibility of philosophical progress be assured.

Early romanticism in Germany has been rightly valued as an innovative new approach to aesthetic theory. Yet, precisely because it takes art, expression and feeling so seriously, it is also far more than an aesthetic. The introduction of an objectivist perspectivism, the insistence on the essentially social and dialogical nature of philosophy, and an appreciation of the value of methodological irony in philosophy that critically interrupts it when it claims success – all of this is what gives Novalis', Schlegel's and Schleiermacher's philosophies a sweeping significance that transcends a mere theory of art. For these poets and friends, aesthetics was an all-encompassing philosophical activity. Each in their own way was aware of the gap between science and morality, and between nature and human freedom. Each saw the aesthetic as a means to bridge and even unify these aspects of human experience. But this was not a *reduction* to aesthetics, nor was it an elevation of the aesthetic over the practical/moral and theoretical/scientific. Rather it was seen as a method for mediating these two fundamental functions of reason in the service of a progressive, dynamic philosophy. Thus, far from attacking reason, early German romanticism addresses challenges to reason positively, with wit and irony, and with reason itself. The romantics produced a new way of philosophizing that was capable of building as many bridges and discovering as many eccentric paths as there are creative individual imaginations and intellects to pursue them in concert with each other. This accomplishment of early German romantic philosophy has yet to be fully appreciated, and the fulfillment of its promise remains a challenge to this day. It will require a re-evaluation of what it is for individuals to *do* philosophy *together* in the twenty-first century.

References

Barzun, J. (1961) *Classic, Romantic and Modern*, Garden City, NY: Doubleday & Co.

Behler, E. (1993) *German Romantic Literary Theory*, Cambridge: Cambridge University Press.

Beiser, F. (2003) *The Romantic Imperative*, Cambridge, MA: Harvard University Press.

—— (ed.) (1996) *The Early Political Writings of the German Romantics*, Cambridge: Cambridge University Press.

—— (2005) "Schleiermacher's Ethics," in Jacqueline Marina (ed.) *The Cambridge Companion to Schleiermacher*, Cambridge: Cambridge University Press.

Böhme, G., and H. Böhme (1985) *Das Andere der Vernunft: Zur Entwicklung von Rationalitätsstrukturen am Beispiel Kants*, Frankfurt am Main: Suhrkamp.

Constantine, D. (1988) *Hölderlin*, Oxford: Clarendon Press.

Crouter, R. (2005) *Friedrich Schleiermacher: Between Enlightenment and Romanticism*, Cambridge: Cambridge University Press.

Eichner, H (1970) *Friedrich Schlegel*, New York: Twayne.

Eldridge, R. (2001) *The Persistence of Romanticism: Essays in Philosophy and Literature*, Cambridge: Cambridge University Press.

Fichte, J. G. (1992) *Foundations of the Transcendental Philosophy*, edited, trans. Daniel Breazeale, Ithaca, NY: Cornell University Press.

Frank, M. (1989) *Einführung in die frühromantische Ästhetik: Vorlesungen*, Frankfurt am Main: Suhrkamp.

—— (2005) "Metaphysical Foundations: A Look at Schleiermacher's *Dialectic*," in Jacqueline Marina (ed.) *The Cambridge Companion to Schleiermacher*, Cambridge: Cambridge University Press.

—— (1995) "Philosophical Foundations of Early Romanticism," in Karl Ameriks and Dieter Sturma (eds) *The Modern Subject: Conceptions of the Self in Classical German Philosophy*, Albany, NY: SUNY Press.

Hardenberg, F. (2003) *Novalis: Fichte Studies*, edited by Jane Kneller, Cambridge: Cambridge University Press.

Foley, P. (2006) *Friedrich Schleiermacher's Essay on a Theory of Sociable Behavior (1799): A Contextual Interpretation*, Lewiston, NY: Edwin Mellen.

Horstmann, R.-P. (2000) "The Early Philosophy of Fichte and Schelling," in Karl Ameriks (ed.) *The Cambridge Companion to German Idealism*, Cambridge: Cambridge University Press.

Kant, Immanuel (1902–) *Gesammelte Schriften: Preußische Akademie der Wissenschaften Ausgabe*, Berlin: Walter de Gruyter & Co.

—— (1986) *Critique of Judgment*, trans. Werner Pluhar. Indianapolis, IN: Hackett.

Kneller, Jane (2009) "Novalis' View of Sociability in 'Christianity or Europe'," in *Das Neue Licht der Frühromantik*, edited by Bärbel Frischmann and Elizabeth Millán-Zaibert, Paderborn: Ferdinand Schöningh.

Larmore, C. (1996) *The Romantic Legacy*, New York: Columbia University Press.

Millán-Zaibert, E. (2007) *Friedrich Schlegel and the Emergence of Romantic Philosophy*, Albany, NY: SUNY Press.

Neuhouser, F. (1990) *Fichte's Theory of Subjectivity*, Cambridge: Cambridge University Press.

Novalis (1983) *Schriften*, edited by Richard Samuel, with Hans-Joachim Mähl and Gerhard Schulz, Stuttgart: W. Kohlhammer.

—— (2003) *Fichte Studies*, edited by Jane Kneller, Cambridge: Cambridge University Press.

—— (2007). *Notes for a Romantic Encyclopaedia: Das Allgemeine Brouillon*, edited, trans. David Wood, Albany, NY: SUNY Press.

O'Brien, W. (1995) *Novalis: Signs of Revolution*, Durham, SC: Duke University Press.

Reinhold, K. L. (1978) *Über das Fundament des philosophischen Wissens*, Hamburg: Meiner.

Schlegel, F. (1967) *Kritische Friedrich-Schlegel-Ausgabe*, vol. 2, edited by Ernst Behler, with Jean-Jacques Anstett and Hans Eichner, Munich: Schöningh.

Schleiermacher, F. (1996) *On Religion: Speeches to its Cultured Despisers*, edited by Richard Crouter, Cambridge: Cambridge University Press.

Schulte-Sasse, J. (ed.) (1997) *Theory as Practice: A Critical Anthology of Early German Romantic Writings*, Minneapolis, MN: University of Minnesota Press.

Zöller, G. (2000) "The Self-limitation of Idealist Thinking in Fichte, Schelling, and Schopenhauer," in Karl Ameriks (ed.) *The Cambridge Companion to German Idealism*, Cambridge: Cambridge University Press.

11

SCHOPENHAUER

David E. Wellbery

Although his niche in the *musée imaginaire* of canonical philosophers is assured, Arthur Schopenhauer (1788–1860) certainly doesn't owe his historical significance to the sponsorship of a vital tradition of philosophical work. Oblivion long ago engulfed his nineteenth-century acolytes (Philipp Mainländer, Eduard von Hartmann), and his most agile reader, Friedrich Nietzsche, found his own philosophical voice by emancipating himself from the thrall of Schopenhauerian pessimism. Scrutiny will also show that those philosophers of the twentieth century who drew inspiration from Schopenhauer's writing (Ludwig Wittgenstein, Arnold Gehlen, Max Horkheimer) could do so only while rejecting his central themes. Today Schopenhauer's thought, in contradistinction to the work of his master Kant and his antipode Hegel, no longer provides a conceptual frame for serious philosophical inquiry. The twin pillars of his systematic edifice (the skeptical reconstruction of Kant's epistemology and the doctrine of the metaphysical Will) are generally dismissed as erroneous or whimsical; the scholarship devoted to his work is, for the most part, antiquarian. One wonders wherein his importance lies.

A possible answer is that Schopenhauer presents us with the intriguing case of a philosopher whose work elicits conviction primarily through the force of aesthetic presentation. The achievement of his masterpiece *The World as Will and Representation* (1996 [1818], hereafter *WWR*) and its companion publications is to project a compelling, albeit dark and slanted, image of the totality of life. The single thought that Schopenhauer means his system to exfoliate – the thought that the world is Will and representation *throughout* – is most aptly interpreted as an encompassing metaphor. A variant of that metaphor opens book 2 of *WWR*: as long as we endeavor to grasp the essence of things along lines set down by the principle of sufficient reason (*Satz vom Grunde*), we resemble someone circling a castle, in vain seeking an entrance, and occasionally sketching – as if that could help! – the façade (*WWR* I, Par. 17). It is a telling fact that the core thought of a philosophical system could find perspicuous formulation in a single conceit. And it is equally telling that Franz Kafka consigned the protagonist of his novel *The Castle* (published 1926) to an existence within the space of meaning limned by this very figure. The conspicuous feature of Schopenhauer's legacy is that it has been most fecund not in academic philosophy (for which his contempt was boundless), but in a tradition of literary writing that includes, along with Kafka, other artists of staggering achievement such as Melville, Tolstoy, Hardy, Machado de Assis, Mann, Proust, Pessoa, Borges, Beckett and Cioran. As long as the worlds their works disclose remain compelling, Schopenhauer's philosophical vision will continue to exert its fascination.

An interpretation of Schopenhauer that accentuates the aesthetic purport of his thought finds support in his own understanding of philosophical activity. Schopenhauer did not endorse a conception of philosophy as deduction from a self-authorizing first principle in the fashion of Reinhold or Fichte, nor as the self-explication of the Notion in the manner of Hegel. Indeed, he judged any construal of philosophy as governed by the principle of sufficient reason to be misguided from the outset. Although certainly affine to science (in the capacious sense of *Wissenschaft*) by virtue of the fact that it takes shape within a conceptual medium, philosophy, properly understood, is not a science, but an art. The task of art is to communicate the content of an aesthetic intuition (*Anschauung*), something typically accomplished in such media as stone, pigment, word-conveyed imaginings, or musical tones. Just this, according to Schopenhauer, is what the philosopher ought to do with concepts. Schopenhauer's sense of his own originality has one of its roots here. He believed that subservience to and inappropriate application of the principle of sufficient reason had hobbled most of philosophy before him. Aristotle serves as the paradigm for this misunderstanding of philosophical activity, while Plato, together with Kant Schopenhauer's most revered precursor, provides the cherished counter-example. Apart from Plato, though, Schopenhauer could point to few "intuitionist" predecessors and it may very well be that Goethe was the source, with regard to this key theme, of Schopenhauer's most sustaining inspiration. Beyond matters of influence, however, the crucial interpretive point is that Schopenhauer saw the ultimate warrant of philosophical claims as deriving not from reasons proffered (rational argument), but from insights acquired in aesthetic intuition. Philosophy explains nothing. The significance of this quietism as regards philosophical inquiry emerges from Schopenhauer's systematic project, which this essay sets out to survey.

I

The first, and in many ways the most familiar component of Schopenhauer's philosophical system is the theory of knowledge. It is developed in Schopenhauer's dissertation, *On the Fourfold Root of the Principle of Sufficient Reason* (2003 [1813]), in the first book of the first volume of *WWR*, in chapters 1–22 of the second volume of *WWR* (1844) and in the appendix to *WWR* I entitled "Critique of the Kantian Philosophy." It should be said at the outset that Schopenhauer's originality in this domain resides in his larger view of cognition as serving the ends of animal survival, one might say: as an adaptive mechanism, but this dimension of Schopenhauer's thought only comes into view once the metaphysics of nature that he develops in the second book of *WWR* is in place and we shall return to it later. Even from a distance, however, a dissonance between the naturalization of epistemology and the transcendental method inherited from Kant is audible. This dissonance can be regarded as a philosophical weakness, as we shall see, but also as the symptom of an historical transition. It is useful to recall that, although his fundamental conceptual commitments were firmly established by 1818, Schopenhauer's career extended from the heyday of post-Kantian idealism during the first three decades of the nineteenth century to the advent of materialism and positivism in the century's latter half, the phase of his belated renown.

Schopenhauer's version of transcendental idealism achieves expression in two principal claims. The first bears on the primacy of representation (*Vorstellung*) as the form of all cognitive relations. The term representation is common in Kant, but its titular function in Schopenhauer's work may have its source in Karl Leonhard Reinhold's effort to systematize Kant's theory by starting from a first principle, namely, that all consciousness is structured as a "representation" distinguishing and relating subject and object (*Attempt at a New Theory of the Human Faculty of Representation*, 1789). Representation, for Schopenhauer, is the universal form of world-relation. It expresses the fact that all experience is of objects *for* the subject and hence conditioned by the subject. One of the allegations that Schopenhauer raised against Kant was that he had slipped into thinking of the thing in itself as an object in itself. For objects are always and only objects "of" or "within" representation; the notion of an object in itself makes no sense. Schopenhauer of course maintains the Kantian distinction between appearances and the thing in itself, but he holds that the thing in itself is heterogeneous to objecthood generally (it is, as we shall see, Will). The second major claim of Schopenhauer's transcendental idealism is that the subjective conditions under which objects appear – space, time, and causality – are species of the same generic principle: the principle of sufficient reason that "nothing is without reason why it is rather than not." The principle of sufficient reason, on Schopenhauer's construal, expresses the structural fact that any object stands in necessary relations to other objects by which it is determined and which, in turn, it determines. The mode of determination, however, varies according to the class of objects to which it is applied. The achievement of Schopenhauer's dissertation, the findings of which are integrated into *WWR*, is to have distinguished four such "roots" or variants of this single *a priori* principle: (1) the *principle of sufficient reason of being* which governs the determination of spatial location and temporal sequence; (2) the *principle of sufficient reason of becoming* or the law of causality; (3) the *principle of sufficient reason of knowing* which determines concepts through justification; (4) the *principle of sufficient reason of acting* which determines the will through its relation to a motivation. One can understand how the inventor of this classification might consider it an advance over Kant in terms of both simplicity and systematicity.

An important consequence of Schopenhauer's two claims is that, taken together, they delimit the sphere of legitimate application for the principle of sufficient reason. For this principle holds *exclusively* for relations among objects, which, of course, are objects for the subject. The subject, however, is not determined according to the principle, nor does it determine anything. The subject eludes both spatial-temporal individuation (it is neither many, nor one) and causal dependency. It is the cognizing instance, but never itself cognized. Circumscribing the domain of applicability of the principle of sufficient reason exposes, in Schopenhauer's opinion, the incoherence of dogmatism. Dogmatism has two varieties, the first of which, realism, posits the causal determination of the subject by the object. Since causal relations obtain only among objects, however, this move is hardly licit. The second variety of dogmatism is idealism of the sort promulgated by Fichte. Schopenhauer was well aware of the fact that Fichte had contrasted his own "critical" philosophy with dogmatism and the attribution to him of dogmatic confusion is as bitingly sarcastic as it is, in all likelihood, erroneous. For it is not at all clear that Fichte, as Schopenhauer claims, conceived the object as "an effect of the subject" (*WWR* I, Par. 5) or that the positing (*Setzung*) of the non-Ego by the self-positing Ego has the status of an empirical fact. Be that as it may, the contention is typical of Schopenhauer's assessment of his major idealist contemporaries. He is no less dismissive of Schelling's philosophy of identity, grounded in the "intellectual intuition" of the Absolute. Schelling is seen as stepping outside the structure of representation altogether and claiming philosophical authority for a merely fantastic faculty (the intuitive grasp by reason of the unity of subject and object). Interestingly, Schopenhauer also argues that the strictures on the applicability of the principle of reason expose the inadequacy of skepticism. The skeptic demands that something *more* than representation be known. But this demand fails to see that determinate representation – say, the cognition of the causal relations among perceived objects – exhausts those objects in their being, hence that there is nothing more of the object to grasp. To know empirical reality just is to know in this way. Echoing Kant, Schopenhauer insists that the represented world, determined by time, space, and causality, has "empirical reality" and that this is in no way incompatible with its "transcendental ideality." To understand this distinction is to see worries about the purchase of knowledge on the real world evaporate (*WWR* I, Par. 5). Nevertheless, Schopenhauer's larger view will drive him toward an account of the world as representation that has a highly skeptical tonality.

A further divergence from Kant underlined by Schopenhauer himself is his parsing of the faculties. On his account, the understanding (*Verstand*), although it apprehends causal relations, is an intuitive faculty. In fact, intuitive perception (*Anschauung*) comes about by projecting a causal source for immediately felt, pre-objectival sensations. Causality has its first application, we might say, in object constitution; subsequently it organizes patterns of determination among objects. In this way, understanding suffuses the perceived world, where it functions for the most part with unperturbed efficiency. All intuition is intellectual, although not in the sense of the special cognitive capacity declared inaccessible by Kant and variously celebrated by Fichte and Schelling. Moreover, since animals intuitively cognize objects that serve as the motives of their behavior, they, too, possess understanding. What distinguishes human beings is reason (*Vernunft*), which Schopenhauer conceives not in the elevated manner of Kant or Hegel, but in the mode of empiricism: as the capacity to operate with concepts abstracted from intuitions. Intuitive engagement with the world has its criterion of success in reality, as opposed to appearance. Reason, on the other hand, produces abstract judgments (generalizations) sufficiently grounded in other judgments. Its standard of success is truth, its predicate of failure error. The striking feature of Schopenhauer's formulation of the issues here is the privileging of intuitive experience – one might say: of our ordinary goings about – over and against the alembicated results of ratiocination. Hegel's contemporary exaltation of the Notion (*Begriff*) provides the telling contrast case. For Schopenhauer, reason is not only parasitic on intuition (in the sense that its justifications must finally come to rest in intuitive evidence); its very constitution (abstraction) depletes experiential content. Reason distinguishes human beings from the animals, but it by no means dignifies them. Very quickly Schopenhauer's doctrine of the faculties shades into an anthropology that, as we shall see, is among the bleakest in our tradition.

It remains to bring out the special character of the principle of sufficient reason, what Schopenhauer calls its "inner essence" (*WWR* I, Par. 3). This essence reveals itself most clearly in the simplest form assumed by the principle, namely temporal sequence. For just as each present moment of time is merely a limit between past and future, without extension and without substance, so too with each item known as proceeding from causes or motives within space and time: it is what it is solely by virtue of something else and therefore has a merely "relative existence" (*WWR* I, Par. 3). Considered as the object of everyday experience and of science, the world exhibits a "thoroughgoing relativity" (*WWR* I, Par. 7), and this in two senses. As representations, the objects of the world are relative to the subject, for such is the very structure of representation. As subsumed beneath the principle of sufficient reason, they are relative to other representations of the same class, indeed to a network that spreads out endlessly and thus suggests an infinite regress. It may very well be that, from a perspective internal to our ordinary epistemic practices, the world is "empirically real" and skeptical doubt otiose. From the transcendental perspective as Schopenhauer conceives it, however, the represented world, because it is entirely relational, evinces a thoroughgoing insubstantiality (*Nichtigkeit*). The ontological hollowness of the represented world is dramatized in Schopenhauer's writing through a number of figures and catch phrases. The most famous, perhaps, is the metaphor of "the veil of Maja" that Schopenhauer borrowed from the Hindu *Vedas*. But the skeptical surmise is also evidenced in the picture of an "inside" to which our knowledge, merely a sketch of the "external" façade, can never gain access. Like the skeptic before him, Schopenhauer is moved to demand *more* than representation: a "what" instead of the endless concatenation of "how's" the principle of sufficient reason furnishes us with, something *beyond* merely relational being. This yearning for substance directly apprehended impels the transition from the theory of knowledge to the metaphysics of nature.

II

Schopenhauer's metaphysical reflections are unfolded principally in the second book of *WWR* I, in the treatise *On the Will in Nature* (1994 [1836]), and in chapters 18–28 of *WWR* II. The basic thesis is well known: the inner nature of the world is Will. The status of that claim, however, is not obvious. An effort to unpack its significance must start by inquiring who asks the metaphysical question. Importantly, it is not the investigator *qua* subject-of-knowledge, for that subject is anyone and no one, a "pure" subject, as Schopenhauer puts it, an "angel's head with wings" (*WWR* I, Par. 18). Rather, it is the investigator considered as a mortal *individual*, an incarnate denizen of that very world whose internal nature and meaning are metaphysically at issue. As we have seen, everything within that world is given to the individual as a representation, as object, but among all those objects one constitutes an epistemic exception, and that is the individual's body. Of course, it too is given to her as an object: extended in space, enduring in time, possessed of a surface that blotches when exposed to excessive sunlight. But it is also given as *her* body (*Leib*), and to her own body she relates not only as subject to object, but, as it were, in radical intimacy, in the mode of identity. Schopenhauer calls this self-awareness "immediately familiar" (*unmittelbar bekannt*). It is the mode in which the individual's will becomes manifest to her. Every bodily action – waving to someone, for example – is immediately familiar to her as an act of her own will. The act of will and the waving of her hand do not become present as distinct phenomena, one the cause, the other the effect. They are one and the same. That the lived body is given in terms of these two aspects – as will and as objective appearance – is for Schopenhauer the immediately intuited and absolutely self-evident fact upon which his entire metaphysics rests. Reason can abstract from it, generalize it to an account of the world, but it can never replace the evidence of self-awareness with derivation from a first principle. For this reason, Schopenhauer refers to the identity of the dual aspects as the philosophical truth *kat' exochen*. It is the inaugural revelation that the world is Will and representation throughout.

What might be called Schopenhauer's corporeal *cogito*, the locating of a secure philosophical starting point in the evidence of the body's two-sided givenness, deserves recognition as a seminal moment in intellectual history. Although its methodological significance is kindred to that of intellectual intuition in Fichte and Schelling, its formulation seems less mysterious. It possesses a descriptive concreteness that anticipates phenomenological accounts of the lived body from Max Scheler to Maurice Merleau-Ponty and Hermann Schmitz. It also resonates in the distinction between observational (mediate) and non-observational (immediate) knowledge that since Anscombe has become a cornerstone of action theory as well as the theory of self-consciousness. This is not the place to explore these affiliations in detail. One matter, however, deserves emphasis. For Schopenhauer, the term "will," in its application both to human action and to the metaphysics of nature, does not refer to an antecedent intention, to a resolve to do this or that at some point in the future, to a potency preceding accomplishment. The will does not weigh alternatives or hover between options. Rather, the mark of the will is actuality, execution, realization (*WWR* II, Ch. 21). Schopenhauer himself attributed particular importance to this conception of the will's actuality and considered it a major philosophical achievement to have unfettered the notion of will from that of an antecedent representation (motive, goal, reason for). Faust's rewriting of the first words of the Gospel of John is relevant here (and may have influenced Schopenhauer): "In the beginning was the Deed." That I will this or that is, of course, dependent on and explainable in terms of the motive in question, but that I will at all (*überhaupt*) is not (*WWR* I, Par. 20; II, Ch. 20). This dimension of the will as Faustian primordial deed – one might say: as the very existence of willing and the willing of existence – constitutes the metaphysical datum that becomes manifest in incarnate self-awareness.

If my body is given to me externally as representation (as an object in space and time causally determined by other objects) *and* internally as will, then charity would seem to demand that all other objects, although they are given to me to know exclusively under the aspect of representation, be conceived transcendentally not merely as the stuff of dreams or the veil of Maja, but rather as having the very same core reality I do: namely will. This is exactly the step Schopenhauer takes in constructing his metaphysics. He generalizes from the case of bodily self-awareness to the entire world. The result is a series of claims that will strike most readers as speculatively stretching the concept of will beyond any recognizable shape (e.g. the force of gravity evinced in falling bodies is a willing). For this reason, it is important to stress that Schopenhauer himself considered his metaphysics to be post-Kantian in the sense of having taken the Kantian strictures on the limitation of knowledge to heart. The doctrine of the metaphysical Will (the capitalization specifies the Will abstracted from the philosopher's individual experience and projected onto the entirety of nature) is not theoretical or scientific; it offers neither causal explanations nor rational derivations (deductions). Rather, it is an interpretation (*Deutung*, *Auslegung*) that originates in puzzlement or wonder (Aristotelian *thaumazein*) and has as its task to decipher (*entziffern*) the totality of experience, which is to say: the articulation of its meaning (*Bedeutung*) (*WWR* II, Par. 17). Schopenhauer's answer to the question how metaphysics might be possible after Kant is: as an interpretation of my experience *qua* existing being, as a hermeneutics of existence. In this respect, Heidegger's fundamental ontology in *Being and Time* (1927) is a methodological descendent of the metaphysics elaborated in *WWR*.

Perhaps the most obscure dimension of Schopenhauer's analysis is the explication of the term "Will" itself. The Will is the Kantian thing in itself, the inner being of every phenomenon, whereby the predicate "inner" is not to be taken as designating a spatial determination. On the contrary, the characteristic feature of the Will is its featurelessness, the inapplicability to it of predicates drawn from the vocabulary of representation. Thus, the Will is one, but in a sense of "one" that excludes plurality or countability; it is timeless and without extension; it has no outside and there is nothing to which it is opposed. Schopenhauer's language often tempts one into thinking of the Will as a kind of combustion engine, energizing the world from within, but the category of causality is as inapplicable to the Will as is spatial location. Teleological concepts (final causes) are equally without pertinence. The Will is without reason (*grundlos*); it has no goal or aim. This is perhaps its most enigmatic quality: that it is Will and nonetheless *doesn't want or desire or strive for anything* (*WWR* I, Par. 29). We are left with a formulation haunted by tautology: the Will wills its own being and its being is willing. To capture this absence of motivation, Josiah Royce characterized the Schopenhauerian Will as "the inexplicable caprice of inner life" (Royce 1926: 252), but the connotations of lightness and playfulness at the heart of "caprice" hardly do justice to the oppressive pointlessness that imbues Schopenhauer's account. Rather than lift our puzzlement, his hermeneutics of existence roots experience in an obdurate absurdity.

It would seem that the notion of the Will does not allow for descriptive richness, but Schopenhauer nonetheless manages to evoke a rather detailed and even colorful account of the natural world and of human experience. Two features of his thought are crucial in this regard. The first is the conviction that the Will, having no outside or other, must be in conflict with itself. At the heart of things is a self-cannibalizing hunger, the dynamics of which Schopenhauer exhibits with a plethora of examples drawn from the natural and social worlds. The second feature generating descriptive complexity is the doctrine of "objectification" (*Objektität*), which characterizes the relationship of the Will to the represented world. As noted previously, the Will is not the cause of the world of appearances, for all causes fall within representation and the Will, as thing in itself, is by definition heterogeneous to this field. Nonetheless, the Will is *expressed* in phenomena. In fact, the phenomenal world – this is its metaphysical "meaning" – is the configuration the Will assumes under the aegis of representation. And here a certain hierarchy is observable, extending from the basic configurations of the physical world through chemical and biological processes to plant and animal life and finally to the life of human beings. The Will "objectifies" itself, in other words, in terms of certain eternal types, which Schopenhauer equates with the Platonic Ideas. These are intuitively available universals and they reflect, in addition to the hierarchical order of increasing complexity, the Will's inexplicable arbitrariness. For although the laws appropriate to each level of nature are employed in causal explanations, they are themselves not explainable in terms of efficient or final causes. They just are the various ways nature is organized, expressions of a Will that wills its own existence in this contingent fashion.

Schopenhauer's metaphysics of nature is unique by virtue of its intertwinement with empirical research, something especially visible in his book *The Will in Nature* and in the second volume of *WWR*. Schopenhauer assiduously followed the international scientific developments of his day, often finding what he held to be compelling confirmation of his views in the work of such researchers as Cabanis and Bichat. Perhaps the most notable aspect of Schopenhauer's ruminations on nature is his emphasis on what might be termed the economy of survival. Nature exhibited itself to him as a "universal strife" (*allgemeiner Kampf*) in which individual forms compete not merely for resources, but, as it were, for occupation of the space of being. Every organism marks a tenuous submission of more primitive forms, which nonetheless press toward dissolution of the supervening organizational pattern. Schopenhauer also had a keen eye for the survival-conducive fit between organism and environment, which he called "adaptation" (*Anpassung, WWR* I, Par. 28). There can be little doubt but that his popularity in the second half of the nineteenth century is in part attributable to the semantic compatibility between his philosophy and Darwinism. Philosophically, the most interesting feature of Schopenhauer's naturalism, if it may be so called, is the articulation of an "external" view of cognition. Internally, of course, cognition is described transcendentally in terms of the *a priori* forms and concepts it brings to every experience, but it is also possible – and, Schopenhauer felt, philosophically obligatory – to account for cognition as one would any other natural phenomenon. From this perspective, it appears as the function of a specific level of biological development, and indeed of a specific organ. Thus, in addition to the array of transcendental statements that describes the order of the represented world in terms of its *a priori* conditions of possibility (subject–object structure, principle of sufficient reason), a second group of statements conceptualizes the same world as an artifact of the brain. The interference of these two vocabularies often makes Schopenhauer sound like an empirical (as opposed to transcendental) idealist. Moreover, Schopenhauer embeds his neurological account within a larger story. The brain stands in the service of the organism's self-maintenance and reproduction. Cognition – including human cognition – is an instrument for the accomplishment of the life-tasks of higher-order organisms. Its role is not to know how it stands with things "objectively," but to support the overriding project of life, which is, above all, the continuation of the life of the species. In this story, mind appears as a device for the management of sensate complexity, as an alarm system that identifies potential dangers, above all as an instrument for the focalization of objects of desire (what Schopenhauer termed "motives"). One could call Schopenhauer's position a naturalism regarding knowledge, or perhaps a biological pragmatism. Whatever term one settles on, however, it is evident that *this* analysis of knowledge is not compatible with the transcendental account reviewed above. Early in the twentieth century, both the Neo-Kantian Ernst Cassirer and the philosophical anthropologist Arnold Gehlen made this point forcefully, although with divergent recommendations as to which component to jettison. For Schopenhauer, however, the important issue was the metaphysical-interpretive one: that cognition (*Erkenntnis*) is in *servitude* to the Will, which in the higher forms of the Will's objectification expresses itself as the will-to-live.

Retrospectively, part of Schopenhauer's historical significance can be said to rest on the fact that the picture of human life (the anthropology) emergent from his doctrine of the Will stripped mankind of the last remnants of its godlike status. While all his great idealist contemporaries accorded a privileged role in their philosophical visions to some avatar of the Christian God, Schopenhauer prepared the way for the robust atheism typical of later nineteenth-century thought. In his view, the human being is, like all animals, principally concerned with maintaining its existence and prolonging the life of the species (affirming the will-to-live). To be sure, humans are distinguished from their fellow creatures by their capacity to reason, but this is hardly an ennobling qualification. Far from affording insight into the way things are or reflecting our divine heritage, reason merely enables us to extricate ourselves from immediate experience through the use of language and concepts and thereby to establish a framework of orientation that embraces past and future events and allows for cooperative endeavors. Reason expands the terrain, but remains nonetheless an instrument in the service of self-perpetuation; it complicates, but by no means elevates the character of animal life. On the contrary, the advent of reason exposes the human animal to dimensions of risk and perfidy unknown to the speechless species. Human beings are unique among the creatures for their cunning and mendacity, for the burden of guilt they inevitably bear, for the fear of death that shadows their every thought. The suffering (*Leiden*) that permeates all of natural life, and, indeed, Being in general, finds its most extreme expression in human life (*WWR* I, Par. 57). There remains, as Nietzsche recognized, a deeply Christian strain in Schopenhauer's philosophy, but it has little to do with theology. Its sources, rather, are anguish over our fallen condition and a longing for salvation.

The disillusioned assessment of our anthropological specificity bespeaks an important philosophical tradition that flows into and, in turn, is transformed by Schopenhauer's thought. With elegance and acumen, such seventeenth-century moralists as La Rochefoucauld in France and Balthasar Gracián in Spain had drawn a picture of human action as driven by dissimulated self-interest. Schopenhauer knew and admired their work. He brilliantly translated Gracián's *Hand-Oracle* (the translation was posthumously published in 1862) and attained stunning mastery of the moralists' preferred literary form, the aphorism, but he also recast the moralist idea of pervasive egotism in metaphysical terms that deepened their vision and profoundly influenced modernist conceptions. In particular, Schopenhauer argued that the ubiquitous conflicts arising from the pursuit of self-interest express the unappeasable strife at the core of our very being. Having no object, the metaphysical Will can assert itself only by turning against itself; its every affirmation is at once a negation; its forms are pitted against one another in unremitting antagonism. To be, on this account, is to be avaricious. Human beings are individuated centers of relentless craving, acting out the drama of the Will's autophagy (*WWR* I, Par. 60). The insatiable and conflict-ridden character of natural desires that Hegel thought overcome in the mutual recognition of self-legislating moral agents remained for Schopenhauer the primary (unsublatable) datum of human affairs. For this reason, he had no social philosophy worthy of serious attention, although his comments on the perniciousness of human interaction do provide an effective antidote against insouciant eudaimonism and naive utopianism. Moreover, his transformation of the moralist tradition disclosed convoluted networks of residually natural motivations, especially as regards sexuality, and such modern moral psychologists as Nietzsche and Freud owe much to his teaching.

III

The two components of Schopenhauer's system thus far inspected, his theory of knowledge and his metaphysics of nature, project an image of the normal condition of human life. Against this background, Schopenhauer's axial thought – the very hinge of his philosophical system – can be formulated as follows:

(1) Available to the human being are two spheres of experience that, in some sense, "emancipate themselves from" or even "negate" the usual Will-driven character of activity and of the world.
(2) These possibilities of experience come about by virtue of an alteration of the normal relationship between Will and cognition (*Erkenntnis*).
(3) The intentionality of each of the two types of experience can be characterized in terms of the metaphysical content it exhibits.

These three claims frame Schopenhauer's treatment of aesthetic experience, on the one hand, and moral experience, on the other. Aesthetic and moral experience, in other words, are not thought of as integrated within an encompassing unity of human practice, which they in one fashion or another perfect, but rather as exceptional anthropological possibilities. Their heterogeneity to ordinary experience expresses the fact that each in its own way provides a kind of "salvation" (*Erlösung*) from the normal conditions of life, yielding a state of mind Schopenhauer does not hesitate to call beatitude (*Seligkeit*, *WWR* I, Par. 68). The sphere of aesthetic experience is discussed in the third book of *WWR* I and in the corresponding chapters (29–39) of *WWR* II. Moral experience is the topic of the fourth and final book of *WWR* I, of chapters 40–9 of *WWR* II, and of the two essays *On the Freedom of the Human Will* and *On the Basis of Morality*, which were published together under the title *The Two Fundamental Problems of Ethics* (1841). However contested, the aesthetic and ethical components of Schopenhauer's thought constitute the zone of his most profound philosophical contribution.

Among the classical aestheticians, it was Schopenhauer who most sharply accentuated the feature of aesthetic isolation and this concept provides the quickest access to his thought on beauty, art, and aesthetic experience. Isolation is characteristic of any object attended to aesthetically, and it is radical. We might say that it is the isolation not of things, beyond whose edges there is always something more, but of worlds, whose edges have no other side. Expressed in Schopenhauer's vocabulary, this means that aesthetic attention detaches its object from the nexus of relations that ramify along the paths set down by the fourfold manifestations of the principle of reason. Although a representation, the aesthetic object is relevantly determined neither by spatial-temporal relations to other objects, nor by causal relations, nor by reasons, nor by its role as a motive for action. Since, however, all empirical objects are by definition individuated within such relational networks, the object contemplated in aesthetic isolation cannot be an empirical object at all. What is it then? Schopenhauer's answer is that it is an Idea or, as he sometimes specified, a Platonic Idea. This contention hooks up, of course, with his metaphysics of nature. Indeed, here we hit upon the core thought of what Schopenhauer called his metaphysics of the beautiful. For in contradistinction to Kant and along a very different path of thought from that taken by Hegel, Schopenhauer set out to demonstrate that aesthetic contemplation discloses a truth about the inner nature of the world.

The exact link between aesthetic isolation and metaphysical content is difficult to bring out clearly. Following a line of interpretation sketched in entries Wittgenstein made in his diary on 7 and 8 October 1916, we might say that, just because aesthetic contemplation sequesters its object in the manner just described, it apprehends that object against the background of the entire world. This would give us the universality Schopenhauer's notion of Idea seems to presuppose; each aesthetic object discloses, from a certain perspective, the character of the world. Wittgenstein takes as an example the stove in the corner of his room, which, when regarded aesthetically, comes to stand in for the world *tout court*. Perhaps (Wittgenstein's notes don't make this explicit) the stove gives us a world that is burning within, that is slowly but relentlessly rusting, that requires our labor and repays that labor with warmth, and that looks back at us opaque and mute and a bit awkward. Aesthetically contemplated, these stove-features become world-features, and something like this seems implied in Schopenhauer's notion of Idea. For the Idea is an intuited universal; it is perceptually grasped, but has concept-like generality. That generality captures one of the archetypes according to which the Will shows itself, a mode of the Will's manifestation. And for Schopenhauer, of course, the Will is the inner nature of the world.

It is clear that Schopenhauer's conceptualization of the aesthetic object as Idea is rooted in the broader context of post-Kantian thought. Especially important in this connection, as noted above, is Goethe's work, in which the concepts of an intuitive method, of natural archetypes, and of the unity of art and nature are developed with originality and consistency. Schopenhauer knew Goethe personally and acquired the techniques of Goethe's scientific method in jointly conducted experiments on color that eventuated in the study *On Vision and Colors* (1816). It is hardly surprising, then, that their writings exhibit affinities. But even in the case of contemporaries whose philosophical differences with Schopenhauer are flagrant, one also finds an emphatic concept of Idea. A case in point is Hegel, whose definition of the Idea as the realized unity of the Notion and its Other bears structural similarities to Schopenhauer's usage and whose theory of art rests on the assertion that the beautiful is the appearance of the Idea in the mode of intuition (*Anschauung*). Much could be learned from a detailed examination of the similarities and differences that emerge across this entire intellectual field, which includes thinkers such as Jean Paul, Friedrich Schlegel and Karl Ferdinand Solger. One feature of Schopenhauer's aesthetic theory that would stand out in such a comparative study is its uniquely unhistorical character. Worries about the ancient/modern distinction or about the end of art or about its future just don't appear on the theoretical agenda. This neglect is motivated by Schopenhauer's view that historical change lacks philosophical importance altogether, but it also has to do with the fact that art for Schopenhauer is not an expression of spirit, not, that is, the *articulation of configurations of historical-cultural self-awareness*, but rather the *revelation of the forms of Being*. Art, in other words, is the disclosure of a metaphysical content that is, to be sure, already there (it is not a human creation), but that is inaccessible to human cognition otherwise than in aesthetic experience. We can glean the basic outlines of Schopenhauer's aesthetics of revelation (his term is *Offenbarung*) from his treatment of architecture, the lowest art because the Ideas it discloses are those governing the simplest and crudest levels of the Will's objectivity. These are such qualities of the building material (stone) as weight, cohesion, rigidity, and hardness, as well as the opposed Idea of light. Such qualities are omnipresent in experience, but, in the normal course of things, they recede into inconspicuousness. The artwork brings these phenomenal features into a relationship of tension with one another such that they manifest themselves as and within the artistic array. As regards architecture in particular (Schopenhauer's paradigm is probably the Greco-Roman use of columns), what is revealed is the strife (*Kampf*) between gravity and rigidity, secondarily between opacity and light. The aesthetic (as opposed to, say, the political) task of architecture is to produce arrangements in which this strife is disclosed in a perspicuous and manifold fashion (*WWR* I, Par. 43). Such disclosure takes place in each of the arts, although in each art a different level of the Will's objectification – a different Idea – is brought to revelation.

Reader's of Heidegger's *Origin of the Work of Art* (1936) will have noticed in the foregoing a number of striking echoes, for example the emphasis on disclosure, the insistence on art's metaphysical or ontological import, and the conception of artistic unity as strife. (These suggest that Heidegger's frequent dismissals of Schopenhauer were either blind or self-serving.) Be that as it may, the important point in the present context is that Schopenhauer's conception of art as revelation allows us to see the specific link between aesthetic experience and philosophy, which was the starting point of our investigation. Recall in this connection the characterization of metaphysical inquiry as a hermeneutic enterprise the task of which is to decipher or interpret a meaning. What art provides is an intuitive apprehension of just such meanings. For the Idea art discloses and enables me to apprehend is not, Schopenhauer insists, the spatial array deployed before the viewer, but rather the "pure meaning" (*reine Bedeutung*) informing that spatial configuration, something that is itself without extension (*WWR* I, Par. 41). Full appreciation of this claim would require examination of the Neo-Platonic background of Schopenhauer's concept of Idea, a matter that we cannot delve into here (see *WWR* II, Ch. 30). But we can take a stab at characterizing the pure meaning that art, in all its objectival forms from architecture to tragedy, makes intuitively accessible, such that it "speaks to me" (*WWR* I, Par. 41). It is the conflict within the Will (hence within all of Being) or the character of Will (and Being) as self-conflict. If this meaning speaks to me, it is because I, too, am Will, which is to say that, in art, the Will comes to know itself in its meaning (*WWR* I, Par. 34). It is also to say that all art, since its meaning is unavoidable and unappeasable conflict, is, broadly speaking, tragic, and that tragedy, narrowly speaking, is the objectival art form where this tragic character is most fully revealed. In this sense, tragedy marks the transition from aesthetics to ethics.

A brief consideration of the subjective side of aesthetic experience is in order. The metaphysical interpretation of nature had shown that cognition is a function of the higher forms of the Will's objectification; that sensory mechanisms, nerves, and brain, just like all other components of the organism, are in service to the Will; and that their artifact representation – is likewise a means for the fulfillment of the manifold needs emergent at this level of development. Moreover, the entire relational network established according to the principle of sufficient reason, which is to say, the world of spatially and temporally differentiated objects, is centered on one such individuated entity, the animal or human body, with its desires and needs. One's very sense of oneself as an individual, then, is inseparable from the project of self-maintenance. Viewed against this background, the noteworthy feature of aesthetic experience is that all the pertinences that hold for a given individual identity – the needs, desires, cares, anxieties, sufferings – fall away *within this experience*. The aesthetically relevant subject, Schopenhauer infers, is not the individual at all, but, as it were, a disembodied, impersonal cognitive function, what he calls the "pure, will-less, painless, timeless subject of cognition" (*WWR* I, Par. 34). The thesis is obviously derived from Kant's notion of disinterested pleasure and it may be that the overcoming of individuation Schopenhauer attributes to aesthetic experience is influenced by what Kant called the "universal voice" authorizing the judgment of taste. But Kant's use of these notions bears on the procedures of justification attached to a certain form of judgment, while Schopenhauer's account tends toward the hypostatization of a trans-individual subjective being, a kind of disembodied mind to which, in aesthetic experience, humans find some sort of access. It is hard to know how to make sense of this. A charitable interpretation might argue that references to the pure subject of cognition attempt to capture salient aspects of the phenomenology of aesthetic experience. The world of the artwork, after all, seems to concern me only insofar as it reveals itself to me. I contemplate the aesthetic object not from a position within a world I share with it, but as if from out of an absence. My activity is replete with contemplation in the sense that I forget all else, even and especially *myself*. This last point is especially important to Schopenhauer, who sees the cardinal feature of aesthetic experience in what might be termed the identity of consciousness and content: the subject is completely taken up by or absorbed in the object such that "it becomes the object" or "is nothing but the object's distinct image" (*WWR* I, Par. 34). With such phenomena in view, to speak of the subject of aesthetic experience as the "limpid eye of the world" (*klares Weltauge*, WWR I, Par. 36) might very well seem to have descriptive traction.

But of course Schopenhauer is not interested just in phenomenology. The point of his entire discussion bears on what I referred to above as the *exceptionality* of aesthetic experience. He wants to make out in aesthetic experience not merely a way of relating to a particular class of objects (say, beautiful ones) within the world, but a *categorically different* sort of experience. Aesthetic experience is not continuous with the experiences human subjects have under normal (one might say: natural) conditions. Rather, it is the momentary suspension of that normality, which is to say: of experience as the apprehension of individuated objects from the stand-point of incarnate subjectivity. The categorical difference at issue rests, then, on a realignment of the metaphysical relationship between Will and cognition. Aesthetic experience occurs when cognition (*Erkenntnis*) "suddenly tears itself loose" (*WWR* I, Par. 34) from its subservience to the Will and contemplates its object *independently of the principle of sufficient reason*. Both the suddenness and the violence highlighted by Schopenhauer's language are suggestive of the radical heterogeneity of aesthetic experience. Getting there requires, as it were, a metaphysical *saltus*. Commentators have pointed out that Schopenhauer's description of aesthetic experience is one of the most nuanced and perspicacious in the philosophical literature. For Schopenhauer, however, the philosophical task is not, to repeat, to get the phenomenology right, but to solicit its metaphysical meaning. From this hermeneutic perspective, aesthetic experience provides compelling *evidence that emancipation from our Will-tethered condition is a real possibility*. Employing a formulation that stresses the proximity of aesthetics and morality, but also brings out the religious sensibility that animates Schopenhauer's thought, one might also say: aesthetic experience has the metaphysical significance of *episodic salvation*. Seldom has art been expected to carry such a heavy burden.

IV

The kindred argument for morality takes its start from the condition of egoism, which is the normal attitude of the animal/human as it goes about its life's tasks. Such creatures are lashed to their desires, perpetually in quest of fulfillment, hence condemned eventually to suffer either the pain of disappointment (since every satisfaction proves chimerical) or the anguish of boredom (when no "motive" capable of stimulating willing shows itself). Schopenhauer's works spin off several versions of this tune, set pieces in his pessimistic litany, all quite drastic, all composed with cantankerous verve. The philosophical basis will strike most readers as dubious due to Schopenhauer's tendentious view of what constitutes human aspirations and fulfillments. His model is natural desire, where it does seem clear in standard cases such as hunger or sex that consumption of the desired object provides abatement of the urge but no lasting gratification. It is of the nature of desire to return. A characteristic move in Schopenhauer's philosophizing is to infer from such serial recrudescence that the essence of life is suffering, since desire is lack and lack is suffering (*Leiden*). A correlate inference is that the satisfactions occasionally available to humans are without substance, being mere, and merely ephemeral, palliatives. The philosophical usefulness of this overall account lies in the fact that it provokes counter-proposals that have a better chance of getting things right. Certainly no one will deny that satisfaction is subject to erosion or that desire is recidivist, but Schopenhauer claims too much when he takes these facts of life to trump even cautiously affirmative assessments. His pessimism shows its threadbare quality when one notes the degree to which it rests on the fact that process goes on, that *no lasting state* is ever achieved. Is that where our problems lie? Could one even coherently want only permanent fulfillments? But perhaps the root weakness of Schopenhauer's thinking here is the strategy of generalizing from natural or animal desires, which doesn't allow the truth to emerge that not all or even most human ends are straightforward seizures-of-possession. The model is just too simplistic to capture the complexity of human projects and achievements. On the other hand, there are deep human thirsts that just won't be slaked and to erase these from our picture of human experience would be folly. Schopenhauer's tendentiousness at least prevents that from happening.

To act egoistically is to act for the sake of one's *own* gratification, hence with reference to one's own individuated will, for it is the will that has wants and feels satisfaction or disappointment, pleasure or pain. On Schopenhauer's analysis, this attitude is rooted in what might be termed a natural ontology that is emergent with individuation. As we have seen, the genuinely real is given to the individuated subject in and through the actions of her body (willing), while all the rest is given, in the normal case, as representation, hence as dependent for its very existence on the subject. Egoism, we might say, interprets this twofold givenness as the very structure of the world. However minute and insignificant the individual might be, she nonetheless places her own existence and well-being above all else, indeed she is capable of sacrificing all else, even of willing destruction of the entire world, in order to maintain her own existence. For it *seems* that the entire Will – reality itself – is within her, while the rest is ontologically pallid. But individuation, of course, brings forth countless individuals, and each one holds the same intuitively convincing ontology and draws from it the same consequence: the priority of her own existence and well-being over that of all others. This situation, resonant of the Hobbesian state of nature, is the visible manifestation of the Will's self-contradiction (*WWR* I, Par. 61).

Obviously there's much to be said about this construction of things. Schopenhauer's views, first formulated in 1818, anticipate themes that would dominate the second half of the nineteenth century. One thinks of Max Stirner, of George Meredith, of the egoism/altruism issue that becomes virulent after Darwin. Perhaps, too, Schopenhauer's egoist has something of the capitalist, ever eager to maximize profits, a hypothesis that would lead very quickly to a comparison of Schopenhauer and Marx. One could also rehearse the classification of actions Schopenhauer generates out of the thesis of egoism, with its morally indifferent actions (egoistic, but not detrimental to others), its just and unjust actions, its evil actions and acts of philanthropy. Such a summary of Schopenhauer's views would stress his opposition to Kant's moral rationalism, his advocacy of a virtue approach, and the importance of character in his ethical thinking. Finally, one would want to note that Schopenhauer, as the account of willing sketched in Section II above suggests, had little tolerance for the notion of freedom of the individual will. In the context of the present discussion, however, these matters can be safely ignored in order to bring out the issue that primarily concerns us: the internal relationship between aesthetics and ethics.

A useful starting point is the *interpretive* conception of egoism just reviewed. If egoism rests, as Schopenhauer claims, on a natural ontology, then it is not solely the function of a drive. Egoism, in other words, takes the *appearance* of the individuated world – the world submitted to the principle of sufficient reason and centered on incarnate (willing) subjectivity – as true. To be egoistic just is to be committed to the ontology (I am real, all else pales) suggested by our natural, individuated standpoint. Consider the *evil* person. On Schopenhauer's account, she is an individual who, given the opportunity and in the absence of deterrence, will always wrong another to aggrandize her own position. That is to say, she holds to the egoist's ontology in a thoroughgoing fashion, not only affirming the will-to-live as it appears in her own body, but also going so far as to negate (*verneinen*) the will-to-live as it appears in others. The normal person's commitment to the egoist ontology is desultory by comparison. If evil is the most extreme form of egoism, then *cruelty* is the outer reach of evil. For cruelty wills the pain and suffering of other individuals not for the sake of the ego's own well-being, but in order to take pleasure in the other's suffering. The suffering of the other is its aim. It is worth mentioning that the analysis of pathological cases shows Schopenhauer's gifts of moral-psychological discrimination at their most sharply honed. His full account of cruelty, in which *envy* and the *anguish of boredom* also play a role, still deserves careful study (*WWR* I, Par. 65). Perhaps unfortunately, we have other prey in sight.

Soliciting the interpretive component of Schopenhauer's theory allows us, somewhat surprisingly, to recognize in it a Socratic element. Pace Royce, human beings are not driven by an utterly capricious will; even in the most extreme form of egoistic behavior (evil), they act according to a belief about what it is right to do. That belief results from a practical syllogism the minor premise of which is what we have been referring to as the natural ontology of individuation: the conviction that I am real and that others are "masks without reality" (*WWR* I, Par. 65). But this ontology is erroneous and evil behavior therefore, just as in Socrates' account, has its source in ignorance. In this connection, metaphors such as the Veil of Maja acquire a secondary usefulness, marking no longer the *purely phenomenal* character of our cognitive takings, but the *deceptive* character of the world of individuated entities, which the principle of sufficient reason lays out before us. The egoist is not only entangled in and deceived by the latticework of space, time, and causality; she is committed to the *truth* of the natural ontology that her two-sided experience as a willing/representing individual suggests to her. Of course, Schopenhauer did not hold, as Socrates did, that the ignorance and confusion at the root of egoism could be overcome through the dialectical process. Abstract reasoning is far too delicate an instrument to extirpate a conviction rooted in the very core of vital self-perpetuation, in Schopenhauer's terms: in the will-to-live. Such conviction is not a purely intellectual matter. To live just is to affirm the will-to-live and therewith to underwrite the egoist ontology. That ontology is not a mistake we make in thought, it is the mistake that we are.

If philosophy traditionally conceived is not in a position to loosen the grip of egoism, then what practice can? Schopenhauer's answer is that emancipation from the hold of the egoist ontology is available in the form of immediate and intuitive insight that won't be "reasoned away" (*WWR* I, Par. 66). Such insight comes in various degrees and has various consequences for action. Consider the pangs of conscience that even the evil person sometimes feels. Why? Not because, Schopenhauer avers, she knows she has violated some moral proscription, nor because she fears punishment. Rather, the anxiety tormenting her conscience (*Gewissensangst*, *WWR* I, Par. 65) is brought about by the dawning recognition: (a) that the *principium individuationis* that sustains the distinction between the perpetrator and her victim is an illusion, hence that perpetrator and victim are one; and (b) that what is manifested in her acts and hence in her very self is the Will in its vehement self-rapaciousness. Conscience, at least of this Macbethian strain, is metaphysical insight coupled with a sense of horror at ones own monstrosity. A final twist: a component of the evil person's insight bears on the fact that that very insight is not strong enough to effect any change in her behavior, that she is tethered (Schopenhauer would say: for all eternity) to the voracious will-to-life.

A qualitatively different level of insight is the source of philanthropy. That word has been dulled in English to mean something like institutionalized charitable giving and for this reason it is important to emphasize that Schopenhauer's term is *Menschenliebe* and that he indeed intends with it something like "love of mankind" or what he also calls "pure love" (Gk *agápe*, Lat. *caritas*) as opposed to sexual love or eros, which springs from the loins of egoism and, in fact, is the nerve of the will-to-live. All love of the pure sort – such is Schopenhauer's admittedly "paradoxical" thesis – is *compassion*, a "suffering with" (*Mitleid*, *WWR* I, Par. 67). Compassion is clearer and more compelling than the crepuscular intuitions of conscience. It apprehends the suffering of the other as equivalent to its own and *acts* to alleviate that suffering. Compassion, then, rests on a metaphysical insight that shatters the illusory surface of the natural ontology of egoism. Note that in the case of both conscience and compassion the metaphysical content of the affect is not explicitly reflected on. The compassionate person does not reason: "Because we are metaphysically one, I shall assuage that person's pain." Rather, she just does it; does it, as we say, out of compassion. Schopenhauer's method is not to give compassion the reasons it needs, for it needs none. The philosopher, as it were, always comes later. His task is to interpret the implicit intentionality of the compassionate act in terms of its metaphysical significance. The project is the same as in the case of aesthetic experience.

The internal relationship between aesthetics and ethics comes especially to the fore when we reach the highest stage of moral experience, the stage of the ethical virtuoso. (This term is borrowed from Max Weber, but it covers the phenomena Schopenhauer has in view.) Not accidentally, the best introduction to this region of Schopenhauer's thought is to be found in the remarks on tragedy in book 3 of *WWR* I. As remarked above, tragedy (apart from music, which we must ignore here) is the zenith of art by virtue of the fact that it discloses the Idea of the human being, which is to say: the most complex archetype of the Will's objectification. The internal dissension (*Widerstreit*) that characterizes the Will at all levels of its objectification and thus manifests itself in every art finds in tragedy its fully exfoliated revelation (*Offenbarung*). It sounds surprisingly Hegelian but is nonetheless an accurate rendering of Schopenhauer's thought to say that in tragedy the Will achieves its clearest and truest self-awareness. Due to the depth and clarity of the metaphysical intuition it affords, tragedy produces an effect in the spectator so unique that Schopenhauer feels compelled to describe it with a technical vocabulary of his own invention. Rather than functioning as a motive (*Motiv*) that stimulates an act of will, the tragic revelation functions as a "quiescent" (*Quietiv*) that stills willing altogether. Tragedy, in short, leads to *resignation*, and it is resignation that characterizes the attitude (the stance toward life, let us say) of the ethical virtuoso. For Schopenhauer, the systematic link between aesthetics and ethics consists in the fact that the ethical virtuoso looks on life – this is his metaphysical intuition – as it is revealed in tragedy. He sees the same truth tragedy displays. For this reason, a philosophy that is intended to have ethical import, as Schopenhauer's certainly is, will do well to model itself not on science but on art. It will present something like a conceptual rendition of tragic insight, at least on a certain understanding of what constitutes the tragic.

The ethical virtuoso represents a step beyond compassion. For him, it is not a question of recognizing his identity with another individual but of knowing his identity with all of Being in its suffering, and of making that suffering his own. According to Schopenhauer, this is metaphysical insight of the most profound sort, an apprehension of the essence of the entire world. Just such insight realigns the normal metaphysical relationship between Will and cognition, thus bringing about another variant of anthropological exceptionality, the possibility of which Schopenhauer's aesthetic and ethical arguments seek to establish. In this case, that exceptionality could hardly be more extreme. After some five hundred pages of prose that had demonstrated the tenacity of the Will's hold on human life, the advent of the ethical virtuoso in the final four paragraphs of *WWR* I strikes the reader as miraculous. In fact, it may very well be that "supernatural" is the appropriate category to capture the event in question. In these paragraphs, Schopenhauer picks up the terminology of his theory of tragedy, describing the virtuoso's metaphysical intuition of the rapaciousness of the will-to-life as a "quiescent" the effect of which is expressed as *asceticism*. True to the pattern we have been tracing, ascetic practices such as fasting and sexual abstinence are taken as evidence of a metaphysical event. The interpretation of this event finds Schopenhauer at his most boldly speculative, and his most obscure. The important, although only dimly intelligible point is that we are not talking about something that a few scattered individuals – the saints, ascetics, and mystics Schopenhauer cites – heroically achieve in their encounter with a monstrous metaphysical antagonist. Rather, what happens in and through the ethical virtuoso is the *conversion* of the metaphysical Will itself: "the Will turns away from life" (*WWR* I, Par. 68). Since life just is the affirmation (*Bejahung*) of the Will, the conversion in question has the status of a denial or negation (*Verneinung*). This act of negation is an *act of the metaphysical Will*, and, as such, *expressive of the Will's freedom*. Recall: affirming itself, the Will freely (without reason, motive, aim: *grundlos*) calls this world of woe into being. In the virtuoso, that same Will, quiesced by the forceful intuitive cognition of its self-cannibalizing nature, freely chooses non-being, nothingness. In this sense, the ethical virtuoso is the sole appearance of freedom in the represented world (where all else is necessity). It is one of the doleful features of Schopenhauer's pessimism that the only *real choice* his philosophy has room for is that between Being and Non-Being. Yet more dismaying is the fact that, of those alternatives, the latter is clearly preferable. In the end, then, the figure of the ethical virtuoso shows us that Schopenhauer's philosophy so severely restricts the possibilities of meaningful experience, both aesthetic and ethical, that it is impossible to find within his world a place for human living. Even the bliss or beatitude attributed to the beholder of art and the ethical virtuoso is attenuated to an angelic stillness. This austerity was beautifully captured in the one-sentence review of *The World as Will and Representation* the novelist Jean Paul published in 1819 (cited in Royce 1926, p. 244). This first word on Schopenhauer's philosophy deserves to be the last as well· "A book of philosophical genius, bold, many-sided, full of skill and depth, – but of a depth almost hopeless and bottomless, akin to that melancholy lake in Norway, in whose deep waters, beneath the steep rock-walls, one never sees the sun, but only the stars reflected; and no bird and no wave ever flies over its surface."

References

Royce, Josiah (1926) *The Spirit of Modern Philosophy*, Boston; New York: Houghton Mifflin.

Schopenhauer, Arthur (1996 [1818]) *The World as Will and Representation*, trans. E. F. J. Payne, 2 vols, New York: Dover.

—— (2003 [1813]) *On the Fourfold Root of the Principle of Sufficient Reason*, trans. E. F. J. Payne, La Salle, IL: Open Court.

—— (1994 [1836]) *On the Will in Nature*, trans. E. F. J. Payne, edited by David E. Cartwright, New York: Berg.

Further reading

German edition of Schopenhauer's works: Arthur Schopenhauer, *Sämtliche Werke*, edited by Wolfgang Freiherr von Löhneysen, 5th edn, 4 vols (Frankfurt am Main: Suhrkamp, 1995). This most widely accessible German edition of Schopenhauer's published philosophical works includes critical apparatus and translations of all foreign citations. *English editions of Schopenhauer's major works*: Arthur Schopenhauer, *The World as Will and Representation*, trans. E. F. J. Payne, 2 vols (New York: Dover, 1996); *On the Fourfold Root of the Principle of Sufficient Reason*, trans. E. F. J. Payne (La Salle, IL: Open Court, 2003); *Parerga and Parilopomena*, trans. E. F. J. Payne (Oxford: Clarendon, 2001); *On the Will in Nature*, trans. E. F. J. Payne, edited by David E. Cartwright (New York: Berg, 1994); *Prize Essay on the Freedom of the Will*, trans. E. F. J. Payne, edited by Günter Zöller (Cambridge: Cambridge University Press, 1999); *On the Basis of Morality*, trans. E. F. J. Payne, edited by David E. Cartwright (Indianapolis, IN: Hackett, 1997). *Secondary Literature*: David E. Cartwright, *Historical Dictionary of Schopenhauer's Philosophy* (Lanham, MD: Scarecrow Press, 2005) includes entries on the key concepts of Schopenhauer's philosophy as well as various individuals significant in Schopenhauer's life and an excellent English-language bibliography. See also Ernst Cassirer, "Schopenhauer" in *Gesammelte Werke*, vol. 4/3: *Das Erkenntnisproblem in der Philosophie und Wissenschaft der neueren Zeit: Die nachkantischen Systeme*, edited by Marcel Simon (Hamburg: Meiner, 2000), pp. 396–430; Arnold Gehlen, "Die Resultate Schopenhauers," in *Gesamtausgabe*, vol. 4: *Philosophische Anthropologie und Handlungslehre*, edited by Karl-Siegbert Rehberg (Frankfurt am Main: Klostermann, 1983), pp. 25–49. Excellent collection of English-language contributions on Schopenhauer's aesthetics and related issues is Dale Jacquette (ed.) *Schopenhauer, Philosophy, and the Arts* (Cambridge: Cambridge University Press, 1996). Christopher Janaway (ed.) *The Cambridge Companion to Schopenhauer* (Cambridge: Cambridge University Press, 1999), contains contributions on all major aspects of Schopenhauer's thought. Bryan Magee, *The Philosophy of Schopenhauer* (New York: Oxford University Press, 1997) is a highly readable overview of Schopenhauer's thought. See also Brian O'Shaughnessy, *The Will: A Dual Aspect Theory*, vols 1 and 2, 2nd edn (Cambridge: Cambridge University Press, 2008); Clément Rosset, *Schopenhauer, philosophe de l'absurde* (Paris: Presses Universitaires de Frances, 1993). Josiah Royce, *The Spirit of Modern Philosophy* (Boston; New York: Houghton Mifflin, 1926), contains lectures Royce gave on German thought originally in 1892 and includes an appreciative, if critical, account of Schopenhauer's thought. Rüdiger Safranski, *Schopenhauer and the Wild Years of Philosophy*, trans. Ewald Osers (Cambridge: Oxford University Press, 1990), is a briskly written, well-informed biography of Schopenhauer.

12

KIERKEGAARD AND GERMAN IDEALISM

Merold Westphal

Søren Kierkegaard (1813–55) is rightly read as a religious thinker, as a founding father of existentialism, and as a postmodern philosopher. In all these aspects his thought is in dialogue with German Idealism, especially Kant and Hegel. Often this relation is that of sharp critique, overt or implied, but sometimes it is more a matter of convergence and overlap.

Kierkegaard lived a dramatic life that included a complex relation with his father, a broken engagement, a spectacular spat with the "tabloid" media, and a bitter denunciation of the state church in the person of its primates. For a full-length biography, a short biographical overview, or an even shorter one, see Hannay (2001), Collins (1983: 1–32), or Westphal (1996: 3–7). It is important not to get carried away with the biographical background of Kierkegaard's authorship, however fascinating. It is all too easy to become distracted. But if we are serious about the truth claims he presents, we'll have to focus on what is said rather than who says it.

This is especially true since often enough Kierkegaard is not the author of his writings. Many of his most important writings are pseudonymous, and it is clear that we can identify the various pseudonymous authors neither with each other nor with Kierkegaard. To assume *a priori* that this multi-authored authorship is either a coherent whole or nothing but disparate fragments is to refuse the hard hermeneutical task of exploring the complex relation of the parts to the whole. So it will be important to respect his emphatic request: "Thus in the pseudonymous books there is not a single word by me ... if it should occur to anyone to want to quote a particular passage from the books, it is my wish, my prayer, that he will do me the kindness of citing the respective pseudonymous author's name, not mine" (Kierkegaard 1992: 626–7). The pseudonyms relate to their creator in the way in which characters in a novel or play relate to their author. Of course it would be foolish to assign to the writer the views of all the characters in a novel or play. Shakespeare is neither Lear nor Hamlet, though perhaps there is a little Lear and a bit of Hamlet in each of us.

Why did Kierkegaard write pseudonymously? It was not to hide identity but rather to communicate more effectively with his reader, whom he often spoke of as "that single individual." Negatively speaking, he wanted to distance himself from the work so that the reader would neither be distracted by his personality, for he was all too well known in his native Copenhagen, nor take him to be an authority of some kind. He regularly insisted that he spoke "without authority," whether it be that of the preacher, the professor, the genius, or the apostle. He wanted to leave the reader alone with the ideas presented in the work, and ultimately alone with the work – before God.

There is also a positive rationale for using pseudonyms. By creating such characters Kierkegaard is able to present us persons not unlike ourselves, or at least aspects of ourselves, who are either (1) the embodiment of a philosophical or religious world view (life world, language game), or (2) persons caught up in serious engagement with such ideas, not as abstractions but as claims upon and possibilities for their own lives. The young man known only as A in the first volume of *Either/Or* and Judge William in the second volume are examples of the first case. They embody, respectively, the aesthetic and the ethical modes of being-in-the-world. Johannes de Silentio, trying to understand Abraham in *Fear and Trembling,* and Johannes Climacus, trying to understand what is involved in becoming a Christian in *Philosophical Fragments* and *Concluding Unscientific Postscript,* are examples of the second case. The existentialism of Kierkegaard – "This is about you, dear reader. What is your response?" – is served by rendering ideas concrete in these ways while removing himself from the scene.

The theory of the stages or existence spheres

The titles just mentioned, along with others, belong to Kierkegaard's theory of the stages on life's way or existence spheres: the aesthetic, the ethical, and the religious. They can be thought of as distinct life worlds, complex combinations of basic beliefs and behaviors. They are perhaps best distinguished as different criteria for what is to count as successful living.

For the aesthetic stage the criteria are pre-ethical. That is to say that the distinction between right and wrong, good and evil, plays no role in one's concept of the good life. The aesthetic stage is sometimes identified with hedonism, but this would be true only on a very expansive understanding of pleasure. It certainly is not restricted to the realm of the physical pleasures of eating, drinking, and sex. Nor should 'aesthetic' be restricted to the realm of the arts, although A, the young aesthete of part 1 of *Either/ Or,* is a lover of opera and the theater. In some of his writing the dominant criterion is the distinction between the interesting and the boring. As long as I don't lose interest in what I'm doing or what is going on around me, however trivial it may be, I'm having a "good" day. Since the aesthetic stage involves many different criteria and thus many different lifestyles, it should be defined by what they have in common: they are pre-ethical in the sense defined above.

The aesthetic stage is regularly identified with immediacy. One meaning we might give to this is that we don't have to learn the aesthetic; we are born into it and are always already there. Thus, for as long as the infant has a full tummy and a dry bottom, life is good. But as in Hegel, the opposite of immediacy is reflection, and since two paradigms of the aesthetic, the young man A and the seducer whose diary he cherishes (Is it his own?), are highly reflective individuals, this is puzzling. They are so reflective that they can be described as spectators of their own lives, about which they think and write extensively. In what sense can they be called immediate?

Hegel's usage, which Kierkegaard follows, is helpful. He defines immediacy as the absence of alterity. Thus mediation is defined as "a beginning, and having advanced to a second, in such a way that this second is only there because one has come to it from something that is other vis-à-vis this second" (Hegel 1991: §12). It consists "in having already left a first behind, to go on to a second" because "at the beginning we have as yet no other" (Hegel 1991: §86 including *zusatz* 1). Kierkegaard agrees and writes, "In immediacy there is no relation, for as soon as there is a relation, immediacy is cancelled. *Immediately everything is true*, but ... then the question of truth is cancelled" (Kierkegaard 1985: 167).

Were such a condition possible, the category of truth and falsity would be inoperative precisely because the difference (otherness, alterity) between appearance and reality, opinion and fact, has been eliminated. Similarly, the aesthetic life is an immediacy, not because aesthetes are never highly reflective persons, but because the difference between action and rightness, character and goodness has been eliminated (or never allowed to emerge). Another way to put this would be to say that what common sense would describe as other to the aesthete, the plays and operas that A loves and the young woman whom the seducer seduces, on close inspection are not really other. They are but grist for his mill, means toward his ends. Like the clothes I wear and the food I eat, they belong to me and not to themselves. Their only *raison d'être*, in his eyes, is to make his day pleasant or interesting.

This is why when Judge William pleads with the young man to choose the ethical over the aesthetic, he writes, "What, then, is it that I separate in my Either/Or? Is it good and evil? No, I only want to bring you to the point where this choice truly has meaning for you ... my Either/Or designates the choice by which one chooses good and evil or rules them out. Here the question is under what qualifications one will view all existence and personally live" (Kierkegaard 1987: 168–9). In other words, will good and evil, right and wrong, replace the pleasant and the interesting as the highest criteria for successful living?

One enters the ethical stage by redefining the good life in this way. But this is not the elimination of aesthetic values; it is rather their subordination to moral values, which are taken to be higher. Thus Judge William affirms that in marriage sex "is by no means repudiated but is ennobled" (Kierkegaard 1987: 61; cf. 21, 30, 57). Marriage is "the transfiguration of the first love and not its annihilation" (31; cf. 56–7, 94, 253).

This "ennoblement" and "transfiguration" have the character of an Hegelian *Aufhebung*. That which at first is taken to stand alone, self-sufficient and not essentially related to anything other than itself, comes to be seen as part of a larger whole of which it is not the first principle. It is thus cancelled so far as its primacy is concerned but preserved in a subordinate position. The best Oscar it could hope to win would be for Best Supporting Actor. But that, of course, is not nothing, and in the case that interests Judge William, there is an important place for sex in the good life, not as an autonomous value but as something to be "ennobled" and "transfigured" in marriage.

On this particular point Judge William is a good Hegelian. On Hegel's view, in marriage "physical passion sinks to the level of a physical moment" and "the sensuous moment, the one proper to physical life, is put into its ethical place as something only consequential and accidental" (Hegel 1945: ¶¶163–4). But sex is raised to new meaning as well as being lowered to a subordinate role. In marriage "the *natural* sexual union ... is changed into a union on the level of *spirit*, into self-conscious love" (Hegel 1945: ¶161; emphasis added and translation altered). Where nature is *aufgehoben* in spirit, sex is "the external embodiment of the ethical bond" (Hegel 1945: ¶164). When the emphasis is placed on 'external', sex is demoted to a secondary role; but when the emphasis is place on 'embodiment', sex is promoted to an important role in the life of spirit. The point is not to choose between this demotion and promotion, as if they were options on a menu, but to see them as two aspects of a single truth, two sides of the same coin. This is a specific instance of a general formula: by losing its presumed autonomy *nature* finds its truest fulfillment as a dimension of *spirit*.

So far Kierkegaard's presentation of the stages is Hegelian in two senses. First, the aesthetic stage is seen as an Hegelian immediacy, the autonomy and self-sufficiency of amoral values. Second, the ethical stage is its mediation through moral categories that are genuinely other in relation to it; moreover this mediation has the structure of an Hegelian *Aufhebung*, a contextualizing in which what purports to be autonomous is reinterpreted as a subordinate part of a larger whole.

The ethical stage is Hegelian in another important sense. One enters into it by giving primacy to the moral categories of right and wrong, good and evil. But these terms are purely formal. Where do their get their content so as to become substantive? Kierkegaard's idealist predecessors offered two answers. Like Plato, Kant appeals to pure practical reason, the power to rise above the contingencies and contaminations of the realm in which natural desire and social convention rule (Plato's cave), so as to apprehend unconditioned, universal and necessary truth analogous to mathematics. Kierkegaard and his pseudonyms don't think humans have any such ability to rise by the power of their own thought above their embeddedness in the contingency and particularity of some specific culture. So the ethical stage is never to be understood in Platonic/Kantian terms.

Hegel's answer to the question of where the ethical categories get their substantial content is *Sittlichkeit*, usually translated as ethical life. It signifies the laws and customs of some particular society and culture. We learn what right and wrong are not by shedding our concrete historical identity so as to become pure reason but by being socialized into some specific form of ethical life. Our moral values are relative to the social institutions from which we have learned them; our teachers are the family, the school, the work place, the government and the culture (high and/or low) to which we turn for inspiration and entertainment. In Marxist language, ethics is the ideology of a specific society.

In Hegel's view each mode of *Sittlichkeit* is an expression, partial and to that degree untrue, of the eternal Idea. The definitive, final moral norms that Plato and Kant thought could be accessed by an ahistorical, pure reason are only possible, on Hegel's view, at the end of history when that idea has fully unfolded and has become fully self-conscious in speculative philosophy. As the ideology of some specific society, moral knowledge could be ultimate rather than perennially penultimate only if it is the ideology of the ultimate social order, the one in which the historical process reaches its appointed end, just as the full growth oak tree is the final destiny of the original acorn in which its being is at once fully achieved and fully manifested. Hegel talks as if this has happened in his time and in his philosophy (Westphal 1998).

Kierkegaard and his pseudonyms think Hegel got it half right. Human knowledge, both moral and metaphysical is always embedded, perspectival, relative to the social order from which it arises and which it in turn sustains. But the finitude of human temporality precludes the possibility of any closure or finality within history. Thus the ethical stage is Hegelian, rather than Platonic or Kantian, in that ethical life gets its content from the laws and customs of a particular people at a particular time.

But it is anti-Hegelian insofar as no version of ethical life can justify any claim to be ultimate and complete rather than penultimate and partial. In many ways Kierkegaard's writings will be critical of the *Sittlichkeit* in which he finds himself and which he calls Christendom. His work, like Marx's, belongs to the tradition of ideology critique. Any critique of the ethical stage will be either (1) a formal critique of the tendency of any ethical life world to treat itself as absolute and ultimate or (2) a substantive critique of a particular mode of ethical life.

Like Hegel, Judge William talks a lot about God. But he appears as an embodiment of the ethical stage, not the religious. The reason is hinted at in a sermon that appears at the very end of *Either/Or*. It is entitled "The Upbuilding That Lies in the Thought That in Relation to God We Are Always in the Wrong" (Kierkegaard 1987: 339–54). The basic idea is that there is always a gap between the human and divine, whether the human is taken individually or collectively. The irony is that Judge William sends this homily to his young, aesthetic friend A, who doesn't believe in God or at least doesn't think God matters, while the force of the sermon is directed, as the reader is supposed to notice, at the Judge himself. For all his talk about God there is a smug complacency about his relation to God. It seems never to occur to him that there could be any difference between what God expects of him and what his society expects. God appears to have been dissolved without remainder into the social morality, what Nietzsche will call the morality of mores, by whose standards he is an upright citizen. Salvation is nothing more than socialization, righteousness than respectability.

The move to the religious stage comes as the recognition that there is a God who transcends both the individual and society, who is not reducible either to natural desire or to cultural convention. While neither of these is necessarily evil, neither is automatically good. The texts we will be looking at will be explications of the religious stage, for they represent the very heart of Kierkegaard's authorship both pseudonymous and in his own name. Looking back on his authorship in a little volume that was to be published posthumously, he writes, "The content, then, of this little book is: what I in truth am as an author, that I am and was a religious author, that my whole authorship pertains to Christianity, to the issue: becoming a Christian, with direct and indirect polemical aim at that enormous illusion, Christendom, or the illusion that in such a country all are Christians of sorts." In other words, the mission is "to introduce Christianity again – into Christendom" (Kierkegaard 1998: 23 and 42).

Before turning to specific texts, we should note two more ways in which the theory of the stages relates to Hegelian thought. Calling them stages might suggest an essentially temporal sequence, as if Kierkegaard were giving a developmental psychology of the spirit. But the sequence is more basically structural than temporal, and in this respect it is like the account of various forms of consciousness found in the first five chapters of Hegel's *Phenomenology of Spirit* (Westphal 1996: 20–1). The movement of the phenomenological modes of being-in-the-world is not from earlier to later but from abstract to concrete. As in Hegel's Logic, the "earlier" forms are abstract because they have been isolated or abstracted from the more complex whole to which they belong, while the "later" ones are more concrete because they include or presuppose the "earlier" ones in a richer and more determinate context. Thus, to use Hegelian language, the ethical stage is the *Aufhebung* or contextualizing of the aesthetic, which it presupposes and includes; and the religious stage is the *Aufhebung* of the ethical in just the same sense. The claim is always that the "later" is the proper fulfillment of the "earlier" – its truth or telos. The whole is the ground of the parts, and, contra Descartes, we find the foundation at the end, not the beginning of thought's journey.

But there is a crucial difference between Hegel's journeys, whether phenomenological, logical or even historical, and the journey through Kierkegaard's stages. Hegel always claims that there is some kind of necessity at work, though it is very difficult to says just what this necessity signifies. Kierkegaard's presentations, by contrast, are less interested in conceptual relations than in actual, existential movement from one sphere to another. Accordingly, he speaks of choosing; it is a matter of personal freedom and responsibility rather than conceptual necessity.

In looking at several interpretations of the religious stage we will have to take seriously the integrity of the pseudonymous authors; so we shall look at specific texts rather than at "Kierkegaard's account" of the religious stage. Five themes will be worth taking into account in the attempt to relate Kierkegaard's various writings to each other and to the idealisms of Kant and Hegel.

(1)   The overcoming of metaphysics.
(2)   The critique of theoretical reason.
(3)   The primacy of praxis over theory.
(4)   Historicism or historical relativism.
(5)   The relation of individual and society.

As it turns out, these issues are closely intertwined and tend to bleed into each other. Running throughout them we will find a post-Hegelian Kantianism. The Kantianism will consist both of a primacy of practical reason and an emphasis on the ways in which human understanding is mediated by the all too human lenses through which we interpret reality. Kant calls these lenses the *a priori* element in understanding; they simultaneously give us access to the real and keep us from merely mirroring it as it truly is. Other names for them include presuppositions, perspectives, horizons of expectation, pre-understanding, prejudices (in the etymological sense of pre-judgments), and control beliefs.

What makes this a post-Hegelian Kantianism is the fact that Kierkegaard and his pseudonyms see the *a priori* as historically and culturally particular rather than ahistorically universal. Like so much of what has been called the "aftermath" to Hegel, they follow Hegel in taking human experience to be essentially historical, and they depart from him in denying the possibility of an all-inclusive closure. With Kant they affirm that while reason may demand totality, it is incapable of achieving it.

Fear and trembling

The first sustained interpretation of the religious stage in the Kierkegaardian corpus is *Fear and Trembling*. It was published in 1843, the same year in which the aesthetic and ethical stages had been presented in the two long volumes that make up *Either/Or*. It is a multifaceted meditation on the faith of Abraham. In relation to the project of introducing Christianity into Christendom, it will be noticed that Abraham's faith is not Christian faith. But he is presented as a paradigm of faith in three New Testament books: Romans, Galatians, and Hebrews. So Johannes de Silentio, the pseudonymous author, can legitimately take him to exhibit the form, if not the content, of Christian faith. He does so in such a way as to pose quite sharply the following question: in the context of a Christendom and an Hegelian philosophy that assume that *everyone* has faith, can it be seriously maintained that *anyone* has a faith like Abraham's?

In *Fear and Trembling* the focus is on the story of the *Akedah*, the binding of Isaac, in Genesis 22, the last of God's seven conversations with Abraham. God tests his faith by telling him to offer his son Isaac as a sacrifice; but Isaac is not merely the son of his old age but also the son of promise, through whom Abraham is to be a blessing to all nations. Abraham agrees, makes the three-day journey to the appointed place, places Isaac on the altar, draws the knife, and only at the very last minute is deterred by a divine voice from going through with it. This is not the only chapter in the story of Abraham's faith, but it is surely the most intense. Silentio is not the first to spend time thinking about it.

If we are to find an overcoming of metaphysics in his meditations, and we should, we must not overlook the fact that Abraham's faith includes a number of beliefs that can only be called metaphysical. He believes in a God who is not merely the personification of the forces of nature or the traditions of his culture. His God is a personal agent and a speaker, one who makes promises and gives commands. He takes himself to have an absolute duty to this God, but only because God is worthy of absolute trust in relation to the promises and absolute obedience in relation to the commands. As an agent, God is able to raise the dead. According to Silentio, what distinguishes Abraham as the knight of faith from the (stoical) knight of infinite resignation is not the willingness to sacrifice his dearest for the highest. This they share. Beyond this, the knight of faith believes that he will get Isaac back from the dead *in this life* if it comes to that. This cluster of beliefs belongs to what we might call the metaphysics of monotheism.

So the overcoming of metaphysics does not consist in the elimination of metaphysical beliefs. In any case the naturalisms, materialisms, and pantheisms that would preclude belief in a God like Abraham's embody an alternative metaphysics, not an escape from metaphysics. The overcoming consists in the denial that philosophical speculation is the source of monotheistic belief and that the latter requires the former for its justification and proper interpretation. Metaphysics as an autonomous discipline is denied hegemony over theology and over the faith that theology seeks to support.

There is a Kantian dimension to this denial. The very first words of the *Critique of Pure Reason* are "human reason" (*Die menschliche Vernunft*), and the crucial differences between appearances and things in themselves and between phenomena and noumena is regularly drawn in terms of the difference between the ways human and divine minds see the same reality (Westphal 1968). When contrasting Abraham as the knight of faith to the knight of infinite resignation, Silentio says that Abraham has faith "by virtue of the absurd." He says this in a Kantian tone of voice. Faith is absurd insofar as it goes beyond "human calculation" and one's own understanding and the realm of "everything finite, for which it is the stockbroker." Abraham believes he will get Isaac back in this life, if he actually has to go through with the sacrifice, because "for God all things are possible." But this is absurd "within the proper domain of the understanding," or "humanly speaking," for "the understanding continues to be right in maintaining that in the finite world where it dominates this having was and continues to be an impossibility" (Kierkegaard 1983: 35–6, 46–7). Faith is not inherently absurd, but only in relation to a finite faculty that is in principle incapable of apprehending what faith affirms. For Silentio the terms 'paradox' and 'madness' have the same logic as 'absurd'. Abraham's faith is paradoxical and sheer madness from the standpoint of a human understanding equipped only to deal with the finite; but Abraham's God is not a finite substance in causal reciprocity with other finite substances, as Kant would define the domain proper to human understanding.

Even more important is the anti-Hegelian dimension of the denial of philosophical speculation's sovereignty over the metaphysics of monotheism. Of course the Kantian thesis of the finitude of human understanding is part of the critique of Hegel. So when Hegel says that Kant is right about the *understanding*, but not about human *reason*, a higher faculty that is capable of absolute knowledge (Hegel 1991: §§79–82), Kant and Kierkegaard will join in accusing him of confusing the human with the divine, of deifying the philosopher.

But when Silentio satirizes "our age" because of its infatuation with *speculation* and the *system* that will achieve the status of *science*, as presented, for example, in the Preface to the *Phenomenology of Spirit*, there is more at stake (Kierkegaard 1983: 5–7). The Hegelians and an all too willing Christendom, at least among the educated elite, assume that everyone has faith and are eager to "go further" than faith to understanding in the mode of the scientific, speculative system of philosophical thought. The *hoi polloi* may "walk by faith, not by sight" (2 Cor. 5:7), but the philosophical elite go beyond faith to speculative insight in which all is manifest and nothing mysterious (Westphal 2004: 80–3). But Silentio suggests that the kind of faith Abraham exhibits and that he himself does not possess, is "a task for a whole lifetime." It would be silly, he suggests, to pretend to go further than something one has not yet attained. In fact, this theme stands like bookends at the beginning and end of Silentio's analysis (Kierkegaard 1983: 6–7, 121–3).

The fact that faith is a task tells us that in addition to a Kantian critique of the scope of theoretical reason, there is a quasi-Kantian primacy of praxis over theory at work. (It is only quasi-Kantian because the ultimate guide for action is God, not the autonomous, self-legislating faculty of practical reason, which would never have put Abraham to this kind of test.) As we have seen, Abraham's faith includes metaphysical beliefs, but these are its presuppositions, not its essence. His faith consists primarily in his obedience to God's commands based on his trust in God's promises. In the language of Kierkegaard's Lutheranism, faith is one's personal response to divinely revealed Law and Gospel. Belief is important. In an atheist Abraham we would find neither this obedience nor this trust. But belief is not an end in itself; it needs to be *aufgehoben* in practice. That is why Silentio can treat faith as a putative moral virtue, inextricably intertwined with courage and humility (Kierkegaard 1983: 33–4, 48–9).

At this point overcoming metaphysics sounds more like Pascal than like Kant, with Pascal's distinction between the God of the philosophers and the God of Abraham, Isaac, and Jacob. Or like Heidegger. For him overcoming metaphysics means overcoming onto-theology and thereby the "god" of speculative philosophy, described in impersonal categories under the principle of sufficient reason with the goal of eliminating anything mysterious (Westphal 2004: Ch. 1). Philosophy allows the deity to be spoken of only on its terms and in the service of its project. But when "god" is reduced to playing the role of *causa prima*, *ultima ratio*, and *causa sui*, "Man can neither pray nor sacrifice to this god. Before the *causa sui*, man can neither fall to his knees in awe nor can he play music and dance before this god" (Heidegger 1969: 60, 72). Heidegger has his own philosophical reasons for wanting to overcome metaphysics in its onto-theological constitution. But he expects those whose deepest identity derives from some form of Abrahamic monotheism to be on his side. For him as for Silentio, Hegel is the paradigm of the metaphysics to be overcome, and he thinks that the "god" of speculative philosophy is an irreligious alternative to the God of Abraham, not a superior understanding and interpretation of that God.

In satirizing those who would "go further" than faith without noticing that they haven't gotten as far as faith, Silentio identifies them with "our age" and speaks of "the kind of self-deception the present generation needs" (Kierkegaard 1983: 5, 121). He thinks that the "Reason" to which the Hegelians appeal is an all too contemporary world view masquerading as absolute knowledge as if it were not relative to the particular culture that originates and sustains it.

We are in the neighborhood of historicism or historical relativism. Later on, when a series of post-Hegelian Kantianisms has developed the idea that "Reason" comes in many different versions, each relative to a particular language game or form of life, a "vertigo of relativity" (Berger and Luckmann 1966: 5) will give rise to the question, "But where are the means to overcome the anarchy of opinions that then threatens to befall us?" (Dilthey 1996: 389).

Silentio does not have this worry. The idea of a universal, entirely objective Reason, whether in a Kantian or Hegelian or some other form, was so dominant, so self-evident to those for whom he wrote, that it was enough for him (and for Kierkegaard in other writings) to call it into question. The clear and present danger, as he saw it, was the complacent arrogance that mistook the rationale of an historically particular and contingent culture for the universality and necessity of a Reason that was not or at least no longer (as Hegel would have it) one among others.

We have seen how the theme of the overcoming of metaphysics bleeds into three other themes: the critique of theoretical reason, the primacy of praxis over theory, and historicism or historical relativism. That leaves the fifth theme mentioned above: the relation of individual and society.

Some tellings of the story of the *Akedah* focus on Abraham's willingness to give up his dearest earthly love for the sake of God. This seems to be the focus of the biblical story. God says, "Because you have done this, and have not withheld your son, your only son, I will indeed bless you" (Gen. 22:16–17). This willingness is what unites the knight of faith with the knight of infinite resignation. (The difference, that Abraham believed he would get Isaac back in this life, is Silentio's gloss, without explicit warrant in the biblical narrative). But Silentio labels the discussion of this issue "preliminary." It is preliminary to the three problems that make up more than half of his book and which he considers the heart of the matter. The preliminary issue concerns whether Abraham will relinquish Isaac, give him up without resentment; the three problems concern the even more pressing question, whether Abraham will kill Isaac.

The first of these problems is expressed in the question, "Is there a Teleological Suspension of the Ethical?" (Kierkegaard 1983: 54–67). The other two problems are best conceived as corollaries to the first, attempts to make clearer its meaning. We have already met the structure of a teleological suspension. It is what Hegel calls an *Aufhebung*. Without using either name, Judge William argues for a teleological suspension or *Aufhebung* of the aesthetic in the ethical. Now Silentio argues that the Abraham story involves this same structure, only this time it is the ethical that is recontextualized in the religious, which is its telos. He will argue that the ethical is not invalidated or abolished but relativized (Kierkegaard 1983: 70–1). It has an important role to play, but not the lead role. It can be trumped.

Silentio makes it abundantly clear that by the ethical he does not mean the Platonic/Kantian ethical consisting of eternal principles discovered by pure practical reason. He rather shares the view of the ethical we found embodied in Judge William, the essentially Hegelian view of the ethical as *Sittlichkeit*, the laws and customs of a particular people. He shows this in three ways. First, he uses the Danish equivalent of Hegel's term, *det sædlige* or *Sædelighed* (Kierkegaard 1983: 55n7). Second, although he calls the ethical the universal, he makes it clear that this signifies not some abstract principle like Kant's categorical imperative, but a concrete universal, a social whole of which the individual is a part. Thus the universal is the nation, the state, society, or even the church or the sect (Kierkegaard 1983: 57–9, 62, 74, 79). Third, he mentions Hegel by name as the target of his analysis. Each of the three problems begins with the same formula: if the ethical as the universal is the highest (that is, if the laws and customs of one's people are the highest criterion for one's behavior), then Hegel is right – but Abraham is lost (Kierkegaard 1983: 54–5, 68–9, 82).

Abraham would be lost because his faith involves "the prodigious paradox … that makes murder into a holy and God-pleasing act" (Kierkegaard 1983: 53). But if it is a holy and God-pleasing act, it is not murder. A more careful formula says, "The ethical expression for what Abraham did is that he meant to murder Isaac; the religious expression is that he meant to sacrifice Isaac – but precisely in this contradiction is the anxiety that can make a person sleepless, and yet without this anxiety Abraham is not who he is" (Kierkegaard 1983: 30). Silentio stipulates what is not immediately clear from the biblical text, that the *Sittlichkeit* in which Abraham finds himself forbids child sacrifice. So as Silentio tells the story, it is not just paternal affection but the moral values of his society that makes this act so dreadful. As the founding father of Abrahamic monotheism for Jews, Christians, and Muslims, he can be a hero of faith only if there is a teleological suspension of the ethical. This means, as it is put in the second problem, that there is an absolute duty to God and only a relative duty to the laws and customs of one's people.

Silentio seems to be thinking along the lines of Augustine. "But when God commands that something should be done which is against the customs or institutions of any people, it must be done, even if it has never been done there before … But when you suddenly command that something unaccustomed and unforeseen should be done – even if this is something which at one time you forebade, and however much you may hide for the time being the reason for your command and however much it may run contrary to the convention of any particular human society – no one can doubt that this command of yours must be obeyed; since the only just society of men is the society which does your will" (Augustine 1963: Bk 3, 8–9).

In the preliminary discussion the knight of faith is contrasted with the knight of infinite resignation; but here the contrast is with the tragic hero. Agamemnon, Jephthah, and Brutus actually kill one of their children. But that is not their essential difference from Abraham. That lies rather in the fact that they do not need to go beyond the ethical to find justification for their act. The laws and customs of their people actually require that in the circumstances in which they find themselves, different in each case, they should kill the child. What they have to do is deeply painful, but they at least have the comfort that family, friends, and nation will see that they did the right thing. By contrast, "Abraham is at no time a tragic hero but is something entirely different, either a murderer or a man of faith" (Kierkegaard 1983 57).

This is why the third problem asks whether it was ethically defensible for Abraham not to tell his family what he was up to (Kierkegaard 1983: 82–123). The answer, of course, is no. Since the ethical is the universal, Abraham must explain to his family and to others how what he is doing is right in terms of the criteria they share. This is what the tragic heroes, Agamemnon, Jephthah, and Brutus can do, while Abraham cannot. But within the religious he is justified because his family, here presumed to be limited to the ethical, will in any case be unable to understand him. Of course, this doesn't mean that they couldn't understand the sentence, "I am going to sacrifice

Isaac." It rather means that within their horizons there is no possible justification for such an act. God has not told them that this is to be done.

We can now see Silentio's view of the relation of individual to society. "The paradox of faith, then, is this: that the single individual is higher than the universal, that the single individual … determines his relation to the universal [society] by his relation to the absolute [God], not his relation to the absolute [God] by his relation to the universal [society]. The paradox may also be expressed in this way: that there is an absolute duty to God, for in this relationship of duty the individual relates himself as the single individual absolutely to the absolute" (Kierkegaard 1983: 70).

In an important respect the knight of faith is like the aesthete. Neither is willing to make the laws and customs of his people the highest norm for his existence; both stand outside the circle of *Sittlichkeit*. But there is a double difference in the way the knight of faith does this. First, while the aesthete does this as an absolute individual, the knight of faith does this as an individual before God as absolute. His "individualism" belongs to an ontology as relational as Hegel's, only he does not conflate God with the social order. Second, for the knight of faith the ethical has an authority that it does not have for the aesthete. So immediately after the passage just cited, Silentio insists that the ethical is not nothing from the standpoint of faith. "This ethical relation is reduced to the relative in contradistinction to the absolute relation to God" (Kierkegaard 1983: 70–1).

The difference between the aesthete and the knight of faith can be summed up in the single word 'after'. "Faith is namely this paradox that the single individual is higher than the universal … so that *after* having been in the universal he as the single individual isolates himself as higher than the universal … it is the single individual who *after* being subordinate as the single individual to the universal, now by means of the universal becomes the single individual who as the single individual is superior, that the single individual as the single individual stands in an absolute relation to the absolute" (Kierkegaard 1983: 55–6; emphasis added). To say that it is "by means of the universal" that the individual rises above the universal is to say that the difference between right and wrong is learned in the school that teaches the importance of obedience to parents, to teachers, and to the laws of the land. Only "after" this learning do we possibly learn that God is an even higher authority.

We can summarize as follows:

- For the aesthetic stage the individual as such is absolute.
- For the ethical stage the social order is absolute.
- For the religious stage God is absolute.

These three views of the highest criterion for one's life signify three different views of the relation of individual to society. Like the aesthetic the religious refuses to make the societal universal the highest criterion; but like the ethical it acknowledges that the social order has an authentic authority over the individual. That is why Silentio can present Abraham as filled with anxiety, with fear and trembling. There are two norms to which he feels a genuine obligation. That one is taken to be absolute and the other only relative does not make it a light matter to violate the latter.

Philosophical fragments

Within the biblical narrative and Silentio's reflection about it the answer to the question how Abraham knew he was to sacrifice Isaac is quite simple: God told him so. But this answer and the concept of revelation it implies cry out for reflection. Where faith signifies the individual's response to revelation, the question of faith and reason immediately becomes the question of revelation and reason. Both philosophy and theology, as reflection on the life of faith, need to give an account.

Nine months after *Fear and Trembling* was published, another pseudonym, Johannes Climacus, provided such reflection in *Philosophical Fragments*. Three philosophical theories form important background for his account: First, there is Lessing, about whom he has a good deal to say in his second book, *Concluding Unscientific Postscript*. He starkly opposes reason to revelation. Revelation is presumed to come in the historical narratives of the Bible, but *"accidental truths of history can never become the proof of necessary truths of reason"* (Lessing 1957: 53), and it is the latter domain to which he assigns his moral and metaphysical beliefs. Accordingly, no matter what the historical record may be, he is not prepared "to alter all my fundamental ideas of the nature of the Godhead," in particular to believe "that God has a Son who is of the same essence as himself," which is an idea "against which my reason rebels" (Lessing 1957: 54). Beliefs that are not produced and ratified by reason are simply ruled out of court.

Like Lessing, both Kant and Hegel find it necessary to allude to various Christian beliefs; but unlike Lessing neither is willing simply to deny them. They find a different way to give reason hegemony over faith and its reflective life as theology. In the language of one of Kant's books, they see philosophy's task as providing "religion within the limits of reason alone." This does not mean ignoring or excluding biblical teachings; it rather means that to philosophy is given the task of giving the definitive interpretation of such materials based on a metaphysics and a morality derived from an autonomous human reason. To call reason autonomous in this context means that it develops metaphysical and moral ideas without dependence on theological interpretations for which the grammatical study of Scripture, the historical study of its context, and the traditions of ecclesial interpretation have normative force.

Taking Kant and Hegel as the two primary representatives of German Idealism, we can say that tradition has given us philosophical theologies with two distinctive characteristics: they differ markedly from the theological interpretations over which they claim hegemony, and they differ markedly from each other (which is not surprising given their sharp disagreements about the nature of reason). For Kierkegaard and his pseudonym this will mean that the appeal to reason as the highest criterion for religious belief will evoke the question: Whose reason? Which version? This is an awkward question for Kant and Hegel, both of whom purport to be *the* voice of reason.

In *Fragments* Climacus poses the question of reason and revelation in terms of the difference between recollection and revelation. Following Socrates' account of recollection in the *Meno*, Climacus presents it as the theory that the truth is already in us, that the knower is "sufficient unto himself," and that the teacher can play only a maieutic role, can be "merely an occasion" for learning at best. Like the midwife, the teacher can assist as knowledge comes to life but cannot give that life (Kierkegaard 1985: 9–12). In the dialogue, Socrates helps the slave boy "discover" a version of the Pythagorean theorem, but he is in principle dispensable. The slave boy might well have turned out to be another Pythagoras who could discover this truth for himself.

Climacus then tries a thought experiment. What would we need to have a theory of knowledge that does not turn out to be but a variation on the model of recollection. The revelation model he develops as an alternative can be expressed in a number of theses (Kierkegaard 1985: 13–20).

Thesis I. The moment must have decisive significance. By the moment is meant the learner's encounter with the teacher, and by decisive significance is meant that this cannot be "merely an occasion," in principle replaceable by the learner's own powers.

Thesis II. This means that prior to the moment the learner does not have the truth within, is outside the truth or is in untruth.

Thesis III. This means, again, that the teacher will have to give the learner both the truth and the condition for recognizing it as the truth. For if the learner has the latter, we are back with the Socratic hypothesis. By suggesting what diagram to draw, he effectively gives the slave boy the answer to the geometrical question. What makes him "merely an occasion" is that the slave boy has the condition; he is able to recognize the truth for himself (though he did not produce it for himself) and is not dependent on the authority of his teacher for knowing it to be the truth.

Consider the following example. Suppose I am trying to remember the name of that little girl I had a crush on in second grade. I can't come up with it, but I remember that it began with L. So I Google the list of girls names beginning with L. I pass by Laura and Lee Ann, but when I come to Linda, I say, "Bingo!" When presented with the truth, I am able to recognize it as such. By contrast, suppose I gave you same question and the same list of names. You would be helpless and could only hazard a guess, with emphasis on 'hazard'. To have the truth within oneself is to be able to recognize it as the truth when presented with it, however that presentation comes about.

This example calls our attention to an important point. By placing emphasis on the condition, Climacus expands the concept of recollection beyond its usual restriction to a priori knowledge. It now includes empirical knowledge in those cases where, when presented with the truth, I am able to recognize it as such. This includes wide swaths of common sense knowledge and knowledge in the various sciences. For while we take most of our scientific knowledge on the authority of experts, the idea of science is that we could, in principle, see for ourselves that it is true. The experts are "merely an occasion." The alternative to recollection that Climacus is developing entails that for religiously significant moral and metaphysical knowledge, we do not have the condition and need a teacher who can give us both the truth and the condition to recognize it as such.

What makes Kant and Hegel examples of the recollection theory rather than the revelation theory is that while they are willing to let the Bible and Christian tradition present them with the truth, these are "merely an occasion." They are not dependent on the authority of these sources but are able to see for themselves what the truth is, truth whose warrant in each case is their own particular version of autonomous reason. Where Lessing rejects, they reinterpret.

Thesis IV. The power to give a person the condition for recognizing truth is not a human power. By giving the condition to recognize religiously significant moral and metaphysical truth God creates humans as more than mere animals. The teacher who by giving the condition will be more than "merely an occasion" will have to be God as Creator.

Thesis V. If we are lacking the condition it cannot be because God didn't give it to us, since we would then not be human. Nor could it be an accident. We could lose our mittens that way, but not the condition. If we lack it, it must be our fault. It must be due to sin.

Thesis VI. The teacher who would be more than "merely an occasion" will therefore have to be God as Savior, Deliverer, and Reconciler as well as Creator. The moment, the encounter with this Teacher, will be utterly indispensable.

Thesis VII. The learner will have to be more than a thinker, for the need is to be transformed and not merely informed. The learner will have to be a new person, one who through repentance has experienced conversion and rebirth.

It might well be objected that these deductions do not strictly follow from the original hypothesis that we do not have the truth within us. Climacus will laugh this off, for deductive rigor was not his purpose. It was rather to present a story that embodies an alternative to the Socratic hypothesis, a story he expects his readers to find familiar. So the objection he raises himself (three times: Kierkegaard 1985: 21–2, 35–6, 53–4) is that he has plagiarized the story whose skeleton the theses are. It is the familiar story of Jesus Christ as the God in time who is Teacher and Savior. Climacus readily gives up all claims to have invented the story, offers to give credit to the objector, and surmises that the objector will not only disavow being the author of the story but will insist that no human thinker is the origin of this story. The point is quite simple. Here is a story about the nature and need of revelation as an alternative to the recollection model, and the story itself can only be the product of revelation. It is not a truth that we already have within us, as I had Linda's name within me and needed only to be presented with it. It is rather the "absolute paradox," that which thought cannot think, especially thought that has been wounded by sin (Kierkegaard 1985: 37–48).

"An alternative to the recollection model." Climacus makes no claim to have shown that this story is true. His point is that this story is irreducibly different from every philosophical theology that rests on the recollection model. This means that the *Aufhebung* of this story in the purely rational, speculative philosophies whose norm is an autonomous reason for which this story is "merely an occasion" is a disguised but dangerous assault on the Christian story and not its highest, most insightful version. That is the meaning of the epigraph from Shakespeare with which Climacus prefaces his own Preface: "Better will hanged than ill wed" (Kierkegaard 1985: 3; cf. 274). Better Lessing, who unambiguously rejects Christianity in the name of reason, than Kant and Hegel who present themselves as friends to that faith but only to replace it with something very different.

361

While not purporting to prove the superiority of the revelation model, there is a threefold critique of the recollection model implicit in Climacus' experiment. First, isn't human reason making claims for itself that belie its finitude? Second, isn't it making claims for itself that don't take seriously enough its fallenness, its insistence on being, in the final analysis, independent of God. Finally, isn't there a certain arrogance, a certain begging of the question in its claim to hegemony over religious faith and its theology, whether that claim is blatant or subtle? The recollection model is a rival of the revelation model, and the *Aufhebung* of the latter in the former is perhaps more an act of violence than of insight.

Like Silentio, Climacus calls the "happy passion" in which the learner welcomes revelation faith. But faith's opposite is offense rather than doubt. Climacus would have welcomed the brief discourse to this effect by Anti-Climacus, a later pseudonym (Kierkegaard 1991: 81). The revelation story replaces the autonomy of the recollection story with a heteronomy in which we are dependent on and responsible to someone quite distinct from our personal or social selves. As with Abraham we are expected to trust in promises that go beyond our abilities and to obey commands that go against our agendas. If we do not welcome this story and its God, we will resent them, will be offended. The question is personal, not merely a matter of disinterested theory.

This offense will express itself in the claim that the Christian story is unreasonable. Whether this verdict comes in the blatant form we find in Lessing or in the more subtle form we find in Kant's and Hegel's offers to provide us with a fully rational version of the story, Climacus detects what he calls an acoustic illusion (Kierkegaard 1985: 49–54). Like the ventriloquist whose acoustic illusion consists in making it seems as if the puppet is speaking, so this acoustic illusion consists in making it seem as if the judgment, "Christianity is in conflict with reason" came from autonomous, philosophical reason. But, Climacus counters, it is Christianity that consistently and from the start has insisted that the "wisdom of God" is at odds with "the wisdom of the world" (1 Cor. 1:18–2:16).

He stages a kind of contest between his two models. Given the choice, the recollection model calls itself Reason; Climacus thinks that 'Reason' often signifies the self-congratulatory self-designation of some human, all too human ideology. Without complaint, the revelation model calls itself the Paradox. Then, when Reason says that the Paradox does not conform to Reason, as if this discredited the former, the Paradox replies, "It is just as you say, and the amazing thing is that you think that it is an objection" (Kierkegaard 1985: 52). That the two are deeply at odds with each other has been the claim of the Paradox from the first. Only an acoustic illusion could lead one to think that it was the voice of Reason that first announced this conflict. Once we see this clearly the question arises for each listener whose side to join; but that question is not answered by the fact that the two options are deeply different.

Although he doesn't mention Lessing until his next book, Climacus agrees with him that the Christian story goes beyond historical knowledge, which cannot justify faith, much less create it. For Climacus, historical knowledge is the access human understanding (a version of "Reason") has to human actions, human events, and human consequences. Like Silentio, he thinks that its proper domain is thus that of a double finitude: both of the knowing subject and the known subject matter. It can be called a realm of immanence, for nothing beyond the human intrudes. But the biblical story involves a double transcendence: divine activities and a knowledge (ingredient in faith) that can only be divinely imparted. So Climacus argues at length (Kierkegaard 1985: 55–110) that historical knowledge can neither produce faith nor provide its justification. The knowledge that the eyewitnesses to Jesus' life had is one thing; faith that he is the Son of God and their Savior is another. They have no essential advantage over later generations, whether they be the next generation, who got the story from eyewitnesses, or the generation of Climacus' contemporaries in 1843. The latter have the advantage of knowing the "consequences," the fact that Jesus was not a stone dropped in a pond whose ripples soon enough disappeared but rather a figure of world historical importance. But this knowledge is one thing; faith is another.

Of the five themes that guided our reading of *Fear and Trembling*, the second is the most central here. *Fragments* is a critique of reason, an analysis of the nature and limits of (unaided, autonomous) human understanding that revolves around the possibility, not to be precluded *a priori*, of revelation and faith as a thoroughly different mode of understanding in which transcendence and its corresponding heteronomy trump immanence and autonomy. But this spills over into the first and third themes. Insofar as the overcoming of metaphysics is not the abandonment of metaphysical beliefs but the repudiation of the hegemony of philosophy over the life of faith and its thoughtfulness in theology, that overcoming is a crucial dimension of *Fragments*. Moreover, faith is not merely a matter of cognition but of conversion as well, just as offense is not just a propositional attitude but a personal response. So the third theme enters as well, the primacy of praxis over theory.

Climacus' Preface consists largely of barbs not too subtly directed at Hegel and his followers. So while it is fitting to explore Climacus' relation to the views of reason espoused by Lessing and Kant, it is doubtless Hegel's version that he has primarily in mind. This brings the other two themes into play at least implicitly. If the reason that stands over against faith is an historical and social version of human understanding two consequences follow. Faith's claim to put the individual in touch with that which transcends history as merely human action and understanding has a bearing on the question of historical relativism. In the same manner it claims to elevate the individual above the social order as did the faith of Abraham. The learner becomes a believer or follower when "the understanding is discharged and he receives the condition. When does he receive this? In the moment. This condition, what does it condition? His understanding of the eternal" (Kierkegaard 1985 64). In the Christian story that concerns Climacus, the eternal has manifested itself as a person in time. But neither ontologically nor epistemologically is the God in time merely a matter of history and its societies.

Concluding unscientific postscript

The full title of Climacus' second book is *Concluding Unscientific Postscript to Philosophical Fragments*. Both titles are satires on Hegel. Whereas he insists that philosophy must be a system and that "The True is the whole" (Hegel 1977: 11), Climacus offers only fragments, or tidbits, as the term might also be translated; and whereas Hegel insists that the system must attain the status of science, Climacus offers an unscientific postscript to some tidbits. The irony is enhanced by the fact that the tidbits take up only a little over a hundred pages (in translation), while the postscript is five and a half times as long – a very big book. There will be much going on in *Postscript* that cannot be presented here, but that is already true of the much shorter texts we've already considered.

The two parts of *Postscript* are devoted, respectively, to objectivity and subjectivity in relation to Christian faith. We get an idea of what concerns Climacus from the table of contents, where we find that the part devoted to subjectivity is fifteen times longer than the part devoted to objectivity! The objective question is whether the truth of Christianity can be verified by historical knowledge or philosophical speculation, both of which purport to give objective knowledge, knowledge attained by the disinterested observer whose work is not conditioned by personal or communal presuppositions and is thus universally valid.

Climacus makes two points here. First, with regard to historical knowledge he insists that it never provides more than an approximation of the truth; it is never finished, but always subject to revision and reworking in the light of new materials and new perspectives. In view of his later claim that the system, too, remains unfinished (Kierkegaard 1992: 106–8), this point applies to speculative objectivity as well. Climacus' position is like that of the philosophical hermeneutics of Hans-Georg Gadamer and Paul Ricoeur in holding that knowledge is interpretation and that interpretation is never either presuppositionless or beyond the need for further revision.

Second, and this point is directed especially at the speculative point of view, which means Hegel above all, Climacus argues that a purely objective approach to Christianity rests on a misunderstanding of what it is. It is the promise of one's own eternal happiness, and to be a disinterested spectator in the face of such a possibility is to confuse its possible truth with truth of a wholly different kind, thereby becoming comical. Only as one with an "infinite, personal, passionate interest" can one engage with Christianity; "Christianity cannot be observed objectively, precisely because it wants to lead the subject to the ultimate point of his subjectivity, and when the subject is thus properly positioned, he cannot tie his eternal happiness to speculative thought" (Kierkegaard 1992: 55–7).

Implicit in the strong contrast between objectivity and subjectivity is a revision of the theory of the stages.

Objectivity	Subjectivity
the aesthetic	the ethical
the speculative	the religious

On this model the speculative joins the aesthetic as a mode of being-in-the-world that effectively eliminates right and wrong, good and evil, as criteria for one's life. More generally, it eliminates the self's relation to itself as more than a matter of the moment (the aesthetic) or a blip on the screen of world history (the speculative). "The speculative thinker ... has become too objective to talk [or think] about himself" (Kierkegaard 1992: 51). Accordingly Climacus devotes a long discussion to the way in which the ethical and religious get ignored and effectively trivialized when the speculative project in a distinctively Hegelian mode, namely the philosophy of world history, becomes the highest task (Kierkegaard 1992: 129–88). Such questions as – What does it mean to die?, What does it mean to be immortal?, What does it mean to pray?, and What does it mean to thank God for the good I have received? – don't even get asked. What makes Climacus an existentialist is not merely the fact that he uses the term 'existence' as a technical term signifying human existence but primarily that he defines the latter in terms of questions like these. To be an ethically and religiously responsible self is not only the highest task I can have (and surely it is the task of a lifetime) but that without which I am not really a human self at all. Selfhood is not a biological, psychological, and sociological *fait accompli*, but an ethical and religious task that is shirked by the aesthete and the speculative thinker.

So Climacus writes, "I, Johannes Climacus, am neither more nor less than a human being; and I assume that the one with whom I have the honor of conversing is also a human being. If he wants to be speculative thought, pure speculative thought, I must give up conversing with him, because at that moment he becomes invisible to me and to the weak mortal eye of a human being" (Kierkegaard 1992: 109).

The very next sentence, set off from what goes before for emphasis reads

> Consequently, *(a) a logical system can be given; (b) but a system of existence* [*Tilværelsens System*] *cannot be given.*

This statement is qualified by the immediately preceding admission by Climacus that he is not speculative thought incarnate but merely a human being. It would be different if he were God. "Existence itself is a system – for God. But it cannot be a system for any existing [*existerende*] spirit. System and conclusiveness correspond to each other, but existence is the very opposite" (Kierkegaard 1992: 118). In a very Kantian voice, Climacus takes the difference between divine and human knowledge to be fundamental. In accusing the Hegelian philosopher of confusing himself with speculative thought he is accusing him of confusing himself with God whose all-inclusive vision makes a conclusive system possible.

Just before denying that a system of existence is possible for a human knower, Climacus satirizes the admission by some speculative thinkers that the system isn't quite finished yet (Kierkegaard 1992: 106–8). But then it wouldn't be a system, would it? For it would have left something out and might better be called a fragment! But now he says, in effect, "Let us suppose that the system is finished to some human being's satisfaction, perhaps with great public acclaim. What would we have?" An abstract, formal conceptual scheme that gives us no specific knowledge about anything. It will be like mathematics, which can tell us that two plus two equals four but not whether there are two bananas or four monkeys anywhere to be found. Not only can it not give us any factual knowledge; it cannot tell us how we should live our lives, which is the most pressing question for thought to wrestle with.

We can read 'existence' here in both a weak and a strong sense. In the weak sense, a logical system or categorial scheme cannot give us any specific knowledge about bananas or monkeys or any aspect of the world. In the strong sense that primarily concerns Climacus, it cannot tell us anything about what it means to be a human being, what my highest task is, and where my highest happiness can be found. For existence (in both senses) is temporal, and therefore open ended. Both the world's story and my own are unfinished. Neither can be fit without remainder into the Procrustean bed of any system.

Were he writing today, Climacus would be targeting the "systems" of the natural and social sciences. Empirically based, they can and do tell us a lot about existence in the weak sense, even if no scientific research can claim to be the final word on its subject matter. But the sciences become reductionist and dehumanizing whenever their practitioners suggest that they can answer the deepest questions about who I am and how I should live.

These questions do not get asked and cannot be answered from the standpoint of the detached, objective observer, but only from the standpoint of "infinite, personal, passionate, interest." To ask these questions from this standpoint is what Climacus means by subjectivity. But this means that my reflection is about me and that any answers I may come up with are to be put into practice until I find better answers. So Climacus famously says, "Truth is subjectivity" (Kierkegaard 1992: 189; for detailed commentary, Westphal 1996). So as not to misunderstand him, we must pay close attention to the following about the truth that is "essentially related to [my] existence."

> When the question about truth is asked objectively, truth is reflected upon objectively as an object to which the knower relates himself. What is reflected upon is not the relation but that what he relates himself to is the truth, the true. If only that to which he relates himself is the truth, the true, then the subject is in the truth. When the question about truth is asked subjectively, the individual's relation is reflected upon subjectively. If only the how of this relation is in truth the individual is in truth, even if he in this way were to relate himself to untruth. (Kierkegaard 1992: 199)

It is important to notice what Climacus does not do here. He does not eliminate the question of objective truth, about which he commented briefly at the beginning of his big book. Nor does he suggest that it is unimportant. Nor does he suggest that the question of objective truth is to be settled subjectively. This is not an "anything goes" or "different strokes for different folks" theory of truth. He thinks I can get it wrong, and that the "what" of my belief may be "untruth." There are two distinct issues here, the "what" issue and the "how" issue. The first issue concerns whether I have the right or wrong answer to the question at issue; the second issue concerns whether I am rightly related to that answer, whether it is right or wrong.

Climacus tells a parable to make his point. He is writing to an audience that takes the Christian idea of God to be the true one.

> If someone who lives in the midst of Christianity enters, with knowledge of the true idea of God, the house of God, the house of the true God, and prays, but prays in untruth, and if someone lives in an idolatrous land but prays with all the passion of infinity, although his eyes are resting upon the image of an idol – where, then is there more truth? The one prays in truth to God although he is worshiping an idol; the other prays in untruth to the true God and is therefore in truth worshiping an idol. (Kierkegaard 1992: 201)

The word 'more' is key here, and Climacus also uses it in the paragraphs immediately surrounding his parable. Both believers have a defect. One has the wrong "how" and one has the wrong "what." Relatively speaking, who is better off? Who is worse off? Who has "more truth?" Climacus leaves this as a rhetorical question, but he does tip his hand. While he doesn't say that the pagan's right "how" is able to correct his wrong "what," he does say that the Christian's wrong "how" is able to destroy his right "what." Both, it turns out, are praying to an idol. It is perhaps no fault of the pagan that he prays to the wrong God, just as it is no credit to the Christian that he prays to the right one. Each is doing what he has been taught. But it is a credit to the pagan that he prays in truth subjectively, and it is a fault of the Christian that he does not.

Climacus offers Socrates as an example of the subjective thinker. Apparently referring to Plato's *Apology* (40c–41b), where Socrates is most emphatic about his ignorance, his relation to the possibility of immortality is best expressed indefinitely – "if there is an immortality." Socrates pretends to no objective certainty about the matter. But he "stakes his whole life on this 'if': he dares to die, and with the passion of the infinite he has so ordered his whole life that it might be acceptable – *if* there is an immortality" (Kierkegaard 1992: 201). He does not have the faith in the resurrection that the Christian has, but he poses the question with an "infinite, personal, passionate interest," and he lets his life be transformed by what he takes to be the best answer.

The account of truth as subjectivity culminates in the following definition of truth: "An *objective uncertainty, held fast through appropriation with the most passionate inwardness, is the truth*, the highest truth there is for an *existing* person" (Kierkegaard 1992: 203). It is the highest truth because (a) it is more important than any truth I may have that does not relate essentially to my existence, even if the later has a higher degree of objective certainty, and (b) in the domain of the truth that really matters, it is the best that is available to us. Kant thinks that when reason aspires to go beyond finitude and to achieve totality it falls into illusion. Climacus thinks the danger to be even greater. When speculative philosophy tries to ascend, Icarus like, beyond its actual powers, it melts and instead of becoming the loftiest it becomes tragi-comically lowly and descends to a sub-human form of life.

Climacus adds that this definition of truth is "a paraphrasing of faith." Faith may have a high degree of subjective certitude, that is, the absence of doubt. But it remains objectively uncertain. It does not have the guarantees of impersonal, disinterested, universally recognized knowledge, the kind of certainty Descartes bequeathed to modernity as a demand if not as a reality. That is why Climacus uses the language of risk, decision, dare, and leap to talk about faith, and why he describes the believer, whatever the belief, as "out on 70,000 fathoms of water" (Kierkegaard 1992: 204).

The contrast between faith and the speculative system in *Postscript* closely parallels the contrast between revelation and recollection in *Fragments*. But Socrates plays very different roles in the two books. In the first, he is the villain, so far as faith is concerned, the perpetrator of the recollection model in terms of which philosophy elevates itself above the life of faith and colonizes theology in the process. But in *Postscript* he is regularly the hero, the paradigm of the subjective thinker.

It is good to keep him in mind when we turn to Climacus' final contribution to the theory of the religious stage, his contrast between Religiousness A and Religiousness B. The latter is Christianity as presented in *Fragments*, the religion of paradox, in tension with any reason that is not itself informed by revelation. The former is religion that stays within the horizons of recollection but in the subjective rather than in the speculative mode. It is the kind of religion we might find in Socrates who, without the benefit of biblical revelation nevertheless relates to the Eternal with an "infinite, personal, passionate, interest," and who "appropriates" or applies objectively uncertain ideas to his own life "with the most passionate inwardness."

Religiousness A is a long, phenomenological description of this passion or pathos, six and a half times the length of the discussion of Religiousness B. It could be read as an alternative to Christianity, as religion within the limits of reason alone. But it is better read, not as another species of religion, but as a genus, to which specific religions belong. It is a formal account of the horizon outside of which what purports to be religion is actually something else. Thus, when Climacus says that to enter into Religiousness B, which is Christianity, "one must first of all exist in Religiousness A" (Kierkegaard 1992: 557), this 'first' does not signify a temporal, developmental priority but a logical priority. A is a necessary condition for B in the sense that if A is absent, B cannot be present. Here is another version of an earlier critique of Christendom and Hegelian speculation: if you haven't even gotten as far as Religiousness A, the formal presupposition of Christianity, you certainly haven't gotten to Christianity, much less "gone beyond" it (Kierkegaard 1992: 361, 370–1, 466). "But if Christianity is perhaps in the wrong, this much is certain: speculative thought is definitely in the wrong, because the only consistency outside Christianity is that of pantheism, the taking of oneself out of existence back into the eternal through recollection" (Kierkegaard 1992: 226). Claiming to be the highest expression of Christianity, Hegelian speculative fails to see that it is antithetical to Christianity.

For Climacus faith is a passion or "existential pathos," not merely the propositional attitude of cognitive assent. The "initial expression" of this passion is the respectful orientation toward the Absolute τέλος, the acceptance of the task "*Simultaneously to Relate Oneself Absolutely to One's Absolute τέλος and Relatively to Relative Ends*" (Kierkegaard 1992: 387). This involves the "renunciation," "surrender" or "resignation" of all finite and relative goods for the sake of eternal happiness, the absolute goal for both Socrates and the Christian. Here again we have an *Aufhebung*, a teleological suspension; for the finite is not to be abandoned but subordinated to what is higher. While relating absolutely to the absolute, I am to relate relatively to the relative. Silentio's Abraham would understand this. Like the knight of infinite resignation he was willing to renounce and surrender the relative for the absolute, which to him was the will of God. But he was no Stoic who systematically dismantled all attachments to the finite. So "the finite tastes just as good to him as to one who never knew anything higher" and his faith makes him "delight in it as if finitude were the surest thing of all." He is the "heir of the finite, while the knight of infinite resignation is a stranger and an alien" (Kierkegaard 1983: 40, 50).

Our immediate position, the default setting as it were, before we respond to the call of the ethical and the religious, is to be absolutely committed to relative ends. The infant is absolutely committed to a full tummy and a dry bottom. So entering into Religiousness A involves the strenuous task "*Dying to Immediacy and Yet Remaining in the Finite.*" Since this is painful, the essential expression of existential pathos is suffering (Kierkegaard 1992: 431). This is not an accidental suffering as if it were some kind of misfortune that might or might not strike. It is rather, as just stated, essential to this existence sphere. But the mediation that moves beyond this immediacy is not that of speculative thought, the move from sensual immediacy to conceptual comprehension. By failing to recognize the "chasmic abyss ... between the *absolute τέλος* and relative ends" and pretending to be the highest truth of the religious it is "forgery by sloth" (Kierkegaard 1992: 409, 396). It flees from the painful strenuousness of the task by assuming that in bourgeois respectability and higher education it has already been accomplished. Once again it confuses the current social order with the Eternal.

If the initial expression of existential pathos is resignation and the essential expression is suffering, "*The* Decisive *Expression of Existential Pathos is* Guilt" (Kierkegaard 1992: 525). This is simply the recognition that the task, the highest task for a human being, is always unfulfilled. As Silentio would put it, it is the task of a lifetime, and the conflict with immediacy is never completely won.

Religiousness A might be the religion of Socrates, especially if one emphasizes the famous Socratic ignorance and irony. The ignorance he professes at his trial means that he does not profess to have that direct intuition of the Eternal, the realm of the Forms, to which Plato will aspire; for him recollection is a task word and not an achievement word. It is Plato, not Socrates, who "loses himself in speculative thought" (Kierkegaard 1992: 205). Socratic irony is the critique that punctures the balloons of any social order, most particularly his own, that confuses itself with the Eternal, taking its norms and its welfare to be the *absolute τέλος* that is the highest task for each individual. His motto might read: to be a good Athenian one must be more than a good Athenian.

Christianity, as Religiousness B, differs from Religiousness A in two ways. First, it is more specific. Whereas A leaves the Eternal quite undefined and indeterminate, Christianity not only defines the Eternal as God but as the God in time, God incarnate in Jesus Christ. Moreover, it makes one's eternal happiness conditioned on one's relation in time to the God in time. Herein lies the second difference. The generic openness of Religiousness A makes it an easy fit for a reason that recognizes the finitude of its powers of recollection. But the specific determinacy of Christianity puts it at odds with reason just as it did in *Fragments*. Here faith involves a "crucifixion of the understanding" (Kierkegaard 1992: 564). The traditional formula is that faith goes "beyond" understanding, but Climacus insists that it goes "against the understanding."

> Consequently the believing Christian both has and uses his understanding, respects the universally human, does not explain someone's not becoming a Christian as a lack of understanding, but … here uses the understanding – in order to see to it that he believes against the understanding. Therefore he cannot believe nonsense against the understanding, which one might fear, because the understanding will penetratingly perceive that it is nonsense and hinder him in believing it, but he uses the understanding so much that through it he becomes aware of the incomprehensible, and now, believing, he relates himself to it against the understanding. (Kierkegaard 1992: 568)

If the content of Religiousness B is not nonsense but only incomprehensible in the sense that recollection could never produce it or penetrate it, how is this against reason? It is against reason if, and to the degree, that philosophy makes the claim that (as with Kant) it can provide us with all we really need for the moral and religious life or (as with Hegel) tells us that it can translate Christian theology in such a way that all mystery is eliminated (Westphal 2004: 80–5). As in *Fragments*, Climacus is not concerned to argue for the truth of Christianity but for its irreconcilable difference from German idealism, especially in its Hegelian form.

Returning to the themes that have been our guide, it is clear that the central one in *Postscript* is the third, the primacy of praxis over theory. There is an overcoming of metaphysics and thus a critique of reason in its speculative mode insofar as its professed hegemony over the life of faith rests on a misunderstanding both of its own finitude (as unfinished, as approximation) and of the religious life. It is the second misunderstanding that takes us to our third theme, for Hegelian speculation fails to understand that religion in general and Christianity in particular is not simply a theory in the domain of objectivity but an existence communication in the domain of subjectivity. The constantly recurring term is 'task'. The religious existence sphere is about selfhood as a task involving decision, dare, and risk. (Nor is the risk merely cognitive. For the meaning of my life and its destiny are at stake.) It is about the "how" – that is the appropriation of what one believes to one's life in infinite passion and interest. It is about how one relates to oneself in relating to one's ends as either absolutely or relatively important. In learning to treat relative ends as only relative and not absolute, it involves resignation, suffering, and guilt. It involves the deepest roots of my existence, not merely my beliefs.

Works of love

The reader of *Postscript* will notice that 'ethics' does not have the same significance there that it had in *Either/Or* and *Fear and Trembling*. In those works the task was to distinguish the ethical and religious stages, while Climacus seeks to remind us that the religious stage has an indispensable ethical dimension, as if the two need to be hyphenated together: ethico-religious. As we have seen, the essential contrast is between objectivity and subjectivity, the pre-ethical domains and those where the right and the good (as opposed to wrong and evil) are dominant. So to be in the religious sphere is to have "passed through the ethical," whereas the speculative involves the loss of both the ethical and the religious and thereby the "*eternal*" (Kierkegaard 1992: 388, 307). Passing through the ethical does not mean getting there first and then leaving it behind. Once again the relation is logical; the ethical is a necessary condition of the religious or, in other words, there can be no right relation with God apart from a right relation with one's fellow humans.

While Climacus talks a lot about the ethical, he gives us no ethics. For him the knight of faith becomes the knight of hidden inwardness. Subjectivity is portrayed as the secret, personal transactions between the individual and the eternal (the soul and God). This emphasis is so strong that public behavior in the family, civil society, and the state seems to fall off the radar screen. Nor can we go back to *Fear and Trembling* to find a Kierkegaardian ethics. All we learn there is that the norms of our society have an important but not unconditional authority over our lives. But what the religious norms are that would trump the *Sittlichkeit* into which we find ourselves thrown we are not told. There is no suggestion that it consists in the practice of child sacrifice.

Kierkegaard was aware of this lacuna, and in the year after he published *Postscript* he published *Works of Love* in his own name. He writes in his journals.

> Despite everything people ought to have learned about my maieutic carefulness, by proceeding slowly and continually letting it seem as if I knew nothing more ... now ... they will probably bawl out that I do not know what comes next, that I know nothing about sociality.

What they fail to understand is

> that continually when I have first presented one aspect clearly and sharply, then the other affirms itself even more strongly.
>> Now I have my theme of the next book. It will be called
>> Works of Love. (Kierkegaard 1995: 409)

It is here that we find the most complete statement of the outward, ethical flip side of the religion of hidden inwardness.

It is unabashedly theistic, for its core is the divine command, "You shall love your neighbor as yourself" (Lev. 19:18). It is also overtly Christocentric, for not only does Jesus repeat this commandment from the Hebrew scriptures in his own twofold summary of the law (Matt. 22: 34–40; Mark 12:28–34; Luke 10:25–28), but he is presented as a model to be imitated. We have here a transition from Religiousness B to what we might call Religiousness C. In the former, Climacus presents Christ as the Paradox to be believed, beyond and thereby against any version of reason that reduces to recollection and claims ultimate authority. But in *Works of Love* and such subsequent works as *Practice in Christianity*, *For Self-Examination*, and *Judge for Yourself!*, Christ is presented as the Pattern, Prototype, and Paradigm to be imitated (Westphal 1992, 1996: 194–200).

This ethics will continue the contrast between revelation and recollection. Neither the God who commands neighbor love nor the Christ who reaffirms and embodies it are presented as "merely an occasion" for us to recollect what we already know. It turns out that the enemy is also the neighbor, whom we are to love as we love ourselves. Kierkegaard knows no pure practical reason (Kant) that will recollect this inconvenient obligation, nor any *Sittlichkeit* (Hegel) that will make civic respectability dependent on loving the enemy. It is revelation that teaches us that we owe this love to the enemy because "God has created him and Christ has redeemed him" (Kierkegaard 1995 67–9).

Moreover, we do not have within ourselves the ability to fulfill this commandment.

> How could one speak properly about love if you were forgotten, you God of love, source of all love ... so that one who loves is what he is only by being in you! ... Just as the quiet lake originates deep down in hidden springs no eye has seen, so also does a person's love originate even more deeply in God's love. If there were no gushing spring at the bottom, if God were not love, then there would be neither the little lake nor a human being's love ... a human being's love originates mysteriously in God's love. (Kierkegaard 1995: 3, 9–10)

Just as in *Fragments* our cognitive limitations are overcome when God gives the condition for recognizing the truth, so here our moral limitations are overcome when we are enabled to love by being in God, hooked up to the spring of divine love.

Of course it is not every kind of human love that can and needs to be spoken of in this way. Neighbor love (*agape*) is to be sharply distinguished from erotic love (*eros*) and from friendship (*philia*). Kierkegaard calls the first of these commanded love, the latter two celebrated love, since the poets love them and sing in their honor.

The two modes of celebrated love share three marks. First, they are spontaneous. We do not have to learn or be taught to seek out those who will be our friends or lovers. When we reach a certain level of development it just comes naturally, whether we are wise or foolish in our choices and whether or not our affection is reciprocated.

Second, celebrated love is preferential. We choose this one rather than that one because we find this one attractive to us, personally, socially, sexually. Third, it is especially for this reason that Kierkegaard describes celebrated love repeatedly as self-love, selfishness, self-willfulness, even self-deification. It is not because I am selfish in my relation to my friend or my beloved. It is rather because they would not be my friend or my beloved if I did not find them attractive, if they did not satisfy some need or desire of my own.

By contrast neighbor love is described as self-denial, self-renunciation and self-sacrifice. This may sound as if there is no room for self-love, but that is not the case. Here again we have a teleological suspension, one in which self-love is not abolished but put in its proper place, which is not the absolute or the highest. It is broken and dethroned, but also opened and transformed. There is such a thing as proper self-love, and the flip side of the command to love one's neighbor is

> *You shall love yourself in the right way* ... To love yourself in the right way and to love the neighbor correspond perfectly to one another ... When the Law's *as yourself* has wrested from you the self-love that Christianity sadly enough must presuppose to be in every human being, then you have actually learned to love yourself. The Law is therefore: You shall love yourself in the same way as you love your neighbor when you love him as yourself. (Kierkegaard 1995: 22–3; cf. 17–18, 45, 112)

This decentering of self-love undermines the preferential character of love. "To be able to love a person despite his weaknesses and defects and imperfections is still not perfect love, but rather this, to be able to find him lovable despite and with his weaknesses and defects and imperfections" (Kierkegaard 1995: 157–8). When we remember that the enemy is also the neighbor whom we are to love as we love ourselves, it will be sufficiently obvious that this love is not spontaneous.

This ethics, accordingly, does not have its basis in human understanding. "Humanly speaking" or from a "merely human" point of view this command is "madness" or "foolishness"; to the "natural man it is an offense." Its only basis is "divine authority" (Kierkegaard 1995: 42, 57–9, 97,108–9, 113–15, 121, 199). For this reason God is the middle term between self and neighbor (Kierkegaard 1995: 57–8, 108, 140–3). Only if we are related to God in a certain way will it occur to us to relate to our neighbors in this way, will we find ourselves categorically obligated to do so, will we be enabled in some degree to do so. Following Jesus' summary of the Jewish Torah as *first* to love God with all our heart and *then* to love our neighbor as ourselves (see reference above), Kierkegaard insists that the God relation comes first and only then all human relations on the basis of the former (Kierkegaard 1995: 108, 140–3).

Kierkegaard expresses this with a visual image. "Shut your door and pray to God – because God is surely the highest." Here we have the religion of hidden inwardness, not because the religious life involves no external, observable actions but because without an inner relation to God in and from the heart such actions are but pretense, hypocrisy, and, most importantly, self-deception. But hidden inwardness is not self sufficient. So "when you open the door that you shut in order to pray to God and go out the very first person you meet is the neighbor, whom you *shall* love" (Kierkegaard 1955: 51).

The engagement with Kant and Hegel is perhaps less direct here than in our earlier texts, but it is still present. This ethic is Kantian in two ways. It belongs to a larger frame of reference in which practice has a primacy over theory, and it revolves around a categorical imperative that obligates unconditionally and infinitely. The obligation is unconditional in that it is binding regardless of my desires and inclinations; and it is infinite in the sense that I can never say I have completed the task assigned. But this ethic is anti-Kantian in that it rests on revelation rather than recollection, on divine authority rather than on the self-legislation of pure practical reason. Whereas Kant draws a sharp distinction in his theoretical philosophy between the human and divine perspectives on matters of fact, physical and metaphysical, that distinction disappears when it comes to practical philosophy, the realm of norms for human behavior. Kierkegaard asks whether a philosophy of reason's finitude might not be as much needed in the latter sphere as in the former. He could also be read as hinting at plagiarism in Kant, taking ideas that his pietist upbringing inherited from biblical revelation and trying to attribute them to autonomous human understanding.

So far as Hegel is concerned, the argument can be read as an extension of *Fear and Trembling*. The unanswered question of what an ethics of biblical faith would look like is answered and in such a way as to reinforce the negative conclusion inherent in Silentio's analysis of faith, namely that the laws and customs of my society are not the highest norms for my moral life. Friendship and erotic love may find their warrant in just about any *Sittlichkeit*, but neighbor love as explicated in *Works of Love* is not to be found in any. By referring to the poets who celebrate friendship and erotic love rather than the politicians, Kierkegaard is only reminding us that culture is as important as society, that ideology is but the other face of institutions.

Kierkegaard doesn't try to prove the superiority of biblical faith to the philosophies of German idealism. But through his pseudonyms and in his own name he highlights the deep differences between them, calling on his reader to employ sufficient intellectual rigor to keep the conceptual oppositions clearly in view and to practice sufficient existential responsibility to choose between them or, perhaps, among other alternatives. Absent the kind of objective guarantees and demonstrations that various forms of reason promise but cannot deliver, he hopes that his reader will recognize that any choice will involve a leap beyond the comfort zone of objective certainty. It will be an act of faith.

Critiques of Kierkegaard

A familiar critique of Kierkegaard is that he is an irrationalist. It is undeniable that he insists that the kind of religious faith that interests him does not merely go beyond reason (or understanding, he doesn't distinguish) but against it. What needs to be noticed is that he doubly qualifies what is meant by reason. On the one hand, it is human reason, a finite capacity whose right to be the ultimate criterion of what God can do or say is not self evident. The Enlightenment claim that reason (unaided human thought) has hegemony over faith (as a response to divine revelation) appears to him just as dogmatic as the theologies it seeks to colonize in various ways.

Second, those various ways betray that the Enlightenment claim to universality for reason is a myth. "Reason" comes in different denominations just as does faith. Thus, for example, religion within the limits of reason alone (the name of an Enlightenment project and not just of a book by Kant) turns out to be quite different when carried out by, say, Spinoza, or Kant, or Hegel. Kierkegaard calls attention to the particular and historically relative nature of "reason" by satirical references to the present age, the new era, the System in a manner that is quite similar to Marx's theory of "reason" as ideology. Kierkegaard, in company with many thinkers in the nineteenth and twentieth centuries, both religious and secular, challenges the notion that reason is or can be pure, universally free from presuppositions and culturally contingent traditions. This does not mean that Kierkegaard's Christian theism is justified, only that noticing the opposition between it and various world views that call themselves "reason" is not an argument in favor of the latter.

Another familiar criticism of Kierkegaard is that he is too individualistic, that he places so much emphasis on subjectivity that he leaves no room for intersubjectivity, that he is an insufficiently social philosopher. There are several things to notice here.

First, it is undeniably true that some of Kierkegaard's writings focus all but entirely on the relation between the individual and God in "hidden inwardness."

Second, this needs to be seen in a context in which the social, the political, and the historical are seen by Kierkegaard to be dangerously overemphasized, especially in Hegelian thought. He seeks to swing the pendulum back toward the responsibility of individuals for their own existence.

Third, this critique tends not to take into account *Works of Love*, where an ethic of self-sacrificial love is developed on the basis of the individual's relation to God, who commands and enables neighbor love. This text has been the subject of much long overdue attention in recent years.

Finally, it remains the case that while Kierkegaard's writings express thoughts about the social order from time to time, there is no sustained and comprehensive social or political philosophy. Perhaps one could develop such a philosophy on Kierkegaardian grounds, but he does not do that for us.

A third challenge to Kierkegaard's thought as presented here is not so much a critique as a reinterpretation. Some recent readings, in the spirit of deconstruction, suggest that Kierkegaard has no positive philosophy or world view to present but rather shows how positive claims cancel themselves out by making his own thought self-de(con)structive. Kierkegaard is surely concerned about the problematics of affirmation and communication. But that is not because he has nothing to put forward but rather because he is aware of the counter-cultural nature of the Christian theism he wants to affirm and communicate.

References

Augustine (1963) *The Confessions of St Augustine*, trans. R. Warner, New York: New American Library.

Berger, P., and T. Luckmann (1966) *The Social Construction of Reality: A Treatise in the Sociology of Knowledge*, New York: Doubleday.

Collins, J. (1983) *The Mind of Kierkegaard*, Princeton, NJ: Princeton University Press.

Dilthey, W. (1996) "Reminiscences on Historical Studies at the University of Berlin," *Hermeneutics and the Study of History*, vol. 4 of *Selected Works*, Princeton, NJ: Princeton University Press.

Hannay, A. (2001) *Kierkegaard: a biography*, New York: Cambridge University Press.

Hegel, G. (1945) *Hegel's Philosophy of Right*, trans. T. Knox, Oxford: Clarendon Press.

—— (1977) *Phenomenology of Spirit*, trans. J. Findlay, Oxford: Clarendon Press.

—— (1991) *The Encyclopedia Logic*, trans. T. Geraets, W. Suchting, and H. Harris, Indianapolis, IN: Hackett.

Heidegger, M. (1969) *Identity and Difference*, trans. J. Stambaugh, New York: Harper & Row.

Kierkegaard, S. (1983) *Fear and Trembling/Repetition*, trans. Howard V. Hong and Edna H. Hong, Princeton, NJ: Princeton University Press.

—— (1985) *Philosophical Fragments/Johannes Climacus*, trans. Howard V. Hong and Edna H. Hong, Princeton, NJ: Princeton University Press.

—— (1987) *Either/Or*, pt 2, trans. Howard V. Hong and Edna H. Hong, Princeton, NJ: Princeton University Press.

—— (1991) *Practice in Christianity*, trans. Howard V. Hong and Edna H. Hong, Princeton, NJ: Princeton University Press.

—— (1992) *Concluding Unscientific Postscript*, vol. 1, trans. Howard V. Hong and Edna H. Hong, Princeton, NJ: Princeton University Press.

—— (1995) *Works of Love*, trans. Howard V. Hong and Edna H. Hong, Princeton, NJ: Princeton University Press.

—— (1998) *Point of View*, trans. Howard V. Hong and Edna H. Hong, Princeton, NJ: Princeton University Press.

Lessing, G. (1957) *Lessing's Theological Writings*, trans. H. Chadwick, Stanford: Stanford University Press.

Westphal, M. (1968) "In Defense of the Thing in Itself," *Kant-Studien*, 59, no. 1: 118–41.

—— (1992) "Kierkegaard's Teleological Suspension of Religiousness B," in G. Connell and C. Evans (eds) *Foundations of Kierkegaard's Vision of Community: Religion, Ethics, and Politics in Kierkegaard*, Atlantic Highlands, NJ: Humanities Press.

—— (1996) *Becoming a Self: A Reading of Kierkegaard's* Concluding Unscientific Postscript, West Lafayette, IN: Purdue University Press.

—— (1998) *History and Truth in Hegel's Phenomenology*, 3rd edn, Bloomington, IN: Indiana University Press.

—— (2004) *Transcendence and Self-transcendence: On God and the Soul*, Bloomington, IN: Indiana University Press.

Further reading

W. Desmond, *Hegel's God: A Counterfeit Double?* (Burlington: Ashgate, 2003), offers an interpretation Kierkegaard would appreciate. C. Evans, *Passionate Reason: Making Sense of Kierkegaard's* Philosophical Fragments (Bloomington, IN: Indiana University Press, 1992), gives a detailed analysis of the philosophical issues raised by this text. See, too, Evans, *Kierkegaard's Ethic of Love: Divine Commands and Moral Obligations* (New York: Oxford University Press, 2004), a reading of *Works of Love* with special attention to the issues involved in a divine command ethics, and *Kierkegaard on Faith and the Self* (Waco: Baylor University Press, 2006), a rich collection of essays on a wide variety of issues in Kierkegaard's work. A detailed and illuminating analysis with special attention to Levinas can be found in J. Ferreira, *Love's Grateful Striving: A commentary on Kierkegaard's* Works of Love (New York: Oxford University Press, 2001). J. Hare, *The Moral Gap: Kantian Ethics, Human Limits, and God's Assistance* (Oxford: Clarendon Press, 1996) is a carefully argued analysis of the relation between Kant's ethics and his theology. Arguments against reading Kierkegaard as an irrationalist and a radical individualist can be found in M. Westphal, *Kierkegaard's Critique of Reason and Society* (Macon: Mercer University Press, 1987), and the essays in Westphal's *Levinas and Kierkegaard in Dialogue* (Bloomington, IN: Indiana University Press, 2008) explore the convergences and divergences between Kierkegaard and Emmanuel Levinas.

13

NIETZSCHE

Ken Gemes and Chris Sykes

Introduction

Placing Nietzsche in the context of nineteenth-century philosophy is difficult for several major and interrelated reasons. First, Nietzsche was not a conventional philosopher. Not only was he not trained as a philosopher – his doctorate and his first and only academic position, at the University of Basel, were in philology. More importantly, he had little time for philosophy as an academic discipline; he eschewed many of its principal concerns such as metaphysics and epistemology. Even moral philosophy, especially as practised in the Anglo-American context, is far from Nietzsche's central concerns – after all, how many moral philosophers are concerned with nihilism and the affirmation of life, arguably Nietzsche's central concerns? Nietzsche was more inclined to diagnose why one would take metaphysics and epistemology seriously than to actually seek answers to the questions typically raised by metaphysicians and epistemologists. Thus he often characterized himself first and foremost as a psychologist rather than a philosopher; in *Ecce Homo* Nietzsche says "[t]hat a psychologist without equal speaks from my writings is perhaps the first insight reached by a good reader" (*Ecce Homo, EH:* "Why I Write Such Good Books," 5). Second, against the trend of nineteenth-century optimism Nietzsche rejected many of the central tenets of Enlightenment thought (the value of reason, the value of science, the value of truth, the inevitability of progress). Indeed, to a certain extent (which we shall examine later), Nietzsche belonged to an esoteric, and now largely lost, line of nineteenth-century thought which might be labelled degenerationist. Third, for a long time Nietzsche's influence was primarily felt outside of philosophy, by psychoanalysts, for instance Adler and, arguably, Freud, and by writers, for instance, Rilke and Mann; and then mostly in the twentieth rather than the nineteenth century – as Nietzsche presciently said of himself "some are born posthumously." Finally, and perhaps most importantly, Nietzsche is what might be called a local rather than a global thinker. Traditionally philosophers have sought final answers to so-called perennial questions, "What is truth?," "What is knowledge?," "What is the good life?," and the like. The answers, once achieved, are meant to have scope over all time and all situations. Nietzsche's thought tends to be much more local, addressing such questions as "What is the value of truth for this kind of person?," "What is the meaning of the ascetic ideal for that kind of person?" For those who think globally this often tends to lead to the conclusion that Nietzsche's philosophy is rife with contradictions; here he denies the value of truth and champions the need for illusions, there he extols the search for truth; here he laments that asceticism is a form of life denial, there he extols asceticism as a form of life affirmation. In reading Nietzsche one must keep in mind that he nearly always has a specific target in mind, so that when he praises X he has in mind one target and when he criticizes X he has another target in mind. For instance, in *The Genealogy of Morality*, a work that today is often treated as his canonical text, he praises the ascetic ideal where it is indulged by a certain type of philosopher as a means for avoiding worldly distractions so he can concentrate on his true task of giving birth to new thoughts and values; yet in the same work he vilifies the ascetic ideal where it is used by certain religious types as a means of denying, indeed slandering the world. Thus for Nietzsche, unlike most philosophers, it is typically pointless to ask does he value the search for truth, since for Nietzsche the question will always be "what does the search for truth mean" in this given context. Even Nietzsche's infamous condemnation of Judeo-Christian values needs to be relevantly contextualized. After all, he is not claiming that those values must be totally destroyed or that they are bad for everyone. Rather, he is claiming that there are certain types of people for whom those values are inimical. This allows him to acknowledge that for other kinds of people, admittedly people he typically deems to be of little interest, Christianity allows for the fullest possible expression they are capable of. Thus he says such things as "the ideas of the herd should rule in the herd – but not reach out beyond it" (KSA: 12.273, repr. WP: 287; see also BGE: 61).

Nevertheless, against all this we should note that as a trained philologist Nietzsche was well versed in the work of the ancient philosophers. Beside his knowledge of Aristotle and Plato, he had excellent knowledge of the pre-Socratics. Furthermore, as an eclectic philosophical autodidact, he had detailed knowledge of Schopenhauer, even if his knowledge of, for example, Kant, Hegel and Hume was less solid. More importantly, while Nietzsche does not fit times where philosophy is becoming an ever more technical specialized subject, his central concerns are close to the perennial, if now unfashionable, philosophical question of what is a good life. Finally, his influence on philosophers has been steadily increasing; on the continent ever since he was taken up by Heidegger, and in the Anglo-American world since philosophers such as Arthur Danto, Philippa Foot and more recently Bernard Williams have claimed that Nietzsche can be seen as addressing, even challenging some of analytic philosophers' central concerns.

We will return to address Nietzsche's relation to philosophy later, in considering his ideas about the death of God, perspectivism, will to power, sublimation, eternal recurrence, affirmation of life, and his notion of the self. For now we will focus on getting an overview of Nietzsche's central concerns and then looking at the particulars of his intellectual career.

It might be claimed that nihilism and its overcoming is the central focus of Nietzsche's philosophy (cf. Reginster 2006 and May 1999). This way of putting things, while essentially correct, needs to be coupled with an awareness of the fact that

Nietzsche did not always have nihilism clearly in his sights. Rather, he slowly came to see the diagnosing and overcoming of nihilism as his central concern. Nietzsche scholars are generally agreed in dividing Nietzsche's writings into three periods. The first period, from 1872–7, might aptly be called the romantic period. The chief writings of this period are *The Birth of Tragedy*, *Philosophy in the Tragic Age of the Greeks* (unpublished in Nietzsche's lifetime), and *The Untimely Meditations*. Simplifying, we may say his central normative concern of this period is that of the prospect of cultural renewal, and in particular cultural renewal in Germany. This is a concern he inherited from the German romantics, in particular from the early Goethe and Hölderlin, and one that was shared with his early mentor Richard Wagner. From Schopenhauer he took over a Kantian metaphysics through which he tended to frame his normative concerns. The middle period, from 1878 to 1882, has often been called the positivist period. Here Nietzsche seeks primarily to understand the nature of man. Here too there is some gesturing at a normative agenda, though the content of that normative project, as witnessed by his vague talk of the need for free spirits, is far from clear. The chief writings of this period are *Daybreak*, *Human All Too Human* and *The Gay Science*. The last period, from 1883 to 1888, might aptly be called the anti-moralist period. Here Nietzsche recognizes the inevitable tyranny of philistine culture and attempts to lessen the hold of what he regards as the deeply nihilistic Judeo-Christian values which sustain that culture, in the hope of fostering conditions that might allow rare individuals to rise above it. The principal works of this period are *Thus Spoke Zarathustra*, *Beyond Good and Evil*, *On the Genealogy of Morality*, *The Anti-Christ*, *Twilight of the Idols*, and *Ecce Homo*.

Throughout his career it is generally normative concerns that drive Nietzsche's thought. To a large degree metaphysics and epistemology are only his concerns to the extent that they are relevant to his various normative projects. Regarding the overall trajectory of his normative thought we might say that in his early romantic period he optimistically aimed for general cultural renewal. His message, in particular his naive assumption that his compatriots, fresh from the victory of the Franco-Prussian war of 1870–1, would recognize the lack of genuine culture that afflicted Germany, fell stillborn: Telling a victorious Germany, one that saw itself as replacing France as the new powerhouse of Europe, that it had no culture was a message almost guaranteed to find no audience. His middle period may then be seen as a kind of retrenchment where Nietzsche seeks psychological insight into human nature allowing him a deeper insight into why his earlier message could not be heard. His final period, weighted with a pessimistic assessment of human nature which posited a deep nihilism to be at the centre of Europe's Judeo-Christian values, aims at the more limited end of finding the means for a few special individuals to overcome nihilism and attain new cultural heights.

The early Nietzsche

The Nietzsche of the early works, *The Birth of Tragedy* (1872), *The Untimely Meditations* (1873–6) and *Philosophy in the Tragic Age of the Greeks* (1873) is perhaps best appreciated through two different lenses that finally may be focused towards a common goal.

Seen through the first lens, these works show a thinker deeply concerned with the romantic problem of how Germany is to achieve an elevated general culture comparable to that achieved by the ancient Greeks. An important theme, which, as we shall see, resonates with themes in his later works, is that modern man lacks a certain unity fundamental to ancient Greek and all higher culture. In the *Birth of Tragedy* this theme is expressed in terms of two forces, the Dionysian and the Apollonian, which the Greeks, or at least the pre-Socratic Greeks, held in a creative balance. The Apollonian represents the intellectual, form-giving faculty. The Dionysian represents the more primordial, instinctive, sexual drives. According to Nietzsche, these two forces achieved their highest synthesis in the Greek tragedies of Sophocles and Aeschylus. However, with Euripides and, more importantly, Socrates, comes a valorization of the Apollonian, the constrained, form giving, rational, over the Dionysian. We moderns are seen as an expression of this victory of the Socratic-Apollonian over the irrational, sexual Dionysian. When one first reads *The Birth of Tragedy* it is natural to think, given the vehemence of Nietzsche's rhetoric, especially when aimed at Socrates, the rationalist par excellence, that Nietzsche is calling for a reversal, for the overthrowing of the Apollonian in favour of the Dionysian. Here again it is vital to understand Nietzsche as a local thinker: He is not championing the Dionysian because he wants it to triumph at the expense of the Apollonian, rather he is championing it because the Apollonian has been thoroughly triumphant and needs no champion to promote its cause. Nietzsche champions the Dionysian because, through the victory of Socratic rationalism, it has become thoroughly repressed and hence is in need of a champion. What Nietzsche really is aiming for is a balance between these two forces. This paean to a higher unity in the early writing is undergirded by Nietzsche's Schopenhaurian metaphysics. The rational, individuating Apollonian is concerned with the world of appearance, what Schopenhauer calls representations (*Vorstellungen*) or Kant calls phenomena. The undifferentiated, irrational, Dionysian is concerned with the world as it is in itself (the Schopenhaurian and Kantian *Ding an sich*). The later Nietzsche dismisses this Schopenhaurian-Kantian framework as simply a youthful naivety – in the 1886 reissue of *The Birth of Tragedy* he appended an "Attempt at Self-Criticism" where he explicitly repudiates his "Schopenhaurian formulations" (BT: "Attempt at a Self Criticism," 6). In fact, there is evidence that already at the time of writing *The Birth of Tragedy* Nietzsche was not really deeply wedded to any such metaphysics but rather saw it, perhaps mistakenly, as a useful means for advancing his polemical purposes. By aligning the Dionysian with the primordial, undifferentiated will, and aligning the Apollonian with the individuating schema of the world of mere appearance, Nietzsche, presumably, hoped to endow the Dionysian with the mantle of ultimate truth and ultimate reality. Those under the influence of the Socratic extreme valuation of truth would thereby be motivated to positively value the formerly despised Dionysian. Either way, the Schopenhaurian Kantian metaphysics can be safely hived off from his fundamental normative project of extolling a higher new unity between the instinctual and the rational in order to achieve an active, creative, life affirming culture.

Seen through the second lens, the central project of his early works is that of overcoming Schopenhaurian pessimism or, as it might be put, that of constructing a secular theodicy (see Geuss 1999; Came 2004). The problem Nietzsche was grappling with was how to reconcile Schopenhaurian pessimism, the recognition that life is irredeemably full of suffering, with an affirmation of life. Schopenhauer combined this descriptive pessimism, his recognition of the ubiquity of suffering, with a normative pessimism, the judgement that the world should not exist (see Soll 1989). Nietzsche attempted to resist this normative conclusion, by concluding in *The Birth of Tragedy* that "only as an *aesthetic phenomenon* is existence and the world externally *justified*" (BT: 5). The principal idea here is that the Apollonian, by giving form through aesthetic creations makes life bearable, and perhaps even beautiful.

In the performance of tragedy, "the terrors and horrors of existence" are "veiled and withdrawn from view, by means of the artistic *middle world* of the Olympians." Reality was "transfigured" by the Apollonian drive into theological terms, and thus "suffused with a higher glory..." (BT: 3).

At the time of BT, Nietzsche believed that Wagner's music-dramas success-fully recaptured this capacity to ennoble reality in mythological terms, at the same time acknowledging the truth of Schopenhauerian pessimism. While the problem of constructing such a secular theodicy arguably remained with him throughout his intellectual career – certainly the question of how one can achieve a truly life affirming stance remained with him to the end – the emphasis on disguising suffering through artistic illusion became notably less pronounced. This shift can in part be explained by Nietzsche's growing ambivalence over whether illusion, once understood as such, can perform in actual life the role it does in tragedy. Self-conscious mytholo-gizing collapses into kitsch, and so the Wagnerian project was doomed to failure by Nietzsche's lights.

The two projects, that of overcoming Schopenhaurian pessimism and that of achieving a unity of the Dionysian and the Apollonian, come together in the story Nietzsche tells of the pre-Socratic Greeks. In their art, principally through Attic tragedy, they allowed a full expression and synthesis of the Apollonian, as represented by the differentiated individual hero, and the Dionysian, as represented by the undif-ferentiated members of the chorus of Attic tragedy. The hero's tragic fate recognized the inevitable suffering of life, at the same time the beautiful representations through which that fate is presented allowed the audience to affirm that suffering.

Nietzsche admired the Greeks for having the strength to embrace Schopenhaurian descriptive pessimism, the recognition of the ubiquity of suffering, without falling into Schopenhauer's condemnation of the world, his prescriptive pessimism.

Nietzsche despised Socrates for his blanket condemnation of the instincts, of the Dionysian, in favour of reason, the Apollonian, since for Nietzsche to condemn the instincts is to condemn life. Moreover he detested what he called the Socratic lie of optimism; the claim that through understanding we may correct "being", that is eliminate suffering.

The project of achieving or paving the way towards a general culture and the project of constructing a secular theodicy are thus deeply related. It is through our failure to properly deal with the problem of suffering, the problem addressed in a secular theodicy, that we fail to create the conditions for a general culture. The modern, post-Socratic way of dealing with suffering is, claims Nietzsche, to repress the Dionysian parts of ourselves. Yet because the Dionysian is an essential part of ourselves, this means that we moderns are deeply divided and for Nietzsche genuine culture essentially involves a unity of all the elements of our nature.

The extolling of unity throughout Nietzsche's intellectual career can seem problematic on two scores. First, it may be viewed as an embarrassing romantic hangover. Second, and relatedly, it may seem like Nietzsche, a philosopher who eschews transcendental philosophy, is promoting unity as a transcendental condition on the possibility of culture and perhaps even genuine selfhood (see fifth and seventh sections, below). While this charge is generally a worry, we think the best answer is that Nietzsche extols unity not because he really sees it as a necessary condition for the existence of culture, or of the existence of a self, but because he believes the fundamental malaise we moderns suffer from is the repression of parts of ourselves; that repression being the product of our Judeo-Christian heritage.

The middle Nietzsche

Nietzsche's works of the middle period, comprising *Human, All Too Human* (1878, with two additional volumes, *Mixed Opinions and Maxims* and *The Wanderer and His Shadow* appended 1879–80), *Daybreak: Thoughts on the Prejudices of Morality* (1881), and *The Gay Science* (1882, with a fifth book added, 1887), are often thought of as primarily transitional works. Often referred to as Nietzsche's positivist period, it is marked by retrenchment from his earlier Romantic aims, severe doubts about the possibility of cultural renewal, as well as gestures towards an alternative normative ideal. Read positively, this ideal of the 'free spirit' involves a conception of an individual who possesses sufficient courage, self-belief and self-sufficiency to pursue his own self-cultivation in the face of general cultural malaise.

Nietzsche now construes cultural malaise as largely owing to a certain cognitive failure, and the unchallenged acceptance of cultural values and institutions as timeless and unchanging. Whereas in the romantic period Nietzsche claimed we require art and illusion in order to live, he now believes such 'higher values', in particular as exemplified in metaphysical speculations, are inimical to human flourishing. The free spirit displays unflinching honesty in the face of such illusions, and in the course of the middle period Nietzsche pursues what he would later call the task of "translating man back into nature" (BGE: 230). Adopting a naturalistic empiricism, Nietzsche suggests that concepts such as morality, the state, art and religion can be exhaustively explained in the historical, evolutionary terms of science, as naturally occurring phenomena. Traditional accounts which rely on metaphysical or supernatural assumptions should be superseded, Nietzsche argues, by an unflinching intellectual honesty and the application of the best scientific methodology, which is suitably rigorous to penetrate illusion, once moral prejudice is set aside.

This naturalistic project has three distinctive elements: a rejection of metaphysics (in particular the possibility of knowledge of the Kantian thing-in-itself); the re-description of values and institutions (in particular morality and moral phenomena) in naturalistic, evolutionary terms; and finally, naturalistic explanations framed in terms of a reductive psychological egoism. The three approaches are interrelated. Nietzsche posits that the appeal to metaphysical values arose primarily owning to ignorance. Lacking a sufficient natural explanation, previous societies posited gods and other metaphysical entities and properties to bridge this explanatory gap. However, if the values and institutions of culture and morality *can* now be explained without the need for such posits, morality's claim to a 'higher' status will wilt.

To take his attack on the metaphysical 'thing-in-itself' first, Nietzsche stops short of arguing for its conceptual incoherence (as he would later do – see TI: "How the True World Became a Fable"). In the middle period, he suggests that while

> there could be a metaphysical world … [t]his is purely a scientific problem and not very well calculated to bother people overmuch …[Its] possibility still remains over; but one can do absolutely nothing with it, not to speak of letting happiness, salvation and life depend on the gossamer of such a possibility. – For one could assert nothing at all of the metaphysical world except that it was a being-other, an inaccessible, incomprehensible being-other; it would be a thing with negative qualities. – Even if the existence of such a world were never so well demonstrated, it is certain that knowledge of it would be of the most useless of all knowledge.… . (HAH: Vol. 1, 9)

Empirical observation gives us knowledge of empirical reality, and any explanation of this reality should be couched in the terms of the empirical world.

A similar strategy seems to be at work in the various reinterpretations of apparently altruistic actions which Nietzsche proceeds to give in egoistic terms. As noted, Nietzsche assumes the appeal of metaphysical concepts and values to derive from their apparent ability to explain what cannot otherwise be accounted for. Altruistic actions go against the behaviour of 'lower' creatures in the animal kingdom. Whereas hunger, sex and self-interest all appear to answer to natural base needs, selflessness and self-sacrifice could only previously be explained as values which issued from a metaphysical realm, of qualitatively distinct values only perceivable to the metaphysician or his forebearer, the priest. Nietzsche argues instead that altruism can be explained as a historically evolved sublimation of the same primitive self-interested drive (HAH: Vol. 2, "Assorted Opinions and Maxims," 91). This reductive egoism has among its influences the work of the French Moralists La Rochefoucauld and Montaigne, as well as the philosophical naturalist and determinist, Paul Ree. Nietzsche would later criticize Ree's psychology as naive. (As he argues in GM, it is implausible that individuals would forget the social utility of acts which are initially praised as such.)

The middle period's evolutionary account of morality has significant value in showing Nietzsche's intellectual development towards his later genealogy of morality. What is called "good" is that which serves the interests of society, and so to the extent that the individual's interests diverge from these, morality acts against the individual's real interests. Nietzsche suggests that by internalizing social mores, the individual succumbs to a form of false consciousness, "[s]o it comes about that through his morality the individual *outvotes* himself" (HAH: Vol. 2, "Assorted Opinions and Maxims," 89; see also HAH: Vol. 1, 95). Potentially great individuals may be stifled by the opinions and values of their peers, both by being shouted down as immoral, and by lacking any alternative source of normative guidance.

Nietzsche's concept of a 'free spirit' is in part a reaction against, and in part a development of, his earlier cultural criticism. German culture, claimed the earlier Nietzsche, was to be united by the propagation, through Wagner, of its 'genuine' expression. This cultural renewal was to stand in contrast to the complacent 'sham culture' of superficiality and philistinism. However, Nietzsche increasingly viewed Wagner as a hypocrite, and merely the latest manifestation of the self-delusional philistinism he was supposed to correct. The belief that Wagner had been corrupted, and effectively absorbed into the culture he had originally set out to challenge, was to have a lasting impression on Nietzsche. In much of the middle period, the need to inoculate his new champions of excellence against a similar fate looms large. He continues to vacillate over whether these so-called "free-spirits" are part of a wider project of cultural renewal, requiring inoculation against the corrupting effects of society before acting to address its ills, or whether they are to be figures operating largely outside the prevalent cultural norms

The late Nietzsche

The later Nietzsche is burdened with knowledge of the inevitably of the triumph of philistine culture. In this Nietzsche was strikingly prescient, but in no way unique. Alexis de Tocqueville in his *Democracy in America* had already warned of the "tyranny of the majority." John Stuart Mill had similar misgivings about the coming democratic age as evidenced in the following:

> None are so illiberal, none so bigoted in their hostility to improvement, none so superstitiously attached to the stupidest and worst of old forms and usages, as the uneducated…[and] no lover of improvement can desire that the predominant power should be turned over to persons in the mental and moral conditions of the English working classes. (CW: Vol. 19, 327, "Thoughts on Parliamentary Reform")

While Mill kept alive some hope for a more elevated general culture with the masses being "guided (which in the best times they have always done) by the counsels and influence of a more highly gifted and instructed One or Few" (CW: Vol. 18, 269, *On Liberty*), Nietzsche saw that battle to be already lost. What he seems to have hoped for is that some individuals could be inspired to rise above the general morass of philistine culture. Brian Leiter (2002), for one, argues cogently that this is a central focus of his later writings.

The idea that the current age is irredeemably philistine is perhaps a recurrent idea throughout history. It is often coupled with a certain romantic nostalgia about some mythical earlier times where life was, at least substantially nearer to, an ideal.

What is particular to the nineteenth-century version of this thought is that it was often coupled with a certain biologism that saw the new masses of the industrial-izing cities as a kind of contagion that would literally, or metaphorically, infect the whole social and political body. Coupled with the influence of neo-Darwinian ideas about the non-inevitability of progress and the dangers of letting the lowest members of the species proliferate, this constellation of ideas led some to a near pathological fear of degeneration (for more on this see Chamberlain and Gilman 1985 and Pick 1989). Even Darwin, generally not one to endorse the pessimistic degenerationist line of thought, indulges in the occasional purple patch of degen-erationist rhetoric:

> Thus the weak members of civilized societies propagate their kind. No one who has attended to the breeding of domestic animals will doubt that this must be highly injurious to the race of man. It is surprising how soon a want of care, or care wrongly directed, leads to the degeneration of a domestic race; but excepting in the case of man himself, hardly anyone is so ignorant as to allow his worst animals to breed. (Darwin 1972: 138–90)

Nietzsche's texts from the beginning to the end contain a veritable avalanche in use of the term 'Entartung' (degeneration). It is worth pausing to note that while much ink has been spilled on the question of Nietzsche's responsibility for his being appro-priated by the Nazi's – much of this debate has centred on the question of whether he was or was not an anti-Semite – causally, at least, his most pernicious influence is perhaps his contribution to furthering the idea that certain elements in society may be seen as contributing to the overall degeneration of the populace. This thought has a notorious logic of its own; unleashing this genie from its bottle near inevitably leads to all kinds of horrors. In fact, Nietzsche's take on degeneration was substantively different than that of other major degenerationist writers such as Cesar Lombroso and Max Nordau (see Nordau 1895 and Lombroso and Ferrero 1899). Generally degenerationists argued that the degenerate elements in society needed to be isolated or eliminated in order to stop them infecting the whole. Their implicit idea of health may be termed Manichean: There are two camps, the intrinsically evil and the intrinsically good, and health involves isolating or eliminating the evil. Against this Nietzsche argued that in fact health consists in incorporating the so-called degenerate elements into a stronger whole. Thus he labels section 225 of *Human all too Human* as "Ennoblement through Degeneration," a title which may seems esoteric today but to a nineteenth-century audience was a clear challenge to their preconceptions about the condition of health. This ties in with Nietzsche's general rejection of the prevalent Judea-Christian prejudice against suffering. For Nietzsche health is not measured in the absence of suffering but in the expression of the will to power. One expresses power by overcoming resistances and resistances in their own turn create suffering. So, for Nietzsche the expressing of power, what for Nietzsche counts as a good healthy life, inevitably involves suffering. Without the suffering engendered by genuine challenges, there can be no real health.

By the later period Nietzsche had identified the Judeo-Christian heritage as the chief force for degeneration since it led to a morality that put the elimination of suffering at the core of its values. Perhaps Nietzsche's most famous attack on the grounds of that heritage occurs in *Gay Science* 125, usually known as the Madman or Death of God passage. There Nietzsche tells of a madman who announces to an audience of apparent atheists that God is dead. After they make fun of him, in a series of rhetorical questions he makes clear to them that even if they do not believe in God they have not truly appreciated the significance of their atheism. For Nietzsche giving up belief in God does not simply mean ceasing to believe in a providential creator. It means losing the grounds for our whole morality. Nietzsche is often regarded as the philosopher of the Death of God precisely because he casts himself as the first to see that in becoming secular we have lost the grounds for our Judeo-Christian morality. Nietzsche maintains that even thoroughly secular moralists, be they utilitarians or Kantian deontologists, have not really abandoned the Judeo-Christian heritage but merely given it a secular makeover. In particular, they take for granted that suffering is something bad that should be to be reduced to a minimum, if not eliminated. For a utilitarian the need to eliminate or at least minimize suffering is straightforward. For a Kantian, arguably, it follows from the fact that one can will it as a universal law that each member of society does what he can to eliminate or at least reduce the suffering of other members of society. What Nietzsche predicts is that when the full realization of the Death of God comes to permeate society we will realize there is no external basis for our values. Faced with this realization we will lapse into nihilism. This, Nietzsche pronounces, is the coming history of Europe for the next two hundred years (KSA: 13:56, repr. WP: Preface, 2).

On first take nihilism is simply the lack of any ultimate values. Today we might consider this the most ubiquitous form of nihilism. But note, Schopenhauer, whom Nietzsche takes to be a paradigm nihilist, empathically condemns the existence of the world. This poses a philosophical problem. How can nihilism, which involves the rejection of all ultimate values, lead to a condemnation of the world, to the judgement that the world ought not to exist? Any such condemnation presumably presupposes certain ultimate values. For instance, Schopenhauer's condemnation of the world is predicated on his descriptive pessimistic judgement that the world will always contain an overwhelming balance of suffering against pleasure, and his normative judgement that the absence of suffering is of ultimate value. In order to finesse this delicate point Reginster (2006) has posited that there are two forms of nihilism for Nietzsche. The nihilism of disorientation involves the rejection of all ultimate values. The nihilism of despair involves the realization that one's ultimate values cannot be realized. Schopenhauer's nihilism is clearly of the later variety. Arguably, nihilism in its deepest manifestation is for Nietzsche an affective rather than a cognitive disorder such as disorientation or despair. It is a matter of the constitution of one's deepest drives rather than a matter of one's overt beliefs. This should hardly be surprising since Nietzsche, following Schopenhauer, tended to treat conscious beliefs as largely epiphenomenal, as more a reflection of deeper causes than as genuine springs of action. For Nietzsche the deepest form of nihilism, what we might called affective nihilism, involves what he calls 'the will turning itself against life' (GM: Preface, 5). Nietzsche, heavily influenced by Schopenhauer's notion of the primacy of the will, saw human beings as constituted by a collection of drives; in *Daybreak* he refers to "the totality of drives which constitute his [a man's] being" (D: 109). Where the drives, for various complicated reasons, turn against their own expression Nietzsche characterized this as nihilism. On this view the more cognitive nihilisms such as disorientation and despair are merely manifestations of this deeper affective nihilism. This account allows us to account for Nietzsche's repeated claim that "Christianity .... is nihilistic in the most profound sense" (EH: §3, "The Birth of Tragedy," 1). The Christian does not suffer from the nihilism of disorientation; he does not believe that there are no higher values; rather he believes that God is the source of all such values. The Christian does not suffer from despair since he believes that ultimately his higher values will be achieved in the next world if not this one. According to Nietzsche, the Christian suffers from a deep rejection of his innermost drives; hence he exhibits the strange phenomenon that Nietzsche labels the will turned against life. It is in this sense that the Christian is deeply nihilistic; he suffers what we have called affective nihilism.

Nietzsche, truth and post-modernism

It is important to realize that Nietzsche is not an advocate of nihilism but its diagnostician. Nihilism for Nietzsche inevitably comes with the recognition of the Death of God. What Nietzsche wants is for his chosen audience to experience the depths of nihilism so that they, like him, may get beyond it. As he modestly puts it

> He that speaks here [is] the first perfect nihilist of Europe, who, however, has even now lived through the whole of nihilism, to the end, leaving it behind, outside himself. (KSA: 13:189, repr. WP: Preface, 3)

At times Nietzsche sounds as if he is a herald of, and hence is in favour of, nihilism. Post-modernists interpreters of Nietzsche have taken up the theme of nihilism in Nietzsche, concluding that Nietzsche himself was some kind of advocate of nihilism in its form as the absence of all ultimate values. A crucial domain where they read Nietzsche as a herald of nihilism is in his writing on truth. Here he has often been interpreted as attacking the very notion of truth. Even some authors who have little sympathy for post-modenists have taken Nietzsche's famous doctrine of perspectivism as an attack on the notion of (correspondence) truth (cf. Schacht 1985: 65). In fact, Nietzsche was more concerned with the high value we give to truth, and the general psychology of the will to truth, than with any philosophical analysis of the nature of, or possibility of determining, truth (see Gemes 1992). The overriding will to truth that characterizes modern scholars, he maintains, stems from the same motivation that fuelled commitment to religious ascetic values, namely, fear of life and feelings of impotence.

The religious person attempts to remove himself from the torments of this world, a world that largely resists his desires. He tells himself that what happens in this life is ultimately unimportant; that what matters is what is in his soul, which will determine his real, eternal life in the world to come. The modern scholar similarly removes himself from life by telling himself that what is of ultimate value is not acting in this world, not what he does, but in understanding the world, in what he knows. Both the religious ascetic and the ascetic scholar believe "the truth will set you free." Nietzsche has realized that here to be free means to be free of the pull of this world, the tumult of earthly passions and desires. Just as the ascetic ideal demands suppression of the passions, so the scholar's emphasis on objectivity and truth demands "the emotions cooled" (GM: Treatise 3, 25). Where the religious take revenge upon the world by denying that it is of ultimate importance, the scholar revenges himself by saying that passive understanding is of greater value than "mere" action. Furthermore, the scholar takes his possession of knowledge to somehow give him a sort of magical possession of the world. Nietzsche seems to countenance two ways in which knowledge can function as a form of revenge against the world. On the first account the valorization of passive knowledge over action is a way of withdrawing from the active life that a healthy nature demands (cf. *Daybreak*, D: 42, "Origin of the *Vita Contemplativa*"). On the second account, through knowledge people attempt to possess the world "as if knowledge of it sufficed to make it their property" (D: 285).

Along with their misreading Nietzsche as rejecting the notion of truth post-modernists take Nietzsche to be one of the earliest opponents of the notion of the unity of the self. Habermas, in his widely debated *The Philosophical Discourse of Modernity*, in which he takes a decidedly critical view of post-modernism, tells us

> Nietzsche appeals to experiences of self-disclosure of a decentered subjec-tivity, liberated from all constraints of cognitive and purposive activity, all imperatives of utility and morality. A "break-up" of the principle of individu-ation becomes the escape route from modernity. (Habermas 1987: 94)

For postmodernists, Nietzsche's perspectivism, his suspicion of metaphysics (ultimate ontology), his radical scepticism and interrogation of conventional notions of truth, all mark him as an agent of dissolution, of polyphony, a practitioner of the hermeneutics of suspicion. Nietzsche is cited as a model of deconstruction; for instance, his genea-logical endeavours are held-up as a paradigm of disclosing the origin in opposites, the unmasking of a facade of unity that hides a congeries of mixed motives. Thus Michel Haar approvingly quotes Nietzsche as saying "We are a plurality that has imagined itself a unity" (in Allison 1985: 18). In this vein the name of Nietzsche travels in the company of Barthes, De Man, Lyotard, Foucault and Derrida. For instance, Alan Schrift in *Nietzsche's French Legacy* says

> The whole Nietzschean project of genealogy directs itself toward deconstructing the foundations of the dominant values of modernity (1995: 24) ... . In dispersing the subject within a system of textual relations, Derrida adopts a Nietzschean strategy of refusing to hypostasize the subject. (1995: 30)

Similarly, Hillis Miller cites Nietzsche as perhaps "the most systematic and cogent" of "all modern *deconstructers* of the idea of selfhood" (Hillis Miller 1981: 248 – emphasis ours).

Yet Nietzsche was careful to describe himself as an affirmative spirit, one who says Yes and Yes again to Life, an opponent of nihilism, a would-be architect of the future. In this affirmative mode Nietzsche typically stresses the importance of finding a unitary voice, of finding a means to retell history as a pathway to one's own constructed self:

> What is meant is that a people to whom one attributes a culture has to be a single living unity and not fall wretchedly apart into inner and outer, content and form. He who wants to promote the culture of a people should strive for and promote this higher unity. (UM: Untimely Meditation 2, 4)

How then are we to reconcile the post-modernists incredulity towards meta-narratives with its resultant polyphony of voices, and Habermas' characterization of Nietzsche as offering a break-up of the principle of individuation, with Nietzsche's insistence that we must learn to appropriate the past, construct a unifying goal and interpret the past in the light of that goal?

The postmodernists and critics of postmodernism who cite Nietzsche as attacking the notion of the singular subject, the unified self, are of course well supported by textual evidence. Thus we have Nietzsche's famous dictum from the *Genealogy* "the doer is merely a fiction added to the deed" (GM: Treatise 1, 13), his observation in *Beyond Good and Evil* (BGE: 26) "our body is but a social structure composed of many souls" and the note from the 1885 *Nachlass* which reads "My hypothesis: the subject as multiplicity" (KSA: 11:650, note 490 in *The Will to Power*, *WP*). Much of the work of the first essay of the *Genealogy of Morality* centres on the claim that the slave's reality principle – his realization that he can not directly attain his desires – has led to a repression of those very desires – the desires for the very qualities and successes of the envied and hated masters. This repression leads to a splitting-off, which renders those desires incapable of direct expression and conscious access. On this model we moderns, as descendants of the slaves, have become, in Nietzsche's memorable expression "strangers to ourselves" (EH: Preface, 1). Our deepest desires and convictions are hidden from us.

However, note that the claim that there is no doer behind the deed need not be taken as a blanket rejection of the notion of a doer. Rather the point of emphasis can be placed on the notion of a doer *behind* the deed. For the Christian there is behind the deed an immutable soul. It is this notion of a free choosing soul that is being rejected here. Thus immediately before saying "the doer is merely a fiction added to the deed" Nietzsche says "there is no such substratum." For Nietzsche the doer is literally in the deeds. While what is directly at stake in Nietzsche's attacks on the notion of a unified, self-transparent Cartesian I, are the very presumptions of unity and self-transparency, his underlying theme is often a replacement notion of unity as a goal. The Cartesian claims to know first and foremost the existence and nature of the I, posing the construction of the external world as a problem. Reversing this formula

Nietzsche problematizes the existence and nature of this I. Yet in problematizing the I Nietzsche is not seeking primarily to expose some kind of metaphysical error. For such a gesture would still fall under the dominion of the Christian inspired will to truth. In offering a critique of the notion of a unified self, as in his critique of the Christian world view that assumes this notion of self, Nietzsche is not primarily aiming to expose a deception, a metaphysical error. As he says of Christianity, "it is not error as error that horrifies me at this sight" (EH: "Why I Am a Destiny," 7). That the notion of the unified self is a deception; this in itself matters only to those with a morality, which shuns all forms of deception. For Nietzsche the desire to escape all deception is another manifestation of the ascetic ideal (cf. GM: Treatise 3, 25). Deception for Nietzsche is an inevitable part of life, thus "[u]ltimately the point is to what end a lie is told" (A: 56). The problem with the notion of the Cartesian self, the Christian soul, is that it is part of a slandering, a poisoning of life:

> That "holy" ends are lacking in Christianity is *my* objection to its means. Only *bad* ends: the poisoning, slandering, denying of life, contempt for the body, the denigration and self-violation of man through the concept of sin – *consequently* its means too are bad. (A: 56 – emphasis Nietzsche's)

The notion of a transparent singular self is, of course, the cornerstone of Cartesian foundationalist epistemology and metaphysics. Now Nietzsche, as postmodernists rightly observe, is a destroyer of all kinds of foundationalisms. They are right to interpret this as the force behind Nietzsche's madman's proclamation of the Death of God (GS: 125). It is not simply the Christian world view that is at stake here but all notions of an external authority that might provide some ultimate guarantor of beliefs. But postmodernists are wrong to take this rejection of the notion of an external, transcendent authority as a rejection of all authority. The postmodern rejection of all authority, all principle of order among the competing modes of representation, presents the very Nihilism that Nietzsche predicts, and warns against, as a natural result of the defeat of dogmatism. For Nietzsche there is still room for an immanent authority, an authority that comes from within. As the *Nachlass* of 1888 reads,

> The multitude and disgregation of impulses and the lack of any systematic order among them results in a "weak will"; their coordination under a single predominant impulse results in a "strong" will: in the first case it is the oscil-lation and lack of gravity; in the later, the precision and clarity of direction. (KSA: 13:394, note 46 of *The Will to Power, WP*)

It is important to recall that while the madman of section 125 of *The Gay Science* begins with the disappearance and then the death of God he concludes with the suggestion that we ourselves, the slayers of God, must become Gods to be worthy of the deed. The importance of the death of God, the ultimate external foundation, is not, primarily, in the revealing of a metaphysical or epistemological error; it is in the task it opens up. We must become our own guarantors. The postmodernists who take Nietzsche's disparaging comments about unity as an endorsement of a decentred pluralism have mistaken the target of Nietzsche's polemic. He is not against unity but rather wants to expose our lack of unity by exposing the myth of the Cartesian unified self. It is by creating such a unity that we can again become, like the ancient Greeks, genuine affirmers of life. Nietzsche agrees with the postmodernist's descriptive claim that there are no pre-given unified selves, but vehemently rejects their prescription that we forgo all attempts at constructing new unities. Such prescriptions he attributes to the nihilism of what he often likes to call "the last man."

Nietzsche on affirmation

Reginster (2006) claims affirmation involves various cognitive stances. Thus he says "To affirm life in general is to recognize that those aspects of it 'hitherto denied' are 'desirable for their own sake'" (2006: 267) and "you affirm life if you react with joy to the prospect of its eternal recurrence" (2006: 202). The later formulation clearly links affirmation with Nietzsche's doctrine of the eternal recurrence which is presented as a test of affirmation; a now prevalent reading of the import of eternal recurrence. A small point to note is that a fervent ascetic Christian who has removed himself from all human interaction and who hates life might well rapturously wish upon himself eternal reliving of his life in all its details. He might do this not because he affirms life itself but because he believes it is his lot to suffer on this earth for his sins. Taking himself to be unworthy of heaven, he might will eternal recurrence as what he takes to be a deserved punishment. This would hardly count as life affirmation in Nietzsche's sense. The best interpretation is not that eternal recurrence is the test of life affirmation such that all and only those who can pass the test are life affirmers. Rather, Nietzsche intends it as an example of life affirmation. For we moderns who, after 2,000 years of self-vivisection imposed on us by Judeo-Christian morality, have no idea of what life affirmation would look like, the joyous affirmer of life's eternal return gives us one possible exemplar of genuine life affirmation. On this reading, as opposed to the more conventional reading, it is not the case that the only way to affirm life is to be able to will its eternal recurrence. Nor is it the case that every one who wills eternal recurrence is a life affirmer.

It is doubtful that the simple masters of the first essay of the *Genealogy of Morality* took the trouble to take such reflexive stances, yet Nietzsche paints them as paradigms of life affirmation. These masters affirm life by living it in a direct, expressive, way. Here the contrast is with the slaves who repress and deny their most basic drives. In fact, Nietzsche's texts complicate this issue for they appear to endorse two conflicting accounts of affirmation. On the first account, to affirm life is to give full and complete expression to one's drives. This might suitably be called naive affirmation. On the second account, to affirm life is to step back from it, reflect upon it, and then endorse it in all its details. It is this kind of reflective affirmation that is rightly identified in Nietzsche's writings on eternal recurrence. It is clearly naive affirmation Nietzsche has in mind when he says, "in all productive men it is instinct that is the creative-affirmative force and consciousness acts critically and dissuasively ..." (BT: 13). Indeed this quotation expresses the idea that reflection is somehow antithetical to genuine affirmation. This idea may also be drawn from other sources in Nietzsche:

> Judgments, judgments of value, concerning life, for it or against it, can, in the end, never be true: they have value only as symptoms, they are worthy of consideration only as symptoms; in themselves such judgments are stupidities. ... For a philosopher to see a problem in the value of life is thus an objection to him, a question mark concerning his wisdom, a piece of un-wisdom. (TI: "The Problem of Socrates," 2)

The tension between Nietzsche's account of naive affirmation and his account of reflective affirmation might aptly be labelled "Nietzsche's paradox of affirmation." While this is not the place to fully articulate an attempt to resolve this paradox we think that a good way to go would be to again pay attention to the temporal factor behind Nietzsche's conflicting accounts of affirmation. Naive affirmation is what Nietzsche ascribes to certain peoples living in more simple times before the slave revolt in morality gave man hidden depths and made him into a more complex, interesting creature. Reflective affirmation is what Nietzsche seems to be recommending for creatures such as ourselves who are victims of the two thousand years of self-vivisection. For us moderns naive affirmation is no longer possible and the best we can aim for is reflective affirmation, with the idea that one day, a long time in the future, we may again be capable of naive affirmation or even a combination of naive and reflective affirmation. As Nietzsche says

> We have to *learn to think differently* — in order at last, perhaps very late on to attain even more: *to feel differently*. (*Daybreak*, D: 103)

Nietzsche and sublimation

Nietzsche, like Freud and like their common predecessor Schopenhauer, takes individual humans to be, at some fundamental level, collections of drives. Schopenhauer was more prone to speak of the will (*Wille*) rather than drives (*Triebe*). How much this is merely a terminological difference is a difficult question to answer. For Schopenhauer, beyond individual time located willings, there is, notoriously, the transcendental notion of *Wille*, for which the Nietzsche of the middle and later periods had no sympathy. However Freud's notion of Eros may, arguably, be seen as a return to a more transcendental picture.

According to Nietzsche, most modern humans, as members of what he denigratingly calls the herd, are simply disorganized collections of competing drives, with different drives having relative ascendancy at different times

> In the present age human beings have in their bodies the heritage of multiple origins, that is opposite and not merely opposite drives and value standards that fight each other and rarely permit each other any rest. Such human

beings of late cultures and refracted lights will on the average be weaker human beings. (BGE: 200)

In many cases drives, particularly aggressive drives, are treated, as per the Freudian model, by repression,

> All instincts which are not discharged to the outside are turned back inside. This is what I call the internalization of man. From this first grows in man what people later call his "soul." The entire inner world, originally as thin as if stretched between two layers of skin, expanded and extended itself, acquired depth, width, and height to the extent that the discharge of human instinct out into the world was obstructed. (GM: Treatise 2, 16)

Central to Nietzsche's account is the notion of splitting off. Aggressive drives, which are not viewed as acceptable, typically because acting on them would exact a painful retribution, are repressed to the point that one does not even acknowledge that one has such drives. These drives may nevertheless find their outlet; often in disguised form. Indeed, often in a form that contradicts their very nature. Thus Nietzsche claims that the Christian value of brotherly love was originally in fact a transformed expression of hostile drives to dominate one's fellow man. By successfully preaching brotherly love the weak get their oppressors to voluntarily disarm themselves and become subservient to the values of the weak. In doing so they, both the weak and the strong who have been converted to the values of the weak, split-off their contrary aggressive drives from conscious apprehension, so that at the same time they harbour both unacknowledged aggressive drives and acknowledged beneficent drives. This repression and splitting-off of drives makes us sick creatures of what Nietzsche calls *ressentiment*.

For Nietzsche in certain rare cases drives rather than being split-off are harnessed into a centered, unified, whole. At one point Nietzsche took Wagner to be such a case:

> The dramatic element in Wagner's development is quite unmistakable from the moment when his ruling passion became aware of itself and took his nature in its charge: from that time on there was an end to fumbling, straying, to the proliferation of secondary shoots, and within the most convoluted courses and often daring trajectories assumed by his artistic plans there rules a single inner law, a will by which they can be explained. (UM: Untimely Meditation 3, 2)

The story of Wagner's achievement of a higher unity borne from some master-drive is of course the story Nietzsche would repeat about himself in the dramatic section of *Ecce Homo* where Nietzsche elaborates the subtitle of that work "How One Becomes What One Is":

> To become what one is, one must not have the slightest notion of what one is... The whole surface of consciousness – consciousness is a surface – must

be kept clear of all great imperatives...Meanwhile the organizing "idea" that is destined to rule keeps growing deep down – it begins to command; slowly it leads us back from side roads and wrong roads; it prepares single qualities and fitnesses that will one day prove to be indispensable as a means towards the whole – one by one, it trains all subservient capacities before giving any hint of the dominant task, "goal," "aim," or "meaning." (EH: "Why I am So Clever," 9)

This notion of training of subservient drives is to be explicated in terms of the redirection of those drives away from their initial, primary, goal towards a secondary goal that is more in line with that of the master-drive. This idea is partially expressed in the following passage from *Human, All too Human*:

> *Microcosm and macrocosm of culture.* Man makes the best discoveries about culture within himself when he finds two heterogeneous powers governing there. Given that a man loved the plastic arts or music as much as he was moved by the spirit of science, and that he deemed it impossible to end this contradiction by destroying the one and completely unleashing the other power; then, the only thing remaining to him is to make such a large edifice of culture out of himself that both powers can live there, even if at different ends of it; between them are sheltered conciliatory central powers, with the dominating strength to settle, if need be, any quarrels that break out. Such a cultural edifice in the single individual will have the greatest similarity to the cultural architecture of whole eras and, by analogy, provide continuous instruction about them. For wherever the great architecture of culture developed, it was its task to force opposing forces into harmony through an overwhelming aggregation of the remaining, less incompatible powers, yet without suppressing or shackling them. (HAH: Vol. 1, 276)

A point to be emphasized here is that on Nietzsche's ideal weaker drives are not suppressed or shackled. Rather, they are to be harnessed to allow their expression in service to a higher aim. Thus in his notebooks Nietzsche writes,

> Overcoming of the affects? No, if that means their weakening and annihilation. But instead employing them; which may mean a long tyrannizing of them .... At last they are confidently given freedom again: they love us as good servants and happily go wherever our best interests lie. (KSA: 12:39)

This gives us the material we need to affect a Nietzschean account of the distinction between repression and sublimation – a distinction Freud greatly relied upon but notoriously failed to clarify. Sublimation is what happens when a drive's primary aim is substituted for by a secondary aim that allows for expression of the drive in a manner consonant with the master drive. Repression is what happens when a drive is denied its immediate aim and is then split off from other drives in the sense that its aims are not integrated with the aims of other drives and it must battle, often unsuccessfully, for any opportunity to achieve expression.

The Nietzschean solution to the problem of differentiating sublimation from pathological symptoms may be summed up in the slogan that sublimations involve integration or unification, while pathological symptoms involve splitting-off or disintegration, as we might call it. What is disintegrated is of course the (possibility of a) unified self. For Nietzsche the difference between repression and sublimation is that in sublimation the stronger drive co-opts a weaker drive as an ally and this allows the weaker drive expression, albeit to an end that contains some degree of deflection from its original aim; whereas in repression the stronger drive attempts to stifle any expression of the weaker drive so that its expression is either fully stifled or can only be achieved in a heavily disguised form which often represents the inverse of the original aim (the Christian's hate and envy of, and desire to have power over, his fellow man being expressed as professions of brotherly love). The relation between sublimation and repression is that often but not always sublimations have repressions as antecedents. If a stronger drive does not at first have sufficient strength to co-opt a weaker drive to it own ends it may simply act to stifle that weaker drive. As the stronger drive gains in strength, opportunities for co-option rather than stifling may arise.

For Nietzsche unified selves, what he takes to be genuine persons, are rare achievements; hence he cautions "one should not at all assume that many humans are 'people'" (KSA: 12:491; translation ours), and " [m]ost men present pieces and fragments of man: one has to add them up for a complete man to appear" (KSA: 12:519). Similarly, Nietzsche sees the achievement of free will as something open to a limited few. (For more on both these themes see Gemes (2006)). It is Nietzsche's aim to foster the development of such genuine persons. In the same vein his Zarathustra says "it is my art and aim, to compose into one and bring together what is fragment and riddle and dreadful chance" (Z: Pt 2, 21). Sublimation, for Nietzsche, is the primary means to a unified self. Nietzsche, like Freud, takes sublimation as a mark of health. "Health" is a term that both Freud and, especially, Nietzsche, who more than Freud explicitly pronounces a strong normative agenda, positively valorize. However, while for Freud health is measured in more utilitarian terms of relative contentment, for Nietzsche health is measured in terms of such interrelated vectors as freedom from *ressentiment*, creative agonal struggle between drives, self overcoming, and superabundance of expressive energy.

Nietzsche's important and difficult normative ideas of *amor fati*, eternal recurrence, and affirmation of life are all strongly related to his aim of overcoming *ressentiment* – the French term *ressentiment* is expressly used by Nietzsche, most notably in the first essay of the *Genealogy*. (cf. GM: Treatise 1, 10). *Ressentiment* is directly connected to repression in that where there *is ressentiment* there is some drive that we have been forced to stifle. Nietzsche claims that in order to fully love fate or to fully wish back everything eternally, both of which are exemplary ways of affirming life, we would have to overcome all such *ressentiment*. To affirm all of one's life, to overcome *ressentiment*, would be to affirm all of one's drives; life, for Nietzsche, being nothing but a collection of drives. This does not mean to simply let all of one's drives have free expression. That would involve conflict, chaos and, inevitably, disintegration. It means harnessing one's drives to allow them a form of concerted expression. Sublimation is for Nietzsche the key means to such concerted expression and, hence, to overcoming *ressentiment*.

Perspectivism

So far we have emphasized, in keeping with Nietzsche's own advice, a largely psychological or moral psychological reading of Nietzsche. In particular, we have downplayed epistemological and metaphysical elements in Nietzsche's texts. It was suggested above that even where Nietzsche addresses, or seems to be addressing, metaphysical and epistemological issues he does so primarily in order to further his normative aims. In this and the next section we will consider what are generally taken to be Nietzsche's best known epistemological and metaphysical claims and show how they fit this reading.

Nietzsche's most well-known epistemological claim is his so-called perspectivism. In fact, the term 'Perspektivismus' (perspectivism) occurs only on a handful of occasions in Nietzsche's writings (including his notebooks). What is widely taken to be the canonical passage on perspectivism occurs in the twelfth section of the third essay of Nietzsche's *On the Genealogy of Morality*:

> There is *only* a perspectival "knowing"; and the *more* affects we allow to speak out about a matter, the *more* eyes, different eyes, we know how to bring to bear on one and the same matter, the more complete will our "concept" of this matter, our "objectivity" be. (GM: Treatise 3, 12)

Using this passage and other texts some take Nietzsche's perspectivism to be a claim about truth. Thus Schacht (1985), Nehamas (1985) and Danto (1965) have taken it as a denial of the correspondence theory of truth. Some readings, including occasionally those of some of the above mentioned authors, suggest it is a blanket denial of truth. Besides having little textual support – note the key text does not even mention truth – the anti-truth readings quickly lead to paradox inducing questions "Is it true that there is no truth?" Similar problems arise for readings which suggest that perspectivism is the claim that there is only perspectival truth. This claim invites the facile response "Well that's not true from my perspective." Danto argues that Nietzsche was offering a pragmatic theory of truth. However there are plenty of texts that demonstrate that Nietzsche allowed for a clear distinction between that which is useful and that which is true (cf. BGE: 2–4, and KSA: 12:317, repr. WP: 487).

More recent readings in Janaway (2007) and Leiter (2002), sticking more closely to the text, take perspectivism to be a claim about the nature of knowledge.

They interpret perspectivism to consist of both a strong and a weak claim. The strong claim is that one's interests (stressed by Leiter) or one's affects (stressed by Janaway) are constitutive of one's knowledge. But exactly how this is so is not at all explained, and the examples they give simply suggest the weaker reading that what interests/affects one has plays a causal role in the knowledge one has. The problem here is that this seems to make perspectivism a fairly banal claim. No one would dispute, for instance, that a given sports fan's interest in golf plays a causal – note, not a justificatory role – in his knowing that Tiger Woods won the 2002 US Open.

If we turn to the following text from Nietzsche's notebooks we gain material that allows for a more fruitful reading of his perspectivism:

> As far as the word "knowledge" has sense, the world is knowable: but it is interpretable otherwise, it has no meaning behind it, but countless meanings – "Perspectivism." It is our needs that interpret the world: every drive and its for and against. Every drive is a kind of attempt to dominate; each has its own perspective, which it wants to force as a norm on the other drives. (KSA: 12:315)

This suggests that perspectivism involves the following descriptive component

> Descriptive Component of Perspectivism: Each drive has its own perspective/ interpretation of the world and seeks to express that perspective/interpretation of the world, often at the expense of other drives.

We have previously seen that Nietzsche's idea of health is to let as many drives as possible be expressed. To ensure concerted expression, rather than a debilitating chaos, such expression is to be achieved, not by stronger drives repressing weaker ones, but by sublimating them. Now the above passage attributes perspectives to drives. So we may conclude that Nietzsche's idea of health involves letting as many perspectives as possible be expressed. This thought is implicit in such a passage as the following:

> The highest man would have the greatest multiplicity of drives, in the relatively greatest strength that can be endured. Indeed, where the plant "man" shows himself strongest one finds instincts that conflict powerfully (e.g., in Shakespeare), but are controlled. (KSA: 11:289)

It is worth noting that the passage from GM Treatise 3, 12, cited above occurs immediately after a passage in which Nietzsche introduced the key exponent of what he sees as the debilitating life hating ascetic ideal which is the focus of Treatise 3, namely the ascetic priest. The ascetic priest in the GM specifically preaches a pacification, that is repression of one's sexual, aggressive, and various other, drives. This suggests the following normative component to perspectivism:

Prescriptive Component of Perspectivism: The healthiest (highest) life involves the maximal expression of the richest set of drives, each of which has its own perspective, interpretation of the world.

Why then does Nietzsche present perspectivism as a thesis about knowledge in both the notebook passage quoted above and the passage from GM Treatise 3, 12? First it is worth noting that he puts quotation marks around the term "knowable" in the notebook passage, and around both "knowledge" and "objectivity" in GM Treatise 3, 12, thereby suggesting these notions are not his real concerns. The greater context makes clear that one of his targets is Schopenhauer's idea of a certain form of alleged disinterested knowledge that Schopenhauer claims, in aesthetic contemplation at least, allows us to escape the world of willing. Yet here again, arguably, the principal target is not Schopenhauer's actual account of disinterested knowledge; rather it is Schopenhauer's valorization of the ascetic injunction to escape the world of the will, or what Nietzsche calls the drives. Finally, given that Nietzsche takes his audience to be labouring under the modern form of the ascetic ideal which puts an extreme value on truth and knowledge (this is a key point of emphasis in GM Treatise 3, 23) it is not surprising that Nietzsche should disguise his anti-ascetic injunction in terms such as "knowledge" and "objectivity" which he takes to be overly valued by his audience.

Will to power

Nietzsche's most well-known metaphysical, or at least ontological, doctrine is that of the will to power. Partly this is the result of the fact that his sister after his death published a selection from his notebooks under the title *The Will to Power*. Nietzsche himself planned but scrapped several attempts to write a book with that title. Some authors, most notably Martin Heidegger, and more recently John Richardson, have argued that will to power is indeed Nietzsche's central idea. At its extreme will to power can be read as an all-embracing metaphysical doctrine according to which everything is will to power, as others have claimed that everything is composed of atoms or everything is composed of forces. This reading is suggested by the following rhetorically powerful last lines of *The Will to Power*:

> *This world is the will to power and nothing besides!* And you yourselves are also this will to power – and nothing besides! (KSA: 11:610, repr. WP: 1067)

While Heidegger takes this grand metaphysical interpretation, Richardson (1996) takes a more plausible approach which limits will to power to all organic phenomena. As Richardson and others have noted, in his published texts Nietzsche develops only the more limited scope claim. Richardson's interpretation deals with the seemingly problematic attribution of wills to all organic phenomena, which obviously would include non-sentient life such as plant life, by emphasizing the role of drives in Nietzsche's philosophy. Drives have a telic structure; each drive comes with its own aim and in talking of a will to power Nietzsche, according to Richardson, is really talking of each drive's disposition to find expressions that further that drive's aim, often at the expense of other competing drives.

This biologistic account of will to power in terms of organically based drives "striving" for dominance fits in nicely with the account of perspectivism given above. There it was claimed that part of Nietzsche's perspectivism is that each drive perspective comes with an interpretation or perspective and seeks to express that often at the expense of other drives. Indeed, in a section of his book entitled "Wills to Power as Perspectives", Richardson points to a passage in *The Will to Power* where Nietzsche speaks of

> this necessary perspectivism according to which every center of force – and not only the human being –construes the rest of the world from itself, i.e. measures, touches, forms, according to its own nature. (KSA: 13:373, repr. WP: 636)

To give an example: Imagine a middle sized animal (a hyena) that sees a similarly sized animal (say a small boar) not too far away. His drive for sustenance may incline him to attack the distant animal, thus interpreting it as prey, as a source of food; his drive for survival may at the same time incline him to flee, thus interpreting the distant animal as a potential predator. Thus we have the renowned fight or flight syndrome as an expression of the conflict between two competing drives. The example of the hyena explains how life can be said to have drives that interpret. Here interpretation comes through a certain complex functional relation and does not necessarily involve consciousness or even sentience, so even a plant may in some attenuated sense be seen as interpreting its environment. This combination of perspectivism with Nietzsche's concept of will to power is neatly and concisely expressed in the following passage from *The Will to Power*:

> Perspectivism is only a complex form of specificity. My idea is that every specific body strives to become master over all space and to extend its force (– its will to power). (KSA: 13:373, repr. WP: 636)

One may be tempted to see Nietzsche's reliance on the notion of drive, and, indeed, his general biologistic outlook, as a reflection of particularly nineteenth century preoccupations. Certainly many readers will have just such a dismissive attitude to Nietzsche's preoccupations with the notion of degeneration – though perennially popular debates about nature versus nurture, genetic determination, the dumbing down of culture etc., continue to this day. Even more generally, while authors such as Leiter (2002) and Richardson (1996) have made much of Nietzsche's naturalism, one may wonder how central this is to what we along with Leiter see as Nietzsche's central concern, namely, his normative agenda. However if we strip Nietzsche of his drive psychology, while we may be left with his high appraisal of the value of creative individuals, his whole diagnosis of the conditions that prevent such individuals from flourishing will be stripped of much of its force and plausibility. The same will be true of his whole diagnosis of the nihilism in our current Judeo-Christian morality. Even if we resist Richardson's very plausible attempt to domesticate will to power by interpreting it in terms of a drive ontology, it is hard to see what status many of Nietzsche's explanations of human phenomena would have if his notion of drives were rejected.

Nietzsche's politics

Given Nietzsche's strident critiques of democracy, equalitarianism, liberalism and the like, as promoters and manifestations of philistine culture, and his emphasis on the need for a new philosophy of life affirmation, it is a striking to many modern readers that no positive political program issues from his philosophy. Even one who shares his extreme valorization of the importance of great, creative individuals is in the end left with no clear vision of how Nietzsche thinks society might be arranged to promote the development of such individuals. Indeed, one can imagine that one sympathetic to liberal democracies, even capitalist liberal democracies, might argue that even if one shares Nietzsche's extreme valuation of great individuals, liberal democracies, with their extreme tolerance for individual expression, actually afford the best current political landscape for the development of such individuals. Such an advocate might ask "Does Nietzsche seriously believe a return to dictatorships or an aristocratic society would provide more opportunities for individual development?" And those many readers with a more humanist bent will, as they always have, shudder at Nietzsche's seemingly wholesale rejection of many basic enlightenment values, in particular that of active compassion towards those born into less favourable circumstances. As we share in many of those enlightenment humanist values we are glad that Nietzsche's aristocratic, elitist values remain uncongenial to the vast majority of those who are exposed to them. And yet we believe there is nothing here that Nietzsche himself could seriously object too. The key to seeing this is an appreciation that Nietzsche is ultimately an esoteric thinker. He took his real, his ideal audience, to be very few in number. His ideal readers are not ordinary members of enlightened liberal democratic states, not even the intelligentsia of such states, indeed, not even the philosophy professors of such states. What he sought were rare gems, still in a relatively uncut state, who might be inspired by his texts to find their own unique voices. And on this matter, like so much else, Nietzsche was wonderfully prescient, despite his occasional moment of pessimism about ever finding true readers. Nietzsche's heritage is to be found in the myriad of creative artists and thinkers, from poets such as Rilke, W. B. Yeats and Stefan George, novelists such as Thomas Mann, Herman Hesse, and D. H. Lawrence, playwrights such as Eugene O'Neill and George Bernard Shaw, psychologists such as Freud, Jung and Adler, and philosophers such as Heidegger and Foucault who were crucially inspired by Nietzsche and often liberated through his influence to find their own unique voices. It is a cutting irony that the philosophers cited here, who are often quite inaccurate in much of what they write directly on the subject of Nietzsche, are in a Nietzschean sense better heirs of Nietzsche's influence than those more careful Nietzsche scholars who have, especially most recently, effectively and successfully, laboured to accurately get to the depth of Nietzsche's enigmatic thought.

References

Works by Nietzsche

Nietzsche (A) *The Antichrist*, trans. R. J. Hollingdale (with *Twilight of the Idols*), Harmondsworth: Penguin, 1969.

—— (BGE) *Beyond Good and Evil*, edited by Rolf-Peter Horstmann and Judith Norman, trans. Judith Norman, Cambridge: Cambridge University Press, 2002.

—— (BT) *The Birth of Tragedy*, edited by Raymond Geuss and Ronald Speirs, trans. Ronald Speirs, Cambridge: Cambridge University Press, 1999.

—— (D) *Daybreak*, edited by Maudemarie Clark and Brian Leiter, trans. R. J. Hollingdale. Cambridge: Cambridge University Press, 1997.

—— (EH) *Ecce Homo*, in *On the Genealogy of Morals and Ecce Homo*, trans. by W. Kaufmannn and R. J. Hollingdale, New York: Vintage, 1969.

—— (GM) *On the Genealogy of Morality*, trans. Maudemarie Clark and Alan J. Swensen, Indianapolis, IN: Hackett, 1998.

—— (GS) *The Gay Science*, edited by Bernard Williams, trans. Josephine Nauckhoff and Adrian del Caro, Cambridge: Cambridge University Press, 2001.

—— (HAH) *Human, All Too Human*, edited by Richard Schacht, trans. R. J. Hollingdale, Cambridge: Cambridge University Press, 1996.

—— (KSA) *Sämtliche Werke: Kritische Studienausgabe in 15 Einzelbänden*, 15 vols, edited by G. Colli and M. Montinari. Berlin: de Gruyter, 1988.

—— (TI) *Twilight of the Idols*, trans. R. J. Hollingdale (with *The Antichrist*), Harmondsworth: Penguin, 1969.

—— (UM) *Untimely Meditations*, trans. R. J. Hollingdale, Cambridge: Cambridge University Press, 1986.

—— (WP) *The Will to Power*, edited by Walter Kaufmann, trans. Walter Kaufmann and R. J. Hollingdale, New York: Vintage Books, 1968. This work was not published in Nietzsche's lifetime and consists of writings taken from his notebooks. All references to this work are accompanied by corresponding references to the relevant notes from the KSA (see above).

—— (Z) *Thus Spoke Zarathustra*, trans R.J. Hollingdale. Middlesex: Penguin, 1969.

Works by others

Allison, David (1985) *The New Nietzsche*, Cambridge, MA: MIT Press.

Came, Daniel (2004) "Nietzsche's Attempt at a Self-Criticism. Art and Morality in *The Birth of Tragedy*," *Nietzsche-Studien* 33: 37–67.

Chamberlain, J. E., and S. L. Gilman (1985) *Degeneration*, New York: Appleton.

Clark, Maudemarie (1998) "Nietzsche's Empiricism and Debt to Schopenhauer," in Janaway (1998).

Danto, Arthur (1965) *Nietzsche as Philosopher*, New York: Columbia University Press.

Darwin, Charles (1972) *The Descent of Man and Selection in Relation to Sex*, New York: AMS Press.

Gemes, Ken (2006) "Nietzsche on Free Will, Autonomy, and the Sovereign Individual," *Proceedings of the Aristotelian Society Supplementary Volume* 80: 321–38.

—— (1992) "Nietzsche's Critique of Truth," *Philosophy and Phenomenological Research* 52: 47–65; reprinted in J. Richardson and B. Leiter (2001).

Geuss, Raymond (1999) Introduction to *The Birth of Tragedy and Other Writings*, edited by Raymond Geuss and Ronald Speirs, trans. Ronald Speirs, Cambridge: Cambridge University Press.

Habermas, Jürgen. (1987) *The Philosophical Discourse of Modernity*, Cambridge, MA: MIT Press.

Hillis Miller, J. (1981) "The Disarticulation of the Self in Nietzsche," *Monist* 69: 247–61.

Janaway, Christopher (ed) (1998) *Willing and Nothingness: Schopenhauer as Nietzsche's Educator*, Oxford: Oxford University Press.

—— (2007) *Beyond Selflessness: Reading Nietzsche's Genealogy*, Oxford: Oxford University Press.

Leiter, Brian (2002) *Nietzsche on Morality*, London: Routledge.

Lombroso, C., and G. Ferrero (1899) *The Female Offender*, New York: Appleton.

May, Simon (1999) *Nietzsche's Ethics and His "War on Morality,"* Oxford: Clarendon Press.

Mill, John Stuart (CW) (1963–91) *Collected Works of John Stuart Mill*, edited John M. Robson, Toronto: University of Toronto Press.

Nehamas, Alexander (1985) *Nietzsche: Life as Literature*, Cambridge, MA: Harvard University Press.

Nordau, Max (1895) *Degeneration*, London: William Heinemann.

Richardson, John (1996) *Nietzsche's System*, Oxford: Oxford University Press.

Reginster, Bernhard (2006) *The Affirmation of Life: Nietzsche on Overcoming Nihilism*, Cambridge, MA: Harvard University Press.

Pick, Daniel (1989) *Faces of Degeneration*, Cambridge: Cambridge University Press.

Schacht, Richard (1985) *Nietzsche*, London: Routledge & Kegan Paul.

Schrift, Alan (1995) *Nietzsche's French Legacy*, London: Routledge.

Soll, Ivan (1989) "Pessimism and the Tragic View of Life: Reconsiderations of Nietzsche's *Birth of Tragedy*' in Solomon, Robert and Higgins, Kathleen, *Reading Nietzsche*, Oxford: Oxford University Press.

—— (1998) "Schopenhauer, Nietzsche, and the Redemption of Life through Art," in Christopher Janaway (ed.), *Willing and Nothingness: Schopenhauer as Nietzsche's Educator*, Oxford: Oxford University Press.

Further reading

As well as the books by Reginster, May, Leiter, Janaway, Nehamas, and Richardson mentioned above, we also strongly recommend: Maudemarie Clark, *Nietzsche on Truth and Philosophy* (Cambridge: Cambridge University Press, 1990), a ground breaking treatment of Nietzsche's stance on the notion of truth and knowledge; John Richardson and Brian Leiter (eds) *Nietzsche* (Oxford: Oxford University Press, 2000), a collection of some of the best articles on Nietzsche, mainly from the late twentieth century; Christa Davis Acampora (ed.) *Nietzsche's On the Genealogy of Morals: Critical Essays* (Lanham, MD: Rowman & Littlefield, 2006), a collection of important articles on what is now often taken to be Nietzsche's canonical text; Richard Schacht (ed.) *Nietzsche, Genealogy, Morality: Essays on Nietzsche's Genealogy of Morals* (Berkeley: University of California Press, 1994), another excellent collection of important articles on GM; and M. S. Silk and J. P. Stern, *Nietzsche on Tragedy* (London: Cambridge University Press, 1981), somewhat fragmentary in style, but nevertheless still one of the best books devoted to BT's argument, style, and intellectual context.

14
BERGSON
Keith Ansell-Pearson

Introduction

Henri Bergson (1859–1941) is widely recognized to be France's greatest philosopher of the modern period. He was the author of four classic texts of philosophy, three of them characterized by a combination of exceptional philosophical gifts and impressive mastery of extensive scientific literature. Each text offers readers a number of theoretical innovations. *Time and Free Will* (1889) provides a novel account of free will by showing that time is not space and that psychic states do not lend themselves to treatment as magnitudes. *Matter and Memory* (1896) provides a non-orthodox (non-Cartesian) dualism of matter and mind, seeking to show that whilst the difference between matter and perception is one of degree (unless we construe it in these terms the emergence of perception out of matter becomes something mysterious and inexplicable), that between perception and memory is one of kind (unless we construe it in these terms memory is deprived of any autonomous character and is reduced to being a merely diluted form of perception, a secondary perception as we find in Locke). *Matter and Memory* offers an extremely rich and novel account of different types of memory that philosophical psychology is still catching up with today. In *Creative Evolution* (1907) Bergson endeavours to demonstrate the need for a philosophy of life in which the theory of knowledge and a theory of life are viewed as inseparably bound up with one another. In the text Bergson seeks to establish what philosophy must learn from the new biology (the neo-Darwinism established by August Weismann) and what philosophy can offer the new theory of the evolution of life. It is a *tour de force*, a work of truly extraordinary philosophical ambition. In *The Two Sources of Morality and Religion* (1932), his final text, and where the engagement with scientific literature is not as extensive, Bergson outlines a novel approach to the study of society (sociology) with his categories of the "closed" and the "open" and the "static" and the "dynamic." He advances a criticism of the rationalist approach to ethics that merits being taken as seriously as Nietzsche's critique of attempts to establish ethics on a rational foundation (Nietzsche 1998: §186). Finally, there are two important collections of essays: *Mind Energy* and *Creative Mind*.

Bergson's philosophy has a number of unique features to it. He has an impressive grasp of the history of science and of new scientific development such as thermodynamics and neo-Darwinism. His ambition was to restore the absolute as the legitimate object of philosophy and to accomplish this by showing how it is possible to think beyond the human condition. Although he contests Kant's stress on the relativity of knowledge to the human standpoint in a manner similar to Hegel, his conception of the absolute is not the same. This is the surprise of Bergson, and perhaps explains why he appears as such an unfamiliar figure to us today: he seeks to demonstrate the absolute – conceived as the totality of differences in the world, differences of degree and differences of kind – through placing man back into nature and the evolution of life. That is, he uses the resources of naturalism and empiricism to support an apparently Idealist philosophical program. Indeed, Bergson argues that "true empiricism" is "the real metaphysics" and held that the more the sciences of life develop the more they will feel the need to reintegrate thought into the very heart of nature (Bergson 2007a: 22). In his own day he was read primarily as an empiricist whose thinking amounted, in the words of his former pupil and later harsh critic, Jacques Maritain, to a "wild experimentalism." Maritain accused Bergson of realizing in metaphysics "the very soul of empiricism," of producing an ontology of becoming not "after the fashion of Hegel's panlogism" but rather "after the fashion of an integral empiricism" (Maritain 1943: 65). Julien Benda vigorously protested against Bergson's demand for new ways of thinking and new methods in philosophy and called for a return to the hyper-rationalism of Spinoza (see Benda 1954). Bergson does not readily fit into the two main camps that define the contemporary academic institution of philosophy: neither the continental one which insists on keeping apart philosophy and science and regards any interest in science as philosophically suspect, nor the analytic one which cheerfully subsumes philosophy within the ambit of the natural sciences and renders metaphysics otiose.

In histories of modern philosophy it is standard to place Bergson alongside Friedrich Nietzsche (1844–1900) and Wilhelm Dilthey (1833–1911) as a philosopher of life and to portray him, along with Nietzsche, as an irrationalist (see Grogin 1988: 73–6, Lehan 1992: 324–5; on Bergson and irrationalism see Höffding 1915: 232; Maritain 1943: 57–61; Schwartz 1992: 289–91). This standard criticism of Bergson amounts to a caricature. As in Nietzsche, reason is promoted by Bergson; what is subjected to critique is a self-sufficient reason and intellectualism. Bergson is not anti-rationalist but anti-intellectualist (see Gutting 2001: 73). Like Nietzsche, Bergson wants a philosophy that can do justice to contingency, to particularity, to individuality, to spontaneous forces and energies, to the creation of the new, and so on. A philosophy of history is found in neither and Hegel's panlogism is anathema to both. Nietzsche famously advocates translating the human back into nature (Nietzsche 1998: §230); we find this echoed in Bergson when he argues in favor of a genetic approach to questions of morality and religion that places "man back in nature as a whole" (Bergson 1979: 208). Those phenomena that have been denied a history and a nature must be given them back.

What stands in the way of our intellectual development and growth? Bergson's answer is the same as Nietzsche's: the prejudices of philosophers with their trust in immediate certainties and penchant for philosophical dogmatizing (Nietzsche 1998: Preface and 43; Bergson 2007a: 40). Both accuse Schopenhauer's will to life of being an empty generalization that proves disastrous for science. For Nietzsche, Schopenhauer's doctrine can only result in a "false reification" since it leads to the view that all that exists empirically is the manifestation of one will (Nietzsche 1986: Vol. 2, pt 1, §5). For Bergson, the "will to life" is an empty concept supported by a barren theory of metaphysics (Bergson 1979: 115). It is impossible, he argues, to cite a biological discovery due to pure reasoning, whilst all the molds in which we seek to force the living crack, being too narrow and too rigid for what we try to put into them. Both thinkers practice historical philosophizing and identify this with the intellectual virtue of modesty. Both insist on the need to provide a genesis of the intellect as a way of ascertaining the evolutionary reasons as to why we have the intellectual habits we do. At certain points in his development Nietzsche is willing to sacrifice metaphysics to history and hands over to science the task of coming up with a history of the genesis of thought and concepts (Nietzsche 1986: Vol. 1, §§10 and 16; Vol. 2, pt 1, §10). For Bergson this is a task that can only be adequately performed by a reformed metaphysics that proceeds via a new method of intuition. This is, in essence, Bergson's response to Kant's Copernican Revolution. In 1878 Nietzsche insists that there is only representation (*Vorstellung*) and that no hunch can take us any further. By 1886, however, Nietzsche commits himself to the view that there is, in fact, a dimension of the world outside of representation – the will to power as a pre-form (*Vorform*) of life – but insists that this is to be approached through the "conscience of method" (Nietzsche 1998: §36), a critical project which, like all others in Nietzsche, denotes the method of the "intellectual conscience" that seeks to replace the theological motivations of Kant's critical project with properly scientific ones (Nietzsche 2005b: §12). Bergson's response to Kant is equally critical and focuses attention on the soundness of the decisions Kant has made about the nature and extent of theoretical knowledge.

There are two main criticisms that have traditionally been advanced against the kind of project undertaken by Bergson. One is that naturalism cannot account for differences in kind insofar as it reduces modes of existence to differences of degree, especially between the human and the rest of nature. The other is that Bergson's thinking is guilty of the error of biologism (a criticism also leveled at Nietzsche's work), that is, of making an illegitimate extension of the biological to all spheres of existence such as the moral and the social (on biologism see Heidegger 1987: 39–48; Troeltsch 1991: 55). This criticism is, in effect, implied in the first concern. In the course of this essay I shall suggest that neither point has purchase when applied to Bergson.

Bergson's reception of Kant

Bergson does not accept two key theses of Kant's Copernican Revolution: (a) the claim that knowledge is relative to our faculties of knowing, and (b) the claim that metaphysics is impossible on the grounds that there can be no knowledge outside of science (Newtonian mechanism) or that science has correctly determined the bounds of metaphysics. For Bergson a new relation between philosophy and science is called for and knowledge of the absolute is to be restored:

If we now inquire why Kant did not believe that the matter of our knowledge extends beyond its form, this is what we find. The criticism of our knowledge of nature that was instituted by Kant consisted in ascertaining what our mind must be and what Nature must be *if* the claims of our science are justified; but of these claims themselves Kant has not made the criticism. I mean that he took for granted the idea of a science that is one, capable of binding with the same force all the parts of what is given, and of co-ordinating them into a system presenting on all sides an equal solidity. He did not consider … that science became less and less objective, more and more symbolical, to the extent that it went from the physical to the vital, from the vital to the psychical. (2007b: 229)

Bergson contends that the physical laws of scientific knowledge are, in their mathematical form, artificial constructions foreign to the real movement of nature since its standards of measurement are conventional ones created by the concerns of the human intellect and its attachment to utilitarian groupings. This does not prevent Bergson from appreciating the success of modern science; on the contrary, it is his insights into the specific character of science that enables him to appreciate the reasons for its success, namely, the fact that it is contingent and relative to the variables it has selected and to the order in which it stages problems. For Bergson, philosophy needs to involve itself in special problems as we encounter in the positive sciences. The true difficulty is to create the unique solution of the problem which the philosopher has posed anew in the very effort of trying to solve it, and this involves abstracting oneself from language (from order-words) which has been made for conversation and which satisfies the requirements of common sense and social action, but not those of thinking. The genuine philosopher, as opposed to the amateur, is one who does not accept the terms of a problem as a common problem that has been definitively posed and which then requires that s/he select from the available solutions to the problem (the example Bergson gives to illustrate his point is that of Samuel Butler rejecting Darwin's solution in favour of Lamarck's) (Bergson 2002: 370).

Bergson makes two major claims contra Kant: the first is that the mind cannot be restricted to the intellect since it overflows it; and second, that duration has to be granted an absolute existence, which requires thinking time on a different plane to space. According to Bergson, Kant considered only three possibilities for a theory of knowledge: (i) the mind is determined by external things; (ii) things are determined by the mind itself; (iii) between the mind and things we have to suppose a mysterious agreement or pre-established harmony. In contrast to these three options, Bergson seeks to demonstrate the need for a double genesis of matter and the intellect. It is not that matter has determined the form of the intellect or that the intellect simply imposes its own form upon matter, or even that there is some curious harmony between the two we can never explain, but rather that the two have, in the course of evolution, progressively adapted themselves one to the other and so attained a common form. He regards this adaptation as coming about naturally, "*because it is the same inversion of the same movement which creates at once the intellectuality of mind and the materiality of things*"

(Bergson 2007b: 133). Both science and the intellect for Bergson concern themselves with the aspect of repetition. The intellect selects in a given situation whatever is like something already known so as to fit it into a pre-existing schema; in this way it applies "its principle that 'like produces like'" (2007b: 19). It rebels against the idea of an original and unforeseeable production of forms. Similarly, science focuses its attention on isolable or closed systems, simply because anything "that is irreducible and irreversible in the successive moments of a history eludes" it (*ibid.*). In cases of organic evolution, Bergson insists, foreseeing the form in advance is not possible. This is not because there are no conditions or specific causes of evolution but rather owing to the fact that they are built into, are part and parcel of, the particular form of organic life and so "are peculiar to that phase of its history in which life finds itself at the moment of producing the form" (*ibid.*: 18). There is a need to display a readiness to be taken by surprise in the study of nature and to appreciate that there might be a difference between human logic and the logic of nature. The scientist has to cultivate a feeling for the complexity of natural phenomena. In this respect we cannot approach nature with any *a priori* conceptions of parts and wholes or any *a priori* conception of what constitutes life, including how we delimit the boundaries of an organism and hence define it. We must resist the temptation to place or hold nature within our own ideas or shrink reality to the measure of them. Contra Kant, therefore, we should not allow our need for a unity of knowledge to impose itself upon the multiplicity of nature. Moreover, to follow the sinuosities of reality means that we cannot slot the real into a concept of all concepts, be it Spirit, Substance, Ego or Will (Bergson 1965: 35 and 49).

Bergson argues that it "is not enough to determine, by careful analysis, the categories of thought; we must engender them" (2007b: 133). A theory of knowledge and a theory of life are to be viewed as inseparable since if the critique of knowledge is not accompanied by a philosophy of life – which will study the emergence of the human intellect and the habits of the mind in its evolutionary context of adaptation – we will blindly accept the concepts that the intellect has placed at our disposal and enclose our facts within a set of pre-existing frames. We need to show how the frames of knowledge have been constructed and how they can be enlarged and gone beyond. Instead of ending up with a split between appearance and reality, or between phenomenon and noumenon, we now approach epistemological issues in terms of the relation between our partial perspective on the real, which has evolved in accordance with the vital needs of adaptation, and a mobile whole. The sensible intuition of a homogenous time and space that Kant establishes as transcendental forms, for example, presupposes a "real duration" and a "real extensity": the former are stretched out beneath the latter in order that the moving continuity can be divided and a becoming can be fixed (Bergson 1991: 211).

Thinking beyond the human condition

Bergson conceives philosophy as the discipline that "raises us above the human condition" ("*la philosophie nous aura élevés au-dessus de la condition humaine*") and makes the effort to "surpass" (*dépasser*) it (Bergson 1965: 50; 2007a: 45).[1] Philosophy provides us with the methods for reversing the normal directions of the mind (instrumental, utilitarian), so upsetting its habits. Because it finds itself having to work against the most inveterate habits of the mind, Bergson compares philosophy to an act of violence (2007a: 33, 40; 2007b: 19). The aim of the enterprise is to expand the humanity within us and allow humanity to surpass itself by reinserting itself in the whole (it recognizes it is part of nature and the evolution of life) (*ibid.*: 124). Intelligence is reabsorbed into its principle and comes to know its own genesis. In spite of what one might think, this makes the task of philosophy a modest one (*ibid.*: 123). If we suppose that philosophy is an affair of perception, then it cannot simply be a matter of correcting perception but only of extending it. Like Nietzsche before him, Bergson is seeking to draw attention to fact that humanity has constituted itself on the basis of a set of errors without being aware of this (Nietzsche 1974: §§110–12, 115). We find ourselves born or thrown into a world that is "ready-made" and that we have not made our own, and it is when we recognize this that we are motivated to think beyond the human condition.

Bergson was motivated by what he saw as the need to correct the wandering and aimless nature of much of our research into the workings of the mind, in which there is an absence of a guiding thread (Bergson 1965: 53). The supposition he sees at work in psychology is that the mind has fallen from heaven in which its subdivision into functions and faculties (memory, imagination, conception, and perception) needs only to be recognized. Only an inquiry into the fundamental exigencies of life will enable us to raise the most important questions, such as, for example, whether the ordinary subdivision into various faculties is natural or artificial. Should our divisions be maintained or modified? Moreover, if one of the results of the research conducted is that the exigencies of life are found to be working in an analogous fashion in humans, animals and plants, what will be the consequences for all kinds of disciplines and modes of inquiry? Our reliance on an unconscious metaphysics has led us to cut up and distribute psychological life in an inadequate manner, one that cannot do justice to the complexity of our evolution and how the mind has been formed. There is, therefore, a need to dig down to sources and roots. Both Nietzsche and Bergson share this commitment to archaeology as a way of opening up the human condition and subjecting the mind and its habits of thinking to a genetic history.

Bergson insists that the "whole" cannot be approached in terms of ready-made criteria of an organic totality. Neither is the whole of nature or the evolution of the fundamental directions of life, such as the divergent tendencies of instinct and intelligence, to be thought in dialectical terms of contradiction, negation, and sublation. It is not necessary to ascribe to evolution, whether natural or historical, a logical or dialectical development. On this point Bergson has clearly been inspired by the Darwinian revolution. Bergson considered Darwin to be the greatest of all modern naturalists and held that the doctrine of evolution would impose itself on our thinking. The conception of the "whole" he has in mind is that of a universal mobility. True evolutionism, he says, must focus on the study of becoming but this requires that we do not follow the path of perception which would reduce an "infinite multiplicity of becomings" to the single representation of a "becoming *in general*" (Bergson 2007b:

194). For Bergson the whole enjoys neither interiority nor totality; individuated forms of life have a tendency towards closure but this is never accomplished. As Bergson puts it in *Creative Evolution*, "finality is external or it is nothing at all" (*ibid.*: 27). That the whole is never given but is a pure virtual should meet with our delight since it is only our habitual confusion of time with space, and the assimilation of time into space, that makes us think the whole is given, if only in the eyes of God (see Deleuze 1991: 104). We could say: on the level of life there is only actualization and differentiation but to make adequate sense of this we need to appeal to a conception of the whole, and what matters is the conception we evince of it. For Bergson it is the *élan vital* conceived as a "virtual" power of self-differentiation; for Nietzsche it is the will to power conceived as a pre-form (*Vorform*) of life (a potential of energy), which is also a power of self-differentiation. Without a conception of the whole we can only posit what comes into existence in mysterious and inexplicable terms of so many brute eruptions of being.

The "human condition" refers, then, not to an existential predicament but to accrued evolutionary habits of thought that prevent us from recognizing our own creative conditions of existence and restricts the domain of praxis to social utility. Bergson believes that there is a basis for a novel alliance between metaphysics and the new post-Newtonian sciences, insofar as both, working in concert, are able to discover the natural articulations of the universe that have been carved artificially by the intellect. The categories of stable being are not simple illusions but have their anchorage in the conditions of our evolutionary existence; space, for example, is a schema of matter that represents the limit of a movement of expansion that would come to an end as an external envelope of all possible extensions. On account of its ever more complete demonstration of the reciprocal action of all material points upon each other science produces an insight into the universal continuity between things. We might suppose that all we need to do is to replace the notion of matter with that of force, but this is still insufficient, for what is decisive are "movements and lines of force whose reciprocal solidarity brings back to us universal continuity" (Bergson 1991: 200). It should, therefore, be the task of a theory of matter to find the reality hidden beneath our customary images of it and that are relative to our adaptive needs. This attempt to think beyond our customary images of matter explains why Bergson claims that "every philosophy of nature ends by finding the discontinuity that our senses perceive incompatible with the general properties of matter" (*ibid.*: 201).

In a letter of 1903 to William James Bergson speaks of the need to transcend "a simple logic" and "the methods of over-systematic philosophy which postulates the unity of the whole." If a "truly *positive* philosophy is possible," he adds, it "can only be found there" (Bergson 2002: 358–9). This would be the opposite of a closed system of metaphysics which one could decide to take or leave. Indeed, Bergson commits himself to the possibility of a metaphysics that could "progress indefinitely" (Bergson 1972: 652). The reformed metaphysics will advance by the gradual accumulation of obtained results. In other words, metaphysics does not have to be "a take-it-or-leave-it system" that is forever in dispute and doomed to start afresh, thinking abstractly and vainly without the support of empirical science. Not only is it the case for Bergson that metaphysics can be a true empiricism, but it can also work with science in an effort to advance our knowledge of the various sources, tendencies, and directions of life. Bergson outlines what is in effect his "superior positivism" in his Huxley lecture of 1911 on "Life and Consciousness": "… we possess now a certain number of *lines of facts*, which do not go as far as we want, but which we can prolong hypothetically" (Bergson 2007c: 4). This is taken up again in the *The Two Sources* where he states that the different lines of fact indicate for us the direction of truth but none go far enough; the attainment of truth can only take place when the lines are prolonged to the point where they intersect (1979: 248). He makes it clear that the conception of a vital impetus and of a creative evolution were only arrived by following the evidence of biology. Furthermore, he stresses that his conception is not simply a hypothesis of the kind that can be found at the basis of all metaphysical systems; rather, it aims to be "a condensation of fact, a summing up of summings up" (*ibid.*: 249). The knowledge we wish to develop and advance concerning evolution must "keep to ascertained facts and the probabilities suggested by them" (*ibid.*: 273).

Duration

To think duration is to think "beyond the human condition" (Bergson 2007a: 45). My existence, including my duration, is disclosed by objects "inferior" and "superior," though in a certain sense interior, to me (*ibid.*: 33). Take the example Bergson gives of mixing a glass of water with sugar and waiting until the sugar dissolves, which he says is a "little fact big with meaning" (2007b: 6 and 216–17). The time I have to wait is not a mathematical time which we could apply to the entire history of the material world as if it was spread out instantaneously in space; rather, it coincides with an impatience that constitutes a portion of my duration and which I cannot protract or contract at will. This is an experience that is lived and denotes not a relative but an absolute. Furthermore, my duration has the power to disclose other durations and to encompass them *ad infinitum*. Bergson gives the example of a simultaneity of fluxes in which while sitting on the bank of a river, the flowing of the water, the flight of a bird, and the uninterrupted murmur in the depths of our life, can be treated as either three things or a single one (Bergson 2000: 36). Bergson admits that "to conceive of durations of different tensions and rhythms is both difficult and strange to our mind simply because we have acquired the useful habit of substituting for duration an homogeneous and independent time" (1991: 207).

Bergson argues that time involves a coexistence of past and present and not simply a continuity of succession as in Kant. Pure duration "is the form which the succession of our conscious states assumes when our ego lets itself *live*, when it refrains from separating its present state from its former states" (Bergson 2001: 100). Duration can be defined as "the continuous progress of the past which gnaws into the future and which swells as it advances" (Bergson 2007b: 2). It is irreversible since, "consciousness cannot go through the same state twice. The circumstances may still be the same, but they will act no longer on the same person, since they find him at a new moment of his history" (*ibid*: 4). Even if states can be repeated and assume the character of being identical, this is merely an appearance, so we cannot live over and over again a single moment. We may think we can efface memory but such effacement would work on the level of our intellect, not our will. If we take time to be something positive then we have to treat it as both irreversible and unforeseeable. This conception of duration, which is that of a "becoming" which flows out of previous forms while always adding something new to them, is very different from Spinoza's conception of the "one complete Being" which manifests forms. For Bergson this conception denies "effective action" to duration (*ibid.*: 225). Both Cartesian and Spinozist physics seek to establish a relation of logical necessity between cause and effect and in so doing "do away with active duration" (Bergson 2001: 208–9).

Duration cannot be made the subject of a logical or mathematical treatment. This is owing to its character as a continuous multiplicity, as opposed to one made up of discrete parts or elements. In *Creative Evolution* Bergson addresses the status of his construal of life in terms of an impetus. He conceives it in terms of a "virtual multiplicity" (*virtuellement multiple*). He acknowledges that describing life in terms of an impetus is to offer little more than an image. The image, however, is intended to disclose something about the essential character of life, namely, that it is not of a mathematical or logical order but a psychological one: "In reality, life is of the psycho-logical order, and it is of the essence of the psychical to enfold a confused plurality of interpenetrating terms" (Bergson 2007b: 165). The contrast he is making is with space in which the multiplicity posited or found therein will be made up of discrete elements or components that are related to one another in specific terms, namely, relations of juxtaposition and exteriority.

In *Time and Free Will* Bergson argues that the different degrees of a mental state correspond to qualitative changes that do not admit of simple measure or number. When we ordinarily speak of time we think of a homogeneous medium in which our conscious states are placed alongside one another as in space, and so form a discrete multiplicity. The question is whether the evolution of our psychic states resembles the multiplicity of the units of a number and whether duration has anything to do with space. If time is simply a medium in which our conscious states are strung out as a discrete series that can be counted, then time would indeed be space. The question Bergson poses is whether time can legitimately be treated as such a medium.

One way of opening the issue is to reflect on the nature of a psychic state and question the validity of treating it as a magnitude. Does it make sense, for example, to say that today I am twice as happy or joyous as I was yesterday? While we can distinguish between experiencing a twinge of jealousy and being obsessed by a jealous passion, would it make sense to say that the jealousy of Othello should be understood as being made up of innumerable twinges of jealousy? (see Moore 1996: 45; Bergson 2001: 73). Bergson asks: "why do we say of a higher intensity that it is greater? Why do we think of a greater quantity or a greater space?" (2001: 7). His contention is that states of consciousness cannot be isolated from one another but should be approached in terms of a multiplicity in which there is fusion and interpenetration, in short, a qualitative heterogeneity. The reason for this fusion and interpenetration is that the states of consciousness unfold themselves in duration and not, like the units of arithmetic, in space. An increasing intensity of a mental state is inseparable from a qualitative progression and from a becoming of time. The notion of an intensive magnitude "involves an impure mixture between determinations that differ in kind" with the result that our question "by how much does a sensation grow or intensify?" takes us back to a badly stated problem (see Deleuze 1991: 19). It is not that we do not count in duration; rather, we count the moments of duration by means of points in space. We perfectly comprehend the sense of there being a number that is greater than another, but can the same be said of an intensive sensation? How can a more intense sensation contain one of less intensity? Unlike the law of number the relations among intensities cannot be adequately approached in terms of those of container and contained with different intensities being superposed upon one another. Adequately understood intensity cannot be assimilated to magnitude.

Looked out from the perspective of pure duration our states can be seen to permeate and melt into another without precise outlines and without any affiliation with number, in which past and present states form a whole, "as happens when we recall the notes of a tune, melting, so to speak, into another" (Bergson 2001: 100). These are involved in qualitative changes that disclose a "pure heterogeneity" (continuous variation). When we interrupt the rhythm of a tune by perhaps dwelling longer than is customary on one note, it is not the exaggerated length that signals the mistake to us but rather the qualitative change caused in the whole of the piece of music.

> We can thus conceive of succession without distinction, and think of it as a mutual penetration, an interconnexion and organization of elements, each one of which represent the whole, and cannot be distinguished or isolated from it except by abstract thought. (*Ibid.*: 101)

When we reduce time to a simple movement of position we confuse time with space. It is this confusion between motion and the space traversed which explains the paradoxes of Zeno. The interval between two points is infinitely divisible, and if motion is said to consist of parts like those of the interval itself, then the interval can never be crossed. But the truth of the matter is different:

> … each of Achilles's steps is a simple indivisible act … after a given number of these acts, Achilles will have passed the tortoise. The mistake of the Eleatics arises from their identification of this series of acts, each of which is *of a definite kind and indivisible*, with the homogeneous space which underlies them. (*Ibid.*: 113)

Because this space can be divided and put together again according to an abstract law, the illusion arises that it is possible to reconstruct the movement of Achilles not with his step but with that of the tortoise. In truth, we have only two tortoises that agree to make the same kind of steps or simultaneous acts so never to catch one another! Within any posited motionless trajectory it is possible to count as much immobility as we like. What we fail to see is that "the trajectory is created in one stroke, although a certain time is required for it; and that although we can divide at will the trajectory once created, we cannot divide its creation, which is an act in progress and not a thing" (Bergson 2007b: 197). Whilst the space traversed is a matter of extension and quantity (it is divisible), the movement is an intensive act and a quality. Bergson is insistent that it is "through the quality of quantity that we form the idea of quantity without quality," not the other way round. Qualitative operations are even at work in the formation of numbers. The addition of a third unit to two others alters the nature (the rhythm) of the whole, even though our spatial habits lead us to disregard the significance of these varying aspects (Bergson 2001: 123). We can appreciate why Bergson holds that metaphysics, in the negative sense of the term, begins not with Plato but with Zeno: "Metaphysics ... was born of the arguments of Zeno of Elea on the subject of change and movement. It was Zeno who, by drawing attention to the absurdity of what he called movement and change, led the philosophers – Plato first and foremost – to seek the true and coherent reality in what does not change" (Bergson 1965: 141; see also 17).

Mechanism is not wholly illegitimate or simply false in Bergson's view (he does not embrace finalism since this is merely an inverted mechanism that also reduces time to a process of realization). It is a reflection of our evolved habits of representation and these are habits that conform in large measure to certain tendencies of matter. The intellect is the product of a natural evolution and has evolved as an instrument of action that exerts itself on fixed points. Intelligence, for example, does not consider transition, but prefers instead to conceive movement as a movement through space, as a series of positions in which one point is reached, followed by another, and so on. Even if something happens between the points the understanding intercalates new positions, an act that can go on *ad infinitum*. As a result of this reduction of movement to points in space, duration gets broken up into distinct moments that correspond to each of the positions (this is what we can call a discrete or actual multiplicity). Bergson writes:

> In short, the time that is envisaged is little more than an ideal space where it is supposed that all past, present, and future events can be set out along a line, and in addition, as something which prevents them from appearing in a single perception: the unrolling in duration [*le déroulement en durée*] would be this very incompletion [*inachèvement*], the addition of a negative quantity. Such, consciously or unconsciously, is the thought of most philosophers, in conformity with the exigencies of the understanding, the necessities of language and the symbolism of science. *Not one of them has sought positive attributes in time.* (1965: 95)

If we say that time merely glides over these (material) systems then we are speaking of simple systems that have been constituted artificially through the operations of our own intellect. Such systems can be calculated ahead of time since they are being posited as existing prior to their realization in the form of "possibles" (when a possible is realized it simply gets existence added to it, its fundamental nature has not changed). The successive states of this kind of system can be conceived as moving at any speed, rather like the unrolling of a film: it does not matter at what speed the shots run; an evolution is not being depicted. The reality here is more complex, but the complexity is concealed. An unrolling film, for example, remains attached to consciousness that has its own duration and which regulates its movement. The more duration marks the living being with its imprint, the more the organism must differ from a mere mechanism (Bergson 2007b: 24).

One of the difficulties we have in accepting this conception of duration as the invention of the new is due to the way in which we think of evolution as the domain of the realization of the possible. We have difficulty in thinking that an event – whether a work of art or a work of nature – could have taken place unless it were not already capable of happening. For something to become it must have been possible all along (this is a conception of logical and spatial possibility). As Bergson points out, the word possibility can signify at least two different things and we often waver between the two senses. From the negative sense of the word, such as pointing out that there was no known insurmountable obstacle to something coming into being, we pass quickly onto the positive sense of it, in which we hold that any event could have been foreseen in advance of its happening by a mind with adequate information. In the form of an idea this is to suppose that an event was pre-existent to its eventual realization. Even if it is argued that an event, such as the composition of a symphony or a painting, was not conceived in advance, the prejudice still holds sway that such an event *could have been*, and this is to suppose that there exists a transcendent realm of pre-existing possibles. In *The Two Sources of Morality and Religion* Bergson applies this critique of the pre-existence of the possible in the real, which he now calls "retrospective anticipation," to the domain of history. The supposition at work in our thinking of history is that things are approximating some ideal or norm – one that must stand outside history to make the judgment possible – as in the view that: "... the conceptions of justice which followed one another in ancient societies were no more than partial, incomplete versions of an integral justice as we know it today" (Bergson 1979: 72). But this is to deny that something new comes into existence in history, often by taking possession of something old and absorbing it into a new whole. It is always possible to interpret a forward movement as a progressive shortening of the distance between the starting-point and the end, and then to claim that when the end has been reached the thing in question was either possible or that it had been working towards this end all along. But there is nothing that warrants this inference; it is the result of the error of "thinking backwards." For Bergson, this is a "metaphysical doctrine" (in the negative sense) that sets the theory of knowledge insoluble problems. Bergson is attacking, in part, the philosophy of history that would identify in a thing's development a linear or logical progress towards a goal, and the proximity of his criticism to that evinced by Nietzsche in *On the Genealogy of Morality* is striking (Nietzsche 2006: II, 12).

The reduction of the real, and of real complexity, to mathematical calculability or computation is one that Bergson locates in both nineteenth-century physics and biology. He quotes the following passage from Du Bois-Reymond's *Über die Grenzen des Naturerkennens* ("On the Limits of Our Knowledge of Nature") of 1892: "We can imagine the knowledge of nature arrived at a point where the universal process of the world might be represented by a single mathematical formula, by one immense system of differential equations, from which could be deduced, for each moment, the position, direction, and velocity of every atom of the world" (*ibid*: 25). Time is positive for Bergson in the sense that it introduces indetermination into the very essence of life. However, our natural bent is always to construe this indetermination in terms of a completion of pre-existent possibles. The intellect, which has evolved as an organ of utility, has a need for stability and reliability. It thus seeks connections and establishes stable and regular relations between transitory facts. It also develops laws to map these connections and regularities. This operation is held to be more perfect the more the law in question becomes more mathematical. From this disposition of the intellect there have emerged the specific conceptions of matter that have characterized a great deal of Western metaphysics and science. Our mind conceives the origin and evolution of the universe as an arrangement and rearrangement of parts that simply shift from one place to another. This is what Bergson calls the Laplacean dogma that has informed a great deal of modern enquiry, leading to a determinism and a mechanism in which by positing a definite number of stable elements all possible combinations can be deduced without regard for the reality of duration (*ibid*.: 24–5).

In *Time and Free Will* Bergson also aims to show the limitations of physical determinism by arguing that the science of energy rests on a confusion of concrete duration and abstract time. Modern mechanism holds that it is possible to calculate with absolute certainty the past, present, and future actions of a living system from knowledge of the exact position and motion of the atomic elements in the universe capable of influencing it. It is this quest for certainty that informed the science built up around the principle of the conservation of energy. To admit the universal character of this theorem is to make the assumption that the material points which are held to make up the universe are subject solely to forces of attraction and repulsion that arise from the points themselves and have intensities that depend only on their distances. Thus, whatever the nature of these material points at any given moment, their relative position would be determined by relation to the preceding moment (Bergson 2001: 151).

Bergson's main concern is to demonstrate why it is illegitimate to simply extend this conception of matter to a deterministic and mechanistic understanding of psychic states (perhaps by making them reducible to cerebral states). Bergson does not deny that the principle of the conservation of energy appears to be applicable to a whole array of physico-chemical phenomena, especially the case, he notes, since the development of the mechanical theory of heat. The question he wants to pose for science, however, is whether there are new kinds of energy, different from kinetic and potential energy, which may rebel against calculation (he is thinking in particular of physiological phenomena). His principal point is to argue that conservative systems cannot be taken to be the only systems possible. For these conservative systems time does not bite into them. Without duration can these systems be said to be *living* systems? On the model of modern mechanism the isolable material point can only remain suspended in an eternal present (*ibid*.: 153). Whilst a conservative system may have no need of a past time (duration), for a living one that exists in a metastable state it is a prerequisite. For Bergson the setting up of an abstract principle of mechanics as a universal law does not, in truth, rest on desire to meet the requirements of a positive science, but rather on a "psychological mistake" derived from treating the duration of a living system to the "duration which glides over the inert atoms without penetrating and altering them" (*ibid.*: 154).

The antinomies of modern thinking, for example of determinism and freedom, stem in large measure from our imposition of symbolic diagrams upon the movement of the real, which serve to make it something uniform, regular, and calculable for us. To break free of these mental habits would make it possible to transcend space without stepping outside extensity. There is no fixed logic or established law that compels us to equate a continuous and diversified extensity with the amorphous and inert space that subtends it, and within which movement can only be constructed in terms of a multiplicity of instantaneous positions. In arguing that movement is something absolute and place is relative Bergson is claiming it to be something real and not merely an effect of measurement (the mathematical symbols of the geometrician are unable to demonstrate that it is a moving body that is in motion and not the axes and points to which it is referred). But if motion is merely relative then change must be an illusion (Bergson 1991: 194–5).

Intuition

What is involved in restoring the absolute? For Bergson it centres on recognizing that reality is made up of both differences of degree (the tendencies of matter) and differences of kind (the tendencies of life). We can divide a composite or mixture according to qualitative and qualified tendencies, such as the way in which it combines duration and extensity defined as directions of movements, giving us "duration-contraction" and "matter-expansion." Such a method of division might be compared to a form of transcendental analysis in that it takes us beyond experience as given toward its conditions. However, we are now dealing not with the conditions of all possible experience, but rather with conditions that are neither general and abstract nor broader than the conditioned (see Deleuze 1991: 26–7). Once we make the turn in experience beyond the bias directed towards utility we reach the point at which we discover differences in kind and no longer subsume reality within utilitarian groupings. We frequently locate only differences in degree (more or less of the same thing), when in actuality the most profound differences are the differences in kind. Experience itself offers us nothing more than composites, such as time imbued with space and mixtures of extensity and duration. To think beyond our mental habits, which give us only badly analyzed composites, we require a special method, and for Bergson this is the method of intuition. Without this method duration would remain a simple psychological experience. Intuition is not itself duration but rather "the movement by which we emerge from our own duration" and "make use of our own duration to affirm ... and recognize the existence of other durations" (Deleuze 1991: 33).

Given our finitude Kant claims that our mode of intuition can only be of a derivative kind and not an original one. By this he means that we have no access to an intellectual intuition. Kant allows for the fact that the way the human being intuits time and space may not be peculiar to it alone but may be something to be found among all finite beings that have a capacity of self-representation. But what he will not allow for is the possibility that we could overstep the bounds of our finitude and attain a higher intuition such as an intellectual one. This can only belong to the primordial being (Kant, *Critique of Pure Reason*, B72). We can only know matter in terms of its outer relations; the inward nature of matter, that is matter as it would be conceived by the pure understanding independently of sensuous intuition, is a phantom. The most we can do is to posit a "transcendental object" (*Objekt*) which may be the ground of the appearance we call matter, but this is an object without quantity or substance, it is "a mere something of which we should not understand what it is, even if someone were in a position to tell us" (A277/B333). To be able to intuit things without the aid of our senses would mean that we could have knowledge "altogether different from the human, and this not only in degree but as regards intuition likewise in kind" (A278/B334). But of such non-human beings we do not know them to be possible or how they would be constituted. Kant does not deny that through observation and analysis it is possible that we can penetrate into "nature's recesses," but he insists that this is nature conceived only in the aspect or dimension of its *appearance*: "with all this knowledge, and even if the whole of nature were revealed to us, we should still never be able to answer those transcendental questions which go beyond nature," that is, beyond nature qua appearance. Ultimately, Kant is led to positing a problematic noumenon, which is not the concept of any determinate object but rather bound up with the limitation of human sensibility. This provides a place for speculation with regard to there being objects outside of our specific field of intuition, objects other and different to what we are able to intuit through our particular *a priori* intuitions of time and space, but of their existence nothing can either be denied or asserted (A288/B344).

Bergson argues that in order to reach a higher mode of intuition it is not necessary, as Kant supposed, to transport ourselves outside the domain of the senses: "After having proved by decisive arguments that no dialectical effort will ever introduce us into the beyond and that an effective metaphysics would necessarily be an intuitive metaphysics, he added that we lack this intuition and that this metaphysics is impossible. It would in fact be so if there were no other time or change than those which Kant perceived ..." (Bergson 1965: 128). By recovering intuition Bergson hopes to save science from the charge of producing a relativity of knowledge (it is rather to be regarded as approximate) and metaphysics from the charge of indulging in empty and idle speculation. Although Kant himself did not pursue thought in the direction he had opened for it – the direction of a "revivified Cartesianism" Bergson calls it – it is the prospect of an "extra-intellectual matter of knowledge by a higher effort of intuition" that Bergson seeks to cultivate (2007b: 229). Kant has reawakened, if only half-heartedly, a view that was the essential element of Descartes' thinking but which was abandoned by the Cartesians: knowledge is not completely resolvable into the terms of intelligence. Bergson does not, let it be noted, establish an opposition between sensuous (infra-intellectual) intuition and intellectual (what he calls an "ultra-intellectual") intuition but instead seeks to show that there is a continuity and reciprocity between the two. Moreover, sensuous intuition can be promoted to a different set of operations, no longer simply being the phantom of an inscrutable thing-in-itself:

> The barriers between the matter of sensible knowledge and its form are lowered, as also between the "pure forms" of sensibility and the categories of the understanding. The matter and form of intellectual knowledge (restricted to its own object) are seen to be engendering each other by a reciprocal adaptation, intellect modelling itself on corporeity, and corporeity on intellect. But this duality of intuition Kant neither would nor could admit. (*Ibid.*: 230)

For Kant to admit this duality of intuition would entail granting to duration an absolute reality and treating the geometry immanent in space as an ideal limit (the direction in which material things develop but never actually attain).

In Bergson intuition denotes neither a vague feeling nor a disordered sympathy but a method that aims at precision in philosophy (see Bergson 1965: 11, 79, 88; 2007a: 43n53; 2007b: 153, 172; 2007c: 26). As Deleuze points out, duration would remain purely intuitive, in the ordinary sense of the word, if intuition in Bergson's sense did not exist as a method (Deleuze 1991: 14). It is a complex method that cannot be contained in single act. Rather, it involves an "indefinite series of acts," the diversity of which "corresponds to all the degrees of being" (2007a: 33). The first task is to stage and create problems; the second is to locate differences in kind; and the third is to comprehend real time, that is, duration as a heterogeneous and continuous multiplicity. Bergson acknowledges that other philosophers before him, such as Schelling, tried to escape relativism by appealing to intuition (1965: 30). He argues, however, that this was a non-temporal intuition that was being appealed to, and, as such, was largely a return to Spinozism, that is, a deduction of existence from "one complete Being."

Regarding the first task, we go wrong when we hold that notions of true and false can only be brought to bear on problems in terms of ready-made solutions. This denotes a negative freedom that reflects manufactured social prejudices where, through social institutions such as education and language, we become enslaved to "order-words" that identify for us ready-made problems that we are forced to solve. True freedom lies in the power to decide through hesitation and indeterminacy and to constitute problems themselves. This might involve the freedom to uncover certain truths for oneself, but true freedom is more to do with invention than it is with discovery that is too much tied to uncovering what already exists, an act of discovery that was bound to happen sooner or later. In mathematics and in metaphysics the effort of invention consists in raising the problem and in creating the terms through which it might be solved but never as something ready-made. As Maurice Merleau-Ponty notes in a reading of Bergson, when it is said that well-posed problems are close to being solved, "this does not mean that we have already *found* what we are looking for, but that we have already invented it" (Merleau-Ponty 1988: 14).

False problems are of two kinds: first, those which are caught up in terms that contain a confusion of the "more" and the "less"; and, secondly, questions which are stated badly in the sense that their terms represent only badly analyzed composites. In the first case the error consists in positing an origin of being and of order from which nonbeing and disorder are then made to appear as primordial. On this schema order can only appear as the negation of disorder and being as the negation of nonbeing (see Bergson 2007b: 143). Such a way of thinking introduces lack into the heart of Being. The more or less errs in not seeing that there are kinds of order and forgetting the fact that Being is not homogeneous but fundamentally heterogeneous. Badly analyzed composites result from an arbitrary grouping of things that are constituted as differences in kind. For example, in *Creative Evolution* Bergson contends that the cardinal error that has vitiated the philosophy of nature from Aristotle onwards is identifying in forms of life, such as the vegetative, instinctive, and rational, *"three successive degrees of the development of one and the same tendency, whereas they are divergent directions of an activity that has split up as it grew."* He insists that the difference between them is neither one of intensity nor of degree but kind (*ibid.*: 87–8). Life proceeds neither via lack nor the power of the negative but through internal self-differentiation along divergent lines.

It is through a focus on badly analyzed composites that we are led, in fact, to positing things in terms of the more and the less, so that the idea of disorder only arises from a general idea of order as a badly analyzed composite. We are the victims of illusions that have their source in aspects of our intelligence. However, although these illusions refer to Kant's analysis in the *Critique of Pure Reason*, where reason is shown to generate for itself in exceeding the boundaries of the understanding inevitable illusions and not simple mistakes, they are not of the same order. There is a natural tendency of the intellect to see only differences in degree and to neglect differences in kind. This is because the fundamental motivation of the intellect is to implement and orientate action in the world. For the purposes of social praxis and communication the intellect needs to order reality in a certain way, making it something calculable, regular and necessary. As Nietzsche notes, in order for a certain species to maintain itself and increase its feeling of power over the world it is necessary that it develop a conception of calculable and constant reality in order to establish a schema of behavior on it (Nietzsche 1968: §480).

If intuition is to be conceived as a method that proceeds via division – the division of a composite into differences of kind – is this not to deny that reality is, in fact, made up of composites and mixtures of all kinds? For Bergson, the crucial factor is to recognize that it is not things that differ in kind but rather tendencies. It is not things (their states or traits) that differ in nature, but the tendency things possess for change and development. A simple difference of degree would denote the correct status of things if they could be separated from their tendencies. The tendency is primary not simply in relation to its product but rather in relation to the causes in time that are retroactively obtained from the product itself. For example, if considered as a product, then the human brain will show only a difference of degree in relation to the animal brain. If it is viewed in terms of its tendency, however, it will reveal a difference of nature. Any composite, therefore, needs to be divided according to qualitative tendencies. Again, this brings Bergsonism close to Kant's transcendental analysis, going beyond experience as given and constituting its conditions of possibility. However, these are not conditions of all possible experience but of real experience (for example the inferior and superior durations we discussed above). Living systems in the universe are open systems in which liberty and contingency are real empirical features. As Deleuze notes: "Indetermination, unpredictability, contingency, liberty always signify an independence in relation to causes ..." (Deleuze 1999: 25).

Bergson's metaphysics of change aims to operate via "differentiations and qualitative integrations," and in an effort to reverse the normal directions of the workings of thought enjoys a rapport with modern mathematics, notably the infinitesimal calculus:

> Modern mathematics is precisely an effort to substitute for the *ready-made* what is in process of *becoming*, to follow the growth of magnitudes, to seize movement no longer from outside and in its manifest result, but from within and in its tendency towards change, in short, to adopt of the mobile continuity of the pattern of things. (2007a: 41; see also 1991: 185)

Metaphysics differs from modern mathematics (the science of magnitudes), however, in that it has no need to make the move from intuition to symbol. Its understanding of the real is potentially boundless because of this: "Liberated from the obligation of working practically for useful results, it will indefinitely enlarge the domain of its investigations" (2007a: 41). Metaphysics can adopt the generative idea of mathematics and seek to extend it to all qualities, "to reality in general" (*ibid.*: 42). The aim is not to bring about another Platonism of the real, as in Kant's system he contends, but rather to enable thought to re-establish contact with continuity and mobility (*ibid.*: 49–50). A form of knowledge can be said to be relative when, through an act of forgetting, it ignores the basis of symbolic knowledge in intuition, and is forced to rely on pre-existing concepts and to proceed from the fixed to the mobile. Absolute knowledge by contrast refuses to accept what is pre-formed and instead cultivates "fluid concepts," seeking to place itself in a mobile reality from the start and so adopting "the life itself of things" (*ibid.*: 13, 43), able to follow "the real in all its sinuosities" (2007b: 232). To achieve this requires relinquishing the method of construction that leads only to higher and higher generalities and thinking in terms of a concrete duration "in which a radical recasting of the whole is always going on" (*ibid.*). Bergson calls for experience to be "purified" of intellectualism and released "from the moulds that our intellect has formed" (*ibid.*: 231).

Bergson insists that his method of intuition contains no devaluation of intelligence but only a determination of its specific facility. If intuition transcends intelligence this is only on account of the fact that it is intelligence that gives it the push to rise beyond. Without it intuition would remain wedded to instinct and riveted to the particular objects of its practical interests. The specific task of philosophy is to introduce us "into life's own domain, which is reciprocal interpenetration, endlessly continued creation" (*ibid.*: 115). This is different, though not opposed, to what science does when it takes up the utilitarian vantage point of external perception and prolongs individual facts into general laws. The reformed metaphysics Bergson wishes to awaken commits itself to an "intellectual *expansion*" of thought and intuition is, in fact, "*intellectual sympathy*" (2007a: 32 and 40; my emphases).

Merleau-Ponty notes that for Bergson many traditional questions of philosophy, such as "Why have I been born?," "Why is there something rather than nothing?," and "How can I know anything?," can be held to be "pathological" in the sense that they fail to acknowledge that we are subjects already installed in being; they are the questions of a doubter who no longer knows whether he has closed the window (Merleau-Ponty 1988: 12). A strictly "positive philosophy," therefore, notes Merleau-Ponty, will not aim to "resolve" classical problems, but rather "dissolve" them. It is not a question of losing ourselves in Being, of being absorbed into it, but of being transcended by it: "It is not necessary for him [the philosopher] to go outside himself in order to reach the things themselves; he is solicited or haunted by them from within" (*ibid.*: 14–15).

Bergson's critique of ethical rationalism

On a cursory reading Bergson's statement in *The Two Sources of Morality and Religion* that "all morality is in essence biological" would seem to lend support to the criticism that his project amounts to biologism. In this final section I want to show that this is not in fact the case, and to do so by looking at the critical points he makes against the rationalist approach to ethics and as found largely, but not only, in Kant.

Nietzsche famously challenges any and all attempts to establish morality on a rational foundation (*Begründung*) (Nietzsche 1998: §186). Bergson makes virtually the same point. For him it is the ease with which philosophical theories of ethics can be built up that should make us suspicious:

> … if the most varied aims can thus be transmuted by philosophers into moral aims, we may surmise, seeing that they have not yet found the philosophers' stone, that they had started by putting gold in the bottom of their crucible. Similarly it is obvious that none of these doctrines will account for obligation. For we may be obliged to adopt certain means in order to attain such and such ends; but if we choose to renounce the end, how can the means be forced upon us? And yet, by adopting any one of these ends as the principle of morality, philosophers have evolved from it whole systems of maxims, which, without going so far as to assume an imperative form, come near enough to it to afford satisfaction. The reason is quite simple. They have considered the pursuit of these ends … in a society in where there are peremptory pressures, together with aspirations to match them and also to extend them … Each of these systems then already exists in the social atmosphere when the philosopher arrives on the scene.... (Bergson 1979: 90–1)

Bergson's contention is that moral philosophers treat society, and the two forces to which it owes its stability and mobility (pressure and aspiration), as established facts. At the same time they take for granted the matter of morality and its form, all it contains and the entire obligation with which it is clothed.

Bergson wishes to expose what he regards as the essential weakness of a strictly intellectualist system of morality, which he holds to include the majority of the philosophical theories of duty. The error of intellectualism is that it fails to appreciate the extent to which morality is a "discipline demanded by nature" (*ibid.*: 269; compare Nietzsche 1998: §188). Moreover, intellectualism supposes that there is a difference of value between motives or principles and that there exists a general idea to which the real can be estimated. It is led to take refuge in Platonism in which the Idea of the Good dominates all others. For Bergson there are essentially two forces acting upon us and to which we respond as duties, namely, impulsion and attraction. Without this emphasis on *forces* moral philosophy has great problems in explaining how a moral motive could take over our soul and impel it to action.

> That reason is the distinguishing mark of man no one will deny. That it is a thing of superior value, in the sense in which a fine work of art is indeed valuable, will also be granted. But we must explain how it is that its orders are absolute and why they are obeyed. Reason can only put forward reasons, which we are apparently always at liberty to counter with other reasons. Let us not then merely assert that reason, present in each one of us, compels our respect and commands our obedience by virtue of its paramount value. We must add that there are, behind reason, the men who have made mankind divine, and who have thus stamped a divine character on reason, which is the essential attribute of man. (*Ibid.*: 68)

Bergson is keen to share in philosophy's promotion of reason: "the rational alone is self-consistent" and cannot be devalued; in civilized society morality is essentially rational (*ibid.*: 81). The danger of reason, however, must equally be recognized: it can give us only a diagram of action and in so doing it runs the risk of rendering our decisions and deliberations automatic. As part of living a vital life we need the joy and exuberance of moral inventions and transformations. Any morality that claims reason as its basis in the guise of a pure form without matter is deluding itself; it is metaphysical in the bad sense of the word (*ibid.*: 87). Social life cannot be taken as a fact we begin with but requires an explanation in terms of the vital necessities and imperatives of life itself. If we pursue matters of morality purely in intellectualist terms we reach a transcendental dead-end; if we place the emphasis on life, we can explain both the static and the dynamic dimensions of life, as well as both the closed and the open forms of morality and religion:

> Let us then give to the word biology the very wide meaning it should have, and will perhaps have one day, and let us say in conclusion that all morality, be it pressure or aspiration, is in essence biological. (*Ibid.*: 101)

Bergson's final text is an inquiry into the sources and origins of morality. Such an approach is possible according to him because in spite of the development of civilization and the transformations of society that have taken place in history the tendencies that are organic in social life have remained what they were in the beginning. There is an "original nature," the bedrock of which is covered over by a "thick humus," namely all the acquisitions of culture or civilization such as the deposits of knowledge, traditions, customs, institutions, syntax and the vocabulary of language, and even gestures (*ibid.*: 83). If we scratch the surface and abolish every-thing we owe to education we find in the depth of our nature primitive humanity, or something near it. Although society and education make all the difference and overlay the natural, "let a sudden shock paralyse these superficial activities, let the light in which they work be extinguished for a moment: at once the natural reappears, like the changeless star in the night" (*ibid.*: 127). It is intelligence and its pride that will not admit our original subordination to biological necessities. The illusion is that intelligence is pure, unrelated to either nature or life, with no correspondence to vital needs. Intelligence wants man to be superior to his actual origins, higher than nature. And yet intelligence, in the form of science, shows man to be part of nature. However, neither Nietzsche nor Bergson is wedded to origins. Nietzsche argues that he who grows wise about origins will seek out sources of the future and new origins and he appeals to a new earth and new peoples to come (Nietzsche 2005a: "Of Old and New Tablets"). For Bergson there are two moralities, one of pressure and one of aspiration. Whereas the former is one of social constraint, the morality of the city as he calls it, the latter concerns humanity's expansion that brings into existence new ways of living and new emotions.

The natural morality of pressure is a "screen" in which the possible immorality that lies behind the exterior through which humanity presents itself to the world is not seen under normal circumstances. As Bergson notes, we don't become misanthropes by observing others but on account of a feeling of discontent with ourselves; only then do we come to pity or despise mankind: "The human nature from which we then turn away is the human nature we have discovered in the depths of our own being" (Bergson 1979: 11). For Bergson the social imperative has a religious source. The first effect of religion is to sustain and reinforce the claims of society. Society needs religion because it "knows" that its execution of the law is imperfect and without divine authority; it dishes out rewards and punishments and needs to believe that these are justly sanctioned. Religion helps here since it gives us the idea of an order that is perfect and self-creative, which is the image society wishes for itself (to hide the effect that in actuality all is imperfect, arbitrary, and so on). In this respect it is like the realm of Platonic ideas in the sphere of knowledge: it enables us to replace the uncertain with the certain, and the empirical with the eternal.

Kant's ethics rest on an absolute distinction between inclination and duty, or between nature and reason, which for him amounts to the difference between heteronomy and autonomy. Contra Kant, Bergson maintains that obligation is not a unique fact incommensurate with others, "looming above them like a mysterious apparition" (*ibid.*: 20). Moreover, he argues that when we seek to define the essence and origin of obligation by laying down that obedience is primarily a struggle with the self, a state of tension or contraction, "we make a psychological error which has vitiated many theories of ethics" (*ibid*). Here there is confusion over the sense of obligation – which Bergson defines as "a tranquil state akin to inclination" – with the violent effort we exert on ourselves now and again to break down possible obstacles to obligation:

> We have any number of particular obligations, each calling for a separate explanation. It is natural … a matter of habit to obey them all. Suppose that exceptionally we deviate from one of them, there would be resistance; if we resist this resistance, a state of tension or contraction is likely to result. It is this rigidity which we objectify when we attribute so stern an aspect to duty. (*Ibid.*: 21)

Bergson appreciates that when we resist resistance – the temptations, passions and desires – we need to give ourselves reasons. There is the call of an idea, and autonomy (the exertion of self-control) takes place through the medium of intelligence. However, "from the fact that we get back to obligation by rational ways it does not follow that obligation was of a rational order" (*ibid.*: 22).

Bergson stresses the social origins of obligation. When we neglect this we posit an abstract conception of our conformity to duty (we obey duty for the sake of duty, Kant says). The "totality of obligation," by which Bergson means our moral habits taken as a whole, represents a force that if it could speak would utter: "You must because you must" (23). What intelligence does is to introduce greater logical consistency into our lines of conduct. However, is it not the case that we never sacrifice our vanity, passions, and interests to the need for such consistency? We go wrong not when we ascribe a spurious independent existence to reason but when we conceive it as the controlling power or agency of our action: "We might as well believe that the fly-wheel drives the machinery" (*ibid*). Bergson is not denying that reason intervenes as a regulator to assure consistency between rules and maxims. His point is that it oversimplifies what is actually taking place in moral agency. Reason is at work every-where in moral behavior. Thus, an individual whose respectable behavior is the least based on reasoning, as someone who acts in accordance with sheepish conformity, introduces a rational order into his conduct from the mere fact of obeying rules that are logically connected to one another.

Bergson makes the striking claim that "an absolutely categorical imperative is instinctive or somnambulistic, enacted as such in a normal state…" (*ibid.*: 26). The "totality of obligation" is, in fact, the *habit of contracting habits*, and this is a specifically human instinct of intelligence. Let us imagine that evolution has proceeded along two divergent lines with societies at the extremities of each. On the one hand, the more natural will be the instinctive type (such as ants or bees). On the other hand, there is the society where a degree of latitude has been left to individual waywardness. For nature to be effective in this case, that is, to achieve a comparable regularity, there is recourse to habit in place of instinct. Bergson then argues:

Each of these habits, which may be called "moral," would be incidental. But the aggregate of them, I mean the habit of contracting these habits, being at the very basis of societies and a necessary condition of their existence, would have a force comparable to that of instinct in respect of both intensity and regularity. (*Ibid.*: 26–7)

No matter how much society progresses through refinement and spiritualization this original design will remain. For Bergson then, social life is immanent, if only as a vague ideal, in instinct and intelligence. The difference in human societies is that here it is only the necessity of a rule that is the cardinal natural thing (rules are not laid down by nature). Obligation can be treated as a kind of "virtual instinct" similar to that which lies behind the habit of speech. Obligation needs to lose its specific or sublime character in our thinking so that we recognize it as among the most general phenomena of life (*ibid.*: 29).

The other morality Bergson inquires into is the morality of aspiration, which can be regarded as "anti-natural" in the sense that it takes humanity beyond what nature prescribes for it. The primitive instinct, hidden under the accretions of civilization, is love of our community or tribe: "it is primarily as against all other men that we love the men with whom we live …" (*ibid.*: 33). To proclaim love of humanity is to decree that each and every human being possesses an inviolable dignity and this is to take a (spiritual) leap since, Bergson argues, it is impossible to arrive at such ideas by degrees. There is a difference in kind between the two moralities: the former consists in impersonal rules and formulae, the latter incarnates itself in a privileged personality who becomes an example, such as exceptional human beings, be they Christian saints, sages of Greece, prophets of Israel, or the Arahants of Buddhism. Whereas the first morality works as a pressure or propulsive force, the second morality has the effect of an appeal. In it new life is proclaimed that goes against what nature prescribes, be it the survival of the fittest or the will to power of the strongest or the weakest. Here Bergson departs from Nietzsche's often brutally naturalist approach to ethics that must struggle harder to meet the charge of biologism (see Amrine 1992: 135–8; on Bergson's alleged reduction of the spiritual to the biological see Maritain 1943: 79).

Bergson insists that in the second morality it is not simply a question of replacing egoism with altruism. It is not simply a question of the self now saying to itself, "I am working for the benefit of mankind," simply because such an idea is too vast and the effect too diffuse. So what is taking place and being asked of the self? In the closed morality of pressure the individual and social are barely distinguishable: it is both at once and at this level spirit moves around a circle. Can we say that operative in the open soul subject to the open morality of aspiration there is the love of all humanity? For Bergson this would not go far enough since the openness can be extended to animals, plants, and all nature. It could even do without these since its form is not dependent on any specific content: "'Charity' would persist in him who possesses 'charity', though there be no other living creature on earth" (Bergson 1979: 38). It is a "psychic attitude" that, strictly speaking, does not have an object. It is not acquired by nature but requires an effort and transmits itself through feeling. Think, for example, of the attraction or appeal of love and its passion in its early stages. It resembles an obligation (we must because we must) and perhaps a tragedy lies ahead, with a whole life facing the prospect of being wrecked, wasted, and ruined. This does not stop our responding to its call or appeal. We are entranced, as in cases of musical emotion which introduces us into new feelings, and as passers-by are forced into a street dance. The pioneers in morality proceed in a similar fashion: "Life holds for them unsuspected tones of feeling like those of some new symphony, and they draw us after them into this music that we may express it in action" (*ibid.*: 40).

The error of intellectualism is to suppose that feeling must hinge on an object and that all emotion is little more than the reaction of our sensory faculties to an intellectual representation. In music, Bergson notes, the emotions are not linked to any specific objects of joy, of sorrow, of pity, or of love. The difference he wants us to think about is between an emotion that can be represented (in images and through objects) and the creative emotion that is beyond representation and amounts to a real invention. States of emotion caused by certain things are ordained by nature and are finite or limited in number; we recognize them quite easily because their destiny is to spur us on to acts that answer to our needs. Bergson is not blind to the illusions of love and our propensity to psychological deception. However, he maintains that the effect of creative emotion is not reducible to this because here we are faced with emotional states that are distinct from sensation, that is, they cannot be reduced to being a psychical transposition of a physical stimulus. For Bergson such an emotion informs the creations not only of art but of science and civilization itself. It is a unique kind of emotion, one that precedes the image, virtually containing it, and is its cause (*ibid.*: 47). His position is not equivalent, he insists, to a moral philosophy of sentiment, simply because we are dealing with an emotion that is capable of crystallizing into representations, even into an ethical doctrine. Moreover, he insists that if a new emotion, such as charity, wins over human beings this is neither because some metaphysics has enforced its moral practice nor because the moral practice has induced a disposition towards its alleged metaphysical claims. It is an "attraction" we are freely responding to in such cases and on the level of *both* intelligence and will (*ibid.*: 49).

Bergson acknowledges that many will find this account of the second morality difficult to accept: is it not the domain of the irrational par excellence? Is it not the domain of fanatics and of sad cases desperately in need of a doctrine of redemption? With Nietzsche, however, Bergson is keen to challenge the assumption that the superhuman can be born only out of reactive forces or energies and he credits the inspirers of humanity with "overflowing vitality" (*ibid.*: 95; admittedly Nietzsche does not see such vitality in the examples that inspire Bergson! For Nietzsche's suspicion of intoxicating states experienced by moral and religious geniuses, see 1997: §50). Neither of the two moralities exists in a pure state today: the first has handed on to the second something of its compulsive force, whilst the latter has diffused over the former something of its aroma. Nevertheless, analysis will find it useful Bergson thinks to hold onto the salient differences between the two. The first, for example, finds its essential character in remaining fixed to self-preservation: "the circular movement in which it carries round with it individuals, as it revolves on the same spot, is a vague imitation, through the medium of habit, of the immobility of instinct" (it is one rendition of the eternal return of the same) (Bergson 1979: 51). In this morality we attain pleasure, such as the well-being of individual and society, but not joy. By contrast, in the open morality we have progress that is experienced in the enthusiasm of a forward movement. There is no need to resort to a metaphysical theory to account for this difference since it is not necessary to picture a goal we are trying to achieve or envisage a state of perfection we wish to approximate. Rather, it is an opening out of the soul and a breaking with nature. Such an open soul expresses Bergson's commitment to a pure movement that cannot be conceived as a series of discrete stages, as in Zeno's paradoxes, since this is incapable of producing real movement. Rather, real movement involves an action in which we find the impression of a coincidence, real or imaginary, with the generative effort of life (*ibid.*: 55).

Bergson's thinking has its normative dimension in this positing of an open morality. Whilst the first morality has its source in nature, the second has no place in nature's design. Nature may have foreseen a certain expansion of social life through intelligence but only of a very limited kind:

> Nature surely intended that men should beget men endlessly, according to the rule followed by all other living creatures; she took the most minute precautions to ensure the preservation of the species by the multiplication of individuals; hence she had not foreseen, when bestowing on us intelligence, that intelligence would at once find a way of divorcing the sexual act from its consequences, and that man might refrain from reaping without forgoing the pleasure of sowing. It is quite another sense that man outwits nature when he extends social solidarity into the brotherhood of man .... . (*Ibid.*: 56–7)

For Bergson the two forces of pressure and aspiration are to be treated as fundamental data and are not exclusively moral; rather, they have their sources in the twin tendencies of life: preservation and enhancement or overcoming (*ibid.*: 96). There cannot be an absolute break with nature since this is never possible. Rather: "It might be said, by slightly distorting Spinoza, that it is to get back to *natura naturans* that we break away from *natura naturata*" (*ibid.*: 58). If the human is part of nature, then it is not far fetched to claim that our moral inventions amount to a nature expressing itself and as freedom.

Conclusion

Bergson's texts have exerted an influence on several generations of French thinkers, including some of the most important philosophers of the twentieth century, such as Jean-Paul Sartre, Simone de Beauvoir, Maurice Merleau-Ponty, Emmanuel Levinas, Paul Ricoeur, and Gilles Deleuze. In contrast to Nietzsche who accurately predicted that he would be born posthumously, Bergson was born in his own lifetime, being the most celebrated philosopher of his time with an influence on intellectual life that extended far beyond the academy. However, his reputation fell into serious decline after his death and the end of the Second World War where existentialism became the new intellectual fashion. Today, however, we are witnessing something of a renaissance of interest in Bergson's writings, and his contributions figure in new research in philosophy of mind (McNamara 1999, Ricoeur 2004), the philosophy of time (Durie 2000a, b; Turetzky 1998), and the philosophy of biology such as complexity theory (Durie 2002). In addition, he is now granted a place of crucial significance in histories of twentieth century thought (Gutting 2001; Ansell Pearson 2010). Gary Gutting, for example, locates Bergson's enduring greatness as a philosopher in the combination of descriptive concreteness and systematic scope and metaphysical ambition that characterizes his work (Gutting 2001: 384). In a recent review of the publication of Bergson's correspondence in the *Times Literary* Supplement, the eminent critic George Steiner wrote of the sense of delight and philosophical scruple one experiences in returning to Bergson after decades in which French philosophic debate was conduced in a jargon of almost impenetrable pretentiousness and opportunistic obscurity (Steiner 2003: 7). Although Bergson possessed tremendous knowledge of the history of philosophy – he was in his lifetime a professor of both ancient philosophy and modern philosophy – he was primarily interested in problems and in ascertaining whether our problems are good ones or ones badly posed. All of Bergson's major concerns closely correspond to today's practice in philosophy, and there is nothing that is peculiarly "continental" about his interests (freedom, consciousness and mind, time and memory, evolution and life, morality and religion).

A number of important thinkers have found liberation in Bergson's new modes of thinking. These include William James who said that it was Bergson who liberated him from intellectualism (James 1909: Lecture 6). James compared what Bergson accomplished in *Matter and Memory* to a Copernican Revolution and considered it a work to be ranked alongside Berkeley's *Principles of Human Knowledge* and Kant's *Critique of Pure Reason*. Upon its publication he hailed *Creative Evolution* as marking a new era in thought. Gilles Deleuze locates in Bergson's writings a "superior empiricism" that can prove its contemporary worth and relevance (Deleuze 1991 and 1999). Emmanuel Levinas argues that against our pan-logical civilization Bergsonism brings to bear an inestimable message, namely, its perception of a mode of change which does not stop at any identity and teaches that time is something other than a mobile image of an immobile eternity, which is what it has been in the history of Western thought, signifying the forfeiture of the permanence of being and the privation of eternity. Levinas wishes to underline the importance of Bergsonism "for the entire problematic of contemporary philosophy" on account of the fact that it is no longer a thought of a "rationality revealing a reality which keeps to the very measure of a thought." In effecting a reversal of traditional philosophy by contending the priority of duration over permanence, Bergson has provided thought with "access to novelty, an access independent of the ontology of the same" (Levinas 1987: 132). There is a Bergsonian revolution and it amounts to an upheaval in philosophy comparable in significance to those we encounter in Kant, Nietzsche, Heidegger and Wittgenstein, and with which we are much more familiar. Bergson occupies an important place in intellectual modernity and his work remains highly relevant today.

Note

1 For Bergson in his original French I have used the edition of his works, *Oeuvres*, published by Presses Universitaires de France (Paris) in 1959.

References

Amrine, F. (1992) "'The Triumph of Life': Nietzsche's Verbicide," in F. Burwick and P. Douglass (eds) *The Crisis in Modernism: Bergson and the Vitalist Controversy*, Cambridge: Cambridge University Press, pp. 131–53.

Ansell Pearson, K. (ed.) (2010) *A History of Continental Philosophy*, vol. 3: 1890–1930, Stocksfield, UK: Acumen Press.

Benda, J. (1954) *Sur le success de Bergsonisme*, Paris: Mercure de France.

Bergson, H. (1965) *Creative Mind*, trans. M. L. Andison, Totowa, NJ: Littlefield, Adams & Co.

—— (1972) *Mélanges*, Paris: Presses Universitaires de France.

—— (1979) *The Two Sources of Morality and Religion*, trans. R. Ashley Audra and C. Brereton, with the assistance of W. Horsfall Carter, Notre Dame, IN: University of Notre Dame Press.

—— (1991), *Matter and Memory*, trans. N. M. Paul and W. S. Palmer, New York: Zone Books.

—— (2000), *Duration and Simultaneity*, edited by R. Durie, Manchester: Clinamen Press.

—— (2001), *Time and Free Will*, trans. F. L. Pogson, New York: Dover.

—— (2002), *Key Writings*, edited by K. Ansell Pearson and J. Mullarkey, London: Continuum.

—— (2007a), *Introduction to Metaphysics*, trans. T. E. Hulme, edited by J. Mullarkey and M. Kolkman, Basingstoke: Palgrave Macmillan.

—— (2007b), *Creative Evolution*, trans. A. Mitchell, edited by K Ansell Pearson, M. Kolkman, and M. Vaughan, Basingstoke: Palgrave Macmillan.

—— (2007c), *Mind Energy*, trans. H. Wildon Carr, edited by K. Ansell Pearson, and M. Kolkman, Basingstoke: Palgrave Macmillan.

Burwick, F., and P. Douglass (eds) (1992) *The Crisis in Modernism: Bergson and the Vitalist Controversy*, Cambridge: Cambridge University Press.

Deleuze, G. (1991) *Bergsonism* (1966), trans. H. Tomlinson and B. Habberjam, New York: Zone Books.

—— (1999) "Bergson's Conception of Difference" (1956), trans. M. McMahon, in J. Mullarkey (ed.) *The New Bergson*, Edinburgh: Edinburgh University Press, pp. 42–66.

Durie, R. (2000a), "Splitting Time: Bergson's Philosophical Legacy," *Philosophy Today* 44, pp. 152–68.

—— (ed.) (2000b), *Time and the Instant*, Manchester: Clinamen Press.

—— (2002) "Creativity and Life," *Review of Metaphysics* 56: 357–83.

Grogin, R. C. (1988) *The Bergsonian Controversy in France 1900–1914*, Calgary, Canada: University of Calgary Press.

Gutting, G. (2001) *French Philosophy in the Twentieth Century*, Cambridge: Cambridge University Press.

Heidegger, M. (1987) *Nietzsche*, vol. 3: *The Will to Power as Knowledge and Metaphysics*, trans. J. Stambaugh, D. F. Krell, and F. A. Capuzzi, San Francisco: Harper.

Höffding, H. (1915), *Modern Philosophers and Lectures on Bergson*, trans. Alfred C. Mason, London: Macmillan.

James, W. (1909) *A Pluralistic Universe*, London; New York: Longmans, Green & Co.

Lehan, R. (1992) "Bergson and the Discourse of the Moderns," in F. Burwick and P. Douglass, *The Crisis in Modernism: Bergson and the Vitalist Controversy*, Cambridge: Cambridge University Press, pp. 306–30.

Levinas, E. (1987), *Time and the Other*, trans. R. A. Cohen, Pittsburgh: Duquesne University Press.

Maritain, J. (1943), *Redeeming the Time*, London: The Centenary Press.

McNamara, P. (1999) *Mind and Variability: Mental Darwinism, Memory, and Self*, London: Praeger.

Merleau-Ponty, M. (1988) "Bergson," in *In Praise of Philosophy and Other Essays*, trans. J. Wild and J. Edie, Evanston, IL: Northwestern University Press, pp. 9–33.

Moore, F. C. T. (1996) *Bergson: Thinking Backwards*, Cambridge: Cambridge University Press.

Nietzsche, F. (1968) *The Will to Power*, trans. W. Kaufmann and R. J. Hollingdale, New York: Random House.

—— (1974) *The Gay Science*, trans. W. Kaufmann, New York: Random House.

—— (1986) *Human, All Too Human*, 2 vols, trans. R. J. Hollingdale, Cambridge: Cambridge University Press.

—— (1997) *Daybreak*, trans. R. J. Hollingdale, edited by M. Clark and B. Leiter, Cambridge: Cambridge University Press.

—— (1998) *Beyond Good and Evil*, edited, trans. M. Faber, Oxford: Oxford University Press.

—— (2005a) *Thus Spoke Zarathustra*, trans. G. Parkes, Oxford: Oxford University Press.

—— (2005b) *The Anti-Christ*, trans. J. Norman, edited by A. Ridley and J. Norman, Cambridge: Cambridge University Press.

—— (2006) *On the Genealogy of Morality*, 2nd rev. edn, trans. C. Diethe, edited by K. Ansell Pearson, Cambridge: Cambridge University Press.

Ricoeur, P. (2004) *Memory, History, Forgetting*, trans. K. Blamey and D. Pellauer, Chicago: University of Chicago Press.

Schwartz, S. (1992) "Bergson and the Politics of Vitalism," in F. Burwick and P. Douglass (eds) *The Crisis in Modernism: Bergson and the Vitalist Controversy*, Cambridge: Cambridge University Press, pp. 277–306.

Steiner, G. (2003) "Mystic Master," *Times Literary Supplement*, 28 Feb, pp. 6–7.

Troeltsch, E. (1991) *Religion in History*, trans. J. Luther Adams and W. F. Bense, Edinburgh, T. & T. Clark.

Turetzky, P. (1998) *Time*, London: Routledge.

Further reading

K. Ansell Pearson, *Philosophy and the Adventure of the Virtual: Bergson and the Time of Life* (London: Routledge, 2002), features essays on TFW, MM, and CE and insights into Bergson's relation to Kant. Both G. Deleuze, *Cinema 1: The Movement-Image*, trans. H. Tomlinson and B. Habberjam (London: Continuum Press, 1986), and his *Cinema 2: The Time-Image*, trans. H. Tomlinson and R. Galeta (London: Continuum, 1989), draw heavily on Bergson's ideas to produce a startlingly novel and wide-ranging appreciation of cinema. See also E. During, "'A History of Problems': Bergson and the French Epistemological Tradition," *Journal of the British Society for Phenomenology* 35 (2004), pp. 4–24, in a special issue devoted to "Bergson Now." D. Emmet, "'Open' and 'Closed' Morality," in *Function, Purpose, and Powers*, by Emmet (London: Macmillan, 1972), pp. 137–68, contains important insights into Bergson's distinction between the closed and the open. M. A. Gillies, *Henri Bergson and British Modernism* (Montreal, Canada: McGill-Queen's University Press, 1996), is a study of Bergson's influence on British writers such as Virginia Woolf; and contains a helpful introduction on Bergson and his philosophical antecedents. S. Guerlac, *Thinking in Time: An Introduction to Henri Bergson* (Ithaca, NY: Cornell University Press, 2006), is a fine new introduction, written with the needs of students in mind, and focused on TFW and MM. D. R. Griffin, J. B. Cobb Jr, M. P. Ford, P. A. Y. Gunter, and P. Ochs (eds) (1993), *Founders of Constructive Postmodern Philosophy: Peirce, James, Bergson, Whitehead, and Hartshorne* (Albany, NY: SUNY Press, 1993), contains an essay on Bergson by renowned specialist P. A. Y. Gunter. To date the only full-length study of Bergson and political philosophy, an important study, is E. Kennedy, *Freedom and the Open Society: Henri Bergson's Contribution to Political Philosophy* (New York: Garland, 1987). A short and helpful introduction is L. Kolakowski, *Bergson* (Oxford: Oxford University Press, 1985). A volume in the 'Arguments the Philosophers' series is A. R. Lacey, *Bergson*, London: Routledge, 1989). An advanced appreciation is L. Lawlor, *The Challenge of Bergsonism* (London: Continuum Press, 2003). A. D. Lindsay, *The Philosophy of Bergson* (London: Dent, 1911), is superb on Bergson's reworking of Kant. M. S. Muldoon, *Tricks of Time: Bergson, Merleau-Ponty and Ricoeur in Search of Time, Self and Meaning* (Pittsburgh: Duquesne University Press, 2006), is a valuable new study that brings Bergson into rapport with two other major thinkers on questions of time. J. Mullarkey, (ed.) *The New Bergson* (Manchester: Manchester University Press, 1999), is a collection of essays presenting new work and insights. D. Papineau, *Thinking about Consciousness* (Oxford: Clarendon Press, 2006), argues against dualism in favor of the view that our general concept of phenomenal consciousness must depend on material properties and contains an appendix on the completeness of physics that discusses the principle of the conservation of energy that was of such interest to Bergson; alas, Bergson is nowhere mentioned and his important contribution goes unacknowledged. A. E. Pilkington, *Bergson and His Influence: A Reassessment* (Cambridge: Cambridge University Press, 1976), contains valuable insights into Bergson's influence on important French intellectual figures and writers, such as Julian Benda, Charles Péguy, Marcel Proust, and Paul Valéry, as well as Bergson's key concepts. T. Quirk, *Bergson and American Culture* (Chapel Hill: University of North Carolina Press, 1990), focuses on the influence of Bergson on the novels of Willa Cather and the poetry of Wallace Stevens. M. Sachs, *Objectivity and Insight* (Oxford: Oxford University Press, 2000), features a chapter on James and Bergson. J.-P. Sartre, *Imagination* (Ann Arbor: University of Michigan Press, 1962 [1936]), has an important chapter on Bergsonism. W. J. Scott, "Bergsonism in England," *Monist* 27 (1917): 179–204, presents Bergson as an enemy of scientific naturalism but argues that his philosophy is one that should appeal to scientifically minded philosophers. See also A. Styhre, "Knowledge as a Virtual Asset: Bergson's Notion of Virtuality and Organizational Knowledge," *Culture and Organization* 9 (2003): 15–27, in a special issue on "Bergson and Creative Social Science." A. Tarkovsky, *Sculpting in Time: Reflections on the Cinema*, trans. K. Hunter-Blair (Austin: University of Texas Press, 1999), contains reflections by one of the most original film-makers of European cinema on how the art of cinema can capture time and memory, echoing Bergson's insights into them. H. Wickham, *The Unrealists* (London: Sheed & Ward, 1933), presents Bergson as a supreme and laughable irrationalist.

Part IV

ENGAGING NATURALISM

15
COMTE'S POSITIVIST DREAM, OUR POST-POSITIVIST BURDEN

Robert C. Scharff

Introduction

Given his view of humanity's future, Auguste Comte might be considered the poster child for scientific optimism. Scientific (i.e. "positive") knowledge is, for him, the only real knowledge; its application to real-world situations will make us safe and happy; and becoming fully aware of these facts about science and about technology (he would have approved of calling them, together, "technoscience") will make safety and happiness come all the more quickly. In other words, for Comte technoscience is nothing short of a consummating occurrence or world event – that is, the practical as well as theoretical "ending" or fulfillment of the Western intellectual tradition. According to his famous "law of the three stages," we all begin as theologians, and under the right conditions we graduate first to abstract or metaphysical thinking, and then finally to science. Following after this intellectual development, given the necessary time lag, come the appropriate socio-political transformations – from primitive, militaristic, and theocratic communities, to societies reflecting increasingly secular and material interests organized by abstract principles, and finally to peaceful, fully industrial societies guided by a genuine knowledge of the human condition and supported by a Religion of Humanity. The task for philosophers in the current age is therefore to become positivists – that is, to become fully and reflectively aware of the historically palpable, ever more pervasive character of the emerging technoscientific era, to explain it, justify it, and see that this is taught to others.

Yet Comte's positivist interpretation of history and its three-stage theory of development have been widely misunderstood. On the one hand, because he is famously the "founder" of sociology (he originally called it "social physics"), his account of the rise of science and its technologies is often assumed to be a causal account. It is not. Comte does not think the coming technoscientific age entails either the complete suppression of other (i.e. non-technoscientific) possibilities or a specific and predictable future state produced by our antecedent socio-historical conditions. The three-stage law is a developmental law; it is no more causally necessary that everyone ends up a perfectly positive thinker than it is that everyone ends up making identical and maximally sophisticated use of their native language. On the other hand, because of the "meta-narrative" reach of his account, Comte's law is often construed as the linchpin of an old-fashioned speculative philosophy of history. His position, however, is neither teleological nor essentialist in the requisite sense. Although he happily regards all non-scientific possibilities as regressive and eagerly depicts philosophy's future in scientistic terms; he does not think that progress toward this future is the actualization of something like humanity's technoscientific entelechy. Comte's account of the rise of technoscience is, I shall argue, something much more interesting than any of these mistaken interpretations can tell us.

Yet my aim is not just to encourage the idea that Comte's account is interesting. In my view, Comte's progressivist, technoscientific optimism is no mere relic of the nineteenth century. Nor should we see it as merely a theoretical stance, still held by some people, applied on some occasions, to some experiences. Comte's account of the rise of an age of technoscience is more even than a "world view" – that is, more than a general conceptualization of the present age that we might choose or reject. It is, and Comte advertises it to be, his projection of how the good life is destined to be experienced and understood in our increasingly post-theological and post-metaphysical circumstances. As he describes it, the third stage is working itself out as the ultimate way for us to *be*, in its full, philosophical and practical articulation. Comte's language sometimes makes his account seem a bit exaggerated and out of place today, yet it should also sound very familiar. It is the sort of language that many philosophers of technology (e.g. Mumford, Ellul, Adorno, Marcuse, Heidegger) complain is all too often used to define what "philosophy" has come to be since the Greeks – namely, a guardian's discipline whose main job is to analyze and defend a "scientific" sort of rationality because it allegedly provides the best intellectual access to and power for handling everything "real" that we encounter.

Comte seems to me, then, to have contemporary rather than just historical significance. He asks what it means to "be" in an increasingly technoscientific world, and he offers an answer that is by no means dated. Indeed, Comte's paean to technoscientific life – his portrayal of our last and most "mature" condition – still serves quite well as a description of the background understanding of most Western technocrats, as well as many Anglo-American epistemologists and philosophers of science and technology. In a way, it is entirely fair to call Comte the last honest positivist. He actually identifies and defends a human condition many others, for various reasons, still embrace but only silently and as if its normativity were self-evident.

Some thinkers, most famously Heidegger, have complained loudly that this technoscientific way of being and understanding everything does not deserve its current hegemony. Yet their complaints are usually met with the objection that they are overheated and romanticist – or worse, that they are complaints typical of cultures that are already technoscientifically "developed" and eager to retain their monopoly on the social and political benefits this accords them. It is one thing to criticize this or that technoscientific excess, so goes the argument; it is another to condemn technoscience itself. Near the end this essay, I come back briefly to this controversy over technoscientific optimism and pessimism. Mostly, however, I talk about Comte. I argue that when Comte's understanding of the scientific age is carefully recounted, it is hard to sustain the usual assumption that his conception of either the present world or philosophy's primary tasks in this world has been surpassed. Indeed, I think Comte is the one positivist who retains his contemporary relevance after positivism as a movement has run its course (Scharff 1995). I begin from this last remark, with some comparisons between nineteenth and twentieth-century positivism.

Comte's positivism

How can I claim that positivism has real presence in the twenty-first century, let alone that its nineteenth-century version is now its most relevant form because it still deeply affects alleged post-positivists, when it is hard to find anyone who admits to being even sympathetic to positivism? The answer is obvious but not simple. Rejecting the doctrines of positivism – and even its world view – need not entail rejecting the orientation that produces them. Let me explain this point somewhat indirectly.

According to the famous logical empiricist manifesto of 1929 (Neurath et al. 1973) – the so-called Yellow Brochure composed by Neurath, et al., to celebrate Schlick's return to Vienna from Stanford – philosophy has one main task, namely, to rationally reconstruct the epistemology of science. In carrying out this task, philosophers need make only two commitments. They must produce a formal analysis of the scientific method, and they must be empiricists about the range of this method's application. Together, says Neurath, these two commitments express "the scientific world view" that is appropriate to philosophy.

It is, of course, this self-portrait of logical empiricism that has received the bulk of the critical attention (Neurath et al. 1985: Translator's introduction). There is, however, another side to the manifesto that was suppressed by its authors and is less considered by its critics. After defining the scientific world view, Neurath observes that those who embrace it also typically share similar ethical, social, and political opinions. But he assures us that this fact, however interesting, is not a topic for philosophy. Philosophy is about the rational reconstruction of the method for testing propositions. It is about meaning and truth, not about the "shared sentiments" of those who happen to pursue this topic.

If we take Neurath at his word, then it is easy to conclude that logical positivism – to quote Passmore – is as about as dead as a philosophical movement ever becomes (Passmore 1967: 56). Today, no one admits to being a logical empiricist. Rational reconstruction, the stress on theory verification but never discovery, the tendency to model all knowledge on nineteenth-century physics, emotivism in ethics and politics – all the main features of the positivist program have been rejected. Yet how thorough has this rejection really been? How genuinely "post-positivist" is the general opposition to logical empiricism's scientific world view, let alone the understanding of life and world that underlies it? The answer, I think, is much less so than practicing post-positivists tend to assume. The reason has little to do with the rejection of the specific tenets of the logical empiricist program and everything to do with Neurath's allegedly irrelevant "sentiments."

Note first that many of the objections to logical positivism have involved criticizing some of its overt features precisely by silently perpetuating its underlying conception of science and its epistemic status. To object, for example, that the "discovery" of scientific theories is just as important philosophically as their justification, does nothing to challenge the more basic assumption that confirming predictive theories is the "essence" of scientific practice and that warrantability is the essence of the meaningfulness of all language. Similarly, to argue that there are "other" sciences with "other" purposes using "other" methods that logical empiricism ignores does nothing to dislodge the epistemic prejudice in favor of the mathematical and physical sciences, or in favor of quantification as the primary mode of scientific conceptualization. Or to give one more example, for all the criticism of logical empiricism's explicit program, it is still not part of the mainstream agenda to ask such questions as who does science, for what purposes, at what costs, and for whose benefit. Philosophy of Science, I recently heard an American Philosophical Association official say, must never degenerate into Science Studies.

In short, opposing logical positivism's program often remains a vehicle by means of which many philosophers, willingly or not, continue to share logical positivism's general "sentiments." But of course, "sentiments" is not the right term. It implies reference to something subjective and thus, at best, of ancillary interest to philosophers. The label undoubtedly served logical empiricists well, but in the glare of subsequent developments, we can no longer accept it at face value. It is just too obvious that promoting a "scientific" method of inquiry, an empiricist semantics, and an objectivist stance toward the surrounding world was important for political as well as for epistemological reasons (Richardson and Uebel 2007; Reisch 2005; Howard 2003).

More precisely, then, "sentiments," is a philosophical misnomer. It is the term logical empiricists use to denigrate something they do not want to think about – something that nevertheless influences their thoughts on science much more profoundly than mere sentiments ever could. In spite of their disclaimers, their supposedly irrelevant "shared opinions" – opinions about the proper place of science in human affairs and about the superiority of science-mindedness in dealing with those affairs – are much more than just an accident of similar political or social attitudes. They express the general understanding of *how to be philosophical in a technoscientific age* – that is, they articulate a global sense of how to think about our dealings with whatever is real that has made positivists positivists since the early nineteenth century. From at least John Stuart Mill to the last logical empiricist, all would agree with what Carnap wrote in 1928. Whenever our world view faces theological or metaphysical opposition, he asserts, we can be sure that science will in the end be "set free" from religion and metaphysics. Our confidence

> stems from the knowledge, or to put it somewhat more carefully, *the belief that those opposing powers belong to the past.* We feel that there is an inner kinship

438

between the attitude on which our philosophical work is founded and the intellectual attitude which presently manifests itself in entirely different walks of life … .We feel all around us the same basic orientation, the same style of thinking and doing. It is an orientation which demands clarity everywhere. (Carnap 1967: xvii–xviii, my emphasis)

This is, of course, a funny sort of belief – philosophically irrelevant, and at the same time definitive of the right sort of post-religious and post-metaphysical thinker.

Unlike the later positivists, however, Comte has a name for "the intellectual attitude which presently manifests itself" everywhere. He calls it the positive spirit, and he is eager to make it THE philosophical topic. Being "oriented" toward "clarity" is of course essential to it. When positivists after Comte attempt to interpret their scientific world view in overt and entirely epistemic terms, they may succeed in deflecting attention from the "spirit" they "feel all around them," but it is precisely because they already understand their circumstances in terms of this spirit that their world view seems self-evident to them. Here is the reason I want to call Comte philosophically more "honest." How the logical empiricists actually understand the present age is not so different from Comte's own. For Comte, however, it is a philosopher's obligation to reflect upon and defend this understanding – to answer the question, as one might phrase it, of how one becomes and why one should be a positivist in a post-metaphysical age. Later positivists "believe" and want us to "share" their objectivistic conviction that a contemporary philosopher's proper outlook is formalist, neutral, decontextualized, and epistemically "monological" – that, in Thomas Nagel's phrase, one must aspire to philosophize from Nowhere (Nagel 1986).

The hard truth is that the more firmly and unreflectively the later positivists embraced the "scientific world view" and suppressed their "sentiments" as extra-philosophical, the more obvious it became that their neutral/objectivist standpoint is nothing of the kind. Positivism was never a philosophy from Nowhere. It has always been in fact a very determinately historical movement. This is what has come to seem obvious from the doctrines it produced. All of the logical empiricist doctrines – the formalistic reconstructions, the verificationism, the pinched and dated accounts of scientific practice, the reduction of values to expressions of feeling – are out of fashion. Yet all of them can and have been rejected … by self-described post-positivists who remain just as objectivistic as any positivist.

The harder truth is, then, that if there is no objectivist epistemology, there can also be no critique of it in objectivist (or what ontologically amounts to the same thing, anti-objectivist) terms. Critics who do not see this end up arguing positivistically against the logical empiricism program – as, I think, many post-positivist, phenomenological, and pragmatist philosophers have in fact unwittingly done. Hence, the title of my book on Comte is also a slogan. I reconsider Comte "after positivism." My point is that even if all the items in logical empiricism's explicit program have been thoroughly trashed, and even if its underlying "sentiments" have been criticized as well, one might still be tempted to conclude that positivism merely failed to become as ahistorical and objectivistic as it intended or that such a View from Nowhere is only appropriate when scientific concerns are at issue – and thus keep alive in one's own criticisms the idea that such a world view is possible.

Here is where a reconsideration of Comte can help. In the first place, for him positivism expresses a general intellectual orientation, not just a belief, feeling, or sentiment. As such it is something to explicitly reflect upon, and when we do so, we see that rather than constituting a rejection of the earlier orientations of theology and metaphysics, it accomplishes its purpose by preserving and transforming them. Indeed, precisely by recognizing that all three are general orientations rather than theories or beliefs, we see that none of them are "options" that one might choose or set aside at will. Hence, Comte regards positivism as the articulation of an orientation that he already discovers himself to be developing *in the midst of socio-historically determinate surroundings* – rather like the way we discover at a certain point that we have and are developing a native language. We can use it, adapt it to perceived new circumstances, become reflective about it, even imagine having a different one, but we cannot simply walk away from it in favor of another choice. Considering positivism in this way can help us to think through what even the loudest critics of positivism have often seemed insufficiently radical to acknowledge. No only do both positivistic and anti-positivistic "sentiments" belong to the same basic philosophical orientation, but both encourage the idea that the philosophy might still actually come to be conducted as if from Nowhere if we only try harder.

Two further preliminary remarks. First, in this essay I approach Comte primarily through the epistemically oriented and scientifically interested arguments he lays out in his earlier *Cours de philosophie positive*, and I relate them primarily to recent work in the Anglo-American tradition. Another recent study begins with Comte's later conception of a secular "Religion of Humanity" (developed especially in the *Système de politique positive*) and relates it primarily to recent work in the French and German traditions (Wernick 2001). For any approach to Comte, however, one's companion should be the indispensable intellectual biography now being completed by Pickering (Pickering 1995, and forthcoming).

Second, I have been talking so far as if Comte and the later positivists all focus first and foremost on science – which might suggest that "technology" is simply their blanket term for all the applications of science. This is indeed the view of many positivists, but I will try to show that it is not Comte's. Technology is, for him, actually the prior phenomenon because it is in our technological practices – both before and after the rise of modern science – that human beings express their most fundamental ontological sense of what there is and what they want. What we now call science is simply the last and the most successful vehicle for enacting this sense of things. Hence, I will use the term "technoscience" wherever the context is contemporary, with the assumption that it is no longer possible to imagine a world in which technology in any sense might still be experienced as a phenomenon separate from science.

Comte's three-stage law

How does Comte understand the present age? John Stuart Mill, in his correspondence with Comte, complains that telling the story of what came before science is a waste of time. We are already *in* the age of science, Mill asserts. Explaining how we got here is a bit like reporting on a finished race as if we did not know its winner. Mill, like the logical empiricists, "feels" the scientific spirit all around him. But Comte does not. The present age, he says, is *going to be* the age of science. He thinks of himself as living in the period of transition between metaphysical and scientific understanding. A positive philosopher is therefore obliged to defend this transition, by explaining what scientific thinking is and why it is superior to the thinking typical of previous ages.

Yet defending the transition to a scientific age is not the only reason Comte has for discussing theology and metaphysics. Making "science" intelligible depends upon comparing it with these earlier sorts of intellectual practice. Ideas, he says, can only be understood through their history. The idea of science is no exception. Science did not and does not result from merely turning our collective backs on, in Carnap's phrase, what belongs to the past. Scientific thinking is actually a transformation of theological and metaphysical thinking, not a rejection of them. The superiority of scientific theories lies precisely in the fact that they do the same thing as theological and metaphysical theories, only better. All our thinking, from the very start, has had two related aims – namely, to make it possible for us to control nature and organize peaceful societies. As it turns out, only the "positive" knowledge generated by science can fulfill these aims.

Comte's conception of the "positivity" of positive philosophy is rich and multi-faceted, in comparison to the pinched and reductive meaning given to it by later positivists and reinforced by the expositions of them by their critics. In the *Discours*, Comte explains that "positive," as it applies to his philosophical orientation, should be understood as having at least six interrelated senses – that is, positivism is concerned with what is (a) real (i.e. actually accessible to the human intellect), (b) useful (to the genuine improvement of the human condition), (c) certain (as opposed to encouraging indecision), (d) precise (as opposed to vague), (e) constructive (as opposed to the "negative," or merely critical, divisive, or skeptical), and (f) relative (in the sense of always responsive to the degree and kind of evidence, not prone to make absolute and unmodifiable claims) (DEP: 126–30 [64–71]). Comte's *Système*, in keeping with his later addition of benevolent love to the earlier slogan of "order and progress," adds "sympathetic" as a seventh meaning (SPP1: 58/45). His point, of course, is that only third-stage, mature reasoning is in a position to fully recognize the meaning and value of all these characteristics taken together. For example, by ignoring the sixth and seventh meanings, one can exaggerate Comte's view of the power of social scientific laws – claiming they tell us what is "bound to occur" and thus making the idea of social reorganization either deterministic or "prescriptive" in a way that Comte would have found metaphysical (Singer 2003: 9–10, 32–5).

Cognition in the positive sciences is successful, then, because it seeks the kind of theories that *affirm* the results of disciplined observation, rather than merely *criticize* and *oppose* the claims of others or engage in abstract and *empirically ungrounded* specu-lation. As the italicized words and phrases suggest, evaluation of both the structure and the function of science must include a careful and sympathetic analysis of how prescientific philosophy tries but falls short of achieving these same aims. Comte defends this position in many places over several decades, but always in terms of his famous three-stage law. Here are some of the details (Scharff 1995: 73–91, 1991: 184–99).

According to Comte's law, "by its very nature … human intelligence in all its inquiries must of necessity pass successively through three different theoretical stages: the theological or fictive, the metaphysical or abstract, and the scientific or positive" (CPP1: 1/1–2). Though of course, Comte could not yet explicitly say so, his conception of human intelligence is what we now call developmental. When he calls science, like theology and metaphysics, an "*état*," it is therefore better to translate this "stage" rather than "state," since he conceives of all three as a series of emerging, not static conditions, both in themselves and with respect to earlier and later conditions. Hence, simply criticizing theology and metaphysics in the name of science would be a bit like criticizing the grammatical limitations of a two-year-old from the standpoint of an adult language user. Moreover, although the law is undoubtedly first and foremost about human intelligence, it is not exclusively about cognition. To really know the comings and goings of our surroundings involves cognition, imagination, feeling, volition – in a word, all the capacities that function together to constitute human intelligence. Moreover, the aim of knowledge is to give us "prevision," that is, comprehension of the principles of natural and social activity. The practical employment of these principles as we have come to know them so far has already begun to dramatically improve our lives and promises to continue to do so.

Comte's account of the rise and development of the extant natural and life sciences, and his projection of the possibility of genuine social science as well, must be under-stood within the context of his larger story about human biological, social, cultural, and political development. The three-stage law shows us what we may still become, given what we have already been. It is not just about human thought considered abstractly or structurally or in itself. It is about the way strictly intellectual (he sometimes uses the older term, "spiritual") developments ultimately influence practical and social ("temporal") activity. "From science," says Comte, "comes [genuine and efficacious] prevision; from prevision comes [genuinely productive and satisfying] action." I have added in brackets what applies specifically to the third stage. The positivist slogan, "Order and Progress," articulates this principle. In 1889, "Ordem e Progresso" was incorporated into the new national flag of Brazil by an intelligentsia that was at the time strongly influenced by Comte's social theory. The idea is that science provides knowledge of the natural and social "order," and the applications of this knowledge facilitate "progress" in real life. In the *Système*, Comte goes still further, adding a third idea to the slogan. He comes to think that from the improvement of our natural and interpersonal circumstances, there will eventually arise a similar improvement in our affective life, and self-centeredness will begin to give way to universal and benevolent "love." The reason is simple enough, he explains. "We grow tired of thinking, and even of acting; we never tire of loving" (SPP1: 1/1).

Regarding the original positivism of Comte, then, it would be wrong to interpret his analysis of human rationality as an "epistemology" in today's familiar sense of providing a theory of knowledge, truth, and/or warranted belief. He would find what we now call epistemology deficient in at least three ways – namely, as suffering from an excessive tendency toward formalization (i.e. where the topic is *the* way to reason and *the* criteria of rationality), as overemphasizing the present (i.e. where only what we twenty-first century Westerners in "developed" countries think about the topic carries real philosophical weight), and finally as displaying a certain narrowness and reductiveness (i.e. by typically starting with the proper functioning strictly of cognition and deeming the consideration of "contextual" issues at best optional and at worst diverting). For Comte, by contrast, the most important philosophical feature of any thinking – theological, metaphysical, or scientific – is that it is a human activity, a way of interacting with our surroundings. We must understand that it *occurs* successively in three ways, and that these represent three successive global "approaches" to our overall circumstances. Comte calls these approaches "*ways* of philosophizing." Each arises from a distinctive sense of experiential encounter with our natural and social surroundings, and this general sense is articulated in a distinctive type of theorizing (Comte uses the old-fashioned term, "speculation" for all three types). The later stages build on the strengths and struggle to overcome the weaknesses of the previous ones, and the ultimate measure of their success is what they enable us to do with the natural and social world.

Comte's law is designed to illuminate these developments from several perspectives. Psychologically, it identifies the main stages of individual intellectual growth. Epistemologically, it explains how each science realizes its ultimate aim by passing through the stages appropriate to it. Socio-politically, it depicts the rise of human societies in their religious, military, industrial, and legal activities as following, with a time lag, intellectual progress. Historically, it depicts the stages and their socio-political expressions in the whole of humanity over time. Finally, behind all these analytical perspectives, there lies an idea of human progress that Comte himself may be happy about but which he believes in any case represents the inevitable developmental tendency of our species. In discussing each stage below, I emphasize especially Comte's general historical articulation of them, but also mention in passing some of the manifestations of these stages in the lives of individuals, in the development of the specific sciences, and the socio-political changes.

Pre-scientific history: theology

For Comte, famously, theology constitutes our necessary intellectual "childhood." Yet if his claim is well-known, his interpretation of it is often misunderstood. Primitive cultures, young human beings, and fledgling disciplines may all begin by thinking theologically, but for Comte, this does not mean either that their fundamental motivations are different from those of mature cultures, adults, and established sciences or that their superstitions and god-talk are merely about some non-existent entities in which grown-ups eventually stop believing. For Comte, as I explained above, all human thinking in all three of its stages, whatever else it may be about and whatever other effects it may have, is rooted in the same basic motivation – namely, a markedly optimistic desire to sustain or restore natural harmony and social peace.

Between the lines of all Comte's descriptions of intellectual and social development, one can see this implicit understanding of how it has been and how it is supposed to be between human beings and their surroundings. Under primitive intellectual conditions, we confidently assume that nature is predictable and at least benign, if not always actually supportive. Day is supposed to follow night. Mountains are at worst supposed to rumble, but not to spew lava over whole villages. There is supposed to be enough to eat. People are supposed to be able to live together. Pleasure is supposed to supplant pain. It is not that there are no surprises or mysteries; but what surprises and mysteries we do encounter are supposed to be either enjoyable or soluble or at least tolerable.

Of course, just a few days of life and a few years of social existence tell us that things are not always so easy; and in "maturity," we know very well what a struggle it always is to make things right and how rare it is when harmony and peace really predominate. For Comte, however, human beings never regard this struggle as completely devoid of a sense that things can be fixed. In other words, what we now call scientific optimism is for him not something essentially scientific at all. We might better call it ontological optimism – that is, Comte's interpretation of how humans always understand things to "be." As I will explain in a moment, this positive sense of things is easiest to detect in his defense of the "maturity" of the scientific stage; but it also informs, if not so obviously, even his conception of the religious ideas and practices of our youngest selves and most remote ancestors.

In primitive human life, according to Comte, cognition begins in experiences of mysterious and disturbing ruptures in what is otherwise taken to be a predictable world. Things just keep doing the unexpected and threatening. Reactions to these events are at first spontaneous – and, of course, largely a matter of instinct and emotion. Both historically as a species and as individuals, we initially lack both reliable theories about our surroundings (which, after all, would have to be based on previous observations) and fruitful observations (which would need guidance from reliable theories). We would thus have forever remained in an intellectual "vicious circle," were it not for the "spontaneous conceptualizations" of primitive minds. In the beginning, instinctual/emotional reactions to the unexpected encounters serve as the substitute for the sort of disciplined, data-collecting "observations" that could provide us with real science; and the imaginative speculations to which these reactions give rise are the substitute for what scientists call "theories." Afraid or awestruck in the presence of some apparently uncontrollable natural force (e.g. an eclipse, earthquake, or epidemic), people are excited by these feelings into thinking about the actually experienced thing itself as having a frightful or awesome countenance. And since at this point we lack the needed theoretical repertoire, all of our resulting conceptualizations of such experiences tend to depict the frightful or awesome thing as alive with power or energy analogous to but (given the evidence of the present encounter) greater than the human will. The formation of such analogies is the first sign of philosophical activity. It is designed to "explain" the strangeness of unexpected events; and primitive speculation makes variations on the image of the human will because what is sought is the "cause" of the occurrence, and the only causally effective power with which the primitive mind is directly familiar is experienced in its own acts of choosing.

Animism, or *fetishism*, is thus the earliest form of theology. It emerges as a direct, experience-based, imaginative response to surprising and disturbing encounters with our otherwise routine and predictable surroundings. Like all subsequent forms of philosophy, it is also thoroughly practical-minded in its intention. It aims to restore sense and order to a temporarily disrupted existence – so that we can get on with life. By giving us guidance for ritual and social interaction, theological speculation, even in this most archaic form, thus grounds our original form of universal praxis. It is no exaggeration to say that, for Comte, prayer and ritual are essentially our first technology – i.e. our first global effort to accommodate and restore the disrupted relations that stimulate our initial speculations.

Over our lengthy period of "infancy," however, the ultimately unacceptable character of these spontaneously produced, fetishistic "theories" becomes all too evident. As accounts of disruptions in our "normally" harmonious relations, they imply that our true condition is one of total subordination to arbitrary external powers. If these disruptions are in fact just manifestations of a world full of entities with "wills" of their own, then fetishism neither explains this world nor promises any relief from undesirable surprises. According to its theories, things just do what they do, and we are powerless to stop them. Such a conclusion, argues Comte, is both intellectually unsatisfying and pragmatically intolerable. Indeed, in the aggregate, our experience does not seem to square with this negative double conclusion. It is not clearly the case that unexpected events "just happen" (i.e. are always merely arbitrary expressions of power); nor does it seem obvious that events are always out of our control. As the mind ponders these matters, it gradually turns from fetishism to *polytheism*.

Polytheistic philosophizing differs from fetishism in several ways. As just noted, it is stimulated not only by feelings of awe or fear but also by a growing sense of dissatisfaction with fetishistic responses to these feelings. As a result, the mind begins to employ the imagination to speculate about other more promising conceptual responses and eventually settles on the possibility of explaining events by conceiving them as driven by "hidden causes" – that is, invisible gods that control not just this or that particular event but whole classes of similar events (e.g. the sun god is responsible for the behavior of the sun generally, not just one eclipse). For the polytheist, it is not the experienced thing that has the mysterious power; it is the god or gods "of" such things that is controlling them. Eventually these controlling hidden causes are systematized into a pantheon of invisible gods who are pictured as presiding together over the natural and social world.

In Comte's account of polytheism, and especially in his comparisons of it backwards toward fetishism and forward toward monotheism, we can already see the outlines of the case he ultimately wants to make for scientific thinking. On the one hand, in contrast to fetishism, polytheism shifts the focus away from the "existent" things we experience to the "phenomenal generalities" (i.e. the awe- or fear-inspiring *kinds* of actions or motions) whose manifestation in the appearance of these things catches our attention in the first place (or so we imagine). This alteration of attention is crucial for all later cognitive advancement, because it suggests for the first time the possibility of systematic intellectual abstraction: Never mind the things we see. What *makes* them the kinds of things we see?

At the same time, this abstractive move seems paradoxically to draw the world closer to us both theoretically and practically than fetishism does. Theoretically speaking, if control of the phenomenal generalities of things is a function of divine wills instead of arbitrary material forces, this suggests that the true course of things is determined by beings (i.e. the hidden gods) analogous to ourselves (for we know from our own case what it is like to will something according to a plan or purpose). And practically speaking, if what we experience are not just the things themselves operating mysteriously and arbitrarily, but things that are under the hidden control of the wills of gods who seem in principle to be comprehensible, then the world is a potentially predictable place after all. Perhaps, with sufficient reverence for these gods and some understanding of their purposes, they may modify the course of future events in a friendly direction, especially if one suspects that these gods might care about us. However, the deepest *scientific* implication of this theoretical and practical transformation does not fully come to light until much later. For when the polytheistic mind conceives the restoration of satisfying relations between ourselves and the world as depending on our understanding the wills and purposes of the gods, it makes spontaneous use of what we in retrospect recognize to be the prototype of the modern epistemic model of thinking subjects seeking the right theories about the world regarded as external object(s). In our terms, the polytheistic mind is learning how to think representatively and how to set up a correspondence model of truth.

On the other hand, the speculations of polytheism are still at best mere creations of the imagination, intimately expressive of and responsive to our immediately felt everyday experiences. If this makes polytheistic theories practically appealing, it also causes them to remain conceptually unclear and inconsistent. (Think of Socrates asking Euthyphro if he really believes all those stories about the gods, their enmities, and their follies.) When dissatisfaction with the conceptual limitations of polytheistic theory grows strong enough (e.g. when the very idea of more than one "supreme" being comes to seem hopelessly illogical), genuinely rational concepts begin to displace imaginative "images," and the transition is made to *monotheism*. According to Comte, even monotheism, like all forms of theology, originates from feelings or instincts stimulated by everyday experiences of the unexpected, but unlike the earlier forms of theology, its theories reflect reason's success in gaining the upper hand in responding to these experiences. Even superstitions that survive into monotheism are given some sort of "rational" gloss; and the imagination is only permitted to contribute to the production of accounts of divine causality that are logically and coherently organized and in which the whole surrounding world is conceived as a single cosmos.

For the first time, the developing human mind succeeds in working out a genuine "system" of knowledge. There is a cosmos, or universe, and it is created by, or is at least under the power of a single god who acts, not capriciously as in earlier theologies, but in accordance with a set of universal and invariable laws.

From one angle, then, monotheistic theology is an obvious "intellectual" improvement. Its cosmology is rational and systematic – at least to the extent allowed by whatever feelings and commitments to superstition and authority are definitive for a given religion – and its rituals and codes of behavior allow for more consciously rule-governed and orderly communities. In the end, however, Comte is not very kind to monotheism. He admits that against the imaginative and illogical character of earlier forms of theology, monotheism is the inevitable corrective; yet its resulting picture of things is, in ways that are not obvious at first, deeply unsatisfying both theoretically and practically. On the one hand, although monotheism's theories about how God's laws work may be logical, these theories themselves remain incurably vague and abstract – which is not really surprising, since for monotheists the whole point is simply that they are God's laws. "God did it" may comfort those who feel that their ultimate divinity, being ultimate, is by definition capable of doing anything; but it is not much of an "explanation." On the other hand, speaking in terms of practice, the god who applies these laws seems increasingly remote from human affairs. It is with monotheism, not polytheism, that cosmological and ethical theories grow "other-worldly." Indeed, in Comte's unflattering portrayal, the very point that the monotheistic mind comes most to insist on – namely, that there is an essential disjunction between divine and human natures – virtually guarantees that its theories will undermine all sense of fundamental (albeit sometimes disrupted) intimacy which lies at the heart of our original experiences of the surrounding world.

Nevertheless, Comte's purpose in these criticisms is not to denigrate monotheism; it is rather to sympathetically reconstruct its place in our intellectual development in order to see how it is both necessary and surpassable. It is therefore important to see both that monotheism is, from the standpoint of what comes before, a kind of completion of this first intellectual stage, and also from a developmental standpoint, the beginning of inevitable "decay" for the theological era. Once the polytheistic imagination awakens reason, monotheistic speculation is ultimately forced on us by our sense that, for all its mystery and variety, the surrounding world is one "connected" whole. In the theological stage, however, the search for an intellectual system that articulates this "urge to unity," is almost wholly abstract and purely conceptual, and it is actually achieved at the expense of our more primitive and lived experience of the connectedness of all things. Comte sees monotheism as thus both intellectually unavoidable and a kind of betrayal of the admirably concrete and intimate sort of original relatedness to our natural and social surroundings – a betrayal that will not be undone until the mind matures enough to understand the need and the value of experimental observation.

Signs of such maturity are, of course, only rudimentary at this stage. Unavoidably, the stimulus of instincts, feelings, and reliance on superstition still functions in place of genuine "observation." To the immature mind, the "mere" recording of resemblance and succession, which scientists understand is the key to real knowledge, simply cannot seem important enough to attract any sustained attention. At this point, Comte explains, the mind must be "overstimulated" – that is, feelings and imagination must stir our intellectual powers sufficiently to make it seem possible for us to understand our surroundings *by* solving life's greatest mysteries (e.g. why things happen, what's "behind" the appearances we see, why we're here, what happens after we die). No answers to these Big Questions are ever found, yet the search for them is what drives our first attempts to subdue the unknown and mysterious by means of thought. Monotheistic speculation shows the mind that logical and systematic theorizing is possible, just as the earlier theological substages made us aware of our feelings and the power of our imagination. All of these powers will eventually figure properly together in the pursuit of scientific knowledge; but if we are ever to understand what this means, we must develop and maintain an appreciation of the functioning of all our intellectual powers, not just focus on rationality in the narrow sense of cognition. (So, for example, Comte would side with post-positivist and science studies critics of logical empiricism's rigid, internalist division between the "mere" discovery of scientific theories and the philosophically "essential" issue of their justification. For him, as for these critics, this division is based on a bloated and unhistorical sense of the power and role of cognition in scientific practice.)

In the end, no theological conception of our surroundings can be intellectually satisfying, since it inevitably depends more on feeling and imagination than on reason; and it is precisely monotheism that demonstrates this. Consider this final form of theology long enough, and it will gradually dawn on us that if there is such a thing as cosmic necessity, then the mind's real subject must be the laws of this necessity and not the fact that any god happens to make use of them. The political parallel of this intellectual insight is, of course, the idea – worked out especially in Christian terms – that it is possible to conceive of a viable social order independently of a divine one. Out of the distinction between the City of Man and the City of God arises the Enlightenment idea of an entirely secular state that God does not supervise. In secularizing the ideas of cosmic and social order, the mind begins to experience its power to overrule all appeals to feeling, superstition, and religious authority. With the emergence of this theoretical – and eventually also practical – realization, thinking turns metaphysical.

Pre-scientific history: metaphysics

Comte's idea of metaphysics and the metaphysical era has also been widely misinterpreted. Unlike the later positivists, he does not define either theology or metaphysics in dismissive scientistic terms, or regard their theories as cognitive nonsense. His conception of observation is more Jamesian than Humean (William James famously described British empiricism as "not very empirical"), and he is no semantic monist about worldly knowledge. He "observes" that both theology and metaphysics are products of historically developed, perfectly meaningful activities that ultimately prove unsuccessful but without which there could have been no science. Indeed, to put this issue in more pointed form, what Comte says about the necessity and limitations of theology and metaphysics actually provides the rationale for the later positivists' silent and ungratefully dogmatic assumption of the superiority of science.

To Comte, the most important thing to notice about metaphysical thinking is that it helps the mind liberate itself from its original tendency to invest all speculation about our surroundings with the feeling that something extra-natural – something divine rather than worldly – controls them. In a word, metaphysics helps the mind make the transition from supernaturalism to naturalism. To see how this liberation takes place, one must understand why the metaphysical era has earlier and later phases, but no actual substages like theology.

In its earlier phase, the intellectual tendency already discernible in the movement from polytheism to monotheism is simply brought to completion. Monotheism itself is criticized in the same way that monotheism criticized polytheism, namely, by showing that monotheism's own theories are no less vague and inconsistent than those of polytheism. Reduced to its barest essentials, "God did it" is no more intellectually satisfying than "the gods did it." Monotheistic ideas of how these forces operate must therefore be rejected in favor of detailed, logically coherent, naturalistic theories. At first, however, metaphysical theories still shared the theological assumption that worldly events are run by hidden (i.e. unobservable) forces, and that these forces are manifestations of God's power.

In the later phase of metaphysics, "Nature" tends to replace "God" as the entity possessing this ultimate power, but this Nature continues to be understood, as God had been, as a "vague, universal bond of connection for all phenomena." On the positive side, however, this substitution completes the revolt of reason against supernaturalism. It not only naturalizes the idea of ultimate power, but it shifts the focus away from this power and toward the law-likeness of natural phenomena themselves. Even in early metaphysics, the topic of greatest theoretical interest is not God or Nature – call it what you will – but the specific "laws" that explain systematically how all the particular hidden forces actually operate. Theological systems always stress that the laws of the cosmos are the laws *of God*, and wonder why God wants things the way they are. Metaphysical systems tend to focus on the laws themselves since, cognitively speaking, it adds little to say they are laws *of* Someone or Something.

Yet in Comte's view, it is ultimately not the substantive theories of metaphysics but what happens to the mind in developing them that matters most. To understand the "transient utility" of metaphysics is to see how its 'hybrid concepts" – that is, its naturalistic ideas about hidden powers – prepare the maturing mind to concentrate exclusively on the world's phenomena themselves. Metaphysics, in its "essential instability," presents a Janus-face. Its reasoning is too independent to be theological; yet its theories are too theological to be scientific. On the one hand, metaphysical concepts differ profoundly, and positively, from theological ones insofar as they subordinate feelings and imagination to purely rational-logical considerations. Theology has substages, because theological reasoning is related to feelings and instincts in three different ways. Looking back on all this with a liberated metaphysical mind, feelings and instincts obviously do not qualify as a genuinely "observational" basis for theorizing. Yet they did at least guarantee for all theology a concrete, experiential relation with the world. And that, on the other hand and negatively, is precisely what is not true of metaphysics. No metaphysical system expresses any kind of experientially distinctive relationship to worldly phenomena. In spite of its often irreverently naturalistic tone, metaphysics remains at bottom simply a collection of naturalistic variations on theological themes – expressed, to be sure, through concepts that are clear and logically related, but also with no empirical anchor to sustain them. In metaphysics, the abstract systems of theology simply morph into equally abstract but largely secular conceptual schemes.

It is this combination of intellectual irreverence and emotional-experiential remoteness that makes metaphysics interesting to Comte. For in these two characteristics, one can recognize both the positive developmental significance of the metaphysical era and also its inability to ever mark more than a "transitional period." Freed from all constraints but those of reason, the metaphysical mind is at home with mathematics and logic; but this is also the sort of mind that produces theoretical systems whose wildly unsatisfactory character eventually becomes too obvious to miss. The problem is that there will inevitably be too many such systems. For once a metaphysical theory is deemed "reasonable," there is no further means for deciding between it and any other equally reasonable metaphysical theory. With nothing analogous to theology's feelings or instincts or superstitious reliance on authority to hold them back, liberated metaphysical minds are able to produce an endless stream of complete, logical, coherent ... but also incompatible ... conceptual systems. During the time of its initial ascendancy, metaphysicians can rightly brag about the intrinsic educational value of being able to reason abstractly and independently while at the same time maintaining a naïve, realist faith in one or another favored theoretical system about the world's causes and purposes.

Yet later, when intellectual ties with theology grow "feeble," the nominalistic character of all metaphysics becomes glaringly obvious – its ideas having become "so empty through overly subtle qualification that all right-minded persons consider them to be only the abstract names of the [natural] phenomena in question" (CPP1: 14/8). For example, Comte would have regarded all the later realism/anti-realism debates and skeptical arguments about the existence of an external world incurably pre-scientific, i.e. metaphysical. "If popular good sense had not long ago pushed aside the absurd metaphysical doubts ... [for example] as to so fundamental an idea as that of the existence of external bodies we may be sure they would still survive in one form or another; for they have certainly never been decisively dissipated by any argument" (DEP: 11/17). The point, of course, is that "metaphysical" doubts can never be dissipated, because they are not anchored in anything that really matters to life. How could they be? Comte shares Kant's view that the scandal is not that we have failed to find but that we are still looking for, say, proves that there is an external world. He does not, however, agree with Kant's response. To actual people, busy discovering what the world is like and how to live in it, who cares?

In short, the metaphysical spirit is best regarded "as a kind of chronic distemper [*maladie chronique*] naturally inhering in our individual and collective mental evolution between infancy and manhood" (DEP: 11/17). It is the spirit of the teenager. Of course, it is a good thing to learn to think against the influence of feelings, imagination, dogma, and appeals to authority; but a mind that is merely liberated can never successfully be anything more than critical. It is always "reasonable" to doubt and to argue, even in the face of "good sense," for it is always "logically possible" for real situations to be otherwise. Yet when a metaphysical mind continues to insist on this point – when it continues to argue about the logically possible even when it is a question of explaining our natural and social relations as we actually (or might realistically) live them – human reason reveals that it is ultimately unfit to be its own authority. Strictly speaking, "the metaphysical spirit properly so called ... can never be *anything but* critical," which is both its glory and ultimately its undoing (DEP: 42/68, my emphasis).

Comte stresses, however, that it is easy to misinterpret this observation. John Stuart Mill, whose own writings dwell almost exclusively on the unscientific character of metaphysical theories, concludes that the sort of "dialectics and negative criticism" necessary to a liberated mind must be features of scientific, not metaphysical thinking. He takes Comte to task for giving metaphysics too much credit (Mill 1969: 278, 404). In this, Mill foreshadows the later positivist tendency to collapse the distinction between theology and metaphysics, relegate them both to the pre-scientific past, and move on to the epistemology of science. We have seen the consequences of this philosophical tunnel vision: At first, the only sort of reason that subsequently seems to deserve the name is the cognitive/calculative rationality one utilizes in mathematics and empirical science. One's earlier experiences of theological and metaphysical thinking are simply suppressed – until at some point, they re-emerge in the form of a free-floating urge to be "skeptical" or in certain moods, to turn away from Rationality in order to "believe" or poetize.

Even without the benefit of our hindsight, however, Comte could see Mill's mistake and told him so. If one simply begins with an analysis of scientific epistemology, one takes no note of how the mind learns to accept the "relativity" of positive knowledge (limited as this knowledge always is to the degree of assurance afforded us by the amount of evidence we have gathered); and in the absence of an understanding of this point, one may fail to appreciate the fundamental difference between the empirically based cautiousness of positive knowledge and the ultimately metaphysical character of skepticism. Comte would thus have been amused by the twentieth-century obsession with the "problem of skepticism" among analytic philosophers. An epistemology that makes this problem a central issue is the product of a mind that never grew up. It is the problem of a metaphysical mind – one that is still more in love with certainties of logic and abstraction than with the probabilities of laboratory experiment and field research, a mind that in its "obstinate proneness to argue rather than observe," remains more interested in the dissolution of theoretical claims that in "truly scientific work" (DEP: 8–10/12–15). For a mind that continues to mature, however, the power to remain obstinately logical eventually becomes an embarrassment; for it reveals the dirty little secret about "pure reason" – namely that, left entirely on its own, it can always find "grounds" for undermining every affirmation. Provided they are not suppressed in a futile effort to achieve instant maturity, experiences of this limitation eventually drive stubborn adolescents toward adulthood … and inquiring minds spontaneously toward science.

The coming scientific era

In Comte's view, then, it is philosophically (not just psychologically) important to see why the move toward embracing the value of "observation" cannot be a Carnapian leap to positivity at the expense of theology and metaphysics. Even in the earliest portions of the theological stage, we develop a generalized awareness that at least in some of our experiences, there are obvious, "perceivable" regularities requiring no special explanation. The world and other people are usually there, where and when I see them; things usually happen in expected ways; I can usually raise my arm when I want to, and so forth. Hence, Comte sees the move toward scientific reasoning as a conscious but radically chastened return to an early, "instinctively" employed savvy about our surroundings – or more formally, as a deliberate and "methodological extension of universal sensibleness [*sagesse universelle*]" (DEP: 44–5/71–2). Experiential encounter is now developed into, not replaced by "observation"; and attention to how things "usually" are is transformed into an appreciation for statistical probability. Occasionally, Comte even calls the turn toward observation in disillusion with metaphysics a "radicalization of fetishism" (SPP4: 204/180).

To explain what genuine observation is, Comte describes positivism as steering a middle course between the extremes of "mysticism" and "empiricism." Positivism is opposed, of course, to abstract speculation. As Comte famously asserts, "All competent thinkers agree with Bacon that there can be no real knowledge except that which rests upon observed facts" (CPP1: 8, 34/4, 20). Reason's efforts to transcend sense never lead to anything but mysticism. Yet this does not mean that Comte's positivism is either inductivist nor sensationalist. Contrary to long-standing opinion, he is just as opposed to the "[mere] empiricism" of eighteenth-century thinkers like Condillac (or Hume) as he is to mysticism (CPP3: 626–7). The false assumption about Comte's allegedly Humean empiricism begins early and runs through the entire development of later positivism and beyond (e.g. Carnap 1936: 420; Sellars 1939: 26–7; Peirce 1984: 126–7; Habermas 1971: 74–5).

The problem, says Comte, is that mysticism and empiricism both distinguish too sharply between scientific theory (i.e. third-stage "speculation") and observation (i.e. third-stage "experience"), because each in its own way misunderstands what these are. We can put the point this way. Cartesians and Baconians are each right in what they affirm and wrong in what they reject. On the one hand, Descartes is right to stress that reason has the power to free itself from feeling, prejudice, and authority – as it already started to do in the second stage, for the sake of logic and mathematics. Yet the *Meditations* can seduce us into believing the mind has the power to discover nature's most fundamental laws all by itself, and believing this, we fall back into metaphysical or even theological speculation. On the other hand, Bacon is right that pre-scientific rationality falls hopelessly prey to various (theoretical) "idols." Yet a purely Baconian inductive procedure – by itself and without the independent resources of reason – is little more than a "barren accumulation of unconnected facts," a "mere" empiricism and not yet science. When the mind reaches maturity, it already understands that Descartes-plus-Bacon cannot be the model for truly productive knowledge; for even in pre-scientific times, reason and experience work *together* in human affairs – for example, in solving the vicious circle of being initially without either facts to guide theory or theory to inform the gathering of facts.

In Comtean positivism, then, mature/scientific reasoning is not more or less but only differently dependent on experience, and not more or less but only differently speculative. "Observation" has for its "objects" everything from stars and molecules to language and social customs – in a word, anything and everything that can, albeit under ever improving technical conditions, actually be encountered. The problem with "experience" as it is understood in pre-scientific times is that it is often a sloppy combination of observation plus felt, imagined, or dogmatically assumed extras. The tree really does burst into flames when lightening hits it, but that doesn't mean the tree's spirit is threatening us. The sun actually does rise in the East and set in the West, but that doesn't mean it's being carried across the sky in a chariot. And it really does seem as if everything hangs together with everything else, but that doesn't mean Somebody planned it or Something has this as Its purpose. Conversely, the problem with "experience" as it is understood in early modern times (and by those later so-called empiricists who, like Russell, wish Kant had never lived), is that it is still based more on an anti-metaphysical urge to avoid sloppy combinations of observation and assumed extras than it is on a scientifically informed idea of what observation can actually be. No one, for example, actually encounters only redness-here-now, so that one then faces the daunting task of "inferring" that this sense data belongs to a ball. One must be trained to think this way – by ignoring what one already observes in favor of abstract theories of sensation and perception. Comte likes to imagine that such theories will some day be ridiculed in plays.

In the end, then, once we have struggled through the successes and failures of theology and metaphysics – and thereby learned the difference between actually encountering something and feeling, imagining, or abstractly speculating about it – we can understand what it is like to pay greater attention *just to the experiential encounter*, before and without allowing ourselves to have an attitude toward or draw any conclusions about it. Once the mind understands, in a positive spirit, the value of experiential encounters as such, it also sees what successful theorizing about these encounters must be. From our individually and collectively having been theologians and metaphysicians, we realize that what we have always wanted is a system of knowledge that facilitates a predictable and livable future; but we also see from the failures of our theological and metaphysical speculations that obtaining this knowledge really has nothing to do with worshipping mysteries or finding hidden powers behind what we observe. Instead it involves attentive and thorough processing of what we actually encounter, which is a matter of seeing and recording the comings and goings of encountered things and then calculating what we might expect from them (and things like them) in the future.

Comte's conception of observational *procedures* is thus interestingly different from that of logical empiricism (Scharff 2002: 30–4). He is no rational reconstructivist, bent on telling practicing scientists what they are doing methodologically when they get it right; nor is he a special advocate of mathematical models of reasoning and "experimental" methods of observation. Indeed, Comte regards any systematic formalization of the method of science as metaphysical. One can of course study, say, how induction works in experimental physics, or classification, in biology. But no general account of induction or classification can do more than "supply general indications" and "mark out a direction to follow," and it will always remain "incompetent … to furnish solutions" for how scientists should conduct their research (SPP1: 518/419). It is essential to positivism, says Comte, that "logic never be separated from [the actual practice of] science." Only in this way can we make certain that scientific procedures run the gamut from ordinary (but instrument-aided) perception, to experimentation, classification, and historical reconstruction, depending upon the kind of observation most suitable to the particular science, and given its current level of maturity and its specific subject matter. So, for example, there is a time when a developing science can do no better than carefully record phenomenal events in the hope that this at least might suggest to us an hypothesis that (in the early modern sense of systematically synthesizing the results) "verifies" them. Astronomy begins to separate itself from astrology in this way. In the earlier parts of his *Cours*, Comte identifies three basic scientific procedures, namely, the direct examination of phenomena as they "naturally present" themselves ("observation proper"), experimentation, and comparison (e.g. CPP2: 7–8, 19–21). In later discussion of social science, however, he identifies the "historical method" (i.e. the "comparison of the various consecutive states of humanity") both as the "last part of the comparative method" and as a separate "fourth mode" that forms the "very basis" of social science (CPP4: 449–68), making it in the latter case the model for Mill's "inverse deductive" method in his *Logic* (Mill 1973–74, VI: x, pars. 4–8).

It is not anachronistic to depict Comte arguing about the dangers of methodological formalism a century before there were any logical empiricists. He already had Mill's *System of Logic* in front of hilm, and he makes it perfectly clear why he thinks there can be, at most, only temporary value to works like Mill's. Mill complains that Comte gives the *Logic* "high approval," without becoming "indebted to it for a single idea, or influenced [by it] in the smallest particular." Instead, he says, Comte continues to take a largely descriptive and often anecdotal approach to the scientific method, and this shows that he is "not so solicitous about completeness of proof as becomes a positive philosopher" (Mill 1969: 293n, 294). Comte, however, takes this rebuff as a complement. Sounding more like a twenty-first-century post-positivist than a colleague of Mill or the great-grandparent of Reichenbach and Hempel, Comte opposes in principle the very intention of works like Mill's *Logic*, if such works are understood to be setting forth (in Mill's phrase) an "organon of proof." Such projects are misconceived both theoretically, for implying that there is an "essential" set of formal-logical rules for the conduct of science, and also practically, because the very offering of such an organon threatens to straitjacket scientific activity itself (Scharff 2002: 61–3).

To see what is at stake here, consider the following. In his introduction to the *Logic*, Mill addresses the potential objection (probably originating with Thomas Carlyle) that just as we cannot learn how to use our muscles by studying anatomy, we cannot learn to think scientifically by studying logic. Mill replies by rejecting both ends of the analogy. In thinking as in exercising, he argues, we must learn to distinguish those moves we ought to make from those we ought not to make. This reply is, in its own way, perfectly sensible, but for Comte it misses a crucial point. Granted that, for example, weightlifters can save themselves a lot of grief by exploiting the knowledge of physical therapists. But this knowledge can only make them healthier, not better weightlifters. (And I assume that Mill would agree that injecting steroids does make them "better" in the requisite sense.) Similarly, knowing the rules of reasoning cannot make a scientist good at anything except maybe those canned experiments in Physics 101.

For Comte, an appropriate analogy to use against Mill would be that of a budding scientist to, say, a chess novice who imagines that competent (not to mention expert) play can come from knowing and applying all the game's rules. At the very time when, as Comte tells it, a nascent scientific mind is finally learning that the power of reason must be neither underestimated nor let loose on its own but rather always be coordinated with observation, the last thing this mind needs to hear is that scientific activity is a matter of following "rules." As usual, it is the *emerging* positive mind in the context of its socio-historical *development* – not, say, a Cartesian ego objectivistically setting out a foundation for itself in a self-possessed mental Nowhere – that Comte is describing when he offers his lengthy accounts of actual episodes of scientific observation, experimentation, and theory construction instead of pushing organons of discovery or proof.

In keeping with this anti-formalistic stance, Comte urges that all observational procedures be understood as nothing more than "perfections and extensions" of ordinary practices. Thus, on the one hand, every mind sensually encounters its natural and social surroundings. Scientists, however, are guided in these encounters not by feelings or imaginings of what must be there but by the idea of carefully and directly examining what is "phenomenally" present. On the other hand, all of us try to explain what we encounter. As Comte says, true science "dispenses with observation as soon as phenomena permit," since its ultimate aim is to "deduce the greatest number of results from the smallest amount of immediately given data." Scientific explanations are better at this simply because, instead of letting their encounters be interpreted in light of common prejudice, superstition, authority, or mere logical coherence, scientists always "attach" observations, at least hypothetically, to some law. It is in the nature of this *connection* (i.e. between experience construed as observational encounter and speculation, as attaching hypotheses) that the principal difference lies between the theorizing of scientists and ordinary persons (CPP4: 417–19). Like the ordinary person does implicitly, the positive scientist embraces explicitly the primary aim of all knowledge, namely, "seeing for the sake of foreseeing" – "studying what *is*, in order to infer what *will be*, in accordance with the dogma that natural laws are invariable" (DEP: 17/26). It's just that scientific hypotheses actually make successful inferences.

Comte's use of "dogma" here is revealing. Science, he explains, routinely employs a dogmatical method (*méthode dogmatique*). For example, when a scientific theory (or set of theories) is employed as a starting point for further research, *at that moment* one treats the theory as if it were sacrosanct – that is, as if (a) it were already complete and had sprung fully developed into the mind, and as if (b) it were never to need modification on the basis of further research. But of course this is never really the case. There is in fact a "genuine imperfectness" to all theorizing. No matter how "natural" a scheme may seem to be, it has and continues to have a genesis, and it necessarily involves cognitive selection – that is, a kind of intellectual impounding (*renfermer*) of actual phenomena that depicts them, "if not arbitrarily, then at least somewhat artificially" (CPP1: 78/46; see Scharff 2002: 100–5).

Here, Comte's sort of positivism pays large dividends by taking a "descriptive" rather than a (re)constructive approach to scientific practice. For he can explain why it is methodologically acceptable in scientific practice but epistemologically unacceptable for philosophers reflecting on this practice to "forget" the artificiality and selectivity of its speculations. When philosophers of science lose or suppress the fact that all thought arises out of and constitutes a response to our encounters – or worse, when they develop justifications for doing this on purpose – they also obscure the fact that the real point of "seeing for the sake of foreseeing" is not theoretical. To carry forward the image from my earlier discussion of theology, we might say that as a substitute for monotheism, metaphysics is ultimately a practical failure and science, a success. The metaphysical ideal of universal praxis is at best (and revealingly, mostly in its earlier period) the "contemplative" life and at worst (and especially toward the end), the love of analysis, argument, unified systems, and formal rules as such. Hence the inevitable practical result of metaphysics is that, whenever changing hearts and minds is the goal, force must replace intellect. Appeals to reason come to nothing by themselves. Even crazy or paranoid world views can be completely "logical." And there is no real difference between fighting wars of conversion because God is on our side and fighting wars of liberation because we know what True Freedom is. Neither theological nor metaphysical abstractions can make human existence better.

As noted above, however, Comte argues that for a mature mind, although reason is not destined to be a slave to feelings or to alleged revelations, it is unfit to be its own authority. Field by field, scientific naturalism (which explains mechanistically *how* things work) replaces metaphysical naturalism (which can only conjecture teleologically *why* things work). Here again, there is an interesting contrast between Comtean and later positivism. One might argue that to the extent that current philosophical talk about naturalism rests on dated images of science and scientific procedure – images that owe more to the epistemic dogmas of logical empiricism than to any socio-historical information about science as it is currently and successfully practiced – today's so-called naturalism has in fact remained metaphysical (Rouse 2002b). For Comte, in contrast, the "naturalistic turn" in the scientific enterprise develops and continuously transforms itself primarily in response to experiences of the limited socio-historical efficacy of metaphysical (and later, fledgling scientific) reasoning, not out of any general respect for formal epistemological demands.

Central to this developmental process is the organization of the individual sciences in a hierarchy – starting with mathematics, the simplest and most abstract, and ending with sociology, the most complex. *Philosophically* speaking, concludes Comte, it eventually becomes clear that sociology is destined to constitute the most important science. In two ways, this conclusion shows how Comte gives life not epistemology the last word. We have already noted that he interprets all science in terms of an ultimately practical motivation. Now we see that he treats the hierarchical arrangement of the sciences in a way that reflects this motivation. Sociology (or really, what we would now call social science) gets its special significance not, as he puts it, "objectively" – that is, from some epistemic criteria of right reason – but "subjectively," from the needs of feeling, social sensibility, and altruistic love. For it is the understanding of social behavior that will ultimately lead to the establishment of peaceful, prosperous societies (Grange 1996: 267–332; Wernick 2001: 27–36). Comte's life-long "subjective" (i.e. ethico-political) interest in fostering the establishment of sociology is only one of several indications that his conception of the hierarchy of the sciences is not reductivist, in the manner of logical positivism (Manicas 1987: 60–2). Not only do astronomy, physics, chemistry, biology, and social science all have their own (increasing) levels of complexity and their own distinctive methodological forms of observation; their ultimate worth lies not in the knowledge they obtain but in what, taken all together, can be done with it. Positive/scientific knowledge thus forms the basis of the third and final form of universal praxis – namely, a truly global and scientific technology that effectuates the sort of normalizing of natural and social relations that we have always sought.

I have stressed here, as Comte often does himself, what we might call the intellectually "revolutionary" character of the transition to the positive stage; but we should remember the generally developmental character of his interpretation of this transition – and thus, in contrast to later positivism, the greater sophistication of his account of the rise of science. He insists upon recognizing, for example, that there is a sense in which the mathematicization of nature, so crucial for the move to science from theology and metaphysics, was already a prominent medieval idea (Dear 1995). He knows also that this same medieval era was already a time full of mechanical devices and displays of the love of gadgetry that had (as yet) nothing to do with the desire to obtain instrumental knowledge of the surrounding world (White 1962). Nevertheless, Comte argues that the "sense" of all this in the present age is ultimately to be understood by recognizing that the scientific stage constitutes the fulfillment of an ultimately practical aim through a surpassing of the intellectual methods used with limited success in the first two stages. It is its superior capacity to fulfill our desire for harmonious natural and social relations – not something "essential" about the positive method or style of thought – that justifies the coming dominance of scientific thinking. There is nothing fundamentally misbegotten about metaphysics or theology. In every phase of intellectual development, the goal is "a conceptual system concerning the totality of phenomena" that would permit us to understand our surroundings well enough to order our lives effectively. In each phase, this goal is pursued by the best means thought to be available at the time.

For a Comtean positivist, then, the familiar stories about philosophy's origin are quite misleading. Theologians and metaphysicians tell us that philosophy originates in feelings of mystery or in intellectual wonder, respectively, and it is undoubtedly true that for a time, both motivations are indispensable stimulants to speculation. In the theological stage, the mind is stirred by the great unknown to overcome the vicious circle of being initially without either theories or data and to set our faculties to work making sense of things. Metaphysics, once begun, ultimately succeeds in showing us the power and possibilities of genuinely free reasoning. Yet in the final analysis, both theology and metaphysics are just as much pursued for the sake of prevision and for the sake of satisfying human needs as science. Thus, science is related to modern technology as theology and metaphysics are related, respectively, to worship/ritual and contemplation – namely, as a comprehensive theoretical basis for a universal form of praxis. Without passing through these two ultimately unsuccessful stages, science can neither be successful nor self-aware of what makes its success possible; and once scientists become reflective about the nature of their success, they will also understand that human nature is at bottom neither theological nor metaphysical nor even scientific but ... practical.

Comte's dream: a technoscientific "ending"

Here, then, is my (much abbreviated) case for the superiority of Comte's positive philosophy over that of the later positivists. For everyone from Mill and Mach to Reichenbach and Ayer – and for many others later, albeit less militantly – philosophy's main topic is the epistemology of science, and this is no place for something like Comte's three-stage law. From their viewpoint, his law expresses an interest extraneous to science. Either it is part of some master-narrative about what science means (in which case it is merely abstract speculation), or it makes a cluster of empirical-sociological claims about science. In the latter case, it is asserting factual claims about real events that must be evaluated *by* science; and even if (as seems unlikely) these claims turn out to be true, they can offer no grounds for philosophical judgments *about* science. In a word, later positivists turn their internalist guns on the likes of Comte. To them, his "defense" of positive philosophy can only amount to confusing either empirical or "subjective" (i.e. introspective, personal, or anecdotal) beliefs about science with the "objective" reconstruction of what science *essentially is*.

Comte, however, would not recognize this forced option between "mere" personal/socio-historical accounts and "genuine" epistemic analysis, and to the extent that it makes sense at all, he would object that it has things backwards. When Mill banishes all "outlying" historical issues from his "correct analysis of reasoning," or Reichenbach vows to "look through" the "superstructure of mists and wishes" lying "above" ongoing scientific research so that he can analyze the latter's "supporting structure" (Reichenbach 1938: 403–4) – that is, when later positivists restrict themselves to analyzing scientific rationality "in itself" or in its "essence" and ignore what they define as the merely "subjective origins" of knowledge in order to develop a "constructional system ... identical for all observers" (Carnap 1967: 7) – they behave as if becoming philosophers of science means transcending the very life in which science could even matter, and conducting the analyses of scientific procedure as neutral and decontextualized minds. For Comte, however, this behavior is both irresponsible (because it abdicates positivism's duty to defend itself) and ultimately self-deceiving. Comte might even be amused by the irony in the fact that philosophizing about science in the manner of the later positivists is clearly "metaphysical" in his sense of the term. No actual phenomenon answers to the name, "scientific reasoning *as such*"; and there is no such thing as a contextless analytical mind.

For Comte, then, our only real option is to philosophize about positive thought from within, not from above, life in the present era. His talk of the positive stage as one of intellectual maturity is often taken to mark him simply as a somewhat more candid analytic epistemologist – one who knows, as Habermas puts it, that positivism's "real job" is to "justif[y] the sciences' scientistic belief in themselves by construing the history of the species as the history of the realization of the positive spirit" (Habermas 1971: 72). But this PR conception of positivism – though it captures the spirit of the self-reports of later positivists – is un-Comtean in two ways. First, it mistakenly assumes that Comte thought of his era as *already in* the third stage, so that a good positivist is just representing an extant condition. As explained above, however, Comte in fact sees us as living toward, or making the transition into the third stage; and he regards the defense of positive philosophy as facilitating this process. Second, the PR interpretation assumes Comte thought there could *actually be* a formal/ahistorical organon of proof (Mill) or a rational reconstruction of the "essentials" of the scientific method (the logical empiricists). This is simply false. Sounding more like a contemporary post-positivist, Comte argues that the analysis of scientific rationality is inseparable from a determinate philosophical understanding of scientific practice as a distinctive sort of human activity. In his view no philosophy, not even positivism, succeeds in placing itself after, or beyond its inheritance; hence, no fully "mature" philosophy sees itself establishing the "essence" of anything in abstraction from its surroundings and inheritance.

Comte's reflective candor makes him more interesting today than his successors. He is not more or less committed to a substantive philosophical position than the later positivists; rather, he thinks it is wrong to be silent about it. Yet perhaps even more significant is the nature of the position Comte defends as positivistic. Like the later positivists, Comte does of course think science is epistemically superior to theology and metaphysics. Yet from his earliest writings, he describes this superiority in expansively worldly and humanistic terms. Instead of sometimes confessing to having "sentiments" about it, Comte argues that scientific reasoning is the form of thinking which can truly satisfy our deepest desires – but only if we cultivate an explicit awareness of what we are doing. His argument thus has two parts, one historical, the other analytical.

First, look at any culture in any part of our history. We humans have always wanted to know what makes things be and act as they do. Indeed, says Comte, this craving for an understanding of the laws of phenomena is so strong that in the midst of any particular struggle for it, we tend to block out every extraneous condition and immediate practical interest in order to focus solely on the matter before us. Even now, were we to find it impossible to "arrange facts in an easily comprehended order" using scientific concepts, we would inevitably resort to theological or metaphysical ones, so that at least we had some sort of explanatory scheme for what we observe. Yet our "natural desire" for knowledge and our displays of single-mindedness in the actual pursuit of the truth are not evidence of our desiring "knowledge for its own sake." Obtaining knowledge – and this is the second part of Comte's position – always has a practical *point* – namely, to facilitate our control of nature and social reorganization. Once this control and reorganization are well under way, we can expect a civilization in which "feeling gains primacy over intellect," a shift occurs from self-centered and individualistic social theories to a more communal viewpoint, and a "Religion of Humanity" begins to form where love, altruism, fellow-feeling, and respect come to be understood as higher values than Order and Progress alone (Wernick 2001: 32–47).

All of this may not be what one thinks about in the midst of searching for knowledge, but it is what gives the search its fundamental sense. Scientific understanding is thus the mark of intellectual maturity precisely because its kind of comprehension of the natural and social world makes possible a technology that really works. It is in relation to this practical technoscientific dream that I think Comte is most worth reconsidering – precisely because we still share it, but no longer with our whole hearts (Scharff 2003; Scharff 1998). In closing, then, let me reconsider Comte's dream, not from his viewpoint but from ours.

A technoscientific "ending": our burden?

Comte, to repeat, interprets his third stage as the final stage. This seems to him settled by the fact that science is a *culminating* occurrence – that is, a successful resolution, at least in principle, of all the insoluble problems of the earlier stages. The Big Questions are retrospectively understood to deserve responses of awe, wonder, a sense of mystery, and good literature, not a vain search for The One Theoretical System. Real knowledge involves the proper combination of all our faculties, and these faculties cannot properly function together if there is nothing to observe. Yet when the Big Questions are simply appreciated and the whole quest for knowledge is confined to the comings and goings of the observable world, the payoff becomes obvious. The third state is an end*ing* that cannot and need not ever *end*, because one finally understands that real knowledge is only "relative" to whatever evidence we have so far obtained from whatever observations we have so far recorded. Lacking a Divine Perspective from which everything could be observed completely and simultaneously, we see that our knowledge is never "absolutely" guaranteed by the *a priori* authority of feeling, faith, or reason; and realizing this leaves us with the benefit of always being ready to handle new disruptions to the natural and social order with modified theories and further observation.

Yet there is in retrospect something disconcerting about the way Comte conceives the third stage. It is not that he refuses to think past the age of science; he never entertains the thought at all. He never asks, Could there be a fourth stage? and then answers No. He never considers "after the third stage," even as a purely logical possibility. There is, I think, a very good reason for this. Put bluntly, Comte has no experiential reason to conceive such a possibility, and it would never occur to him to do philosophy by entertaining purely logical ones. For him, there is nothing to observe that seems to fall outside the pattern of explanation set up by the three-stage law. He speaks out of an understanding and at a time when technoscience is still more promise than actualization, and when pre-scientific thinking is still mostly seen as ill-fated and ineffectual rather than meaningless. It is not that Comte is theoretically or socio-politically committed to thinking dogmatically only in terms of three stages and no more. Rather, in keeping with his sense that philosophizing happens within the living of life not from above it, he carefully conceptualizes the arrival of the third stage entirely in terms of an experienced sense of its arrival; and in this "culminating" form of its arrival, there simply *is* no fourth stage.

In a word, he simply has no *real* motivation to think beyond an internalist vision of the third stage. "Within" the context of Comte's experience and thus "for" his philosophical reflection, the third stage is what life predominantly promises to "mean" – ontologically, epistemologically, and practically. For him, science is *actually becoming* the successful, comprehensive cognitive response to that sense of Reality (i.e. the world as mostly benign, predictable, and thus at least restorable to an accommodating condition given our proper response) which originates in primitive life. For him, the scientific response promises to really *be* a global, open-ended articulation without a terminal point. He thus understands the move from theological/metaphysical to scientific responsiveness as what Heidegger calls an eventuation, not an event. For Comte, when practice is guided by a scientific rather than a theological or metaphysical articulation of our experience, life can really *be* what it most deeply and essentially *is* when we make ourselves part of this endless "maturation" process. In Comte's milieu, the very idea that in its eventual unfolding, the positive stage might mark out an essentially oppressive and occlusive ontological site would have seemed like utter nonsense to him. Slogans like "science doesn't have all the answers, yet," and "every human problem has a technological fix" still retained their innocence.

Today, of course, these slogans do not seem so innocent. For Comte, the prospect of an entirely technoscientific age could still be an entirely "positive" projection; and it is unfair to call this idea utopian. But today, it is no longer a projection, and it is hard to depict its realization as anything better than ambiguous. In a late essay, Heidegger asks whether "the world civilization just now beginning might one day *overcome* its technological-scientific-industrial character as the *sole criterion* of our journey through the world" (Heidegger 1993: 437, my emphasis). Comte could never ask such a question, because he could not consider the "overcoming" of what had not yet arrived. It would have made no sense to him to ponder the need for additional, *post*-technoscientific "criteria" for our journey through the world. To him, the emergence of science and its technologies could only be a happy and thoroughly progressive eventuation. With nineteenth-century eyes, he happily concludes that a "scientific view of the world" is therefore the only plausible position for enlightened minds.

Today, however, this same conclusion – whether actually defended or simply assumed – seems strikingly old-fashioned and out of touch. It is difficult to ignore the depressing, retrograde, and dystopian threats that often seem just as constitutive of technoscientific life as the many happy outcomes Comte predicted. It now makes very good sense indeed to ask if there are technological problems that do not have technological fixes. Can we, for example, just engineer our way out of air and water pollution? Is human mentality really best understood by closely following the latest conceptual revisions in cognitive science? (Is it e.g. an accident that the currently most popular idea of "intelligence" tends to define it reductively in terms of manipulating abstractions and rapidly processing information – as if we were just fleshy computers?) Are there important ways of thinking about human health that a scientistic or "medical" model of care can never articulate? (Is it e.g. merely a correctable bad choice that the US health care system is built around the idea of fixing what goes wrong rather than preventing it in the first place?) Or, finally, are there perhaps what used to be called spiritual concerns for which "artistic" celebrations of awe and mystery are really beside the point?

For Comte – and for many of his later sympathizers and inheritors, candidly or not – these questions are just "immature." The very idea that there could be *extra*-technoscientific issues in life tends to be seen as ontologically unworthy and regressive. To be really educated and informed, one simply must be, as contemporary analytic philosophers often say, some sort of naturalist. For the only "known" alternative to naturalism is the return to some sort of *super*-naturalism. Yet in my view, one need not be a Heideggerian – or something like one of Comte's recalcitrant theologians or metaphysicians – to be suspicious of this line of reasoning. Should we continue to assume that positivism – that is, a position that rests upon the idea that something like Comte's ever-improving technoscientific existence is the ideal human situation – still constitutes the appropriate philosophy, now that this age has *arrived*? Not, as Heidegger nicely puts it, if our experience of *being in it* has become at least as "distressing" as it is satisfying.

It is often objected that Heidegger's take on the Western tradition, allegedly like that of his whole generation of anti-Enlightenment romantics, is incurably and unjustifiably dystopian. Yet surely it is now possible – in life, not in the head – to find Comte's brand of technoscientific optimism profoundly unsatisfying. Is it really self-evident that we humans are *by nature* primarily interested in manipulating the cosmos and fostering social control, and *by nature* ultimately satisfied to reduce the Big Questions to artistic mysteries? Much of humanity's interest in order and control seems driven more by circumstance and by power-hungry people than by something hard-wired into human nature. Comte assumes that, in line with the idea that every problem will eventually have a technological fix, social science will finally inform us about how to live, and the political task of bringing such science to the rest of us will be accomplished by "experts" whose only motive is a desire to improve humanity's lot. Comte can still, with a straight face, call these experts social engineers (CPP1: 67/41) – just as Marx a little later will call them scientific socialists. These are nineteenth-century ideas, but they are also strong parts of our continuing inheritance. To the extent we find their technoscientific optimism overdrawn, we need to ask, Can there to be something genuinely "beyond" the era Comte regarded as an ending that can never end? What would this mean?

Unlike the later positivists, a twenty-first-century Comte would in fact understand and welcome this *kind* of question. He would recognize it as a properly philosophical question about how to interpret what he calls a "stage" of human life – that is, a whole general way of existing, involving a pervasive sense of what things mean and what we should do about it. He would even agree that if it were ever to become necessary to ask whether the positive stage is really the sort of "ending" it initially seemed to be, this is not a question that can be addressed piecemeal, occasionally, between the lines, in strategic discussions focused primarily on how to plan, control, or conceptually clarify this or that specific methodological or practical problem. Of course, taken one way, a global critique of this vision is a silly one. Even in the capitalist/democratic West, there is obviously something profoundly right about Comte's projection. It remains, in some sense, both a true and a "developmentally" necessary picture of what is in fact occurring. Indeed, it is doubtful whether it even makes sense to consider remaking the world so that it is not (or is no longer) technoscientific. As Heidegger says, one can imagine or logically cognize the idea of an entirely non- or post-technoscientific existence; but one cannot really think it. Moreover, depending upon who asks and who is listening, the question can also sound arrogant and chauvinistic. It is easy for North Americans and Western Europeans to sit in the comfort of their "developed" world and convince themselves that their experience of the drawbacks of the kind of life they already live is a good reason to stop the rest of the world from becoming more technoscientific. I start, however, from the Comtean premise that a thoroughly technoscientific existence, extended to ever more of the world, is no longer merely an option. Yet even supposing Comte is right about developmental necessity of such an existence, it is hard not to notice that today – for pretty much everyone, everywhere – it is virtually impossible not to see a threatening and destructive side of *the very same eventuation* that simultaneously promises – and in fact already delivers – so much good.

But isn't all of this obvious? Do we really need elaborate references to Auguste Comte and his law of three stages to consider the matter? Here, I think, Comte's own observation is telling. No idea, he says, can be understood apart from its history – and this is no more powerfully true than when it is denied. Comte's positivistic idea of humanity's third stage might therefore best be seen, not so much as dead as something that continues to function underground, as a legacy. It still represents, we might say, a general way of being oriented in the world that is so widely and routinely "sensed" that it often disfigures contemporary debates about science and technology without being noticed. Despite all the recent fuss about the necessary demise of grand narratives, we might well regard positivism as such a grand narrative – as indeed THE current grand narrative of most of the developed world. Rather than dismiss it as merely a latter-day version of the old speculative philosophies of history, we might better call it a kind of philosophical vampire, something "undead that still haunts our concepts and interpretations of nature, culture, and science" (Rouse 2002a: 63). Rouse's description of the haunting process lends itself well to the sort of global diagnosis I have in mind. With increasingly malignant results, the Comtean idea of technoscientific life as the age of humanity's "maturity" continues to impede critical inquiry about the problematic character of our age – not because the idea is still widely embraced or because many

—— (2002a) "Vampires: Social Constructivism, Realism, and Other Philosophical Undead," *History and Theory* 41: 60–78.

—— (2002b) *How Scientific Practices Matter: Reclaiming Philosophical Naturalism*, Chicago: University of Chicago Press.

Scharff, Robert C. (1991) "Comte, Philosophy, and the Question of Its History," *Philosophical Topics* 19, no. 2, 184–99.

—— (1995 [2002]) *Comte after Positivism*, Cambridge: Cambridge University Press.

—— (1998) "Comte and Heidegger on the Historicity of Science," *Revue Internationale de Philosophie* 52, no. 1: 29–49.

—— (2002) "Comte and the Possibility of a Hermeneutics of Science," in *Hermeneutic Philosophy of Science, Van Gogh's Eyes, and God: Essays in Honor of Patrick A. Heelan, S.J.*, edited by Babette Babich, Dordrecht: Kluwer, pp. 117–26.

—— (2003) "On Philosophy's 'Ending' in Technoscience: Heidegger vs. Comte," in Robert C. Scharff and Val Dusek (eds) *Philosophy of Technology: The Technological Condition – An Anthology*, Oxford: Blackwell, pp. 265–76.

Sellars, Roy Wood (1939) "Positivism in Contemporary Philosophic Thought," *American Sociological Review* 4: 26–42.

Singer, Michael (2005) *The Legacy of Positivism*, New York: Palgrave Macmillan.

Verbeek, Peter-Paul (2005) *What Things Do: Philosophical Reflections on Technology, Agency, and Design*, trans. Robert P. Crease, University Park: Pennsylvania State University Press.

Wernick, Andrew (2001) *Auguste Comte and the Religion of Humanity: The Post-Theistic Program of French Social Theory*, Cambridge: Cambridge University Press.

Zammito, John H. (2004) *A Nice Derangement of Epistemes: Post-Positivism in the Study of Science from Quine to Latour*, Chicago: Chicago University Press.

16
DARWIN'S PHILOSOPHICAL IMPACT

Richard A. Richards

Synopsis

Darwin's philosophical impact derives from his naturalism and explanatory pluralism. His naturalism is constituted by the requirement that causes be observed and to the degree observed; the requirement that causes unify phenomena by explanation; and a continuity thesis that humans are part of nature and are to be explained on the same principles as other organisms. His explanatory pluralism not only appeals to natural selection, but also to sexual selection, evolutionary ancestry and more. The philosophical impact of this naturalism can be seen in the pragmatic naturalization of inquiry, the development of a historical metaphysics, and the contemporary evolutionary accounts of human psychology and social ecology. These pose challenges to traditional philosophical ways of conceiving human psychology, moral judgment and normativity, based on among other things, the assumptions about the nature of value, the roles of reason and emotion, and the functioning of moral judgments.

1. Introduction

The scientific significance of Darwin and his theory of evolution is obvious. Evolutionary theory has become the foundation of modern biology, and has been extended to a variety of other fields. We find, for instance, evolutionary explanations and models beyond the traditional biological disciplines into psychology and social psychology, anthropology, economics and linguistics. Recognition of this influence has lead many commentators to classify Darwin with Newton and Einstein in the pantheon of scientific greats.

The philosophical impact of Darwin and his theory of evolution, on the other hand, is less obvious and more controversial. Introductory philosophy textbooks typically include few if any readings on, or references to evolution. Consequently, an introductory course in philosophy might never even have a discussion of Darwin or his theory of evolution. This suggests that many philosophers might well agree with Ludwig Wittgenstein in his *Tractatus*: "The Darwinian theory has no more to do with philosophy than has any other hypothesis of natural science" (Wittgenstein 1960: 4.1122). For Wittgenstein, Darwinism was irrelevant to philosophy because philosophy was restricted to "the *logical* clarification of thoughts" (Wittgenstein 1960: 4.112 emphasis added). If so, we can understand why an *empirical* theory such as Darwin's would seem irrelevant. But not everyone conceives philosophy in this narrow way, and Darwin's views have been incorporated by a variety of philosophical thinkers from the American Pragmatists, to the many philosophers who write and work in a variety of the contemporary disciplines and subdisciplines of philosophy, from philosophy of biology, philosophy of mind, to evolutionary ethics and evolutionary epistemology. Among those who see the relevance of Darwinism, there are some who think its influence to be pervasive. Daniel Dennett, for instance, claims that "The Darwinian Revolution is both a scientific and philosophical revolution ..." and "In a single stroke, the idea of evolution by natural selection unifies the realm of life, meaning, purpose with the realm of space and time, cause and effect, mechanisms and physical law" (Dennett 1995: 21). More centrist are the views of philosophers such as Philip Kitcher who see a role for Darwin, but a relatively modest one. In a recent essay he tells us: "Philosophers should find it worthwhile to read Hume and Darwin, Kant and Einstein, Descartes and Chomsky ... I want to make a particular case for bringing Darwin on to the philosophical team, not as the star player who wins the day all by himself, but as a contributor to a much larger effort" (Hodge and Radick 2003: 400).

The central question for this essay is the extent and nature of Darwin's impact on philosophy. But first, we should notice that there are really two questions here. First is an historical question: to what extent did Darwin and his theory of evolution actually affect the practice and content of philosophy? This question is to be answered by reference to threads of actual influence. There is also a second, more philosophical question: what is the philosophical impact of Darwin when we trace out its proper consequences – whether or not this impact has been fully recognized? This is more a question about what the impact of Darwinism should be if understood correctly. I shall not treat these two questions separately, although I hope it will be clear throughout this essay which sort of impact is in question.

As we shall see, there are three main sources of Darwin's philosophical influence. First is his naturalistic treatment of humans and their activities. This has a substantive component: we should explain humans and their activities as we explain other parts of nature *because humans are part of nature*. There is also a methodological component: we should use the methods of science to understand humans *because science is the best way to approach our understanding of a natural phenomena*. And because Darwinism is grounded on a scientific approach, it is often not philosophers, but scientists who have come to be most engaged in teasing out the philosophical consequences of Darwinism. The second area of influence is in the use of evolutionary models to conceptualize and understand various phenomena. We can, for instance, treat scientific, conceptual or ethical change as instances of selection based processes, even though strictly speaking they are not biological processes. Third, Darwinism has impact in that it provides a way to think about philosophical issues historically and scientifically, providing an alternative to the traditional philosophy of the last century or so that focuses on linguistic practices, intentional explanation and self-conscious introspection.

It would be possible to approach the question of Darwin's philosophical impact strictly through the traditional philosophic divisions – epistemology, metaphysics, ethics and aesthetics. Darwin's naturalism, however, suggests a slightly different approach, one based on the questions he began with, his methodology, and how it led to the answers he gave. We can then trace the implications of his answers to various questions, and see how they influence more recent thinkers and cross traditional philosophical divisions. On this approach, we will be able to see, for instance, how a Darwinian account of reason and emotion has implications for epistemology, ethics, and aesthetics. The organization of this essay will on that basis be as follows: The second section is a brief sketch of Darwin's life, his work, and his context. Following that is a section on Darwin's philosophical naturalism. The fourth section, "The Pragmatic Naturalization of Inquiry," addresses the influence of Darwin on Pragmatic conceptions of philosophical inquiry, truth and meaning. In the fifth section, we briefly look at the implications of Darwinian naturalism on more recent metaphysical speculation. The sixth section sketches out a Darwinian account of human nature in terms of human psychology and social ecology. Finally I consider some standard philosophical objections to Darwinism and conclude with a few thoughts about the scientific challenge posed by Darwinism to traditional philosophy.

Darwin and his context

Darwin was born in 1809, the fifth of six children, to a wealthy and well-educated British family. His father, Robert Darwin, was a successful physician. His grandfather, Erasmus Darwin, was a poet and evolutionist. His mother, who died when Charles was eight years old, was the daughter of Josiah Wedgewood, founder of the Wedgewood ceramics dynasty. While both sides of Darwin's family were largely Unitarian, his father was free thinker, and his mother's side had Anglican sympathies. Darwin himself was baptized into the Anglican Church.

Darwin's early education was as an unenthusiastic boarder at the Shrewsbury School. In 1825, he attended the University of Edinburgh, with the intention of studying medicine. But his interest in medicine studies was diminished by the brutality of unanaesthetized surgery. While in Edinburgh, he joined the Plinian Society, a group of students interested in natural history, sat in on a course in geology, and received training in systematics. In 1827, Darwin left the scientifically oriented University of Edinburgh for Cambridge University. At the time, there was little formal scientific education at Cambridge. One could not major in a science, although there was a smattering of optional lectures on scientific topics. Those with scholarly ambitions could enroll in honors, but studies there were limited to math and the classics. In the 1820s Oxford and Cambridge were just beginning to appoint chairs in the sciences, but often those appointed would have little scientific experience. Adam Sedgewick, for instance, was elected chair of geology without a background in geology, on the promise that he would learn some (Ruse 1999: 22).

Even though the formal science training at Cambridge left a lot to be desired, there were other opportunities. Darwin learned about beetle collecting from his cousin, W. Darwin Fox, who introduced him to the Reverend John Stevens Henslow, professor of Botany. Darwin became good friends with Henslow, attended his lectures on botany, and enjoyed evening discussions with him and others on a variety of scientific topics. Through Henslow, Darwin also became acquainted with some of the most important scientific thinkers of his time: Sedgewick, who, true to his promise, learned geology; the mineralogist and historian of science William Whewell; and the astronomer John Herschel. By the time Charles Darwin left Cambridge in 1831, his informal studies and connections with the scientific community put him well on his way to a career in the sciences.

During this time at Cambridge, Darwin's enthusiasm for a scientific career was reinforced by his reading of Herschel's newly published *Preliminary Discourse on the Study of Natural Philosophy* – a systematic theory of scientific method; and Alexander von Humboldt's *Personal Narrative of Travels to the Equinoctial Regions of the New Continent* – a romanticized account of a scientific expedition to Tenerife and South America. Inspired by Humboldt's travel narrative, Darwin planned a trip to Tenerife that was sadly waylaid by the death of his intended travel companion. Shortly thereafter, Darwin was chosen to accompany a young Captain Fitzroy on a journey aboard a ship named "The Beagle" to South America, that left England on 11 Dec. 1831. On this voyage Darwin brought along and read the first volume of Charles Lyell's *Principles of Geology*, and received the anxiously awaited second volume in Montevideo in 1832. Through his continuing correspondence with Henslow, Darwin was also maintaining and expanding his scientific network back in England, impressing both Sedgewick and Lyell, who wanted to meet him on his return. On the Beagle voyage Darwin visited with John Herschel, who was mapping the heavens at the Cape of Good Hope. When Darwin returned to England in 1836, it was to a supportive and respectful network of scientists.

In the year following his return, Darwin began thinking seriously about Herschel's "mystery of mysteries" – the origin of species. In 1837, he began his transmutation notebooks to organize his thoughts on the topic. While Darwin was already well on his way to accepting the transmutation of species, he believed that he lacked an adequate mechanism of change. In 1838, he read an essay by Thomas Malthus, and concluded that he finally had a mechanism. In this essay, Malthus highlighted the differential between normal reproduction rates and the resources required for survival. As Malthus put it: population increases geometrically, while food supply can only increase arithmetically. But while Malthus seemed to be arguing for the necessity of reproductive limits, Darwin concluded something very different.

> In October 1838, that is, fifteen months after I had begun my systematic
> enquiry, I happened to read for amusement Malthus on *Population*, and being
> well prepared to appreciate the struggle for existence which everywhere goes

on from long-continued observation of the habits of animals and plants, it at once struck me that under these circumstances favourable variations would tend to be preserved and unfavourable ones to be destroyed. The result of this would be the formation of new species. Here, then, I had at last got a theory by which to work. (A: 120)

This was a watershed moment. Darwin had been looking for a mechanism of change, and Malthus gave it to him – natural selection. For the next four years Darwin worked on his transmutation hypothesis, and put together his ideas in a "sketch" in 1842. He elaborated on these ideas in a longer essay in 1844. But while Darwin engaged in correspondence with his friends about many of his ideas, he published nothing advocating his transmutationist ideas.

In 1846 Darwin set aside his evolutionary theorizing for a detailed study of barnacles. This study lasted eight long years, and resulted in an extremely detailed and careful manuscript that earned Darwin a Royal Society medal. Darwin's barnacle study did two things. First it established him as a legitimate authority among scientists. This would later help him in the initial reception of his Origin of the Species. Second, it gave him a much clearer idea of the extensive variability in nature. Before his study on barnacles, he thought variability within a species to be the exception rather than the rule. In 1854 Darwin returned to his theorizing and began gathering his notes and thoughts for a manuscript he described as "The Big Species Book." But in 1858, while this book was still less than half finished, he received a letter and essay from the naturalist Alfred Russell Wallace, arguing for a theory of transmutation almost identical to his own. A crisis in priority for Darwin was averted when Charles Lyell and Joseph Hooker arranged to have Wallace's essay read before the Linnaean Society along with an abstract of Darwin's manuscript. At the time this meeting attracted relatively little attention, but it prompted Darwin to devote himself full time to the production of a longer abstract of his big species book (Browne 2002: 33–42). In November of 1859 this abstract was published under the title: "On the Origin of Species by Means of Natural Selection."

In the Origin, Darwin argued for three main hypotheses. First was the transmutation hypothesis: new species originate from the modification of other species. Second was common ancestry: speciation occurs through a branching process in a tree like structure. All species therefore share a common ancestor at some point in the evolutionary past. Third, was a causal mechanism: natural selection was the main, but not exclusive mechanism for change. Here Darwin argued: (1) there is variation among all organisms; (2) because more organisms are born than can survive and reproduce there will therefore be a struggle for existence; (3) some individual organisms will be better adapted to survive and reproduce; (4) these individuals will pass on their traits to offspring; (5) this will result in a gradual modification of the species. At the end of the Origin, Darwin turned to the explanatory power of these three hypotheses – transmutation, common ancestry, and selection as mechanism – arguing that they could explain a variety of phenomena from geographical distribution, embryological development, rudimentary organs, to the patterns of morphological similarity among species.

The response to the *Origin* was all the publisher could have desired. The first printing sold out in one day and a second printing was issued a month later. There were numerous reviews, many positive, and even those that were not were often sympathetic, based on Darwin's reputation and previous work (Browne 2002: 101). Those in Darwin's network were particularly impressed. Lyell, for instance, called it "A splendid case of close reasoning & long sustained argument ..." even though he could not agree with all of its conclusions (Browne 2002: 90). When there was criticism, it was typically not based on conflict with the account of origins in Genesis. Familiarity with German "literary" Biblical criticism precluded this sort of literalism among most educated British (Ruse 1999: 239). Criticism instead often focused Darwin's methodology. One standard objection was that Darwin was not being inductive enough, and was dabbling in hypotheses (Hull 2003). The rhetorical value of this was well entrenched. After all, it was long known that the great Isaac Newton himself "feigned no hypothesis" and the proper method was "Baconian" – based on the prescriptions of Francis Bacon. There was also a second question about the adequacy of natural selection to produce the obviously adapted forms we observe in nature. Lurking here was the assumption that a divine "designer" was required. This question was raised both by Darwin's critics and his most loyal supporters.

In the *Origin*, Darwin had little to say about human evolution, knowing full well the controversy it would create. Only at the very end does he explicitly address the topic:

> In the distant future I see open fields for far more important researches. Psychology will be based on a new foundation, that of the necessary acquirement of each mental power and capacity by gradation. Light will be thrown on the origin of man and his history. (O: 488)

Darwin does not elaborate further in the *Origin*. His conscious avoidance of this topic, however, did not prevent both his critics and supporters from addressing it. There seemed to be three main issues. First was the question of common ancestry. In the *Origin*, Darwin seemed to be implying that humans descended from apes and monkeys. (It was perhaps too subtle to insist that he instead implied humans shared a common ancestor with modern apes and monkeys.) This was the focus of a famous debate in 1860 between T. H. Huxley – "Darwin's Bulldog" and Bishop Wilberforce (Browne 2002: 122). The second issue was the matter of the differences between humans and other primate species. Richard Owen claimed that humans were different in kind from other species, by virtue of a unique structure in the human brain – the hippocampus minor. This particular claim was quickly rejected by 1861, based on Huxley's article in the *Natural History Review* demonstrating that the hippocampus minor is also found in nonhuman primates (Browne 2002: 119).

The third issue was whether the existence and nature of humans could be explained in the same way other species were explained. Lyell, in his 1863 *Antiquity of Man*, gave natural selection a role, but seemed to reserve a place for a "guided saltatory mechanism" (Ruse 1999: 145). He could just not give up the idea that man's creation was guided by, and explained by a greater power – even if this creation was still subject to the laws of nature. Wallace was similarly inclined. He worried that the higher mental faculties of humans could not be explained through natural selection alone. Even "savages," according to Wallace, possessed mental faculties in excess of what was needed for survival. He concluded: "a superior intelligence has guided the development of man in a definite direction, and for a special purpose, just as man guides the development of many animal and vegetable forms" (Ruse 1999: 246). But Darwin had little sympathy for those who, like Lyell and Wallace, wanted to bring God back into the explanation. In 1871 he published his *Descent of Man and Selection in Relation to Sex*, which addressed human evolution naturalistically and in much more detail.

In the introduction to the *Descent of Man* Darwin explained his reticence in discussing humans in the *Origin*, and indicated that given the widespread acceptance of evolution, there was no longer a need to put off discussion of man. His goals, he claimed, were first to establish that man has descended from some pre-existing form; second, to explain the manner of his development; third to consider the differences in the "so-called races of man" (DM: 3). The evidence he gave in chapter 1 for human descent will be familiar to anyone who has read the *Origin*: homologous structures in man and lower animals, development, and rudimentary structures. More important for purposes here however, is Darwin's discussion of mental powers in chapter 2. Here he argued that the differences between humans and the higher apes are only of degree, and relative to all aspects – instincts, curiosity, imitation, attention, memory, imagination, reason, tool and weapon use, language, self-consciousness, sense of beauty, belief in God, spiritual agencies and superstitions.

In chapter 2, Darwin also addressed the origin and development of languages, proposing his own evolutionary explanation.

> We see variability in every tongue, and new words are continually cropping up; but words, like whole languages, gradually become extinct … As Max Muller has well remarked: – "A struggle for life is constantly going on amongst the words and grammatical forms in each language. The better, the shorter, the easier forms are constantly gaining the upper hand, and they owe their success to their own inherent virtue." (DM: 60)

Darwin concluded: "The survival or preservation of certain favoured words in the struggle for existence is natural selection" (DM: 60–1). What is important in this passage is that instead of just explaining the appearance of language through the biological evolution of humans, Darwin was applying an evolutionary model to linguistic processes. He was using the conceptual framework he applied to biological evolution to the non-biological change and development of languages.

At the beginning of the *Descent* then, we have Darwin laying out two different strategies for using evolution to understand human phenomena. The first is to treat humans and all their physical, mental and social traits as products of biological evolution. This is a thoroughgoing naturalism. The second is to use a model of change, derived from biological evolution but not itself biological, to explain historical origins and processes of change. In the remainder of the *Descent*, Darwin employed these strategies to explain human psychological faculties such as reason, emotion and the social instincts. Here Darwin also employed a *continuity* assumption that human faculties and social nature are to be explained in terms of the same causes we explain the faculties of other species. Finally, he adopted an explanatory pluralism. While natural selection explained some human features, other features were explained by sexual selection, ancestry, effects of the environment, use and disuse, and learning.

The *Descent* sold well and Darwin made a substantial profit. In 1872, the year after the publication of *Descent*, Darwin wrote and published his *Expression of the Emotions in Man and Animals*. He laid out his general principles of expression in the first three chapters, with illustrations from man and other species, cats and dogs in particular. The means of expression occupy the next several chapters. Specific emotions are addressed in the remainder – anger, sadness, grief, love and so on. The *Expression* initially sold well, but after a second edition appeared in 1889, seven years after Darwin's death, it more or less disappeared from the intellectual landscape for nearly a hundred years. What is important here is that first, in both the *Descent* and *Expression*, Darwin was pursuing his project of understanding all things human naturalistically – including the "higher" human faculties such as reason, imagination, and the moral sense. Second, Darwin saw human nature as continuous with nonhuman nature. Humans may differ from other species, but they are also similar, in part because of shared ancestry.

Darwin's naturalism

The first sources for Darwin's naturalism likely came from the books noted above, that he read in the year or so before his Beagle voyage. The *Personal Narrative*, a record of Humboldt's expedition to South America, so enchanted Darwin that he would copy and read aloud passages to his fellow students, as he planned his own voyage (Richards 2003: 93). Part of the influence here on Darwin was surely its imaginative and romanticized description of travel to unexplored lands. But Humboldt's voyage was not mere tourist travel, but an investigation into the "unity of nature." At the onset of this voyage, he wrote:

> In a few hours we sail around Cape Finisterre. I shall collect plants and fossils and make astronomic observations. But that's not the main purpose of my expedition – I shall try to find out how the forces of nature interact upon one another and how the geographic environment influences plant and animal life. In other words, I must find out about the unity of nature. (Humboldt 1995: ix)

In the introduction to his *Personal Narrative*, Humboldt tells us that this unity of nature is to be reflected in the interconnections of science. In particular, he was interested in connecting the laws of life with those governing inanimate nature (Humboldt 1995: 6–7). Throughout his *Personal Narrative*, Humboldt makes it clear that he includes humans in this "unity of nature." It was with this book and its picture of a grand interconnected nature, that Darwin later undertook his voyage on the Beagle. He described its significance in a diary entry written during his voyage back to England: "As the force of impression frequently depends on preconceived ideas, I may add that all mine were taken from the vivid descriptions in the Personal Narrative which far exceed in merit anything I have ever read on the subject" (Richards 1987: 93).

At about the same time Darwin was reading Humbold's *Personal Narrative*, he was also reading Herschel's *Preliminary Discourse on the Study of Natural Philosophy*, just published in 1830. John Herschel, son of the astronomer William Herschel, was the most prominent scientist in England. His *Preliminary Discourse* was widely read, with twelve published editions, and translations into French, German, Italian, Russian, Chinese and Arabic (Herschel 1996: xi). What was distinctive about this book was not just its systematic approach to scientific method, but also its account of scientific induction.

At the time, the term "induction" was associated with the views of Francis Bacon and Isaac Newton. But it was a slippery term, often meaning different things to different people at different times. Like many of his day, Herschel claimed to be advocating an inductive method along the lines used by the great Isaac Newton in the derivation of the universal law of gravitation. Induction, for Herschel, seemed to involve two main processes: first, the rise by inductive generalization from the observation of particular facts to empirical law, followed by the subsequent inference of higher level theoretical laws; second, the establishment of *verae causae* – true causes – by direct observation and analogy. The first process, begins with observation and generalizes to empirical laws, then derives higher level, more theoretical laws. The second process is, in effect, a rule governing causal inference. Science, according to Herschel is at its best when it explains phenomena in terms of already established causes. Herschel explains, then credits Newton:

> Experience having shown us the manner in which one phenomenon depends on another in a great variety of cases, we find ourselves provided, as science extends, with a continually increasing stock of such antecedent phenomena, or causes ... To such causes Newton has applied the term *vera causae*; that is, causes recognized as having a real existence in nature, and not being mere hypotheses or figments of the mind. (Herschel 1996: 144)

What is important here is how these *vera causa* are established. Herschel identifies two ways – direct observation and analogy. We can observe directly, for instance, the force exerted by whirling around a stone in a sling, and we can apply that by analogy to the orbit of heavenly bodies.

> If the analogy of two phenomena be very close and striking, while at the same time, the cause of one is very obvious, it becomes scarcely possible to refuse to admit the action of an analogous cause in the other, though not so obvious in itself. For instance, when we see a stone whirled round in a sling, describing a circular orbit around the hand, keeping the string stretched, and flying away

the moment it breaks, we never hesitate to regard it as retained in its orbit by the tension of the string, that is, by a force directed to the centre; for we feel that we do really exert such a force. We have then a direct perception of the cause. When, therefore, we see a great body like the moon circulating around the earth and not flying off, we cannot help believing it to be prevented from so doing, not indeed by material tie, but by that which operates in the other case through the intermedium of the string-a force directed constantly to the centre. (Herschel 1996: 149)

The details of Herschel's views here are beyond the scope of this essay, but the main significance of his *vera causa* requirement is that we can postulate new causal hypotheses *only if* there is a sufficiently close analogy with already observed causes.

Charles Lyell, in the two volumes of his *Principles of Geology* (read by Darwin in 1831 and 1832), seemed to endorse the Herschellian methodology of science. This is clear in his rejection of "catastrophism," that asserts geological features are to be explained in terms of a variety of catastrophic processes of biblical proportions – volcanoes, floods, earthquakes, rapid climate change. Lyell's rejection of catastrophism was based on first, his *actualism* – we are to explain geological phenomena only in terms of the kinds of causes and processes that we observe around us; second, his *uniformitarianism*: we are to explain only in terms of causes *to the degree that we observe them*. We can explain in terms of floods and volcanoes, but only on the scale we observe. Lyell was clearly in agreement with Herschel about methodology – as both recognized in print (Ruse 1999: 59–61).

The fourth influence on Darwin was William Whewell, who was quoted by Darwin before the title page of his *Origin*. Whewell disagreed with Herschel about the *vera causa* requirement, arguing that it implied we could not discover new causes. For Whewell, induction consisted in the superimposition of a concept or idea on the phenomena via the "colligation" of empirical facts. Gravity, for instance, was a concept that colligated facts about the motion of heavenly bodies. But what was important for Whewell was explanatory power through *consilience*. A consilient hypothesis was one that not only explained the phenomena it was invented to explain, but predicted and explained additional phenomena. Not only could gravity explain the motion of the planets, but it could also explain the orbit of the moon around the earth, the ocean tides, and the descent of stones on earth (Whewell 1989: 328–30). In effect, the consilience requirement is a rule of *explanatory unification*.

It is beyond the scope of this essay to work out in detail the actual historical influence of Humboldt, Herschel, Lyell and Whewell on Darwin. Nonetheless, we can easily find the broad themes outlined above throughout Darwin's work. Humboldt's holism and treatment of humans as part of the interconnected unity of nature are seen in the broadest and most important features of Darwin's work – in his application of the same laws to all of life from barnacle to humans. Similarly, Herschel's views are echoed in Darwin's attempt to establish that natural selection is a *vera causa* by direct observation in domestic breeding. Because breeders do not select for the benefit of the individual organisms, they typically reduce the fitness of the organisms being bred. It is possible to observe the elimination of the less fit in natural selection, as Darwin thought had happened with the highly modified Niata cattle in South America (Richards 1997). Lyell's methodological prescriptions can similarly be seen in Darwin's work. At the same time Darwin was establishing that natural selection was a Herschellian *vera causa*, he was also conforming with his gradualism to Lyell's requirements that postulated causes must be among those known to operate and to the degree observed. Finally, Whewell's consilience requirement was satisfied in the penultimate chapter of the *Origin*, where Darwin argues first that his theory can explain various and different "classes of facts" from classification and comparative morphology, to rudimentary organs, embryology and geographic distribution; and second, that this explanatory ability is sufficient reason to accept it as true (O: 457–8).

One implication of Darwin's naturalism is that it seems to rule out a variety of the "exemptionalist" theories that treat human nature as unique and requiring unique *kinds* of explanations. Theistic exemptionalism, for instance, might explain human nature by reference to a God that created man in his own image. Darwin's rejection of this sort of explanation not only put him at odds with opponents of his evolutionary theory, but many of his supporters, including A. R. Wallace, the co-discoverer of natural selection, as well as Charles Lyell and Asa Gray (Richards 1987: 178–85). Darwin's rejection of these theological tendencies would be expected given his methodological commitments. Unless God could be observed, or shown to be a close analogy to an observed cause, then he could not be established as a Herschellian, empirical *vera causa*.

Other exemptionalist approaches seem to be ruled out by Darwin's naturalism as well. Approaches that conceive humans as different in kind from other animals, based on the uniqueness of human reason, language or culture violate Darwin's continuity principle. Human divergence from animals in terms of reason is a matter of degree, to be explained as a variation on the same faculty possessed by animals. While humans may differ from the great apes in terms of the degrees of reason, ability to communicate or form culture, there are also obvious similarities. And, as Darwin noted, the differences are even greater between the great apes and fish. So if we are to say humans and apes are different in kind, should we not also say that of apes and fishes?

> If no organic being except man had possessed any mental power, or if his powers had been of a wholly different nature from those of the lower animals, then we should never have been able to convince ourselves that our high faculties had been gradually developed. But it can be clearly shewn that there is no fundamental difference of this kind. We must admit that there is a much wider interval in mental power between one of the lowest fishes, as a lamprey or lancet, and one of the higher apes, than between an ape and man; yet this immense interval is filled by numberless gradations. (DM: 34–5)

It is also important to notice that Darwin did not focus exclusively on natural selection as the causal force for change. He employed explanations based on a variety of factors including the "conditions of existence," "use and disuse" and "correlation of parts." Perhaps most importantly, he recognized a second form of selection – sexual selection. The title of his book on human evolution is, after all, *The Descent of Man, and Selection in Relation to Sex*. Here Darwin first introduced sexual selection in humans as a possible explanation for the differences among the human races (DM: 250). He then laid out the general principles governing sexual selection, giving examples from molluscs, crustaceans, butterflies, moths, birds, reptiles, and dogs. The idea behind sexual selection is simple. First, just as there is a struggle to survive, in sexual species there is also a struggle to reproduce, primarily but not exclusively, a struggle among males for females. This struggle takes two forms – a physical struggle with other male rivals, and a struggle for the attention of the female (DM: 398). Second, those individuals that do best in this struggle are more likely to reproduce, passing their traits on disproportionately to the next generation. Sometime the traits that are useful in the struggle to reproduce are not useful in survival. The peacock's tail, for instance, is useful in attracting the attention and charming peahens, but it is also a hinderance in survival, reducing the ability of peacocks to avoid predators. Sexual selection can potentially explain traits not explainable by natural selection. This suggested to Darwin that sexual selection might be able to explain the excess human cognitive abilities that Wallace, Lyell and Gray thought inexplicable by natural selection (DM: 402).

What we have here in Darwin's naturalism, then, is first an approach based on an assumption about the continuity of nature from invertebrates to birds, apes and humans; second, a methodological, empirical *vera causa* rule that allows only observationally grounded hypotheses; and third, an explanatory unification *vera causa* requirement. And finally, we have an approach that is pluralistic, employing explanations based on natural selection, sexual selection, common ancestry and more.

The pragmatic naturalization of inquiry

In the years following the publication of the *Origin*, Darwinian evolution was much discussed in broader philosophical contexts. Nowhere was this more apparent than in "pragmatism," the most openly Darwinian of philosophical movements. The pragmatists did not typically embrace Darwin's naturalism in its entirety, but they applied its insights to important philosophical topics. Darwin's influence on the pragmatists came through Chauncey Wright, a mathematician and student of Asa Gray. Wright adopted Darwin's views shortly after reading the *Origin* in 1860. He corresponded with Darwin, defended Darwin in print, and earned the respect of Darwin (Wiener 1949: 31). Wright was also part of a group of young philosophers who began meeting regularly in Cambridge, Massachusetts in the early 1870s. This group, called the "metaphysical club" by Peirce, consisted of Wright, Charles Peirce, William James, Oliver Wendell Holmes, Frank Abbott and Nicholas St John Green. According to Peirce, Wright was the central figure in this club, and its most powerful and assertive intellect:

> Chauncey Wright, something of a philosophical celebrity in those days, was
> never absent from our meetings. I was about to call him our corypheus; but he

will better be described as our boxing master whom we – I particularly – used to face to be severely pummeled. (Wiener 1949: 19)

Wright's significance here was, of course, less his pugilistic skills, than the fact that he was a tireless advocate of Darwin's theory of evolution.

Charles Peirce was clearly influenced by Wright's Darwinism, but he also went far beyond a Darwinian naturalism into sometimes obscure metaphysical musings (Wiener 1949: 70–96). Nonetheless, Peirce's views about philosophical inquiry are Darwinian. According to Peirce, "logicality" is an adaptation produced by natural selection, useful in survival.

We are, doubtless, in the main logical animals, but we are not perfectly so ... Logicality in regard to practical matters is the most useful quality an animal can possess, and might, therefore, result from natural selection. (Menand 1997: 10)

Inquiry is something that "logical" organisms (such as humans) do in response to problems posed by their environment that generate doubt. Since this doubt is uncomfortable, producing a kind of irritation, the organism tries to eliminate the doubt. It does this through an inquiry, the proposal of an hypothesis to dispel the doubt. If the hypothesis succeeds, it results in belief – the satisfaction of doubt, that then guides our actions (Menand 1997: 13–14, 33). A satisfactory belief will bring us into a state of adaptation to our environment, until some problem forces us again into a state of doubt, and we begin a new inquiry.

Like Peirce, William James applied Darwinian ideas to inquiry. According to James, *beliefs* are tools or instruments of action to guide our living in the world (Menand 1997: 114). True beliefs are those that work, false beliefs are those that don't. Where James disagreed with Peirce is his view that the success of beliefs depends not just on the world, but also on individual tendencies, preferences, and pre-existing belief. A particular belief might work well for me, but not for you (Menand 1997: 101). This is because each person has a different set of background beliefs, tendencies and preferences, and for a belief to work, it must work relative to both an environment and the organism, as James explains:

A new opinion counts as "true" just in proportion as it gratifies the individual's desire to assimilate the novel in his experience to his beliefs in stock. It must both lean on old truth and grasp new fact .... (Menand 1997: 102–3)

The functioning of beliefs not only varies among individuals, but may change over time. As an environment or an individual changes, the utility of a belief may change.

Oliver Wendell Holmes applied Darwinian ideas to the law, arguing that we should conceive of laws as tools, and interpret and evaluate them based on how well they work. What are the consequences of conceiving a law in a particular way? Is a law, interpreted in a particular way, adaptive in the sense that it works well in social circumstances (Menand 1997: 156–7)? We can think of this in more general evolutionary terms. Humans, like other social species, adopt rules of social interaction. For humans, these rules are not purely instinct, but learned through interaction in the social environment. And for humans they get expressed in language and institutionalized in legal systems.

Darwinian ideas were also applied pragmatically by John Dewey in his conception of *experience*. Instead of thinking of experience as the passive reception of sensory experience, we should think of it as an interaction with a world of danger and risk. We act on the world, get a response, then act again. In effect, we experiment with our environment, and good experiments are those that are apt – help us adapt. Knowledge, for Dewey is a "mode of participation" in experience.

> … The living creature is a part of the world, sharing its vicissitudes and fortunes, and making itself secure in its precarious dependence only as it intellectually identifies itself with the things about it, and forecasting the future consequences of what is going on, shapes its activities accordingly. If the living, experiencing being is an intimate participant in the activities of the world to which it belongs, then knowledge is a mode of participation, valuable to the degree to which it is effective. (Menand 1997: 210)

Like Peirce, James and Holmes, Dewey asked us to think about philosophical activities in Darwinian terms – as instruments for functioning in environments. In the time since Dewey pragmatism has become less explicitly Darwinian. Nonetheless, similar Darwinian ideas have been adopted and developed by contemporary philosophical thinkers.

A Darwinian metaphysics

If we think of metaphysics as that which lies beyond experience – and define it in these terms – then Darwin had little to say relevant to metaphysics. His naturalism precludes it. But if we instead think of metaphysics as the study of the fundamental kinds of things that exist and processes that operate, then there is much he could say. First, Darwinism seems to rule out the traditional essentialist view that species are "natural kinds." Second, Darwin's selection-based causal mechanisms provide a probabilistic and non-teleological explanation of order that requires no appeal to intentions – human or theistic. Third is an implicit conception of value that is naturalistic and relational, and based on contextual facts about functioning.

The usual story told by philosophers is that before Darwin, species were conceived as natural kinds with essences. These essences have often been identified with a set of necessary and sufficient properties. Elliott Sober explains this approach:

> *Essentialism* is a standard philosophical view about natural kinds. It holds that each natural kind can be defined in terms of properties that are possessed by all and only members of that kind .... (Sober 2000, 148)

As the story goes, this "property essentialism" is the view of Aristotle and Linnaeus (Dennett 1995: 36–7). Unfortunately this story is not accurate. Aristotle was more interested in classifying functional features of organisms to get at the important functional principles, than in classifying organisms into species on the basis of essential traits. And Linnaeus was a species essentialist only in the first editions of his *Systemae Natura*. In later editions he was a "genus" essentialist and then an "order" essentialist, where species were hybridizations from the God-created genera or orders. Furthermore, Linnaeus did not identify a particular set of properties with an essence. Essences were instead something *underlying* the changing form that was passed on in reproduction. Species had essences not because of their distinctive properties, but because of a genealogical connection to some original form created by God (Richards 2007).

Both versions of species essentialism seem incompatible with Darwinism. First, Darwin's naturalism ruled out appeals to causes that could not be observed or connected to observation by analogy. Genealogical essentialism is ruled out if the essences passed on in reproduction cannot be observed. Second, Darwin's gradualism implies that change is continuous and there is therefore no single set of unchanging properties to be associated with a species over time. Moreover, Darwin's "population thinking," that conceives of species as variable populations implies that at a single time there is no set of invariable properties associated with a species. All this caused Darwin to worry in the *Origin* that maybe there were really no such things as species (O: 52).

In the last fifty years, there has been a heated debate over how to best conceive species. The *biological species* concept many of us learn in introductory biology courses, asserts that species are groups of interbreeding or potentially interbreeding organisms. This concept is clearly inadequate, however, applying only to sexually reproducing species. In recent years, the number of species concepts in use has expanded to well over twenty. But while there is no consensus about which species concept is best, there is consensus that whichever concept we adopt, species are ultimately *historical population lineages* – groups of organisms connected by reproduction and ancestry that change over time (Richards 2007).

On the basis of this idea, David Hull has argued that species are like individual organisms – with origins and endings, cohesion and change over time – and should therefore be conceived as "historical individuals" (Ereshefsky 1992: 293–316). The advantage of this is that it focuses attention on the nature of change and the processes that govern the origin and endings of species lineages. Criticism of this proposal has centered on whether *groups* of organisms ever have sufficient cohesion to count as individuals and what would be required. Ruse, for instance, argues that species lack sufficient cohesion (Ereshefsky 1992: 343–62). Undeterred, Hull has extended this idea of individuality beyond its strict biological domain, arguing that we can conceive disciplines, conceptual systems and theories as individuals as well, since each sort of thing has a beginning and ending, cohesion and change over time (Ereshefsky 1992: 310–13). What is important with historical individuals is that they cannot be defined and don't have essences. This has obvious implications for debates about human nature. If *Homo sapiens* is like any other species, and is conceived as a historical individual, then it has no essences and cannot be defined. And since the members of the human lineage have changed over time, and exhibit variability at any single time, then the best we can do is identify the distributions of particular changing traits at a given time and geographic location.

The second area of Darwinism's metaphysical significance is its commitment to fundamental processes and explanations of order. Before Darwin, a standard explanation of order, exemplified by William Paley, was by divine intention. Nature has order because God gave it order. If we wanted to explain the vertebrate eye, for instance, we would have appealed to the design intentions of God. Darwin knew Paley's argument well, but argued that order – apparent design – could instead arise spontaneously from the undirected processes of natural and sexual selection. This idea has two important implications. First, it suggests a general explanation of order that is non-directed, and spontaneous. Second, it seems to undercut Paley's argument from design to the existence of God. If selection processes can explain apparent design in nature, we need not appeal to a designing God.

This second implication of Darwinian naturalism has been the source of much debate. Theists fear – while atheists celebrate – its apparent atheistic implications. As John Dupre puts it: "Darwinism undermines the only remotely plausible reasons for believing in the existence of a God" (Dupre 2005: 56). In Dupre's view, Darwinism does not just imply an agnosticism – a suspension of belief, but an atheism – a denial of the existence of God. This view, however, is at odds with Darwin's attitude and naturalism. While Darwin was never particularly religious, neither was he atheistic, even though his belief gradually weakened. By the time he wrote his *Autobiography*, he was resigned to an agnosticism: "The mystery of the beginning of all things is insoluble by us; and I for one must be content to remain an agnostic" (A: 94). This is just the attitude we should expect, given that his methodological naturalism not only prohibited the appeal to a God or a God's intentions for any sort of explanation, but also seemed to rule out claims that go beyond observation to deny the existence of God.

Whatever its implications for theism, natural selection is now seen by many, not just as a fundamental *biological* process, but as an instance of a more general causal process. Daniel Dennett, for instance, has argued that natural selection is a universal, algorithmic and substrate neutral process for generating order. Selection, according to Dennett does not just work in the biological realm, but throughout nature, "promising to unite and explain just about everything in one magnificent vision" (Dennett 1995: 82). Richard Dawkins extends this idea of universal selection to culture by highlighting the similarities between genes and *memes* – ideas, habits, skills, behaviors, inventions songs and stories. Susan Blackmore explains:

> Genes are instructions for making proteins, stored in cells of the body and passed on in reproduction. Their competition drives the evolution of the biological world. Memes are instructions for carrying out behavior, stored in brains (or other objects) and passed on by imitation. Their competition drives

the evolution of the mind. Both genes and memes are replicators and must obey the general principles of evolutionary theory and in that sense are the same. (Blackmore 1999: 17)

If Dennett, Dawkins and Blackmore are right, then the same fundamental processes that govern biological evolution to produce biological order, govern conceptual and cultural evolution to produce order there as well.

This idea of extending selection beyond biology is made possible partly through the general theory of selection formulated by David Hull. According to Hull, selection really consists of two component processes – replication and interaction. Adopting this model, he argues is a better way to understand both biological and non-biological selection processes. Hull proposes that we replace the hierarchy of genes, organisms and species, with the more general *replicators*, *interactors*, and *lineages*, that can apply anywhere there is selection (Hull 2001: 2).

Replicators are things that produce copies of themselves. Genes are the paradigm case, but some organisms can replicate themselves as well. Interactors are "those entities that interact as cohesive wholes with their environments in such a way as to make replication differential" (Hull 2001: 22). Organisms are paradigm interactors, but genes and chromosomes can interact in their environments as well. Higher levels can also serve as interactors, in the instances where colonies, hives, and other kinship groups function as cohesive wholes. Lineages can be constituted by either interactors or replicators. Selection then, "can be characterized generally as any process in which differential extinction and proliferation of interactors causes the differential perpetuation of the replicators that produced them" (Hull 2001: 22).

Critics have responded to Hull's analysis by arguing that such a general theory is not possible because genes, organisms, cultures and concepts are too different to be subsumed under one general theory. One worry is that in biological evolution transmission is always "vertical," from parent to offspring, but in processes like conceptual evolution there is "horizontal," cross-lineage transmission. Hull replies that this sort of cross-lineage transmission does occur in nature, in particular among bacteria and viruses as well as throughout the plant kingdom (Hull 2001: 34). A second worry is that cultural and conceptual change occurs much more rapidly than evolutionary change. But as Hull notes, bacterial and viral evolution can occur much faster than much cultural or conceptual change. A third worry is that intentionality is a fundamental part of cultural and conceptual change, but not evolutionary change. But Hull sees intentionality in the "artificial selection" of the breeders (Hull 2001: 37). But sexual selection similarly introduces intentionality into selection.

Darwin thought the struggle for mates important enough to include it in his title for his book on human descent. Its significance is partly in the fact that it is "intentional." Where female choice drives sexual selection, the beliefs, desires and preferences of the female help determine the outcome of selection and of evolution. Evolutionary psychologist Geoffrey Miller has recently revived sexual selection, using it to explain a variety of human phenomena. Miller explains this intentionality of sexual selection:

> ... We were neither created by an omniscient deity, nor did we evolve by blind, dumb natural selection. Rather our evolution was shaped by beings intermediate in intelligence: our own ancestor, choosing their sexual partners as sensibly as they could. We have inherited both their sexual tastes for warm, witty, creative, intelligent, generous companions, and some of these traits that they preferred. (Miller 2000: 10)

The details of Miller's account are beyond the scope of this paper, but we should recognize in it a naturalism that represents both a return to Darwin's pluralism, and a recognition of intentionality in biological evolution.

Before we go further though, a caution is in order. Dennett, Dawkins and Hull have all argued that selection processes are fundamental, general features of the world, and should be understood to apply beyond narrow biological evolution. This should not be confused with the use of a selection based *model* that is not just an instance of a more general selection process. We could for instance, think about the "survival" of theories, but without invoking a general theory of selection. Karl Popper and Thomas Kuhn both seem to be doing this. Popper, for instance, claims that his falsificationist model of science is based on "Darwinian *selection*" (Popper 2002: 194). And at the end of his *Structure of Scientific Revolutions*, Kuhn argues that science proceeds by revolution, and that,

> ... the resolution of revolutions is the selection by conflict within the scientific community of the fittest way to practice future science. The net result of a sequence of such revolutionary selections, separated by periods of normal research, is the wonderfully adapted set of instruments we call modern scientific knowledge .... (Kuhn 1970: 172–3)

Neither Popper nor Kuhn seem interested in incorporating theory fitness and selection into a more general theory of selection. Rather than instances of a universal selection process, these seem to be mere models of selection.

A third area of significance here is in the conception of value. Ethicists have long argued over the nature of value. Often it is conceived in terms of non-natural, secondary or supervenient properties (Richards 2005: 271–3). In these terms "goodness" is usually conceived as a property of an action, person or state of affairs. Darwin did not develop a general evolutionary theory of value, but he did provide the resources for thinking about value naturalistically – as a relation between an organism and an environment. The basic value concept for Darwin was "fitness." One version applies to survival: an organism is better than another in some way if its traits provide a better fit with its environment so as to function better. Another version applies to reproduction: an organism is better than another in some way if its traits provide a better fit with the preferences of its potential mates so as to reproduce better.

In Richards (2005) is a Darwinian framework for thinking about these notions of fitness. The basic idea begins with *mattering*: A feature of an organism can matter in an environment in an indefinite number of ways and relative to survival and reproduction.

Value is generated by this mattering. But mattering is complex: A feature may be good relative to one organism, but bad relative to another. It may be good relative to one respect, but bad to another. And it may be good relative to one environment, but bad to another. This can be represented in a simple valuation schema: *w is good (or bad) with respect to x for y in z*. The significance of this schema is that it represents mattering and value as relations between an individual organism and an environment, rather than as a simple property. This implies first, that value is subjective in that it is always relative to a subject; second, that it is nonetheless objective – based on facts about functioning and mattering. This is a Darwinian conception of value first, in that it is based on fundamental Darwinian processes. Second, value is fully naturalistic and explainable in terms of the processes we observe in the world around. Third, it conforms to Darwin's continuity principle, applying both to humans and nonhuman species.

Part of the legitimate philosophical impact of Darwinism is its historical metaphysics. Darwin gave us the resources to think about the things in the world that change and the processes that cause change. Darwinism can therefore be seen as challenging the metaphysical picture we got first from Parmenides and Plato, that valued the unchanging "essences" over the changing. While Darwin was not the first or only thinker to focus on change, surely he was one of the most successful, and surely this success is partly a consequence of his naturalistic approach. This success of Darwinian naturalism is apparent in contemporary evolutionary approaches to human psychology, and the functioning of humans in their environment – "human social ecology." These are the topics of the next section.

Darwinian psychology and social ecology

In the *Descent of Man*, Darwin treated the emotions and "higher" faculties – reason and the moral instincts – naturalistically and as continuous with the same faculties in other species. Human reason and sympathy, for instance, were explained on the same principles as canine reason and sympathy. As we might expect, given his naturalism, he also looked to the brain and nervous system as the physiological basis for human psychology. The most important fact for Darwin was that behavior, the brain and nervous system are all products of evolutionary processes – natural selection, sexual selection, inheritance and the effects of the environment, etc. We can then understand human psychology by understanding how a feature conferred a survival or reproductive advantage; how a feature was inherited from evolutionary ancestors; or how a feature was acquired through interaction with an environment.

Darwin began his inquiry into the higher, intellectual faculties with the assumption that they are adaptations that confer a survival and reproductive advantage (DM: 159). More recent approaches, from the pragmatists to contemporary philosophers of biology and brain scientists, typically begin with the same basic assumption, leading to Darwinian accounts of epistemology, ethics and aesthetics. The basic idea is that the *capacities* associated with the acquisition of knowledge, the norms and standards of good behavior, and the creation and appreciation of art, are understandable in terms of the advantage they confer for survival and reproduction.

Michael Ruse applies this idea to epistemology – the study of knowledge. He takes scientific knowledge as a paradigm instance of knowledge, then argues that scientific knowledge is a product of "epigenetic rules" or developmental tendencies.

> … In order to understand why science is as it is – why laws, why predictions, why falsifiability, why consiliences – we need to look at the principles of scientific reasoning or methodology. … What I argue is that these principles have their being and only justification in their Darwinian value, that is in their adaptive worth to us humans – or at least to our proto-human ancestors. In short, I argue that the principles which guide and mould science are rooted in our biology, as mediated by our epigenetic rules. (Ruse 1998: 155)

Ruse argues for a Darwinian explanation of the developmental tendencies that cause us to think in terms of scientific law, to value predictions, to demand falsifiability, and to look for consilience in our reasoning (Ruse 1998: 164–8).

Ellen Dissanayake has similarly argued that the capacities and tendencies under-lying our appreciation and construction of art are to be understood on a Darwinian basis. The adaptive value in art behavior is its ability to make things "special." This ability to make things special is a general enabling mechanism, based on the motiva-tional force of pleasure, and directed towards activities associated with survival and reproduction.

> The principal evolutionary context for the origin and development of the arts was in activities concerned with survival. As we look back through the eons, we see abundant evidence of humans making things or experience special. Overwhelmingly what was chosen to be made special was what was considered important: objects and activities that were parts of ceremonies having to do with important transitions, such as birth, puberty, marriage, and death; finding food, securing abundance, ensuring fertility of women and of the earth; curing the sick; going to war or resolving conflict; and so forth. (Dissanayake 1992: 61)

While survival and reproduction enhancing activities have been the focus of this "making special," Dissanayake argues that the same capacities and tendencies can be directed to other types of activities, and explain the pervasiveness of art.

Ruse, Dissanayake, and many other contemporary thinkers have focused almost exclusively on natural selection. Geoffrey Miller, however, sees potential explanations of a variety of human phenomena, including the arts, in sexual selection, and based on the idea that some behaviors are "fitness indicators." The selection of a mate that has these fitness indicators guarantees fit offspring. And the sorts of traits that indicate fitness are also those that function in the arts. This avoids the problem that,

> … Nobody has been able to suggest any plausible survival payoffs for most the things that human minds are good at, such as humor, story-telling, gossip, art,

music, self-consciousness, ornate language, imaginative ideologies, religion, and morality. How could evolution favor such apparently useless embellishments? (Miller 2000: 18)

If Miller is right about all this, he is giving a Darwinian account that supplements the evolutionary epistemology and aesthetics of Ruse and Dissanayake.

We can be Darwinian not just in our explanations, but also in our *conceptions* of psychological states, faculties and capacities. Recently, philosophers and neuroscientists have argued for an approach to conceiving human psychology based on evolutionary functions (not to be confused with the non-evolutionary "functionalism" in recent cognitive psychology and philosophy of mind). Emotions are conceived functionally by the philosopher Paul Griffiths, who describes them as "affect programs," comprised of a coordinated system of responses, physiological, muscular-skeletal, and expressive (Hodge and Radick 2003: 91). The neuroscientist Joseph LeDoux similarly advocates a functional conception of the emotions.

> I view emotions as biological functions of the nervous system ... This approach contrasts sharply with the more typical one in which emotions are studied as psychological states, independent of the underlying brain mechanisms. Psychological research has been extremely valuable, but an approach where emotions are studied as brain functions is far more powerful. (LeDoux 1996: 12)

The functional concepts of Griffiths and LeDoux contrast with more traditional conceptions of the emotions based on feeling, cognition or perception.

Another kind of explanation used by Darwin was in terms of evolutionary ancestry or *phyletic conservativism*. Many of the features of an organism are present not because of natural selection, but because of inheritance from an ancestor. Humans for instance, have vertebral columns not because of some direct adaptive advantage to humans, but because their ancestors had a vertebral column. Similarly the human brain is a product of the pre-human evolutionary past, and the specifically human functioning is built upon the functioning of evolutionary ancestors. This is largely a process of addition rather than modification. Neuroscientist David Linden explains:

> The brain is built like an ice cream cone ... Through evolutionary time, as higher functions were added, a new scoop was placed on top, but the lower scoops were largely unchanged. In this way, our human brainstem, cerebellum and midbrain are not very different in overall plan from that of a frog. It's just that the frog has only rudimentary higher areas in addition (barely more than one scoop). All those structures plus the hypothalamus, thalamus and limbic system are not that different between humans and rats (two scoops), which have a small and simple cortex, while we have all that plus a hugely elaborated cortex (three scoops). When new, higher functions were added, this did not result in a redesign of the whole brain from the ground up; a new

scoop was just added on top. Hence, in true kludge fashion, our brains contain regions, like the midbrain visual center, that are functional remnants of our evolutionary past. (Linden 2007: 21–2)

The fact that humans have functional remnants of their evolutionary past seems to vindicate Darwin's continuity principle – we share brain structure with other species so we can explain our psychologies similarly – but it also has philosophical implications.

The fact that newer brain structures and faculties were just layered upon old structures and functions has several consequences. The first is that there are multiple parallel networks: Older networks pass through the emotion, memory and motor systems but not through the newer regions of the cortex associated with consciousness. Newer networks also pass through the newer "conscious" regions of the cortex. Significantly, the older systems are typically faster, so we can get sensory input processed by the emotion centers in the amygdala, and memory centers in the hippocampus, and have motor output and action before we are even consciously aware of the sensory input. A sensory experience, therefore, may produce a particular emotional response and an action *prior to and without conscious awareness or reason*. Neuroscientist Michael Gazzaniga tells us that "by the time any of us consciously experience anything the brain has already done its work" (Gazzaniga 2006: 89). This implies that conscious deliberation often plays a role only in inhibition – stopping an action in its early stages. As Gazzaniga describes it, we may not have free will here, but we might have "free won't" (Gazzaniga 2006: 93). The philosophically important point of all this is that the causal sequence of psychological events may often not involve conscious deliberation at all, or only after the fact. If so, it is unclear that self-conscious introspection can have access to the true causal picture.

Recent experiments with split brain patients indicate that there is another barrier to our abilities to understand psychological functioning through introspection, based on the presence of a system in the left cortex that constructs narratives to explain actions – after the fact. Patients with severe epilepsy sometimes have surgery to cut the corpus callosum and anterior commissure that connect the left and right hemispheres of the brain. This surgery leaves each side of the cortex functioning normally, but unable to communicate. It is then possible to give directions to just the right cortex, which can then initiate action without communicating the stimulus to the left side. But the left side of the cortex, responsible for speech, when asked why the action was undertaken will typically fabricate a response, instead of expressing ignorance. Linden explains:

If, in a split-brain patient, the (mute) right brain receives the instruction "Go take a walk," the subject will push the chair back and prepare to leave. If, at that point, the (speaking) left brain, which had no access to the instruction, is asked "What are you doing?" it will manufacture a seemingly coherent response to make sense of the body's action, such as "I was feeling thirsty and decided to get a drink" or "I had a cramp in my leg and needed to work it out." This is not just of fluke of one or two split-brain patients.

> The narrative-constructing capacity of the left cortex has now been clearly observed in more than 100 split brain patients in many different situations. (Linden 2007: 229)

Linden claims this narrative functioning is at work in dreaming and religious belief as well. But the important point here is that we may all be constantly subject to the misleading narration of this "confabulator," or "baloney generator" as Steven Pinker calls it.

> The spooky part is that we have no reason to think that the baloney-generator in the patient's left hemisphere is behaving any differently from *ours* as *we* make sense of the inclinations emanating from the rest of *our* brains. The conscious mind – the self or soul – is a spin doctor, not the commander in chief. (Pinker 2002: 43)

If Pinker and Linden are right, then our own psychology may not just be inaccessible to us in important ways, but we may in fact be systematically mislead by our own accounts.

The philosophical significance of this understanding of brain function has not been explored in detail, so it is hard to be very precise here. There are, however, some fairly obvious ways that it might impact philosophy. First, it challenges the view, usually associated with Descartes, that the operation of the mind is transparent and discoverable by introspection. But the implications go further, suggesting that introspection may actually be misleading. The left-brain "baloney generator" tells a satisfying but incorrect story of motivations and causes. Second, this approach also challenges the view that for humans, reason plays a primary causal role in action and reaction – we do things as a result of conscious deliberation about principles or means and ends. Human psychology instead seems to be based on an animal foundation that functions to a significant degree independently of conscious deliberation and reason.

Rather than focusing on individual psychology, a Darwinian approach might also begin with social ecology – the study of humans in a social environment. Owen Flanagan does this in his approach to ethics.

> As I conceive it, normative ethics is part of the science of ecology. Ecology is the discipline that tells us what conditions lead to the flourishing of various natural systems (wetlands, orchids, beavers) in certain environments. Ethics is ecology for humans and other sentient beings. Ethics, so conceived, is both empirical and normative. It asks: what are the conditions that led to fitness and flourishing for humans and other sentient beings? To answer, we need to look and see what sorts of environments lead to flourishing and what don't. (Hodge and Radick 2003: 381)

Flanagan sees this as a Darwinian approach in that it is naturalistic and appeals to selection processes (Hodge and Radick 2003: 381). He begins by quoting a long passage from Darwin's *Descent of Man*.

In order that primeval men, or the ape-like progenitors of man, should have become social, they must have acquired the same instinctive feelings ... They would have felt uneasy when separated from their comrades, for whom they would have felt some degree of love, they would have warned each other of danger, and have given mutual aid in attack or defense. All this implies some degree of sympathy, fidelity, and courage ... The love of approbation and the dread of infamy, as well as the bestowal of praise or blame, are primarily due ... to the instinct of sympathy, and this instinct no doubt was originally acquired, like all the other social instincts, through natural selection ... With increased experience and reason, man perceives the more remote consequences of his actions, and the self-regarding virtues, such as temperance, chastity, &c., which during earlier times are ... utterly disregarded, come to be highly esteemed or even held sacred ... Ultimately a highly complex sentiment, having its first origin in the social instincts, largely guided by the approbation of our fellow-men, ruled by reason, self-interest, and in later times by deep religious feelings, confirmed by instruction and habit, all combined, constitute our moral sense or conscience. (Hodge and Radick 2003: 383)

There are three important ideas here: the moral sentiments and instincts, the "approbation of fellow-men," and "religious feelings."

The moral sentiments, according to Darwin, are based on the sympathy humans have for, and pleasure they get from the company of their conspecifics. We need and enjoy the company of other humans, and we "feel their pain." This social nature is likely a product of our evolutionary past. As primatologist Frans de Waal has persuasively argued, our closest primate relatives seem to have the same social sentiments and preferences, and enjoyment of conspecifics that we see in humans (de Waal 2006). What is important here is that we are moral because we have in our nature certain emotions and preferences. We are not moral *just* on the basis of our reason or ability to form maxims that guide our actions. As Flanagan argues, emotions are "essential to morality, even when experience, habit and reason enter the picture" (Hodge and Radick 2003: 384).

But emotion, habit and reason are not enough for Flanagan. Morality requires norms, and norms presuppose evaluations. This is the *approbation* component of morality. Flanagan explains:

... Norms – moral ones, at any rate – express evaluations and make appeals that certain practices creating protecting or maintaining what is valuable to be observed. When I display anger, I express a desire that you back off. If you get the message you will do so, and if you are smart you will continue to do so in relevantly similar situations. Supposing you do so, you now govern your behaviour by a norm, consciously or unconsciously. (Hodge and Radick 2003: 385)

For Flanagan, moral expressions and associated judgments function to guide behavior.

490

When a parent gets angry at a child and tells him that what he did was wrong, the parent is trying to get him to act in accordance with a particular norm – one that rules out the behavior that produced the disapproval. Flanagan sees this as a fitness enhancing move:

> The Darwinian genealogy of morals I am sketching ties the origin of morality very closely to Darwinian fitness. A basic emotional expression communicates the wish that others behave in certain ways, ways that will promote the survival and reproductive success of the expressor. (Hodge and Radick 2003: 386)

This idea that we can understand moral judgments in light of their evolutionary functioning to guide behaviors has also been developed by Richard Joyce. First, he allows that it is not the actual behavior that would be adaptive, but the underlying psychological tendencies. So it is not particular moral judgments that function to enhance survival, but the tendency to make moral judgments. What is important for Joyce is that moral judgments have *practical clout*: "Calling an action 'morally correct' or 'virtuous' or 'wrong' or 'just' is (putatively) to draw attention to a deliberative consideration that cannot be legitimately ignored or evaded" (Joyce 2006: 57–8). This practical clout functions as motivation – "probabilifying" action: "a moral judgment in favor of an action is no *guarantor* that the action will be performed, but so long as it increases the likelihood of the performance then this may be its evolutionary function" (Joyce 2006: 114).

According to Joyce, moral judgments motivate in a special way, coordinating the actions of both the person making the moral judgment and the person who hears it. First, the expression of approval commits the expressor to a particular attitude that motivates that person's action. For instance, if a person publicly claims that "recycling is morally required," or that "premarital sex is forbidden," then that public commitment motivates that person to act in accordance with the norm expressed. And it likewise serves as a motivator for the person who is the target of the moral judgment. This bridging function produces a coordination of norms and behavior:

> ... We should now see that one of the adaptive advantages of moral judgment is precisely its capacity to unite these two matters. By providing a framework within which both one's own actions and others' actions may be evaluated, moral judgments can act as a kind of "common currency" for collective negotiation and decision making. Moral judgment thus can function as a kind of social glue, bonding individuals together in a shared justificatory structure and providing a tool for solving many group coordination problems. (Joyce 2006: 117)

In the last sentence here, Joyce raises an important question to be asked of a Darwinian framework – the justification of moral judgments. Moral judgments won't serve their function to coordinate behavior if they are not regarded as expressing more than mere preference. Joyce argues that we have this tendency to objectify moral facts from a young age, treating some judgments as expressions of mere preference, and others as independent of preferences. If so, there must be some fundamental feature of human psychology, based on an emotional response, that treats some kinds of judgments as independent of preference and with special normative force (Joyce 2006: 128–30).

Michael Ruse has also addressed this question of normative force and given it an evolutionary explanation. According to Ruse, evolution has made us such that we naturally cooperate. And to make us cooperate better, we have acquired the attitude that moral prescriptions are not mere preferences or conditional requirements, but obligations: "Epigenetic rules giving us a sense of obligation have been put in place by selection, because of their adaptive value" (Ruse 1998: 223). The belief that moral principles have special authority, perhaps from God, is one, but not the only way for this to function. Ruse describes this as the illusion of ethics.

> The Darwinian argues that morality simply does not work (from a biological perspective), unless we believe that it is objective. Darwinian theory shows that, in fact, morality is a function of the (subjective) feeling; but it shows also that we have (and must have) the illusion of objectivity. In other words, we 'objectify' moral claims … The point about morality (says the Darwinian) is that it is an adaptation to get us to go beyond regular wishes, desires and fears, and to interact socially with people. How does it get us to do this? By filling us full of thoughts about obligations and duties, and so forth. And the key to what is going on is that we are then moved to action, precisely because we think morality is something laid upon us … In a sense, therefore, morality is a collective illusion foisted upon us by our genes. (Ruse 1998: 253)

This passage may seem shocking and dangerous. But if Ruse is right, then that would be expected. Evolution has made us so that we *cannot* regard our moral principles as anything less than objective.

This conclusion gestures toward what might be regarded as a useful function for Darwinism in philosophy – as the foundation of an "error theory." If Darwinian approaches can tell us *why* we think the way we think about topics central to philosophy – knowledge, ethics and human nature, perhaps it can also tell us where we tend to go wrong, and why. The preceding discussion has suggested several ways that Darwinism can unmask typical errors. First, the fact that much of psychological functioning occurs subconsciously in the older parts of the human brain, prior to conscious deliberation and introspection implies that we typically cannot understand the causes of our own action by introspection. Second, the functioning of the left-brain confabulator suggests that the story we tell ourselves may be positively misleading. Third, the account of the functioning of norms and moral judgments we get from Flanagan and Joyce suggests that at least sometimes a focus on the content of the norms – what they value or disvalue, has missed what is important – the functioning of norms and judgments to guide and coordinate behavior. Finally, the special normative force that we associate with ethical principles seems to get "explained away" as an illusion favored by evolution, an illlusion that gets us to act in certain ways. The philosophical implications of all this have yet to be worked out with care, so I will not try to draw a specific conclusion, but surely any philosophical view that makes assumptions about human psychology or social ecology should revisit those assumptions in light of this Darwinian error theory.

Conclusion

Darwin's philosophical impact begins with his commitment to a methodological naturalism and explanatory pluralism, and how that has played out relative to philosophical discussions and issues. From Humboldt, Darwin took the view that nature is interconnected and that humans are part of, and continuous with nature. From Herschel and Lyell he adopted the empiricist requirement that causes be directly observed and be to the degree observed. And from Whewell he adopted the view that a good explanation unifies phenomena. Finally, Darwin adopted an explanatory pluralism that may have emphasized natural selection, but also incorporated sexual selection and phyletic conservativism, as well as a variety of other processes.

This naturalism has obvious philosophical impact in the commitments of the pragmatists, who argued that we can understand doubt, inquiry, meaning and truth on a Darwinian approach. Its impact is also obvious in the naturalistic and historical metaphysics that conceives of species as "historical individuals" rather than natural kinds with essences, and views selection as a general process for generating order. Perhaps less obvious in terms of philosophical impact, Darwinism has provided the resources to understand the functioning of human psychology in terms of evolutionary history and the selection processes that formed the human brain. And it has also provided a naturalistic framework for thinking about ethics as a natural feature of human social behavior in an environment – as "human social ecology." On the basis of its insights into human psychology and social ecology, the Darwinian approach has also seemed to promise an understanding of the processes at work in our acquisition of knowledge, and in our use of moral judgments and belief in their normative force. Finally, Darwinian naturalism suggests a naturalistic "error" theory that might tell us ways we are likely to go wrong in our philosophical thinking about reason, emotion and moral principles.

There are, however, two enduring philosophical concerns about Darwin's naturalistic approach. First is a concern about its continuity thesis that humans are to be understood on the same explanatory principles as other species. The concern is that humans are so different from other species that it becomes a difference "in kind," requiring a different kind of explanation. Christine Korsgaard expresses this concern:

> ... Kant speculated that the form of self-consciousness that underlies our autonomy may also play a role in the explanation of some of the other distinctively human attributes – including culture, romantic love, and the capacity to active from self-interest. Other philosophers have noticed the connection of self-consciousness of this sort of capacity for language. I can't go into those

arguments here, but if they are correct they would provide evidence that only humans have this form of self-consciousness ... If that is right, then the capacity for normative self-government and the deeper level of intentional control that goes with it is probably unique to humans beings. (de Waal 2006: 116)

The idea is that because of the distinctive human functioning based on self-consciousness, we should explain human behavior in terms of things like principles, values and ideas, rather than emotion and instincts.

A form of life governed by principles and values is a very different thing from a form of life governed by instinct, desire and emotion – even a very intelligent and sociable form of life governed by instinct, desire and emotions ...We have ideas about what we ought to do and to be like and we are constantly trying to live up to them. Apes do not live in that way ... Even if apes are sometimes courteous, responsible and brave, it is not because they think they should be .... (de Waal 2006: 117)

If Korsgaard is right, the proper way to explain human behavior is unique to humans, and Darwin's continuity principle fails.

The Darwinian has obvious responses to Korsgaard's exemptionalist objection. The first is that modern science has proven Korsgaard's Kantian assumptions wrong about both human and ape psychology. Humans are not as governed by self-consciousness and intentional control as claimed, while apes are not as different from humans as claimed. Korsgaard's claims are, after all, empirical and must be backed up by evidence. Unfortunately the best evidence is against them. The second response is based on the fact that Darwinian metaphysics does not recognize the "differences in kind" assumed by Korsgaard and others. While humans may differ from other species in dramatic and significant ways, because there is common ancestry and gradual divergence the differences are still only of degree. And if the basic units of biodiversity and evolution are "historical individuals" rather than natural kinds, then it is unclear that there *can be* essential differences in a metaphysically significant way. Korsgaard and the Darwinians seem to be starting from fundamentally different metaphysical stances.

The second concern is about naturalism and the commitment to a 'scientific' approach: doesn't the Darwinian approach just rule out by fiat, non-naturalistic explanations that may in fact be better? Alvin Plantinga expresses this worry from a theistic standpoint:

... It could be that the best scientific hypothesis was evolution by common descent – that is, of all hypotheses that conform to methodological naturalism, it is the best. But of course what we really want to know is not which hypothesis is the best from some artificially adopted standpoint of naturalism, but what is the best hypothesis *overall*. (Plantinga 1998: 694)

Plantinga makes it clear that he thinks the best explanation is likely to be of a non-natural sort – an explanation in terms of God (Plantinga 1998: 695).

One need not be a theist like Plantinga, however, to reject the naturalistic restriction of Darwinism. Korsgaard also seems to be rejecting the naturalistic approach in favor of an "intentional" approach based self-conscious reasons, principles and a "deeper level of intentional control." For those, like Korsgaard, who think human behavior is to be explained in terms of unique human intentions, Darwin's naturalism is simply the wrong approach.

It may be that ultimately, the Darwinian cannot refute Plantinga or Korsgaard. But what the Darwinian can do is to appeal to the explanatory power of science in general. If we take a scientific approach seriously in other domains of inquiry, why would we not apply it to human psychology, social ecology and inquiry? And the Darwinian can also appeal to the explanatory power of science relative to the phenomena discussed here. Does it successfully explain human inquiry, cognition and ethical behavior? The ultimate philosophical significance of Darwinism may well be in the foundation it provides for a naturalistic, "scientific" alternative to recent philosophical approaches based on the primacy of reason, linguistic practices and self-conscious introspection. In this sense, Darwinism is in part a return to an older approach that saw what we would now call science as "natural philosophy," and conceived it as just another branch of philosophy. On this approach, we use whatever resources we have, be they scientific, logical or linguistic, to understand the philosophical aspects of human nature. Surely there are good reasons to use a scientific, Darwinian naturalism to answer our philosophical questions, and illuminate our philosophical practices.

References

Works of Darwin

Darwin, Charles (A) (1958) *The Autobiography of Charles Darwin*, New York: W.W. Norton and Co.
—— (DM) (1981) *The Descent of Man and Selection in Relation to Sex*, Princeton, NJ: Princeton University Press.
—— (O) (1964) *On Origin of Species: a Facsimile of the First Edition*, Cambridge MA: Harvard University Press.

Other citations

Blackmore, S. (1999) *The Meme Machine*, Oxford: Oxford University Press.
Browne, J. (2002) *Charles Darwin: The Power of Place*, Princeton, NJ: Princeton University Press.
de Waal, F. (2006) *Primates and Philosophers: How Morality Evolved*, Princeton, NJ: Princeton University Press.
Dennett, D. C. (1995) *Darwin's Dangerous Idea: Evolution and the Meanings of Life*, New York: Simon & Schuster.
Dissanayake, E. (1992) *Homoaestheticus: Where Art Comes from and Why*, New York: Macmillan.
Dupre, J. (2005) *Darwin's Legacy: What Evolution Means Today*, Oxford: Oxford University Press.
Ereshefsky, M. (ed.) (1992) *The Units of Evolution*, Cambridge, MA: Bradford Books.
Gazzaniga, M. S. (2006) *The Ethical Brain*, New York: HarperCollins.
Herschel, J. (1996) *Preliminary Discourse on the Study of Natural Philosophy*, London: Routledge/Thoemmes Press.

Hodge, M. J. S., and G. Radick (eds) (2003) *The Cambridge Companion to Darwin*, Cambridge: Cambridge University Press.

Hull, D. L. (2001) *Science and Selection: Essays on Biological Evolution and the Philosophy of Science*, Cambridge: Cambridge University Press.

—— (2003) "Darwin's Science and Victorian Philosophy of Science," in Hodge and Radick (eds) *The Cambridge Companion to Darwin*, Cambridge: Cambridge: University Press, pp. 168–91.

Humboldt, A. van (1995) *Personal Narrative*, trans. Jason Wilson, London: Penguin.

Joyce, R. (2006) *The Evolution of Morality*, Cambridge, MA: Bradford Books.

Kuhn, T. S. (1970) *The Structure of Scientific Revolutions*, Chicago: University of Chicago Press.

LeDoux, J. (1996) *The Emotional Brain*, New York: Simon & Schuster.

Linden, D. (2007) *The Accidental Mind,* Cambridge, MA: Belknap Press.

Menand, L. (ed.) (1997) *Pragmatism*, New York: Random House.

Miller, Geoffrey (2000) *The Mating Mind*, New York: Anchor Books.

Pinker, S. (2002) *The Blank Slate: The Modern Denial of Human Nature*, London: Penguin books.

Plantinga, A. (1998) "When Faith and Reason Clash: Evolution and the Bible," *The Philosophy of Biology*, Oxford: Oxford University Press.

Popper, K. (2002) *Unended Quest: An Intellectual Autobiography*, London: Routledge.

Richards, R. A. (1997) "Darwin and the Inefficacy of Artificial Selection," *Studies in the History and Philosophy of Science* 28, no. 1: 75–97.

Richards, R. J. (1987) *Darwin and the Emergence of Evolutionary Theories of Mind and Behavior*, Chicago: University of Chicago Press.

—— (2003) "Darwin on Mind, Morals and Emotions," in Hodge and Radick (eds) *The Cambridge Companion to Darwin*, Cambridge: Cambridge University Press, pp. 92–115.

—— (2005) "Evolutionary Naturalism and the Logical Structure of Valuation: The Other Side of Error Theory," *Cosmos and History: The Journal of Natural and Social Philosophy* 1, no. 2: 270–94.

—— (2007) "Species and Taxonomy," *Oxford Handbook of the Philosophy of Biology*, Oxford: Oxford University Press.

Ruse, M. (1998) *Taking Darwin Seriously: A Naturalistic Approach to Philosophy*, Amherst, NY: Prometheus Books.

—— (1999) *The Darwinian Revolution: Science Red in Tooth and Claw*, Chicago: University of Chicago Press.

Sober, Elliott (2000) *Philosophy of Biology*, 2nd edn, Boulder, CO: Westview Press.

Whewell, W. (1989) *Theory of Scientific Method*, ed. Robert E. Butts, Indianapolis, IN: Hackett.

Wiener, Philip P. (1949) *Evolution and the Founders of Pragmatism*, Cambridge, MA: Harvard University Press.

Wittgenstein, L, (1960) *Tractatus Logico-Philosophicus*, London: Routledge & Kegan Paul.

Further reading

The authoritative biography of Darwin's life during and after the publication of his *Origin* is J. Browne, *Charles Darwin: The Power of Place* (Princeton, NJ: Princeton University Press, 2002). The authoritative biography of Darwin's life up to the writing of the *Origin* is J. Browne, *Charles Darwin: Voyaging* (Princeton, NJ: Princeton University Press, 1995). M. Ereshefsky (ed.) *The Units of Evolution* (Cambridge, MA: Bradford Books, 1992), is an edited volume containing essays about the nature of species from important systematists and philosophers of biology. M. J. S. Hodge and G. Radick (eds) *The Cambridge Companion to Darwin* (Cambridge, Cambridge University Press, 2003), is an edited volume covering a variety philosophical and historical topics relating to Darwin and his development to modern Darwinian metaphysics, epistemology, and ethics. A philosophically sophisticated, evolutionary account of moral judgment and behavior can be found in R. Joyce, *The Evolution of Morality* (Cambridge, MA: Bradford Gooks, 2006). R. J. Richards, *Darwin and the Emergence of Evolutionary Theories of Mind and Behavior* (Chicago: University of Chicago Press, 1987), offers an authoritative, historical account of biological accounts of mind and behavior from the seventeenth and eighteenth centuries to Darwin and beyond to the twenty-ninth century. A careful historical and philosophical account of the "Darwinian Revolution," by the most prominent philosophical expert on Darwin is M. Ruse, *The Darwinian Revolution: Science Red in Tooth and Claw* (Chicago: University of Chicago Press, 1999), and Ruse's *Taking Darwin Seriously: A Naturalistic Approach to Philosophy* (Amherst, NY: Prometheus Books, 1998), sympathetically explores the implications of Darwin for philosophy.

17
THE PHILOSOPHY OF RACE IN THE NINETEENTH CENTURY

Robert Bernasconi

The task of a philosophical history of race

Even though a number of major philosophers have contributed to writing the history of race in the nineteenth century – Eric Voegelin in *The History of the Race Idea*, Georg Lukács in *The Destruction of Reason*, Hannah Arendt in *The Origins of Totalitarianism* (1979), and Michel Foucault in "*Society Must Be Defended*" – this history is still not well known among philosophers today. Nevertheless, the study of the history of the concept of race is indispensable for all those pursuing the philosophical task of a critique of racism in all its myriad forms, and the nineteenth century in particular was the age when race came of age. In mid-century Benjamin Disraeli, who would become Prime Minister of Britain in 1868, could write: "All is race. In the structure, the decay, and the development of the various families of man, the vicissitudes of history find their main solution" (Disraeli 1852: 331). This was not an isolated claim. It was a view shared by others, such as Robert Knox, an anatomist who had also studied the transcendental philosophy of Immanuel Kant and the *Naturphilosophie* of Lorenz Oken, and who wrote "Race is everything: literature, science, art – in a word, civilization, depends on it" (Knox 1850: v).

Any account of the history of the concept of race needs to be broad. A critical philosophy of race cannot confine its historical component to listing what the canonical philosophers have had to say about race: their contributions can only be assessed if they are seen in their context, that is to say, as interventions in ongoing scientific debates and responses – or failures to respond – to the social movements of the day: such as calls for the abolition of slavery, the pursuit of Empire, and demands for segregation.

Another reason why any such study cannot limit itself to those who are now regarded as canonical philosophers is because the boundary line between philosophers and scientists was a great deal less clear in the nineteenth century than it became later. The nineteenth century was a time of growing specialization in philosophy as a result of the birth of a number of new disciplines such as biology, ethnology, anthropology and sociology, all of which made race central to the definition of their task. However, because these disciplines were not as isolated from each other, and especially from philosophy, as they tend to be today, they cannot be altogether omitted even from a brief account.

The history of race thinking in the nineteenth century is a great deal more complex than is usually recognized and it seems that what is needed more than anything else today is an account that offers a richer sense of that complexity, an account that conveys both how foreign the racial thinking of that time is to the conceptual structures dominant at the beginning of the twenty-first century and yet one that poses the question as to whether we have yet learned the lessons that history conveys. I will organize my remarks around four issues with which philosophers were deeply involved, leaving aside many other questions that a broader survey of racial issues would need to address. The four are: firstly, the debate between monogenesis and polygenesis as the source of the scientific concept of race; secondly, the place of race mixing in the philosophy of history; thirdly, the role of Lamarckianism in inhibiting a full-blooded debate between racial essentialists and racial environmentalists; and, finally, eugenics both in its relation to Darwinism and in its introduction of the distinction between nature and nurture.

The introduction of the scientific concept of race as a response to polygenesis

At the beginning of the nineteenth century there was little clarity about what the simple sounding word "race" meant. There was as yet no consensus that this would become the preferred term dividing humanity into usually four or six varieties according to certain inherited characteristics, both physical and mental. Even when the term "race" usually referred to these few main races, it was also often used as a synonym for "people." For example, when Herder's *Ideas* was translated into English at the beginning of the century, *Volk* was sometimes translated as "race," even though Herder in that text explicitly rejected the term "race" (*Rasse*) which he associated with Kant (Herder 1800: 166). The term "race" continued to be used throughout the nineteenth century to refer to "peoples," like the English, the French, or the Italian. Because of the ambiguity of the term, I will, when it seems important, specify whether I am talking about the few main races, on the one hand, or the subsidiary or secondary races on the other hand, but it should be remembered that this was not a firm division for most of these theorists. Much depended on the context: in the United States the focus tended to fall on a few main races, whereas the imperial project led Europeans, particularly in the final years of the nineteenth century, to highlight differences between the subsidiary races.

The passion for classification among natural historians in the seventeenth and eighteenth centuries meant that they wanted to record and find a place for all human varieties. The attention of Northern European scientists in particular was fixed initially on gypsies and Laplanders, although in England the Irish were often singled out too.

Native Americans also long presented a problem because the apparent geographical isolation of the continent made it unclear how it came to be populated. In the same period, Africans were subjected to investigation because of their color. All skin colors had to be explained, but the frameworks that had been devised had the consequence that black skin was understood to present special problems: for example, those who believed that skin color was simply a consequence of the heat of the sun or lack of it had to contend with the fact that it was virtually impossible to find instances where black skin was eradicated (Mitchell 1745: 148). The burgeoning debate over chattel slavery toward the end of the eighteenth century provided another reason why the focus of natural historians fell increasingly on Africans, but the information reaching Europe was supplied by partisan observers who had already taken sides in the debate. The ease with which, in the same period, Indians and Chinese were lumped together in the same main racial category, in spite of the lack of any obvious resemblance between them, is an indication of the fact that the primary focus of European scientists fell elsewhere. Africans were believed to be on the margins of humanity and, for that reason, at the center of all discussions of race.

Francois Bernier in 1684 seems to have been the first to use the word "race" to refer to a few main human varieties, but Immanuel Kant was the first to single out the term and give it a precise sense (Bernasconi 2001). Kant defined races as "deviations that are constantly preserved over many generations and come about as a consequence of migration (dislocation to other regions) or through interbreeding with other deviations of the same line of descent, which always produces half-breed offspring" (Kant 2000: 9). Racial characteristics as such were inheritable and derived in equal measure from both parents (Kant 2001: 41).

Kant had insisted on the word "race" as part of his attempt to respond to the challenge posed by polygenesis, the idea that human beings did not descend from a single pair, as the Bible maintained, but were the result of several local creations. Isaac de la Peyrere had promoted polygenesis in the middle of the seventeenth century in an effort to defend the authority of the Bible from the challenge presented by the fact that the Chinese, Chaldeans, and Egyptians recorded a longer history than could be found in the Bible (La Peyrere 1655: 164–70). These peoples then must have been created before Adam and Eve, who were not therefore the original parents of all human beings but only of the Jews (La Peyrere 1655: 118–28). However, by separating the Jews from the rest of humanity in this way La Peyrere did not think of himself as demeaning them: they were in his eyes God's chosen people (La Peyrere 1655: 90). The planters in the West Indies, who, already in the seventeenth century adopted polygenesis to justify slavery, had an entirely different perspective, using this and other ideas derived from the Bible, including the so-called curse of Ham, to "infer their Negro's Brutality; justifie their reduction of them under Bondage; disable them from all Rights and claims even to Religion itself" (Godwyn 1680: 14).

In the middle of the eighteenth century a strong form of what we today would call environmentalism seemed the only way to reconcile monogenesis, the idea that human beings derived from a single pair, as the Bible maintained, with the limited time frame the Bible seemed to allow for the history of humanity. As late as 1766

Buffon thought that what would later be called racial characteristics, such as skin color, were largely a product of the environment and that as one moved from one climate to another those characteristics would completely change, perhaps in as little as ten generations (Buffon 1766: 314). However, because the evidence increasingly seemed to suggest the permanence of racial characteristics, there was a revival of polygenesis, particularly among those who wanted to cast doubt on the Bible, like Henry Home, also known as Lord Kames, and Voltaire (Home [Lord Kames] 1774: I 38–9, II 70–5; Voltaire 2000: 5).

Kant resisted their conclusions by appealing to Buffon's role of species identification, according to which only members of the same species could propagate fertile offspring across successive generations. This established the unity of the human species, but his main contribution was to do so in such a way as to explain the permanence of racial characteristics, even if that explanation seems somewhat artificial. Kant posited the existence of four seeds or germs that were allegedly present in the first human beings and that corresponded to the four main races that he had identified. The actualization of these seeds, together with the corresponding racial characteristics, depended on the climate and other environmental conditions that human beings encountered as they spread throughout the world. As one set of racial characteristics developed, the possibility of realizing the other characteristics disappeared (Kant 2000: 21). Race mixing and the fact that in the course of these early migrations a certain group might move from a warm climate to a cold climate before the germ had been fully actualized explained the existence of intermediary forms.

Kant went far beyond natural description, which is what occupied most of his contemporaries. He acknowledged that he was engaging in speculation, but he believed that this was forced on him, given the limitations of knowledge of the past at that time. Somewhat misleadingly, he borrowed the phrase "natural history," which his contemporaries used to refer to what he called "natural description," and employed it to differentiate the kind of inquiry he was engaged in from what they were doing. However, he increasingly recognized that many scientists were also going beyond simple description in their work: he saw this, for example, in Johann Friedrich Blumenbach's account of a formative drive (*Bildungstrieb*) (Kant 2001: 51n6; 1987: 311). Unlike Kant, Blumenbach believed that the divisions that could be drawn among the human varieties were somewhat arbitrary; the human varieties formed a continuum and to that extent he was no racial essentialist (Blumenbach 1865: 264). And, unlike Kant, he used the term "race" in earlier works, but as a synonym for variety (Klatt 2007: xxiii–xxiv). However, in 1797 Blumenbach adopted Kant's distinction between "race" and "variety," as well as his claim that when two races mate their offspring is a half-breed that shares equally in the racial characteristics of both parents (Blumenbach 1797: 23 and 14; Bernasconi 2006: 84–5).

Blumenbach cited Kant as a scientific authority. Skin color was Kant's primary example of an inherited characteristic that borrowed equally from both parents, and surprisingly, Blumenbach in 1795 accepted this claim from Kant, even though he had dismissed the reliability of skin color as an indicator some years earlier and even though Georg Forster, who had traveled with Captain Cook, had earlier made the point that Kant knew little on this topic at first hand (Blumenbach 1865: 207). The boundary line between philosophers and scientists was not yet fixed, and this remained the case until at least the middle of the nineteenth century. Franz Theodor Waitz, Professor of Philosophy at the University of Marburg, presents a clear example of a philosopher who devoted a significant portion of his energies to the study of race, in addition to his innovative work on pedagogics and psychology. In his multivolume *Anthropologie der Naturvölker*, the first volume of which was translated into English, he not only showed a remarkable knowledge of the ethnological data, but in his defense of the unity of mankind he exercised all of his philosophical skills in a field where rigorous argumentation was often lacking (Waitz 1863).

One of the most prominent advocates of monogenesis and a strong opponent of Lord Kames was the American, Samuel Stanhope Smith. In 1787, while Professor of Moral Philosophy at Princeton, he published *An Essay on the Causes of the Variety of Complexion and Figure in the Human Species*. In line with the speculations of another North American, John Mitchell, more than half a century earlier, but asserted more decisively, he supplemented the account of the impact of climate with a recognition of the role of the "state of society" in modifying the influence of climate (Mitchell 1745: 148; Smith 1787: 52–88). He published a heavily revised and expanded edition of his book in 1810 while President of the College. It incorporated some of the insights of Blumenbach into his defense of monogenesis and thus did more than anyone before him to integrate North American ideas of race with those in Northern Europe (Smith 1810).

The impact of the Kantian formulation of race on subsequent thinking is evident from a thinker like James Cowles Prichard, who was perhaps the leading racial scientist in Europe in the first half of the nineteenth century. Prichard often gave credit to Blumenbach, but, unlike Blumenbach and like Kant, Prichard established the unity of species by reference to hybridity, defined race in terms of hereditary permanent characteristics, and, when pressed on the issue of how races with permanent characteristics arose from an original pair, he resorted to the Kantian language of germs and predispositions. However, he made this last point only in the second edition of his *Researches into the Physical History of Mankind* (Prichard 1826: Vol. 2, 544; Augstein 1999: 113). Like most monogenists, his preferred way of negotiating the problem was by choosing to ignore it, beyond general statements of the kind found in Samuel Stanhope Smith about how racial characteristics are transformed as a race becomes more civilized (Prichard 1813: 239).

The significance of Kant's essays on race is more evident in the German context. In 1799 at the beginning of his *First Outline of a System of the Philosophy of Nature*, Friedrich Schelling embraced the notion of race, understood, following Christoph Girtanner, in terms of the action of Blumenbach's *Bildungstrieb* on the Kantian seeds, which then give rise to inherited characteristics (Girtanner 1796; Schelling 2004: 44–6). Indeed, Schelling seems to have seen how Kant's attempt to justify his doctrine of races led him to write the *Critique of Teleological Judgment* which was the inspiration for his own philosophy of nature. Nevertheless, Schelling progressively abandoned the concept of race that reflects significant changes in racial thinking in the first half of the nineteenth century. In 1827 he proposed that Europeans no longer be thought of as constituting a race, restricting the term only to those parts of humanity that are "degraded" (Schelling, 1920: Vol. 6, 100), and by the time of his death, in 1854, when he was still working on the philosophy of mythology, he fell under the influence of the increasingly racist developments in natural history. In late works, he cited Georges Cuvier and Samuel Morton to support a crude version of polygenesis. This led him to go back on his earlier endorsement of the term *Rasse*, preferring now *Geschlecht*, except in special cases (Schelling 1927: Vol. 5, 668).

Polygenists in general had little use for the term "race," given that, strictly speaking, they recognized many species rather than many races, a point Prichard had made earlier (Prichard 1836: Vol. 1, 109). However, by this time the term "race" had a life of its own and was not easily eradicated, even as polygenesis came to dominate, first in France, then in North America, and finally, more generally. Already in 1864 Alfred Russel Wallace used Darwin's theory of natural selection to declare the debate between monogenists and polygenists to be an irrelevancy, because one could believe both that man was once a homogenous race, and that man only became man strictly speaking when the higher faculties developed. There was thus a sense in which both monogenesis and polygenesis could be true, but this argument was not widely accepted (Wallace 1864: clxvi).

Race mixing and the philosophy of history

In the 1820s Georg Wilhelm Friedrich Hegel already set aside the debate between monogenesis and polygenesis as one that lay outside philosophy (Hegel 1978: I 113). He accepted as the teaching of natural history that races are permanent and have different characteristics (Hegel 1978: II 53–5 and 68). In this way, he retained the concept of race, vacillating between Kant's division between four races and Blumenbach's five varieties, although he usually preferred the former (e.g. Hegel 2007: 90–1; Hoffheimer 2000: 44–6; 2005: 197–8). However, Hegel's main significance for the history of race thinking was the way in which he incorporated race into his philosophy of world history. History proper was the history of the Caucasian race (Hegel 1956: 173; Bernasconi 2000). He excluded Africa proper – that is to say, sub-Saharan Africa – from history and in the process he seems to have deliberately distorted his sources to produce a wicked caricature of Africans (Hegel 1975: 173–90; Bernasconi 1998). Somewhat surprisingly, given what he had said about the exclusion of Africa, sub-Sarahan Africans do make an appearance in world history in such a way as to make world history's transition to Greece necessary. This took place in Egypt and was associated with the fact that its attempted fusion of the African element with the Oriental burst out in the form of monstrous productions (Hegel 1956: 207). It was only with the introduction into Egypt of the Caucasians, initially in the form of the Persians and then the Greeks themselves that history could progress further (Hegel 1956: 198–222; Bernasconi 2007b).

Hegel's view of non-European peoples as either excluded from history or largely static had a major impact on subsequent nineteenth-century theorists, including Karl

Marx. Less attention has been given to the impact of Hegel's views on the historical role of race mixing. Although he believed that race mixing led to the downfall of Egypt, his history has a number of examples where mixing within the Caucasian race contributed to fruitful transformations. He celebrated purity only when he turned to "Germany proper," that is to say, Germany without the portions colonized by the Romans (Hegel 1956: 349 and 421).

By the middle of the nineteenth century, the Northern European obsession with race mixing had been turned into a law of history based in biology. Northern Europeans had previously objected to race mixing on theological, social, or personal grounds: it was against God's plan, disrupted the clear divisions between "types" of people, and offended the brute racism of those who found the very idea repulsive. However, strictly biological objections to race mixing became widespread only in the early 1840s. There were only a few who anticipated this idea, such as Friedrich Ludwig Jahn, sometimes called the father of gymnastics. He was a strong advocate of German racial purity and in 1810 in his *Deutsches Volkstum* he issued a warning: "Just as hybrid animals have no genuine power of reproduction, mixed peoples have as little capacity for natural survival" (Jahn 1884: Vol. 1, 164).

As long as one focused on the view that the human varieties were permanent – it did not matter whether they had been formed monogenetically by germs or polygenetically by direct creation – racial inequality would serve as the ultimate reference point of historical explanation. But within the context of the philosophy of history the focus shifted to explaining change: races and peoples arose in history and then declined or disappeared. In the late eighteenth century the decline, disappearance, or even the static character of certain races led to questions like the one Kant posed to himself in his response to Herder: "Why do the Tahitians exist?" (Kant 1995: 219–20). It seemed that the disappearance of inferior races was necessary for progress. But in the nineteenth century the approach was more proactive. The extermination of races whose usefulness was not apparent was a strong temptation, if they stood in the way of progress, and, if it was going to happen anyway, one was merely hastening the inevitable (Bernasconi 2005).

It was in the context of the writing of history that the focus shifted decisively from a largely static portrayal of races to an account which highlighted the fashioning or making of races. To be sure, the experience of animal breeders had already been applied haphazardly by slave owners seeking to improve their "stock" and satisfy their sexual desires at the same time. But for the nineteenth-century philosophers of history who denied that any pure races existed, except perhaps among the Jews or in isolated parts of the world, the picture was more dynamic. Racial purity was not so much something to be preserved as something to be produced by breeding out variation.

The injection of a specifically biological notion of race into the writing of history in an effort to explain its development seems to have been the contribution of the Saint-Simonians. The biological notion employed was that of William Fréderic Edwards, who in 1829 argued that when neighboring races mix, as had happened in France, the differences were preserved. It was mixing between the main races alone that produced a hybrid that shared the racial characteristics of the parent races equally (Edwards 1829: 22–9). Two more Saint-Simonians, Victor Courtet de l'Isle and Gustave d'Eichthal, incorporated this insight into a program that advocated race mixing (Courtet de l'Isle 1838: 389–91; d'Eichthal 1839: 18–19 and 62–9). In 1835 Wolfgang Menzel called for a universal mixing of the colored and White races in order to secure the victory of Christianity and civilization. He believed that after a time race mixing leads to the production of a new race with its own purity and in this vein he proposed that the mixing of Whites and Blacks would lead after eight generations to a totally white population (Menzel 1835: 160, 84–5). In a somewhat different idiom, but with a somewhat similar conclusion, Gustav Klemm, director of the library at Dresden, maintained that the blending of the originally separate active and passive races promoted the fulfillment of the aim of nature and the completion of mankind in the blossoming of culture (Klemm 1843: 204). Prichard also argued, albeit more soberly, that race mixing was as advantageous among human beings as it was among animals (Prichard 1836: Vol. 1, 146).

The biological argument against the efficacy of race mixing was put by Honoré Jacquinot (Blanckaert 2003: 49) and especially Josiah Nott. In 1843 Nott published a short essay in the *American Journal of the Medical Sciences* whose title said everything: "The Mulatto A Hybrid – probable extermination of the two races if Whites and Blacks are allowed to intermarry" (Nott 1843). Foucault traced the introduction of biopolitics to eighteenth-century *Polizeiwissenschaft*, and although it already had a racial application at that time – for example, Johann Frank in his *System of Complete Medical Police* advocated the mixing of races on health grounds and explained the weakness of American Indians on their lack of opportunity to mix (Frank 1784: 404–11; Eigen 2006) – Nott took it in the reverse direction and to another level. Nott, a physician based in Mobile, Alabama, was looking for ways to defend what was euphemistically called "the Southern way of life." By co-editing with George Gliddon *The Types of Mankind*, an enormously successful volume dedicated to the memory of Samuel George Morton, whose cranial studies were widely respected, and by soliciting for this volume a contribution from Louis Agassiz of Harvard University, Nott found a way to give his own research a high level of respectability it did not deserve (Nott and Gliddon 1854). Paul Broca, founder of the Societé d'Anthropologie de Paris, frequently cited Nott. Georges Pouchet had the work of Nott and his collaborators in mind when he wrote that "At present France and England walk entirely in the scientific path opened by the American school" (Pouchet 1864: 7). Nott's claim was that mixed race populations were more susceptible to diseases, including decreased fertility. The result was that hybridity – at least in the case of mulattoes, the mix of Blacks and Whites – came to be considered a medical condition that should be prevented: the health of society called for measures to prevent it.

The suspicion that those of mixed race were less vital than other people contributed to the rejection of monogenesis, precisely because its defense, as in Buffon and Kant, had been based on fertility across the races. Nott succeeded in persuading many of the leading scientists in Europe that, because the offspring of Blacks and Whites were supposedly shorter-lived and less fertile, they must constitute two different species. Although there was a much more open response to race mixing in South America than North America, and even some idealism, as in the case of Simón Bolivar (Lynch 2006: 284), by the final quarter of the century attitudes had changed. Even Brazil's cultural elite had been persuaded by the North American school of polygenists that miscegenation was a disease (Daniel 2006: 37).

Racial amalgamation would never entirely disappear as a proposed solution to alleged racial inequality, but, after Nott, it was less likely to be promoted on biological grounds as it had been with, for example, d'Eichthal and Prichard. Long after Darwinism had rendered Nott's advocacy of polygenesis virtually irrelevant, the impact of Nott's promotion of racial purity on biological grounds would persist. However, most theorists acknowledged that, insofar as races were made, not given, then racial purity itself was to be created, as one might develop a new breed. This dynamic conception left a constant uncertainty about when a race in this sense was constituted. Did the label "White" embrace a number of such races? There were numerous controversies over whether the people of a given nation were made up of a single race, a mixture, or more than one distinct race.

Like Menzel, Count Arthur de Gobineau believed that race mixing was the key to history. Gobineau's *Essai sur l'inégalité des races humaines* was published between 1853 and 1855. His thesis statement went far beyond the assertion of a static racial hierarchy: "the racial question overshadows all other problems of history, that it holds the key to them all, and that the inequality of the races from whose fusion a people is formed is enough to explain the whole course of its destiny" (Gobineau 1915: xiv). He believed that race mixing had been essential for the development of civilization. Artistic genius, for example, arose only as a result of mixing between the White and Black races (Gobineau 1915: 208). Civilization had reached its zenith in his own time and the history of humanity was moving into its second half, that race mixing was a clear cause of decline (Biddiss 1970: 175). Gobineau posited a law of revulsion, which led all races to be repelled by the prospect of race mixing, but he immediately supplemented it with a law of attraction that led the conquering races to disregard the first law and instead seek to mix (Gobineau 1915: 30). This observation, with its suggestion that in the North American context the desire White slave owners felt for their Black female slaves was unreciprocated, was clearly too much for some Southerners to bear. When Nott promoted Gobineau's racial theories in the United States, this idea was omitted from the translation. (Gobineau 1856: 157–8).

Gobineau's impact was strongest not in his own time but in the 1920s and 1930s. When a second posthumous edition of the *Essay* was published in 1884, it needed a subvention from Richard Wagner's circle in Bayreuth. By the time Gobineau appeared in German translations, between 1897 and 1900, his theories were eclipsed by those of Houston Stewart Chamberlain, a member of the Bayreuth Circle, whose books, *Foundations of the Nineteenth Century* and *Immanuel Kant*, were more highly regarded than Gobineau's.

In 1850 Knox, a strong opponent of race mixing, had already proclaimed race war as a reality (Knox 1850: 16–17, 266). By the end of the nineteenth century the idea had become an obsession among intellectuals and Chamberlain was one of its main exponents. He feared the Russians and the so-called "busy soulless yellow race," but above all he feared "the millions of the blacks poverty-stricken in intellect, bestially inclined, who are even now arming for the war of races in which there will be no quarter given" (Chamberlain 1914: II 332). He saw the alternative as follows: "our human society must either enter upon the most brutal barbarism which ever presided, the barbarism of artificially civilized superstitious races, hostile to nature, debilitated, intellectually poverty-stricken – as dreamless as so many cattle, or it must, boldly conscious of its aims, prepare for a further step and climb a new stage, a markedly higher stage of culture" (Chamberlain 1914: II 339). Chamberlain declared that Kant had shown the way to the second path, but he believed that the Aryan race could pursue that path only by leaving the other races behind. The Aryans should try to progress on their own, as the Jews had done.

Chamberlain was not troubled by those who cast doubt on the existence of an Aryan race. An Aryan race could be made (Chamberlain 1913: I 266n): "Race is not an original phenomenon, it is produced; physiologically by characteristic mixture of blood, followed by interbreeding (*Inzucht*); psychically by the influence which long lasting historical and geographical conditions exercise upon that special, specific, physiological foundation" (Chamberlain 1913: I, 354). He believed that race mixing should be a matter of social policy. He even cited Benjamin Disraeli's celebration of the racial purity of the Jews and turned it around to present them as threatening the preeminence of the Germans, who were less pure racially. Whereas Disraeli had thought of the Jews as belonging to the Caucasian race, Chamberlain shared the growing conviction that the Jews were a separate race (Disraeli 1844: II 138. Chamberlain 1913: I 271).

The process by which the Jews became a race is not easy to determine, in part because of the ambiguity in the source literature between main and subsidiary races. As we have seen, La Peyrere already isolated the Jews in mid-seventeenth century by arguing that the Jews were the result of a distinct creation. Indeed, the Purity of Blood Statutes in Spain in 1492 had already indicated that inheritance could surpass religion in importance (Popkin 1980: 79) and this language of purity was exported by the Spanish into colonial Mexico where it was applied to give Indians as well as the Spanish-Indian mestizaje, a special status almost equal to that of the Spanish, in contrast to anyone of African descent, with only very few exceptions (Martinez 2004). But the racialization of the Jews is probably best thought of as having been accomplished in the nineteenth century. Already in 1816 Jakob Fries, while Professor of Philosophy at Heidelberg, wrote a virulent attack on the Jews and identified them as "a race," but it is not entirely clear what he meant by this (Fries 1816: 12). Even Ernest Renan, who seems to have done as much as anyone to establish the Jews as the Semitic race par excellence and the Semitic race as distinct from the Indo-European race, thought that they could not be distinguished on a physiological basis but only on the basis of their language, literature, and religion (Renan 1947: 577; Marrus 1971: 11–15). Renan had a major influence on Moses Hess, an early figure in Zionist thought, who, in 1862, was among the first to present the Jewish race as one of the primary races of mankind, unchanging in spite of changes of climate (Hess 1918: 59; Rose 1990: 321). Nevertheless, as late as 1880 Hermann Cohen proposed assimilation as an answer to the racial issue and in terms that suggest that this included for him becoming physically more German (Cohen 1880: 15).

Race mixing proved a decisive issue. In 1843, Bruno Bauer wrote an essay on the Jewish Problem, to which Marx responded. He returned to the theme in 1863 when he dramatically differentiated the Jews and Germans, denying that a true mixture was possible on the grounds that a Jew cannot be Germanized, whereas a German can take on certain Jewish qualities (Rose 1990: 273–4). This turned the Jews into a remarkable exception because, at least up until 1853, Bauer had insisted that only race mixing would supply the intellectual and moral elasticity that would give a people the force needed for world domination (Bauer 1853: 9). Concern about Germans mixing with Jews became even more pronounced in the writings of Eugen Dühring. Dühring acknowledged that healthy neighboring races could produce healthy offspring, but he did not put the Jews and the Germans together in that category. Indeed, he considered the "Judaisation (*Verjudung*) of the blood of modern peoples" to be a great evil (Dühring 1881: 144–5).

Concerns about race mixing within the White community in the United States and about the effects of race mixing on the Black community came to a head in the 1890s and gave rise to one of the classic texts of the critical philosophy of race, W. E. B. Du Bois's "The Conservation of Races." The context was the publication of Frederick Hoffman's *Race Traits and Tendencies of the American Negro*. Hoffman, a leading statistician, updated Nott's argument that people of mixed Black and White ancestry had less vitality than people of either pure Black or White ancestry. He drew the further conclusion that, given that most of those who were designated African American were mixed, they were destined for extinction, although he did allow that there might be a reprieve if they changed their moral nature (Hoffman 1896: 310–11 and 328–9). Both Kelly Miller (Miller 1897) and W. E. B. Du Bois responded in 1897 at the inaugural meeting of the American Negro Academy, although on that occasion Du Bois did not mention Hoffman by name.

Some philosophers today have tried to impose their question of whether "race" is a legitimate concept onto W. E. B. Du Bois's "The Conservation of Races" but this is anachronistic (Appiah 1992: 28–46). There were certainly questions about the usefulness of the term "race" within biology at that time, but the complaint was that the multiple uses of the word had left it with sufficient precision for it to have a scientific utility that matched its social usefulness and not that there was nothing in the world to which it corresponded. Du Bois was not concerned about whether the word should be maintained, but rather whether the races themselves should conserve their identity. It was his answer to segregation which, by 1897, Whites had blocked the path of assimilation, and the argument of Frederick Douglass that, because many African Americans were already mixed, and could neither be expatriated, nor annihilated, they should look forward to being absorbed through further race mixing (Douglass 1886: 438). The context establishes that Du Bois was not defending a narrowly scientific concept of race, but arguing for race loyalty, and doing so in the context of the philosophy of history.

Du Bois, Miller, and Hoffman all embraced Social Darwinism in some form or another, and that meant that survival was meant literally, as when Du Bois asked his fellow African Americans: "Have we in America a distinct mission as a race – a distinct sphere of action and an opportunity for race development, or is self-obliteration the highest end to which Negro blood dare aspire?" (Du Bois 1986: 821). It is this that gives the essay its almost existential feel as when Du Bois asks "What, after all, am I? Am I an American or am I a Negro? Can I be both? ... Does my black blood place upon me any more obligation to assert my nationality than German, or Irish or Italian blood?" (Du Bois 1986: 821). The fact that Du Bois wrote of conservation rather than preservation, suggests that he was not averse also to applying physical principles to philosophy and history, as Herbert Spencer and Walter Bagehot had done.

Whereas Alexander Crummell and Edward William Blyden had preached the duty to preserve the Black race on theological grounds (Blyden 1971: 201; Crummell 1992: 195), Du Bois presented the same claim in the language of the philosophy of history. It is in terms of the philosophy of history, with its heavy reliance on the concept of race, that his contribution (including his so-called definition of race) can best be understood. To be sure, Du Bois's philosophy of history employed arguments that relied heavily on references to Providence, as did those of Kant and Hegel. For Du Bois "the duty of the American Negro descent, as a body, to maintain their identity" was addressed not in terms of racial purity, but race ideals and once those ideals had been incorporated within history, then and only then, would "the ideal of human brotherhood" become possible (Du Bois 1986: 825). Strong echoes of both Herder and Hegel have been found in Du Bois's essay, even though these two German philosophers are usually understood as occupying opposing positions within the philosophy of history. Herder explicitly rejected Kant's model of Europe giving law to the other continents and proposed in its place a kind of latent multiculturalism according to which each people had its own model and that all these forms contributed to the whole framework of humanity (Kant 1995 52; Herder 1800: 224, 227). By contrast, Hegel believed that each race or people was assigned its own time in which to play a central role in world history (Hegel 1975: 196–209). By discounting the view, upheld by many African Americans, that Egypt was African, and by overlooking the fate of American Indians, Eskimos, and South Sea Islanders, who seemed not to have a moment in history (Du Bois 1986: 818), Du Bois held out the prospect that the time of the Black race still lay in the future.

Eighteenth-century environmentalism and nineteenth-century Lamarckianism

In 1809 in *Philosophie zoologique* Jean-Baptiste Lamarck challenged Buffon's rule, which in any case Buffon himself had already put into question by questioning the sterility of the offspring of a horse and an ass (Buffon 1764: 223). Lamarck argued that hybridization across species led through time to the formation of new races and then through time to new species (Lamarck 1984: 39). He did not exempt humanity from this process (Lamarck 1984: 169–71). This would be important for theorizing the human races, but its impact was completely overshadowed by Lamarck's doctrine of the inheritance of acquired characteristics, according to which an organism's environment (*circonstances*) imposed needs upon it in response to which it developed characteristics which were then passed on to its offspring (Lamarck 1984: 113). This too was not an altogether new idea, but he had generalized it and his name came to be attached to it. Because it is the environment that is credited with making the changes that subsequently became permanent, some commentators call this a form of "environmentalism" (Harris 1968: 83–4), but it is very different from what was thought of as environmentalism in the eighteenth century, which was understood to operate more quickly and was usually thought of as reversible. In the eighteenth century, environmentalism, understood as the attempt to refer the existence of races to climate and nutrition, was an idea that had failed because it did not explain the kind of issues that led Kant to posit races, such as why, after a time, races seemed to stop changing or changed only minimally. Environmentalism became a viable explanation of the human races again only as the time-frame allowed for human evolution became massively extended, but this new environmentalism was a very different kind of theory. Meanwhile, so long as it held sway, Lamarckianism excluded any straightforward application of the nature-culture distinction to the topic of race, and this is why nineteenth-century discussions of race do not readily conform to the categories that philosophers have tended to employ at least since the end of the Second World War.

I have already indicated that what we today call "racial essentialism," at least in its core sense, was not as widespread in the nineteenth century as is often thought. Some commentators have been tempted to cast John Stuart Mill as one of its early opponents, but there is a danger that this reading may distort the terms in which he saw the debate. It is perhaps better to use Mill to show how the framework which determined how race was viewed in the middle of the nineteenth century was very different from what it is today, and that is why I shall give it more attention than perhaps it deserves in its own right. Mill's contemporaries observed that he was relatively silent on the question of race and they attributed this to his focus on the individual (Varouxakis 2005: 159). Mill wrote at the time of the triumph of organism epitomized by Carl Carus's essay on Goethe (Carus 1849). The separation of body and mind, which had already been challenged in the eighteenth century by such thinkers as Charles Bonnet and Herder, seemed less and less relevant in this context. But it should be remembered that whereas what Mill called "national character" could change, it was still consistent with what many, if not most, of his contemporaries would have called "race," in one of its many senses.

Mill's main public statement on the question of race was made in response to his dispute with Thomas Carlyle in a debate that was conducted in mid-century in the pages of *Fraser's Magazine*. The controversy is often presented as pitting Carlyle's crude racial determinism and Mill's enlightened environmentalism, but this would be anachronistic and overdetermined. Mill attributed to Carlyle the view that there was "an original difference of nature" between the races (Mill 1984: 93), but when he caught Carlyle describing "the Negro" as born to be the servant of Whites, Mill refused to hold Carlyle to it, saying only that the latter did not know what he was saying (Carlyle 1849: 676–7; Mill 1984: 92). Mill did not rule out the possibility of some form of essentialism; he simply dismissed the evidence available at that time as sufficient to prove it. Furthermore, he knew that Carlyle's essay was not a theoretical piece but an intervention within the ongoing debate about British policy toward the West Indies. Indeed, Carlyle described it on its first publication as "an occasional discourse." He was less interested in addressing the question of the nature of the different races than promoting his "gospel of work," and it was for this reason that he presented Blacks as having been happy and indolent under slavery, whereas, since emancipation, they had become hard-pressed and beleaguered. Because Mill observed that two trees from the same stock may grow to different sizes because of differences of climate (Mill 1984: 93), commentators, even in the late nineteenth century attributed to him a form of environmentalism (e.g. Hoffman 1896: 310), but the application of that label to Mill was a projection made possible by a shift in the intellectual horizon. In fact, although Mill believed that many of his contemporaries exaggerated the importance of race, he himself did not deny "the great influence of Race in the production of national character" and used it, for example, to explain the similarities between the French and Irish in spite of their different histories and social circumstances (Mill 1985: 235–6; Mill 1972: 691, 1093, 1563).

Mill was inclined to highlight education more than either race or environment. In a letter he wrote to Charles Dupont-White in 1860, he explained that in place of the indelible differences of nature, "the influence of both education and of the social and political milieu" should be highlighted (Mill 1972: 691). Initially he had supported d'Eichthal's proposals for uniting or fusing Europeans and Orientals (Mill 1963: 329) and Whites and Blacks (Mill 1963: 404 and 456) on the grounds that their character-istics were complementary. As time went on his thinking took a somewhat different direction. In "The Subjection of Women," he proposed that education and culti-vation should be the main means for "correcting … the infirmities incident" to the temperament of women or races. However, it seems that, at least on this occasion, he was talking about the fact that some European races, such as the French, the Greeks, and the Italians, were "excitable" and yet still capable of excellence and did not have a broader view in mind (Mill 1984: 309–10). In "On Liberty" Mill had described despotism as a legitimate mode of government in dealing with barbarians, provided it was directed toward their improvement in such a way that the means employed were both appropriate to the end and effective in bringing it about (Mill 1977: 224). This is what makes Mill's response to Charles Dilke's book *Greater Britain* so disappointing. Mill complained to the author about his tendency to reduce the sources of national character to race and climate "as if whatever does not come from race must come from climate, and whatever does not come from climate must come from race" (Mill 1972: 1563). But he said nothing about Dilke's celebration of the Saxon as "the only extirpating race on earth" (Dilke, I 308). It is shocking to find that Mill could let such comments pass unchecked. Nor is this an isolated case of Mill turning a blind eye: in 1831 he judged that "The conduct of the United States towards the Indian tribes has been throughout, not only just, but noble" (Mill 1986: 236).

511

A generation later, Henry Sidgwick also exhibited attitudes that it is virtually impossible for us to avoid thinking of as racist (B. Schultz 2007: 123–30). He granted that drastic and permanent segregation would be appropriate, if "the social amalgamation of two races would be debasing to the superior race," but like Mill, he allowed that additional evidence might lead him to modify his view. He simply doubted that that had yet been shown and he thus favored only temporary separation as a transitional measure toward complete social amalgamation of "the inferior race" with the colonizing race (Sidgwick 1891: 313–14). This is not the place to try to differentiate the various forms of imperialism that philosophers sought to justify in the final years of the nineteenth century, but mention should be made of the fact that Carl Peters, one of the most vicious imperialists of his generation, wrote a work of philosophy that was heavily influenced by both Schopenhauer and Darwin (Peters 1883).

Because Herbert Spencer in his synthetic philosophy linked biological evolution to sociocultural evolution, in such a way that moral intuitions were understood to be biologically inheritable, he can be seen as a representative of Lamarckianism. Spencer's short essay on "Personal Beauty," which was intended for a popular audience, was a defense of the proposition that beauty of character is related to facial beauty. It began with a statement of how transitory forms produce permanent forms, but instead of leading to a discussion of how facial characteristics might in this way reflect personal character, Spencer immediately introduced the phenomenon of hereditary transmission together with the recognition that changes in functions lead to changes in forms. In this way, progressive civilization can be correlated with the remaking of features, including changes in the facial angle of the kind that Petrus Camper had studied with regard to the races at the end of the previous century. Even more interesting for our purposes is the way in which Spencer in the second part of his essay addressed the anomalies and exceptions to this general rule. Spencer observed that when pure races mix with those that are already mixed, the features of the unmixed race tends to predominate. And yet, Spencer noted, all civilized races at least are of mixed origin. The point of these observations was to establish a framework in which exceptions to the law that "all forms of feature are related to forms of mind" could be seen as contingencies that would over time disappear, just as hybrids would "dwindle away in a few generations" (Spencer 1858: 423, 427).

One final feature of Spencer's brief discussion merits attention, his observation that when two pure races mix the result is "not a homogenous mean between the two constitutions, but a seemingly irregular combination of characteristics of the one with characteristics of the other" (Spencer 1858: 425). This of itself was not new, although it contravened Kant's original claim that racial characteristics were those that derived equally from both parents. However, it led Spencer to the further point that certain traits might disappear for a few generations only to reappear, even if only for a single generation. It is remarkable, albeit not untypical, that Spencer would draw attention to this fact in what was in many ways a popular essay because, it was a phenomenon for which the dominant biology of the day did not yet have a ready explanation.

Darwinism, eugenics, and the miscegenation debate

So far as the topic of the human races is concerned, Charles Darwin is less important for what he wrote than for what others made of his writings. The full title of his 1859 book – *On the Origin of Species by Means of Natural Selection, or the Preservation of Favored Races in the Struggle for Life* – already indicated the direction in which others would take his thought, but he himself decided not to address racial issues there on the grounds that the book was already controversial enough. By the time he decided to address these questions in *The Descent of Man*, which appeared in 1871, his opinions were no longer on the cutting edge. In this later book he largely restricted himself to a cautious review of the literature on race without adding much that was new. For example, he questioned the findings of Nott and Broca about the relative sterility of the mixed races, but did so by relying mainly on the findings of John Bachman, a clergyman from Charleston, South Carolina, who had been Nott's most vociferous opponent in the 1850s.

What one does not see so clearly in Darwin himself, but which is manifest in his contemporaries, is how the effort to come to terms with Darwin's theories intensified philosophical interest in racial theories. In Germany, Fritz Schultze argued that Kant was a forerunner of Darwin and called for greater interest in Kant's essays on race, a call that was answered by Johannes Unold and Ernst Haeckel, the foremost Darwinist in Germany, particularly in later editions of *The History of Creation* (F. Schultze 1875; Unold 1886; Haeckel 1903: Vol. 1, 102–5, 172–5). In France, Georges Pouchet, a French polygenist, issued a second edition of his *The Plurality of the Human Race* and among the changes was a new paragraph which made clear that evolution had become a genuine philosophic topic: "philosophy commences where science ends, and it belongs to it to give us an explanation of the matter." It was a question not just of the past, but of the future: "The genius of man has no bounds, who can say to what it may reach? Who knows whether, like a new Prometheus, a creator in his turn, he may not one day breathe life into some new species, which will suddenly appear from his laboratories?" (Pouchet 1864: 133). Perhaps because he was not persuaded that geology had yet resolved enough of the questions to leave the field open to the philosopher, he turned to studying the history of science and published a study of Aristotle's *De generatione animalium* (Pouchet 1885).

Clemence Royer, as the first French translator of Darwin's *Origin of Species*, supplied a long introduction that insisted that Darwin's theory of natural selection showed that the superior races would supplant the inferior races. In her view, Darwin had shown the equality of races to be a dangerous and impossible idea (Royer 1866: lvii). Royer's use of Darwin to advocate racial inequality is of particular interest because it provoked a strong response from Anténor Firmin, a Haitian member of the Société d'Anthropologie de Paris. Frederick Douglass had already addressed racial ethnology in 1854 (Douglass 1982), but Firmin's *The Equality of Human Races* was not only at that time the most detailed response by a Black thinker to White racial theories, but it is a philosophical statement of some significance in its own right. Firmin aligned himself with the positivist philosophy of Auguste Comte, sharing the latter's celebration of progress and perfectibility, and its conviction that racial differences were less salient than usually thought. But Firmin drew the implications of a belief in human progress for racial equality more clearly than anyone, including Comte himself. Whereas Comte called for "intimate cooperation" between the races, while still giving the leadership role to the Whites (Comte 1875: Vol. 2, 378), Firmin, while acknowledging the special role accorded to the advanced nations at any given time, believed every race had an historical role to play. In this respect, his work resembled the account found later in W. E. B. Du Bois's "The Conservation of Races," albeit Firmin seems to have believed in civilization as "common destiny" (Firmin 2000: 83).

Firmin was aware of the widespread conviction among Europeans that the "inferior races" were destined to die out and that for the sake of human progress exterminating them could sometimes be tolerated. For example, Alfred Russel Wallace already in 1864 argued that the law of "the preservation of favoured races in the struggle of our life" led to "the inevitable extinction of all those low and mentally underdeveloped populations with which Europeans come in contact" (Wallace 1864: clxiv-clxv). With the displacement of the lower races by the more intellectual and moral races, there would be continuing improvement until "the world is again inhabited by a single homogenous race" (Wallace 1864: clxix). That Wallace sought to reconcile Darwinism with a belief in the equality of the human races is historically significant. Firmin attempted to arrive at the same result but by emphasizing the influence of the environment, rather than natural selection, in the development of the human races.

Firmin's belief in the equality of the human races was a belief in the idea that under the right conditions all the races could attain the same high levels of virtue and intellectual development (Firmin 2000: 450). He denied that race should be understood in terms of permanent characteristics, a conception which led to ideas of destiny (Firmin 2000: 449). For him the only destiny is human perfectibility, which was why an exclusive focus on the accomplishments of the White race was misleading. His attempt to redress this imbalance led him to celebrate the contribution of Blacks to the history of civilization (Firmin 2000: 393–404).

Because discussions of evolution were concerned with how nature contributed to the making of races, it was inevitable that they would recognize that, once evolution had become conscious, human beings might dictate to nature at least in part the subsequent course of evolution, thus leading to eugenics. In *The Origin of Species* Darwin relied heavily on the evidence that the scientist would amass from the experience of animal breeding, and it is hardly surprising that this led to a heightened focus on the breeding of human races.

The term "eugenics" was coined by Francis Galton, Darwin's cousin, in 1883. By "eugenics" Galton meant the science of improving stock, both in the sense of "judicious mating" and taking "cognisanse of all influences that tend in however remote a degree to give to the more suitable races or strains of blood a better chance of prevailing speedily over the less suitable than they otherwise would have been" (Galton 1883: 24–5n). Although Galton was arguably more interested in class than race, he made a significant contribution to the understanding of race through his challenge to the notion of the inheritance of acquired characteristics, both physical and mental. With Galton race comes to be identified with nature and opposed to nurture. Galton defined the terms in this way: "Nature is all that a man brings with himself into the world; nurture is every influence from without that affects him after his birth" (Galton 1874: 12). The former includes the latent faculties of growth of body and mind; the latter includes "the environment in which the growth takes place, by which natural tendencies may be strengthened or thwarted, or wholly new ones implanted." Everything is hereditary (Cowan 1977: 176–7). The equation of race with nature prepared the way for the resolution that would emerge towards the middle of the twentieth century, in which anthropology would confine itself to culture, leaving race to biology, in the knowledge that biology had already renounced the concept as too imprecise to be useful (Bernasconi 2007a: 128–30).

Friedrich Nietzsche owned – and read – Galton's *Inquiries into Human Faculty and its Development* and at certain points there are clear resemblances in their positions (Moore 2002: 134–5, 145–6, 160–3), although Nietzsche tended to understand "breeding" indeterminately in both its moral as well as its biological sense, whereas Galton emphasized simple inheritance. Nietzsche seems not to have read Darwin at first hand and, not surprisingly, his polemic against Darwinism is marked by a number of misunderstandings, although it should be added that Darwin was at that time also misunderstood by many who had read him. Nevertheless, these misunderstandings are nothing compared with the widespread confusion about Nietzsche's ideas of race. There is still a tendency on the part of some commentators to describe Nietzsche's remarks on race as original or transgressive, whereas greater familiarity with the historical context challenges that perception (Schank 2000). For example, when Nietzsche referred to the Jews as "the strongest purest, most tenacious race living in Europe" and only four sentences later acknowledged that none of the European nations were yet a race because they were still in a state of becoming, this was not a unique perspective, but reminiscent of ideas we have already seen in Disraeli (Nietzsche 2002: 142). Similarly, when Nietzsche described the German people as composed of "the most enormous assortment and combination of races (perhaps even with a preponderance of the pre-Aryan element" (Nietzsche 2002: 135), he was merely taking sides in an ongoing debate in anthropology, not engaging in a novel deconstruction of racial concepts. Indeed, at one point he referred to Rudolf Virchow's study of the races of Germany that established this (Nietzsche 1989: 30; Ackerknecht 1953: 207–19).

Earlier, in 1878, Nietzsche had foreseen the abolition of European nations as a result of trade and industry and, in consequence, the production through continual crossing of a European mixed race. In spite of his complaint that Jews were "dangerous and repellent to an exceptional degree," Nietzsche thought they would be as "usable and desirable as an ingredient" of this European mixed race as any other national residue (Nietzsche 1986: 174–5). It was against this background that Nietzsche in an attack on anti-Semitism, proposed, in response to the desire of many Jews to be absorbed and assimilated into Europe, that they marry into the families of the "more strongly delineated types of new Germanism," the Prussian officers of noble rank (Nietzsche 2002: 143). These comments are an important corrective to the misuse subsequently made of his writings by the Nazis. However, his proposal that Jews marry into some of the best German families was far from being the transgressive gesture some commentators like to imagine it to be. Bismark famously proposed bringing together Christian stallions of German upbringing with Jewish mares (Busch 1878: II 218).

For Nietzsche race was fundamentally about inheritance: "it is utterly impossible that a person might *fail* to have the qualities and propensities of his elders and ancestors in his body." This led him in the same place to describe education and culture as the art of deception with its need "to deceive about lineage about the inherited vulgarity in body and soul" (Nietzsche 2002: 161). One can see here the impact on Nietzsche of the racial histories of the mid-nineteenth century. So in *On the Genealogy of Morals* he not only took Negroes as representatives of prehistoric man, but he also speculated that physiological inhibition might be traced back to such factors as the crossing of very different races and classes and the migration of races to climates for which they were not suited (Nietzsche 1989: 68 and 130). His belief that values are passed through the bloodline is reflected in his claim in *Beyond Good and Evil* that when races that had long been separated mix, the resulting hybrids are indecisive and lack a sense of balance. He applied this analysis to offer a diagnosis of contemporary Europe in terms of its "radical mixing of classes and *consequently* of races" (Nietzsche 2002: 100–1). Nevertheless, he shared with many of his contemporaries the idea that races are not given but made. That is why he insisted that "There are probably no pure races but only races that have become pure" (Nietzsche 1982: 149). Presenting himself as a philosopher of the future and contrasting himself with the English biologists, Nietzsche insisted that the focus should not be the persistence of a race or even the enhancement of its power to adapt to a certain climate: the task was to produce a stronger type (Nietzsche 1989: 55–6). For example, when in 1888 in *Twilight of the Idols* he proposed that doctors were morally obliged to suppress degenerate life so as to promote ascending life (Nietzsche 2005: 210), he was rehearsing the criticism of Darwin by contemporaries like W. H. Rolph where it was not about preserving what already existed, but creating or enhancing what was yet to be attained (Moore 2002: 46–55).

Conclusion

Today philosophers tend to view race in terms of its opposition to culture, an opposition that can readily be related to other familiar conceptual pairs: nature and history; what is inherited and what is acquired; body and mind; blood and spirit; and, in institutional terms, biology and anthropology. This approach may be popular among philosophers today, but historians of the nineteenth century are liable to judge it to be anachronistic for understanding the history of the concept of race, not only because the relation of biology and anthropology was very different then, but also because of the dominance within nineteenth-century science of the Lamarckian idea of the inheritance of acquired characteristics. It is no easy matter to separate the biological and cultural conceptions of race in the nineteenth century, and well into the twentieth century scientists found it hard to distinguish the influence of physical inheritance from the impact of environment (B. Schultz 2007: 120, 129; Cooke 1998: 267–8).

But this is not the only way in which readings of nineteenth-century philosophers of race tend to be anachronistic. We too easily forget that for most of the nineteenth century races tended not to be thought of as given by nature but as made by human intervention, largely through the policing of race mixing. Galton placed race on the side of nature, but in a sense he could only do so because his whole project was concerned with the influence that human beings themselves exercised on the formation of races through race mixing and emigration (Galton 1883: 308–17). The races were therefore even on this model a product of culture, including a culture either prohibiting or promoting race mixing, and it was this possibility that the African American philosopher Alain Locke explored in 1924 with his notion of "culture-heredity" (Locke 1989: 192; Bernasconi 2007a: 131).

Throughout the nineteenth century the idea of race was fundamentally always about race mixing. At the beginning of the century the possibility of race mixing established the unity of the human species. In mid-century, with the dominance of polygenesis, that was placed in doubt, and as a result races were also regarded as species, but in such a way that they could but should not mix. The medicalization of race mixing, particularly when it was united with Social Darwinism, led to segregation and apartheid, as well as laws against miscegenation and some of the uglier aspects of eugenics. But this was far from the end of the story. In spite of doubts about the scientific usefulness of the concept of race in the face of the complexity of the phenomena it was called upon to describe, during the first two decades of the twentieth century race science was at its most prolific and self-confident, particularly in Germany. It was a question of making the races conform to an ideal of purity that had come to be associated with strength, survival, and victory over other races.

The rediscovery of Gregor Mendel's theory of inheritance at the beginning of the twentieth century provided a fuller explanation of the problem of regressive traits that had already been observed, for example, by Spencer. The half-breed or blending theory proposed by Kant that had long been under strain finally had to be abandoned. This gave rise to a new account of race, according to which an inheritable variation, the so-called Mendelian trait, once introduced, cannot be bred out of a given population, and can only be eliminated by the death of those who carried it (Fischer 1916: 281). In the United States this led to increased anxiety about passing and thus to the one drop rule, which became law in some states in the late 1920s, but was already socially in effect a decade earlier. In Germany it led to a massive sterilization program which eventually gave way to a policy of extermination. Already in 1905 William Bateson, who would become recognized as one of the leading authorities on Mendelism, saw the writing on the wall. He posed the question: "What will happen when civilized society thoroughly grasps what heredity means?" His answer was that "in some country, at some time, not, perhaps, far distant, that power will be applied to control the composition of a nation" (Bateson 1926: 456, 459). The roots of that disaster were firmly planted in the nineteenth century and to this day it is shocking how few were the voices that were raised in an effort to halt what was coming. The study of the history of race thinking not only helps us understand our current intellectual problems by exposing their genealogy, but calls for greater scrutiny of current ideas on the topic and a suspicion of quick conceptual fixes.

References

Ackerknecht, E. (1953) *Rudolf Virchow*, Madison, WI: University of Wisconsin Press.
Appiah, K. A. (1992) *In My Father's House*, Oxford: Oxford University Press.
Arendt, H. (1979) *The Origins of Totalitarianism*, New York: Harcourt Brace.
Augstein, H. (1999) *James Cowles Prichard's Anthropology*, Amsterdam: Rodolpi.
Bateson, W. (1928) Review of G. Archdall Reid, *The Principles of Heredity*, in *William Bateson, Naturalist*, by B. Bateson: Cambridge: Cambridge University Press, pp. 456–9.
Bauer, B. (1853) *Russland und das Germanenthum*, Charlottesburg: Egbert Bauer.
Bernasconi, R. (1998) "Hegel at the Court of the Ashanti," in S. Barnett (ed.) *Hegel after Derrida*, London: Routledge, pp. 41–63.
—— (2000) "With What Must the Philosophy of World History Begin? On the Racial Basis of Hegel's Eurocentrism," *Nineteenth-Century Contexts* 22: 171–201.
—— (2001) "Who Invented the Concept of Race?" in R. Bernasconi (ed.) *Race*, Oxford: Blackwell.
—— (2005) "Why do the Happy Inhabitants of Tahiti Bother to Exist at All?" in J. Roth (ed.) *Genocide and Human Rights*, New York: Palgrave Macmillan, pp. 139–48.
—— (2006) "Kant and Blumenbach's Polyps," in S. Eigen and M. Larrimore (eds.) *The German Invention of Race*, Albany, NY: SUNY Press, pp. 73–90.
—— (2007a) "Ethnic Race," in J. Gracia (ed.) *Race or Ethnicity?* Ithaca, NY: Cornell University Press, pp. 123–36.
—— (2007b) "The Return of Africa: Hegel and the Question of the Racial Identity of the Egyptians," in P. Grier (ed.) *Identity and Difference*, Albany, NY: SUNY Press, pp. 201–16.
Biddiss, M. (1970) *Gobineau: Selected Political Writings*, New York: Harper & Row.
Blanckaert, C. (2003) "Of Monstrous Métis? Hybridity, Fear of Miscegenation and Patriotism from Buffon to Paul Broca," in S. Peabody and T. Stowall (eds) *The Color of Liberty*, Durham, NC: Duke University Press, pp. 42–70.
Blumenbach, J. (1797) *Handbuch der Naturgeschichte*, 5th edn, Göttingen: Johann Christian Dieterich.
—— (1865) *Anthropological Treatises*, trans. T. Bendyshe, London: Longman, Green, Longman, Roberts & Green.
Blyden, E. (1971) *Black Spokesman*, edited by H. Lynch, London: Frank Cass.
Buffon, G.-L. L., Comte de (1764) *Histoire naturelle*, vol. 12, Paris: Imprimière Royale.
—— (1766) *Histoire naturelle*, vol. 15, Paris: Imprimière Royale.
Busch, M. (1878) *Graf Bismarck und seine Leute*, 2 vols, Leipzig: Grunow.
Carlyle, T. (1849) "Occasional Discourse on the Negro Question," *Fraser's Magazine* 40: 670–9.
Carus, C. G. (1849) *Denkschrift zum Hundertjährigen Geburtsfeste Goethes*, Leipzig: Brockhaus.
Chamberlain, H. S. (1913) *Foundations of the Nineteenth Century*, 2 vols, London: John Lane.
—— (1914) *Immanuel Kant*, 2 vols, London: John Lane.
Cohen, H. (1880) *Ein Bekenntnis in der Judenfrage*, Berlin: Dümmler.
Comte, A. (1875) *System of Positive Polity*, trans. F. Harrison, 4 vols, London: Longman.
Cooke, K. J. (1998) "The Limits of Heredity: Nature and Nurture in American Eugenics before 1915," *Journal of the History of Biology* 31: 8, 263–78.
Courtet de l'Isle, V. (1838) *La science politique*, Paris: Arthur Betrand.
Cowan, R. S. (1977) "Nature and Nurture: The Interplay of Biology and Politics in the Work of Francis Galton," in W. Coleman and C. Limoges (eds.) *Studies in History of Biology*, vol. 1, Baltimore, MD: Johns Hopkins University Press, pp. 133–208.
Crummell, A. (1992) *Destiny and Race*, edited by W. J. Moses, Amherst, MA: University of Massachusetts Press.
Daniel, G. (2006) *Race and Multiraciality in Brazil and the United States*, University Park, PA: Pennsylvania State University Press.
d'Eichthal, G. (1839) *Lettres sur la race noire et la race blanche*, Paris: Paulin.

Disraeli, B. (1844) *Coningsby*, London: Henry Colburn, 3 vols.

—— (1852) *Lord George Bentinck: A Political Biography*, London: Colburn.

Douglass, F. (1886) "The Future of the Colored People," *North American Review* 134: 352, 437–40.

—— (1982) "The Claims of the Negro Ethnologically Considered" *Speeches, Debates, and Interviews*, vol. 2: 1847–54, edited by J. Blassingame, New Haven, CT: Yale University Press, pp. 497–525.

Du Bois, W. E. B. (1986) *Writings*, edited by N. Huggins, New York: Library of Liberal Arts.

Dühring, E. (1881): *Die Judenfrage als Racen-, Sitten- und Culturfrage*, Karlsruhe: H. Reuther.

Edwards, W. (1829) *Des caractères des races humaines*, Paris: Compère Jeune.

Eigen, S. (2006) "Policing the *Menschen=Racen*," in S. Eigen and M. Larrimore (eds.) *The German Invention of Race*, Albany, SUNY Press, pp. 185–202.

Firmin, A. (2000) *The Equality of Human Races*, New York: Garland.

Frank, J. (1784) *System einer vollständigen medicinischen Polizey*, 3rd edn, Vienna: Johann Thomas Edlen.

Fries, J. (1816) *Über die Gefährdung der Wohlstandes und Charakters der Deutschen durch die Juden*, Heidelberg: Mohr & Winter.

Galton, F. (1874) *English Men of Science*, London: Macmillan.

—— (1883) *Inquiries into Human Faculty and Its Development*, London: Macmillan.

Girtanner, C. (1796) *Über das Kantische Prinzip für das Naturgeschichte*, Göttingen: Vandenhoeck & Ruprecht.

Gobineau, A. de (1856): *The Moral and Intellectual Diversity of Races*, trans. H. Hotz, Philadelphia: J. B. Lippincott.

—— (1915) *The Inequality of Human Races*, trans. A. Collins, London: William Heinemann.

Godwyn, M. (1680) *The Negro's and Indians Advocate*, London.

Haeckel, E. (1903) *The History of Creation*, 2 vols, trans. E. R. Lankester, New York: Appleton.

Harris, M. (1968) *The Rise of Anthropological Theory*, New York: Harper & Row.

Hegel, G. W. F. (1956) *The Philosophy of History*, trans. J. Sibree, New York: Dover.

—— (1975) *Lecture on the Philosophy of World History*, trans. H. B. Nisbet, Cambridge: Cambridge University Press.

—— (1978) *Philosophy of Subjective Spirit*, edited by M. J. Petry, Dordrecht: Reidel.

—— (2007) *Lectures on the Philosophy of Spirit*, trans. R. Williams, Oxford: Oxford University Press.

Herder, J. (1800) *Outlines of a Philosophy of the History of Man*, trans. T. Churchill, London: J. Johnson.

Hess, M. (1918) *Rome and Jerusalem*, New York: Bloch.

Hoffheimer, M. (2000) "Hegel, Race, Genocide," in T. Nenon (ed.) *The Contemporary Relevance of Hegel's Philosophy of Right, Southern Journal of Philosophy* 39 (suppl.): 35–62.

—— (2005) "Race and Law in Hegel's Philosophy of Religion," in A. Valls (ed.) *Race and Racism in Modern Philosophy*, Ithaca: Cornell University, pp. 194–216.

Hoffman, F. (1896) *Race Traits and Tendencies of the American Negro*, New York: Macmillan.

Home, H. Lord Kames (1774) *Sketches of the History of Man*, 2 vols, Edinburgh: Creech.

Jahn, F. (1884) *Werke*, edited by C. Euler, 3 vols, Hof: G. A. Grau.

Kant, I. (1987) *Critique of Judgment*, trans. W. Pluhar, Indianapolis, IN: Hackett.

—— (1995) *Political Writings*, trans. H. Nisbet, Cambridge: Cambridge University Press.

—— (2000) "Of the Different Human Races," in R. Bernasconi and T. Lott (eds) *The Idea of Race*, Indianapolis, IN: Hackett, pp. 8–22.

—— (2001) "On the Use of Teleological Principles in Philosophy," in R. Bernasconi (ed.) *Race*, Oxford: Blackwell.

Klatt, N. (2007) "Einleitung" in F. W. P. Dougherty (ed.) *The Correspondence of Johann Friedrich Blumenbach*, vol. 2: 1783–5, Göttingen: Norbert Klatt, pp. viii–xxx.

Klemm, G. (1843) *Allgemeine Cultur-Geschichte der Menschheit*, vol. 1, Leipzig: Teubner.

Knox, R. (1850) *The Races of Men*, London: Henry Renshaw.

Lamarck, J.-B. (1984) *Zoological Philosophy*, trans. H. Elliot, Chicago: University of Chicago Press.

La Peyrere, I. (1655) *A Theological Systeme upon That Presupposition That Men Were before Adam*, London.

Locke, A. (1989) *The Philosophy of Alain Locke*, edited by L. Harris, Philadelphia: Temple University Press.

Lynch, J. (2006) *Simón Bolívar*, New Haven, CT: Yale University Press.

Marrus, M. R. (1971) *The Politics of Assimilation*, Oxford: Oxford University Press.

Martinez, M. (2004) "The Black Blood of New Spain," in *The William and Mary Quarterly* 61: 3, 479–519.

Menzel, W. (1835) *Geist der Geschichte*, Stuttgart: Liesching.

Mill, J. S. (1963) *The Earlier Letters of John Stuart Mill 1812–1848*, edited by F. Mineka, Toronto: Toronto University Press, 2 vols.

—— (1972) *The Last Letters of John Stuart Mill 1849–1873*, edited by F. Mineka and D. Lindley, 4 vols, Toronto: Toronto University Press.

—— (1977) *Essays on Politics and Society*, edited by J. M. Robson, 2 vols, Toronto: Toronto University Press.

—— (1984) *Essays on Equality, Law and Education*, edited by J. M. Robson, Toronto: Toronto University Press.

—— (1985) *Essays on French History and Historians*, edited by J. M. Robson, Toronto: Toronto University Press.

Miller, K. (1897) *A Review of Hoffman's Race Traits and Tendencies of the American Negro*, Washington, DC: American Negro Academy.

Mitchell, J. (1745) "An Essay upon the Causes of the different Colours of People in different Climates," in *Philosophical Transactions* 43: 102–50.

Moore, G. (2002) *Nietzsche, Biology and Metaphor*, Cambridge: Cambridge University Press.

Nietzsche, F. (1982) *Daybreak*, trans. R. J. Hollingdale, Cambridge: Cambridge University Press.

—— (1986) *Human All Too Human*, trans. R. J. Hollingdale, Cambridge: Cambridge University Press.

—— (1989) *On the Genealogy of Morals*, trans. W. Kaufmann, New York: Vintage.

—— (2002) *Beyond Good and Evil*, edited by R.-P. Horstmann and J. Norman. Cambridge: Cambridge University Press.

—— (2005) *The Anti-Christ, Ecce Homo, Twilight of the Idols*, edited by A. Ridley and J. Norman, Cambridge: Cambridge University Press.

Nott, J. (1843) "The Mulatto a Hybrid," *American Journal of the Medical Sciences* 6: 252–6.

Nott, J., and G. Gliddon (eds) (1854) *Types of Mankind*, Philadelphia: Lippincott, Grambo.

Peters, C. (1883) *Willenswelt und Weltwille*, Leipzig: Brockhaus.

Popkins, R. (1980) "The Philosophical Basis of Modern Racism," in *The High Road to Pyrrhonism*, San Diego: Austin Hill, pp. 79–102.

Pouchet, G. (1864) *The Plurality of the Human Race*, trans. H. Beavan, London: Longman.

—— (1885) *La biologie Aristotélique*, Paris: Félix Alcan.

Prichard, J. (1813) *Researches into the Physical History of Mankind*, 1st edn, London: John & Arthur Arch.

—— (1826) *Researches into the Physical History of Mankind*, 2nd edn, 2 vols, London: John & Arthur Arch.

—— (1836) *Researches into the Physical History of Mankind*, 3rd edn, 5 vols, London: Sherwood, Gilbert & Piper.

Renan, E. (1947) "Histoire générale et système comparé des langues sémitiques" in *Oeuvres complètes*, vol. 8, edited by H. Psichari, Paris: Calmann-Lévy.

Rose, P. (1990) *German Question/Jewish Question*, Princeton, NJ: Princeton University Press.

Royer, C. (1866) "Préface de la première édition," in *De l'origine des espèces par Charles Darwin*, Paris: Charles Masson, pp. xv–lix.

Schank, G. (2000) *"Rasse" und "Züchtung" bei Nietzsche*, Berlin: Walter de Gruyter.

Schelling, F. (1927) *Werke*, edited by M. Schröker, Munich: Beck.

—— (2004) *First Outline of a System of the Philosophy of Nature*, trans. K. R. Peterson, Albany, NY: SUNY Press.

Schultz, B. (2007): "Mill and Sedgwick, Imperialism and Racism," *Utilitas* 19: 1, 104–30.

Schultz, F. (1875) *Kant und Darwin*, Jena: Hermann Dufft.

Sidgwick, H. (1891) *The Elements of Politics*, London: Macmillan.

Smith, S. H. (1787) *An Essay on the Causes of the Variety of Complexion and Figure in the Human Species*, Philadelphia: Aitken.

—— (1810) *An Essay on the Causes of the Variety of Complexion and Figure of the Human Species*, New Brunswick: Simpson.

Spencer, H. (1858) "Personal Beauty," in *Essays: Scientific, Political and Speculative*, London: Longman, pp. 417–29.

Unold, J. (1886) *Die Ethnologischen und anthropogeographischen Anschauungen bei I. Kant und J Reinh. Forster*, Leipzig: Dietzsche Hofbuchdruckerei.

Voltaire, F.-M. (2000) "Of the Different Races of Men" in R. Bernasconi and T. Lott (ed.) *The Idea of Race*, Indianapolis, IN: Hackett.

Waitz, T. (1863) *Introduction to Anthropology*, trans. J. Collingwood, London: Longman, Green, Longman & Roberts.

Wallace, A. R. (1864) "The Origin of Human Races," in *Journal of the Anthropological Society of London* 2: clviii–clxxxvii.

Further reading

R. Bernasconi, *Concepts of Race in Eighteenth Century*, 8 vols (Bristol: Thoemmes, 2001), has photomechanical reprints of some of the key original texts for the introduction of a science of race, including those by Kant, Blumenbach, and Girtanner; *American Theories of Polygenesis*, 7 vols (Bristol: Thoemmes, 2002), includes Nott and Gliddon's *Types of Mankind* and Nott's edition of Gobineau's *Essay*; and *Race and Anthropology*, 9 vols (Bristol: Thoemmes, 2003), includes photomechanical reprints of the original editions of the texts cited above by Pouchet, Firmin, and Wallace, among many others. Highlights the role of Nott and responses by African Americans to the miscegenation debate are found in R. Bernasconi and K. Dotson (eds) *Race, Hybridity, and Miscegenation*, 3 vols (Bristol: Thoemmes, 2005). R. Bernasconi and T. Lott (eds) *The Idea of Race* (Indianapolis, IN: Hackett, 2000), includes extracts from Kant, Blumenbach, Hegel, Gobineau, Darwin, Galton, and Du Bois, among others. See also M. Foucault, *Society Must Be Defended*, trans. D. Macey (New York: Picador, 2001). Foucault's apparent ignorance about the history of race thinking surfaces at various points, but the notion of biopower elaborated here is indispensable. By focusing on the material available in English, the survey, I. Hannaford, *Race: The History of an Idea in the West* (Baltimore, MD: Johns Hopkins University Press, 1996), lacks balance. A number of the essays address the place of race among the utilitarians in B. Schultz and G. Varouxakis (eds) *Utilitarianism and Empire* (Lanham, MD: Lexington, 2005). N. Stepan, *The Idea of Race in Science* (Hamden, CT: Archon, 1982), offers a good survey, but it largely focuses on Britain between 1800 and 1960. E. Voegelin, *The History of the Race Idea: From Ray to Carus* (Baton Rouge: Louisiana State University Press, 1998), is the most philosophical of the histories of race, but focuses mainly on the late eighteenth century. R. J. C. Young, *Colonial Desire: Hybridity in Theory, Culture and Race* (London: Routledge, 1995), highlights the crucial relation of race to sexuality.

18
PSYCHOLOGY AND PHILOSOPHY

Gary Hatfield

Psychology studies the mind and its operations, including sense perception, action, imagination, attention, and thought. Philosophers and scientists have studied such psychological phenomena since the time of the ancient Greeks. The nineteenth century was an important period in the development of psychology. As the century opened, psychology was mainly studied either within medical physiology or as a part of philosophy. By the end of the century, psychology was on the way to establishing itself in university departments as an experimental natural science. The new experimental psychology appropriated the experimental techniques of sensory physiology and the empirical observations and theoretical constructs of philosophical psychology.

In order to understand the development of psychology during the nineteenth century, we must consider psychology during the eighteenth century, when it separated itself from the study of living things in general and became a specialized discipline of its own. In the mid-eighteenth century, several thinkers, both philosophers and medical physiologists, proposed that psychology should be a natural science. They meant that psychology should use careful observations, including some quantitative observations, to study the phenomena of mind and chart the laws of such phenomena. At this time, most authors classified psychological phenomena as products of various mental faculties or mental powers, including sensory capacities, imagination, and memory. Over the course of the century, theorists came more and more to emphasize the laws of association as explanatory factors within psychology. According to such laws, the contents of mental states become "associated" so that, subsequently, when one occurs (in thought or sensation) the other comes forth through association. The law of contiguity says that sensations or ideas that are constantly conjoined (spatially or temporally) in experience become associated; the law of similarity says that sensations or ideas with resembling content become associated. At the start of the nineteenth century, some theorists proposed resolving all psychological phenomena into the laws of association and foregoing any talk of faculties.

During the nineteenth century, psychological thought developed in several distinct contexts. Within the universities, psychology was taught as a distinct subject matter in the faculty (or school) of philosophy. German philosophical psychology often situated itself in relation to the thought of Immanuel Kant, although alternative viewpoints soon arose. Also at universities, but within the medical faculty, physiologists continued to work on the physiology and psychology of sensorimotor and mental functions. Sensory physiologists, together with some physicists, invented sophisticated laboratory techniques for measuring sensory phenomena (especially visual phenomena) and for testing theories. Initially in Germany, this work was synthesized into a new, self-avowedly "scientific" and ultimately "experimental" psychology.

Outside the universities, the work of Herbert Spencer and Charles Darwin provided a new impetus for allying psychological thought with biology. Spencer's *Principles of Psychology* offered a view of the mind as a faculty for adapting the organism to its environment. Darwin applied evolutionary thinking especially to the emotions. The work of these "gentleman scholars" soon had an impact within the universities. In Germany, the sensory physiologist Ewald Hering immediately applied Darwinian thinking to the senses. In Britain and America, Darwin's evolutionary psychology was taken up and developed into a comprehensive outlook toward psychological phenomena.

In the latter part of the nineteenth century, the new experimental psychology gained recognition as a distinct subject matter in German and American universities. The new discipline found especially fertile soil in North America, where by the beginning of the twentieth century forty-two universities and colleges had founded psychological laboratories in the arts and sciences faculty. The discipline continued to grow in North American universities, but it took longer to establish itself in Germany, Britain, and France. Indeed, in the early decades of the twentieth century some German authors were proclaiming a "crisis" in psychology concerning its ability to become a natural science while also addressing central aspects of human thought (Ash 1991). In institutional terms, European psychology gained a similar status to American psychology only after the Second World War.

In subsequent sections, this chapter first enlarges on psychology in the eighteenth century. It then recounts developments within German psychology, British psychology, evolutionary psychology, and American psychology, followed by a discussion of introspective methods in the laboratory. The final three sections discuss conflicting opinions on the existence of unconscious mental states, review relations between philosophy and psychology, and survey the state of psychology in the early twentieth century.

Psychology before 1800

As a discipline taught in school, psychology arose in Aristotle's curriculum as the study of the soul (*psyche, anima*). The Aristotelian conception of the soul included vegetative (nutritive and reproductive), sensitive (sensorimotor: perception and action), and rational aspects. Aristotle grouped the study of such phenomena within the larger discipline of physics, broadly defined as the study of nature in general. Accordingly, Aristotelian psychology entered the European universities during the middle ages as a branch of physics, a position that it retained in the standard university curriculum into the eighteenth century. This Aristotelian discipline of psychology had a broader scope than later psychology, because it included vital or biological aspects as well as sensorimotor and rational aspects. All the same, the focus in this psychology was on the cognitive and appetitive functions of the soul, as found within the sensitive and the rational powers.

The term "psychology" first appeared in print (in Latin and Greek) during the sixteenth century, as a name for this Aristotelian discipline (Lapointe 1972). "Psychology" became fixed in its modern meaning during the eighteenth century, especially after the German philosopher Christian Wolff published textbooks (1732, 1734) separating psychology from biology and restricting its purview to sensory, cognitive, and appetitive (emotional and volitional) phenomena. Wolff's follower, Michael Christoph Hanov, sealed this distinction by using the term *biologia* for the science of life as distinct from the science of the soul (Hanov 1766). Especially in German-speaking lands, the second half of the eighteenth century saw the establishment of regular courses in empirical and rational (i.e. theoretical) psychology, and thus the production of numerous textbooks in the subject. Scottish universities also often taught psychological subject matter, but usually under another title, such as "philosophy of the mind." As the eighteenth century progressed, physics came more and more to be equated with its later, narrower meaning – as mechanics and allied sciences, such as optics, astronomy, and hydrostatics – and psychology sought another disciplinary home. It was sometimes treated as a science coordinate with physics, sometimes as a part of metaphysics, and sometimes, especially in Scotland, as a "moral" science, that is, pertaining to the nature of human beings (Hatfield 1995).

From around 1750, many authors proposed that the science of mind or soul should become an empirical natural science. These included the English physician David Hartley (1749), the Swiss naturalist Charles Bonnet (1755), the French physician Guillaume-Lambert Godart (1755), and the German physician Johann Gottlob Krüger (1756). Hartley placed "psychology," or the theory "of the human mind" and "of the intellectual principles of brute animals" within natural philosophy, along with mechanics and the like (1749: 354). He elaborated an associationist psychology based in the physiology of neural vibrations, in which nerve fibers that vibrate together on one occasion are more likely to vibrate together on another occasion, so that a few vibrating fibers can set the other (associated fibers) in motion. Without denying that the vibrations act on an immaterial soul, Hartley attributed all psychological operations, including rational choice, to associations established through neural vibrations. Bonnet also developed a psychology of association as depending on neural vibrations, but he differed from Hartley in granting to the soul the ability to affect the vibrations through psychological functions such as attention. Godart, by contrast, worked within an Aristotelian framework, treating the soul as a vivifying principle responsible for vital, animal, and intellectual functions. His approach was "physical" in that he treated the soul not according to its substance, a topic that he relegated to pneumatology (the science of spirits), nor according to the merit of its actions (which belongs to morals), but in relation to its bodily operations. Krüger sought to justify an "experimental" psychology, by which he meant a psychology based on controlled observation and mathematical description. He used clinical observations from brain-damaged patients to examine theories of normal psychological function. Despite the real differences among these authors, the topics covered in their psychologies were remarkably similar: sensory, cognitive, and appetitive functions, as divided into further categories such as the external senses, bodily motion, passions or emotions, imagination, memory, will, and reason or intellect.

Although the discipline of psychology remained within the arts faculty in the eighteenth century (as also today), many of its advocates were trained in medicine (as were Hartley, Godart, and Krüger). The empirical study of mental phenomena in connection with the nervous system had been a part of medicine from antiquity, and it continued to be so throughout the nineteenth century, as it remains today. As medical thinkers developed empirical and experimental techniques for studying physiology, they included sensory and behavioral functions within their ambit. In antiquity, Galen performed an experiment on instinct by delivering a goat through cesarean section and finding that, in the absence of contact with its mother, it immediately chose a bowl of milk over other comestibles (reported in E. Darwin 1794–6: Vol. 1: 142). During the eighteenth century, physicians offered clinical observations that they or others used to support theoretical accounts of visual perception. In 1728, the English physician William Cheselden reported observations on a newly sighted blind person, which observations were deemed to support Molyneux's and Locke's speculations that such a person would lack form and distance perception (Degenaar 1996). The Scottish physician William Porterfield published an anatomical and physiological treatise on the eye in 1759, in which he ascribed binocular single vision to innate anatomical structures, discussed spatial perception in detail, and contradicted Locke and Molyneux on the newly sighted blind.

During the eighteenth century, some philosophers located explanations for human belief and conduct in a naturalistic psychology of association. Among the best known are David Hume (1739–40) and the French philosopher Etienne Bonnot de Condillac (1754). Hume's associationism was more influential for some nineteenth-century authors, such as Thomas Brown, than was Hartley's. Condillac's famous statue-come-to-life captured the imagination of many subsequent authors. Condillac modeled human psychological and cognitive development by imagining that his statue was awakened through its sense perceptions, acquiring one sensory modality at a time (starting with smell). His naturalistic approach to human belief and conduct inspired the French "Ideologues," including the physician Pierre Cabanis (1802), who developed a monistic vitalism, and the philosophers Destutt de Tracy (1817) and Maine de Biran (1803), the latter of whom ultimately rejected organic vitalism for dualism so as to account for the activity of the self in free will.

Psychological topics were also addressed in the science of optics. From antiquity into the eighteenth century, "optics" was the discipline that investigated the sense of vision as a whole, including mathematical, anatomical, physiological, and psychological aspects. During the eleventh century, the Arabic-speaking author Ibn al-Haytham (1989) combined mathematical, medical, and natural philosophical approaches to vision in a comprehensive treatise, which covered the cognitive aspects of the perception of colors, spatial properties, and other properties of objects. He used mathematics (in the form of geometry) not only in analyzing the propagation of light in physical media and its reception by the eyes, but also in examining the perception of distance, size, and shape, thereby applying mathematics to psychological topics. Optical theory, conceived as a theory of vision, was pursued in the Latin middle ages by Roger Bacon, John Pecham, and Witelo (Lindberg 1976). Although optics itself was typically classified as a "mixed mathematical science," and so was ranged under mathematics rather than natural philosophy, optical content made its way into commentaries on Aristotle's *De anima* and so into the ambit of natural philosophy (Hatfield 1998b).

In the seventeenth century, Descartes published a *Dioptrics* that was both natural philosophical and mathematical, including extensive analyses of the perception of size and distance, and his followers discussed these topics in the psychological portions of their physics textbooks (Hatfield 2005b). Early in the eighteenth century, the Irish philosopher George Berkeley denounced the theoretical practice of imputing to the mind unnoticed geometrical operations in the visual perception of size, shape, and distance. His *Essay towards a New Theory of Vision* (1709) provided an associationist account in which touch educates vision. Berkeley held that, originally, our visual experience does not include distance but our tactual ideas do. Through touching or walking to visual objects, associative (or "suggestive") connections form, so that visual ideas incorporate tactual ideas of distance and solidity. Berkeley's theory was widely discussed and frequently adopted, but some also dissented. The English "experimental philosopher" Robert Smith published a two-volume work on optics, focusing on mathematical and physical aspects of light, microscopes and telescopes, and astronomical observations. It also contained a "popular" treatise on how vision works, which explained distance perception through variations in apparent size: a larger size, as determined by visual angle, indicates a closer distance (unaided by tactual ideas). This treatise offered an account of the moon illusion, which occurs when the horizon moon appears larger than does the moon when overhead (Smith 1738: §§164–9). Smith measured the way observers experience the shape of the vault of the sky. He found that they experience it as flattened rather than truly hemispherical. Accordingly, the moon illusion arises because observers perceive the moon as following this flattened path, which makes it appear farther away and so larger at the horizon (assuming it subtends a constant visual angle). Smith (1738: Remarks 333–43) distinguished his account from that of Berkeley, who proposed that the horizon moon is perceived as larger when the comparatively greater extent of intervening atmosphere makes it appear dimmer, since, in his theory, comparative dimness directly indicates greater size if "visible magnitude" (or visual angle) is held constant.

At the close of the eighteenth century, psychology as a discipline was taught in the arts faculty, and was especially well represented in German-speaking lands, as can be seen by the large number of university courses and textbooks. Indeed, the first appointment of a professor of psychology may have been Jacob Friedrich Abel, during the 1780s at the Karlsschule in Stuttgart (during its brief history as a university). Abel's (1786) textbook surveyed the normal range of eighteenth-century psychological topics, including the existence and immateriality of the soul, the senses, imagination, attention, thought, feeling, will, and bodily motion. He excluded the problem of mind–body interaction from psychology as a metaphysical question that was empirically intractable. As was often the case in psychology manuals, he showed awareness of a wider body of literature, including optical experiments such as that of Patrick d'Arcy to determine the duration during which visual impressions in the retina remain before fading – although he provided no reference to show how he became aware of d'Arcy's result, which was widely cited (Hatfield 1995: 210, 216).

Carl C. E. Schmid's textbook contained a lengthy bibliography of "psychological literature" (1796: 142–56), both in the original languages of Latin, French, German, and English and in German or Latin translation. His section on "general psychology" included, in a subsection on human nature in general, the works by Wolff, Hartley, Bonnet, Krüger, and Abel that I have mentioned and many others as well, including German translations of Hartley and Hume. A subsection on the "faculty of knowledge" listed two translations of Locke's *Essay Concerning Human Understanding*, further translations of Hume's works, Leibniz's *Nouveaux Essays*, another edition of Hartley, and a translation of Condillac. Another subsection contained works on the relation between mind and body – also known as "anthropological" writings because they treated the whole human being (body and soul) – and included works in medical physiology, by Albrecht von Haller, Johann Friedrich Blumenbach, and Samuel Sömmerring, among others, as well as Godart's book as mentioned above and a second reference to Bonnet's writings; the bibliography contained several other subsections as well. Schmid's work is representative of the state of German scholarship at the time, in which his readers could be assumed to read Latin and French if not English, the latter deficiency often remedied by the translation of English-language works into German. It also reveals the connection between psychology and medical physiology, which consisted mainly, but not exclusively, in the citation of basic anatomical and physiological findings in the psychological literature.

Psychology in German-speaking lands

As the nineteenth century opened, Kant's influence and legacy loomed large in psychological discussions in German-speaking lands, as it did throughout much of the nineteenth century. Philosophers, psychologists, and sensory physiologists made conflicting claims about Kant's relation to psychology and about the relevance of psychological considerations in evaluating or replacing Kant's epistemological system.

Early in the century, several philosophers addressed what they perceived to be the psychological basis of Kant's critical philosophy. Jakob Friedrich Fries contended that Kant had intentionally made psychology the basis for his epistemological findings about the scope and limits of human knowledge. In Fries's estimation, Kant's basis was inadequate and he sought to replace it with a better one. Scholars still disagree over how Kant intended to support his "transcendental" claim that the law of cause is a synthetic *a priori* principle that applies to all experience with necessity and universality (Anderson 2001). Kant's justifications appealed to mental structures and processes, such as space and time as "forms of intuition," and to the categories as *a priori* concepts that serve to unify our sensory experience according to principles such as the law of cause.

Fries (1807) contended that such transcendental claims need not achieve the status of "proofs" but can be justified through an "exposition" of the principles of thought that starts from the "fact" of our knowledge. Fries's "exposition" is psychological in that it seeks to explain the empirically given fact of our knowledge of, say, geometry by positing causally described mental structures and processes. These structures and processes were counterparts to Kant's forms of intuition and processes of judgment. Fries then used this empirically grounded transcendental theory of the mind to account for other domains of knowledge, including geometry and philosophical or metaphysical principles such as the law of cause. In the end, by basing his arguments on the "facts" of consciousness, Fries arrived at a subjective idealism that restricted each individual's knowledge to the contents of their own consciousness – a position that Kant would have rejected, as did most of Fries's contemporaries. Nonetheless, Fries rendered prominent the question of how Kantian epistemology, or epistemology in general, is related to empirical psychology.

Johann Friedrich Herbart also believed that Kant's critical philosophy ultimately rested on psychology, but he considered this to be a failing. Herbart (1813) developed a conception of philosophy as the "reworking" of concepts that describe the fundamental "givens" of experience – initially, a spatio-temporal world of objects undergoing alterations. Philosophy takes such concepts as "cause" and "space" and reworks them into a self-consistent whole, which then constitutes a foundational metaphysics for the other disciplines, including psychology. Rejecting the transcendental idealism of Kant, Herbart believed that his metaphysics provided a description of things as they are in themselves. These things in themselves, or "Reals," are simple substances, akin to Leibnizian monads but differing from them because they are in causal interaction. Such causal interactions provide the basis for and are described by the continuous space of geometry as applied physically to the world as it is in itself.

Starting from his metaphysics, Herbart (1816, 1824–5) sought to develop a natural-scientific psychology. The fundamental entities in his psychology were soul-Reals, which are simple substances endowed with perception. Herbart rejected innate conceptual structures and mental faculties. Originally, a soul-Real experiences only a single quality at a time, which has intensity but no spatial structure. He deemed such experienced qualities *Vorstellungen* or representations. The representations experienced by a given soul-Real change due to its causal interactions with other Reals. Herbart developed a mathematical mental-mechanics to describe the interaction of successive representations within a soul and momentary interactions among various representations that "strive" to enter consciousness simultaneously (arising from multiple causal interactions with other Reals). As hitherto unconscious representations seek to enter consciousness at the same time, they may "fuse" or become associated. Through such interactions, all forms of representation, including spatiality, and all psychological structures and capacities arise. Herbart founded all psychology on his mental mechanics.

Herbart's program was not adopted in its details, even if it encouraged subsequent applications of mathematical description in psychology. His postulation of interactions among unconscious sensory representations was influential. Finally, his psychology and metaphysics highlighted the question of how spatial representations might originate from a presumed basis of nonspatial sensory representations, a question that came to dominate psychological, metaphysical, and epistemological discussions of spatial perception in Germany for a period (Hatfield 1990: Chs 4–5).

German philosophical psychology remained robust throughout the nineteenth century (Sachs-Hombach 1993). Some authors were inspired by Herbart, such as F. E. Beneke, Theodor Waitz, and the young Wilhelm Wundt. Hegel's discussions of the unfolding of the world spirit, in which he portrayed the reciprocal interactions between sensory and conceptual mental structures, made assumptions and assertions about such structures without intending to present a natural scientific or "empirical" psychology (an enterprise that he shunned). The German philosophers who had the most impact on subsequent psychology and on the relations between philosophy and psychology were those who interacted with and even contributed to the ongoing work in sensory physiology and psychology.

German sensory physiology was a vigorous field of research and writing. In the first half of the century, original contributions came from physicians working on their own, as in the case of Johann Georg Steinbuch in Hildesheim or Caspar Theobald Tourtual in Münster, or in connection with university research groups, such as that of Johannes Müller and his students in Berlin. After mid-century, such contributions were more likely to come from medically trained sensory physiologists who held university appointments, which might be in physiology, as with Hermann Helmholtz and Ewald Hering, or in philosophy, as with Gustav Fechner and R. H. Lotze, or in physiology and then philosophy, as with Wundt.

German sensory physiology was important for the development of psychology in several ways. First, this work continued to show that systematic observation and precise experimental methods could be marshaled to support psychological theories. The types of observations included clinical reports of visual deficits (such as the effect of strabismus or squint on binocular single vision) but also, and increasingly after mid-century, experiments involving quantitative measure. The most renowned applications of quantitative techniques were by E. H. Weber and Fechner, who developed generalizations about sensory acuity that related stimulus values, especially intensities such as weight, loudness, and brightness, to the resulting sensations. They used a method of "just noticeable differences" in stimulus magnitude in assessing acuity. This approach, called "psychophysics," was by no means the only sort of experimental work on sensory perception. Wundt, Helmholtz, and Hering made experimental observations on visual experience of depth, which related physical locations to experienced locations. Helmholtz and Hering performed experiments on the perception of color (Turner 1994). In the last quarter of the century, many areas were subject to experimental research, including attention, memory, and word recognition. The experimental techniques included, in Wundt's laboratory, the measurement of reaction times in order to identify various stages in psychological processes (Robinson 2001).

Second, German sensory physiology and psychology reached a high level of theoretical development. There were several theoretical questions at stake, including the relation between neural activity and sensations (experienced qualities); the basis for spatial perception (whether innate or acquired); the types of processes involved in the perception (judgmental or associative); and the epistemological significance of perception (whether it reveals the real world or is merely subjective).

Steinbuch (1811) adopted a radical *empirism*, which holds that even the bare form of spatial representation is acquired as a result of fetal motions in utero. Steinbuch accepted the common (but not universal) assumption that each sensory nerve fiber produces a single sensation. But he rejected the view that these sensations are naturally ordered in the same spatial arrangement as the nerves themselves, so that the fibers leading from the skin or the retina would naturally produce a two-dimensional spatial mosaic of sensations (on the assumption that epidermal and retinotopic order are preserved as nerves enter the brain). Rather, Steinbuch regarded the ability to represent space as a product of learning, in which the motor commands that govern the motions of the limbs provide the initial spatial framework for the sense of touch (developed in utero) and the motor commands that control eye-motion develop into a two-dimensional visual representation. He also ascribed to learning the subsequent mapping of external world locations into this two-dimensional visual matrix and the yet further ability to perceive depth and distance through the usual cues (accommodation, convergence, known size, intermediate ground intervals, atmospheric perspective, and clarity of details). In this way, perceptual space develops so as to produce an experienced copy of real space. Steinbuch believed that he had refuted Kant's nativist account of spatial perception as well as Kant's idealism – but one may question whether the Kantian *a priori* should be equated with the psychologically innate and also whether Steinbuch provided adequate arguments for his realism (Hatfield 1990: Chs 3–4).

Tourtual (1827) agreed with Steinbuch's basic assumption that each nerve fiber produces a single sensation, which, in the case of vision, would vary in quality and intensity (color and brightness). But he posited an innate mechanism for ordering nonspatial sensations into two-dimenaional spatial representations. He maintained that the perception of distance is partly innate (depending on accommodation) and partly learned (using the usual cues). He assumed that spatial representation gives us the world of things as they are, but he merely asserted a kind of common sense realism in opposition to Kantian idealism, without attempting to argue for his position.

By contrast, Müller (1833–7) held to a more traditional position regarding visual sensation, according to which vision innately begins from a two-dimensional spatial representation. In effect, he held that the mind "feels" the spatial extension of the retina (or of a corresponding sheet of neurons in the brain). From there, distance perception is learned through the usual cues. Müller receives credit for proposing the law of specific nerve energies, according to which each type of nerve fiber produces its own characteristic type of sensation, no matter what the external stimulus might be. Thus, fibers in the optic nerve always produce sensations of color and brightness, even if their retinal terminals are stimulated by pressure, or cold, or electricity, or in any other manner. In fact, Müller merely made this principle prominent; previously, Descartes had explicitly affirmed it and most sensory physiologists held to it, at least tacitly (Hatfield 2000). In philosophy, Müller followed Herbart's brand of realism, starting from basic concepts found in experience and then speculatively applying those concepts to form a consistent picture of reality.

The theoretical development of German sensory physiology and psychology continued in the work of Lotze, Wundt, Helmholtz, and Hering. Lotze advanced the analysis of spatial perception in his *Medicinische Psychologie* (1852). Wundt (1862) and Helmholtz (1867) drew especially on the associationist tradition in developing their accounts of spatial perception, although Wundt came to believe that associationist explanations were not adequate for higher cognition. Hering (1861–4), who was trained by Weber and Fechner, was less tied to traditional psychological theory and saw the limits of associationism more quickly than did Wundt.

Finally, sensory physiology helped to develop psychology by drawing attention to the manner in which psychological research might be relevant to philosophical questions. Certainly Müller, Steinbuch, Tourtual, and many subsequent theorists, including Helmholtz, Wundt, and Ernst Mach, affirmed the relevance of sensory physiology and psychology for epistemology. The extent to which they fell prey to the supposed fallacy of "psychologism" will be taken up in a subsequent section.

German psychology was by no means limited to sensory perception. From the 1880s onward, work on attention, memory, and motor reaction expanded vigorously. Wundt's Leipzig laboratory, founded in 1879, served as a haven for experimental work. Wundt had furthered the disciplinary basis of physiological, or experimental, psychology by publishing his *Grundzüge der physiologischen Psychologie* in 1874. In the subsequent four decades, he oversaw the laboratory, supervised many doctoral dissertations in both psychology and philosophy, and published voluminously on a wide range of psychological and philosophical topics. In the 1860s, Wundt had suggested that the higher cognitive functions can be studied through their objective cultural products, including language, literature, myth, and the historical record. During the 1880s, he was convinced that higher cognitive functions are unsuited to experimental study and should be studied through their cultural products in what he called *Völkerpsychologie*, a term variously translated as "ethnopsychology," "psychology of peoples," and "social psychology." Whereas the early Wundt of the 1860s had seen psychology as a natural science, by 1874 he viewed it as occupying a middle ground between the natural sciences and the *Geisteswissenschaften* ("social," "moral," or "human" sciences), adopting the methods of the former but serving to ground the subject matter of the latter. Subsequently, he assigned psychology to the *Geisteswissenschaften* alone, while acknowledging that in its experimental portion it still drew on the methods of the natural sciences. Throughout this period, and certainly from 1874 onward, Wundt never doubted that psychology was and should be an autonomous discipline distinct from philosophy, even as he argued in the early decades of the twentieth century that, for pragmatic, academic-political reasons, it should remain administratively tied to philosophy (Hatfield 1997).

In 1883, Wundt's laboratory became the Institute for Experimental Psychology at Leipzig, thereby achieving independent status among the other institutes and seminars of the university. Wundt was not alone in gaining "institute" (effectively, disciplinary) status for the new experimental psychology. During the 1880s, Georg Elias Müller, a student of Lotze and his successor at Göttingen, investigated perception, attention, and memory, while equipping an excellent laboratory, which became part of an Institute for Psychology in 1887. Hermann Ebbinghaus, who pioneered experimental work in memory, started the laboratory at Berlin during the 1880s; Carl Stumpf, who was appointed in 1893 to head the Psychological Seminar, was named Director of the newly formed Institute for Psychology in 1900. A Psychological Laboratory was founded at Freiburg in 1889, an Institute in Würzburg in 1896, a Seminar at Bonn in 1898, and a Laboratory in Copenhagen (a university having strong intellectual connections to Germany) in 1886. Wundt started the journal *Philosophische Studien* in 1881, which, despite its title, was an organ for publishing theoretical, methodological, and experimental work in psychology. Ebbinghaus and Arthur König founded the *Zeitschrift für Psychologie and Physiologie der Sinnesorgane* in 1890, as a journal outside the Wundtian sphere. In 1904, Müller helped found the German Society for Experimental Psychology. Beyond these developments, but interacting with them, the Austrian philosopher Franz Brentano had in 1874 issued his own call for an empirical psychology, which was in fact to be a phenomenological psychology (see Chapter 28 of this volume). In any event, after its initial fast start, in the twentieth-century Germany psychology developed slowly as a natural science, not fully achieving independent institutional status in many universities until the 1930s (Geuter 1987).

Psychology in Great Britain

British psychology of the early eighteenth century was the heir to two traditions, the associationist psychology of Hartley and Hume and the common sense psychology of Thomas Reid and Dugald Stewart. Whereas Hartley and Hume made the principles of association into the engine of human thought and behavior and their regularities, Reid and Stewart explained human beliefs and actions as the product of innate faculties and powers, including a faculty of reason or common sense that innately produces a belief in the existence of the external world. With this psychological opposition between associationism and faculty psychology was frequently paired an epistemological divide: some associationists, following Hume, tended to be phenomenalists about human knowledge, whereas those in the common-sense tradition tended to be realists. Reid and the common-sense tradition ascribed the phenomenalism and skepticism of Berkeley and Hume to their uncritical acceptance of "images" or "ideas" as perceptual intermediaries that form an impenetrable veil of perception between the observer and the external world.

At first, the psychological opposition played out between the Scottish psychologists Thomas Brown and William Hamilton, who successively taught at Edinburgh.

Brown, who took medical training at Edinburgh but also studied with Stewart and succeeded him as Professor of Moral Philosophy, became a radical opponent of Reid and a supporter of associationism. Brown (1820) accused Reid of foisting an implausible version of the representative theory of perception onto his predecessors, whose positions were in fact similar to Reid's own in rejecting separately existing "images" or "ideas." He also accused Reid of misdiagnosing the basis for skeptical challenges to perceptual knowledge. According to Brown, any theory that distinguishes perception and object is open to such a challenge; perception can always be imagined to occur without the object and so skepticism does not require "images" or "ideas" distinct from perception. Like Reid, Brown was committed to realism; he posited mind and matter as unknown permanent substrates of mental and physical phenomena. But he did not found his realism on innate faculties or intuitions. Instead, he proposed an associationist account of perception and cognition and of the development of beliefs in an external world, which beliefs subsequently *seem* to be intuitive (or "commonsensical"). He forged an empiricism of spatial perception as radical as that of Steinbuch and Herbart, with muscle feelings as the basis of all spatial representation. He also invoked the notion of "mental chemistry," according to which the elements that are associated may not be recognizable in the resulting compound, any more than hydrogen and oxygen are recognizable in water. Such a "chemical" joining might explain how muscle feelings can provide the basis for distance perception, and yet phenomenally we don't seem to feel our ocular muscles but rather to see houses and trees at a distance.

Brown's associationism, which he preferred to call a theory of "suggestion" (Berkeley's term), was built on both simple and "relative" laws of suggestion. The simple laws were those of resemblance, contrast, and spatio-temporal contiguity (or "nearness"). The relative suggestions divide into relations of coexistence and succession. Unlike simple laws of suggestion, in which one may be aware of a single product of association, as in remembering something without being aware of what provoked the memory, relative suggestion involves awareness of both terms of the relation. The species of relative suggestion include: position; resemblance and difference; degree; proportion; and comprehensiveness, or part–whole relations. From simple and relative relations, Brown sought to build all powers of thought, including memory, imagination, and reasoning. In allowing the direct perception of relations, he exceeded the simplest forms of association. He was not alone; Hume's account of relations gave precedent (1739–40: Bk 1, pt 1, §5).

When Brown died in 1820, Hamilton applied for his position as Professor of Moral Philosophy at Edinburgh but was not selected. He turned to other pursuits, published some important articles, and in 1836 assumed the Chair in Logic and Metaphysics at Edinburgh and became a defender of Reid. Hamilton edited Reid's works, adding learned historical appendices that remain useful. His own "lectures on metaphysics and logic" (a title to match his Chair) were published posthumously (1861–6), invoking a lengthy response from John Stuart Mill (1865b) on behalf of Brown's account of perception and in defense of association. The lectures were divided into two parts, metaphysics and logic; Hamilton equated the first or metaphysical part with psychology, which he further divided into three parts: phenomena of psychology; laws of psychology; and inferences concerning ontology (the existence of souls and God). Against Brown, Hamilton defended Reid's "natural realism" in perception, and he elaborated Reid's common-sense account of reason with a more rigorous logical analysis of the rational faculty. Hamilton also defended, contrary to Brown, the view that some mental states are unconscious, using arguments that hailed Leibniz's postulation of unconscious *petites perceptions* as the ingredients of conscious perceptions (as the sound of individual waves, singly imperceptible, make up the roar of the sea).

The torch of associationism in Britain passed on to James Mill and his son, John Stuart. The elder Mill was educated in Scotland and made a career with the East India Company in London. He engaged in literary pursuits and published a two-volume work on the human mind (Mill 1829). In that work, he expounded an associationist psychology of perception and cognition in which he explained the perception of distance through the association of light and color with muscle feelings, and he treated belief in the existence of bodies as so many associations among sensations, in effect endorsing phenomenalism. This work became a point of departure for the subsequent efforts of his son and his son's friend and sometime collaborator, Alexander Bain. The younger Mill was not without reservations about associationism. After endorsing an associationist account of logical inference in the first edition of his *Logic*, he subsequently raised doubts about whether association alone could account for inference (Mill 1973–4: 664). As regards external objects, in the *Logic* he treated matter as an unknown cause of sensations (1973–4: 56–63); subsequently, in responding to Hamilton (Mill 1865b: Ch. 11), he analyzed the idea of matter into Permanent Possibilities of Sensation, a position he dubbed "Berkeleian" (presumably minus divine causation of sensations), thereby adopting his father's phenomenalism. Also in that work, he defended Brown and Bain against Hamilton on the view that touch (through the muscle sense) educates vision and yields the perception of depth and distance (Mill 1865b: Ch. 13).

Alexander Bain brought systematic psychology to a new level in Britain, publishing a comprehensive two-volume survey (1855, 1859), with an overview of the relevant neurophysiology. He created the journal *Mind* in order to promote scientific psychology and to improve scholarly standards in philosophy. In his psychology, or "science of mind," he defined the mind as having three attributes or capacities: feeling, including sensation and emotion; acting according to feeling; and thought (1855: 1). Consciousness is always annexed to feeling, but may not be to action and thought. He rejected mental faculties in favor of an exposition that proceeded "entirely on the Laws of Association" (1855: vi), which in his estimation comprised two simple laws, of contiguity and similarity, and two instances of the joint effects of the laws, which occur in compounding and constructing intellectual states. In addition to these laws of association, Bain recognized various instincts, which are expressed in motor coordination and movement, the emotions, and inborn volitional tendencies. Nonetheless, the central feature of his psychology is its reliance on association in explanations of perception and intellectual cognition, including a psychological account, similar to that of J. S. Mill, of belief in an independent material world.

British psychology after mid-century saw four theoretical or methodological innovations. First, physiologists such as William Carpenter and Henry Maudsley, along with the biologist T. H. Huxley, promoted the notion that brain activity, in the absence of consciousness, might undergo processes that account for conscious mental products or, more radically, that some brain activity might constitute unconscious mental processes. Second, James Ward and George F. Stout introduced phenomenological psychology into Britain. Third, Francis Galton developed psychometric techniques that he put largely in the service of his studies of hereditary "genius." Finally, Spencer, Darwin, and others promoted an evolutionary psychology, which I will discuss in the next section.

Carpenter (1874) was an avowed dualist who nonetheless argued for the necessity of positing automatic, unconscious mental activities that were carried out by the brain, which he called "unconscious cerebration." Such brain activity was mental and psychological not because of its ontological status but because of its functional character. Carpenter did not include vital functions such as digestion within the ambit of the mental, but he did include sensorimotor adjustment of behavior to current circumstances. In effect, he adopted the standard functional divide between "vegetative" or "organic" functions and "animal" functions involving sensation and movement (1874: 29). Sensorimotor functions might or might not be accompanied by consciousness, depending on the phylogenetic level and whether the instance in question was reflexive and automatic. Carpenter admitted into his psychology both "subjective," introspective data and "objective" observations of animal and human behavior. Further, human psychology brought in will or voluntary control, which Carpenter regarded as undetermined and so as causally independent of the brain (in accordance with his dualism). Nonetheless, brain processes carry out automatic mental functions. Carpenter treated consciousness and will as mental properties that interact with brain processes, but he did not restrict the mental to the conscious or the volitional: unconsciously mediated instincts, motor processes, and brain-based habits may all be deemed "mental" (1874: Chs 1–2, 13).

Maudsley, by contrast, was an avowed materialist who contended that all mental functioning, conscious and unconscious, was nothing but brain activity. Maudsley (1876) considered the introspective method in psychology to be woefully inadequate. He complained that within the intended sphere of its application – the description of a subject's conscious mental states – investigators disagree, largely because the act of introspecting interrupts the mental phenomena under study. His complaint was sustained by ongoing disputes concerning the number of items that one can attend to at the same time (Hatfield 1998a, 2005a). Maudsley did not propose abandoning introspection altogether, but supplementing it. Introspection cannot reach many mental states and processes, including those of small children and nonhuman animals; but the behavior of infants and animals under various conditions can be observed and compared. In adult humans, introspection fails to penetrate the many unconscious mental operations; but the existence of such operations can be inferred from observable behavior. Maudsley urged the use of "objective" methods that do not depend on introspective self-observation, which included physiological, comparative, and developmental observations, and the study of pathological cases, biography, and history. Such objective data are equally available to multiple observers.

In a second new development, phenomenological psychology was introduced to Britain by Ward (1886), who had studied in Germany and was influenced by Lotze and Brentano. Ward took individual consciousness to be the sole subject matter of psychology. He posited an active ego apart from the "presentations" that fill consciousness, and he declared attention to be the fundamental psychological activity, more basic than association. Stout, who was Ward's student at Cambridge, presented the psychological work of Stumpf, Brentano, Christian Ehrenfels, and Alexius Meinong to a British audience (Stout 1896).

The nineteenth century saw the development of statistics and its application to social, historical, biological, physical, and psychological subject matters (Porter 1986). As the century opened, astronomers regularly calculated the mean value of repeated observations of the same phenomenon, regarding the mean as the true value and deviations from it as observational errors. The Belgian statistician Adolphe Quetelet extended the notion of error to explain the observed distribution of properties in a population of individuals: the observed values are deviations from the naturally specified ideal type. The nature of the human male specifies that all men should be a certain fixed height, but the effects of perturbing causes ("errors"), randomly distributed to yield the normal curve, yield the actually observed distribution of male heights. Galton applied these statistical ideas in his study of psychological variations in the British population, especially to the distribution of "genius" or exceptional ability. His motives for doing so led him to found the British eugenics movement in order to encourage good breeding. Through his technical acumen, he developed the formal apparatus of regression and correlation, which Karl Pearson applied in biometrics and R. A. Fischer extended further in experimental design and the analysis of variance. Galton's methods were taken up in the psychological testing movement of the late nineteenth and early twentieth centuries, in Britain, France, Germany, and the United States.

An institutional basis for experimental psychology developed slowly in Britain. Ward's repeated efforts to start a laboratory at Cambridge met limited success, but in 1893 Michael Foster created a Lectureship in Experimental Psychology and Physiology of the Senses and he provided the lecturer with permanent laboratory space in 1897. Laboratories were established at University College London in 1897 and at Edinburgh in 1907. Also in 1907, William McDougall obtained rooms from an Oxford physiologist to use as his laboratory. McDougall was the second Wilde Reader in Mental Philosophy at Oxford. Henry Wilde, who funded the readership, did not expect its recipient to pursue experimental investigations and attempted to have McDougall removed for doing so; McDougall left Oxford for Harvard in 1920. In the meantime, James Sully, W. H. R. Rivers, and others founded the British Psychological Society in 1901, and Ward and Rivers started the *British Journal of Psychology* in 1904. The founding of that journal, added to American journals specializing in psychology started in 1887 and 1894, resulted in a decline in psychological contributions to *Mind* after 1910, and also of philosophical discussions of psychology. These declines reflected a hardening of attitudes among some British philosophers about the potential contribution of empirical psychology to philosophy and even doubts about the scientific credentials of mentalistic psychology, to be discussed below.

Evolutionary psychology

The functional organization of human and nonhuman animal bodies had been a topic of discussion from antiquity, evoking appeals to intrinsic ends-directed processes that govern the growth and vital processes of organisms. The role of the senses and of instinctual behaviors in adjusting animal behavior to the environment was also well remarked. During the seventeenth century, Cartesian theorists sought to explain both the instinctual and sense-guided behaviors of animals by appeal to mechanical processes, in accordance with the hypothesis that animal bodies are intricate machines. Others appealed to vital forces or animal souls to explain the physiological and psychological abilities of animals.

These discussions sometimes raised the question of the origins of animals and of the innate instinctual processes and sensory capacities that serve the ends of animal survival. Many authors from the seventeenth into the nineteenth centuries invoked a designing creator, who bestowed animals with well-adjusted sense organs and effective behavior-guiding instincts. At the same time, some authors in the seventeenth and eighteenth centuries revived the ancient Epicurean idea, found in Lucretius' poem *On the Nature of the Universe*, that human beings and other animals are natural objects that have arisen by natural processes. Lucretius (1997: Bk 5) ascribed the natural origin of all species to spontaneous generation, which produced many forms that are no longer extant; he described a process in which unsuccessful forms are weeded out because their bodies are not well adapted. Hume referred to Epicurus' (hence Lucretius') account of the natural origin and subsequent culling of animal forms, and speculated that this process might explain the "uses of the parts" of plants and animals and the apparent "adjustment of means to ends" of those parts (1779: Pt 8). In this way, the innate functional organization of animals, including their instinctual behaviors, might be explained through a wholly natural process.

Other eighteenth-century naturalists, including Georges Buffon and Erasmus Darwin, avoided the Epicurean hypothesis of the spontaneous generation of all present forms by attributing present species to the interbreeding of a few original forms to create new forms. Darwin (E. Darwin 1794–6, Vol. 1: 480, 502–5), as well as Cabanis and Antoine Lamarck, wedded this view to the inheritance of acquired characteristics, in that way explaining the adaptedness of current species to their environments without appealing to special creation: animals pass on to their offspring acquired physiological responses to the environment and learned strategies for coping with that environment, thereby transforming the species (Richards 1987: Ch. 1).

Such evolutionary ideas were rife in nineteenth-century Britain and were, as in the earlier literature, applied not only to the anatomical structure of the sense organs but to behavior-guiding psychological processes. Herbert Spencer, in his *Principles of Psychology* (1855), elaborated the notion that psychological traits evolve through the inheritance of acquired characteristics so that mental structures become adjusted to environmental circumstances. Spencer defined life as "the continuous adjustment of internal relations to outer relations" and intelligence as "the adjustment of inner to outer relations" (1855: 374, 486). In the second edition of 1870–2, he distinguished "objective" psychology, dealing with material organismic processes, from the study of "subjective" processes available to consciousness (Pt 1, ch. 7). Objective psychology concerns the adaptive adjustment of behavior-guiding internal states to external circumstances. Subjective psychology describes consciously available mental states that correspond to some of the processes of objective psychology. Spencer's methodological recommendation, that the relation of behavior to circumstances might be studied "objectively" without appeal to introspection, was subsequently championed by Charles Mercier (1888).

Charles Darwin, in his *Origin of the Species* (1859), added his theory of natural selection to discussions of the origins of adapted species, while also accepting the inheritance of acquired characteristics as a mechanism of evolution. In the *Origin*, Darwin foresaw applications of his theories to psychology: "In the distant future I see open fields for far more important researches. Psychology will be based on a new foundation, that of the necessary acquirement of each mental power and capacity by gradation. Light will be thrown on the origin of man and his history" (1859: 488). Indeed, the *Origin* devoted an entire chapter to instinct, that is, to inherited behavioral traits "performed by many individuals in the same way, without their knowing for what purpose it is performed" (1859: 207). Darwin discussed examples of variation in instinctive "mental qualities" among domesticated and wild species, with the aim of making it plausible that the traits of individual species have arisen through natural selection or by the inheritance of acquired habits (1859: Ch. 7). His 1872 book on the emotions (human and nonhuman) was greatly influential in early evolutionary psychology. Indeed, as an area of evolutionary psychology, work on the emotions forms a continuous research tradition from the nineteenth century until today.

Darwinian explanations of mental adaptation, including the mechanisms underlying both instinct and learning, were soon found in Germany and England. In Germany, Hering applied Darwin's insight to account for innate structures that mediate spatial perception, thereby countering Helmholtz's charge that innate mental structures could only be explained by appeal to obscure "spiritual" factors (Hatfield 1990: Ch. 5). In England, George Henry Lewes (1874–80) treated mind as a biological function of the organism. As had Spencer, Lewes made association the engine of psychological development; but as had Spencer and Bain, he also recognized a fixed organic component in psychological responses. Lewes saw that evolutionary theory could explain innate mental adaptations in organisms, including human beings (1879: Chs 1, 9).

Darwin encouraged the British naturalist George J. Romanes to apply evolutionary thinking to the mind. Romanes (1883, 1888) divided adaptive behavioral responses into innate reflexive behaviors and those guided by choice. He used consciousness as the criterion for the presence of mind, proposing as an "objective" sign of consciousness the manifestation of choice in novel environmental circumstances. He held that much animal behavior arises from reflexes, which are subject to organic hereditary transmission, which do not require consciousness, and which, when unaccompanied by consciousness, are nonmental. Methodologically, Romanes contended that mental states beyond the confines of one's own consciousness must be inferred from the behavior of other organisms (human and nonhuman) by analogy with one's own conscious mental life. Another naturalist, C. Lloyd Morgan, sought to constrain such inferences through his celebrated "canon": "In no case may we interpret an action as the outcome of the exercise of a higher psychical faculty, if it can be interpreted as the outcome of the exercise of one which stands lower in the psychological scale" (1894: 53). Morgan was a great advocate of the power of "trial and error learning" for explaining an animal's adjustment to environmental circumstances, a line of thinking that was adapted by the behaviorist psychology of the early twentieth century.

American psychology

For the first three-quarters of the nineteenth century, psychology was treated as a branch of moral philosophy in American colleges and universities. The Scottish tradition stemming from Reid and Stewart dominated. Psychology was often taught by the Provost or Vice Provost of the college, who frequently was a minister. There were some exceptions, such as Benjamin Rush's lectures on the mind (1981), which were part of his course on physiology in the School of Medicine at the University of Pennsylvania from 1791 to 1813.

In the final quarter of the nineteenth century, psychology grew rapidly as a discipline in the United States. This growth coincided with a period of general expansion of the arts and sciences, as American universities extended research and graduate education beyond the traditional "higher" faculties of law, medicine, and theology by founding graduate schools in arts and sciences. This transformation resulted in the division of the "philosophy faculty," as the arts and sciences faculty was typically known, into separate academic departments and degree programs. Although a few institutions had previously developed schools or institutes to support work in natural science, the general expansion of graduate education in the period after 1890 opened up the possibility of founding new departments and research laboratories in all disciplines, and psychology was frequently included. Indeed, between 1883 and 1900, forty-one psychological laboratories were founded at American colleges and universities. By 1912, there were more than twenty independent departments of psychology at these and other institutions (Ruckmich 1912). By 1926, the number of laboratories reached 100 (Garvey 1929), the great majority of which had produced research publications (the few exceptions being laboratories devoted only to undergraduate instruction).

Initially, there were three trends in American psychology. The first continued the old moral psychology, as represented by McCosh (1872), who nonetheless helped to foster the new psychology and who sought to reconcile Darwin with religion (McCosh 1871). The second was a transplantation of Wundt's physiological and experimental psychology without his ethnopsychology. Indeed, a large plurality (nearly half) of the founders of American laboratories had been trained by Wundt in Leipzig (Hilgard

1987: 32–4). E. B. Titchener (1896) represents this trend. George Ladd (1887) produced his own counterpart to Wundt's textbook, but remained a philosopher and metaphysician at heart (1895). The problems and methods of Titchener led to the development of an "American" Wundt, or an allegedly "Wundtian" structuralism that was more atomistic and associationist than Wundt himself (Danziger 1980). Titchener (1896) may not have been far off the mark when he described his psychology as a combination of traditional English psychology with the most recent German experimental psychology.

The third trend, which yielded a distinctively American brand of psychology, was the American functionalism that continued the evolutionary psychology spawned by Darwin and Spencer. James's monumental *Principles of Psychology* (1890: Chs 24–5, 28) exhibited this evolutionary psychology with respect to the emotions but also more widely. James Mark Baldwin, who had been trained by McCosh, was soon publishing in this vein (1894, 1902), and John Dewey (1896a, b) adopted a functionalist stance during the 1890s. Dewey and James collectively trained James Angell, who in 1894 joined Dewey at the University of Chicago in the Department of Philosophy, Psychology, and Education. Psychological functionalism flourished at Chicago, as also at Columbia.

American psychology quickly came to describe itself as distinct from philosophy and as willing to engage with philosophy on metaphysical and methodological questions. Indeed, some of its founders wore both disciplinary hats: James was avowedly both a psychologist and a philosopher, and in his early years Dewey could claim both titles. James and Titchener, among the leaders of American psychology as the century turned, agreed in distinguishing the study and explanation of psychological phenomena from metaphysical questions about the nature of mind and matter (James 1890: Vol. 1, vi; Titchener 1896: Ch. 15). Psychology would study the relations between physiological processes and psychological states, and might even adopt as a methodological principle that all mental states have a neural counterpart. Philosophy would address the substantial natures and causal relations between mind and matter. Even Ladd, who believed it unwise to keep metaphysics out of psychology, recognized that the two disciplines were distinct (1887: 7, 668; 1895: viii–ix).

Introspective methods in the laboratory

Introspection, or *Selbstbeobachtung* (self-observation) in German, was widely discussed as a scientific method in the psychology textbooks of the latter eighteenth century (well prior to the systematic use of introspection in the laboratory). Schmid treated introspection as one among several recognized empirical sources for psychology, the others including: behavioral expressions of mental states; the organization and structure of the body in relation to the production of mental states; and products of mentality, such as institutions, inventions, writings, and mechanical as well as artistic artifacts (1796: 107). He recognized introspection as the primary source for psychology narrowly defined, that is, for studying the "inner" states of human beings, or what "appears" to "inner sense" (1796: 11). Schmid's textbook thoroughly discussed the methods of psychology, focusing on the difficulties involved in introspection, which arise from the fact that the mind is seeking to observe itself, and also from the complexity and fleetingness of mental states and the lack of a naturalistic vocabulary for describing mental states (1796: 105–31).

The first two-thirds of the nineteenth century saw periodic discussion of the difficulties of introspection. August Comte (1830–42) contended that psychology could never be a science because it must rely on introspection. He cited a standard objection from the eighteenth century, that introspecting is rendered difficult by, or else itself interrupts, the very inner states that are supposed to be its objects (his objection was known to Maudsley). If, for instance, one were seeking to attend carefully to an intense emotion, the emotion would prevent the intellectual detachment needed for good observation. J. S. Mill defended introspection by arguing that it can be effective if based on memory (1865a: 64). The observer introspects by attending to psychological events and processes after they have occurred but while they are still fresh in memory. By contrast, Hamilton (1861–6: Vol. 1, 266) simply affirmed that we have infallible knowledge of our own conscious states.

Some investigators of psychological states, such as Fechner and Helmholtz, in effect ignored these methodological discussions and simply proceeded with the study of sensory and perceptual experience in psychophysics or in color and spatial perception. But as experimental psychology became institutionally grounded in psychological laboratories, and as experimental methods became more varied, introspection increasingly attracted discussion and debate as a laboratory method. Indeed, part of this discussion arose because different laboratories refined and developed differing introspective methods, depending on the types of psychological processes that investigators wanted to study and the experimental apparatus that they built for collecting observations.

The question of what constituted introspection in late nineteenth-century experimental psychology can receive no simple answer. We may look for help in discussions of introspection by its main practitioners, such as Wundt and Titchener. On the eve of the behaviorist onslaught against introspective methods and mentalistic constructs, Titchener (1912a, b) published two articles reviewing past controversies surrounding introspection and discussing current methodological attitudes. He distinguished the commonsensical introspection of the diarist or moralist, along with the precritical introspection of earlier psychology, from the critical introspection of the new experimental psychology. Experimental conditions limit the range and focus of introspection. He argued that introspection in experimental psychology meets the standards of natural scientific "observation and experiment" (1912b: 486). He denied that introspection must be self conscious or even a conscious act: psychological observers may become intent on the contents of consciousness and prepared to describe or respond to those contents, without remaining consciously aware that their attention is thus focused. One can watch the ball into the mitt and consciously perceive the ball the entire time, without being consciously or self-consciously aware of the act of attending.

Introspection in early experimental psychology was carried out by knowledgeable observers who understood the point of the experiment and knew the relevant descriptive and theoretical vocabulary. The experimental subject introspects on behalf of scientific psychology: "the ideal introspective report is an accurate description, made in the interests of psychology, of some conscious process" (Titchener 1912b: 486). Titchener cautioned that introspective descriptions must be kept distinct from causal or explanatory hypotheses. But he did not mean that the descriptive vocabulary would be theory neutral: "the categories of description" in introspection are "the last terms of analysis, the elementary processes and their attributes; and consciousness has been described when analysis is, qualitatively and quantitatively, complete" (1912b: 495). Of course, depending on what one considers the least elements of consciousness to be, one will bring one or another attitude to the introspective task. Indeed, James (1890: Vol. 1, 158–9, 172–3), among others, protested against Wundtian psychological atomism, contending that conscious experience has a continuity and holistic structure that the atomists artificially seek to decompose into elements that they in effect create during the act of introspection (as in treating attentionally isolated auditory sensations as more "real" than complex sounds).

Titchener writes as if introspection is largely a matter of verbally describing the contents of consciousness using a special "analytical" vocabulary. In fact, this sort of free verbal description was not extensively employed in psychological experiments, save those that sought to investigate higher thought processes by the method of "systematic experimental introspection" (associated with the "Würzburg school"). With the latter method, subjects were given a brief task requiring thought and then, immediately afterwards, they described the contents of their consciousness during the task. The tasks varied, but might include the interpretation of a proverb or even of aphorisms read from Nietzsche, or associations to various words or numerals. As subjects described their experiences experimenters could ask questions. Use of this method led to the imageless thought controversy, in which the Würzburg school claimed that, during some tasks, subjects reported mental contents that were not in the form of images (whether visual images, or the sounds of words in inner speech). Titchener, who was an opponent of imageless thought, contended such reports arose from a failure to distinguish conscious content from underlying meanings. Meaning, in his view, does not require images, but also is not a part of conscious content. Others held that imageless thought consists in the nonimagistic awareness of meaning (Woodworth 1938: Ch. 30, contains a good discussion.) Wundt rejected outright the method of systematic experimental introspection. As previously mentioned, he did not believe that higher thought processes *per se* could be studied experimentally, and he promoted instead the methods of *Völkerpsychologie* for studying thought and its products.

Most of the introspective experiments that Titchener describes in his textbooks (1901–5), and that Wundt promoted in his laboratory, did not involve free verbal description, and many required no overt verbal response at all. Many experiments concerned sense perception, attention, and memory. In those involving sense perception and attention, subjects might simply report whether they saw something, or push a button when they saw something, or they might manipulate an apparatus until they achieved a match between two stimuli. Wundt preferred to limit introspective experimentation to conditions in which the conscious states of the subject are closely controlled by physical stimuli that are themselves controlled by the experimenter. Studies of sense perception, in which the subject is shown a stimulus and responds by affirming its presence and perhaps naming it, or by matching stimuli, fit this bill. Such experiments were "introspective" in Wundt's sense because subjects responded in accordance with what they experienced. Their responses depended on the quality, intensity, structure, or content of their experiences.

Wundtian introspection is thus far removed from the mere verbal description of passing states in one's consciousness. Furthermore, in Wundt's conception, the objects of introspection are not special "inner" entities, but are one with everyday perception. Terminologically, Wundt spoke of "inner" perception and experience, which he contrasted with "outer" perception and experience. Such talk did not mark off two separate types of perceptual objects, but two different attitudes toward one and the same objects. Introspection takes the same (phenomenal) objects as ordinary perception, but approaches them with a different attitude: "the expressions outer and inner experience do not indicate different objects, but *different points of view* from which we take up the consideration and scientific treatment of a unitary experience" (1901: §1). Wundt rejected the definition of psychology as the "science of inner experience" because "it may give rise to the misunderstanding that psychology has to do with objects totally different from the objects of so-called 'outer experience'" (1901: §1). When a subject is looking at an object, he engages in introspection when he engages in "deliberate and immediate observation of inner processes" (Wundt 1888: 297). The processes are "inner" because the observer does not intend, as a physicist or biologist might, to abstract from the subjective aspect of the appearance, but instead considers the momentary contents of consciousness to be the object of his observation. Stout, Wundt's contemporary in Britain, observed that in such experiments subjects are not asked "What process do you, by introspection, find to be going on in your mind?" but simply "What do you see?" The question is to be answered by responding to the objects seen, the same objects as are found in the "other sciences" and in "ordinary knowledge" (1896: Vol. 1, 12).

The introspective practices of Wundt and Titchener subsequently underwent criticism on several fronts. I have mentioned James's protests against psychological atomism. The American behaviorist J. B. Watson (1913) later charged that introspection could not yield stable results, citing the imageless-thought controversy along with disagreements over the number of different "levels" of attentive awareness. The Gestalt psychologists subsequently added their voice to that of James. Wolfgang Köhler devoted a chapter of his *Gestalt Psychology* (1929) to a thorough critique of the atomism of standard psychological introspection. In this critique, he used the term "introspection" as synonymous to the analytical introspection of Wundt and Titchener, which he rejected. If we remove the search for atomic elements from the account of introspection given by Wundt and Titchener, we are left with the "deliberate and immediate" description of the contents of consciousness, or a deliberate response to the contents of experience. Under that description, the Gestaltists frequently relied on introspection in their writings, and psychological research in perception, attention, and memory still does so, when it asks subjects to respond based on what they consciously perceive or remember (although subjects now usually remain unaware of the purpose of the experiment and may not be apprised of the theoretical concepts in play). Wundt and Titchener did not invent the experimental use of introspection as a basis for psychological data, but they rendered its use widespread, and introspective data remains an important part of scientific psychology today.

Unconscious mental states

Throughout the nineteenth century, theorists of the mind debated the question of whether there are unconscious mental states. Herbart, Hamilton, Helmholtz, Wundt, Bain, Carpenter, and Maudsley affirmed that such states exist, whereas Brown, J. S. Mill, and James denied them. Those who countenanced unconscious mental states invoked them for various reasons. Many sensory physiologists and psychologists used them mainly to account for processes in sensory perception that mediate between the stimulation of individual nerve fibers and the production of conscious perceptual experience. These unconscious sensations were ascribed the qualitative characteristics of conscious perceptions: they were conceived as sensations of sound or color, having the qualitative features that we experience as sounds and colors, and yet as existing outside consciousness. Such unconscious sensations enter into unconscious psychological processes that combine them to form conscious perceptions. All of the theorists mentioned as favoring unconscious mental states allowed unconscious associations.

Hamilton recalled a case in which apparently unrelated thoughts arose one after the other in his mind, and explained the succession as the result of unconscious associations.

> Thinking of Ben Lomond, this thought was immediately followed by the thought of the Prussian system of education. Now, conceivable connection between these two ideas in themselves, there was none. A little reflection, however, explained the anomaly. On my last visit to the mountain, I had met upon its summit a German gentleman, and though I had no consciousness of the intermediate and unawakened links between Ben Lomond and the Prussian schools, they were undoubtedly these, – the German, – Germany, – Prussia, – and, these media being admitted, the connection between the extremes was manifest. (1861–6: Vol. 1, 353)

Hamilton posits that associative connections may exist in the mind between conscious thoughts, such as his thought of the Scottish mountain Ben Lomond, and unconscious mental states, such as his memory of having met a German man on his last trip up the mountain. These unconscious mental states may have further associative connections, such as between being German and Germany, between Germany and Prussia, and between Prussia and its system of schools, which become activated without becoming conscious, but which deliver up to consciousness a later member in the chain of associations: the Prussian schools.

Other theorists appealed to unconscious processes to account for cognitive acts that yield appropriate behavior. Bain argued that the environmentally appropriate behaviors of lower organisms, including one-celled animals, presumably are not accompanied by consciousness and yet the behavior exhibits the characteristics of mentality: the behavior is appropriate to the circumstances. Carpenter and Maudsley pointed to higher cognitive functions, such as problem-solving activity that may occur while one is asleep or thinking about something else, with the result that the solution simply appears in consciousness.

The opposing theorists, such as Brown, Mill, and James, did not deny these phenomena. Depending on the specifics, they either refused to count these as cases of mental activity or else argued that the mental states were not truly unconscious but rather went unnoticed because they were forgotten as soon as they occurred. Thus, Brown and Mill both argued that, in sensory perception, sensations may occur to which the mind responds but which are immediately forgotten. In their view, the sensations are conscious but unnoticed.

James (1890: Vol. 1, 162–76), who rejected atomistic accounts of sensory perception, rejected these unnoticed atomic sensations. But he did allow that associations may occur among sensory or cognitive states, and he repeated Brown and Mill's solution: the associative links are conscious but forgotten. He gave the same response to problem solving while asleep or distracted: the thoughts are conscious but forgotten, just as dreams may be conscious but are easily forgotten. He used neural mechanisms to explain situationally appropriate behavior that arises without conscious thought. He envisioned two sorts of mechanisms: reflexive, and acquired through habit. James held that reflexive behaviors could arise through natural selection. Such behaviors serve the end of preserving the organism, without involving an awareness of that end. Similarly, in the case of apparently "intelligent" processes underlying spatial perception, James allowed that "certain results, *similar* to results of reasoning, may be wrought out by rapid brain-processes to which no ideation seems attached" (1890: Vol. 1, 170). In his psychological scheme, *mind* is restricted to states that are accompanied by consciousness and that exhibit an awareness of ends (1890: Vol. 1, 8).

The relation of conscious and unconscious to thought and perception raises several questions. First, if the criterion of the mental is not consciousness, what is it? We have seen Carpenter invoke a distinction among types of organic processes to distinguish mentality from vitality: merely vegetative processes, such as digestion, are not mental products, but processes that yield properly adjusted behavioral responses (sensorimotor adjustments) are. Spencer also defined mind in terms of the adjustment of inner relations to outer relations. Still, the question remains of what allows *mentally* based adjustments to be distinguished from other physiological adjustments, such as the release of digestive fluids into the stomach when food is present. Second, what was driving theorists such as James when he refused to allow that merely physiological processes, even if yielding results "similar" to mental processes, are not really mental? Third, Sigmund Freud's work may now seem, retrospectively, as if it originated the notion of unconscious mental states. Freud's work, as pertaining to psychiatry and psychoanalysis, lies outside the scope of this chapter on philosophical and experimental psychology. Still, we may ask, given that uncon-scious mental states were widely discussed during the nineteenth century, what did Freud add that rendered his discussions so prominent in the twentieth century?

Relations between philosophy and psychology

Philosophy and psychology were variously related throughout the nineteenth century. Philosophers such as Fries believed that psychology should provide the basis for theoretical philosophy, including metaphysics and epistemology. Other philoso-phers, such as Herbart, contended that metaphysics must provide the basic theory of reality that grounds psychology. Still others, such as Helmholtz, Wundt, and James, recognized autonomous spheres for philosophy and psychology, but believed that psychological findings were relevant for the theory of knowledge.

In the latter part of the nineteenth century, some philosophers claimed that applying psychology to epistemology involved a fallacy, which they labeled "psychologism." J. E. Erdmann (1870: Vol. 2, 636) used that term in his history of philosophy to characterize the (in his view) mistaken attempt by Beneke to ground philosophy, and especially the theory of knowledge, on psychology (a respect in which Beneke allied himself with Fries rather than Herbart). Other philosophers, including the neo-Kantians Hermann Cohen and Wilhelm Windelband, took up the charge (whether they adopted the term or not), and faulted anti-Kantian philoso-phers with attempting to use psychology to settle epistemological questions. This, they contended, psychology could never do, because it offers descriptions of mental events and natural laws of their succession, whereas epistemology is concerned not with how we *in fact* reason but with how we *should* reason. The normative standards of epistemology are, accordingly, independent of actual human psychology. From this point of view, Steinbuch and Tourtual were simply in error in believing that the psychology of spatial perception could address Kant's theory of space as an *a priori* form of perception. Subsequently, the dispute about psychologism widened to include Gottlob Frege's charge that J. S. Mill had committed the psychologistic fallacy in attempting to ground arithmetic in psychology, and Frege similarly denied that formal logic could rest on psychology (see Chapter 30 of this volume). The debate grew after 1900 and was bound up with academic politics in Germany concerning whether chairs in philosophy should be assigned to experimental psychologists (Kusch 1995).

The possible contribution of psychology – and especially the psychology of perception – to epistemology was addressed in British philosophy. The British Idealist T. H. Green (1882), who was educated and taught philosophy at Oxford, asked whether there can be a natural history of man and answered negatively. He argued that all natural sciences, including perceptual psychology, must rely on notions of objectivity and fact, which, he held on quasi-Kantian grounds concerning the condi-tions for objective thought, cannot be explicated naturalistically. The Cambridge philosopher G. E. Moore, who initially adopted but subsequently abandoned British Idealism, was skeptical about the potential contribution of empirical psychology to epistemology, contending that in a proper description of judgments "there must ... disappear all reference to our mind" (1899: 193). At Oxford, H. A. Prichard took aim at the science of psychology as a whole, saying that "The statements of psychologists cannot fail to arouse misgiving in the mind of any one who has not been bred as a psychologist and whose interests are chiefly philosophical" (1907: 27). This disparaging attitude toward the relevance of psychology – and of scientific developments in general – to philosophy became widespread, and was especially forceful at Oxford in the guise of "ordinary language" philosophy. Not everyone agreed. Bertrand Russell sympathetically drew on psychology in his epistemological writings and in his *Analysis of Mind* (1921). Ludwig Wittgenstein, who is sometimes described as a logical behaviorist because of his skepticism concerning private knowledge of mental states, shows a deep and sustained interaction with the data and theories of perceptual psychology after 1930.

The question of the relevance of psychology to philosophy is still debated today under the name of "naturalism" in epistemology, metaphysics, and philosophy of science. "Naturalism" can mean several things. It can mean simply that the findings of the sciences are relevant to epistemological and metaphysical disputes. So understood, the outlook is hard to dispute. Consider the metaphysics and epistemology of color perception. It is difficult to imagine that anyone would make philosophical headway in this field without close knowledge of psychological theories of color perception (Hardin 1988). By contrast, naturalism may be taken to mean that scientific findings directly decide all questions of interest in metaphysics and epistemology. So understood, the outlook is questionable. In the case of the metaphysics of color qualities, scientists disagree among themselves and are unlikely to achieve an understanding of the metaphysical issues without engaging in dialogue with philosophers (Mausfeld and Heyer 2003).

Throughout the nineteenth century, philosophy and psychology came into contact in considering the nature of mind, body, and their interaction. Herbart (1813), Lotze (1856–64), and Ladd (1895) engaged the traditional questions concerning the substantial nature of mind and body. They each adopted a variant of monism, according to which there is only one type of underlying substance. They each viewed this substance as mind-like, with material properties arising from the external relations of mind-like substances. Nonetheless, psychological writers increasingly left the traditional mind–body problem to philosophers and metaphysicians. Bain (1888), Wundt (1901), and James (1892) each insisted that psychology's disciplinary concerns are distinct from those of philosophy and metaphysics. They adopted a provisional psychophysical parallelism, according to which for each mental or psychological state there exists a corresponding neurophysiological state. Within psychology, they did not seek to determine the substantial nature of such states or to solve the question of how mind and body interact. Rather, they sought to determine the empirical relations between mental states and brain states. In the latter decades of the century, philosophers took up the question of how physiology and psychology are related, and that question became more prominent in philosophy than the mind–body relation. For a time, the physiology–psychology question eclipsed the mind–body problem.

Psychology in the early twentieth century

As the twentieth century opened, experimental psychology was most firmly entrenched in the United States, where the number of laboratories and departments was growing rapidly. Germany, which initially had led experimental psychology, was losing prominence. Great Britain, which provided important theoretical discussions in the associationist tradition, on brain activity and psychological processes, and in evolutionary psychology, expanded its position in experimental psychology slowly. In France, after the Ideologues, Victor Cousin and others led a resurgence of traditional dualistic psychology. From about 1870 on, Hippolyte Taine and Théodule Ribot introduced the "new psychology" from Britain and Germany into France. Soon, Alfred Binet made original contributions to the psychology of testing. All the same, the disciplinary development of psychology was slow in France.

In addition to the rapid deployment of experimental laboratories, psychology in the United States exhibited two other characteristics that distinguished it from the situations in Germany and Great Britain. First, relations between philosophers and psychologists remained relatively cordial. When the American Psychological Association first met in 1892, philosophers also attended. As the meetings progressed, philosophers and psychologists came to agree that the philosophers needed a separate association, and the American Philosophical Association met for the first time in 1902. All the same, intense interchanges between philosophers and psychologists continued (with some scholars contributing on both sides, in the style of James), both in the journals and at the meetings of the respective associations. The *American Journal of Psychology* and the *Psychological Review*, from their foundings in 1887 and 1894, published occasional philosophical papers into the first or second decades of the twentieth century. Similarly, the *Philosophical Review* and the *Journal of Philosophy, Psychology, and Scientific Methods*, from their foundings in 1892 and 1904, published on psychology from a theoretical and methodological perspective. In fact, the *Journal of Philosophy* at first published experimental reports, but soon articles on experimentation took the form of reviews and discussions of work reported elsewhere. The journal regularly reviewed the literature in experimental psychology and reported on meetings of the American Psychological Associations and related societies. Its extensive discussions of psychological topics contrasted with the rapid decline of such discussions in *Mind*, which, although founded in part to secure the scientific status of psychology, only rarely published on scientific psychology in the decades following 1910.

Even before Watson proclaimed his behaviorist manifesto in 1913, the philosophical journals contained discussions on the role of consciousness in psychology and the desirability of "objective" (i.e. behavioral) psychological data (e.g. Singer 1911). Watson's behaviorism proclaimed not merely that behavioral data was acceptable or desirable in psychology, but that it was the only scientifically acceptable form of data. He restricted psychology's subject matter to behavior alone and declared that its explanations would eschew mentalistic notions in favor of physical descriptions of the conditions for behavior. A wide-ranging and lively discussion ensued, with both psychologists and philosophers publishing in the philosophical and the psychological journals (see Roback 1923 for a review). The interchange between philosophers and psychologists over behaviorism continued beyond the first three decades of the new century, but it was not as extensive. The notion that behaviorism and philosophy primarily interacted through the unity of science movement during the 1930s is a retrospective fiction. In fact, the neobehaviorists E. C. Tolman, C. L. Hull, and B. F. Skinner showed little ongoing interest in logical empiricism or the unity of science (Hatfield 2003).

The immigration of the Gestalt psychologists Köhler, Kurt Koffka, and Max Wertheimer to the United States between 1927 and 1934 instigated new interactions between psychologists and philosophers. The Gestalt psychologists defended the role of mentalistic constructs in psychology and they were strong critics of behaviorism and the older analytical introspection. Further, even at the height of behaviorism others in the United States continued to study mental phenomena while using only behavioral evidence (as with Tolman) or even retaining introspection (Woodworth 1938). The issues that the Gestaltists and neobehaviorists raised were discussed in journals, anthologies, and monographs into the 1950s, when the first stirrings of the "cognitive revolution" marked the beginning of yet another period of intense interactions between philosophy and psychology (Hatfield 2002).

References

Abel, Jacob F. (1786) *Einleitung in die Seelenlehre*, Stuttgart: Metzler; repr., Hildesheim: Olms, 1985.

Anderson, R. Lanier (2001) "Synthesis, Cognitive Normativity, and the Meaning of Kant's Question, 'How are synthetic cognitions a priori possible?'" *European Journal of Philosophy*, 9: 275–305.

Ash, Mitchell G. (1991) "Gestalt Psychology in Weimar Culture," *History of the Human Sciences*, 4: 395–415.

Bain, Alexander (1855) *The Senses and the Intellect*, London: Parker.

—— (1859) *The Emotions and the Will*, London: Parker.

—— (1888) "Definition and Demarcation of the Subject-Sciences," *Mind* 13, o.s.: 527–48.

Baldwin, James Mark (1894) *Mental Development in the Child and the Race: Methods and Processes*, New York: Macmillan.

—— (1902) *Development and Evolution*, New York: Macmillan.

Berkeley, George (1709) *Essay towards a New Theory of Vision*, Dublin: Rhames & Papyat.

Bonnet, Charles (1755) *Essai de psychologie; ou, considerations sur les operations de l'ame, sur l'habitude et sur l'education*, London.

Brown, Thomas (1820) *Lectures on the Philosophy of the Human Mind*, 4 vols, Edinburgh: Ballantyne.

Cabanis, Pierre (1802) *Rapports du physique et du moral de l'homme*, 2 vols, Paris: Crapart, Caille and Ravier; trans., Margaret Duggan Saidi, as *On the Relations Between the Physical and Moral Aspects of Man*, 2 vols, Baltimore: Johns Hopkins University Press, 1981.

Carpenter, William (1874) *Principles of Mental Physiology*, London: Kegan Paul.

Comte, Auguste (1830–42) *Cours de philosophie positive*, Paris: Rouen; trans., Harriet Martineau, as *The Positive Philosophy*, New York: Blanchard, 1855.

Condillac, Etienne Bonnot, Abbe de (1754) *Traité des sensations*, Paris: de Bure; trans., Franklin Philip and Harlan Lane, as *Treatise on the Sensations*, in vol. 1 of Condillac's *Philosophical Writings*, 2 vols, Hillsdale, NJ: Lawrence Erlbaum, 1982.

Danziger, Kurt (1980) "Wundt and the Two Traditions in Psychology," in R. W. Rieber (ed.) *Wilhelm Wundt and the Making of a Scientific Psychology*, New York: Plenum.

Darwin, Charles (1859) *On the Origin of Species*, London: Murray.

—— (1872) *Expression of the Emotions in Man and Animals*, London: Murray.

Darwin, Erasmus (1794–6) *Zoonomia, or, the Laws of Organic Life*, 2 vols, London: Johnson.

Degenaar, Marjolein (1996) *Molyneux's Problem: Three Centuries of Discussion on the Perception of Forms*, trans. Michael J. Collins, Dordrecht: Kluwer.

Destutt de Tracy, Antoine (1817) *Elemens d'ideologie*, Paris: Courcier.

Dewey, John (1896a) "The Reflex Arc Concept in Psychology," *Psychological Review* 3: 357–70.

—— (1896b) "Review of *Studies in the Evolutionary Psychology of Feeling*, by H. M. Stanley," *Philosophical Review*, 5: 292–9.

Erdmann, Johann Eduard (1870) *Grundriss der Geschichte der Philosophie*, 2nd edn, 2 vols, Berlin: Hertz.

Fries, Jakob Friedrich (1807) *Neue Kritik der Vernunft*, 3 vols, Heidelberg: Mohr and Zimmer.

Garvey, C. R. (1929) "List of American Psychology Laboratories," *Psychological Bulletin* 26: 652–60.

Geuter, Ulfried (1987) "German Psychology During the Nazi Period," in Mitchell G. Ash and William R. Woodward (eds) *Psychology in Twentieth-Century Thought and Society*, Cambridge: Cambridge University Press.

Godart, Guillaume-Lambert (1755) *La physique de l'ame*, Berlin: La Compagnie.

Green, T. H. (1882) "Can There Be a Natural Science of Man?" *Mind* 7, o.s.: 1–29, 161–85, 321–48.

Hamilton, William (1861–6) *Lectures on Metaphysics and Logic*, 4 vols, Edinburgh: Blackwood.

Hanov, Michael Christoph (1766) *Philosophia naturalis sive physica dogmatica, vol. 3: Geologia, biologia, phytologia generalis et dendrologia*, Halle: Renger.

Hardin, Clyde L. (1988) *Color for Philosophers*, Indianapolis, IN: Hackett.

Hartley, David (1749) *Observations on Man, His Frame, His Duty, and His Expectations*, London: Leake and Frederick; repr., Theodore L. Huguelet (ed.) Gainesville: Scholars' Facsimilies, 1966.

Hatfield, Gary (1990) *The Natural and the Normative: Theories of Spatial Perception from Kant to Helmholtz*, Cambridge: MIT Press.

—— (1995) "Remaking the Science of Mind: Psychology as a Natural Science," in Christopher Fox, Roy Porter, and Robert Wokler (eds) *Inventing Human Science*, Berkeley: University of California Press.

—— (1997) "Wundt and Psychology as Science: Disciplinary Transformations," *Perspectives on Science*, 5: 349–82.

—— (1998a) "Attention in Early Scientific Psychology," in R. D. Wright (ed.) *Visual Attention*, New York: Oxford University Press; repr., *Perception and Cognition: Essays in the Philosophy of Psychology*, Oxford: Clarendon, 2009.

—— (1998b) "The Cognitive Faculties," in Michael Ayers and Daniel Garber (eds) *Cambridge History of Seventeenth Century Philosophy*, Cambridge: Cambridge University Press.

—— (2000) "Descartes' Naturalism about the Mental," in Stephen Gaukroger, John Schuster, and John Sutton (eds) *Descartes' Natural Philosophy*, London: Routledge.

—— (2002) "Psychology, Philosophy, and Cognitive Science: Reflections on the History and Philosophy of Experimental Psychology," *Mind & Language* 17: 207–32; repr., *Perception and Cognition* (2009), Oxford: Clarendon.

—— (2003) "Behaviorism and Psychology," in Thomas Baldwin (ed.) *Cambridge History of Philosophy, 1870–1945*, Cambridge: Cambridge University Press.

—— (2005a) "Introspective Evidence in Psychology," in Peter Achinstein (ed.) *Scientific Evidence: Philosophical Theories and Applications*, Baltimore: Johns Hopkins University Press; repr., *Perception and Cognition*, Oxford: Clarendon, 2009.

—— (2005b) "Rationalist Theories of Sense Perception and Mind–Body Relation," in Alan Nelson (ed.) *Blackwell Companion to Rationalism*, Oxford: Blackwell.

Helmholtz, Hermann (1867) *Handbuch der physiologischen Optik*, Leipzig: Voss; trans., J. P. C. Southall, as *Treatise on Physiological Optics*, 3 vols, Rochester, NY: Optical Society of America, 1924–5.

Herbart, Johann Friedrich (1813) *Lehrbuch zur Einleitung in die Philosophie*, Königsberg: Unzer.

—— (1816) *Lehrbuch zur Psychologie*, Königsberg: Unzer.

—— (1824–5) *Psychologie als Wissenschaft neu gegründet auf Erhfahrung, Metaphysik und Mathematik*, Königsberg: Unzer.

Hering, Ewald (1861–4) *Beiträge zur Physiologie*, Leipzig: Engelmann.

Hilgard, Ernest R. (1987) *Psychology in America: A Historical Survey*, San Diego: Harcourt Brace Javanovich.

Hume, David (1739–40) *Treatise of Human Nature*, 3 vols, London: Noon.

—— (1779) *Dialogues Concerning Natural Religion*, London.

Ibn al-Haytham (1989) *Optics*, 2 vols, trans. A. I. Sabra, London: Warburg Institute (originally written in Arabic, eleventh century).

James, William (1890) *Principles of Psychology*, 2 vols, New York: Holt.

—— (1892) "A Plea for Psychology as a 'Natural Science,'" *Philosophical Review* 1: 146–53.

Köhler, Wolfgang (1929; 2nd edn 1947) *Gestalt Psychology*, New York: Liveright.

Krüger, Johann Gottlob (1756) *Versuch einer Experimental-Seelenlehre*, Halle: Hermerde.

Kusch, Martin (1995) *Psychologism*, London: Routledge.

Ladd, George Trumbull (1887) *Elements of Physiological Psychology*, New York: Scribner's.

—— (1895) *Philosophy of Mind: An Essay in the Metaphysics of Psychology*, New York: Scribner's.

Lapointe, Francois H. (1972) "Who Originated the Term 'Psychology'?" *Journal of the History of the Behavioral Sciences* 8: 328–35.

Lewes, George H. (1874–80) *Problems of Life and Mind*, 5 vols, Boston: Osgood.

—— (1879) *Problems of Life and Mind, 3rd Series: The Study of Psychology*, Boston: Houghton, Osgood.

Lindberg, David C. (1976) *Theories of Vision from Al-Kindi to Kepler*, Chicago: University of Chicago Press.

Lotze, Rudolf Hermann (1852) *Medicinische Psychologie, oder Physiologie der Seele*, Leipzig: Weidmann.

—— (1856–64) *Mikrokosmus: Ideen zur Naturgeschichte und Geschichte der Menschheit: Versuch einer Anthropologie*, 3 vols, Leipzig: Hirzel; trans., Elizabeth Hamilton and Emily Elizabeth Constance Jones, as *Microcosmus: An Essay Concerning Man and His Relation to the World*, 2 vols, Edinburgh: Clark, 1885.

Lucretius (1997) *On the Nature of the Universe*, trans. Ronald Melville, Oxford: Clarendon Press (original work of first century BCE).

McCosh, James (1871) *Christianity and Positivism*, New York: Carter.

—— (1872) *Intuitions of the Mind Inductively Investigated*, 3rd edn, New York: Carter.

Maine de Biran, Pierre (1803) *Influence de l'habitude sur la faculté de penser*, Paris: Henrichs; trans., Margaret Donaldson Boehm, as *Influence of Habit on the Faculty of Thinking*, Baltimore: Williams & Wilkins, 1929.

Maudsley, Henry (1876) *Physiology of Mind*, London: Macmillan.

Mausfeld, Rainer, and Heyer, Dieter (eds) (2003) *Colour Perception: Mind and the Physical World*, Oxford: Oxford University Press.

Mercier, Charles (1888) *The Nervous System and the Mind: A Treatise on the Dynamics of the Human Organism*, London: Macmillan.

Mill, James (1829) *Analysis of the Phenomena of the Human Mind*, 2 vols, London: Baldwin & Cradock.

Mill, John Stuart (1865a) *August Comte and Positivism*, London: Trübner.

—— (1865b) *Examination of Sir William Hamilton's Philosophy*, London: Longman.

—— (1973–4) *System of Logic*, ed. J. M. Robinson, 2 vols, Toronto: University of Toronto Press (originally published in 1843, with seven subsequent revised editions).

Moore, G. E. (1899) "Nature of Judgment," *Mind* 8, n.s.: 176–93.

Morgan, C. Lloyd (1894) *Introduction to Comparative Psychology*, London: Scott.

Müller, Johannes (1833–7) *Handbuch der Physiologie des Menschen*, 2 vols, Coblenz: Holscher; trans., William Baly, as *Elements of Physiology*, 2 vols, London: Taylor & Walton, 1838–42.

Porter, Theodore M. (1986) *Rise of Statistical Thinking: 1820–1900*, Princeton, NJ: Princeton University Press.

Porterfield, William (1759) *Treatise on the Eye: The Manner and Phenomena of Vision*, 2 vols, Edinburgh: Balfour.

Prichard, H. A. (1907) "A Criticism of the Psychologists' Treatment of Knowledge," *Mind* 16, n.s.: 27–53.

Richards, Robert J. (1987) *Darwin and the Emergence of Evolutionary Theories of Mind and Behavior*, Chicago: University of Chicago Press.

Roback, A. A. (1923) *Behaviorism and Psychology*, Cambridge, MA: University Book Store.

Robinson, David K. (2001) "Reaction-Time Experiments in Wundt's Institute and Beyond," in Robert W. Rieber and David K. Robinson (eds) *Wilhelm Wundt in History: The Making of a Scientific Psychology*, New York: Kluwer Academic/Plenum.

Romanes, George J. (1883) *Mental Evolution in Animals, with a Posthumous Essay on Instinct by Charles Darwin*, London: Kegan Paul, Trench.

—— (1888) *Mental Evolution in Man*, London: Kegan Paul, Trench.

Ruckmich, Christian A. (1912) "History and Status of Psychology in the United States," *American Journal of Psychology* 23: 517–31.

Rush, Benjamin (1981) *Lectures on the Mind*, edited by Eric T. Carlson, Jeffrey L. Wollock, and Patricia S. Noel, Philadelphia: American Philosophical Society.

Russell, Bertrand (1921) *Analysis of Mind*, London: Allen & Unwin.

Sachs-Hombach, Klaus (1993) *Philosophische Psychologie im 19. Jahrhundert: Entstehung und Problemgeschichte*, Munich: Alber.

Schmid, Carl C. E. (1796) *Empirische Psychologie*, 2nd edn, Jena: Cröker.

Singer, Edgar A., Jr (1911) "Mind as an Observable Object," *Journal of Philosophy, Psychology and Scientific Methods*, 8: 180–6.

Smith, Robert (1738) *Compleat System of Opticks*, 2 vols, Cambridge: printed for the author.

Spencer, Herbert (1855) *Principles of Psychology*, London: Longman, Brown, Green & Longmans.

—— (1870–2) *Principles of Psychology*, 2nd edn, 2 vols, London: Williams & Norgate.

Steinbuch, Johann Georg (1811) *Beytrag zur Physiologie der Sinne*, Nuremberg: Schrag.

Stout, George Frederick (1896) *Analytic Psychology*, 2 vols, London: Sonnenschein.

Titchener, E. B. (1896) *Outline of Psychology*, New York: Macmillan.

—— (1901–5) *Experimental Psychology: A Manual of Laboratory Practice*, New York: Macmillan.

—— (1912a) "Prolegomena to a Study of Introspection," *American Journal of Psychology* 23: 427–48.

—— (1912b) "Schema of Introspection," *American Journal of Psychology* 23: 485–508.

Tourtual, Caspar Theobald (1827) *Die Sinne des Menschen*, Münster: Regensberg.

Turner, R. Steven (1994) *In the Eye's Mind: Vision and the Helmholtz-Hering Controversy*, Princeton, NJ: Princeton University Press.

Ward, James (1886) "Psychology," in *Encyclopaedia Britannica, vol. 20*, 9th edn, Philadelphia: Stoddart.

Watson, John Broadus (1913) "Psychology as the Behaviorist Views It," *Psychological Review* 20: 158–77.

Wolff, Christian (1732) *Psychologia Empirica*, Frankfurt: Renger.

—— (1734) *Psychologia Rationalis*, Frankfurt: Renger.

Woodworth, Robert S. (1938) *Experimental Psychology*, New York: Holt.

Wundt, Wilhelm (1862) *Beiträge zur Theorie der Sinneswahrnehmung*, Leipzig: Winter.

—— (1874) *Grundzüge der physiologischen Psychologie*, Leipzig: Engelmann.

—— (1888) "Selbstbeobachtung und innere Wahrnehmung," *Philosophische Studien*, 4: 292–309.

—— (1901) *Grundriss der Psychologie*, 4th edn, Leipzig: Engelmann; trans., Charles Hubbard Judd, as *Outlines of Psychology*, Leipzig: Engelmann, 1902.

Further reading

Edwin G. Boring, *History of Experimental Psychology*, 2nd edn (New York: AppletonCenturyCrofts, 1950), is an older history, containing much useful information. Friedrich A. Carus, *Geschichte der Psychologie* (Leipzig: Barth & Kummer, 1808; repr., Rolf Jeschonnek, ed., Berlin: Springer, 1990), offers a window into the topics and authors, from antiquity to the early nineteenth century, considered to form the history of psychology from an early nineteenth-century perspective. Kurt Danziger, *Constructing the Subject: Historical Origins of Psychological Research* (Cambridge: Cambridge University Press, 1990), includes experimental methodologies in psychological research from Wundt's laboratory into the twentieth century.

An excellent introductory textbook in the history of psychology, from the seventeenth into the twentieth century is Raymond E. Fancher, *Pioneers of Psychology*, 3rd edn (New York: Norton, 1996). Michael Heidelberger, *Nature from Within: Gustav Theodor Fechner and His Psychophysical Worldview*, trans. Cynthia Klohr (Pittsburgh: University of Pittsburgh Press, 2004), gives the intellectual context, philosophical background, and scientific development of Fechner's psychophysics. Serge Nicolas, Anne Marchal, and Frédéric Isel, "La psychologie au XIXème siècle," *Revue d'Histoire des Sciences Humaines* 2 (2000): 57–103, surveys the history of nineteenth-century psychology, focusing on Germany, Great Britain, and France. An interesting account of the development of psychology as a science in the nineteenth century can be found in Edward S. Reed, *From Soul to Mind: The Emergence of Psychology, from Erasmus Darwin to William James* (New Haven, CT: Yale University Press, 1997). Robert W. Rieber and Kurt D. Salzinger (eds) *Psychology: Theoretical-Historical Perspectives* (Washington, DC: American Psychological Association, 1998), contains essays in the history of psychology, with many on the nineteenth century. Daniel N. Robinson, *Intellectual History of Psychology*, 3rd edn (Madison: University of Wisconsin Press, 1995), offers a history of psychology, with its relations to philosophy. William R. Woodward and Mitchell G. Ash (eds) *The Problematic Science: Psychology in Nineteenth-Century Thought* (New York: Praeger, 1982), has essays on various themes in nineteenth-century psychology. Robert M. Young, *Mind, Brain and Adaptation in the Nineteenth Century: Cerebral Localization and Its Biological Context from Gall to Ferrier* (New York: Oxford University Press, 1990), offers a study of the interactions among evolution, psychology, and theories of brain function in the nineteenth century.

19

DILTHEY AND THE NEO-KANTIANS: THE DISPUTE OVER THE STATUS OF THE HUMAN AND CULTURAL SCIENCES

Rudolf A. Makkreel and Sebastian Luft

Introduction

The topic concerning the status of the human and cultural sciences was at the forefront of the work of Wilhelm Dilthey and the neo-Kantians in the latter third of the nineteenth century. In order to understand the discussion concerning these sciences, its ramifications and broader implications, one needs to consider the history of philosophy and science prior to that period. The issue to be dealt with in this chapter derived its urgency from the very successes of the natural sciences at the time. Indeed, it was a *reaction* to the rise of the experimental natural sciences.

The so-called "collapse of Hegelianism" around the middle of the nineteenth century gave rise to a plethora of new developments in philosophy as well as the sciences. The most immediate result of this widespread disdain for grandiose systems and idealistic constructions was an immense proliferation of the *natural sciences*. The German Idealists devoted significant amount of time and energy to what they called *Naturphilosophie* as part of their speculative systems. Here one may mention Fichte, Schelling and Hegel, who made variegated attempts to "deduce" nature and natural science from an intellectual standpoint; attempts, which seem entirely dated from the perspective of modern science. Indeed, it was precisely this "speculative" manner of doing natural science, which became the main target of critique around 1850 as well.

Instead, researchers turned to much more modest aims in natural science, thereby hoping to leave behind the legacy of Idealism. The new natural sciences proceeded empirically in proving their hypotheses through experiments. This quickly led to an entire re-conception of the nature and understanding of science in general. This can be seen in a seemingly slight semantic shift, indeed a narrowing, of the German term science, *Wissenschaft*, to mean primarily the *natural* sciences. Up until Hegel, the terms "philosophy" and "science" were interchangeable, as witnessed in the titles of works such as Fichte's *Wissenschaftslehre* ("*Doctrine of Science*") and Hegel's *Enzyklopädie der philosophischen Wissenschaften* ("*Encyclopedia of the Philosophical Sciences*"). In the second half of the nineteenth century, the meaning of the German term *Wissenschaft* had changed, tipping the meaning entirely to the side of the *natural* sciences and, as a result, the term became identical to the meaning of the English term *science*. This was a significant shift that had occurred over only a brief period of time. While the scientists at the time, aptly called the age of "scientism" or "positivism," celebrated this move as an achievement in its own right, it led philosophers to ponder its meaning and virtue. For, this meant more than just a terminological alteration, but an eminent change in the way science was conceived, how it was carried out, and most importantly, its relation to philosophy and the cultural world at large. Indeed, one immediate result was a fundamental mistrust in philosophy as a "science" in its own right. Philosophers themselves felt compelled to step up to meet the challenge posed by the new sciences.

What *was* the meaning of science after all? Had not the meaning of science been, in Antiquity as well as the Enlightenment, a self-empowering of humankind, as the human mind penetrated *all* areas of the knowable world? How could such a shift from science in this grand tradition to the narrow sense of experimental natural science have occurred in the first place? If the word "science" pertained mainly to *nature*, was there something left out and what exactly was it? This was precisely the question concerning the sciences of those areas which seemed to fall *out* of the framework of science in the new sense of the term: the "regions" of spirit (*Geist*), hence the *Geisteswissenschaften*, literally translated as *spiritual sciences*, but more aptly as *human sciences* (to avoid too much affinity with Hegel). Whereas strict Hegelians used the monistic term *Geistwissenschaft*, Dilthey uses the plural term *Geisteswissenschaften*. Neo-Kantians used both Dilthey's term as well as the term *Kulturwissenschaften* that can be related back to Kant's concept of culture. What was *their* status, what kind of sciences are we talking about, what kind of "regions" define their subject domain, and what methods did they use?

From a twenty-first-century perspective, these questions might seem confusing. For one, it sounds rather odd to consider what we might today call "disciplines" as sciences. History, literary criticism, music, art history, sociology to name only a few of the candidates, are considered disciplines that in Anglo-American universities are grouped under the Liberal Arts. Literary critics and philologists consider themselves part of the Humanities and would not call their work "*scientific*." Yet history and sociology departments are usually classified as being part of the Social Science division of universities. Dividing the natural sciences from the socio-historical or cultural sciences presents a juxtaposition that could suggest a more generally "speculative" scenario, roughly between "nature" and "spirit" or the "real" versus the "ideal." Thus, put in this manner, it means that there might be an Idealist legacy lingering here after all. This, too, would seem unappealing for contemporary philosophy of science, which would not even consider cultural, human sciences as *sciences* to begin with.

Yet it is clear that there are disciplines pertaining to "culture" or "human affairs," and it is equally clear that their methods and their goals, though perhaps similar, are not the same as those in the natural sciences. Hence the question arises: what exactly *are* the subject domains, tasks and methods of these sciences of the "spirit"? May they even claim superiority over the natural sciences, which seem to quantify everything in numbers and formulae? This was already the complaint of the Romantics as a reaction to the Enlightenment: "*nicht mehr Zahlen und Figuren sind Hüter aller Kreaturen*" ("no longer numbers and figures are masters of all creatures," Novalis). Was this concern not all the more virulent in view of the meteoric rise of the natural sciences at the end of the century?

Hence, the discussion of the status of the cultural and human sciences in the last decades of the nineteenth century reflects the general circumstances of the time and can only be understood in this context. This does not mean, however, that this discussion is dated and of historical interest alone. Quite to the contrary, in a time such as ours, where the dazzle of Postmodernism seems to have passed and the natural sciences more than ever assert their dominance in our cultural, especially academic, landscape, the question of these other "sciences," their methods for world orientation and their goals at elucidating meaning merit philosophical attention more than ever. Both tendencies presented here – Dilthey and the neo-Kantians – reflected on these issues in an overarching philosophical view; not attempting to forge a philosophical "system" (none of them wanted to revive Hegel), but in trying to understand human life and the world it shapes, and the place of scientific endeavor *in* this life. Their discussions concerning the scientific status of the *Geisteswissenschaften* have timeless values for anybody working in these areas. Yet, their work was not merely theory of science; to the contrary, their reflections on the scientific status of the *Geisteswissenschaften* stemmed from their general philosophical concerns.

The main philosophical figures in Europe dealing with this issue were the neo-Kantians on the one hand, and Wilhelm Dilthey, on the other. (While there were some philosophers working in this area in countries such as France [Boutroux, Brunschvicq] and Italy [Comte], Germany was the main country where the thinkers relevant for this discussion were located.) Neo-Kantianism was the most dominant philosophical movement in Central Europe between ca. 1880 and 1920 (see Köhnke 1991). The main schools were the Southwest School, located in the university towns of Heidelberg and Freiburg and the Marburg School located in this small university town north of Frankfurt in the State of Hessia. The main figures of the Southwest School (also called the "Baden" School due to both cities' location in this State, after World War II called "Baden-Württemberg," and sometimes also referred to the "Value School" of neo-Kantianism due to their specific focus) relevant for this discussion were Wilhelm Windelband and Heinrich Rickert. In Marburg, the representatives of this school were Hermann Cohen, Paul Natorp, and Ernst Cassirer, the latter being the most famous heir of the Marburg School. While he is sometimes seen as having left behind or "overcome" the Marburg School, it is more appropriate to consider his

"Philosophy of Culture" the most profound and broadest expression of his teacher Cohen's method. And, it is arguably the most promising systematic attempt to couch the cultural sciences in a broader philosophical reflection on "culture."

Though Wilhelm Dilthey's life (1833–1911) is squarely set in this time period, he is typically *not* considered part of the neo-Kantian movement. The reasons for this exclusion seem, in retrospect, rather arbitrary and can mainly be traced back to academic fault lines at the time. In this sense, other contemporary figures, such as Edmund Husserl or Nicolai Hartmann, both of which taught in Freiburg and Marburg respectively and were in close contact with the neo-Kantians, are not counted as part of neo-Kantianism either. The fact that the gulf between the work of the neo-Kantians and Dilthey is not so great as it might have seemed at the time justifies treating them together in one combined article on the hotly debated status of the human or cultural vis-à-vis the natural sciences. Indeed, Dilthey was deeply immersed in the topics that his contemporary neo-Kantians worked on, and their mutual relations were cordial, though their disagreements are not to be overlooked.

Neo-Kantianism arose in the second half of the nineteenth century as the project to revive the "spirit" of Kantianism, against its distortions in German Idealism and, indeed, in Kant's writings themselves. In this sense, they attempted to not only go *back* to Kant but also to *update* him in the light of the challenges posed by the contemporary natural sciences. As one of the most famous interpreters of Kant and the founder and head of the Marburg School, Hermann Cohen, alleged, Kant received his insights into the need for a "Copernican Revolution" through a meditation on Newton's *Principia Mathematica* (Cohen 1987: 2f.). In the same sense, the neo-Kantians believed, they could only resuscitate the spirit of Kant by closely studying and monitoring the developments in the sciences of their day. However, this attention merely provided the starting point for their philosophical endeavors. For, as mentioned, dealing with the status of the natural sciences also brought that of the *Geisteswissenschaften* into special focus. Corresponding to the two main schools, the manner and the direction in which this topic was discussed differed significantly. While the achievements of neo-Kantianism extends far beyond merely the issue of the cultural sciences, indeed *culture* at large, it is arguably this topic that remains the most well known of their legacy. And, it is fair to say that it is, from a historical standpoint, also the most important one, judging from its reception in twentieth-century thought, where representatives of Phenomenology (Husserl, Scheler, Heidegger) and Hermeneutics (Gadamer) intensively discussed and criticized the neo-Kantians.

What distinguishes Dilthey's approach to the *Geisteswissenschaften* is his concern to define the nature of historical knowledge. From early on he was interested in many of the themes that define the richness of Hegel's work: the relation of art, religion and philosophy as they develop in the history of mankind. However, Dilthey rejected the speculative ways in which Hegel systematized the contents of human life. He called Hegel's dialectic a kind of panlogism that rid the development of human history of its facticity. Trained in Berlin by historicists like Boeckh who were also influenced by the hermeneutical approach of Schleiermacher, Dilthey conceived of a Critique of Historical Reason that would examine historical knowledge along more Kantian lines.

Are there, he asked, limits inherent in the explanative goals of the natural sciences that make them less appropriate for the human sciences and their overriding goal to understand the meaning of human life and productivity? As a consequence, the human sciences will be less concerned with determining the general laws that explain historical development than with articulating the distinctive structural relations that allow us to reflect on the overall significance of human culture. Combining the full scope of the Hegelian conception of spirit with the critical modes of analysis of Kantian epistemology, Dilthey developed a *sui generis* theory of the human sciences that especially influenced the work of Heidegger, Gadamer and Ricoeur.

But to get our discussion about Dilthey and the neo-Kantians started, let us go back to Kant and see where and how one can derive such a discipline as "human sciences" stemming from his philosophy. Judging from the first two *Critiques*, it might seem impossible to see how something like a theory of the human sciences could emerge from transcendental philosophy. The *Critique of Pure Reason* establishes the domain of theoretical or scientific knowledge and the *Critique of Practical Reason* the domain of moral practice. Kant's main concern in these two works is how to reconcile the possibility of doing natural science with the practical postulate of freedom. Do the laws of nature that determine human beings from without undermine the possibility of taking moral responsibility? But the *Critique of Practical Reason* delimits this question very narrowly by focusing purely on the decision to act. It considers how the moral law can be the incentive to act, but does not really confront the problem of how this affects human practice in a behavioral or public sense. Even the actualization of the highest good is couched in relation to the postulate of the immortality of the individual soul rather than in historical and social terms. This changes in the *Critique of Judgment* where taste and the arts are treated in communal and cultural terms. Now Kant defines humanity as involving a "universal feeling of participation" and a capacity to "communicate one's inmost self universally" (Kant 2001: 5:355). But this is a region where methods of inquiry that would count as science have not been developed. In §60 of the *Critique of Judgment*, Kant speaks of a quasi-cognitive sense of humanity, but not of human sciences. However, by tracing the increasingly skeptical questions that Kant poses about the status of psychology and whether it can ever become a proper natural science, we can see that Kant opens up the possibility of another kind of science.

Kant: replacing a psychology of the soul with a cultural anthropology

In the *Critique of Pure Reason*, Kant undermines the possibility of rational psychology by warning that speculations about the metaphysical status of the soul are untrustworthy. The transcendental unity of consciousness needed to legitimate epistemic claims about the world does not justify the inference that this unity is grounded in a spiritual substance that is simple and immortal.

Giving up on the traditional rational psychology of the soul, Kant was left with questions concerning the status and location of its empirical counterpart. Any psychological claims about mental processes will have to be restricted to an empirical psychology. If empirical psychology relies on introspection, it will confront difficulties in determining the status of the soul and our states of mind. Kant regards inner experience as less reliable than outer experience and holds out little hope that empirical psychology can make good on its cognitive claims. Yet, because the questions raised by psychology remain important, Kant allows it to retain its place in metaphysics as a temporary abode until it gradually finds its more permanent dwelling place in what he calls an *anthropology*.

In the *Metaphysical Foundations of Natural Science* of 1786, Kant expresses further doubts about psychology's ability to provide more than a "natural description (*Naturbeschreibung*) of the soul" (Kant 1902–97: 4:471). This is because mathematical measurement is not readily applicable to the temporal phenomena of the life of the soul. These ephemeral phenomena of inner sense need a spatial reference to make them more determinate. They flow into each other and are hard to keep distinct. Their indeterminacy is unfortunate, according to Kant, not only because it makes the analysis of psychic phenomena difficult, but also because it makes their *a priori* synthesis impossible. He thinks that any theory about natural phenomena can only be scientific insofar as it contains an *a priori* foundation, and that the only *a priori* cognition we can have about nature is mathematical (Kant 1902–97: 4:470).

A few years later, Kant writes in the *First Introduction* to the *Critique of Judgment* that "psychological explanations are in a wretched state compared with physical ones" (Kant 2001: 20:238). This is because psychological explanations are

> endlessly hypothetical [*hypothetisch*] so that given three different explanations a fourth, equally persuasive one can easily be conceived … . To make psychological observations, as Burke did in his treatise on the beautiful and the sublime, thus to collect material for a future systematic connection of empirical rules without striving for their comprehension [*begreifen*], is probably the sole true duty of empirical psychology, which can hardly even aspire to rank as a philosophical science. (Kant 2001: 20:238)

Psychology should avoid hypothetical explanations, not because they are difficult to construct, or because they lack persuasive power, but rather because there is no way of testing the many alternate persuasive accounts that they produce. From the fact that no valid explanation of psychological processes is possible, Kant concludes that no definitive scientific comprehension of them can result. All we can expect are preliminary psychological descriptions.

Despite these initial doubts about the value of psychological description, we find that in §78 of the *Critique of Judgment*, Kant develops a reflective conception of descriptive elucidation (*Erörterung*) and exposition (*Exposition*) in relation to teleological judgment that provides a kind of intelligibility, although it falls short of full comprehensibility. In exploring the problem of reconciling mechanism and teleology, Kant points out that each proposes a mode of explanation. Although mechanistic explanation can be applied indefinitely – even to organisms – it will, given the limits of the human understanding, always leave something unaccounted for. We must, therefore, appeal to a principle of final causality as well. But the overall relation between the principle of mechanical determinism and the principle of purposive activity cannot be comprehended, for the two principles mark out irreconcilable approaches to reality. Since "one kind of explanation excludes the other," their inter-relation is only "intelligible (*verständlich*)" reflectively (Kant 2001: 5:412–13). The two principles cannot be united in a determinant explanatory manner, but if we apply the principle of purposiveness merely descriptively (Kant 2001: 5:417), then we can reflectively coordinate it with the principle of mechanism. Kant now seems willing to assign his reflective use of description a systematic intelligibility, if not a full architectonic comprehensibility.

Kant's new willingness to link intelligibility with reflective exposition can be related to a more liberal attitude toward what counts as science. This new attitude becomes evident in the preface for the *Anthropology from a Pragmatic Point of View*, published in 1798. While admitting that there are many obstacles to anthropology rising to "the rank of a formal science," (Kant 2006: 7:121) Kant maintains that it can be made systematic enough to count as a mode of world cognition. Anthropology may not be able to rise to the level of the universally valid (*allgemeingültige*) sciences, but it can become a "generally useful (*gemeinnützige*) science" (Kant 1902–97: 7:122). The term *gemeinnützig* suggests that anthropology cannot ignore *Gemeinsinn* or common sense. It is thus not a doctrinal science in the academic sense (*Schulbegriff*), but one that is oriented to the world and our participation in it. Anthropology relates to philosophy as a mode of world-cognition (*Weltkenntnis*). It brackets the traditional academic question of psychology whether we possess a soul, and instead studies human beings as they relate to the world. Anthropology is "physiological" if it merely observes and explains human behavior – it then tells us what *nature* makes of human beings. Anthropology is "pragmatic" if such observations are used to investigate what a human being "as a free-acting being makes of himself, or can and should make of himself" (Kant 2006: 7:119). To show why anthropology should be pragmatic rather than physiological, Kant considers the difficulties in explaining human memory. He points out that many have, like Descartes, speculated that memory is caused by "traces of impressions remaining in the brain" (Kant 2006: 7:119). But this is an untested natural hypothesis.

Pragmatic anthropology avoids such explanative speculation and focuses instead on what reflective descriptions and assessments of human practices can teach us about the nature of memory and about ways to improve it. Memory, being a form of reproductive imagination that is volitional, can be cultivated and efforts to improve it can proceed either: (1) by mechanical repetition, (2) by ingenious associations, or (3) by the judicious use of classifications. It is the third approach that Kant approves of, and his elucidation of it discloses what is pragmatic about his anthropology:

> *Judicious* memorizing is nothing other than memorizing, in thought, a *table* of the *divisions* of a system (for example, that of Linnaeus) where, if one should forget something, one can find it again through the enumeration of the parts that one has retained; or else through memorizing the *sections* of a whole

made visible (for example, the provinces of a country on a map, which lie to the north, to the west, etc.) ... Most of all, the judicious use of *topics*, that is, a framework for general concepts, called *commonplaces*, facilitates remembering through *class division* .... (Kant 2006: 7:184)

The reference to a "topics" of "commonplaces" (*Gemeinplätze*) indicates that Kant is operating at the level of common sense (*Gemeinsinn*), not at the level of universal theory. A pragmatic science serves to orient us in the world by providing a kind of topological outline of it. The parallel with judicious memorization is that both build on our general feeling of orientation to the world and articulate it into a more specific worldly mapping, within which divisions can be made to systematically order things.

Anthropology as a pragmatic worldly endeavor is not aimed at a theoretical understanding of the psyche based on inner sense or speculation about the soul, but considers the full human being's proper orientation to the world through common sense. Whereas Kant had rejected common sense as a source of theoretical content in the *Prolegomena*, it is allowed to reassert itself formally as a *sensus communis* in the *Critique of Judgment* where it becomes relevant to value considerations, whether they be aesthetic or practical. Kant's *sensus communis* projects an ideal normative consensus, which cannot ground our understanding of nature, but which can orient us in interpreting the world as the sphere of human action. The *sensus communis* is defined by Kant as the *a priori* sense that allows us to compare our own private judgments based on feeling with the "possible judgments of others" (Kant 2001: 5:294). The commonality involved here is not among the senses, but among human beings. In the Aristotelian tradition, the imagination has been considered as a common sense that mediates among the outer senses. By contrast, Kant's *sensus communis* orients inner sense to the human community.

Whereas Kant's theoretical subject of understanding adopts a kind of view from nowhere on nature, the subject of anthropological reflection is situated amidst the world as the horizon of action. There is a complementarity between these two subjects. The former is concerned with scientific observation and constructs nature in accordance with universal laws, the latter is concerned to orient itself in its sphere of action and instead appeals to "a topics of commonplaces" (Kant 2006: 7:184). The theoretical subject surveys the world discursively, allowing its phenomena to appear successively or stepwise so that they can be properly determined. To say that the human subjects of anthropological reflection by contrast are situated in their worldly surroundings, means that they possess a direct, but less determinate, sense of the whole. Kant's anthropology supplements our discursive scientific understanding of the successive parts of the human world with a topological outline of the whole for pragmatic purposes.

What Kant promises at the beginning of his anthropology is not a theoretical description of human nature, but a complete account of "the headings under which this or that observed human quality of practical relevance can be subsumed" (Kant 2006: 7:121). His aim is not a detailed description of each of the aspects of human life, but a characterization of the whole. To characterize is to use description to point to more than what is directly given. With reference to life, Kant writes that "the character of a living being is that which allows its vocation to be cognized in advance" (Kant 2006: 7:329). Characterization allows us to be prepared for the future and is thus more pragmatic than mere description.

Just as the concept of description was expanded teleologically, so the concept of characterization allows us to relate pragmatic anthropology to the *telos* of culture as Kant defined it in §83 of the *Critique of Judgment*. There he states that human beings can only be considered as an end of nature if we consider their common culture rather than their individual happiness. Human beings as mere natural creatures have no intrinsic superiority to other living beings. But they can be the ultimate end (*letzter Zweck*) of nature to the extent that they alone among living beings have the power to set final ends (*Endzwecke*) that transcend nature (see Makkreel 1990: 136–41). The paradox here is that nature considered teleologically prepares us to become practically self-activating and independent of nature. What makes us worthy of being the ultimate end of nature is not some mere natural end such as happiness, but a moral end to be achieved through culture.

There are two kinds of culture according to Kant: (1) the culture of skill, which is the aptitude for the promotion of ends in general, and (2) the culture of discipline, which liberates "the will from the despotism of desires" (Kant 2001: 5:432). The culture of skill cultivates the natural capacities of human beings to find the means to satisfy their desires. This culture of skill allows natural life to become more organized in terms of economic and political life. Skills can produce goods that are indispensable to life as well as luxuries that are dispensable. They lead to social inequalities that need to be limited. In so far as we are members of the culture of skill we must operate under the external constraints of law. As Kant puts it: "the formal conditions under which alone nature can attain its final aim is that constitution in the relationships of human beings with one another in which the abuse of reciprocally conflicting freedom is opposed by the lawful power in a whole, which is called *civil society*" (Kant 2001: 5:432). The culture of skill needs to be regulated from above.

It is the culture of discipline that entitles human beings to be the ultimate end of nature. The culture of discipline denotes the capacity to voluntarily curb our natural desires and be "receptive to higher ends than nature itself can afford" (Kant 2001: 5:433). Whereas the culture of skill needs the external limits of the state, the culture of discipline sets its own bounds from within. An argument could be made that the self-binding higher ends of the culture of discipline lead to a *cosmopolitan society* where cooperation replaces competition. If the rules of civil (*bürgerliche*) society can be correlated with Kant's theory of right, then those of cosmopolitan (*weltbürgliche*) society may be correlated with his theory of virtue. Speaking of the virtues of social intercourse, Kant writes: "It is a duty to oneself as well as to others not to isolate oneself but to use one's moral perfections in social intercourse … While making oneself a fixed center of one's principles, one ought to regard this circle around one as also forming a part of an inclusive circle of those who, in their disposition, are citizens of the world" (Kant 1996: 6:473). Virtues of social intercourse such as agreeableness and tolerance are described in terms that evoke the idea of culture, namely, as the cultivation of a disposition of reciprocity in human life.

To the extent that culture includes the development of skills, the pragmatic retains its usual association with the prudential interest of the individual "to use other human beings skillfully for his purposes" (Kant 2006: 7:322). But to the extent that culture becomes the culture of discipline, the pragmatic moves beyond the prudential concern for individual happiness and aims at the civilizing of the human species. Now the pragmatic cultivates "social relations" and generates human "concord" (Kant 2006: 7:323). Although culture is not yet truly moral, it allows for a mutual use of human beings for their common good.

The way that Kant's pragmatic anthropology responds to the doubts about psychology raised in the first *Critique* will be especially relevant to Dilthey's theory of the human sciences and to what he has to say about descriptive psychology and anthropological reflection. On the other hand, the fact that Kant's anthropology is oriented by the *telos* of culture as developed in the third *Critique* helps to explain why the Baden school neo-Kantians – Windelband and Rickert – preferred the term "cultural sciences" over "human sciences." Marburg neo-Kantians such as Cohen and Cassirer used both terms. Cohen in fact comes closest to the more traditional term "moral sciences" in that he focuses on how Kant's philosophy of right fits with the standpoint of the second *Critique*. For Cohen a properly critical approach to the human sciences requires that they be legitimated in an *a priori* fashion.

Dilthey's theory of the human sciences

It was Dilthey's goal to supplement Kant's three *Critiques* with a Critique of Historical Reason. The first important theoretical work within that project is the *Introduction to the Human Sciences* of 1883. Its task is to delineate the intellectual globe into two domains – that of the natural sciences and that of the human sciences. The latter domain encompasses what we more commonly call the humanities and the social sciences. The human sciences range from disciplines such as philology and linguistics, literary and art criticism, religious and cultural studies, to political science and economics. According to Dilthey "the human sciences as they exist and as they are practiced according to the reason of things that were active in their history ... contain three classes of assertions" (Dilthey 1989: 78). These are (1) descriptive and historical statements, (2) theoretical generalizations about partial contents and (3) evaluative judgments and practical rules. The human sciences are more obviously normative than the natural sciences, where formal norms related to objective inquiry suffice. The fact that human scientists are forced to confront substantive normative issues puts a limit on the kind of theoretical regularities that can be established in the human sciences. Given the core role that human beings play in the socio-historical world, the understanding of individuality is as important in the human sciences as are the explanations to be found through generalizations.

The role that individuals can play in history becomes a vexing problem for Dilthey. He can no longer adopt the Lockean or Kantian position that regards individuals as the building blocks of social history. Individuals are not self-sufficient atoms nor should we attribute too much to their rational autonomy. On the other hand, Dilthey is suspicious of those like Hegel who allow individuals to be simply submerged by communities like nations or peoples. Concepts that posit the spirit or soul of a people "are no more usable in history than is the concept of life-force in physiology" (Dilthey 1989: 92). Individuals are at the same time the carriers of human history and points of intersection of contextual socio-political and cultural forces that they can partly set in motion, but cannot fully control.

For Dilthey most of the human sciences analyze human interactions at a level that can mediate between individual initiative and communal tradition. These sciences deal with what he calls "cultural systems" and "external organizations of society." Cultural systems are associations that individuals join voluntarily for certain purposes that they can only achieve through cooperation. These systems are cultural in the widest possible sense and include all aspects of our social life. They can be political, economic, artistic, scientific or religious in nature and are not bound by local or national interests. External organizations of society by contrast are those institutional structures like a family and a state that we are born into. Here "enduring causes bind the wills of many into a single whole" (Dilthey 1989: 94) within which relations of power, dependence and property can be established. It is important to cross-reference cultural systems and institutional organizations. Enlightenment thinkers had focused on cultural systems and their potential universal scope while overlooking how they are rooted in real life. Although Dilthey received his training from members of the Historical School, he recognized that many of them had been equally one-sided by stressing the distinctive institutional organizations that separate different peoples while ignoring the role of generalizations made possible through the analysis of cultural systems.

By combining these two approaches Dilthey hopes to liberalize the historicist perspective and give it a methodological rigor. To understand the role of the law in historical life we must consider it both as a cultural system that frames legal issues in universal terms and as an external organization of society that examines them in terms of the positive laws of particular institutions. The Historical School was wrong to regard individuals as completely subordinate to the bonds of family and state and to think that the positive laws of institutions define the full reality of life. The authority of the state "encompasses only a certain portion … of the collective power of the populace" and even when state power exerts a certain preponderance it can do so only "through the cooperation of psychological impulses" (Dilthey 1989: 132).

What then is the role of psychology in Dilthey's system of the human sciences? The answer changes somewhat over time. We can start by disclosing that Dilthey agreed with Kant that psychological explanations are untestable and to be avoided as much as possible. But the fact that for inner experience we have to content ourselves with description is not seen as a problem at all. This just reflects the more complex material that the human sciences have to deal with. From the natural science standpoint of causal explanation, the inability to measure inner states makes prediction difficult. But the human sciences are more concerned with understanding the meaning of experience and for that the description of the inherent coherence of our inner experience is important.

Dilthey's explanation-understanding distinction has much in common with Kant's determinant-reflective judgment distinction. Thus he agrees with Kant that the natural sciences must derive their determinant explanations from a discursive understanding (*Verstand*), which posits an ideal mathematical continuity among the empirical contents of outer experience that would otherwise remain discrete. However, the human sciences must appeal to a descriptive psychology to bring out the real continuum that inheres in inner experience and provides the basis for a reflective understanding (*Verstehen*) of human relations. Dilthey agreed with Kant that the traditional associationist psychology was too hypothetical, and proposed a new descriptive and analytical psychology that could delineate in psychic life the very "immanent purposiveness" that Kant had assigned to organic life. Whereas Kant wanted to replace psychology with a culturally oriented anthropology, Dilthey expanded the function of description to articulate the immanent structures of experience. Instead of limiting psychological description to introspective observation, Dilthey recognized that the very interconnectedness of our states of mind brings out their social embeddedness and historical indebtedness. The nexus of consciousness is thus not fully intelligible on the basis of introspection. To understand our inner experiences we must recognize what has been assimilated from without. Any psychological description of inner experience must use not only first-order psychological concepts like sensation, feeling, emotion, impulse, and desire, but also second-order psychological concepts like ambition, thrift and courage, which only make sense in economic and military contexts.

In his "Ideas for a Descriptive and Analytic Psychology" of 1894, Dilthey claimed that psychology could be the first of the human sciences if it rejects the hypothetical and explanative approach of the natural sciences and remains primarily descriptive. Whereas outer experience proceeds from parts to wholes, inner experience is essentially holistic. For ordinary lived experience, which is both inner and outer, the relations among contents are as real as the contents themselves. Our lived experiences possess an inner coherence and continuity that is directly available in reflexive awareness (*Innewerden*). Reflexive awareness is the way consciousness is present to itself and occurs at a pre-reflective level where the act-content and subject-object distinctions of representational consciousness are not yet made. Reflexive awareness brings out the self-given feltness of consciousness before any reflective self can be posited. What links both the volitional and cognitive aspects of the self as it develops in time is the life of feeling. Only when the interest of feeling attaches itself to the play of sense impressions do they attract our attention as serious perceptions and are we likely to act on their basis. Feelings play an essential evaluative role in the structuring of lived experience and instead of just passively assimilating every impression that comes our way, we filter out what is not worth perceiving by a process of apperception. But this apperception is not focused by a mere cognitive I-think, but brings about an I-think-feel-will structure that gets embodied in what Dilthey calls the "acquired nexus of psychic life."

This concept of an acquired nexus makes the case that individuality is not something we are born with, but gets historically generated over time. Individuality must be conceived structurally rather than in terms of unique qualities. Even when people share the same qualities their relative intensity will differ. Sometimes qualities are present to such a small extent as to be, in effect, unnoticeable. Prominent qualities, however, tend to reinforce certain related qualities and suppress others. Each individual can thus be understood as a structural configuration of a set of dominant qualities in tension with some subordinate qualities. This tension may be unresolved for a long time until finally some articulation or *Gestalt* is reached that defines a person's character. Dilthey gives the example of strong ambition leading someone to gradually overcome shyness in public if it stands in the way of an important goal being fulfilled.

Windelband attacked Dilthey's attempt to reconstitute psychology as a descriptive human science. Thinking that Kant's doubts about psychology as a natural science could be overcome by the new experimental methods pioneered by Wilhelm Wundt and others, Windelband claimed that psychology would soon establish itself as a proper nomothetic natural science and arrive at general laws. Moreover, the resulting psychological laws would have no bearing on ideographic historical studies interested in unique patterns. Dilthey in turn responded by casting doubt on the adequacy of an ideographic approach to history. What psychological and historical understanding have in common is a concern with structures that link the general and the particular. The description of singular historical data only becomes meaningful if understood in the framework of regularities: "What is most characteristic of the systematic human sciences is their consideration of individuation in connection with general theories …" (Dilthey 1924, 258). Not only is it the case that universal considerations are as important as ideographic specificity, but also the understanding of individuality is not possible without reference to some broader context.

The final phase of Dilthey's theory of the human sciences begins with his 1900 essay "The Rise of Hermeneutics," where he comes to the realization that the "experience through which I obtain reflexive awareness of my own condition" does not yet constitute self-understanding. Lived experience had been considered as sufficient to provide us an understanding of ourselves, but now Dilthey asserts that we understand ourselves only by means of our objectifications. The understanding of self requires me to approach myself as others do, that is, from the outside to the inside. "The process of understanding, insofar as it is determined by common conditions and epistemological means, must everywhere have the same characteristics" (Dilthey 1996: 237). To the extent that rules can guide the understanding of the objectifications of life it constitutes interpretation. Hermeneutics is the theory of interpretation that relates to all human objectifications, which include not only speech and writing, but all other palpable forms of expression and any publicly accessible human activity.

This new way of proceeding from the outside to the inside also alters Dilthey's conception of psychic structure. In a 1904 study entitled "The Psychic Structural Nexus," Dilthey considers what linguistic expressions can teach us about the intentionality of consciousness. No longer merely explicating the scope of psychic life through the interweavings of acts of cognition, feeling and willing, Dilthey uses the linguistic schema "I am worried about X" to disclose the referential structure of a lived experience. Psychic acts have contents that are related to the objects of the world by means of attitudinal stances. These stances toward the world are "indefinite in number. Asking, believing, presuming, claiming, taking pleasure in, approving, liking and its opposite, wishing, desiring, and willing are such modifications of the psychic attitude" (Dilthey 2002: 43). Attitudinal stances are not just cognitive, but predelineate something more encompassing, which Dilthey calls "knowledge." Knowledge (*Wissen*) adds to the conceptual cognition (*Erkenntnis*) of reality, "the positing of values" and "the determination of purposes and the establishment of rules" (Dilthey 2002: 25).

The representational epistemology (*Erkenntnistheorie*) established by Kant suffices for the natural sciences, but the human sciences require a more full-blooded theory of knowledge (*Theorie des Wissens*). Knowledge is to be "distinguished from a mere representation, presumption, question or assumption by the fact that a content appears here with a sense of objective necessity" (Dilthey 2002: 27–8). This objective necessity is to be located in the evidentness that accompanies thinking that is properly executed and reaches its goal whether through the self-given reality of lived experience or the "givenness that binds us to an outer perception" (Dilthey 2002: 28).

The human sciences are not content merely to cognize things as phenomenal objects, but aim to know them as real for our life-concerns (*Lebensbezüge*). Referring to the files in his study, Dilthey writes:

> I worry about their unfinished contents, whose completion demands incalculably more work from me. All this "about," "of," and "toward," all these references of what is remembered to what is experienced, in short, all these structural inner relations, must be apprehended by me, since I now want to apprehend the fullness of the lived experience exhaustively. And precisely in order to exhaust it, I must regress further in the structural network to the memories of other lived experiences. (Dilthey 2002: 50)

The attempt to understand this experience of worry leads beyond it to other structurally related experiences that ground it. This involves not just an observational process of willful attention, but also an involuntary "being-pulled-along by the state of affairs itself" to ever more constituent parts of the nexus of human knowledge.

The next major work to be considered is Dilthey's *Formation of the Historical World in the Human Sciences* of 1910. Here the same kind of structural analysis that we saw him develop for lived experience is applied to the understanding of history. The human sciences give form to the historical world by analyzing the structural systems in terms of which human beings participate in history. In the *Introduction to the Human Sciences* Dilthey had conceived the psychic nexus, cultural systems and the external organizations of society as purposive systems. Now a more neutral covering concept is used to capture all the ways the forces of life can converge, namely, the concept of the "productive system (*Wirkungszusammenhang*)." The efficacy of life and of the historical world is to be understood in terms of productivity before any causal or teleological analysis is applied. The carriers of history, whether they be individuals, cultures, institutions, or communities, are productive systems capable of producing value, meaning, and, in some cases, realizing purposes. Each productive system is to be considered structurally as centered in itself.

Even individual human beings can be regarded as psychic productive systems inherently related to other more inclusive productive systems that are also at work in history. These larger productive systems come about because of the need for communication, interaction and cooperation among individuals. But they can also take on a life of their own and survive the individuals that formed them. In the *Introduction to the Human Sciences*, Dilthey had been unwilling to consider these larger groupings as subjects or carriers of history. In *The Formation of the Historical World*, he qualifies his opposition to transpersonal subjects by allowing them to be considered as logical rather than real subjects. It is possible to regard cooperative productive systems as logical subjects that transcend individuals without positing them as superempirical real subjects.

On the one hand, individuals only give part of themselves to the more inclusive productive systems in which they participate, leaving them a certain amount of independence. On the other hand, they can express their whole being through this part and in this way make a difference. But there is no doubt that in this late work the psychological contribution to historical understanding is less prominent than before. Now Dilthey warns that when hermeneutics refers outer sensory phenomena back to a reality that is inner, we should not assume that the latter is psychological in nature. The inner content that is expressed in the laws of a state is not the mental states of its legislators, but a normative relationship among human beings. Similarly, what is expressed in a drama is "not the inner processes in the poet; it is rather a nexus created in them but separable from them. The nexus of a drama consists in a distinctive relation of material, poetic mood, motif, plot, and means of presentation" (Dilthey 2002: 107).

Interpretations of history must deal with all manifestations of life, not merely expressions that are intended to communicate a state of mind. In an important supplement to the *Formation of the Historical World* entitled "The Understanding of Other Persons and Their Manifestations of Life," Dilthey distinguishes three classes of life-manifestations. The first class consists of concepts, judgments and larger thought-formations. They are intended to communicate states of affairs, not states of mind. Thus the proposition "two plus two equals four" means the same in all contexts and says nothing about the person uttering it. Actions form a second class of manifestations of life. Actions as such are not meant to communicate anything, but they often do reveal something about the intentions of the actor. Thus if someone puts on a coat, it is appropriate to assume that he or she is getting ready to leave and go outside. There is a third class of life-manifestations that Dilthey calls "expressions of lived experience" and which disclose more about the individual uttering them. Expressions of lived experience can range from simple exclamations and gestures to personal self-descriptions and reflections to works of art. Often these expressions betray more than was intended:

> An expression of lived experience can contain more of the nexus of psychic life than any introspection can catch sight of. It draws from the depths not illuminated by consciousness. But at the same time, it is characteristic of the expression of lived experience that its relation to the spiritual or human content expressed in it can only be made available to understanding within limits. Such expressions are not to be judged as true or false but as truthful or untruthful. (Dilthey 2002: 227)

A work of art often reveals more of human life in general than of the specific life of the artist. It may disclose something about the state of mind or the attitude of the artist, but a work of art will only be great if its "spiritual content is liberated from its creator" (Dilthey 2002: 228).

These three classes of life-manifestations can be called theoretical, practical and disclosive respectively. Dilthey then goes on to distinguish two modes of understanding that can be applied to them: elementary and higher understanding. Elementary understanding goes back to the associative relation that normally exists between an expression and what is expressed in it. It assimilates the meanings that are commonly attached to expressions in the community that we grow up in. Dilthey uses Hegel's concept of "objective spirit" to account for this commonality of meaning. Objective spirit embodies "the manifold forms in which a commonality existing among individuals has objectified itself in the world of the senses," allowing the past to become "a continuously enduring present for us" (Dilthey 2002: 229). Whereas Hegel restricted objective spirit to the legal, economic and political aspects of historical life, Dilthey expands the concept to also include religion, art and philosophy, which Hegel had located in absolute spirit. But most of all, objective spirit embodies the everyday, mundane aspects of life that we grow up with.

> From earliest childhood, the self is nurtured by this world of objective spirit. It is also the medium in which the understanding of other persons and their life-manifestations takes place. For everything in which spirit has objectified itself contains something that is common to the I and the Thou. Every square planted with trees, every room in which chairs are arranged, is understandable to us from childhood because human tendencies to set goals, produce order, and define values in common have assigned a place to every square and every object in the room. (Dilthey 2002: 229)

The commonality of objective spirit suffices for the elementary understanding of everyday life. But whenever the common meaning of life-manifestations is called into question for some reason, higher understanding becomes necessary. This can occur because of an apparent inconsistency among judgments or expressions, or because of an ambiguity that attaches to them or because of a complexity that we have not come upon before. Higher understanding cannot continue to rely on the common meanings of an expression that derive from a shared local background between speaker and listener, writer and reader. Higher understanding must replace the sphere of commonality, where inference by analogy suffices, with that of universality, where inductive inference must take over. Here the human sciences become relevant by offering the appropriate universal disciplinary contexts that can help to deal with uncertainties of interpretation. Thus literary scholars may be able to clarify a puzzling poetic passage by showing it to contain a literary allusion to a classical work with an unfamiliar vocabulary. Or they can perhaps clarify it by seeing it as a way of accommodating certain technical demands of the genre as such. But the context that higher understanding appeals to need not be merely literary or cultural. It may also be legal, political or economic. In certain cases, these contexts may even allow for explanation. Although Dilthey considered the primary task of the human sciences to be that of furthering the understanding of human affairs, he never ruled out that within well-defined and limited contexts, explanations could be achieved. Thus within the system of economic relations it may even be possible to discover laws of historical stages, but for history in general no such laws are possible (Makkreel 1975: 314–22).

Higher understanding can either expand the context of reference beyond the sphere of familiarity or contract it. Thus to better understand the work of an author it may focus on his or her life-situation. But the late Dilthey warns that this kind of psychological specification of context should come only at the conclusion of the interpretive process and represents a shift from exploring the relation "of expression to what is expressed" toward the relation "of what has been produced to productivity" (Dilthey 2002: 233). Here we move from meaning relationships to something like a productive relationship to which biographical information about an author becomes relevant. But the first recourse here should be to consult more of the products of the author. How does a sentence fit into a paragraph, a chapter, a whole work, or a corpus as a whole? Only if these contexts fail to resolve the problem may we consider psychological claims about the author.

Elementary understanding can be said to be pre-discursive and higher understanding the kind of discursive operation that many human sciences make possible. However, history is not just a human science; it is also an art that requires judgment. Only historical reflection can create the right balance that will transform the conceptual cognition of the human sciences into adequate historical knowledge.

This shift to historical knowledge is the main theme of the notes for a second volume of *The Formation of the Historical World* which were published posthumously as *Drafts for a Critique of Historical Reason*. Here Dilthey analyzes the categories of life that are relevant to historical knowledge. He distinguishes between formal and real categories. Formal categories stem from elementary logical operations that are at work in all apprehension: they include the processes of comparing, noting sameness, differentiating and relating. Although such elementary operations are prediscursive, they provide the basis for discursive thought. The prediscursive noting of sameness prepares the way for the unifying concepts of discursive thought and the process of relating provides the basis for synthetic procedures. These prediscursive and discursive modes of thought account for the formal categories of unity, plurality, identity, difference, degree and relation that are shared by the natural and human sciences.

But the real categories begin to differentiate themselves in the natural and human sciences. Whereas time as a Kantian ideal form suffices for the natural sciences, for the human sciences it must involve experienced content. Time is experienced as advancing into the future and "always contains the memory of what has just been present" (Dilthey 2002: 216). The relation between the past and the present becomes the source for the category of meaning which is Dilthey's main historical category. The present never *is* in the sense of being observable, but it can be understood meaningfully to the extent that the past asserts its *presence* in it. When the present is merely lived, "the positive or negative value of the realities that fill it are experienced through feeling. And when we face the future, the category of purpose arises through a projective attitude" (Dilthey 2002: 222). Each of these three central categories of life is rooted in a response to temporality. What is valued by feeling focuses on the momentary present, but for the will everything in the present tends to be subordinated to some future purpose. Only the category of meaning can expand the present into a presence that overcomes the mere juxtaposition or subordination of the various aspects of life to each other. The understanding of meaning involves the encompassing sense of knowledge that attempts to relate cognition to evaluation and the setting of goals.

Windelband claimed that Dilthey's distinction between the natural and human sciences involved a metaphysical distinction. But Dilthey denies this by claiming that he is not creating a dualism between nature as the domain of causality and history as the domain of freedom. There are indeed determining forces at work in history because it cannot be divorced from natural conditions. But to understand how individuals participate in history we must replace the purely external relation of cause and effect with the integral relation of "agency and suffering, of action and reaction" (Dilthey 2002: 219).

The overall task of Dilthey's Critique of Historical Reason is to bring out the reciprocal relation between the doing of human subjects that makes it possible for "the connectedness of the world of human spirit" to dawn in them and the undergoing that makes it necessary for them to find the actual connections in an independent "progression of spirit directed at an objective knowledge of this world" (Dilthey 2002: 213). Such knowledge is rooted in the elementary understanding of lived experience and the higher understanding of the objectifications of spirit made possible by the human sciences. But ultimately historical knowledge requires a third kind of understanding, namely, a reflective understanding of life itself. For the sake of historical knowledge, psychology and epistemology must go over into what Dilthey calls "anthropological reflection" (Dilthey 2002: 259–60). Dilthey never renounced his descriptive psychology, but like Kant he came to place increasing emphasis on a broader notion of anthropological reflection. Psychology can no longer be the first of the human sciences, but as we saw it can be appealed to as a last resort.

Anthropological reflection looks to history for how it cultivates life and defines its goals, yet history remains dependent on life. There is a circularity here that could only be overcome "if unconditioned norms, purposes, or values set the standard for contemplating an apprehending history" (Dilthey 2002: 281). Unlike his neo-Kantian contemporaries Cohen and Rickert, Dilthey does not accept unconditional values and transcendent goals. The spiritual nexus of history "is that of life itself insofar as life produces connectedness under the conditions of its natural environment" (Dilthey 2002: 280). Life is the ultimate context behind which we cannot go. It is the horizon of productivity which encompasses the organic and the mental, but cannot be defined by either. Since "life is intimately related to temporal fulfillment" (Dilthey 2002: 249) historicity is part of its essence. Consequently, the objective validity that is to be attached to any value cannot be separated from our temporal engagement with life. Values are not derivable from on high nor are they simply given by life. Values are produced as part of the human process of explicating the meaning of history. Dilthey's project of the formation (*Aufbau*) of the historical world is to be distinguished from an *a priori* grounding that imposes form determinantly. Yet the formative project is critical in not simply assimilating the connectedness of life and in giving it a reflective articulation that can be objectively analyzed.

Neo-Kantianism I: the Southwest School's distinction between idiographic and nomothetic sciences and philosophy as theory of values

We have already seen how Dilthey and the neo-Kantians have dealt with common issues and have mutually criticized one another. These were mainly about the *methods* to be employed for the different types of sciences and about the *value* attached to human life. Now it is time to turn to the neo-Kantians themselves. While this presentation of the neo-Kantian movement is restricted to the issue of the cultural or human sciences, this discussion will lead to the heart of their overall philosophical concerns. (Other topics that have to be passed over but were important topics in the neo-Kantian movement shall be mentioned briefly: for the Marburg School, its contributions to the philosophy and theory of the natural sciences [Helmholtz and his contemporaries in the nineteenth century, Einstein in the twentieth]; its concern with social and political issues; Cohen's late interest in the philosophy of religion, especially Judaism. For the Southwest School, one might call attention to Emil Lask's [1875–1915] meta-philosophical reflections and his doctrine of categories [*Kategorienlehre*] of philosophy itself.)

Unlike the Marburg School, the Southwest neo-Kantians, especially Rickert, favored the historical or spiritual sciences over the natural ones. To condense their overall philosophical concerns into one term, it would appropriately be that of *value* as the main category of human life. This term was so determinative of this school that it was oftentimes also referred to as the "value theoretical" (*werttheoretische*) or simply "value school" of neo-Kantianism. With this paradigm of value they remained closer to Kant's practical concerns in the Second Critique and also, in effect, to Plato's theory of the forms when it came to determining the ontological status of values.

But before discussing the issue of value, a good entryway into the Southwest School is to introduce what was the main occupation especially of Windelband, namely, historiography of philosophy. Writing the history of philosophy was no trivial matter for Windelband. While Dilthey wrote about the history of religion, philosophy and literature in ways that bring out pervasive world views (*Weltanschauungen*) and how individual thinkers relate to their temporal context, Windelband made his initial mark as an historian of philosophy and is, to this day, most known as an historian of philosophy, but unfairly reduced to a mere historian. To put the matter differently, he is one of the first to raise the issue of what it means to write the history of philosophy. After Hegel, it can no longer be done naively (or "positivistically"), as a simple story-telling of what happened when. But after Hegel the idealistic treatment seemed overly speculative. Hegel himself attempted a reconstruction of the stages of consciousness's experience, a "story" in which "inner" and "outer" history seem to have been collapsed (or have been sublated). Windelband's method of philosophical historiography is both "positivistic" in the sense of working on original sources and "idealistic" in the sense of being a highly reflected method, that of being oriented to *problems*. Windelband inaugurated, in other words, a type of philosophical historiography that seems perhaps the most obvious today, called *history of problems* (*Problemgeschichte*).

Windelband became known to a wider philosophical audience through his two-volume work *History of Modern Philosophy* (*Geschichte der neueren Philosophie*), which was first published in 1878–1880 but was re-edited an astonishing twelve times until 1928. There, Windelband devised and put to use this new way of writing the history of philosophy, as the history of *problems*. At the time this was quite innovative; namely, to write the history as a development of philosophical problems, not *primarily* of thinkers. This way of doing the history of philosophy would become paradigmatic for all neo-Kantians who worked in the history of philosophy, besides Windelband, especially Cassirer in his impressive four-volume work *The Problem of Cognition in Modern Philosophy and Science* (*Das Erkenntnisproblem in der Philosophie und Wissenschaft der Neueren Zeit*), drawing an arch from the Renaissance up until the first three decades of the twentieth century. Indeed, one can cite a passage from Cassirer's first volume of *Das Erkenntnisproblem* that captures the spirit of Windelband's method of philosophical historiography and demonstrates its highly reflected nature. I have attempted, Cassirer writes,

> to combine the systematic and the historical interest. From the very start it was for me a necessary and self-evident [*selbstverständliche*] demand to study the emergence of the fundamental concepts in the *historical sources* themselves and to justify every step of the presentation and the consequences immediately from them. Individual thoughts should not only be reproduced in historical fidelity; they should at the same time be viewed and grasped from within the intellectual horizon [*Gesichtskreis*] to which they belong. ... The history of philosophy, to the extent that it is science [*Wissenschaft*], can be no mere collection through which we get to learn facts in a colorful succession; it strives to be a *method* through which we learn to understand them. (Cassirer 1994: viif.)

Hence, Windelband's historiological method takes the emphasis away from individual philosophers and a quasi-biographical reconstruction of their work and instead places them into a rich historical "horizon," which enabled them to be seen as working in a historical-scientific-philosophical setting. This setting is the process in which "European mankind" exposes its view of world and life (*Welt- und Lebensauffassung*). It is not a Hegelian scenario, in which history is the process of increasing knowledge of freedom, but rather a process of communicating thinkers and scientists. The way this communication operates is again not to be understood as some sort of dialectical process of thesis and antithesis. Instead, in this historical process, Windelband discerns *three* relevant factors that need to be taken into account: *pragmatic*, *cultural* and *individual*. A *pragmatic* consideration of the history of problems emphasizes that it is the same philosophical problems that always re-emerge in Western history with a certain consistency in changed circumstances. The *cultural* aspect asserts that culture is the binding continuum that holds together seemingly incoherent scientific or philosophical discussions. And finally, the focus on *individuality* highlights the import on the part of individual characters in the history of philosophy; while important – and the only real focus in earlier philosophical historiography – this consideration comes at the *end* of this historical reconstruction (see Holzhey 2004: 59f.). However, the individual is highlighted not for the sake of the person itself, but to the extent to which its life is relevant for the work it produced.

The manner in which an individual's life counts as part of his or her work in science or philosophy (an artificial distinction anyway to Windelband and his followers) can best be exemplified, again, in Cassirer's *Kant's Life and Thought* (Cassirer 1918). This book, originally intended as the introductory volume to his edition of Kant's collected works, ingeniously shows how Kant's philosophical development intersects with his life and how his critical philosophy emerged as an extension of his character. Cassirer is thereby taking a "view from within" in trying to recapture the spirit of Kant's character by immersing oneself in it. In demonstrating how his philosophy arose "from within," it also seeks to find the *unity* of life and work, stemming from a hidden center of gravity. While Kant's philosophy can certainly not be *reduced* to his life, it is nevertheless a meritorious historical task to ground philosophy in life, as compared to an anonymous "spirit" that evolves mysteriously. In other words, this method of writing the history of philosophy along the lines of problems that concrete persons pondered in their "lifeworld" and their scientific and academic circumstances is intended to provide a most circumspect opening up of the horizon of understanding in which these scientists dwelled. The history of thought does not evolve according to some blind "force," but as a conversation of thinkers in their concrete circumstances. There are no gaps or leaps in this history; or if there are, it is the task of the faithful historian to explain them away.

This type of philosophical historiography – in conjunction with the scrupulous and meticulous efforts that neo-Kantian philosophers carried out concerning the "hard" work, such as editions of the original sources that helped canonize Kant – has become the standard for any historical writings in philosophy. But it has also been the main target of subsequent attempts to overturn this traditional way of doing the history of philosophy. For instance, Heidegger's "History of Being" and Gadamer's "History of Effects" are direct critiques of the neo-Kantian method of doing history of problems. Both Heidegger and Gadamer knew this neo-Kantian method intimately. Gadamer's critique is, like Hegel's critique of philosophy of reflection (*Reflexionsphilosophie*), that the attempt to reflect oneself out of history is neither possible nor desirable (Gadamer 1990: 281). Therefore, one has to make recourse to an individual's "presuppositions" (*Vorurteile*), rather than her "judgments" (*Urteile*), as the former determine "the historical reality of her existence" (*ibid.*). Hence, Gadamer wants to move from the overt discourse of scientists and immerse himself in the "rich bathos" of concrete life. Whether Gadamer's project is successful is another story; to criticize the neo-Kantian method for stopping at the judgments that the individuals made, as *scientists* or *philosophers*, however, is justified. Yet one has to keep in mind that the neo-Kantian context was explicitly to write the history of ideas, not of concrete individuals. This "existentialist" tendency to go back to the ultimate concretion of human life was univocally repudiated by the Southwest School, especially Rickert. (Perhaps a different story could be told for the Marburg School and Natorp's ultimate recourse to "Life" as "primal concreteness" [*das Urkonkrete*].)

Hence, doing the history of philosophy is itself an activity that can be construed as a performative act of pursuing philosophy as science. Consequently philosophy's relation, its "essential connection [*Lebenszusammenhang*] to all other disciplines" (Windelband 1924: 138) itself becomes a problem. This issue is exacerbated when the relation of philosophy as a *method* is considered in conjunction with the methods of the sciences, and in this manner Windelband comes to consider the methods of the sciences *themselves*, especially the theory of the human sciences vis-à-vis the natural sciences. Here, the neo-Kantians intersect most with Dilthey's concerns. Indeed, perhaps the most famous Southwest legacy is Windelband's distinction between *idiographic* and *nomothetic* sciences, already mentioned above (as a distinction Dilthey took issue with). Rickert on his part expanded upon this distinction and added some further details, but went beyond Windelband in his own systematic value theory. (One reads occasionally, and incorrectly, that this idiographic-nomothetic distinction was introduced by Rickert; it was Windelband who conceived it.) Windelband lays out this influential distinction in his Presidential Address (*Rektoratsrede*) *Geschichte und Naturwissenschaft* (*History and Natural Science*) in Strasbourg in 1894.

His starting point is a critique of the traditional (Leibnizian-Kantian) distinction between rational and empirical sciences. Windelband begins his reflections by asserting that this distinction is no longer satisfactory; indeed, the development of certain sciences – most notoriously psychology and physics – has shown that the true results of these disciplines are neither just rational nor just empirical. The problematic discipline is, as Kant saw initially and as Windelband agrees, psychology, which cannot be a rational discipline with claims to *a priori* cognition, nor is it thereby merely an empirical discipline. An overview over the scientific activities of his day reveals a different distinction that seems to fit better the actual status quo, namely that between sciences of nature (*Naturwissenschaften*) and sciences of the human world (*Geisteswissenschaften*). They *are* both sciences – *Wissenschaften* – but neither's character can be grasped by considering them purely rational nor purely empirical. They distinguish each other, not with regard to different subject domains, but in terms of *method*. Indeed, such a distinction undercuts that of rational and empirical sciences and is an advance over the former. For, the traditional distinction between rational and empirical sciences seems to rest on an ontological predicament – the ontic regions of nature and spirit – which has its problems, as witnessed in the case of psychology. This is the launching pad for Windelband's original contribution to this issue. Psychology reveals the problem with the distinction between natural and human sciences: What kind of science is one to group it under? Having the human psyche as its object, one would be inclined to call it a human science. Yet insofar as its goal is experimentally verifiable general results, it has the character of a natural science:

> It is impossible to group a discipline of the importance of psychology amongst natural science and human science [*Naturwissenschaft und Geisteswissenschaft*]: according to its object [*ihrem Gegenstand nach*] it can only be characterized as human science and is in a certain sense a foundation of all others; but its entire method [*Verfahren*], its methodological style [*Gebahren*] is from beginning to end that of the natural science. It is for this reason that it had to allow itself to be called at times the "natural science of the inner sense" ["*Naturwissenschaft des inneren Sinnes*"] or even "spiritual natural science" ["*geistige Naturwissenschaft*"]. (Windelband 1924: 143)

Hence Windelband moves from a thematic to a methodological criterion: *all* sciences, since they have an object of experience, are "*empirical*" in a broad sense of the term. The question is only, *how* and *as what* one *interprets* these empirically ascertained results. It is clear that this new distinction is not ontological, but must be a methodological one. Hence, the principle for distinguishing sciences is

> the formal character of their goals of cognition [*Erkenntnisziele*]. The one set of sciences seek general laws, the others special historical facts: in the language of formal logic, the goal of the former is the general, apodictic judgment [*Urteil*], that of the latter is the singular, assertoric proposition [*Satz*]. (Ibid.: 144)

Hence, the focal points of cognition are, in principle, the individual or the general, which is a fundamental relation of the human mind, Windelband remarks, since the days of Socrates/Plato and Aristotle (and their known disagreement on the "locus" of the universal). These focal points are, however, not absolute but merely *relative* terms. Scientific cognition oscillates between these extreme focal points of interpreting its findings. The scientific cognition of something individual Windelband calls *idiographic* (i.e. describing the individual, singular), that of something general, *nomothetic* (i.e. positing the general, lawful).

> The latter are sciences of laws [*Gesetzeswissenschaften*], the former are sciences of events [*Ereigniswissenschaften*]; the latter teach what is always the case, the former what occurred only once. Scientific thought is – if one may be

permitted to use new and artificial terms [*Kunstausdrücke*] – in the one case *nomothetic*, in the other *idiographic*. (*Ibid.*: 145)

For instance, if one wants to, as historian, work on the French Revolution, one has to describe the individual characters and individual events that took place etc. Its focus is on concrete intuitability (*Anschaulichkeit, ibid.*: 150). On the other hand, if one wants to understand, as chemist, the manner in which certain chemicals react together, one has to find out the general laws by which they function and react – always and in a reliable, repeatable pattern; its tendency is towards abstraction (*ibid.*). However, in both cases, the focus on the individual and general, respectively, is a matter of *degree*. The historian cannot avoid certain generalizations, whereas natural science cannot disregard individual specimens that might contradict the hypothesis underpinning the experiment. Here what we saw Dilthey make as an objection to the nomothetic-ideographic distinction is acknowledged as a limitation.

The fact that both do not rest on an ontological premise can be seen in that the tendency towards individuality and generality can even be *reversed*. Indeed, the nomothetic and idiographic standards can be applied to one and the same ontic field. The classic example for this is, according to Windelband, the science of organic nature:

> As systematics, it is of nomothetic character, insofar as it describes the always fixed types of living creatures, which have been experienced within the millennia of human observation as their lawful form. As developmental history, where it presents the order of earthly organisms as a process of descent and transformation of species [i.e. in evolutionary theory] ... there it is an idiographic discipline. (Windelband 1924: 146)

This distinction stakes out a new *type* of science in the wake of the positivistic predicament that was rampant at the end of the nineteenth century. Contrary to the notion that human "disciplines" cannot be *sciences* precisely because they yield no general results, Windelband's emphasis was that the human sciences can indeed have the character of science with no less dignity than natural science *if* one has a different scientific ideal. His interest is in staking out a scientific task for the human sciences, not *privileging* them over their natural counterparts. The idiographic sciences are of no lesser importance for the understanding of our world, to the contrary; indeed, if by "world" we mean more than nature but *culture*, the idiographic sciences even have an edge over the former. Windelband's distinction was, in effect, an assertion of the importance of a genuine "science of culture" over a sell-out of the grand notion of science as *Wissenschaft* if its sense be reduced to that of natural science. What distinguishes idiographic sciences is, indeed, that they are an extreme point of concretion. Thus, both methods must not be understood as dialectically opposed, where the scientist would be faced with an either/or. Rather, they are extreme points on a flexible scale, which satisfy the human desire for abstract knowledge and concrete intuition. The individual and the universal are merely abstract focal points of the human mind and "cannot be led back to a common source" (*ibid.*: 157), as Windelband asserts with Kantian humility. Hence, again, absolute abstraction on the one hand and absolute concretion on the other are neither possible nor desirable; they are abstract extremes of the human mind in orienting itself in the world (much like Thomas Nagel defines the relation between the first and third person perspective). In navigating between the two, they yield a world view (*Weltbild*) for the scientist:

> The fixed frame of our world view is provided by this general lawfulness of things which, elevated above all change, expresses the eternally same essence of reality; and within this frame unfolds the living nexus of all individual formations [*Einzelgestaltungen*] of their species that are valuable for humanity. (*Ibid.*: 157)

Hence, to view nomothetic and idiographic sciences as two static and distinct methods is, though often asserted, an incorrect rendering of their relation. No science is ever completely abstract and can dispense with concrete facts, nor can it ever be completely concrete and do without at least some degree of generalization, of which *a priori* cognition (necessary and universal) is merely the extreme. Both are the extremes between which the human mind, in its attempt to gain cognition, moves back and forth. Finally, circumscribing this scope of the human mind also marks the limit of what philosophy proper can do, furthering the critique that the neo-Kantians had reduced philosophy to the "handmaiden of the sciences":

> Philosophy is capable of showing how far the cognitive power [*Erkenntniskraft*] of the different disciplines reaches. Beyond that, it cannot itself reach any substantial insight [*gegenständliche Einsicht*]. The law [*Gesetz*] and the event [*Ereignis*] remain as the ultimate, incommensurable quantities of our representation of the world [*Weltvorstellung*]. (*Ibid.*: 160)

Hence, what is circumscribed in this distinction is, generally speaking, the character of the human mind in its opposing directions, and more specifically, two groups of sciences, the natural and the human or cultural sciences. They are distinguished by the two opposed tendencies, whereby neither is fully the one or the other, but more "inclined" towards one tendency. Thus, the difference between both types of sciences comes down to a question of how much a given discipline chooses to strive for generality or individuality. Seen in this light, the difference between natural and cultural sciences is merely relative. However, when it comes to the relevance of things in our lives, the emphasis lies on the uniqueness and incomparability of individual objects, which determine our interests and feelings for *value*. Hence, the recognition of individual things that we deem valuable is the trajectory into the Southwest value theory, which was worked out specifically in Rickert.

As mentioned, this distinction was the touchstone for the critiques stemming mainly (though not exclusively) from Dilthey and the phenomenological camp, especially Husserl and Heidegger, all of which, albeit for different reasons, rejected this distinction when it came to describing what is the proper object of the human sciences. Dilthey's critique is known from the previous section. Husserl's attempt at an *eidetic science* of subjectivity goes further than Dilthey by asserting the possibility of a "rigorous" (i.e. *a priori*) science of subjectivity after the phenomenological reduction. In other words, Husserl's phenomenology purports to be an eidetic (= universal) science of concrete subjectivity, a science of the third person perspective *precisely of* the first person perspective. Finally, Heidegger's sketch of a hermeneutic of factical *Dasein* is predicated on a wholesale rejection of the (Platonic) distinction between the individual and the universal, with which Windelband is operating. Heidegger thereby also rejects Husserl's notion of an "eidetic science" of human subjectivity.

The idea of an idiographic science as the proper method of accessing the life of human culture was especially emphasized by *Rickert*. Philosophically and systematically more ambitious than his teacher, he was introduced to philosophy through Windelband's lectures covering the history of philosophy. Ironically, his own systematic aspirations were spurred by Windelband's modesty. As Rickert recalls his first encounter with Windelband:

> Here, no system was offered or even imposed, and that was good ... . [With Windelband], I rather had to immerse myself into the thinkers of the past and now a rich world opened up before me, which I was not to believe in, but which had merely to be understood. It was not *one* philosophy that was offered here, but rather *the* European philosophy in its totality, and all that I encountered previously in singularity I now grasped as a moment of an encompassing totality, including my earlier relativism and skepticism. This totality meant to me more than a system ... . (Quoted in Ollig 1979: 60)

This reminiscence indicates that Windelband's lectures set the young Rickert on the path of his own system, which can appropriately be called a system of values. It is to be seen how Rickert arrives at this system, which articulates at the same time his position on the status and task of the human sciences.

Rickert initially followed Windelband in accepting the idiographic-nomothetic distinction, but radicalized it. Instead of seeing idiographic and nomothetic sciences as equally viable methods for cognition, Rickert clearly *privileges* the idiographic over the nomothetic sciences. In this move he was influenced by Lotze's famous Plato interpretation in his *Logic* (*Logik*, 1843). This is the origin of Rickert's philosophy of value. In the mentioned work, Lotze alleges that Plato's ideas ought properly to be conceived as *values*. Their status is that they are valid (*gelten*) as opposed to things that exist (*sind*) in the sensuous and the mental world. Values occupy a "third realm" above these two forms of existence. Lotze's interest was merely in clarifying the *ontological* status of values, but this distinction between being and value was to become the cornerstone for Rickert's own approach relevant for the present context. (It deserves mention that Lotze's interpretation of ideas as values also became important for Paul Natorp, who was inspired by Lotze to interpret Platonic ideas as universally valid *natural laws* in the Newtonian sense.)

Following Lotze, Rickert asserts in his influential *Der Gegenstand der Erkenntnis* (*The Object of Cognition*, first published in 1891 and re-edited six times, each time vastly reworked; see Rickert 1928) that *all* cognition is in its core a form of *valuing*. In agreement with Kant's thesis of the primacy of practical reason, this primacy asserts itself, to Rickert, already in the field of theoretical cognition insofar as cognizing is not a mere passive apprehending but a *forming* of the object of cognition as something to be integrated into culture, i.e. the world of values. What is at stake, for Rickert, is nothing less than a redefinition of the traditional task of epistemology. The object that is represented in cognition is not only something *independent*, but is something that is being *formed* by the subject, and this object of cognition is essentially a value. Reality, which to Kant was mind-independent, is hence dependent on the *culturally creative* subject, who, in its activities, creates values. This, concomitantly, also changes the traditional notion of the cognizing subject. That all activities of the subject would be value-creating in effect undercuts the nomothetic-idiographic distinction, according to which only idiographic *events* (*Ereignisse*) could be interpreted as yielding any value for our individual existence. That means, nomothetic science, too, is a form of *valuing*.

Hence, epistemology itself takes on a new sense, and with it the notion of the knowing subject, as Rickert clarifies with a series of rhetorical questions:

> Can an epistemology, which is erected upon the opposition of non-conscious real being and representing consciousness, be carried out, or must not rather the object of cognitions be seen as a transcendent reality beyond consciousness [*bewußtseinsjenseitige, transzendente Realität*] and cognition, accordingly, not as its mere representing? Is, hence, not a complete transformation of the traditional notion of cognition necessary, if cognition of reality is to be understood with regards to its measure [*Maßstab*]? In this question we find the *basic problem of epistemology*, and the following treatise has the task of answering it. It wants to show that one cannot carry through with a notion of cognizing as a *representing* of a *reality* independent or transcending consciousness. Instead, we must form a different notion of the cognizing subject as only that of *representing* consciousness and, consequently, also a different notion of the object and the measure of cognition as that of a *transcendent reality*. (Rickert 1928: 2)

Given these two poles of cognition, cognizing subject and reality as value, one can approach the problem from both angles, subjective and objective. The subjective path leads to a transcendental psychology, the objective one to a transcendental logic; both are disciplines within transcendental philosophy. However, the empirical approach to the object of cognition remains valid in the empirical sciences; hence Rickert maps Kant's idealism-realism distinction onto that of philosophy and the empirical sciences. This dual approach is Rickert's restatement of Kant's transcendental idealism. This is the formal framework of Rickert's epistemology. It becomes relevant for the current context if one understands the relation between subject and object to be essentially a *value* relation, whereby the subject is framed in terms of value-creating (through culture) and the "cognized" object as an object of value.

Hence, if the subject's relation to reality is a *value* relation, the subject's relation to this objective value sphere becomes a *normative* one. Our relation to values can only be affirmative or rejective; conversely, the status of values is their ought (*Sollen*) or, in the opposite case, their non-ought (*Nichtsollen*). Values, while universally valid in the form of ought, can only be valued by the valuing subject in the form of his or her *individual* act of valuing. In fact, it is *primarily* in the individual valuing act in which values can be apprehended, not, in other words, in the general judgments of the nomothetic scientist, which merely establish causal relations (Rickert 1928: 420). The way Rickert construes the relation between the individual act of valuing and the universal value, as content of the act, is quite analogous to how Husserl relates conscious intentional acts and their logical (ideal) content in his refutation of psychologism – and Rickert admits as much in later editions of *Der Gegenstand* (Rickert 1928: 271). Thus, value judgments render objects *goods* (*Güter*), i.e. the former attach value to the latter. It is these judgments, in other words, in which objects are grasped as *culturally relevant*.

In his second famous work, *Die Grenzen der Naturwissenschaftlichen Begriffsbildung* (*The Limits of Concept Formation in Natural Science*, first published in 1896; see Rickert 1929), Rickert expands on the epistemological foundations while further drawing from Windelband's idiographic-nomothetic distinction. As the title indicates, concept formation in the natural sciences *has* limitations. It ends up, if pursued to its extreme, in a dead end of a purely naturalistic world view. Contrary to Windelband, who considered both forms of scientific research to be on a *relative* scale, Rickert emphasizes the fundamental difference between both (hence, the critique that is typically leveled against this distinction really only targets Rickert). Nomothetic research winds up in a dangerous abstraction that threatens to cover up or to make obsolete the historical life of culture (here anticipating Husserl's famous critique of mathematization of science and the idealization of the lifeworld in the *Crisis*). This is the negative part of this work. The positive part is Rickert's description of the inner functioning of the cultural sciences. The latter science establishes values; philosophy's task is to establish a *system* of values that correspond to the various cultural sciences. Rickert prefers the term "cultural sciences" over "human sciences" because he wants to preserve the implication that they are products of human making, just as culture itself (from Latin *cultura*, which stems from *collere*, to build, care, honor).

How, then, can Rickert call these cultural disciplines dealing with the cultural world *sciences*? They are not sciences because they are idiographic; to the contrary, Windelband's criterion would not allow us to account for the ideality of values. What makes them distinctly scientific in their own right, vis-à-vis the natural sciences, is that they establish a *relation* to supra-individual *values*. Values, to Rickert, are neither physical nor mental, but occupy an altogether different realm, "*das dritte Reich*," the "third realm." (The term was not exclusively used by the neo-Kantians; it was also used, in the same sense, by Frege.) Reminiscent of Lotze, this realm is ontologically distinct from the former as both are forms of *being*, while the ontological status of values is their *validity*. Cultural-scientific judgments, hence, are characterized by making reference to this "world" of values. Hence the peculiarity of cultural-scientific

Table 19.1. Rickert's system of values

Field	Value	Good	Subjective Comportment	World View
Logic	Truth	Science	Judging	Intellectualism
Aesthetics	Beauty	Art	Intuiting	Aestheticism
Mysticism	impersonal	All/the One holiness	Idolatry	Mysticism
Ethics	Morality	Community	Autonomous Acting	Moralism of free persons
Erotics	Community	Community of Happiness	Attraction/Devotion of Love	Eudaimonism
Philosophy of Religion	Personal Holiness	Divine Realm	Piety	Theism/ Polytheism

work is not primarily that it focuses on the individual – this is, as it were, taken for granted – but instead that *in* this individual attention it makes a connection to an independently existing realm of values. In connecting the individual human being to the universal realm of values, Rickert comes close to Cassirer's cultural anthropology, which defines the human being as a cultural being precisely in its capacity to lift itself out of the "crude" realm of nature and to become part of the world of spirit, which is intersubjective and universal.

This realm, moreover, must be systematically organized. Correct cultural and also moral judgments can be discerned in their adequacy to the systematic hierarchy and order of values. Cultural sciences, hence, are expressions of the ideal order of values. Therefore, the task of philosophy is to draft and describe this ideal system of values. In his last years, Rickert drafts a "system of values" based on the distinction of six different *domains* (*Gebiete*) of values: logic, aesthetics, mysticism, ethics, the erotic and religion. To each is correlated a specific value, a good (*Gut*), a subjective comportment (*Subjektverhalten*) and, finally, a world view (*Weltanschauung*) (see Ollig 1979: 63; Table 19.1).

Hence, the true meaning of transcendental philosophy as providing a system of values is redeemed in this overview. It is clear that the scientific fields sketched above provide, in their entirety, the system of cultural sciences. What they are to work out is the system of values in a transcendental register, i.e. following the correlational aspect of subjective acting in the human being's individual existence and the objective value system that this individual realizes in her actions. Yet Rickert – more than Windelband, who was oriented to science and its different methods – is more focused on the individual's comportment in culture as such. The cultural sciences merely ground theoretically the meaningful life of the individual in culture. As he says in his "Theses on the System of Philosophy": "Philosophy is a matter of the theoretical human being, while the entire human being, in his intuiting, willing, feeling, his life and his existence, is always limited to a particular world" (quoted in Ollig 1979: 65). Whereas Dilthey's life-philosophy attempts to address all these aspects of the human being in reciprocal and this-worldly terms, for Rickert philosophy must ground these forms of life by means of higher or transcendent values. The unity of this life of culture is not to be found in a transcendental subject, but in the "third realm" of values, which we are directed to in any "cultural" activity which instantiates values. Rickert thereby draws from Kantian as well as Platonic elements in his epistemology, which can properly be described as a theory of values and their manner of (a) apprehending them, and, more importantly, (b) realizing them in the fields of culture listed above.

Rickert began composing this sketch in his *System der Philosophie* (*System of Philosophy*, Rickert 1921), of which only volume one appeared and which has remained – despite Rickert's reputation in Germany at the time – largely unnoticed (for a recent recognition of Rickert's systematic philosophy, see Krijnen 2001). What dominated his work after finishing the first volume of his System was, not surprisingly, a scathing critique of life-philosophy and the emerging movement of Existentialism (*Die Philosophie des Lebens*, *The Philosophy of Life*, 1922). This critique stemmed from the heart of his positive philosophical concerns: The Existentialists' focus on individuals and their concrete existence *without* taking into consideration the ideal, eternal system of values that provide the framework for any meaningful existence in a culture, is irresponsible and ultimately unphilosophical. Not surprisingly, in turn, it was Rickert who was ridiculed by the young Heidegger, Rickert's pupil in Freiburg, in his early lectures at the University of Marburg, where he chastised Rickert for positing a problematic Platonic *topos huperouranios* and then having to dig himself out of the hole that he got himself into: namely, (a) to artificially construct a connection between the individual subject and these supra-individual values and (b) to have to explain how values "inhere" or are "attached to" valuable *objects*. In a similar critical vein, Max Scheler's material ethics of values seeks to locate values in the factual world and the person construed as instantiating certain ideal value personalities (ideal types). "Seeing" these values requires no mysterious value intuition but simply the "eidetic intuition" professed by the phenomenologists and already put to use in their analyses of intuition of mathematical objects and external perception.

In sum, the Southwest School's theory of the cultural sciences is based largely on a methodological distinction between idiographic and nomothetic sciences, where the former are solely capable of understanding and justifying the activities of human beings in the world as *culture*. These sciences are, accordingly, the cultural sciences, which seek to locate the individual in the universal sphere of culture. Whereas for Windelband, there was to remain an equilibrium between both scientific methods, with their respective individualizing and generalizing tendency, Rickert tipped the balance clearly to the side of the idiographic sciences as the cultural sciences. In Rickert's estimation, only sciences which establish value relations deserve to be called cultural sciences. But with these cultural sciences, he meant something slightly different than Windelband. The cultural sciences, to Rickert, are about the expression of a-temporal, transcendent values. As shown, all cognitive statements come down to value statements of one form or another. As expressing values, however, they are not merely subjective or arbitrary, but must be seen as corresponding to a universal sphere of values and its systematic order. The systematic laying out of this order of values is the task of transcendental philosophy in Rickert's understanding of the term, modifying Kant's. Rickert, however, was not so much concerned with the internal – lawful – workings of individual cultural-scientific disciplines, as was the focus of the Marburg School, but rather with the internal coherence of the system of values *itself*. A cultural science is what it is, not because it establishes lawful relations and structures, but because its work helps articulate the values of a certain cultural activity itself, for instance, in aesthetics it articulates how the value of beauty emerges in the world of art.

Neo-Kantianism II: the Marburg School: critical philosophy as philosophy of culture

To understand the Marburg School's approach to the cultural or human sciences, their method needs to be presented as it was conceived by the head of this school, Hermann Cohen. This method, which Cohen first develops in his interpretation of Kant's First Critique, becomes further modified as Cohen's own systematics takes on shape, culminating in his three-volume "System of Philosophy," consisting in *Logik der reinen Erkenntnis* (*The Logic of Pure Cognition*), *Ethik des reinen Willens* (*Ethics of Pure Willing*) and *Ästhetik des reinen Gefühls* (*Aesthetics of Pure Feeling*). Despite this systematics covering ethics and aesthetics besides theoretical philosophy, his contribution to philosophy in general, the human sciences in particular, is oftentimes reduced to his reading of the First Critique. Nevertheless, his interpretation of Kant's "treatise on method" is the bedrock of his overall method and must, hence, be expounded first. This method is the *transcendental method* and it is within it that the cultural sciences become situated. Its focus is on the *lawful formations* that obtain and govern all sciences, including the cultural sciences. Cassirer is sometimes considered as having abandoned the tenets of the Marburg transcendental method. However, upon closer inspection, this verdict is incorrect. While he modifies the transcendental method to a certain extent, he remains within its framework in important ways.

Hence, in order for Cohen's theory of the historical or cultural sciences – the Marburg School used both terms interchangeably – to become understandable, the overall doctrine of the "transcendental method" shall be presented first as it functions in theoretical cognition; but from here, one can easily make the transition to the cultural sciences.

Cohen's influential work on Kant's First Critique is characteristically entitled *Kants Theorie der Erfahrung* (*Kant's Theory of Experience*, first published in 1871 and expanded to more than thrice its original size by the third edition in 1885). The title indicates the thrust of the interpretation: in his critique of reason, Kant discovered a new concept of *experience*. Kant forged this new sense, Cohen claimed, as he meditated over the meaning of Newtonian physics. Newton had laid the foundation of modern mathematical physics in that he canonized the system of mathematical laws by which nature functions. The experience that Newtonian physics utilizes, and can only utilize, for forming the laws of nature is not the experience in the pre-scientific sphere; instead, experience is the observation on the part of the scientist in her laboratory, much in the original sense of the Latin *experimentari*.

Kant's question was, according to Cohen, how these results – the laws of nature – were justified as having the status of *a priori* (universal and necessary) cognition. This is the transcendental question, as to the *quid facti*: how is *a priori* cognition possible? But Kant's critique provided most importantly a *justification* of these claims to *a priori* cognition (*quid iuris*). This type of cognition and the principles by which it proceeds had to receive, asserts Cohen, a philosophical "certification" (*Beglaubigung*). This was, to him, the (first) task of transcendental philosophy: a justification of the claims of the modern natural scientist, insofar as these claims can rightfully claim the status of *a priori* laws. Hence, generally speaking, philosophy, to Cohen, is about the justification of laws in every domain of culture, of which Newtonian physics was but one, from an accepted *factum*. This is the general scope of Cohen's system, which has three parts, in analogy to the Kantian critiques (epistemology, ethics, aesthetics), and which was intended to be completed with a fourth part, a psychology that was to articulate the "unity of cultural consciousness" (*Einheit des Kulturbewusstseins*), but Cohen passed away before ever beginning its composition. But to close the system with an account of the consciousness of *culture in general* indicates both his overriding concern with culture as well as an unfair reduction of his attempt as merely justifying Newtonian science. But what is it that justifies a science as being truly scientific? To answer this, let us again turn to his Kant interpretation.

Indeed, Cohen's interpretation of the Kantian intention in his first Critique sets the tone. The basic claim is that experience in the pregnant and *only* epistemically relevant sense of the term is that of the scientist, and the *objects* of this experience are the laws of nature ascertained in the method of modern science.

> Not the stars in the heavens are the objects that this [transcendental] method teaches us to contemplate, but the astronomical calculations; those facts of scientific reality are, as it were, the real which is to be accounted for, as that at which the transcendental gaze is directed. What is the basis of this reality that is given in such facts? What are the conditions of this certitude from which visible reality derives its reality? Those facts of laws are the objects, not the star-objects. (Cohen 1877: 20f.)

Preferring Kant's analytic manner of presentation (from the *Prolegomena*), Cohen conceives of the transcendental question as proceeding *regressively* from an established fact. Hence, the "*factum*" from which transcendental philosophy must take its departure – in each case – is precisely this *factum* that Kant sought to justify, the *factum of science* (*das Faktum der Wissenschaft*). The analytic method hence clarifies how these *facta* become possible, which means answering the question, 'which are the laws that rule the objects of the scientific subject domain', in the present case, nature? Nature is the reality that becomes understood through science *as governed by* a priori *laws*. The reality is hence itself of lawful character, and is *understood* only *insofar as* these laws have been discovered. Hence, Cohen is not talking about nature as a *factum brutum*, but as that which has come to be cognized through science, which is itself a cultural activity. As he writes polemically:

What nature may actually be does not matter to us in so far as we want to philosophize, not write poetry. (Cohen 1987: xi)

The discovery occurs in the experiments that constitute the scientist's experience and further her knowledge of nature. Hence, experience in this technical sense *constructs* reality as an increasing cognitive mastery of the world in its progressively continuous research, since nature has been understood by the scientist as standing under *a priori* laws. As Kant already said, the world is not *given*, instead, it is *given as a task* to be discovered; punning on the German simplex *geben*, reality is not *gegeben* (given), but *aufgegeben* (given/posited as a task). Experience constructs reality, and the transcendental-analytical method ascertains the laws by which this construction takes place in any science. This is the essence of the transcendental method as Cohen conceives it in his interpretation of Kant's First Critique: the construction of the laws that obtain in a given field of human activity, in this particular case, natural science. But one must emphasize that this is but one field of human activity.

To understand how this yields a "philosophy of culture," as the Marburg School's intention can be described in general, one must see how philosophy itself relates to the particular sciences. Relating each science to the overall transcendental framework will give each individual science its position within this system. While science in general deals with the construction of reality (= laws), philosophy concentrates on the *cognition* of the lawfulness of this construction and the "*securing*" of this lawfulness in its objective formations (the laws in their systematic order). The sciences are empirical products of human beings in a culture. But their objective achievements cannot be reducible to empirical findings (generalities); they must be *a priori*, otherwise we are not dealing with lawfully governed science, which legitimately assigns *a priori* status to its findings ("constructions"). The scientific results, though achieved by empirical agents, must indeed be *a priori*. How is this justifiable? Certainly, *a priori* laws cannot be reducible to empirical generalities of the human mind. Hence the transcendental method is decidedly anti-subjectivistic or anti-psychologistic. Cohen deliberately excludes any kind of psychological notion of consciousness precisely for this reason, that it jeopardizes the *a priori* character of scientific facts. The transcendental method is a justification of the already existing *a priori* cognitions without considering empirical subjectivity as the agency that achieves them. Psychological accounts are *epistemically irrelevant*. Hence Cohen has a highly formalized notion of consciousness, not because he does not believe a psychology to be possible (see the planned fourth part of his system), but because a consideration of the "living" side of consciousness threatens to disintegrate pure cognition into subjective, psychological occurrences of the human mind. This anti-subjectivistic, constructive notion of consciousness is characteristic of the Marburg School.

Reality is – consciousness, not the material content of consciousness, but a lawful basic formation [*gesetzliche Grundgestalt*] of scientific consciousness, a form of conscious unity, a principle of cognition. Thus, the psychophysical problem is done away with through the epistemo-critical [*erkenntniskritische*] determination of reality. (Cohen 1968: 229)

Philosophy as theory of knowledge hence becomes critique of *a priori* cognition. Terminologically, Cohen insists that transcendental philosophy is not epistemology, *Erkenntnistheorie*, but *Erkenntniskritik*, as critical justification of the *facta* of the sciences. Cohen calls his version of idealism a "scientific idealism," as its transcendental function is the clarification of the condition of the possibility of objective cognition. Consciousness thus, as the formal and law-giving structure of pure thought, constructs reality as we know it ("knowing" = *a priori* cognizing). As constructive, consciousness is productive, it brings forth the laws in its scientific activity, and these laws are the true objects of science – not the stars in the heavens, but the laws by which they evolve. Laws of cognition are not created *ex nihilo*, but reveal themselves in ongoing scientific work. Scientific progress is only to be measured in constructions of new objects, and hence the scope of *a priori* cognition expands constantly. The sphere of *a priori* is dynamic, not static (something inconceivable to Kant).

However, *natural* science is only one, though the most prominent and dignified, activity of mankind. Mankind's activity – "culture" – *in general* is productive as constructing novel formations. As Natorp asserts, commenting on Cohen's transcendental method:

> Such producing of the object is precisely "experience," as it is carried out in genuine science, genuine human action, and in all culture in ever-continuing progress. (Quoted in Holzhey 1986: 55)

This producing, carried out by empirical agents, is to be found in "printed tomes," but this is merely the locus where these objects are encountered. Their origin lies not in an empirical subject (*any* subject), but in thinking as such, which Cohen terms "pure thought" (*reines Denken*), as their origin. This is the "unacknowledged Hegelianism" of the Marburg School, as Gadamer once termed it (Gadamer 2000: xvi). Pure thinking does not proceed dialectically, as in Hegel, but there is a Hegelian motive in Cohen that he also takes issue with Kant's dualism between intuition and thought and overcomes it in positing "pure thinking," pure conceptuality as the only "true" reality. Human beings construct culture insofar as they construct lawful relations by finding (creating) concepts for its contingent experiences. Only then *are* they objects for us. This means that while these objects are encountered in empirical intuition, they do not *collapse* into the acts in which they manifest themselves. In their manifestation, they can modify themselves over the course of their discovery, but the object itself is the *law*, though it is only discovered piecemeal. Thereby Cohen produces a highly original interpretation of the thing-in-itself: it is a limit concept of the object of pure cognition, which is a law, ultimately the entire lawfulness of the world. Hence, the law appears to the experiencing-producing agent as appearance, but as the appearance of the law itself. "The experience, *conceived as special case of the law*, is itself the thing-in-itself" (Cohen 1877: 28). The law is, hence, the human interpretation of the thing-in-itself to which we approximate ourselves in the concrete work of science, thereby proving ourselves as a cultural humanity, expanding our culture itself. We only have true cognition of the world if we understand the laws by which it is governed, the totality of which is an idea lying in infinity. The world of laws, as the totality of the things in themselves, is reality as *objective* reality is the *terminus ad quem* of all cultural work. The process of cognition, hence, is constantly dynamic and expanding. Discovering new laws is the measure of the "cash value" of cultural progress. This uncovering is achieved in observation, thought and other mental activities, to be precise in *all* mental activities insofar as they discover and construct their objects; this is what makes them *cultural* in the sense described. Pure thought is the foundation and the basis for all cognition; it can have no origin outside itself. "Experience," hence, is constructive and "conceptual" all the way down.

Cohen thus calls his brand of transcendental philosophy a "logic of origin" ("*Ursprungslogik*"), as all cognition must be grounded in pure thought. The *terminus a quo* to the thing-in-itself as law, hence, is the process of grounding in pure thought in the laws of each cultural domain. Pure thought is not concerned with a special body of foundational knowledge – this would be a matter of speculative metaphysics – but with actively grounding laws in pure thought, which anticipate pure laws. Hence, philosophy, to Cohen, is not the discipline of foundations (*Grundlagenwissenschaft*), which is *divorced* from the progress of the sciences and winds up in empty speculation. Instead, philosophy anticipates this progress itself; it is part and parcel of the cultural activities itself. Transcendental philosophy is a grounding science (*Grundlegungswissenschaft*) which must be confirmed or negated by the scientific experiment, in the case of natural science, but can equally be modified in other domains (hypothesis is, in other words, not a method specific to the natural sciences). This means, just as the progress of the sciences modifies and further refines the laws it discovers, so, too, are the grounding categories that we use to cognize the scientific results subject to constant revision and modification. Philosophy, concerned with the grounding of pure thought (concepts), acknowledges the necessary incompleteness and essential extendibility of the system of categories, since new scientific problems will necessitate new categories and concepts. This renders philosophy not a discipline with its own domain and problems, but a meta-theory of the existing sciences that takes account of the progress of the sciences and how they discover laws, refine them, and establish new laws that require new grounding categories. Philosophy and the sciences work together at all times.

How does this program now become applied in the cultural sciences? From what has been said, the answer is fairly easy. Though this program has so far been developed mainly with respect to scientific cognition, the same constructive process occurs in all cultural activities. The principle of all cultural progress is, for Cohen, "pure thinking" in the sense specified above: ascertaining the pure laws that drive any progress. Yet "culture" is an encompassing concept, which includes the natural sciences. Hence, there are also other sciences, following the Kantian triad: besides natural science the science of ethics and that of aesthetics. Yet it is clear that what makes these scientific, and what defines the philosopher's task in studying them, is to determine *the types of laws* that obtain in these domains, or to scrutinize them according to the elements of "pure thinking" inherent in them.

> We feel the demand for a law for all these *three basic directions of culture.* ... It is not our opinion that only mathematical thinking could be understood as thinking. Thinking [*das Denken*] also pertains rightfully to *morality* and to *art*. In these disciplines, determinations and rules, too, obtain that have the character of laws. (Cohen 1977: 40)

Which of these two disciplines now, ethics and aesthetics, can be the basis for human sciences in the narrower sense (insofar as natural science is part of culture writ large)? Cohen's answer is unambiguous: ethics. Cohen recognizes the limitations of theoretical thought, which results in modern natural sciences. Cultural life in general, however, involves human beings' *practical* behavior, and this is the focus of the human sciences.

> Since ethics establishes the laws that are to be found for the human sciences [*Geisteswissenschaften*], in whose matter [*Material*] ethics has to search for them, we may be permitted, in the narrower sense of law, to refer to ethics as the logic of the human sciences. (Cohen 1977: 607)

Since here, too, we must be dealing with laws, we must look at the *factum* of that science, where these laws have become institutionalized: this is jurisprudence. (The reason why aesthetics cannot be the logic of the human sciences is because the "laws" it establishes e.g. that of genius and aesthetic production, can only be called "laws" in a very loose sense; see Cohen 1977: 608. Cohen's aesthetics has also been the least well-received part of his system.) Cohen thereby reject's Kant's distinction between a doctrine of right or law (*Recht*) and a doctrine of virtue (*Tugend*) and posits the laws established in the already existing science of jurisprudence as the constructions that govern our lives as moral persons. This is not the place to discuss Cohen's ethics, which constructs a highly original I–Thou relation at the core of human interaction, a basic idea that was influential for the "dialogical" thinkers Buber and Levinas (for a presentation and critique, see Gibbs 2004). What is important for the present context is that moral life, as the object of the human science of ethics, should also be governed by lawful structures, which cannot come forth from something individual (the moral law in us, as in Kant), but from a *science* in which these laws are established as *facta*, and this is jurisprudence. Again, the task for philosophy is the justification of the *factum* of this juridical science by tracing the constructive activities that went into forming these laws.

In sum, all sciences are, insofar as they construct laws, *cultural activities, cultural sciences*. They are and can be so *only insofar* as they establish laws. Laws are structures of "pure thinking" that philosophy must keep watch over, and this means *justifying* their status as lawful, grounded in pure thinking. In this sense, what makes sciences sciences is the fact that they are law-governed, and as establishing *facta* of knowledge, they are all *cultural* sciences. The laws in the human domain more specifically are established in jurisprudence as science of laws of permissible human behavior. In his aesthetics, Cohen struggles to find laws as well, though one should assert critically that they can hardly be described as being "*a priori*" laws of "pure thinking," presumably because one can describe "laws," say of aesthetical production, as individual at best (the "law" that governed Shakespeare). Cassirer was to seize on this problem in his philosophy of symbolic formation.

In defining science as a contribution to culture, Cohen's focus on law and "purity" in each scientific domain, the totality of which defines culture, comes to the fore. Philosophy helps the sciences wrest this purity of concepts and the laws that govern each specific subject domain. In this sense, the verdict of philosophy playing the role of the handmaiden of the sciences is correct, but unfair if one thereby suggests that philosophy is left to irrelevance. To the contrary, the specific sciences can only assume their role in culture if placed within an overarching structure, which is provided by philosophy. Philosophy hence becomes, already in Cohen but more prominently in Cassirer, a philosophy of culture. Humanity, in raising itself above brute nature, is cultural in creating lawful structures and thereby establishing value for human beings, value structures in which they can dwell as cultural beings. Hence, "culture" is the operative term for the Marburg School. A helpful definition of culture as it is understood in the Marburg School is the following:

> Culture is a process which produces values and does not reflect them. Culture is by definition a process of creating value and cultural values are valuable because they have come out of this process and not the other way around. (Renz 2004: 331)

Cohen's focus on culture becomes the cornerstone but also critical point of departure for Cassirer. Cassirer agrees on the systematic structure of the sciences as having to be part of an overarching system that is provided by philosophy. But Cassirer is critical of Cohen's exclusive focus on laws governing cultural domains. While expanding Cohen's original method, but also broadening it, he nevertheless arrives at his own system from a different angle. Hence, Cassirer's first original contribution to critical philosophy was his *Substanzbegriff und Funktionsbegriff* (*Substance and Function*, Cassirer 1910), which discusses a seemingly remote problem in scientific concept formation, but in fact raises an issue that will be the basis of his philosophical systematic: the distinction between a substantial and functional ontology and its epistemological implications. This basic insight, stemming from the groundwork laid by Cohen, was exploited in Cassirer's three-volume *Philosophy of Symbolic Forms* (*Philosophie der Symbolischen Formen*, 1922–9). Besides these substantial tomes, Cassirer wrote the above mentioned 4-volume study *The Problem of Knowledge in Modern Philosophy* and a plethora of articles and smaller studies on mythology, linguistics, modern physics and intellectual history. He was the most prolific philosopher of the Marburg School as well as the most widely knowledgeable thinker of this group. Once in the United States, where he emigrated in 1943 to seek shelter from the Nazis, he summarized his system in the popular book *An Essay on Man*. His last work, *The Myth of the State*, offers a penetrating critique of modern fascism based on his interpretation of the role of myth in the hierarchy of cultural achievements and its relation to modern totalitarianism.

In the first systematic work, *Substance and Function*, Cassirer takes his cue from Cohen's paradigm of *construction*, but here Cassirer traces this constructive activity of the human mind specifically in the distinction between substantive and functional concepts in scientific nomenclature. Opposed to a substantial paradigm, following Aristotle's substance ontology according to which concepts mirror things as substances, a new type of concept formation has emerged in Modernity, that of *functional* concepts. (Cohen had actually analyzed such a functional "system" in his interpretation of the mathematical method of infinitesimals, but had not actually arrived at Cassirer's conclusion.) Functional concepts place the objects that they mirror into a *function*, as in mathematical functions ($F(x)$). What functional concepts mirror, hence, are not substantial things, but functions, i.e. relations. The functional concept formation actually *constructs* the object of a particular scientific endeavor. In simple terms, the object *is* nothing besides its relation to others ("3" is nothing in isolation from its order in the series of natural numbers pre- and succeeding it, "2," and "4"). It is the relational "system" that defines its "existence," and such a system is nothing occurring in nature, but created by the onlooker. Hence, Cassirer discovered Cohen's constructive principle at the heart of scientific concept formation itself.

This was only the first step of Cassirer's move beyond Cohen. For, Cassirer asserted, such a constructive activity is not just present in scientific concept formation – an activity of the human spirit, to be sure – but in *all* cultural activities. Construction, hence, takes on a new meaning in Cassirer, namely as functional formation. It is neither merely nor primarily a construction according to *laws*, but according to a formation of a certain progression (*Reihe*). What human spirit achieves in *general* is, hence, a formation of a progression (*Reihenbildung*) in different cultural contexts in analogy to the mathematical notion of the term. The rigid notion of "law," which was paradigmatic for Cohen, thusly becomes relaxed by the idea of a function, i.e. a certain "logic" (again in a loose sense) obtaining in different cultural domains. Construction is, in other words, a form of *interpretation* of something that can be completely different depending on the manner in which it is constructed. The sine curve (Cassirer's example) in the mathematical context is, in an artistic manner of seeing, an ornament, and may represent yet another meaning depending on the context. Prior to such an interpretation – *any* interpretation – the thing is simply nothing for us. What a thing is depends on its context, and the context is something *constructed* through the human mind.

Cassirer calls the agent of this activity *spirit*, echoing Hegel; i.e. it is not a matter of single individuals but a community of subjects interacting, creating culture. That which is constructed, or the medium of construction, he calls, alluding to Kant's Transcendental Aesthetics, a *form*, as a "manner of intuiting." There is no simple object given (as a substance or substratum) that *then* receives a supervening interpretation, but there are only objects-in-contexts. There is no "raw" datum. In searching for a term for such an object within a form Cassirer makes recourse to his favored author, Goethe, in calling it a *symbol*. Hence, each spiritual activity takes place within a "symbolic form." Here is Cassirer's general definition of a symbolic form:

> By a "symbolic form" shall be understood every energy of spirit through which a spiritual meaning-content is connected to a concrete sensual sign and is intrinsically bound to that sign." (Cassirer 1983: 175)

There are several symbolic forms that Cassirer discerns. In the following passage, he introduces them for the first time, and he also clarifies how they stem from Kant's transcendental background but, indeed, go beyond Kant. We must, Cassirer asserts,

> accept in all seriousness what Kant calls his "Copernican Revolution." Instead of measuring the content, meaning, and truth of intellectual forms by something extraneous which is supposed to be reproduced in them, we must find in these forms themselves the measure and criterion for their truth and intrinsic meaning. Instead of taking them as mere copies of something else, we must see in each of these spiritual forms a spontaneous law of generation; an original way and tendency of expression which is more than a mere record of something initially given in fixed categories of real existence. From this point of view, *myth, art, language and science* appear as symbols ... in the sense of forces each of which produces and posits a world of it own. (Cassirer 1953: 8, italics added)

Hence Cassirer calls his system that of *Symbolic Forms*. They are the forms of manifestation in which human spirit's activity become "crystallized." Indeed, we live in a plurality of meaningful "contexts." The three symbolic forms that Cassirer discusses in this important work are language, myth, and scientific cognition, but the above citation also mentions art. Symbolic forms can be regarded as more broadly conceived analogues of Dilthey's socio-cultural systems. Whereas Dilthey's socio-cultural systems are treated as historically generated "productive" systems, Cassirer's symbolic forms are derived from the "productive-constructive activity" of the human spirit. Cassirer's adaptation of the transcendental method is to trace the manner of construction in each form, respectively, while breaking with Cohen's exclusively scientific-logistic paradigm and moving to an understanding of "form" to be more freely described as different "logics" inhering in them. Cassirer's system can also be described as a methodology of symbolic formation, by which formation occurs by different "methods"; he is decidedly a methodological pluralist. But his methodological pluralism is incomprehensible without the fundamental constructive paradigm that is the signature of the "Marburg Method."

Philosophy hence becomes a scrutiny and analysis of these different symbolic forms. It is in these forms that human beings live in their world as "culture." Hence, in keeping with the Kantian paradigm alluded to in the last quotation, Cassirer writes in a famous passage in the first volume of the *Philosophy of Symbolic Forms*:

Thus the critique of reason becomes the critique of culture. It seeks to understand and to show how every content of culture, in so far as it is more than
a mere isolated content, in so far as it is grounded in a universal principle of
form, presupposes an original act of the human spirit. Herein the basic thesis
of idealism finds its true and complete confirmation. (Cassirer 1955: 80)

Hence, as a study of symbolic forms, it becomes clear, and more plausible than in
Cohen's account of a "philosophy of culture," what the relation between philosophy
and the individual sciences is to be. Indeed, as a study *of* the different symbolic forms,
philosophy of culture in Cassirer's understanding *replaces* the individual cultural
sciences. It does not make the work of the chemist or biologist on the one hand,
the linguist or sociologist on the other obsolete, but it breaks their monopoly as the
only providers of "knowledge." As studies of domains of culture within the universe
of symbolic formation, all sciences construct certain symbolic forms, i.e. establish
functional series about individual things, i.e. things that are seen in a certain symbolic
"light" as contexts in which they can become understood. In a different terminology,
all sciences proceed by the method of "subsumption" of the individual under the
general. In this broad sense, this is the "logic" of symbolic formation, of which all
sciences are part as forming culture.

However, despite this general characteristic of scientific activity, Cassirer does
draw a distinction between the natural and cultural sciences. The cultural sciences
in the narrower sense, as human sciences (though Cassirer prefers the term "cultural
sciences"), differ from the natural sciences in the way in which they construe this
relation of subsumption of the individual under the general. In the natural sciences the
method of subsumption strives to bring individual findings under theoretical concepts:

If this is achieved, then there is in principle no longer an individual determination of an empirical concept. We thus possess, as in pure mathematical
concepts, one basic determination from which all others follow and from
which they can be inferred. (Cassirer 1994: 70)

Contrary to natural sciences, the cultural sciences differ from the former in precisely
not allowing for "one" basic determination of cultural phenomena, but in pluralizing
the notion of what counts as a "basic determination." Cassirer quotes approvingly
the Renaissance scholar Walser's conclusion on what might count as "basic determination" of the Renaissance: "The life and striving of the entire Renaissance cannot
be derived from *one* principle, that of individualism or sensualism" (quoted in Cassirer
1994: 72). The subsumption, hence, is not one of placing something individual –
Leonardo da Vinci, Michelangelo – under a *single* general concept, but a *plurality*
thereof, "the more the merrier."

Every one of them collaborates in his way in the construction [*Aufbau*] of that
what we call the 'spirit' or the culture of the Renaissance. We thus bring to
expression a unity of *direction*, not a unity of *being*. (*ibid.*: 73).

This constitutes what one might call the "meaning" of the Renaissance, to remain with this example. Hence: "All genuine stylistic concepts of cultural science lead back to such meaning concepts [*Sinnbegriffe*]" (*ibid.*), as opposed to *determinate* concepts. But note that "unity of direction" is understood in a very loose sense: it is a "unity" that is constituted by several, perhaps innumerable determinations. To determine something as complex as "the Renaissance," might be an inexhaustible task. This is not a weakness of the cultural sciences, but precisely their strength if they understand and embrace this principle. Cultural sciences pay attention to the plurality of symbolic formation, of which natural science is but one. Their cognitive goal is to widen contexts, even create new ones – e.g. if one thinks of newly emerging scientific disciplines and methods – rather than adhere to one paradigm only.

Hence, natural and cultural sciences differ methodologically, analogous but not identical to an idiographic or nomothetic distinction, namely in the sense of two different directions of spirit, *unification* and *pluralization*. Whereas natural science aims at single determinations, cultural science gives us a richer image of its symbolic form the more determinations it is able to discern. Cassirer summarizes both the activity of culture as well as that of philosophy and science as follows:

> Culture creates, in an uninterrupted stream, ever new linguistic, artistic, religious symbols. Science and philosophy, however, must break down this symbolic language into its elements in order to make it comprehensible for itself. It must treat analytically that which was synthetically produced. Hence there is a constant flux and reflux. Natural science teaches us, in Kant's phrase, "to spell out appearances in order to be able to read them as experiences"; cultural science teaches us to interpret [*deuten*] symbols in order to decipher [*enträtseln*] the content that lies hidden in them, in order to make visible once again the life from which they have originally sprung. (Cassirer 1994: 86)

The natural and cultural sciences account for the different, opposing "directions" of spirit and thus help us orient ourselves in the world as a "symbolic universe." Humans dwell in it in the form of symbolic creatures; accordingly, Cassirer terms the human being in his late work an "*animal symbolicum.*" As a symbolic "spirit," the individual has the capacity to do science, and in scientific activity merely spells out the directions of spirit in its always already ongoing creation of culture. Although Cassirer did not follow Cohen in finding a juridical basis for the human sciences, his allegiance to the Marburg School's brand of idealism still comes to the fore in the construction of a symbolic universe, in which individuals can become human beings, lifting themselves out of brute and finite nature to participate in infinite tasks. Being a human being in this sense means to have the capacity to contribute to culture in its main directions of symbolization. The sciences merely trace the different directions in which spirit moves. Science, in general, thus brings the individual under the general, but the general that Cassirer has in mind here is nothing but the symbolic forms themselves, which operate with different internal logics. Consequently, the "general" results that different sciences ascertain will differ according to the different internal "logics" of the cultural domains, such as science, art, religion, and language (and perhaps others).

Cassirer's claims that the cultural sciences are pluralistic and that their interpretations must revive the life from which they stem make it evident that of all the neo-Kantians he comes closest to Dilthey. Both thinkers were inspired by Kant's *Critique of Judgment* – Cassirer by its conception of aesthetic symbols and Dilthey by its discussion of immanent purposiveness. Their main difference is that Dilthey places more stress on the historical nexus in which the cultural systems are generated. It is for this reason that when Dilthey speaks of the way the human sciences establish the *Aufbau* of the historical world by means of cultural systems, we translated this term as "formation." Dilthey explicitly differentiates an *Aufbau* (formation) from an *a priori Konstruktion* (construction).

By contrast, Cassirer is willing to conceive of the *Aufbau* of Renaissance culture as a construction that makes use of Burckhardt's idea of the Renaissance man. Such an individual is defined by "his delight in the senses, his turning to nature, his being rooted in 'this side of existence,' his openness on behalf of the world of forms, his individualism, his paganism, his amoralism" (Cassirer 1994: 71). In that Cassirer acknowledges that no one has been found who actually embodies this complex of traits, Burckhardt's Renaissance man must be considered as an ideal type that only indirectly illuminates the life of the Renaissance. As early as 1862 Dilthey had criticized Burckhardt's approach to the Italian Renaissance as too aesthetical and schematic. "Everything is shown only in outline, as though in the distance, nothing with the patience and plain detail of the foreground" (Dilthey 1996: 274). What is characteristic of Dilthey's approach to history is the use of more real types. Thus in order to characterize what distinguishes the German Enlightenment from the French Enlightenment, he focuses on the lives and works of Lessing and Voltaire as typical. Whereas Lessing used the light of reason to breathe the spirit of toleration into religions, Voltaire used it to ridicule religion altogether.

Both approaches have their advantages as well as limits. By focusing on so-called "real types" we can attain a proximity to a historical period, yet we may fail to exhaust the full significance that an ideal type can suggest. An ideal type can point to the aspirations of an age that were never realized yet help us to understand that age better. But it may also overreach its intended target, as when Dilthey complains that all of the conceptual characteristics given by Burckhardt "can be applied just as well to analogous periods of culture, such as post-Periclean Athens or Rome in the transition period into the empire" (Dilthey 1996: 275). Whereas the neo-Kantians make the case that a complex of concepts is essential for individuating human life, Dilthey's hermeneutical approach to the human sciences also sees the need to specify a temporal worldly context.

References

Cassirer, E. (1910) *Substanzbegriff und Funktionsbegriff: Untersuchungen über die Grundfragen der Erkenntniskritik*, Berlin: Cassirer; trans., W. C. Swabey and M. C. Swabey, as *Substance and Function and Einstein's Theory of Relativity*, New York: Dover, 1953.

—— (1918) *Kants Leben und Lehre*, Hamburg: F. Meiner; trans., J. Haden, as *Kant's Life and Thought*, New Haven, CT: Yale University Press, 1981.

—— (1953) *Language and Myth*, trans. S. K. Langer, New York: Dover.

—— (1955) *The Philosophy of Symbolic Forms*, vol. 1: *Language*, trans. R. Manheim, New Haven, CT: Yale University Press.

—— (1983) *Wesen und Wirkung des Symbolbegriffs*, Darmstadt: Wissenschaftliche Buchgesellschaft.

—— (1994) *Zur Logik der Kulturwissenschaften. Fünf Studien*. Darmstadt: Wissenschaftliche Buchgesellschaft.

—— (1996) *The Philosophy of Symbolic Forms*, vol. 4: *The Metaphysics of Symbolic Forms*, trans. J. M. Krois, New Haven, CT: Yale University Press.

Cohen, H. (1877) *Kants Begründung der Ethik*, Berlin: Dümmler.

—— (1968 [1883]) *Das Prinzip der Infinitesimal-Methode und seine Geschichte*, edited by Bruno Cassirer, Frankfurt am Main: Suhrkamp.

—— (1977) *Logik der reinen Erkennntis*, New York: Olms (*Collected Works*, edited by H. Holzhey, vol. 6.1).

—— (1987) *Kants Theorie der Erfahrung*, New York: Olms (*Collected Works*, edited by H. Holzhey, vol. 1.1).

Dilthey, W. (1924) *Gesammelte Schriften*, vol. 5: *Die geistige Welt: Einleitung in die Philosophie des Lebens. Erste Hälfte: Abhandlungen zur Grundlegung der Geisteswissenschaften*, edited by G. Misch, Göttingen: Vandenhoeck & Ruprecht.

—— (1985–2002) *Selected Works*, edited by R. A. Makkreel and F. Rodi, Princeton, NJ: Princeton University Press.

—— (1989) *Introduction to the Human Sciences*, vol. 1 of *Selected Works*, edited by R. A. Makkreel and F. Rodi, Princeton, NJ: Princeton University Press.

—— (2002) *The Formation of the Historical World in the Human Sciences*, vol. 3 of *Selected Works*, edited by R. A. Makkreel and F. Rodi, Princeton, NJ: Princeton University Press.

—— (1996) *Hermeneutics and the Study of History*, vol. 4 of *Selected Works*, edited by R. A. Makkreel and F. Rodi, Princeton, NJ: Princeton University Press.

Gadamer, H.-G. (1990) *Wahrheit und Methode: Grundzüge einer Philosophischen Hermeneutik*. Tübingen: Mohr/Siebeck.

—— (2000) "Die Philosophische Bedeutung Paul Natorps," in P. Natorp (ed.) *Philosophische Systematik*, Hamburg: Meiner, pp. xi–xvii.

Gibbs, R. (2004) "Jurisprudence is the Organon of Ethics: Kant and Cohen on Ethics, Laws, and Religion," in R. Munk (ed.) *Hermann Cohen's Critical Idealism*, Heidelberg: Springer.

Holzhey, H. (1986) *Cohen und Natorp*, vol. 1: *Ursprung und Einheit: Die Geschichte der "Marburger Schule" als Auseinandersetzung um die Logik des Denkens*, Basel; Stuttgart: Schwabe.

—— (2004) "Der Neukantianismus" in H. Holzhey and H. Röd (eds.) *Geschichte der Philosophie*, vol. 12, Munich: Beck.

Kant, I. (1902–97) *Kants Gesammelte Schriften*, Berlin: Walter de Gruyter.

—— (1996) *The Metaphysics of Morals*, trans. M. Gregor, Cambridge: Cambridge University Press.

—— (2001) *The Critique of the Power of Judgment*, edited by P. Guyer, trans. P. Guyer and E. Matthews, Cambridge: Cambridge University Press.

—— (2006) *Anthropology from a Pragmatic Point of View*, trans. R. Louden, Cambridge: Cambridge University Press.

Köhnke, K.C. (1991 [1986]) *Entstehung und Aufstieg des Neukantianismus: Die Deutsche Universitätsphilosophie zwischen Idealismus und Positivismus*, Frankfurt am Main: Suhrkamp; abridged trans., R. J. Hollingdale, as *The Rise of Neo-Kantianism: German Academic Philosophy between Idealism and Positivism*, Cambridge: Cambridge University Press, 1991.

Krijnen, C. (2001) *Nachmetaphysischer Sinn: Eine Problemgeschichtliche und Systematische Studie zu den Prinzipien der Wertphilosophie Heinrich Rickerts*, Würzburg: Königshausen & Neumann.

Makkreel, R.A. (1975) *Dilthey, Philosopher of the Human Studies*, Princeton, NJ: Princeton University Press.

—— (1990) *Imagination and Interpretation in Kant*, Chicago: The University of Chicago Press.

Ollig, H.-L. (1979) *Der Neukantianismus*, Stuttgart: Metzler.

Renz, U. (2004) "Critical Idealism and the Concept of Culture: Philosophy of Culture in Hermann Cohen and Ernst Cassirer," in R. Munk (ed.) *Hermann Cohen's Critical Idealism*, Dordrecht: Springer.

Rickert, H. (1921) *System der Philosophie*, vol. 1, Tübingen: Mohr/Siebeck.

—— (1928) *Der Gegenstand der Erkenntnis. Einführung in die Transzendentalphilosophie*, Tübingen: Mohr/Siebeck.

—— (1929) *Die Grenzen der Naturwissenschaftlichen Begriffsbildung: Eine Logische Einleitung in die historischen Wissenschaften*, Tübingen: Mohr/Siebeck; edited, trans., G. Oakes, as *The Limits of Concept Formation in Natural Science: A Logical Introduction to the Historical Sciences*, Cambridge: Cambridge University Press, 1986.

Windelband, W. (1924) "Geschichte und Naturwissenschaft," in *Präludien: Aufsätze und Reden Zur Philosophie und Ihrer Geschichte*. Tübingen: Mohr.

Part V

UTILITARIANISM AND BRITISH IDEALISM

20

MILL: LOGIC AND METAPHYSICS

Fred Wilson

Introduction

John Stuart Mill (20 May 1806–8 May 1873) was born in Pentonville, then a suburb of London. He was the son of James Mill. The young Mill never attended school, nor went to university: he was home educated by his father. The educational practice was guided by the learning theory, associationism, of James Mill and Jeremy Bentham, one of the leaders (James Mill was another) of the radical reformers who defended reform principles on the basis of utilitarianism in ethics and political philosophy, Ricardo's theory in classical economics, and associationism in psychology. A remarkable education it was – beginning with Greek at three, and proceeding rapidly through history, mathematics, Latin, economics and logic – certainly by the age of seventeen he was the best educated young man in Great Britain. He always held up his own person to give an example of what a good education could achieve and what the existing systems of education at public schools and universities in England certainly did not achieve. He was educated to be the leader of the utilitarian party, which in due course he did become, though not without reworking its doctrines and principles, in major works such as his *System of Logic* (1843) and *Principles of Political Economy* (1848). These went through many editions, and both shaped discussions for years to come. His essays on "Utilitarianism" (1861) and "On Liberty" (1859) were important in their own day, and continue to this day to be of interest to philosophers and political scientists. His argument in "The Subjection of Women" (1869a) was important in the strong impetus it gave towards the movement for women's liberation. His major work in metaphysics was his *Examination of Sir William Hamilton's Philosophy* (1865); this deserves greater attention than it has received, but so thoroughly demolished the philosophy it was attacking that it is now little read. He wrote many essays and reviews for Victorian journals, including major essays on "Bentham" (1838) and "Coleridge" (1840) which re-shaped the utilitarianism of the radical reformers, and a review on the published lectures on moral philosophy and its history by William Whewell in which Mill critically attacked intuitionism in ethics. His posthumously published *Autobiography* (1873) is a classic of Victorian literature.

He died 8 May 1873, and was buried in Avignon, next to the grave of his previously deceased partner Harriet Taylor.

Mill studied logic, guided by his father, early in his education, and later studied it further with some friends. His reading was essentially scholastic logic, followed by Hobbes. Richard Whatley published his text on *Elements of Logic* in 1826 (second edition, 1827). It was a great improvement upon other texts then available, and Mill praised it in one of his earliest reviews (1828 – the review is of both the first and second editions of Whatley). Mill himself then undertook the task of writing a logic that would cover not only deductive logic, as did Whately, but also the logic of inductive inference and what we would now call the philosophy of science. The *System of Logic* was the result of this work.

While Mill worked on his *Logic*, William Whewell (1794–1866) published his massive studies on the *History of the Inductive Sciences* (3 vols.) and the *Philosophy of the Inductive Sciences* (2 vols.) in 1837 and 1840 respectively. These gave Mill many examples, but more importantly became a foil for Mill's argument. Whewell replied to Mill in the next edition of his work, and Mill replied to Whewell in his next edition. The debate continued through several exchanges.

That was not the only debate Mill had with Whewell. Whewell was a trades-man's son, and through hard work as a scientist, as an historian of science, and as a college don at Cambridge he secured a professorship at that university and finally was appointed Master of Trinity College by the Tory Prime Minister Sir Robert Peel. He argued that natural laws were, or at least came to be known *a priori* (contrary to Mill, who argued that they were matter-of-empirical-fact generalizations arrived at through inductive inference); he defended a form of moral intuitionism in ethics, and argued that utilitarianism in ethics was not only mistaken but was morally vicious (with which Mill naturally enough disagreed); he defended innate ideas against the associa-tionist views of Locke, Bentham and James Mill (where the younger Mill vigorously defended the associationist account of the human mind); he thought that the Reform Bill of 1832 had gone far enough (where Mill pressed for a thoroughly democratic franchise, and further for the vote for women); and he defended the unreformed universities of Oxford and Cambridge (where Mill pressed for extensive reforms). It has been said of Whewell that if he had not existed Mill would have had to invent him.

The issues that divided them were theoretical in nature, but also moral and ethical. Mill argued that Whewell's logic of science and his intuitionism in ethics were both unreasonable and that both stood in the way of the progress in the social realm that the utilitarians defended. Whewell conversely argued that Mill's philosophy of science and utilitarian ethics were undermining the moral foundations of the English social order.

Mill had as his aim the "improvement of mankind." His writings and other work, such as his brief parliamentary career, were in his own mind parts of an effort to provide humankind with the tools that would enable people to secure on their own that improvement in their lot. There were positive aspects such as, for example, his work in logic and the philosophy of science which he hoped would provide humankind with the tools that were needed to better find the truth about the matter of fact world in which humans find themselves existing. And there were negative aspects, such as, for example, his work in metaphysics which embodied his criticisms of outdated metaphysics which on the one hand hindered the advancement of science by giving a false view of how to find the truth about the world and on the other hand provided spurious intellectual support for moral and political doctrines which held back the improvement of humankind. We should take his arguments defending his positions in logic and metaphysics for what they are worth – and they are usually worth a good deal, philosophically – but also view them in the context of his overall programme for the improvement of humankind – what are in effect his moral concern for the general well-being of humankind.

Associationism

Whewell argued that the roots of the philosophy to which he was opposed was its associationist theory of learning in psychology. This theory was understood to be an empirical scientific theory. It had its roots in Locke's empiricist epistemology, but the latter in Locke's own work remained largely undeveloped; Locke was in fact largely content to merely assert that our ideas derive from our sensible experiences without giving any detail about how the process of association proceeds from sensible antecedents to complex ideas. Associationism as an empirical psychological theory was first developed in some detail by David Hartley in his *Observations on Man* (1748). To be sure, Hartley included a speculative Newtonian physiology, and a rather strange linkage to theology; but the structure of the theory of mind was certainly clear – certainly clearer than the presentation in Hume, who understands the theory as well as Hartley but develops it in the context of a series of philosophical concerns, ontological, epistemological, and moral. Joseph Priestly prepared a version of Hartley (*Hartley's Theory of the Human Mind* [1775]); this was Hartley's book shorn of the physiology and the theology, and it became the version that was more or less standard.

The theory (which is still plausible as a starting point for psychological theorizing) is roughly this: We live in a world which, in our sensory experience, as it were impresses itself upon us. Our ideas derive from these impressions. Our basic ideas are images produced by the impressions, replicas of but fainter than the latter. Impressions of certain sorts go together in our experience, either simultaneously or successively. If A and B are regularly presented to one in relation R, then the impression of A will call up the idea of B, or the idea of A will call up the idea of B, that is, A and B will become associated and indeed fused in the mind of the learner. (Behavioristically, this is classical conditioning.) Mill argued that objects with the property S all resemble each other; if we take R to be this relation of resemblance then the association formed is the fusion of ideas that constitutes the concept that refers to the property S. Alternatively, if R is the relation of immediate successor in space and time then the association formed is the judgment that A causes B. Or again, if R is the relation of co-presence or simultaneity the association that is formed is the (abstract) idea of a kind or sort of thing or material object. James Mill laid out the theory in his *Analysis of the Phenomena of the Human Mind* (1829). This, in outline, was accepted by the younger Mill, who edited and published a second edition (1869b), to which he added extensive notes. On one central point he disagreed with his father, this in a way that enabled him to meet some of the points emphasized by the critics of associationism. On this theory, it is usually possible to analyze the product of an association to recover the genetic antecedents from which it arose. Indeed, James Mill argued that this held for all cases: any complex could be analyzed into its genetic antecedents in sense experience: the complex idea was simply the genetic antecedents added together as parts. Here the younger Mill disagreed. There are, he argued against his father, cases where the fusion is sufficiently strong that analysis proves impossible, the associated parts have become inseparable. In any case, however, the production of ideas through association is not simply a matter of adding separable parts; the processes are not in this way merely mechanical and additive but are, rather, more akin to chemical processes. Just as water has properties that are different in kind and are logically irreducible to the properties that define hydrogen and oxygen, so the products of association are characteristically different from their genetic antecedents. (This distinction between processes which are mechanical or additive in nature and those which are chemical is defended at length in the *Logic*.) The elder Mill had argued that the sensible antecedents were present in the product as literal parts – implausibly argued in the case of ideas of almost any sort of complexity. The younger Mill availed himself of the notion that the associational processes are chemical in nature, not merely additive, and argued that they are not in this sense integrant parts but rather metaphysical parts, not normally present as parts to consciousness where only their fusion is given, but are there dispositionally, ready to be called up if one attends under an analytic set. Whether associationism, even as in this way importantly modified by the younger Mill, can do all the work in detail that he asks of it is a good question – he clearly inserts elements of a reinforcement account of learning – and the higher cognitive processes such as reasoning likely need a stronger theory, probably more is innate than Mill allows – but for all that the theory can do a great deal. As a theory it is simple enough, yet in fact it is quite powerful, and with considerable evidence in its favour as scientific theory of the human mind. Its concepts are fairly simple, yet used judiciously they can be argued to generate a not implausible account of not only our complex sensory awareness or perception of things in the world, but also our higher mental processes.

Thus, for example, in ethics it could be argued that the only basic motivator consists of feelings of sensory or bodily pleasure. Nothing else is intrinsically an end in itself. Other things are sought as ends only if pleasure becomes associated with the idea of such a thing and that thing thereby becomes part of the person's pleasure. Acquisition of gold is normally a means to pleasure, but in the miser has become so associated with pleasure that it has become part of the miser's pleasure. Or again, for the scientist, knowledge is not sought only as a means, but is sought for its own sake: knowledge has become a part of the pleasure of such a person. Noble ends such as that of seeking the general happiness or even such an end as seeking the happiness of members of our family are not among the ends we seek as a matter of native human motivation, but they can become ends sought for their own sake by becoming through association part of an individual's pleasure; they are first sought as mere means to pleasure, but the association of that means and that end makes the means into part of what constitutes a person's happiness.

Platonism and anti-Platonism

For the generation that came of age at the end of the eighteenth century, the combination of associationism as (the outline at least of) a causal explanation of human behaviour and utilitarianism which set the seeking of the general happiness as our ultimate moral end provided a series of arguments justifying and directing the form of political and social change, and was seen as justifying the hopes for reform in Britain that were raised by the French revolution in 1789. These principles were embraced in particular by the young poets William Wordsworth and Samuel Taylor Coleridge. (Coleridge named his eldest son "Hartley"). Bentham provided a rigorous argument to support reform of such things as English law, but Wordsworth and Coleridge, with Hartleyan associationism in the background, found their inspiration in William Godwin's much more readable presentation in his *Elements of Political Justice* (1793). But there were some strange features in Godwin's utilitarianism. Thus, he argued that one ought never to seek an end because one simply felt it was right, for example, one should never act on one's feelings of moral approbation or one's special feelings for one's own family; one ought to focus on, and seek solely as one's end the general happiness of humankind. John Stuart Mill was later to argue, contrary to Godwin, that it is reasonable from a utilitarian point of view that these are to be sought for their own sake and not as means to other ends; pursuing them as ends in themselves is justified through such action being in fact a means to the general happiness. It was, however, more Godwin's social philosophy, the liberation from old constraints, and the defence of democracy that was greeted with enthusiasm by a younger generation that found revolution, or maybe just the idea of revolution, exhilarating. In particular, where Locke and even Bentham looked to a rational and beneficent group among the upper classes to take the lead in securing reforms, Wordsworth and Coleridge (and many others) found Godwin's utilitarian defence of liberty and democracy both moving and consonant with their views on the liberating power of the French revolution.

Until, that is, the Revolution turned into the Reign of Terror and the negation of all liberty. They became former enthusiasts both of revolution and of Godwin, coming to the view that one can avoid such things as a Reign of Terror only by strengthening the social ties that bind the citizens into a stable community in which alone, it now seemed, liberty was secure. Utilitarianism, particularly Godwin's version, but also Bentham's, deemed action on any motive given by our moral sentiments or by such feelings as love of family, or love of one's community to be immoral; action aimed at the general happiness alone was virtuous. Thus, the social ties essential to any social stability were deemed immoral by utilitarianism. But acting on the rule of seeking the general happiness does not secure the general happiness, as the Terror demonstrated; utilitarianism thus declares itself to be an immoral doctrine. Moreover, associationism held that the moral sentiments and such sentiments as love of family or of country were all reducible to searching for general happiness; morality and other social ties are in effect nothing more than means to attaining a sort of pleasure that is equally attainable by playing pushpin. However, moral sentiments and other ties that bind are basic and ineliminable parts of human nature. Trying to run counter to them, as Godwin recommended, was not only degrading but also an attempt to avoid the inescapable, something which is fraught with social danger, again as the Terror made clear.

The poet-philosopher Samuel Taylor Coleridge took the lead philosophically (see his *Biographia Literaria* [1817] and *Aids to Reflection* [1825]). In effect, he revived the Platonic tradition to counter the newer philosophy of associationism and utilitarianism. Platonism in metaphysics had in fact formerly been strong in Britain: it was defended in the sixteenth century by Hooker (Locke's "judicious Hooker") and later in the seventeenth and eighteenth centuries by, for example, Ralph Cudworth and the Newtonian Samuel Clarke. It was defended by these philosophers as a metaphysical position in defence of an intuitionism in ethics. It was used to defend the established moral and social order against the criticisms especially of Hobbes. Locke and Hume had extended the Hobbesian critique of things established and accepted as right, and had largely triumphed over earlier Platonists by the end of the eighteenth century.

On the Platonic tradition, modified by Aristotle, the basic entities are substances. Sensible events are separable in themselves, but occur in substances, where these latter are active entities that bind separable events as parts into metaphysical wholes. Substances have forms or essences, which determine the direction the activity takes. This activity explains, by tying together, the events we experience by sense, events which as we sensibly experience them are separable. The substance and its form are not given in sense experience, they are metaphysically real though not real to sense. In order to understand the link that explains sensible events one must go outside the realm of sense to another realm beyond or behind the events we know by sense. In Coleridge's terms, it is our faculty of Understanding that knows sensible events. It is our faculty of Reason that gives us knowledge of the ideal forms or essences that explain ordinary experience.

The ideal forms or essences are unanalyzable powers. The substance is inseparable from its form or essence. The essence of Socrates is to be human, that is the basic ordering behind the events as we ordinarily experience them, and if Socrates ceases to be human he ceases to be, his form is something he is essentially or necessarily.

The whole substance tradition is subject to criticism by Mill as it had been by Hobbes and Locke and Hume and as it was later to be by Bertrand Russell. These philosophers argued that, for humans at least, their behaviour is to be explained not in terms unanalyzable powers but by the laws of association. In terms of the Platonic metaphysics, this is to limit oneself to the Understanding, ignoring what Reason tells us about the world. For the critics of Platonism, this is true but they deny that there is any realm of ideal forms or essences or active substances or any faculty of Reason that reveals such a realm to us; one explains the world of sense by appeal to regularities that describe the events in that world, and one does not have to fly off to an imaginary world of timeless entities that lies above or behind the world of ordinary sense experience.

For the associationist one explains ends other than simple pleasure in terms of associations that come to be in the world we inhabit as incarnate beings. Such motives as love of family or love of country, like the miser's love of gold, are not native to human beings but are acquired. This means, therefore, from the point of view of the Platonist tradition that humans are no better than dogs, as seekers of pleasure; insofar as people seek other ends, they do so, not intrinsically, but only as a matter of the contingencies of association. What is essentially human has been lost. That at least is the charge.

There is something further, according to the Platonists. The ideal form or essence necessarily determines the end towards which the substance strives to be in its sensible appearances. Now, one must make a virtue of necessity. That at least is which the reasonable person does; such a one does not strive to do the impossible, but rather acquiesces in what is necessary and inescapable, what is fated. So the ideal form or essence does not only determine what the substances *does* or *is* but also what it *ought to be*. The patterns the active substance brings about in the world as we observe it are thus not only *descriptive*, but also *normative*. The patterns, in other words, are *natural laws*, both in the sense of empirical science, but also in the moral sense.

It follows that, where for the associationists like Locke, Hume and Mill, explanation is purely descriptive, in terms of matter-of-fact regularities, explanation for the Platonist tradition inevitably involves values: for the former there is a fact-value distinction, where for the latter there is no such fact-value distinction.

Further, since the ideal form or essence is normative as well as descriptive, when Reason grasps this ideal form in the case of our own humanity it is grasping the *moral law*, the immutable moral standards by which we *ought to live*. The associationists, in arguing against ideal forms or essences, are thus arguing for the abolition of the moral law. What could be more immoral than that? Far from seeking the orientation as humans towards the "improvement of mankind," these philosophers teach the violation of our eternal moral rules and reduce humanity to base seekers after pleasure. No wonder that revolutionary action based on something like Godwin's *Political Justice* should lead to a Reign of Terror.

Mill vs. the metaphysics of intuition: the ontology of virtue

Mill argued that all our empirically meaningful concepts are derived from our sensory experiences through processes of association. There were those metaphysicians, deriving originally from Plato who held that we have ideas, innate or from some other source, that give us access to a world outside of or beyond the world we know by way of our senses (and inner awareness). Mill argued that such a metaphysics was at bottom quite without empirical meaning, and, indeed, quite without meaning. He was concerned to rebut it, since, as he saw these things, it was nothing more than support of illusory ways of coming to know truths deeper than can be found out by experience, and support for retrogressive moral doctrines – and in either case, hindrances to his overall task of the "improvement of mankind." Mill's critique, while formulated in terms of a psychological theory of learning, was at bottom a matter of metaphysics: neither knowledge nor morality could be found to have an ontological ground beyond the empirical world.

Hobbes had preceded Mill in the associationist critique of Platonism and its doctrine of abstract, non-empirical forms. Several British philosophers, e.g. Henry More, undertook a defence of Platonism and argued that the associationist theory was not only wrong but also a source of moral depravity. Locke and Hume renewed the defence of a philosophy of experience, in its defence of an empirical methodology in science and its the critique of any moral theory that claimed to be rooted in some sort of transcendental forms.

The Platonist critique of the associationist-utilitarian position was revived, as we said, by Coleridge. Nearer to John Stuart Mill was Whewell who was also a Platonist in this tradition, developing while critically analyzing the ideas of Coleridge. For Coleridge, the opposition was the associationists and utilitarians, Hobbes, Locke, Hume and Godwin. Whewell opposed the same things, now represented by Bentham; for whom he had hardly a good word to say, and it later became John Stuart Mill. Whewell's Platonism determined his view in moral philosophy and ethics. He argued in his *Elements of Morality, including Polity* (1845) and his *Lectures on the History of English Moral Philosophy* (1852) that our moral principles are justified by virtue of stating truths about the ideal form of human being which we know by intuition of the natural law rooted in the human essence or ideal form. These intuitions, our moral sentiments, cannot, he argued, agreeing with Coleridge, be reduced to some sort of awareness derived through association of feelings given in our experience of the world of sense: these intuitions are irreducible. Mill reviewed these two works in his essay on "Whewell on Moral Philosophy" (1852), arguing that the moral principles Whewell was defending were in fact an impediment to the "improvement of mankind," and that the metaphysical basis upon which the defence depended was mistaken

Whewell, in his defence of intuitionism in ethics, offered little by way of positive argument. He more or less simply asserted that there was universal agreement on various moral and political principles, and proposed that this amounted to a set of intuitions of the transcendent ground of value. That the principles largely coincided with those standard in Victorian England, even when they seem clearly wrong, e.g. the prohibition on divorce, did not strike him as odd. They struck Mill as odd and in fact as morally perverse. He argued that Whewell's moral "intuitions" arose through association and in fact were merely entrenched prejudice that had to be subjected to critical evaluation rather than taken as given. To take them as given amounted to nothing more than unquestioning acceptance of the existing order, and a denial that any improvement was either needed or possible.

For Mill, there was no human essence or form or Idea, intuitions of which by some mythical faculty of Reason judged human action. He argued that there is at bottom only one motivator, namely, pleasure: one aims at happiness and happiness consists in maximizing pleasure and minimizing pain. But other things come to be sought after as ends in themselves. This happens through association. For the miser, having money is part of his happiness; for him money, originally a means to other ends, comes through the contingencies of life to be associated with pleasure, and with this fusion becomes an end in itself, part of the happiness of this person. Or, to take another example, we search for true matter-of-fact generalizations because knowing those generalizations is to know causes, and to know causes is to know that means to things that are parts of our happiness: such knowledge is itself such a means. But like the miser's gold, knowing causes can become associated and even fused with pleasure. In this way, the search for causes, the impulse behind science, can become part of a person's happiness and disinterested curiosity an end in itself. Whewell argued that such motivations have a peculiar character that makes it clear that they are not mere associations where pleasure is simply externally added to something else. In this the younger Mill agreed, differing on this point with his father and with Bentham. But it does not follow, he argued, that the associationist account is false; there is no need to retreat into innatism as Whewell suggested, following Coleridge. For, associations can have as their products conscious states that are characteristically different from their genetic antecedents: the processes are chemical in nature, not merely mechanical or additive. Mill can grant that our moral sentiments are irreducible in kind to more basic elements of pleasure, while holding that they are nonetheless also the genetic products of associations of such elements. Whewell may have successfully replied to Locke and perhaps even to Bentham, but he provides no reply to the critique of the younger Mill.

It is Mill's argument that through experience we have learned that our own happiness is best found in concert with others with whom we live together in an order in which people are as reasonably happy as they could be under the circumstances (various sorts of such order possible, though some are clear improvements on others). In general, the individual leads a more satisfying life if the end of all is the general happiness. That makes human virtue to be the pursuit of the general happiness. And for any individual person, through association, in a way similar to the case of the miser, the general happiness can become part of the happiness. Here he agrees with Godwin.

At the same time Mill also disagrees with Godwin. For, unlike Godwin, Mill acknowledges that the general happiness is best sought by pursuing other ends, e.g. love of one's family or the disinterested pursuit of knowledge. If many of Whewell's moral intuitions do not pass the test of utility, there are in fact many that do, and these ought to be pursued, not because we have an intuition that they are right but because the principle of utility so judges them. The point is that each of these motives, including feelings of moral approbation and disapprobation, has its own peculiar character, but that does not imply that they are somehow innate and forms of insight into the oral structure of the universe; rather each is the product of a process of association acquiring its special character through the chemical nature of the association, and is justified or unjustified by appeal to the ultimate standard of the general happiness.

The general happiness, that is, the utilitarian end, becomes the standard by which other moral rules are tested. Many of the principles that Whewell claimed were intuitive, innate, and self-evident turn out to fall short of the utilitarian standard. Mill's argument begins, it is clear, with the challenge to the Platonic metaphysics – there are no necessary ideal forms or essences beyond the world of sense, no form of humanity that determines our eternal moral ends – and, as part of this challenge, with Mill's claim that all our concepts about the ordinary world arise by way of processes of association from our experience of it, either by sense or by inner awareness. Whewell thus makes the claim in his lectures on moral philosophy and its history that we do in fact have *a priori* moral concepts for which association can give no account. But there is in fact no argument, just assertion, that associationism as it derives from Hobbes and Locke can't do this or that, and insofar as it leads one to question the moral principles we take as given it is evil. Mill, of course, has a reply, first, that associationist theory is in fact a well-confirmed empirical theory about human beings (which indeed it is); second, that our moral sentiments can be the products of association even though they are characteristically different from their genetic antecedents; and third, that accepted standards Whewell claims to know intuitively are simply ways of behaving that have willy-nilly through the exigencies of history become ends through being associated with pleasure. They are often felt to be different from, and more firmly grounded than the principles proposed by the utilitarians; it but does not follow that they are innate and necessary parts of some metaphysically defined human nature. Whewell's moral theory is thus nothing more than a begging of the question, disguised as a spurious Platonistic metaphysics, and is in fact a defence of the ingrained habits and laws of the English squirarchy of which Whewell struggled to become a member – Tory ideology rather than reasoned philosophy. By making the accepted standards to be natural laws deriving from the transcendent ideal forms Whewell builds those taken-for-granted values into the necessary ontological structure of the universe, and thereby shields them from critical evaluation and from the need for human beings to take responsibility for the moral codes they adopt as they try to live together in some sort of harmony: if it is God's law and built into His universe, who then are we to question it? and, indeed, is not such questioning presumptuous and does it not come close to blasphemy? (Nor is it any accident that laws against blasphemy are part of the social order that Whewell is defending.)

Mill vs. the metaphysics of intuition: Coleridge

Coleridge, when he took the lead philosophically, turned to German philosophy. In his *Biographia Literaria*, he makes clear his view that on the Locke-Hartley associationism the world consists of sensory atoms – sensory impressions – that are independent logically and ontologically of one another, unconnected save for relations of resemblance and of proximity in space and time, and our ideas insofar as they derive from sense share in this ontological and logical independence. As for our complex ideas, including our abstract ideas of things, they are "mere" "conjunctions" of separable parts: associationism is a "mechanical" theory which applies to only those ideas the parts of which are "additive." The same holds for the ideas that motivate us, our more noble sentiments are hardly noble after all; at best they mark not ends but merely prudential judgments; and our real ends are simply various sorts of bodily pleasure. Our human dignity, moral and cognitive, dissolves into the habits of beasts.

The solution to the problems generated by associationism and utilitarianism, Coleridge argues, is to recognize that beyond sense experience and association, which at best yields an empirical understanding, the mind also has the capacity, Reason, to grasp real structures in the world, necessary connections that lie outside the world of sense but which nonetheless provide the reasons for things. In reality sensible appearances are linked into more substantial realities which are the underlying causes of things, and which bring it about that they form structured wholes rather than mere conjunctions. Since in the end everything is related to everything else, there is only one true reality. (There is only one such whole: for, if there were two, then they would still be related, at least in being not each other, and so there would be, beyond them, a more substantial whole which is wholly One.) The one complete substantial whole is the Hegelian Absolute, or what Coleridge, in the *Biographia Literaria*, (with Biblical implications), called the great "I AM."

These wholes are known by Reason, via its own Ideas. These Ideas, which are the ideal forms or essences of things, are themselves connected wholes, not the sort of "abstract ideas" derived by association from sense and to which the understanding is restricted. The Ideas in our mind reflect in their necessary structures the necessary structures in things which account for the appearances of things given to us in sensible experience and the Understanding. Since the Ideas are not derived from sense experience, they are *a priori*, and innate to us – though (Whewell argued) they only gradually in the history of the individual become present to consciousness.

In looking for an *a priori* element to knowledge, Coleridge turned to Kant, but, like Schelling and Hegel, insisted that if there is a whole that is known then, *one*, the form of that whole is made to be as it is by the way it is connected to other forms, each of which derives its form and being from its location in the greater and greater systems of wholes culminating in the ultimate whole which is the Absolute, and, *two*, your Idea and mine of some whole themselves share the same form with each other and with that whole through a coordination deriving from the Absolute – such coordination of Ideas and the wholes they make known itself constitutes a whole, a whole with the form of knowing, and which has its own place in the whole which is the great I AM in which everything has its place and from which it derives its meaning.

Just as cognitive relations bind things into knower-known wholes irreducible to sense encounters with the world, so also our moral sentiments unite people into social wholes. Far from ends being merely utilitarian, there is an Idea of community in-dwelling in each individual and in the community as a whole. Social practices and social institutions could be studied only in the context of such an Idea, and not merely as habits acquired through associational learning. The state does exist for the sake of the individual, as the utilitarians assert, but the individual also exists for the sake of the state. No person is an atom, independent of all others, but in a society becomes something different, the self as part of a greater whole. ("Each man in a numerous society is not only coexistent with, but virtually organized into, the multitude of which he is an integral part. His *idem* is modified by the *alter*. And there arise impulses and objects from the *synthesis*, of the *alter et idem*, myself and my neighbour" [cf. Coleridge, *First Lay Sermon*, App. F {1815–17}].). There are bonds that unite not only the living with one another, not merely with the living, but also with those who have gone before and are now dead and those who will come, the yet to be born. The same holds for our duties. We have our duties to others, but also our duties determined by the greater whole for the parts which we are. Contrary to what the utilitarians assert our felt moral sentiments which bind us into these greater wholes are not reducible to forms of searching after pleasure. They are innate parts of our human nature, that is, parts of that Idea which forms us, and which we know through our Reason: we know our duties intuitively rather than through prudential calculations in our search after bodily contentment.

For Mill, his project for the "improvement of mankind" demanded a rejection – to be sure, a reasoned rejection – of this ethical intuitionism and of the mystical Platonistic metaphysics that provided spurious support for this system of ethics.

Mill vs. the metaphysics of intuitionism: logic and philosophy of science

Mill's system of logic should be seen as part of this critique of the Platonism of Coleridge and Whewell. But it should also be viewed as part of his efforts to secure a methodology appropriate to the project of the "improvement of mankind."

Coleridge had a wide influence. Tutors at Oxford and Cambridge spread his Germanic metaphysics and ethical intuitionism in defence of the established order in church and state, the existing political and social institutions, parliament as it then was, unrepresentative and almost archaic, and unreformed universities, all those things criticized by the utilitarians. ("If it was good enough before the war, it is good enough now.") (One can get a feel for these teachings in Charles and Augustus Hare, *Guesses at Truth* [first edition 1827, second edition 1838] – the Hares were tutors at Oxford.) Coleridgian ideas were carried into public life by Mill's friends F. D. Maurice and John Sterling. Dr. Thomas Arnold spread his ideas among his students at Rugby; they were already converts when they arrived at university. It was in this air of Germanic philosophy that Whewell developed his ideas at Cambridge.

John Stuart Mill's father, James Mill, wrote various long essays, including ones "On Government" (1820) and "On Education" (1819), and Bentham wrote on legal matters such as the law of evidence and the rational structure of the British legal system, arguing for reform on utilitarian and associationist grounds. But they were unpersuasive, their arguments were lost in the pervasive air of German mysticism and philosophy that Coleridge had introduced. Mill's *Analysis of the Phenomena of the Human Mind* (1829) was meant to re-establish on a secure basis the associationist psychology derived from Hartley and which formed the basis of utilitarian arguments for a changed social order. It was in this context that the younger Mill emerged as the leading advocate for reform. His first major work was his *System of Logic* (1843) which turned out to be immensely popular. It had as its aim to establish on firm grounds the empiricist account of logic and of science, including psychology and including the social sciences, political economy in particular (defending Ricardo's economics had been a central concern of the utilitarians, it was argued that it showed various economic practices are contrary to the general welfare, though they served the interests of a smaller group or class, e.g, how import tariffs on wheat served the narrow interests of landowners but kept the price of bread high contrary to the interest of the majority): the reformers' arguments were to be made methodologically secure.

Mill's account of logic was thoroughly empiricist; it presupposed an empiricist metaphysics and, where necessary, defended that perspective. Mill's *Logic* is therefore more than a logic: it is also a philosophy of language, a theory of evidence, and a metaphysics – an empiricist metaphysics to counter the Platonism of Coleridge and Whewell. To understand what Mill is doing it is therefore necessary to look at the sort of logic of which he was critical, and the metaphysical context of that earlier account of logic – an account which also fit in with Coleridge's metaphysics: both took for granted what Mill denied, that there are objective necessary connections in the world which we know but which are not given in sense experience.

The traditional metaphysics derived from Plato, but the traditional logic, while rooted in a metaphysics of ideal forms or essences, derived more specifically from Aristotle. It concentrated on the syllogisms of the sort

	All M are P
(s)	*All S are M*
	so, All S are P.

S and P are known as the subject and predicate terms of the conclusion, and M which appears in the premises is known as the middle term. Mill argued that the premises and therefore also the conclusion were about classes of individuals, where these individuals are located in the ordinary world that we know through sensible experience and inner awareness. The terms S, P, and M connoted empirical properties of these individuals, and the classes of the syllogism were the sets of individuals which exemplified these properties; the terms are said to denote the members of these classes. The properties connoted by the terms are, at least the ones that are basic or undefined, also given in sense, and so far as our ordinary experience goes, the relevant properties and individuals are logically and ontologically self-contained: there is nothing about their intrinsic being that connects them logically or necessarily to any other entity. While these entities need not be separate, they are all logically and ontologically separable – at least so far as our sense experience of these entities is concerned. But, Mill asks (rhetorically), rejecting any appeal to Coleridgean Reason or Whewellian rational intuition, what other kind of experience is there?

From all this, it follows that any proposition of the form

(a)   All S are P

makes an assertion about a population S. But all we ever observe is a sample. And what holds in a sample is not guaranteed to hold in the population. The generalization is therefore uncertain, relative to the evidence; we may assert it, and have good evidence from our observed sample, but there is no guarantee that the generalization is true. In particular, no syllogism of the sort (s) can ever guarantee that a proposition

like (a) is true, for the premises are themselves generalizations which are also inductively uncertain.

Mill argued for this position against a long tradition, also going back to Aristotle
and beyond that to Plato, but defended by Coleridge and Whewell, which held that
some syllogisms are demonstrative in the sense that their premises and therefore
their conclusions, while making substantive statements about the ordinary world,
are nonetheless necessary truths. This means that the terms of the syllogism cannot
be logically self-contained, that there must be necessary connections amongst them
that make them necessary truths rather than merely contingent and uncertain.
Since things and their properties that are given in ordinary experience are logically
self-contained, it follows that on this view the properties to which the terms of
the syllogism refer cannot be simply given in ordinary experience; they must exist
external to the world as transcendent ideal forms, and must be known by some sort of
non-empirical intuition. Thus, the form of a syllogism cannot be (s) so much as

$$
\begin{array}{ll}
& \text{M is P} \\
(s') & \underline{\text{S is M}} \\
& \text{so, S is P,}
\end{array}
$$

where the propositions state necessary relations amongst transcendent ideal forms, or
Ideas, as Coleridge and Whewell put it.

Now, if a syllogism like (s') is to give information about the empirical world, then
the (ideal) forms mentioned in (s') must have the empirical properties mentioned in (s)
as their instances, and in addition we must have a necessary connection implying that

(e)   S is P → All S are P

and similarly for the other two propositions in (s) and (s'). The proposition on the left
is known by Reason or non-sensory intuition, that on the right by the Understanding
or sense experience. It is the truth of (e) that guarantees that the world as we know
it by sense presents itself to us exemplifying in its patterns the structure among the
ideal forms that is discerned by Reason. As Mill points out in his *Logic*, the truth
of (e) is what is asserted by the thesis of the *dictum de omni et nullo* of traditional
logic ("whatever can be affirmed [or denied] of a class can be affirmed [or denied] of
everything included in the class"). This maxim states a fundamental principle or law
about the ontological structure of the universe to the effect that the entire nature
and properties of the ideal forms constituted the nature and properties of each of the
individual things called by the same name.

Note that if the proposition

(a')   S is P

is necessary by virtue of being about the transcendent ideal forms of things, and if (e)
is also a necessary truth, then so is the proposition (a)

All S are P.

If, therefore, we know as necessary the truth (s') and the principle (e) then we know that there is a necessary connection that guarantees the truth of (a). (a) is not, as the Understanding would have it, contingent but necessary, as Reason would have it, and therefore does not partake of the inductive uncertainty that attaches to (a) if the only evidence for its truth is that of an observed sample: if we know a truth about ideal forms like (a') then it is guaranteed that what holds in a sample also holds in a population, even if it is a sample of one. We know with certainty that the future will resemble the past.

We may refer to the view that there are ideal forms or essences of the sort we are talking about as "Platonism," since Plato held something like that view. It was a view common among English philosophers, but apparently demolished by Hobbes, Locke and Hume. Mill's critic, William Whewell, was a Platonist in the older tradition, developing while critically analyzing the ideas of Coleridge, except that the opposition was now Bentham and later John Stuart Mill. His Platonism determined not only his views on ethics, but also his views on logic and, as we shall now see, his philosophy of science. In both logic and the philosophy of science he affirmed the existence of demonstrative arguments. It was his Platonist metaphysics that supported his claim that there are demonstrative arguments. Mill rejected both that metaphysics and the claim that there are demonstrative arguments in logic and in science.

In the philosophy of science, Whewell held with Mill that explanation among individual events was by way of subsumption under natural laws. Explanations of individual events, why, say, this x which is S is also P, took the form,

$$\text{(p)} \quad \frac{\begin{array}{l}\text{All S are P}\\ \text{x is S}\end{array}}{\text{so, x is P,}}$$

which is also the form of a prediction. In more recent terms, Mill adopts the "deductive-nomological" or "covering law" model of explanation. Whewell adopts much the same model. There is a difference, however, between Mill and Whewell. For Mill the major premise (a) of (p) is a matter-of-empirical fact contingent generality. For Whewell in contrast, if (p) is to count as an explanation the major premise (a) must be a necessary truth, a generalization about matters of fact but backed by a truth like (a') about the ideal forms.

At the same time, since such backing proceeds by way of principle (e), we must note that there are difficulties with this principle. If the ideal forms are truly transcendent, outside the world of sense, as they must be, then how can any truth about them guarantee, as (e) asserts them to guarantee, a truth about the sensible particulars of this world? Whewell charges that Coleridge runs into this difficulty [in his essay on Coleridge appended to the second edition of his *Lectures on the History of Moral Philosophy in England* (1852, second edition 1862), with reference to his essay on the distinction, which is also Kant's, between the Understanding, which knows the world of sense, and Reason, which knows the ideal forms, in Coleridge's *Aids to Reflection*]. But Whewell does not notice that Coleridge has a solution of sorts to the problem: the coordination of sensible things with our Ideas is effected by those events being located appropriately in a greater whole, ultimately in the Absolute. It is the activity of the Absolute that guarantees the truth of (e) and thereby effects the coordination of our Ideas or forms, on the one hand, and sensible things on the other: it is the Absolute that guarantees the necessity of the principle (e), which asserts that patterns among sensible things imitate structures among the ideal forms. In any case, Whewell does object to the apparent separation in Coleridge of Reason from the Understanding. Whewell suggests that he (Whewell) has a solution to the problem. However, if Coleridge does not solve the problem, it is hard to say that Whewell does much better. For, what he argues is that what solves the problem is the fact that God, as an active creator of the world, acts to create in this world entities which replicate the structure of the world of ideal forms. It is God's activity that guarantees that the implication (e) holds true, or, what is the same, that the traditional *dictum de omni et nullo* holds true. This means that the explanation of why this x which is S is also P is in the first instance by way of the pattern (p), where the major premise is a pattern with a necessity deriving from the ideal forms, because that guarantee is made through the activity of God, it is the latter which does the real explaining.

One can see that Whewell's account of the necessity of (e) had the further consequence that the ultimate explainor of everything is an, or the, active deity no doubt appealed to Anglican dons and bishops; nonetheless, it still holds true in general, and certainly holds for Mill, that the appeal to the activity of God to solve a problem creates more mystery than it solves. Whewell's appeal to God to bridge the logical gap between a sample and a population is no more plausible than Descartes' appeal to God to establish that the desk upon which he was writing really did exist.

Mill denied the Platonist claim that there are ideal forms or essences; he follows earlier empiricists in rejecting, because he cannot find any in his inner awareness, any such "abstract ideas" that are not derived from things given in our sensible experience of the world. Nor, given the power of associationist theory to account for the ideas we do find in our inner awareness is there any need to postulate innate ideas that give us non-sensory intuitions of such entities. It was Mill's argument, based on his associationism, that all our ideas derive from sense experience or inner awareness. He therefore argued in particular that the class interpretation of the propositions in the syllogism is the correct one. Since he argued that there are no entities like the ideal forms which transcend our ordinary experience of the world, and that there are therefore no necessary connections amongst the properties of things, there can be no matter-of-fact generalization which does not partake of inductive uncertainty and no syllogism can be demonstrative in the traditional sense. There is no guarantee that the future will resemble the past.

There is one further point about Platonism that requires notice. This is the connection between the theory of ideal forms and moral philosophy.

First, we must recognize that, if (a′) is to guarantee the truth of (a), then an individual x which is S must be S necessarily. For if it is only contingently S then it is also only contingently P, and the proposition (a) is itself only contingently true: it might be false since x being S will be no guarantee that x be P. But the point of the scheme at least in part is to effect necessary connections among the changing facts of the empirical world. Hence, if an individual is S then it is S necessarily.

With this, it becomes clear, as we have already seen, that the ideal forms also define a moral order: the form not only describes what human beings *are* but also what they *ought to be*. This is because x's being S, where S is an essence or ideal form, is something that x must necessarily be, and for the reasonable person, if it is necessarily the case that x is so and so then it ought to be the case that x is so and so. So, given (a'), the regularity (a) not only describes how things are, and must be, and in that sense is a natural law, but also says how things ought to be and is therefore a natural law in the moral sense of that term. The moral order of things, including human beings, is thus an objective order built into the necessary ontological structure of the world.

On the Platonist scheme, human beings are rational animals, in the sense that they have the capacity to grasp the reasons for things, that is, they have intuitions of the reasons for things being as they are and not another way, or, in other words, intuitions of the essences or ideal forms. Among those ideal forms they can in particular know their own form or essence, that of humanity. Human reason thus grasps how humans ought to be, that is, the natural law to which they ought to conform. Human reason in grasping the real end of the human being is thus sovereign over the passions, giving them their proper directions, organizing them so the human being can become what it ought to become.

Mill's rejection of Platonism pervades his philosophy. It is evident that his account of concept formation excludes any transcendent ideal forms or essences and claims that we have intuitive knowledge of them. As a consequence, as we have seen, there are therefore no objective necessary connections, and no demonstrative syllogisms. It is the class interpretation that is the correct understanding of deductive reasoning. Whewell, naturally enough, disagrees: the principles of a science like mechanics as defined by Newton are objectively necessary and can be known *a priori* by rational intuition. Such a science is therefore demonstrative. To be sure, Whewell acknowledges, these laws have not always seemed self-evident, and in fact such knowledge grew out of ignorance by the accretion of empirical data until their necessity finally dawned to human consciousness. But having dawned, such principles are beyond questioning and the inconceivability of their contraries is a mark of their necessity. In fact, Whewell does not offer much of an argument for his position. In his essay on "Truth" ("The Nature of the Truth of the Laws of Motion" [1835], reprinted in the *Philosophy of the Inductive Sciences*) with regard to the principles of mechanics, he advances no argument for the truth of these principles being *a priori* beyond the fact (again more asserted than argued for) that we are all now agreed that their contraries are inconceivable. Is that not so, he asks, expecting one answer – which may be correct, but does not, Mill argues, establish that they are *a priori*. Whewell does not eliminate other possible causes for such inconceivability. Mill offers such an account. To wit, the concepts forming such principles have become so firmly associated with one another and fused together that of course we can no longer imagine how they could be false: their contraries are indeed inconceivable but it does not follow that their truth is grounded in transcendent ideal forms or essences nor that they are not, logically speaking, simple matter-of-empirical-fact truths.

Here, as in ethics, Mill's reply to Whewell depends crucially on his associationism. And again, as in ethics, Whewell simply asserts that he is right and Mill is wrong and that the associationist account of human being is inadequate to account for the higher aspects of human being – and that it is not only wrong, inadequate to our cognitive faculties and therefore pernicious, but that it is also and thereby a moral evil. But Whewell cannot escape the fact that associationist theory is a well confirmed theory, and that the explanation that it proposes or at least sketches for the unimaginability of the contraries of first principles of empirical sciences such as mechanics is entirely plausible. Thus, Whewell's appeal to the felt necessity of certain principles does not address and certainly does not eliminate Mill's psychological account of how first principles of well confirmed sciences such as mechanics come to have a felt necessity; Whewell's claim is therefore quite unreasonable.

Mill also offers a similar explanation of the felt necessity of the axioms of (Euclidean) geometry. This challenged the dogma of centuries, and was a stronghold of Platonism. Naturally enough Whewell used geometry as another example of a demonstrative science resting on objectively necessary truths. Given that tradition Whewell's criticism of Mill's account of geometry as an empirical science had a certain strength. But Mill's account of geometry as an applied empirical science now, in the light of the discovery of non-Euclidean geometries, is widely seen to be entirely correct, in outline at least if not in the details. No longer can one find that the case for a demonstrative science is made to rest on geometry: Whewell's appeal is now simply rejected, or, worse, deemed irrelevant.

Mill's account of arithmetic has less to be said for it. Again Whewell was an opponent, and Mill attempted to give an account of arithmetic as an applied science. G. Frege's suggestion that Mill's analysis is merely psychologistic is misleading. Mill did attempt to deal with its supposed necessity as he handled the supposed necessity of geometry and mechanics, in terms of deeply rooted associations making contraries unimaginable, but that is not to hold that they are to be understood as somehow laws of thought, that is, generalizations about how we think about the world. But Mill has difficulty saying exactly how arithmetical truths are truths about the world of things of ordinary experience. However, prior to Russell, everyone had trouble with this so to hold Mill guilty of any grave sin here would be equally to condemn most preceding philosophers, including even Whewell.

Certainty and the methods of science

In general with regard to any science, Whewell in effect argued that, unless something like his view were true then no certainty would ever be possible. In the absence of any objective necessary connections, then, since the only evidence for a generalization like (a)

All S are P

about a population S could be an observed sample, it is both logically and ontologically possible that the evidence be as it is and yet the generalization be false. For Europeans, all observed swans were white and so they inferred that all swans are white – which they found out was false, upon the discovery by Dutch sailors landing in Western Australia and discovering black swans. So, in spite of what has happened in the past, maybe the sun won't rise tomorrow. And maybe, as Pliny suggested, there can be people with their heads below rather than above their shoulders. This is the so-called problem of induction. Whewell can claim he has a solution for it. But of course it is no solution if the required ideal forms or essences do not exist. Which they do not, Mill insists: careful attention shows clearly that all our (meaningful) concepts are derived from sense experience or inner awareness. So Whewell does not have a solution to the (so-called) problem of induction.

But, Mill points out, the logical gap is there and there is in fact no way in which it can be eliminated: it is a fact about ourselves, the world and our knowledge of it, and must simply be accepted. In that sense, the problem of induction is not a problem, or anyway not a problem that we can do anything about. The real task is to get on with the task of coping with a world in which we are thus situated.

We do not come to this task devoid of beliefs that help us to anticipate what the world will bring, beliefs like "Fire burns" or "Food nourishes." But as we discover in our interactions with the world, these are not exactly true: fire burns only if we get too close and not everything edible nourishes. We come to adjust our beliefs in the light of this further evidence that experience brings. We even come to formulate rules for changing our beliefs in the light of incoming evidence. We find out that the rule of induction by simple enumeration

From All observed S are P infer All S are P

is not a very safe rule: it often leads us to accept generalizations that later turn out to be false. We observe all S so far are P, and infer that all S are P, but discover soon enough that we have an S which is not P but rather P′. Simple enumeration does not take account of the fact that the variety in the world must be accommodated, or at least we must make allowances for it. Instead of thinking only of

(a)   All S are P

we should think also of possible alternative hypotheses, such as

(b)   All S are P′
(c)   All S are P″.

The task then becomes that of finding data that will eliminate all alternatives but one. Only then can one conclude that the uneliminated hypothesis is true. Induction must proceed not by simple enumeration but through the *elimination* of all but one of a set a competing hypotheses. Mill carefully articulated these rules in what have come to be called *Mill's Methods* of *eliminative induction*.

Since no syllogism can ever be demonstrative, deductive logic can never establish as true some principle we did not already, at least implicitly, know. Knowledge is genuinely increased only through inductive inference. The role of deductive logic is to keep our reasoning consistent. Deductive logic is the *logic of consistency*, the *logic of truth* is inductive logic, the principles of which Mill argues are to be found in the methods of eliminative induction which he adumbrates.

But a description of those methods is not the whole of inductive logic. Mill is also careful to note that in, for example, our simple example above, one can conclude that the unelimineated hypothesis (a) is true upon the elimination of (b) and (c), only if one assumes that this set forms a complete list of alternatives (*Principle of Limited Variety*), and only if one assumes that at least one member of the set is true (*Principle of Determinism*). That these Principles hold in some area of investigation is, as Mill says, a *law about laws*. These laws about laws are themselves matter of fact generalizations, and are subject to the infirmity that affects any inductive inference. We do, however, accept such laws as true, and in fact take for granted *abstract generic theories* that assert such laws for a variety of systems, and therefore that *there are* specific laws of a certain generic form in these various specific areas – without, of course, saying specifically what those laws are – finding those laws that *are there* (determinism) and of the relevant *generic sort* (limited variety) is the task of experiment: the theory yields gappy knowledge of the new areas, and it is the task of the experimenter, guided thus by the theory, to eliminate those gaps. We use our generic theories (often now called "paradigms" or "research programmes"), as laws about laws, to guide us in our research: we accept them on the basis of our experience in actually finding specific laws of the sort the theory asserts to be there, waiting as it were to be discovered – guided by the theory we have been successful, so far as we can tell, in discovering new laws. Guided by them, we have come to be able to eliminate the imperfections and gappiness in our primitive beliefs about the world. The laws we have discovered, and the data that support those laws, support our acceptance of these theories as laws about laws.

Note that we rise up a generic hierarchy of laws, from specific laws to laws about laws to the law of the highest level, the Law of Universal Causation, that for every sort of event there is a law for its occurrence. At the specific level there are many competing alternatives: the world is full of variety. At this level we must rely upon the rules of eliminative induction to guide us in our search for generalizations we can accept as laws. But as we move up the hierarchy the variety becomes less, until one arrives at the Law of Universal Causation, which, Mill argues, is so generic that there is no competitor. It may be false, but if it is there is no alternative *law* that could be true. Nor is it easy to eliminate it: it predicts that *there is* a law in a certain area, but a failure to find such a law does not falsify it – maybe we have just not searched hard enough. From the logic of existence statements, claims such as "there is a unicorn" or "there is a law" cannot be falsified by a failure to find what is asserted to be there – not finding an example does not amount to a falsifying counter-example – it may be just that we have not located an example, that we have just not looked hard enough – such is the logic of "there are" statements. But while such statements cannot be falsified, they can be confirmed – by finding an example of what is asserted to be there. So the inference from the discovery of various laws to the Law of Universal Causation proceeds by the rule of induction by simple enumeration. At the specific level, this rule of inference is unsafe because of competing alternatives, but at the generic level, in the absence of competing alternatives, reliance upon this rule is reasonable, and we can reasonably accept on that basis the Law of Universal Causation – and, accepting it, we can use it to further guide our research as we use the rules of eliminative induction in the search for specific laws in new areas, areas that are as yet unexplored or only partially explored. Indeed, not only may we accept the Law of Universal Causation as reasonable, we may accept it as morally certain, as strongly confirmed as any inductive inference could be.

Which is not to say it has anything like the certainty of something known *a priori*. To the contrary, assuming the absence of ideal forms and of a principle like (e) to connect them to the world of ordinary experience, then, like any generalization, the Law of Universal Causation is subject, if not to doubt, then at least to the cautionary thought that it is still possible that contrary evidence might be found. It is our psychological instinct to make inferences to and anticipate the future, or in other words to draw generalizations; indeed, how else could we exist in the world? It turns out that some of these primordial inferences are more reliable than others. We can, however, upon reflection formulate rules to locate those upon which we are better able to rely. These rules serve to separate science from superstition. The rules we select as those upon which we can reasonably rely are those of eliminative induction at the specific level, that of induction by simple enumeration at the most generic level. It is these that have stood the test of experience. That experience may take them beyond reasonable doubt but does not take them beyond all doubt. But we cannot do better – there are no transcendent ideal forms nor any objective necessary connections and there is therefore no test other than experience – and since that is the best that we can do, it is the only reasonable thing to do.

(Mill is careful to note that the Law of Universal Causation, while holding in regions of the universe where we have collected evidence, might, for all we know, break down in parts of the universe that are very distant, too far for us to see, as yet at least, or parts that are very small, too little for us to see, as yet at least. There seems to be no reason to suppose that the Law breaks down for things very distant, but for the very small, Mill's conjecture has turned out to be correct: quantum mechanics has shown that the basic entities there do not conform to the law of causation but to laws that are irreducibly statistical.)

Material objects

With the disappearance of the transcendent ideal forms, Mill gives a revised account of individual facts such as are represented by statements like

(g)   That apple is green.

Traditionally, individual things were understood to be substances, entities that continued to exist identically through change, and which instanced substantial essences or ideal forms which determined the sorts of properties that are to be predicated of them. So, with regard to (g), 'that' refers to a substance instancing an essence or ideal form referred to by 'apple' and having in it the property referred to by 'green'. But there are no ideal forms and so for Mill there are no substances to instance those forms. Since there are no substances, there is no reference to them, nor are sensible qualities predicated of them. A sentence like (g) is now understood as saying something simply about how the world appears, and not about what metaphysically transcends this world, not about substances or ideal forms. Formerly, on the old view, but also on the new, the predicate 'green' refers to a sensible quality that is in the thing of which it is predicated. But where the subject term 'that apple' was formerly taken to refer to a substance in which sensible qualities inhere, including the one that is predicated of it, it is taken, as before, to refer to the thing that remains the same through change, which now, however, can only be the whole itself of all the sensible properties predicated of it. Where formerly the relation of predication represented the tie of inherence, it now represents the relation of a part to a whole. As for the term 'apple', where this formerly was taken to refer to the active substantial essence or ideal form of the substance, it is now taken to describe the *pattern* of appearances characteristic of apples, the pattern that distinguishes those wholes from other wholes such as sticks and rainbows.

But this is not the end of the story. As science comes further to investigate the regularities that give the causal structure of the world it locates the sensible appearances of things as rooted in a common source, a "material object," which is unlike the sensible appearances to which it gives rise, unlike them in quality but like them in having a similar structure. These material objects are not traditional substances: the supposition that there are such entities is not a matter of metaphysical speculation but rather is rooted in the inferences from sensible experience of empirical science: the evidence for their existence is empirical, not metaphysical. Mill defends this view in the *System of Logic*, and in still greater detail in the *Examination of Sir William Hamilton's Philosophy*. As he states his view, "When … I say, The sky is blue, my meaning, and my whole meaning, is that the sky has that particular colour …. I am thinking only of the sensation of blue, and am judging that the sky produces this sensation in my sensitive faculty; or (to express the meaning in technical language) that the quality answering to the sensation of blue, or the power of exciting the sensation of blue, is an attribute of the sky" (*Examination of Sir William Hamilton's Philosophy*, 1865: 386).

Mill sketches out an associationist account of how we form the concept of a material thing, that is, how we come to locate the sensation blue externally to our body as part of a set or collection of qualities which jointly exemplify a pattern defining the collection to be the relevant sort of material object. Naturally enough, Whewell, agreeing with Kant (and Coleridge), holds that our knowledge of the space in which we locate such bodies is innate. Mill allows that the two-dimensional spatial order among the sensible entities given to us in experience is irreducibly relational, but that our knowledge of depth, the third dimension, is learned through complicated processes of association. Little of philosophical importance turns on this: even if the concepts are innate they are concepts of things in the world of ordinary experience and the laws of geometry are still matter-of-fact generalizations about this world.

The collections which constitute the material thing consist of qualities which, in the relevant circumstances, cause us to become aware of sensations exemplifying certain sensible qualities. Often it seems to us that the relevant quality attributed to the object is in fact the sensible entity of which we are aware. But reflection soon shows that the quality is of a sort different from the sensible property awareness which it causes. This is not terribly paradoxical, it is in fact quite common that causes do not resemble their effects – hydrogen and oxygen are both different in kind from the water they produce, smoke is different from fire, rainbows are unlike rain, and the shadow is quite different from the flagpole of which it is the shadow. Some of the qualities corresponding to our sensations are transitory, but others are more permanent. These permanent qualities bundled together form the material object to which they are attributed in our judgment. A material object is thus, as Mill puts it, the "permanent possibility of sensation."

We start out as we become reflective upon the world and of ourselves as part of it with beliefs about patterns of objects and their effects: "Fire burns" and "Food nourishes." These patterns we take to be of qualities which are the sensible properties which are given to us in our awareness of the world. But this knowledge of causal patterns, while serviceable up to a point, is imperfect and gappy, and we would like to eliminate those gaps, make our knowledge less imperfect. As we rummage through the world, and even come to undertake consciously to explore experimentally the patterns among and defining the things we encounter in the world, then we come to recognize that the permanent quality corresponding to our sensation is not like the quality of the sensation: the stick that presents us with a straight shape when out of water presents a bent shape when situated in water, but the permanent quality that causes both these visual sensations is the straight shape we know by touch. In fact, we eventually come to the conclusion that none of the permanent qualities is like any of our sensations, at least in their specific properties. Mill allows that we have among our concepts the very general, indeed most abstract generic concept, of an entity or existent. There are specific properties of the qualities of material objects, they are existent, but they are not given to us in sensation: they are thinkable but not sensible. In more recent ways of speaking we use a definite description to apply to these events and these qualities that we do not know by acquaintance: using the generic concepts of "event" and "property," we think of *the* event characterized by *the* definite property which causes me to have the present sensory awareness.

Thus, a watch when wound sometimes works and sometimes does not. Why is there this difference? what fills the gap? The law of universal causation determines that there is a cause, and we speak of *the* cause for the watch not working. We do not know specifically what it is, but we can think of it, using generic concepts, and the inference to its existence is licensed by the well-confirmed law of universal causation. Failure to see that cause does not invalidate our inference: we have just not looked hard enough.

In the case of the watch we can imagine that the jeweller with his or her lens finally finds the speck of dust which is the cause. But this sort of outcome often does not happen: often we hypothesize such causes that we have never brought into our sensible awareness either directly or by the instruments that extend our senses. And Mill accepts the atomic hypothesis that the causes of the entities given to us in our sensible experience are congeries of atoms, small things too small for us ever to see. The concept of such an atom is easily formed, it is (as the theory had it in Mill's time) the concept of something like a billiard ball only much reduced in size. This is the generic concept of an entity as a congeries of unsensed parts which effect my sensible awareness of the world.

When Mill, in his *Examination of Sir William Hamilton's Philosophy*, characterizes the material objects as the "permanent possibilities of sensation," he is often interpreted as endorsing a form of phenomenalism. And when he endorses the atomic hypothesis, he is taken to be simply inconsistent. But the inconsistency is not there: Mill is not a phenomenalist. His view is more like that of the American Critical Realists, or the later Bertrand Russell. Certainly, there is nothing about his views on concept formation and about how we causally investigate the world that make it impossible for him to accept the theory that the entities which cause our sensations are congeries of the small entities that scientists like Dalton called atoms.

Other minds

One can say about Mill's account of our knowledge of other minds, as with his account of material objects, that it is often misunderstood and unfairly criticized. Like his detailed account of material objects, Mill's discussion of our inferences to other minds also appears in the *Examination of Sir William Hamilton's Philosophy*.

Mill's account of our inferences to other minds, that is, to the mental states of others, goes something like this. Whenever I stub my big toe and feel a pain there, in my toe, I say something like "Ouch, my toe." There is a regularity:

(m) Whenever there is an awareness from within one's body that there is a pain located within the skin of one's big toe, then and only then one says "Ouch, my toe."

I have confirmed this generalization, and many others like, many times in my own case. When one observes analogous behavior from another human being, when we have, for example,

Jones says "Ouch my toe,"

we infer by means of (m) that

There is an awareness from within Jones' body that there is a pain located within the skin of his or her big toe.

This affirms the existence of an inner awareness of an inner state. The inference from analogous behavior to an analogous inner awareness is by way a well-confirmed law. The inference is to an inner state of the other person, a state of which he or she is aware but of which I am not aware, since I am not aware from the inside of any body but my own (though I am constantly aware of my own body from the inside). Given the law (m), the privacy, so-called, of the experience of the other person is precisely what one would expect: on Mill's account, there is no "problem" of other minds. Certainly, as in the case of material objects, there is nothing about Mill's views on concept formation and about how we causally investigate the world that make it impossible for him to accept that the entities which cause the behaviour of other persons are mental states, private to that person, analogous to our own.

The science of human being

Material objects and minds thus both find a secure place within the logic and methodology of science that Mill defended – a methodology that presupposes, as we have seen, his empiricist ontology and his critique of Platonic ideal forms and objective necessary connections. What he aimed to defend was not just a methodology, however, but more strongly a science of human being in the same sense in which there is a science of stones or of chemical compounds. Such a science would not only be of theoretical interest, but also of interest to the social reformer (one who wished for, and worked for, the "improvement of mankind") who wished to find the means appropriate to his or her ends – which, if Mill was correct, would be the utilitarian end of the general happiness. (For discussion of Mill's defence of the utilitarian principle as the correct moral standard, see the following article on Mill's moral theory by P. Kitcher in this volume.)

The psychological theory of associationism was part of this science of human being – but only a part. It dealt with human beings as learners with little, indeed almost no reference to their interaction with others. What was needed was not just psychology but a *social science*, a science of human being in social contexts. Here Mill was concerned to locate those methods which are appropriate to such a social science.

The reformers such as James Mill had appealed to the political economy of David Ricardo. This economic theory began with the assumption that people were motivated by material self-interest and by this interest alone. From this and certain other assumptions various theorems were deduced. These axioms and theorems were taken to be laws of nature, in the scientific sense of 'law'. Among other theorems were some which dealt with rents. The reformers argued that, given these "laws," certain practices with respect to, for example, rent-taking were contrary to furthering the general happiness, and that reform was therefore needed. The rent-takers to which this pointed were the landed aristocracy and lesser members of the squirearchy – who were disinclined to think that such things needed to be changed.

One way to resist the argument was to suggest that Ricardo's science was methodologically inadequate. Whewell was among those who came thus to the defence of those with the landed interests – another aspect of his commitment to the established order and to Tory values. He urged, together with his Cambridge colleague Richard Jones, that one could not establish empirical truths for such social facts as rent-taking by trying to establish them as parts of a demonstrative science – which clearly economics was not. Ricardo began from false premises; he assumed, for example, that people are motivated solely by self-interest – when in fact there were other, more noble motives in human nature. And from such false premises one cannot establish warranted conclusions. What was needed was plain ordinary induction from observed facts. If one attended to different patterns of rent-taking in different cultures then it quickly became evident that the patterns described by Ricardo's purported demonstration were clearly false in general, and were therefore unsafe grounds for policy recommendations. Ricardo's error was to treat economics as if it were a deductive science. It could be that – any good science eventually becomes that, on Whewell's view, as the relevant Ideas come to the fore in consciousness – but as yet we have no clear Idea for the laws of people in groups. In the absence of such an Idea, the best that we can do is simple induction by enumeration. And this reveals that the conclusion of Ricardo's inferences regarding rent were simply not laws.

The younger Mill defended Ricardo by withdrawing from the idea that the patterns Ricardo was describing were universal. One had to distinguish, Mill argued, between distribution and production. The latter are inviolable patterns of natural law. But the patterns of distribution are dependent upon social custom. Moreover, although it is true that people have motives beyond self-interest, when it comes to economic matters the restrictive assumption of Ricardo is reasonable. And Mill also argued that, when taken as restricted to economic behavior and social custom in England, then Ricardo's assumptions held true, so therefore did his conclusions regarding rent to that extent also held, and so therefore the policy recommendations of the utilitarian reformers were justified.

Whewell and Jones were not the only ones to attack the social science that the utilitarians such as Rocardo and James Mill were attempting to develop.

T. B. Macaulay in an essay, "Mill on Government" (*Edinburgh Review*, 1829) raised objections to James Mill's "Essay on Government" (1820). The elder Mill argued for democratic reforms for government based on what he claimed were scientific considerations. His argument, like Ricardo's in economics, purported to be demonstrative from premises such as the assumption that the relevant human motive was self-interest with these premises taken to be in effect self-evident. With masterly prose Macaulay ridicules Mill's argument, suggesting that the premises, far from being self-evident, are clearly false, and the implications clearly absurd. Richard Jones had already noted the connection between the accumulation of capital and technological advance. The contribution to the general welfare depended on motivating such innovation by appropriate rewards. Macaulay argued that if, as Mill supposed, there are no motives other than self-interest, then any democratic government so founded would destroy innovation and saving since it would immediately expropriate all capital and capital gains from those who have profited by innovation or simply accumulated savings and then distribute that capital equally to all – thereby both destroying any motive to innovation or saving and ruining the economy. But there are motives other than self-interest, and these provide the ties that bind people into groups and serve to control the urgings of self-interest. Changes were certainly needed in society; the means, however, were not to be found in revolutionary democracy, but, as the Whigs argued, working slowly within the established constitutional framework. And if we are to find the truth about forms of government and the possibility of social change, then (as Whewell and Jones argued) we must use simple induction based on a thorough analysis of the facts of history.

The younger Mill, in his *Logic*, defended his father's argument. (He defended the economics of the reformers in his *Political Economy*.) Mill responded to Macaulay that the latter had to assume that the citizens of a democratic society would not be reasonable enough and responsible enough to recognize the role of innovation and the accumulation of capital in the process of economic production. Self-interest does not imply either stupidity or irresponsibility – though critics such as Coleridge and Whewell did suggest that the utilitarian assumptions deprived humans of all their higher faculties – but these critics were wrong, and so was Macaulay. There is no reason to suppose that the citizens of a democratic society would not recognize that the accumulation of capital and the rewarding of innovation contributed in essential ways to the general welfare. The younger Mill did allow, however, that his father was somewhat simplistic in his attempt to use the pure deductive method which was in fact not adequate to the social sciences. Macaulay was correct in so arguing, but the alternative he proposed – simple enumerative induction – was hardly any better: as Mill argued in the *Logic*, at the level of specific laws that method is seldom conducive to truth, and its use is therefore to be judged unsound.

Mill argued that the laws of social groups involved many variables and were therefore very complex. The experimental method of induction by elimination was therefore not viable when there were so many relevant variables. But one can take for granted that people in groups do not become different in kind from individuals considered in themselves. Here he disagreed most strongly with Coleridge. He praised Coleridge for making people aware of the role of custom and institutions in shaping the individual. The individualism of Bentham and his father was inadequate in this respect. But contrary to Coleridge, humans do not as it were become different in kind when they enter into social relations that define social and group behaviour. The behaviour of people united in social wholes can be studied by using the tools available to what Coleridge called the understanding; there was no need to invoke some higher faculty such as Coleridge's Reason to grasp the reasons for things. As Mill emphasized in the *Logic*,

> The laws of the phenomena of society are, and can be, nothing but the laws of the actions and passions of human beings united together in the social state. Men, however, in a state of society, are still men; their actions and passions are obedient to the laws of individual human nature. Men are not, when brought together, converted into another kind of substance .... (Mill, *System of Logic*, 1843: 879)

Coleridge's metaphysics proposed that social relations bring about social wholes where the individuals in them are different in kind and therefore obey laws that are irreducible to the laws that apply to those individuals taken in isolation. Knowledge of such wholes was not accessible to the mere understanding; it was known by Reason since those wholes are not be found in the world of sensible experience. Mill argued the empiricist claim that such qualities that cannot be understood as underivable from sense simply do not exist: we are not acquainted with them, that is, acquainted with them in our sensible awareness of the world: Coleridge's ontological claims about social wholes are to be rejected.

The method for a social science is this: one assumes the laws for human beings as individuals – essentially the laws of association, that is, the laws of a scientific psychology. One assumes as initial conditions that individuals are responding to events in the social context. They will respond to those conditions in ways that they have learned – which learning is explained by the laws of scientific psychology. One then adds these responses together to obtain the behaviour of the group or social whole. One then takes the pattern thus inferred and compares it to history as actually recorded. Either the pattern is confirmed, in which case one may tentatively assert it as a law – tentatively because one has not, as one has where the methods of elimination are used, eliminated the possibility that there are variables that one has not (yet) noticed; or the pattern one has inferred is falsified, in which case one looks for variables that have been omitted from one's calculations. This is what Mill calls the "inverse deductive method." It is not the simplistic use of history and simple enumeration that Macaulay proposed.

Mill is correct against Coleridge that the laws describing social wholes are not of the same sort as the laws of chemistry, dealing with properties that cannot be under-stood in terms of the properties of the parts, that is, the individuals that are part of the social whole. Social relations involve the coordination of the behaviour of two (or more) individuals. Consider a simple case, that of promising. There is the promisor on the one hand and the promisee on the other. The promisor has the intention of delivering what he or she has promised; in fact, there is present in the promisor the feeling that so acting is morally obligatory. As for the promisee, he or she has the moral expectation the what was promised will be done. Then there is the act which brings the relation into existence – in this case, the promisor saying to the promisee "I promise to do such and such." Coleridge correctly argues that in such a case *idem* and *alter* are modified differently than they would be had the relation not existed: if *idem* ceases to be a promisor with regard to *alter* as promisee, then *alter* will not have the property of being a promisee: the two become inseparable in that respect – together they constitute a whole in which their behaviour is coordinated and not a pair of individuals each of whom would be unchanged if the other ceased to exist. More schematically, if a stands in relation R to b, then a has the property of R-ing b while b has the property of being R-ed by a; if b ceased to exist then a would be changed, it would lose the property of R-ing b: if b ceased to exist then a would be different in its being. So, if a and b are in relation R to one another, then they are not separable individuals, they are not atoms where the being of one does not affect the being of the other. In the case of social relations such as promising, the relevant coordination of the one to the other is effected by moral and other feelings directed towards and from the other: the social bond is constituted by these feelings.

Coleridge argues that these feelings that constitute the bond cannot be reduced to what is true of the related individuals when they are not so related. Mill argues to the contrary. Again consider our example. The *saying* by *idem* that "I promise that so and so" *causes* these feelings, peculiarly characterized, in *idem* and *alter*. There is no reason to suppose that persons, starting out knowing nothing of promising, cannot *learn* to respond in these ways to that speech act. Such learning will be in accordance with the laws of association. Moreover, though the feelings have their own peculiar characters – they are feelings of moral approbation – there is no reason to suppose that such feelings cannot be generated by association out of simpler feelings quite unlike them in their characteristics – for, the processes of association are chemical in nature, not mechanical. The laws of people taken as individuals, that is, the laws of association can thus explain the coming to be of social bonds such as promising but also any other of the many – extremely many – social relations into which people can enter.

However, it is important to note that the effect of saying "I promise" is *not* a mere *conjunction* or simple *sum* of individual behaviours. It is true that if we have

a R b

then we have

a is R-ing b & b is R-ed by a,

but this is different from ordinary conjunctions such as

a is red & b is green,

where the being of a is independent of the being of b: in the case of the relation, one does have a conjunction but it is a conjunction of facts where the being of each fact implicates the being of the other. In the one case, the conjoined facts are logically independent and in that sense separable, but in the case of the relational fact the conjoined facts are inseparable: in that sense, the latter is not a *mere* conjunction.

Now, Mill argues that in physics, mechanics in particular, one can obtain the law for a complex system, say a four-body system, from the laws that apply in the simpler two-body systems into which it can conceptually be decomposed. The effect on an object of the other objects in the four-body system is the sum of the effects on the objects when taken to be in the two-body systems. The inference to the law for the complex system is therefore a straightforward deduction from the laws for the simpler systems. But Mill is wrong. The effects in the four-body system depend not only on the effects in the two-body system, but also on the relations of the objects in the four-body system: the effects will be different depending on whether, for example, the objects form a square or a rhombus. One needs a further premise concerning how to determine what the effects will be given the effects in the simpler systems. Such a premise will be an *empirical law*, relating the laws for complex systems to those of simpler systems; it will be a *law about laws*. Such a law has been called a *composition law*.

In mechanics the composition law is the law for the vector addition of forces. Mill fails to recognize the need for this rule as an additional matter-of-fact premise for the deduction of the laws for complex systems from the laws for simple systems. The term 'addition' in 'vector addition' undoubtedly is what misleads Mill. But vector addition is neither conjunction nor a sum in the arithmetical sense. So he fails to recognize that the connection of the laws in the simpler systems to the laws for more complex system is itself an empirical law. The inference to the laws for complex systems requires the composition law as a premise additional to the assumptions about the laws for the simpler systems, and to mistake that inference for a deduction from the laws for the simpler systems alone is, in effect, to ignore the fact that the relations that define the complex system are relevant variables: it is to suppose that so far as concerns the law for the complex system, the relation that define the system do not exist. (It is perhaps worth noting that Whewell, like Mill, failed to recognize that the rule for the vector addition of forces, that is, the composition law in mechanics, is an empirical law.)

Mill makes just this error in his characterization of what he calls the inverse deductive method. He supposes that effects of behaviour in groups is the *sum* of the effects of the behaviour when the persons are taken to be separate individuals, and the inference to the law for the complex system is a mere deduction from the laws about the individuals taken alone. As in mechanics, the laws for complex systems are *additive*. But in the social sciences, as in mechanics, Mill is in error: he fails to recognize that the inference to the laws for complex systems requires a composition law as an additional matter-of-fact premise.

And this is to deny in effect that the social relations that define the complex systems are relevant variables.

We have, then, some irony. On the one hand, Mill praises Coleridge for recognizing the importance of social relations, where his predecessors such as Bentham and his father had affirmed an atomism that denied their existence. On the other hand, in his own characterization of the methodology of the social sciences, Mill himself, when he ignores the need for a composition law, in effect denies the existence of those relations.

But Mill was surely correct in his criticism of Coleridge: the existence of social relations does not imply that empirical science breaks down and that one must resort to some mystical sort of intuition or Reason with a capital R. Indeed, not only are the laws for social systems empirical in exactly the way laws for stones or planets are empirical, but further there is no reason to suppose that there is no composition law relating the laws about complex systems to the laws about individuals. Mill is basically correct in his defence against Coleridge of methodological individualism in the social sciences.

References

Works by John Stuart Mill

Mill, J. S. (1828) "Whatley's Elements of Logic," in J. S. Mill (1963–), vol. 21, pp. 3–35.

—— (1838) "Bentham," in J. S. Mill (1963–), vol. 10, pp. 75–115.

—— (1840) "Coleridge," in J. S. Mill (1963–), vol. 10. pp. 117–63.

—— (1843) *System of Logic, Ratiocinative and Inductive*, in J. S. Mill (1963–), vol. 7–8.

—— (1848) *Principles of Political Economy*, in J. S. Mill, (1963–), vol. 2–3.

—— (1852) "Whewell on Moral Philosophy," in J. S. Mill (1963–), vol. 10, pp. 165–202.

—— (1859) "On Liberty," in J. S. Mill (1963–), vol. 18, pp. 213–310.

—— (1861) "Utilitarianism," in J. S. Mill (1963–), vol. 10, pp. 203–59.

—— (1865) *An Examination of Sir William Hamilton's Philosophy*, in J. S. Mill (1963–), vol. 9.

—— (1869a) "The Subjection of Women" in J. S. Mill (1963–), vol 21, pp. 259–341.

—— (1869b) Notes to James Mill (1829, 1869).

—— (1873) *Autobiography*, in J. S. Mill (1963–), vol. 1, pp. 1–290.

—— (1963ff) *Collected Works of John Stuart Mill*, ed. J. M. Robson (Toronto: University of Toronto Press).

Works by other authors

Coleridge, Samuel Taylor, (1815–17) *First Lay Sermon*; 2nd edn, in *On the Constitution of Church and State, and Lay Sermons*, London: Pickering, 1839.

—— (1817) *Biographia Literaria*, 2 vols, London: Fenner; repr., edited by J. Shawcross, 2 vols, Oxford: Oxford University Press, 1962.

—— (1825) *Aids to Reflection*, London: Taylor and Hessey; 2nd edn, London: Hurst, Chance, 1831.

Godwin, William (1793) *Enquiry concerning Political Justice*, 2 vols, London: G. G. J. & J. Johnson; repr., edited by F. E. L. Priestly, 3 vols, Toronto: University of Toronto Press, 1946.

Hare, John, and Augustus Hare (1827) *Guesses at Truth by Two Brothers*, London: Taylor; 2nd edn, London: Macmillan, 1st pr., 1838; repr. 1889.

Hartley, David (1748) *Observations on Man*, London: J. Johnson.

Macaulay, T. B. (1829) "Mill's *Essay on Government*, Utilitarian Logic and Politics," *Edinburgh Review* 59 (Mar 1829): 159–89; repr. *Macaulay's Miscellaneous Writings and Speeches*, New York: Longmans, Green & Co., 1889, pp. 205–55.

Mill, James (1819), "On Education," in *Supplement to the Encyclopedia Britannica*; repr., edited by J. Burston, *James Mill on Education*, Cambridge: Cambridge University Press, 1969.

—— (1820), "On Government," in *Supplement to the Encyclopedia Britannica*, repr., in James Mill, *Political Writings*, edited T. Ball, Cambridge: Cambridge University Press, 1992, pp. 1–42.

—— (1829, 1869), *Analysis of the Phaenomena of the Human Mind*, 1st edn 1869, London: Baldwin & Craddock; 2nd edn, edited by J. S. Mill, London: Longman, Green, Reader & Dyer; repr., New York: A. Kelly, 1967.

Priestly, Joseph (1775) *Hartley's Theory of the Human Mind, on the Principle of the Association of Ideas, with Essays Relating to the Subject of It*, London: Johnson.

Whatley, Richard (1826) *Elements of Logic*, London: Mawman; 2nd edn, London: Mawman, 1827.

Whewell, William (1835) "The Nature of the Truth of the Laws of Motion," *Transactions of the Cambridge Philosophical Society*, vol. 5, pt. II, pp. 149–72; repr. Whewell (1840), *Philosophy of the Inductive Sciences*, pp. 573–94.

—— (1837) *History of the Inductive Sciences*, 3 vols, London: John W. Parker.

—— (1840) *Philosophy of the Inductive Sciences*, 2 vols, London: John W. Parker; 2nd edn, London: John. W. Parker, 1847.

—— (1845) *Elements of Morality, including Polity*, London: John W. Parker.

—— (1852) *Lectures on the History of English Moral Philosophy*, London: John W. Parker; 2nd edn, London: J. W. Parker & Son, 1862.

Further reading

For further reading on this topic, see A. Bain, *John Stuart Mill: A Criticism, with Some Personal Reflections* (London: Longmans, 1882); M. St John Packe, *The Life of John Stuart Mill* (London: Secker and Warburg, 1954); Nicholas Capaldi, *John Stuart Mill: A Biography* (Cambridge: Cambridge University Press, 2004). *General evaluations*: J. M. Robson, *The Improvement of Mankind* (Toronto: University of Toronto Press, 1968); J. Skorupski, *John Stuart Mill* (London: Routledge, 1989). *Secondary literature*: B. Bosanquet, *Philosophical Theory of the State* (London: Macmillan, 1889); M. Brodbeck, "Methodological Individualisms: Definition and Reduction," in M. Brodbeck (ed.) *Readings in the Philosophy of the Social Sciences* (New York: Macmillan, 1968), pp. 280–303; W. L. Courtney, *The Metaphysics of John Stuart Mill* (London: Kegan Paul, 1879); W. Donner and Richard Fumerton, "Mill" (Chichester, West Sussex: Wiley-Blackwell, 2009); R. Jackson, *The Deductive Logic of John Stuart Mill* (Oxford: Oxford University Press, 1941); P. Kitcher, *The Nature of Mathematical Knowledge* (Oxford: Oxford University Press, 1983); O. A. Kubitz, *The Development of John Stuart Mill's System of Logic* (Urbana, IL: University of Illinois Press, 1932); Hugh Lehman, *Introduction to the Philosophy of Mathematics* (Totowa, NJ: Rowman & Littlefield, 1979); J. L. Mackie, "Mill's Methods of Induction," in P. Edwards (ed.), *The Encyclopedia of Philosophy*, 8 vols (New York: Macmillan, 1967), vol. 5, pp. 324–32; J. L. Mackie, *The Cement of the Universe* (Oxford: Oxford University Press, 1974); G. Scarre, *Logic and Reality in the Philosophy of John Stuart Mill* (Dordrecht, The Netherlands: Kluwer, 1989); J. Skorupski, "J. S. Mill: Logic and Metaphysics," in C. L. Ten (ed.) *The Nineteenth Century*, vol. 7 of *Routledge History of Philosophy* (London: Routledge, 1994), pp. 98–121; (ed.) *The Cambridge Companion to John Stuart Mill* (Cambridge: Cambridge University Press, 1998); Laura Snyder, *Reforming Philosophy: A Victorian Debate on Science and Society* (Chicago: University of Chicago Press, 2006); G. H. von Wright, *A Treatise on Induction and Probability* (London: Routledge & Kegan Paul, 1951); J. W. N. Watkins, "Methodological Individualism and Social Tendencies," in M. Brodbeck (ed.) *Readings in the Philosophy of the Social Sciences* (New York: Macmillan, 1968), pp. 254–68; John Watson, *Comte, Mill, and Spencer* (Glasgow: John Maclehose & Son, 1895); *Hedonistic Theories from Aristippus to Spencer* (Glasgow: John Maclehose & Son, 1896); F. Wilson, "The Logic of John Stuart Mill," in Dov Gabbay and John Woods (eds) *British Logic in the Nineteenth Century*, vol. 8 of *Handbook of Philosophical Logic* (Amsterdam: Elsevier, 2007), pp. 231–84; "Mill's Autobiography," in T. Mathien (ed.) *Autobiography in Philosophy: Philosophical Uses of Self-Representation* (London: Routledge, 2006); "John Stuart Mill and the Social Sciences," in Skorupski (ed.) *The Cambridge Companion to John Stuart Mill* (Cambridge: Cambridge University Press, 1998), pp. 203–54; "Mill and Comte on the Method of Introspection," *Journal of the History of Behavioral Science* 27 (1991): 107–29; 'Mill's Proof of Utility and the Composition of Causes', *Journal of Business Ethics* 2 (1983) 135–58; *Psychological Analysis and the Philosophy of John Stuart Mill* (Toronto: University of Toronto Press, 1990); "William Wordsworth and the Culture of Science," *Centennial Review* 33 (1989): 322–92; and "John Stuart Mill," in *The Stanford Encyclopedia of Philosophy* (2007 edn), edited by Edward N. Zalta, http://plato.stanford.edu/archives/win2003/entries/davidson/

21

MILL'S CONSEQUENTIALISM

Philip Kitcher

The tangles of Utilitarianism

Utilitarianism is one of the most popular, and perhaps the most prominent, of all secular approaches to ethics, and John Stuart Mill's *Utilitarianism* is typically viewed as the classic formulation of the position. Its canonical status is slightly odd. For Mill was not the originator of Utilitarianism: that honor must go to Jeremy Bentham, whose *Principles of Morals and Legislation* appeared decades before *Utilitarianism*. (Bentham's *Principles* was published in 1781; *Utilitarianism* originally came into print in three issues of *Fraser's Magazine* in 1861; the essays were collected into a single volume in 1863.) Nor did Mill offer the most elaborate and wide-ranging exposition and defense of Utilitarianism: that work was done by Henry Sidgwick, whose *Methods of Ethics* ran through seven editions, from 1874 to 1907. Sidgwick explored many fundamental questions about Utilitarianism, issues that had not been addressed by the writings of Bentham and Mill, and it is no overstatement to claim that his book is "the clearest and most accessible formulation of what we may call 'the classical utilitarian doctrine'" (John Rawls, in Sidgwick 1981: v). Given Bentham's concern with questions of social theory (many of which are entangled with features of late eighteenth-century Britain), it is hardly surprising that we do not go to the originator to learn about Utilitarianism. Yet Sidgwick's concentration on the philosophical questions might seem to favor his work as the canonical source. Why then do those concerned with Utilitarianism turn so immediately to Mill?

There is one obvious reason. Mill was *supposed* to be the apostle of Utilitarianism – that was part of the point of the peculiar (and monstrous) educational regime to which he was subjected. In fact, Mill was more of an apostate than Sidgwick, and, as I shall be trying to show, he broke with the framework of classical Utilitarianism far more radically than commentators usually recognize. Yet his book (or essay, or sequence of essays?) has two features that make it a good candidate for the canon. It is short (as Sidgwick's is not) and it is written in that clear, yet elegant, prose that makes Mill a joy to read.

Mill's refinement and defense of the earlier version of Utilitarianism, articulated by Jeremy Bentham and by James Mill (J. S. Mill's father and Bentham's close friend), is apparently transparent. The simplicity is, however, deceptive. In his efforts to respond to previous objections to Utilitarianism and to articulate the most plausible form of the theory, Mill produces statements that are apparently at variance with one another. *Utilitarianism* is powerful and suggestive, in large measure because it is often sensitive to the central problems that subsequent critics have raised for its official ideas, but that very sensitivity easily generates an impression that no consistent account has been given. Indeed, *Utilitarianism* has a third feature, shared by many canonical texts, a cluster of puzzling passages that provide ample room for reflection and interpretation. If we attend to these puzzles, we find, I believe, that Mill's version of ethics is rather different from the views we typically ascribe to him.

Very early in his presentation, Mill provides a concise formulation of the doctrine to be defended:

> The creed which accepts as the foundation of morals, Utility, or the Greatest Happiness Principle, holds that actions are right in proportion as they tend to promote happiness, wrong as they tend to produce the reverse of happiness. By happiness is intended pleasure, and the absence of pain; by unhappiness, pain, and the privation of pleasure. (Mill 1963–91: Vol. 10, 210)

Strictly speaking, the principle given here provides only the first stage in the theory Mill intends to expound, for it only gives a criterion for appraising the value of actions, leaving the assessment of agents and of traits of character to subsequent discussion. Yet there are already important sources of ambiguity and future difficulty. One that is relatively easy to amend stems from the fact that Mill fails explicitly to consider the range of options available to an agent: a better version of the Principle would state that an action is right if and only if it produces at least as much happiness as any alternative action available to the agent. In unlucky circumstances, even the best available action may lead to considerable unhappiness, while, for someone more fortunately situated, just about anything that could be done might produce abundances of bliss. Mill's standard, inherited from Bentham, is that rightness is always a matter of causing as much happiness as possible.

My suggested amendment of the Principle flattens out a crucial ambiguity, on which later passages in *Utilitarianism* appear to trade. Instead of talking directly about producing (or "promoting") happiness, Mill adverts to *tendencies* to yield happiness or unhappiness. His proposal can be read either as recognizing that an individual action may have multiple effects, some positive, others negative, and that the "tendency" of that individual act is to be measured by the sum of the happiness engendered across all these causal pathways, or as focusing instead on *types* of acts and thinking of their "tendency" as the average total happiness they produce, when a range of contexts is considered (West 2004: Ch. 4; Berger 1984). Imagine that someone endows an annual prize for the best new opera written by a composer under forty. In the spirit of the first version of the Principle, we would appraise the action by looking at the various ways in which this particular endowment affects human happiness: maybe there are positive effects in the fortunes of winners and enhanced opportunities for opera-lovers, perhaps negative effects in intensified rivalries among younger musicians and the distortion of budding careers. On the basis of the second version, we'd consider a far broader class of actions and their total consequences, looking perhaps at the general trend of instituting prizes for artistic achievement and the broad effects on human happiness. (So we could consider prizes offered to people under forty, prizes offered for composing operas, prizes offered to musicians, and so on.) We might then explore the consequences of a *rule* enjoining acts of this general type. Which perspective does Mill have in mind?

Utilitarianism can easily give the impression that Mill is undecided. Sometimes, particularly when he wants to commend the flexibility of Utilitarianism to allow for divergence from supposedly exceptionless moral principles, the emphasis is clearly on appraising particular actions. Thus, in replying to the objection that Utilitarianism promotes the Expedient at the expense of the Right, Mill explains that an individual breach of principle, telling a lie to avoid damaging consequences, say, has a number of different effects: it may contribute to happiness by saving human lives, but we must always set this against the damage done to the general institution of requiring people to tell the truth: "... in order that the exception may not extend itself beyond the need, and may have the least possible effect in weakening reliance on veracity, it ought to be recognised, and, if possible, its limits defined; and if the principle of utility is good for anything, it must be good for weighing these conflicting utilities against one another, and marking out the region within which one or the other preponderates" (Mill 1963–91: Vol. 10, 223; see also p. 259). The principle deployed in the imagined instance is plainly one that considers the varied effects of individual acts. Elsewhere, however, Mill seems to judge actions according to the *type* to which they belong. In considering cases in which the public interest is served by general abstinence from behavior that would be individually beneficial – as in famous examples about the use of common land – Mill recognizes that a few isolated people might enjoy additional private interest, without any diminution of the general good. Applying the principle in the form that concentrates on particular actions seems to commend free riding: instead of a situation in which all those involved receive the same large utility derived from the public good, we have an outcome in which the majority receives the same high level of happiness as before and the small minority of free riders does even better. Mill backs away from this conclusion:

> In the case of abstinences indeed – of things which people forebear to do, from moral considerations, though the consequences in the particular case might be beneficial – it would be unworthy of an intelligent agent not to be consciously aware that the action is of a class which, if practised generally, would be generally injurious, and that this is the ground of the obligation to abstain from it. (Mill 1963–91: Vol. 10, 220; see also Ch. 5)

Here, Mill specifically does *not* say that the individual action of a member of the minority has two different effects on overall happiness, a small boost for the agent and a large loss in terms of undermining a social practice. Instead he focuses on a type of act, abstention, and on the overall consequences of rules that either require acts of this type or else permit deviations from it. Sometimes, apparently, the *inflexibility* of rules is valuable.

A second tangled issue in *Utilitarianism* derives from Mill's principal amendment to Bentham. In the wake of his famous breakdown, poignantly described in the *Autobiography*, Mill came to believe that his own education had been misconceived, precisely because of its neglect of an important dimension of human value (Mill 1963–91: Vol. 1, 136–55; see also the paired essays "Bentham" and "Coleridge" in Mill 1963–91: Vol. 10). Bentham had insisted that pleasure and pain are to be measured with respect to two factors: intensity and duration. Even at this stage, there's a technical difficulty, since it's not evident how one is to collapse the two dimensions into a single measure of happiness. When exactly is a shorter, but more acute, pleasure preferable to a longer, less acute, one? Mill compounds this difficulty, it seems, by introducing a third dimension. Responding to the frequent objection that Bentham, like Epicurus before him, represented "human nature in a degrading light," Mill suggests, in direct opposition to Bentham's refusal to distinguish allegedly "higher" pleasures from "lower" ones, that "some *kinds* of pleasure are more desirable and more valuable than others" (Mill 1963–91: Vol. 10, 210, 211). Poetry, it turns out, is superior to pushpin or to other delights of the alehouse. We now appear to have more difficult issues to settle: how are we going to rate this higher pleasure of its particular intensity and its duration against another lower pleasure of somewhat greater intensity and somewhat longer duration?

A preliminary question concerns how to discriminate the higher from the lower pleasures in the first place. Mill offers a simple answer.

> Of two pleasures, if there be one to which all or almost all who have experience of both give a decided preference, irrespective of any feeling of moral obligation to prefer it, that is the more desirable pleasure. (Mill 1963–91: Vol. 10, 211)

There are already danger signals. Although Mill will often write as if these were topics on which complete consensus can be expected, he hedges here, and requires only the agreement of "almost all" (although the very next sentence ignores the qualification). Moreover, as we read further in *Utilitarianism*, we should begin to wonder whether the competent judges who decide on the grading of pleasures are exempt from suasion on other grounds than those of happiness, even when they have "no feeling of moral obligation." After reading chapter 3 of *Utilitarianism*, an unrepentant Benthamite might well suppose that the supposed hierarchy of pleasures is foisted upon the unsuspecting youth by the moral authorities who educate them.

In light of Mill's solution to the problem of distinguishing higher from lower pleasures, it might seem that he has a way to resolve the difficulties of constructing a single measure of utility from the three-dimensional approach to happiness. Given two pleasures, of particular intensities, durations, and qualities, the first will have higher utility than the second just in case competent judges who have experienced both prefer the first to the second. Yet to extend the proposal in this way only makes the requirement of complete consensus appear more problematic, for our experience of human variation teaches us that different individuals rank pleasures quite differently (as we might expect that the author of On Liberty would appreciate). Constructing a utility-scale in this fashion loses something important at which Mill is aiming, a measure of human happiness that is objective and applicable to all, in favor of an indefinitely large collection of orderings of subjective preferences. This is, of course, the approach adopted in contemporary uses of utilitarian ideas within economics and other social sciences, where the subjective turn, derived from the supposed non-comparability of individual utilities, has serious consequences for normative theorizing.

Unfortunately, Mill's efforts to explain his gradations of pleasures appear to undermine his own program. First, he acknowledges that earlier champions of utilitarianism have met the charge of recommending a swinish mode of existence, by arguing that the distinctively human pleasures have "circumstantial advantages" that lie in their "greater permanency, safety, uncostliness, &c." (Mill 1963–91: Vol. 10, 211). The concession threatens to concede the dispensability of the distinction Mill advocates, for if the circumstantial advantages give the right results in all instances, there's no need to go beyond Bentham's two-dimensional approach to value. Mill goes on to deny that the appeal to these indirect benefits of "higher" pleasures really identifies what makes them so particularly important, and, in doing so, he introduces an explanatory idea that deviates from his official position. Just before his famous comparison between "a pig satisfied" and "Socrates dissatisfied," he proposes that the extra significance for us of the higher pleasures lies in a feeling of distinctively human characteristics and aspirations: "... its most appropriate appellation is a sense of dignity, which all human beings possess in one form or other, and in some, though by no means in exact, proportion to their higher faculties, and which is so essential a part of the happiness of those in whom it is strong, that nothing which conflicts with it could be, otherwise than momentarily, an object of desire to them" (Mill 1963–91: Vol. 10, 212). Not only does this suggest that human beings might differ in their tendencies to give priority to a "sense of dignity," with the prospect that there might be important differences in the ways that pleasures were ranked, but we also have to wonder if the sense is introduced by prevalent modes of acculturation, so that what Mill is pointing to will turn out to be a sociocultural artifact, one that, from a genuinely hedonist perspective, might make us far less happy than we might have been. If happiness is our true concern, why don't we aim to develop techniques that can *suppress* this "sense of dignity," and avoid the dissatisfactions it brings in its train? Mill would quite reasonably insist that this option would be rejected, but the real question is whether he can argue that the grounds for dismissal are purely hedonistic. Most people probably would endorse his judgment that Socrates is better off than the contented pig, but it's not at all evident that the ground of the judgment is our appreciation of Socrates' superior state of overall *pleasure*. The connection between the sense of dignity and the development of faculties is telling, for it does seem more plausible that what contributes most to the judgment of Socratic superiority is the development of distinctively human capacities, rather than the greater hedonic tone of the philosopher's experiences.

Mill's own vivid example leads him quickly to further worrisome formulations. Socrates was, of course, unusual in his ability to disavow the pleasures Mill views as "lower" in favor of their "higher" counterparts. Others often do less well, and we find an all-too-common pattern in human lives: the "youthful enthusiasm for everything noble" gives way to indulgence in "lower" pleasures (Mill 1963–91: Vol. 10, 212–13). Mill responds with a straightforward explanation:

> Capacity for the nobler feelings is in most natures a very tender plant, easily killed, not only by hostile influences, but by mere want of sustenance; and in the majority of young persons it speedily dies away if the occupations to which their position in life has devoted them, and the society into which it has thrown them, are not favourable to keeping that higher capacity in exercise. (Mill 1963–91: Vol. 10, 213)

I suspect that Oscar Wilde had this magnificently high-minded Victorian pronouncement in mind, when he had Lady Bracknell declare "Ignorance is like a delicate exotic fruit: touch it and the bloom is gone."

The psychology implicit here is surely controversial, for we might suppose that genuine happiness requires variety, that an exclusive diet of "higher" pleasures might equally well dull human sensibilities, and that not every occasion on which someone prefers a "lower" pleasure to a "higher" reflects the agent's weakness. Perhaps Mill drew the wrong moral from the one-sidedness of his own education, and temporarily forgot the emphasis placed on cultivating difference in On Liberty. Moreover, if the desire for variety is sufficiently widespread, then the test of distinguishing "higher" from "lower" pleasures by appealing to the experts will be in trouble.

With the recognition of human diversity clearly in view, Mill's next paragraph develops more explicitly the hedge that he had originally introduced. When we're differentiating pleasures, he tells us, "… the judgment of those who are qualified by knowledge of both, or, if they differ, that of the majority among them, must be admitted as final" (Mill 1963–91: Vol. 10, 213). If, however, the pattern of decline from the noble aspirations of youth to hankering after grosser forms of indulgence is a common one, then, at any given time, most people are likely to be, from Mill's perspective, corrupted in their judgment, so that the verdict of the majority will probably be *wrong* rather than "final." Although Socrates received from the jury of Athenians a larger number of votes than he expected, he was, as Mill reminds us in his famous discussion of the "tyranny of the majority," still condemned (Mill 1963–91: Vol. 18, 219).

I've explored, rather briefly, two areas in which, with respect to crucial aspects of the position to be defended, the surface clarity of *Utilitarianism* dissolves under scrutiny. As commentators have made very clear, the same sorts of difficulties attend other parts of Mill's position – his explanation of the "sanction of morality," his notorious attempt to give a proof of the principle of utility "of the sort of which it is susceptible," and his treatment of issues regarding justice and legal interventions (see Chs III–V of *Utilitarianism*, Mill 1963–91: Vol. 10, 227–59; sensitive commentary is offered in West 2004; Berger 1984; and Skorupski 1994). Given the subtle shifts of Mill's discussions, it is very hard to see what *consistent* position *Utilitarianism* presents. Matters only become worse, when we set this classic work in the context of Mill's other writings.

Broader complexities and contradictions

The most famous objection to Utilitarianism focuses on its relentless indifference to anything except aggregate happiness. So long as an action generates the maximal amount of happiness that could have been produced in the circumstances, then the action counts as right (at least if we endorse that version of the principle that focuses on individual acts). Mill appears to be committed to the view that a future in which maximal happiness were achieved, even though some people were cast into lives of utter misery, would be better than one in which slightly less total happiness was gained with everyone living at the same high level (a level which, by simple arithmetic, must be somewhat less than that enjoyed by the most fortunate individuals in the first state of affairs). The fundamental difficulty is familiar from staples of contemporary philosophy: utility monsters (people who gain enormous amounts of happiness if they are given resources that might have been assigned to others), lifeboat cases (where forcibly taking the life of a single person would enable several others to survive), participation in executions (where someone has the opportunity to gain a reprieve for some victims by killing one, in a situation where all are likely to be innocent), and many more (for excellent presentations of these concerns, see Scheffler 1988). Late in *Utilitarianism*, Mill almost seems to invite the objection, when, in a note, he describes utilitarianism as proposing that "equal amount of happiness are equally desirable, whether felt by the same or by different persons" (Mill 1963–91: Vol. 10, 257–8 and 258n). The phrase is easily interpreted as expressing indifference to distributional concerns: two states of the world are equivalent if their total amounts of happiness are the same, even though two people, A and B are equally happy in the first, while in the second all B's happiness is assigned to A. Perhaps, however, Mill has something much weaker in mind, to wit that two worlds with exactly the same distribution of happiness (or value) are equivalent, whatever people get assigned different levels of happiness. A world in which your role and mine are reversed, with no change in the distribution of happiness, is neither better nor worse than the actual state of affairs.

It is profoundly strange that the author of Mill's other works should have endorsed the stronger conclusion usually attributed to him, that expresses indifference to the distribution of happiness. Consider first the most widely read of his other essays (at least among philosophers and political theorists) *On Liberty*. Early in *On Liberty*, Mill is careful to explain that he foregoes "any appeal to the notion of right independent of utility," maintaining that his arguments for his social principles are purely utilitarian (Mill 1963–91: Vol. 18, 15). Philosophers have wondered how one might develop a utilitarian argument for the principles of tolerance advocated in *On Liberty*, principles that advocate permitting people to "pursue their own good in their own way," provided that they do not harm others, and that defend the liberty of thought and discussion (Mill 1963–91: Vol. 18, 226, and Chs 1 and 2 *passim*; Lewis 2000). Even more perplexing, however, is the obvious fact that *On Liberty* is overwhelmingly concerned with the *good of each*, where this is plainly not to be subsumed in some grand sum that measures the happiness of a total state. This essay, published two years before *Utilitarianism*, and judged by Mill to be the work, besides his *System of Logic*, most likely to endure (Mill 1963–91: Vol. 1, 259), seems to have at its center just that sensitivity to issues of distribution that the apparently aggregative obsession of *Utilitarianism* lacks. How could an author who saw it as one of his most important works go on, a mere two years later, to defend a theory that ignores its main thrust?

The mystery only deepens if we turn from *On Liberty* to another of Mill's major writings, albeit one less studied by philosophical commentators. (Major exceptions to the trend of neglecting Mill's "non-philosophical" works are recent pioneering efforts to take Mill whole: Skorupski 1994, 2006; Donner 1991, 2006.) Two of the significant innovations of Mill's *Principles of Political Economy*, a work that was republished many times in different editions during Mill's lifetime, are his explicit commitment to addressing questions of economic distribution and his atypical reaction to what his predecessors and contemporaries feared as "the stationary state" (a state in which the economy neither grows nor declines). Instead of supposing, as Adam Smith for example had done, that political economy has no need to consider distributional questions, since, when the growth rate is high, the accumulation of wealth will automatically be transmitted to the working population – a mechanism Smith calls the "liberal reward of labor" (Smith 2000: 79–91; 2002: 216–18) – Mill entitles the second book of his treatise "Distribution," and begins with the thesis that the allocation of resources among individuals or groups is determined by social rules (Mill 1963–91: Vol. 2, 200). Mill proposes a reform, based on a normative evaluation of existing rules, at the heart of which is a reconceptualization of property. Allowing the differential successes of individuals to give rise to inequalities *within* generations, he suggests that intergenerational transfers should be used as devices for restoring effective equality with respect to the assets with which people begin their lives (Mill 1963–91: Vol. 2, 225–6). His defense of the suggestion rests on a clear vision of what is socially and individually valuable: "it must be apparent to every one, that the difference to the happiness of the possessor between a moderate independence and five times as much, is insignificant when weighed against the enjoyment that might be given, and the permanent benefits diffused, by some other disposal of the four-fifths" (Mill 1963–91: Vol. 2, 225). The existing practice of permitting the accumulation of dynastic wealth errs, he argues in two ways, most evidently by depriving a large segment of the population of any serious opportunity for being prepared to "find their own good" and to "pursue it in their own way" (adapting the later language of *On Liberty* to crystallize the points made in Mill's socio-economic analysis), but also in "over-enriching" the few, who thereby become equally deprived of the capacity to realize the most important goods (Mill 1963–91: Vol. 2, 226). The message is that the best parents can do for their children is to provide them with a thorough education that enables the young to find their *métier*, and enough initial resources to begin to pursue it, and that the best societies will foster equal access to education and "life preparation" so that citizens are in a state of fair equality of opportunity to pursue what they, individually and freely, regard as best for them (subject, of course, to the requirement that they don't thereby interfere with the projects of others).

The concern with distribution and redistribution, exemplified in the revised conception of rights to private property, is echoed in Mill's discussions of the "stationary state." Smithian orthodoxy supposed that cessation of economic growth would automatically lead to a situation in which the wages of workers were reduced to subsistence levels (this being the obverse of the "liberal reward of labor"), and that a central problem for affluent societies is thus to stave off the "stationary state" as long as possible, by expanding markets for example, so that they could avoid the situation attributed to China (conceived, without much detailed knowledge, as a stagnant society, bereft of innovation and with a large population of abysmally poor workers). Mill, however, thinks that, given an enlightened commitment to avoiding population growth, the "stationary state" would be "on the whole, a very considerable improvement on our present condition" (Mill 1963–91: Vol. 3, 754). He continues:

> I am not charmed with the ideal of life held out by those who think that the normal state of human beings is that of struggling to get on; that the trampling, crushing, elbowing, and treading on each other's heels, which form the existing type of social life, are the most desirable lot of human kind, or anything but the disagreeable symptoms of one of the phases of industrial progress. (Mill 1963–91: Vol. 3, 754; compare Vol. 21, 254)

Implicit here is a denial of any purely aggregative conception of what is valuable, for Mill is asserting that the value of a social arrangement should be understood, in part, by examining the relations among the citizens.

There is no way in which the author whose conception of political economy depended so thoroughly on the distribution of goods could have subscribed to the simple aggregative approach typically viewed as the main commitment of *Utilitarianism* – and also no way in which the conception of what is valuable in life, a conception that underlies the critique of existing socio-economic arrangements, could have adopted the hedonism, even the qualified hedonism, that commentators on *Utilitarianism* usually ascribe to Mill. These judgments are reinforced by study of other important works. In *Considerations on Representative Government*, he is interested in the functional design of governments, understood as constrained by the stage of development of the citizenry, to promote what is most valuable for the citizens. Valuable lives are taken to be those in which the "moral, intellectual and active powers" are developed, but, instead of taking the exercise of such powers to be some state of "higher" pleasure, he explicitly focuses on the development of a sense of sympathy with others, ultimately perhaps with the whole of humanity, and supposes that the primary purpose of government is "educative" in enabling people to overcome their myopia and selfishness (Mill 1963–91: Vol. 19, 390, 417, 442–4, 467–9). These emphases are quite different from the official hedonistic approach to utility adopted in *Utilitarianism*, although they do resonate with some of Mill's discussions there (Mill 1963–91: Vol. 10, 231–3).

Similarly, in his seminal essays "Bentham" and "Coleridge," Mill takes great pains to identify the complementary achievements of an oversimplified radicalism and a sensitive conservatism. In framing the diagnosis of the shortcomings of Bentham's Utilitarianism, Mill writes:

> That the morality of actions depends on the consequences which they tend to produce, is the doctrine of rational persons of all schools; that the good or evil of those consequences is measured solely by pleasure or pain, is all of the doctrine of the school of utility, which is peculiar to it. (Mill 1963–91: Vol. 10, 111)

Moreover, as a previous passage had suggested, the dangers of oversimplification threaten *any* attempt to provide a complete specification of what utility is: "We think utility, or happiness, much too complex and indefinite an end to be sought except through the medium of various secondary ends ..."; the significance of trying to articulate some "first principle" of utility lies in the need for resolution when "secondary principles conflict" (Mill 1963–91: Vol. 10, 110, 111). Viewed from this perspective, the entire project of the distinction between "higher" and "lower" pleasures begins to look different – rather than being an articulation of a decisive fundamental principle, the appeal to "expert judges" looks as though it is a pragmatic device for responding to the conflicts among "secondary" values. Mill's assessment of Coleridge connects the complexities of the identification of utility with the general terms in which he characterizes value in *On Liberty*, *Principles of Political Economy*, and *Considerations on Representative Government*. He declares that "the culture of the inward man" is "the problem of problems," contrasting Coleridge's recognition of this point with the oversimplifications of Bentham's approach to social issues (Mill 1963–91: Vol. 10, 140, 154). Effectively, Coleridge is taken to have understood the complexity of the individual human good, and to have described some of its principal elements, while Bentham is viewed as having focused on the need for a conception of the general good, in which individuals are treated equally; each lacks an insight that the other supplies, even though the combination of those insights is not yet sufficient for a fully developed theory.

When we place *Utilitarianism* in the context of Mill's other writings (and the embedding could be extended much further than I have done here), it becomes evident that a simple reading of the essay, one that interprets it as offering a complete and final specification of utility and a principle that enjoins maximizing aggregate utility, is seriously at odds with the nuanced ways in which Mill writes about particular social and ethical projects, and with the conception of ethical and political theorizing he deploys on other occasions. Commentators are inclined, perhaps, to suppose that an ethical theory ought to supply a sharp and definite principle, so that we should prefer the apparent specificity of *Utilitarianism* to the suggestive, but vague, remarks of other texts, as an interpretation of Mill's ethical views. Yet the perspective from the other writings is sufficiently precise to show that they are at odds with the various definite principles interpreters have extracted from *Utilitarianism* – the emphasis on distribution, for example, contradicts any reading of utility-maximizing as a purely aggregative affair – and, in any case, as we saw in the first section, each definite candidate is in tension with some passages in that essay. Instead of supposing that one of the candidates represents his preferred ethical views, and that the wide-ranging social discussions are just aberrations, we do better to explore Mill's ethics by taking clues from a spectrum of his writings, and, eventually, explaining the formulations of *Utilitarianism* as adaptations of a more complex, if vaguer, consequentialism to a specific project. I shall start by considering the structure of a consequentialist theory, and the options that it makes available.

Varieties of consequentialism

The central idea of consequentialism is that the rightness of actions depends on their consequences: a thought Mill takes to be the "doctrine of rational persons of all schools" (Mill 1963–91: Vol. 10, 111). In a discussion of Kant early in *Utilitarianism*, Mill suggests that attempts to avoid assessing actions in terms of consequences fail, and he interprets the test supplied by the Categorical Imperative as tacitly relying on exposing the bad consequences of universalized maxims (Mill 1963–91: Vol. 10, 207; Kantians would surely protest that this is a distorted reading of the *Groundwork of the Metaphysics of Morals*, but, in Mill's defense, it should be conceded that the "contradictions" Kant claims to derive are extraordinarily elusive). There is, however, a more fundamental and systematic objection to ethical systems that focus on obedience to prior rules in a way that ignores consequences, and, in his discussion of self-sacrifice, Mill comes close to formulating this objection. He tells us that someone who sacrifices himself typically does so for "the sake of something which he prizes more than his individual happiness," and that, if this is not the case, the alleged hero "is no more deserving of admiration than the ascetic mounted on his pillar" (Mill 1963–91: Vol. 10, 217). There is no ethical justification for following a rule unless one has grounds for viewing that rule as authoritative, and those grounds cannot come from labeling the source – either as a divine lawgiver or as its de-theologized counterpart "the moral law within" – but only from recognizing that the rule is well-adapted to producing good outcomes. As I read Mill's discussion of self-sacrifice, he takes deontological theories in ethics simply to be residues of divine-command approaches (themselves vulnerable to devastating objections delineated by philosophers from Plato to Kant), that have substituted a supposedly *a priori* rule for the absent deity. In claiming that the only legitimate grounding for ethical rules lies in their promotion of good consequences, Mill was, I suggest, completely correct: this is the "doctrine of rational persons of all schools."

There are alternative schools because there are very different ways of measuring the value of consequences. When someone acts, she changes the way the world would have been in the absence of the action, or would have been if she had done something different. At its most inclusive, consequentialism can compare the different total world-histories, the courses of the world that run from the beginning to the end, and can, in principle, focus on any or all of the features of those histories. That is not, of course, how consequentialist accounts are typically presented. Such accounts concentrate more narrowly on very special features of the world-histories – so, for Bentham and even for the amended version of Bentham that *Utilitarianism* appears to endorse, the relevant points of comparison are the subjective experiences of sentient beings, specifically their pleasures and pains, and, in practice, the states that occur in a small group of sentient beings who are relatively immediately affected by the action. (Bentham does not suppose that human beings are the only animals that count in evaluating consequences. In a famous passage [Bentham 1948: 310–11 and 311n], he claims that animal abilities to suffer have to be considered in ethical appraisals. Mill does not explicitly endorse this thesis, but in a review, published in 1852, he refers to this passage in Bentham and criticizes Whewell for suggesting that it is a *reductio* of Utilitarianism [Mill 1963–91: Vol. 10, 185–6].) In moving from the general idea of consequentialism to the particular Benthamite version, various important assumptions play a role: (1) The only aspects of the world that need to be considered in evaluating the consequences of an action are those that are subsequent to the action. (2) These pertinent aspects are properties of the lives of existing beings, all of whom belong to a particular class. (3) The existing beings in question are sentient beings. (4) The relevant facts about their lives can be assessed by considering the stream of their subjective experiences. (5) The subjective experiences can be conceived as momentary (or fleeting) states, to which value can be assigned. (6) The relevant states are experiences of pleasure and pain. (7) The value of a pleasure (or pain) is measured by its intensity. (8) The intensities are summed across the intervals through which they persist. (9) The value of an individual's life-course is calculated by summing the values of pleasures and subtracting the values of pains across all moments of the person's life (with, in Mill's case, an adjustment for the quality of the pleasures and pains). (10) The value of a world-history is calculated by aggregating the values of the lives of all the individuals from the point of the action on. (11) In practice, comparisons can typically be made by using small segments of the lives of a few people as proxies for the values of world-histories and viewing the actions to be compared as irrelevant to aspects of the world that lie beyond these segments. (12) Strictly speaking, an action is right if the value of the world-history it generates is at least as high as the values that would have resulted from any of the available alternatives (but using the proxy calculations identified in [11] will almost always provide an accurate test).

Each of these assumptions deserves scrutiny, for none of them is immediately self-evident. Initially, you might think that both (1) and (2) are extremely plausible. After all, an agent can do nothing to change the past, so why can't we simply concern ourselves with what happens after her action? The answer is that our task is to *evaluate* the consequences, and it shouldn't be taken for granted that the value of an event or state of affairs is always independent of the causal history that led up to it. It is open to consequentialists to hold that an effect has greater or lesser value in virtue of its relation to past actions: even if your spending time with the sick would promote greater happiness than expressing your gratitude to someone who has helped you, a consequentialist might adopt an approach to value that viewed the relation between your overt gratitude and the past aid as conferring sufficient value to outweigh the benefits you might provide by hospital visiting. Once this point is appreciated, it's easy to see that (2) is similarly vulnerable. Consequentialism isn't committed to the view that you can consider lives in isolation from one another: it's quite possible that relations among lives, and relations of living beings to other constituents of reality are sources of value. It's even possible that non-living things, and the relations among them, could be sources of value.

At this point, it should be evident that there's a very general reason for worrying about almost all the assumptions that generate utilitarianism from consequentialism. In effect, utilitarianism derives from consequentialism by a series of reductionist moves. We aim to compute the values of the worlds that would flow from our envisaged actions. We reduce the problem to one of summing the values of the lives of a class of individuals; we reduce it further by considering only sentient individuals, and further still by ignoring most of these and concentrating on those we suppose immediately affected by the actions under scrutiny; we reduce the problem of measuring the values to be assigned to the individual lives by decomposing those lives into a sequence of momentary states; now we assign values to those states by reducing the aspects we consider to the intensities (and maybe qualities) of pains and pleasures; having reduced the problem in this way, we can start summing, and arrive at the measure utilitarians commend. Any or all of the reductions could be questioned. For there's no reason to think that the value of a world will always consist in the sum of the value of the lives of the individuals we consider one by one, no reason to suppose that the value of an individual life can be generated by summing the values of momentary states (or even longer experiences that occur in people) taken in isolation from one another. Benthamite utilitarianism, even in the amended version apparently offered by Mill in *Utilitarianism*, is a systematically *reductionist* form of consequentialism. There are other, alternative, versions of reductionism that could be applied to the fundamental consequentialist idea, but the really interesting rival developments are those that introduce *holistic* considerations at one or more of the points where Bentham's assumptions come into play.

For the many passages, both within *Utilitarianism* and in his social, political and economic writings, in which Mill offers ideas that seem at odds with the official emendation of Bentham's view, share a more holistic way of conceiving value. Central to *On Liberty* is the thought of a human life as something that should be directed by the free choices of the person whose life it is, as something that is given a coherence by that individual conception of the good. However pleasurable a sequence of disjointed experiences (even a repetitive sequence of experiences) might be, it would fail against the standard *On Liberty* offers unless it had certain global properties. Similarly, in both *On Liberty* and *Considerations on Representative Government*, Mill conceives the valuable social state as one in which individuals, pursuing a wide diversity of projects for their lives, are nonetheless bound together in relations of dialogue, joint action, and mutual sympathy. Both the heterogeneity of the whole, and the interconnections among the individuals, are sources of value. In more concrete terms, *Principles of Political Economy* views an approximate equality of material resources as obtaining value in terms of its contribution to the possibilities of all members of society having fair chances to fashion and to pursue their life plans.

Mill's holism ought to be apparent in the most obvious modification *Utilitarianism* makes to the classical Benthamite position. Plainly his guiding example in insisting on differentiating "higher" from "lower" pleasures is poetry, about whose significance Mill thought that Bentham was profoundly wrong. This particular form of "higher" pleasure had played an important role in Mill's recovery from the "crisis" of his early twenties – Wordsworth, he tells us, was "exactly" what suited his condition (Mill 1963–91: Vol. 1, 151, 153). Reading Wordsworth was surely not a pleasurable experience like that of a good meal, or even a soother of pain, like an analgesic. Mill didn't look back on his education, and view his father as having withheld some crucially important pleasure or as having failed to supply the medicine his state of dejection required. Rather he saw the encounter with Wordsworth, like the later encounter with Harriet Taylor, as reshaping and redirecting his entire life. The Benthamite calculus of assigning values to passing experiences, based on intensity and duration, is inadequate to measuring the value of Wordsworth, not because these fleeting experiences come in various types, some "higher," others "lower," but because the Wordsworth encounter has resonances that continue in Mill's subsequent life, modifying the ways in which individual experiences cohere with one another. Treat Mill's life as a sequence of states with an assortment of pleasures and pains, and you just can't capture the significance of reading Wordsworth or conversing with Harriet Taylor. Their value lies in the difference they made to everything, not in the instantaneous quality of experience. Mill's own writings on their impact make it absolutely clear that he knew that.

In the house of consequentialism there are many mansions, and Mill doesn't belong in the Benthamite annex to which he has traditionally been assigned. This leaves us with two important questions: What is his version of consequentialism? Why does *Utilitarianism* appear to propound a modified form of Bentham's position? To answer these questions, we'll need to understand some facets of Mill's views that I have so far not emphasized.

Three Millian themes

Empiricism

Mill is famous (notorious?) for being the most radical of the great empiricists. In the *System of Logic*, he advances a view of mathematics as founded in experience, thereby avoiding the concessions made by Locke and Hume, both of whom had accommodated mathematics by treating it as *a priori* in virtue of being concerned solely with conceptual relations (Kitcher 1999). Hence it is unsurprising that *Utilitarianism* opens with an attack on the thesis that ethics has general first principles that are immediately knowable *a priori*. This is set within a conception of human knowledge that emphasizes the uncertainty of "first principles," which identifies them as "the last results of metaphysical analysis, practiced on the elementary notions with which the science is conversant" (Mill 1963–91: Vol. 10, 205). Someone who adopts that conception of human knowledge in general, and ethics in particular, should not expect to be able to "prove" his favorite fundamental ethical principle, and, as Mill explicitly warns his reader, the "proof" he offers in chapter 4 doesn't really count as "proof, in the ordinary acceptation of the term" (Mill 1963–91: Vol. 10, 110, 111). The commitment to empiricism cuts deeper than this, however.

Canvassing the alternative possibilities to appraising actions by their consequences convinces Mill that some form of consequentialism is correct, but that judgment is itself defeasible because it rests on the supposition that the catalog of rivals considered exhausts the possibilities. Just as in the natural sciences, a change of perspective might reveal that there are alternatives that the arguments so far provided fail to eliminate. But, as we have seen, there is a significant gap between the basic idea of consequentialism and the principle that emerges from Bentham's sequence of reductionist assumptions. By his own empiricist principles, therefore, Mill should not suppose that whatever tentative credibility accrues to consequentialism is transmitted either to Bentham's version of the Greatest Happiness Principle or to his own.

Nor does he. In evaluating Bentham's life work, Mill sets up the status of the first principles of ethics in a fashion entirely concordant with his empiricist approach to knowledge. He describes "utility, or happiness" as "too complex and indefinite an end to be sought except through the medium of various secondary ends," and proposes that the fundamental principle of ethics comes into play only when these secondary ends conflict (Mill 1963–91: Vol. 10, 110, 111). It would be quite contrary to Mill's empiricism to conclude that the appeal to that principle can be anything other than a fallible attempt to shed light on a difficult conflict, and, in view of his reference to the complexity and indefiniteness of the notion of utility, he could hardly suppose that any more specific version of the consequentialist view could amount to more than a tool to be currently employed in our tentative efforts to resolve tensions in our ideas about what is valuable.

Bentham's own development of the consequentialist idea took him out of "the right path," and Mill emphasizes the difficulties of not going astray: "... to go far in it without wandering, there was needed a greater knowledge of the formation of character, and of the consequences of actions upon the agent's own frame of mind, than Bentham possessed" (Mill 1963–91: Vol. 10, 111, 112). Any temptation to read this judgment as a boast to have been able to succeed where Bentham failed should be curbed by Mill's commitment to empiricism. He is not suggesting that he, a shrewder judge of important nuances in human life, can succeed where Bentham failed, but that he can nudge consequentialism in a progressive direction by correcting an error in Bentham's version of the position. As I interpret him, Mill believes that ethics, like a natural science, is unfinished, that we are not yet ready to articulate anything more than a tentative first principle, and that the consequentialist tradition is best viewed as a method for improving our ethical practices.

This means that a confident specification of human happiness – *any* such specification, and not just Bentham's inadequate one – is premature. Rationalist philosophy might dream of a finished system of ethical precepts, founded in a completely articulated first principle ready for application; but empiricists see the project as one in which generalizations are built up slowly, and are always vulnerable to revision, so that, although we can glimpse the form of the most basic principle (through seeing it as the only available alternative – though even that is defeasible), our attempts to give it content are preliminary efforts that will, we hope, lead to progress.

By Mill's own empiricist lights, it would have been a bad idea for his contemporary chemists to offer a "metaphysical analysis," give final definitions of 'acid', 'element', and 'molecule', and thus announce the "first principles" of their science. The closing lines of the *System of Logic* make it apparent that he regards the project of developing "the moral and social departments of science" as even more difficult than that of advancing the major natural sciences, and hopes that errors can be eradicated and a significant "intellectual achievement … forwarded" (Mill 1963–91: Vol. 8, 952). We'll see shortly that these same pages offer an important disanalogy between the project of developing ethics and the ventures of the natural sciences, one that is to the disadvantage of the former.

Egalitarianism

As already noted, Mill's principal innovations in political economy lie in claiming that the accounts of economic growth offered by his predecessors, principally Smith and Ricardo, need to be supplemented by a positive theory of distribution, designed to transfer wealth from the affluent to the poor. From the first edition of *Principles of Political Economy* to the "Chapters on Socialism" (edited posthumously by his stepdaughter, Helen Taylor), Mill confronts the free-market capitalism of the most wealthy nations with the theories and experiments of a variety of egalitarian reformers (his principal representatives of socialism being French thinkers like Fourier and Saint-Simon, not the then relatively obscure figure who has come to stand for us as the chief voice of nineteenth-century socialism). The problem is defined in *Principles of Political Economy*, where Mill notes that free-market capitalism seems to assign monetary rewards in inverse proportion to the labor actually done, and concedes that, if a choice had to be made between "the present state of society with all its sufferings and injustices" and "Communism," then "all the difficulties, great or small, of Communism would be but as dust in the balance." He continues:

> But to make the comparison applicable, we must compare Communism at its best, with the régime of individual property, not as it is, but as it might be made. The principle of private property has never yet had a fair trial in any country; and less so, perhaps, in this country than in some others. (Mill 1963–91: Vol. 2, 207)

His immediate diagnosis of the ills of British capitalism is that it is not only founded in allocations of property by "conquest and violence," and by making "property of things that never ought to be property," but that it has "purposely fostered inequalities, and prevented all from starting fair in the race" (Mill 1963–91: Vol. 2, 207). Here we have the heart of the egalitarian ideal that guides Mill throughout his career. The task is to provide for each person, at the start of his or her life, the resources to thrive physically and intellectually, so that he or she may decide among a range of worthwhile options for life, and, where there is competition for pursuing some of these options, may have a fair chance of succeeding. Talent, and talent alone, is to decide this competition. (This is evident in his discussion of opportunities for women, in *On the Subjection of Women*.)

Mill suggests a variety of means for realizing this goal: a reconceptualization of property that debars intergenerational transfers of large amounts of wealth, a rich system of public goods to care for, and develop, the faculties, both physical and mental, of citizens, and, perhaps most emphatically, heavy investment in education (see, for example, Mill 1963–91: Vol. 4, 376, 382; Vol. 3, 783 ff.; Vol. 5, 743). He situates his position between the *laissez-faire* capitalism, of which Smith and Ricardo are the chief theorists, and socialism, by offering a very specific egalitarian ideal. While it would be mistaken to insist on exact equality of economic resources at all times, or even to apportion those resources strictly according to need, Mill holds that inequalities in the conditions of young people, that affect their ability to prepare themselves for a freely chosen plan of life they take to be worthwhile and to have equal chances of pursuing that plan successfully, must be eradicated.

This ideal dovetails with the central themes of *On Liberty* in important ways. The project of *On Liberty* is to remove those *social* and *legal* forces that prevent individuals from deciding freely for themselves what matters in life, and having the opportunity to pursue their chosen goals (subject, of course, to the proviso that their choices and pursuits don't infringe on the similar choices and pursuits of others). The egalitarianism that pervades Mill's socio-economic writings is born from the recognition that, without the dismantling of *economic* barriers, the thought of promoting the good life for all would be idle. His egalitarianism could be characterized as demanding equal opportunity for the good life, where that is interpreted as resting on a rich period of education and preparation for making a free decision about what one's own version of the good life should be.

In this light, it's relatively easy to understand why Mill rejects the more apparently straightforward egalitarianism of requiring equal distribution of material resources. He thinks that is irrelevant to what really matters (namely the development of the individual), and that it introduces difficult problems of management (Mill 1963–91: Vol. 5, 743ff.). Moreover, Mill agrees with a psychological assumption emphasized by Smith and Ricardo, to wit that economic health depends upon incentives for working hard (Mill 1963–91: Vol. 3, 794–6, 941–2; Vol. 5, 742). Considerations of economic efficiency are subordinated to those connected with the pursuit of the good life, but they play a role which becomes comprehensible in light of the next (and last) theme.

Progressivism

When Mill announces that the argument of *On Liberty* will make no appeal to the notion of abstract right, except insofar as it is grounded in the concept of utility, he adds a telling phrase – utility must, however, be understood "in the largest sense, grounded on the permanent interests of man as a progressive being" (Mill 1963–91: Vol. 18, 224). Although the phrase is vague, it's already evident that some work must be done if this conception of utility is to be made congruent with the "official" notion, defined in terms of pleasure and the absence of pain and presented in *Utilitarianism*. In fact, Mill's formulation in *On Liberty* captures both his holistic approach to the value of lives, and also adds a distinctive thought – that the possibilities for a worthwhile human life are different at different stages of history, and that the opening up of new possibilities counts as an extremely important kind of progress.

Mill's vision that history unfolds ever richer possibilities for human existence receives a vivid presentation in the penultimate paragraph of the *System of Logic*.

> The character itself should be, to the individual, a paramount end, simply because the existence of this ideal nobleness of character, or of a near approach to it, in any abundance, would go further than all things else towards making human life happy; both in the comparatively humble sense of pleasure and freedom from pain, and in the higher meaning, of rendering life, not what it now is almost universally, puerile and insignificant – but such as human beings with highly developed faculties can care to have. (Mill 1963–91: Vol. 8, 952)

The language here is far closer to that of Aristotle's *Nicomachean Ethics* than to the idiom of Benthamite Utilitarianism: happiness (in the less humble sense) is a property of ways of human living. Mill adds the thought that the available ways are limited by socio-historical conditions. The "universal puerility" of nineteenth-century lives results from the obvious fact that, as in Aristotle's Athens, most people have to struggle to stay alive, and they must perform monotonous and dreary tasks to do so. History can liberate human beings from this predicament, and, in light of *On Liberty*, *Considerations on Representative Government*, and his socio-economic writings, we can understand some of the ways in which it does so. First, we can emancipate ourselves from the thought that there is one right way, or a few right ways, to live, and cultivate "experiments of living" (Mill 1963–91: Vol. 18, 261). Second, economic arrangements can provide the material basis, on which the needed public goods and system of redistributing resources would enable fair equality of opportunity for a worthwhile life, within a society or (ultimately) for the entire species. Systems of cooperative work can lead both to a more equal division of goods and to involvement with the tasks that are required to maintain this basis, and that interaction and cooperation are introduced in the ideal of democracy that Mill takes to develop our sympathies and faculties (Mill 1963–91: Vol. 19, 411–12). Mill's egalitarianism leads him beyond the Greek question of the good life as an issue for a small class of privileged males: he supposes that that question can be taken up again in societies that have achieved a particular level of wealth and political stability, and that it can be viewed as a serious question for *all* members of those societies. Moreover, as opportunities for the good life are more widely extended, and as further "experiments of living" are encouraged, the way will be opened for further developments of human faculties and ideals of humanity, than are so far inconceivable. The "permanent interests of man as a progressive being" cover both the prospect of participating in those forms of the good life that have been made available at a particular historical stage and contributing to the project of bringing forth yet higher forms of human existence.

In the Preface to the *Principles of Political Economy*, Mill offers an account of the socio-economic history of the world, which discerns, as in the writings of some of his predecessors, most evidently Adam Smith, a series of stages. The replacement of one economic arrangement by another is seen as opening up new possibilities for human life, possibilities that are not always exploited. The theme is developed more fully in the discussion of the stationary state, where Mill envisages "much room for improving the Art of Living, and much more likelihood of its being improved, when minds [cease] to be engrossed by the art of getting on" (Mill 1963–91: Vol. 3, 756). Technology, he suggests, might have liberated human beings from drudgery, but the effects have so far been insignificant in comparison with what is possible: "mechanical inventions," he tells us, "have not yet begun to effect those great changes in human destiny, which it is in their nature and in their futurity to accomplish" (Mill 1963–91: Vol. 3, 756, 757). Mill's project of reforming capitalism is driven both by the wish to liberate people from competition for the unimportant goods that *laissez-faire* systems see as the principal ends, and to ensure that economic efficiency is retained to the extent it is needed to preserve the material basis on which "improved Arts of Living" can proceed, to guard against return to the enslavement of meaningless toil.

The thought of a series of socio-economic stages, through which the species can progress, is, however, linked to an aspect of Mill's thought that has inspired much recent scorn and condemnation. In several of his writings, most notably in the *Considerations on Representative Government*, he suggests that societies in different parts of the world pass through the sequence at different rates, and that it may be necessary for the more "advanced" nations to guide those that are more "backward," if the latter are to ascend to the next level (Mill 1963–91: Vol. 18, 272–3; Vol. 19, 393–4, 396–7, 408–9, 569–77). There are two different grounds for concern about this picture: on the one hand, Mill might be criticized for thinking of distant cultures (about which he displays little detailed knowledge) as inferior with respect to the "Art of Living" to the European nations, and as in need of political shepherding into capitalism and democracy; on the other hand, one might reject the whole picture, with its claims about progress towards higher forms of human existence. With respect to the former issue, the criticism seems entirely justified. It is a sad irony that the eloquent defender of variety in modes of life should have failed to appreciate the possibility that the societies he assigned to be led by allegedly benign colonizers might be pursuing "experiments of living" from which the supposed "educators" could learn, and that he viewed the colonies as analogs of children, in their "nonage." On the second score, however, Mill can be vindicated. His ideal of progressive human development is not tied to any belief in the intrinsic superiority of some nations, but in the much more compelling thought that the ability to be uncoerced in choosing from a wide range of life possibilities is an important ideal of human freedom.

Mill's commitment to human progress pervades his writings, and surfaces in *Utilitarianism* in ways that subvert the "official" approach to utility. In response to the objection that a "life of rapture" is impossible, Mill concedes the point, and explicitly considers happiness, not in terms of individual experiences, but in the shape of a whole life (Mill 1963–91: Vol. 10, 215–17). In this discussion, he reiterates the thought that humanity has progressed to a stage at which a genuinely worthwhile life is possible for the many: "The present wretched education, and wretched social arrangements, are the only real hindrance to its being attainable by almost all" (Mill 1963–91: Vol. 10, 217). As at the end of the *System of Logic*, Mill holds out the prospect of a "long succession of generations" that will generate a wider ability for people to pursue an increasingly diverse and refined set of options for their lives (Mill 1963–91: Vol. 10, 217, 231–2).

Given Mill's progressivist picture of utility, it's now possible to see why his empiricism should lead him to avoid premature efforts at precise definition. The ethical theorist, like the chemist, has incomplete evidence, so that any attempt to offer articulate foundations for theory would be fallible. Yet the predicament of ethical theorizing is worse, in that the phenomena to be understood under the rubric of utility are not fixed and constant. Rather there are types of valuable human life that we can, almost certainly, not yet conceive. With luck, those "higher" forms of the "Art of Living" will be brought into being by our efforts to improve our own situation, but, as Mill says, again and again, our progress so far has been limited and our conceptions are likely to be "puerile and insignificant." Any attempt to state a fundamental principle – or, better, to craft a tool for working through present conflicts in "secondary" values – should be acknowledged as tentative and provisional.

Mill's consequentialism

Is it then possible to identify a form of consequentialism that would accord better with all Mill's considerations and concerns than the modified version of Bentham that *Utilitarianism* seems to commend? In closing, I'll try to show how we can start to identify something more specific than a general commitment to consequentialism with an indefinite conception of the value to be maximized. I'll also explain briefly how my understanding of Mill's consequentialism resolves the exegetical problems raised earlier, and how it can explain the project undertaken in *Utilitarianism*.

An important clue to understanding Mill's consequentialism comes from his struggles with a problem that occupied his contemporaries, the Malthusian problem of overpopulation. Fear of the stationary state often resulted from the thought that, without economic growth, an ever-expanding human population would have to subsist on the same total of resources, with the result that average material well-being would inevitably decline. Political economy was driven by a search for methods of postponing the dreaded state as long as possible, typically on the grounds that the Malthusian solution of "restraint in propagation" would be impossible. Mill, by contrast, embraces the stationary state, commits himself to a program for limiting the size of the population, and objects to *regulated* control, not on the grounds that this is impractical but rather because it would require an illegitimate intrusion into people's lives (Mill 1963–91: Vol. 3, 752–7; Vol. 4, 365–89). The solution lies in education, and in the provision of social conditions that will provide for all the opportunity for valuable lives, since Mill believes, perhaps optimistically, perhaps plausibly, that the citizens of his envisaged society will recognize the advantages of their situation and the dangers that population growth would bring.

This apparently particular issue illuminates Mill's consequentialism in general because, in conjunction with the other elements I've discerned in his thought, it enables us to understand how he envisages the recent past of the progression of human life, and how the next stages are supposed to go.

Most of human history consists of a simple struggle for survival by all, or almost all, the people alive at any one time. In its early periods, there are only occasional opportunities for a few individuals to pursue lives that are genuinely worthwhile, and the options available even to them are limited. With economic development, together with increased social, political, and philosophical understanding, comes the chance for all members of certain societies to be prepared for the free choice of a plan of life, and to have genuine chances of carrying out their projects. At this point in history, it becomes possible for those societies to make the transition to a situation of higher value, where their citizens lead lives that are not "puerile and insignificant – but such as human beings with highly developed faculties can care to have" (Mill 1963–91: Vol. 8, 952). From that period on, further progress is made, as what has been achieved by these first societies spreads to the whole of humanity, as further possibilities for human living are included in the catalog of options, and, perhaps, new ideals come into our purview.

The significance of this picture for Mill's general account of value resides in the fact that utility must be at least two-dimensional. One dimension is Benthamite, based on the aggregation of pleasures and subtracting the total of pains; the second dimension embodies those more holistic concerns to which Mill adverts in his nuanced discussions of the value of human lives. Along this dimension, lives are assessed for their significance, and they either pass the test or fail it. Unlike the Benthamite dimension, whose formal structure is that of the real line, the higher dimension is discrete: when the issue of genuinely significant lives comes into play, the value of each life can be represented by a pair of numbers $<x, y>$, where y is 1 if the life goes well and -1 if it goes badly, and x is a real number generated from the balance of pleasures and pains. History divides into phases at which different quantities are to be maximized. When the conditions for significant lives are simply unattainable, Benthamite calculations are basically correct, and the aim is to make lives go well, as judged by the balance of pleasures and pains – although in computing the total value of a state of affairs, Mill's egalitarianism might inspire him to maximize something other than the simple sum, Σx. When the conditions for significant lives are attainable for all members of a society, but not yet attained, then there will be a *secondary* imperative to institute those conditions, resulting from the thought that the second dimension is genuinely higher and that the aim is now to maximize the number of significant lives, Σy. Once those conditions are in place, Mill's consequentialism rests on the maximization of this sum (until further, even higher, dimensions of value come into play) and the Benthamite aggregate, Σx, is no longer relevant. In the transitional stage, however, the secondary imperative to bring about the conditions for significant lives has to be weighed against the sacrifices (in terms of pains and the forfeiture of pleasures) by people who, *ex hypothesi*, do not yet have the opportunity to live the sorts of lives Mill takes to be distinctively valuable.

An account of value of this sort is a prerequisite for exposing the solution to the problem of the stationary state. Mill's discussion supposes that population must be limited to that number of people for whom the material resources of the world could provide opportunities for lives of genuine significance. In effect, he deploys an analog of the ecologist's notion of the carrying capacity of an environment (the size of a population that the environment could support), supposing that the institutions for promoting significant human lives, and the individual lives they make possible, have material requirements, which could not all be met if the human population were to grow too large. Characteristically, he doesn't think of these material requirements as simply generated by the basic human requirements of food and shelter, but also by the needs of the "higher" forms of human life. Thus, for example, in reflecting on the limits imposed by the surface of our planet, he writes:

> A population may be too crowded, though all be amply supplied with food and raiment. It is not good for man to be kept perforce at all times in the presence of his species. A world from which solitude is extirpated, is a very poor ideal. Solitude, in the sense of being often alone, is essential to any depth of meditation or of character; and solitude in the presence of natural beauty and grandeur, is the cradle of thoughts and aspirations which are not only good for the individual, but which society could ill do without. (Mill 1963–91: Vol. 3, 756)

Out of this idea of a limited population of significant lives, required by Mill's egalitarianism to be available to all, comes his concern for the maintenance of the material basis on which the opportunities rest – and from that the defense of a humane form of capitalism that will avoid the erosion he fears from more radically egalitarian proposals.

In contemporary discussions of utilitarianism, the difficulty of simple aggregation of value has emerged as a serious difficulty, precisely because of the issue that worried Mill and his contemporaries – the expansion of the population with a decline in the average quality of each life (Parfit 1984: Pt 4). Suppose any account of human value you please, so long as it has the formal structure of the real numbers. Then, because of a simple property of the real numbers – the Archimedean property that, for any two positive real numbers, a, b, there is a natural number n such that $na > b$ – for any population of people whose lives have some particular high value, there will be a larger population of people with a lower value for which the aggregate value is greater than that of the first population. Any consequentialist proposal that identifies the value of a state to be the sum of the values of individual lives will thus lead to a "Repugnant

Conclusion" (Parfit 1984). The natural reaction is to suppose that consequentialism must find some other way of computing the value of a state from the values of the lives lived in that state, but, given plausible assumptions, this is probably impossible, so long as the Archimedean assumption is retained (Kitcher 2000). Mill's approach to value, however, solves the problem in a very natural way, by denying that you can indefinitely increase the value of a world by multiplying the number of people who live in it. He sets a limit to the value we can achieve, since there is a maximum number of people who can live significant lives, given the basic resources of our planet, and the best state of affairs is where all those lives succeed.

The first section offered two exegetical puzzles about *Utilitarianism* that we can now begin to resolve. First, does the first principle of Utilitarianism consider the consequences of individual actions or the consequences of rules about types of actions? Strictly speaking, given Mill's empiricism and his progressivism, no sharp "first principle" can be expected at our historical stage. We should think of consequentialist thinking as a tool, given content for us by the incomplete account of value just outlined. When that tool is applied to the problems that arise at certain historical stages, as when the lives of individuals are threatened unless someone lies, the proper focus is on individual acts. With respect to other stages, and other kinds of problems, the emphasis is properly on rules, for the goal that is of concern is that of creating, or maintaining, institutions that allow for the higher dimension of value. In the transitional stage, for example, when the possibility of significant lives for all members of a society arises, public rules for various kinds of abstinences are critical. Moreover, once the transition has been accomplished, the structure of the problem is changed: individuals who are leading significant lives no longer have anything to gain from the supposed "extra benefits" of not abstaining (for them, the lower dimension of value has become irrelevant); if there are people for whom the success or failure of their lives would turn on breaking the rule and acquiring the small material advantages, then the situation would be exactly analogous to the example of lying – but it is reasonable to believe that such situations would be extremely rare.

Second, the distinction between "higher" and "lower" pleasures should be viewed as an inadequate way of expressing Mill's progressivism and his two-dimensional approach to value. The disastrous idea of deferring to judges to estimate the quality of pleasures, of worrying whether the judges will agree and whether they become jaded and corrupted as they age, is an artifact of his attempt to present an important distinction as a correction to Benthamite Utilitarianism. The distinction properly belongs within the framework of Mill's progressivism, as resting on the importance of coherence in people's lives and of their free choice of a life plan, something that is far more aptly illustrated by the example of Socrates and the pig than the implausible suggestion that this contrast is all about different sorts of pleasure, and something he could reasonably expect his readers to conclude on the basis of the arguments of *On Liberty*. Once the distinction has been drawn in this way, the élite judges vanish from the picture, and the emphasis is on individual people, properly prepared for choice from a wide range of possibilities, expressing their own reflective preferences.

Why, then, if I am correct, does Mill so mislead us by assimilating his position closely to Bentham's and thus encouraging the simple and straightforward reading with which we began? The right answer begins with a counter question: What is the function of Mill's essay? Philosophers typically treat it as a stand-alone treatise, one in which Mill gave a systematic account of his ethical position. Yet we can read it differently, as an attempt to defend the deployment of an unfinished tool that Mill was using throughout his entire corpus of writings to address large issues in social and political theory. During the early nineteenth century, objections to Bentham's Utilitarianism had accumulated, and the obvious structure of Mill's essay is to take these objections, one by one, and to respond to them. For that, rather than try to articulate a many-sided and subtle version of consequentialism that he had never synthesized from his writings (and that he might reasonably believe, given his empiricist commitments, it would be premature to synthesize), he defended the position that had actually been attacked, rebutting what he took to be misguided criticisms. To do that successfully, he believed that Bentham's blindness to particular valuable features of human lives had to be corrected, and he tried to introduce the corrections without making large and difficult changes in the Benthamite formulations. That strategy is responsible for the distortion of some of his most seminal ideas, and for the tensions that arise within *Utilitarianism*, but it is also worth noting that the strategy does enable Mill to express very clearly what he takes to be incorrect in some of the most important criticisms leveled against consequentialism in his day.

For the last fifty years, however, much philosophical ink has been spilt on the indifference of Utilitarianism to issues about the distribution of happiness: for many commentators that has been *the* problem. On my reading of his consequentialism, egalitarian considerations must play a role in the determination of overall value. Mill is plainly impatient with the idea that some people should have the opportunity to live significant lives, while others are consigned to lives of meaningless drudgery, possibly to privation and disease. There are situations in which he would concede that Benthamite calculations are entirely to the point, as he does at the end of the *System of Logic* (Mill 1963–91: Vol. 8, 952). If you are concerned, as Bentham was, with what to do in a situation where large numbers of people, already poor, are being deprived of the limited opportunities to feed and clothe themselves, and forced by the nascent industrial revolution to live in squalid and unhealthy conditions, working for more than half the day for bare subsistence, then simple summation of pleasures and relief from pain is completely appropriate as a guide to action. This context is at a far remove from utility monsters, rogue trolleys and the other staples of philosophical fiction that have been recently used in challenges to Utilitarianism – and I strongly suspect that neither Bentham nor Mill would see contrived scenarios as raising serious questions about the consequentialist tools they applied to social reform.

Whether Mill's consequentialism can be articulated to handle all the variants of the distributional puzzle that have arisen in contemporary discussions of ethical theory is not clear. Yet even in the form I have outlined, it does have resources to cope with some important cases of the objection. For example, given Mill's assumption that significant lives, typically if not invariably, involve cooperation with others and the extension of sympathies, a scenario in which someone is forced to choose between executing a single prisoner and allowing a larger number to be killed will present just that conflict between the total value of the lives saved and the committed project of the decision-maker that critics of utilitarianism have emphasized. But, even if he is successful with examples like these, Mill's own progressivist picture does introduce distributional questions of its own, both across time and across societies: What sacrifices of mundane pleasures and experiences of pain should people accept in order to bring about the institutions that allow for genuinely significant lives? Should the development of the social and material bases for worthwhile lives proceed in some societies, even if that would entail abstaining from opportunities to increase the basic welfare of people in other societies who are struggling to survive? Empiricist consequentialism maintains that we have much still to learn about how to characterize the good. Perhaps, as we continue with the project of improving our vision, Mill's complex ideas, rather than being reduced to the simple forms of the common interpretations of *Utilitarianism*, and then summarily dismissed on distributional grounds, will come to seem valuable resources for our endeavors.

References

Bentham, Jeremy (1948) *The Principles of Morals and Legislation*, New York: Hafner.

Berger, Fred (1984) *Happiness, Justice, and Freedom: The Moral and Political Philosophy of John Stuart Mill*, Berkeley: University of California Press.

Donner, Wendy (1991) *The Liberal Self: John Stuart Mill's Moral and Political Philosophy*, Ithaca, NY: Cornell University Press.

—— (2006) "Mill's Theory of Value," in Henry West (ed.) *The Blackwell Guide to Mill's Utilitarianism*, Oxford: Blackwell, pp. 117–38.

Kitcher, Philip (1999) "Mill, Mathematics and the Naturalistic Tradition," in John Skorupski (ed.) *The Cambridge Companion to Mill*, Cambridge: Cambridge University Press.

—— (2000) "Parfit's Puzzle," *Noûs* 34: 550–77.

Lewis, David (2000) "Mill and Milquetoast," in *Collected Papers*, vol. 3, Cambridge: Cambridge University Press.

Mill, John Stuart (1963–91) *Collected Works*, 33 vols, edited by J. H. Robson, Toronto: University of Toronto Press.

Parfit, Derek (1984) *Reasons and Persons*, Oxford: Oxford University Press.

Scheffler, Samuel (1988) *Consequentialism and Its Critics*, Oxford: Oxford University Press.

Sidgwick, Henry (1981) *Methods of Ethics*, Indianapolis, IN: Hackett.

Skorupski, John (1994) *Mill*, London: Routledge.

—— (2006) *Why Read Mill Today?* London: Routledge.

Smith, Adam (2000) *Wealth of Nations*, New York: Modern Library.

—— (2002) *Theory of Moral Sentiments*, Cambridge: Cambridge University Press.

West, Henry (2004) *An Introduction to Mill's Utilitarian Ethics*, Cambridge: Cambridge University Press.

22
BRITISH IDEALISM: THEORETICAL PHILOSOPHY

Stewart Candlish

Introduction

The last great English-language philosophical work of the nineteenth century was Bertrand Russell's *The Principles of Mathematics*, whose first draft was completed on that century's last day, 31st December 1900. Earlier the same year, he had published *A Critical Exposition of the Philosophy of Leibniz*. Both books exhibit an uncompromising rejection of British Idealism, to a form of which he had previously adhered (see e.g. Russell 1897). This break, partly because of Russell's own eventual influence, marked the start of the decline of Absolute Idealism in Britain. (In this chapter, all unqualified references to idealism should be understood as references to Absolute Idealism as exemplified in Britain.) We shall see that, to grasp the dialectic of the debate between idealists and the critics who were responsible for their eclipse, it is just as important to understand Russell's conception of what he was breaking with, as it is to understand idealism itself.

The causes of the break are complex; we shall consider them in more detail later. But a crucial element in them is the question of the truth of mathematics. As Russell conceived idealism, its adherents denied the absolute and unqualified truth of any statement, whether it be one of, for example, common discourse, of science, or of mathematics, no matter how carefully phrased, how conscientiously established, or how simple, these may be.

For various reasons, Russell came to hold that mathematical statements are simply and absolutely true: not just partly true; not merely temporarily true as one moment of a dialectical transition; not just true as part of a wider whole; not merely empirically true while being transcendentally false; not just relatively or conditionally true. This view of the status of mathematics, Russell thought, requires a certain kind of metaphysics, whose components can look as if they have been formulated by denying their idealist counterparts. This metaphysics is marked by a lack of epistemic restrictions: the mind has direct and unmediated contact with many separate propositions and their many separate constituents; propositions are truth-bearers; they are real entities, not linguistic, ideal or mental, as much part of the world as cats and dogs, and can be quantified over; they are objective and independent of our formulating them; their constituents are likewise real, and include not only physical objects but universals which in turn include relations such as (to use Russell's favorite example) *greater than*. The question of the status of relations, in particular, became the principal issue between the idealists and their critics.

The arguments Russell used in justifying his repudiation of his former views display in perhaps their clearest form the theoretical questions on which the fate of idealism turned, in metaphysics, the philosophy of logic, and what was eventually to become known as the philosophy of language. His chosen focus of criticism was the most famous of the idealists, F. H. Bradley, whom he treated as their representative. Although Bradley himself was too idiosyncratic for this role, his arguments shaped the beliefs of later idealists, e.g. Bernard Bosanquet (1895, 1911), H. H. Joachim (1906) and Brand Blanshard (1939). And clearly discernible in his writings are some of the views of his idealistically more orthodox Oxford teacher, T. H. Green. Russell's focus, then, is not completely misplaced. Evident in both Green and Bradley is a conscious rejection of the tradition of their earlier compatriots, such as Locke, Hume and Mill, together with a positive though not uncritical response to the work of Kant and Hegel.

T. H. Green

In so far as there is a single event which can be regarded as the origin of British Idealism, it is the introduction of Hegel to Anglophone philosophers. The crucial date seems to have been around 1857, when Green first encountered Hegel's writings at Oxford through his tutor Benjamin Jowett, one of the first people to have brought a set of them into Britain. It was principally because of the activity of Green that the idealists came to prominence in the closing decades of the nineteenth century (Quinton 1971).

The theoretical issues which the idealists themselves emphasized resulted in part from something they shared with Russell. This was a natural, though from the point of view of more recent logicians, naïve account of the nature of logic: "[L]ogic," Russell held, "is concerned with the real world just as truly as zoology, though with its more abstract and general features" (Russell 1919: 169). It is universal, ranging over everything, and its aim is to find the most general truths of all. This conception, shared despite their more obvious differences with Russell over e.g. technical apparatus and formal methods, gave rise to what the idealists themselves called the problem of the relation of thought and reality. The problem takes two principal forms: truth and inference. In the case of truth, the question arises, how is it possible for a mind to attain truth about a reality that is non-mental? In the case of inference, the question is, how is it possible to infer with deductive validity from one matter of fact to another when the reality about which the deduction is being made does not itself contain logical relations between its components? J. S. Mill (1843) e.g. had in effect responded to the latter question by answering that it is not so possible: valid deductive inference is circular and any inference to new knowledge must be inductive. Hume's thought that deductive inference could relate only ideas gives the same answer: one cannot validly reason from one matter of fact to another.

It should not, then, be particularly surprising that Green chose Hume as the focus for his first and most significant contribution to the discussion of these matters (Green 1874), nor that his lectures contained a comparably searching examination of Mill (Green 1885–8: Vol. 2, 195–333). But Hume had an extra significance for Green, who regarded him as the culmination of the empiricist tradition (by this stage a kind of orthodoxy in British philosophy), the first philosopher to think through with rigor the consequences of the school's fundamental assumptions and to eradicate completely the inconsistencies arising from Locke's attempts to reconcile those assumptions with common sense (Green 1874: 5).

Green argued that Hume's view, that there is nothing in the mind but the "impressions" of experience and "ideas" derived therefrom, makes it impossible to give an account of relations between the mind's ingredients. For example, after quoting a famous passage in Hume's *Treatise of Human Nature* (1739: Bk 1, pt 1, §6), in which Hume criticizes the traditional account of substance by arguing that it cannot "be deriv'd from the impressions of sensation or reflexion," Green later draws the same conclusion concerning the idea of a relation, asking,

> [C]an there be an idea of relation at all? Is it not open to the same challenge which Hume offers to those who talk of an idea of substance or of spirit? … What, then, is the one impression from which the idea of relation is derived? … [W]hat passion or emotion is a resemblance, or a proportion, or a relation of cause and effect? (Green 1874: 174)

Hume had inferred further that the notion of substance was illegitimate. But Green did not draw the parallel inference about the notion of relation: on the contrary, he maintained that the very beginnings of knowledge involve "the processes of discerning, comparing, and compounding ideas, which mean nothing else than bringing them into relation" (*ibid.*: 42). This is not to deny that knowledge comes from experience. Rather, following Kant, he argued that experience itself is conceptually impregnated. He believed that "formal conceptions" cannot be derived from simpler ideas because even the simplest ideas presuppose some such relational concepts: to attribute experience to an external object, for example, is to rely on the understanding of the relation of cause and effect, an understanding which cannot then be supposed to arise from that experience itself (*ibid.*: 57). Relations, then, are in his view essential to thought, so Green took his adaptation of Hume's own argument to show, not that the notion of a relation is illegitimate, but rather that Hume can give no coherent account of articulated, propositional thought. Green denied that "his [Hume's] doctrine would account for any significant predication whatever, as distinct from exclamations prompted by feelings as they occur" (*ibid.*: 185).

But Green's objections to Hume were not intended to be merely *ad hominem*: he held Hume's failure to be of the utmost significance, since it reveals two things. The first, because of Hume's status as the empiricist *par excellence*, is the bankruptcy of this entire approach to understanding thought and its relation to reality in terms of passively received feelings. The second, more surprisingly, is that "the import of the proposition becomes the central question of philosophy" (*loc. cit.*). Following Hume, then, it becomes philosophy's central task to account for the possibility of structured, propositional thought. This bringing to the fore of the question of the nature of the proposition is characteristic of idealism (Green's treatment of Mill argues the same point), and it persists as a kind of unquestioned axiom in the thought of Russell and Moore following their defection from the movement, forming a fulcrum on which turned the struggle between the idealists and their pluralist critics. It is significant that Moore's first publication after his defection (Moore 1899) is concerned with just this theme, and that Russell at the same turning point says explicitly, "That all sound philosophy should begin with an analysis of propositions, is a truth too evident, perhaps, to demand a proof" (Russell 1900: 8).

"A proposition," however, as Russell was to say later (1903: §54) "is essentially a unity." That is, it differs crucially from a mere list of its constituent elements, just as a sentence is not a list of its component words: it *says* something. For example, the sentence "Desdemona loves Cassio" has a unity which the string of words, "Desdemona," "loves" and "Cassio," does not. The former, unlike the latter, expresses a proposition. And the question arises, what is the source of this unity? Green in effect agreed with Kant that that which unifies the proposition cannot itself be amongst the unified elements, but is "an act of the understanding" (Kant 1787: 151; B130). And Kant had claimed further that "The same function which gives unity to the various representations *in a judgment* also gives unity to the mere synthesis of various representations *in an intuition*" (*ibid.*: 112; B104–5), so that not merely thought but experience in general is, one might say, propositional. In this way the idealists saw Kant as, in effect, giving a solution to the first form of the problem of the relation between thought and reality: truth is possible because both the reality and the judgment about it share a conceptual organization.

But Green, typical of the idealists in reading Kant through Hegelian eyes (so that what is important in understanding idealism is a grasp, not of Kant's doctrines themselves, but of what the idealists believed they were), thought him still wedded to a conception of the world which his own arguments had rendered untenable. For Kant had drawn the distinction between phenomena, the world of experience, and noumena, the world as it is in itself, which for human beings is not a possible object of experience; it is only the former which is conceptually impregnated. Lying beyond all possible experience, the world of noumena (so the idealists reasoned) would be one impenetrable to understanding, of which nothing can be said, not even that there is such a world. The idealists thought this doctrine incoherent, and concluded that reality cannot transcend experience, indeed that in some sense they must be identified. It would be absurd, however, to think of such experience as that of any individual finite consciousness, such as a human being (Green 1883: §36). That way lies subjective idealism and its inherent threat of solipsism. Rather, "there is one spiritual self-conscious being, of which all that is real is the activity or expression;

[and] we are related to this spiritual being, not merely as parts of the world which is its expression, but as partakers in some inchoate measure of the self-consciousness through which it at once constitutes and distinguishes itself from the world" (Green 1880: 146), so that the phenomenal world does not reappear as an alien other whose postulation threatens to re-pose the problems about truth which it was meant to help solve.

For Green, "this participation is the source of morality and religion" (*loc. cit.*); it thus provided a basis for the vindication of the evangelical Christianity which informed his life, preserving its essence from the increasing threat to its traditional historical claims posed by a combination of German biblical scholarship and the rise of geology and paleontology: together with the earlier revolution in astronomy, the discovery of the fossil record and the growing acceptance of an evolutionary account of the origins of humankind had not only displaced humanity from the centre of the universe but undermined biblical chronology. And it was clearly important to Green's religious commitments, with their promise of personal salvation for individual human beings distinct both from each other and from the creating God, that his ontology was pluralist. For Bradley, following Green but instead reacting against just such conventional Christianity, especially in its evangelical form, there was no necessity to hold on to any of its components no matter how central to faith. As we shall see, he diverged from Green at just this point, outlining a monist version of idealism which excluded the possibility of ultimately distinct entities, and setting up the main point of disagreement within idealist ranks. (McTaggart was to become the most prominent exponent of the pluralist version; and, again, it seems that religious commitment was at the root of the difference.)

F. H. Bradley

Prominent in Kant's thought had been what he termed antinomies (such as that the world as a whole either has, or lacks, a cause – or again, either is, or is not, finite), inevitable inconsistencies posing forced choices neither of which can be rationally preferred to the other. Kant's own resolution of the antinomies had relied on the distinction between noumenal and phenomenal worlds: it is, he had thought, the unrestricted application of the categories of the understanding, so that they are taken to apply to both worlds, which gives rise to the problems. Applied only to the phenomenal world, Kant alleged, the categories produce no such difficulties. Rejecting the noumena/phenomena distinction, the idealists were forced to give the antinomies a different significance. Taking them seriously as a demonstration of the inadequacies of conceptual thought set a pattern for later idealists of detecting inconsistencies in our thinking.

We find just this pattern, for example, in Bradley's best-known work, *Appearance and Reality*. Bradley accepted Kant's critique of rationalist metaphysics and his restriction of knowledge to appearances. In line with the standard idealist reading of Kant, Bradley rejected the division of the universe into noumena and phenomena. The Kantian thing-in-itself is unintelligible; experience is all there is. Nevertheless, as the title of his book suggests, Bradley accepted the distinction between appearance and reality and the possibility of an account of both. Consistently, he redrew the distinction within the realm of experience (1893: 127). As a result, although we are denied full access to the real, this is not because, like a noumenon, it is utterly beyond all possible experience; and we may intelligibly talk about it, if only by resort to analogy with, and extension from, familiar if elusive aspects of everyday experience. Bradley thus provided in a most original way the possibility of constructive metaphysical thinking within a framework that might have seemed to preclude it.

Appearance and Reality is divided into two books. The second, "Reality," constitutes the bulk of the text: its aim is to provide a positive account of the Absolute – the ultimate, unconditioned reality as it is in itself, not distorted by projection through the conceptual mechanisms of thought. A large proportion of his discussion is devoted to consideration of natural objections to this positive account. The two main features of this account are its idealism ("reality is experience") and its monism ("reality is one, not many"). The first book, "Appearance," is brief, and its aim destructive, arguing that "the ideas by which we try to understand the universe" (1893: 9) all bring us ultimately to contradictions when we try to think out their implications. Much of this destructive argument involves ideas based on the antinomies: he alleges, for example, that contradictions can be found in the notions of space and time, of motion, change, causation, the self, even that of *thing*. Bradley rejected on these grounds the view that reality can be understood as consisting of many objects existing independently of each other (pluralism) and of experience (realism). These are familiar suggestions, and make only part of his case. But preceding and inspiring them is chapter 3, entitled "Relation and Quality," which is uniquely Bradleian and alarming in the breadth of its implications; it has caused intermittent controversy ever since. In generalized form, its contention is that relations are unintelligible either with or without related terms, and, likewise, terms unintelligible either with or without relations. Bradley himself says of the arguments he wields in support of this contention,

> The reader who has followed and has grasped the principle of this chapter, will have little need to spend his time on those which succeed it. He will have seen that our experience, where relational, is not true; and he will have condemned, almost without a hearing, the great mass of phenomena. (Bradley 1893: 29)

This is fighting talk: it makes clear that his views on relations are at once highly controversial and central to his thought; from them he derives his main doctrines fairly directly. First, he arrives at monism (*ibid.*: 25, 124–6), by arguing that pluralism requires, but cannot provide, a consistent account of relations between its objects, so that the only reality can be a unified whole. Secondly, he reaches idealism (*ibid.*: 127–9), by arguing that the universe cannot intelligibly be supposed to exist independently of experience, drawing on a general principle enunciated earlier: "... if [something] is non-existent for us except in one relation, then for us to assert its reality away from that relation is more than unwarranted. It is ... an attempt in the end without meaning" (*ibid.*: 11). He concludes that "to be an integral element in a whole which is experienced, this surely is itself to be experience" (*ibid.*: 129).

Attacks on his positive views accordingly tended to proceed by undermining their basis in his discussion of relations.

Bradley and Russell on propositions

But questions concerning the nature and status of relations were also, independently, important to Russell. The consequence was that, for an extended period, they formed one of the most-debated matters between the two. Before dealing with these questions directly, we should look at how they arose for both philosophers, a process which reveals how prescient was Green's remark that "the import of the proposition becomes the central question of philosophy." For in Bradley's *Principles of Logic* (1883) we see in his treatment of the proposition (or, as it was often called at the time, judgment) an anticipation of his later, developed and notorious views on relations. Bradley rejected the long-standing belief that judgments are formed by somehow conjoining ideas: for example, the claim of the venerable textbook, the Port-Royal *Logic*, that they are "necessarily composed of three elements – the subject-idea, the attribute, and the joining of these two ideas" (Arnauld and Nicole 1662: Bk 2, ch. 3). Bradley, for whom, like Green, the proposition was primary, attacked such doctrines on several fronts, drawing the radical conclusion that in every judgment there is but one idea (1883: Bk 1, ch. 1, §11).

He argued, for instance, that those who, like Hume, think judgments to consist of separable ideas, fail to identify the sense of "idea" in which ideas are important to logic: ideas in this sense are not separate, datable psychological events (such as my now visualizing an apple) but abstract universals. Once ideas are properly understood, he suggested, they can no longer plausibly be thought of as individual and mutually independent entities which can be combined to create a judgment, as Locke had maintained (Locke 1706: Bk 4, Ch. 14): the order of dependence is the opposite, ideas being abstractions from complete judgments.

Further, given that ideas are universals, accounts like that of Port-Royal make it impossible to see how judgment can be about reality, since its ideas represent *kinds*, not particular real things; so long as judgment is confined to ideas, there can be no unique identification of any item about which we judge. Bradley applied the point to language, arguing that even grammatically proper names and demonstratives are disguised general terms.

Surprisingly for those who subscribe to the common view, first broadcast by Russell (1900) and much repeated thereafter, that Bradley thought all judgments to be of subject–predicate form and accordingly failed to recognize relational judgments as a distinct kind, Bradley's treatment of inference included the complaint that the mathematical logics of his time could not represent valid relational inferences (indeed, paradoxically enough, this was not to be possible until the Russellian developments in logic with which Bradley himself took issue). After a long and tangled consideration of the question of how it is possible for a deductive inference to be reflected in reality, in the second edition he came up with an account of inference: "Every inference is the ideal self-development of an object taken as real" (Bradley 1922: 598). Bradley seems here to be following the Humean idea that there are no logical relations between distinct existences: the reason that valid inference can be reflected in reality is that it can never take one beyond the original subject matter.

However, we shall concentrate here on propositions rather than inferences, for it is over this matter that the battle lines between Bradley and Russell begin to be drawn.

First, as we have seen, Bradley held that judgments are "ideal," being constituted of idea, that is, of meaning in the sense of something belonging to thought and possessing intentionality. Secondly, although Bradley, like Frege, was against psychologism in logic (Bradley 1883: 7), he nevertheless held that judgments are in some sense psychological: they belong to thought and "every idea ... has an aspect of psychical event" (Bradley 1922: 38n). Further, he maintained that judgments were not stitched together from a gaggle of individual meanings: on the contrary, the unified judgment is the real entity, and the individual meanings are derived from it.

In *The Principles of Mathematics*, Russell opposed all these components of Bradley's thinking. Judgment, he claimed, is a single primitive binary relation between two entities, a judging mind and a proposition. A proposition does not consist of words; "it contains the entities indicated by words" (Russell 1903: §51). These Russell called "terms," and they include, for example, men, chimaeras, numbers and relations (*ibid.*: §47). This gave Russell a very striking account of the nature of propositions: they consist of the very objects about which we speak. I shall call this the *doctrine of real propositional constituents*. The motivation for Russell's adopting this unusual view is epistemological: if our propositions consist of ideas (or of senses, he said, too, arguing against Frege) rather than of the actual things we are talking about, then the ideas themselves will form an impenetrable barrier to knowledge of those things (Russell 1904; 1911; CP6: 155). A consequence of these views is that the existence of a proposition does not depend on any mind, or anyone's formulating it – they are all out there waiting for us.

"Every term," he decided, "... is a logical subject ... possessed of all the properties commonly assigned to substances" (1903: §47). This view, that everything is at bottom an object, and of the same sort, is, Russell thought, unavoidable: the attempt to deny it leads to self-contradiction (*ibid.*: §49). His explanation of the contradiction looks to be a version of Frege's notorious problem concerning the concept *horse* (Frege 1892: 45). Frege had argued that "not all of the parts of a thought can be complete; at least one must be 'unsaturated,' or predicative; otherwise they would not hold together" (*ibid.*: 54). It turns out that if one regards the proposition in this way, as composed of both saturated and unsaturated elements (in Frege's vocabulary, of objects and concepts), the saturated element being what we talk about and the unsaturated element what we say about it, then it is impossible to talk about the unsaturated ones; for as soon as one puts the unsaturated, predicative, element into subject position in order to say something about it, then it becomes something else, something saturated. Thus the concept *horse*, as it occurs in "The concept *horse* is unsaturated," is not a concept but an object (whereas it is a concept as it occurs in "Shergar was a famous horse").

This not only makes it impossible to talk about concepts, but looks inconsistent. Had Russell used Fregean terminology, then, he would have held the constituents of propositions to be, all of them, saturated. For Bradley, in contrast, a proposition is like something carved from a single continuous piece of wood, whose individual pieces are notional rather than real, all of them unsaturated and derivative upon the whole (as e.g. we might for purposes of calculating the carving's volume regard it as a collection of adjacent small cubes); but for Russell, it is like a model assembled from pieces having a prior existence in their own right.

But Russell also thought that propositions, as well as being composed of entities, are themselves entities, because he recognized their unity (1903: §54), and subscribed to the principle that being and unity are interchangeable (*ibid.*: §47). His view of what makes a proposition a unity, though, was utterly opposed to Kant's mind-involving account; rather, Russell held, constituents are related by the proposition's verb: "the true logical verb in a proposition may be always regarded as asserting a relation" (*ibid.*: §53). That is, Russell openly committed himself to the claim that every proposition asserts the holding of a relation. Moreover, the verb, Russell said, "when used as a verb, embodies the unity of the proposition" (*ibid.*: §54). (We should not take this as inconsistent with the doctrine of real propositional constituents: at this stage, he thought of English as, by and large, a transparent medium through which reality's ingredients may be inspected – I shall refer to this as the *transparency thesis* –, and talked indifferently of "verbs" whether he meant words or the "entities indicated by words" [*ibid.*: §51], that is, terms.)

As we have seen, the phrase "unity of the proposition" is a way of remarking what distinguishes a proposition from a list of its constituents, so that unlike a mere list it "holds together" and says something. For both Bradley and Russell, this is a given. But this seemingly undeniable unity, when combined with Russell's principle that "Every constituent of every proposition must, on pain of self-contradiction, be capable of being made a logical subject" (*ibid.*: §52), makes apparently unanswerable the question of how unity is achieved. The verb must, according to this principle, itself be a term, something capable of appearing as a logical subject; in Frege's parlance, saturated. But it must be a very unusual kind of term, for it must simultaneously be unsaturated too, the source of the proposition's unity, relating all its constituents while itself being one of the related items. That is, the verb is unlike other terms in that it has, he says, a "twofold nature ..., as actual verb and verbal noun, [which] may be expressed ... as the difference between a relation in itself and a relation actually relating"(*ibid.*: §54). Yet as soon as we make the verb a logical subject, we are forced to identify it as "a relation in itself" rather than as "a relation actually relating," destroying the unity of the original proposition in which it was the source of that unity. Russell illustrated the point like this (*loc. cit.*):

> Consider, for example, the proposition "A differs from B." The constituents of this proposition, if we analyze it, appear to be only A, difference, B. Yet these constituents, thus placed side by side, do not reconstitute the proposition. The difference which occurs in the proposition actually relates A and B, whereas

the difference after analysis is a notion which has no connection with A and B. ... A proposition, in fact, is essentially a unity, and when analysis has destroyed the unity, no enumeration of constituents will restore the proposition. The verb, when used as a verb, embodies the unity of the proposition, and is thus distinguishable from the verb considered as a term, though I do not know how to give a clear account of the precise nature of the distinction.

Russell's problem, then, was that while he could not deny propositional unity, he could find no account of the proposition which could do justice to it. Anxious to get on with mathematical matters, he left the matter unresolved. But Bradley saw that the trouble was serious, that Russell was making inconsistent demands of relations, as we see in this extract from his critique of *The Principles of Mathematics*:

Mr. Russell's main position has remained to myself incomprehensible. On the one side I am led to think that he defends a strict pluralism, for which nothing is admissible beyond simple terms and external relations. On the other side Mr. Russell seems to assert emphatically, and to use throughout, ideas which such a pluralism surely must repudiate. He throughout stands upon unities which are complex and which cannot be analysed into terms and relations. These two positions to my mind are irreconcilable, since the second, as I understand it, contradicts the first flatly. If there are such unities, and, still more, if such unities are fundamental, then pluralism surely is in principle abandoned as false. (Bradley 1910b: 281)

And Bradley thought this difficulty was fundamental. While Russell, after some prevarication, had just put it on one side, for Bradley the unity of the proposition formed the basis of an overwhelming objection by *reductio* to the idea that a relation could be thought of in Russell's way, as another constituent of propositions and capable of appearing as logical subject. This idea, for Bradley and Russell alike, entailed what may be called the *reality thesis*, that all relations are real (we may also call the opposing claim, that all relations are unreal, the *unreality thesis*), which was the focus of much of Bradley's critical attention right up to his death in 1924. We shall see that, as he understood externality, any relation that is independently real is thereby external. Thus in Bradley's mind Russell's attachment to the idea that any relation is a logical constituent of a proposition, one which could in principle appear as subject term, committed him to what I shall call the *externality thesis*, the extreme and rarely held view that all relations are external.

Bradley and Russell on relations

It is, then, apparent that the topic of relations began to be a crucial issue between Bradley and Russell because on it is going to turn the question of whose account of the proposition can be defended. But it went on to become an issue of far greater significance, so that even as late as 1924 Russell could still say this:

> The question of relations is one of the most important that arise in philosophy, as most other issues turn on it: monism and pluralism; the question whether anything is wholly true except the whole of truth, or wholly real except the whole of reality; idealism and realism, in some of their forms; perhaps the very existence of philosophy as a subject distinct from science and possessing a method of its own. (Russell 1924, CP9: 170; LK: 333)

What Russell does not mention here is something of special importance to him: his account of the nature of mathematics had put relations at its heart. Developments in nineteenth-century mathematical thinking (the important figures include Cantor, Dedekind, Gauss, Hilbert, Peano and Weierstrass) had resulted in the replacement of *quantity* by *order* as the fundamental concept in mathematics, and required a concomitant emphasis on the significance of relations. Russell's work after his break with idealism explicitly reflected these changes, whose influence appeared repeatedly in the first statement of his logicism (the reduction of mathematics to logic), *The Principles of Mathematics*: from, for example, §1's definition of pure mathematics through §187's explanation of the importance of order to §208's insistence that "all order depends upon transitive asymmetrical relations." A threat to the status of relations thus imperiled Russell's greatest intellectual achievement by undermining what he himself thought were its metaphysical foundations.

Relations, then, formed the chosen battleground, and Russell's view of what was at issue subsequently became entrenched in philosophical memory. This standard account includes the claims that Bradley was opposed to relations (the vocabulary varies in revealing ways: instead of "opposed" we may get any of "rejected," "was hostile to," "attacked," and "denied"); that this opposition was because he just assumed the only possible propositional form to be subject–predicate (the *subject–predicate assumption*); that his attempted *reductio* of relations treats them illegitimately as objects; that he believed that all relations are internal, and what this means is either that all relations are reducible to properties (the *reducibility thesis*), or alternatively that no relation holds contingently (the *necessity thesis*).

Perhaps Russell's most noticeable argumentative tactic is his frequent appeal to the allegation that various philosophers, especially idealists, made the subject–predicate assumption. For example, he identified that assumption as the key to understanding Leibniz's metaphysics. Russell argued both that it is false and that its falsity is a matter of utmost philosophical significance. It is significant, first, because the assumption is very widely held:

> In the belief that propositions must, in the last analysis, have a subject and a predicate, Leibniz does not differ either from his predecessors or from his successors. Any philosophy which uses either substance or the Absolute will be found, on inspection, to depend upon this belief. Kant's belief in an unknowable thing-in-itself was largely due to the same theory. It cannot be denied, therefore, that the doctrine is important. Philosophers have differed,

not so much in respect of belief in its truth, as in respect of their consistency in carrying it out. (Russell 1900: 15)

To Kant and Leibniz, Russell explicitly added Descartes, Spinoza and Bradley as adherents of the subject–predicate assumption, but it is clear from the above that he held that almost every philosopher thought likewise and that the assumption has major metaphysical consequences, so that its falsity is doubly significant. But there is something special *for him* about the error, which we can find in his adherence to the transparency thesis and the doctrine of real propositional constituents. Adding the subject–predicate view to these would entail the conclusion that relations are not real, objective, non-mental entities (Hylton 1990: 155). And this, he thought, would make all relational judgments false. Given what he held to be the consequences for mathematics and logic, the subject–predicate view has to go.

This diagnosis is borne out by the fact that over several years Russell used his allegation, that almost every philosopher had made the subject–predicate assumption, in an attempt to refute a range of different views on the subject of relations. Here is its occurrence in *Our Knowledge of the External World*:

> Traditional logic, since it holds that all propositions have the subject–predicate form, is unable to admit the reality of relations: all relations, it maintains, must be reduced to properties of the apparently related terms. There are many ways of refuting this opinion; one of the easiest is derived from the consideration of what are called "asymmetrical" relations. (Russell 1914: 56)

After explaining his classification of relations, Russell went on to produce his refutation (1914: 58–9). Russell attached a great deal of weight to this argument. It was given a prominent place in chapter 26 of *The Principles of Mathematics*, where it represents his attack on what he called the "monistic" version of the reducibility thesis, which he attributed to Bradley. It is rehearsed briefly in the famous lectures on logical atomism (1918: Lecture 3). It also occurs in his famous and influential paper to the Aristotelian Society (1907), from which Russell reprinted the relevant passages in his 1959 book *My Philosophical Development*, and again in his contribution to *Contemporary British Philosophy: Personal Statements* (Russell 1924). It has accordingly been a formative influence on how later philosophers have conceived the dispute between the two. We shall try to come to a verdict on its significance later.

Russell, as we can see in the above quotation, was clearly concerned to oppose Bradley over the *reality* of relations, one holding the reality thesis, the other the unreality thesis. But one of the various puzzling things about all this is that what is commonly assumed to be in dispute between them is something else: what we may call the *internality thesis*, namely the view, which Russell also attributed to Bradley, that all relations are internal to their terms. This attribution appeared alongside that of the unreality thesis, in the Aristotelian Society paper, where he said "[Bradley's] argument explicitly assumes what I have called the 'axiom of internal relations'" (Russell

1907: 138n). Thereafter the attribution turned up in similarly influential places (e.g. Russell 1924: 172; Moore 1919: 79) and eventually entered the secondary literature as something so uncontroversial that it needed only to be mentioned to be accepted (e.g. Warnock 1958: 10; Wollheim 1959: 104 and 1969: 102; Rorty 1967: 126; Findlay 1984: 275; Blackburn 1994: 2 and 325; Griffin 1998: §2; Irvine 2004).

What then, *was* the argument over relations about? And what role was played by Russell's attribution to the idealists of the subject–predicate assumption?

The first prerequisite for answering these questions adequately is to realize that the unreality and internality theses have been run together in the minds of most participants in the discussion. For example, the passage from Russell 1924 which we quoted earlier, beginning "The question of relations is one of the most important that arise in philosophy," is surrounded with confusion about what this question actually is. Russell, although he preceded these remarks with reference to "arguments for and against the reality of relations," went on to say that what he means by the "question of relations" is the question which is preferable: his own "doctrine of external relations," that is, "what Mr Bradley denies when he asserts the doctrine of internal relations," or Bradley's view (1924: 172). But if we ask, what exactly is this doctrine of external relations?, it turns out that it is the denial of (what Russell took to be) Bradley's axiom of internal relations. Given this tight circle, it is thus important to obtain some more direct understanding of what the internality thesis is supposed to be.

Interpreting the internality thesis

There are two standard interpretations in the literature. One is that to assert the internality of all relations amounts to asserting that no relational statement is contingently true; and this in turn is treated as entailing that all are necessary. As any statement can be cast in a relational form, this version amounts to the necessity thesis. The other interpretation has it that the doctrine is that, because the subject–predicate thesis holds, so does the reducibility thesis. And we can find remarks in *Appearance and Reality* which lend themselves variously both to the necessity (e.g. Bradley 1893: 347) and to the reducibility interpretation (*ibid.*: 125–6, 322).

But these two accounts seem not to amount to the same thing, for on the face of it a subject–predicate statement that a certain object has a certain property can be just as contingent as a relational statement. Bradley is certainly hostile to the notion of contingency, yet he seems to move from one interpretation to the other quite indiscriminately, as though he saw no significant difference between them.

However, even if Bradley had made the subject–predicate assumption, this would not have meant that he accepted the reducibility thesis, for he thought that subject–predicate propositions themselves involved relations between subject and predicate, so that any problems with relations would hardly be solved by attempted elimination of them in favor of subjects and predicates. Noting this important qualification, let us suppose for the sake of argument that he was committed to some sort of equivalence between relational and subject–predicate propositions, even though his actual view was that all propositions had the same subject, namely reality itself, and was unlike the conventional subject–predicate analysis in supposing that this subject did not feature in the proposition's conceptual content (Bradley 1883: 13).

Given his hostility to contingency, then, did Bradley think at this time that every property of a thing belonged to it essentially? The best way to address this question is through a passage which Bradley appended to the second edition of *Appearance and Reality* in an attempt to articulate his views more clearly. In it, he imagines someone defending the claim that spatial relations are external by urging that it is just common sense that, for instance, a man or a billiard ball is unaffected in itself by a mere alteration of place. His response is significant:

> But an important if obvious distinction seems here overlooked. For a thing may remain unaltered if you identify it with a certain character, while taken otherwise the thing is suffering change. If, that is, you take a billiard-ball and a man in abstraction from place, they will of course – so far as this is maintained – be indifferent to changes of place. But on the other hand neither of them, if regarded so, is a thing which actually exists; each is a more or less valid abstraction. But take them as existing things and take them without mutilation, and you must regard them as determined by their places and qualified by the whole material system into which they enter. And, if you demur to this, I ask you once more of what you are going to predicate the alterations and their results. The billiard-ball, to repeat, if taken apart from its place and its position in the whole, is not an existence but a character, and that character can remain unchanged, though the existing thing is altered with its changed existence. Everything other than this identical character may be called relatively external ... but absolutely external it cannot be. (Bradley 1897: 517–18)

It is sometimes suggested that this reply is fallacious, moving from the essentiality to a material object of some spatial relations or other, to the essentiality of the particular relations it happens to be in. But Bradley's claim is that to think of the total particular situation in terms of *a billiard-ball* is already to have abstracted without argument, to have divided that total situation into object plus (possibly unmentioned) surroundings. Once we have made that abstraction, then of course some relations will be external to the object; but unless we do, none can be singled out in any principled way as external. The crucial point, though, is that the very process of abstraction involved in thinking this way itself relies upon supposing some relations to be external to the object, for without such externality, no conception of an object at all is possible. As an argument for the externality of some relations, this appeal to common sense is plainly circular: one party attempts to conduct the argument in terms whose very legitimacy the other is questioning, while the other party is unable to provide any other terminology in which the question can even be framed.

Although this dialectic ends in stalemate, its assessment does put us in a better position to say something useful about the connection between the two interpretations of internality. For there is such a connection; it can be seen in Bradley's distinction between *existences* and *characters*. Suppose that relations are indeed reducible to properties. The question asked earlier is, why should these properties be any more essential to their terms than the original relations were? The answer is, of course, that they need not; but this lack of necessity depends on a division of the properties of the object in question into the essential and the non-essential. And to make the assumption that this division is possible is already to abstract an aspect of the whole, to treat the object "as a character," not as an existence. If we refuse to make this division, then we can plausibly be supposed to be committed to the denial of contingency. There is no doubt that Bradley did so refuse, albeit with a vital quali-fication: as he repeatedly insisted, he was not opposed to such division for practical purposes; it can give us everyday truths, but not the final truth about things. And, in the end, we must assess Russell's allegation (1907: 138), which goes to the heart of idealism, that there is no difference between what is true and what is true "in the end."

Bradley on relations: a closer look

We have seen that the reducibility interpretation of the internality thesis is unjustified, and that the remarks which appeared to justify it support, at best, a claim of equiva-lence between some relational statements and others, not a reducibility claim but instead one closely connected to the necessity interpretation. This latter appears to reflect Bradley's hostility to contingency. What we have yet to answer is the question of whether Bradley held either, or both, of the internality and unreality theses.

Bradley does appear to be explicitly committed to the internality thesis in the first and second editions of *Appearance and Reality* in 1893 and 1897. But by the time of the essays of the period 1909–11 which make up a substantial part of *Essays on Truth and Reality*, the commitment has disappeared and, with some qualifications, he repudiated the thesis (1909a: 190; 1909c: 238–9; 1911a: 290–1; 1911b: 312). At the end of his life he was still disputing its attribution to him (1924: 641, 646, 665 and 667–8).

What explains this seeming change of mind? And why did Russell vacillate over what he thought were Bradley's views on relations? These questions have the same answer. Bradley's wavering commitment to the internality thesis was based to a significant extent on a confusion with another doctrine about relations which he did firmly hold to for most of his life, namely the unreality thesis. In *Appearance and Reality*, he moved, seemingly unawares, backwards and forwards between them. This confusion is understandable in the light of genuine logical relationships between the two doctrines. (We find the same confusion in later commentators.) Bradley was never, then, the archetypal theorist of internal relations. He gained the reputation of being so for two principal reasons. First, over-attention to *Appearance and Reality* and neglect of his later writings (understandable, when the book was intended to be the canonical statement of his metaphysical views, and when his clearest repudiation did not appear in print until 1935, by which time the philosophers with whom the future lay were unlikely to have been even remotely interested). Secondly, the effect produced by controversy: Bradley, holding Russell to be committed to the reality of external relations, criticized him for this (see e.g. Bradley 1909c: 237n). It would only be natural, even if fallacious, to infer from this criticism some commitment on Bradley's part to the internality thesis.

Even *Appearance and Reality* itself, where the internality thesis is most prominent, is not the unequivocal source of that thesis it is commonly assumed to be. In the section normally assumed to be an argument for the thesis, chapter 3, most of what Bradley says is about relations in general, without qualification. (There are two occurrences of the phrase "internal relation" in the chapter, but neither has anything to do with the internality thesis; Bradley merely used the phrase casually to distinguish intra-propositional relations from relations between propositions and outside things.) The following remark, particularly when read in context, is surely definitive:

> The object of this chapter is to show that the very essence of these ideas [sc. "the arrangement of given facts into relations and qualities"] is infected and contradicts itself. Our conclusion briefly will be this. Relation presupposes quality, and quality relation. Each can be something neither together with, nor apart from, the other; and the vicious circle in which they turn is not the truth about reality. (Bradley 1893: 21)

However, in the middle of the discussion we find evidence of confusion about what it is supposed to be proving:

> It is possible for many purposes to accept and employ the existence of processes and relations which do not affect specially the inner nature of objects. But the very possibility of so distinguishing in the end between inner and outer, and of setting up the inner as absolutely independent of all relation, is here in question. (*ibid.*: 23)

This second quotation's first sentence suggests that it is external relations which are in question, and that the conclusion is going to be that all relations are internal; but in the second sentence we immediately return to part of the original issue: whether there can be terms without any relations at all. If we read carefully, though, we can see that the main theme here is that there is something in principle wrong with the whole distinction between the external and the internal. This is a view to which Bradley always adhered: it recurs in his writings right up to his death. But he was not consistent. Consider this passage:

> But the "this" certainly is used also with a negative bearing. It may mean "this one," in distinction from that one and the other one. And here it shows obviously an exclusive aspect, and it implies an external and negative relation. But every such relation, we have found, is inconsistent with itself (Chapter iii). For it exists within, and by virtue of an embracing unity, and apart from that totality both itself and its terms would be nothing. And the relation also must penetrate the inner being of its terms. (*ibid.*: 201)

Not only does this look like an unequivocal affirmation of the internality thesis, via the assertion of the inconsistency of *external* relations, it also refers to the very chapter of *Appearance and Reality* which specially dealt with relations as proving this. Add to this the book's index entry, "Relations are all intrinsical," which Moore chose to quote at the start of his influential essay "External and Internal Relations" (Moore 1919), and it is no wonder that Bradley was credited with the thesis by both followers and opponents. Moreover, in the important Note B to the Appendix in the second edition of 1897, Bradley was explicitly hostile to external relations, and apparently makes the extreme claim that starting from, say, one's own hair color one would, in principle, be able to infer every other truth about the universe, which implies that everything is internally related to everything else.

But Bradley himself was later to say of *Appearance and Reality*'s treatment of relations "I have perhaps fallen in places into inconsistency" (1909c: 224n), and it was not long after its publication that he started to clarify his views. In a letter to Russell of 28 January 1901 he insisted "I don't hold *any* relational system can be consistent," and thereafter he adhered to the claim that his hostility to externality is based on a rejection of the external/internal distinction and includes the internality thesis as well:

> Criticism therefore which assumes me committed to the ultimate truth of internal relations, all or any of them, is based on a mistake. (1909c: 239)

> Mere internal relations, then, like relations that are merely external, are untenable if they make a claim to ultimate and absolute truth. But taken otherwise, and viewed as helpful makeshifts and as useful aids in the pursuit of knowledge, external and internal relations are both admissible and can be relatively real and true. (1924: 645)

Here we see Bradley committing himself to the idea that it is all right in everyday contexts to appeal to both internal and external relations, but nevertheless both are "ultimately" unreal. To understand what this means, we need to look at the key terms involved, and especially at their interconnections. First, what condition did Bradley think a relation would have to meet to be external?

> What should we mean … by a relation asserted as simply and barely external? We have here, I presume, to abstract so as to take terms and relations, all and each, as something which in and by itself is real independently. (1924: 642; cf. 1911a: 291; 1897: 507 and 559)

One thing that is obvious from this passage is the close connection in Bradley's mind between the externality and the reality of a relation. Now Bradley's conception of what it is to be real was a very traditional one: to be real is to be a substance, that is, complete, independent or individual (1883: 52, 71 and 187; 1893: 9; 1897: 509; 1909c: 227n; 1911a: 289–90). For example: "… what is real must be self-contained and self-subsistent and not qualified from the outside" (1897: 509). We have already seen Russell, in his account of propositions, claiming that "Every term ... is a logical subject ... possessed of all the properties commonly assigned to substances" (1903: §47), and committing himself to supposing that "verbs" (i.e. relations) are terms like any other constituent of a proposition. It follows, then, that Russell at this time was committed to the reality thesis. So the central dispute between Russell and Bradley over the reality of relations can be summed up as a dispute over the proper account of propositions.

But it looks as though far more is at stake than this. McTaggart, making a typical idealist point about the unreality of matter, had claimed, "So Matter is in the same position as the gorgons and the harpies" (1906: 95). John Wisdom (1942: 439), commenting on G. E. Moore's appeal to this passage, pointed out that people who say this kind of thing "expect to shock us." And a natural interpretation of the suggestion that relations are unreal is that it amounts to the claim that no relational statement is true, the exaggerated rhetoric of the monists lending credibility to this thought, one that they half-believed themselves. It is clear that Russell's anxiety over relations and their importance for mathematics was based on some such idea. But in fact, Bradley's claim of unreality is simply that relations are not objects, which he conceived of as independent substances. As relations are not objects, there are no names of relations. It is not obvious that, without the aid of the commitments to transparency and real propositional constituents, such a doctrine entails that all relational statements are false.

Internality and unreality

All this said, however, Bradley was nevertheless more sympathetic to internal than to external relations, and he was careful to deny only their *ultimate* reality. The following remark reveals this: "As to what has been called the axiom of internal relations, I can only repeat that 'internal' relations, though truer by far than 'external,' are, in my opinion, not true in the end" (1911b: 312). We may contrast this with his far harsher view of externality:

> And Pluralism, to be consistent, must, I presume, accept the reality of external relations. Relations external, not relatively and merely in regard to this or that mode of union, but external absolutely must be taken as real. To myself, such relations remain unthinkable. (1909c: 237)

In view of this lingering sympathy, and of Bradley's own inclination to confuse the doctrine of internality with that of unreality, a confusion which others have been only too willing to adopt, one may suspect some close logical connection between the two doctrines.

In a metaphysical system one of whose governing concepts is that of reality in the sense of substantiality, the internality thesis occupies an unstable position. It is unstable because things that are internally related do not have – by definition – the kind of independence that is logically required of substances, and yet without such independence they cannot be thought of as related *things* at all. Russell, in his classic exposition of logical atomism, says that each of his particulars "stands entirely alone and is completely self-subsistent," having "that sort of self-subsistence that used to belong to substance," so that "each particular that there is in the world does not in any way logically depend upon any other particular" (1918, CP8: 179; LK: 201–2). Such independence can be achieved only via the elimination of complexity arising from internal relations. Russell's logical atomism displayed one way of doing this: complexity is shifted from objects to facts; complexes lose their status as objects and the substances are independent in virtue of their simplicity. Bradley's monism displayed another: complexity is absorbed, so that the eventual sole substance has its independence in virtue of there being nothing else. But what systems of both kinds agree on is that internal relations not only are unreal themselves because all relations are, but also undermine the reality of their terms.

Once it is understood that the internality of relations entails their unreality, it should be no surprise that Bradley was more sympathetic to internality than externality, for internal relations are, by Bradley's criterion of reality, *obviously* unreal: their necessary mutual connectedness with their related terms precludes independence. Neither should it be surprising that he was at one stage inclined to confuse the two, and sometimes seems indifferent as to whether he is trying to show that relations are internal or that they are unreal. For the former is but an indirect route to the latter. Also understandable is that he eventually got clear enough on the point to be able to make it explicit that the rejection of the claim that there are external relations did not commit him to the doctrine of internality, and that, when rejecting the doctrine of internality, he did so by stipulating carefully that it does not express the "ultimate truth" about things, is not true "in the end." Even when, as we saw, he dismissed as "ludicrous" the idea that he would accept the doctrine of internality, he described the doctrine as that of "a relation which is asserted to be real ultimately and internal merely" (1924: 642).

Russell, internality and unreality

We saw earlier that Bradley himself suffered temporary confusion about the nature of his own views on relations. By the time he had sorted this out, it was too late: the controversy with Russell had become muddled, with fatal consequences for idealism. To reinforce this point, and bring out the consequences of what I have shown, let us examine the best known, most straightforward, and most historically influential, of Russell's arguments against Bradley. This argument is the appeal to asymmetrical relations, that is, those of which, for example, if it is true that *a* bears the relation to *b*, then it is false that *b* bears the relation to *a*. We saw that Russell used it repeatedly, and that the notion of an asymmetrical relation was essential to Russell's account of order, which itself was vital to his account of mathematics (Russell 1903: §216; 1919: Ch. 4).

In a later version, though, Russell gave the argument an even greater importance:

> Asymmetrical relations are involved in all series – in space and time, greater and less, whole and part, and many others of the most important characteristics of the actual world. All these aspects, therefore, the logic which reduces everything to subjects and predicates is compelled to condemn as error and mere appearance. To those whose logic is not malicious, such a wholesale condemnation appears impossible. And in fact there is no reason other than prejudice, so far as I can discover, for denying the reality of relations. When once their reality is admitted, all *logical* grounds for supposing the world of sense to be illusory disappear. (Russell 1914: 59)

What, then, is the argument? The *Principles of Mathematics* version is the fullest and most carefully elaborated, concluding that "the distinction between an asymmetrical relation and its converse" is something "the monistic theory of relations is wholly unable to explain" (Russell 1903: §215). But the later version is clearer (1914: 58–9): "the question whether all relations can be reduced to predications" is to be answered in the negative, since it is clearly impossible to express propositions concerning asymmetrical relations (such as "*a* is greater than *b*") in terms of properties; the best attempts we can make at such expression, for example, through propositions such as "The whole *ab* contains difference in magnitude," are "formally incapable of explaining the facts" because they lose the information as to which of the objects is greater. Restoring this information requires that we say which of the magnitudes is greater, and this means that the original relation, which was to be reduced, reappears. Let us grant for the moment that the argument refutes what Russell called "the monistic theory" of relations. Two questions are pertinent in this context. First, what exactly is this theory? And second, did Bradley hold it?

By this stage it should not be surprising to find that Russell himself wobbled on the answer to the first question. In some places (Russell 1907, 1924, 1959), what is under attack is the internality thesis. In others (Russell 1903, 1914), it is the unreality thesis. On occasion (Russell 1918), the matter is entirely unclear.

What, though, about the second question? As we saw, Bradley's commitment to the internality thesis was a temporary muddle which was sorted out by 1901, so that Russell's 1907, 1914 and 1959 versions of the refutation are apparently misdirected. Bradley did, on the other hand, consistently subscribe to the unreality thesis. But this latter was interpreted by Russell as the monistic account given, for example, in the above quotation from *The Principles of Mathematics*. And in fact this was also how Russell interpreted the *internality* thesis. But we have already observed that Bradley, in holding that relations were unreal, was not committed to maintaining that relational propositions were reducible to subject–predicate propositions. There are two reasons for rejecting the attribution to Bradley of such a commitment: first, he held both that subject–predicate propositions require a relation between the subject and the predicate so that relations turn out to be ineliminable even if any relational proposition is replaceable by a subject–predicate proposition; second, he held also that in any case subject–predicate propositions too are problematic, so that no problem with relations would be resolved by reducing them to predicates. He made this plain in his most considered treatment of relations, which directly addressed Russell's argument, but was unfortunately left unfinished at his death, appearing in print too late to make any serious contribution to the debate:

> Asymmetrical relations are said to disprove Monism, because Monism rests on *simple* inherence [sc. predication] as the only way in which there is ultimate reality.
> The argument, if right, is improperly limited – because *any* relations, *if so*, disprove Monism.
> But Monism does not rest on simple inherence as the one form of reality. It even (in my case) says that that form is unsatisfactory (see *Appearance*).
> [...] In short, far from admitting that Monism requires that all truths can be interpreted as the predication of qualities of the whole, Monism with me contends that all predication, no matter what, is in the end untrue and in the end unreal .... (Bradley 1924: 670, 672; his italics)

What was at stake for Bradley was the ontological status of relations; and a *locus classicus* of the sort of view that he was rejecting in urging that relations are unreal, is Russell's *Principles of Mathematics*. What is in question, that is, is whether relations can be thought of as terms in the Russellian sense, the reality thesis that we uncovered earlier. It is possible, as we shall see from Russell's own example, to reject the idea that a relation is a term in a proposition, on an ontological par with its other constituents, without embracing what Russell calls "the monistic theory" of relations (or any comparably problematic alternative).

In the sense that Bradley intended the claim that relations are unreal, then, Russell's appeal to asymmetrical relations was neither here nor there. It was no concession of defeat for Bradley to admit that relational expressions are ineliminable from sentences like "*aRb*," nor can be converted into monadic predicates without loss of information. What is at issue here is how such expressions function: do they function by introducing a kind of object into the proposition, or not? Russell held (at this stage) that they do; Bradley denied this. Russell thought that something important was at stake. In *The Principles of Mathematics* he opens §212 with a reference to "the philosophic dislike of relations," and immediately goes on to describe this "dislike" as the view that "no relations can possess absolute and metaphysical validity." In case it is not obvious what this means, we can discern it in Russell's rehearsal of the same theme in his famous essay "The Monistic Theory of Truth," where he glosses it as "the denial that there are any relations" (1907: 142; 1959: 57). These telling phrases reveal his thinking far more clearly than his explicit arguments. It takes the form of a *reductio*: "Both the internality and the unreality doctrines come to the same thing: there are no relations. Consequently, every proposition invoking a relation is appealing to something that does not exist. Hence, every such proposition (and mathematics is full of them) is false." And this is an argument on which, as we shall see, Russell came to change his mind, by changing his views about meaning. In fact, the real issue between the two philosophers, for which the confused dispute over relations goes proxy, is that of how to think about meaning. For Russell, but not for Bradley, meanings were individual objects; without such objects, there would be no objectivity.

Nevertheless, however justified it may be to say that Bradley remained unrefuted by Russell's argument, this of course leaves open the possibility that his view is still mistaken, or at least undemonstrated, or even unmotivated. We must now investigate this possibility.

Bradley's arguments for the unreality of relations and their terms

Bradley's various arguments on this subject were a team effort. No one of them on its own was meant to show conclusively the unreality of relations or of terms, but each closes off one of the possible positions which an opponent might adopt. (The point is well made by Mander, 1994: 108–9.) This systematicity is most evident in chapter 3 of *Appearance and Reality*. The question informing Bradley's arguments is, "Are relations and their terms real?" This question is the same as "Are relations and their terms substances?"; its linguistic counterpart is "Do names of relations and their terms figure in a language which accurately mirrors reality?"

Bradley's most notorious argument (1893: 27–8) is the second member of a pair which works by excluding in turn each component of this disjunction: Either relations essentially relate their terms (in the sense that there can be no term-free relations) or they do not. The first member alleges that if they do, then they do not exist independently of their terms and are thus unreal. The second member alleges that the consequence of denying this conclusion and supposing that relations are real is that they would be themselves extra terms which would require further relations in order to link them to the terms which they were supposed to be relating (and so on *ad infinitum*).

Given the technical sense which Bradley attaches to "real," and the assumptions common to all participants in the dispute, this dilemma is unavoidable, whether it is taken as a point in the philosophy of language about the analysis of propositions – that apparent names of relations are in principle eliminable (as Wittgenstein independently showed in *Tractatus*, 1921: 3.1432) – or as a point in metaphysics about the constituents of the world, that relations are not substances. Our modes of expressing relations are not names, and the relations themselves are not objects. One may respond that nothing is or could be a substance in the required sense, for the notion itself is muddled; but to take this line is to repudiate the mutually agreed terms of the dispute as it was conducted at the time. This is all very clear in the debate of 1910–11 between Bradley and Russell in the pages of *Mind* (e.g. Russell 1910a: both sides appear in CP6), and in the contrast between Russell's 1903 commitment to the reality of relations in *The Principles of Mathematics* and the eventual ontological parsimony of his 1924 essay "Logical Atomism": it is strange that Bradley is still blamed for treating relations illegitimately as objects when it was just that treatment that he was disputing by displaying its consequences. When Russell wrote, "Bradley conceives a relation as something just as substantial as its terms, and not radically different in kind" (Russell 1927: 263), he himself was writing retrospectively and from the comfortable position of having abandoned the ontology of *The Principles of Mathematics*, in which relations were just so conceived. No wonder that Russell, having surreptitiously switched sides to become the new champion of the insubstantiality and unreality of relations, could make his long–standing opponent appear to have subscribed to their substantiality and, via this, to the denial of ordinary facts. (Notice too that, despite the earlier fears which had fueled his opposition to those who held relations to be unreal, Russell, perhaps because of his Wittgenstein-influenced shift away from a conception of logic as the most highly generalized description of reality to a "linguistic" view, managed to change sides on the issue of relations without worrying about catastrophic consequences for mathematics; which casts an interesting light on the earlier wrangle.)

The second component of the disjunctive argument is often thought to stand alone (as, for example, by Russell in the debate summed up in the last paragraph), and is sometimes described accordingly as "Bradley's regress argument." This is, of course, to misrepresent its function; it is giving only one half of an argument by dilemma. And there is a standard reply to it which originated with Russell (1903: §99). It is that the regress is indeed endless but not vicious, being merely one of implication and not requiring the actual completion of an infinite series before anything can actually be related. (Thus "A and B are alike" implies "A is like something which is like A," and this pair implies further "A is like something which is like something which is like B," and so on *ad infinitum* but trivially.) This reply, if it is to be effective, must be based on the idea that the goal of the argument is to prove the internality rather than the unreality of relations. If we keep it in mind that the question at issue is whether or not relations are real, we can see that the argument's point is that an infinite series of actual *objects* is generated, not just an infinite series of possible names, so that even if the argument does not prove a vicious infinite regress, it still shows that the reality of relations requires an embarrassingly generous ontology.

We can see the appropriateness of Bradley's argument to the ontology of *The Principles of Mathematics*, and accordingly in the context of his debate with Russell, by putting together the following two extracts:

> Among concepts, again, two kinds at least must be distinguished, namely those indicated by adjectives and those indicated by verbs. ... [T]he latter are always or almost always relations. (Russell 1903: §48)

> [T]he theory that there are adjectives or attributes or ideal things ... which are in some way less substantial, less self-subsistent, less self-identical, than true substantives, appears to be wholly erroneous, and to be easily reduced to a contradiction. Terms which are concepts differ from those which are not, not in respect of self-subsistence .... (*ibid.*: §49)

Bradley's argument, then, was applicable to the position at which it was directed, even if Russell, always a fast-moving opponent, had already left it; and the regress the argument demonstrates is in fact far from innocent. To see what it succeeds in showing, take a familiar analogy. Suppose I am given the task of making a chain out of some loose metal rings, and when I come to join any two of them, I ask for a third ring to do the job. The most I can achieve in this way is just the addition of more rings to the collection. It is obvious that no matter how many rings I add, I shall never get a chain unless I do something "radically different in kind" (to repeat Russell's own words) from merely collecting more rings, something that I could just as well have done with the first pair of rings as with any of those subsequently added. Now as long as we think of relations as real, that is, as substantial in the sense which we have seen was common ground between Russell and Bradley, we are in an analogous situation. A relation needs to be something "radically different in kind" from its terms.

A parallel analogy can be constructed to meet the objection that the problem is not to relate previously unrelated things but to understand actual relational facts: suppose I have a chain and I want to understand its principle of construction. It is clear that I am already on the wrong track if I begin by pointing out that the two end rings of an existing chain are linked by the intervening ones, for this account of linking does not explain how two adjacent rings are linked; and if I try to pretend that it does, once more an infinite regress appears.

Nevertheless, the conventional wisdom that Russell's response was sufficient became so entrenched that, for example, one commentator felt able to write of Bradley's arguments concerning relations, without further explanation: "The defects of these arguments are by now well-known" (Griffin 1983: 199). But it should now be obvious that matters are by no means so clear. Certainly, it would be an *ignoratio* to suggest that Bradley ignores the fact that it is a matter of sheer common sense that there are related things in the world; for this is not in contention. What *is* in contention is a philosophical account of the world's variety and relatedness, a fact obscured by the same word, "relation," having to do double duty as identifying *both* the problem *and* an unsatisfactory solution to it, so that rejecting a proffered solution looks like denying the fact to be explained. (This phenomenon appears in other contexts and is a common source of philosophical confusion.)

So far these arguments have concentrated on relations themselves, and their conclusion is that relations are unreal. This means that they do not constitute elements out of which complex wholes are constructed but instead are "abstractions" from those wholes, creatures of intellectualization. Provided that we do not forget that this conclusion is not that reality contains no differences, merely that these differences are not to be understood in the reifying way that some philosophers have supposed, it can and should be accepted with equanimity. Russell, in asserting that "the axiom of internal relations is incompatible with all complexity ... lead[ing], as we saw, to a rigid monism" (1907: 145), mistook his target. Bradley's view has a lot in common with those whom Russell thought of as allies: applied to judgment, then, apart from its generalization from some to all propositional constituents, it is reminiscent of Frege; and both Bradley and the Wittgenstein of *Tractatus* 3.1432, despite their different ways of expressing the point, could be said to be at one on the unreality of relations even though the latter held the same sort of absolutist conception of truth as Russell did himself. Of course Bradley and Wittgenstein, the former a monist, the latter a pluralist, diverge dramatically in their ontology. But this was nothing to do with their views on relations. It was a consequence of their differences concerning the status of related objects. Wittgenstein, rejecting the tradition of thinking of objects in terms of independent substances, thought it possible to name objects even though they could occur only in combination with others so that this naming could be achieved only in the context of a proposition. Bradley thought this not possible: objects, no less than relations, turn out to be unreal. And his arguments to *this* effect cannot be accepted with equanimity by those who wish to draw back from monism. It is on his treatment of *things*, not of relations, that Russell should have focused his attention.

Consider, for example, another argument, which Bradley deployed on various occasions (1893: 25–7; 1924: 634–5), and is intended to prove the unintelligibility of related terms. (It is again the second of a pair of arguments whose first member is a proof of the unintelligibility of terms devoid of relation. The first needs no special attention, because any two terms whatever are related by similarity or dissimilarity.) The key claim is that "in order to be related, a term must keep still within itself enough character to make it, in short, itself and not anything diverse" (1924: 634). The point is this. Imagine two numerically different objects of which the same relational predicate holds true. By virtue of their diversity, they must differ in some other respect. That is, each term must have some other predicate holding true of it which the other lacks. (This other predicate, although it may itself be relational too, must hold independently of the original relational one, or the terms would have no character of their own.) But then the question of the relation between the relational predicate and the other predicate arises, and a familiar regress begins: an endless multiplicity of relations breaks out within the term itself.

This argument has a metaphysical significance far beyond that of the attack on the reality of relations. It attacks the reality of terms, albeit – as Bradley himself saw – using the attack on the reality of relations as a model (so that the issue of relations could easily have had its significance overestimated), and its consequences are far-reaching. Of comparable significance, it may seem, is the logical atomist attack on the reality of complex objects; but the comparison is inadequate, for the logical atomists remained content with simple objects while Bradley rejected the reality of these too. And of course, after the reality of relations eventually became a non-issue for Russell because of his surreptitious switch of sides on the question, he came around to the view that mathematics and logic can survive on the reality of terms alone. Hence, of course, a threat to the reality of terms would equally be a threat to Russell's class-based account of number (a threat which would have persisted despite all the twists and turns in that account in reaction to the discovery of Russell's Paradox: it is by no means clear how to reconcile monism and the axiom of infinity); and this, together with the idea that mathematical truths are at best less than wholly true, should have been the primary focus of his hostility which, in its early concentration on relations, misidentified its target. It is on the rejection of the reality of terms, rather than that of relations, let alone on his muddled and temporary commitment to the doctrine of internality, that we should regard Bradley's more extravagant monistic conclusions as having been based.

Truth

We have seen that it was a standard idealist tactic to appeal to the distinction between everyday truth and ultimate truth, and Bradley extended the use of this tactic by claiming that truth comes in an infinite range of degrees. But it was hard for subsequent philosophers, mostly reared in the ideology of classical logic, and trained to assume that the truth/falsity distinction is a matter of black and white and not to think too hard about such awkward sentences as the not-quite-true "The earth is round," to keep in mind that the idealist account of truth includes such talk of partial and temporary truths: those which suffice for everyday business, and for the practice of science, logic and mathematics, but are metaphysically inadequate in that they lead to contradiction when fully thought through. And even an idealist would hardly have embraced a metaphysics which treated the statements "The earth is round" and "The earth is not round" as both just plain false, with nothing to choose between them when it comes to making a practical decision on, say, whether to take the Flat Earth Society seriously. Thus Moore's saying that it is just obvious that there are contingent truths, and even Russell's demonstration that propositions expressing transitive asymmetrical relations are irreducible and essential for mathematics, were neither of them direct refutations of Bradley's considered views on relations which could always be defended by admission of the claims but denying that they expressed any ultimate truth.

But Russell, as we saw, was inclined to think that such appeals to ultimate truth were just attempts to have one's cake and eat it too, saying dismissively "[A]s though what is true 'in the end' were anything different from what is true" (1907: 138). And this brings out the fact that another major issue between the idealists and those who displaced them is the nature of truth. Russell was inclined to hold that simple isolated judgments such as "I am now seeing a red patch" could be absolutely true, moving from a primitivist (1903: §52) to a correspondence account (1910b). Bradley, in keeping with his monism, thought such detached statements utterly misrepresented the way things are in a reality which is not composed of detachable fragments (1909b): scientific laws, because more inclusive, would for him rate far higher on the scale of truth; but nothing but the whole truth, encapsulating the entire world, would count as absolutely true. Consistently with his monism, however, he rejected the distinction between the world and its representation so that such a complete truth could not in the end be separate from the world itself. Starting with Russell himself (1907: 136, 140), it became standard to refer to Bradley as holding a coherence theory of truth (e.g. Blackburn 1984a: 235, and 1984b: 155–6; Kirkham 1998), and to take seriously Russell's original objection that there are indefinitely many coherent sets of propositions with which a patently false proposition will cohere (e.g. Walker 1989); in fact, though, Bradley thought coherence to be only a test of truth, not its nature – coherence was a test because the world itself is a coherent whole, but the *nature* of truth consists in identity with that world (Bradley 1907: 112–13), and propositions are more true the closer they approach that inexpressible ideal. (Likewise those other alleged coherentists, Blanshard and Joachim.)

So Bradley evaded the quick refutations provided by Moore's appeal to contingency and Russell's appeal to mathematics, by ensuring that his metaphysics was in competition only with rival metaphysical positions, not with common sense or any of the disciplines. Yet, as we have seen, idealists, including Bradley himself, were happy to employ the rhetorical device of appearing to provide vigorous competition for absolutely everybody, so that such quick criticisms were inevitable. Rival metaphysicians, however, are all in the same boat: as soon as one leaves the level of common sense and gets into metaphysics at all, some doctrine which has the same purpose as this idealist one of partial truth is going to have to be deployed at some stage. Russell affected to believe that it was just plain false "that there are no relations and that there are not many things, but only one thing," jibing that "Idealists would add: *in the end*. But that only means that the consequence is one which it is often convenient to forget" (Russell 1959: 56–7, quoting his 1907: 141). Yet those who deploy the weapon of common sense against others' metaphysics have no defense when it is turned against their own, and *in the end*, Russell too, who said "I do not believe in complex entities of this kind," a kind exemplified by "all the ordinary objects of daily life" (1918, CP8: 170; LK: 190), had to face the task of giving an account of their status that would preserve (at least many) ordinary truths about them while discarding ordinary falsehoods. Russell's account appealed to the notion of logical construction: statements apparently about ordinary things are *really* about quite different, metaphysically approved, things; but this strategy for saving the appearances is just the counterpart of the idealist's appeal to partial truth. And the program of logical constructions, which stumbled at the first hurdle of Russell's Paradox in its paradigm application, namely logicism, proved in the end to be no more satisfactory a working philosophical tool than that of partial truth. But things must have looked different at the outset, and the eclipse of the latter by the former must be explained at least in part by the notion of the logical construction's at least appearing to offer a workable program, which its predecessor did not, completely lacking as it did a metric for determining whether, say, Snell's Law is more or less true than Boyle's Law.

Conclusion

We have seen that the history of the debates between idealists and their most influential critics is one of confusion, misunderstanding and inconclusiveness. It should by now be clear that the gradual replacement in Anglophone philosophy of idealist logic and metaphysics by the range of doctrines, methods and attitudes that we have come to think of as characteristic of the various forms of analytic philosophy was not the result of any clear refutation of some central tenets of the former (although the early analytic philosophers, and perhaps even some of their readers, might have thought the opposite). Indeed, the dubious benefit of hindsight makes it look puzzling that this major shift in philosophy should ever have taken place. How did the near-total, if gradual, collapse of monistic idealism come about?

What begins to emerge as one considers the intellectual, social, and political changes which preceded and accompanied the decline of idealist metaphysics is that it was as it were overtaken by events, increasingly looking like a philosophy of the past. Consider, for example, the developments in nineteenth-century mathematics already mentioned. These had largely taken place without reference to, let alone support from, German philosophy, the inspiration of the British Idealists. While there might be argument about whether idealism could *in principle* give a sensible account of mathematics, there is no doubt that, as Russell pointed out in §4 of *The Principles of Mathematics*, Kant's treatment of the subject could no longer stand; nor can it be disputed that the idealists had given it little explicit attention let alone the veneration with which it was regarded by Russell. Mathematics came to provide both fresh problems and fresh methods for philosophy, and the idealists, lacking a philosophical program to rival that of e.g. logical empiricism, could not keep up.

But general disenchantment with idealist metaphysics was also founded, historically speaking, on taking seriously what might seem one of its strongest recommendations, that is, its apparent ability to provide a substitute for the consolations of religion in the face of the weakening of traditional Christianity. To understand why it began to fall out of favor more generally, we should observe that, once the lessons of Darwin had been fully absorbed, the need for a replacement began to wane, and room became available for metaphysical views less overtly uplifting. Indeed, spiritual uplift began to look positively distasteful in the aftermath of the Great War. Appeal to idealism had played a prominent role in justifying the University of Oxford's training the servants of the British Empire (Quinton 1971). But after the War's prolonged agony of organized mass killing in the clash of imperial ambitions, British Idealism's central tenet of the spirituality of the universe was offensive when not merely laughable, particularly in the light of its Germanic origins and their unfortunate association with the ideology of the lately demonized Prussian state. The world had become a bleaker place, and Moore's mockery – "Reality may be spiritual, for all I know; and I devoutly hope it is" (Moore 1903: 3) – began to find a wider audience among philosophers, for whom Absolute Idealism could eventually become an object of derision (e.g. Ayer 1936: 36).

References

Apart from the lists of convenient abbreviations, in each case the citation date shown following the author's name is the date of original publication. A separate date is shown for the edition cited only where this differs from the original. Page references in the main text are, unless otherwise stated, to the latest edition cited.

Bradley's writings

Bradley, F. H. (ETR) *Essays on Truth and Reality*, Oxford: Clarendon Press, 1914.
—— (WLM) *Writings on Logic and Metaphysics*, edited by James W. Allard and Guy Stock, Oxford: Clarendon Press, 1994.
—— (1883) *The Principles of Logic*, London: Oxford University Press, 1922.
—— (1893) *Appearance and Reality*, Oxford: Clarendon Press, 1930.
—— (1897) Appendix, Index and Explanatory Notes to *Appearance and Reality*, 2nd edn, Oxford: Clarendon Press, 1930.

—— (1907) "On Truth and Copying," *Mind*, repr. ETR, pp. 107–26, and WLM.

—— (1909a) "On Our Knowledge of Immediate Experience," *Mind*, repr. ETR: 159–91, and WLM.

—— (1909b) "On Truth and Coherence," *Mind*, repr. ETR, pp. 202–18, and WLM.

—— (1909c) "Coherence and Contradiction," *Mind*, repr. ETR, pp. 219–44, and WLM.

—— (1910a) "On Appearance, Error and Contradiction," *Mind*, repr. ETR, pp. 245–73.

—— (1910b) Supplementary Note to 1910a, *Mind*, repr. as "Supplementary Note II," in ETR, pp. 276–88.

—— (1911a) "Reply to Mr. Russell's Explanations," *Mind*, repr. as "Supplementary Note III," in ETR, pp. 288–92. (This may also be found in *The Collected Papers of Bertrand Russell*, vol. 6: *Logical and Philosophical Papers 1909–13*, London: Routledge, 1992, 394–7.)

—— (1911b) "On Some Aspects of Truth," *Mind*, repr. ETR, pp. 310–52.

—— (1922) "Additional Notes" and "Terminal Essays," in *Principles of Logic*, 2nd edn, London: Oxford University Press, 1922.

—— (1924) "Relations," in *Collected Essays*, Oxford: Clarendon Press, 1935, pp. 629–76. (This uncompleted but important essay was not in fact published until 1935, but I have given the date of its final form as this is a better indication of when Bradley was writing: in 1935 he had been dead for more than ten years.)

Russell's writings

Russell, B. (CP6) *The Collected Papers of Bertrand Russell*, vol. 6: *Logical and Philosophical Papers 1909–13*, London: Routledge, 1992.

—— (CP8) *The Collected Papers of Bertrand Russell*, vol. 8: *The Philosophy of Logical Atomism and Other Essays 1914–19*, London: George Allen & Unwin, 1986.

—— (CP9) *The Collected Papers of Bertrand Russell*, vol. 9: *Essays on Language, Mind and Matter 1919–26*, London: Routledge, 1994 (repr. of Unwin Hyman, 1988).

—— (LK) *Logic and Knowledge*, edited by Robert C. Marsh, London: George Allen & Unwin, 1956.

—— (PE) *Philosophical Essays*, London: George Allen & Unwin, 1966; originally published with somewhat different contents and different pagination, 1910.

—— (1897) *An Essay on the Foundations of Geometry*, London: Routledge, 1996.

—— (1900) *A Critical Exposition of the Philosophy of Leibniz*, London: Allen & Unwin, 1937.

—— (1903) *The Principles of Mathematics*, London: Allen & Unwin, 1937.

—— (1904) Letter to Frege 12 Dec 1904, in G. Frege, *Philosophical and Mathematical Correspondence*, Oxford: Basil Blackwell, 1980, pp. 166–70.

—— (1907) "The Monistic Theory of Truth," in PE, pp. 131–46.

—— (1910a) Letter to Bradley of 9 Apr 1910, in CP6, pp. 349–51.

—— (1910b) "On the Nature of Truth and Falsehood," in CP6, pp. 116–24 (also in PE).

—— (1911) "Knowledge by Acquaintance and Knowledge by Description," in CP6, pp. 148–61.

—— (1914) *Our Knowledge of the External World*, rev. edn, London: George Allen & Unwin, 1926.

—— (1918) "The Philosophy of Logical Atomism," in CP8, pp. 160–244 (also in LK).

—— (1919) *Introduction to Mathematical Philosophy*. London: George Allen & Unwin.

—— (1924) "Logical Atomism," in CP9, pp. 160–79 (also in LK).

—— (1927) *An Outline of Philosophy*, London: George Allen & Unwin.

—— (1959) *My Philosophical Development*, London: George Allen & Unwin.

Other writings

Arnauld, A., and P. Nicole (1662) *The Art of Thinking* [the Port-Royal *Logic*]. Indianapolis, IN: Bobbs-Merrill, 1964.

Ayer, A. J. (1936) *Language, Truth and Logic*, 2nd edn, London: Gollancz, 1946.

Baldwin, T. (ed.) (1993) *G. E. Moore: Selected Writings*, London: Routledge.

Blackburn, S. (1984a) *Spreading the Word*, Oxford: Clarendon Press.

—— (1984b) "Is Epistemology Coherent?," in Manser and Stock (1984), pp. 155–72.

—— (1994) *The Oxford Dictionary of Philosophy*, Oxford: Oxford University Press, 1996.

Blanshard, B. (1939) *The Nature of Thought*, 2 vols, London: George Allen & Unwin.

Bosanquet, B. (1895) *The Essentials of Logic*, London: Macmillan.

—— (1911) *Logic*, 2 vols, Oxford: Clarendon Press.

Craig, E. J. (ed.) (1998) *The Routledge Encyclopedia of Philosophy*, 10 vols, London: Routledge.

Edwards, P. (ed.) (1967) *The Encyclopedia of Philosophy*, 8 vols, New York: Macmillan.

Findlay, J. N. (1984) "Bradley's Contribution to Absolute-Theory," in Manser and Stock (1984), pp. 269–84.

Frege, G. (1892) "On Concept and Object," in *Translations from the Philosophical Writings of Gottlob Frege*, edited, trans. Peter Geach and Max Black, 2nd edn, Oxford: Basil Blackwell, 1960, pp. 42–55.

Green, T. H. (1874) Introductions to Hume, *Treatise of Human Nature*, in Green (1885–8), vol. 1.

—— (1880) "Review of J. Caird: *Introduction to the Philosophy of Religion*," in Green (1885–8), vol. 3.

—— (1883) *Prolegomena to Ethics*, ed. A. C. Bradley, Oxford: Clarendon Press (5th edn, 1906).

—— (1885–8) *The Works of Thomas Hill Green*, edited by R. L. Nettleship, 3 vols, London: Longmans, Green (6th impr., 1911).

Griffin, N. (1983) "What's Wrong with Bradley's Theory of Judgment?" *Idealistic Studies* 13: 199–225.

—— (1998, 2003) "Russell, Bertrand Arthur William," in E. Craig (ed.), *The Routledge Encyclopedia of Philosophy Online*, London: Routledge, http://www.rep.routledge.com/article/DD059.

Hume, D. (1739) *A Treatise of Human Nature*, Oxford: Clarendon Press, 1888.

Hylton, P. (1990) *Russell, Idealism, and the Emergence of Analytic Philosophy*, Oxford: Clarendon Press.

Irvine, A. (2004) "Bertrand Russell," in E. Zalta (ed.), *The Stanford Encyclopedia of Philosophy* (Fall 2004 edn), Stanford, CA: Centre for the Study of Language and Information, Stanford University, http://plato.stanford.edu/archives/fall2004/entries/russell/ (first posted 1995, last revised 2004).

Joachim, H. H. (1906) *The Nature of Truth*, London: Oxford University Press.

Kant, I. (1787) *Critique of Pure Reason*, trans. N. Kemp Smith., 2nd edn, London: Macmillan, 1974.

Kirkham, R. L. (1998) "Truth, coherence theory of," in Craig (1998), vol. 9, pp. 470–2.

Locke, J. (1706) *An Essay Concerning Human Understanding*, 5th edn, London: Dent, 1965.

Mander, W. J. (1994) *An Introduction to Bradley's Metaphysics*, Oxford: Clarendon Press.

Manser, A. R., and G. Stock (eds) (1984) *The Philosophy of F. H. Bradley*, Oxford: Clarendon Press (repr., corrections 1986).

McTaggart, J. M. E. (1906) *Some Dogmas of Religion*. London: Edward Arnold, 1930.

Mill, J. S. (1843) *A System of Logic*. London: Longmans, Green, 1900.

Moore, G. E. (1899) "The Nature of Judgment," in Baldwin (1993), pp. 1–19.

—— (1903) "The refutation of idealism," in Baldwin (1993), pp. 23–44.

—— (1919) "External and Internal Relations," in Baldwin (1993), pp. 79–105.

Quinton, A. (1971) *Absolute Idealism*, Dawes Hicks Lecture on Philosophy, British Academy, Oxford: Oxford University Press, 1972.

Rorty, R. (1967) "Relations, Internal and External," in Edwards (1967), vol. 7, pp. 125–33.

Walker, R. C. S. (1989) *The Coherence Theory of Truth*, London: Routledge.

Warnock, G. J. (1958) *English Philosophy since 1900*. London: Oxford University Press.

Wisdom, J. A. T. D. (1942) "Moore's Technique," in P. A. Schilpp (ed.) *The Philosophy of G. E. Moore*, La Salle, IL: Open Court, pp 421 50.

Wittgenstein, L. (1921) *Tractatus Logico-Philosophicus*. London: Routledge & Kegan Paul, 1933. (1921 is the date of publication of the original *Logisch-philosophische Abhandlung*; the first English translation appeared in 1922.)

Wollheim, R. (1959) *F. H. Bradley*, 1st edn, Harmondsworth: Penguin.

—— (1969) *F. H. Bradley*, rev. edn, Harmondsworth: Penguin.

Further reading

J. Allard, *The Logical Foundations of Bradley's Metaphysics: Judgment, Inference, and Truth* (New York: Cambridge University Press, 2005), offers an interpretation of Bradley's *The Principles of Logic*, focusing on the problem of inference and connecting his logic with his metaphysical monism and account of truth. P. Basile, *Experience and Relations: An Examination of F. H. Bradley's Conception of Reality* (Berne: Paul Haupt, 1999), gives a remarkably clear, accurate and wide-ranging account of Bradley's thought.

S. Candlish, *The Russell/Bradley Dispute and Its Significance for Twentieth-Century Philosophy* (London: Palgrave Macmillan, 2007), offers an extended discussion of several of the central themes of this article, with full attention to detail and context. P. T. Geach, *Truth, Love and Immortality* (Berkeley and Los Angeles: University of California Press, 1979), gives a clear and readable account of McTaggart's philosophy. A thorough account of Russell's views in his idealist period, i.e. prior to his criticisms of idealism discussed in this chapter, can be found in N. Griffin, *Russell's Idealist Apprenticeship* (Oxford: Clarendon Press, 1991). P Hylton, *Russell, Idealism, and the Emergence of Analytic Philosophy* (Oxford: Clarendon Press, 1990), is the standard source for this topic, unusually strong on the idealist background, including T. H. Green. Early chapters of J. Passmore, *A Hundred Years of Philosophy*, 2nd edn (London: Duckworth, 1966; 1st edition, 1957), provide good, orthodox accounts of idealism and its critics. (There is a 1968 paperback of the second edition under the Penguin imprint.) A. Quinton, *Absolute Idealism*, Dawes Hicks Lecture on Philosophy, British Academy, 1971 (Oxford: Oxford University Press, 1972), is a standard source for this topic, brief and well written. T. L. S. Sprigge, *James and Bradley: American Truth and British Reality* (Chicago; La Salle: Open Court, 1993), contains a long discussion of these two philosophers and their interactions, giving insight into the comparisons and contrasts between idealism and pragmatism. D. Stove, *The Plato Cult* (Oxford: Blackwell, 1991), contains several chapters severely and amusingly critical of idealism.

23

BRITISH IDEALISM: PRACTICAL PHILOSOPHY AND SOCIAL RESPONSIBILITY

David Boucher

Introduction

British Idealism became the pre-eminent philosophy in Great Britain and most of the English speaking world for four decades from the early 1870s until the First World War. Even when under attack from the new generation of Realists such as Bertrand Russell, the early Wittgenstein and G. E. Moore, it could still muster its heavyweight battalions in the form of F. H. Bradley and Bernard Bosanquet until the mid-1920s. Beyond that its philosophical influence waned, but was never completely extinguished. R. G. Collingwood picked up the baton, for example, but distanced himself somewhat from the philosophical principles of the school of T. H. Green, by relying for inspiration on the critical Idealist philosophy of the Italians Giovanni Gentile, Benedetto Croce and Guido de Rugierro. Collingwood passionately opposed the Realist critics of Green, among them Moore and Russell from Cambridge, but also John Cook Wilson, E. E. Carritt, H. H. Prichard, W. D. Ross and H. W. B. Joseph from Oxford. While fundamentally it was their philosophies with which he disagreed, it was their practical consequences of which he despaired.

In his view, both Prichard and Joseph had become radical sceptics, the former more so than the latter which resulted in pernicious tendency to part company with all positive doctrines by a process of critical disintegration. In relation to moral philosophy this entailed rejecting over two thousand years of believing that its purpose was to think out more clearly the issues involved in conduct in order to act better (Collingwood 1978: 47). Prichard contended that moral philosophy was purely theoretical, focusing upon the workings of the moral consciousness, without interfering with its practice, and Russell had jettisoned ethics altogether from the body of philosophy. The implication was fundamental. The generation of students brought up on T. H. Green's idealism had been taught that clear philosophical thinking is essential to informing and improving conduct, whereas those exposed to Realism were told that philosophical thinking is a disinterested activity with no contribution to make to practical conduct. It was, then, the separation between theory and practice to which Collingwood objected, and not least of which because it denied the role of the committed intellectual, and absolved philosophy of social responsibility.

Even though the School of Green was often called British Hegelianism, it nevertheless rejected a fundamental component of his philosophy, that is, the view that the philosopher comes on the scene too late to make any practical difference to that about which he philosophises. Collingwood admired in British Idealism the crusading spirit in sending young men and women out into the world to make a practical contribution to eradicating social ills. Green's adeptness in working through abstract issues and threading them through practical situations was a quality often remarked upon by his associates (Leighton 2004: 73). It should be cautioned, however, that the relationship between theory and practice is complex. Green believed that political and moral theories will always be slow to a catch-on and provide direct practical guidance. They may nevertheless have an indirect effect especially in providing obstacles to reform, as in Green's view utilitarianism was doing in his own day (see Wempe 2004: 155–91).

In rejecting the individualism upon which British Empiricist philosophy was posited, the British Idealists rejected the atomistic conception of society that they associated with utilitarianism, but also the metaphor of a naturalistic organism that Herbert Spencer popularized.

The social responsibility of the philosopher

Although critics constantly blamed Hegel for the practical implications of his political philosophy, he contended that it had no such contribution to make to practical life. In *The Philosophy of Right* he contends that the philosopher, like the owl of Minerva takes flight only with the coming of dusk. He arrives on the scene only to make sense of it in retrospect. For most of the British Idealists, with a few exceptions, notably F. H. Bradley, his follower Michael Oakeshott and J. M. E. McTaggart, this was simply a mistaken view; philosophy was integrally related to practical life and should be directed to improve the condition of society. It was a crusading philosophy in which the universe was implicated, and the work of the philosopher was to raise the mind of the working man to the level of considering principles (see Jones 1906: 20, and 1910: x).

The British Idealists were the dominant group in developing social work and in demonstrating the relevance of philosophy to ordinary life by positing the unity of theory and practice (Vincent and Plant 1984: 116). They believed that personal sacrifice was necessary for the betterment of society. Enjoyment of the higher pleasures, Green argues, if they are not somehow pertinent to social reform cannot be condoned, "while the mass of men whom we call our brethren, and whom we declare to be meant with us for eternal destinies, are left without the chance, which only the help of others can gain for them, of making themselves in act what in possibility we believe them to be" (Green 1899: §70).

Theirs was an ethical view of society in which a social purpose was constantly in the process of realisation through the individuals whose good was identical with that of society. In ethics they subscribed to the normative theory of "perfectionism" in answering the question of the ultimate good or supreme value in human life (Sullivan 2007: 233). Their answer was the realisation of the potential or capacity, inherent to different degrees in every individual, assisted by a system of rights recognised by the community or state, and valued because of their contribution to the common good.

Knowledge was for them a prerequisite to developing one's capacities, and education, in its broadest sense, the great social leveller that was to empower everyone. The Idealists were passionately engaged in extending university education to women, and through extension schemes, out into the broader community. In this and in Public Administration, for example, the spirit of Idealism endures. Jose Harris has argued that the Idealist frame of reference became dominant in the inter-war period (Harris 1992: 123), and indeed remains at the centre of the modern welfare state.

Idealism and the state

The state is a notoriously amorphous concept and no more so than in the writings of the British Idealists. It may among them refer to nothing more than the apparatus of government, but more often than not it encompasses everything that we think of as society and the nation, and all of the associations that comprise them. It even takes on a spiritual, or a quasi-religious character in being the agent through which freedom reveals itself in the world. Those who wish to ridicule or vilify the Idealists refer to the sometimes expressed remark that the state is the march of God on earth.

Some critics of the Idealists such as C. E. M. Joad, L. T. Hobhouse and J. A. Hobson, have with some justification stood in awe and trepidation at the mighty Leviathan that emerges out of the torrent of prose devoted to its all enveloping and pervasive purview. The tendency has been to view the language of absolutism, talk of its higher purpose, and its moral personality as a license for the arbitrary infringement of citizen's rights. Hobson, for example, complained that the Prussian theory of the state of which he thought British Idealists exponents, compelled the individual to regard himself, his will and activity as subservient to the state; the instrument of its super-personality (see Hobhouse 1951; Hobson 1915; Joad 1924).

It is true that for the Idealists the state is a moral agent with ideals and purposes which it formulates and pursues for the good of society as a whole in its capacity as the sustainer of rights and the most adequate representative of the general will (Ritchie 1891: 138; and Bosanquet 1997: 276–7). This does not mean that the individual must be blindly obedient. It is important, as Bosanquet suggests, to distinguish the ideal character of the state, and states as they exist empirically (Bosanquet 1997: 274–6). The state for the Idealists could only be a moral absolute when acting in conformity with its purpose of promoting and sustaining the common good. The state cannot make people moral and no individual can delegate responsibility for making judgements about what is right and wrong (Jones 1919). States that do not conform to their purpose, and instead promote factionalism invite moral resistance.

There could be no unconditional duty on the citizen to obey the law, "since those laws may be inconsistent with the true end of the state, as the sustainer and harmoniser of social relations" (Green 1917: 148). Similarly for David Ritchie, a law that is so contrary to person's conscience must be disobeyed at any cost, or one's self respect and character are degraded (Ritchie 1997: 153–4). Bosanquet, despite his reputation for restricting the compass of the state, believed that it had an important role to play in ensuring equality of education. Such equality of chances that education provides was ten times more important than any other (Nicholson 2007: 214). To achieve this Idealists such as Green, Caird, Jones, Haldane, Bosanquet, Muirhead and others agitated for legislation; assisted government commissions by giving evidence and serving on them; held offices on school boards; actively extended university education to women; and enthusiastically supported extra mural, or university extension schemes and the Workers' Educational Association by organising and delivering lectures.

The role of philosophy in social reform and practical politics was indispensable because it provided a vision of the whole against which the social reformer could measure the shortcomings of society. Philosophy and morality are the ways in which we confront the world in order to make our intellectual and practical life intelligible (Jones 1909: 22). No static and fixed philosophy can do justice to a subject matter as complex as society whose elements are constantly changing. Idealism, in comparison with other creeds is a philosophy "which distorts reality less; which finds reasonable room for more of its facts; which leaves over fewer incoherencies; and which does not forget Spirit, which alone is omnipresent where truth is in question" (Jones 1909: 297).

The philosopher should not be confused with the preacher. The London Ethical Society that sought to bring university education closer to the public, including the working man, should have as its aim, Bosanquet contended, "not moral suasion", which is merely medicinal, but instead the provision of new resources in "life, intellect, and feeling – which one may compare with wholesome food – not so much to help our hearers as to put them in a position to help themselves" (Muirhead, ed., 1935: 48). In other words, the state should only do so much as to enable individuals to act, and not try to bring about substantive ends on their behalf. In that motivation is at the heart of a moral act, state compulsion takes an action outside of the moral sphere. State action must comply with three conditions for its justification. In the first place there must be an impediment frustrating the capacity for potential action. Second, enabling the individual to harness the resources of character and intelligence must outweigh the restrictions imposed. And third, that it is better that an act be done, even if it is compelled through fear of legal reprisal, than it is not done at all (Bosanquet 1923: 179–80; also see Sweet 1997: 172). This is not a magical formula that can be mechanically applied to impose *a priori* limits on state activity. Each case is different and experience and judgement have to be brought to bear in weighing the consequences against the benefits (Nicholson 2007: 223–4). There can be no presumption, even in Bosanquet's case, that there would be *per se* a predisposition among Idealists to individualism in preference to collectivism.

Individualism and socialism

Individualism and Socialism, or liberalism and collectivism, at the end of the nineteenth and the beginning of the twentieth century, were the reference points to which the activity of the state was referred (Greenleaf 1983: vol. 2). The British Idealists, whose ethical concerns embroiled them in all the leading political controversies of the times, were naturally drawn towards this debate. Their predisposition to overcome contradictions by transcending them in a synthesis led them to conclude that the opposition of individualism and socialism was false, and that each in some way, implied, or absorbed into itself, the other (Caird 1888, 1997; Jones and Muirhead, 1921: 317–31; Ritchie, 1902: 43–65; Bosanquet 1893). The extension of the role of the state, for them, if guided by the right principles, constituted a move away from recalcitrant freedom, or the idea of negative liberty, towards reconciliatory freedom, or positive liberty. Even though Bosanquet is often viewed as more resistant to state socialism than his fellow Idealists, and more of an advocate of private property and *laissez-faire* capitalism he was nevertheless committed to the same principles by which to judge whether a social ill was best left to individual enterprise or state legislation. He was not in sympathy with either the subjectivist, nor hedonist justification of the free market because he believed that both justifications rested on an impoverished view of human nature in which individuals are viewed as isolated sentient appropriators driven by demand and motivated by calculating consumption. Such a view neglects the capacity of humans to realise a higher self through participation in art, religion, philosophy and social morality. The achievement of the elevated life, or highest good, may well be best facilitated by private property and a free market. Indeed, in terms of the individual trajectory in life private property gives an outward unity and continuity that is necessary for the inward unity of the person's moral life (Bosanquet 1895: 310). Bosanquet's support for allowing free market forces to prevail, or for social or state intervention was always based on the capacity of whatever institutional arrangements were in place to facilitate or impede individuals in realising their natures. On the whole he tended to think that private property and *laissez-faire* capitalism performed the task adequately (see Sullivan 2007: 238), but where they did not, as Muirhead remarks, Bosanquet was "prepared for any amount of collectivism" on the condition that it was guided by "the essentials of happiness and character" (Muirhead 1935: 48).

Some of the Idealists were happy to term the extension of state activity as socialism, but on condition that it be differentiated into what they called the "right" and "wrong" types. The right type is that which equates morality with freedom of choice. It is the justification of this right type of intervention that came to influence the Christian Socialism of R. H. Tawney, who was as closely associated with Idealism as some of its main exponents, including Bosanquet, Jones and Haldane (Carter 2003).

Jones and his fellow idealists sought to give theoretical credibility to the view that the opposition between individualism and socialism was false. Starting from the assumption that society is a unity in diversity he suggests that the individual and society are mirror images of each other. The person is nothing less than "society individualized, its impersonal forces focussed" (Jones 1910: 284). The individual and the state are mutually inclusive and thus the person is "society individuated" making social criticism "the most difficult of all criticism, for it is self-criticism" (Jones 1910: 34). Ritchie maintains that society develops into a synthesis of the opposites of individualism and socialism, retaining what is precious in individualism while at the same time facilitating a social stability which individualism had destroyed (Ritchie 1917: 69). "True" individualism, that is the self-realisation of one's capacities in the context of society, is promoted by the true or "right" kind of socialism which uses the state to advance freedom of choice by removing the obstacles to the development of individual freedom. On this conception of organic unity the welfare of the whole is inseparable from the welfare of the individuals who comprise it. Whatever the environment brings to bear upon the individual it is the latter whose consciousness is penetrated and who transmutes the forces that permeate his, or her, life. The organism is not a mechanical entity whose forces collide like billiard balls, but a self-conscious unity in which individuals realise themselves as ethical beings, and society realises itself in them. "My volitions are my volitions, they issue from the secret places of my will; but if I examine my will, from which they emanate, I find it saturated with that portion of the world which has been the object of my experience" (Jones 1912: 32). The State is not able to make men moral, and it is up to individuals to make the most of external conditions. It was the role of the state to ensure that those external conditions were available for all to seize. The large cities, suffering the consequences of rapid industrial growth, had to answer the question of the extent to which the community should intervene in order to improve the condition of the disadvantaged (Caird 1997: 180).

Both individualists and socialists presuppose that any increase in the activity of the state limits the opportunities for individual enterprise: they agree that the extension of the state encroaches upon individual will. They differ about whether the encroachment is desirable. Both, however, are mistaken, and the controversy itself absurd because the individual is through and through social. The coming of socialism could with equal credibility be viewed as the coming of individualism. Measured against the criterion of what the state can do for the individual, and what the individual can do for himself, or herself, and society, it is self-evident that individual freedom (not capricious choice), and increased state activity have grown hand in hand. Socialism, rightly understood, provides the individual with opportunities, deepening the personality, and facilitating the conception and pursuit of higher purposes. The "true" socialism, then, empowers individuals and generally makes them stronger and better citizens. Socialism does not diminish individualism but enables more people to enjoy opportunities arising from an advanced social life.

It would be a mistake to think that the British Idealists were all equally and strongly in favour of state intervention. Green and Bosanquet, for example, were much less so than the more politically radical Ritchie, Jones, Haldane or Muirhead. Their differences over this issue amount to achieving the right balance between individual and collective responsibility. Bosanquet applauds the necessity of civilised societies exercising their wills through the state in order to encourage progress in the condition and quality of its members' lives, but not to the extent that it weakens the character of the individual by transferring responsibility to the state. It is the point at which individual responsibility may be undermined by too much state intervention over which the Idealists differ. It is not a matter of applying abstract principles, but of taking each case on its merits and examining the empirical conditions in the light of the general principles of what may or may not contribute. Bosanquet and Green err on the side of self-reliance. Without the will for moral self-improvement moral character would not be improved by state interference by providing better housing conditions. They both took a hard line on Poor Relief because they believed that there was a strong possibility of it undermining individual character. Bosanquet, for example, believed that there must be a judicious balance between the voluntary private actions of individuals to effect social reform and legislative and public provision. He was not at all averse to the latter because he thought it the responsibility of a civilised society "to exercise initiative through the State with a view to the fullest development of the life of it members" (Bosanquet, 1895: 290). On the other hand, Jones and Muirhead were less sceptical of the efficacy of state intervention. They nevertheless believed in the gradual, or evolutionary approach, rather than the revolutionary extension of state activity. As Muirhead cautioned: "What the state could do was to remove hindrances to the free action of what for lack of a better name moralists call 'conscience' – a faculty that might be deadened rather than quickened by a hasty ill-considered collectivism ..." (Muirhead 1942: 160).

The state and social justice

Social Justice for the Idealists is not merely equated with redistributive justice. They advocated redistribution not to uphold principles of fairness, impartiality, mutual benefit, desert or entitlement -- those most commonly used today – but instead to secure the economic, social and moral conditions necessary for self-realisation. They are not talking about a procedural theory of justice which is neutral between different conceptions of the good. Social justice had to steer a judicious course between character and circumstances. The success of altering the circumstances had always to be measured in terms of the opportunities provided for the development of character. Because this was always a pragmatic judgement requiring detailed knowledge of the problem Idealists would always disagree on what was the most appropriate course to steer (cf. Carter 2003: 83).

Their concern for physical well-being was to lay the foundation for spiritual development, and where the material interests conflict with the moral the former must give way to the latter. Rights, then, were not always trumps. The British Idealists hold, with Aristotle, that justice "is a sort of equality," requiring that equals be treated equally. But this begs the question, as Aristotle acknowledged, equal in respect of what? (Aristotle 1988: 1282b). For the Idealists each person is equal in so far as he or she has capacities for self-realisation, but does not possess these capacities to the same degree. In other words, their attainments may be different according to their capacities, but each person should have an equal opportunity to make the best of himself or herself.

The aim of social justice must be the removal of impediments to such attainments. This may require active state intervention on the condition that it enhances human freedom by enabling individuals to exercise their capacities. At a time when society is becoming ever more complicated Green believed that "social justice" demands that society should be so organised that: "whatever his station, whether peer or peasant, capitalist or labourer, townsman or countryman, should have a fair chance of making the best and most of himself" (Green 1997: 385). The advantages and disadvantages of society must be distributed impartially. Individuals have claims and these must be at the basis of social justice in taking account of relative circumstances, acknowledging inequalities and asking what if anything should be done to adjust them. Justice, while important, may not always and in all circumstances be the social ideal.

For Bosanquet, for example, justice has two components. The first is that of keeping a rule, ensuring that likes are treated alike, and unalikes differently, with no arbitrary exceptions to the rule. The second is the justice of the rule itself. Individual claims have to be seen in their social context. It is these claims that form the basis of social life, but to acknowledge some may undermine that very social life itself. The demands of the safety and preservation of the state, of patriotism, and of strong community responsibility require an ideal justice that does not manifest itself in equality of treatment. Ideal justice transcends the claims and rights of individuals and posits the idea of obligations to the whole. What Justice requires is the impartial development of individual capacities, balanced with social stability which requires the prudent management of necessary social performances by individuals (Bosanquet 1968: 195, 198 and 229).

There is no suggestion of an egalitarian theory of justice in terms of equality of outcomes. Idealists condone inequalities of outcomes because each person has different capacities. Inequalities of income can be justified if the competition for, and rewards of office can be shown to be reasonable and fair. Inequalities in social goods are acceptable if they are consequent on merit, that is, if they are deserved. Social justice attempts to eradicate the undeserved inequalities which result from social circumstances. It is a threshold theory of social justice in which each person should have the social impediments removed that hinder the development of his or her talents. No one should be disadvantaged by age, sex, social class, or race.

The limits of state intervention could not be determined by abstract principles. Rapid industrialisation and a political apparatus ill-equipped to respond to the new social squalor and deprivation that mitigated against spiritual growth had to be addressed by enlarging the functions of the state. The need for social reform was urgent and there was an imperative need for the community to "interfere" in order to ameliorate the sorry condition of the poor and disadvantaged (Bosanquet 1968: 195, and Caird 1997: 173).

The state is a deliberative personality, and has rights. T. H. Green, for example, devotes much more space in *The Principles of Political Obligation* to justifying the rights of the state than he does the rights of the individual (Green 1917: 160–243, §§157–246). As with the individual person the justification for the exercise of such rights is that they contribute to the common good. The purpose of exercising its right to legislate is not simply to play the role of the policeman in keeping order and preventing individuals colliding, but also to make a positive contribution to the growth of human personality (Jones and Muirhead 1921: 324; and Caird 1997: 180–1).

What this means is the development of a character that is disposed to do good because it is good, and that this good that is common is the same for everyone. It is a disposition on each person's part to perfect, or make the best of, the humanity in himself, or herself, and in every other person. It is not a matter of satisfying material interests because they may conflict and those of one person may be satisfied at the expense of another. The common good is spiritual, or moral, and in which all individuals must participate if the full realisation of human potential is to be attained. The moral interest may conflict with the material, and should it do so the latter must give way to the former.

In an age when social welfare and state intervention in all aspects of life are unquestioned assumptions from which very few dissent, the radical politics of the British Idealists in the latter part of the nineteenth and early part of the twentieth centuries is difficult to appreciate. Education, sanitation, regulation of the externalities of production, social welfare and health and safety were all areas into which the state feared to tread. The social reformer had to combat not only deep-seated inertia, but also modern scientific thought. The pervasiveness of evolutionary theory and the political uses to which it was put constituted a significant barrier to state "interference" in natural processes. Advocates of state interference had to counter the arguments of those, such as Herbert Spencer, who believed that it was at once impractical and immoral to interfere with the natural processes of evolution because the unintended consequences of allowing the unfit to survive were imponderable. In order to give credibility to their social policies Idealists had first to enter into the technicalities of evolutionary and heredity debates. Put in its starkest form, they denied social determinism, and particularly the Lamarkian idea of inherited character that Spencer tended to favour. They also denied genetic determinism which was gaining credibility from the powerful theories of August Wiesmann and his germ plasm theory. The Idealists contended that we inherit certain capacities, and that these do indeed limit the extent of our potential, but that nevertheless those capacities require the right social environment in which to flourish. The state's role, then, was to ensure that the social environment did not constitute an impediment to the development of those capacities, and therefore it should endeavour to remove the obstacles, or hinder the hindrances, to human attainments. It had to do this without, at the same time diminishing individual responsibility (see Boucher and Vincent 1993: 61–86).

The test of any extension of state activity must always be the question of whether the individual personality was being offered a wider opportunity to develop, and development in this sphere could never be effected by a weakening of individual responsibility. Henry Jones expressed this best in his Dunkin Lectures on Sociology delivered at Manchester College, Oxford, 1904. There he argued that: "The limits of Socialism are not to be fixed by any abstract opposition of State and Individual. The criterion of State action is the good life of the individual: and, the criterion of individual action the good of the State. The common good must always assume a personal form" (Jones 1904: fols. 8–9).

The idea of citizenship is central to the social philosophy of British Idealism because it is integral to freedom and individuality. Citizenship is a moral category that implies self development within a civilised state. The freedom associated with citizenship is not that of the absence of constraints, but of acting in conformity with the higher good, or general will of the community. Choice is of the essence of freedom, and to act rationally is to make the right choices consistent with one's higher interests. The existence of poverty, social deprivation and degrading conditions of work are simply not compatible with these ideals. In opposition to classical liberalism British Idealism made economics subordinate to morality, and viewed the state not as a referee in a free-market society, but as the institution charged with sustaining the moral community and system of rights that make social life possible.

Take, for example, the issue of temperance. It raises a series of questions that go to the heart of British Idealism. W. Vernon Harcourt – one of two Liberal MPs for Oxford – objected to such legislation on the grounds that it restricted freedom of choice, and that no one could be forced to be moral. Indeed, how could the restriction or abolition of the availability of alcohol increase the capacity of the individual for moral growth, when the opportunity for such growth, namely temptation, was being taken away? From the point of view of idealism, however, to be a slave to drink is to be a slave to one's passions; and to diminish one's capacity for freedom of choice. The degeneracy into which excess in drink drives the individual has social consequences in the inability to provide and sustain a loving moral family environment in which children may grow and flourish, and which arouse passions in men that make them a danger to women. With the diminution of drunkenness, the incidence of child neglect, poverty, and the sexual abuse of women would be much less (Green 1997: 223–4).

Intemperance imposes a heavy burden on society in the form of crime and pauperism, and society has every right to intervene to lessen the burden (Green 1997: 450). Green was not averse to the use of legislation to diminish temptation, especially in relation to the sale of alcohol. For Green limiting the sale of intoxicating liquor was one of the most pressing social issues because "drink is the greatest impediment to freedom that exists in England" (cited in Nicholson 1985: 517). Intemperance, he believed, was a "horrible evil" and that those who wish to eradicate it by persuading others of the error of their ways should lead by example and develop the habit of total abstinence (Green 1997: 321–2). Education and "comfortable habits" were unlikely to check the vice among the degraded and hopeless (Green 1997: 451). Liquor legislation would remove one of the obstacles to moral improvement. In this respect education needed a helping hand before it could transform social (or antisocial) values.

Lord Haldane, too, believed in a multifaceted approach that involved legislation and better social conditions. He believed that the provision of adequate housing, a living wage, and education would considerably alleviate most social problems. If the problems of poverty, housing and ignorance were properly addressed, Haldane optimistically predicts, "Temperance will follow" (Haldane 1918: 11). In Haldane's view the state should give every man and women the right to such education capable of liberating them from circumstances that were not of their making and which prevent "them individually from having a real chance in life" (Haldane 1929: 301). Jones, a disciple of Caird and admirer of Green, thought the function of the state in the last resort was educative. He maintained that: "… the State itself is, in the last resort, an educational institution" (Jones 1910: 58) charged with teaching only one thing, that is, "the nature of the good" (Jones 1919: 117). This did not mean merely formal education through schools and universities, but through every institution of the nation, including the economy (Jones 1910: 58). Every social relation must be moralised as it stood, and every workshop was to be a school of virtue.

Idealism and human rights

We have seen how the Idealists conceived of the state as a sustainer of rights, and how the state itself is a bearer of rights and responsibilities. The relationship in which the state stands to the individual rights holder is very different from that posited in social contract and natural rights theories. The abstractness of natural rights made them susceptible to being harnessed in the service of any cause, and the radical heritage from which they sprang was no impediment to their adoption by extreme right-wing radicals vehemently opposed to state "interference", championing individual responsibility against the state erosion of liberties. This, in Ritchie's view, is a fault of abstract theorising in general: "it is the characteristic of an abstract theory to admit of quite opposite applications" (Ritchie 1891: 87). Ritchie complained that "the theory of natural rights is used by Anarchists to condemn the existing inequalities of social conditions, and by Conservatives to check attempts on the part of government to remedy these inequalities" (Ritchie 1894: 15).

The British Idealists were politically astute enough to know the importance of taking popular ideas which were evaluative/descriptive in their character, and extending their descriptive meaning, while retaining favourable evaluative connotations. They were able to take popular ideas alien to their way of thinking and transform them into something consistent with the Idealist world view. They very effectively appropriated the language of their opponents, while transforming its meaning in the process.

The Idealist theory of rights consciously attempts to overcome the deficiencies in the individualism of both social contract and utilitarian theories. Idealists explored not individuals as such, but the relations of individuals to each other and to the state which they saw as essential to, or even constitutive of, individuality (Jones 1997: 3 and 25). Rights belong to individuals as members of a community. They are justifiable claims recognised as rational and necessary for the common good of society. The common good is inconceivable apart from membership in a society (Green 1899: §183), and the self that is to be realised through moral activity is "determined, characterised, made what it is by relation to others" (F. H. Bradley 1927: 116; cf. Green 1899: §184).

The British Idealists were hostile to Natural Rights traditionally conceived, but not fundamental rights *per se*. They took issue over the source of such rights, but nevertheless believed that they could be a convenient fiction (Ritchie 1998: 440). In so far as there are fundamental rights necessary for the life of a community and which could be justified as contributing to the common good those rights could legitimately be termed "natural rights" providing they were not attributed to an abstract individual independent of communities. Green marvellously epitomised the Idealist position when he contended: "without society, no persons" (Green 1899: §288; cf. Ritchie 1894: 102, and Bosanquet 1923: 144). Green's objection against Natural Rights theorists such as Spinoza, Hobbes and Locke was that they fail to appreciate the development of a person through the development of society. They mistakenly believe that the higher essence of the person is somehow separable from society and its norms (Tyler 1997: 174).

There is a remarkable degree of agreement among the British Idealists on the shortcomings of natural rights theories. They reject the equation of might and right that you find in descriptive versions of Natural Rights, as for instance in Hobbes's conception of a pre-social state of nature in which rights have no correlate obligations. They also reject intuitionism in Natural Rights theories which posit an external law standing above and outside of social existence, discoverable through the exercise of right reason, and to which our actions must conform – as, for example, in Locke's normative theory of Natural Law and Natural Rights. The Idealists all agree that rights are powers or capacities to do or desist from doing something, or to require something of others. In addition, there are no rights without social recognition, whether by society or the state, or both. This is part of what it means to have a right. The justification for such rights can only be made with reference to their contribution to the common good (see Gaus 2006: 209–35). In other words, they must link up with the real interests of individuals, and have palpable and demonstrable benefits or utility for the community. The requirement that they are socially recognised and contribute to the common good counters the charge that they are capricious and arbitrary, or so abstract that they are incapable of being translated into moral injunctions.

Let's take Green as a starting point. The Idealists were conceptually clear in distinguishing descriptive and prescriptive Natural Rights. Hence, in criticism of Hobbes and Spinoza, for example, Green denies that what they call rights are rights at all because they have no second-party duties attached to them. Green wants to distinguish between what Hobbes and Spinoza call rights in a state of nature, and rights proper. The former are mere natural powers or liberties, whereas the latter imply or are correlated with duties (Martin 1986: 108 and 110). For him rights exist, not independently of society, but independently of political society, in, for example, the family or even among a group of slaves in their relations with each other, and with the wider community in which they live. Rights are those powers of an individual that are recognised by others as being necessary for the attainment or achievement of a good in which they all share. Rights are, for Green, made by recognition. This is not, of course a sufficient condition, because rights must also be powers, and contribute to the common good. The possession of such powers, or capabilities, guaranteed by society, and those that society exercise over the individual, are justifiable only on the grounds that they are a necessary prerequisite to fulfilling "man's vocation as a moral being"

(Green 1917: §21, 41). This social conception of rights entails, for Green, correlative obligations.

What is pernicious about the idea of pre-social natural rights is the idea that they are not derived from society and that the state is created to protect them. It encourages irreverence to the state on the assumption that the individual has rights against society irrespective of fulfilling any duties that he or she may have towards society. It encourages the corrosive view that powers exercised by the state are restraints upon individual freedom that may rightly be defied as far as is safely possible (Green 1917: §32; also see Richter 1996: 232).

The justification for any particular right is that it tends to promote the true or common good. This differs from the utilitarian justification for respecting civil rights. The utilitarian thinks that rights are useful in that they assist in the attainment of pleasure or the avoidance of pain. We ought to respect them because "the ultimate sanction is fear of what the consequences would be if we did not" (Green 1917: §23, 43). What both theories have in common, Green maintains, is that neither grounds actual rights in prior Natural Rights. Instead, they are grounded in the conception of an end, the greatest happiness of the greatest number, or of moral self-realisation, to which the maintenance of a system of rights contributes. The justification of rights in terms of social ends is for Green teleological. Here he acknowledges that utilitarianism is able to avoid the defects of social contract theories by offering a justification of rights in terms of the ends which they sustain, but it ultimately fails because of its hedonism in refusing to acknowledge that there can be any other object of desire than pleasure (Green 1899: §373, and 1919: §23). Utilitarianism fails to account for moral actions which cannot be reduced to the pursuit of pleasure or happiness.

David Ritchie presses the relation between Idealism and Utilitarianism, suggesting that the former has transformed and incorporated the insights of the latter by allying it with advances in evolutionary theory. Some elements of Benthamism could be retained, particularly its critical spirit of questioning existing institutions and proposing radical reconstructions (Ritchie 1891: 80). However, Ritchie argues, that when people appeal to justice against society what they are really doing is claiming that a higher form of society should replace the lower, and it would be better if they were honest about it rather than appeal to abstract justice and Natural Rights (Ritchie 1894: 106–7). One of the faults of intuitionism in ethics is that people are likely to disagree over matters of conscience, but they are just as likely to disagree on what is useful as they are on what is right or just. Ambiguity is the hallmark of both what is just and what is useful. The latter, however, is capable of further elaboration because something is useful only in relation to something else. Useful for what is the question that utilitarianism stands in need of reformulating. Although Benthamism famously rejects the rhetoric of Natural Rights it nevertheless clings to the abstract individualism that is characteristic of both doctrines

Utilitarianism in its traditional forms homogenises individuals as moral atoms, attributing to them similar feelings which can be quantified, and a quantity of pleasures to be distributed among them. Institutions are required to justify themselves in terms of their contribution to the general happiness. In Ritchie's view, Benthamist utilitarianism is susceptible to the same range of criticisms as Natural Rights theories. The appeal to nature in Natural Rights and social contract theories attempts to reconcile the abstract individualism of the multiplicity of isolated instincts with the abstract universalism of the consent of humanity. Utilitarianism similarly appeals to nature in assuming a uniformity of human nature over time and place. It combines the abstract individualism of treating every person as a discrete unit, with the abstract universalism of the greatest happiness which is taken to have an existence divorced from the concrete individuals who are singularly capable of experiencing it.

The truth of Utilitarianism does not emerge until its errors are corrected by the doctrine of evolution, and in particular that of natural selection. While Bentham and Austin contributed significantly to the divorce of jurisprudence and ethics from vague appeals to Natural Law, their constructive ethical theories remained too closely allied to hedonism. The positive side of utilitarianism needed to be separated from hedonism by being reinterpreted in the light of evolutionary theory, and their jurisprudence needed to be impregnated with an evolutionary and historical spirit (Ritchie 1998: 127).

Ritchie contends that in relation both to nature and each other, societies are engaged in a struggle for existence. Good and bad are judged in relation to what contributes to success or failure in the struggle. Mutual dependence or inclusiveness of society and the individual means that the good of a community provides us with the only criterion of what an individual ought to do, because it is identical with the good of the individual. The good associated with a community changes over time and the standard of our moral judgement progresses in relation to it. In an allusion to Green Ritchie argues that as the range of persons we take into account when we think of the common good broadens, our moral judgements develop. Moral judgements vary because societies are variable in character, and conflicts of duties and of moral judgements occur in complex societies because each individual belongs to many overlapping communities. In the course of the evolution of societies, among self-reflective and intelligent human beings, natural selection becomes transformed into rational selection. It is at once feasible and desirable that some social organisms cease to be fit for purpose and become superseded by more sophisticated types into which individuals become absorbed. This constitutes a transition from Individualistic Utilitarianism to Evolutionary Utilitarianism and comprises a Copernican revolution in perspective from the eighteenth-century view that society was instituted to secure the protection of pre-existing Human Rights to the modern view influenced by advances in scientific thinking that "natural rights" are those fundamental rights that *ought* to be recognised by a society, and judged wholly from the point of view of society. Social cohesiveness requires any society to adhere to certain ground rules or conditions which inform the actions of their individual members: "In order to hold together, every society formally or informally agrees to observe, or let us say, finds itself compelled to observe these conditions of common life, and thereby creates rights and duties for its members" (Ritchie 1891: 39; also see 1917: 106).

The point that Green wants to make is that even if civil and political rights could be shown to derive from Natural Rights, we are still left with the question why certain powers are recognised by people in their relations with others as powers that ought to be exercised, or secured for possible exercise. In other words, it is no justification of a right to maintain that it is natural. A right presupposes that the right holder is a member of society, in which some common good is recognised by its members as their ideal which is pertinent to each of them. The powers or rights that are recognised, and indeed regulated by that recognition, are deemed necessary for, or contributory to, the common good (Green 1919: §26, 45). The foundation of rights, then, is not that they are natural, but that the individual has a capacity to conceive of a good that is common, the same for himself, or herself, as for others, and in being moved to act by that conception. Rights are what enable that capacity to be realised (Green 1919: §29, 47). It is this capacity to conceive of a good that is the same as that of others and to act upon it that for Green defines the moral person. The rights or powers necessary to the fulfilment of such a conception of the moral person are innate or natural in a different sense from that associated with the Natural Law and Natural Rights traditions. People are not born with them. They do not have them outside of society, and they do not inhere in individual persons. Furthermore they are not the creation of law or custom. They are "natural" because "they arise out of, and are necessary for the fulfilment of, a moral capacity without which a man would not be a man" (Green 1919: §30, 47; cf. Watson 1919: 222–3; Jones 1919: 148; Ritchie 1894: 270).

What then determines rights? The British Idealists basically follow the same pattern. The idea of recognition is crucial to their arguments. This aspect of their theory was criticised by W. D. Ross who argued that in order for something to be recognised, it must already exist (Ross 1930: 51). Gaus maintains, however, that by recognition Green means it in the sense that is used when the chair of a committee recognises the floor, or a speaker, that is, gives the person recognised a certain status (Gaus 2006: 211).

David Ritchie, like Bosanquet and the rest of the British idealists, was concerned to advance our understanding of rights beyond the negative conception of liberty. The individual in Natural Rights theories, and indeed in utilitarian criticisms of them, was nothing but an abstraction (Otter 1996: 160–6). Even though Spencer advanced a form of Natural Rights theory, he nevertheless adhered to the negative conception of liberty held by Jeremy Bentham and J. S. Mill (Sweet 1997: 11–16).

With advances of our understanding of society in terms of evolutionary theory, and by use of the historical method in exploring institutions and problems, it was now possible to think of the ideal associated with Natural Rights theories, not as something fully formed and definitive, but as something whose revelation is gradual in the education of the human race. Following Hegel, Ritchie maintained that any satisfactory theory of rights or of the state must rest upon a philosophy of history (Ritchie, 1894: 286). For him philosophical reasoning went hand in hand with historical studies. In Ritchie's view, the common good which acts as the criterion of appropriate conduct changes from age to age and depends upon what actions and virtues contribute to the realisation of the well-being of society at different stages of its evolution.

The state and international relations

The social recognition theory of rights and its dependency on a moral community with a state apparatus to promote and enforce claims, along with the elevated place that the state has in Idealist theory has led many critics to the conclusion that British Idealism was not internationalist in its scope, nor capable of transcending state borders. Indeed, critics have tended to take what they believe to be the implications of Hegel's view of international relations, and transpose them onto the thought of the British Idealists. Among the more extreme critics, the British Idealists are regarded as worshippers of the state, supporters of militarism, and realists in international politics (see Hobson 1909: 248–61, and 1916: 307–8). These criticisms were directed at all of the Idealists, but Bosanquet came in for special attention because of the obtuseness of his language. Even one of his staunchest supporters regretted this tendency in his writings (Jones 1896: 206). Lord Haldane, as a prominent Liberal politician, of course, bore the brunt of public disapproval for his "Prussianism" in popular newspapers and magazines (Koss 1969: Chs 3 and 6).

It is important, however, not to misunderstand their method of analysis. Idealism is a philosophy that is committed to giving a rational account of what is here and now. That does not mean that they were committed to justifying everything that exists here and now, but they nevertheless had to account for everything. As Caird, suggests: "Men have come to see the necessity of realising the nature of the universe in which they live, and of dealing with the facts as they are, and not as they would like them to be" (Caird 1907: 193). Hence when they explained the condition of international relations in their day, such explanations could easily be taken as justifications. There is a big difference between giving an account of things as they are, and things as they might be. The state and its relations were facts of life, and stood in need of rational explanation, but that did not mean that it was not possible or desirable to transcend the state. Although the idealists differ on the extent to which morality at an international level had already transcended the state, they did not differ on the desirability of ever increasing the moral community beyond the state to include everyone in the human race among those we treat as our neighbours. Even David Ritchie, who was less internationalist than most of the Idealists, could argue that it was an arbitrary arrest in thought to suppose that the nation state was "the highest and final type of political society" (Ritchie 1901: 150). The modern invention of federalism, coupled with representative democracy, opens up new ways of pressing toward peace. Smaller states can now become parts of larger political units without compulsion by despotic emperors. Within the federation peace becomes possible by means of international arbitration, and a federal army to enforce decisions and police possible rebellions (Ritchie 1901: 156–7). In one of the most widely read political tracts of the 1890s Ritchie made it quite clear that his Hegelianism did not preclude a league or federation of nations.

The general will, he argued, "realises itself in different forms, in the family, the clan, the city, the nation, perhaps some day in the federation of the world" (Ritchie 1894: 69–70).

British Hegelians like Ritchie, Bradley, Bosanquet, Watson and Sorley maintain that the morality of states is different in kind, and not only in degree, from that of individual or private morality. Sorley, for instance, argues that "National morality is not the same thing – cannot be expressed by the same laws – as individual morality" (Sorley 1890–1: 433; cf. 1916). Bosanquet suggests that the state, unlike the individual person, sustains the moral world and does not itself act in one. Its moral function and duties are different from private morality (Bosanquet 1968: 284, and 1915: 137).

Some of the British Hegelians, J. S. Mackenzie, A. C. Bradley and Jones, for instance, held views much closer to those of Leonard Hobhouse and J. A. Hobson who believed that the morality of states must conform to that of individuals. While there might be differences in detail there could be no differences in kind. An honourable man would not do anything for the state that he would not be prepared to do in his private conduct, acting on the same moral principles (Hobhouse 1972: 204–6; also see Clarke 1978: 68). Hobson, for example, thinks that there are considerable differences to be observed between the actual moral conduct of states and individuals, but maintains "that does not imply any essential difference in the actual ideal of the conduct of the two" (Hobson 1909: 259–60). Mackenzie maintains that in passing from the morality of the individual to that of the state "we need not introduce any change in our fundamental principle" (Mackenzie 1901: 20). On the issue of individual and national self-sacrifice he suggests that in both cases a lesser good may be sacrificed for a higher where the criterion is the greater good of mankind and the preservation of the ancient and eternal values upon which the best in humanity depends. Furthermore, the power of the state, for Mackenzie "is simply an organised extension of the power of individuals" (Mackenzie 1916: 78; cf. A. C. Bradley 1915: 46–59). To give another instance Jones maintains that all occupations or stations in life afford men opportunities for acting morally or immorally. The only difference between the office of a statesman and that of the ordinary individual "is that it gives him opportunities of doing right and wrong on a larger scale" (Jones 1910: 122). Nations and individuals share a spiritual destiny in a world that is morally one, and "there cannot be one morality for men, and another, or none at all, for the state" (Jones 1916: 56).

Irrespective of the differences among the British Hegelians over the question of the identity of individual and state morality, they all maintain that the state is a moral agent performing a moral function in relation to its citizens. They maintain that morality is relative to one's situation and that the functions and duties of any moral individuality, including the state, are commensurate with its station and the capacity and purpose with which it is charged.

There was, many of the British Idealists believed, in their different degrees, a genuine possibility of a General Will emerging out of the existing international cooperative ventures, such as the Empire, or in the relations which Canada, the United States of America and Great Britain enjoy with each other (see for examples,

Haldane 1928: 49–93; and Watson 1919: 273). Internationalism was perhaps more to the forefront of those Idealists who had emigrated as ambassadors of Idealism to Australia and Canada, and who felt the social sinews of a common sympathy stretch over continents and oceans (Hughes-Warrington and Tregenza 2008: 89–108). For all of the Idealists there is no opposition between political right and cosmopolitan right, that is, the obligations of a citizen and the obligations of the person towards humanity, because it is through the state that we most effectively contribute to the development of higher ideals and the establishment of a general will among nations.

There was nothing sacrosanct about the organisation of the state and there was no reason with the development of a wider morality why sovereign states could not be superseded by a gradual extension of the community within which a common will prevailed. Green maintains that there is a consciousness of a good and of participators in it even in the most primitive of communities, Reason and the consciousness of the unfulfilled potential of a common rationality lead us to acknowledge wider and wider circles of people who have claims upon us and who are capable of participating in the common good. He contends that: "It is not the sense of duty to a neighbour, but the practical answer to the question Who is my neighbour? that has varied" (Green 1899: 247). Furthermore, it is not the idea of a cosmopolitan humanity that needs to be explained, but the retreat from it by sectional interests and privileged classes who are prepared to lend their weight to any counter-theory that furthers their exclusive ends. The existence of conventions and usages functioning as and constituting a code of morality in the international sphere is considered to be already far advanced by Caird, Sorley, Mackenzie, MacCunn, Jones, Watson, A. C. Bradley and Haldane. Bosanquet and Bradley, however, are more sceptical. They acknowledge that the unifying process of individuals in organised wholes would eventually supersede the limits of the state, but that there had been very little advance in that direction so far (F. H. Bradley 1927: 205). Bradley did not doubt that right existed between states, but it was not in the context of "a visible community," and to take moral rules that pertain to citizens and turn them into abstractions by applying them everywhere was indefensible (F. H. Bradley 1927: 205, and 1935: 22).

Conclusion

I have tried to show that while Idealists may differ in their conclusions on substantive political issues, they were nevertheless united on the level of principles. Applying these principles always required a thorough knowledge of the circumstances; necessitating fine judgements about the balance required, for example, between altering the social environment, while at the same time affording character the opportunities for moral development. The British Idealists were committed to the idea of the social responsibility of the public intellectual, which entailed taking a position on pressing practical political issues. They believed that it was the role of the philosopher to take a lead on social and moral issues.

References

Aristotle (1988) *The Politics*, edited by Stephen Everson, Cambridge: Cambridge University Press.

Bosanquet Bernard (1893) "The Antithesis between Individualism and Socialism Philosophically considered," (1890), repr. *The Civilization of Christendom and Other Studies*, London: Sonnenschein.

—— (1895) *Aspects of the Social Problem*, London: Macmillan.

—— (1915) "Patriotism in the Perfect State" in Eleanor Sidgwick *et al.*, *The International Crisis in Its Ethical and Psychological Aspects*, London: Humphrey Milford; Oxford University Press.

—— (1918) *Some Suggestions in Ethics*, London: Macmillan.

—— (1923) *The Philosophical Theory of the State*, 4th edn, London: Macmillan.

—— (1968) *Social and International Ideals*, London: Macmillan, 1917; New York: Krauss repr. 1968.

—— (1997) "The Function of the State in Promoting the Unity of Mankind," in D. Boucher (ed.) *The British Idealists*, Cambridge: Cambridge University Press.

Bosanquet, Bernard (1997) "The Function of the State in Promoting the Unity of Mankind" (1997), in D. Boucher (ed.) *The British Idealists*, Cambridge: Cambridge University Press.

Boucher, D., and A. Vincent (1993) *A Radical Hegelian: The Political and Social Philosophy of Henry Jones*, Cardiff: University of Wales Press; New York: St Martin's.

Bradley, A. C. (1915) "International Morality," in Eleanor Sidgwick *et al.*, *The International Crisis in Its Ethical and Psychological Aspects,*, London: Milford.

Bradley, F. H. (1927) *Ethical Studies*, 2nd edn, Oxford: Clarendon Press.

—— (1935) "Limits of International and National Self-sacrifice," in *Collected Essays*, 2 vols., Oxford: Clarendon Press.

Caird, Edward (1888) *The Moral Aspect of the Economical* Problem, Glasgow: Maclehose.

—— (1907) *Lay Sermons*, Glasgow: Maclehose.

Caird, Edward (1997) "The Present State of the Controversy between Individualism and Socialism," in D. Boucher (ed.) *The British Idealists*, Cambridge: Cambridge University Press.

Carter, Matt (2003) *T. H. Green and the Development of Ethical Socialism*, Exeter, UK: Imprint Academic.

Clarke, Peter (1978) *Liberals and Social Democrats*, Cambridge: Cambridge University Press.

Collingwood, R. G. (1978) *An Autobiography*, Oxford: Oxford University Press.

Dimova-Cookson (2000) "T. H. Green and Justifying Human Rights," *Collingwood and British Idealism Studies*, 7: 97–115.

Gaus, Gerald (2006) "The Rights Recognition Thesis: Defending and Extending Green," in Maria Dimova-Cookson and W. J. Mander (eds) *T. H. Green: Ethics, Metaphysics, and Political Philosophy*, Oxford: Clarendon Press, pp. 209–235.

Green, T. H. (1899) *Prolegomena to Ethics*, 4th edn, Oxford: Clarendon Press.

—— (1917) *Lectures on the Principles of Political Obligation*, Bernard Bosanquet (ed.) London: Longmans Green.

—— (1997) *Collected Works of T. H. Green*, vol. V, *Additional Writings*, edited by Peter Nicholson, Bristol, UK: Thoemmes Press.

Greenleaf, W. H. (1983) *The British Political Tradition*, vol. 2 of *The Ideological Heritage*, London: Methuen.

Haldane, R. B. (1918) *The Future of Democracy: An Address*, London: Headley.

—— (1928) "Higher Nationality: A Study in Law and Ethics," repr. *Selected Addresses and Essays*, London: Murray. (The essay was written in 1913.)

—— (1929) *An Autobiography*, London: Hodder & Stoughton.

Harris, Jose (1992) "Political Thought and the Welfare State 1870–1940," *Past & Present*, 135: 116–41.

Hobhouse, L. T. (1951) *The Metaphysical Theory of the State: A Criticism*, London: Macmillan. (First published 1918.)

—— (1972) *Democracy and Reaction*, edited by Peter Clarke, London: Harvester. (This edition includes Hobhouse's introduction to the second edition of 1909.) (First published 1904.)

Hobson, J. A. (1909) *The Crisis of Liberalism: New Issues of Democracy*, London: King.

—— (1916) "The War and British Liberties," *The Nation*, 10 Jun.

—— (1915) *Democracy after the War*, London: Allen & Unwin.

Hughes-Warrington, and Ian Tregenza (2008) "State and Civilization in Australian New Idealism, 1890–1950," *History of Political Thought* 29: 89–108.

Joad, C. E. M. (1924) *Modern Political Theory*, Oxford: Clarendon Press.

Jones, Henry (1896) *Browning as a Philosophical and Religious Teacher*, Glasgow: Maclehose.

—— (1904) "The Dunkin Lectures on Sociology," R.V. Lennard's notes, Nov 1904. Ms. TOP OXON e 417, Bodleian Library, Oxford.

—— (1906) *Francis Hutcheson, a Discourse Delivered in the University of Glasgow on Commemoration Day, 18 April 1906*, Glasgow: Maclehose.

—— (1909) *Idealism as a Practical Creed*, Glasgow: Maclehose.

—— (1910) *The Working Faith of the Social Reformer*, London: Macmillan.

—— (1912) *The Immanence of God and the Individuality of Man*, Manchester: Rawson.

—— (1919) *The Principles of Citizenship*, London: Macmillan.

Jones, Henry, and J. H. Muirhead (1921) *The Life and Philosophy of Edward Caird*, Glasgow: Maclehose, Jackson & Co.

Koss, Stephen E. (1969) *Lord Haldane: Scapegoat for Liberalism*, New York: Columbia University Press.

Leighton, Denys P. (2004) *The Greenian Moment: T. H. Green, Religion and Political Argument in Victorian Britain*, Exeter, UK: Imprint Academic.

Mackenzie, J. S. (1901) "The Use of Moral Ideas in Politics," *International Journal of Ethics* 12: 1–23.

Mackenzie, J. S. (1916) "Might and Right," in Louise Creighton *et al.*, *The International Crisis: The Theory of the State*, London: Milford; Oxford University Press.

Martin, Rex (1986) "Green on Natural Rights in Hobbes, Spinoza and Locke," in *The Philosophy of T. H. Green*, edited by Andrew Vincent, Aldershot, UK: Gower Publishing.

Muirhead, J. H. (1900) "What Imperialism Means," *Fortnightly Review*, no. 404, n.s. (1 Aug).

—— (ed.) (1935), *Bosanquet and His Friends*, London: George Allen & Unwin.

—— (1942) *Reflections by a Journeyman in Philosophy*, London: Allen & Unwin.

Nicholson, Peter (1985) "T. H. Green and State Action: Liquor Legislation," *History of Political Thought* 6: 517–50.

—— (2007) "Bosanquet and State Action," in William Sweet (ed.) *Bernard Bosanquet and the Legacy of Idealism*, Toronto: University of Toronto Press.

Otter, Sandra den (1996) *British Idealism and Social Explanation*, Oxford, Clarendon Press, 1996.

Richter, Melvin (1996) *The Politics of Conscience: T. H. Green and His Age*, Bristol, UK: Thoemmes Press.

Ritchie, David George (1891) *The Principles of State Interference*, London: Swan Sonnenschein.

—— (1894) *Natural Rights: A Criticism of Some Political and Ethical Conceptions*, London: Swan Sonnenschein.)

—— (1900–1) "The Moral Problems of War – In Reply to Mr. J. M. Robertson," *International Journal of Ethics* 11: 493–514.

—— (1901) "War and Peace," *International Journal of Ethics* 11: 137–58.

—— (1902) "Law and Liberty: The Question of State Interference" (1891), repr. *Studies in Political and Social Ethics*, London: Sonnenschein.

—— (1917) *Darwinism and Politics*, 4th edn, London: Swan Sonnenschien.

—— (1997) "The Rights of Minorities," in D. Boucher (ed.) *The British Idealists*, Cambridge: Cambridge University Press.

—— (1998) *Collected Works*, vol. 6: *Miscellaneous Writings: Articles and Discussion, Book Reviews and Critical Notices Letters*, edited by Peter Nicholson, Bristol, UK: Thoemmes Press.

Ross, W. D. (1930) *The Right and the Good*, Oxford: Clarendon Press.

Sorley, W. R. (1890–1) "The Morality of Nations," *International Journal of Ethics* 1: 427–46.

—— (1916) "The State and Morality," in Louise Creighton *et al.*, *The International Crisis: The Theory of the State*, London: Milford; Oxford University Press.

Sullivan, Kevin (2007) "Bosanquet, Perfectionism, and Distributive Justice," in William Sweet (ed.) *Bernard Bosanquet and the Legacy of British Idealism*, Toronto: University of Toronto Press.

Sweet, William (1997) *Idealism and Rights: The Social Ontology of Human Rights in the Political Thought of Bernard Bosanquet*, Lanham, MD: University of America Press.

Taylor M. W. (1993) *Men versus the State: Herbert Spencer and Late Victorian Individualism*, Oxford: Clarendon Press.

Tyler, Colin (1997) *Thomas Hill Green (1836–1882) and the Philosophical Foundations of Politic*, Lewiston, NY: Edward Mellen.

Vincent, Andrew, and Raymond Plant (1984) *Philosophy, Politics and Citizenship*, Oxford: Blackwell.

Watson, John (1919) *The State in War and Peace*, Glasgow: Maclehose.

Wempe, Ben (2004) *T. H. Green's Theory of Positive Freedom: From Metaphysics to Political Theory*, Exeter, UK: Imprint Academic.

Further reading

Colin Tyler, *Idealist Political Philosophy: Pluralism and Conflict in the Absolute Idealist Tradition* (London: Continuum, 2006), addresses some of the more common misapprehensions of some of the ideas of selected thinkers. David Boucher and Andrew Vincent, *British Idealism and Political Theory* (Edinburgh: Edinburgh University Press, 2000), relates important themes in British Idealism to modern political philosophy. A scholarly, reliable and thorough study of the key thinkers and ideas is Peter

Nicholson's *The Political Philosophy of the British Idealists: Selected Studies* (Cambridge, Cambridge University Press, 1990). Andrew Vincent and Raymond Plant, *Philosophy, Politics and Citizenship* (Oxford: Blackwell, 1984), is an excellent integration of the relation between the philosophical and social issues.

Part VI

AMERICAN PRAGMATISM AND IDEALISM

24

C. S. PEIRCE

Vincent Colapietro

Charles Sanders Peirce was born in 1839 into a prominent family in Cambridge, Massachusetts, graduated from Harvard College in 1859, received a master's of science from the Lawrence Scientific School in 1862, taught at the newly founded Johns Hopkins University from 1879–84 (when he was dismissed under mysterious circumstances in the middle of the academic year), and died as a recluse in his home (named Arisbe in honor of the pre-Socratic cosmologists) in Milford, Pennsylvania, in 1914. That is, he was born in the same year as was Ludwig Mond (d. 1909), a German-English chemist, who founded Mond Nickel Company, was born (Mond's company symbolizing scientific technology being subordinated to commercial interests); the year in which Charles Goodyear (1800–60), an American inventor, made possible the commercial use of rubber by his discovery of the process of "vulcanization"; and that in which John D. Rockeller (d. 1937), an American industrialist who preached the gospel of social Darwinism, was also born. Moreover, Peirce graduated from Harvard College the year in which Charles Darwin's *Origin of Species* was published, also the one in which the philosophers Henri Bergson, Edmund Husserl, and John Dewey were born. Finally, he died shortly before the First World War, also during the years in which not only the geopolitical world but also the scientific one (especially theoretical physics) was undergoing cataclysmic upheavals.

Portrait of the philosopher as a young scientist

Peirce was the second and favored son of a prominent father (Benjamin Peirce), born into the intellectual capital of the United States in the nineteenth century. He was a child of privilege who in terms of worldly success squandered many of his inherited advantages. Especially in his later years, however, Peirce exemplified nothing less than intellectual heroism, devoting himself indefatigably (without much of an audience and with little hope of a publisher) to work on a variety of topics, including cosmology, pragmatism, semeiotics (or the theory of signs), and most of all logic. The scientifically trained philosopher was, until the end, a philosophically speculative experimentalist who devoted himself to nothing less than offering a guess at the riddle of the Sphinx, that is, the enigma of the universe.

We obtain a sense of the household in which this experimentalist was reared by recalling what he wrote years later in retrospect:

> My father was universally acknowledged to be by far the strongest mathema-
> tician in the country, and was a man of great intellect and weight of character.
> All the leading men of science, particularly astronomers and physicists,
> resorted to our house [in Cambridge, on the edge of Harvard College]; so that
> I was brought up in an atmosphere of science.

Despite the tremendous influence Benjamin wielded over his precocious son, he could
not dissuade Charles from devoting himself to logic. While his father encouraged
Charles to develop his other intellectual talents, ones more likely to secure a means
of livelihood, the son could never take up a subject without ultimately focusing on
questions of methodology – how the study of this subject ought to be conducted. In
one of his earliest but also most famous articles, "The Fixation of Belief" (1877), he
claimed, "each chief step in science has been a lesson in logic" (CP: 5.363; also in EP:
Vol. 1, 111). He was ultimately more interested in the lessons in logic to be learned
from the history of science than the inherently fascinating discoveries made by experimental inquiries, including the most pivotal discovery in the nineteenth century:
"The Darwinian controversy is, in large part, a question of logic" (CP: 5.364; also in
EP: Vol. 1, 111). Specifically, it involved applying the statistical method, so successful
in explaining the behavior of gas molecules, to the fate of biological populations.

Peirce's lifelong love for logic is traceable to a fateful but chance encounter at a
tender time. In another letter, he reported: " ... at the age of twelve or thirteen I took
up, in my elder brother's room a copy of Whately's *Logic*, and asked him what logic
was, and getting some simple [and thus unsatisfactory] answer, flung myself on the
floor and buried myself in it ..." (Wiener [ed.]: 408). Thus began a romance with this
subject lasting a lifetime. Peirce tended to think of himself primarily as a logician,
but for him this word carried a much broader and deeper meaning than it ordinarily
is intended to convey. At the very least, logic in Peirce's sense extends to the logic
of science, of those processes of inquiry in which certifiable discoveries about real
features of the empirical world are, unquestionably, made.

Thus, he was even more concerned with the logic of science than the dazzling
discoveries of specific branches of experimental investigation. His self-defined task
might be described as an endeavor "to take skillful soundings of the experimentalist's
minds" (CP: 5.411; also in EP: Vol. 2, 331) to reveal thereby the depths of such minds.

But Peirce did so *as a philosopher*, steeped in various traditions of philosophical
reflection. In the letter to Victoria Lady Welby (14 March 1909), a rich source of
biographical detail, Peirce noted, immediately after asserting that his "very unusual
gift was for logical analysis":

> I began with German philosophy, having read hardly any of the great English
> school and not very much of such French writers as Maine de Biran, Jouffroy,
> Cousin, etc. For several years I studied the *Kritik der reinen Vernunft*, and
> knew it almost word for word, in both editions [the A or earlier edition and
> the B or later one]. Even now, I fancy there are few who know it better.
> Then I devoted myself for some years chiefly to the scholastics and after that

to Locke, Hume, Berkeley, Gay, Hartley, Reid, Hamilton, etc. I had already read the most readable part of Cudworth & all of Hobbes. Gradually, I gained independent views. (Wiener [ed.]: 417)

Peirce did not begin his study of German philosophy – what for him was his initiation into philosophy – with Kant's first *Kritik*, but with Friedrich Schiller's *Aesthetic Letters*. He recalled in a letter: "the first book of philosophy I ever read (except Whately's *Logic*, which I devoured at the age of twelve or thirteen) was Schiller's *Aesthetische Briefe* where he has so much to say about the *Spiel-Trieb* (or Play-Impulse); and it made so much impression on me to have thoroughly soaked my notion of 'play,' to this day ..." (Wiener [ed.]: 401).

His youthful encounter with philosophical texts was mediated by the imposing presence of Benjamin Peirce. He later recalled:

> When, in my teens, I was first reading the masterpieces of Kant, Hobbes, and other great thinkers, my father, who was a mathematician, and who, if not an analyst of thought ... would induce me to repeat to him the demonstrations of the philosophers, and in a very few words would usually rip them up and show them empty. In that way, the bad habits of thinking that would otherwise have been indelibly impressed upon me by those mighty powers, were, I hope, in some measure, overcome. Certainly, I believe the best thing for a fledgling philosopher is a close companionship with a stalwart practical reasoning. (CP: 2.405)

Benjamin Peirce's influence was firmly, but not narrowly, scientific.

> But my father was a broad man and we were intimate with literary people too. William Story, the sculptor, Longfellow, James Lowell, Charles Norton, Wendell Holmes, and occasionally Emerson, are among the figures of my earliest memories.

Moreover, Benjamin was a deeply religious man who saw no inherent or inevitable conflict between science and religion. Especially in his later life, Charles strove strenuously to show how scientific inquiry might be envisioned as a form of religious worship and, in turn, a religious life as an ongoing attempt to plumb the depths of human experience.

The son of such a father went so far as to describe his philosophy as "the attempt of a physicist to make such conjecture as to the constitution of the universe as the methods of science may permit, with the aid of all that has been done by previous philosophers" (CP: 1.7). Hence, he decisively broke with the deductivist tradition of the dominant schools in Western thought, judging the "demonstrations of the metaphysicians" to be "moonshine," and he advocated an experimental approach in which deductive (or demonstrative) arguments play a subordinate role to the systematic elaboration of conjectures or hypotheses, acknowledged as such. In philosophy as well as elsewhere, the "best that can be done is to supply a hypothesis, not devoid of all likelihood, in the general line of growth of scientific ideas ..." (CP: 1.7). This meant for him taking seriously, far more seriously than even most of his contemporaries were doing, evolution and continuity, two of the ideas most dramatically in line with the actual growth of scientific understanding in the nineteenth century, at least as appraised by Peirce.

Though some prominent thinkers in the nineteenth century (most notably Friedrich Nietzsche) have suggested that science is as much a figment of our minds as any other mode of interpreting the data of our experience, Peirce cannot be counted among them (see CP: 6.503). At least, the natural sciences have effectively and undeniably disclosed certain real features of the empirical world. In calling these features *real*, Peirce is stressing that they do not depend on what you or I or any other finite mind or even some circumscribed community of such minds happens to think.

Except for less than a handful of years, Peirce's life was not that of a professor or instructor. By training and (for much of his life) by occupation, Peirce was a scientist. Shortly after graduating from Harvard College, he took a position as a regular aide (or consultant) with the US Coast Survey. Around this time, he also met William James and married Harriet Melusina (Zina) Fay (16 October 1863), He worked at the Harvard Observatory and the only authored book by him published during his lifetime was *Photometric Researches* (1878), a study growing out of his work at the Observatory. Arguments with Charles W. Eliot, the President of Harvard, over the publication of this work, led to a lasting enmity between the young scientist and this powerful figure. From 1861 to 1891 Peirce was employed as a scientist by the US Coast and Geodetic Survey. His work at the Observatory and the Survey compelled him to come to terms with the practices of measurement within the exacting context of painstaking scientific observation. Of the various facets of such practices with which he thereby became familiar, the pressing need for critical attention to the probability of errors made in such observations was arguably foremost.

Sketch of a "system" as an interminable task

In sketching Peirce's "system" I will provide an overview of his thought. But, the very attempt to do so invites the question: To what extent was Peirce committed to erecting a philosophical edifice, to constructing a philosophical system? Much depends on how we understand the expression *philosophical system*. I would argue that Peirce was primarily a systematic philosopher and (at most) only secondarily a speculative thinker committed to constructing a philosophical system. There are, however, important passages in which he claims either to have articulated the outlines of a philosophical system or to be engaged in the work of accomplishing nothing less than this. But a philosophical *system* suggests a degree of conceptual closure, finality, and completeness that Peirce denied was attainable by the human mind. The most we can ever hope to attain, at any historical juncture, will always be open-ended, provisional, and in no small measure fragmentary. Precisely because human knowledge is such a patchwork affair, woven out of the fabric of approximations, human knowers must commit themselves in a deliberate manner to *systematic* inquiry, connecting as intimately and effectively as they can seemingly disparate spheres of investigation, for the sake of advancing inquiry in these spheres. The hope of a grand synthesis of these disparate fields is, for the most part, not only a vain but also a debilitating hope. The work of systematic inquiry is nonetheless facilitated by the hope of there being genuine affinities between (or among) apparently disparate undertakings. Just as the isolated fact, insofar as such a matter is even conceivable, is of far less heuristic value than connected facts (see CP: 5.594), so insular inquiries carrying no heuristic implications for other research programs are of far less importance than those fecund fields whose organizing concepts have not only immediate applicability to a circumscribed range of experimental questions but also an as yet unknown potential for illuminating the footpaths of other experimental investigators.

Of the various unresolved tensions in Peirce's philosophical authorship, none is more important or illuminating than the one concerning his systematic aspirations. Peirce took from Kant an architectonic conception of philosophical investigation (architectonic being defined by Kant as "the art of constructing systems" [p. 653; see Peirce, CP: 1176–9]). He derived from the inescapable influence of the nineteenth century, however, the need to conceive our defining endeavors as unfinished processes open to radical transformation. In a manuscript written in the last decade of the nineteenth century, Peirce wrote: "As this Century is drawing to a close, it is interesting to pause and look about us and to ask ourselves in what great questions science is now most interested" (CP: 7.267n7). His answer says a great deal about both him and the century in which he was born, for it is that "*the* question that everybody is now asking, in metaphysics, in the theory of reasoning [i.e. in logic], in psychology, in general history, in philology, in sociology, in astronomy, and perhaps even in molecular physics, is the question *How things grow*" (see Darwin 1993: 212; also Peirce, EP: Vol. 2, 373). He immediately goes on to stress the evolution of science itself, thereby providing a crucial piece of evidence for John Dewey's claim that Peirce, living "when the idea of evolution was uppermost in the mind of his generation," "applied it everywhere" (LW: Vol. 11, 482–3). His application of this idea to science and, more broadly, meaning is a defining feature of Peirce's philosophical project.

Insofar as Peirce was a systematic philosopher or engaged in the interminable task of systematic inquiry, he was so by virtue of formulating, refining, and applying a categoreal scheme of indefinite generalizability. Like Aristotle, Kant, and Hegel, he was self-critically committed to such a scheme.

In light of his immense learning and practical involvement in several experimental sciences, Charles Peirce returned, time and again, to several fundamental questions, not least of all "What *guess* are we, at this stage in the history of inquiry, most entitled to make about the nature of the cosmos?" and, "What are we, in addition, entitled to say about this seemingly insignificant species of animal which lacks an intuitive capacity to know anything whatsoever and thus must rely solely on its apparently instinctual ability to guess more or less correctly, enough of the time, at least when conjectures bear upon circumstances related to motility and sociality?" In addition to this *cosmological* and this *anthropological* question, he posed a *methodological* one and, indeed, devoted even more attention to this question than the other two. With respect to these and indeed all other questions, he took his categories to be indispensable aids in goading and guiding in promising directions. Far more than his answers to these questions, these questions themselves define his philosophical interests. Even so, his answers (in a sense, his "doctrines" or positions) help to flesh out our portrait of Peirce as a philosopher.

In the course of addressing these questions, then, Peirce identified and defended a handful of substantive positions. Peirce's evolutionism, tychism (the doctrine of chance) and synechism (the doctrine of continuity) are central to his answer to the cosmological question, whereas his fallibilism, semeiotic, and pragmaticism are most relevant to his largely implicit portrait of the human animal, at least in its unique stance as a logical agent or experimental inquirer. From a Peircean perspective, the human animal is first and foremost a social actor whose practical involvements (including those in the practice of theory, in the work of inquiry) ineluctably assume a dramatic form and thus call for narrative depiction. But the very efforts of this animal to offer such narratives are themselves integral parts of an ongoing dialogue, if only the conversation of the self with itself. The story of such animals, bound together in transformative associations of critical dialogue, is that of agents acquiring and refining the ability to exercise appropriate control over their cognitive processes and heuristic (or theoretical) practices. That is, it is a tale of the increase and refinement of methodological self-consciousness.

Without the resources of later thought, in particular those bearing on our understanding of the forms and functions of narrative as well as the ineliminability and power of metaphor, such a story cannot be adequately told. But the resources of Peirce's philosophy, as critically sharpened in his efforts to provide detailed answers to the cosmological and methodological questions identified above, also at least an implicit response to the anthropological question, represent the monumental achievement of a scientifically trained and metaphysically literate philosopher to offer a wild yet intelligent guess at the riddle of the sphinx. Given the cast of his mind and the range of his interests, it should hardly come as a surprise that this guess took a reflexive turn. For it extended to the *logic* of guessing as central to adequate understanding of experimental inquiry and, moreover, the cosmos as a perfusion of signs (CP: 5.448n1). It is necessary to see Peirce's efforts on these fronts not only in conjunction with those of post-Kantian idealists such as Schelling and Hegel, but also in anticipation of much later theorists striving to formulate a defensible form of anti-reductive naturalism. In this, he was paradigmatically representative of the nineteenth century.

To read Peirce in light of the nineteenth century is to read him, in part, as he invited us to do so. For he was a self-consciously historical thinker who was acutely aware of the tangled history of philosophical thought – moreover, one who took pains to situate his own project vis-à-vis certain especially prominent predecessors, influential contemporaries, and imagined successors. His first public address in 1863, at the age of twenty-four, was entitled "The Place of Our Age in the History of Civilization"! He was deeply engaged in both an ongoing, critical dialogue with a wide array of historical figures and (selected from among these figures) an intense, innovative engagement with a handful of authors, several of whom were themselves pivotal figures in the nineteenth century (including here Schiller and Hegel). Though decidedly a champion of transforming philosophy into a discipline akin to science in the modern, experimental sense, Peirce was equally an advocate of traditional theism and, eventually, a thinker for whom the aesthetic dimensions of our rational pursuits came to assume a fundamental importance.

Peirce at times seemed devoted to nothing more than piecemeal analysis of disparate questions. For example, he once stressed in a letter to William James, "the only thing I have ever striven to do in philosophy is to analyze sundry concepts with exactitude" (Perry 1935: Vol. 2, 438). At other times, however, his commitment to something far less modest is unmistakably in evidence. There are occasions when he announced to his readers his aspiration to erect an edifice outlasting the vicissitudes of time (CP: 1.1). It may seem difficult to square these two sides of his intellectual temperament, but the irrepressible drive of historical agents to transcend not only the confines of their actual history but also the limits of time itself is a dominant tendency in human thought. In Peirce's writings, this drive is discernible.

A high faith in knowledge and a contrite sense of fallibility

Peirce took our scientific knowledge of the real world to be exceedingly slight: "notwithstanding all that has been discovered in Newton's time, his saying that we are little children picking up pretty pebbles while the whole ocean lies before us remains as substantially true as ever, and will do so though we shovel up the pebbles by steam shovels and carry them off by cartloads" (CP: 1.118). He makes this definitive point with utmost precision: "An infinitesimal ratio may be multiplied indefinitely and remain infinitesimal still" (*ibid.*). The character of our knowledge needs to be appreciated no less than the slightness of our knowledge. What Peirce writes of philosophy is also true of science: "Approximation must be the fabric out of which our philosophy [more, generally, all of our knowledge] has to be built" (CP: 1.404).

Peirce's fallibilism makes – or, at least, appears to make – his claims about our knowledge of reality paradoxical, since we can never be absolutely certain that what we claim to know we do in fact know. In one sense, our second-order knowledge (our knowledge about what we claim to know) appears to be more certain than our first-order knowledge (our claims about this or that feature of the world). Indeed, fallibilism is itself the doctrine, rather certainly held and forcefully advocated by Peirce, that we can never be completely certain about what we presume or profess to know. That is, it is an instance of second-order knowledge. In another sense, however, Peircean fallibilism insists that, while we know any number of truths about the world, we are never in the position to know with unqualified certainty or clarity what truths will remain fixed or stable in the ongoing course of human inquiry. Part of the difficulty here is that Peirce is trying to incorporate a historical dimension into his normative account of human knowledge. Truth is, for him, what would in the course of history prove itself to be reliable to an infinite community of experimental investigators. Of course, we live in the meantime, not at the end of history. But the conception of us as participants in an unfolding historical process is critical for carrying on our practices in a responsible and intelligent manner. An abiding mindfulness of our ineliminable fallibility is a defining feature of the experimental attitude, whatever paradoxes might be generated in our efforts to underscore this feature with the emphasis it demands.

One of the most remarkable features of the Peircean approach to understanding experimental inquiry is Peirce's insistence upon studying, in the spirit of science itself, the history of science. The point of this study is that only such an orientation opens the possibility of grasping what science actually is. Long before Thomas Kuhn revolutionized our approach to science, stressing that scientific traditions are just that – traditions, historically evolved and evolving practices prone to theoretical crises, the responses to which involve paradigm shifts in the research programs of these intergenerational communities – Peirce insisted upon a self-consciously *historical* approach to understanding experimental science.

Peirce's understanding of science as first and foremost inquiry informed his vision of education. This point is best made in reference to an institution with which he was all too briefly associated, one representing an institutional innovation in the nineteenth century of immense significance. The first president of Johns Hopkins University Daniel Coit Gilman asked, in his installation address, "What are we aiming at?" He responded to his own question by asserting: "The encouragement of research … and the advancement of individual scholars, who by their excellence will advance the sciences they pursue, and the society where they dwell." For Peirce, however, the advancement of science ought to be the primary and direct goal of such an institution, that of society only a secondary and indirect aim. To be sure, a society in which institutions devoted to the advance of science, for its own sake, have a respected and secure place is, in Peirce's judgment, a society worthy of high praise. But the value of science must be determined, for the most part, on the basis not of external, societal considerations, but of internal, theoretical ones. The integrity of society no less than that of science requires that the influence of science on society and, in turn, the influence of society on science ordinarily be anything but direct and immediate. Scientists ought to be allowed to pursue their inquiries quite apart from supposed benefits to the social order. It is almost certain that many of their investigations will lead to discoveries benefiting not only the wider society but also the specific communities of experimental inquirers to which these inquirers owe their primary allegiance. But the work of scientists is impeded when it is tied too closely to the demands of society. Such, at least, is the strongly held position of Peirce.

As already intimated, this has bearing on his vision of the university. " … the function of a university is the production of knowledge, and … teaching is only a necessary means to that end …" (Wiener [ed.]: 334) "The great mediæval universities, the modern German universities, the new science colleges of England, were never in the least founded for their students' individual advantage, but, on the contrary, because of the expectation that the truths that would be brought to light in such institutions would benefit the state" (Wiener [ed.]: 333). Peirce is quick to stress: "Yet even this is a low view of learning and science." Even (perhaps especially) the readers of a journal such as *Science* are not likely "to be content with the statement that the searching out of ideas that govern the universe has no other value than that it helps human animals swarm and feed" (333–4).

Students "should be made to feel they are doing which was to appear in the digests [or journals] of science and for the accuracy of which they were responsible" (328). They should be accorded the status, and hence the responsibility, of co-inquirers: "instructors and pupils ... compose a company who are all occupied in studying together, some under leading strings and some not" (Wiener [ed.]: 334).

It is important to recall that, in the context of defining the function of the university, Peirce framed his discussion in terms of an adequate conception of human practice. He noted that, in his youth, he "wrote some articles to uphold a doctrine I called Pragmatism. ... That is all very well, when properly understood. I do not intend to recant it." When it is however improperly understood – in particular, when it is taken to assert or imply that theory is for the sake of practice and, in turn, practice is conceived in a narrow and superficial sense, bearing upon merely the egoistic interests of isolated or separable individuals – then pragmatism is as pernicious a doctrine as it is an erroneous one. "Subsequent experience of life has taught me," Peirce confessed in his reflections on education, "that the only thing that is really desirable without a reason for being so, is to render ideas and things reasonable" (Wiener [ed.]: 332), insofar as this is possible. The continuous growth of concrete reasonableness is alone worthy of being identified as the *summum bonum* (the highest good). Reasonableness is rendered concrete by becoming embodied in habits and artifacts, including institutions, not least of all institutions of learning.

However narrow it might appear to us, the function of a university is, above all else, to foster the growth of experimental science. This is a communal task of a self-consciously historical character. As we have already seen, Peirce came to intellectual maturity precisely at the time when profound institutional transformations were taking place in higher education in the United States. This is nowhere more apparent in the founding of the Johns Hopkins University in 1876 and, to a less extent, such institutions as Clark University. The very kind of institution for which he was ideally suited (the research university modeled on German precedent) turned out to be the one from which he would soon be expelled, increasingly living his last years in intellectual exile from any institutional home. His ideal of an unlimited *community* of scientific inquirers became more central to his philosophy as the actual circumstances of his personal life forced him to become ever more reclusive and isolated. Equally, his ideal of the continuous growth of concrete reasonableness took on greater importance as the contingencies, accidents, and absurdities afflicting him threatened not only his survival but also his sanity. But neither his ideal of community nor that of reasonableness was merely a compensatory illusion (or delusion) spun to enable him to cope with crushing circumstances. Each one needs to be considered on the basis of its philosophical merits, not simply in reference to the putative psychological function each one might have had in enabling an isolated genius to carry on in exceedingly straightened circumstances. In addition, each of these ideals is intimately connected to the other.

The ideal of an unlimited community of experimental inquirers is, from Peirce's perspective, inseparable from that of deliberative or dialogic rationality (the form of reasonableness to which he was primarily committed). In other words, the community of such inquirers is the matrix (from the Latin word for womb) from which truly rational intelligence emerges. On this view, rationality is not so much an individual possession as a communal achievement. It is achieved in and through one's participation in those forms of community or association in which the rigorous demands of mutual account-ability are instituted, refined, and enlarged. The members of the community hold one another accountable for what is said and done, especially in the name of the community (that is, in the name of those who profess to be devoted to the discovery of unknown truth). In turn, the ideal of concrete reasonableness involves the explicit recognition of the growth of traditions, institutions, and practices in which unfettered, uncoerced exchanges among the participants define the innermost life of these traditions, institu-tions, and practices. The flourishing of community enjoins the growth of reasonableness. Conversely, the growth of reasonableness demands the emergence and evolution of forms of dialogue in which appeals to ideals and adherence to norms effectively guide conduct.

As a participant in such a community, however idealized in imagination, Peirce offers what might be read as an *apologia pro sua vita* when he asserts:

> The first step toward *finding out* is to acknowledge you do not satisfactorily know already; so that no blight can so surely arrest all intellectual growth as the blight of cocksureness; and ninety-nine out of every hundred good heads are reduced to impotence by that malady – of whose inroads they are most strangely unaware! Indeed, out of a contrite fallibilism, combined with a high faith in the reality of knowledge, and an intense desire to find things out, all my philosophy has always seemed to me to grow.
>
> (CIP 1.13)

Logic: a normative theory of objective inquiry

One of the principal preoccupations of Peirce's intellectual life was logic, but logic conceived first and foremost as a theory of inquiry (more fully, as a normative theory of objective inquiry). What is meant by describing this theory as *normative* is this: Peirce ultimately desired to offer an account of how the conduct of inquiry *ought* to be undertaken. His task was not simply descriptive or even explanatory; it was irreducibly normative, since Peirce strove to specify the norms and ideals defining this mode of conduct. The most pressing question for him was always, how ought humans to conduct an investigation? He addressed this question as a practitioner, that is, as a participant in a number of practices uncontroversially recognized as sciences (e.g. physics, chemistry, and various branches of mathematics). These practices were sciences in the distinctively modern sense, a sense somewhat obscured by the name of *science*, a late English coinage derived from the Latin word *scientia* (the Latin translation of the Greek word *epistemé*). In the discourse of scientists themselves, *science* does not so much designate established knowledge (much less absolutely certain knowledge) as it signifies an ongoing pursuit to discover unknown truths. In brief, *science* signifies inquiry. What distinguishes scientific inquiry from other investigative procedures is, more than anything else, the spirit in which the endeavor is carried on. Science is an investigation undertaken in the spirit of seeking to know what is presently unknown, not to certify pre-existing beliefs. The defense of truths already in our possession is incidental to the work of the scientist; the establishment of absolutely certain truths, rather than experimentally supported hypotheses, is no part of this work.

Such a spirit tends to prompt inquirers to be methodologically reflexive and, indeed, formally critical. The question of *how* to conduct a specific inquiry is one with which engaged inquirers are inevitably confronted, at least when their efforts are unsuccessful. When doing the done thing – following established procedures – proves to be ineffective, then methodological innovations are required. The felt need for the exercise of methodological ingenuity arises, time and again, in the course of inquiry, so that the activity of scientific inquirers involves, (at least) in effect, the cultivation of methodological self-consciousness (though ordinarily only within a somewhat narrow sphere). In Peirce's case, however, we observe a scientist who deliberately committed himself to the cultivation of such self-consciousness, moreover, not simply in this or that sphere of investigation but with regard to any pursuit properly designated as *scientific* in its distinctively modern sense.

The cultivation of methodological self-consciousness, sought primarily to serve methodological self-criticism and self-control, was for Peirce inseparable from the acquisition of historical self-consciousness. Science is a practice that tends to efface its history, at least insofar as its most exemplary practitioners are pressing forward to use the cumulative achievements of previous inquirers to make novel discoveries. While a workaday disregard of many of the notable achievements of one's scientific predecessors might do little or nothing to impede one's work as a scientist, a painstaking, detailed acquaintance with the effective methodologies of various sciences might prove to be illuminating and beneficial to the working scientist. Such, at least, was Peirce's hunch. Accordingly, he devoted considerable attention to the actual history of scientific inquiry. His interest was far from antiquarian: his concern was not with the past for its own sake alone. Rather it was truly scientific: he conjectured that a detailed historical knowledge of the methods actually used by scientists would benefit inquirers in his own time, especially on those occasions when such practicing scientists were pressed by circumstances to exercise methodological ingenuity. "All men who are now called discoverers, in every matter ruled by thought," in the words of Augustus De Morgan, "have been men versed in the minds of their predecessors, and learned in what had been before them" (A *Budget of Paradoxes*, vol. 1, p. 5).

One way to read Peirce's philosophical authorship is to see his writings as radiating from this center of concern. He typically identified himself as a logician, but in turn he identified or, more accurately, redefined logic as the theory of inquiry. So understood, logic is concerned with methods of inquiry and, more generally, the conditions facilitating the work of inquiry (conditions extending to the acquisition of certain dispositions and even certain sentiments).

More than anything else, the love of truth, particularly truths not yet known but experimentally knowable, defines the scientist. Such love either withers or flowers into increasingly refined methods of effective inquiry. The refinement of such methods is the conscientious work of intergenerational communities. There is, in the foreground of such communities, the pressing work of carrying to fruition specific investigations; but, in the background (if often only slight so), there is inevitably the augmentation, modification, and creation of methods potentially having applicability to other spheres of inquiry. The refinement of methods is unquestionably the work of individuals, but only as self-conscious and self-critical participants in such communities. (This connects, more generally, to the pragmatist conception of human individuals as social selves, albeit ones whose sociality provides opportunities far more than posing threats to the realization of individuality.) Accordingly, science does not so much name a species of knowledge as a distinctive form of human community.

Conceived in communal terms, the defining traits and human significance of our scientific practices (including the inherent significance such practices have for scientific investigators themselves) are unknowable apart from the evolved and evolving forms of those human associations animated by an overarching love (what Peirce does not hesitate to call "scientific Eros"). The human significance of scientific inquiry is to be ascertained not only in reference to the impact of science on other human practices but also in terms of this practice itself (what it means for scientists themselves who are devoted to a lifetime of inquiry). In Peirce's judgment, the subordination of science to other practices cannot but corrupt science. This is especially true when those practices or concerns are admirable or noble. For this reason, Peirce went so far as to characterize science as the study of useless things! Against a powerful tendency in the nineteenth century to press science into the service of the betterment of society, Peirce voiced extreme skepticism about the wisdom of such a construal. If science is conceived exclusively or even just principally in reference to its benefits to society (no matter how valuable or momentous are these benefits), the integrity of scientific practice would, he believed, be put at risk of being violated or denigrated. Moreover, the authority of traditional practices, such as traditional morality and traditional religion, would be unfairly but effectively undermined. Peirce's position here is a complex and nuanced one, far more so than is ordinarily appreciated. At the very least, he wanted, simultaneously, to protect science from the external pressures of the encompassing society in which the work of scientists inevitably took place but also to protect society from the immediate impact of "scientific" reforms. Underlying both of these endeavors, Peirce was engaged in the task of clarifying the meaning of *science*, but also explicating the means by which scientists in the context of inquiry clarify the meaning of the terms on which their efforts so critically turn.

The pragmatic clarification of meaning and the Peircean ideal of community

Though Peirce's synechism (doctrine of continuity), tychism (doctrine of chance), evolutionism, and other cosmological doctrines are not likely to be known outside of a narrow field of academic specialists, Peirce's pragmatism and semeiotics (or theory of signs) are today widely recognized as significant contributions to debates in contemporary thought. The deeply communitarian cast of Peirce's thought needs, ultimately, to be conjoined to its equally deep pragmatic character. But, first, Peircean pragmatism demands a detailed explication.

(1) Peirce's Pragmatism

Though outside of philosophy Peirce is likely best known for his theory of signs, he is among philosophers still most famous for his contribution to pragmatism. Primarily based on several early essays (above all, "The Fixation of Belief" [1877] and "How to Make Our Ideas Clears" [1878]), the dominant view among professional philosophers is almost certainly distorted. Even so, Peirce's mature views unquestionably grew out of his youthful work. In particular, his eventual reformulation of his pragmatic position owes much to its original formulation. First at meetings of the Metaphysical Club (an informal discussion group including Chauncey Wright, Oliver Wendell Holmes, Jr., and William James) and, then, in two essays in *The Popular Science Monthly*, Peirce presented a theory of inquiry and, in conjunction with this theory, a maxim designed to assist inquirers in clarifying the *meaning* of terms.

Following the Scottish psychologist Alexander Bain, he conceived a belief to be that upon which a person is willing to act (CP: 5.12; also in EP: Vol. 2, 399). Conscious assent or verbal expression turns out to be incidental to belief, whereas habit is essential: pragmatically defined, a belief *is* a habit or disposition to act in certain ways in certain circumstances. Belief concerns first and foremost how agents comport themselves in the world, not what takes place in consciousness or what is expressed in words. The opposite of belief is doubt: to be in doubt is not to know what to do or how to act. The experience of doubt signals the disruption of our habits. It makes dramatically clear that how we habitually go on has, in some context, proven to be ineffective or, worse, counterproductive. Such doubt prompts a process in which agents struggle to regain their fluency of action. Only restoring or replacing the challenged belief can accomplish this. Thus, the struggle begins in doubt and drives toward the overcoming of such uncertainty, by the re-establishment of a belief. Peirce takes *inquiry* in its most basic sense to be just this struggle. It is generated by the disruption of genuine doubt and brought to closure in the establishment of an effective habit. Against Descartes' universal, hyperbolic, and methodic doubt, Peirce (anticipating Ludwig Wittgenstein and J. L. Austin) argues that there must be a specific motive or inducement to doubt any one of our beliefs. "There must be," in other words, "a real and living doubt, and without this all discussion is idle" (CP: 5.376; also in EP: Vol. 1, 115). At any rate, he is said by expositors to offer a doubt-belief theory of inquiry.

In "The Fixation of Belief" (1877), Peirce distinguishes four ways of overcoming doubt by fixing (or establishing) belief. The first is the method of tenacity. This involves clinging as tenaciously as possible to whatever an individual happens to believe. But this purely individualistic manner of fixing belief is doomed to fail, since "the social impulse is against it" (CP: 5.378; also in EP: Vol. 1, 116). "The man who adopts it will find that other men think differently from him, and it will be apt to occur to him, in some saner moment, that their opinions are quite as good as his own, and this will shake his confidence in his belief" (5.378; 116). Human beings are social animals to such an extent that what is required is a communal method.

The second method is that of authority. An established authority in a human community wields the power to dictate what is creditable or tenable. But the social impulse of human beings as effectively undermines this method as it does that of tenacity: "in the most priest-ridden states some individuals will be found who are raised above that condition [of being intellectual slaves]." Such individuals "possess a wider sort of social feeling; they see that men in other countries and in other ages have held to very different doctrines from those which they themselves have been brought up to believe; and they cannot help seeing that it is the mere accident of their having been taught as they have ... that has caused them to believe as they do ..." (CP: 5.381; also in EP: Vol. 1, 118). As it turns out, the scope of such feeling is, in principle, boundless, for it extends to nothing less than an infinite community of human inquirers. Historically, however, the understandable reaction to the brutal methods of institutional authority exemplified by the Roman Empire and, later, the Catholic Church (to cite Peirce's own paradigms of this method) were not only eloquent pleas for intellectual tolerance but also an unqualified endorsement of individual rationality. Whatever appears to be agreeable to the rationality of individuals, apart from the coercions or even pressures of institutional authority, is taken to be the surest route to tenable belief. This method "makes of inquiry something similar to the development of taste; but taste, unfortunately, is always more or less a matter of fashion" (CP: 5.383; also in EP: Vol. 1, 119). To draw out the implications of this, we can say that, for Peirce, this method falls far short of obtaining an adequately communal form (the circle of interlocutors is not an infinite community, but a more or less insular cluster of contemporaneous inquirers). Moreover, we can say that this method fails to accord experience a sufficiently central or critical role in inquiry. Consequently, the third method, that of apriority or agreeableness to reason, is fatally flawed.

As it turns out, all three of these methods are, from the perspective of Peirce's pragmatism, unable to distinguish in a sufficiently strong manner the way things are from the way they are taken to be by us. For advocates of the method of tenacity, this is most obviously the case: what is tenable is simply whatever one tenaciously holds to be so. It is, however, equally (though less manifestly) true of the other two methods.

The fourth method is that of science. It alone secures a basis for differentiating what is the case from what I or we happen to take to be the case. Even more radically, only the method of science (or experimentation) "presents any distinction of a right and a wrong way" (CP: 5. 385; also in EP: Vol. 1, 121). It does so because it is a practice instituted on the hypothesis that there are real things, that is, things whose traits or characteristics are independent of what anyone happens to take them to be. Reality in its otherness – in its independence from what any finite individual or finite community happens to believe – is, in effect, effaced by the other three methods. The role of experience (in particular, experience as a confrontation with what is other than, or independent of, what I or we happen to believe) is effectively denied by these methods. Science or experimentalism alone accords experience the central and critical role it deserves in the drama of inquiry.

In "How to Make Our Ideas Clear" (1878), Peirce turns from the basic question of fixing our beliefs to the even more fundamental one of clarifying our meanings (see e.g. CP: 5.410; also in EP: Vol. 1, 141). But the second essay ("How to Make Our Ideas Clear") joins the first one ("The Fixation") by also concluding with an appeal to reality. While in "The Fixation" reality enters primarily as a hypothesis securing the basis for differentiating between reality and our accounts of reality, it is in "How to Make Our Ideas Clear" introduced as the last example of a concept calling for clarification. The clarification of the concept of reality turns out to be a refinement of the hypothesis on which a truly experimental method of responsible inquirers is based. The argument for the superiority of the scientific method is, in "How to Make Our Ideas Clear," strengthened by a pragmatic clarification of its most fundamental hypothesis (the conjecture that there *are* real things having discoverable properties).

In "The Fixation" Peirce distinguishes four rival methods of inquiry, while in "How to Make Our Ideas Clear" he differentiates three hierarchically ordered grades of clarity. At the lowest level, there is the familiarity indicative of our ability to use a word (or other sign) properly (our capacity to utter or interpret a word or sign in an appropriate or intelligent manner). Such largely tacit familiarity is itself a sign of our minimal competence (our linguistic or, more generally, semiotic competence). At the intermediate level, there is the grade of clarity obtained by abstract definition. At the highest level, there is that attained by pragmatic clarification. Such clarification is achieved by the application of a maxim, rather cumbrously formulated by Peirce in this essay:

> Consider what effects, that might conceivably have practical bearings, we conceive the object of our conception to have. Then, our conception of these effects is the whole of our conception of the object. (CP: 5.402; also in EP: Vol. 1, 132)

What might easily be missed is that effects having practical bearings are ones exerting a transformative influence on human conduct in a very wide sense. From Peirce's perspective, experimental inquiry is a distinct sphere of human conduct. Things are what they disclose themselves to be in the context of experience and, more narrowly, experimentation. The disposition of, say, salt and other substances to dissolve in water and other liquids is an observable effect making up the core meaning of solubility. Our conception of these effects is, in Peirce's judgment, the whole of our conception of this property.

The practice of inquiry tends, according to Peirce, to outstrip the theoretical self-understanding of inquirers. That is, the level of heuristic sophistication characteristic of the actual procedures employed at any historical moment is higher than that of theoretical understanding: we are better investigators than our "logic" portrays us. If we take "logic" (as Peirce did) to designate a theory of inquiry (more precisely, a normative theory of experimental inquiry), then the logic embodied in the actual procedures, practices, and indeed habits of the most effective investigators are more refined than the logic articulated in formal theories. This was nowhere more evident than in reference to the mode of clarification on which experimental investigators continually rely, in contrast to those forms of definition to which theorists of inquiry gave formal recognition. Hence, he stresses in "How to Make Our Ideas Clear," "the doctrine that familiar use and abstract distinctness [or definition] make the perfection of apprehension [of meaning] has its only true place in philosophies which have long been extinct; and it is now time to formulate the method of attaining to a more perfect clearness of thought, such as we see and admire in the thinkers of our own time" (CP: 5.390; also in EP: Vol. 1, 125). The pragmatic clarification of terms is, accordingly, a formalization of what experimental investigators have discovered to be, for their purposes, the highest grade of conceptual clearness.

While philosophers in particular have been content with abstract definitions, they ought to attend to the practice of experimentalists and to see the necessity of moving beyond such definitions. Put positively, they ought to insist upon pragmatic clarification of the pivotal terms on which these various disputes turn.

In "How to Make Our Ideas Clear" Peirce illustrated the value of his maxim by showing how four concepts (hardness, weight, force, and reality) can be pragmatically clarified. Let us consider here only the least and the most controversial of these examples. What we, as experimentalists, *mean* by ascribing hardness to a substance is that this substance "will not be scratched by many other substances. The whole conception of this quality, as of every other, lies in its conceived effects" (CP: 5.403; also in EP: Vol. 1, 132). What we mean by reality, at the level of abstract definition, is "that whose characters [or properties] are independent of what anybody may think them to be" (CP: 5.405; also in EP: Vol. 1, 137). But, at the level of pragmatic clarification, reality is what would be disclosed in the course of inquiry. Hence, "reality is independent, not necessarily of thought in general, but of what you or I or any finite number of men may think about it" (CP: 5.408; also in EP: Vol. 1, 139). On the one hand, there is here a robust affirmation of reality as possibly other than how anyone or any community happens to conceive it. On the other, there is an equally strong insistence on reality as intelligible, as what reality would, given enough time, resources, and ingenuity, disclose itself to be. As he will eventually state the matter, it is what *would* disclose itself to an unlimited community of experimental inquirers.

As Peirce makes clear in "The Fixation of Belief," experimental inquiry rests upon the hypothesis that there "are real things, whose characters are entirely independent of our opinions [and beliefs] about them" (CP: 5.384; also in EP: Vol. 1, 120). They have the capacity to act on us as percipient, active, and intelligent beings in such ways that "we can ascertain by reasoning [on the disclosures of our experience] how things really and truly are" (CP: 5.384; also in EP: Vol. 1, 120). But, as he tries to show in "How to Make Our Ideas Clear," such an abstract definition of real things is inadequate. A pragmatic clarification of the meaning of the term on which experimental investigation rests defines this term by its power to sustain and, to a greater extent, disrupt the beliefs (at bottom, the habits) of embodied agents engaged in the passionate quest to discover what is not yet known. The observable effects of environing realities are most telling in their power to undermine existing habits and to facilitate the acquisition of new habits (ones more fully and finely in accord with the dispositions of the things encountered in experience).

In 1898, William James presented a paper entitled "Philosophical Conceptions and Practical Results" to Philosophical Union of the University of California at Berkeley.

On this occasion, he announced to his audience his desire to identify "the most likely direction in which to start upon the trail of truth." He immediately added:

> Years ago this direction was given to me by an American philosopher whose home is in the East, and whose published works, few as they are and scattered in periodicals, are not fit expression of his powers. I refer to Mr. Charles S. Peirce, with whose very existence as a philosopher I dare say many of you are unacquainted. (1975, 258)

After briefly explaining Peirce's views, as expressed in conversations in the Metaphysical Club as well as several early articles, James adapted them to his own purpose. But 1898 marks the moment when pragmatism and Peirce's role in its inauguration first came to be recognized, thanks to James, by philosophers and scholars in the United States and elsewhere. For very quickly American pragmatism became, somewhat paradoxically, an international movement. Peirce became an increasingly audible voice in the re-inauguration of pragmatism, twenty years after its original formulation in *The Popular Science Monthly*

In 1903, for example, Peirce presented at Harvard a series of lectures on pragmatism and, beginning in 1905, published a series of articles in *The Monist* on this topic ("What Pragmatism Is" [1905], "Issues of Pragmaticism" [1905], and "Prolegomena to an Apology for Pragmaticism" [1906]). In his own lectures on pragmatism several years after Peirce's, James described his predecessor's efforts as "flashes of brilliant light relieved against Cimmerian darkness!" (1975: 10). In the first article in this *Monist* series, however, Peirce bemoaned "the merciless way" in which words are treated "when they fall into literary clutches" (CP: 5.414; also in EP: Vol. 2, 334). As a result of finding pragmatism used "to express some meaning that it was rather designed to exclude," Peirce felt the need "to kiss his child goodbye and relinquish it to its higher destiny; while to serve the precise purpose of expressing the original definition, he begs to announce the birth of the word 'pragmaticism,' which is ugly enough to be safe from kidnappers" (CP: 5.414; also in EP: Vol. 2, 334–5). Moreover, there are among his unpublished manuscripts in the period from 1898 until his death in 1914 numerous attempts to reformulate his pragmatic position. For far too long, professional philosophers have discussed Peircean pragmatism in terms of its original formulation, paying little or no attention to its mature reformulation. Especially in light of Peirce's own dissatisfaction with his earlier attempts, such an approach is unjustified.

One of the most striking features of his later efforts is their drive toward integration (e.g. toward showing how his categories, theory of signs, and pragmatism are to be integrated with each other). There is, however, an ongoing debate about the extent to which Peirce was actually successful in weaving together the disparate strands of his philosophical inquiries into a coherent fabric. Some (e.g. Justus Buchler and Murray Murphey) argue that his actual achievement fell short (perhaps far short) of his architectonic or systematic aspirations, while others (e.g. Paul Weiss, John E. Smith, Christopher Hookway, and Sandra Rosenthal) contend that at least the sufficiently charitable interpreter can discern the outlines of a philosophical system or systematic approach to philosophical questions.

What cannot be disputed is that, in his later thought, the meaning of pragmatism tended to go beyond that of a maxim designed for clarifying the meaning of troublesome words and unduly abstract conceptions. To be sure, he would at times even then insist that his "pragmatism is, in itself, no doctrine of metaphysics, no attempt to determine any truth of things. It is merely a method of ascertaining the meanings of hard words and of abstract concepts" (CP: 5.464 [c. 1906]; also in EP: Vol. 2, 400). But he did so mostly in response to the looseness with which such authors as James, F. C. S. Schiller, and Giovanni Papini were using this word. The context in which he set forth this maxim was a theory of inquiry demanding acknowledgement of the defining features of our rational agency. This is unmistakably clear in such later texts as "What Pragmatism Is" and "Issues of Pragmaticism."

It thus might be helpful to distinguish Peirce's pragmatism in its narrowest sense and its more encompassing meaning. In its narrowest sense, it merely designates a method of clarification. In its broader meaning, however, it at least implies a normative portrait of human agency, one in which the ideal of self-control is of utmost prominence. The connection between the two senses is that we cannot obtain mastery over our selves without also obtaining control over the meanings of our words and other signs, insofar as this is possible. The pragmatic maxim in its most restrictive sense is, accordingly, only one example of a more general commitment to rational autonomy. Stated positively, then, pragmatism in its broader sense is integral to Peirce's attempt to reconstruct our understanding of rationality. In "Issues of Pragmaticism" (1905), "the secret of rational consciousness is to be sought ... in the review of the process of self-control in its entirety" (CP: 5. 440; also in EP: Vol. 2, 347). In Peirce's reformulation of pragmatism (i.e. in his pragmaticism) the maxim publicly articulated in 1878 is explicitly connected to an understanding of rationality, fashioned in reference to such monumental figures in Western thought as Plato, Aristotle, Thomas, Scotus, Descartes, Kant, Hegel, and Darwin but (arguably to an even greater degree) to the practice of inquiry, especially as exemplified by the dramatic achievements of natural science.

(2) Community, Meaning, and Truth

While Peirce refused to separate the task of clarifying meaning from that of discovering truth, he devoted considerable attention to the thorny question of, "What is meaning?" and (inseparably connected to this), "How are the meaning of our words and indeed other signs most effectively clarified?" Meaning in general and the clarification of meanings in the context of inquiry (or science) were matters of the greatest interest to this philosophical inquirer.

There is, as a constitutive feature of any truly scientific community, something analogous to a code of honor (Ransdell 1986 [1979] 240). The ethics of inquiry takes the form of mutual accountability (Polanyi) extending to an ethics of terminology. A scientific code of honor encompasses a conscientious use of words, a use enforced by no authority other than that of the experimentalists for whom clarity means nearly as much as truth. Peirce was simultaneously devoted to explaining how the clarification of terms within the discourse of scientists is to be accomplished and how the very meaning of *science* is, in light of its history, to be clarified.

Peirce provides the warrant for reading him in this manner. But he also suggests other ways of interpreting him, not least of all one inspired by a line from one of R. W. Emerson's poems ("The Sphinx") ("Of thy eye, I am eyebeam"), also several lines from one of Shakespeare's plays ("Most ignorant of what we're most assured / Our glassy essence"). "Each man has," Peirce insists, "an identity which far transcends the mere animal – an essence, a *meaning* subtle as it may be. He cannot know his own essential significance; of his eye it is eyebeam" (CP: 7.591). Such significance is transcendent: it concerns individual agents not as separable beings or at any determinate time in their unfolding lives but as communal beings contributing to an encompassing development (see e.g. CP: 5.403n3).

We are, apparently, never in the position to ascertain our place in history or (except perhaps in vaguest intimations) the ultimate meaning of our defining commitments and lifelong work. Our peculiar fate, especially after the profound transformations inaugurated in the nineteenth century, is a paradoxical one: we cannot avoid seeking what we cannot attain – a historical self-consciousness adequate to our pursuits and situation (though an awareness of this very inadequacy is, paradoxically, part of our distinctive form of historical self-consciousness and, in addition, a chastened sense of our invincible finitude requisite for the humane engagement in our defining practices). The ongoing course of human history and of the broader processes in which human history is enveloped is driving toward, without exaggeration, *unimaginable* transformations and upheavals. There is in evidence, at least, something akin to a mystical faith in the benevolent movement of an encompassing Spirit. On this score, Peirce is far closer to Hegel than Nietzsche.

But, those facets of the century in which Peirce was born, reared, and educated on which he tended to place the greatest emphasis are ones that work at exposing what A. N. Whitehead called the fallacy of simple location. Being located in, and representative of, the nineteenth century by no means confines Peirce to this period. His conceptions of growth, development, and evolution, also time, history, and transformation, so deeply a part of his inheritance from his time, imply that Peirce was self-consciously writing for posterity, all the more so as he advanced toward death and came increasingly to realize the extent to which he was both at odds with and unheeded by his contemporaries. His appreciation of the open-ended, prospective, and fallible dimensions of any human endeavor, including his own philosophical reflections, informed his vision of community: to be a responsible inquirer is to participate self-consciously and self-critically in an intergenerational community, stretching back to ancient times and driving forward into an unknown future. One's contemporaries are not necessarily the most important or worthwhile interlocutors. Thus, in many late manuscripts, Peirce explicitly imagined and formally addressed his Reader, sometimes as "your Honor," not infrequently as a person living in a faraway future. Hence, Peirce invites us to read him as a figure wrestling with Hegel and Darwin, Herbert Spencer and William James, Alexander Bain and Karl Pearson, along with countless other nineteenth-century thinkers, but in doing so he is in effect thrusting himself beyond the limited confines of his particular time and self-consciously addressing future generations.

If we derive a theory of science from the practice of scientists, as we ought to derive such a theory, then the *reality* of community cannot be gainsaid. The isolated individual is never a competent inquirer, let alone an omnicompetent one. Only the self as a participant in a community, but not a bounded or limited association of finite, fallible investigators – rather an infinite community of rational agents bound together by nothing less than love, hope, and faith (what Peirce calls the "three logical sentiments") – can rightfully be accorded the status of inquirer. To be an inquirer is to be a participant in a certain form of community and to be transformed by participation in the work of that community. Though the focus of Peirce's concern tended to foreground a particular form of human community (the unlimited community of experimental inquirers), he was far from overlooking other forms of human association, for instance, the community of worshippers so central to an adequate understanding of the religious life or the community of citizens so crucial for a compelling account of our political existence. Sometimes Peirce's communitarianism seems to drive in the direction of collectivism, to a reductivist conception of human association in which human individuality is justifiably sacrificed for collective goals more or less externally related to the character and, thus, the individual(s) making the sacrifice. But, far more often, a critical distinction between community and collectivity is implicit in Peirce's discussions of the associations in and through which human individuals acquire their various competencies and realize their distinctive capacities.

The reality of community is evident in a range of phenomena, not just the exemplary practice of experimental inquirers exerting mutual accountability in their ongoing pursuits. For Peirce at least, a community of scientists clearly exemplifies the reality of community, but so does simply a community of speakers sharing a language by which they can share much more. The notion of an invincibly *private language* (one with which the self might communicate its thoughts to itself but one in principle unintelligible to anyone else) is, for Peirce no less than the later Wittgenstein, self-defeating or self-contradictory. Meaning is inherently and irreducibly general in the sense that what is meaningful to you must be, in principle, meaningful to me. It may turn out that meaning is not only irreducibly general but also irreducibly vague. In fact, Peirce held that this is indeed the case. But, for certain purposes in certain contexts, meaning can be rendered sufficiently determinate in both respects so that effective communication is a humanly realizable goal.

We are always already members of a community of meaning, caught up in complex exchanges as often as not initiated by parties other than our selves. There is, in Peirce's writings, a vision of human actors as sign-using and sign-making animals who instinctually are responsive to the import of some signs. In his emphasis on these points, Peirce as much anticipated one of the central developments in twentieth-century philosophy as he gave eloquent expression to a particular vision of human life.

The question of meaning was near, or arguably at, the very center of his concern. On the one hand, he was principally interested in this question as it arises in the context of science. His pragmatic maxim was initially formulated as the practical counsel of an experimental inquirer addressed to other such inquirers but also those (including philosophers) who aspire to carry out the exacting work of responsible investigation. On the other hand, he devised a theory of signs by which the meaning of not only scientific terms but also virtually any other one might be illuminated. That is, he desired to articulate a truly *general* theory of signs, one providing the resources for identifying, analyzing, and evaluating signs and, more narrowly, symbols in their myriad manifestations, not merely their scientific roles. But he designed this general theory primarily for a specific purpose – to offer a normative account of objective inquiry. In order to understand science, we have to understand signs, in particular, how certain semiotic functions become integrated in complex signs and, beyond this, become integral to the interwoven forms of logical inference. But, in order to understand signs sufficiently for this task, we have, somewhat paradoxically, to go beyond the rather narrow sphere of scientific investigation. The theoretical imagination must be allowed to take sweeping flight, gliding over (often high above) the fields of science but also those of the various other forms of human practice.

For Peirce, the question of meaning is, in any event, bound up with a far-reaching, deep-cutting investigation of signs. The nineteenth century is not only a time in which historical consciousness assumed a dramatically reflexive form, but also one in which semiotic awareness (a consciousness of the role and indispensability of signs in the acquisition of experimental knowledge and in other domains of human experience or practice) assumed such form. Such semiotic consciousness was in no small measure due to Peirce's own Herculean efforts to articulate a general theory of signs, principally in light of the painstaking contributions of various medieval logicians and the exacting demands of providing a convincing account of objective investigation (the kind of inquiry in which general laws as much as particular facts are experimentally discovered and thereby objectively established). The parallels and, of greater significance, the differences between this North American philosopher, scientist, and logician, on the one hand, and the Swiss linguist Ferdinand de Saussure, on the other, make it clear that, already in the closing decades of the nineteenth century and the opening ones of the twentieth, the linguistic turn (the turn toward language – the explicit, critical appreciation of the role and indeed centrality of language in resolving various disputes, including philosophical controversies) had been taken. But the linguistic turn as taken at least by Peirce (if not also by Saussure) was more than this: it was in the same breath a semiotic turn, a turn toward signs in their myriad forms (not just in their linguistic or verbal forms).

The claims of rationality and experience / the relationship of theory to practice

"The story of modern thought is," as John E. Smith so insightfully notes, "largely the story of the criticism of reason undertaken from many points of view and prompted by diverse motives" (1992: 103–4). The story of nineteenth-century philosophy is an important chapter in this unfolding history, but it is decidedly an intensification of this critique, one wherein the constructive and creative functions of reason are accorded at least as central a place as the self-critical and self-restraining requirements on which the responsible exercise of human rationality insists. The Kantian project of theoretical reason subjecting itself to a systematic critique resulting in severe strictures regarding metaphysical speculation generated a variety of reactions, not the least of which involved attempts to recover a more robust conception of human reason than that offered by the author of the first *Kritik*.

To place reason within the limits of experience alone, as Kant so forcefully argued in this work, might have to be radically modified if the very *meaning* of experience is itself altered or transformed. This is, in any event, precisely what Peirce proposed. Peirce's transformation or reconstruction of our conception of experience begins by stressing that experience is far from exhausted by the role it plays in the acquisition of knowledge. Experience is, first and foremost, the course of our lives, all that we have lived through (a sense expressly captured in the etymology of the German word *Erlebnis*). As valuable and informative as the differential perspective of the theoretical inquirer is, it is only one perspective among various other ones. This is indeed the point in characterizing this perspective as differential. Quite simply, it makes a difference whether one adopts a theoretical perspective or some other viewpoint. Here is a difference that truly makes a difference. But, there is, in the story to which Smith refers, the one in which the criticism of reason is undertaken from diverse perspectives and animated by diverse impulses, a strange oscillation between uncritically privileging theoretical reason and harshly denigrating it.

Beginning in the nineteenth century – more accurately, gaining clarity and force in this century – there has arisen the tendency to grant primacy to practical reason. Sometimes this has meant enslaving theory to practice, at least, to subordinating theoretical reason to the demands of some form of practical reason (be it technological, moral, or some other form of such rationality). At other times, however, the effort to grant primacy to practice has been done in the hope of honoring theory as a distinctive form of human practice. On this construal, theory is not said to be for the sake of practice but rather is itself conceived as a form of practice, possessing an integrity of its own. Theoretical reason turns out to be the somewhat misleading name for an extended family of human practices oriented toward the discovery of unknown truths. What is true of any human practice is also true of our theoretical investigations (or heuristic practices – practices having as their purpose the advancement of *inquiry* at least in some specific domain and possibly in providing models, strategies, and tools applicable to yet other domains). These investigations are evolved and evolving practices ordinarily stretching across a number of generations (newly instituted fields of inquiries are almost always ones generating work to be accomplished not in the course of a single lifetime but for the indeterminate duration of successive generations). Granting primacy to practice, at least in this sense, need not entail undermining the authority of theory. It does however entail squaring the authority of theoretical reason, as established within particular fields of human practice, with the authority of other forms of human rationality or, more broadly, other forms of human experience and engagement. The authority of scientific reason cannot immediately or decisively discredit the authority of religious sentiment. That is, the differential perspective of religious consciousness is simply not of such a character that it can be laid alongside the viewpoint of science and thereby judged to be fatally flawed or defective. Certain historical forms of religious consciousness can certainly be challenged by the discoveries of science (e.g. those depending on a literal interpretation of the creation story found, say, in *Genesis*). But religious consciousness as such is not inherently opposed to scientific rationality. The extent to which such consciousness, in this or that historical or cultural configuration or articulation, needs to be modified because of the findings of science is itself an experimental question, moreover, one requiring hermeneutic sensitivity as much as intellectual candor. This was, at least, Peirce's position regarding such questions.

The story of philosophy – not only modern philosophy but also at least Western thought in its full sweep – conceived as the story of the critique of rationality attained, nonetheless, a heightened form of *critical* consciousness with Kant in the eighteenth century and a sharpened sense of *historical* consciousness with Schelling, Hegel, Fichte, and others in the nineteenth. The critique of reason is never anything less than the self-critical exercise of our remarkable capacity to form judgments and draw inferences. The critical exercise of human reason generates a potentially unlimited series of reflexive judgments and critical inferences (we judge a certain judgment or even an entire manner of judging to be mistaken or irresponsible, just as we infer that certain patterns of forms or inference are defective or unreliable).

In turn, the story of Peirce's philosophy is a decisive intervention into this ongoing history. It represents a unique contribution to the Kantian project, in the broadest sense of this term. For it represents a contribution to the critique of reason in all of its forms. Like Kant, Peirce's project grants, in a certain respect, *primacy to practice*. But, unlike Kant, it does so not by increasing the split between theory and practice, science and sentiment (though there is, in reference to Peirce, a need to qualify this claim). Rather it grants primacy to practice partly by subsuming theory under the rubric or heading of practice. And it does so without erasing the integrity of our theoretical investigations. Such investigations are like other practices in some respects (e.g. they are historical through and through) but unlike other practices in at least equally important respects.

The critique of reason is bound up with the task of philosophy. While philosophy cannot be reduced to this critique, it also cannot be relieved of the responsibility to determine the forms, functions, scope, and status of rationality. But, like so many other prominent figures in the nineteenth century, Peirce connected his critique of rationality with a defense of autonomy, above all, autonomy in the etymological sense of this highly contested term (the sense of giving laws to oneself). What most sharply distinguishes Peirce's vision of reason from Kant's view is the extent to which human autonomy is understood in uncompromisingly historical terms. Peirce replaced the antecedently fixed structures and principles of the human mind by historically emergent and operative forms and procedures. Hypothesis in philosophy ceases to be viewed as (in Kant's words) "contraband" ("Everything ... which bears any measure of resemblance to an hypothesis is to be treated as contraband; it is not to be put up for sale even at the lowest price, but forthwith confiscated, immediately upon detection" [1965: 11]) and comes to be honored as the only reliable means of extending human knowledge. This goes for philosophy as much as any other field of inquiry.

735

The extent to which Peirce was himself engaged in a transcendental project in a Kantian sense, even a greatly modified Kantian sense, is a thorny question. It seems plausible to assert that Peirce was devoted to determining the conditions for the possibility of science, for that sort of objective inquiry in which intersubjectively established discoveries are unquestionably made. Since this seems to be what Kant defined as a transcendental justification, Peirce appears to have been engaged in just such a justification of science. But the precise character of these conditions is not anything Kant himself would recognize as underwriting a transcendental justification in the strict sense, since these conditions are not to be found in *a priori* forms of sensibility or categories of understanding (or anything else *a priori*), but in historical inheritances, innovations, and accomplishments.

This is, however, to jump ahead of the story. What most deserves to be emphasized at this juncture is that Peirce's philosophy encompasses a contribution to the critique of reason and, as this critique was actually carried out by him, it further includes a defense of autonomy. These facets of Peirce's project become most visible when seen against the background of earlier thought, above all, those German philosophers with whom he was caught up in a lifelong debate.

However, the towering figure of Charles Darwin is no less important than philosophical authors for appreciating the distinctive character of the Peircean project. Peirce's undertaking represents, at once, many of the unresolved tensions of the nineteenth century and (at least as much) vivid intimations of the emergent agenda of the twentieth century in its full expanse and the twenty-first in its opening decade. These tensions are nowhere more evident than in Peirce's Kantian tendency to conceive human reason as a capacity for heroic self-restraint and his Hegelian tendency to envision our rationality as nothing less than an integral part of a cosmic development. Connected to this tendency, there is, on the one hand, the insistence that our historical locatedness for the most part precludes ascertaining in any precise manner the defining characteristic or our particular epoch and, on the other, the confidence as a young man and ever afterwards of identifying just these characteristics!

Accordingly, Peirce's unique contribution to the unfolding account of human rationality needs to be set in its immediate context. This means that it must, at the very least, be seen in reference to Kantian and post-Kantian idealism. The critique of reason launched by Immanuel Kant in the eighteenth century and carried forward by such figures as Schelling, Hegel, and Fichte in the nineteenth is a project to which Peirce and, indeed, the other pragmatists are committed in their own way. The pragmatic reconstruction of intelligence unquestionably takes shape against the background of the Kantian and post-Kantian efforts to determine the scope, forms, functions, and status of reason (or Reason). Above all, it takes shape against the Kantian endeavor to delimit the scope of reason within the bounds of possible experience and the post-Kantian projects to expand this scope to include a theoretically legitimate account of the divine Being and human freedom. Kant argued that God, freedom, and immortality pose theoretically undecidable questions (taken as strictly theoretical questions, human reason is in principle barred from arriving at a rational answer). But, for the "king of modern philosophy" (as Peirce dubbed him), each of these is a necessary postulate of practical reason, where practical reason means moral reason (the specific form of human rationality requisite for the exercise of our moral agency). Moral agents as practical beings must postulate the existence of God, for such a Being alone guarantees that injustice and immorality will be punished, justice and morality rewarded. Such agents must also postulate freedom or autonomy and immortality.

The postulates of practical (or moral) reason are, thus, not based on the disclosures of theoretical reason. What moral reason most deeply needs, theoretical reason cannot provide. But, for Kant, this does not spell the defeat of rationality. For he does not take moral reason to be utterly dependent on theoretical reason. Indeed, he contends that moral rationality itself has a degree of autonomy from theoretical reason. The autonomy virtually identifiable with rationality is, on Kant's account, even more evident in moral (or practical) than in theoretical (or scientific) reason. For Kant, reason is, at bottom, the capacity to give laws to oneself. This is the justification for suggesting that, from Kant's perspective, rationality is virtually identifiable with autonomy.

In its theoretical form, the most severe challenge confronting Kant is to show how scientific reason is a self-legislative power, meaning that our reason gives laws to nature, but comes thereby to discover experimentally what reason does not dictate or construct, at least in any strong sense. Whatever nature comes specifically to mean for theoretical or scientific reason (e.g. a domain in which explicable patterns are identifiable and effective explanations discoverable), it generally means only what falls within the boundaries of possible experience. The limits of sensory experience hence define, for Kant, the limits of human knowledge. In this, he is in accord with empiricism, with such thinkers as John Locke, David Hume, and George Berkeley. But the possibility of experience in the relevant sense – the sense in which our sensory experience can serve to ground our scientific knowledge of the natural world, a knowledge in some respects universal and necessary (e.g. all bodies of a certain mass, etc.) – requires us to reject the equation between sensory experience and the allegedly unrelated data of sensory intuition. Put simply, experience cannot be what such empiricists as Locke and Hume claim it is, at least if experience is to serve as the basis of knowledge, taking our paradigm of knowledge to be physics (more precisely, natural science – what he typically called natural philosophy – as reformed by Isaac Newton).

At the very least, the possibility of experience in the relevant sense demands the categorization of enduring objects identifiable in and through their locus in causal networks (e.g. this billiard ball colliding with this other one in such a manner – with such force and at such an angle – to propel the second ball in this direction, at this velocity). From Kant's perspective, the categorization of the items or data of experience is the conjoint work of sensory intuition (or input), on the one hand, and rational activity, on the other. The work of theoretical (or scientific) reason extends to organizing sensory data into recognizable objects (thus, relatively stable and enduring objects) standing in discoverable relationships to one another. Accordingly, the possibility of experience encompasses the possibility of encountering identifiable (by implication, re-identifiable) objects connected in multiple yet for the most part unknown ways with one another. Only experience in this sense can serve as the basis of knowledge. But experience so conceived is itself possible only because reason brings to experience – to the sensory intuitions spontaneously given to human reason – *a priori* forms of intuition (namely, time and space) and *a priori* categories of the understanding (e.g. substance and property or cause and effect). Theoretical reason is able to read out of sensory experience intelligible patterns and illuminating connections only because such reason reads into such experience a coherence and stability the sundered bits of sensory impressions, in their chaotic, atomistic upsurge, could never secure. Such reason defines the terms in which experience must be cast, legislates the forms in which objects-in-relation must appear.

The conflict between rationalists and empiricists points to the need to square the claims of rationality against those of experience. For Kant and even more for Hegel, this meant overcoming the dualism between reason and experience. But this is not by any means the only dualism to be transcended. The dualism between *praxis* and *theoria* – the domain of human practice and that of strictly theoretical investigation – a dualism already evident in René Descartes' writings (see e.g. his *Meditations on First Philosophy*), assumes a peculiarly sharp form in Kant's critical project (his endeavor to limit theoretical reason to the domain of possible experience while freeing practical or moral reason from such narrow confinement).

In Peirce's hands, however, the critique of human reason does not assume, at the outset, the form of a critique of *pure* reason, but rather that of experimental intelligence. Peirce's critique of experimental intelligence does indeed trace its roots to the Kantian project, but with arguably even greater significance issues fruits resembling Hegel's speculative venture far more than Kant's critical philosophy. "My philosophy," Peirce came eventually to see, "resuscitates Hegel, though in strange costume" (CP: 1.42).

In its theoretical form, then, human reason is, from a Kantian perspective, a self-legislative power, properly exercising its rights to give laws to nothing less than nature. This characterization of rationality is, however, easily misunderstood. It does not mean that reason dictates how nature must, in particular, disclose herself, only how nature must be approached in order for discoveries to be made. Put otherwise, it means that theoretical reason defines the sphere in which scientific inquiry, as a responsible undertaking (not least of all, an empirically responsive undertaking – i.e. responsive to the promptings, pressures, and revelations of experience), takes place and, indeed, alone can take place. In order for reason to take anything at all away *from* experience, it must bring much *to* experience – nothing less than those principles of organization technically identified by Kant as the *a priori* forms of sensibility and the *a priori* categories of the understanding. In this sense, theoretical or scientific reason is self-legislative.

In its practical or moral form, however, human reason is, if anything, even more decidedly self-legislative. Moral agents do not as such follow the dictates of their sensuous natures or even the commands of a divine lawgiver, but the demand of the categorical imperative. Such agents are acting morally, in Kant's judgment, when they are acting not only in accord with duty but also out of an explicit, conscientious sense of duty, a sense obtainable only by means of a rigorous adherence to the categorical imperative. Just as the self-legislative function of theoretical or scientific reason is not intended by Kant to deprive nature of its autonomy, so too the self-legislative function of practical or moral reason is not understood by him as denying the authority of God. In giving laws to nature in the sense of conceiving the natural world in accord with the organizational principles of human reason, Kant takes theoretical reason to be establishing not only an intelligible but also an autonomous sphere. The world is knowable in large measure because it is *our* world, a world of appearances organized in accord with the demands we make upon what is given to us in sensation. But, Kant nonetheless insists, our world is truly a world (the world of theoretical reason is an arena for responsible inquiry), not merely the fabrication of private fancy or even the projection of collective delusion. It stands over against us with such solidity and degree of opposition, not only coherence and intelligibility, that empirical realism becomes an integral part of the Kantian position. That is, Kant is, in a sense, a realist (specifically, an *empirical* realist). While he certainly does not grant that we can know what things-in-themselves are (what things independent of our forms of sensibility and categories of understanding are), he insists that things as they appear to us in our experience can only be known on the basis of this experience. Empirical reality cannot be known *a priori*, even if the very possibility of there being such reality is dependent on the organizational work of human rationality. It must be known empirically and, in many cases, this means it can only be known experimentally (on the basis of delib-erately designed and carefully executed experiments). While Kant is a *transcendental idealist* because he insists that the defining features of *pure* reason (theoretical reason in its self-legislative character) are not known empirically or experimentally, but rather transcendentally, he is an *empirical realist* because he insists empirical reality is only knowable by empirical processes or procedures.

But Peirce encountered Schiller's *Aesthetic Letters* even before reading Kant's first *Kritik* (Peirce insisted upon translating *Kritik* as *Critic* rather than *Critique*, presumably stressing thereby one of the controlling metaphors presented very early in the Kantian text, that of the judge, in effect, the critic whose role is responsibly discharged only to the extent that certain canons of self-criticism are followed). Peirce came to philosophy by way of a scientific training and rather extensive reading in classical, medieval, and modern philosophy, with special attention paid to certain paradigmatic medieval logicians and modern authors. He was as deeply, if not more deeply, steeped in the German tradition of philosophical writing as any other.

Decisive steps toward a historical critique of experimental reason

Peirce was, at once, a representative figure of the nineteenth century (that is, he was a representative man in the Emersonian sense) and a thinker deeply at odds with many of the dominant tendencies of his time and place. The defining conflicts, contradic-tions, and aspirations (in all their ambiguity and ambivalence) of this century virtually define Peirce himself. For example, he could not have been more strenuously opposed to individualism, mechanism, scientism, materialism, agnosticism, and reductive conceptions of evolutionary development. As any thinker whose genius is receptive no less than innovative, Peirce was a child of his times and an exile from them. But he was in fundamental respects more our contemporary than Herbert Spencer's or Karl Pearson's (that we are far more familiar with his writings than theirs is indicative of this). But he is a contemporary whose style and even thought can, at times, seem quaint or dated, but more often one whose insights and suggestions are not yet fully appreciated or even understood.

The image of a recluse in Milford, Pennsylvania, spending his last years filling page after page contrasts sharply with that of us less than a hundred years later sitting in front of a computer screen. But the words in those manuscripts can sound stunningly contemporary. For him, methodological self-consciousness encompassed historical self-consciousness. In this, Peirce was far more a child of Vico than a child of Descartes (MacIntyre 1980 [1977]).

Experimental mind leans on historical consciousness. In turn, historical awareness today is infused with an experimental spirit: it takes itself to be never more than an attempt – a guess – at obtaining insights into what eludes definitive articulation or final reckoning. The narrative turn is only implicit in Peirce's writings. But his turn toward history, so characteristic of the nineteenth century, implies a turn toward narration, toward the process by which the past is re-appropriated and also re-framed or reconfigured. The example of Hegel is unmistakably that of a philosopher who tries to appropriate the reconfigurations of his predecessors.

But his approach (although in modified form) is relevant to our understanding of more than philosophy. Peirce worked indefatigably to offer a compelling account of scientific inquiry. He did so in a manner somewhat reminiscent of Hegel. But, at the same time, he worked with equal persistence to transform philosophy into a science, going so far in a letter to William James as to proclaim, "philosophy is either a science or it is balderdash" (Perry 1935: Vol. 2, 438). One of the unresolved tensions at the very center of Peirce's philosophical project bears directly upon his status as a representative thinker of the nineteenth century. For his writings both embody the tendency to privilege scientific knowing (in the sense of experimental inquiry) as the only reliable form of human knowing and provide the resources for (indeed, exhibit the impetus to) frame a comprehensive theory of human practices in which scientific inquiry is but one among numerous other forms of human symbolization. While he was in so many arenas of debate an astute critic of the reductivist impulse of so much nineteenth-century thought, he appears to be in his principal preoccupation an advocate (however unwitting) of reductivism. For is not scientism an instance of reductivism, in that it reduces all human knowing to the accredited forms of scientific inquiry? But the matter is more complex than this, since what Peirce means by science is more humane and encompassing than what is ordinarily meant by this word, especially in the mouths of the more militant defenders of the scientistic faith.

What emerges from Peirce's efforts to understand science on its own terms, from within the sensibility and Eros of those passionately devoted to a life of investigation, is a reconstructed understanding of human rationality. This understanding traces its roots partly to the classical vision of *logos*, but partly to a Darwinian (or, more broadly, evolutionary) conception of animal intelligence or cunning. In it, we clearly hear echoes of especially Aristotle and, in a more muted but still audible form, those of Kant and Hegel. In Peirce's writings, we encounter in a somewhat implicit, but in no small measure also an articulated, form a deliberative, dialogical understanding of human reason. Experimentation is itself understood, at bottom, as a dialogue between a sign-using and making animal, on the one hand, and a sign-generating nature, on the other. Animals are in the business of uttering and interpreting signs, quite apart from their intention or consciousness of doing so. Humans are animals for whom the utterance and interpretation of signs have evolved in the direction of self-consciousness, self-criticism, and self-control. Humans cannot think *without* signs; but we also cannot, at least at certain junctures in the tangled histories of our various practices, avoid thinking *about* signs. Human semiosis is virtually destined to become a reflexive operation, one ineluctably generating and extending semiotic awareness (our consciousness of signs as sign). The emergence and evolution of science are examples of nothing less than the development of methodological self-consciousness, self-criticism, and self-control, as these have taken shape in the various exchanges constituting the life of intergenerational communities of experimental inquirers. But the development of such awareness, assessment, and autonomy are not exhausted in the forms observable in the practices of science.

Experimental intelligence (the capacity not only to learn haphazardly from experience but also – and more decisively – to learn deliberately from experimentation) must inevitably lean on narrative consciousness. An experiment in the true sense is as much a drama as a dialogue; and, as a drama, the import and teachings of an experiment are available only by means of narration (an agent undertook a course of action and, as a consequence of these actions, certain results – some of which were likely unanticipated or unexpected – ensued). While experimental intelligence inescapably relies on narrative consciousness, narrative awareness drives beyond all inherited limits. The prefix *re-* is, in any pragmatically inflected discourse (thus in Peirce's own characteristic diction), as critical and central as the prefix *trans-* (as, for example, in such words as transmutation, transactions, transition, transformation, and translation). But this inflection is not only audible in such terms as reconstruction, renovation, reparation, and recovery but also in such words a re-narration and reconfiguration (especially when *reconfiguration* signifies the replacement of one figure or metaphor by another – e.g. the metaphor of constructing the edifice of knowledge on an unshakeable foundation with that of a journey, a process of making our way through largely unmapped terrain). The vitality of any tradition depends on a series of renewals and, in turn, these renewals often themselves depend on our narrative ingenuity, an ingenuity exhibited nowhere more dramatically than in our ability to re-narrate inherited stories in novel ways and, more radically, to revise what might count as an intelligible form of human storytelling.

Peirce took great pains to tell the story of the emergence and evolution of science. In doing so, he reformed our understanding of science, unquestionably anticipating the revolution inaugurated by Thomas Kuhn in academic circles a hundred years later. But his narration could not help but be a re-narration and even a counter-narrative, a story crafted and defended in the teeth of previous and rival accounts. In the course of unfolding this story, however, Peirce also articulated a reconstructed understanding of human rationality in which the ideal of demonstrative proof (animated by a demand for apodictic certitude) is replaced by the ideal of dialogical suasion (infused with the spirit of contrite fallibilism). Paradoxically, the severe self-restraint characteristic of the Kantian approach to theoretical reason is combined by Peirce with an abiding confidence in the irrepressible self-transcendence of our rational pursuits, in any of their actually realized forms (including their most authoritatively established ones at the present time), so central to the Hegelian account of living Reason.

Peirce's *evolutionary cosmology* was an attempt to envision a cosmos in which the myriad forms of living beings in their *ongoing* evolution are far from incidental or insignificant. This is, more than anything else, a universe in which life has emerged, evolved, and continues to evolve. Life – thus, growth and evolution – are not cosmic anomalies or (even more paradoxically) metaphysical impossibilities, but among the most salient features of the empirical world – phenomena to which our attention is drawn at every turn, though ones rendered inexplicable by the very theories whose function it is to illuminate – rather than deny – such phenomena.

"What the true definition of Pragmatism may be," Peirce once confessed, "I find it very hard to say; but *in my nature* it is a sort of instinctive attraction for living facts" (CP: 5.64; emphasis added). In my judgment, a deft feel for living facts, beginning with the phenomena of life themselves, is the deepest mark of Peircean pragmatism. In any event, scientific inquiry is, for Peirce, "a *living* thing" (CP: 1.234; emphasis added). But, to be in the position to conceive adequately the life of science, we must appreciate that "the woof and warp of all thought and all research is symbols, and the life of thought and science is the life inherent in symbols" (CP: 2.220). But it is all too easy to miss how seriously Peirce intends this point. Hence, it is helpful to stress that, for him, "every symbol is a living thing, in a very strict sense that is no *mere* figure of speech" (CP: 2.222; emphasis added), even if it is inescapably such a figure. In order to offer an account of the life of science, Peirce elaborated a general theory of signs, one applying to much more than linguistic signs or even the specific functions fulfilled by various signs in the vastly extended family of experimental inquiries. The phenomena of life in the cosmos – taken as telltale and undeniable signs of an irreducible and irrepressible reality – pointed Peirce toward an acknowledgement of the life of signs. His intellectual response to vital phenomena, extending to the life of science and more broadly signs, not just that of plants and animals, was the self-conscious articulation of an evolutionary perspective, albeit one in which social Darwinism and even the Darwinian theory of biological evolution were contested. Peirce was a thoroughgoing evolutionist but, in some respects, a half-hearted Darwinian.

In this and numerous other ways, he was a representative thinker in the Emersonian sense of the nineteenth century. Indeed, his deeply ambivalent relationship to this other paradigmatic figure – this other exemplar of the century in question – is nowhere more apparent than in his deep agreement with Emerson (Nature is a manifestation of Spirit and thus the study of Nature is a form of worship) linked to his equally deep dissatisfaction with approaching the study of Nature in the manner of *litterateurs*. But, regarding the principal function of the various forms of human symbolization, Peirce can only be read as being in the deepest agreement, moreover one unmarked by ambivalence, with Emerson's claim in "the Poet":

> the quality of the imagination is to flow, and not to freeze. ... Here is the difference betwixt the poet and the mystic, that the last [i.e. the mystic] nails a symbol to one sense, which was a true sense for a moment, but soon becomes old and false. For all symbols are fluxional; all language is vehicular and transitive, and is good, as ferries and horses are, for conveyance [or transport], not as farms and houses are, for homestead. (Ziff [ed.]: 279)

The life of science, so central to Peirce's own life of inquiry, manifests more than anything else the growth of symbols. The growth of symbols is one with the series of transitions facilitated by our use of symbols. In the context of science, the transitions of greatest importance are those contributing to the movement of thought *from* what is presently known, on the basis of our commonsensical inheritance and, on *this* basis, on that of the cumulative results of our deliberate experiments, *to* what is unknown. But, in the contexts of art, religion, ethics, politics, everyday life and erotic attachments (to name equally important domains of human practice), symbols as fluxional – as the indispensable means by which the requisite transitions, transformations, and transactions alone can be made by situated agents shaped by intersecting histories – are no less important than in the context of science. Peirce's general theory of signs and dialogical understanding of rationality potentially contribute a great deal to grasping the life and functions of symbols in all of these domains, even if Peirce himself focused somewhat narrowly on the context of science.

Peirce's writings are nothing less than a site in which some of the most powerful currents of nineteenth-century thought intersect and, in intersecting, reconfigure themselves in complex patterns, at times patterns of mutual support, at one times ones of explicit opposition, and yet other times patterns of unresolved tensions and unacknowledged ambivalence. Is it still possible to envision Nature as a manifestation of Spirit or does whatever can properly be called spirit, mind, or consciousness emerge out of natural processes in such a random manner that any attempt to configure Nature as a revelation of Spirit is unwarranted? Or does this very opposition – the tendency to pit Nature as manifestation of Spirit against Spirit as the offspring of Nature – itself betray an inability to reconfigure in an adequately contemporary manner the terms of the debate? Whatever may be the answers to these questions, what is certain is that Peirce, at once, defended an evolutionary cosmology and provided indispensable resources for developing an anti-reductive naturalism. He conceived his efforts to craft such a cosmology to be itself an evolution of the positions of such predecessors as Aristotle, Kant, Schelling, Hegel, and Darwin. His opposition to mechanistic determinism or, to stress the most salient positive point in his opposition to this doctrine, his insistence on absolute chance (or *real* spontaneity) marked a decisive break with the dominant approach in the nineteenth century, continued throughout much of the twentieth and indeed into the twenty-first, to the physical world.

The attempt to square our scientific understanding of the natural world with our moral self-understanding, so central to Kant's critical project but also to post-Kantian thought, was ingeniously reconfigured by Peirce with respect to both our vision of nature and our portrait of our own agency. Chance is as objectively or really characteristic of nature as is lawfulness or regularity. Chance might in truth be an even more prominent and pervasive trait of nature than law. Indeterminacy marks being, what is no less than our thoughts and efforts to know what is. That is, reality itself is in some respects and to some degree indeterminate. The intelligibility of the cosmos implies the presence – in the end, nothing less than the reality – of continuity. The world *is* intelligible and the degree to which it is such can only be determined experimentally. The tendency to pronounce this or that inexplicable or unknowable amounts to the suicide of thought. For thought in the relevant sense here is primarily imagination transfigured by demands of rendering phenomena explicable. For thought to insist upon inexplicability amounts to thought in the pertinent sense destroying itself.

Logical agency – the form of deliberative rationality exerted and refashioned by the experimental inquirer, moreover, the form explored and explicated by the logician in the uniquely Peircean sense of that word – is, according to Peirce, only a species of moral agency. The principal task confronting human beings in their role as logical agents is neither to construct demonstrative arguments (or deductive proofs) nor to secure reliable inductions, but to generate fruitful hypotheses (and this practically means putting forth somewhat wild but not unintelligent guesses carrying the promise to illuminate facets or features of what presently eludes understanding or explanation).

For many of the impulses unleashed or at least intensified during this time are ones that define arcs and trajectories extending all the way into the present. C. S. Peirce's efforts to come to terms *with* his own time, partly in terms inherited from his most immediate predecessors (most notably, Kant, Schiller, Schelling, Hegel, and Darwin) and partly in ones improvised by him, provides us with a model for coming to terms with Peirce himself *in* his time. That his physical life extended beyond the limit of the century in which he was born might be taken as a symbol of not only the unfinished task embodied in his voluminous writings but also (more broadly) the ongoing work of considering anew numerous pivotal figures in the nineteenth century. What Schelling and Hegel were to the three inaugural decades of the nineteenth century, arguably Peirce and James were to the concluding decades of that century and the opening years of the twentieth – at the very least, disparate attempts to square the natural world with human freedom, to reconcile the claims of religious consciousness with the discoveries of experimental inquiry, and finally a sustained interrogation of the *meaning* of science (*Wissenschaft*) encompassing a reflexive account of meaning itself. An understanding of science articulated self-consciously in light of the history of science – one aiming to display the meaning of science – turned out to be impossible apart from a science of meaning or, more exactly, the study of signs. But such a study, especially when conjoined to an unqualified acceptance of unconscious mind, an insistence upon the evolutionary continuity between the human species and other species, a conception of intelligibility inhering in networks of relationship as much discovered as created by the symbolific propensities of the human mind, and finally an acute awareness of the metaphorical character of all innovative thought, could not avoid directing attention (regarding the unconscious mind) from Eduard von Hartmann to Sigmund Freud and beyond, (regarding evolutionary continuity) from Charles Darwin, Louis Aggasiz, and Asa Gray to contemporary biologists and (more broadly) evolutionary theorists in various fields (e.g. Terrence Deacon [1997]), from Saussure and Peirce himself to Ernst Cassirer, Susanne Langer, and other theorists of signs today, finally from (again) Peirce to Mary Hesse, Paul Ricoeur, George Lakoff, Mark Johnson and other theorists of metaphor. That is, one cannot but trace the trajectories of thought originating or intensifying in the nineteenth century into, and beyond, the twentieth. This is one of the insights we have inherited from this century regarding the meaning of meaning itself: significance is irreducibly and irrepressibly historical and, thus, it is, no matter how firmly consolidated or authoritatively instituted, ineluctably driving toward an unending series of more or less radical transformations.

Meaning is, first and foremost, *in the making* – meanings made (those established and integrated, adumbrated and codified) are ultimately in the service of meanings in the making. The value of symbols is that they insure the growth of symbols and, ultimately, their own self-overcoming or self-overturning. Peirce's vision of the cosmos, so intimately connected to his understanding of signs (or semiosis – i.e. sign-activity or sign-process) and, more specifically, to the experimentally controlled use of signs in methodically deliberate investigations, exemplifies this growth. It also offers one of the most penetrating analyses of this dramatic process to be found in a writer from this epoch or, for that matter, from any other one. The manner in which meaning and evolution are creatively linked here is emblematic of this thinker and the century in which he was born. This is so not least of all because we can observe, as a sign of the times, the unresolved tension between rational control of our use of signs and the uncontrollable growth of signs in their myriad forms – more precisely, between the ideal of rational control and the recognition of ungovernable evolution.

The exercise of rational agency as much as anything else leads to a vision of staggeringly complex, intricately interwoven processes (biological, cultural, political, economic, and ultimately cosmic) in which humans are ineluctably caught up. The historical situatedness of human rationality is, at once, a disclosure of rationality itself and an apparent threat to even the minimal requirements for rational control over our various pursuits (including experimental inquiry). Part of the story is, arguably, the transition from conceiving reason as a transcendent capacity (indeed, the tendency to identify reason with the capacity to transcend the contingencies and particularities of time and place, personality and culture, animal life and human finitude) to envisioning reason as an immanent force (at least, an immanent presence) in the actual world in all of its unfinished and alterable character.

Does human reason truly possess the powers it presumes to exercise? The most troublesome threats to human rationality emerge – or, perhaps more accurately, erupt – from within the life of reason itself. As a result, reason appears to be divided within itself. The efforts of Kant and subsequently such thinkers as Schelling, Fichte, and

Hegel to portray human rationality as an ultimately harmonious unity were taken up and carried forward by Peirce and the other pragmatists (to name but one significant movement tracing its roots to the nineteenth century and, more specifically, staking its identity in part on offering an radical revision of human reason). Peirce and the pragmatists no more offered a definitive solution to the internal conflicts befalling human reason by virtue of its most dramatic achievements than did Kant or the post-Kantian idealists. But like these and other predecessors, they provide profound insights into the situated and thus conditioned character of rationality, also the critical function and dialectical developments so much a part of the evolution of reason. These insights alert us to the possibilities of distortion in such expressions as "the evolution of reason" and "the intelligibility of nature," without necessarily forcing us to abandon such expressions. The work of reason is unending, the evolution of rationality and thus autonomy is full of unpredictable twists and turns, and our alliances with nature are intimate and fateful, making our estrangement from nature inescapable but (whenever frozen into a permanent posture) destructive beyond imagination.

Can acknowledgement of the historicity of reason be conjoined to an unblinking recognition of the ultimately irrational character of human history (at least, the possibility of this being true of history), without losing reason? Peirce and other pragmatists, along with other movements inaugurated in the century of Marx, Kierkegaard, Darwin, and Nietzsche, are as important for pressing this question as they are for providing resources to address it. Perhaps Peirce is more a child of the century in which he was born than the one in which he died by being more preoccupied with showing the rationality of evolution and history than exhibiting the historicity and evolution of reason. But the unresolved tensions evident even in his most carefully developed positions suggest he represents that century not so much in the positions he advocated as in the problematics he embodied, with all their jagged edges and unanswered questions.

References

Darwin, Charles (1993) *The Portable Darwin*, edited by Porter M. Porter and Peter W. Graham, New York: Viking.

Deacon, Terrence W. (1997) *The Symbolic Species*, New York: W. W. Norton & Co.

Dewey, John (LW) "Charles Sanders Peirce," *New Republic* (3 February 1937): 415–16; repr. *Later Works of John Dewey*, vol. 11, Carbondale: Southern Illinois University Press, 1987, pp. 479–84. (Review of volumes 1–6 of *Collected Papers*.)

Kant, Immanuel. 1965. *The Critique of Pure Reason*, trans. Norman Kemp Smith, New York: St Martin's Press.

Peirce, C. S. (CN) *Charles Sanders Peirce: Contributions to "The Nation,"* edited by Kenneth Ketner and James Cook, 3 pts, Lubbock, TX: Texas Tech Press, 1975–9.

—— (CP) *The Collected Papers of Charles Sanders Peirce*, vols 1–6, edited by Charles Hartshorne and Paul Weiss; vol. 7 and 8, edited by Arthur W. Burks, Cambridge, MA: Belknap Press of Harvard University Press, 1931–58.

Perry, Ralph Barton (1935) *The Thought and Character of William James*, 2 vols, Boston: Little, Brown & Co.

Ransdell, Joseph (1986 [1979]) "Semiotic Objectivity," in John Deel, Brooke Williams, and Felicia E. Kruse (eds) *Frontiers in Semiotics*, Bloomington, IN: Indiana University Press, pp. 236–54.

Smith, John E. (1992) *America's Philosophical Vision*, Chicago: University of Chicago Press.

25

WILLIAM JAMES

Robert Burch

A brief biography of James

William James was born on the eleventh of January 1842, into a wealthy family in which intellectual endeavor was highly valued. From 1857 until 1860 his education took place in France and Switzerland. Upon returning to the United States at age 18, he undertook various studies. These included art (his first and possibly his greatest passion), science, and finally (in 1863) medicine. In 1865 he traveled with the notable paleontologist and zoologist Louis Agassiz to the mouth of the Amazon River to collect biological specimens. During this trip he began to experience a variety of health problems, which continued to plague him thereafter and which seemed to have the result that he was always very attentive to his own bodily sensations and perhaps also somewhat prone to hypochondria. James continued his medical studies, going to Germany to do so in 1867 and 1868; there he studied physiology with Herman Helmholtz, and became friends with psychologist Carl Stumpf. James discussed with Stumpf many of the ideas of Wilhelm Wundt, who was widely regarded at the time as the greatest of all of the contemporary psychologists.

After returning to the United States, James received his medical degree from Harvard in 1869. Soon after receiving his degree, James experienced (in 1869 and early 1870) a serious case of major depression. He ultimately recovered from this depression, and he associated his recovery with acquiring a new way of thinking about three philosophical problems: the problem of monism, the problem of determinism, and the problem of pessimism versus optimism. James's depressive episode and his recovery from this episode will be looked at more closely in the following section of this article.

In 1871 and 1872 James took part in philosophical discussions with a group of exceptionally able graduates of Harvard, including Oliver Wendell Holmes, Chauncey Wright, and Charles Sanders Peirce. The group called themselves "the Metaphysical Club." Many of James's later ideas had an origin in one way or another amidst the Metaphysical Club's discussions. For example, Darwin's theory of evolution was a major focus of interest of the Club. So also was Peirce's novel account of cognition and scientific research, which James later called "pragmatism." James always regarded Chauncey Wright's careful analytic criticisms of monism to be some of the most acute thinking he ever encountered.

In 1873 James became instructor in anatomy and physiology at Harvard, but his main focus of attention was already turning in the direction of psychology and philosophy. In 1875 he offered his first course in psychology at Harvard and established the first psychology research laboratory in America (1875 was also the year that Wundt established the first psychology research laboratory in Europe). In 1876 James became assistant professor of physiology. He married Alice Gibbons in 1878, and over the following years the husband and wife raised five children. In 1878 also James wrote a treatise on psychology. In 1879 he offered his first course in philosophy. It was also in 1879 that he published the paper, "The Sentiment of Rationality" in which psychology and philosophy are closely intertwined. After 1879 James's attention was totally absorbed by psychology and philosophy. In 1880 he became assistant professor of philosophy at Harvard. By 1885 he had become full professor of philosophy.

In 1890 James's first major published work appeared: *The Principles of Psychology*. In 1892 he published *Psychology: the Briefer Course*, which soon became known as "the Jimmy" on account of its ability to open up the meaning of the earlier and much larger book. Soon James was as hard at work on philosophy as was on empirical psychology. *The Will to Believe and Other Essays on Popular Philosophy* was published in 1897. In 1899 his interest in education resulted in *Talks to Teachers*. In 1901 and 1902 James gave the Gifford Lectures in Edinburgh. These lectures were published as *The Varieties of Religious Experience*. In 1906 he gave the Lowell Lectures at Harvard; these were published as *Pragmatism*. In 1908 at Oxford he gave the Hibbert Lectures, which were published as *A Pluralistic Universe*. In 1909 he attempted to clarify his much criticized – and in James's view much misunderstood – ideas about truth in *Pragmatism* by publishing a new work on truth called *The Meaning of Truth*.

James died of heart disease on August 26, 1910.

Difficulties in interpreting James

As a philosopher James is widely regarded, along with Peirce, as one of the founders of American pragmatism. James in particular is regarded as putting forward his own novel, but still pragmatic, theory of truth. Beyond these general assertions, however, there is not universal agreement as to what exactly and in detail James's pragmatic theory involves. It is not unusual to find almost opposite interpretations of James. There are those who consider James's pragmatism a relativistic position, and there are those, including James himself, who deny that his position is relativistic. There are those who consider that James had a "coherence theory" of truth, somewhat akin to theories of truth often found in German and English idealists (for which truth is a matter of the internal coherence of a system of ideas). There are those, including James himself, who assert that he had a "correspondence theory" of truth, according to which truth is a matter of a correspondence between thoughts or assertions on the one hand and facts on the other hand. Interpretations of James have thus varied widely. A number of factors have contributed to this situation.

One factor that contributes to making James not always easy to pin down in detail is his writing style, which is more typical of a novelist than of a philosopher. Like

David Hume, James exercised a strong literary bent in writing philosophy, which makes him, like Hume, usually easy to read at a casual level but often difficult to grasp in precise detail.

Aside from the literary flavor of James's writings, a second factor in much of his philosophical writings contributes to the difficulty of getting at a precise account of James's doctrines. Before saying what this second factor is, we can take note that the immediate effects of this second factor are prominent in much commentary on James's thought. From the time of publication of Ralph Barton Perry's comprehensive, two-volume work *The Thought and Character of William James* (1935) to the present day, scholarly commentary on William James has often exhibited the following special property: in it discussion of James's philosophical thought and discussion of James's personal biography are extremely closely intertwined with each other. The philosopher's doctrines and arguments, on the one hand, and the man's psychology, character, and life history, on the other hand, appear almost as one and the same thing. Thus, it is difficult to separate in this commentary the doctrine from the man.

The aforementioned "second factor" that makes it difficult to pin James down exactly – and which has the result that man and doctrine are often merged in commentary on James – is James's own tendency, especially in the decade or so following 1870, to write essays that essentially, if not always formally, were to some extent self-referential. This self-referential character of his writings was connected with the previously mentioned period of major depression into which James had fallen and from which he had then subsequently recovered. Accordingly, it is useful to look further into this period.

Several years before his entering medical school James had struggled to find his own path in life and had ardently wanted to become a painter. His father, however, went to extremes to prevent James from pursuing an artistic vocation and urged upon him a career in science and engineering. Medicine was perhaps a compromise, and James received his MD degree from Harvard in 1869 at age twenty-seven. The depressive episode followed shortly afterwards. It was connected in James's mind with his attachment at the time to the philosophical ideas of monism, determinism, and pessimism. The depression lasted several months before it began to resolve itself. The lifting of the depression in February of 1870, moreover, was connected in James's mind with his reading of the French philosopher Charles Bernard Renouvier (1815–1903). It was Renouvier who led James to become increasingly convinced of the genuine reality and efficacy of human free will. Many of James's Renouvier-influenced writings in the decade or so after this episode were efforts to describe the personal attitudes and beliefs that contributed both to his recovery and to the sustaining of it. These writings took the form of general and somewhat abstract discussions of the relation between the individual human will and the constitution of reality. They had on the whole an optimistic note: there is some relation of "congeniality" between the world and the human will. In fact, the writings describe patterns of thinking that led James into recovery, but they do so in a rather disguised way, as philosophical points that on the surface of things have the appearance of being far removed from James himself.

A third factor that makes James's thought hard to grasp in detail and that also contributes to the merging of James the philosopher and James the man is the ongoing attention James himself gave to empirical and introspective psychology. As was mentioned earlier in this article, although James was professionally trained as a medical doctor, specializing in anatomy and physiology, his attention quickly turned to psychology as his area of special interest. As was also said: James established a psychology laboratory at Harvard in 1875; his earliest writings (c. 1878) were concerned with psychology; and his first major published work was *The Principles of Psychology* (1890). Many commentators have considered *The Principles* to be James's masterpiece; and, indeed, it made James the premier psychologist of the time in American and perhaps also – along with Wilhelm Max Wundt (1832–1920) – in the world. James's theory of sensations and emotions as being felt bodily conditions is even nowadays still cited as "the James (or: James-Lange) theory of the emotions." (For a while at Harvard even James's professional title was Professor of Psychology. Philosophy and psychology at the time were not clearly demarcated from one another in the university.) *The Varieties of Religious Experience* is almost purely a work in descriptive psychology of religion, and in particular it contains lengthy discussions of the psychology of religious conversion, which according to James are convulsive revolutions in opinion that appear suddenly but that are nevertheless quite long in preparation.

James the psychologist will be looked at further in the fifth section of this article. For now the point is merely to note that from the outset James was as much empirical psychologist as philosopher, and that in some ways, perhaps, he was even more empirical psychologist than philosopher. Now, this fact – especially when it is coupled with his introspective approaches to psychology of the sort that are associated (rightly or wrongly) with the name of Wundt – had a powerful influence on the details of many of James's philosophical arguments. In particular this fact, conjoined with James's flair for literary narrative, made James appreciative of concrete and down-to-earth exposition and examples. In almost all of his writings, James tends to distrust abstract and general philosophical doctrines; he prefers to avoid excessive reliance on "ism" words. As the point is put in *Pragmatism*, along with (James) Clerk Maxwell James's desire was to understand "the particular go" of things. (It was, by the way, James's down-to-earth concreteness that made him one of the very few philosophers of whom the mature Wittgenstein had anything positive to say.) But the avoidance of abstract doctrine in favor of concrete examples often makes it difficult to say, abstractly and generally, exactly what James was thinking.

James and the problem of epistemic responsibility

In addition to the three aforementioned factors, which make it hard to pin James down in detail, and which often lead commentators to identify doctrine and man, there is a fourth such factor. Indeed, in connection with the issue whether James was or was not a relativist, it is perhaps the most important factor of them all. This factor is the peculiar nature of one of the central philosophical problems with which James wrestled throughout his career. The present article submits, prior to specifying exactly what the problem is, that this problem is at the core of much of James's philosophy;

it is a problem by reference to which most of James's philosophical and psychological writings can be, in one way or another, clarified.

A title for this problem is not easy to provide. One would be tempted to call it something like the problem of "epistemic ethics," or the problem of "the ethics of belief," or some such phrase with the word "ethics" in it. But the problem in question is not exactly an ethical problem, for reasons that will be specified in the material to follow. Most generally this problem is an offshoot from the trunk of the general problem of epistemology, but it is not any straightforward part of epistemology. It is also an offshoot of ethics but not a part of ethics. Clearly, it is concerned with some sort of evaluation, and clearly this sort of evaluation is connected with justification in epistemology. But it is not the same thing as the problem of justification in epistemology. Most generally, it is the problem of *what a person has a right to believe*; or perhaps more accurately: it is the problem of what a person does not have an obligation not to believe. It is the problem of determining one's epistemic responsibilities and rights. It concerns what is intellectually to be allowed and what is intellectually respectable in connection with belief. It is the problem of determining to what extent one is free of some or other kind of "culpability" for arriving at one's beliefs as one does arrive at them and for believing what one does believe. This kind of culpability is not the same thing as ethical culpability, but it opens the possessor of it to certain kinds of negative evaluations. It is not to be reduced to believing-without-justification, for issues other than purely epistemic ones of justification are involved in it. For lack of any other suitable name for the problem, let us call it the problem of "epistemic responsibility."

This problem that herein is being called the problem of epistemic responsibility is hardly a new problem, even though it seems not to be discussed as a separate theme nowadays by either epistemologists or ethicists. One must admit that tangential or glancing references to it are sometimes made in epistemology in the course of discussions concerning the role in knowledge played by justification, but the subject is not taken up in its own right. The problem, nevertheless, traces at least to Plato's metaphor in the *Republic* of the mutiny on shipboard, where the mutineers are clearly presented as being epistemically culpable. The problem is involved in St Paul's argumentation in the first chapter of the *Epistle to the Romans* that non-believers have no excuse for themselves. The problem is connected with doctrines of the medieval period, when certain sorts of refusal to accept what was put forward as rationally compelling argumentation were classified as "invincible ignorance," which was attributed to a person as a severe epistemic criticism of a quasi-moral sort. In the early modern period Descartes took up the problem of epistemic responsibility vigorously in several much-neglected passages in the *Meditations*, especially in the fourth *Meditation*. There, Descartes does not treat the problem as merely one more of the problems of epistemology. Rather, he treats it as an epistemic analogue of the classical problem of evil. Descartes considers the question of how it is possible that God, who is not a deceiver, made human beings with epistemic faculties that so often lead them into false judgments. His answer is that God made human beings not only with epistemic faculties but also with will; and that when the will is allowed to overpower the epistemic faculties and lead them to overhasty judgment, then the case resembles sinful behavior. The resultant evil of false judgment is not owing to any deceptiveness or any other sort of imperfection in God, but rather is owing to the culpable failure of human beings to control their own wills in an epistemically responsible manner. Human beings, when they fall into error, are thus culpable in some sense of "culpability" that, though it is not the very same thing as moral culpability, is still more or less like the sin involved in falling into temptation.

Even a short reading of James's autobiographical accounts will show the great extent to which this problem that is here being called the problem of epistemic responsibility was involved in James's depressive episode of 1869–70. Having long been deeply committed to what he conceived of as the highest standards of rational appraisal of reality, James found himself in 1869 unable to avoid the conclusions that the world, along with us in it, is totally determined by causal laws. Freedom of action and moral endeavor, then, appeared to James to be nothing but an illusion. To believe in free will, contrary to all the deliverances of rational appraisal and contrary to the highest standards of epistemic justification, would have been an abrogation of epistemic responsibility: a sin against rationality. The resultant conflict in James's inner life, and the accompanying pessimism of his deterministic ideation, were both intricately involved in the depression he experienced in his emotional life.

The problem of epistemic responsibility explicitly appeared early in James's philosophical writings; indeed it was the central theme in one of his earliest papers. This paper was written in French in 1878 for the journal *Critique philosophique* and it was entitled "*Quelques considérations sur la méthode subjective.*" The paper's second paragraph states (as here translated) the crucial problem to be considered in the paper: "It treats of knowing whether one has the right to reject a theory that is apparently confirmed by a very considerable number of objective facts, simply because it does not at all answer to our interior preferences." The central question, then, of the essay is "whether one has the right" to believe the opposite of something that is strongly supported by empirical evidence, and for no other reason than that this something fails to harmonize with one's inner preferences. In the essay James allows that in some cases one does have that right. In those cases in which it is possible to settle matters by reference to empirical data, by empirical data the matters should be settled. But there exists a kind of issue that is different from one that can be clearly settled by empirical evidence, and this kind of issue is exemplified strikingly in the problem of monism, the problem of determinism, and the problem of optimism and pessimism. Such problems as these are not of a nature to admit anything like clear settlement on the basis of empirical data. Doctrines concerning them are not empirical. Rather they are of the nature of fundamental principles: *postulates* in terms of which we choose, subsequent to adopting these postulates, how to interpret *all* of our empirical experience. James argues in connection with such problems and doctrines that a person has the epistemic right to adopt or not adopt philosophical positions concerning them solely on the basis of what responds to that person's interior preferences. That is to say, James argues that believing in certain principles, just because one deeply wants to believe in them, is sometimes within a person's sphere of epistemic right. Quite apart from the acceptability of James's arguments for this point, James clearly identifies the question of epistemic responsibility as central to philosophy in general. And he clearly allows much greater latitude for being within one's epistemic rights than most other philosophers would allow. (It seems to be this great latitude of allowance that is largely responsible for the tendency of some readers of James to consider James a relativist.)

One of the critical features of epistemic responsibility is that evaluating it is placing a value on neither a belief nor a process of arriving at a belief; rather, it is evaluating, either negatively or positively, a *person* who has a belief or arrives at a belief by using a given process. But evaluating epistemic responsibility is evaluating a person insofar and only insofar as that person has a certain belief or engages in a certain process of arriving at that belief. Evaluation of epistemic rights and responsibilities, then, is always epistemic evaluation of *persons* in their epistemic context. (Later in this article it will be noted that James the philosopher's wide latitude of allowance for belief is, then, connected with James the man's wide tolerance of and respect for persons.)

It is interesting that, when James did finally begin to pull out of his depression, he made remarks to the effect that he had simply *chosen* to believe in free will, completely independently of any evidence. As his depression lifted, James wrote in his diary that his first act of free will would be to believe in free will. A remarkable jotting this was, and one that has not failed to capture the attention of virtually every James scholar. It and many more like it in the course of James's career have urged upon many readers of James the question whether James was what we might call an "epistemic voluntarist." An epistemic voluntarist, in the sense here intended, is someone who holds that in general, if a person's sole or main reason for believing in a doctrine is that believing in it will make that person happy or prosperous or otherwise in some felicitous and desirable state, then that person is within his or her epistemic rights. If James is an epistemic voluntarist in this sense, then, it is hard to see how he could not also be some sort of relativist. If merely wanting to believe something were always sufficient grounds for epistemic non-culpability, then it is difficult to see how anyone, believing anything for any reason, could be epistemically culpable in any way at all. In other words epistemic voluntarism seems not to allow one to make any substantial distinction between conditions of epistemic culpability and conditions of epistemic non-culpability. In epistemic voluntarism, then, epistemic responsibility would seem to be abrogated altogether.

Those who do see James as an epistemic voluntarist are also quick to associate this view with a specific understanding of James's theory of truth. That is to say, they are likely to understand his theory of truth, which is that truth is what in some sense "works," to mean that truth for a person is what makes that person, or perhaps all of us, happy, prosperous, and successful. This doctrine, that truth is simply what works for us, in the sense of what makes us happy or prosperous, has often been associated with James. Clearly, however, this is a doctrine that is pretty wide of the mark of the notion of truth as we ordinarily understand it. Bertrand Russell called it the doctrine of "transatlantic truth," attributed it to James, and dismissed outright both the doctrine and James. The notion that truth for James is what makes us prosper is thus an interpretation of James's view that is at least problematic.

James himself, however, was adamant that Russell did not in the least understand his theory of truth; he also wrote a whole volume (*The Meaning of Truth*) to explain his theory of truth and to insist that he did not hold that truth is what makes us happy and prosperous. James also tried to detach himself totally from the relativist label. The sixth ("James's Pragmatism") and especially seventh section ("James's Theory of Truth") of this article will attempt to show that James's theory of truth is indeed very different from the "transatlantic truth" that Russell was talking about. In these sections it will also emerge that James is far from being an epistemic voluntarist or relativist. But we can already see one thing that has gone wrong in the philosophical motivation for interpreting James in these common ways. James argues forcefully that we *sometimes* have the epistemic right to believe a proposition merely because it accords with our inner preferences. Very fundamental and overarching propositions of the sort that he called "postulates," can be believed on this basis without the believer being epistemically culpable. Now, if one holds that what James had to say about postulates (like monism, pluralism, determinism, and free will) applies as well to every doctrine of every kind, then the result is epistemic voluntarism and relativism. James, however, did not hold that what one can say about postulates can also be said about propositions in general.

Renouvier, radical empiricism, the reality of relations, and a pluralistic universe

As was mentioned previously, the earliest formations of James's mature ideas are connected with his depressive episode of 1869 and 1870 and with the relation between his recovery and his study of Renouvier. Moreover, James cited Renouvier approvingly throughout his career, and it is hard to overestimate the importance of Renouvier for understanding James's so-called "radical empiricism." For this reason it is important for understanding James to have a good idea of Renouvier's philosophy.

However much James's depression might have been caused in its full concreteness by his troubled relation with his father or by James's exhaustion after the completion of a difficult education, this depression – as we have seen – was animated by ideation connected with James's having accepted a monistic metaphysics whose deterministic implications were inconsistent with human free will. James was intellectually too honest not to see that compatibilism – the view that causal determinism is after all consistent with human free will – was no genuine way out and was in fact a cheat as a doctrine. (In his later essay "The Dilemma of Determinism" he would call compatibilism "soft determinism" and characterize it as nothing but a "quagmire of evasion.") In James's view there was always a clear dichotomy: either the doctrine of determinism is true and there is no real human freedom, or human freedom is real and the doctrine of determinism is false. James's intellectual problem during his depression was that he could see no way to avoid monism and determinism. It was at this point in his intellectual development that James turned to Renouvier.

Renouvier was what he himself called a "neo-critical" philosopher. By this label Renouvier meant that his point of departure was the Kantian philosophy, but that his intent was to transform significantly the standard doctrines of Kant as they were at the time often understood. Effecting such a transformation became Renouvier's lifelong work.

Renouvier took extremely seriously Kant's insistence (in the later editions of the *Critique of Pure Reason*) that the notion of the noumenal (as introduced in the first edition) had no positive content and was purely a "boundary concept" (*Grenzbegriff*), correctly usable only to set strict limits to all possible empirical thought. For Renouvier, then, there is no noumenal/transcendental self or noumenal/transcendental reality that presents itself or "gives" itself in experience (*Erfahrung*). There is only the phenomenal. There is merely the presentation, and not also something else beyond it that the presentation presents. The presentation presents merely itself and nothing more. It follows that phenomenal experience is all there is. The existence of experiences, of presentations: this is the ultimate metaphysical bedrock. The world is a world of pure experience. Nothing more. James would come to develop the epistemic and metaphysical implications of this sort of thoroughgoing phenomenalism under the heading of "radical empiricism." James's radical empiricism will be discussed further in the ninth section ("James's Radical Empiricism and Pluralism") of this article.

Experiences, however, in their most immediate phenomenal nature have both a subjective and an objective aspect. On the one hand experiences are experienced; on the other hand experiences have an experiential object of some sort. From this bedrock we move to a somewhat orderly but still complex picture of the world and of ourselves as experiencing it. But never in the whole process is there any leap into any noumenal realm. Renouvier maintained an absolutely strict phenomenalism. From this basic premise two points follow. First, the validity of all individual human experiences as genuine experiences of something is not to be denied: if experiences are the bedrock of all knowledge, there is nothing more basic than experiences by which the content of experiences can be negated. Second, the self and all its aspects are phenomenal and not noumenal. This point implies that freedom itself is phenomenal and not, as Kant thought, noumenal. We experience ourselves as free, and when there is no phenomenal experience to the contrary, the experience of ourselves as being free implies that we are genuinely free. In general, then, freedom of the will is not to be denied. Most especially, freedom is not to be denied on the basis of some abstract, philosophical line of argumentation that is divorced from actual, phenomenal experiences.

Experiences, moreover, do not come as already metaphysically interpreted. They most certainly do not display any kind of metaphysical monism. In themselves and as experienced, they are inherently diverse: "plural" in nature. No form of monism, then, is a direct deliverance of experience. In fact the immediate deliverance of experience is that the world is a vast plurality of things that are related to one another but not on that account unified into one substance. In the experiences, the relations among things are as fully given as the things themselves. Thus relations are as real as the things related, and they are as diverse as, or even more diverse than, the things related. Relations cannot, then, all be collapsed into the identity relation. What experience serves up is a metaphysically diverse world, a (to use James's words) "pluralistic universe."

Since all individual human experiences are basic in the way above indicated, it follows for Renouvier that each human being is unique and is of unique value; each human being has free will. Each human being is thus free to develop himself or herself in a process of dynamic self-determination and self-creation. As James later elaborated this idea, it came to have clear affinities with themes in what would later appear as, for example, the existentialism of Albert Camus.

These are the new doctrines that James juxtaposed against his former, deterministic monism; and, not surprisingly, the new doctrines simply swept away James's previous view with a mighty whisk. What James saw in Renouvier was that he, James, had a perfect epistemic right to believe in free will and to engage in his own process of dynamic, even Promethean, self-determination. This was a sea change in James's intellectual life and in his psychological wellbeing. And, as we shall see, James came to endorse heartily most of the other major points of Renouvier's philosophy. The ninth section of this article will focus on James's radical empiricism and pluralism.

James as psychologist

It was emphasized in the foregoing material of this article that James was as much a psychologist as he was a philosopher. We are now in a position to begin to appreciate the fact that for James being a psychologist and being a philosopher essentially amounted almost to one and the same thing. For if the unsurpassable bedrock of metaphysics and epistemology is pure experience, and if experience is always a plurality of diverse experiences, then the investigation of metaphysics and epistemology just *is* the investigation of experiences in all their concrete detail. But such concretely detailed investigation is what James understood to be the business of psychology. So the fact that psychology and philosophy were combined in James's thinking was much more than a mere artifact of the arrangement of academic departments in James's day. It was a matter for James of the proper methodology of philosophy. When coupled with James's pragmatism (to be discussed in the following section of this article), James's commitment to the idea of a pluralistic universe of pure experiences makes psychology an indispensable part and the chief tool of philosophy.

Before looking more closely at any features of James's psychology that are related to James's philosophy, let us very briefly consider (again) James simply as an empirical psychologist, quite apart from any special philosophical implications of his psychology.

In the topics they explore, James's psychological studies in *The Principles of Psychology*, *The Varieties of Religious Experience*, and other psychological works are extraordinarily wide-ranging. Habit, emotion, exertion, religious conviction and conversion, all figure prominently and are deeply explored. But we also find James exploring virtually everything imaginable: the sentiment of rationality, the sense of dizziness, the sensation of extension, the feelings of effort and relaxation, sensations from "phantom" limbs, and so on and on. Nothing in conscious life seemed to be alien to James's interest. And consciousness itself, which James described as an onrushing stream with a center and a periphery rather than as a static container with sharp boundaries, was a major focus of his psychology. In this stream, not only individuals are directly experienced but also relations among individuals. It would not be incorrect to describe consciousness itself as the main focus of James's psychology.

Aside from a few specific doctrines that divided James and Wundt, James's psychology is remarkably similar to that of Wundt. Both men were trained in physiology and both viewed psychology as causally continuous with physiology. Neither, however, was a reductionist of the psychological to the physical: both held that psychology deals with the world of consciousness and that consciousness is metaphysically *sui generis*. Mind is intimately connected with body, but the two are not the same thing. Wundt's psychology of consciousness and its properties is not unlike James's discussions of consciousness in *The Principles of Psychology*. Both Wundt and James championed the use of experimental method in psychology, and both considered the right experimental method to be based on the examination of consciousness by means of introspection. By "introspection," however, both meant something very different from the ideas later promulgated by the extreme introspectionist Edward Bradford Titchener (1867–1927). Titchener, an Englishman who had studied with Wundt and had come to the United States to teach at Cornell, represented himself as merely spreading Wundt's ideas. But by "introspection" Titchener meant little more than private internal mental examination of oneself. This understanding of "introspection" is not the understanding of either Wundt or James. For both Wundt and James, "introspection" was understood to be examination of consciousness by *any* possible legitimate means, including but certainly not limited to private internal mental examination of oneself. Among other things, "introspection" for them meant investigating the causal origins and effects of mental events and states.

Indeed, without this wide understanding of the meaning of "introspection" for both Wundt and James, it is impossible to understand one of the well-known points of disagreement between them: the disagreement concerning the causal relationships between the "external" world and our emotions. For Wundt an emotion is the *intermediary* between a perception of something and the bodily manifestations of that emotion: perception immediately causes emotion, and emotion causes bodily manifestations. But for James perception immediately causes bodily manifestations, which in turn are felt as emotions: perception causes bodily manifestations, which cause emotion. In this so-called "James-Lange" theory of the emotions, emotions are the third link in the causal chain, not the second or middle link. One should note here once again that neither Wundt nor James held that emotions are *identical with* bodily manifestations.

In *The Principles of Psychology*, James is concerned with a wide variety of phenomena that cannot be "introspected" at all in Titchener's sense, because these phenomena are not merely internal mental objects, states, or events. For example, one of James's most prominently investigated psychological phenomena is the phenomenon of "habit." James understands habit, not as anything internal to consciousness, but rather as a certain sort of dispositional relational property that is connected with action toward an external world. The investigation of habit, then, cannot be accomplished by any internal peering at some entity, state, or event that is a content of one's own consciousness. Rather, it is unavoidably the investigation of the relations between the self and the world. For James psychology is typically an investigation of such relations, a study not merely of internal objects of the mind but also and most importantly of the total set of relations between a conscious self and the world. For James, such relations are central in both psychology and epistemology; they must be investigated in all their concrete detail both by the psychologist and by the philosopher. More accurately, they must be investigated by the psychologist-philosopher.

It is ironic to the point of tragedy that, by progressive indirection and ever-increasing distortion, James's emphasis on experimentalism and the investigations of the conscious self's relations with the external world would lead, in the 1930s and thereafter, to the dominance in American academic psychology of the doctrines (and by the practitioners) of "behaviorism," such as the behaviorism of B. F. Skinner. Behaviorism is the doctrine that psychology can dispense altogether with any concern for understanding consciousness and should simply attend to the physical inputs to and the physical outputs from behaving organisms. The behaviorist understands the organism as nothing more than a kind of "black box" which accepts physical inputs and in response to them generates physical outputs, which the behaviorist calls "behaviors." For the behaviorist, then, consciousness simply disappears from the field of psychology. In ignoring consciousness altogether, behaviorism is virtually the opposite of any doctrine that James ever held or to which he would be sympathetic. Behaviorism is not (as it is often wrongly represented to be) an extension of James's views.

Nowadays, behaviorism has fallen out of vogue among academic psychologists. Indeed, behaviorism seems to have been relegated almost entirely to the wayside or wastebasket of the subject of psychology, and a new understanding of psychology has taken center stage in academic life. This new psychology makes *cognition*, in the broadest sense that relates to all the acts and states of conscious life, its special topic of investigation. The new psychology goes by the name of "cognitive psychology." Not at all surprisingly, in large measure it simply represents a return to the older, pre-behavioristic ideas of Wundt and James. Psychology is all about consciousness once again. James's style and methods in psychology are back in business again.

James's pragmatism

Coming so soon after James's recovery from depression, being so much in accord with themes in the thinking of Renouvier, and being so clearly concerned with proper methods of inquiry in the empirical sciences, the discussions of the Metaphysical Club must have struck James like great flashes of light. Abundantly obvious is the fact that the deterministic monism that had led James's into his painful depression had been the polar opposite of the views favored by the Metaphysical Club. That sort of monism had been motivated only by empty *a priori* metaphysical considerations, as Chauncey Wright argued forcefully. That sort of monism had prevented James from seeing his own way out of his dilemma of depression; it had blinded him to the powerful case for human freedom; it had led him prematurely to block the path of inquiry. Not surprisingly, James would always remain heavily influenced by the discussions of the Metaphysical Club.

In particular the thought of his close friend Charles Sanders Peirce had an enormous influence on the philosophy of James. One feature of Peirce's thought played a special role for James: James adopted this feature with enthusiasm but then molded it in ways so that it diverged significantly from Peirce's own understanding. For this feature James seems to have introduced the name "pragmatism" in the 1890s, attributing the original ideas to Peirce. Pragmatism, though without use of the word "pragmatism," appeared in Peirce's earliest thought as a method of clarifying concepts and thus of clarifying the meanings of judgments that involve the use of these concepts. At the end of the second section of his famous paper "How to Make Our Ideas Clear" (1878) Peirce expressed in the following way the basic maxim of pragmatism for achieving the highest possible grade of clarity about a "conception": "Consider what effects, which might conceivably have practical bearings, we conceive the object of our conception to have. Then our conception of these effects is the whole of our conception of the object." By "conception" here Peirce meant to include both concepts and judgments.

The core idea in the pragmatic maxim is the idea that meaningful concepts and judgments must have genuine empirical content, which for Peirce consists of real and concrete empirical manifestations, specific discernible "effects," when the concept applies or the judgment is true. The maxim as understood by Peirce has often been likened to the verifiability principle of the logical positivists and to "operationalism" in the philosophy of science. Such assimilations are not entirely wide of the mark, but they are far too strong to be accurate. (Peirce vehemently attacked the operationalism of Karl Pearson's philosophy of science as expressed in *The Grammar of Science*, for example, and vigorously defended the reality of "hypostatic abstractions," which are metaphysical constructs.) Peirce's pragmatism does not in the least try, as logical positivism did try, to rule out all judgments involving metaphysical notions.

What pragmatism, whether that of Peirce or that of James, insists upon is that a meaningful concept should not be some mere bag of metaphysical wind; it may be a metaphysical construct, but it should have at least some concrete empirical criteria by which it may be judged applicable or inapplicable in particular circumstances. An alleged concept, for the application of which no empirically determinable conditions exist, is simply no meaningful concept at all. In addition to the idea that meaningful conceptions must have empirically determinable "effects," there is also the idea of pragmatism that exact meaning depends on a multitude of empirical details that are fully concrete and not mere abstractions. Pragmatists are happy enough to allow metaphysical concepts like "mass" and "force," and they can accept (with certain reservations about alleged deterministic implications) judgments like Newton's laws, along with a host of other metaphysical notions and propositions. But what they insist upon is that there should always be some well-specified relation of concepts and judgments to clearly specifiable, empirically determinable conditions if the concepts and judgments are to be accepted as meaningful. These conditions are what is meant by the "practical bearings" of (the effects of) the concept. (It is to be strenuously emphasized that having practical bearings does not mean – as some distorters of pragmatism have alleged – the same thing as having effects that make someone wealthy, happy, or powerful.) One philosophical consequence of the requirement of "practical bearings" for meaningful conceptions is the rejection by both Peirce and James of all rationalist *a priori* methods and of all *a priori* metaphysical systems – in the style for example of Descartes – for totally determining the contents of the world. This rejection does not involve renouncing mathematics or metaphysical conceptions as scientific tools, but it does involve eschewing any procedure that involves nothing other than reasoning *de more geometrico*. Pragmatism, then, is a strict and rigorous form of empiricism. James labeled it "radical empiricism."

It should not be thought that James's exact idea of the practical bearings of a concept is identical with Peirce's. Peirce and James came at experience from almost opposite starting positions. Peirce approached experience as a mathematician and physical scientist. James approached experience as an artist and descriptive psychologist. Naturally, what each emphasized as being practical bearings differed somewhat from what the other emphasized. For Peirce what is paramount is fertility for the sort of physical experimentation that one finds in the chemistry laboratory or the site of geodesic investigation. For James what is paramount is fertility for infusing life with meaning and meaningful action. Peirce relished the quantitative and mathematical. James relished the qualitative and aesthetic. This is not to say that Peirce ignored the qualitative and aesthetic: indeed, he placed aesthetics as the most basic of all cognitive areas. And this is not to say that James ignored the quantitative and mathematical: indeed, in a late chapter of *The Principles of Psychology* he discusses with admiration the Peano axioms for arithmetic. The point is that Peirce and James have different emphases in their notions of the practical bearings of concepts.

Peirce developed his earliest pragmatic ideas into a full-blown philosophy of science, elaborated along mathematical lines with relentlessly rigorous mathematical logic. James developed his earliest pragmatic ideas into a tendency toward exact and concrete narrative description of experiences: into, that is to say, his radical empiricism. By 1905 Peirce realized that his own views were so sharply different from the pragmatism of James (and of others who were calling themselves pragmatists) that he insisted on using the word "pragmaticism" to label his own highly technical position. James continued to use the word "pragmatism."

Along with the radically empiricist nature of James's version of pragmatism is its insistence on the tentativeness, fallibility, and non-finality of all inquiry. Although James and Peirce agree as to the fallibility of all inquiry, still with regard to the extent and implications of this fallibility the opinions of Peirce and James differ from one another.

For Peirce, empirical evidence will tend in the long run to converge toward some one cognitive limiting point, which Peirce calls "the truth." This one limiting point is never actually and finally reached for Peirce: it exists only as an ideal point of convergence. There is not and cannot be any guarantee that the empirical evidence that has been obtained up to some particular point in time in an inquiry, and which indicates powerfully a certain direction of convergence toward the truth, will continue in the future to steer in the same direction. At some point in the future the facts might simply begin to veer off and indicate another direction of convergence. Nevertheless, even though knowledge is only something that exists at an ideal limiting point and is a goal that is continually sought but never finally attained, there is still for Peirce a single limiting point at which inquiry strives. Peirce's only requirement, in order that the convergence of inquiry toward that single point be guaranteed, is what Peirce called "the first rule of reason": Do not block the path of inquiry.

By contrast with Peirce, James's understanding of the implications of fallibility is much more diffuse, diverse, and open. James does not insist that there is one single point of epistemic convergence that is valid for everyone. Indeed, because James allows that two inquirers might have different postulational starting points in their inquiries, James seems to be sympathetic to the idea that there might be various points of convergence for various inquirers. What is certainly the case is that James did allow for the possibility that multiple inquirers might reach differing results and all of them still might be well within their epistemic rights. In connection with the issue of inquiry's converging, we might say that James's theory is more like W. V. O. Quine's theory than like Peirce's theory.

Peirce's first rule of reason, however, was a cornerstone of James's philosophy. James considered that the lowest ebb of epistemic irresponsibility is prematurely or arbitrarily to close off epistemic possibilities and epistemic rights: with *a priori* dogmatism, with the closed-mindedness of unexamined presuppositions, with refusal to be open to novel experiences. By contrast, a chief epistemic duty of any person who is committed to epistemic responsibility is to be open to and even to seek out the widest possible diversity of experiences: the new, the novel, and even the unusual. The highest standards of rational appraisal of reality require for James that a person allow himself or herself maximum access to experience. Any procedure that stops short of such openness to experience fails to do justice to all the possibilities that have not yet been sufficiently explored. Such a procedure refuses to allow access to areas of experience that might provide refutations of cherished intellectual possessions. Such a procedure for James amounts to little more than cowering in a redoubt of dogmatism. It fails to live up to the highest standards of epistemic responsibility. It blocks the path of inquiry.

James's tenacious rejection of dogmatism and his extraordinary openness to the widest variety of experiences is one of the features of James's thinking that have led some very able commentators on James to regard James as some kind of relativist. As we have seen, with regard to the fundamental *postulates* by which we interpret all experiences, James is akin to an epistemic voluntarist. In a very restricted sense of the word "relativist," then, the claim that James is a relativist is correct. The position of the present article, however, is that "relativist" in the *usual* and unrestricted sense is not the right concept to apply to James, because in its usual signification "relativism" involves a general abdication of standards of epistemic appraisal – that is to say appraisal that is relevant to the truth of doctrines. James's openness to experience, however, was not at all a stance in the service of dispensing generally with epistemic standards; rather, it was in the interest of embracing, wherever applicable, the strictest possible standards for epistemic appraisal, as James understood them. When his colleague Hugo Münsterberg and others accused James of being a relativist, James strenuously rejected this interpretation of his views.

James's theory of truth

Probably no area of James scholarship has been so much vexed as that concerned with James's theory of truth, as James first put it forward in *Pragmatism* (1907) and then, in order to try to clarify his ideas and respond to objections, as he elaborated it in *The Meaning of Truth* (1909). Almost immediately upon the publication of *Pragmatism*, James's theory came under withering attack from all quarters. Already mentioned has been Bertrand Russell's characterization of it as a theory of "transatlantic truth," which characterization assimilated it to everything philistine that some Englishmen are apt to find so abundantly displayed in American culture. An American Russell, John E. Russell, kept up a debate with James on the theory of truth, a debate somewhat more respectfully maintained than the criticism of the English Russell but still highly critical. John Russell thought that James's theory confused the quality of truth that is possessed by some propositions with the activity of verifying propositions that are performed by some persons. Even into the present, the discussion about what exactly James's theory of truth is has continued. Some commentary on James even holds that James has two different notions of truth – one being the ordinary notion of truth and the other being a special "pragmatic" notion of truth not unlike the notion of "transatlantic truth" that Bertrand Russell had in mind. Some detractors claim that James's whole account of truth is just confused. Certainly it must at least be admitted that a number of James's assertions about truth, for example his claim that truth is something that *happens* to an idea, are very difficult to deal with and are perhaps open to a diversity of interpretations.

As with so much in James scholarship, however, part of the general difficulty of pinning down James's theory in detail seems to be attributable not to James's own lack of clarity but rather merely to James's lively and artistic writing style. In the case of the theory of truth, this general difficulty in James scholarship seems to have inflated to huge proportions for this reason. It is submitted in this article that, although James did have a clear theory of truth, a theory that might have been (and perhaps should have been) expressed precisely, James did not do so mainly because he did not like to write dryly and technically.

Another and more important source of difficulty in connection with James's theory of truth has already been mentioned. This has to do with a contrast between types of theories of truth that by James's time had gained such a toehold in philosophical discussions of the difference between realists and idealists that it might well be called something like "the canonical contrast" between theories of truth. This canonical contrast is that between so-called "correspondence" theories of truth and so-called "coherence" theories of truth. Correspondence theories of truth are often associated with realist metaphysical positions, whereas coherence theories of truth are often associated with idealist metaphysical positions. Crudely put, correspondence theorists hold that the truth of a proposition consists of some sort of correspondence or agreement between that proposition and reality. By contrast, coherence theorists hold that truth of a proposition consists of its being a part of a system of propositions among which there is some sort of special mutual logical coherence. Now, pragmatists are often contrasted with realists and, although they are not exactly identified with idealists, they tend to be somewhat more assimilated to idealists than to realists. An unfortunate conclusion commonly drawn, then, has been that there must be a sharp contrast and mutual opposition between a correspondence theory of truth and a pragmatic theory of truth.

But if we think along these lines, we shall immediately fall into confusion about James's theory of truth. For James, who is avowedly and without doubt a pragmatist, nevertheless explicitly describes himself as a correspondence theorist of truth: truth, he holds, is indeed an agreement between a proposition and reality. But, James argues, to say this much and no more is not to give a theory of truth but rather is merely to begin it. For, as the agreement formula stands without further explication, it is so devoid of content as to be virtually meaningless pragmatically. The pragmatic content of the notion of agreement of a proposition with reality still remains to be given. The issue for James, then, is what the pragmatic meaning is of "agreement" in the context of a correspondence theory of truth.

James makes clear that as a pragmatist he must apply the pragmatic criterion of meaning in order to spell out clearly the "cash value" of the concept of "agreement" here. In turn, doing so requires giving a detailed account of what the agreement in question comes to when it is described in concrete, empirically significant terms of direct experience. James wants to provide (what he calls) "the particular go" of truth.

To this end James discusses a number of examples. In them the chief issue is not that of the nature of predication or that of the correctness of predication, both of which James tends to take for granted in the discussion. Rather, the chief issue is that of how a proposition can be *about* the world. The central problem, that is to say, that gradually emerges in James's discussion of cases in giving a pragmatic account of the agreement between a true proposition and reality is the problem of the *aboutness* of judgments. How is it, for example, that we can use the phrase "the tigers in India" actually to talk *about* the tigers in India (and say *about* them things that are true)? How can we *mean* the tigers in India when we speak or think. The central focus of James's pragmatic account, then, turns out to be the nature of *reference*.

James's account of the nature of reference is given with many metaphors, and it is this fact, in part, that has made his intentions in regard to his theory of truth very hard to understand and all too easy for his detractors to repudiate or mock. James speaks of truth as involving "prosperous workings and leadings," and such language is very suggestive of a special pragmatic notion of truth, in which the truth of a belief is understood as its ability to promote the happiness and success of its believer. The present article, however, submits that in so understanding James's language, James's actual thinking is seriously misrepresented. Rather than defining a special pragmatic notion of truth, James is offering, as the heart of his pragmatic theory of (the ordinary notion of) truth, a pragmatic theory of reference.

In what, then, for James does reference consist, when it is spelled out pragmatically, that is to say in full, concrete detail? James's point is that reference to an item consists in a chain of concrete links – which are usually causal links – that lead in an unbroken manner from the act of intending to refer to an item (or to the vicinity or context of an item) that is the object of reference. When there exists such an unbroken chain, the referential intention succeeds and truth is then possible. When such a chain does not exist or when the chain is broken in certain ways, then the referential intention fails, and truth is not possible. In his 1895 essay "The Knowing of Things Together" James already makes his ideas abundantly clear: "The pointing of our thought to the tigers [in India] is known simply and solely as a procession of mental associates and motor consequences that follow on the thought, and that would lead harmoniously, if followed out, into some ideal or real context, or even into the immediate presence, of the tigers … [our mental images'] pointing to the tigers is a perfectly commonplace physical relation, if you once grant a connecting world to be there" (1975 [1911]).

James's sort of theory is nowadays called a "causal theory of reference." Specific causal theories of reference were defended in the latter parts of the twentieth century by philosophers like Saul Kripke and Keith Donnellan. The Kripke-Donnellan theory of reference, as it is usually called – rather than the James theory of reference (or perhaps the Peirce-James theory of reference) as it ought to be called – is difficult to describe briefly because of the many and various ways in which the referentially necessary causal chain may be constituted. The theory is difficult to describe in brief because of the many and various ways that such a causal chain can be constituted or broken. But James did an excellent job of laying out the general scheme and some of the details of such a theory. It is the core of his account of truth: the heart of his correspondence theory that is *also* a pragmatic theory. That his theory was and still is, so often misunderstood is *in part* owing to James's language: but *only* in part.

The earliest presentations in the late 1970s of James's theory of truth as basically being a pragmatic theory of reference tended to stress the temporally backward-looking nature of the causal chain connecting referring acts with referents and stressed the similarities between James's account of reference and the Kripke-Donnellan account. Recent work along these same lines (Boersema 2009: Ch. 4) rightly argues that there is also in James's account an important temporally forward-looking component. This forward-looking component has the potential to allow us to explain some of James's otherwise puzzling metaphorical language. For example, it may allow us to interpret James's point that truth is something that happens to an idea. (For example, we might say that for James truth is something like sustainable reference and predication in the court of all future inquiries.) The forward-looking component in James's theory of truth may also provide ways in which James's account of reference differs from the Kripke-Donnellan account and, indeed, might even be preferable to the latter.

Despite a century of hard work by scholars to understand in detail James's theory of truth, there remains a great deal of work left to be done in making his theory more detailed and precise.

Scientific methodology and the open universe

James's thought is incomprehensible apart from his interest in science and conse-quently in the methodology of the sciences. He had turned initially away from studying art to studying medicine as a way into the study of general science. Many of his writings show him to have been in touch with the writings of the outstanding physical scientists of the nineteenth century, including James Clerk Maxwell, Charles Darwin, and others. The apparent determinism of the sciences was one factor leading to his depression of 1869 and 1870. The issue whether determinism is a guiding principle of science in general, and of the social sciences in particular, was one of the most-often debated issues of the nineteenth century. Renouvier had shown James the way out of determinism, and a way out moreover that is provided by a commitment to experience as the most basic element of all knowledge, including scientific knowledge.

It might seem, however, that James's commitment to freedom and an open universe conflicts with his respect for science. For it might seem to be the case that actual scientific practice, especially in the really "hard" sciences of physics, astronomy, chemistry, and geodesy, showed that determinism must be the guiding principle of the philosopher who is respectful of science. Do the hard sciences reinstate the determinism that James so abhorred? The astonishing answer, coming initially to James perhaps from Peirce, but echoed by many others like Ludwig Boltzmann and perhaps also Josiah Willard Gibbs, was: Not necessarily. The long-known and constant experience of the physics laboratory and of the astronomical observatory is that many measurements of one and the same physical quantity, no matter how carefully these measurements may be taken, always yield values that are not simply duplicates of another but rather are values that are distributed throughout a range, usually in accord with the so-called "error curve" (which is now called the "normal distribution"). The "probable error" of such measurement results (the fraction .6745 of what is now called the "standard deviation") can be reduced, perhaps, but never eliminated.

The idea behind calling the normal distribution the "error curve" is the idea that, independent of the actions of measuring a physical quantity, there exists some definite value that the physical quantity already really has; and that in taking measurements we are trying to ascertain this real value. According to this idea, the deviations from each other of individual measurement results are also indicative of deviations from this real value. Hence, according to this idea, the observed deviations from each other of measurement results indicate various errors in getting the right measurement.

But note: the idea that there is some single, definite, and "real," physical quantity that is being measured (with errors) is not a direct deliverance of laboratory experience. Rather it is a postulate. This postulate is fleshed out by choosing to regard some statistical value of the distribution curve of measurement results – typically but not necessarily the so-called "mean" of the distribution – as the postulated real, exact value. Thus the idea of a single, real, exact physical value is not an immediate datum of experience at all: rather, it is only an intellectual construct that is based on interpreting in a special way many experiences. It is an intellectual postulate as to how we should interpret the many experiences. So also, then, the "laws" of physics and the precise differential equations that encode them (and which lead through the notion of Laplace's Demon to determinism) are constructs, based on postulates. Determinism and realism themselves, then, are only postulates. Moreover, they are postulates with which science can dispense, at no harm to itself.

Thus, for James, science need not be out of harmony with the idea of an open universe.

James's radical empiricism and pluralism

James labeled his own fundamental philosophical position "radical empiricism" for reasons that were described in the foregoing material: the radical empiricist takes as ultimate epistemic bedrock pure experiences, just as they are phenomenally given.

Radical empiricism, however, was never for James a precise, technical doctrine or set of doctrines. Rather, it was what he himself called an "attitude" or a "*Weltanschauung.*" Moreover, his descriptions of radical empiricism, and the emphases in his descriptions, varied somewhat (although not widely) over the years from 1897 to 1909. In his earlier descriptions he mainly associated his empiricism with the sort of fallibilism that characterizes Peirce's pragmatism; and he defined its being radical as its refusal to presuppose any form of monism as either an axiom or first principle with which all experience has ultimately to square. Monism itself was regarded by radical empiricism as nothing but an hypothesis with which empirical evidence does not happily cohere. For *prima facie* the world of experience is inherently a plurality of presentations that display only here and there the possibility of reduction of different phenomena to one "thing."

A few years later James took the main point of radical empiricism to be its opposition to "rationalism," by which term he understood a philosophy that makes wholes and universals to be both logically and ontologically prior to parts and particulars. (By examples of "rationalism" James understood the philosophies of the absolute idealists, and in particular the idealism of Hegel and the idealism flourishing in England around such thinkers as F. H. Bradley.) Thus the main point of radical empiricism, as he described it in these years, is to insist on the ontological priority of parts, particulars, and individuals. Laying stress on parts and particulars as ontologically prior to wholes and universals means that wholes are to be regarded merely as classes of particulars and that universals are to be regarded merely as abstractions from particulars. Wholes have no existence except as collections of particulars, and universals have no existence except as abstractions from particulars. Radical empiricism is, James said, "a mosaic philosophy, a philosophy of plural facts."

By 1904, however, James added a new dimension, or at least a new emphasis, to radical empiricism. This is a sharp distinction between radical empiricism and the traditional empiricism of the sort that we find, for example, in Hume. Traditional empiricism tended to fragment experience by failing to recognize within it real "conjunctive relations," like causal or cause-like connections. Instead of recognizing such relations as real, traditional empiricism regarded them as non-existent. Causation in Hume, for example, is reduced to nothing but a certain species of constant conjunction, and so is not any sort of real nexus between cause and effect. The "incoherencies" of the unconnected world of traditional empiricism, James held, invited "rationalistic philosophers" (i.e. absolute idealists) to correct them by positing for the world "trans-experiential agents of unification" – like special substances or unique Selves – or by insisting upon special intellectual categories and powers. Radical empiricism, by contrast, recognizes that real, "conjunctive relations" are found in experience. Hence, it has no need for some sort of special unifying agent to bring experience together: experience is already together because it already contains the real relatedness of things. The relations are as real as the things related. Indeed, in some sense the relations constitute, or at least help to constitute, the natures of the things related. Radical empiricism still insists that experience is of a plurality, but it is a plurality of things and relations, of things that are necessarily genuinely interrelated.

In James's descriptions of radical empiricism, one increasingly sees the influence not only of Renouvier and Peirce, but also of Rudolf Hermann Lotze, who like James opposed the absolute idealists for somewhat the same reasons as Renouvier. The idealists had ignored Kant's understanding of the noumenal realm as being nothing but a boundary concept (*Grenzbegriff*). They had seized on hints in Kant's third *Kritik* to the effect that some teleological principle of unity must underlie the phenomenal world, and then they had provided some principle (*Geist*, the Absolute, etc.) to provide once and for all for this unity. Lotze, like Renouvier, insisted that there was nothing but the phenomenal world. Additionally, he had argued vigorously for the reality and direct apprehensibility of relations. James's account of relations in his later descriptions of radical empiricism is quite similar to the account of Lotze.

The pragmatic principle that philosophy should deal only with material that is definable in terms of concrete, direct experience meant from the outset of James's adapting it that one should not admit into philosophical discussion anything that cannot be defined in terms that hook onto direct experience. But increasingly we find James extending this principle in an obvious way: James also holds that one should not exclude from philosophical relevance any element, term, or relation that is directly experienced. In this way James reached the conclusion that all genuine and direct experiences are philosophically important and cognitively relevant. This extension of the pragmatic principle provides another reason why the study of philosophy and the study of psychology are not to be separated: psychology provides evidence of the widest ranges of direct experience and thus cognitively significant data. We also can understand more deeply James's interest in wide-ranging, unusual and even odd, experiences. It is not surprising that in his last great volume, *The Varieties of Religious Experience*, we find a compendious catalogue of human experiences connected with religious conversion and commitment.

This new twist on the pragmatic principle in James's radical empiricism also allows us to understand a special kind of ethical quality that pervades all of James's writings, but especially his popular essays on what makes a life worth living, what is good teaching, and the like. This ethical quality is what we might call "respect for persons." James thinks that every person carries his/her own "inner candle," so to say, which is what makes that person, at the deepest level, what he/she is. This inner light is the basic thing for judging any person's epistemic rights and responsibilities. Seldom or never should a genuine philosopher say, "Thou fool," to anyone; for everyone's own direct experience has its own high dignity and its own cognitive worth. James cared greatly for good teaching, and he argued that the good teacher is not the person who is most knowledgeable; it is the person who most understands how to fan the student's inner fire and, without deforming it, to make it grow.

A year before his death James wrote of radical empiricism as consisting of a postulate, a statement of fact, and a generalized conclusion. The postulate is essentially the expanded pragmatic principle that anything that is material for discussion and debate in philosophy must be definable in terms of actual experience, and that all actual experience is material for philosophical discussion and debate. The statement of fact is that relations, including "conjunctive relations," are directly experienced and indeed are every bit as real as the things of which they are the relations. The generalized conclusion is that the directly apprehended universe does not need any sort of trans-experiential connective support; it hangs together on its own, in its own right. As directly experienced, it is already concatenated, conjoined, and continuous. The parts of experience are held together by relations that are themselves parts of experience. It follows that resorting to trans-empirical entities in order to obtain such unity as the world has is entirely unnecessary. What experience directly gives us is a pluralistic but still genuinely interconnected universe.

References

Boersema, David (2009) *Pragmatism and Reference*, Cambridge, MA; London: MIT Press, 2009).
James, William (1975 [1911]) "The Meaning of Truth," in *The Meaning of Truth*, edited by Frederick H. Burkhardt, Cambridge, MA: Harvard University Press.

Further reading

Primary sources: The Works of William James (Cambridge, MA: Harvard University Press, 1975–88); *The Correspondence of William James* (Charlottesville, VA, and London: University Press of Virginia, 1992–). John J. McDermott (ed.) *The Writings of William James: A Comprehensive Edition* (Chicago and London: University of Chicago Press, 1977). *Secondary sources:* Gay Wilson Allen, *William James* (New York: Viking Press, 1967); Graham Bird, *William James* (London and New York: Routledge & Kegan Paul, 1986); Gerald E. Meyers, *William James, His Life and Thought* (New Haven, CT: Yale University Press, 1986); Ralph Barton Perry, *The Thought and Character of William James*, 2 vols (Boston: Little, Brown & Co., 1935); Hilary Putnam, *Pragmatism: An Open Question* (Oxford: Blackwell, 1995); Robert D. Richardson, *William James: In the Maelstrom of American Modernism* (Boston and New York: Houghton Mifflin, 2006); Charlene Haddock Seigfried, *William James's Radical Reconstruction of Philosophy* (Albany, NY: SUNY Press, 1990); H. S. Thayer, *Meaning and Action: A Critical History of Pragmatism* (Indianapolis, IN: Hackett Publishing, 1981).

26

JOSIAH ROYCE
David P. Schweikard

Josiah Royce's prominence in the history of philosophy is based on two facts about his life and thought. First, he was a part of the first *Golden Age* of philosophy at Harvard University, where he taught from 1882 until his death in 1916. Having arrived, with the help of William James, as a promising young scholar from Berkeley, he helped to shape what became *the* department of philosophy and to professionalize the discipline in the United States (see Kuklick 1977 and 2001). Second, he is known to have been the leading proponent of so-called *American Idealism* at the turn of the twentieth century (see Randall 1966). This is interesting in at least the following two respects: one regards the geography of the subject, for at that time especially Great Britain, Germany and Italy witnessed lively discussions about the tenability of idealism; the other regards the topology of philosophy as a subject influenced by the rise of such diverse movements and paradigms as pragmatism, phenomenology, existentialism and analytic philosophy. Royce's idealism relates to these movements in manifold and somewhat complex ways and, by seeking to incorporate insights gained from those other perspectives, constitutes a rich and multifaceted view.

However, while defining Royce's prominence in terms of his institutional role and in terms of a vague label for his position might be useful for historiographic purposes, this strategy alone would be insufficient for grounding an assessment of Royce's systematic contributions to the philosophical debates in which he was involved. But there is an alternative to such a primarily historical approach to Royce's thought, one which can perhaps be called more empathetic and that is itself Roycean. It consists in taking the stance towards Royce's thought that he himself took towards the masters of modern philosophy whose work he studied extensively and on whom he lectured throughout his career, and involves examining the academic setting in which he worked, the systematic philosophical problems he sought to solve and the shape and plausibility of the solutions he proposed. Royce's exceptional studiousness and breadth of reading made him an expert on the history of philosophy, but it is characteristic of his historical work that he treated thinkers such as Spinoza, Kant, Hegel and Schopenhauer not just as historical figures, but as partners in a dialogue about philosophical problems and as inspiration for his own thinking. Royce would have agreed with the claim that the greatness of a past thinker depends largely on the extent to which both the way he conceived of a philosophical problem and his solution thereto can continue to influence theorizing about the respective problem. This interleaving of historical study and systematic interest marks an interesting parallel between Royce's work and Hegel's lectures on the history of philosophy insofar as this approach rests on the hypothesis that one can track leitmotifs and systematic progress in the history of thought.

The attempt at such a Roycean approach to Royce made in the following begins with a brief look at the academic setting in which he worked and developed his most received and most provocative views (first section, "Colleagues and Contexts"). The main parts of the portrait will consist of brief reconstructions of Royce's idealism (second section) and Royce's ethics (third section); a conclusion provides a sketch of the reception of Royce's thought and a survey of challenges awaiting further research (fourth section, "Remaining Challenges").

Colleagues and contexts

One can describe Royce's way into and his role within the philosophical community of his time as a struggle for recognition and, after achieving a highly successful outcome, as a professional life spent in the forceful development of a philosophical system that provoked more critique and opposition than it attracted adherents and disciples. Both in his formative years and at the height of his fame as a professor in an epochal department at Harvard, Royce's profile as a philosopher was shaped by the relations to his colleagues and his reception of the scientific movements of his time. It is worth highlighting some of the most important influences on his thinking rather than undertaking a more comprehensive biographical sketch (see Clendenning 1999). The focus here is laid on those topics and works which later serve to reconstruct some of his most important themes and theses.

After completing a Classics degree at the University of California in 1875, Royce received a grant that enabled him to go to Germany and immerse himself in the study of German and German philosophy. This included extensive reading of German literature and philosophy, especially Kant and Schopenhauer, as well as the attendance of lectures in Heidelberg, Leipzig, and Göttingen, where psychologist Wilhelm Wundt, and neo-Kantians Kuno Fischer and Hermann Lotze impressed him most. Royce returned after a year, entered the first graduate program in the United States at Johns Hopkins University, continued his studies of Kant's epistemology, and received a PhD in 1878. Part of the research for his dissertation was carried out in Boston in the summer of 1877, there Royce also convened with William James, whom he had first met on the way to Europe. During that summer and the following academic year, when James served as a part-time lecturer in psychology at Johns Hopkins, Royce impressed James with his philosophical talent. James encouraged Royce to pursue a career in philosophy and so began a relationship that was substantial, at least to Royce's subsequent life.

For want of vacant positions in philosophy, Royce returned to the University of California, Berkeley to teach English literature and composition. Although personally he experienced this period as an exile from philosophical life, he pursued his research and produced a manual for his students, entitled *Primer of Logical Analysis* (1881), as well as a number of critical essays and studies on various philosophical topics. James, whose work he followed closely and with whom he regularly exchanged letters about philosophical matters, had called Royce's attention to Charles Sanders Peirce's first formulations of the view that was later termed *pragmatism*. Royce longed to be part of a department and those circles in the east in which the most vibrant discussions were held. Aside from the people, mostly non-philosophers, whom he gathered around him in Berkeley, an appearance at the Metaphysical Club in Baltimore stood out as a step towards recognition as a scholar to be reckoned with. In the talk he gave there in May 1880, entitled "On Purpose in Thought" (reprinted in FE: 219–60), he sought to elaborate on his reception of both Kantian epistemology and of James' and Peirce's most recent work on the practical nature of belief. On that occasion, Royce and Peirce, the latter a lecturer at Johns Hopkins at the time, must have met for the first time, but no further exchange of ideas followed. It took some three decades until Peirce's influence on Royce reached its full extent (see Oppenheim 2001a: 19; see also 2005).

Thanks to William James' effort and the need for a replacement of James during a sabbatical in the academic year 1882/3, Royce was eventually able to move east and take up a temporary position at Harvard. The one-year contract and the lectureship were extended twice before he was appointed assistant professor in 1885 and Professor of the History of Philosophy in 1892. The years leading up to his first appointment were dedicated to working out a lecture series entitled *The Religious Aspect of Philosophy* accompanying a monograph by the same title. This work, rightly seen as Royce's breakthrough in the field, embraced most of the historical and assimilative material he had assembled, starting with his PhD thesis at Johns Hopkins. This first statement of idealism received considerable attention, was critically reviewed by William James, and grounded his reputation. While we shall return to the main argument of this work in the next section, it is worth noting that the young Royce was not trying to buttress his ties with his colleagues at Harvard or an affiliation with some school or movement, but endeavoring to find his own voice. And this earned him wide recognition.

The next philosophical milestone in Royce's biography grew out of a series of public lectures published in 1892 as *The Spirit of Modern Philosophy*. After his early success, Royce had suffered a breakdown caused by overwork and been forced to slow down on writing assignments. Reviving his strength, he used these lectures both to narrate the history of modern philosophy, pursuing a path from Spinoza through Kant, the Romanticists, the German Idealists and Schopenhauer to the doctrine of evolution and to expound his own view constructively. Topically speaking, this work covers metaphysical and epistemological as well as ethical questions, thus prefiguring the *opera magna* yet to come.

Though Royce may seem to have concentrated on his earlier specialization, the 1890s were in fact characterized by extensive involvement in at least two lively debates. On the one hand, he took part in debates on psychology with his colleagues James and the newly arrived Hugo Münsterberg and contributed to incipient discussions on what was later called *social psychology;* he was interested in the genesis and the anomalies of consciousness, the social constitution of self-consciousness and the relation between consciousness and external reality. Dealing with the latter problem led Royce to determine the relation between his metaphysical idealism and his psychology, a task that was to occupy him for at least fifteen years. On the other hand, in the years from 1895 to 1900 saw the culmination of the so-called *Battle for the Absolute* (see Clendenning 1999: Ch. 6), an influential controversy between James and Royce on the conception of the absolute and thus on the metaphysical framework of their theories. Royce's idealism found its initial expression in a compilation of lectures and discussions entitled *The Conception of God* as well as in his Gifford Lectures, delivered in Aberdeen and Edinburgh. The lectures given by Royce in 1899 and 1900 were published in two volumes as *The World and the Individual* (WI 1 and 2) and can be seen as the pinnacle of his development of an idealistic philosophical system. But this work of more than 1,100 printed pages constitutes not only an amplified, but also a considerably refined, statement of his idealism in that it reflects Royce's logical studies and his critique of Francis Herbert Bradley's idealistic views. While the first volume is taken up by refinements and discussions, the second volume – subtitled *Nature, Man, and the Moral Order* – comprises statements of Royce's views on social ontology, the nature of self-consciousness and moral life, and the "union of god and man" (WI 2: 415). The success of the Gifford Lectures established Royce as America's leading proponent of philosophical idealism, an honor with advantages and disadvantages. On the one hand, he was subsequently elected president of both the American Psychological Association (1902) and the American Philosophical Association (1903), each one a hallmark of institutional recognition. But on the other hand, to many contemporaries it seemed as though idealism as a philosophical doctrine belonged to the just bygone century, and was an intellectual edifice of the past – so in this respect Royce did not receive the recognition he can be assumed to have hoped for (see the reviews collected in Auxier 2000).

Royce dedicated the years following the Gifford Lectures to working out the problems they had brought up. This included intensive studies of the foundations and principles of logic, to which he was urged by Charles Sanders Peirce (see Peirce 1900 and 1902), the compilation of a text book on psychology, and a critical appraisal of George Herbert Spencer, deepened discussions with pragmatist and humanist philosophers, and a revived and growing interest in ethical issues. The papers in philosophical logic written by Royce during that period, some of which were encyclopedia entries (all collected by Robinson in Royce 1951), and represented Royce's prevailing enthusiasm and analytic ambition, did not receive as much attention and are, notwithstanding C. I. Lewis' appraisal (Lewis 1916), still largely unexplored. Throughout his career, Royce was fascinated by abstract discussions and formal analyses, but he shared the basic contention of his pragmatist and humanist contemporaries, that such purely theoretical endeavors should not be taken as ends in themselves, but that they need a foundation in practical life. Conceiving of the questions concerning knowledge, being and the good life as closely intertwined had already been a core feature of *The Religious Aspect of Philosophy* and of the Gifford Lectures and would remain characteristic of Royce's later works, i.e. those composed after 1901.

Among these, his *Philosophy of Loyalty*, presented as public lectures in Boston in 1907, stands out as Royce's first book-length statement of an ethical theory that complements his metaphysical and religious studies of the previous decades. As in numerous other lecture series he gave before and with which he at least partially addressed a wider audience, Royce here attempted to combine the presentation of philosophical reflections and theorizing with the treatment of problems known and accessible to non-specialists. In this vein, he both diagnosed and criticized an upcoming individualism in the American society of his day and the progressing devaluation of community in social life it implied. Royce opposed any form of individualistic liberalism in ethics and social philosophy and, as we shall see below, sought to develop the so-called principle of "loyalty to loyalty" as an ideal by which individual lives could be oriented towards a socially embedded and conditioned form of self-realization. The pronounced emphasis on the practical life of the individual, which did not betray the metaphysical underpinnings Royce's had spelt out before, grounded his recognition as a precursor of twentieth-century existentialism (see Marcel 1956).

This work, published in 1908, marked the beginning of a phase of immense productivity and originality in which Royce wrote and published four more monographs. The first two of these, *Race Questions, Provincialism, and Other American Problems* (1908) and *William James and Other Essays on the Philosophy of Life* (1911), were collections of essays in which Royce outlined the political dimension of his ethical views and explained the commonalities with and divergences from James' pragmatism. The seemingly complete scholarly immersion masks the fact that between 1907 and 1910 Royce suffered the illness and loss of his oldest son Christopher and William James, his former protégée, a close friend and colleague for almost three decades. The homage to James paid expressly with the second of the mentioned volumes is continued in *The Sources of Religious Insight* (1911), in which Royce responded to James' *Varieties of Religious Experience* (James 1985) with a renewed statement of his religious and ethical views. Roughly speaking, in contrasting these two works one can individuate outlines of debates that would remain central to twentieth-century philosophy: debates between rationalists and empiricists in terms of the foundation of knowledge, and between collectivists and individualists in terms of social ontology, where Royce represents the first and James the second of the groups mentioned.

While Royce's works up to 1911 can be read as developments of a single philosophical program based on a largely stable set of underlying theoretical commitments, to some extent he altered this systematic foundation during the preparation of *The Problem of Christianity*, his last major work, which was published in 1913. This alteration or reorientation of his philosophy was mainly due to a reconsideration of Peirce's theory of knowledge in the light of reflection on the connections between epistemological and ethical problems; alluding to his own paraphrasing of moral and the religious insights (see RAP), this has been termed Royce's "Peircean Insight" (Oppenheim 2001a: 19). Royce himself explained this late shift in his thought, which most probably occurred in 1911–12, to an audience at a summer session at Berkeley in 1914:

there were some aspects of Peirce's theory of knowledge which I never understood until ... I was lead to reread some of Peirce's early logical contributions, and to reconsider the way in which these his earlier theories had worked themselves out in the form which some of his later studies indicate. ... When I hereupon tried to restate these central ideas of Peirce, I found that, if once grasped and held before one's mind, they supply one with a theory of knowledge which I ought to have understood and used long ago. ... Then indeed, I observed its close connection with what I had been seeking to formulate in my philosophy of loyalty. I saw also how many aspects of philosophical idealism, when this Peircean theory of knowledge was brought to bear upon the[m], got a new concreteness, a new significance and a new relation to the methods and to the presuppositions of inductive science. (Oppenheim 2001b: 3–4)

Here, Royce was looking back on a shift that had found expression in the second volume of *The Problem of Christianity*, in which the social community is taken to constitute the horizon of both ethics and scientific knowledge, of endeavors to live a good life and to formulate true theories. Some have regarded this shift as Royce's finally completed turn away from absolute idealism, marked by the replacement of the Absolute by the Community; but "turn away" may be too drastic a description for a move that can also be read as providing a new way of expounding essentially the same metaphysical foundations. This remains contested ground among Royce scholars.

After publishing *The Problem of Christianity*, Royce's physical strength and intellectual capacity for innovative work both deteriorated progressively. Except for a highly contextual commentary on international politics, essays collected in *War and Insurance*, and several lecture series and courses on already published material, some of which were also published posthumously, he had completed his remarkable philosophical œuvre.

The rest of this portrait is divided into two main sections, reconstructing some of Royce's crucial and most influential ideas under the headings of his *idealism* (second section) and his *ethics* (third section) respectively. This exposition of Royce's thought proceeds chronologically, starting from the epistemological and metaphysical questions he dealt with in his first writings and moving on to the ethical and social philosophical ideas he developed in the last decade of his career.

Royce's idealism

It is hard if not entirely pointless to divide Royce's philosophy into a theoretical and a practical branch. While especially the monographs he wrote at the height of his career are indeed dedicated to more specific areas – for instance, *The Philosophy of Loyalty* to ethics and social philosophy and *The Sources of Religious Insight* to the philosophy of religion – Royce was a thinker whose views were intended to cohere in an all-encompassing philosophical system. He never explicitly propounded his view *as* such a system, although the views of the system-building German idealists deeply fascinated him. But the case for the claim that in the course of his career Royce did develop, refine and alter a philosophical system can be made, and we shall keep this in view in the reconstruction now following.

For the purpose of reconstructing Royce's idealism in this section, we will trace aspects of its development from an early programmatic essay to the grand exploration he gave it in his Gifford Lectures. One leitmotif in this development is the connection between epistemological and metaphysical questions. Royce did not isolate problems such as those about the structure of mental states or the individuation of material objects. Rather, he would start from a question of the form "How should human thinking be conceived?" and would be lead to interleaving reflections about the structure of thought and judgments as well as the constitution of the objects and contents of thoughts and judgments.

The purposive nature of thought

In line with his idealist predecessors, Royce's first formulations of idealistic philosophical views grew out of interlocking discussions of the nature of thought on the one hand and of the nature of truth and error on the other. Before we look at two expositions of these views, let us try to picture how such discussions can lead one to adopt idealism.

In a very basic sense, an individual's act of thinking can be described as consciously relating to some object. In thinking the thought or in making the judgment "There is a tree," for instance, she enters into a relation with what then becomes the content of her thought: the tree she is thinking of. Studying thought-processes of this and more complex kinds requires, at least, accounting for the status of the entities involved; in particular, it requires answering the question as to whether it is conceivable that the objects one can think of can be entirely independent of being thought. Here we ask whether it is the case that the objects of thought exist and have all their constitutive properties regardless of whether they are thought of. Besides this, the study of thought-processes seeks to account for the conditions under which judgments of the form mentioned are true or false.

As will be clear, one's answer to the independence question has far-reaching implications for one's conception of truth, for there is a difference between saying that some statement about a thought-independent entity is true and saying that some statement about a thought-dependent entity is true. But, intuitively, both variants are problematic, given that the distinction between thought-dependent and thought-independent entities can only be drawn and employed from a standpoint external to the relation between the thinking subject and the object being thought of. Guided by interests in both the structure of thought processes and the constitution of objects of thought, the challenge taken up by Royce is to develop a comprehensive account of the processes and of the terms of the relations mentioned.

A first premise of Royce's theorizing about thought and being is that thought should be conceived as a purposive activity. It is important to note that with this conviction, which he had already acquired in his graduate years, he combined fundamental insights of Kant, Fichte and Hegel on the one hand and a main tenet discussed among the early pragmatists, especially Charles Sanders Peirce (see Oppenheim 2005), on the other. All these thinkers are united in the idea that thinking is not detached from practical motives or interests, not to be seen as an abstract process of contemplation or as an end in itself, but as an intentional and, to some extent, constructive activity by which the thinking subject engages with the world.

In an essay written in 1880, entitled "On Purpose in Thought" (reprinted in FE), Royce contrasts the sort of study of the purposes of thought-processes he terms "teleological analysis," with psychological and logical analyses of thinking. He intends to lower the importance of neither of the following two approaches: the first consists of giving "a history of the evolution of mental processes" (FE: 220), which is what the psychological analysis of thought provides; the seconds seeks to offer an "exhaustive logical analysis of the principles, assumptions, methods, and great results of thought" (*ibid.*). But Royce aims at going beyond these efforts. He envisages a teleological analysis which is focused on "the final end of purely theoretic thought" and on the relation between this final end and "the fundamental axioms or principles of human reasoning" (*ibid.*).

But what is this final end in which the fundamental purposes of all thought are captured? And what does it mean to say that the study of thought should go beyond the structures and principles highlighted in the other two approaches and attend to the end to which all thought is directed? Royce's answers, which are stated programmatically in this early essay and which are taken up and elaborated on several later occasions, have implications for the conception both of the subject matter and of the method of epistemology.

The first candidate for a final end of all thought Royce considers is the *attainment of truth*. What else could be more plausible than to say that whenever we think or judge, we strive to think true thoughts and make true judgments? But this first answer can very quickly be confronted with a far-reaching problem, for it does not specify what the attainment of truth is taken to consist in. It may be correct to say that with the statement "There is a tree outside my window," I mean to make a true statement, but what also seems to be required is that I be aware of the truth of my statement. As Royce puts it, I cannot really have reached my end of making a true statement without knowing that I have done so. But how do I arrive at this second, reflective sort of knowledge and know that my statement is true? Again, an intuitively plausible understanding of truth suggests that what I need to know in order to know that my statement is true is whether its content corresponds to the external fact it refers to. So what I would need to do is to compare my statement, "There is a tree outside my window," with the stated fact, i.e. the tree outside my window. On the basis of this comparison I could then affirm (or deny) the correspondence between by statement and the fact it is (meant to be) a statement about, which would amount to affirming the truth (or falsity) of my statement. Royce points out that any comparison between two terms requires that they both be given to the comparer, so that in this case the problem arises that I, as the one who makes statement or judgment, cannot carry out the required comparison between my judgment and the external thing, since only one of its terms, the judgment but not the external thing, is given to me. Royce concludes that this version of the definition of the end of all thought as the attainment of truth is useless, for this end is inconceivable. For if the truth to be attained in thought-processes is defined as an agreement between thought and an external reality, an agreement that cannot be established by the thinker, then thought can in fact never attain its goal and it is pointless to call such a goal thought's end.

While Royce himself would later focus on the aspect of this criticism that regards the conception of external reality, for the sake of argument at this stage he turns to a different reading of the phrase "attainment of truth." If the idea of agreement between thought and external reality cannot be given a coherent interpretation, Royce considers the view that there may still be "some meaning in the expression that the end of thought is the attainment of confidence in the agreement of the thought with external reality" (FE: 225). Here, the search for subjective confidence regarding the truth of a statement replaces the requirement of correspondence between thought and fact that cannot be ascertained by the judging subject. The attainment of such *subjective certainty* is the second candidate for the end of thought.

It is characteristic of this view that it describes the goal to be attained as a state of consciousness, in which thoughts cohere and in which there is confidence as to their correspondence with external reality, whereas this correspondence is not positively cashed out. In a word, this view suggests seeking axiomatic certainty and confiding in some kind of correspondence between a coherent set of beliefs and external reality. Consequently, on this account, the purpose of thought-processes is "to change uncertainty into confidence, and beliefs that appear as though they might not be in harmony with reality into beliefs of which we are mysteriously but perfectly convinced that they are in harmony with reality" (FE: 227). However, can the confidence regarding correspondence crucial to this account be taken seriously? Royce thinks not, for it remains mysterious to him how such correspondence should ever be ascertained. But, he continues, if the idea of correspondence is subtracted from that account, what remains is the important insight that at least part of the end of thought lies in attaining knowledge about the relations between different facts of experience. This next candidate for a definition of the purpose of thought appeals to a conception of possible experience relying on an interpretation of the so-called "principle of uniformity." Instead of analyzing the instantaneous relation between a thought and its object, this conception is focused on the cross-temporal relations between the thoughts of an epistemic subject at different times. Roughly, the idea is that if I have perceived a certain object as having acted in a certain way in certain circumstances, then I am in principle warranted to believe that like objects in like future circumstances will act likewise. As much as I rely on an object's identity with itself, I rely on the uniformity of its behavior under relevantly similar circumstances. I am, as any epistemic subject is, bound to my present conscious thoughts which relate to past and future experiences on the assumption that the bases of all experiences, in particular the time-flow and the laws of succession and uniformity, remain stable.

Royce's view at this stage is that epistemologists should neither skeptically undermine nor generally underestimate the force of this assumption. So on the one

hand, expectations about the future behavior of objects should not be labeled fictitious, even though the exact course of events cannot be predicted with certainty;
on the other hand, the epistemic conception of uniformity as guiding the anticipation of future experience should not be deflated to the recognition of an absolute
contingency of events, which either do or do not confirm the subject's expectations.
Rather, he concludes, the "end of thought in assuming the axiom of uniformity is the
construction of an ideal picture of a world of experience that shall be seen as One"
(FE: 259–60).

But if the task of the subject is thus described as constructing such an ideal picture
of a uniform and internally coherent world of experience, how could it possibly err
about what it experiences? Does this view not eliminate the practically all too familiar
difference between truth and error? Royce responds that what is meant by error is the
disappointment of "an expectation of experience, possessed by [the epistemic subject]
in the past" (FE: 256). The idea is that when I, for instance, become aware that my
judgment that there is a tree outside my window is false, I realize that my expectation
concerning the existence or the position of the tree, an expectation I formed on the
basis of earlier experience, is now disappointed. Between then and now the tree may
have been cut down, say. Looking forward, I can, analogously, fear error in imagining
that an expectation I now have regarding a future state of affairs will be disappointed.
In both cases it is the background of an ideally uniform world of experience and
beliefs, in view of which, present and anticipated future experiences are assessed.

This view – which is roughly in line with the early pragmatist conception of
belief – seems to account successfully for the way epistemic subjects seek to form a
system of beliefs on which they act and which they adjust in the light of new experiences. But if what is called experience, belief or knowledge is not conceived as an
affair entirely relative and internal to an epistemic subject – an account that is much
harder to defend than the ones Royce criticizes in the study cited – then the idea of
correspondence between thought and object, which was allegedly overcome, is still in
play. For what makes the disappointment of an anticipated experience plausible if not
the object's *in fact* behaving (or being) otherwise than expected? And how else should
the (possibly fallaciously) expected and the actual state of affairs be related if not by
somehow comparing them in order to assess their correspondence?

The possibility of error

Although Royce did not confront this objection in this early study, he was aware of
the problems created by limiting the originally epistemological investigation to the
perspective of a single and finite epistemic subject, for whom its singularity and its
finitude pose distinguishable problems. That perspective allowed accounting for a
subject's awareness of error, but it had to be transcended in order to overcome the idea
of correspondence, an idea Royce knew could not plausibly be made sense of within a
framework based on the subject-object-dichotomy assumed in epistemological reflections. Up to that point, Royce had expressed the practical and voluntaristic nature
of belief and thus subscribed *avant la lettre* to central pragmatist tenets. But, setting

out from those commitments, he was onto something more. The reflections he built on the problem of accounting for truth and error in the famous chapter 10 of *The Religious Aspect of Philosophy* (= RAP) were to ground his reputation as a proponent of idealism. One way of approaching what has been called Royce's "Argument from Error" (see Trotter 2001) is to read it as shifting the focus of investigation from the subject's consciousness of error to the "*conditions that determine the logical possibility of error*" (RAP: 385), i.e. as a shift from an epistemological inquiry to an inquiry one might also call transcendental or metaphysical.

Royce starts out from the almost trivial fact that in both theoretical and practical endeavors epistemic subjects and agents like us err or commit errors. I can be wrong in judging that there is a cube lying on a bookshelf when it is in fact only rectangular pieces of paper arranged upright, and I can fail to cook a delicious meal when I add salt instead of sugar. Furthermore, I can be wrong in such matters as saying that my friend Tom believes that there is a cat on the mat. Any theory of knowledge must, Royce is convinced, account for the existence of such errors. And any theory that precludes even the possibility of error is to be rejected.

On Royce's account, even the epistemological positions *skepticism* and *relativism*, although their proponents claim not to invoke general propositions or standards of truth, cannot be formulated without recourse to the existence of error. For being skeptical about the existence of error would amount to acknowledging the possibility of a higher order error, an error about the existence of error; nor can claiming that the truth of a judgment is dependent only on making it do away with invoking (relative) standards that can either be met or violated. Moreover, Royce continues, both the *commonsensical* view and the *subjective idealist* view of what it means for a judgment to be true can be shown to lead to the denial of the possibility of error. These latter views, as Royce (re-)constructs them, deal with the question of truth by analyzing the relation between a judgment and the object about which it is a judgment. Here, the idea is that a judgment picks out its object, thus representing what is (so to say) in or before the mind of the judging subject when the judgment is made; beyond this there is no question as to the truth of the judgment. But such a conception pre-empts the whole consideration of the possibility of error, since whatever is picked out in the judgment is picked out correctly. According to Royce, we are then led to acknowledge that either there is no error or that this conception of judgment needs to be supplemented. Given that the existence of error is practically undeniable, by *modus tollens*, the task is to provide the supplement missing so far.

One of Royce's central examples, used to establish a theory that can successfully account for the possibility of error, can be reconstructed in the following way. Suppose two individuals, John and Thomas, are in the same room and form beliefs about one another (or even one another's beliefs). We can integrate the commonsensical take on such a situation by saying that each cannot refer to the other's real self but only to his own image of the other, so that besides the real John and the real Thomas, Thomas's image of John and John's image of Thomas are also present – as if there were four individuals in the room. Let us next face the question as to how John's judgment that Thomas is thinking of a tree can be false. We have acknowledged that John cannot refer to the real Thomas and what he (Thomas) is thinking, but only to his own (i.e. John's) image of Thomas and to whatever that image contains. But then it seems that whatever John's judgment about Thomas is, it cannot be false, since it is in fact nothing but John's judgment about his own image of Thomas. To avoid this spinning in the void, Royce inserts, we need to extend the picture so as to include a third subject, one to whom all four individuals in the room are present, one that can assess whether John's judgment about John's image of Thomas corresponds to the real Thomas. But this third subject should, for this extension of the picture to have a point, not be like John and Thomas. If it were, say, just their common pal Paul, he again would be limited to his images of John and Thomas and thus in the very same way limited to comparing just these images without access to the respective real persons and their properties. So instead of the neutral and unconstrained perspective on the situation there would follow a regress of limited perspectives, none of which would be sufficient for determining the truth of a judgment such as John's judgment about Thomas.

Evading this threat of regress – which he takes to arise not just for judgments about other subjects but also for judgments concerning facts in the outside world and judgments about the future – Royce suggests "that John and Thomas are both actually present to and included in a third and higher thought" (RAP: 422). What the study of the possibility of error is to overcome, argues Royce, is the presupposition that entities such as John and Thomas, as well as present and future facts, have a separate, unconnected existence. In other words,

> let us overcome all our difficulties by declaring that all the many Beyonds, which single significant judgments seem vaguely and separately to postulate, are present as fully realized intended objects to the unity of an all-inclusive, absolutely clear, universal, and conscious thought, of which all judgments, true or false, are but fragments, the whole being at once Absolute Truth and Absolute Knowledge. (RAP: 423)

Instead of positing an independent, but equally finite observer of the situation involving John and Thomas, and instead of a single subject's judgment concerning an external fact, Royce thinks the possibility of error can only be conceived by acknowledging the existence of a higher, all-encompassing thought. This Absolute – with a capital "A" – is understood as a whole including all facts and factive judgments so that where a finite mind can only vaguely refer to something beyond its finite perspective, be it spatial or temporal, this "Beyond" is present to the infinite thought of the Absolute. According to Royce, who is here drawing an inference to what he takes to be the best explanation, this makes the puzzles about the nature and possibility of error disappear, "because any one finite thought, viewed in relation to its own intent, may or may not be seen by this higher thought as successful and adequate in this intent" (RAP: 423).

In contrast to the skeptical and relativistic accounts Royce criticizes, this absolute idealism is meant to provide an answer to the question about the possibility of error.

In formulating the transcendental conditions of erroneous judgments (and beliefs), it does overcome the limitations of the other views. But even without reconstructing the theistic conclusions Royce subsequently draws from his understanding of the Absolute, one might query whether (i) introducing the Absolute is without alternatives and whether (ii) this equips ordinary individuals with a strategy to determine the truth of judgments. While Royce himself, as we shall see below, repeatedly returns to the first of these questions, nowhere does he give a genuinely epistemological answer to the second one. Approaching the question of truth and error, as Royce conceives of it throughout his writings on this subject, is taken to require ascending to transcendental conditions or, put differently, to the metaphysical foundations of thought and existence. In line with the intersubjective scenario involving John and Thomas, one of Royce's main themes in 1890s is not to determine the relations between the individual, taken singly, and the Absolute, but the conception of individuality as such. Taking it primarily not as a logico-metaphysical category, but as an empirically informed conception of "being an individual," Royce approaches this topic in the classical idealistic fashion, i.e. as a theory of self-consciousness.

Self-consciousness and social consciousness

Subsequent to his early success with *The Religious Aspect of Philosophy* and his effort to combine historical and systematic studies in *The Spirit of Modern Philosophy*, Royce's interest extended to psychology. It is characteristic of Royce's way of thinking that in the essays in which this new interest found expression – collected in his *Studies of Good and Evil* – he connects the ambition to integrate insights from the rising field of developmental psychology on the one hand and the traditional idealistic treatment of the respective issues on the other. What emerges is an innovative take on the classic topic of self-consciousness. In line with his idealistic predecessors, Royce understands this topic as not just asking for an empirical explanation of the genesis of self-consciousness, but also for an account of the relations between self-conscious beings, nature and the Absolute; in other words, he combines the questions "How does an individual become self-conscious?" and "What is the deeper (metaphysical) meaning of self-consciousness?" We shall start with his treatment of the first question and then proceed by tracing Royce's conclusions regarding the second one.

Royce opposes the view that an individual is a subsistent and self-conscious being before it interacts with others and the natural world around it. In (our) contemporary terms, he criticizes social atomism as the view according to which the development of an individual's mental capacities is independent of its external relations. But any opponent of this kind of atomism needs to give an account of whether only the acquisition of certain capacities is thus relationally constituted or whether this also holds for the continuous engagement in their application. Concerning the acquisition of mental capacities, which includes the capacity of conceiving of oneself as a self-conscious being, Royce introduces the notion of *social consciousness*. Drawing on psychologist J. Mark Baldwin's work on imitation (see Baldwin 1894), Royce explains that a child's imitative behavior is to be seen as the key to its self-conception. In imitating, for instance, its siblings' or its parents' actions, the young child is seen as becoming aware that others react to their common environment in ways similar to its own. In view of these similarities it realizes both that it is in important ways like these others and, at the same time, that it is yet individual in instantiating its own responses to the common environment. On Royce's view, it is due to these processes of assimilating its own behavior to and contrasting it with the behavior of others that the child becomes aware of there being other conscious life around it and of being such a conscious individual itself. Thus the child's imitative behavior is taken to be the key to its reflective awareness of being a conscious self. "[T]here is," as Royce puts it, "on the whole, in us men, no self-consciousness apart from some more or less derived form of the social consciousness. I am I in relation to some sort of a non-Ego" (SGE: 203). In this passage, Royce asserts not just the *genetic dependence* of self-consciousness on the consciousness directed at other agents like us, but also the *constitutive dependence* of selfhood on being related to a "non-Ego."

Especially in the context of nineteenth-century philosophy, one is reminded of the classical analyses of recognitive relations in Fichte and Hegel. And with respect to the aforementioned constitutive dependence between self-conscious individuals, we can trace a degree of continuity from Royce's view back to what Hegel, for instance, had condensed into the picture of mutually recognizing self-consciousnesses. Royce himself later acknowledged this continuity in the sixth and seventh of his *Lectures on Modern Idealism* (published in 1919).

But Royce's account of the relational constitution of self-consciousness includes another step which cannot be situated as straightforwardly in the history of idealistic thought. For the function of social relations is not limited to the constitution and affirmation of the selfhood of the individuals involved, but extends to the conception a thinking subject has of all external reality, both conscious and unconscious, animate and inanimate. Royce phrases this as "the assertion that what you and I mean by Nature is, as a finite reality, something whose very conception we have actually derived from our social relations with one another" (SGE: 204). These social relations comprise not just mutual observation and imitation, as suggested by the first illustrations above, but in their most elaborate form they consist in the communicative exchange between individuals with the aim of exchanging and aligning experiences.

Royce gains three important insights from the reflections on these processes: first, since self-conscious thought is dependent on social interaction with other thinkers, and since this interaction is characteristically carried out in language, we seem to be entitled to claim that "nearly all our thinking, not only about the *non-Ego*, but also about the Ego, is notoriously carried on in language" (Royce 1894: 534). Second, if such interaction is to play the constitutive role for an individual's self-consciousness, the element of contrast between its own and the others' experiences, Royce presupposes that those others are conceived as being conscious thinkers and intentional agents, too. We can thus understand Royce's insistence on the importance of social consciousness for self-consciousness as one way of expressing the close connection between knowledge of other minds and self-knowledge. However, emphasizing these close connections does not, as Royce notes, do away with the asymmetry between ascribing (third-personal) beliefs to others and having (first-personal) beliefs oneself. Moreover, third, the social interaction and exchange of experiences presuppose a common point of reference. If Tim and Jim, for instance, report to one another that what they are seeing in front of them is a grizzly bear, they align their perceptions of one and the same object. They each see the bear and by communicating they find out that what each sees is (more or less precisely) what the other sees, too. Their mutual assurance of this perception may ground not just a definite perceptual judgment but also a decision concerning subsequent (possibly joint) action. At least in so far as it concerns the judgment about the external object, the process involves a triangle spun up between Tim, Jim, and the object; this process was later (and famously by Donald Davidson [2001]) termed *triangulation*. For Royce, it is a characteristic function of social communication to provide this (re-)assurance of external facts: "There is no evidence for the reality of nature-facts which is not defined for us by the very categories of the social consciousness" (SGE: 230). It is on this view only through some form of social consciousness that one can arrive at the cognitive realization of "the existence of a finite non-Ego" (SGE: 228).

From these reflections on the nature of self-consciousness emerges Royce's idealistic conception of nature. It is idealistic in not presupposing a dualism of consciousness and external fact, of mind and world, but in seeking to establish continuity between the perceiving and judging epistemic subject and the objects of perception and judgment. Dualism is incomprehensible, for

> [n]o evidence [.] can indicate nature's inner reality without also indicating that this reality is, like that of our own experience, conscious, organic, full of clear contrasts, rational, definite. We ought not to speak of dead nature. We have only a right to speak of uncommunicative nature. Natural objects, if they are real at all, are *prima facie* simply other finite beings, who are, so to speak, not in our own social set, and who communicate to us, not their minds, but their presence. For, I repeat, a real being can only mean to me other experience than mine; and other experience does not mean deadness, unconsciousness, disorganization, but presence, life, inner light. (SGE: 230)

So, regarding the question as to how judgments about such idealistically conceived nature-facts can be true or false, this view of nature seems to be quite in line with Royce's earlier argument for the possibility of error: it is through the integration of all being into a totality of life that a meaningful linkage between subjects, acts and objects of judgment is constituted, and it is precisely in virtue of this totality that judgments can err.

But Royce does not go as far as drawing the metaphysical consequences of these views at this stage. In the 1890s, he limited his arguments to asserting both the social nature of knowledge and the essentially social character of any knowledge of nature. He can there be read as beginning to expound a *social ontology*, in which an analysis of the constitution of social entities such as the self and the community have as much a place as an ontological account of the existence of nature-facts through their presence to socially communicating individuals. "Social" here means, in the first place, the individual's immersion in imitative, contrastive and communicative exchange with fellow individuals, and, in the second place, the contrast with nature-facts, where these are conceived as belonging to what he calls the "non-Ego," i.e. everything outside the Ego. Royce conceived it as his task for later works to proceed from the thus articulated relational conception of self-consciousness and nature, where social consciousness functions as a mediating instance, to an inquiry into the nature of being. To what extent insights from the study of self-consciousness helped to mold his ontological view, we can only tell by taking a closer look at Royce's discussion of what he called "conceptions of being."

Conceptions of being

Royce's studies in metaphysics and epistemology, the philosophy of religion, philosophical psychology, and the history of philosophy and logic, as he had undertaken them in his writing and teaching since he first turned to philosophy, culminated in his Gifford Lectures, published as the two volumes of *The World and the Individual*. While the twenty lectures and the famous "supplementary essay" contained in these volumes can, or indeed should, be read as an exposition of a philosophical system, an exercise in *prima philosophia* forms their core. Royce describes his "precise undertaking" in those lectures as showing "what we mean by Being in general, and by the special sorts of Reality that we attribute to God, to the World, and to the Human Individual" (WI 1: 11). The "we" here refers not just to the professional philosopher, but to anyone ready to critically reflect on the most basic structures of being. Paying tribute to the sponsor of the lectures, Lord Gifford, who had declared the study of religion to be the focus of the lectures, Royce interpreted the study of religion as "a branch of the Theory of Being" and set out to investigate "the ultimate problems of Ontology, laying due stress upon their relations to religion" (*ibid.*). Especially in the first volume, Royce proceeds by way of reconstructing, reassessing and re-appropriating "some of the principal conceptions concerning the ultimate nature of Being," thus sketching "the history of what one might call the ontological predicate of the expression *to be*, or *to be real*, used as a means of asserting that something exists." Asserting that something exists leads to such an ontological study "because to assert that God is, or that the World is, or even, with Descartes, that I am, implies that one knows what it is to be, or in other words, what the so-called existential predicate itself involves" (WI 1: 12).

Of the many paths that lead to and through Royce's *opus magnum* – reading it as a history of metaphysics or as a renewed statement of the above-mentioned argument from error, to name just two such paths – we shall here restrict ourselves to a summary of Royce's conception of being, the argument for which takes up the first volume. The introduction and discussion of three alternative types of ontological theory serve to establish Royce's own idealistic conception as the one that best accounts for the meaning of the ontological predicate that is expressed by "exists," "is," or "is real." Approaching the question concerning the nature of being via an analysis of the ontological predicate gives center stage to the determination of the relation between an idea and its object. The analysis of judgments in which the existence or reality of objects is predicated, in which objects are said to exist or to be real, is one part of the study of this relation; more generally formulated, the inquiry is focused on the relation between thought and reality.

Royce frames his discussion of ontological theories by specifying his understanding of the concept "Idea" as "any state of mind that has a conscious meaning" (WI 1: 24). Nowadays this is referred to as a kind of *intentional state*, in which the subject of this state actively refers to some (intentional) content. The direction of this reference, or intentionality, points to the content of the state, as it is the case when a subject – to use Royce's examples – sings a melody, appreciates a picture or has the memory of a friend present to its mind. Royce calls the capturing of such contents in states of mind the *embodiment* of the content, which he regards as a partial fulfillment of a purpose. By forming the intention to write a letter to my friend, for instance, I grasp and explicitly pronounce what I want to do, but this constitutes just a partial fulfillment of the purpose I want to pursue, for only the successful act would make it complete. Such a "purpose, in so far as it gets a present conscious embodiment in the contents and in the form of the complex state called the idea, constitutes what [Royce calls] the *Internal Meaning* of the Idea" (WI 1: 25, emphasis added). But this internal aspect does not exhaust what is commonly (or even commonsensically) referred to as the meaning of an idea. As Royce continues, such states have another "sort of meaning," they refer "beyond themselves to objects," bear a "cognitive relation to outer facts," and they are characterized by an "attempted correspondence with outer facts, which many accounts of our ideas regard as their primary, inexplicable, and ultimate character" (WI 1: 26). Royce calls this aspect of the nature of ideas their *External Meaning*. When I think of an absent friend, say, this idea has an internal meaning insofar as I have this friend present to my mind, but it can, in the external sense, also be regarded as meaning the real being that is my friend. Royce seeks to distinguish sharply between these aspects of an idea and takes it to illustrate "the problem of the whole relation between Idea and Being" (WI 1: 27). We shall now use this distinction to briefly review the conceptions of being discussed by Royce.

In its pure form, the first conception of being, which Royce calls *realism*, is characterized by the claim that the objects of knowledge exist totally independently of any knowledge of them, as well as of one another. *Mysticism*, as Royce calls the second conception of being, in contrast, asserts that "to be means, simply and wholly, to be *immediate*, as what we call pure color, pure sound, pure emotion, are already in us partly and imperfectly immediate" (WI 1: 80). With respect to the aforementioned distinction, "the mystic knows only Internal Meanings, precisely as the realist considers only External Meanings" (WI 1: 176). Within both of these positions, the distinction between idea and object – or, as Royce also puts it, between content and reference, between the *essence* and the *existence* of whatever there is – is drawn in the sharpest conceivable way. Where the realist, according to Royce's portrayal, asserts the total independence of existent entities, the mystic asks us to limit ourselves to that which is immediately before our consciousness and not to seek any relevant reference beyond. Both these views are judged one-sided and inadequate to account for the relation between the idea viewed as an intentional state and its object, the relation crucial to determining the truth of a belief or a judgment.

But this extreme form of realism can be amended so as to be committed only to a weaker claim than that regarding the total independence of idea and being. A weaker, relative independence is asserted when it is said "that the Real is essentially *such that, under conditions, it would become knowable and known*" (WI 1: 196). The conditions under which such a relatively independent object becomes real are fulfilled if an epistemic subject, as it were, turns and attends to it, accommodating it by making it an object of judgment and knowledge; the existential predicate *to be* is then interpreted as involving this possibility of becoming an object of knowledge, i.e. the object's knowability.

The third conception of being mentioned by Royce is foreshadowed in this modified form of realism. It stresses the tight relation between being and knowledge by asserting that what is "is there as *that which, if known, is found giving to ideas their validity*, as *that to which ideas ought to correspond*, and as that whose essential relation to ideas is that it is their *model*, and is adapted to their nature as such model" (WI 1: 201–2). Royce depicts this *critical rationalism* as offering the following definition of being: "To be real [.] means, primarily, *to be valid, to be true, to be in essence the standard for ideas*" (*ibid.*). Ideas understood as intentional states are thus taken to have the criterion of validity as a standard external to themselves, one to which they must correspond in order to be true. On the whole, this critical rationalist conception declares as real that which can be grasped by ideas, where this grasping includes the modes of conceiving and of experiencing.

Against these three conceptions Royce places a fourth, his own conception of being, to whose elaboration he devotes more than two thirds of the entire lecture series. The dialectics with which Royce prepares and then carries out the exposition of this fourth conception is exemplary for his understanding of the dialogue with the history of philosophy. He intertwines the systematization of conceptions of being with reconstructions and interpretations of historical positions, giving priority to critical scrutiny and the incorporation of tenable systematic claims. Given the breadth and depth of the topic envisaged, these heuristics require the restatement of earlier views in light of Royce's own understanding of the key phenomena and problems.

Against this methodological background, Royce's introduction of the distinction between the internal and external meanings of ideas, drawn sharply, serves as an argumentative tool in the defense of his conception of being. Despite the fact that the first three conceptions had not been spelt out either in the light of this distinction or on the basis of Royce's definition of its terms, he takes the question about the relation between Idea and Being essentially to boil down to the question: "How is the internal meaning of ideas consistent with their apparently external meaning?" (WI 1: 32) Ideas appear, *prima facie* and according to a commonsensical introduction of the problem, to refer to things entirely distinct and independent of themselves. In analyzing the conditions of application of the predicate "to be," the first three conceptions seem, on Royce's account, not to be able to account for the relation between the internal and external meanings of ideas. Indeed, mysticism and realism are both depicted as assigning being only to immediate or independent facts respectively, thereby excluding either the one or the other and defining those facts as fictional or reducible. Critical rationalism seems to do better in not being as one-sided, but its definition of being in terms of validity ultimately gives priority to an external standard for ideas that seek correspondence. Royce, by contrast, follows neither the mystic in resorting only to immediate, inner facts, nor the realist in his exclusive recourse to so-called independent, outer facts; and he does not join the critical rationalist in claiming that being is tied to the possibility of validating or verifying ideas.

Nevertheless, in a Hegelian sense of *aufheben*, all three preceding conceptions do articulate true insights, which the fourth conception is intended to synthesize and incorporate. *Firstly*, Royce takes the truth of the realist conception to lie in the claim that, in a judgment, say, the object of an idea is an other that is "authoritative over against the finite idea" (WI 1: 353). The purpose of judging is to grasp an object that is, at the moment of judgment, not yet present to the consciousness of the judger; so it is to be affirmed that, in judging, an internal idea points beyond itself. But the realist, argues Royce, goes too far in claiming that the object pointed to is in itself wholly separated from the internal idea it is sought by. Rather, "the idea submits to no external meaning that is not the development of its own internal meaning" (WI 1: 354). Accordingly, in the realist conception of being what is to be rejected is the "isolation of the idea from the object, and of the object from the idea (*ibid.*)".

Secondly, Royce agrees with the mystical conception of being that "the object is for us simply the completely embodied will of the idea" (WI 1: 355). This insight assigns a crucial role to the purposiveness of the cognitive relation between idea and object. But the mystic is presented as and criticized for tying this purposiveness to the present finite will, whereas Royce takes the purposive nature of finite ideas to be just particular instances, or fragments, of the general relation between ideas and objects. In contrast to the mystic, Royce claims that the momentous fulfillment of a finite idea, as exemplified in a single judgment, is not "founded in heaven," but that such a fulfillment, which Royce calls embodiment, provides a glimpse "of the genuine and eternally present truth of the one real world" (WI 1: 356). Royce thereby seeks to resist restricting being to the momentous, present internal meaning of an idea, to which external reference, taken as pointing both beyond the particular instant and beyond the internal idea, is of no importance.

Thirdly, the critical rationalist conception is affirmed in the assertion that "Being essentially involves what gives the validity to ideas" (*ibid.*). But if this is accepted, the crucial question becomes "what conditions are necessary to constitute validity" (*ibid.*). Royce's own view is that the introduction of validity as a criterion of being needs to be grounded in something that is more than merely valid, for validity is "nothing [.] unless it takes an individual form as an unique fulfillment of purpose in a completed life" (WI 1: 358). The critical rationalist is thus charged with limiting the realm of being to that which is possibly experienceable, thereby subscribing to a view that refers to nothing but fragmentary single experiences, without seeking to account for that of which particular experiences are fragments.

Royce's meta-claim in this discussion is that his own conception of being retains all the true insights listed and, at the same time, avoids the listed criticisms. Thus Royce affirms that

> What is, is authoritative over against finite ideas, as Realism asserted, is one with the true meaning of the idea, as Mysticism insisted, and is valid as Critical Rationalism demanded. (WI 1: 358)

And he continues as follows:

> What is, presents the fulfillment of the whole purpose of the very idea that now seeks this Being. And when I announce this as our Fourth Conception of Being, I do not mean to be understood as asserting a mere validity, but as reporting facts. I do not any longer merely say ... Being is that which, if present, would end your finite search, would answer your doubts, would fulfil your purpose. ... [Overcoming the language of validity] I now say, without any reserve, What is does in itself fulfil your meaning, does express, in the completest logically possible measure, the accomplishment and embodiment in your finite ideas. And I say, that this embodiment means in itself precisely what your present embodiment of purpose in your rational experience means, just in so far as your purposes are not mere fragments, but are also, even in their transiency, results known as, relatively speaking, won, as possessed, as accomplished. The accomplishment of your purpose now means that your experience is viewed by you as the present and conscious expression of a plan. Well, what is, precisely in so far as it is, is in the same way a whole experience finally expressing and consciously fulfilling a plan. And the Being of the real object of which you now think means a life that expresses the fulfillment of just your present plan, in the greatest measure in which your plan itself is logically capable of fulfillment. (WI 1: 358–9)

This statement is exemplary of what Royce calls his *synthetic* or *constructive idealism*. It is synthetic on two levels: in synthesizing the first three conceptions in the way sketched above and in claiming that the internal and external meanings of an idea do not fall apart or represent distinct realms, but are rather aspects of the notion of a complete idea. What is thus complete, either in terms of the embodiment of a purpose on the part of a subject, or in terms of an object (or content) embodied therewith, is called an *Individual* by Royce. This concept of "individual" subsumes the notion of an individual self and the notion of an individual thing. In *The World and the Individual*, Royce uses the reflection on the relation between the single instance – be it an individual self, a particular judgment or idea, or the present content of a conscious state – and the totality of which it is an instance and an expression, as the principle of individuation. Accordingly, he programmatically claims that "that is real which finally presents in a completed experience the whole meaning of a System of Ideas" (WI 1:

61). According to Royce, none of the preceding conceptions of being possess the conceptual tools for articulating what is here referred to as a "completed experience."

With respect to the distinction between the internal and external meanings of ideas, Royce's view is that

> the final meaning of every complete idea, when fully developed, must be viewed as wholly an internal meaning, and that all apparently external meanings become consistent with internal meanings only by virtue of thus coming to be viewed as aspects of the true internal meaning. (WI 1: 34)

This view, although metaphysically much more ambitious, is continuous with Royce's understanding of thinking as a purposive activity. In other words, we can read Royce's defense of his conception of being as fleshing out the metaphysical presumptions of his reflections on the nature of thinking and the possibility of error. As for the nature of thinking, he declares it to be misleading to impose an ontological gap between thought and object, between internal and external meaning. Indeed, in his view, experience remains crucial to thought and judgment, but he understands experience not as a form of passive intake, but as a constructive activity of testing and reformulating the internal meaning of ideas. As for the possibility of error, he invokes the (*per se* reflective) distinctions between finite and infinite, between incomplete and complete. A particular judgment can be erroneous in that it only incompletely represents the external meaning of the idea expressed by it. But the finitude and incompleteness of such a particular judgment are sublated in what Royce calls a "System of Ideas," which comprises the totality of meanings and in which the distinction between internal and external is overcome.

Within this idealistic conception of being, the aforementioned claims about the *social* nature of knowledge and the *sociality* of individual selves (see the subsection, "The Possibility of Error," above) are also maintained. Royce restates and refines the respective arguments in his second set of Gifford Lectures (WI 2). We will come back to these reflections in the third section, where we will also take a brief look at how Royce reformulates the argument for his conception of being in terms of interpretation as a kind of knowledge. Although this constitutes part of Royce's idealism, we will postpone the discussion of this new argument, thereby retaining the chronological order of exposition.

But before we proceed, we should briefly note one further point about Royce's idealism. Throughout his life, Royce was fascinated by the precision and intricacies of logics. His first monograph, the *Primer of Logical Analysis*, and a number of essays on both informal and formal logics and the foundations of mathematics and philosophical methodology – collected in the volume *Royce's Logical Essays* (edited by Robinson in 1951) – amply certify this interest. As was typical for Royce's systematic philosophizing, there is a deep and complex connection between his logical studies and the metaphysical idealism being defended. In Royce's published work, this connection is most apparent in the essay "The One, the Many, and the Infinite" that was supplemented to the first volume of *The World and the Individual*. In this essay, whose tone and method reflect the influence of Peirce (see Cotton 1954: 217), Royce pursues two interconnected goals: he discusses Bradley's metaphysics as an alternative idealistic position and seeks to spell out his conception of being in terms of the analysis of so-called "self-representative systems." While this is not the place to enter into the details of this treatise, it *is* the occasion to emphasize that Royce's philosophy does not fall short of paying attention to the methodological standards later associated with analytical philosophy. Already at the time of the Gifford Lectures, Royce incorporated the pragmatist tenets concerning the practicality and sociality of thought into his view, but he also – albeit in less received works – sought to answer for the logical and structural foundations of his metaphysics. The question as to how logics and metaphysics relate in Royce's idealism is surely one that will attract interest in future Royce scholarship.

Royce's ethics

What is nowadays commonly called "practical philosophy" always played an important role in Royce's thought, not only in terms of his pragmatic, action-oriented conception of belief, but also in the sense of normative reflections on what makes for a good life, a just structure of social arrangements, and the importance of an harmonious ethical life in the community. In his early works, especially in *The Religious Aspect of Philosophy*, ethical deliberations grew primarily out of a preoccupation with the tenability of religious moral doctrines, or were presented as reviews or criticism in journal articles (see FE, SGE and Rand 1916). When Royce intensified his ethical studies in the years after publishing *The World and the Individual*, second series of which had already contained an account of "The Moral Order" (WI 2: Lecture 8), this was not just motivated by an interest in elaborating that part of his philosophical system, but also by his ongoing concern with the state and fate of the American society of his day. With respect to both social theory and political life, Royce diagnosed that diverse tendencies towards what he called *individualism* threatened the social bonds essential to all individuals living meaningful and successful lives. In a very basic sense, Royce objected to modern appeals to the individuality of a person as her outright independence of all social relations and community life. He judged views based on this premise to be inadequate concerning both their metaphysical and epistemological underpinnings and their conception of what counts as a good life. In his more specifically ethical and social philosophical works – of which we will here concentrate on *The Philosophy of Loyalty* (= PL, 1908) and *The Problem of Christianity* (= PC, 1913) – Royce sought to counter these individualistic tendencies of his time by developing accounts of social relations and social communities.

The normative branch of Royce's philosophy is largely taken up by deliberations on the moral dimension of religious doctrine and the value of community life. While Royce was still immersed in working out and teaching his ideas on these matters, the outbreak of the First World War provided occasion to contribute to the concrete and, he felt, pressing political discussions in his country. These contributions – especially those contained in *War and Insurance* – are interesting as Royce's testimony of the historical developments, but he did not live to justify and elaborate the political principles he referred to therein. We shall not consider these political writings here, but restrict the discussion to the two core elements of Royce's ethical theory.

The virtue of loyalty

Royce's ethics as he developed it in his 1907–8 Lowell Lectures, published as *The Philosophy of Loyalty*, is centered on the question as to what constitutes a meaningful life. How, Royce asks, should, an individual living in a modern society orient his life? What is it that gives life worth and sense? As indicated by the title, an analysis and understanding of the concept of *loyalty* are crucial to Royce's reply. Although Royce touches on a wide range of topics in the fields of ethics, metaethics and political philosophy, his arguments are developed in direct reference to concrete ethical practices and they are addressed not just at scholars, but at everyone to whom the mentioned questions occur. Contrary to the abstractness of idealistic thought that William James incessantly opposed by calling it "intellectualist" (see James 1975), Royce here sets out to "justify the philosophy through its application to life" (PL: 9). Nevertheless, the lack of explicit references to the traditions of or familiar views within ethical theory makes it difficult to precisely determine the place of Royce's ethics on the spectrum of ethical positions.

Royce defines loyalty as the "*willing and practical and thoroughgoing devotion of a person to a cause*" (PL: 16–7). Thus loyalty concerns a person's will and actions, precisely those spheres through which a person seeks to attain and realize her freedom and autonomy. But according to Royce's account, such autonomy is not a precondition of loyalty, but rather, the realization of an individual's autonomy is dependent on the degree to which the individual thoroughly devotes herself to a cause. To fill in the details of this explanation, we need to take a closer look at the other elements of Royce's definition.

The basis for the definition of loyalty is the view that individual persons seek to live their lives in accordance with a plan, an overarching goal they strive for and whose pursuit gives structure and meaning to those activities that are conducive to that goal. Royce calls such an overarching goal a person's "cause." A loyal person, as stated in the definition, is one who consistently and effectively pursues his goal(s) in life. But these specifications of a purposeful life are insufficient for grounding an ethical theory if they do not include a principle for distinguishing between different kinds of cause, since it would seem at least implausible if not dangerous to regard just any thoroughly pursued life-plan as constituting a valuable and good life. This challenge is best illustrated by a contrast that we will take up again in the course of this section. Consider the difference we intuitively make between the life of a man who, in addition to his regular job, works on a voluntary basis for a charity organization where he helps to educate orphans, and the life of a Mafioso who engages, equally devotedly, in a variety of criminal activities including fraud, smuggling, and murder. Here we have two individuals whose devotion to their respective causes *prima facie* fulfills the definition of loyalty. But it seems safe to assume that we would not regard both of these ways of life as equally worthy ideals. So if loyalty is to have any bite as an ethical principle – one that can be generally accepted or even universalized to be applicable to all persons at all times – we need a principle for identifying good causes.

In developing this principle, Royce invokes the conception of sociality he developed in his studies on the relationship between self-consciousness and social consciousness. A personal life, as he now applies those earlier insights, is not to be viewed as being the life of a self-sufficient and independent individual who sets and pursues her own goals to the detriment of everything and everyone around her. From Royce's perspective, such an atomistic view is characteristic of the American society of his time; by opposing it he intends to revive values and principles for which there is a need in his time. The first step towards an anti-atomistic view of personal life consists in claiming that loyalty "concerns other men. Loyalty is social" (PL: 20). Instead of being a merely private affair, the devotion of cause is seen as concerning other persons both in so far as others are affected by or even addressed with one's own actions and in so far as there will in most cases be others pursuing the same goals. Loyal persons are thus to acknowledge the social interleaving of their individual actions and life-plans with those of others; dedicating one's life to a goal that others share therefore grounds the existence of community. In Royce's terminology, loyalty is not just personal but includes an *impersonal*, other-regarding dimension as well as a *superpersonal*, community-regarding dimension. Yet loyalty remains personal in so far as it is the person's individual life that is significantly enriched by the acknowledgement of social relatedness and community (see PL: 52–3).

At this stage, Royce incorporates elements of his epistemological and social psychological studies (see "The Possibility of Error," in the second section, above), which formed the basis of his conceptions of self-consciousness or "the human self" (see SGE and WI 2: Lecture 6). For him, the single person is not a self-contained and self-sufficient atom, but a social entity whose immersion in social relations enables her to lead a meaningful life. In the ethical realm, Royce's opponent is not the atomist, but the individualist, the defender of individuals' claims to independence and particularity. Royce does not deny the legitimacy of these characteristically modern claims, but from his perspective the individualist's defense rests on a misapprehension. For Royce, *individuality* is not attained by abstraction from relations to other or to a community to which one is a member, but consists precisely in acknowledging one's dependence on others, on one's role as a member of a community; being an individual in the sense specified by Royce in the context of the metaphysical argument sketched above means acknowledging one's sociality and living a life in harmony with others and the community.

But our clarifications concerning the social dimensions of loyalty do not yet provide the principle we asked for. A social and communal form of loyalty can plausibly be ascribed to, say, the members of a mafia family of which all members are thoroughly devoted to defending the honor and the status of the family. Formally, all the lives of these Mafiosi seem to be loyal in line with the foregoing definition, but these lives would not be accepted as general examples for good and valuable lives. The crucial element of an ethics of loyalty must lie in the definition not of loyalty as an attitude but of the object of loyalty, i.e. the cause to which one is loyal. Replying to the thus crucial question as to what constitutes a good cause. Royce defines it as follows:

> a cause is good, not only for me, but for mankind, in so far as it is essentially a *loyalty to loyalty*, that is, is an aid and a furtherance of loyalty in my fellows. It is an evil cause in so far as, despite the loyalty that it arouses in me, it is destructive of loyalty in the world of my fellows. My cause is, indeed, always such as to involve some loyalty to loyalty, because, if I am loyal to any cause at all, I have fellow-servants whose loyalty mine supports. But in so far as my cause is a predatory cause, which lives by overthrowing the loyalties of others, it is an evil cause, because it involves disloyalty to the very cause of loyalty itself. (PL: 118–19)

This counters the provocation according to which any devotedly and thoroughly pursued life-plan represents a loyal life and is therefore justified. The further and indeed decisive requirement Royce introduces here means that the cause to which one is loyal should be such that it aids and furthers the loyalty of others. The "fellows" thereby supported should, if this principle is to have any bite, not just be fellow conspirators as in the mafia-case but simply all those fellow individuals who strive to lead a balanced and meaningful life. While the Mafiosi do show a kind of loyalty on the first level, on a higher level the cause they pursue is bound to involve disloyalty to the loyalty of others, namely the victims of their crimes. The criterion thus put forth demands a kind of loyalty that retains its value under consideration of the value it has for everyone else. In so mutually supporting not necessarily the same causes but, essentially, the loyal pursuit of good causes, loyal persons may regard each other as "fellow-servants" and in this way constitute an ethical community.

Classifying Royce's ethical theory is not exactly an easy task, for he repeatedly rephrases the demands of loyalty in terms of the duties of loyal persons and, at the same time, requires the consequences of activities that are part of the pursuit of one's life-plan to be taken into account. Put this way, Royce's seems to make use of deonto-logical as well as teleological or consequentialist arguments, which are commonly taken to be mutually exclusive. What is more, Royce claims *"that all the commonplace virtues, in so far as they are indeed defensible and effective, are special forms of loyalty to loyalty"* (PL: 129–30). Whereas the cited principle of loyalty to loyalty appears to have the form of the Kantian *Categorical Imperative*, demanding reasonable insight into the moral law on the part of the moral person, it also regards both the consequences of actions for others and the virtuous character of the loyal person as essential to the fulfillment of this moral law. In the light of this constellation the task is not to find one particular label for Royce's ethical views but to determine which of these aspects of his views takes center stage. Given the set-up and style of the lectures that constitute *The Philosophy of Loyalty*, especially their orientation towards the everyday quest for a "true ideal of life" (PL: 24), the inquiry into the elements of a *good life* seems to be the central topic of Royce's ethics. And if what constitutes a good life is the extent to which it is lived in pursuit of a good cause, one that relates to and furthers the wellbeing of others and made possible through and in harmony with a social community, the character traits that enable a person to live such a life appear to be crucial. This line of consideration of the basic elements of Royce's ethical theory justifies calling it a *virtue ethics*, albeit one that integrates the concept of duty and the weighing of possible consequences of actions. Analyzing how exactly this latter integration is carried out and justified would make for an extensive interpretive study.

In the two closing lectures of *The Philosophy of Loyalty*, Royce elaborates the main claims of his ethical theory in two directions. The first regards the foundation of the doctrine that loyalty itself is a good. "In what sense is this good of loyalty real?" or "Does it need to be real?," one may ask. Royce understands these questions as challenges to his view insofar they express a sort of skepticism about the foundation of loyalty that is derived from general skepticism about knowledge and truth. Here, the skeptic raises the question as to whether the good of loyalty is not a mere illusion, on the whole arbitrary and contingent; he is on the verge of either defending moral relativism, the doctrine that there are no universal principles such as "loyalty to loyalty," or of resorting to outright amoralism, the view that there is no point in leading a moral life or in engaging in the ethical justification of one's actions. In brief, Royce's reply is that loyalty does not just serve to unite persons in interest or purposive groups, groups whose members happen to share certain ends which can better be achieved when they are organized, but that loyalty links human lives "in some genuine spiritual unity" (PL: 307). It assigns individual persons a place in a community of loyal persons and thus, at the same time, in a social world in which they can lead a meaningful life. The truth of this good of loyalty lies not in the mere practicality or practical necessity of finding some social arrangement with others, but in the spiritual unification it helps to realize.

In the context of this clarification, Royce explains the difference between the pragmatist conception of truth, as developed by William James, and his own idealist conception of truth (see WJOE: Essay 4). The argument against the pragmatist conception makes use of the same idea that inspired the earlier "argument from error" (see above). Here it is combined with allusions to the "fourth conception of being" and stated in the following passage:

> whoever talks of any sort of truth whatever, be that truth moral or scientific, the truth of common sense or the truth of a philosophy, inevitably implies in all his assertions about truth, that the world of truth of which he speaks is a world possessing a rational and spiritual unity, is a conscious world of experience, whose type of consciousness is higher in its level than is the type of our human minds, but whose life is such that our life belongs as part to this living whole. (PL: 313)

So, if it is claimed that some moral ideals are superior to others, or that one way of life is more valuable than another, then this claim invokes a truth that is not merely relative. Indeed, Royce says here, such assertions presuppose that there is a "world possessing a rational and spiritual unity." Besides expressing a specific brand of *cognitivism* about moral judgments, a version of the view that moral judgments are true or false in virtue of their structure and the constitution of their objects, this passage expresses a *moral holism*, according to which the moral life of individuals is part of and essentially related to a "living whole." As prefigured in *The World and the Individual*, Royce's idealist conceptions of reality, being and truth are revealed as being the foundation of his moral doctrine.

The second dimension in terms of which Royce explicates his ethics of loyalty concerns the relation between loyalty and religion. From *The Religious Aspect of Philosophy* onwards, Royce had been concerned with philosophical reflections on the justificatory status of religious ethics. While he expounded a more extensive and elaborate *philosophy of religion* in later works – especially in *The Sources of Religious Insight* (1912) and *The Problem of Christianity* (1913) (see Oppenheim 1987) – it is in the closing lecture of *The Philosophy of Loyalty* that he first explains the religious dimension of his ethics. Up to the two final lectures of this work, Royce had bracketed discussion of metaphysical foundations and the religious motives of his doctrine, approaching moral issues from a commonsensical understanding thereof. The key to the religious dimension is the aforementioned recourse to the spiritual unity realized through the loyal life of individuals in a community. Connecting the elements of the definition of loyalty developed up to that stage, Royce undertakes a reformulation of his definition of loyalty, one he terms metaphysical and considers final:

> Loyalty is the will to manifest, so far as is possible, the Eternal, that is, the conscious and superhuman unity of life, in the form of the acts of an individual Self. (PL: 357)

From the point of view of an individual self, without presupposing his own metaphysical background theory, but echoing the vocabulary William James used in his Gifford Lectures (James 1985), Royce paraphrases this definition as follows: "*Loyalty is the Will to Believe in something eternal, and to express that belief in the practical life of a human being*" (ibid.). Whether or not this relation to the eternal, conscious and superhuman unity of life is consciously aimed at by the loyal person is, in Royce's view, not essential to the fact that the truth of loyalty lies in this unity. Here the realm of loyal action is not limited to morality, but also pertains to science and to all human activities which are thus integrated into a life as a whole. As Royce summarizes:

> Whoever seeks any truth is loyal, for he is determining his life by reference to a life which transcends his own. And he is loyal to loyalty; for whatever truth you try to discover is, if true, valid for everybody, and is therefore worthy of everybody's loyal recognition. The loyal, then, are truth seekers; and the truth seekers are loyal. And all of them live for the sake of the unity of all life. And this unity includes us all, but is superhuman.
>
> Our view of truth, therefore meets at once any ethical and a logical need. The real world is precisely that world in which the loyal are at home. Their loyalty is no pathetic fallacy. Their causes are real facts in the universe. The universe as a whole possesses that unity which loyalty to loyalty seeks to express in its service of the whole of life. (PL: 376)

Royce goes on to use this renewed statement to ask whether the real world thus described is not "also the world which religion recognizes" (PL: 376–7). If this is true, then the ethics of loyalty and religious doctrine converge in their final and overarching claim. And this is precisely Royce's view. Accordingly, he completes his discourse – remember that the Gifford Lectures were read before a wider, not exclusively academic audience – by defining religion in "its highest forms" as "*the interpretation both of the eternal and of the spirit of loyalty through emotion, and through a fitting activity of the imagination*" (PL: 377).

The close connection Royce draws between loyalty and religion should, however, not be misunderstood as the claim that loyalty presupposes religious belief. What loyalty does require is that a person devote her striving to a cause and that she further the causes of others. Royce explains that she may, but need not do this in virtue of a belief in the spiritual unity she thus serves to constitute; she may, but need not recognize that her fragmentary experience and her individual life are completed in a higher, superhuman "world-life" of which hers is a part (see PL: 392 ff.).

By rounding off the exposition of his ethical theory with explanations regarding the dimensions of truth and religion, Royce shows how his metaphysical doctrine provides the foundation of his normative views. He repeatedly sides with the pragmatists of his time by saying that there is no such thing as a merely theoretical truth and that "[t]rue is that which successfully fulfils an idea" (PL: 392). There is, for him, no point in developing a philosophical theory just for its own sake. But with thinkers such as Kant, Fichte and Hegel, who also believed in the primacy of the practical, he defends the view that moral action is justified in being subject to a standard beyond the immediacy of the particular action. Royce interprets the moral law as being grounded in the unifying life of the spiritual whole – this is his idealist ethics as formulated in *The Philosophy of Loyalty*.

The ethical community

In the years after the publication of *The Philosophy of Loyalty* in 1908, years in which he was extraordinarily productive both in terms of writing and in terms of public lecturing, Royce intensified his research on logical and ethical issues as well as on the philosophy of religion. His last *opus magnum*, *The Problem of Christianity*, can be read as comprising the last full-fledged exposition of his views on these matters. Yet, the term "logical" here in fact stands for a complex of issues, interleaving epistemological questions, questions from the philosophy of science, the theories of signs and interpretation, and, more specifically, formal problems. And as was pointed out in the first section, the so-called "Peircean Insight" also falls into these years. This is not the place for trying to capture how Royce dealt with and incorporated all these topics in his final works. We shall instead look at *The Problem of Christianity* with regard to the question of how the theory of the universal community contained therein continues and complements the exposition of Royce's ethics. Royce's ethical theory of the community is deeply influenced by Peirce's theory of signs and interpretation, so, besides taking the main argument of *The Problem of Christianity* into account, we should also keep that in mind as we go along.

In the work now under consideration, Royce once again undertook complex treatment of a variety of philosophical issues. As its title indicates, and as Royce makes clear in the opening passage of the main text, *The Problem of Christianity* is devoted to the defense of "certain theses regarding the vital and essential characteristics of the Christian religion" (PC: 57). He goes on to characterize his approach to the Christian religion as

> regarding it, at least provisionally, not as the one true faith to be taught, and not as an outworn tradition to be treated with an enlightened indifference, but as a central, as an intensely interesting, life-problem of humanity, to be appreciated, to be interpreted, to be thoughtfully reviewed, with the seriousness and with the striving for reasonableness and for thoroughness which we owe to every life-problem wherewith human destiny is inseparably interwoven. (PC: 61)

A philosopher would be ill-advised – so we can paraphrase Royce's stance – if he either uncritically affirmed religious or specifically Christian doctrines, or if he shunned critical engagement with religion altogether by appealing to achievements of enlightened thought. If philosophy is instead to be important to people outside academia, and if it upholds the claim to capturing the character of its respective age, it has to take into account that the reflection on the nature and value of religious belief is and remains important even in post-enlightenment modernity. What Royce here calls the "life-problem of humanity" is the problem of developing an understanding of one's place in the world and the deeper meaning of one's life, a problem even the modern individual cannot avoid being confronted with. The main question Royce deals with in this work is the question of whether the answer Christian religion gives to this life-problem is acceptable under critical scrutiny. In other words, the question is "whether the modern man can consistently be in creed a Christian" (PC: 64). Royce takes this question as requiring both philosophical analysis and an account of the history of Christianity, including the historical role of religion in society. Accordingly, he defines *the problem* as follows:

> When we consider what are the most essential features of Christianity, is the acceptance of a creed that embodies these features consistent with the lessons that, so far as we can yet learn, the growth of human wisdom and the course of the ages have taught man regarding religious truth? (PC: 65)

Royce identifies three central Christian ideas that represent the "essential features" in view of which Christianity is to be reflected upon: (i) "the idea of the divinely significant spiritual community of the faithful," (ii) the idea that the "individual human being is by nature subject to some overwhelming moral burden from which, if unaided, he cannot escape," and (iii) the idea that "the only escape for the individual, the only union with the divine spiritual community which he can obtain, is provided by the divine plan for the redemption of mankind. And this plan is one which includes an Atonement for the sins and for the guilt of mankind" (PC: 72–3). Systematically, these ideas raise the issue of determining the structure and significance of relations within the individual self as well as those between individual and community (see Humbach 1962).

For our present purposes, we need not go into the details of Royce's discussion of these ideas, which takes up the first part of *The Problem of Christianity* (see Cotton 1954: 253–5; Kuklick 1985: 227), but can focus on the background of this discussion provided in the second part. In this second part, titled "The Real World and the Christian Ideas" (PC: 229–405), Royce explicates his conception of the community. Here, he develops the conceptual background of his answer to the problem of Christianity by showing on what sort of understanding of the community – one based on epistemological, metaphysical *and* ethical arguments – it can play the requested role in modernity.

Central to Royce's theory of the community is the reference to a third kind of knowledge (or cognitive processes) besides *conception* and *perception*, i.e. *interpretation*. The first of these three captures conceptual activity of the mind in forming judgments, the second captures the experiential dimension of thought processes. In Royce's view, this twofold distinction does not exhaust the spectrum of activities of the mind, even though conceiving and perceiving seem to be complementary, for both conception and perception are dyadic relations between thought and object. Royce deems as mistaken any attempt to characterize a synthesis of conception and perception as presupposed by pragmatism. The true basis of pragmatism, including his own "absolute pragmatism," is instead, Royce claims, an understanding of cognitive processes as triadic, as relating three terms instead of two.

Now, let us try to reconstruct Royce's train of thought in more detail. The reflection on the nature of cognitive processes aims at accounting for the constitutive elements of an individual's epistemic grasp of the world. Such processes are crucial to both knowledge and action, categories the consideration of which as strictly distinct would be resisted by Royce. "What happens when an individual forms a judgment or tries to understand what someone else said?" This sort of question could be tentatively answered by referring to pre-experiential processes, e.g. logical inferences, or by referring to a processing of sense data. But these approaches to the question are not complex enough because they limit the scope of reflection to a two-place relation between thinking subject and object as well as to the very instant of (conceptual or perceptual) judgment. If we want to retain the idea that thinking and judging are essentially related to actions, we should go beyond these limitations.

In a first step, we do this by introducing a third term to the relational description of cognitive processes. Here, the guiding idea is that cognitive processes such as judgments are not just *about* objects but are also *directed at someone*, where this someone can be the judging individual herself or another individual. Thus, cognitive processes are described as being essentially reflective and social – an idea we came across when discussing Royce's relational conception of self-consciousness. In the terminology of interpretation, the idea so far developed is this: When I judge that there is a tree outside my window or seek to express the meaning of a road sign, I *interpret* a fact – which I grasp partly through perception and partly through exercising linguistic and conceptual capacities – to myself or, given a social context, to another person. The stated fact, whether it involves inanimate objects, other (i.e. third) persons or institutional facts, thus becomes common knowledge of the two (or more) individuals who thereby constitute a prototypical community.

The second step of transcending the limited picture described above consists in acknowledging the temporal dimension of interpretation. In the individual case, it is through interpretation that individuals relate to themselves over time; they do this, for instance, by reflecting on beliefs formed in the past, by being aware of promises given in the past or of commitments undertaken for the future. In Royce's view, an individual that "extends his life" (PC: 252) by relating to his own past and future selves constitutes a form of community, the community of Annie-in-the-past, Annie-now and Annie-in-the-future, say. Being a self essentially requires this sort of cross-temporal self-relation. Communities of several individuals basically instantiate the same structure as do individual selves: What guarantees their cohesion is the fact that the individual members share attitudes concerning past and future, e.g. memories of the past and hopes for the future. In Royce's words,

> a true community is essentially a product of a time-process. A community has a past and will have a future. Its more or less conscious history, real or ideal, is a part of its very essence. A community requires for its existence a history and is greatly aided in it consciousness by a memory. (PC: 243)

Royce takes communities to exist, to be meaningful and to instantiate the structure of a self by having consciousness and a history. While it is true that concrete acts of remembering past events relevant to the community are carried out by individual members – again, by interpreting the past to themselves or others – this does not render metaphorical the talk of the community's consciousness. What is needed to ensure the community's cross-temporal existence, its stability and integrity, is that individuals fulfilling certain roles perform such acts expressing the consciousness and identity of the community. This applies especially to larger, extended communities which Royce characterizes as having

> an organic life of their own. ... [W]e can compare a highly developed community, such as a state, either to the soul of a man or to a living animal. A community is not a mere collection of individuals. It is a sort of live unit, that has organs, as the body of an individual has organs. A community grows or decays, is healthy or diseased, is young or aged, much as any individual member of the community possesses such characters. Each of the two, the community and the individual member, is as much a live creature as is the other. Not only does the community live, it has a mind of its own – a mind whose psychology is not the same as the psychology of an individual human being. (PC: 80)

The nucleus of community, conceptually, is a triad of cooperating and mutually inter-preting individuals. Take the individuals A, B, and C, all endowed with a will and a life-plan of their own, and all members of a community: For instance, what prevents A and C from living in some parallel and unconnected fashion is B's effort to interpret the one to the other and thereby unite their individual wills into one. As explained in the analysis of loyalty, pursuing a life-plan is itself a social affair insofar as the loyal cause of an individual already involves and is meant to support and further the loyalty of others; within a community that is at base such a community of interpretation, these social bonds are rendered transparent to all members of community, since, through interpretation, they all gain an understanding of their respective individual and joint strivings. It is through continuous interpretation, that a community develops into what Royce calls "a live unit," a social entity that integrates many individual lives into one organism.

With this reconstruction we have moved from the structural aspects of community, i.e. the fundamental processes of interpretation, to the social and ethical significance of communal life (see Cotton 1954: Chs. 6 and 7; Fuss 1965: Ch. 8). In Royce's social philosophy, the claim that communities are irreducibly social entities comes with a specific understanding of the role they play in the lives of their members. This role is, at base, twofold: on the one hand, communities provide contexts within which their members carry out meaningful interaction, i.e. individuals need communities to engage (interpretive) interaction that supports the pursuit of their individual causes; on the other hand, communities themselves, understood as comprising the lives of many, can constitute causes, i.e. at least some communities are such that individuals direct their lives towards the realization of a common purpose shared by fellow members. In this way communities are, or can be, both the *basis* and the *purpose* of the moral lives of individuals.

However, there are different sorts of communities and we would do injustice to Royce's account if we depicted the concept of community solely in this universal and idealized manner. Families and small groups as well as clubs and provinces can be described as communities, where it is obvious that they are particular and, under normal conditions, exclusive. And it is especially in the essays contained in *War and Insurance* (1914) that Royce distinguishes more local and functional social arrangements, such as the "judicial community," the "banker's community" and the "community of insurance" (see Blau 1956). In different ways, these special or, as Royce sometimes calls them, "practical communities" are designed to harmonize conflicting wills and interests of individuals or opposing groups. The degree of integrity they achieve is consequently limited to the extent to which they establish such harmony. It is through the balancing of conflicting interests that practical communities can function as spheres within larger societies, spheres that are designed to guarantee the stability of, for instance, the judicial, financial and insurance systems of a society. But Royce does not define social institutions in terms of their procedures and the norms governing them, but in terms of the individual members, or office holders, and their interpretive relations to others.

Since the claim that individuals can only realize their individual life-plans within communal life is crucial to Royce's normative account of communities, the relation between individual and community can be regarded as pivotal to Royce's social philosophy (see Humbach 1962). The main principles Royce uses for explicating this relation are love and, again, loyalty. In the context of *The Problem of Christianity* – as in *The Sources of Religious Insight* – it is again the virtue of loyalty on which the relation between individual selves and the community in which they are a member is modeled. The pursuit of true causes unites individuals into a community. According to Royce, the community of loyal individuals is not restricted to specific practical purposes or societal functions; it is an encompassing community whose members value it as giving support and meaning to their individual and collective endeavors. In this ethical community, for whose members "loyalty to loyalty" is the fundamental principle, individuals do not give up but retain their individuality. As individual selves have a biography, so do communities: they exist through time in virtue of the shared memories and hopes or the expectations of their members, and in virtue of the traditions they maintain and cultivate. In this respect, the structural characteristics of communities are taken as having an ethical dimension, so that the structural integrity realized through interpretive processes turns out to be the basis of an ethical integrity realized through social relations of loyalty.

Royce's point in *The Problem of Christianity* is that the Pauline Church can be understood as the best illustration of such an ideal ethical community (see PC: Ch. 10; Cotton 1954: 256). In so far as this community, the Pauline Church, instantiates a community of interpretation, one that exists through time, that is of ethical integrity, that is "beloved" by its members, and whose purpose is the guidance and salvation of its members, that it is reasonable for the modern man to be Christian. The understanding of community thus outlined forms the core of Royce's answer and solution to the problem of Christianity.

Although we have not here sought to reconstruct the details of Royce's philosophy of religion (see Oppenheim 1987), and have therewith bracketed an account of the ethical views implied in those reflections, we have gained an overview of Royce's idealistic ethics. It is an ethical theory, for it offers an account of what constitutes a meaningful and good life in accordance with principles that are available for justification. And it is idealistic, since it appeals to an encompassing and synthesizing instance which gives reality and meaning to life of individual selves. Scholars have been puzzled by the question of whether Royce not only changed his terminology when he replaced talk of the Absolute (up to PL) by talk of the Universal Community (in PC), but also fundamentally revised his metaphysics. Put more drastically, the question is whether Royce gave up idealism when he inaugurated the Community as being foundational to meaningful life. However – to offer a daringly brief assessment of this dispute – those who see a discontinuity between Royce's earlier and later views seem to overlook that Royce's later conception of an ideal and universal community does not free him of the justificatory task connected with his earlier expressions. Even after publishing *The Problem of Christianity*, Royce continued to teach the metaphysics of *The World and the Individual* and the ethics of loyalty basic thereon as an alternative and indeed complementary approach to the one based on the theory of interpretation and the category of the community (see Royce 1998).

To conclude the overview of Royce's idealism and ethics, we should return to the claim that Royce can be read as having developed a *philosophical system*. To be sure, Royce did not pursue such an ambition as explicitly as some of the authors he is said to be most indebted to, especially Hegel, had done. But he did continually take up the question of the relation between his treatments of issues on different fields, and he answered it by emphasizing the stability of his basic metaphysical assumption and his synthetic method. He did not regard his *opera magna* as constituting singular and self-contained systems. It would need extensive further studies of his logical writings to assess whether and how, for instance, the principles and structural analyses developed there, and especially the analysis of self-representative systems, can be regarded as the systematic foundation of his thought. In any case, this question regarding the systematicity of Royce's thought seems to have been well addressed.

Remaining challenges

Although Royce spent most of his career right at the center of attention within the philosophical community and thus enjoyed a very high reputation in the field, interest in Royce's philosophy decreased soon after his death. Despite being highly regarded as a public lecturer and as a teacher at Harvard, Royce did not found a school of disciples who would carry on defending his views after his death. This may also be due to the fact that the absolute idealism defended by Royce was considered out-of-date when the foundations of critical reception could have been laid. In addition, some of Royce's works, e.g. *The Philosophy of Loyalty*, went out of print and were not reprinted for long stretches of the twentieth century, so that he was barely present within academic circles. Since his death in 1916, there have been several, albeit local returns to Royce's thought and it is not an exaggeration to say that interest in his philosophy is now increasing. The effort of publishing a critical edition of his works, supported by the *Josiah Royce Society*, will certainly fuel this interest and provide it with solid reference material.

By way of conclusion, I would like to list topics that seem to me particularly worthy of the attention of contemporary scholars and future interpretive and systematic studies relating to Royce's philosophy. The basis for closer scrutiny is surely given in the many biographical and synoptic studies of Royce already available (e.g. Buranelli 1964; Powell 1967; Oppenheim 1980 and 2005; Kuklick 1985; Clendenning 1999; Trotter 2001; Parker 2004). The now increasing interest in the origins of pragmatism and analytic philosophy could and probably should also extend to Royce, especially given how closely he interacted with Peirce and William James and the extent to which he followed discussions about the logical foundations of science and philosophical sub-disciplines. Considering the historical setting in which he lived and worked, the relation between his thought and the thought of British Idealists such as Bradley and McTaggart can be taken to reveal a better insight into the constellations within philosophy at the turn of the nineteenth to the twentieth century.

Royce pursued and argued for positions on a number of systematic problems; he was aware of the history and the historicity of certain problems and respective answers and despite being reproached as an old-fashioned idealist and intellectualist he was innovative in developing his own views. It seems apt to scrutinize what roles exactly these two features of his own thought play with respect to the defense of virtue ethics, to epistemology, logics, the theory of self-consciousness, social ontology, and to the philosophy of science. Even the philosophical study of semantics could profit from a return to Royce based on a semantic reading of the distinction between internal and external ideas and paralleling Frege's distinction between meaning and reference, discussed above.

But Royce was also a historian of philosophy. He lectured extensively on modern idealist theories of being and knowledge, taking into account the then contemporary debates in philosophical psychology and the theory of evolution. Studying his interpretation of Kant and his reading of Hegel's *Phenomenology*, for instance, would contribute significantly to our understanding today of the history of the reception of philosophy around 1800, a reception whose main tenets were conveyed to influential theorists such as George Santayana and C. I. Lewis. Although he was not the founder of a school, Royce exerted a rather implicit influence on his students by upholding the gestus of Kant's transcendental philosophy and the German Idealist tradition. How this influence is to be individuated and how far-reaching it was would need to be explored.

These remarks are meant as guidelines for recasting Royce's idealist thought in the historical setting in which it was formed and in view of the logical, metaphysical, and ethical claims he sought to defend systematically. They are hints towards reanimating and preserving Royce's prominence in the history of philosophy.

Acknowledgements

I wish to thank Randy Auxier, Dean Moyar, Kelly Parker, Michael Quante, Chris Skowroński, Andreas Vieth and Matthias Wille for support and helpful suggestions during the work on this essay.

References

Writings of Josiah Royce

Royce, J. (FE) *Fugitive Essays*, Cambridge, MA: Harvard University Press, 1920.
—— (PC) *The Problem of Christianity*, Washington, DC: Catholic University of America Press, 2001 [1913].
—— (PL) *The Philosophy of Loyalty*, New York: Macmillan, 1908.
—— (RAP) *The Religious Aspect of Philosophy – A Critique of the Bases of Conduct and of Faith*, New York: Harper, 1885.
—— (SGE) *Studies of Good and Evil: A Series of Essays upon Problems of Philosophy and of Life*, New York: D. Appleton & Co., 1898.
—— (WI 1) *The World and the Individual*, 1st Series: *The Four Historical Conceptions of Being*, New York: Dover, 1899.
—— (WI 2) *The World and the Individual*, 2nd Series: *Nature, Man, and the Moral Order*, New York: Dover, 1901.
—— (WJOE) *William James and Other Essays in the Philosophy of Life*, New York: Macmillan, 1912.

—— (1881) *Primer of Logical Analysis*, San Francisco.

—— (1892) *The Spirit of Modern Philosophy*, New York: Dover, 1983.

—— (1894) "The External World and the Social Consciousness," *Philosophical Review* 3: 513–45.

—— (1912) *The Sources of Religious Insight*, New York: Charles Scribner's Sons.

—— (1914) *War and Insurance*, New York: Macmillan.

—— (1919) *Lectures on Modern Idealism*, New Haven, CT; London: Yale University Press, 5th printing, 1967.

—— (1951) *Royce's Logical Essays*, edited by Daniel S. Robinson, Dubuque, IA: W. M. C. Brown.

—— (1998) *Metaphysics*, edited by Richard Hocking and Frank Oppenheim, New York: SUNY Press.

Collections

Auxier, Randall E. (ed.) (2000) *Critical Responses to Josiah Royce*, vol. 2: *Reviews and Articles*, Bristol, UK: Thoemmes Press.

Oppenheim, Frank M. (2001a) *Josiah Royce's Late Writings: A Collection of Unpublished and Scattered Works*, vol. 1, Bristol, UK: Thoemmes Press.

Oppenheim, Frank M. (2001b) *Josiah Royce's Late Writings: A Collection of Unpublished and Scattered Works*, vol. 2, Bristol, UK: Thoemmes Press.

Further references

Baldwin, James Mark (1894) "Imitation: A Chapter in the Natural History of Consciousness," *Mind* 3, no. 9, n.s.: 26–55.

Blau, Joseph L. (1956) "Royce's Theory of Community," *Journal of Philosophy* 53, no. 3: 92–8.

Buranelli, Vincent (1964) *Josiah Royce*, New York: Twayne.

Clendenning, J. (1999) *The Life and Thought of Josiah Royce*, rev. exp. edn, Nashville, TN: Vanderbilt University Press.

Cotton, J. Harry (1954) *Royce on the Human Self*, Cambridge, MA: Harvard University Press.

Davidson, Donald (2001) *Subjective, Intersubjective, Objective*, Oxford: Clarendon Press.

Fuss, Peter (1965) *The Moral Philosophy of Josiah Royce*, Cambridge, MA: Harvard University Press.

Humbach, Karl-Theo (1962) *Das Verhältnis von Einzelperson und Gemeinschaft nach Josiah Royce – Eine Untersuchung zum Zentralproblem der Sozialphilosophie*, Heidelberg: Carl Winter.

James, William (1975) *Pragmatism: A New Name for Some Old Ways of Thinking*, vol. 1, *The Works of William James*, edited by Frederick H. Burckhardt, Fredson Bowers, and Ignas K. Skrupskelis, Cambridge, MA: Harvard University Press.

—— (1985) *Varieties of Religious Experience*, vol. 13, *The Works of William James*, edited by Frederick H. Burckhardt, Fredson Bowers, and Ignas K. Skrupskelis, Cambridge, MA: Harvard University Press.

Kuklick, Bruce (1977) *The Rise of American Philosophy*, New Haven, CT: Yale University Press.

—— (1985) *Josiah Royce – An Intellectual Biography*, Indianapolis, IN: Hackett.

—— (2001) *A History of Philosophy in America 1720–2000*, Oxford: Clarendon Press.

Lewis, C. I. (1916) "Types of Order and the System Σ," in R. E. Auxier (ed.) *Critical Responses to Josiah Royce*, vol. 3: *Papers in Honor of Josiah Royce on his Sixtieth Birthday (1916)*, Bristol, UK: Thoemmes Press 2000.

Marcel, Gabriel (1956) *Royce's Metaphysics*, trans. Virginia Ringer and Gordon Ringer, Chicago: Regnery.

Oppenheim, Frank M. (1980) *Royce's Voyage Down Under: A Journey of the Mind*, Lexington, KY: University Press of Kentucky.

—— (1987) *Royce's Mature Philosophy of Religion*, Notre Dame, IN: Notre Dame University Press.

—— (2005) *Reverence for the Relations of Life – Re-Imagining Pragmatism via Josiah Royce's Interactions with Peirce, James, and Dewey*, Notre Dame, IN: University of Notre Dame Press.

Parker, Kelly A. (2004) "Josiah Royce," in E. N. Zalta (ed.) *The Stanford Encyclopedia of Philosophy* (2004 edn), http://plato.stanford.edu/entries/royce/

Peirce, Charles Sanders (1900) "Review of *The World and the Individual* (First Series)" *The Nation* 70 (1900); repr. R. E. Auxier (ed.) *Critical Responses to Josiah Royce*, vol. 2: *Reviews and Articles*, Bristol, UK: Thoemmes Press 2000.

Peirce, Charles Sanders (1902) "Review of *The World and the Individual* (Second Series)" *The Nation* 75 (1902); repr. R. E. Auxier (ed.) *Critical Responses to Josiah Royce*, vol. 2: *Reviews and Articles*, Bristol, UK: Thoemmes Press 2000.

Powell, Thomas F. (1967) *Josiah Royce*, New York: Washington Square.

Rand, Benjamin (1916) "A Bibliography of the Writings of Josiah Royce," *Philosophical Review* 25, no. 3: 515–22.

Randall, John Herman, Jr (1966) "Josiah Royce and American Idealism," *Journal of Philosophy* 63, no. 3: 57–83.

Smith, John E. (1950) *Royce's Social Infinite – The Community of Interpretation*, New York: Liberal Arts Press.

Trotter, Griffin (2001) *On Royce*, Belmont, CA: Wadsworth.

Part VII

NEW DIRECTIONS IN PHILOSOPHY OF MIND AND LOGIC

27
POST-KANTIAN LOGICAL RADICALISM

Stephan Käufer

LOGICAL RADICALISM

Canonical histories of logic, such as that of I. Bochenski or William and Martha Kneale, ignore the work of nineteenth-century philosophers working on traditional logic. This disregard is somewhat justified. Mainstream philosophers working on logic in the nineteenth century make no enduring or significant changes to the old scholastic syllogistic logic; and their concerns do not seem to be properly logical at all, but metaphysical, methodological, or epistemological. Kant's work illustrates this approach to logic. In his logic lectures Kant adheres to the Aristotelian syllogistic and states that "from Aristotle's time on, logic has not gained much in content, nor can it by its nature do so" (1800: 534). This echoes his assessment of the syllogistic in the *Critique of Pure Reason*, that logic is correct and complete, and further improvements are neither necessary nor possible (1781: Bviii). At the same time, however, Kant develops his astoundingly complex and innovative "transcendental logic," which radically changes metaphysics and epistemology, but whose title seems misleading from the point of view of modern logic.

Recently historians of logic and philosophy have begun to re-examine the logical writings of the post-Kantian philosophers. The early and middle decades of the nineteenth century are unprecedented in the intensity and breadth of challenges to precisely the traditional logic that Kant had proclaimed complete. Immediately following Kant's work, and indeed *because* of Kant's work, philosophers call for a complete overthrow of logic. In 1812 Fichte demands that "general logic be destroyed to its very foundation" (Martin 2003: 36). Hegel writes in his *Science of Logic* that "if logic has not undergone any changes since Aristotle ... then we should rather conclude that it requires a total reworking" (1831: 46). With such provocations Fichte and Hegel invigorate contemporaneous logical thought. They initiate a three-way debate between Kantian, Hegelian, and other logicians about what comes to be known as "the logic question," a debate that dominates the middle decades of the century. In Wayne Martin's phrase, this is a period of deep and pervasive "logical radicalism," of attempts to rework the entire edifice of logic from the ground up.

The importance and core interests of the logical radicalism of the nineteenth century do not consist of technical advances in formal or symbolic logic; before Frege such advances are few and modest and, like Frege's work, they take place at the margins of post-Kantian philosophy. The same philosophers who want to overthrow logic in debating the logic question, reproduce much of the entrenched logic of terms and syllogisms in their lectures and textbooks. This is also true for philosophers with a greater penchant for symbolic logic. For example, William Stanley Jevons, who works on extending Boole's and Hamilton's innovations in symbolic logic, publishes a short and elegant vademecum called *Lessons in Logic*, in which he exhorts students to recite the "ingenious, yet wholly unscientific" medieval mnemonic verse "Barbara, Celarent, Darii, Ferioque ..." and practice reducing valid syllogisms to those of the first figure (1881: 145). Logical radicalism runs alongside continued adherence to the traditional syllogistic. Its historical and philosophical importance lies in its attempts to understand the nature and bounds of logic and to provide it with metaphysical grounding and epistemological import.

LOGIC IN THE NINETEENTH CENTURY
Theories of concepts, judgments, and inferences

In the nineteenth century a standard exposition of logic comprises three parts: the theories of concepts, judgments, and inferences. They reproduce the ancient stock of logical analyses whose core goes back to the syllogistic logic first developed by Aristotle in the books of his *Organon*, especially the *Prior Analytics*. The theory of inferences (*Schlusslehre*) consists of the Aristotelian theory of syllogisms. It contains the list of valid syllogisms divided into moods and figures and examples of how to reduce some syllogisms to others. It usually also discusses hypothetical syllogisms, induction, and modal syllogisms. From a modern perspective the theory of inferences looks hopelessly outdated. But nineteenth-century philosophers consider it complete and do not devote much effort to overhauling it.

The theory of judgments (*Urteilslehre*) analyzes the logical form of judgments. Since syllogisms require premises and conclusions to be in subject–predicate form, much of the theory of judgments consists of proposals for shoehorning the grammatical variety of sentences into this logical mould. Some such proposals are fairly complicated, especially in the case of existential judgments ("God exists"), and impersonal judgments, which abound in German ("it rains"). Among the better known views is that of Sigwart, who claims that there is only a single form of judgment, "S is P," and that all variation derives from the content of its component concepts; or the view proposed by Trendelenburg that precisely impersonal judgments reveal the original unified judgment-form from which the subject–predicate distinction arises.

The theory of judgments also contains the analysis of negation and quantification. It divides judgments into universal ("all S are P"), particular ("some S are P"), and singular ("this S is P"), in both affirmative and negative modes. Like the syllogisms, this analysis derives from Aristotle, who also first points out the inferences that obtain between some pairs of judgments. "All As are Bs" implies that "some As are Bs" and that "no As are not Bs" and so forth, and Aristotle uses these operations to reduce all valid syllogisms to the ones he considers basic. These "immediate" or "direct" inferences, i.e. inferences which do not require a third term beyond the two contained in a given judgment, are also expounded in the theory of judgments. A common mode of presenting them is the traditional square of oppositions, which organizes contraries, contradictories, subcontraries, and subaltern inferences in a diagram. Unlike syllogistic inferences the immediate inferences are the cause of some disagreement among logicians. Stoic and medieval logicians already know that some immediate inferences are problematic and among the logical radicals of the nineteenth century these problems provide a touchstone for rejecting old views of logic and proposing new ones.

The third part of traditional logic, the theory of concepts, analyzes the logical structure of concepts, or terms, that can take the place of a logical subject or predicate. Syllogistic logic is often referred to as "term logic," because much of the inferential significance modeled in a syllogism derives from the structure and content of its major, minor, and middle terms. Hegel's counter-intuitive claim that "the inference is the completely posited concept" (1816: 351) amounts to this: a syllogism is nothing but an articulation of one aspect of the content of its terms. This part of logic has no specific predecessor in ancient and medieval logics and there is limited overlap between its many expositions. Most authors agree that there is not much to be said in general about the structure of concepts *per se*. Conservative authors focus on the idea that concepts are aggregates of attributes or marks (*Merkmale*) and that the conceptual relations articulated in logic are grounded in the inclusion or exclusion of these attributes. They adduce illustrative examples from the hierarchies of genera and species being developed by botanists and zoologists, who, in turn, find their systems of classification validated by its "logical" structure. Most of the logical radicals of the nineteenth century find this attribute analysis of concepts either true, but empty (Herbart 1813: 88; Drobisch 1836: 16); or misleading (Lotze 1874a: 47); or false (Hegel 1816: 295; Trendelenburg 1870: 250; cf. Käufer 2005: 273). Many logicians supplement this analysis with accounts of the formation of concepts, or the *a priori* status of some concepts. Here they find themselves in a gray area in which they commonly stray into psychology, epistemology, or transcendental philosophy.

Virtually all logic books of the nineteenth century consist of these three parts. Normally they begin with the theory of concepts, followed by the theory of judgments, and end with the theory of inferences. This order indicates a commitment to a type of *Aufbau* view, according to which concepts are the most elemental components of logic, which are then combined into judgments, which, in turn, make up syllogistic inferences. This view itself also comes to be challenged. Hegel thinks that none of the three parts is logically more elemental; instead they constitute a system each part of which articulates an aspect of the others. Others argue that judgments are logically more fundamental than concepts, because they, not concepts, are the unit of cognition. Regardless, the division into the three theories persists even in texts that challenge the presumptions inherent in it. Famously, the transcendental logic, which makes up the vast majority of Kant's *Critique of Pure Reason*, is organized by a plan

811

that reproduces this same division. Hegel's *Science of Logic* also includes the theories of concepts, judgments, and inferences in its second book, the Subjective Logic, even though they only make up a part of the book and he makes radical changes to the content of each.

Main authors and texts

The most important authors and most influential positions of logical radicalism fall into three main camps: Kantians, Hegelians, and a group of philosophers who sought to develop positions on the middle ground between these two.

The Kantian school consists of philosophers who claim to teach general logic in his sense within the framework of his critical philosophy. They do not take themselves to be radicals and do not advocate an overthrow of logic. Much of the work of the Kantian school of logic consists of logic textbooks, such as Herbart's 1813 *Lehrbuch zur Einleitung in die Philosophie* or Moritz Drobisch's 1836 *Neue Darstellung der Logik nach ihren einfachsten Verhältnissen*. In the course of the evolving debate these Kantians are forced to defend their overall position against challenges from the other camps. Often these defenses are integrated into successive editions of textbooks. Drobisch's book is a prime example of this, both because of its longevity and the diligence of its author. His explanation of the nature and unity of a concept, for instance, changes in each edition, from the second in 1851 to the fifth in 1887. The view of the Kantian school is also called "subjective logic" or "formal" logic.

Hegel scholars today debate how to interpret the role of Hegel's logic in his overall system. The book is clearly concerned with more than logic, and it may not have much to say about logic at all, especially given our contemporary understanding of that discipline. Philosophers in the early nineteenth century, by contrast, do not question the status of Hegel's *Wissenschaft der Logik* as logic. From the moment Hegel publishes it until the decline of the first wave of Hegelianism, philosophers agree that this work is at least *supposed* to be a logic and that it should be interpreted as such. Of course, these philosophers presume that it is more than an amendment to the technical apparatus of syllogistic logic. They see its scope and ambition as on par with Kant's transcendental logic. Indeed, roughly speaking Hegel's overall goal is to unify general and transcendental logic, and in doing so to overcome a number of Kantian distinctions that Hegel deems untenable.

Hegel inspires a lot of devoted followers and acolytes, such as Karl Ludwig Michelet, Karl Rosenkranz and Johann Eduard Erdmann, many of whom are enthralled by his style and language. A few philosophers defend and refine what they take to be Hegel's central insights into logic by engaging in a reasoned and reasonably clear debate with other logical radicals. Most important among these is Kuno Fischer, whom Windelband credits with the "art of translating Hegel into German" (1904: 180). In two very different editions of his *Logik und Metaphysik*, Fischer defends Hegel's view that the structures of logic are the structure of being. These works constitute a Hegelian school of logic and their position is also called the "metaphysical logic."

A third, somewhat looser group of philosophers explores middle ground between the Kantian and Hegelian schools. They agree with Hegel's basic insight, that Kant's transcendental logic must be reconciled with general logic into a single, coherent discipline. They also agree that this unification of the two logics requires a fundamental rethinking of the metaphysics and epistemology of logic. However, this third group of philosophers strictly opposes the style and much of the substance of the Hegelian attempts. Hegel, they claim, goes too far and in effect abandons logic as such by conflating it with his ambitious metaphysics. His "metaphysical logic" is no longer a logic at all. Trendelenburg first articulated a forceful and detailed version of this opposition to Hegel's logic in his 1840 *Logische Untersuchungen*. In response to the pugnacious and disdainful replies this book evokes from Hegelian devotees he reiterates the main outlines of his criticisms in his 1843 essay *Die Logische Frage in Hegel's System*. This essay initiates the three-way debate on the nature of logic and gives this debate its name. Trendelenburg's work is enormously important for its detailed criticisms of Hegel's logic and for bringing the "logic question" into focus. However, Trendelenburg's positive proposals, which he develops in great detail and at length in the two volumes of his *Logical Investigations*, do not gain many adherents. A more influential middle view is that of Hermann Lotze, who defines logical reality as its own realm. While metaphysics is concerned with being, logic articulates the realm of *Geltung*, validity. Truth and falsity, the coherence, unity, and structure of a proposition or syllogism are all structures of the realm of validity. We should not say that they "are" but that they "are valid." Other authors in this middle group are Friedrich Ueberweg and Hermann Ulrici.

These authors are not neo-Kantians, strictly speaking. The neo-Kantian movement, which has been the topic of some exciting historical scholarship lately, starts later. It is rallied by Otto Liebman's slogan "back to Kant" in his 1865 *Kant und die Epigonen* and produces its first serious Kant interpretation in Hermann Cohen's influential 1871 *Kants Theorie der Erfahrung*. It grows, ramifies, and blossoms in the writings of Heinrich Rickert and the Southwest school and Ernst Cassirer and the Marburg school. The work Lotze, Trendelenburg and others do on logic in the 1840s and 1850s prefigures but predates such an explicit and programmatic return to Kant. Trendelenburg's Kant-criticisms are part of an attempt to develop his own middle view of metaphysics that he associates with a return to Aristotle. More than a proto-neo-Kantian, he is a product of the classical scholarship in nineteenth-century German philosophy. He studies classical languages at the *Gymnasium* and at the Universities of Kiel and Berlin and his first scholarly work is an attempt to reconcile Aristotle and Plato on ideas and numbers.

Trendelenburg (1846 and 1867), Kuno Fischer (1852 and 1865), and Ueberweg (1857) write histories of logic in addition to their contributions on the logic question. Scholarly work on the continent has always emphasized the history of an issue; even today a good part of a typical philosophy book published in Germany is dedicated to a critical exposition of the history of its topic. And the nineteenth century witnesses an especially broad and important increase in historical awareness and historicist approaches. But in Ueberweg's *Geschichte der Logischen Lehren* or Trendelenburg's *Geschichte der Kategorienlehre* more is at stake than scholarly diligence. Their historical overviews are intended to show the range of different approaches to logic since

Aristotle and hence position their own reform efforts in the grand tradition of innovations in logic.

THE TRANSCENDENTAL TURN IN PHILOSOPHICAL LOGIC

Kant and Hegel

Kant on transcendental and general logic

"General logic" is Kant's name for the traditional syllogistic logic. He frequently lectures on general logic, elaborating on available textbooks. While Kant never writes a logic textbook, his student Christian Jäsche edits and publishes Kant's lecture notes in 1800. According to Kant, general logic contains the principles of the correct use of the understanding and reason, "without which no use of the understanding takes place." It studies the laws of thought without any regard for the objects it is about, or even whether it is about objects at all. A more specific task is taken up by types of logic that study "the rules for correctly thinking about a certain kind of objects." So a particular logic might study the rules for thinking about motion or plants and hence be the logic of physics, or the logic of botany. As Kant puts it, such a particular logic is always the "organon of this or that science" (1781: A52/B76). It presumes prior knowledge of the objects studied in that science and consists of rules for ordering the body of knowledge about those objects. General logic is not bound by any such orientation towards objects and hence governs more widely than just this or that science.

With his critical philosophy, Kant develops the idea of transcendental logic, which he contrasts to general logic. Object cognition requires twin contributions of sensibility and the understanding. The former provides intuitions of the object and the latter provides concepts under which to cognize the object. In the *Critique of Pure Reason* Kant argues that there are pure intuitions that are not received by the senses and pure concepts that are not derived from empirical experience. Pure concepts applied to pure intuitions yield cognition of a pure object, one that is devoid of specific content and that does not belong to "this or that science." The rules governing the understanding's contribution to such cognition of pure objects do not fall into any particular logic bound to an empirical science. Nor do they fall into general logic which studies thinking irrespective of its directedness towards objects. Kant therefore develops the "idea of a science of pure understanding and of the pure cognition of reason, by means of which we think objects completely *a priori*. Such a science, which would determine the origin, the domain, and the objective validity of such cognitions, would have to be called transcendental logic" (1781: A57/B81). Kant's transcendental logic is superficially similar to general logic, as it, too, is divided into chapters on concepts (the Analytic of Concepts), judgments (the Analytic of Principles), and inferences (the Transcendental Dialectic). But the content of these chapters differs radically from general logic. Instead of the "brief and dry science" required by the "scholastically correct presentation" of syllogisms and forms of judgments (A54/B78), the transcendental logic makes substantial claims about what we can experience objectively.

The difference between these two logics lies in the pure content of cognition. General logic "abstracts from all contents of the cognition of the understanding" (1781: A54/B78). Kant expresses the same point by saying that general logic abstracts from the "difference of its objects" (A54/B78), or from "any relation of [cognition] to the object" (A55/B79), or from the "matter" of cognition (A59/B83). He treats this criterion as the definition of generality. A science, a statement, or a criterion is *general* with respect to cognition precisely if it applies to "all cognitions without any distinction among their objects" (A58/B83). Transcendental logic, on the other hand, does "not abstract from *all* content of cognition" (A56/B80, emphasis added). It excludes the empirical content of cognition, but focuses precisely on the pure content. It is thus sensitive to certain kinds of distinctions among the objects of pure cognitions. For instance, it distinguishes between pure objects that are possible or impossible, or between objects that are something and those that are nothing (A290/B346).

However, transcendental logic shares two crucial features with general logic. First, both are normative for thought, or, as Kant puts it, both are a "canon of the understanding." A canon is "the sum total of the *a priori* principles of the correct use of certain cognitive faculties in general" (1781: A796/B824). One can think, or "use the understanding," correctly or incorrectly. Whether a given act of thinking is correct *as thinking* is determined by its adherence to the principles contained in the canon of the understanding. These principles are thus normative; they prescribe features to which a mental act must conform if it is to count as thought. General logic is "a canon for understanding and reason in general," i.e. it contains norms for all of thought, and it is a canon "only as far as form is concerned, since it abstracts from all content" (A796/B824). It is silent on cognitions whose content is false, or even nonsensical. "For although a cognition may be in complete accord with logical form, i.e., not contradict itself, yet it can still always contradict the object" (A59/B84). Transcendental logic is "a canon for the assessment of empirical use [of the understanding]" (A63/B88) and "the canon of the pure understanding" (A796/B824). Cognition of objects is subject to the normative constraints of transcendental logic. These constraints concern the *content* of empirical judgments, insofar as this content includes the general features of an object. "For no cognition can contradict it without at the same time losing all content, i.e., all relation to any object, hence all truth" (A62/B87).

Second, transcendental logic, too, is formal, though it does not abstract from all content. Kant uses "form" in two different senses. First, he contrasts it to the sensible matter of cognition. "I call that in appearance which corresponds to sensation its matter, but that which allows the manifold of appearance to be intuited as ordered in certain relations I call the form of appearance" (1781: A20/B34). Transcendental logic is formal in this first sense, since it abstracts from objects as they are given in intuition. Second, in his definition of general logic, Kant contrasts form to the content of cognition, where this content itself is constituted by form (in the first sense) and matter. General logic is formal in this second sense. As regards transcendental logic, Kant warns against "the danger of making a material use of the merely formal principles of pure understanding" (A63/B88) and points out that pure concepts contain "only the form of thinking of an object in general" (A51/B75). This warning is directed at an undisciplined use of the transcendental logic that would aim to spin it into results beyond possible experience, a tendency that the Transcendental Dialectic is meant to reign in. All intuition is particular, so what transcendental logic abstracts from is *particular* content, or material content. It is directed at a pure object, or an object in general, and outlines the form of possible objectivity, which needs to be filled in by intuition in order to yield cognition.

Kant's distinction between general and transcendental logic rests on the idea that the cognitions treated in transcendental logic are a proper subset of cognitions in general. In other words, Kant countenances a class of thoughts that is wider than object-directed thoughts, whether this object is possible or impossible, something or nothing. For Kant the idea of thought without directedness to an object makes sense. Thoughts in this class, sanctioned by the norms of general logic but beyond the scope of the norms of transcendental logic, have no content on grounds of their failure to be object-related. They are formally nonself-contradictory and they are not about anything.

Hegel's logic

In his survey of the century's developments on logic, Wilhelm Windelband writes that "the relationship between [general and transcendental logic], these two logical doctrines that Kant regarded as entirely separate, was the agent that brought enormous ferment into the investigations about the essence of scientific thought, and it triggered a wealth of new movements whose tendencies still are not nearly reconciled and define our position to this day" (1904: 163). As Wayne Martin shows, Fichte may be the first to voice a radical challenge to logic explicitly, and he does so in precisely these terms. After Kant rejects his *Wissenschaftslehre*, claiming that it aims to derive substantial claims from purely formal reflection, Fichte argues that Kant here is mistaken because he confuses the formality of general logic with the method of transcendental philosophy. Indeed, he claims that Kant's "own philosophy requires that general logic be destroyed to its very foundation" (Martin 2003: 36). Put less dramatically, the proposal is to dissolve general logic in transcendental logic. This is what Hegel's logic intends to do.

Hegel rejects the idea of a logic that is more general than a properly conceived transcendental logic. Unlike Kant, he thinks that the idea of non-objective thoughts is incoherent. All thought is at least minimally object-directed. Rules governing object-directed thoughts, found in a transcendental logic, therefore constitute precisely the "canon for understanding and reason in general" that Kant reserves for general logic. It amounts to the same thing that Hegel also rejects Kant's second distinction between the form and content of thought, according to which general logic is concerned only with the form of thought. Hegel denies that it is coherent to conceive of thought *as opposed to* its content in this sense at all, and he criticizes Kant sharply and persistently on this distinction. He says it belongs among the presumptions "on which the conception of logic has rested so far, but that either have already gone under, or whose time has come to disappear completely" (1831: 36). Consequently it makes no sense to think of logic as studying the abstract forms of thought, the way traditional general logic does. Instead, Hegel claims, logic studies the content that all thought necessarily has insofar as it is about objects. It analyzes the most general content of thoughts, not their abstract form. In other words, logic is transcendental logic.

Hegel's overall conception of logic corresponds exactly to Kant's idea of a transcendental logic, in that it analyzes the concepts and principles that make objective thought possible. The details of Hegel's logic, however, are very different. Kant's transcendental logic establishes a table of pure concepts that function jointly and are logically independent from one another. Hegel argues that these concepts are not independent, but imply one another in a sequence of increasingly specific articulation. His logic traces the development of the entire system of concepts and principles through these articulations. The beginning of this process lies in the idea of pure objective thought itself, whose simplest and most immediate content is the idea of being. Logic then proceeds dialectically, i.e. by way of a series of logical arguments that show how every partial concept implies distinctions that go beyond itself; this means that every concept implies a further concept that is distinct from it and a third concept that comprehends this distinction itself. This dialectical sequence covers all pure concepts, types of judgments, and types of inferences and establishes their interrelation. It culminates in a system of the elements of pure thought that Hegel simply calls "the idea."

Kant derives his table of categories from the forms of judgments of traditional general logic. Since Kant conceives of transcendental logic as a restriction of traditional general logic, it does seem consistent that the categories should be based on the traditional forms of judgment. The laws of general logic govern all thought, and therefore also hold for the objective cognitions analyzed in transcendental logic. Hegel, however, finds this approach deeply flawed. "Kant's philosophy is inconsistent when its transcendental logic borrows the categories from subjective logic, which collected them empirically. It may as well help itself empirically to the categories right away" (1816: 289). He points out that traditional logic simply organizes kinds of concepts and judgments as it finds them in experience. It does not derive them logically and therefore remains an "empirical logic," based on experience. This may be acceptable for a mere presentation of forms of thought for the didactic purposes of a school logic. But transcendental logic must establish the possibility of objective experience in the first place, and therefore must provide a derivation of the structures that constitute this possibility. Hegel claims that Fichte's philosophy "has the deep merit of reminding us that the determinations of thought have to be essentially derived and revealed as necessary" (1830: 68). Logic must derive its own structures, as the dialectic aims to do.

Hegel argues that logic is not formal. Kant claims that general logic is formal insofar as it abstracts from all content of thought. This, Hegel claims, is incoherent; there is no thought without content. General logic, at best, amounts to a limited, uncritical survey of structures of thought found in experience. These structures are absorbed in a properly philosophical logic where they have their place in a dialectical derivation that shows their interrelation and demonstrates their necessity. Kant also claims that transcendental logic is formal, in the sense that it does not concern itself with the matter of sensations given in intuition. Hegel agrees that transcendental logic, which for him is the only kind of logic, has this feature. Like Kant, he prefers to call it its "purity." "Logic is the science of the pure idea" (1830: 53), just as Kant's transcendental logic studies the pure concepts and principles of pure reason. Purity is just the formality that Kant attributes to transcendental logic: objective thought shorn of intuitive material content.

Since logic is pure and abstracts from sensations, there is a sense in which it can be called formal. Hegel calls it the "science of the absolute form." However, he points out that "this form is of a completely different nature from what logical form is commonly taken to be" because "it has its own content or reality in itself" (1816: 265). This specific content consists of the structures that enable thought to be about objects. The principles of logic govern all thought not because they abstract from its content, but because they partake in it and constitute it. The logical constitution of objective content, Hegel claims, is ubiquitous and substantial and logical content is therefore not abstract or empty. "This [logical] form must be conceived as being much richer in determinations and content and as having infinitely greater effect on the concrete than is commonly thought" (1816: 267). Hegel says that Kant himself realized that pure concepts are the seed of necessary content. "Kant introduced this point of view through the highly important thought, that there are synthetic judgments *a priori*. This original synthesis of apperception … contains the beginning of the true grasp of the nature of the concept and is entirely opposed to any empty identity or abstract generality" (1816: 260). In Hegel's interpretation, Kant's transcendental logic shows that logical concepts in themselves have concrete content and hence undermines the basic idea of a formal, general logic.

Challenges to the formality of logic

Regardless of its importance to metaphysics and other subjects beyond logic, Hegel's radically new version of logic does not attract philosophical followers beyond the generation of his devotees. His sweeping criticisms of traditional logic and his broad conception of the foundation and scope of logic are influential in less direct ways. They have a liberating effect on the thought of philosophers of logic in the following decades. Trendelenburg begins his logical investigations with a careful and detailed response to Hegel's logic. Lotze follows both Trendelenburg and Hegel in arguing for an epistemological conception of logic. Fischer starts out as a faithful Hegelian, but later departs from his initial strict Hegelianism and develops a looser version that incorporates elements of traditional syllogistic logic more strictly. Due to their Hegelian beginnings these logical radicals share the principle that logic is not formal, although they go on to develop this claim in different ways. Trendelenburg wants to supplement formal logic with a study of the material content of the basic concepts of the sciences. Lotze argues for a conception of logic as the formal structure of cognitive content. Fischer, finally, defends the Hegelian position that logic is transcendental and as such also specifies the basic features of objects.

Herbart and Drobisch: the formality of logic

In one way or another, all major logical radicals after Hegel reject the claim that logic is, or should be, formal. MacFarlane (2000, 2002) has disentangled different senses in which the philosophical tradition claims that logic is a formal discipline, and he has shown that one of these senses originates with Kant. Prior to Kant's critical philosophy, metaphysicians in the Wolffian tradition argue that logical principles can yield substantial insight about some objects, such as God or the soul. Kant rejects such views and begins to maintain that logic is formal in the sense that it must abstract from all content of thought. Although Kant does not produce an explicit argument to this effect, MacFarlane discerns such an argument in the combination of two views that Kant is committed to. First, he claims in his logic lectures that logic is general, i.e. that it covers the rules of all thinking. Second, Kant's critical epistemology implies that if logic is to be general, it must abstract from all relation of thought to sensibility and, therefore, from all content. (MacFarlane 2002: 49ff.). This is a claim about general logic, not transcendental logic. When Kant claims that transcendental logic is formal, he does not use this word in the same sense; for Kant transcendental logic is not general.

In its historical context Kant's claim is both original and controversial. Asserting the formality of logic, he rejects the position of Wolffian metaphysics and is in turn rejected by the logical radicals. However, in challenging the formality of logic, the post-Kantian logical radicals reject neither Kant's critical epistemology, nor the view that logic is general. Both Fichte and Hegel argue that these two views can be reconciled in a conception of logic that is not formal. Indeed, they claim that Kant himself undermines the idea of the formality of logic through his discovery of transcendental logic, which, they argue, implies that the most general concept of thinking is precisely the transcendental notion of thinking an "object in general." In rejecting the formality of logic they both claim to develop Kant's own philosophy to its consistent end. Similarly later philosophers from Trendelenburg to Windelband, who articulate and motivate arguments against the formality of logic, think that Kant's philosophy is amenable to their views. They do not think that they are attacking Kant, even though they occasionally use the label "Kantian logic" as equivalent to "formal logic." Instead they target the logic of Herbart and his followers Twesten and Drobisch.

For the logical radicals the so called Kantian school of formal logic is not Kantian in any straightforward or privileged sense. The debate about the nature of logic implies a debate about the proper interpretation of Kant's critical philosophy. Herbart and Drobisch also base their views about the nature of logic on an interpretation of Kant that rejects some of his most fundamental claims and emphasizes others. Herbart calls his Kant interpretation "realism" in explicit opposition to Fichte and Hegel's idealism. His view insists on the givenness of experience as the starting point of critical analysis and rejects the idea that the transcendental subject can constitute this givenness. The purpose of transcendental philosophy, particularly transcendental logic, is to show how the subject cognizes according to principles that inhere in the given objects themselves and, in particular, to explain how the natural sciences can discern such principles. Consequently Herbart rejects the basic claim of Kant's transcendental deduction, that self-consciousness is grounded in a synthesis that also makes cognition of objects possible. He writes that Kant here provides "the first occasion for the manifold errors in recent philosophy," pointing out that Fichte is particularly indebted to this point (1813: 75).

It is more accurate to draw the distinctions between the three camps of logical radicals in terms of the aspects of Kant's critical philosophy that they most emphasize. Herbart insists on the givenness of experience and maintains that the primary task of philosophy is to analyze and explain this givenness. Fichte and Hegel think that the most important and fruitful insights are contained in the transcendental deduction; and with their analyses of subject-object identity they take themselves to be faithful to the idea of critical philosophy in drawing out the consequences of Kant's argument that the same synthesis constitutes the possibility of subjective self-consciousness and the cognition of objects. Logic, they argue, analyzes the transcendental concepts that constitute object cognition. Trendelenburg's work undermines Kant's strict division between the two sources of cognition. He thinks that the transcendental aesthetic points the way to the foundations of cognition. Kant argues according to a false dilemma when he infers from his arguments that the forms of intuition must belong to a subjective faculty that they could not also be in the objects themselves. Both subjective and objective aspects of space and time, Trendelenburg argues, derive from the metaphysically fundamental principle of Aristotelian original movement. In his view, a complete logic needs to take account of the common origin of both thought and objects in original movement.

Herbart's conception of logic as a formal general discipline follows from his realist interpretation of critical philosophy. Logic is faced with given concepts and should restrict itself to the analysis of the structure and interrelations of these concepts without admixture of sensible content or the forms of sensibility. "Logic posits concepts as known and does not deal with their particular content. Hence it is not a tool of inquiry in which something new is to be discovered, but a guide for expounding what one already knows" (1813: 45). In other words, he insists on the formality that Kant claims for general logic. Drobisch similarly states that the proper subject matter of logic includes only those relations among concepts that "apply to all concepts, independently of what is thought in them" (1836: 3). He underscores this minimal conception of the role and content of logic by suggesting an improvement to Kant's own definition of general logic. Where Kant writes that logic studies the "necessary laws of thinking, but not with respect to specific objects, but all objects in general" (Kant 1800: 9), Drobisch comments that "the only mistake in this explanation is that it relates thinking to objects" (1836: 7). Kant's "object in general" imports more content than formal logic in the Herbartian tradition is willing to admit.

Trendelenburg and material content

A common argument against the formality of logic is that by restricting itself to the mere form of thought, logic is unable to explain some inferences that it should be able to account for. For example, traditional logic licenses the conversion inference from "all As are Bs" to "some Bs are As." This is correct if we consider examples such as "all dogs are mammals" which implies precisely that "some mammals are dogs," no more and no less, presuming, as logicians before the twentieth century do, that "all As are Bs" means that there are at least some As. However, when we infer from "all figures with the Pythagorean property are right triangles" to "some right triangles are figures with the Pythagorean property," the licensed inference is misleading. There are many such cases having to do with conversion inferences and the immediate inferences of the square of oppositions, and logicians from antiquity onwards discuss how best to handle these examples.

One solution in the nineteenth century, developed in detail by Hamilton, is that propositions implicitly quantify both subject and predicate. So the propositions in this example differ logically; the first states that "all dogs are some mammals," while the second states that "all right triangles are all Pythagorean figures." Drobisch proposes that the correct conversion of universal affirmative judgments can only be justified by an analysis of the object itself and hence falls beyond the reach of logic into the domain of a specific science. It is a question of geometry, not of logic, whether right triangles are in fact all the Pythagorean figures (1836: 46). Lotze holds the broader view that all conversion inferences and immediate inferences belong to applied logic (1874a: 101).

Trendelenburg does not look for a particular solution to the problems of conversion inferences. Instead he cites this example as evidence for the vastly more general point that a purely formal analysis of inferences, which abstracts from all content of the concepts involved, is impossible: "They found it significant that *nothing more* follows from the universal form of judgments. We believe that we see in the insufficiency of this whole result an indication that the entire standpoint of the science, in which the form is detached from the content, is itself insufficient" (1870: 336n). Formal logic excludes logically salient information by abstracting from the material content of concepts. Moreover, according to Trendelenburg, the very idea of a form of the concept without consideration of its material content denatures the concept and hence undermines itself. Formal logic, he claims, is not only overly restrictive; it also forces logicians to accept a false view of the structure of concepts.

Traditional logic converges on a quantitative account of concepts, according to which they are aggregates of attributes. Judgments express inclusion and exclusion relations between the sets of attributes of two different concepts, and syllogisms do the same for three or more concepts. According to a purely formal conception of this analysis, any set of attributes forms a concept. Trendelenburg points out that some pairs of attributes, such as "square" and "circular" necessarily exclude one another, for reasons that lie in the objects themselves. Since such exclusion relations between attributes are necessary, they lie within the proper purview of logic and the theory of concepts ought to be able to express them. Similarly, the formal quantitative account does not distinguish between essential and accidental attributes of a given concept. So, in an example Trendelenburg borrows from Hegel, "plant" is an essential attribute of "rose" while "red" is not. Once again, this difference has necessary inferential import, but formal logic does not have the analytic tools for representing it. Trendelenburg generalizes the point and faults formal logic for its inability to conceptualize the "particular connection" that forms the unified whole of a concept and instead reduces it to a senseless aggregate (1862: 21).

Trendelenburg's approach here can be compared to one of the basic principles that Frege establishes for his *Begriffsschrift*, that a logical notation must "fully express everything needed for a correct inference." Like Frege, Trendelenburg and other logical radicals are disposed to revise logic in its entirety. Nevertheless, unlike Frege, Trendelenburg's criticisms issue in proposals for extensions of traditional logic that keep its core intact. Detaching the form of thought from its content is "insufficient," not because the very distinction between form and content is incoherent, but because in some respects the content of thought has logical import. Trendelenburg argues that there is a logical task that goes beyond a purely formal analysis. Logic includes a formal part, but this formal part must be supplemented by some analysis of the content of concepts. In essence, then, Trendelenburg makes the same point that Drobisch and the defenders of formal logic also make: the puzzle about conversion inferences points to material questions about the objects denoted by the concepts in the examples. But where Drobisch draws the limits of logic at formality, Trendelenburg wants to extend these limits to include those aspects of the sciences that contribute to the correct analysis of an inference. The question is motivated by a reconsideration of the nature of logic, not by new discoveries about the structure of inferences.

To make the scope of his proposal clear, Trendelenburg distinguishes between a narrow and a wide sense of logic in his *Logical Investigations*. In the narrow sense logic maintains its formality, but is limited to a mere analysis of contradictions and incapable of making fruitful contributions to the sciences. In the wider sense the domain of logic is defined by necessity, not merely by formal contradictions. Necessity in thoughts and in facts can have logical and metaphysical origins. Therefore Trendelenburg aims for a single theory which must comprise "both domains to understand the inner possibility of knowledge and conceive thought in its striving toward knowledge" (1862: 11). Logic in the wider sense aims to analyze the necessity of scientific knowledge by explaining the metaphysical ground of the objects of scientific knowledge and the structure of thought about such objects. The culminating element of Trendelenburg's theory is that thought and objects have the same metaphysical principle. They both derive from the original "movement" that constitutes the ground of being in space and time as well as the possibility of combining discrete concepts in judgments.

The theory Trendelenburg develops in great detail in his *Logical Investigations* has a fate similar to Hegel's *Logic*, which it criticizes so sharply. The work is influential in stimulating the debates about the status of logic, but no philosopher is persuaded by Trendelenburg's view about movement as a metaphysical ground of thought and being.

Lotze and cognitive content

Lotze writes two editions of his influential logic. The 1843 "small" logic contains a lengthy preface in which he stakes out a position between formal and Hegelian approaches and largely agrees with Trendelenburg's view that the proper boundaries of logic include the conceptual groundwork of the sciences. Lotze's justification for this proposed extension of logic differs from Trendelenburg's. Trendelenburg argues that basic material content belongs to logic because thought and objects share a single metaphysical root and hence cannot be analytically divided without falsifying the structure of concepts and inferences. Lotze, on the other hand, argues that logic can only study the forms of thought insofar as these forms tend to the cognition of real objects. The main body of Lotze's *Logic* consists of a detailed exposition of the theories of concepts, judgments, and inferences with significant changes of emphasis from traditional presentations. In the 1874 "big" logic Lotze completely rewrites the preface, produces a revised version of the body of the small logic in a first volume called "On Thinking" and adds two further volumes, "On Inquiry" and "On Cognition." With its focus on this third volume, the later logic develops the epistemological conception of the small logic explicitly. Unlike Trendelenburg's *Investigations*, Lotze's *Logic* becomes one of the standard logic texts of the nineteenth century, along with Drobisch and Sigwart's books. He is a logical radical who captures the mainstream.

Lotze spreads his revisionist arguments about the nature of logic throughout the presentation of the theories of concepts, judgments, and inferences. He echoes Trendelenburg's arguments that the quantitative analysis of concepts as aggregates of attributes misses the essential nature of concepts (1874a: 47). We only fully grasp a concept when besides its attributes we also grasp why precisely these attributes are connected in precisely this way, to the exclusion of others (1874a: 39). Lotze also agrees that a purely formal treatment of the immediate inferences is useless unless it is merged with an analysis of the basic concepts of the actual sciences in applied logic. He includes a discussion of these immediate inferences only "for the sake of tradition" (1874a: 101).

Lotze's overall conception of logic preserves features of both Herbartian formal logic and Hegelian metaphysical logic. He writes that the discipline is neither formal, nor real. "Logic should be formal in the sense that it is a theory of the operations of thinking by which the subject prepares his thoughts for cognition; but not in the sense that these forms are something factically given without explicit reference to the task of cognizing the real" (1843: 13). The main fault of Herbartian formal logic, according to Lotze, is that it simply takes its tables of forms and laws as given. It is for this reason that logic has become a dry and largely useless discipline. It is precisely such uncritical deference to existing collections of doctrine that leads to the misleading analyses of the structure of concepts and inferences. While Herbart defends this character of logic as the essential expression of its proper boundaries, Lotze finds that such a logic does not fulfill its purpose. "Logic is not supposed to list the laws of thinking, but explain the origin of these laws and their relation to other activities of the mind; this way it should attain more influence on the development of actual knowledge than is possible for an abstract formalism" (1843: 5).

Hegel makes virtually the same criticism of the "dead bones" of formal logic and argues that the task of logic is to systematically derive the forms and laws of logic from the very idea of pure thought. But, Lotze claims, in doing so Hegel's dialectic conflates logical and metaphysical structures and reduces to nothing but a "play on words, which is not far from a logical error" (1843: 11). Nevertheless, much like Hegel, Lotze conceives of the laws of logic as having real significance and as overlapping with the structure of real objects. Only such overlap can ground the cognitive import of logical structures. Lotze indicates his middle position with the claim that "there are motives in the nature of things that force the cognizing mind to produce precisely these shapes of perception and combinations of objects" (1843: 13). On the face of it, this seems to be a naturalistic claim, in that it attributes the laws of logic to the impact of non-logical laws on the mind. Lotze, however, strongly opposes psychological construals of the origins of logical laws. At pains to avoid the appearance of psychologism in his own case, he turns to Kant, and specifically to the schematism of the categories.

According to Kant, the schemata are rules for producing intuition according to patterns of time-determination. The transcendental imagination applies these rules and brings intuited content into patterns that make such content understandable according to the categories. In other words, the transcendental imagination produces patterns in which the mind intuits material as categorically formed. Lotze proposes that in addition to this intuition oriented schematism there is an analogous schematism for logical form. Just as patterns of time determination enable the categorical cognition of intuitable content, so the laws of logic are patterns that enable the cognition of thinkable content. Laws and structures of logic are rules according to which the mind can cognize categorically formed and thinkable, yet intuitively empty, content. "Forming schemata, in this sense, means nothing other than thinking, as opposed to cognizing" (1843: 29). So, for example, Lotze suggests that the logical schema of the category of substance is the concept of the logical subject and the logical schema of the category of inherence is the logical copula (1843: 30).

Of course full cognition requires both intuitive and logical schematization of the categories. In this sense Lotze maintains that logic is a formal discipline. Its structures do not apply to actual objects and do not extend to material content. But logic is not formal in Herbart's sense, because it must contain an account of the origin of logical laws, and this account must be grounded in the role that logical laws play in cognition. And it is not real, or metaphysical, in Hegel's sense, because while the laws of logic are necessary and binding on the thinking subject, they are not themselves constitutive of real objects. Nor, finally, is Lotze's conception that of a transcendental logic, since he distinguishes logical forms from the categories. Transcendental logic is the doctrine of the categories. Logical concepts are not categories, but they presume the categories and explicate how it is possible that the categories apply to thinkable content.

Fischer and transcendental content

Kuno Fischer is one of the few prominent nineteenth-century Hegelians who is not a student of Hegel himself. He comes to Hegel's philosophy after Hegel's death through the influence of his dissertation adviser, Johann Eduard Erdmann. Perhaps it is precisely this separation that enables Fischer to present and defend Hegel's logic in a clear and sober manner, with such distinction that Windelband calls his work the "by far most interesting presentation of Hegel's logic" (1904: 180). Fischer's exposition of Hegel's logic is the rare such work that gains adherents and promotes continuous study of Hegel's philosophy throughout the nineteenth and into the twentieth century. Fischer writes two editions of a logic textbook. The earlier, 1852 edition is a faithful Hegelian work. He prefaces the main body of this text with a survey of the history of logic, which culminates in the development of Kant's critical philosophy into the philosophy of identity in Fichte, Schelling and Hegel. The body of the text is a concise version of Hegel's own logic and covers the entire dialectical development of the categories of thought from pure being to the absolute idea. A small part of this is the exposition of the "subjective logic," which contains the doctrines of concepts, judgments, and inferences. Like Hegel's own exposition of these doctrines, Fischer abstracts entirely from their traditional content in favor of a dialectical demonstration how they arise from one another. In the second, 1865 edition Fischer distances his view from the details of Hegel's logic because, he writes, "even though it set itself the right task, its execution was all wrong" (1865: vi). Even though in its main outlines the exposition still follows Hegel's logic, Fischer now includes a more traditional version of the doctrines contained in the subjective logic, and he frames his conception of the relation between logic and metaphysics in more recognizably Kantian terms. He also defends his Hegelian conception of logic against Herbart and Trendelenburg's alternative proposals.

According to Fischer, logic analyzes concepts that transcend the domains of specific sciences and make scientific cognition possible. In a nod to Kant, Fischer calls these concepts the categories. Fischer thus develops Hegel's argument against the formality of logic, itself derived from Kant's idea of a transcendental logic, that logic is concerned with the constitution of objects in pure thought. Logical concepts and structures are not the form of thought without content, but the function of thought in constituting its objects. While formal logic limits itself to empty concepts, logic ought to aim at necessary concepts (1865: 204). As Fischer puts it, the concepts of logic "do not generalize, but combine; they do not represent, but judge" (1865: 9). Since categories such as being, quantity, or force are also the basic determinations of objects, logic is synonymous with metaphysics. This conception of logic is grounded in Hegel's philosophy, for "the task of logic is solved in the transcendental standpoint of the philosophy of identity" (1852: 46). According to this Hegelian argument, logic is not formal at all. It is transcendental, and its necessity and generality derive from this.

Fischer's logic is similar to Hegel's and thus deviates more radically from the details of traditional logic than Trendelenburg and Lotze. For instance, Fischer adduces an example used by virtually all authors who aim to demonstrate the limits of traditional or formal logic. Traditional logic wrongly finds that the two judgments "the square is white" and "the square is a parallelogram" have the same form (1865: 432). Trendelenburg solves this problem by extending the theory of concepts to include a distinction between accidental and essential attributes. Lotze argues that in this case the different connections imply different interpretations of the copula in the theory of judgments. Fischer mounts a broader criticism that incorporates both of these. He uses this example to challenge the whole theory of judgments that posits a table of quantities, qualities, relations and modalities. These forms of judgments, says Fischer, must first be developed dialectically as determinations of concepts. Such a dialectic development of the forms of judgments yields the logical distinctions between accidental and necessary attributes. Further, this distinction between accidental and necessary attributes of a concept also constitutes a distinction between different forms of judgments.

Indeed, in the later version of his logic, Fischer pretends to go further than Hegel himself. He rejects Hegel's way of integrating the structure of traditional formal logic in his dialectical progression as overly beholden to the received tables of logical forms. "Just as for Kant the judgment forms of ordinary logic served as the guiding thread for the discovery of the categories, so Hegel and his school used it as the guiding thread for the development of judgments" (1865: 433). Instead of merely repeating the table of forms, Hegel makes a dialectic series of arguments that produces a sequential order of the same forms. In effect he, too, uses the existing tables as a guiding thread. But it is an open question, to be resolved by logic itself, whether these forms of judgment appear in the dialectic. The dialectic should unfold according to the necessary content of pure thought, according to the schema that Hegel had identified as the progression from the logic of pure being to pure essence and finally the pure concept. In the same edition, however, Fischer actually returns to a more conservative treatment of the syllogistic than Hegel's. Instead of applying Hegel's schema in the "subjective logic" and reducing all syllogistic figures to a single relation between universal, particular, and individual determinations of a concept, he reproduces an entire theory of inferences according to the traditional figures and types of inference.

In the early edition, Fischer ends his survey of the history of logic with Hegel. In the second edition he takes account of the debates among logical radicals in the intervening decades. Fischer repeats his claim that the task of logic is to explain the possibility of scientific object-cognition. However, he now measures the standpoint of the philosophy of identity against the criticisms leveled at it by Herbart and the "formal" logicians on the one hand, and by Trendelenburg on the other. This additional layer of critical examination of the claims of subject-object identity leads Fischer to formulate his basic conception of logic by appealing to Kant's notion of the synthetic function of the categories, rather than the unity of apperception that he sees as the basic principle in Fichte and Hegel. In other words, for Fischer the nature of logic as transcendental logic is primarily determined by the function of the categories in grounding objective cognition, and only secondarily by the structure of self-consciousness. Although this is only a slight shift of emphasis, it reflects the anti-Hegelian dynamics of the arguments of the logical radicals. To defend his Hegelian logic, Fischer retreats to less controversial Kantian grounds.

Herbart, of course, disagrees with the entire standpoint of subject-object identity. Metaphysics and logic, he maintains, are fundamentally distinct sciences. Fischer's main argument against Herbart's realism consists of a Hegelian refutation of the notion of a mind-independent reality. This notion amounts to a point of view that attempts to "think being as independent of thinking; i.e. being is thought as not thought" (1865: 134). This amounts to a contradiction in the concept of "reality" that Herbart wants to reserve as the domain of metaphysics and oppose to the domain of logic. Self-contradictory concepts, however, need to be developed dialectically and hence Herbart's realism is swallowed up by Hegelian logic.

Fischer's criticisms of Trendelenburg's view are more detailed. Trendelenburg's idea of movement as a substrate that grounds both being and thought resembles Fischer's standpoint of subject-object identity. Trendelenburg, too, aims to be able to explain the cognitive possibility and objective validity of logical structures and he uses his metaphysics of movement as the bridging principle. Fischer argues that in doing so Trendelenburg cannot preserve the unity of his idea of movement. At best he establishes an analogy between the material ground of objects and the logical ground of thought. More importantly, Fischer also criticizes Trendelenburg's "loophole" objection to Kant. Kant's *Critique*, Fischer argues, does not overlook the possibility that space could be objective; on the contrary, Kant proves that this is impossible by demonstrating the possibility of *a priori* knowledge of mathematics. For, Fischer writes, if space were objective, it would be given in experience and hence "mathematical insights would have to be judgments of experience and as such could be neither general nor necessary" (1865: 175). These criticisms of Trendelenburg's loophole objection lead the latter, who has a penchant for such *Auseinandersetzung*, to write a disparaging denouncement of Fischer's understanding of Kant. The resulting exchange plays a significant role in the development of the Kant interpretations of Hermann Cohen, and hence contributes to the views of the neo-Kantian schools, which focus on ways to integrate the transcendental aesthetic with the functions of the concepts of the understanding. Thus Trendelenburg for a second time becomes the catalyst of a debate that shapes nineteenth-century philosophy.

Reactions to symbolic and mathematical approaches to logic

The post-Kantian use of "formal logic" is not universal. In England, where mathematical and symbolic approaches to logic have more influence on philosophy, the phrase is used to denote mathematical or symbolic logic. For example Augustus De Morgan titles his 1847 textbook *Formal Logic*. This is not entirely coincidental. Windelband speculates that "pure formal logic must follow a natural inclination to express its forms in mathematical formulae and to seek its grounding in mathematical relations" (1904: 166). Drobisch experiments with such notation in a "logico-mathematical appendix" to his *Neue Darstellung*. Following Herbart he conceives of judgments as the relation between the spheres of two concepts and writes that therefore "simple judgments can also be represented by algebraic equations" (1836: 132). Hamilton's idea to quantify over both subject and predicate may come from Herbart's discussion of conversion inferences in his *Lehrbuch*. Herbart accounts for the apparent oddness of the fact that "All As are B" converts to "Some Bs are A" by positing the logical principle that propositions never assert the "entire sphere" of the predicate (1813: 104), i.e. that the predicate "B" does not mean "all Bs." Trendelenburg claims that Hamilton "essentially transplanted Kant's German formal logic onto the ground of English philosophy" (1862: 15), giving further evidence of some influence of post-Kantian philosophers of logic on English symbolic logic.

Due to such perceived commonality of Herbartian formal logic and mathematical logic, and in the wake of the influential criticisms of formal logic by the logical radicals, the philosophical mainstream in Germany spurns the idea that mathematical logic can provide new insights, even as such approaches begin to yield results that eventually revolutionize the entire discipline. In a representative gesture, Windelband dismissively credits both the Herbartian and the later British mathematical logics with the same emphasis on mere "acumen" and notes that "in Germany this logical sport which, it cannot be denied, has the merit of exercising formal acumen, has met with little approval." He likens it to attempts to ground logical relations in spatial or geometric relations and writes that in both cases "a successful tool of visualization is confused with the essence of the matter" (1904: 166f.). The upshot of the criticisms of formality in Trendelenburg, Lotze, and the Hegelians is that formal considerations do not get at the heart of logical issues. The thrust of philosophical thought on logic through the middle of the century is to conceptualize the content of judgments in pure and general ways, so as to reinvigorate logic and once again make it relevant to scientific cognition. This tendency is exemplified most dramatically in Sigwart's logic, which is one of the most widely used logic textbooks in the latter decades of the century up into the early decades of the twentieth century. Sigwart in effect reduces the forms of logic to a bare minimum. He argues that there is only a single form of judgment, the categorical affirmative judgment. Other differences amount only to differences in the content of subject or predicate. Similarly, he argues, there is only a single form of inference and the entire array of syllogistic forms derives merely from variations in content.

Mathematical and symbolic logic does flourish in Germany, outside the circle of post-Kantian philosophers of logic and somewhat later than in England. So, for example, a number of mathematicians develop extensive algebraic treatments of logic. Chief among these are the brothers Hermann and Robert Grassmann and, following them, especially Ernst Schröder who produces a systematic synthesis between Boolean algebra and Peirce's discoveries. Some philosophers show genuine understanding of these innovations. One of the earliest is Ulrici's 1855 review of Boole's *An Investigation of the Laws of Thought*. This is a positive and detailed review that displays a good deal of understanding of Boole's technical innovations, but it goes mostly unnoticed by Ulrici's philosophical colleagues. Two decades later the Austrian neo-Kantian philosopher Alois Riehl writes another detailed and appreciative review of Boole's *Investigation* and Jevons' *The Principles of Science* in which he points out the most significant implications of this work. Riehl remarks that a great merit of Boole's system is that it makes clear that the syllogisms only cover a small part of all logically valid inferences, and he points out specifically that mathematical deductions are examples of non-syllogistic inferences (1877: 60). He also maintains that mathematical logic has the great advantage that it develops logical structures independently of grammatical or linguistic structures, which are the basis of traditional syllogistic logic (1877: 53).

Challenges to the traditional analysis of judgments

Arguments that logic ought to include an analysis of the content of concepts in addition to its formal part are, in a sense, conservative. Trendelenburg and Lotze, for example, leave the main structure of traditional logic intact and seek to supplement it in various places to make up for its inadequacies. A more radical strain of logical thought aims to undermine that structure itself. Often the same philosophers deploy both the conservative and radical strains of argument and thus betray a fundamental ambivalence over the status of traditional logic.

Underlying this ambivalence is the fact that the established parts of traditional logic reinforce one another. The form of the syllogisms requires an analysis of judgments as the synthetic combination of two terms. This analysis of the subject–predicate form, in turn, bolsters the analysis of the structure of concepts as conglomerates of attributes that can be subjected to a quantitative analysis of inclusion and subsumption. The theories of concepts, judgments, and inference in traditional syllogistic logic form a unified whole. Consequently criticisms that aim at a single aspect of the entire edifice tend to be formulated within the overall structure of traditional logic. The challenges to the formality of logic are mainly bound up with proposals to amend the theory of concepts, since this is where critics locate the cognitive, material, or transcendental content of thought. But they focus on the logical structure of concepts in such a way as to leave their role with respect to judgments and syllogistic inferences untouched. Fischer and other Hegelians, of course, reject traditional logic in a more wholesale fashion. Fischer even criticizes Hegel's own logic for being too beholden to the traditional table of judgment forms. The logical radicals of the other schools develop arguments of similarly sweeping implications, though these implications are not often made explicit. These arguments, which lead to challenges that question the entire edifice of logic, mostly derive from attempts to reject the traditional analysis of the structure of judgments. Besides the criticisms of the formality of traditional logic, revisionist thought about the logical structure of judgment makes up the second main strain of arguments within logical radicalism.

Post-Kantian philosophical arguments about the logic of judgments cluster around three main topics. First, philosophers question the structure of judgments itself. Second, they debate the priority of judgments over concepts. And third, a few philosophers begin to challenge the role judgments play in inference.

The structure of judgments

Investigations into the structure of judgments begin with widespread recognition that the distinction between subject and predicate owes its origins to grammar and therefore requires careful logical interpretation. Even Herbart and Drobisch, who maintain and defend the traditional analysis of judgments as the combination of two concepts, recognize this need. The main component of the logical interpretation of judgments is the copula, the logical structure that corresponds to the grammatical "is." The different functions of the copula constitute various forms of judgments. To emphasize the independence of the logical notion of the copula from grammatical structures, almost all writers of logic texts consider examples of judgments that do not fit the common "S is P" schema. Standard examples are existential judgments ("S exists") and impersonal judgments ("It rains"), which abound in German (particularly with respect to atmospheric conditions: *"es blitzt," "es regnet," "es donnert," "es friert"* are the usual examples). Traditionalists argue that the logical structure of these judgments is identical to that of less recalcitrant cases, consisting of the combination of logical subject and predicate by means of a copula. Wayne Martin has shown how Kantian logicians struggle with this attempt to conflate judgment forms, and that this very problem motivates a radical restructuring of logical form in Brentano (2006: 58f).

Lotze also analyzes impersonal judgments as subject–predicate compounds. He regards impersonal judgments as "the first act of judging in thought; as it were a preliminary step to categorical judgments" (1874a: 70). But as an act of thought, these judgments must still have a logical subject, which is, however, completely undetermined and vaguely expressed in language by the "it." Despite this conservative strain, he proposes substantial changes to the traditional table of judgment forms. The novelty of Lotze's analysis of judgments lies mostly in his interpretation of the logical copula. It expresses the validity (*Geltung*) of the fact that is thought in the combination of subject and predicate terms. Validity, he argues, is the metaphysical mode specific to logical entities, as opposed to the being of real entities. Lotze argues in general for a robustness and uniformity of the copula; since it expresses validity, it is fundamentally the same in every judgment. Consequently, Lotze's analysis reduces the traditional variety of the forms of judgment, attributing them to differences in terms or content, rather than form. For instance, he claims that difference in quantity between universal, particular, and singular judgments are due to the quantity of the subject term, while the asserted connection between subject and predicate is identical in all three cases.

A particularly interesting line of argument derives from Lotze's consideration of negative judgments. Where the Kantian table of judgments distinguishes affirmative from negative judgments, Lotze maintains that the copula is exactly the same in both cases. In each case the copula joins the subject and predicate to yield a thinkable content. This content as a whole is affirmed in one case and negated in the other (1874a: 61). Affirmative and negative judgments, then, differ not in logical form, but in the content of a second judgment about the first one. This view, which Sigwart later develops even further, initiates a debate about the double nature of judgments. One logical act forms the judgable content and another act affirms, denies, or takes some other evaluative attitude towards this content. This view of the double nature of judgments proves influential in the neo-Kantian *Wertphilosophie* of Windelband and Heinrich Rickert as well as phenomenology through the work of Brentano and Husserl. It may also be at the root of Frege's invention of the judgment stroke in his *Begriffsschrift* (Martin 2006: 75f.).

More radical proposals reject the subject–predicate structure as a basic analysis of judgments. This is Hegel's approach. A judgment, he claims, is an articulated concept, and its synthetic structure is the expression of this articulation. "The judgment is the concept in its specificity, as the distinguishing relation of its moments" (1830: 155). In this view, the underlying concept is the warrant for the unity of the judgment, and consequently there is no need for the synthetic function of the copula. Rather than combining two terms, judgments divide a single concept. "The etymological meaning of judgment [*Urteil*] in our language is deeper and expresses the unity of the concept as the first thing, and its differentiation as the original division [*ursprüngliche Teilung*], which is what the judgment is in truth" (1830: 155). Though this etymology, which Hegel shares with Hölderlin, turns out to be mistaken, the point itself is clear.

Trendelenburg develops a view of judgments that inverts Hegel's, but also resembles it. He, too, finds that rather than producing a unity by means of a logical copula, judgments of subject–predicate form differentiate a more original unity. He rejects the traditional view according to which "thought is only the means, as it were the vehicle, to bring concepts together" (1870: 232). Like Hegel, Trendelenburg claims that this traditional analysis arises from an external perspective that does not grasp the nature of judgment. According to Trendelenburg's metaphysics, the subject–predicate form of thought mirrors the substance-activity form of reality, because both thought and being are constituted by the "original movement" which first makes it possible that thought can be about being. Activity, however, is more basic than substance. At the most fundamental level thought grasps pure activity without substance, reflected grammatically in subjectless predicates. "We think in predicates. This main concept originally arises alone" (1870: 232). Further articulation of thought attributes the activity to a substance. So the intellect fixes a substance "the lightning" to which we can attribute the activity "lightning" and which it then uses as the subject of further judgments, "lightning strikes," etc. Trendelenburg claims that far from being recalcitrant cases, the impersonal judgments best represent this logical structure of judgments. "We judge when we think, and in every complete judgment we distinguish subject and predicate. But this differentiated form points us back to a unity. In language this is represented in the so-called impersonal verbs, such as *es braust, es blitzt, es friert*" (1870: 231). Trendelenburg further draws on etymological evidence from Jacob Grimm that many nouns derive from verbs. So, for instance, *Hahn* (cock) derives from the lost verb *hanan* (to crow) (1870: 236). The activity precedes the substance in thought.

However, the conclusion Trendelenburg draws from this analysis of the original unity of judgment is precisely the opposite of Hegel's. Where Hegel grounds judgments in concepts, Trendelenburg argues that the original unities of thought are themselves judgments. This is the point illustrated by impersonal judgments. "It rains" expresses a full judgment in its structural simplicity. "The beginnings of language lie in verbs, but in such a way that these in themselves form judgments" (1870: 236). Similarly the first names and words uttered by children represent entire sentences, despite their grammatical, and logical, simplicity. Indeed it is the concepts that owe their beginnings to such simple, unified judgments. Concepts, both nominative and predicative, only arise from an original thought and only within the articulated structure of derivative judgments. Here Trendelenburg once again appeals to evidence from etymology, this time from Gruppe, who "has shown that every concept is based on a judgment" (1870: 234). To take the same example, the concept "lightning" is only a concept insofar as it is thought as something to which a predicate can be attached, that it "strikes," "shines" or whatever. Concepts essentially are partial and incomplete judgments. It is noteworthy that Trendelenburg makes this claim for all concepts, not only for logical predicates.

The priority of judgments

The question about the logical structure of judgment has implications for the structure of logic as a whole. In traditional analyses, such as Herbart's, concepts have priority in two senses. First, they have priority in the order of exposition. The presentation of logic proceeds from the most elemental to the most complex, from concepts to inferences. Secondly, concepts have a logical priority, insofar as they make judgments and inferences possible as their constituent parts. Judgments are combinations of concepts, and the validity of inference is explained by the interrelations of the three terms of a syllogism.

In Hegel's logic, too, concepts have priority. This is evident from the structure of his exposition. In the *Encyclopedia* logic, his versions of the three theories that traditionally make up logic, the theories of the concept "as such," of judgments, and of inferences, are all included in the chapter on the "subjective concept," which itself is part of the "doctrine of the concept." Similarly in the *Science of Logic*, the three theories are part of the division on "subjectivity" in the subjective logic, which is also the doctrine of the concept. In its general outline, the same exposition is maintained in Fischer and other Hegelians. However, the logical priority Hegel accords to concepts differs from the traditional account. Whereas the tradition claims that concepts are the component parts of judgments and inferences, Hegel claims that these latter structures are nothing but articulations of particular concepts. Further, these particular concepts are parts of a whole that itself has the structure of a single concept.

Trendelenburg's view, on the other hand, accords logical priority to judgments, not concepts. On his analysis, there could be no concepts without judgments. This shift in understanding logical priority, prompted by his revision of the analysis of the structure of judgments, is representative of the overall epistemological turn of post-Kantian logic. As philosophers debate the cognitive and epistemological import of logic, they focus on judgments as the basic form of cognitive achievement and hence also as the basic logical act. This same shift is evident in Lotze's three-volume logic. In the first volume he adheres to the traditional order of exposition and writes that "without doubt, *pure* logic must posit the form of the concept before that of the judgment" (1874a: 24). However, when he analyzes the cognitive import of logic in the third volume, the fundamental role judgments play in cognition leads him to posit a different kind of logical priority for them. Logical entities, he argues, are distinct from real entities in that their metaphysical realm is validity (*Geltung*) as opposed to being (*Sein*). However, one cannot say of concepts that they are *valid*, because they are only meaningful insofar as they are parts of judgments. "Of concepts we can at most say that they mean something; but they mean something, because sentences about them are valid" (1874b: 521). In other words, concepts only belong to the realm of the logical insofar as they are constituent parts of judgments. It is the judgment that confers logicality onto the concept. So from the point of view of "pure logic," which disregards the application of logical structures to real cognition, concepts show themselves to be elemental constituent parts. But from the point of view of applied logic judgments are the basic logical unit.

This trend becomes pervasive and at the end of the century philosophical logic preponderantly emphasizes the epistemological import of logical structures and consequently focuses more on the theory of judgments. The goal is to develop a thorough classification of the logical forms of judgment as the basic unit of cognition. Windelband, who develops a theory of double judgments, sums up this state of the art: "The theories of concept and inference are only appendices of the theory of judgments, which is the main problem of logic. This we may regard clearly as the foundation for future developments of this science: logic is the theory of judgments" (1904: 169). At this point philosophers of logic entirely lose interest in the bottom-up approach of constructing logic from concepts to judgments to inferences.

Judgments and inference

As Windelband indicates, new work on the theory of judgments also displaces the theory of syllogistic inferences from the center of logical concerns. Traditional syllogisms stipulate that premises and conclusions of an inference must be in subject–predicate form. As new theories of judgment challenge this analysis of judgments, it becomes apparent that traditional syllogisms cover only a small part of scientific deductions and arguments. Indeed from the beginning of ancient logic, logicians recognize that, while it is often possible to state arguments as a series of such syllogisms, some valid arguments resist this form. This is why expositions of the theory of inference usually also contain discussions of hypothetical and disjunctive syllogisms, as well as inductive, modal, and probabilistic inferences.

Further, logicians are aware that in traditional syllogisms the subject–predicate form plays two different roles that can easily be analytically separated. For example, syllogisms with hypothetical premises of the form "If A is B, then A is C" are treated as syllogistic inferences with categorical premises in which the major, minor, and middle terms stand for judgments, not for concepts. In demonstrating the validity of the inference, logicians substitute the entire judgment "If A is B, then A is C" for a premise of the form "S is P," where "If A is B" is substituted for S, "then A is C" is substituted for P, and the copula becomes irrelevant. In such cases "S is P" does not stand for the form of a judgment, but for the schema of a valid inference, whose substitution instances can have many different forms.

This ambiguity of the subject–predicate form in syllogistic logic gives philosophical logicians license to challenge the traditional analysis of judgments. It implies that the inferential significance of judgments is not tied to the subject–predicate form, since other forms of judgment can figure in perfectly valid inferences. Indeed, as philosophers begin to explore different theories of judgment, they also begin to think of inferential schemas along different, non-syllogistic lines. A telling example, here, is once again Sigwart's system of logic, which reduces all syllogisms to a single form of inference and differentiates arguments according to the judgments they involve. While Sigwart and others fall well short of developing a substantial non-syllogistic theory of inference, they nevertheless uncouple the analysis of judgments from the dictates of syllogistic form, leaving the way open toward a radically novel conception of inferential significance.

RESULTS AND INFLUENCES

It is tempting to think that this entire debate is made irrelevant by the discoveries of Frege's *Begriffsschrift* and the development of modern mathematical logic. Judging by the chronological sequence of events, this is certainly not the case. In 1904 Windelband was writing as one of the foremost German philosophers about the work of other prominent philosophers that the central issues in logic were to develop a new theory of judgments and to reconcile the discipline with Kant's notion of a transcendental logic. While he and other philosophers are to a limited extent cognizant of developments in mathematical logic, they regard them as refinements in mode of presentation and training of logical acumen, but not as solutions to central logical problems. As late as 1930 Carnap complains that "the majority of philosophers have even now taken little cognizance of the new logic" (1930: 134). He suggests that the neo-Kantian philosophers who continue to elaborate theories of judgment are laboring on an anachronism. However, such a sweeping dismissal mistakes the substance of the views that make up logical radicalism. They are concerned with questions about what Trendelenburg defines as the "wider sense" of logic, such as the relation between logic and metaphysics and the possibility of objective cognition. Once we survey this wider ambit, a lasting and profound influence is more evident.

To begin with, it has been argued that both Frege and Carnap themselves owe much of their philosophical stance more or less directly to these authors. Sluga (1980) and Gabriel (1986, 1989a, b) show how the intellectual context of Lotze, Trendelenburg, and the neo-Kantians who follow them shapes Frege's work. Similarly, Richardson (1992) and Friedman (1997) trace the origin of Carnap's logical empiricism to neo-Kantian transcendental logics.

Some of this influence derives from early rejections of psychologism. Due to its focus on the mind's cognitive faculties, Kant's transcendental logic prompts a number of early psychologistic interpretations. Jakob Friedrich Fries, for example, claims that Kant's critique is based on the inner experience of cognitive processes. In keeping with Kant's claim that logic is a canon of the understanding, both Herbart and Drobisch oppose such tendencies by insisting that general logic studies how one ought to think, not how one actually thinks. Nevertheless, Herbart claims elsewhere that transcendental arguments are psychological and hence proposes a scientific psychology in place of a critical epistemology. Consequently he, too, becomes a target of Trendelenburg's broad anti-psychologism (1846: 349); the latter was particularly diligent in detecting elements of psychology in the arguments of Hegel's dialectic. Lotze, too, is rigorously anti-psychologistic and he uses his notion of validity to mark a clean separation between the logical and the actual.

However, the central legacy of this period of logic-criticism derives from its novel conception of just what a philosophical logic is supposed to do. In rejecting the formality of logic, the logical radicals search for ways to capture its proper content. As they attempt to reconcile a notion of the cognitive import of logic with a Kantian understanding of the structure of cognition, they in effect redefine the scope and nature of theoretical philosophy. They create a discipline at the area of overlap between transcendental philosophy, critical epistemology, the logic of scientific cognition, and the theory of scientific inquiry. While post-Kantian logical radicalism does not give us modern mathematical logic, it does give rise to the conception of philosophy as the theory of the sciences, a conception that continues to shape theoretical philosophy today.

References

Carnap, Rudolf (1930) "The Old and the New Logic," trans. Isaac Levi, in A. J. Ayer (ed.) (1959) *Logical Positivism*, New York: Free Press.

De Morgan, Augustus (1847) *Formal Logic: The Calculus or Inference, Necessary and Probable*, London: Taylor & Walton.

Drobisch, Moritz (1836) *Neue Darstellung der Logik nach ihren einfachsten Verhältnissen*. Leipzig: Leopold Voß.

Fischer, Kuno (1852) *Logik und Metaphysik oder Wissenschaftslehre*, Heidelberg; repr., edited by Hans-Georg Gadamer, Heidelberg: Manutius Verlag, 1997.

—— (1865) *System der Logik und Metaphysik oder Wissenschaftslehre*, 2nd rev. edn. Heidelberg.

Friedman, Michael (1997) "Overcoming Metaphysics: Carnap and Heidegger," in Ronald Giere and Alan Richardson (eds) *Origins of Logical Empiricism*, Minnesota Studies in Philosophy of Science, vol. 16, Minneapolis, MN: University of Minnesota Press, pp. 45–79.

Gabriel, Gottfried (1986) "Frege als Neukantianer," *Kant-Studien* 77: 84–101.

—— (1989a) "Lotze und die Entstehung der modernen Logik bei Frege," introduction to reprint of Lotze (1874a).

—— (1989b) "Objektivität: Logik und Erkenntnistheorie bei Lotze und Frege," introduction to reprint of Lotze (1874b).

Hegel, G. W. F. (1813) *Wissenschaft der Logik: Die Lehre vom Wesen*; repr. *Werke*, vol. 6, Frankfurt: Suhrkamp, 1986, pp. 13–240.

—— (1816) *Wissenschaft der Logik: Die Subjektive Logik*; repr. *Werke*, vol. 6, Frankfurt: Suhrkamp, 1986, pp. 241–573.

—— (1830) *Enzyklopädie der Philosophischen Wissenschaften im Grundrisse*; repr., edited by F. Nicolin and O. Pöggeler, Hamburg: Meiner, 1959.

—— (1831) *Wissenschaft der Logik: Die Objective Logik*; repr. *Werke*, vol. 5, Frankfurt: Suhrkamp, 1986.

Herbart, Johann Friedrich (1813) *Lehrbuch zur Einleitung in die Philosophie*, Königsberg: A. W. Unzer; repr. Hamburg: Meiner, 1993.

Jevons, William Stanley (1881) *Elementary Lessons in Logic: Deductive and Inductive*, London: Macmillan.

Kant, Immanuel (1781) *Kritik der Reinen Vernunft*, edited by R. Schmidt. Hamburg: Meiner, 1993; trans., P. Guyer and A. Wood, as *Critique of Pure Reason*, Cambridge: Cambridge University Press, 1997.

—— (1800) *Logik*, edited by C. Jäsche, in Wilhelm Weischedel (ed.) *Schriften zur Metaphysik und Logik*, Frankfurt. Suhrkamp, 1996; edited, trans. Young, J. Michael, as *Lectures on Logic*, Cambridge: Cambridge University Press, 1992.

Käufer, Stephan (2005) "Hegel to Frege: Concepts and Conceptual Content in Nineteenth-Century Logic," *History of Philosophy Quarterly* 22: 259–80.

Lotze, Rudolf Hermann (1843) *Logik*, Leipzig: Weidmann'sche Buchhandlung.

—— (1874a) *Logik*, bk 1: *Vom Denken*, Leipzig: S. Hirzel; repr., edited by G. Gabriel, Hamburg: Meiner, 1989.

—— (1874b) *Logik*, bk 3: *Vom Erkennen*, Leipzig: S. Hirzel; repr., edited by G. Gabriel, Hamburg: Meiner, 1989.

MacFarlane, John (2000) *What Does It Mean to Say That Logic Is Formal?* PhD diss., University of Pittsburgh.

—— (2002) "Frege, Kant, and the Logic in Logicism," *Philosophical Review* 111: 25–65.

Martin, Wayne (2003) "Nothing More or Less than Logic: General Logic, Transcendental Philosophy, and Kant's Repudiation of Fichte's *Wissenschaftslehre*," *Topoi* 22: 29–39.

—— (2006) *Theories of Judgment: Psychology, Logic, Phenomenology*, Cambridge: Cambridge University Press.

Richardson, Alan (1992) "Logical Idealism and Carnap's Construction of the World," *Synthese* 93: 59–92.

Riehl, Alois (1877) "Die Englische Logik der Gegenwart," *Vierteljahrsschrift für wissenschaftliche Philosophie* 1: 51–80.

Sigwart, Christoph (1873) *Logik*, vol. 1: *Die Lehre vom Urteil, vom Begriff und vom Schluss*. Tübingen: H. Laupp.

Sluga, Hans (1980) *Gottlob Frege*, London: Routledge.

Trendelenburg, Friedrich Adolf (1843) *Die Logische Frage in Hegel's System: Zwei Streitschriften*, Leibzig: F. A. Brockhaus.

—— (1846) *Geschichte der Kategorienlehre*, Berlin: G. Bethge.

—— (1857) "Ueber Leibnizens Entwurf einer allgemeinen Charakteristik"; repr. Trendelenburg (1867), pp. 1–47.

—— (1862) *Logische Untersuchungen*, vol. 1, 3rd edn, Leipzig; repr. Hildesheim: Georg Olms, 1964.

—— (1867) *Historische Beiträge zur Philosophie*, vol. 3, Berlin: G. Bethge.

—— (1870) *Logische Untersuchungen* vol. 2, 3rd edn, Leipzig; repr. Hildesheim: Georg Olms, 1964.

Ueberweg, Friedrich (1857) *System der Logik und Geschichte der Logischen Lehren*, Bonn: Adolph Marcus.

Ulrici, Hermann (1855) A review of George Boole, *An Investigation of the Laws of Thought*, *Zeitschrift für Philosophie und philosophische Kritik* 27: 273–91.

Windelband, Wilhelm (1904) "Logik," in Wilhelm Windelband (ed.) *Die Philosophie im Beginn des zwanzigsten Jahrhunderts: Festschrift für Kuno Fischer*, vol. 1, Heidelberg: Carl Winter.

Further reading

Kuno Fischer, *Anti-Trendelenburg: Eine Gegenschrift* (Jena: Hermano Dabis, 1870), contains Fischer's response to Trendelenburg's "loophole" argument. Detailed treatment of mathematical and symbolic logic in Germany during this period, with a thorough bibliography can be found in Volker Peckhaus, *Logik, Mathesis universalis und allgemeine Wissenschaft: Leibniz und die Wiederentdeckung der formalen Logik im 19. Jahrhundert* (Berlin: Akademie Verlag, 1997). Friedrich Adolf Trendelenburg, "Über eine Lücke in Kants Beweis von der ausschließenden Subjektivität des Raumes und der Zeit," in *Historische Beiträge zur Philosophie*, vol. 3 (Berlin: G. Bethge, 1867), contains Trendelenburg's "loophole" argument that space may be both objective and subjective; and *Kuno Fischer und sein Kant* (Leipzig: S. Hirzel, 1869), Trendelenburg's vitriolic attack on Fischer's challenge to his loophole argument.

28

FRANZ BRENTANO

Peter Simons

Life and works

Philosophers are creatures of the mind and the circumstances and events of a philosopher's life are usually marginal to their philosophical ideas, achievements and outputs. In the case of Franz Brentano this is not so. His status as a lapsed priest led to his being denied the standard reward of a successful academic, a university chair, a denial which became a *cause célèbre* in late nineteenth-century Vienna. This, his several shifts of country, his blindness in later life, his fraught relationships with former students, and his many and complex changes of mind and doctrine, resulted in his published works being just a small and unrepresentative fraction of his thought. His influence was exerted not through the printed but through the spoken word. An inspiring lecturer and a dedicated mentor, he was perhaps the most successful teacher of philosophy in the history of the subject, inspiring two generations of students with his vision of a rigorous scientific philosophy. His best students filled chairs of philosophy and psychology throughout the Austro-Hungarian Empire and abroad in Germany and Italy: they also numbered two heads of government and the founder of psychoanalysis. The fragmented and chaotic nature of Brentano's scientific *Nachlass* and its initial unscholarly editing and posthumous publication mean that his work is still not properly available to the historian of philosophy. The breadth of his influence on subsequent philosophy is considerable, but his own philosophy remains partly hidden and unknown.

Franz Clemens Honoratus Hermann Brentano was born in 1838 in the Rhineland into a distinguished German literary and Roman Catholic family of Italian ancestry. His father Christian was a writer and Catholic publicist, brother of the noted romantic poet Clemens. Brentano's father died when he was thirteen. His mother Emilia, née Genger, was very pious and strongly encouraged him to enter the priesthood. His aunt Bettina von Arnim was also a notable romantic author famously associated with Goethe.

Brentano early showed an aptitude for study and scholarship. In his teens he was fascinated by Aquinas and scholastic philosophy. He specialized in philosophy and theology, studying, as was the custom, at several universities, including Berlin with the notable German philosopher Adolf Trendelenburg, who had written an influential history of the theory of categories. He completed his doctorate in 1862 with a dissertation called *Von der mannigfachen Bedeutung des Seienden nach Aristoteles* (*On the Several Senses of Being in Aristotle*), a piece which attracted attention for its well-argued defence of the reasonableness of Aristotle's division of the categories against criticisms of Kant and Mill. Following his doctorate Brentano studied theology and took holy orders in 1864. He obtained his *Habilitation* in 1866 at the University of Würzburg, where he was employed as lecturer and later as associate ("extraordinary") professor. His students from the Würzburg period include Anton Marty and Carl Stumpf, both of whom became notable philosophers.

In the period preceding the first Vatican Council, it became clear that the Pope and his supporters wanted to proclaim a dogma of papal infallibility. Brentano was commissioned by liberal Catholic bishops to argue against this proposal. The opposition was unsuccessful, and at the same time Brentano began to have doubts about matters of Catholic dogma including the Trinity and the Incarnation. He delayed acting openly until after the death of his mother, but news of his doubts had leaked out and made his position untenable in Würzburg, where his position was linked with his status as a priest, so in 1873 he resigned his position there and left the priesthood. Being in the middle of writing a book on psychology as a "passport out of Würzburg," he spent several months without a position, contracting then recovering from smallpox, and visiting Herbert Spencer in England, though unable to meet John Stuart Mill in Avignon as planned, due to the latter's death. In his absence he was appointed to a chair of philosophy at the University of Vienna, which he took up in 1874. In the same year the first part of his book *Psychologie vom empirischen Standpunkte* (*Psychology from an Empirical Standpoint*) was published, and this made his reputation.

In Vienna Brentano plunged into teaching and society. Being a brilliant and charismatic teacher, with an imposing appearance and a hint of exotic scandal because of leaving the priesthood, he soon acquired celebrity status, and his lectures, particularly those on practical philosophy (ethics), were heavily attended. Never a fluent writer, his publishing suffered from his other activities, and his ongoing changes of mind made it impossible for him to complete the psychology book. In this period his notable students included Alois Höfler, Alexius Meinong, Sigmund Freud, and Tomáš Masaryk.

In 1880 Brentano married Ida Lieben, member of a wealthy Jewish family. Austrian law apparently forbade ex-priests from marrying. Although juridical opinion was divided on the question, Brentano decided not to risk a court case and revoked the Austrian citizenship he had acquired with his professorship, which entailed resigning his chair. He took Saxon citizenship and he and Ida married in Leipzig. Returning to Vienna in the expectation of reinstatement, having broken no Austrian law, Brentano discovered he had alienated conservative opinion including that of the Emperor, who steadfastly refused to reappoint him despite annual declarations of support from the Vienna faculty. Brentano retained the lowly status of *Privatdozent*, allowed to lecture, but unsalaried and unable to supervise dissertations. His teaching continued to be as popular as before, with his lectures on ethics attended by hundreds of students. His later illustrious students from this period of Vienna teaching included Christian von

Ehrenfels, Edmund Husserl, Benno Kerry, and Kazimierz Twardowski. During this period his publications were mainly confined to short essays.

Ida's death and his continuing frustration with the official blocking of his reinstatement prompted Brentano to retire in 1895 and move to Florence. He married again, his second wife Emilie Ruprecht becoming stepmother to his son Johannes (John, Gio). As time went on his eyesight deteriorated and he became unable to read or write. An eye operation in 1903 failed to restore his sight and he became dependent on his wife reading to him and his thoughts being dictated. He corresponded copiously, in particular with Marty. In this period he acquired a second generation of followers who had been taught by Marty in Prague, but had "defected" to Brentano, notably Emil Arleth, Oskar Kraus and Alfred Kastil. They stepped in to help Brentano in compiling publications. During this period Brentano's ideas underwent a fundamental shift towards the position later called *reism*, and everyone struggled to understand him and catch up with his changes of opinion. After Italy entered the war against Austria-Hungary in 1915, the popular sentiment against Austrians forced Brentano into exile again, in Zurich in Switzerland, where he died in 1917.

As a person Brentano was apparently genial, helpful to his students, and a kind and loving husband and father. His striking photographic appearances as a young man in dark habit, black beard and shock of hair, and occasionally a dashing broad-brimmed hat suggest a certain dandyism, certainly an awareness of the impression he conveyed to others. This is corroborated by the testimony of his student Ehrenfels, who claims Brentano's speaking style was a little self-conscious, retaining something of the tones of the pulpit, and he continued to wear black. In later life, having lost his eyesight, he appears more conventionally the untidy *grand homme*. In social conversation he was effortlessly charming and witty. His wit extended to penning numerous puzzles, some of which he published. He was an accomplished chess player, and published a new opening. In art and music his tastes were by nineteenth-century standards old-fashioned: he loved plainchant and hated Wagner, a difference in taste setting him off from the ardent Wagnerian and Bruckner student Ehrenfels. As an academic polemicist Brentano was quick to take offense and did not readily forgive or try to understand those of his students – the majority – who strayed from the assigned path. As his at times intemperate correspondence with Marty makes clear, had he remained in a position of power and influence in Vienna he might well have become, as Rudolf Haller once remarked, "an impossible tyrant."

After Brentano's death his second generation followers Kraus and Kastil, assisted by generous funding from the new Czechoslovak state, whose first President was Brentano's former student Masaryk, set about organizing and publishing his copious and chaotic *Nachlass*. This caused many more of Brentano's words to enter the public domain, and in some cases, such as in the publication of lecture notes, these were relatively unproblematic. On the other hand, Brentano, realizing that his writings were a mess, explicitly gave his editors *carte blanche* to work with his *Nachlass* in the way Jeremy Bentham's nephew had dealt with his similarly chaotic leavings, by a process which can euphemistically be called "creative editing."

The problems caused by the editors' way of going about this are still with us, in two senses. Firstly, many of the actually published texts are compilations of pieces drawn from different places and periods, put together to give the appearance of a coherent treatise, but in fact no such thing. In some cases, such as the compilation on logic called *Die Lehre vom richtigen Urteil* (*The Theory of Correct Judgement*), edited by Franziska Mayer-Hillebrand and published in 1956, the complication gives a drastically misleading picture of Brentano's thought on the subject, lending it a spurious unity and coherence. The second and not unconnected problem is that Brentano's views underwent a long, complex and tortuous development, resulting in him abandoning or repudiating earlier positions, but sometimes also going back to earlier positions after reconsideration. Without a suitably chronological trail through Brentano's thinking, which is completely covered up by the attempt to provide coherent and convincing unified presentations, we remain largely in the dark about his motives for changing his mind. In this he is very unlike, say, Bertrand Russell, whose similarly copious and radical changes of mind are much more publicly documented in virtue of his fluency and productivity as a writer. The fragmentary nature of Brentano's writings as his eyesight deteriorated also increased the problems, as did his practice of reusing lecture notes more than once and introducing copious revisions and annotations to his manuscripts at different times. The problem is similar to, but if anything worse than, the problem that faced the Wittgenstein *Nachlass*. There is even a genetic link between the two cases, in that Wittgenstein's literary executor Rush Rhees had been in earlier times a Brentanist, and had spent time at Innsbruck with Alfred Kastil, presumably observing Kastil's cut-and-paste editorial methods.

After his death, Brentano's *Nachlass* passed into the possession of his son John, who had trained in Germany as a physicist and worked in Zurich, Manchester and finally at Northwestern University in Evanston, Illinois. Parts of it went to Innsbruck (Kastil) and Prague (Kraus) for working into publication, but after the Second World War John Brentano gathered the manuscripts together and deposited them in the Houghton Library at Harvard, where they were catalogued by Franziska Mayer-Hillebrand and partly microfilmed by John and his wife Sophie. John also set up a foundation to propagate his father's work, and this was led for many years by the eminent philosopher Roderick Chisholm, who assiduously promoted Brentanian ideas and organized further publications and translation into English. In time it became apparent that the only way to preserve Brentano's writings, which were written on highly acidic and rapidly deteriorating paper, was to digitally photograph them, and this work has been largely completed with support from the Brentano Foundation. In the course of this work Mayer-Hillebrand's defective catalogue was revised, enlarged and much improved by Thomas Binder. The more exacting work of transcribing the complex manuscripts into a publishable form, whether print or online, remains to be done. Until much of this writing is in the public domain, any summative assessment of Brentano's philosophy and its complex development will remain interim and incomplete.

Metaphysics

For much of his life, Brentano's primary philosophical interest was metaphysics. This is closely connected with his early work on Aristotle's categories, which constitute the primary divisions of being. Brentano retained throughout his life a concern for the importance of categories, but he radically revised his opinion of which ones are to be employed. Later writings, collected together by Kastil and published in 1933 under the title *Kategorienlehre* (*Theory of Categories*) are critical of Aristotle. These writings are in truth not just about categories, but comprise Brentano's later ontology.

Brentano's metaphysics has very few fixed points throughout his long development. He remained a metaphysical dualist in the Cartesian sense, believing in mental and material substances. He also retained his belief in God despite the loss of his specifically Christian faith. Another feature that remains constant is his acceptance of the Aristotelian distinction between substance and accident, although its interpretation shifts. Finally Brentano remains wedded throughout his career to a conviction of the philosophical importance of the concepts of part and whole and their cognates, of what was to become known as mereology. This is apparent not only in his 1862 dissertation: it is prominent in his Würzburg metaphysics lectures of 1867, repeated in Vienna in 1874, where he speaks of logical parts and metaphysical parts. A logical part of a species is for example its genus or specific difference, so *animal* and *rational* are logical parts of the species *human*. At this stage Brentano agrees with Aristotle that when a substance changes, e.g. when a green apple becomes red, the apple loses an accident or metaphysical part, the greenness, this being replaced by another metaphysical part, the redness, without detriment to the existence and identity of the apple. The theory of part and whole is also prominent in the middle-period lectures on descriptive psychology, and is especially prominent in Brentano's late reism. In this regard Brentano's views seem to speak to us across the decades, since mereological considerations play a much larger part in contemporary metaphysics than they did during the heyday of the linguistic turn, a turn of which Brentano would have thoroughly disapproved.

Brentano's early metaphysics is basically Aristotelian, but he is less convincedly realist than Aristotle, being influenced by Descartes and the British empiricists to consider the existence of the external world uncertain by comparison with the certain existence of myself revealed by introspection. In his middle period, particularly in his work on truth, he appears to swing towards a more expansive ontology comprising something like states of affairs or propositions, what he calls judgement-contents, whose existence or non-existence may be employed to account for truth as correspondence in traditional Aristotelian-scholastic fashion. This is despite the fact that he continued to stress the importance of *Evidenz*, intuitive self-givenness, as the ultimate touchstone of truth and our knowledge of truth. Brentano's middle lectures also seem to lean slightly towards the theory later made notorious by Twardowski and Meinong that some of the objects we think about do not exist. Certainly Brentano later both repudiated this theory severely and claimed that his middle students had plagiarized it from him, but in truth his pronouncements on the subject are sufficiently vague to allow of several interpretations.

The most dramatic phase of development in Brentano's philosophy comes after about 1904, when he progressively worked out an extremely lean ontological position he called *reism*, according to which the only things that exist are concrete individuals, whether material, mental, or divine. Reism, as its name implies, acknowledges only (concrete) things. There are on this view no universals, propositions, states of affairs, events, properties, relations, abstract objects, or any other of a host of items beloved of philosophers. Reism had been foreshadowed by certain medieval nominalists, but never explicitly upheld for fear that it would render them heretically unable to explain the miracle of eucharistic transsubstantiation. Brentano as an ex-Christian was free of that fear. Subsequently, a more extreme materialistic form of reism was formulated independently by the Polish philosopher (and grand-pupil of Brentano) Tadeusz Kotarbiński, who acknowledged Brentano's priority when the coincidence was pointed out to him.

Reism has never had many followers because it is difficult for a reist to explain such elementary phenomena as predication and change. A scholastic nominalist (or Aristotle for that matter) can account for change and accidental predication using dependent accidents or tropes, as they became known: the apple is truly green because a trope of greenness inheres among its other parts, and its changing to red consists in the substitution of a redness trope for a greenness trope. Kotarbinski's reism lacks tropes as they are not material bodies, and late Brentano does not accept them as things. But Brentano's version of reism does have a way to explain change and true predication. Rather than the accident being a (dependent or metaphysical) part of the substance, Brentano reverses the mereology: the red apple is a whole of which the apple is a proper part. Because the red apple exists (and because existential judgments are prior to predicatory ones for Brentano), 'the apple is red' is true. The color change consists in a green apple containing the apple going out of existence to be replaced by a red apple, the apple *simpliciter* existing throughout as a proper part successively of the two larger wholes. Brentano's use of the term 'accident' has a precedent in Aristotle, where such things as the red apple or musical Coriscus are termed 'accidental unities'. Brentano uses this new mereology of concrete things also to give a new account of the mental, of which more below. The respect in which Brentano's theory is definitely non-standard is that he denies the principle of mereology that a proper part must go together with a disjoint supplementary part to make up a whole. Nevertheless, the theory is ingenious and while revisionist, not easy to catch in inconsistency.

Brentano uses his reistic theory to account for our talk of relations, denying them ontological status. In the truth that John is taller than Mary we have a substance, John, and an accident, John-being-taller-than-Mary, where the latter is itself a thing, what Brentano calls relative-like, *ein Relativliches*. In this, the apparent reference to Mary herself is in fact ontologically non-commital or *oblique*. The reason is that John is also taller than Rumpelstiltskin, though there is no Rumpelstiltskin. To express the existence of Mary and her "relation" to John we have to form a true existential judgement: Mary-shorter-than-John exists. This has Mary as a proper part. The "real" relatedness of actually existing John and actually existing Mary is to be expressed by the conjunction of these two existential propositions. It goes without saying that this theory of relations is highly questionable.

The reistic theory of substance and accident is also turned to a final elucidation of the concept of mental intentionality (see below).

Another interesting area of Brentano's late philosophy is his theory of space, time, and the continuum. Brentano followed Aristotle's idea of boundaries as things which are inseparable parts of the things they bound, and developed a complex theory of the properties of parts of boundaries, for example claiming that the infinitesimally thin boundary between a red and a blue surface can be said to be red on one side and blue on the other. Brentano's theory rejected by then prevalent Cantorian accounts of continuity in a way which was taken up independently by such diverse thinkers as Whitehead and Karl Menger Jr. Brentano accepted absolute space, a stance echoed by his grandstudent Kraus in forlorn and near-hysterical criticisms of Einstein. In his final phase Brentano comes close to accepting Kelvin's idea of a moving body as a congeries of qualities successively occupying neighboring locations, akin to the way in which an image moves across the pixels of a display screen. While this remains a thought-experiment, had Brentano fully gone along with it, it would have somewhat undermined the materialistic leg of his dualistic reism, leaving absolute places as the non-mental substances.

Psychology

The work which made Brentano famous and which remains his best known is the book *Psychology from an Empirical Standpoint*. In this book Brentano famously reintroduced to philosophy the Aristotelian–Scholastic concept of the intentionality of the mental. We shall consider this in a moment. It is worth remarking however, that the work as it appeared in 1874 represented only a third of the planned treatise. The 1874 edition and subsequent translations contain only books 1 and 2 out of six that were planned. Book 1 is about Psychology as a science and book 2 is about the primary division or classification of the mental. Three further books were to have dealt in greater detail with the three main classes of mental phenomena, while a final book would have dealt with metaphysical issues such as the mind–body problem and the immortality of the soul. That these metaphysical matters, traditionally central in the philosophy of mind, were to be delayed until the end, was part of Brentano's plan to develop psychology in a way which stayed close to the given phenomena and eschewed metaphysical controversy. This was the point of the otherwise puzzling designation "empirical." This derived from Comte, whose positivistic philosophy Brentano had studied, and whose method of avoiding metaphysics he was here adopting, at least for most of the treatise. By "empirical" Brentano did not mean "experimental," but "based on experience." Brentano did not discount the importance of experimental investigation in psychology. Indeed he did carry out some fairly modest demonstrations. Had he remained a professor in Vienna there is little doubt he would have obtained funding for experimental psychology at the university. As it was, Austria did not get a psychology laboratory and institute until 1894, when Meinong opened one in Graz. So Brentano's fall from grace resulted in Austria falling far behind Germany in experimental psychology, where Wundt's laboratory in Leipzig, founded in the 1870s, led the world.

The antecedents for Brentano's thinking about psychology were the British empiricists, the scholastics, Descartes, and, as ever, Aristotle. Indeed it was in his previous book *Die Psychologie des Aristoteles, insbesondere seine Lehre des* nous poietikos (*The Psychology of Aristotle, in particular his theory of the* nous poietikos), that Brentano first discussed the theory of intentional inexistence, though not under this name. His starting point was the Aristotelian account of sensation and thinking in *De anima*, particularly as filtered through the commentaries of Thomas Aquinas.

In the nineteenth century psychology had not yet emerged as an independent discipline, and there were methodological differences between those who wanted to treat it as solely an objective experimental science dependent on physiology, and those who wanted to preserve a subjective experiential component. Brentano, with his philosophical background, was a major proponent of the later approach. In this regard it was crucial for him to establish the subject matter of the science of psychology and demarcate psychology from physiology. This was the task of book 1 of the *Psychology*.

Sciences may differ in subject matter or in method, or in both. For example mathematics differs from physics in both subject matter and method, while chemistry differs from biology in subject matter but not in method. Brentano in his habilitation theses of 1866 had defended the proposition that the proper method of philosophy does not differ from that of the natural sciences. So whether or not it had a philosophical component, psychology would not differ in method from physiology. Hence to uphold the autonomy of psychology as a science Brentano needed it to differ in subject matter.

There are several ways in which psychology's subject matter, the mental, may be held to differ from others, in particular from human physiology. One is that mental events and processes have as their bearer not the material body but the immaterial soul. Brentano as a Cartesian dualist in fact accepted this. But to make this the basis of the demarcation would have been to entangle psychology in metaphysical controversy from the start, something which Brentano, despite his Aristotelian leanings, was anxious to avoid. Under the influence of the British empiricist philosophers and the French positivist Auguste Comte, he considered a science should deal with *phenomena* and not with metaphysically disputable entities such as an immaterial soul. These phenomena are what we experience, and this is the source of the epithet "empirical" in his book's title. Another characterization of mental processes is that they are thought to be in time but not in space, whereas physical processes are in both time and space. Again, as a dualist Brentano did not deny this, but again it is metaphysically loaded. Further, it defines or demarcates the subject by a partly negative definition, things *not* in space. As a matter of proper definition Brentano held this to be unacceptable. Therefore he fixed on a third, positive characteristic, that of intentionality.

The roots of the notion of intentionality go back to Aristotle. In *De anima* Aristotle theorized that perception and thought consists in the mind taking on the form of a perceived or thought object without its matter. Thus when I see red apple the forms of redness, roundness, shininess, etc., which in the apple are really embodied in matter, exist in the mind divorced from matter, and in this way I mentally apprehend the apple and its characters. This means that when I have an idea of or think about something, that something is in a certain sense literally within my soul, or within my thought. Medieval Arabic commentators on Aristotle compared the relationship to that of an archer drawing a bow at a target, and their simile affected the Latin terminology, *intentio*, deriving from *tensio*, the drawing of the bow, being used by Aquinas and other scholastics. At the same time the form's being in the mind gave rise to the term "in-existence," meaning not "non-existence" but "existence-in." This is the origin of Brentano's term for the characteristically mental relationship of *intentional in-existence*.

At the time of writing the *Psychology* Brentano, under the influence both of Cartesian skepticism about the security of our knowledge about an external world, and the positivist credo to confine scientific investigation to what is unproblematically given, formulated the intentionalist criterion in terms of phenomena. This was not simply a form of words: phenomena are what appear to the individual person, and by Cartesian standards they are secure from skeptical doubt. Brentano thus proceeds to outline a distinction between two kinds of phenomena, physical and mental. Here is the passage in which he broaches the criterion:

> Every mental phenomenon is characterized by what the scholastics of the Middle Ages called the intentional (or mental) *in-existence* of an object and what we might call, though not wholly unambiguously, the reference to a content, a *direction towards an object* (which is not to be understood here as meaning a thing), or an immanent objectivity. Each mental phenomenon includes something as object within itself, although they do not all do so in the same way. In presentation something is presented, in judgment something is affirmed or denied, in love loved, in hate hated, in desire desired, and so on. This intentional in-existence is characteristic exclusively of mental phenomena. No physical phenomenon exhibits anything like it. We can, therefore, define mental phenomena by saying that they are those phenomena which contain an object intentionally within themselves. (Brentano 1973: 88)

The demarcation is thus one between physical phenomena, which simply are as they are and have a certain experienced character, and mental phenomena, which have both a character and a further component, the object or content. Famous as it is, this passage has been grievously misinterpreted on many occasions. It is anachronistic to read back into this early statement either an ontological distinction between mental and physical entities in general, or a distinction between a mental event and an external object, like my perception of the apple and the apple itself. At this stage Brentano is simply subclassifying phenomena, which are all themselves given to individual subjects. A physical phenomenon is not a physical object, independent of us, but what we would now consider the mental representation of a physical object. The object or content of a mental phenomenon is literally contained within it, as a part, though as Brentano notes the forms of containment may vary, and we will see how. This immanentist reading of the phenomenon–object distinction was not stable, even terminologically, and it is not even clear whether Brentano himself subscribed to it wholeheartedly: several of his remarks suggest a less immanentistic reading, even at this early stage. But it is the understanding which is closest to the spirit and letter of the passage, whatever Brentano's or others' misgivings about it later.

Brentano often uses the term "mental act" for mental phenomena. This usage survives the transmutation of intentionality from an immanentist to a realist understanding, and has passed into general terminology via Husserl and others. The term does not connote action or activity on the part of the subject but simply actuality, the opposite of potentiality. It is a scholastic term. It means that Brentano is describing not mental dispositions such as beliefs, which might be considered mere potentialities (to judge or assert), but occurrent mental events.

Given the intentional inexistence of contents in mental phenomena as a defining mark of these over against physical phenomena, the next question is whether all contents inhabit their acts in the same way. Brentano's opinion, as the quoted passage says, is that they do not. The simplest relationship is that between a mental act and a content which is simply and immediately contained in it, and which itself has no further complexity. This is the case of *presentation* (*Vorstellung*). "Vorstellung" is Wolff's concocted term for the Cartesian–Lockean notion of an idea, and like the English word "presentation" it is ambiguous between the act or event on the one hand and the relation between the act and its content/object on the other. These are just two of many senses which were exhaustively separated some years later by Husserl. I shall generally prefer the term "idea."

Brentano's chief complaint about the Cartesian–Lockean notion of idea, carried forward by the other British empiricists, is that it ignores intentional inexistence. An idea is not just an idea: it is an idea-of something. Ignoring this is what made it possible for Locke to slide between treating ideas as mental on the one hand and as composing real objects on the other, and Berkeley to regard complexes of ideas as the very everyday things we perceive. So for Brentano an idea is an act, but it also has a content/object, in a simple and direct way, contained within it. Vorstellung is indeed the most basic kind of mental act, and the foundation for all the others. In an idea, something is simply placed before the mind: a colour, a smell for instance. The colour or smell is itself a physical phenomenon, but its being included in an idea as content makes the idea a mental phenomenon.

Next in complexity comes judgement. A judgement (*Urteil*) is itself also an act, but one in which the subject takes up a cognitive stance, yes or no, to something. The something is the content of a presentation or idea. For example when I look out of the window and judge that the sky is blue, I am taking up a positive cognitive stance to blue sky out there. This positive stance Brentano calls *accepting* (*anerkennen*). It has a negative counterpart, rejecting (*verwerfen*), as when I reject (for example) unicorns or boy wizards. To judge is always to accept or reject something, and what I accept or reject is something presented in an idea. So when I reject boy wizards, I have to have an idea of a boy wizard in order for me to take up the rejecting attitude. Since there really are no boy wizards, the content of an idea need not be the content of anything external that has real existence, yet the content is still mentally present. This is in fact the origin of Husserl's later transcendental phenomenological reduction, as well as the theories of objects of Twardowski and Meinong.

In ordinary language we tend not to express judgements in a way transparent to their nature as conceived by Brentano. We don't say "Blue sky outside – yes!" or "Boy wizards – no!" but rather something much smoother, like "There is a blue sky outside," or "Boy wizards don't exist." Brentano's view of judgements then is that acceptance and rejection are what we standardly express as positive and negative existential judgements. It might seem that existential judgements are rather rare and even exotic, philosophical fare rather than that of the man or woman on the street. But Brentano has two reasons for denying this. The first is that judgements are in fact very common, because most of our conscious waking life is taken up with perception, and perception is typically a positive existential judging of what is presented to us through the senses. We don't isolate these judgements as atomic judgings in the way we might express an existential sentence, but simply "go with the flow" of ideas, endowing the contents of our sensings by default with a blanket positive acceptance, only disturbed by striking exceptions or situations of sensory poverty, like seeing in the fog or listening for a barely discernible rustle in the grass. To find a "naked" idea unjudged is the exception. Secondly, Brentano is not one to conform his theory of mind to the grain of language. This arm's-length attitude to language is one which became much more obvious and prevalent in Brentano's late, *sprachkritisch* phase, but it is already latent in his early work.

The primacy of existential judgement over other forms, in particular over traditional subject–predicate form, is one which Brentano adopted early and from which he did not deviate. He argues in correspondence with John Stuart Mill that existential judgements, including negative ones like "No boy wizards exist" and meteorological and other subjectless predications like "It's hot" or "It's snowing" are irreducible to subject–predicate judgements. On the contrary, traditional categorical judgements like "All men are mortal," "Some men are red-haired" are reducible via nominal conjunction and negation to positive and negative existential judgement, "There are no immortal men," "There are red-haired men." This reduction formed the basis of Brentano's modest reform of traditional logic, of which more below.

The third way in which a content can be in a mental act is when we take a non-cognitive attitude towards it. This may be in emotion or desire. All of these kinds of act are classed together by Brentano as "phenomena of love or hate," an unsnappy expression he later sometimes substituted by "interests" or "affects" (*Gemüts bewegungen*). For example I see a glass of Guinness on the table in front of me and form the desire to drink it: I take up a positive affective or desiderative attitude to the content myself-being-about-to-drink-this-Guinness. I then drink it and enjoy it: I take up a positive or liking attitude to this currently accepted cold-bitter-drink-in-my-throat idea. But I dislike the price: an attitude of dislike to the judgement me-having-paid-so-much-for-this-Guinness.

Brentano's third class of affects was not widely accepted: although Marty and some others accepted it, most of his students preferred to distinguish emotive from desiderative acts as a basic distinction alongside that between ideas and judgements. In this they were following Kant and other philosophers. Another area of mental life that is surprisingly underemphasized by Brentano is the conative or voluntative side:

the mental acts by which we act physically, walking, talking, and so on. In the period of the 1860s and 1870s this might be accounted for by Brentano's general skepticism about our knowledge of the external world, coupled to his Cartesian dualism of mind and body, but once his philosophy began to take on a more common-sense realist tone the omission of action and volition became a glaring gap.

The contortions of linguistic representation aside, Brentano's classification of mental phenomena into three broad classes of ideas, judgements and affects is nothing new: it is to be found in Descartes, who called the whole overarching class "thoughts" (*cogitationes*). In general, affects presuppose judgements and judgements presuppose ideas. A few affects may be non-judgemental, based on ideas directly, but they are the exception. Without exception though, every mental act is either an idea or presupposes ideas. This indeed is a possible characterization of the mental in general, but being disjunctive and relying on the antecedent notion of idea, Brentano did not make it his definition.

Taking the broadest perspective, the project of the *Psychology* is predominantly a taxonomic one, a fact emphasized by Brentano's renaming of the second book of the *Psychology* in the 1911 second edition edited by Oskar Kraus: there it became *On the Classification of Mental Phenomena*. This taxonomic framework sets Brentano's endeavor in the context of Descartes, Spinoza and the British empiricists, as well as other psychological philosophers like Bain and Mill. The role of intentionality as the mark of the mental is as it were artificially prominent because of the fact that only books 1 and 2 of the six envisaged appeared, so it looms larger than it might have done had the full treatise appeared. After Brentano's death, text intended for the third part appeared, edited by Kraus, under the title *Vom sinnlichen und noetischen Bewußtsein* (*On Sensory and Noetic Consciousness*).

Descriptive and genetic

The psychology of the *Psychology* was what we would nowadays call philosophy of mind: concerned with definitional, demarcation and classification of the mental. Despite the title "empirical," Brentano did not offer evidence from any other source of experience than our own reflection on the nature of the mental, a reflection he claimed was possible because every mental act is incidentally self-presenting. In this way he is a true precursor of phenomenology. But he was obviously not unaware of the rise of experimental psychology under Wilhelm Wundt and others in Germany. He occasionally gave rudimentary demonstrations in class, but whatever his interests might have been in transplanting experimental psychology to Austria-Hungary, the loss of his professorship put paid to any plans he might have had. The Austrian education ministry was both less wealthy and less progressive than its German counterparts, and Austria's first psychology laboratory did not get started until 1894 in Graz, under Brentano's former student Meinong.

From around 1880, Brentano began to distinguish between *a priori* facts about the mind and its acts and contents, as instanced in the *Psychology*, and the empirical investigation of causal regularities and successions. He called the former "descriptive psychology" or "psychognosy" and the latter "genetic psychology" because it studies the causal sequence of mental occurrences, and what comes after what. In the 1890s he occasionally used the word "phenomenology" for descriptive psychology, and this is probably where Husserl and others got the word, although it had been used previously by Lambert and Hegel. When "phenomenology" became popular for Husserl's version of philosophical psychology, Brentano rather childishly resorted to "phenomenognosy" for his own version, a term which fortunately failed to catch on. Texts from Brentano's lectures on the subject from 1887/88, 1888/89 and 1890/91 were later edited by Roderick Chisholm and Wilhelm Baumgartner, and appeared as *Deskriptive Psychologie* in 1982. In these lectures Brentano again goes over the questions of classification and method, paying particular attention to questions of the mereology of mental acts. He distinguishes between separable and inseparable parts, a distinction which had been broached by Carl Stumpf in the 1870s and would become generally known through Husserl's *Logical Investigations* in 1901.

In his theory of the mental, as in all other aspects of his philosophy, Brentano's thought underwent a complex development whose detail has yet to be traced. In his middle years he is inclined towards a realism which is opposed to the early immanentist treatment of mental acts and their contents/objects. In the 1890s, whether autonomously or prompted by critiques of Höfler and Meinong, he begins to make a clear distinction between the mental *content* of an act and its (normally) extramental object, a distinction cemented by Twardowski in 1894 and subsequently accepted by nearly everyone, including Meinong and Husserl. Brentano was also more inclined in these middle years to consider judgements to have their own kind of object, called (unhappily) "judgement content" (*Urteilsinhalt*), and widely taken as a precursor or rudimentary version of Meinong's objectives and Stumpf's and Husserl's states of affairs. The extent to which these middle students took the idea from Brentano and the extent to which they worked them out for themselves is still not clear, and investigation is not helped by accusations of intellectual theft from Brentano and his second-generation students that at times border on the hysterical. Another aspect of the middle period was a relatively easy-going tendency to talk of acts having objects that did not exist, again something that looms large in Twardowski and Meinong, but which Brentano swiftly reined in for his own part.

As Brentano's later philosophy began to develop after the turn of the twentieth century, his views on mental acts and their objects and contents swung back in certain respects towards the non-realist position of the early psychology. In the context of his later reism, mental acts, being relatively fleeting and dependent, were treated as at best abstractions or fictions. The only really existent entities were things, including mental things or souls. When I see the red apple, there may well be a real material thing, the red apple, but now there is no separate item called the seeing, or its content. Rather, there is the object which is me-the-apple-seer, or me-*qua*-seeing-the-apple. This object, which contains me myself, the soul, but does not have any supplementary parts making up the difference, is what Brentano calls an accident of the substance which is the simple soul. When I stop seeing the apple, the accident ceases to exist. In the description of the situation as the existence of me-the-apple-seer, the reference to me is genuine and substantial, but the apple is mentioned only indirectly or obliquely, *modo obliquo*, to use Brentano's scholastic term: it is there to make up the description of the content. So it is possible for me to hallucinate a pink apple or think of a boy wizard when there is no such thing, and the description of me as pink-apple-seer or boy-wizard-accepter does not commit anyone to the actual existence of pink apples or boy wizards.

In its final phase then, intentionality becomes a referential device, mentioning *modo obliquo* a descriptive aspect of what a person is a part of when they think, present, judge, love, etc. This is radically different from both the immanentist and the realist phases. So we see that intentionality in Brentano undergoes a complex development, even while it retains its role throughout as the touchstone of the mental.

Logic, truth and language

Brentano was not in the first instance either a logician or a philosopher of language. Language he largely left to his trusty lieutenant Anton Marty, who duly produced a Brentanian philosophy of language, albeit one so embedded in polemic that it is difficult to extract the positive content. Nor was Brentano part of the great logical renaissance and revolution of his time. He completely ignored the advances of mathematical logic, having (rightly) taken umbrage at the Scottish William Hamilton's quantification of the predicate and (wrongly) assuming any mathematical logic would have to embody the same mistake. Nevertheless Brentano's psychology of judgement gave him a perspective on standard syllogistic which was interesting in several ways, and which led him to a modest but elegant reform of Aristotelian logic.

For Aristotle and traditional logic, statements have the form of subject–predicate. A predicate is affirmed or denied of a subject, whether the subject is singular, universal or particular. Brentano's theory of judgement made existential statements prior to predicational ones, as explained above. This has one immediate effect: that the subject-term of a universal proposition like "All cats are carnivores" carries no existential import, since its reduced form "There are no non-carnivorous cats" is true if there are no cats at all. The easiest way to bring the import back is to assert it directly: "There are cats," and conjoin this to the previous proposition, but Brentano also later allows what he calls "double judgements," which acknowledge a subject and secondarily attribute something to the subject so accepted, roughly "There are cats, none of which are non-carnivores." This doctrine is not logically required and is merely a sop to tradition.

To make his term logic work, Brentano first introduces a number of rules for working with terms, e.g. that "red apple" and "apple that is red" mean the same, so the order of terms can be switched, that repetitions and double negations may be eliminated, e.g. red red apple = red apple, non-non-cat = cat. Next he introduces rules for adding terms to negative existentials and dropping them from positive, so the inference "There are no boy wizards, therefore there are no flying boy wizards" is valid, as is "There are poisonous caterpillars, therefore there are caterpillars." He also has two-premise rules which validate inferences involving a term and its negation:

"There are no flying boy wizards and there are no non-flying boy wizards, therefore there are no boy wizards" is one which rejects a term by exhausting both cases, and its partial contrapositive "There are dolphins and there are no purple dolphins, therefore there are non-purple dolphins." Using these rules it is very easy to show that all classical syllogistic inferences are valid, whether the nineteen which are valid without existential import, or the additional ones which require existential import, validated by adding the existential propositions as explicit premises. In addition to these inference rules Brentano has a few simple axioms, notable "*a = a*" and "there is no *a* non-*a*," the former being a law of identity and the latter a law of non-contradiction. The whole system is very simple, and Brentano presents it using a simple notation. He also shows how by treating propositions as fictitious objects one may simulate inferences of propositional logic in the same framework. Although these ideas were not published by Brentano during his lifetime, and only appeared in 1956 in the compilation by Franziska Mayer-Hillebrand, Brentano's student Franz Hillebrand (husband of the former) published a summary in 1891 entitled *Die neuen Theorien der kategorischen Schlüsse* (The new theories of categorial inference). It had little effect on the development of logic.

Brentano's theory of truth is an especially tangled story. He did hold to something like the Aristotelian theory of correspondence early in his work, so that a judgement "There are rabbits" is true if indeed there are rabbits. Brentano expressed this by saying that a judgement to the effect that there are rabbits is *correct* (*richtig*) whereas one to the effect that there are no rabbits is *incorrect* (*unrichtig*). The rabbits themselves are what guarantee the truth, or are, as is now said, *truthmakers* for the judgement. But Brentano was always concerned to ensure the epistemological transparency of truth where possible. He therefore stressed that the most secure truths are those which are self-evident (*evident*). These include the truths of mathematics and logic, which are analytic and therefore do not correspond to anything. Their correctness is guaranteed not by their correspondence but by their *Evidenz*. All evidently correct judgements are by definition true, all evidently incorrect ones by definition false. Some evident judgements are *a posteriori*, for example the correct judgement that I am now thinking about Brentano's theory of truth. This correctness is guaranteed by the infallibility of inner perception, a Cartesian notion upheld by Brentano. So correspondence only comes to bear for *a posteriori* and non-evident propositions and judgements. In his middle period Brentano is inclined to accept special correlates of judgement, e.g. John's loving Mary as the correspondent judgement-content rendering the judgement "John loves Mary" true. Nearly all of Brentano's students maintain this line, including the otherwise fiercely loyal Marty. But in the wake of his reistic turn and rejection of all abstract entities, including judgement-contents, Brentano fully rejects the last remnants of the correspondence theory and reverts to *Evidenz* alone: a correct judgement is one that is *evident* or one which would be judged so by someone judging with *Evidenz* about the matter in question (e.g. God). Indeed since in the final throes of reism even judgements are rejected, the theory of correctness and incorrectness becomes a theory about judgers, who are judging persons, accidents of persons. A correctly judging snow-is-white judger is an evidently-judging snow-is-white judger or a snow-is-white-judger judging as would an evidently-judging snow-is-white judger. Whether these contortions remove all doubts about truth is a moot point.

While as mentioned Brentano did not specialize in the philosophy of language (indeed Marty was perhaps the first specialist philosopher of language), he did perforce have certain opinions about language, which became more marked with time. As would be expected of someone whose views led him to express himself in ways which are to say the least linguistically unharmonious, he considered that ordinary ways of speaking lead the unwary astray, into treating the subject–predicate form of expression as sacrosanct and basic, and in particular into employing all manner of abstract nouns and complex phrases that seem to denote all manner of abstract, ideal and theoretical entities, such as numbers, universals, states of affairs, propositions and the like. Anticipating later ideas of analytic philosophers, Brentano advocated a critique of language (*Sprachkritik*) which aimed to replace misleading forms of expression purporting to designate *irrealia* by ones referring only to concrete individuals. The flavour of his paraphrases may be gathered from some of the examples given earlier. While it is extremely doubtful that this project can succeed if we demand synonymy between the original and the reduced expression, it is not clear that Brentano expected synonymy to hold, or indeed whether we should. In any case, unlike Marty, Brentano had rather little interest in language for its own sake, so his project remains a sketch only.

Practical philosophy

The lectures by which Brentano was best known in Vienna, which brought him contemporary fame and following, were those on ethics or practical philosophy, published in 1952 as *Grundlegung und Aufbau der Ethik* (*Foundation and Construction of Ethics*). This dealt with a wide range of issues including hedonism, freedom of the will, and the difference betweic and personal morality. During his lifetime however, only one piece appeared which gained notice, the lecture "Vom Ursprung sittlicher Erkennthis" ("On the Origin of Moral Knowledge"). Delivered in Vienna in 1889 and published the same year, it subsequently appeared in English translation in 1902, when its strongly influenced the young G. E. Moore. The *Ursprung* bears a relation to the longer work similar to that which Kant's *Grundlegung* bears to the second Critique: it is shorter, clearer, and more accessible.

Brentano's theory of ethics is based on his psychology in just the same way as is his logic. As logic is concerned with correct judgement, so ethics is concerned with correct love and hate. To those who might object to the words "correct" and "incorrect" in this context we must point out that Brentano is neither a subjectivist nor a relativist about ethics, but nor is he a cognitivist – trivially, since love and hate are not cognitive attitudes. The terms "correct" and "incorrect" do not mean the same in connection with affects that they do in connection with judgement, but they are used because of their suggestiveness. The discrepancies go further. In judgement there is no such thing as one true judgement being more correct than another true judgement, even if one is judged with *Evidenz* and the other not. As truths, they are equal. By contrast, one thing may be more loveworthy or more hateworthy than another, for example killing a pig is less hateworthy than killing a person. So there is not only correct love and correct hate, there is also correct preference: it is correct to prefer killing a pig to killing a person, or to put it less positively, it is incorrect to prefer killing a person to killing a pig. Some things are in themselves neither loveworthy nor hateworthy but neutral. In ethics then, unlike logic, there is no excluded middle, and there are degrees of goodness and badness.

Brentano is not afraid to lay the foundation of ethics with some truisms, e.g. that it is correct to prefer pleasure to suffering, or that it is *evident* that more of a good thing is better than less of it, or that less of a bad thing is better than more of it. These truisms and the analogy between cognition and affect in regard to correctness are very suggestive to modern ears: it is as if Brentano is at the threshold of a logic of preference, or of deontic logic. Indeed this was so: Brentano's students Ehrenfels and Meinong both took steps in the direction of a formal theory of value, and Meinong's student Ernst Mally presented the first (albeit defective) deontic logic.

Just as he is unwilling to reify propositions or states of affairs as abstract entities, so Brentano is unwilling to reify values such as goodness or beauty, and this unwillingness became categorical during the final reistic phase of his thought. Brentano is thus an objectivist about valuing while not being an objectivist about values. Things have positive value which are correctly loved, and have negative value which are correctly hated: they are not correctly loved because they have positive value or correctly hated because they have negative value. As with judgement, correctness of love, hate and preference is grounded through cases which are *evident*: these include truisms like those mentioned above p. 851. Again as with judgement, some affects are not experienced as *evident*: for example it is not evidently correct to be vegetarian, i.e. to hate one's eating meat. But it might nevertheless *be* correct to be vegetarian. It would be so if someone in the advantageous position to have affects regarding meat-eating with *Evidenz* would hate meat-eating. Such a person might be a better-informed or more sensitive human being: in default of there actually being such a one, God always loves and hates correctly and with *Evidenz*. So God is an affective as well as a cognitive being, as is particularly clearly portrayed in the Old Testament. For this reason also, Brentano contends that God exists in time. While things are not good simply *because* God loves them, because God always loves with *Evidenz*, he never loves anything not good, so we cannot go wrong if we love and hate as God does.

Brentano raises the question whether there is anything that is good (loveworthy) or bad (hateworthy) in its own right or intrinsically: a very modern question. He answers that it is so: pleasure, knowledge and correct love or hate are intrinsically good, while pain, ignorance and incorrect love or hate are intrinsically bad. All these intrinsic and primary goods are mental in kind. Other goods, such as health, wealth and honour, are secondary: good because of their effects or because they are conducive to increasing intrinsic good and decreasing intrinsic evil. Because of this pluralism of goods and evils, Brentano is no hedonist, though he acknowledges the partial truth of hedonism. His support of pleasure is not without exception: somewhat problematically he contends that *Schadenfreude*, pleasure in what is bad such as the suffering of others, is not intrinsically good. When it comes to what we should do in life, what Brentano calls the practical good, his answer is broadly utilitarian: we should strive to produce and increase that which is good and prevent or decrease that which is bad, to the greatest extent we can, compatibly with our own continued life and welfare and that of our kindred, friends, other human beings and other creatures, in concentric circles (Brentano is not a rigorist: he does not insist on inhuman efforts to do the right thing).

Brentano on the history of philosophy

During his lifetime, Brentano's most numerous publications concern the history of philosophy, his dissertation, habilitation and three further monographs on aspects of Aristotle's thought. He constantly took his bearings from his predecessors, though he owned to no teacher in the strict sense, Aristotle excepted. His heroes included not just Aristotle but also Augustine, Aquinas, Descartes and the British empiricists, though he disliked Hume's skepticism as he disliked that of Ockham. His villains were Kant and the post-Kantian German idealists, but also earlier dogmatists and mystics. The loves and hates were systematic, and Brentano formulated the scheme behind them as his Four Phases of Philosophy. Whereas most historians of philosophy either saw a past golden age (as did Hegel, and later Heidegger), or were unashamed progressivists (such as Comte and many analytic philosophers), Brentano's view is more interesting and complex. He claimed to see a cyclical development in philosophy, cycles of advance and retreat in four phases. In the first phase philosophy is dominated by high theory; in the second practical concerns become prevalent; the third is where skepticism gains the upper hand; while the fourth confronts skepticism with dogmatic and mystical affirmations. Three times the circle had passed around, from the pre-Socratics to Hegel, in ancient, medieval and modern philosophy. Brentano saw his mission in philosophy, in his own person and through his teaching, writing and influence, as attempting to spearhead a new theoretical phase of rigorous, scientific philosophy. While this pattern is no perfect fit for the complexities and vagaries of the history of philosophy, it is better than either the Golden Age or Brave New World models at coping with philosophy's ups and downs, and it can be discerned in more recent mini-cycles on both sides of the analytic/continental divide.

Brentano's influence and legacy

Hubristic as was Brentano's self-estimate of his historic role, it was a source of conviction that was transmitted by his powers as a teacher to his students, inspiring them with the same mission to put philosophy on the firm path of science (the cycle of four phases begins again at just this point). The list of his students comprises astonishingly many of the best minds of the age, and not just among philosophers, and all who wrote about him pay testament to his inspirational sense of mission and his rhetorical gifts.

Among the philosophers we have first Anton Marty, who after studying with Brentano in Würzburg ended up in Prague propagating the Brentanian gospel, though he retained judgement-contents after Brentano had rejected them. Marty predeceased Brentano in 1914, and when his students Kraus and Kastil had finished publishing Marty's relatively simple *Nachlass* they turned to the much tougher case of Brentano. Also at Würzburg Brentano taught Carl Stumpf, who after wandering all over central Europe from post to post ended up in Berlin. He wrote works on the psychology of spatial perception and most notably on sound and music. His later works on epistemology and the theory of states of affairs are undeservedly little known. An early student in Vienna was Tomáš Masaryk, whose interests took him more into sociology and politics than theoretical philosophy. Masaryk was of course the founding President of Czechoslovakia, and he was able to use part of that country's interwar wealth to support the project of publishing Brentano's posthumous writings. Alexius Meinong was taken under Brentano's wing as an historian: Brentano wanted a history of British empiricism. But Meinong was an indifferent historian, far too interested in the theories he wrote about. As time went by his views became more unlike those of Brentano, and they were duly resented and criticised by Brentano and his outriders Marty, Kastil and Kraus. Meinong only reconciled his feelings about Brentano shortly after the latter's death and shortly before his own. Like Brentano, he founded a distinctive and impressive school, which branched out into experimental psychology. Like Brentano too, Meinong was blind, and fiercely protective of his students and views. It was a recipe for discord. Christian von Ehrenfels studied with both Brentano and Meinong and managed, amazingly, to remain on good terms with both. Most of his writing is today forgotten except for the groundbreaking 1891 essay "Über Gestaltqualitäten," generally seen as the origin of Gestalt psychology, but he wrote interestingly on value theory and ethics, held quirky views on eugenics and sexual ethics, and wrote turgidly ghastly neo-Wagnerian opera librettos. His contemporary Edmund Husserl came to Brentano after getting a doctorate in mathematics and working with Weierstrass, but was converted to philosophy and set about applying Brentanian methods to the philosophy of arithmetic and logic. Like Meinong, Husserl wandered far from Brentano's doctrines while retaining the same sense of mission. His influential criticism of psychologism in logic was taken by Brentano as a critique of himself and relations became duly frosty, and Husserl's later manifest success with his phenomenology was resented by Brentano and his clan as a mixture of plagiarism and wrongheadedness. Brentano's last great philosophy student was Kazimierz Twardowski, whose dissertation Brentano could not supervise. Twardowski cemented the content/object distinction, then in 1895 went to Lwów in Poland and thoroughly reorganized and revitalized Polish philosophy along Brentanian lines. Twardowski's own illustrious students included the founders of the Warsaw school of logic and philosophy, and it is rare for a single philosopher to have had such an influence on a single nation.

Among Brentano's many other students were some who like Masaryk made a name for themselves in other fields: Count von Hertling, the penultimate Imperial German Chancellor, and most famously of all, Sigmund Freud, for whom Brentano found some income as a translator of minor writings of John Stuart Mill. The extent to which Freud's views owe anything to Brentano is something on which surprisingly little has been written. Certainly Brentano had no time at all for the idea of the unconscious mind, regarding such concepts as unconscious desires as contradictions in terms. Of other notable figures influenced by Brentano, one of the most important and surprising is Franz Kafka, who absorbed Brentano's ideas in Prague. The tangential solipsism of many of Kafka's characters and the tenuousness of the reality they inhabit is a direct reflection of Brentano's view that only what is evident to inner perception is certain.

Brentano's most loyal followers were not his own students but those of Anton Marty: Alfred Kastil and Oskar Kraus, the "second generation." They were most fervent in support of Brentano's views, most polemical in rebutting opponents, and most intrusive in their editing practices, quarrying the posthumous manuscripts to produce synoptic gospels to convert unbelievers. The religious language is apt: Kastil and Kraus used it between themselves, describing those dissenting from Brentano's views as "fallen." Away from his fanatical defence of everything Brentanian, Kraus was a philosopher of law who wrote interestingly and competently on Bentham and produced a comprehensive and useful (if Brentanian) history of value theory.

Outside the Germanophone world, Brentano's ideas had most echo initially in Italy, where he lived from 1895 to 1915. Brentano carried on correspondence with numerous Italian intellectuals, most notably Giovanni Vailati, who stayed with Brentano, and of whom Brentano wrote to Marty that Austria and Germany needed many more like him. In England G. E. Moore wrote a highly appreciative review of the English translation of Brentano's *Ursprung*, and it is clear that aspects of Brentano's ethics found their way into *Principia Ethica*. Which ones they were is harder to say. In the 1920s Gilbert Ryle took a brief passing interest in Brentano as in other Austrians. It is likely also that Wittgenstein knew of and may have read some Brentano, but how much and what effect such reading may have had is unknown.

The steady stream of publications coming from the efforts of Kraus and Kastil through the 1920s and 1930s kept Brentano's name in the catalogues, but it does not appear that his work was widely read or influential at this time. A second phase of Brentano reception really started in the 1950s and 1960s, when the eminent American philosopher Roderick Chisholm took an interest first in Meinong's then in Brentano's views. An independent interest was fostered by Rudolf Haller in Graz, whose Research and Documentation Centre for Austrian Philosophy possesses Brentano's library as well as a digital photographic copy of his *Nachlass*. Chisholm was energetic in editing and translating Brentano's work and in obtaining translators for it. The *Psychology* appeared in translation in 1973, and numerous other works followed, though by no means all of the published German writings are translated. Chisholm also took on himself both the task of representing Brentano's views to an Anglophone audience and defending many of those views in his own philosophy. Like Brentano a dualist, he subscribed to what he called the primacy of the intentional, regarding all good philosophy as proceeding via a correct analysis of the forms of consciousness in which certain kinds of objects are given. Unlike Brentano and his students however, Chisholm pursued this project via analysis and definition rather than introspection. With Chisholm's death in 1999, Brentano lost his foremost recent advocate.

Brentano's dissertation on the manifold meanings of "to be" first awakened the young Heidegger to philosophy, and while in Heidegger's later work little of Brentano remains, other contemporaries in the wake of Husserl such as Maurice Merleau-Ponty absorbed some of Brentano's views on intentionality and the self, even while disagreeing with Brentano's dualism.

Through the advocacy of Chisholm and others, aspects of Brentanian lore have found their way into contemporary analytic philosophy of mind, through such philosophers as John Searle, Colin McGinn, and Tim Crane. The phenomenon of intentionality is widely seen alongside that of phenomenal consciousness as a severe challenge to a naturalistic account of the mental. Whether intentionality can be "naturalized" remains one of the foremost unanswered questions of philosophy of mind. At the same time, as the prevalence of philosophy of language has receded in analytic philosophy, Brentano's stress on the importance of the mental and its contents and his reservations about the reliability of language have become more congenial and modern-seeming, while his anxiety about reference to the abstract resonates with post-Quinian ontology and some forms of modern nominalism.

In short, while no one subscribes wholeheartedly to Brentano's unique combination of views, his influence in philosophy has managed to jump the chasm between analytic and continental traditions, and his influence is more pervasive than at any time hitherto.

Reference

Brentano, F. (1973) Psychology from an Empirical Standpoint, trans. A. C. Rancurello, D. B. Terrell, and L. McAlister, London: Routledge (2nd edn, with introduction by P. Simons, 1995).

Further reading

W. Huemer, "Franz Brentano," Stanford Encyclopedia of Philosophy (2007) (http://plato.stanford.edu/entries/brentano/), offers a good survey of Brentano's views, comparable to the present article in scope, and available online. The bibliography of writings in German, English translations, secondary literature and online links is the most convenient place to start looking for texts leading to greater depth and breadth of knowledge about Brentano. D. Jacquette (ed.) The Cambridge Companion to Brentano (Cambridge: Cambridge University Press, 2004), is an up-to-date and balanced collection of essays on a variety of aspects of Brentano's philosophy, by leading contemporary commentators. It contains an excellent primary and secondary bibliography. There is, astonishingly, no general introductory monograph on Brentano in English. The nearest to an introduction is A. Kastil's book in German, Die Philosophie Franz Brentanos: Eine Einführung in seine Lehre (Bern: Francke, 1951), which is written with intimate and detailed knowledge of Brentano's views, but published after Kastil's death without benefit of footnotes, references or index. An older collection but still very valuable, L McAlister (ed.) The Philosophy of Brentano (London: Duckworth, 1976), contains authoritative essays including personal reminiscences by Kraus and Husserl.

29
GOTTLOB FREGE
Kevin C. Klement

Introduction

Although primarily a mathematician in both training and employment, German thinker Gottlob Frege's writings are thoroughly philosophical in their outlook, style and significance. He despaired at what he saw as the average working mathematician's inattention to the fundamental questions of their discipline: what the nature of a number is, how our knowledge of them and their properties is possible, what conditions a mathematical argument must meet in order to constitute a legitimate proof, and so on. At least with regard to the proper understanding of arithmetic, he also found the views popular among philosophers of his day severely wanting. Attempting to redress these deficiencies, Frege produced works that, *in time*, profoundly changed the practices of logicians, philosophers and mathematicians, though his influence was slow in gaining ground.

Most of Frege's intellectual endeavors grew out of the attempt to get clear about the nature of arithmetical truth. Frege endorsed a position now known as *logicism*, the thesis that arithmetical truths, when properly analyzed and demonstrated, reveal themselves to be logical or analytical truths. In pursuing this project, Frege developed important and lasting criticisms of rival theories, and innovated a new approach to logic itself so profoundly different from what was prevalent at the time that it is now often described as *the* fundamental point of departure between contemporary approaches to logic and the Aristotelian tradition which had dominated for over two millennia. In thinking about the proper analysis of mathematical propositions, he also developed views about the logical segmentation of language, the distinction between the sense and reference of linguistic expressions, and the nature of truth, which have been profoundly influential in more recent (especially analytic) philosophy of language and metaphysics.

Life and works

Compared to many of his contemporaries, the details of Frege's life are relatively unknown. Friedrich Ludwig Gottlob Frege was born 8 November 1848 in Wismar, Germany. Both parents were educators at a private secondary institution for girls. Frege studied at the *Gymnasium* at Wismar from 1864 until 1869, when he began studies in mathematics at the University of Jena. In 1871, Frege transferred to the University of Göttingen, where he primarily pursued mathematics, but also studied philosophy with the neo-Kantian philosopher and logician, Hermann Lotze. Frege completed his doctoral dissertation, on planar geometry, in late 1873 under the guidance of Ernst Schering. In 1874, on the strength of his *Habilitationsschrift*, devoted to the mathematics of complex functions, and the recommendation of a long-time supporter and benefactor in Jena, the physicist of optics, Ernst Abbe, Frege was granted a lectureship at the University of Jena, where he remained for the rest of his academic life.

At Jena, Frege was in regular contact with other neo-Kantian philosophers, including Liebmann and Windelband, and all in all, Frege seems to have been more sympathetic with their work than with the rival speculative Hegelian tradition. He took from them his anti-psychologism, his apriorism, his esteem for Leibniz, and his distrust of various forms of naturalism. He shared with them the conviction that the logical validity of a deduction is independent of its causal origins, and an understanding of logic as a science of fully general laws of truth. Nevertheless, it is largely in the ways in which his views *deviate* from those of Kant (at least) that Frege has come to be known: in particular, his contention that it is possible for purely logical sources of knowledge to acquaint us with a realm of abstract objects, and more specifically, his contention that the truths of arithmetic could be understood as analytically true.

It is not known precisely when Frege first conceived of his project of attempting to reduce the truths of arithmetic to those of logic, but it may have been as early as the time of his *Habilitation*. Frege's first major work in logic, *Begriffsschrift* (literally "Concept-script,"), published in 1879, is more or less a primer in the logical system he endorsed as an alternative to the then-dominant Boolean algebraist logics. In it, he laid out the first ever fully axiomatic deductive calculus for first- and second-order quantifier logic, and showed its power by defining within it the notion of the ancestral of a relation, used in the logical analysis of series or sequences. Strictly speaking, Frege's system is a function calculus, but the similarity between it and a predicate calculus is so strong that the *Begriffsschrift* is usually seen as the inauguration of modern predicate logic. It stopped short, however, of including the theory of classes as extensions of concepts necessary for Frege's definition of numbers.

It was certainly not an immediate success. In 1919 (p. 25), Bertrand Russell wrote, "[i]n spite of the great value of this work [Frege's *Begriffsschrift*], I was, I believe, the first person who ever read it more than twenty years after its publication." Russell's remark is an exaggeration, but a telling one. This and others of his writings did receive some attention from the leaders in the field, including Venn, Schröder, Cantor and Husserl, and over the next twenty-five years, Frege did correspond with Peano, Löwenheim, Hilbert and other top figures working on the foundations and philosophy of arithmetic. Nevertheless, overall, his works received lukewarm reviews at best. There are no doubt many contributing factors to this. While the still-widespread reputation of Frege's two-dimensional logical notation as being cumbersome or difficult to understand is almost completely undeserved, it is intimidating in its unfamiliar look, and Frege did not – in the *Begriffsschrift* anyway – do much to compare his system to the notations of the Boolean tradition in a way that would encourage those already familiar with the alternatives to take it seriously. Frege did follow up with articles explicitly comparing his logical language to Boolean algebra, but these did not seem to gather much notice, and the harsh criticism they contain of the rival approach would likely have been more alienating than inviting. In general, Frege did not go out of his way to call attention to commonalities between his approach and interests and those of others, rarely acknowledged intellectual debts to philosophers, and even more rarely to other mathematicians. It is small wonder, then, that similar fates were in store for Frege's other major works, and it is entirely possible Frege's name was so unknown in Britain in the early years of the twentieth century that Russell was entirely justified to have leapt to the conclusion he did.

Frege's next major work, *Die Grundlagen der Arithmetik* ("The Foundations of Arithmetic"), appeared in 1884 and represents an attempt on Frege's part – occasioned by the advice of colleagues – to explain the core of his logicist program in ordinary language, in preparation for more technical works which were to follow, along with polemical replies to rival views. Although largely ignored in Frege's day, it is safe to say that this work has since become one of the most influential works in the philosophy of mathematics ever written.

Volume 1 of Frege's magnum opus, *Grundgesetze der Arithmetik* ("Basic Laws of Arithmetic") was published in 1893. Preceding it in the early 1890s, Frege published some important articles in which he outlined certain aspects of how his views on philosophical logic and the theory of meaning had changed since the writing of the *Grundlagen*, including his famous "Über Sinn und Bedeutung" ("On Sense and Reference") in 1892. The *Grundgesetze* itself was devoted largely to actual demonstrations of the most important principles of arithmetic beginning with only logical axioms and inference rules. It added to the logic of *Begriffsschrift* notation and axioms dealing with classes or extensions of concepts necessary for, among other things, defining numbers in Frege's approach. These additions were discovered to make the system of *Grundgesetze* inconsistent by Russell in 1902. Frege received a letter from Russell informing him of the contradiction just as volume 2 of *Grundgesetze* was in the initial stages of being typeset for publication. Frege was, in his own words, "thunderstruck," (PMC: 132) and hastily prepared an appendix to the volume discussing the contradiction and offering a very tentative proposal for revision.

He continued to do important work for a few more years. A series of articles entitled "Über die Grundlagen der Geometrie," ("On the Foundations of Geometry") was published between 1903 and 1906, representing Frege's side of a debate with David Hilbert over the nature of geometry and the proper understanding of axiomatic systems. However, around 1906, probably due to some combination of poor health, the early loss of his wife in 1905, frustration with his failure to find an adequate solution to Russell's paradox, and disappointment over the continued poor reception of his work, Frege seems to have lost his intellectual steam. He produced almost no published work between 1906 and his retirement in 1918, and the initially planned third volume of *Grundgesetze* never appeared.

Ironically, it was during these years that Frege's eventual legacy as an influential figure was fomented. Thanks to an appendix dedicated to Frege's work in Russell's

Principles of Mathematics, Frege began to become known to the English-speaking world, including to Ludwig Wittgenstein, who had been an engineering student in Manchester until discovering Russell's works and, through them, Frege's, in 1910. Wittgenstein wrote to Frege in 1911 concerning the proper solution to Russell's paradox. Frege invited Wittgenstein to Jena, and engaged him in philosophical debate, and eventually recommended him to study with Russell at Cambridge. The two continued in contact for many years to follow, up through till the publication of Wittgenstein's seminal *Tractatus Logico-Philosophicus*, which lists Frege as a major influence. Also, during the years 1911–13, Rudolf Carnap attended Frege's lectures on logic and the foundations of mathematics: Frege thereby influenced Carnap's important works in logic and semantics. Carnap later described these lectures as "the most fruitful inspiration I received from university lectures" while at Jena (Reck and Awodey 2004: 18).

Upon retirement, Frege returned to the Wismar area, and also to an improved pace of writing and publishing, most notably, a series of articles including the important 1918 piece, "Der Gedanke" ("The Thought"). In 1924, having abandoned full-fledged logicism, Frege sought to describe a new approach to understanding the foundations of arithmetic which assigned Kantian pure intuitions of space and time a significant role to play. Frege did not live long enough to pursue this new tack in much detail, however. He died on 26 July 1925 at the age of seventy-six.

It was not until the next generation of philosophical logicians, some of whom had been directly inspired by Frege himself, including Wittgenstein, Carnap, Church, Geach, Quine, Ramsey, etc., recognized and acknowledged the innovation and importance of Frege's logical and philosophical works that his influence became more fully felt. In bequeathing his unpublished work to his son, Alfred, Frege wrote prophetically, "I believe there are things here which will one day be prized much more highly than they are now. Take care that nothing gets lost." Alfred later gave the papers to Heinrich Scholz of the University of Münster for safe-keeping. Unfortunately, however, they were destroyed in a bombing raid in the Second World War. Although Scholz had made copies of some of the more important pieces, a good portion of Frege's unpublished works was lost.

Although a fierce and often satirical polemicist, Frege was a quiet, reserved man. He was right-wing in his political views, distrustful of foreigners and rather anti-Semitic. Himself Lutheran, Frege seems to have wanted all Jews expelled from Germany, or at least deprived of certain political rights. These facts of Frege's personality have gravely disappointed some of Frege's intellectual progeny, the present author included.

Contributions to logic

Frege's logical project

Although Frege agreed with Kant that the truths of geometry are synthetic *a priori*, for most of his career, Frege believed that the truths of arithmetic are analytic. In this, he agreed with Leibniz against both the Kantians, who held that the truths of arithmetic were grounded in "pure intuition," and more empiricist thinkers such as Mill, who thought arithmetic was grounded in observation. Frege defined an analytic truth as one whose ultimate proof relies only on "general logical laws and definitions" (GL: §3). Hence, Frege set about to establish his logicist position by actually providing the requisite proofs in a deductive system whose only axioms and inference rules were purely logical. Frege situated himself within a broader movement towards greater rigor in definitions and deductions in mathematics, no doubt having in mind both Cauchy's, Weierstrass's and Dedekind's work on clarifying the notions of limits and continuity, as well as the push for more systematic proofs in geometry following the discovery of non-Euclidian interpretations (Gauss, Riemann and others).

Again following Leibniz, Frege held that natural language was unsuited to the task, so he sought to create a language that could combine the properties of what Leibniz had called a "*lingua characterica*" (a logically perspicuous language in which the meaning of each symbol is made fully precise) and a "*calculus ratiocinator*" (a language in which precise rules can be set forth to determine what does, and what does not, count as a legitimate inference).

Although there had been attempts, most notably those of Boole and his successors, to fashion logical notations that had some of these features, Frege was not sufficiently pleased with them. For example, under Boole's approach, categorical judgments in forms such as *All A are B* and *Some A are B* were captured by means of operations on classes. Boole interpreted the "logical multiplication" AB, of classes A and B as their intersection, i.e. the class of the members they have in common. He used the numerals "1" and "0" to represent the universal and empty classes, respectively. (The universal class is the class with everything as a member, and the empty class is the class with no members.) Then, the categorical forms, *all A are B* and *some A are B* could be represented, respectively as:

$$AB = A \quad AB \neq 0$$

The former says that the intersection of A and B has precisely the same members as A itself, which can be true (if and) only if all members of A are also members of B. The latter says that the intersection of A and B is not empty, i.e. that they have members in common. The same notations could be reinterpreted to deal with propositional inferences; e.g. if logical multiplication is reinterpreted as conjunction, "1" as representing truth, and "0" as falsehood, the above could be understood as the claims that A (materially) implies B, and that A and B are both true, respectively.

Frege found this approach unsuitable for a variety of reasons: (i) it reused mathematical notation in ways incompatible with their usual mathematical meanings, thereby posing an obstacle for using it to represent mathematical proofs without ambiguity, (ii) with its dual interpretations, it bifurcated its propositional and categorical/quantificational elements, thereby making it impossible to represent deductions involving both kinds of steps, and (iii) without further supplementation, it could not deal with statements of multiple generality (e.g. "*every* person loves *some* city"). It is for these reasons that Frege developed his own logical language, which he dubbed "Begriffsschrift."

Function and argument

Frege's book *Begriffsschrift* is subtitled "a formal language for pure thought, modeled upon that of arithmetic," and in particular it took over the function/argument analysis of mathematical formulæ and utilized it as a replacement for the subject/predicate analysis found in traditional logic. Thus, for example, in the complex expression "5 + 7," "+" represents a function, "5" and "7" represent its two arguments, and the whole expression "5 + 7" represents the value of that function for those arguments – it is another name for 12. According to Frege, a function expression can be understood as "incomplete" in the sense that it affords a place or places for its arguments to be written; hence, it might be better to think of the function expression as "( ) + [ ]" or "$\xi + \zeta$," where "ξ" and "ζ" (or "( )" and "[ ]") are understood as placemarkers for where the names of the arguments would be written. In this regard, function signs differ from proper names of objects, and Frege thought there was a corresponding difference between functions and objects themselves; whereas objects are "complete" functions he said, were "unsaturated" (*ungesättigt*). In a mathematical equation, such as:

$$f(x) = x^2 + 1$$

the function $f(\ )$ is said to take its argument and yield as value the result of squaring the argument and adding 1. The import of the letter "x" here used as a variable, is, according to Frege, to lend generality to the statement, so that this is said to hold for *every* possible argument to this function.

In order to make his logical language applicable more generally, Frege expanded the function expressions it contained to represent functions with arguments and values other than numbers. In his mature views of *Grundgesetze*, this included two special objects, truth-values, "the True" and "the False." A function of one argument, whose value, for every argument, is either the True or the False, Frege called a "concept." Thus, for example, if $H(\ )$ is the function such that:

$$H(x) = \begin{cases} \text{the True, if } x \text{ is human, or} \\ \text{the False, otherwise.} \end{cases}$$

then we can regard $H(\ )$ as the concept *being human*. Hence, if "a" stands for Aristotle, $H(a)$ is the True, but if "b" stands for Boston, then $H(b)$ is the False. An object whose value is the True when taken as argument to a given concept is said to "fall under" that concept. A function with two (or more) arguments whose value is always either the True or the False Frege called a "relation." Thus one way to regard the relation sign "$\xi \leq \zeta$" is as standing for a function whose value is the True in case its first argument is less than or equal to its second, and whose value is the False, otherwise.

Syntax and axiomatization of the core logic

The logical constants in Frege's system were also taken to represent functions. One such constant, called "the horizontal" or "content stroke," is used mainly to transform any term into the name of a truth-value:

$$— x = \begin{cases} \text{the True, if } x \text{ is the True, or} \\ \text{the False, if } x \text{ is anything other than the True.} \end{cases}$$

Notice that if the argument is a truth-value, the value is the same truth-value; otherwise, this yields the False. The reverse of this function is the negation stroke, which is the nearest equivalent in Frege's system to the modern "~ p" or "¬ p," except that, for Frege, this is a function sign that is applied to a term to form a term, rather than a statement operator:

$$─\!\top\, x = \begin{cases} \text{the False, if } x \text{ is the True, or} \\ \text{the True, if } x \text{ is anything other than the True.} \end{cases}$$

Frege's near-equivalent to the material conditional sign "$p \rightarrow q$" or "$p \supset q$" involves a two-dimensional branched array with the antecedent term written below the consequent.

$$\begin{array}{l} \top\, y \\ \llcorner\, x \end{array} = \begin{cases} \text{the False, if } x \text{ is the True and } y \text{ is other than the True, or} \\ \text{the True, otherwise.} \end{cases}$$

The three examples above are all first-level functions, meaning that they take objects as argument. The first two are first-level concepts, the last, a first-level relation.

As in algebra, Frege utilized variables to make quantified or general statements. When Roman letters are used, the generality applies to the entire proposition (as demarcated by the judgment stroke, discussed below). If Frege wished the scope of the generality to apply to only part of the proposition, he utilized Gothic (Fraktur) letters, along with a concavity as a variable-binding quantifier and scope marker, akin to the contemporary "$(x)(\ldots x \ldots)$" or "$\forall x(\ldots x \ldots)$."

$$─\!\underset{\mathfrak{a}}{\cup}\, \phi(\mathfrak{a}) = \begin{cases} \text{the True, if function } \phi() \text{ has the True as value} \\ \qquad \text{for all arguments, or} \\ \text{the False, otherwise.} \end{cases}$$

According to Frege, $\underset{\mathfrak{a}}{\cup} \ldots \mathfrak{a} \ldots$ should be understood as a *second-level concept*, i.e. a concept that takes a first-level function $\phi()$ as *argument* and returns its own value depending on the values of the function it takes as argument. As a second-order calculus, Frege's system also contained apparatus for quantification over first-level functions, written "_f_ ... f ... ."

Notice that the horizontal parts of these last three signs can themselves be regarded as content strokes, since the output is unchanged if arguments or values of the above are fed through this function. In general, making the value of one function into the argument of another is just a matter of attaching the left horizontal line of the term to be made into an argument to the right horizontal line leading to the argument place of the function into which it's fed. For example, the truth-value of its being the case that *if Socrates is human, then if not everything is human, then Boston is not human*, or, $Hs \rightarrow (\neg \forall x H x \rightarrow \neg H b)$, could be represented thusly:

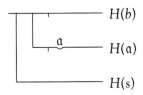

H(b)

H(a)

H(s)

The above, however, remains simply a name of a truth-value, and does not actually assert anything. Frege therefore added a special sign, called *the judgment stroke*, a terminal vertical line which could only appear at the beginning of the expression. Unlike the others, it was not a function sign, and was instead used to *assert* that what followed the sign was a name of the True. In the above case, this would yield:

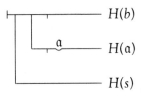

H(b)

H(a)

H(s)

The result is a proposition with assertoric force, rather than just the name of a truth-value.

In what follows, for the convenience of the reader, we shall replace Frege's conditional and negation signs with their near equivalents, "$\rightarrow$" and "$\neg$," and utilize the more familiar notation "$\forall x(...x...)$" for quantifiers, but retain the unique Fregean syntax and semantics, where there is no distinction between terms and formulæ, so that, for example, "$H(\neg a)$" and "$2 \rightarrow 3$" are not ill-formed. The former, for example, represents the truth-value of a truth-value's being human.

Frege did not introduce signs especially for conjunction, disjunction or the existential quantifier, and simply made use of equivalent forms using his primitive signs, e.g. "$\neg(p \rightarrow \neg q)$" for the conjunction of p and q, or "$\neg \forall x \neg \phi(x)$" in place of "$\exists x \phi(x)$." Indeed, Frege was most likely the first to discover these equivalences.

Frege's logical notation also used a primitive sign for the identity relation:

$$(x = y) = \begin{cases} \text{the True, if } x \text{ is the same object as } y, \text{ or} \\ \\ \text{the False, otherwise.} \end{cases}$$

Obviously, this, and the others above, must not be regarded as object-language definitions of Frege's logical signs, but just informal explications of their use.

Frege's *Begriffsschrift* outlined the first modern axiomatic calculus for logic, and indeed, Frege was the first even to suggest that inference or transformation rules ought to be explicitly formulated and distinguished from axioms. The axioms of his 1879 system were:

(1) $\vdash a \rightarrow (b \rightarrow a)$
(2) $\vdash [a \rightarrow (b \rightarrow c)] \rightarrow [(a \rightarrow b) \rightarrow (a \rightarrow c)]$
(3) $\vdash [a \rightarrow (b \rightarrow c)] \rightarrow [b \rightarrow (a \rightarrow c)]$
(4) $\vdash (a \rightarrow b) \rightarrow (\neg b \rightarrow \neg a)$
(5) $\vdash \neg \neg a \rightarrow a$
(6) $\vdash a \rightarrow \neg \neg a$
(7) $\vdash (a = b) \rightarrow (F(a) \rightarrow F(b))$
(8) $\vdash a = a$
(9) $\vdash \forall x F(x) \rightarrow F(a)$; along with similar principles for function variables.

Given the functional nature of Frege's language, ordinary language glosses of the above must be somewhat awkwardly worded, and even then, won't be entirely faithful to his intent. However, the following readings might be suggested.

(1) If A, then B (materially) implies A.
(2) If A implies that B implies C, then if A implies B then A implies C.
(3) If A implies that B implies C, then B implies that A implies C.
(4) If A implies B, then not-B implies not-A. (The principle of transposition.)
(5) If not-not-A, then A. (The eliminability of double negation.)
(6) If A, then not-not-A. (The introducibility of double negation.)
(7) If a is b then any concept that holds of a holds of b.
(8) a is a itself.
(9) Any concept that holds of all objects holds of any particular object.

To these Frege added inference rules of detachment (*modus ponens*) and universal generalization (applicable either to an entire judgment, or within a consequent of the main conditional assuming the variable replaced is not found in the antecedent), and implicitly utilized a rule of replacement (which became explicit in *Grundgesetze*). Together (1)–(6) provide what amounts to a complete axiomatization of propositional logic, in the sense that all truth-functionally tautologous forms can be derived from them, although (3) is redundant (provable from the others). With (7), (8) and the explicitly given form of (9), they constitute a complete axiomatization of first-order quantified logic with identity, and the system as a whole represents a consistent and

Henkin-complete axiomatization of second-order logic. (Henkin completeness is weaker than standard completeness; a standardly complete axiomatization of second-order logic beginning with a finite axiom set is now known to be impossible as a corollary of Gödel's incompleteness theorems.) The development of this system is undeniably one of the watershed events in the history of logic.

Given the extent to which they are taken for granted today, it can be difficult to appreciate the advantages Frege's system offered over its predecessors. Frege's new analysis in terms of scoped variable-binding quantifiers applied to truth-functional forms provided new insights even into the four basic forms of categorical logic (i.e. the square of opposition). By understanding "all A are B" as "⊢ $\forall x(A(x) \rightarrow B(x))$," Frege first made it possible to capture the logical connections between such statement pairs as "either all students are hard-working or all students are intelligent" and "all students are either hard-working or intelligent" (for example, that the first implies the second). Frege's system was not only adequately able to render statements involving multiple generality, but was even able to distinguish adequately the different meanings of such statements as "every person loves some city" in terms of quantifier scope distinctions:

$$\vdash \forall x[Person(x) \rightarrow \exists y(City(y) \wedge Loves(x,y))]$$

means that every person loves some city *or other*, but

$$\vdash \exists y[City(y) \wedge \forall x(Person(x) \rightarrow Loves(x,y))]$$

means that some one city in particular is loved by everyone. When compared to the baroque explanations and theories that other logicians of the time, or even after Frege, invoked to explain the same phenomena (compare even Russell 1903: Ch. 5), Frege's treatment stands out as a model of eloquence and simplicity. And while work was being done from within the Boolean tradition, by such logicians as Peirce, Schröder and Peano, that moved it closer to matching the expressive power and exactness of Frege's approach, including, for example, independent (re)discovery of the universal and existential quantifiers by Peirce around the same time, these efforts were, relatively speaking, fragmented and piecemeal by comparison.

Value-ranges, extensions and Russell's paradox

Frege offered a slightly different axiomatization of his core logic in the 1893 *Grundgesetze* system, which included fewer axioms but additional inference rules. He also added two additional primitives to his logical notation, most importantly, a sign consisting of a Greek vowel written with a *spiritus lenis* accent acting as a variable binding second-level function sign: "ά(...α...)." Frege described the value of this second-level function for a given argument first-level function as the "*Werthverlauf*" of the first-level function – a word translated into English sometimes as "value-range," "course-of-values" or "graph." The word was one of several used widely by German mathematicians at the time for the representation of the arguments and values of a mathematical function, such as on a Cartesian plane (e.g. a wave for the sine or cosine functions or a parabola for a quadratic function). Frege's value-ranges can be understood similarly, but broadened, once again, to include functions whose arguments and values were not numbers. Obviously, Frege did not have in mind a "graph" considered as a physical object, or anything else intuitable, but rather something more like the complete argument-value pairings generated by a function thought of as a single abstract object. Frege identified the value-range of a concept with its *extension*, and sometimes also used the word "class" to describe the sorts of things expressions of the form "$\acute{\alpha}\phi(\alpha)$" name when $\phi()$ is a concept. The label is appropriate, since if $F( )$ and $G( )$ are concepts that pair precisely the same truth-values with the same objects, they would have the same "extension" i.e. have precisely the same things falling under them.

The other added sign was a first-level function sign to be used in conjunction with the value-range notation:

$$\backslash x = \begin{cases} \text{the sole object falling under the concept whose extension is } x, \text{ assuming } x \\ \qquad\qquad\qquad \text{is the extension of such a concept, or} \\ x \text{ itself, otherwise.} \end{cases}$$

Frege called this the "substitute for the definite article," since where $\phi()$ is a concept under which only one thing falls, "$\backslash \acute{\alpha}\phi(\alpha)$" might be read "the ϕ."

Frege added two additional axioms to his system governing these new signs (– recall that Frege had renumbered his axiom list –):

(**Basic Law V**) $\vdash (\acute{\varepsilon} F(\varepsilon) = \acute{\alpha} G(\alpha)) = \forall x(F(x) = G(x))$
(**Basic Law VI**) $\vdash a = \backslash \acute{\varepsilon}(a = \varepsilon)$

The second of these laws basically says that a is *the* thing identical to a, which is relatively straightforward. The first, the notorious Law V of the *Grundgesetze*, also seems straightforward at first blush. Since "=" placed between names of truth-values works more or less as a material biconditional in Frege's system, Law V states that $F( )$ and $G( )$ determine the same value-range (or have the same "graph") if and only if they have the same value for every argument, which, in the case of number-theoretic functions, seems perfectly reasonable. In the case where $F( )$ and $G( )$ are concepts, Law V amounts to the assertion that two concepts have the same extension if and only if they are coextensive. It is not difficult to see why Frege might have taken this to be an analytic truth or basic law of logic, and – although this reading is controversial and somewhat problematic – some read it as an attempted implicit definition of the notion of the value-range of a function, i.e. an attempt to explicate what sort of a thing a value-range would be by giving the identity conditions of value-ranges in terms of already-understood logical vocabulary.

Unfortunately, however, the addition of Basic Law V to the other principles of Frege's system renders it inconsistent due to a version of Russell's paradox. Extensions of concepts are objects, and hence, we may ask of each one whether or not it falls under its defining concept. Some, such as the extension of the concept of self-identity, or the concept of being a class, do so. Others, such as the extension of the concept *being a cat*, will not (since the class of cats is not a cat). Now, however, consider the concept $W(\xi)$, definable as $\exists F[(\xi) = \dot{\alpha}F(\alpha) \wedge \neg F(\xi)]$, i.e. the concept of being a value-range/extension that does not fall under (one of) its defining concepts. This concept has its own value-range, $\dot{\varepsilon}W(\varepsilon)$. Does $\dot{\varepsilon}W(\varepsilon)$ fall under $W(\xi)$? Suppose it does. Then $\dot{\varepsilon}W(\varepsilon)$ must not fall under some concept $F(\xi)$ of which it is the extension. However, since it is also the extension of $W(\xi)$, by Basic Law V, $W(\xi)$ and $F(\xi)$ must be coextensive, and since it doesn't fall under $F(\xi)$, it also must not fall under $W(\xi)$, contradicting our hypothesis. But suppose instead that it doesn't fall under $W(\xi)$. Then it must fall under *every* concept of which it is the extension, including $W(\xi)$, so we are back at contradiction. In a classical logic such as Frege's, a single contradiction in the system explodes so that it then becomes possible to derive every single well-formed proposition in the language as *both* true and false, thereby trivializing his attempt give arithmetic a logical foundation.

After learning of this contradiction, Frege identified Basic Law V as culpable (though this is not altogether a safe assumption; for discussion, see Dummett 1991: Ch. 17; Boolos 1998: Ch. 14). Reflecting on the above argument, it is clear that Basic Law V comes in only once, in allowing us to conclude that because $F(\xi)$ and $W(\xi)$ have the same extension, they must be coextensive. Hence, Frege reached the conclusion that this inference is not always valid, and that it is possible for two concepts to have the same extension *even when they are not coextensive*, or differ with regard to what objects fall under them. In particular, he proposed that if two concepts differed by at most what their values were for their own extension(s), then they have the same extension. After Frege's death, this proposal was later discovered to lead to more complicated contradictions (Quine 1955; Landini 2006). Nevertheless, Frege's general rubric of supposing that two non-coextensive concepts may determine the same "extension" – or something appropriately renamed but playing a similar role within an overall logical theory – has been profitably explored by more recent logicians to develop consistent theories (see, e.g. Boolos 1998: Ch. 11; Shapiro 2003). Moreover, the notation and axioms governing classes can be removed wholescale from Frege's *Grundgesetze* system, leaving a perfectly functioning and (again) Henkin-complete axiomatization of second-order logic, and so Frege's achievement is not altogether marred by Russell's paradox.

The philosophy of logic

Frege understood logic to constitute the *a priori* science of the laws of truth, claiming that "true" points the way for logic "just as 'beautiful' points the way for æsthetics and 'good' for ethics" (Ged: 325). In keeping with the neo-Kantian tradition, Frege resisted psychologism about logic. Logicians need not concern themselves with the psychological processes that underlie thinking, inferring or reasoning. The laws of logic would remain true even if no one's reasoning ever accorded with them, or people in fact reasoned differently than they do. They are laws of *truth* in a descriptive sense, but they are laws of *thinking* only in a prescriptive sense. They tell us which chains of reasoning are truth-preserving, and hence which allow for us to infer the truth of a certain conclusion *justifiably* from certain premises. Frege understood the laws of logic to be general laws, universally and equally applicable to all domains of objects and concepts.

Where Frege differed from some neo-Kantians, Kant himself, and many others since, was in rejecting the understanding of logic as comprising *purely formal* principles, devoid of content and subject matter, and as such, incapable of expanding our knowledge. We have already seen that Frege understood the logical constants of his *Begriffsschrift* as representing concepts, relations and other functions, no less real or substantial than the meaning of the predicate, "… is human." What's more is that by combining such functors to form any complete name of a truth-value, and then removing any one (or more) constituent name(s) or variable(s), one achieves the name of a possibly new concept (or relation). Frege's replacement rule for second-order variables allowed one to instantiate variables for functions to any complex concept expression so formed, and hence is equivalent to the modern (impredicative) *comprehension principle* for second-order logic, i.e. for every open sentence "…x…" containing "x" but not "F" free, Frege held:

$$\vdash \exists F \forall x (Fx \leftrightarrow \dots x \dots).$$

This represents a powerful means for the recognition of new logical concepts, and eventually (along with the recognition of logical objects, described below), the recognition of mathematical concepts as well. According to Frege, logic is *ampliative*; it can extend our knowledge even when the proofs involved start off with self-evident axioms and utilize only transformation rules that guarantee truth-preservation. As Frege put the matter, the truth of the conclusions thereby reached is in one sense "contained within" the truth of the self-evident logical principles with which one begins, but only "as plants are contained in their seeds, not as beams are contained in a house" (GL: §88).

Prior to the discovery of Russell's paradox, Frege even thought that by means of making the transition from concepts to their extensions, or more generally, from functions to their value-ranges, logic could afford us with knowledge of objects, in contradistinction to the Kantian dictum that the content for our reasonings and judgments must be provided by the faculty of sensibility (intuitions, perception, or mental imagery). Frege was explicit that, even when their members are concrete objects, he did not regard classes as aggregates or collections of those members. Instead, he claimed that "the extension of a concept is constituted in being … by the concept itself" (CP: 224–5; cf. PW: 183). This would seem a rather puzzling remark were it not for Frege's understanding of concepts as functions. Frege claimed that functions with the same value for every argument, "coincided," and hence the concepts of *having a heart* and *having a kidney*, which map the same things to the True, and the same things to the False, were the same concept. (Frege could still claim that the two expressions "… has a heart" and "… has a kidney" differ in sense, so long as they have the same referent; see "Sense and Reference," fifth section.) In that regard, Frege's concepts were already extensional in their identity conditions, and it is not unreasonable to think of the extensions or value-ranges of concepts differing from the concepts themselves only insofar as the concepts themselves are "unsaturated" while the extensions are objects. On this understanding, it is natural to think that insofar as logic alone suffices for awareness of the concepts, it can also afford us knowledge of their extensions. Frege, however, came to have doubts about this way of thinking after the discovery of Russell's paradox (PMC: 140–1; GG: II 265).

Frege's philosophy of mathematics

Criticisms of rival views

Although best remembered in the philosophy of mathematics for his positive arguments in favor of logicism, Frege also provided powerful and influential arguments against other positions about the nature of mathematical truth and knowledge.

We have seen that Frege was a harsh critic of psychologism in logic. He thought similarly about psychologism in mathematics. Numbers cannot be equated with anyone's mental images, nor truths of mathematics with psychological truths. Mathematical truths are objective, not subjective (GL: §26; GG: xviii–xxv).

Frege was also a critic of Mill's view that arithmetical truths are empirical truths, based on observation. Frege pointed out that we can just as well count things that cannot be observed, or cannot all be observed together. It would be perfectly possible for us to realize that two distinct tastes and two distinct musical notes constitute four types of experiences altogether without experiencing them all in a unified perceptual state. Moreover, the limited range of observations we have had seem inadequate to make sense of our knowledge of very large numbers, where we are unlikely to have observed precisely that many things together – not to mention that *no one* has ever had an experience of zero things – rendering inexplicable our knowledge of those numbers' mathematical properties (GL: §§7–8, 24). Moreover, if our knowledge of numbers were to be based on observation, numbers would have to be observable properties of external things, or aggregates of things. Frege points out that the same observable conglomerate can be seen as made up of a different number of things depending on how the parts are counted. *One* deck of cards contains *fifty-two* cards, but each card consists of a multitude of atoms. There is no one uniquely determined "number" of the whole conglomeration (GL: §§22–3). He also reiterated the arguments of others: that mathematical knowledge seems apodictic and *a priori*, and hence not the result of (fallible) sense perception.

Frege also takes issue with the Kantian position that arithmetic is grounded in pure intuitions of space and time. Frege notes that the notion of "magnitude" involved in speaking of intuitions of various magnitudes is often too vague to be useful, that "pure" intuition fares little better than direct observation when it comes to zero and large numbers, and that any attempt to explain how intuitive knowledge gained about small numbers could be extended to large ones is liable to draw an arbitrary boundary between large and small (GL: §§5–6, 12). Perhaps Frege's most forceful response to this kind of position, however, is his positive argument that e.g. the basic properties of the kind of succession involved in the series of natural numbers could be defined and proven purely logically, without appeal to a representation of the succession of time or any other form of intuition. Of course, establishing this required giving the proofs: hence the importance of carrying out the project in an artificial logical language with precisely formulated inference rules, where no appeal to intuition could go undetected.

Finally, Frege was an ardent opponent of formalism, the view that arithmetic can be understood as the study of uninterpreted formal systems. While Frege's logical language represented a kind of formal system, he insisted that it was important only because of what its signs represent and its propositions mean (CP: 112ff). Frege believed that at its worst, formalism was guilty of simply conflating the signs with what they represent, e.g. concluding, absurdly, that numbers are signs, or that "5 + 7 = 12" written in Arabic numerals, is not the same truth as the formula, "V + VII = XII" written in Roman numerals (cf. e.g. GG: §100). Even at their best, Frege believed that formalist theories in mathematics were guilty of a kind of confusion of concept and object. By simply laying out a formal system (even a consistent one) and holding its subject matter to be constituted by the fact that it is what is characterized by those axioms, one is really, according to Frege, defining a *concept* (e.g. "object satisfying the axioms") which one, many, or even *no* systems of objects might fall under (GL: §97; CP: 120–1). Without providing a specific interpretation of the vocabulary used in the theory so that it does represent a specific content, the formal system cannot even be thought of as *truth-apt*, much less *actually true*.

Frege suggests that mistaken views in the philosophy of mathematics are often the result of attempting to understand the meaning of number terms in the wrong way, for example, in attempting to understand their meaning independently of the remainder of the propositions (sentences) wherein they appear. If simply asked to consider what "two" means independently of the context of a proposition, we are likely simply to imagine the numeral "2" or perhaps some conglomeration of two things. Thus, in the *Grundlagen* (p. x), Frege espouses his famous *context principle*, "never to ask for the meaning of a word in isolation, but only in the context of a proposition." The *Grundlagen* is an earlier work, written before Frege had made the distinction between sense and reference (see "Sense and Reference," fifth section, below). It is an active matter of debate to what extent this principle coheres with Frege's later theory of meaning, and in particular, the compositionality principle of sense, but what is clear is that it plays an important role in his own philosophy of mathematics in the *Grundlagen*.

The definition of number

According to Frege, most everyday uses of number words place them within propositions that, as wholes, make claims about concepts. In particular, they are used to specify how many times a certain concept is instantiated. Consider, for example:

I have six cards in my hand.

or

There are ten members of Congress from Wisconsin.

These propositions seem to tell us how many times the concepts of *being a card in my hand* and *being a member of Congress from Wisconsin* are instantiated. Thus, Frege concludes that ascriptions of number are statements about concepts. Frege was able to show that it is possible to define what it means for a concept to be instantiated a certain number of times purely logically by making use of quantifiers and identity. To say that the concept F( ) is instantiated zero times is to say that there are no objects that fall under F( ), or, equivalently, that everything does not fall under F( ), i.e.:

$$\vdash \forall x \neg F(x).$$

To say that F( ) is instantiated exactly once is to say that something, *x*, falls under F( ), and that nothing *else* does:

$$\vdash \exists x[F(x) \wedge \forall y(\neg F(y) \vee y = x)].$$

To say that F( ) is instantiated twice is to say that there are *distinct x* and *y* which fall under F( ) and that everything either does not fall under F( ) or is one of them:

$$\vdash \exists x \, \exists y[F(x) \wedge F(y) \wedge x = y \wedge \forall z(\neg F(z) \vee z = x \vee z = y)]$$

and so on. In general, for each natural number *n*, we seem to be able, using logical constants only, to define a formula involving a variable "F" that will hold of a given value if and only if it is a concept instantiated by precisely *n* objects.

However, Frege rejects thinking of this as a complete understanding of what numbers are. The above definitions do not define the number words "1," "2" or "3" but only the second-level concept expressions, "the number of things that fall under … is 1" and "the number of things that fall under … is 2." In mathematics, and even in ordinary language, however, numerals and other expressions for numbers often occur as complete expressions or proper names and hence must be thought of as referring to objects. (See "Objects and the Hierarchy of Concepts," fifth section, below, for explanation of Frege's distinction between objects and concepts of various levels.) Nevertheless, Frege does not think it fruitful simply to ask what object a number word stands for; determining what sorts of objects numbers might be is constrained by the fact that number words typically occur in statements about concepts, and hence any account of their nature must do justice to this fact. Frege then suggests that we might get a better handle on what objects numbers are by considering statements concerning their identity or non-identity. Here Frege appeals to an insight expressed by Hume according to which the number of Fs is the same as the number of Gs if and only if we can pair up each F with a unique G and vice-versa. It is possible, in second-order logic, to define what it means for there to exist a one-to-one correlation between two concepts, which we can call the relation of *equinumerosity*:

$$(F(x) \cong_x G(x)) \quad =_{Df.} \quad \exists R\{\forall x[F(x) \to \exists y(G(y) \land \forall z(R(x,z) \leftrightarrow z = y))] \land$$
$$\forall x[G(x) \to \exists y(F(y) \land \forall z(R(z,x) \leftrightarrow z = y))]\}$$

or, in other words, $F(\xi)$ and $G(\xi)$ are *equinumerous* just in case there is a relation R that correlates each F to one (and only one) G and each G to one (and only one) F. Using the notation "$(\#_x)F(x)$" for "the number of xs such that $F(x)$" (Frege's own notation was $\mathfrak{N}\grave{\alpha}F(\alpha)$), we can then state the following:

(Hume's Principle) $\vdash((\#_x)F(x) = (\#_y)G(y)) \leftrightarrow (F(x) \cong_x G(x))$

i.e. the number of Fs is the number of Gs if and only if F is equinumerous with G. This principle seems to be an analytic statement that just explicates what we *mean* when we speak of numbers. Notice, however, that it does not actually give a definition of the notation "$(\#_x)\phi(x)$" or provide a way of eliminating it in terms of core logical notation. Instead, it only gives us a criterion for the truth or falsity of identity statements formed using such notation. It tells us when one number is identical with another, purely logically, but not yet what a number *is*. It does not even fix the truth conditions for all statements of identity involving numbers since it does not tell us whether or not $(\#_x)F(x) = q$ when q is not given to us *as* the number belonging to some concept. To adapt an example Frege uses in a slightly different context, it does not tell us whether or not the number of Fs is Julius Cæsar. Hence, Frege is unwilling to rest content with this as a "definition" of number words either.

Nevertheless, Frege holds that Hume's Principle is another important step forward, since any account of the nature of numbers must validate it, even if it on its own cannot precisely afford us knowledge of what numbers are. At this point, Frege turns to his theory of extensions of concepts in order to identify objects that can play this role which our understanding of logic alone can make known to us (as explained in the subsection, "The Philosophy of Logic," third section). In the *Grundlagen*, Frege suggests that we can define "the number of Fs" as "the extension of the concept 'equinumerous with F'," thereby making numbers into extensions of second-level concepts. In the later *Grundgesetze*, noting the ready interchange between speaking of a concept and speaking of its extension, Frege modifies this definition so that "the number of Fs" (or "$(\#_x)F(x)$") is taken as the extension of the concept *being the extension of a concept that is equinumerous with F*, thereby making numbers into extensions of concepts applicable to extensions, and anticipating Russell's 1901 definition of numbers as classes of like-membered classes. A (cardinal) *number* generally can be defined as any object that is "the number of" some concept. Since equinumerosity is an equivalence relation, both symmetric and transitive, if we assume that F and G are equinumerous, then (the extension of) any other concept H will be included in the number of Fs if and only if it is included in the number of Gs. Conversely, if anything that is included in the number of Fs is also included in the number of Gs, since this includes (the extension of) F itself, F must be equinumerous with G. Therefore, the proposal validates Hume's Principle (though of course it does so by invoking Frege's problematic notion of the extension of a concept, which eventually was shown to lead to inconsistency.)

Logicism and its prospects

With his conception of number in hand, in the *Grundlagen*, Frege began to sketch how many of the basic arithmetical truths of number theory, beginning with the theory of natural numbers, might be deduced. He gave a list of several basic principles governing them, not identical to, but equivalent with, the Peano-Dedekind axioms. Full axiomatic proofs of these principles, stated in Frege's logical notation, were given in his *Grundgesetze*. Zero is defined as the number of the concept *non-self-identical*, or $(\#_x)(x \neq x)$. For any numbers m and n, m can be said to be the *successor* of n, by definition, just in case for some concept F, $m = (\#_x)Fx$ and there is a y such that $F(y)$ and $n = (\#_x)(F(x) \wedge x \neq y)$. We can say that a concept ϕ is "successor-hereditary" if it's the case that whenever $\phi(n)$ and m is the successor of n, then it also holds that $\phi(m)$. We can say that m follows n in the successorship-series just in case m has every successor-hereditary property that n has. The *natural numbers* can be defined as zero and all those numbers that follow zero in the successorship-series. We can establish that this series never runs out with the observation that, for any member n of this series, the number of natural numbers up to and including it, will be the number m that succeeds n.

Much in keeping with Georg Cantor's theory of transfinite cardinal numbers, Frege points out that there are some concepts whose number is not a natural (finite) number, such as the concept of *natural number* itself. Infinite numbers of various sizes, still definable in terms of equinumerosity or one-to-one correspondence, are also countenanced within Frege's approach. Moreover, Frege believed that integers (including negative numbers), and real numbers, could be defined in terms of natural numbers and certain relations between them, and had been well on his way towards establishing the basic principles governing them when his project was derailed by the discovery of Russell's paradox.

In light of its inconsistency, and the fact that his proposed way out of the inconsistency also failed, it can be difficult to gauge what the lasting significance of Frege's logicist project is, and opinions differ significantly. Of course, the invention of quantifier logic, which remains intact after the inconsistent naive class theory is removed, is no small feat. Yet, there is reason to think that even the mathematical part of Frege's logicist project was in its own way a success. It sketched a methodology for logically defining numbers and proving their basic properties which could be largely retained excepting only various possible modifications to escape inconsistency. Frege's approach directly influenced the approaches to such issues by later mathematical logicians, including Whitehead and Russell, Carnap, Wittgenstein, Leśniewski, Church, Ramsey and Quine, at least *some* of whom took themselves to be offering their own brands of logicism. More recently, it has been stressed by Crispin Wright that Frege's proofs of (what amount to) the Peano-Dedekind axioms stem exclusively from Hume's Principle and the other, consistent and widely accepted, principles of second-order logic (or can be changed to do so), and that the role Basic Law V plays in Frege's treatment of natural number theory, at least, is almost exclusively limited to obtaining Hume's Principle. Hence, Wright has urged that if Hume's Principle can itself be argued to be a logical, or at least analytic, truth, prospects remain for the pursuit of neo-Fregean forms of logicism. Whatever one thinks about this suggestion, Wright is no doubt right that the result that the whole of second-order Peano arithmetic can be derived from Hume's Principle alone is a significant discovery, and it has come to be known as "Frege's theorem."

In 1931, Kurt Gödel discovered that no deductive system that utilizes a finite or recursively specifiable collection of axioms can be both consistent and have every arithmetical truth as a theorem. This has only clouded further the evaluation of Frege's logicism. Notice that the result certainly doesn't establish, at least not in any direct fashion, that there are arithmetical truths that are not logical truths. Indeed, a corollary of Gödel's results show that no finite or recursively specifiable collection of axioms for second-order logic can be both consistent and have every standardly valid or logically true formula as a theorem; this certainly doesn't establish that there are logical truths that are not logical truths! Gödel's results do deal a significant blow to Frege's own method of trying to *establish* the analyticity of arithmetic, insofar as Frege thought this meant finding "*the* proof" of any given proposition, as if there is one preferred, all-encompassing, logical calculus in which this is to be done. Still, the problem persists only if we insist there has to be a *single* such calculus or deductive system, since Gödel's results do *not* show that there are any truths of mathematics which cannot be established in *any* deductive system of logic, only that they can't *all* be established in the *same* one. (And notice that accepting multiple logical *calculi* is not tantamount to believing in multiple "logics.")

Moreover, it is entirely unclear how and to what extent these results give a point in favor of any of the major rivals to logicism. Supposing it were true that Frege or a neo-Fregean had succeeded in capturing all of Peano arithmetic, and the core principles of real number analysis, in a purely logical or analytic deductive system, but was happy to admit that there were some arcane truths involving complex recursive number systems it didn't capture. Still, *all* of the arithmetic we learn in our primary and secondary schools would be included. It would seem odd in the extreme to insist then that there was some *other* metaphysical or epistemological basis for mathematics as a whole, which just doesn't *happen* to be necessary for *any* of the so-called "arithmetical truths," which we make use of in day-to-day calculations or normally associate with the word "arithmetic." It is also very hard to imagine a plausible case being made that some non-logical source of knowledge is precisely what fills the void left by the undecidable sentences posited by Gödel's arguments.

Language and metaphysics

Frege's work in the foundations of arithmetic and logic led him to investigate more fully both the nature of language, and certain fundamental questions about the structure of reality and our knowledge of it. Commentators on Frege disagree about precisely to what extent Frege was interested in metaphysics or the nature of language for their own sakes, and what brought him to these investigations. Nevertheless, it is clear what the primary connection is. Frege's logical language aimed to capture precisely that which was thought relevant to inference – what, early on, he called the "content" – of a premise or conclusion. This led him to investigate how precisely these contents should be understood, and in particular, (i) how they are expressed and logically articulated in ordinary language, (ii) whether the notion of content is univocal or further distinctions are necessary, and (iii) what the nature of these contents is, whether they are the products of the mind, or objective, and whether or not they are the same for all who grasp them.

Objects and the Hierarchy of Concepts

As discussed in the subsection, "Function and Argument," third section, the syntax of Frege's logical language is modeled on the function/argument analysis of complex mathematical terms. Frege believed that ordinary language, to the extent that it is articulated in a logically non-defective way, is capable of the same kind of segmentation. Thus, proper names, descriptions, or other "complete" expressions must be distinguished from "incomplete expressions," such as "the capital of ..." or a predicate phrase like "... plays tennis," which bear the hallmark of function expressions generally, i.e. that they suggest or hold open a spot for the sign for an argument or arguments to be written. Recall that for the mature Frege, a concept is simply a function whose value is always a truth-value. Beginning with any complete proposition, if a constituent name is removed, the result is a concept expression, and the removed name can be considered the sign for its argument. For some propositions, it is possible to divide or decompose them into concept expression and argument in more than one way. Thus, Frege says, "Jupiter is larger than Mars," can equally well be divided into the concept expression, "Jupiter is larger than ..." and the object name, "Mars," or into the concept expression, "... is larger than Mars" and the argument name, "Jupiter."

Frege believed that corresponding to the distinction between complete and incomplete expressions there was an analogous distinction between the kinds of things to which they referred. Objects, the referents of complete expressions, were regarded as "self-standing" or "saturated." Concepts and other functions, the referents of incomplete expressions, were regarded as "unsaturated" somehow. Frege regarded this lack of "saturation" as explaining the "predicative" nature of concepts; it is what makes them *suitable* to be predicated *of* something. Multiple names of objects written in succession cannot form a meaningful proposition; only if one or more of the expressions making up a proposition stands for a function, concept or relation, can a phrase be regarded as a significant whole. (Frege thought there was also a corresponding saturated/unsaturated distinction to be found at the level of the senses of these expressions; more on this in the next section.)

Frege regarded the distinction between objects and concepts (and other functions) that take objects as arguments, i.e. the kind that might be represented by removing a name from a proposition, at the base of an hierarchy of different "orders," or, in his mature terminology, different "levels" of concepts (or other functions). Functions that take objects as argument are called "first-level"; functions that take first-level functions as argument are called "second-level," and so on. The name of a second-level concept might be obtained by removing a first-level function expression from a complete proposition. Thus, if we remove "… is human" from the proposition, "for any x, if x is human, then x is mortal," to obtain "for any x, if … x …, then x is mortal," our new incomplete expression names a concept that will map its argument concept to the True just in case all objects that fall under that argument concept also fall under the concept of mortality. Notice that a second-level function expression, like a first-level function expression, contains a gap or spot to be completed by another expression, except that the kind of expression that would fit that gap is of a different sort. If an argument expression is inserted, the two "fit together" in the appropriate way. At the level of what the expressions stand for, again Frege thinks there is something comparable: the second-level function "mutually saturates" with its argument first-level function to yield an object as value. But notice, however, that a concept expression of any level is never of the right sort to complete, or be completed by, itself or another concept expression of the same level.

Frege takes this distinction to be of utmost philosophical importance. He goes so far as to call the confusion of concept and object, or concepts of different levels, "the grossest possible" (GG: xxv). As we have already seen, he argues that numbers must be considered self-standing objects, and his rationale for this conclusion is that numerals and other number expressions are syntactically complete. He also argues that the concept of existence, as represented by the existential quantifier, "$\exists x(…x…)$," must be understood as, at least at the fundamental level, a second-level concept (GL: §68; FuB: 25), and, alongside other confusions, diagnoses the ontological argument for God's existence as a failure of inattentiveness to this (GL: §53; FuB: 27). Frege admits, however, that our normal ways of speaking about concepts and objects within philosophical contexts is often imprecise, and apt to mislead. Part of this is because any attempt to talk about a concept or other function as if it were an object is doomed to failure. It is natural to think of "the color of the sky" as referring to the same thing as the adjective "blue," but Frege claims that this cannot be so, since the former but not the latter is an object (GL: §106) Notoriously, Frege argues that despite what we might initially assume, the phrase "the concept horse," since it is not itself incomplete or predicative, cannot name a concept, and hence, accepts the *truth* of the following paradoxical-seeming assertion (BuG: 184):

The concept horse is not a concept.

Benno Kerry (1887), Bertrand Russell (1903), and others since have despaired that a result like this renders Frege's position unintelligible at best and inconsistent at worst. Indeed, the issue seems to pose a rather direct problem for interpreting Frege's own language when stating his own theory. How are we to understand the words "object" and "concept" that Frege uses? If "… is an object" is a first-level concept expression, then it is true of everything whatever of which it can be meaningfully predicated, and so doesn't seem to mark off a distinction between objects and other sorts of entities. (And if it is interpreted differently, parallel problems arise.) Frege himself admitted the problem, adding that "by a kind of necessity of language, my expressions, taken literally, miss my thought" and that hence, "I was relying upon a reader who would be ready to meet me halfway – who does not begrudge a pinch of salt" (BuG: 193). This has led some commentators to the conclusion that Frege believes there are insights into metaphysical categories, founded (in his own words) "deep in the nature of things" (FuB: 31) that escape expression in language, and has led others to conclude that Frege regarded his own elucidations of his views of logic as nothing more than nonsense used as a stepping stone on the way to mastering his logical notation, but both groups of commentators find Frege's struggles with these issues to prefigure Wittgenstein's discussion in the *Tractatus* of ineffable truths, those that can be "shown" but not "said."

Sense and reference

Distinct from, and cutting across, the distinction between concept and object is the distinction Frege makes between two components of meaning expressions may possess, the distinction between, in German, "*Sinn*" (sense) and "*Bedeutung*." The proper translation of Frege's "Bedeutung" is controversial, with "meaning," "denotation," "nominatum," "indication" and "significance" all in the running, though here we follow Dummett (1973) in substituting either "referent" or "reference" depending on whether we mean the thing referred to (the referent), or the relationship between the word or phrase and this thing (reference). The distinction was first outlined in Frege's 1891 piece, "Funktion und Begriff," and was expanded upon in his celebrated essay, "Über Sinn und Bedeutung," a year later.

During Frege's time, there was a dispute among certain mathematicians over the sign "=" routinely used in mathematical equations. Consider:

$$4 \times 2 = 11 - 3.$$

A number of Frege's contemporaries (Weierstrass among them) were wary of viewing this as a statement of identity proper, and instead posited some weaker form of "equality" whereby 4×2 and $11 - 3$ could be considered equal-in-magnitude or equal-in-number without being one and the same thing. Their rationale was rather straightforward: the two cannot in all ways be thought to be the same: the former is a product, the latter a difference, and so on. In his early work, 1879's *Begriffsschrift*, Frege apparently put enough credence into this viewpoint to think it worth using a different sign, "≡" for "identity of content" so that "=" could be reserved for mathematical equality instead.

Before distinguishing between sense and reference, Frege merely spoke of the "content" of a word or phrase. He came to the conclusion that a judgment recorded in the form:

$$\vdash (a \equiv b)$$

must not actually be about the contents of the names "a" and "b," but rather about the names themselves, since – assuming the judgment is true – "a" and "b" typically have the same content, and hence the judgment above as a whole would otherwise not differ in content from the analytic judgment $\vdash(a \equiv a)$, whereas the former judgment may be synthetic depending on how these names determine their content.

In his mature work, Frege is an explicit opponent of the view that mathematical equality needs to be distinguished from identity proper, and is usually read as no longer holding the view that identity statements involve claiming something about signs rather than things themselves. (For an exception, see Caplan and Thau 2001.) However, Frege now differentiates two parts of the content of a well-formed expression. In the case of "4×2" and "$11 - 3$," for example, we can make a distinction between the actual number designated – the common referent of both these expressions – and the way in which that number is presented or picked out – the senses of the two expressions, which differ in the two cases. In Frege's terminology, a word or phrase is said to *express* its sense, and *refer to* (i.e. *bedeutet*) its referent. The distinction applies outside of mathematics as well. Another famous example Frege gives is of the pair, "the morning star" and "the evening star," both of which refer to the planet Venus, but in virtue of very different properties that it has. In the case of a proper name or complete expression, the referent is the object that it stands for, and the sense is what contains the "mode of presentation" or "cognitive content" used to represent that object.

Frege is explicit that he believes that the sense/reference distinction can be applied to other kinds of phrases as well as complete propositions. In the case of a concept expression, "... is an equilateral triangle," the referent is a concept, again, understood as a kind of function from objects to truth-values. Frege believes that functions "coincide" (– he reserves the label "identical" for pairs of objects –) when they always have the same value for the same arguments, or in the case of concepts, when the same objects fall under them (PW: 120–2). Because the function mapping all equilateral triangles (and nothing else) to the True is the same as the function mapping all equiangular triangles to the True, the difference in meaning between "... is an equilateral triangle," and "... is an equiangular triangle," must be one of sense rather than reference. Frege concludes that the notion of sense captures what other logicians have in mind when speaking of the "intension" of a concept, though Frege is clear that the referent of a concept phrase – the concept itself – must still be distinguished from its extension, in virtue of the fact that the latter is an object not a function (see e.g. PMC: 63–4).

Frege believes in compositionality principles at both levels. The reference of a complex expression is a function of the referents of the parts; indeed, the referent of one of the parts *is* a function that is applied to the *referent(s)* of other part(s) to yield the referent of the whole. The sense of the whole expression is also a function of the senses of the parts; indeed, Frege often suggests something stronger: that the sense of the complex expression *is* a kind of whole composed of the senses of the parts. (The incompleteness of the senses of function expressions provides the "logical glue" holding the whole together.) He uses this as an explanation for how it is we are able to understand new propositions we've never heard before: we put together the already-understood senses of the individual parts in order to grasp the sense of the whole (CP: 390). There is, however, some uncertainty among Frege commentators as to how this view coheres with the context principle of *Grundlagen*, which seems to put our understanding of the content of parts of a proposition secondary to that of the entire proposition, as well as what's sometimes called Frege's "priority thesis," according to which the parts of a complete judgment are to be found by analyzing the judgment, and not vice-versa (PW: 17, 253; PMC: 101).

Returning to the puzzle about identity, consider the two cases:

(A)   the morning star = the morning star
(B)   the morning star = the evening star.

It seems clear that in (A) the two expressions flanking the identity sign have the same sense, but in (B) the two signs flanking the identity sign have different senses, but in both cases they have the same referent. This latter fact explains why these two claims are both true. However, Frege believes that the "cognitive value" or "informativity" of a proposition is determined by its sense. Hence, we have an explanation of how it can be that (B) is informative whereas (A) is not, despite that each part of one corresponds to a part of the other with the same referent. Frege calls the sense of a complete proposition a "thought" (*Gedanke*), and believes the referent of a complete proposition is its truth-value. Indeed, Frege sometimes defines thoughts as those senses whose referents are truth-values (e.g. GG: §2). Since these are determined functionally, (A) and (B) can differ in the thought expressed, but must have the same truth-value (as they do). Thus, in his mature work, Frege's prior single notion of "content" was replaced by the dual notions of "thought" and "truth-value."

Unfortunately, Frege tells us very little about what senses are and how they are related to the referents they present. A long-standing interpretative tradition (e.g. Kripke 1972) reads him as thinking of the sense of a proper name as involving certain descriptive information, or a condition, which must hold of one individual and one individual alone in order for that individual to be the referent. There is some evidence in favor of this reading. Frege says that each sense "illuminates a single aspect of the referent, supposing it to have one," and that "comprehensive knowledge of the referent would require us to be able to say immediately whether any given sense attaches to it" (SuB: 27), suggesting that which senses present which referents is a function of the properties of those referents. Evidence also comes by way of certain examples Frege gives, such as his suggestion that for some people the sense of the name "Aristotle" can be described in terms of "the pupil of Plato and teacher of Alexander the great" (SuB: 27n; cf. Ged: 65). Nevertheless, it is not entirely clear that this gives the right picture for all Fregean senses. With regard to senses of other kinds of expressions, Frege tells us even less (see Klement 2002: Ch. 3).

One nice thing about the interpretative tradition is that, if correct, it sheds light on something Frege certainly does believe: that it is possible for there to exist expressions that have a sense but no referent. Frege gives such examples as "Odysseus" and "the least rapidly converging series." Given that Frege believes that the reference of a complex expression is a function of the referents of its parts, and that the referent of a complete proposition is its truth-value, he concludes that when a phrase such as these occur within a proposition, while the proposition may be considered to express a thought as sense, as a whole it is devoid of reference, and hence is neither true nor false. If the interpretative tradition is right, the explanation for this is surely that the sense fails to present a reference because no one individual uniquely satisfies the requisite condition. (The thought expressed by the whole doesn't actually assert that there is one such individual; it merely presupposes it – see SuB: 39–40.) Frege regarded the existence of referent-less phrases as a defect of ordinary language to be avoided within a logical language, where stating precise rules of truth-preservation is the goal.

Lastly, Frege thinks that in certain contexts, the reference of words "shift" so that they have as their referents what would ordinarily be their senses. Consider the following two propositions:

(C) Ptolemy believes that the morning star is a planet.
(D) Ptolemy believes that the evening star is a planet.

It seems perfectly natural to suppose that one of these might be true, and the other false, assuming Ptolemy to be unaware that the morning star and evening star are the same. However, if the truth or falsity of (C) and (D) is determined functionally by the referents of their parts, it seems that Frege would be committed to holding that (C) and (D) must have the same truth-value. Worse, he would seem committed to holding that anyone who believes one truth believes all of them. Frege responds to such puzzles with his theory of "*oratio obliqua*" or "indirect speech," according to which, in belief reports and similar contexts, words have as referents what would ordinarily be their senses. Hence, rather than referring to the same truth-value, the dependent clauses in (C) and (D) refer to distinct thoughts, and so Frege is free to regard one of these as true and the other as false without abandoning the principle that the reference of the whole is determined by the referents of the parts. Frege's deliberation on this issue has sparked a lively, and still ongoing debate (over a century later), about whether or not words within such contexts really should be taken as meaning something other than what they normally mean, and whether, if we answer yes to that question, this requires us to posit the existence of a potentially infinite number of distinct meanings (*senses* or *referents*) the same words might have given the possibility of embedding one such indirect speech report within another.

Thoughts and truth

As we have seen, Frege believed that the referent of a complete proposition, when it has one, is its truth-value, either the True or the False. This view comports with, and indeed, is probably the source of, his understanding of concepts and relations as functions whose values, when given arguments, are truth-values. Frege gives two broad reasons in favor of this view. First, he claims (rather cavalierly) that, in general, the reference of expressions becomes important to us precisely when we become interested in the truth or falsity of what we are saying. If simply telling a story for amusement, then it may not matter to us at all whether or not the name "Odysseus" refers to a person, but if we become interested in the historical accuracy of the story, i.e. its truth or falsity, then it will matter (SuB: 32–3). His other reason stems from his conviction that the reference of the whole must be determined by the referents of the parts, adding, rhetorically (SuB: 35), "what feature except the truth-value can be found that belongs to such propositions quite generally and remains unchanged by substitutions" in which "a part of the proposition is replaced by an expression with the same referent"? Frege doesn't give examples, but it seems likely that he meant such transformations as between sentences (A) and (B) in the previous section, although it is not obvious in that case that *nothing* else remains in common between them other than their truth-value. Years later, followers of Frege on this point gave more complicated examples. Assuming that both substitutions of coreferential descriptions preserve reference, and that logically equivalent propositions have the same referent as well, Alonzo Church (1956: 25) argued that we must accept that the following all have the same referent:

(E)   Sir Walter Scott is the author of *Waverly*.
(F)   Sir Walter Scott is the writer of twenty nine *Waverly* novels.
(G)   The number of *Waverly* novels written by Sir Walter Scott is twenty nine.
(H)   The number of counties in Utah is twenty nine.

Since the first and the last seem to have nothing interesting in common except their truth-value, we are lead to Frege's conclusion that truth-values are the referents of propositions. Arguments of this form have come to be called "the Frege-Church slingshot."

Thoughts, the senses of complete propositions, can thus be understood as senses that present truth-values. It is their truth or falsity that is at issue in any inquiry. Frege is clear that the relationship between thoughts and their truth-values must be understood as the relationship of senses to referents, not the relationship of subject and predicate. Frege notes that the words "it is true that ..." adds nothing to the sense of the proposition that would fill the ellipsis; they therefore cannot represent a genuine property. Moreover, Frege does not think that it is possible to give a non-circular account or definition of what truth, or "the True," is. Truth cannot consist of correspondence of a thought with something else, according to Frege, since nothing *completely* corresponds with anything distinct from itself, and if truth relied on correspondence with something in this-or-that respect, we would inevitably be led to the question as to whether it was *true* that there was just such a correspondence, and we would be stuck in a vicious regress. Frege thinks similar remarks apply to any other property we might suggest as our characterization of what truth is, since recognition of the possession of a property is always *ipso facto* the recognition of a thought as being true. Frege concludes that truth is "*sui generis* and indefinable" (Ged: 327). (I note in passing that one might attempt to define a thought as true when the object it presents as referent is —⊥— a = a, keeping in mind that " —⊥— a = a" is, in Frege's notation, considered a name of the True. Although extensionally correct, this definition would be circular, since the logical function expressions involved were characterized in terms of the True.) Rather, Frege thinks that logical activity in a way indirectly spells out what truth is, particularly the activity of forming judgments and making inferences and assertions (over and above merely grasping thoughts and considering them). "The meaning of the word *true* is spelled out in the laws of truth" (Ged: 59; cf. PW: 251–2).

According to Frege, thoughts (and other senses) exist in a "third realm," distinct from both the concrete physical world, and the psychological world of ideas, feelings and sensations. Frege rejects the supposition that thoughts can be thought of as concrete objects or built up out of them, adding that "Mont Blanc with its masses of snow and ice is no part of the thought that Mont Blanc is over 4000m high" (PMC: 187), while noting that thoughts need to be finer grained than the objects they're about. Secondly, Frege strenuously rejects the suggestion that thoughts can be considered as ideas, citing as his reasons that unlike ideas, which are private to the individual who has them and are created by our mental activities and destroyed by their cessation, thoughts are timeless, can be shared by multiple individuals, and exist (and can be true or false) regardless of having been grasped or not by any thinkers. Frege insists that we must not confuse the thought with the act of thinking. If each person's thought were different from another's, like each person's ideas and perceptions differ, then it would be impossible to communicate or disagree with others in a true sense. (Interestingly, however, Frege does acknowledge a certain kind of exception to the communicability of senses and thoughts, by recognizing a special way in which each of us is presented to him or herself which no one else is capable of grasping: the notion of "I" when used in our own cogitations. This has generated significant interest, in part, because it seems out of sorts with the remainder of Frege's theory, and in part because it seems as if it might be an early recognition of the distinctive character of *de se* belief and knowledge, as discussed, for example, in John Perry's work.)

Frege's legacy

Frege is a philosopher whose work has dramatically changed how it is we think about nearly all areas of abstract study: abstract truths, abstract objects and abstract knowledge. In some cases, he did this directly, such as in his groundbreaking work in quantificational logic and the philosophy of mathematics, where his innovations were many and his arguments cogent. In other cases, he did this indirectly, by failing in such a drastic, but such an understandable, fashion, as with his inconsistent theory of the extensions of concepts, that investigating where and how Frege went wrong has been every bit as instructive to ongoing researches as work not so flawed. With his theories of meaning and truth, perhaps, the jury is still out regarding in which category they belong, though I think there is increasing evidence these may go the way of Basic Law V. Either way, his influence, although limited during his own lifespan, is now pervasive. Even 125 years after its publication, Frege's *Grundlagen* is likely still the single most widely read work in the philosophy of mathematics. We find working philosophers of language write about Frege's views in the same way one might write about an esteemed contemporary whose work must be considered as viable as anyone's (e.g. Salmon 1986; Kripke 2008). It is perhaps in the area of logic, however, that the effects of his work are most ubiquitous – indeed, perhaps so thoroughly so that they're almost invisible. First-order predicate logic, extracted out of Frege's function calculus, is now the default standard logical calculus for conducting any technical proof. More complicated logical calculi are almost unthinkable except as building upon, or *intentionally* and systematically deviating from, the Fregean (or "classical") approach. Moreover, while, in practice, most working mathematicians don't construct proofs using the full rigor of a *Begriffsschrift*-style derivation, most do, I think, attempt to fashion their proofs in such a way as to provide enough details that a proof of this level of rigor *could* be constructed out of it, and would regard it as not really a proof at all if this were not possible. To be sure, however, these were not changes that had no hope of being brought about without Frege (given the parallel work of Peirce, Schröder, Peano, etc.), nor are they changes Frege brought about *alone*, or indeed, could have helped bring about at all without the championing of later intellectual heirs who eventually did come to prize his work much more highly than it had been at first.

References

Frege's Principal Works

Frege, G. (BS) *Begriffsschrift, eine der arithmetischen nachgebildete Formelsprache des reinen Denkens,* Halle: L. Nebert, 1879; trans., T. W. Bynum as *Conceptual Notation and Related Articles,* London: Oxford University Press, 1972.

—— (BuG) "Über Begriff und Gegenstand," *Vierteljahrsschrift für wissenschaftliche Philosophie* 16 (1892): 192–205; trans. as "On Concept and Object," in CP, pp. 182–94, FR, pp. 181–93, or TPW, pp. 42–55.

—— (CP) *Collected Papers on Mathematics, Logic and Philosophy,* trans. M. Black, V. Dudman, P. Geach, H. Kaal, E.-H. W. Kluge, B. McGuinness, and R.H. Stoothoff, New York: Basil Blackwell, 1984.

—— (FR) *The Frege Reader,* edited by Michael Beaney, Oxford: Blackwell, 1997.

—— (FuB) *Funktion und Begriff,* Jena: Hermann Pohle, 1891; trans. as "Function and Concept," in CP, pp. 137–56, FR, pp. 130–48, or TPW, pp. 21–41.

—— (Ged) "Der Gedanke." *Beträge zur Philosophie des deutschen Idealismus* 1 (1918–19): pp. 58–77; trans. as "Thoughts," in CP, pp. 351–72, or as "Thought," in FR, pp. 325–45.

—— (GG) *Grundgesetze der Arithmetik,* 2 vols, Jena: Hermann Pohle, 1893–1903; trans., in part, as *The Basic Laws of Arithmetic,* edited by M. Furth, Berkeley: University of California Press, 1964.

—— (GL) *Die Grundlagen der Arithmetik, eine logisch mathematische Untersuchung über den Begriff der Zahl,* Breslau: W. Koebner, 1884; trans., J. L. Austin, as *The Foundations of Arithmetic: A Logico-Mathematical Enquiry into the Concept of Number,* 2nd edn, Oxford: Blackwell, 1953.

—— (GLG) "Über die Grundlagen der Geometrie." *Jahresbericht der Deutschen Mathematiker-Vereinigung* 12 (1903): pp. 319–24, 368–75; 15 (1906): pp. 293–309, 377–403, 423–30; trans. as "On the Foundations of Geometry", in CP, pp. 273–340.

—— (PMC) *Philosophical and Mathematical Correspondence*, trans. H. Kaal, Chicago: University of Chicago Press, 1980.

—— (PW) *Posthumous Writings*, trans. P. Long and R. White. Chicago: University of Chicago Press, 1979.

—— (SuB) "Über Sinn und Bedeutung," *Zeitschrift für Philosophie und philosophische Kritik* 100 (1892): 25–50; trans. as "On Sense and Meaning," in CP: 157–77, as "On Sinn and Bedeutung," in FR, pp. 151–71, or "On Sense and Reference," in TPW, pp. 56–78.

—— (TPW) *Translations from the Philosophical Writings of Gottlob Frege*, 3rd ed., eds. P. Geach and M. Black. Oxford: Blackwell, 1980.

Works by others

Boolos, George (1998) *Logic, Logic and Logic*, Cambridge, MA: Harvard University Press.

Caplan, Benjamin, and Mike Thau (2001) "What's Puzzling Gottlob Frege?" *Canadian Journal of Philosophy* 31: 159–200.

Church, Alonzo (1956) *Introduction to Mathematical Logic*, Princeton, NJ: Princeton University Press.

Dummett, Michael (1973) *Frege: Philosophy of Language*. Cambridge, MA: Harvard University Press.

—— (1991) *Frege: Philosophy of Mathematics*. Cambridge, MA: Harvard University Press.

Kerry, Benno (1887) "Über Anschauung und ihre psychische Verarbeitung IV," *Vierteljahrsschrift für wissenschaftliche Philosophie* 11: 246–307.

Klement, Kevin C. (2002) *Frege and the Logic of Sense and Reference*, London: Routledge.

Kripke, Saul (1972) "Naming and Necessity," in *Semantics of Natural Languages*, edited by D. Davidson and G. Harman, Dordrecht: D. Reidel.

—— (2008) "Frege's Theory of Sense and Reference," *Theoria* 74: 181–218.

Landini, Gregory (2006) "The Ins and Outs of Frege's Way Out," *Philosophia Mathematica* 14: 1–25.

Quine, W. V. (1955) "On Frege's Way Out," *Mind* 64: 145–59.

Reck, Erich H., and Steve Awodey (eds) (2004) *Frege's Lectures on Logic: Carnap's Student Notes 1910–11*, Chicago: Open Court.

Russell, Bertrand (1903) *The Principles of Mathematics*, Cambridge: Cambridge University Press.

—— (1919) *Introduction to Mathematical Philosophy*, London: Allen & Unwin.

Salmon, Nathan (1986) *Frege's Puzzle*, Cambridge, MA: MIT Press.

Shapiro, Stewart (2003) "Prolegomenon to Any Future Neo-Logicist Set Theory: Abstraction and Indefinite Extensibility," *British Journal of the Philosophy of Science* 54: 59–91.

Further reading

Michael Dummett's extensive secondary works on Frege – *Frege: Philosophy of Language, The Interpretation of Frege's Philosophy, The Interpretation of Frege's Philosophy, Frege: Philosophy of Mathematics* (Cambridge, MA: Harvard University Press, 1973, 1981 and 1991, respectively), and *Frege and Other Philosophers* (Oxford: Clarendon Press, 1991) – are perhaps the best known in English. Hans Sluga's *Gottlob Frege* (Boston: Routledge, 1980) and Joan Weiner's *Frege in Perspective* (Ithaca: Cornell University Press, 1990) attempt to place Frege in his historical perspective. Other important general sources include G. Baker and P. Hacker, *Frege: Logical Excavations* (New York: Oxford University Press, 1984) and Tyler's Burge's *Truth, Thought and Reason: Essays on Frege* (Oxford: Oxford University Press, 2005). Frege's mathematical philosophy is addressed in Michael Resnick's *Frege and the Philosophy of Mathematics* (Ithaca: Cornell University Press, 1980) and Crispin Wright's *Frege's Conception of Numbers as Objects* (Aberdeen: Aberdeen University Press, 1983). His theory of meaning is explored in Michael Beaney's *Frege: Making Sense* (London: Duckworth, 1996) and Kevin Klement, *Frege and the Logic of Sense and Reference* (New York: Routledge, 2002). Three large collections of smaller pieces on Frege's work include E. Reck and M. Beaney, eds. *Gottlob Frege: Critical Assessments of Leading Philosophers*, 4 vols. (Abingdon: Routledge, 2006), Hans Sluga, ed. *The Philosophy of Frege*, 3 vols. (New York: Garland, 1993), and M. Schirn, ed. *Studien zu Frege*, 3 vols. (Stuttgart: Verlag, 1976).

30

EDMUND HUSSERL

Christian Beyer

Synopsis

In the last decade of the nineteenth century, the Austro-German mathematician and philosopher Edmund Husserl managed both to bring the predominant "psychologistic" philosophy of mathematics and logic of his time to a culmination and to overcome that philosophy. He did so by developing, in his *Logical Investigations* (LI), a forceful critique of psychologism as well as a positive approach, his "phenomenology of logical experiences (*Phänomenologie der logischen Erlebnisse*)," which he associated with a platonistic ontology of meaning and thought content.

The work of the early (pre-LI) Husserl can be subdivided into three thematic fields, namely (i) the descriptive psychological study of the basic concepts of arithmetic and logic, (ii) the foundations of a logic of contents (*Inhaltslogik*), as opposed to a logic of extensions (*Umfangslogik*), and (iii) the problem of intentional objects and reference. Husserl's early approaches to (i) and (iii), at least, remain of considerable interest today, whilst his work on (ii) (which will be left aside in what follows) has probably been superseded by the development originating from Frege's *Begriffsschrift* and advanced by Russell and Whitehead.

His LI from 1900/1 continue these early approaches in some important respects. LI are the first chief work of phenomenology, which was to become a major current of twentieth-century philosophy, along with analytic philosophy, whose insights have been partly anticipated by Husserl. On the basis of the results achieved in this work, Husserl later developed a method he called "transcendental phenomenology." This method has us focus, in a radically unprejudiced way, on the essential structures of intentional (i.e. object-directed) consciousness that allow the objects naively taken for granted in the "natural attitude" (which is characteristic of both the "personalistic" stance we use to take in our everyday life and the "naturalistic" stance taken in ordinary science) to "constitute themselves."

Life and early work

Husserl was born in Prossnitz (Moravia) on 8 April 1859, as the second of four children of the hatter Adolf Husserl and his wife Julie (for the following, see Schuhmann

1977). His parents were non-orthodox Jews; Husserl himself and his wife would later convert to Protestantism. They had three children, one of which died in the First World War. In the years 1876–8 Husserl studied astronomy in Leipzig, where he also attended courses of lectures in mathematics, physics and philosophy (with Wilhem Wundt, among others). His mentor was the philosophy professor Thomas Masaryk, a former student of Brentano's, who was to become the first president of Czechoslovakia. In 1878 Husserl changed his subject and went to Berlin, to study mathematics with Weierstrass and Kronecker, as well as physics and philosophy. He was particularly impressed with Weierstrass' scientific ethos and was strongly influenced by him (and Kronecker), and also by Brentano and his pupil Stumpf, in connection with topic (i) above (Ierna 2006). As regards topic (iii), the influence of Bolzano and Twardowski, another pupil of Brentano's, was decisive.

Husserl took his PhD in mathematics in Vienna, with a thesis on the theory of variations (1883). After that he returned to Berlin, to become Weierstrass' assistant for a short period of time. Husserl then went back to Vienna. After a brief military service he studied philosophy with Brentano, whose lectures on psychology and logic had a lasting impact on Husserl, as had his general vision of a strictly scientific philosophy (1884–6).

Husserl's academic career continued in Halle, where he submitted his habilitation dissertation *On the Concept of Number* with Stumpf in 1887. That thesis was later incorporated in his first book, *Philosophy of Arithmetic* (PA), published in 1891, which is devoted to topic (i). Despite the high quality and originality of PA, Husserl had to wait for a long time before he got a professorship. He worked as a *Privatdozent* (an unpaid honorary office) at the University of Halle for fourteen years, during which he wrote his major work LI, which appeared in 1900/1 and was widely discussed immediately in the German-speaking world, especially due to Husserl's attack on psychologism.

Thanks to LI, Husserl received an associate professorship in Göttingen in 1901, where he taught until 1916, when he went to Freiburg/Breisgau to become full professor. He retired in 1928. Husserl died on 27 April 1938 in Freiburg. His manuscripts (more than 40,000 pages in total) were rescued from Nazi-Germany by the Franciscan Van Breda, who brought them to Leuven (Belgium), where the first Husserl archive was founded in 1939. Since 1950 the Husserl archives are editing Husserl's collected works, *Husserliana* (henceforth quoted as Hua, [volume number], [page]).

Philosophy of arithmetic

It is widely held that the position developed in PA represents a paradigm example of psychologism, the view according to which the laws of mathematics and logic depend on psychological laws of thinking, deriving from necessary conditions of, or even completely contingent empirical facts about, the human mind. However, the main aim of PA is conceptual clarification regarding the basic notions of arithmetic. (Frege, whose critical review of PA seems to constitute one of the causal factors that eventually led Husserl to turn against psychologism [Føllesdal 1958; cf. Patzig 1958: 131], must have been aware of this aim, as his letter to Husserl from 24 May 1891 indicates, where he even equates Husserl's "concepts" to his predicative "senses"; see Mohanty 1982: 117ff. However, in his 1894 review Frege ignores this point.) Following Stumpf, Husserl is "guided by the methodological strategy" here that the "content of a concept" is to be clarified by investigating into its psychological origins, i.e. the lived experiences which occur when the concept develops in one's own mind (Willard 2003: xvi f.).

It is far from clear how this approach is related to psychologism, as characterized above (p. 888). Mohanty has drawn a helpful distinction between what he calls "strong" and "weak psychologism" in this connection. Strong psychologism claims that logic is a branch of psychology, whilst so-called weak psychologism merely regards psychological inquiry (which would be *descriptive* psychological inquiry in Husserl's case) as an indispensable means for conceptual basic research regarding logic (Mohanty 1982: 20). The author of PA certainly subscribes to the latter view. This leaves it an open question whether there is a sense in which he may look upon logical and mathematical laws as dependent on psychological ones.

In any case, PA is a masterpiece of descriptive psychology in the Brentanian tradition. (Somewhat ironically, then, Brentano did not hold Husserl in high esteem. As Thomas Binder, University of Graz, has pointed out to me, he did not even open the copy of PA that Husserl had sent him; thus, Husserl's dedication to his teacher "with heartfelt gratitude" escaped him.) For instance, Husserl anticipates a central idea of *Gestalt* psychology here, the notion of a "*Gestalt* quality" (Ehrenfels 1890), which is expressed by the label "figural moment" in PA (Husserl arrived at his notion independently of von Ehrenfels):

> One speaks, for example, of a *a file* of soldiers, of a *heap* of apples, of a *row* of trees, of a *flight* of birds, of a *gaggle* of geese, and so on. In each of these examples ... there is expressed a certain *characteristic property* of the unitary total intuition of the [sensible] group, which can be grasped at one glance .... (Husserl 2003: 216; Hua: XII, 203f.)

Intuitions such as this, displaying a figural moment, entitle us to classify something as a sensible group (*Menge*) or collection of objects. The notion of a figural moment thus helps us to solve an epistemological problem not unlike the rule-following problem later discussed by Wittgenstein (in his *Philosophical Investigations*):

> What enables us to know that the process of collection can be continued by only so much as a single step, that beyond what has in fact been colligated there still remains something more to be colligated? What enables us to know that a 'total collection' is to be intended? (Husserl 2003: 209f.; Hua: XII, 197)

By invoking the idea of a figural moment at this point, Husserl relates the formal concept of a group back to its conceptual roots in what he was later to refer to as (the perceptual dimension of) our everyday lifeworld (see the sixth section, "Prospects," below). It is here that the psychological origin of our formal concepts is to be found, according to the author of PA; and it is with reference to that origin that such concepts are to be clarified and their application is to be epistemically justified, in the final analysis. Accordingly, he repeatedly stresses the close relationship between the contents of arithmetical thought and speech, on the one hand, and the practical interests of everyday life, on the other, criticizing Frege's definition of the concept of number for neglecting that relationship, while conceding, importantly, that it yields the right extension (Husserl 2003: 122, 128; Hua: XII, 116, 122).

Husserl regards the intuition of a group of n objects as such by means of a figural moment as an "inauthentic," symbolic representation of that group, where he follows Stumpf in holding that an "authentic" (re)presentation of such a group is only possible for $n \leq 12$ (Husserl 2003: 202; Hua: XII, 192). The distinction between authentic and inauthentic representation is inspired by Brentano (see Husserl 2003: 205n1; Hua: XII, 193), and it continues to play a crucial role in Husserl's phenomenological epistemology as developed in LI (and elsewhere). In PA he writes:

> If a content is not directly given to us as that which it is, but rather only indirectly *through signs which univocally characterize it*, then we have a symbolic representation of it instead of an authentic one. We have, for example, an authentic representation of the outer appearance of a house when we actually look at the house; and we have a symbolic representation when someone gives us the indirect characterization: the corner house on such and such side of such and such street. (Husserl 2003: 205; Hua: XII, 193)

This conception is similar to Bertrand Russell's distinction between knowledge by acquaintance vs. knowledge by description underlying (the epistemological part of) his theory of definite descriptions (Russell 1917) and it is remarkable that in his review of PA, Frege, whose view on the sense of proper names is sometimes associated with that theory, particularly recommends the chapter where Husserl presents the conception in question as containing valuable insights (if mainly psychological ones).

Descriptive-psychologically, and thus conceptually, the relation of collective unity obtaining between the members of a group cannot be reduced to any other relation, such as similarity between those members. (Quite the contrary: in order to determine such similarity one must already presuppose the collective unity in question.) To justify this and many other theses, Husserl invokes what Brentano has called "inner experience," a kind of introspection or inner perception (Husserl 2003: 69; Hua: XII, 66).

Further examples of symbolic representation include cases of multiplying and exponentialization. Thus, to quote Husserl's example, "4^3" symbolically represents (s. r.) "$4 \times 4 \times 4$," which s. r. "$(4 \times 4) \times 4$," which s. r. "$(4+4+4+4)+(4+4+4+4)+(4+4+4+4)+(4+4+4+4)$," where "4" in turn s. r. "$1+1+1+1$" (Husserl 2003: 197; Hua: XII, 187). In this manner, arithmetical concepts can be traced back, regarding both their psychological origin (the way they are formed) and the ultimate justification of their application, to simple additions, i.e. acts of collecting units into sums, which acts are understood to be authentic representations of small groups of objects with at most a dozen members (see above, p. 890). Furthermore, a descriptive psychological analysis such as this obviously serves to clarify the corresponding arithmetical concepts. In addition, it makes it clear how symbols function as non-authentic surrogates for complex arithmetical operations, thereby enabling us to reason in an economical way.

The same holds, *mutatis mutandis*, for the concepts referring to the "numbers (*Zahlen*)," i.e. the concrete forms of groups containing a cardinal number (*Anzahl*) of units, the arithmetical operations in question operate upon. Thanks to "certain instrumentalities," to be studied in semiotics, notably "those of enumerating and calculating, i.e., certain 'mechanical' operations, as it were, the true basis for which lies in the elemental relations between the numbers," these concepts can be applied with ease in a wide range of cases (Husserl 2003: 95; Hua: XII, 90; also see Husserl 2003: 436, where an algorithm is described as "a blind mechanism" of symbols that "can replace and spare us logical thinking"; see Hua: XII, 394). Note that Husserl regards cardinal numbers, which he also refers to as "abstract forms of multiplicities," as types whose instances are "numbers" in the sense of "determinate forms of multi-plicities," where "multiplicities" denotes concrete groups or collections of objects (Husserl 2003: 87; Hua: XII, 83). Thus, for example, he thinks of the cardinal number three as a type, or general concept, which is tokened by the individual form of a group of, say, three birds as such, i.e. by the individual feature that distinguishes this group from a concrete collection of four birds. "1+3=4" then means: quite generally, if we unite a single object and a group of objects instantiating (by its form) the cardinal number three, the resulting collection is a group instantiating the cardinal number four (Husserl 2003: 191f.; Hua: XII, 181f.).

When claiming that psychological description helps to clarify concepts, in the way just illustrated, Husserl does not have in mind traditional definitions, which must not be circular. For Husserl, circular explanations of concepts are perfectly acceptable as long as they shed light on the structure "of the phenomena upon which the abstraction of [the respective] concept rests" (Husserl 2003: 22; Hua: XII, 21). We also have to keep in mind this credo when turning to Husserl's platonistic theory of thought content as developed in LI (see the fifth section, "*Logical Investigations*," below). However, that theory, and indeed the whole point of the phenomenological method introduced in LI, can only be understood properly against the background of his conception of intentional object and reference, which took shape in the 1890s, particularly in the key text "Intentional Objects" (IO) from 1894 (Husserl 1994: 345–78). It is to this conception that we now turn.

Intentional objects

The problem discussed in IO is an antinomy Husserl refers to as "the paradox of objectless representations." He borrows the term "objectless representations" from the great Bohemian philosopher, logician and mathematician Bernard Bolzano, the study of whose major work *Theory of Science* (1837) helped him (along with other pupils of Brentano's) to free himself from the influence of his Viennese teacher. By "representations" he means what Bolzano refers to as "objective representations" or "representations in themselves," i.e. the objective meaning contents of "subjective representations" like, for instance, the mental phenomena of "having something in mind" underlying the use of names (general or singular terms), which phenomena he also calls "nominal" subjective representations. According to Bolzano, these meaning contents are not to be confused with the real objects, if any, the relevant mental phenomena are directed at; for there are subjective representations lacking a corresponding object, such as your thought of a golden mountain. The objective meaning content of such a representation is called "objectless."

Objective representations that are *not* objectless play a crucial role in Bolzano's "logic of variation," whose central notion, called *derivability*, is defined (in §155 of *Theory of Science* [1972]) as a relation in which one or more propositions (what Bolzano calls "sentences in themselves"), the conclusions C, stand to one or more propositions, the premises P, with respect to one or more variable representations in themselves R, if and only if every collection ("*Inbegriff*") of representations in themselves put in the place of the representations R that makes true all premises P also makes true all conclusions C; where it is understood that the representations replacing R are not objectless. For instance, the conclusion that Kant is male is derivable from the premise that Kant is a bachelor, provided that we regard the objective representation *Kant* as variable. For, regardless of which representation we put in the place of *Kant*, we shall always obtain a true conclusion, given only that the representation in question is not objectless (otherwise the resulting conclusion is false, according to Bolzano).

While Husserl found the ontological status of objective representations completely mysterious until he read R. Hermann Lotze's 1874 *Logic* (Lotze 1989a, b; see fifth section, below), he had no doubt that Bolzano was right in holding that they serve an important function in mediating our mental and linguistic reference to objects. This mediating relationship he called "representation."

Here, then, is the paradox.

(1) Every (objective) representation represents an object.
(2) There are objectless representations, ones which have no object they represent.

This even goes for propositions and the "states of affairs" they represent when functioning as propositional thought contents:

> One can say that every proposition, even the false or perhaps absurd, represents a state of affairs (*Sachverhalt*) as its "object," and nevertheless there is not for each proposition a corresponding state of affairs. An invalid proposition represents a state of affairs which does not exist, does not subsist. (Husserl 1994: 346; Hua: XXII, 304)

However, Husserl confines his explicit discussion of the problem to nominal (objective) representations. In this area, proposition (2) is supported by examples like "a round square," "the present King of France" and "(the centaur) Cheiron" (to quote Husserl's examples).

Husserl begins by criticizing two solutions to the problem proposed in a treatise from 1894 (Twardowski 1977) by Kasimir Twardowski, another pupil of Brentano's, notably what might be called (i) the mental image theory and (ii) the immanent object theory of (objectless) representation.

Ad (i) According to the mental image theory, meaning contents represent intra-mental pictorial representations of objects. Like other pictures, such images may exist without there being a depicted object in the actual world. Where proposition (1) is about depiction, (2) concerns depicted objects.

Husserl raises three forceful objections against this proposal. First, he argues that it is a theoretical construction lacking a sufficient descriptive-psychological basis:

I would like to be introduced to those "mental images" which are supposed to reside in the concepts *Art, Literature, Science*, and the like ... I would also like to meet the mental images of objects thought in absurd representations; and, again, those that come before the mathematician in reading a treatise filled with complicated systems of formulae. Veritable cyclones of phantasms must play themselves out in his consciousness. (Husserl 1994: 347; Hua: XXII, 305)

Secondly, he observes that the mental image theory merely shifts the problem it is supposed to solve: The mental image represented is said to always exist, so (1) will be true, or so the theory has it; all right, but how can (2) be true on this assumption? The only option for the mental image theorist at this point is to make a "duplication" of objects represented by postulating that in the veridical case, i.e. when there is an actual object corresponding to the representation, we are dealing with two represented objects, the mental image as well as the extra-mental referent. However, this alleged solution flies in the face of our common conception of objectual reference:

The same Berlin which I represent also exists, and the same would no longer exist if judgement fell upon it as upon Sodom and Gomorrah. (Husserl 1994: 347; Hua: XXII, 305f.)

Finally, the mental image theory already presupposes what an adequate conception of pictorial representation is yet supposed to accomplish: an explanation of what it is that makes the underlying "phantasy content," or phantasm, "the [r]epresenting image *of* something or other" (Husserl 1994: 348; Hua: XXII, 306). It is precisely an objective representation that does the trick here (as in all cases of representation), according to Husserl, in a way to be explained in more detail (see the fifth section, *below*). Consequently, the idea of mental imaging is unhelpful when it comes to explaining the sense in which a given objective representation represents an object, which is exactly what a solution to the paradox of objectless representations would amount to.

Ad (ii) Another proposed such solution, not unlike the first one, and to be found in Brentano (at least on one reading of his notion of "intentional inexistence"), draws upon the distinction between "true" vs. "intentional," alias "immanent," existence; where a representation is supposed to have an "immanent object" even if the representation is objectless in Bolzano's sense of the term. In the latter case, the immanent object is said to exist "merely intentionally"; its "true" existence can be truthfully denied.

Husserl objects that this proposal makes the same "false duplication that also doomed the image theory" (Husserl 1994: 350; Hua: XXII, 308):

> The immanent object can … be none other than the true object in the cases where truth corresponds to the representation … Whether we merely represent Berlin, or judge it to be existing, in *either* case we are dealing with Berlin itself. (*Ibid.*)

The immanent object theorist might answer that this observation does not prove the distinction between immanent and true existence to be illegitimate. In fact, what else could it be whose true existence we affirm or deny, as the case may be, if not an object that in some sense, i.e. "immanently," exists?

This sort of reply has been nicknamed "Plato's beard" (Quine). Husserl criticizes it by pointing out, among other things, that it forces us to concede "the existence of any and every absurdity," such as a round square, since the corresponding objective representations do exist (Husserl 1994: 352; Hua: XXII, 310). In this context, it is notable that in 1902 Husserl planned to send a copy of IO to Alexius Meinong (Hua: XXII, 456n1), whose "theory of objects" seems to lead to consequences of precisely the sort that Husserl warns against (cf. Hua: XXII, 458, note in the margin and 310, lines 35ff.).

Now to Husserl's own solution. He crops Plato's beard in the style of a classic analytical philosopher, by rephrasing sentences (1) and (2) in such a way that their alleged conflict vanishes. He argues that "merely intentional objects" talk, based on the fact that there are representations lacking a ("true") object they represent, must not be taken literally; on his view, this would be just as illegitimate as the classification "of objects into determinate and indeterminate" ones on the ground that representations like "a lion" do not represent determinate objects – which surely has no tendency to show that there are "indeterminate lions running around in the world" (Husserl 1994: 354; Hua: XXII, 313). What is indeterminate is the *representation* (the meaning content), not the represented objects. Similarly, it is representations that we actually classify when we talk about "true" vs. "merely intentional objects." The attribute "merely intentional" modifies the meaning of "object," just as the attribute "painted" modifies the meaning of "fish" (Twardowski's example). By making explicit the intended literal meaning of sentences involving an alleged (successful) reference to merely intentional objects, this reference gets eliminated, such that the paradox of objectless representations becomes resolved, as follows:

(1') For every representation R there is an assumption A such that: if A were true, there would be an object that R represents.

(2') It is not the case that for every representation R there is an object that R represents.

Examples for the kind of assumptions referred to in (1') include the implicit assumptions underlying our talk about fictional characters ("*In Greek mythology*, the centaur Cheiron exists") and the existential assumptions on which a given system of geometry rests ("*Granted that there is a space, a manifold of such-and-such a determinate type (exactly defined in the principles), then in it* there exist these and those structures, for which these and those propositions hold true"; see Husserl 1994: 368; Hua: XXII, 328).

According to Husserl, we normally leave such assumptions implicit, as the respective "circumstances" automatically bring it about that they are taken for granted. Thus, "[i]t is obvious [*selbstverständlich*] that whoever judges about mythological objects places himself upon the grounds of the myth, without actually *claiming* it for himself" (Husserl 1994: 358; Hua: XXII, 317). Our talk about such objects is therefore elliptical; "taken literally and [properly]," the sentences employed (e.g. "the centaur Cheiron exists") are false (*ibid.*).

The same goes for our corresponding thoughts. Here as elsewhere, particularly in science and mathematics, we often think in an elliptical or abbreviated manner, thus conforming to the principle of the "economy of thought" formulated by Ernst Mach (whose 1886 [1897] *Contributions to the Analysis of the Sensations* Husserl studied while preparing his *Habilitationsschrift*), without which "science as an achievement of human thought is not intelligible," on Husserl's view (Husserl 1994: 365; Hua: XXII, 324). Notice that this principle also plays a significant role in Husserl's theory of symbolic representation, as sketched in PA (see third section, "Philosophy of Arithmetic," above, headword: symbolic representation of number); and it continues to do so in later writings, especially in LI (but see Husserl 2001: 123–33; Hua: XVIII, 196–213, where Husserl distances himself from Mach and Avenarius).

So Husserl subscribes to an informed common sense view of intentional, i.e. represented, objects (a view sometimes labeled as "direct realism"), combining it with a conception of objective representation deriving from Bolzano. In LI, Husserl develops the latter conception further, while still adhering to the conception of intentional objects presented in IO – claiming in no uncertain terms that:

It need only to be stated to be acknowledged *that the intentional object of a presentation is the same as its actual object, and on occasion as its external object, and that it is absurd to distinguish between them* … If the intentional object exists, the intention, the reference, does not exist alone, but the thing referred to exists also. (Husserl 2001a: 127; see also *ibid.*: 97ff., 125ff.; Hua: XIX/1, 384–9, 436–40)

This further development would eventually lead to a philosophical conception of objects as "constituted" in intentional consciousness, a conception that is anything but naive, despite the fact that it has the same extension as the common sense view (see sixth section, below, headword: phenomenological reduction).

Logical Investigations

The two volumes of LI were published in 1900/01 (second, revised edition 1913). The official goal Husserl pursues in this work is to develop a general theory of inferential systems, which (following Bolzano) he conceives of as a theory of science, on the ground that every science (including mathematics) can be looked upon as a system of propositions that are interconnected by a set of inferential (logical) relations. Following John S. Mill, he argues that the best way to study the nature of such propositional systems is to start with their linguistic manifestations, i.e. (sets of) sentences and (assertive) utterances thereof.

The first volume of LI contains Husserl's attack against psychologism, whereas the (much larger) second volume consists of six "descriptive psychological" and "episte-mological" investigations into (I) expression and meaning, (II) universals, (III) the formal ontology of parts and wholes (mereology), (IV) the "syntactical" and mereo-logical structure of meaning, (V) the nature and structure of intentionality as well as (VI) the interrelation of truth, intuition and cognition.

Husserl now adheres to a version of platonism that he derived from ideas of Bolzano and Lotze, where he embeds platonism about meaning and mental content in a theory of intentional consciousness.

In his *Theory of Science*, Bolzano draws a sharp distinction between subjective representations, objective representations and represented objects (see fourth section, "Intentional Objects," above), regarding which he holds the following six theses (Beyer 1996: 95–115).

(T_1) For every subjective representation there is an objective representation grasped in that representation, its "matter" or "stuff" (*Stoff*).

(T_2) The matter of a subjective representation is different from the object(s) represented by that representation.

(T_3) The matter of a subjective representation is its meaning content.

(T_4) Two subjective representations are alike if and only if they share the same matter; where likeness entails that the respective representations are composed in the same way out of the subjective representations they contain as parts, if any, such that the matter of any of these components is a part of the common matter of the two representations in question.

(T_5) The object(s) represented by a subjective representation whose matter is not objectless are identical to the object(s) represented by its matter.

(T_6) The matter of a subjective representation mediates its objectual reference in that it uniquely determines the object(s) represented, i.e., two subjective representations sharing that matter are thus bound to represent the same object(s), if any.

And accordingly for judgments, their propositional contents ("sentences in themselves") and the objects judged about (Beyer 1996: 116–30).

As it became clear, at least partially, in the fourth section, above, Husserl subscribed to all of these theses as early as in 1894. However, he was dissatisfied with the lack of positive explanation, in Bolzano, of what the subjective "grasping" of an objective representation, or proposition (sentence in itself), consists in. Here, Lotze's identification of meaning contents with Platonic ideas, in the sense of types that can (but need not) be psychologically tokened, or instantiated, by "thinking" (Beyer 1996: 146f.), filled the bill for him. He writes:

[a] If, like all earlier readers of *Bolzano*, his 'propositions in themselves' previously [notably before studying Lotze; CB] appeared to me as mythical entities, suspended between being and non-being, it then became clear to me, with one stroke, that here we basically have a quite obvious conception which traditional logic did not adequately appreciate. I saw that under "proposition in itself" is to be understood what is designated in ordinary discourse – which always objectifies the Ideal – as the "sense" ("*Sinn*") of a statement. It is that which is explained as one and the same where, for example, different persons are said to have asserted the same thing. Or, again, it is what, in science, is simply called a theorem, e.g., the theorem about the sum of the angles in a triangle, which no one would think of taking to be someone's lived experience of judging.

[b] And it further became clear to me that this identical sense could be nothing other than the universal, the species, which belongs to a certain *Moment* present in all actual assertions with the same sense, and which makes possible the identification just mentioned, even where the descriptive content of the individual lived experiences (*Erlebnisse*) of asserting varies considerably in other respects. The proposition thus relates to those acts of judgement to which it belongs as their identical meaning (*Meinung*) in the same way, for example, as the species *redness* relates to individuals of "the same" red color.

[c] Now with his view of things as a basis, *Bolzano's* theory, that propositions are objects which nonetheless have no "existence," comes to have the following quite intelligible signification: – They have the "Ideal" being (*Sein*) or validity (*Gelten*) of objects which are universals ("*allgemeiner Gegenstände*") ... But they do not have the real being of things, or of dependent, thing-like [*dinglichen*] *Moments* [better: moments of things; CB] – of temporal particulars in general. (Husserl 1994: 201f.; Hua: XXII, 156f.)

Some explanations are in order (for the following see Beyer 1996: 154–71). By an "ideal" object, as opposed to a "real" one, Husserl understands an object (i.e. a logical subject of predications which are literally true) that is "atemporal (*unzeitlich*)," in the sense that it lacks temporal location. Hence, he regards any object as either ideal or real. Ideal objects can be subdivided further into ideal particulars, e.g. cardinal numbers (but see below, p. 902), and ideal universals, such as number concepts (which are said to become instantiated by particular numbers). It is ideal *universals* that Husserl equates with Bolzanian propositions in section [b] of the foregoing passage, characterizing them as "species, which belong [...] to a certain moment present in all actual assertions with the same sense."

What kind of "moment" is meant here? Husserl mentions in [b] that the moment in question belongs to the "descriptive content" of the subjective representation or, more generally, the lived intentional experience whose matter (as Bolzano would call it) is instantiated by that moment. In LI, the descriptive content of an intentional experience is defined as the collection of all "concrete or abstract parts" of the experience. By a "concrete" or "independent part," also named a "piece" of a given whole, or collection, *w*, Husserl understands a part of *w* whose existence does not stand or fall with – a part which is not "founded in" – *w*. By contrast, the terms "abstract part," "dependent part" and "moment" designate parts which are not pieces, whose existence stands or falls, in other words, with the existence of the relevant whole. (These mereological notions are further defined in the third of the LI, where you also find the definition of the notion of foundation given near the end of this section. Some of these notions are already to be found in Stumpf and made use of in PA.)

The elements of an intentional experience's descriptive content are laid bare in what Husserl calls the "descriptive psychological analysis" of the experience, which involves something like inner experience (inner perception) à la Brentano, brought about by psychological reflection performed from the subject's own first-person perspective (introspection). These elements then serve "as our exemplary basis for acts of [i]deation," yielding "ideal [s]pecies of experiencing of differing levels of generality, and ideally valid truths of essence which apply *a priori*, and with unlimited generality, to possible experiences of these species" (Husserl 2001a: 112; Hua: XIX/1, 412). Among those ideal species is the meaning content of the experience, i.e. the representation or sentence in itself building its matter.

The *first step* to lay bare this meaning content consists in describing the experience's "distinguishable parts and aspects" (*ibid.*), i.e. its reflectively available pieces and moments. These include a moment that is responsible for the fact that the subject is inclined to describe under which aspects he represents the object(s) his experience is directed at in a certain manner, with those aspects manifesting themselves both in the formulation he would make use of to this end, which makes clear how the object(s) are symbolically represented, and in what he would regard as an authentic representation of the object(s) represented, i.e. what would count as an "intuitive fulfillment" of that symbolic representation (see the first paragraph of the sixth section, below).

It is this element of the experience's descriptive content that constitutes the "exemplary basis" for the *second step* of the process, which step Husserl refers to as *ideation*; the descriptive moment in question he sometimes calls the *moment of matter* (*Materiemoment*) of the experience under (descriptive psychological) investigation.

This idea is missing in Bolzano (while a similar idea can be found in Lotze). Husserl describes the ideation of meaning content on the exemplary basis of a given moment of matter in the following passage:

> The relation between the meaning and the significant expression (or its "meaning-tincture") [in the sense of an according lived experience, or rather its moment of, matter CB] is the same as the relation, e.g., between the Species Red and a red object of intuitive experience (or the "moment" of red which appears in this object). When we mean Red *in specie*, a red object appears before us, and in this sense we look towards the red object to which we are nevertheless not referring. The moment of red is at the same time emphasized in this object, and to that extent we can again say that we are looking towards this moment of red. But we are not referring to this individually definite trait in the object, as we are referring to it when, e.g., we make the phenomeno-logical observation that the moments of red in the separate portions of the apparent object's surface are themselves separate. While the red object and its emphasized moment of red appear before us, we are rather "meaning" the single identical Red, and are meaning it in a novel conscious *manner*, th[r]ough which precisely the Species, and not the individual, becomes our object. The same would apply also to a meaning in its relation to an expression, and an expression's meaningful orientation, whether this expression relates to a corresponding intuition or not. (Husserl 2001: 237; Hua: XIX/1, 111f.)

If we follow Husserl's instruction from the last sentence of this quotation, we get a characterization of the ideation of a given meaning *m*, according to which it can be thought of as a subjective representation directed at *m* that is founded in a reflection upon another intentional experience and especially its moment of matter (which is in the reflection's focus of attention), such that this moment of matter is particularly "emphasized in" the lived experience reflected upon. Now while that experience appears along with its moment of matter, we are, when performing the relevant ideation, neither "meaning" (having in mind) the experience itself nor its moment of matter, but rather the ideal species instantiated (tokened) by that moment of matter. This ideal species coincides with the meaning content *m* of the experience the reflection underlying the described ideation is directed at, its matter in Bolzano's sense of the term.

If the moments of matter of two lived experiences instantiate one and the same ideal meaning species, then we "may say ..., and with good sense," that we are dealing with "the same presentation, memory, expectation, perception" or the like on both sides (Husserl 2001a: 123; Hua: XIX/1, 432). Husserl basically seems to have in mind here what is asserted in Bolzano's above theses (T_3) and (T_4) (and in their counter-parts for judgments and other sorts of intentional experience). However, Bolzano does not explain the likeness of two experiences sharing the same meaning contents by construing the latter as ideal species of a certain sort, whilst Husserl contends that "wherever things are 'alike', an identity in the strict and true sense of the term is also present"; after all, he argues, we "cannot predicate exact likeness of two things without stating the respect in which they are ... alike," thus relating it to an ideal species (Husserl 2001: 242; Hua: XIX/1, 117f.).

Both thinkers agree, though, that a given meaning content does not depend, for its existence, on its being instantiated in thought. As Husserl puts it:

> [T]he ideal unities of pure logic, ... its concepts, propositions, truths, or in other words, ... its meanings ... are an ideally closed set of general objects, to which being thought or being expressed are alike contingent. (Husserl 2001: 233; Hua: XIX/1, 110)

Thus, true propositions like the Pythagorean theorem can be *discovered*. For Husserl, the ideal species in question must therefore be conceived of along the lines of Lotze's conception of ideas, i.e. as something that can *but need not* be thought (see above p. 897); where Husserl understands "being thought" in the sense explained in his species-theory of meaning content, i.e. in terms of the instantiation of the respective meaning content by an element of a particular thought's descriptive content: its moment of matter.

It is in this sense that Husserl states, in section [b] of the passage we started from, that "the proposition ... relates to those acts of judgement to which it belongs as their identical meaning (*Meinung*) in the same way, for example, as the species *redness* relates to individuals of 'the same' red color." And accordingly for the relationship between objective and subjective representations (Hua: XXVI, 33f.). Note that in both cases it is, strictly speaking, the moment of matter rather than the complete intentional experience that instantiates the ideal meaning. In short: *x* is an ideal meaning if and only if it is possible that there is an intentional experience whose moment of matter is an instance (token) of *x*. In cases where this kind of possibility is realized, Husserl refers to the ideal meaning as the *(ideal) matter* of the respective experience. He holds that:

[a] Identical matters can never yield distinct objective references[; but [b] different matters can indeed yield the same objective reference]. (Husserl 2001a: 122; the second sentence is omitted in the translation by Findlay; see Hua: XIX/1, 430)

In section [a] Husserl asserts a generalized version of Bolzano's thesis (T_6). In [b] he states that the converse does not hold true; a thesis we also find in Bolzano. His argument demonstrates just how fine-grained his descriptive-psychological, or epistemic (see the first paragraph of sixth section, below), identity criteria for ideal meaning contents are (an issue he and Frege discussed in their correspondence; see the appendix in Mohanty 1982: 122–5):

> The ideas *equilateral triangle* and *equiangular triangle* differ in content, though both are directed, and evidently directed, to the same object: they present the same object, although 'in a different fashion'. The same is true of such

presentations as *a length of a+b units* and *a length of b+a units*; it is also true of statements, in other respects synonymous, which differ only in [such] "equivalent" concepts. (Husserl 2001a: 121; Hua: XIX/1, 429)

Because descriptive psychological analysis yields ideal species, it involves what Husserl calls ideation (see above p. 989). In later works he would speak of "eidetic reduction" in this regard, construing it as an unfolding of abstract features shared by appropriate sets of fictitious or real-life examples, by way of free imaginative variation on an arbitrarily chosen initial example (for the method of "free variation," see *Experience and Judgement*, §87).

Descriptive psychological analysis also yields the "moment of quality" of the intentional experience under investigation, i.e. the particular feature instantiating its psychological mode (judgment, deliberation, desire, hope, etc.), which roughly corresponds to the speech act mode of an utterance "giving voice to" that experience. (The intentional experience given voice to by a speaker A in an utterance u of an expression e is the conscious state, or lived experience, s such that (i) A performs u in order to present himself as being in, or undergoing, s and (ii) the respective meaning expressed by e as employed in u is identical with the intentional content of s; where p coincides with the general meaning function of e just in case that e is not an essentially occasional expression.) Husserl gives the following example:

> The two assertions "2×2=4" and "Ibsen is the principle founder of modern dramatic realism" are both, *qua* assertions, of one kind; each is qualified as an assertion, and their common feature is their *judgement-quality*. (Husserl 2001a: 119; Hua: XIX/1, 426)

Furthermore, descriptive psychological analysis yields relations of "foundation" i.e. one-sided or mutual relative existential dependencies between (1) the intentional experience (alias "act") in question and other experiences and (2) the particular descriptive features of the act. Thus, to quote one of Husserl's examples for dependencies of type (1), an experience of pleasure about a given event is one-sidedly founded, relative to the "stream of consciousness" (to use a term Husserl adopted from William James) it belongs to, in a particular belief-state, or judgment, to the effect that this event has occurred. (The relativization to a particular stream of consciousness makes sure that both founded and founding experience occur in the same person's mind.) Like all foundation relations, this one holds in virtue of an essential law, to the effect that conscious pleasure about some state of affairs requires a corresponding (and simultaneous) belief. Quite generally, a given object a of type F is founded in a particular object b of type G (where a is different from b and F is different from G) relative to a particular whole c of type H if and only if (i) there is an essential law in virtue of which it holds that for any object x of type F there is an object y of type G and a whole z of type H, such that both x and y are (proper) parts of z, and (ii) both a and b are (proper) parts of c (Husserl 2001a: 25–8; Hua: XIX/1, 267–72). This definition also allows for foundation relations of type (2), which hold between elements of an act's descriptive content (notably, with respect to that act itself). In particular, Husserl claims with regard to an act's respective moment of matter and quality that:

> [A]ct-quality is undoubtedly *an abstract aspect of acts*, unthinkable apart from all matter. Could we hold an experience possible which was a judging without definite [matter]? This would take from the judgement its character as intentional experience, which is evidently part of its essence.
>
> The same holds of matter. A matter that was not matter for presentation, nor for judgement, nor for … etc. etc., would be held to be unthinkable. (Husserl 2001a: 122; Hua: XIX/1, 430)

In his critique of psychologism, Husserl draws upon the above-described Platonic conception of meaning content (among many other things, he raises about eighteen objections in total; see Soldati 1994: 117ff.). He compares the platonistic ontology of logic with that of mathematics and particularly arithmetic. In the latter regard, he argues that while arithmetical concepts can be clarified by recourse to their "psychological origin" only (just as he held in PA), the mathematical principles containing these concepts are nevertheless far from being psychological laws. For, the "domain of research" of arithmetic "is completely and exhaustively determined by the familiar series of ideal species 1, 2, 3, …" (Husserl 2001: 109f.; Hua: XVIII, 173f.):

> In this sphere there can be no talk of individual facts, of what is temporally definite … The number Five is not my own or anyone else's counting of five, it is also not my presentation or anyone else's presentation of five. It is in the latter regard a possible *object* of acts of presentation, whereas, in the former, it is the ideal *species* of a form whose concrete *instances* are found in what becomes objective in certain acts of counting, in the collective whole that these constitute. (*Ibid.*)

Note that Husserl still subscribes to his analysis of number concepts as presented in PA (see third section, above). However, he now particularly stresses the *atemporal* character of cardinal numbers and the fact that they are *instantiated* by certain moments of particular collections. (This makes it difficult to understand, though, why Husserl wants to classify cardinal numbers as ideal *particulars* rather than as universals; see above, p. 898.) As we have seen already, he also ascribes this atemporal and universal character to the objects with which logic is concerned, i.e. representations and sentences in themselves. Now why, Husserl asks, should the laws of logic be psychological ones, if the laws of arithmetic, which concern ideal species as well, clearly do not qualify as psychological?

Where Husserl's species-theory of meaning content is based upon a descriptive psychological approach, it is thus nevertheless strictly anti-psychologistic in its orientation. But does it allow for a decent analysis of the concept of ideal meaning content? The answer depends on what demands such an analysis is supposed to meet. If what we are after is a traditional (non-circular) concept-definition in the form of logically necessary and sufficient conditions, then Husserl's proposal fails, for it is circular. After all, it explains ideal meaning content as what is instantiated by a certain element of the descriptive content of a given intentional experience whose ideal matter coincides *with that very meaning content*. But then, just like the author of PA (see the third section, above), the author of LI has in view a rather different kind of conceptual analysis:

> Logical concepts, as valid thought-unities, must have their origin in intuition: they must arise out of an ideational intuition founded on certain experiences, and must admit of indefinite reconfirmation, and on recognition of their self-identity, on the reperformance of such abstraction. Otherwise put: we can absolutely not rest content with "mere words," i.e. with a merely symbolic understanding of words ... [W]e must go back to the "things themselves" ...
>
> The phenomenology of the logical experiences aims at giving us a sufficiently wide descriptive ... understanding of these mental states and their indwelling sense, as will enable us to give fixed meanings to all the fundamental concepts of logic. (Husserl 2001: 168; Hua: XIX/1, 10)

Prospects

Much more could be said about the content and philosophical significance of Husserl's LI. Thus, to pick up the thread of the foregoing quotation, an interesting and still largely unexplored claim defended particularly in the sixth of the LI (which in many respects continues the approach taken in PA) is the following:

> Any logically consistent meaning can in principle be subjectively fulfilled, more or less adequately, by a unified intuition (authentic representation), such as an act of continuous perception or intuitive imagination, where the structure and other essential features of the meaning in question can be read off from the respective mode of intuitive fulfillment.

Inconsistent meanings can be singled out and studied by means of (reflection upon) corresponding experiences of intuitive conflict, like for instance the discrete switching back and forth between a duck-head-imagination and a rabbit-head-imagination in the case of an attempted intuitive imagination of a duck-head that is at the same time a rabbit-head. Some meanings are inconsistent for formal-logical reasons. According to Husserl, all analytically false propositions belong to this category. (It should be noted that regarding the question of what is distinctive of this category, Husserl did not improve on the pioneering results arrived at by Bolzano and Frege; nor did he intend to do so.) Other meanings are inconsistent because they conflict with some general material *a priori* truth, also called "essential law." The proposition expressed by the sentence "There are perceptual objects whose surface is both (visibly) completely green and completely red at the same time" is a case in point (although some members of the Vienna Circle were to take issue with this contention).

As for the species-theory of meaning content developed in LI, Husserl seems to have been aware that it faces at least one serious objection. It concerns utterances of "essential occasional" (Husserl), i.e. systematically context-sensitive, expressions like "I am here now" and the (as one could call them) indexical experiences they give voice to. If the meaning content of an indexical experience is to serve as a (sub-)propositional content, it must uniquely determine the object (if any) that the respective experience refers to. That is to say: if two indexical experiences display the same meaning content, they must refer to the same object (if any). It seems, though, that the moments of matter of two such experiences can instantiate the same ideal matter – the same type of (particular) content – whilst representing different objects. If you and I both think "I am here," our respective thoughts share the same type of content, or so it would seem, but they represent different states of affairs.

In order to accommodate this observation, Husserl draws a distinction (in the first of his LI) between, on the one hand, the "general meaning function" of an utterance (which corresponds to what is called "character" in recent semantics, roughly: the linguistic meaning of the expression used) and, on the other hand, the "respective meaning" (i.e. the propositional or sub-propositional content expressed in the relevant context of utterance).

However, it is doubtful whether this distinction really helps Husserl to overcome the difficulty the phenomenon of context-sensitivity (which he considered to be ubiquitous in our empirical thought and speech; see Husserl 2001: 7; Hua: XVIII, 13) poses for his species-theory of content. If intentional contents are ideal matters in the sense of *types* of particular moments of matter, and if this kind of type may remain constant while the intentional object and hence the (sub-)propositional content differs, then surely intentional contents thus conceived cannot always function as (sub-)propositional contents, as Husserl's theory would have it. Rather, there must be another intentional content involved, namely the "respective meaning," which serves as the (sub-)propositional content of the indexical experience. And this content does not appear to be an ideal *species*. (It may be argued, however, that even (sub-)propositional contents of indexical utterances can be *instantiated multiply* in thought and speech, thus qualifying as ideal species after all. But the crucial question is whether this holds true in complete generality: consider the above example "I am here now.")

Anyhow, Husserl construes (sub-)propositional contents ("respective meanings") as two-factored, with the general meaning function plus the relevant context of utterance (if any) determining the content in question. And at least in the case of indexical experiences he seems to identify their meaning contents (intentional contents) with these two-factored contents, for he holds that meaning content uniquely determines the object referred to or represented (in the sense defined in [T$_6$]; see the fifth section, above).

Because Husserl equates meaning content with respective meaning, he is committed to subscribe to a version of *externalism* about intentional content (*pace* Beyer 1996: 175–83; see Beyer 2000). After all, the respective meaning expressed depends on objects located in, or constituting, the relevant context of utterance, according to the author of LI, with these objects usually belonging to the external environment, e.g.

to the perceptual surrounding of the speaker. And externalism can be looked upon as the view that the environment helps determine the intentional content. More particularly, it can be thought of as the claim that the actual referent (if any) helps determine the content in that the latter is dependent, for its very identity, on that referent – provided the lived experience in question is indeed successfully related to an intentional object belonging to the external environment.

Notice, however, that unlike most recent externalists, Husserl does not naively take the existence of an extra-mental referent for granted. Instead, he asks which structures of consciousness entitle us to represent the world as containing particular objects "transcending" what is currently given to us in experience. (It is in these structures of consciousness that the objects in question "constitute themselves.") To achieve this, he introduces the method of "epoché" that requires the phenomenologist to systematically "bracket" his "natural attitude" towards the objects belonging to the real world and thus transcending our (empirical) consciousness. In order to prevent the misunderstanding that this method leads to a genuinely solipsistic conception of intentional consciousness, Husserl stresses that far from distracting our attention from these real, transcendent objects, the epoché is designed to enable us to make coherent sense, in terms of the essential "horizon-structure" of our consciousness, of that very reality and transcendence, i.e. to perform the "phenomenological reduction" (Hua: XIII, 432ff.). To this end, Husserl employs a research strategy in the theory of intentional content and reference that could be called his *dynamic method*:

> Intentional states and experiences are looked upon as momentary components of certain transtemporal cognitive structures – *dynamic intentional structures* – in which one and the same object or state of affairs is represented throughout a period of time during which the subject's cognitive perspective upon that object or state of affairs is constantly changing. (Hua: III/1, 196–9)

Typical examples of dynamic intentional structures include continuous observations, which represent Husserl's standard example, as well as those totalities of successive judgments, or momentary belief-states, that actualize one and the same continuous belief. (For instance, my judgment that yesterday was Thursday actualizes the same belief as the judgment I could have given voice to yesterday by "Today is Thursday.")

The dynamic method has us look upon noematic Sinn under the "functional aspect" (Husserl) of how it enables us to keep the intentional object "in mind (*im Sinn*)" (Hua: II/1, 196ff.), instead of viewing it merely statically as a psychological type or species to be instantiated by isolated moments of consciousness. It makes us regard any content of the latter sort, particularly "static perceptual content," as a mere "abstraction from dynamic content" (Mulligan 1995: 195, 197).

Even objectless subjective representations of spatiotemporal individuals, such as hallucinations, display dynamic content, so that an intentional object appears to "constitute itself" in a dynamic intentional structure. This appearance is deceptive, though. If there is no real object, there can be no successful object-constitution. To be sure, there is still intentional content (and thus thought) even in this case. But the content is going to "explode" once we follow its "intentional implications" in that the horizon-structure it predelineates will eventually turn out to be incoherent (Hua: VIII, 434). As a consequence, the associated dynamic intentional structure will become deactivated. In this way, our cognitive system is constrained by the external environment, at least in the long run.

It should be stressed, though, that Husserl does not regard the external environment as independent from the essential structures of consciousness, with its associated criteria of coherence. In fact, the task of the phenomenological reduction is precisely to study the interdependence between these structures and the environment in a methodologically well-regulated manner.

To achieve this task, Husserl starts from a "solipsistic" abstraction of the notion of a perceptual object which differs from that notion in that it does not presuppose that any other subject can observe such an object from his own viewpoint. But then, the "the crucial further step" (Husserl) towards the phenomenological clarification of the interdependence in question consists in disclosing the dimension that opens up when the epistemic justification, or "motivation," of intersubjective experience, or empathy, is additionally taken into account and made explicit (Hua: VII, 435).

It is worth noticing that Husserl's concept of motivation is more general than the notion of epistemic justification in the traditional ("internalist") sense of the term. His explanation of the concept of motivation runs as follows:

> [H]ow did I hit upon that, what brought me to it? That questions like these can be raised characterizes all motivation in general. (Husserl 1989: 234, with translation change; Hua: IV, 222)

Husserl stresses that whenever an object exercises a motivating "stimulus" on a subject "comporting itself" (*sich verhaltend*) "toward the [o]bject," then an intentional content of consciousness, a "noema," is in play; the object is "immanently constituted" in the subject's consciousness (Husserl 1989: 231; Hua: IV, 219). This even holds true for our practical copings with everyday objects, at least insofar as we are comporting ourselves to these objects as free agents. For, on Husserl's view, the will of such an agent, on a given occasion, is always already embedded in a "volitional context" (*Willenszusammenhang*) predelineating, in the final analysis, the open "future horizon" of a "full individual life" that the agent is currently able to lead (Hua: XXXVI, 252), thus qualifying as a dynamic intentional structure.

The idea of the intersubjective constitution of objects belonging to our common everyday "lifeworld" is one of the many interrelated issues examined in his later works. The term "lifeworld" is employed in Husserl's last work, *The Crisis of European Sciences and Transcendental Phenomenology* (1936/54 [1970]), to denote the way the members of one or more social groups (cultures, linguistic communities) use to structure the world into objects (Hua: VI, 126–38, 140–5). The respective lifeworld is claimed to "predelineate" a "world-horizon" of potential future experiences that are to be (more or less) expected for a given group member at a given time, under various conditions, where the resulting sequences of anticipated experiences can be looked upon as corresponding to different "possible worlds and environments" (Hua: III/1, 100). These expectations follow typical patterns, as the lifeworld is fixed by a system of (first and foremost implicit) intersubjective standards, or conventions, that determine what counts as "normal" or "standard" observation under "normal" conditions (Hua: XV, 135ff., 142) and thus as a source of epistemic justification. Some of these standards are restricted to a particular culture or "homeworld" (Hua: XV, 141f., 227–36), whereas others determine a "general structure" that is "a priori" in being "unconditionally valid for all subjects," defining "that on which normal Europeans, normal Hindus, Chinese, etc., agree in spite of all relativity" (Hua: VI, 142). Husserl quotes universally accepted facts about "spatial shape, motion, sense-quality" as well as our prescientific notions of "spatiotemporality," "body" and "causality" as examples (ibid.). These conceptions determine the general structure of all particular thing-concepts that are such that any creature sharing the essential structures of human consciousness will be capable of forming and grasping them, respectively, under different lifeworldly conditions. If you will, it is this universal "a priori" structure of the lifeworld that makes intercultural understanding possible (Hua: XV, 159).

On Husserl's view, it is precisely the "subjective-relative" lifeworld that provides the "grounding soil" of the more objective world of science (Hua: VI, 134), in the twofold sense that (i) scientific conceptions owe their (sub-)propositional content and thus their reference to reality to the prescientific notions they are supposed to "naturalize" and that, consequently, (ii) when things get into flux in science, when a crisis occurs, all that is left to appeal to in order to defend new scientific approaches against their rivals is the prescientific lifeworld, as manifested in our according intuitive acceptances (for references see Føllesdal 1990: 139f.). This view offers an alternative to the "naturalistic" stance taken by many analytic philosophers today. Husserl's notion of lifeworld should be of interest for contemporary discussions in philosophy of science and epistemology, such as the debate about "contextualist" approaches to knowledge and epistemic justification. However, a more detailed exploration of these issues goes far beyond the scope of an article about Husserl considered as a nineteenth-century philosopher.

Among the most notable of Husserl's other later works are *Ideas Pertaining to a Pure Phenomenology and to a Phenomenological Philosophy – First Book* (1913 [1982]; the second book is important, too [1989]), *Lectures on the Phenomenology of the Consciousness of Internal Time* (1928 [1990]), *Formal and Transcendental Logic* (1929 [1969]), *Cartesian Meditations* (1931 [1988]) and *Experience and Judgement* (1939 [1973]). In the first six decades of the twentieth century his thought had a particularly great impact on German and French philosophy. Members of the phenomenological school include Adolf Reinach, Max Scheler, Edith Stein, Martin Heidegger, Oskar Becker, Roman Ingarden, Alfred Schütz, Helmuth Plessner, Jean Paul Sartre, Maurice Merleau-Ponty and many others. As this list of names indicates, Husserl's work has influenced other disciplines, too, such as sociology, anthropology, linguistics and literary study. More recently, his ideas have been taken up in psychology (recent headwords include "embodied cognition," "mindreading," "[meta-]representation and consciousness," "temporal awareness," "attention," among others).

Finally, there is a growing awareness among analytic philosophers that Husserl has anticipated, at least in part, many of their ideas (e.g. rigid designation, externalism and Twin Earth, the referential/attributive distinction, the distinction between content and character, cognitive dynamics, pre-predicative experience, make-believe and fictional operators, to cite but a few examples from the philosophy of language and mind). His ethics and conception of personhood, closely related to the notion of lifeworld, is still provocative. In any case, it ought to be clear that there is yet a lot to be learned from his challenging writings.

References

Beyer, Christian (1996) *Von Bolzano zu Husserl*, Dordrecht: Kluwer.

—— (2000) *Intentionalität und Referenz*, Paderborn: mentis.

Bolzano, Bernard (1972) *Theory of Science*, trans. R. George, Oxford: Blackwell.

Ehrenfels, Christian von (1890) "Über Gestaltqualitäten," in *Vierteljahresschrift für wissenschaftliche Philosophie* 14: 249–92.

Føllesdal, Dagfinn (1958) *Husserl und Frege*, Oslo: Aschehoug; trans. in L. Haaparanta (ed.) (1994) *Mind, Meaning and Mathematics*, Dordrecht: Kluwer.

—— (1990) "The *Lebenswelt* in Husserl," in L. Haaparanta et al. (eds.) (1990) *Language, Knowledge and Intentionality*, Acta Philosophica Fennica 49 (special issue), Helsinki.

Husserl, Edmund (Hua) *Husserliana – Edmund Husserl, Gesammelte Werke*, The Hague; Dordrecht: Nijhoff/Kluwer/Springer, 1973–.

—— (1969) *Formal and Transcendental Logic*, trans. D. Cairns, The Hague: Nijhoff.

—— (1970) *The Crisis of European Sciences and Transcendental Phenomenology*, trans. D. Carr, Evanston, IL: Northwestern University Press.

—— (1973) *Experience and Judgement*, trans. J. Churchill and K. Ameriks, London: Routledge.

—— (1982) *Ideas Pertaining to a Pure Phenomenology and to a Phenomenological Philosophy – First Book*, trans. F. Kersten. The Hague: Nijhoff.

—— (1988) *Cartesian Meditations*, trans. D. Cairns, Dordrecht: Kluwer.

—— (1989) *Ideas Pertaining to a Pure Phenomenology and to a Phenomenological Philosophy – Second Book*, trans. R. Rojewicz and A. Schuwer, Dordrecht: Kluwer.

—— (1990) *On the Phenomenology of the Consciousness of Internal Time*, trans. J. B. Brough, Dordrecht: Kluwer.

—— (1994) *Early Writings in the Philosophy of Logic and Mathematics*, trans. D. Willard, Dordrecht: Kluwer.

—— (2001a) *Logical Investigations*, vol. 1, trans. J. Findlay, with a new preface by M. Dummett; edited, with a new introduction, by D. Moran, London: Routledge.

—— (2001b) *Logical Investigations*, vol. 2, trans. J. Findlay, edited by D. Moran, London: Routledge.

—— (2003) *Philosophy of Arithmetic*, trans. D. Willard, Dordrecht: Kluwer.

Ierna, Carlo (2006) "The Beginning of Husserl's Philosophy," pt 2: "Philosophical and Mathematical Background," in *The New Yearbook for Phenomenology and Phenomenological Philosophy*, vol. 6, pp. 33–81.

Lotze, Hermann (1989a) *Logik*, bk 1, Hamburg: Meiner.

Lotze, Hermann (1989b) *Logik*, bk 3, Hamburg: Meiner.

Mach, Ernst (1897) *Contributions to the Analysis of Sensations*, trans. C. Williams, Chicago: Open Court.

Mohanty, Jitendranath (1982) *Husserl and Frege*, Bloomington: Indiana University Press.

Mulligan, Kevin (1995) "Perception," in B. Smith and D. Smith (1995).

Patzig, Günther (1958) "Logik," in A. Diemer and I. Frenzel (eds) *Das Fischer Lexikon Philosophie*, Frankfurt am Main: Fischer.

Russell, Bertrand (1917) "Knowledge by Acquaintance and Knowledge by Description," in *Mysticism and Logic*, London: Allen & Unwin.

Schuhmann, Karl (1977) *Husserl-Chronik*, The Hague: Nijhoff.

Soldati, Gianfranco (1994) *Bedeutung und psychischer Gehalt*, Paderborn: Schöningh.

Twardowski, Kasimir (1977) *On the Concept and Object of Presentations*, trans. R. Grossmann, The Hague: Nijhoff.

Willard, Dallas (2003) Translator's introduction to Husserl (2003).
Wittgenstein, Ludwig (1958) *Philosophical Investigations*, trans. E. Anscombe, Oxford: Blackwell.

Further reading

Rudolf Bernet, Iso Kern, and Eduard Marbach, *An Introduction to Husserlian Phenomenology* (Evanston, IL: Northwestern University Press, 1993), is a useful standard work. A clear critical exposition of Husserl's philosophy, with a positive emphasis on his Brentanian background, the position developed in PA and his phenomenology of the lifeworld is David Bell, *Husserl* (London: Routledge, 1989). Hubert Dreyfus (ed.) *Husserl, Intentionality, and Cognitive Science* (Cambridge, MA: MIT Press, 1982), is an important collection of essays that has helped to bridge the gap between phenomenology and analytic philosophy. A collection of high-quality articles introducing the reader to different aspects of Husserl's work is Barry Smith and David Smith (eds) *The Cambridge Companion to Husserl* (Cambridge: Cambridge University Press, 1995). David Smith and Ronald McIntyre, *Husserl and Intentionality* (Dordrecht: Reidel, 1982), is a widely discussed study on Husserl's theory of intentionality, offering a rational reconstruction from the viewpoint of analytic philosophy. A competent exposition of Husserl's transcendental phenomenology is Elisabeth Ströker, *Husserl's Transcendental Phenomenology* (Stanford: Stanford University Press, 1993). Dallas Willard, *Logic and the Objectivity of Knowledge* (Athens: University of Ohio Press, 1984), is a standard reference on the early Husserl. D an Zahavi, Husserl's *Phenomenology* (Stanford, CA: Stanford University Press, 2003), offers a concise introduction covering a wide range of topics, with an eye on related debates within contemporary analytic philosophy.

INDEX

Related titles from Routledge

Routledge Philosophy Guidebook to
Frege on Sense and Reference

Mark Textor

Gottlob Frege is considered the father of modern logic and one of the founding figures of analytic philosophy. He was firstly a mathematician but his major works, including *Conception and Notation*, also made significant conceptual contributions to the philosophy of language. Frege's writings are difficult and deal with technical, abstract concepts. *The Routledge Philosophy Guidebook to Frege on Sense and Reference* helps students get to grips with Frege's thought, and introduces and assesses:

* Frege's life and the background to his philosophy
* Frege's main papers and arguments, including his distinction between sense and reference
* the continuing importance of Frege's work to philosophy of logic and language.

Ideal for those coming to Frege for the first time, this *Routledge Philosophy Guidebook* is essential reading for students of philosophy of language and logic.

Mark Textor is a lecturer in philosophy at King's College London, UK.

ISBN 13: 978-0-415-41961-1 (Hbk)
ISBN 13: 978-0-415-41962-8 (Pbk)
ISBN 13: 978-0-203-84590-5 (Ebk)

Available at all good bookshops
For ordering and further information please visit:
www.routledge.com

Related titles from Routledge

Continental Idealism: Leibniz to Nietzsche
Paul Redding

Paul Redding's *Continental Idealism* is a lucid account of the development of German philosophy in the eighteenth and nineteenth centuries, and a contribution to current philosophical debates. Its originality lies in stressing the foundational importance of Leibniz, and in offering clear and compelling explanations of the different kinds of metaphysical commitments within idealist philosophy. Redding casts new light on the relation of Hegel to Kant and Fichte, situates the German Romantics in this body of thought, and traces the subversion of these traditions in Schopenhauer and Nietzsche. Redding is also attentive to contemporary philosophical issues, arguing that idealism, properly understood, remains viable as an alternative to the reductive naturalism that characterises much current thinking. *Douglas Moggach, University of Ottawa*

Standard accounts of nineteenth-century German philosophy often begin with Kant and assess philosophers after him in light of their responses to Kantian idealism. In *Continental Idealism*, Paul Redding argues that the story of German idealism begins with Leibniz.

Redding begins by examining Leibniz's dispute with Newton over the nature of space, time and God, and stresses the way in which Leibniz incorporated Platonic and Aristotelian elements in his distinctive brand of idealism. Redding shows how Kant's interpretation of Leibniz's views of space and time consequently shaped his own 'transcendental' version of idealism. Far from ending here, Redding argues that post-Kantian idealists such as Fichte, Schelling and Hegel on the one hand and metaphysical sceptics such as Schopenhauer and Nietzsche on the other continued to wrestle with a form of idealism ultimately derived from Leibniz.

Continental Idealism offers a new picture of one of the most important philosophical movements in the history of philosophy, and a valuable and clear introduction to the origins of Continental and European philosophy.

Paul Redding is Professor of Philosophy at the University of Sydney, Australia

ISBN 13: 978-0-415-44306-7 (hbk)
ISBN 13: 978-0-415-44307-4 (pbk)
ISBN 13: 978-0-203-87695-4 (ebk)

Available at all good bookshops
For ordering and further information please visit:
www.routledge.com